FREDERICK LEONG

Contributors

Leslie B. Alexander, PhD, Graduate School of Social Work and Social Research, Bryn Mawr College, Bryn Mawr, Pennsylvania

Godfrey T. Barrett-Lennard, PhD, The Centre for Studies in Human Relations, Perth, Western Australia, Australia

Ariadne P. Beck, MA, Private Practice, Indian Head Park and Des Plaines, Illinois

Lorna Smith Benjamin, PhD, Department of Psychiatry, University of Wisconsin, Madison, Wisconsin

James M. Dugo, PhD, Private Practice, Forest Institute of Professional Psychology, Des Plaines, Illinois

Robert Elliott, PhD, Department of Psychology, University of Toledo, Toledo, Ohio

Albert M. Eng, PhD, Palo Alto Veterans Administration, Palo Alto, California

Sue E. Estroff, PhD, Department of Psychiatry, University of Wisconsin, Madison, Wisconsin

Sharon W. Foster, PhD, Department of Psychiatry, University of Wisconsin, Madison, Wisconsin

Leslie S. Greenberg, PhD, Department of Psychology, York University, North York, Ontario, Canada.

Clara E. Hill, PhD, Department of Psychology, University of Maryland, College Park, Maryland

Mardi J. Horowitz, MD, Langley Porter Psychiatric Institute, University of California, San Francisco, California

Adam O. Horvath, PhD, Department of Counseling Psychology, Simon Fraser University, Burnaby, British Columbia, Canada

Kenneth I. Howard, PhD, Department of Psychology, Northwestern University, Evanston, Illinois

Gillian P. Kerr, PhD, York University, North York, Ontario, Canada

Donald J. Kiesler, PhD, Department of Psychology, Virginia Commonwealth University, Richmond, Virginia

Marjorie H. Klein, PhD, Department of Psychiatry, University of Wisconsin, Madison, Wisconsin

Carol M. Lewis, MS, Community Guidance Center, Mercy Hospital, Chicago, Illinois

Lester Luborsky, PhD, Department of Psychiatry, School of Medicine, University of Pennsylvania, Philadelphia, Pennsylvania

Charles R. Marmar, MD, Langley Porter Psychiatric Institute, University of California, San Francisco, California

Elsa Marziali, PhD, Clarke Institute of Psychiatry, University of Toronto, Toronto, Ontario

Philippa Mathieu-Coughlan, PhD, Wesleyan University, Middletown, Connecticut

Stephanie Samples O'Malley, PhD, Yale University School of Medicine, New Haven, Connecticut

David E. Orlinsky, PhD, Department of Behavioral Sciences, University of Chicago, Chicago, Illinois

J. P. N. Phillips, PhD, Department of Psychology, University of Hull, Hull, England

William M. Pinsof, PhD, Center for Family Studies, The Family Institute of Chicago, Northwestern University, Chicago, Illinois

Laura N. Rice, PhD, Department of Psychology, York University, North York, Ontario, Canada

Laura Giat Roberto, PhD, Department of Psychiatry, University of Wisconsin, Madison, Wisconsin

Harold Sampson, PhD, Mount Zion Hospital and Medical Center, Department of Psychiatry, San Francisco, California

William B. Stiles, PhD, Department of Psychology, Miami University, Oxford, Ohio

Hans Strupp, PhD, Department of Psychology, Vanderbilt University, Nashville, Tennessee

Chong S. Suh, PhD, Vanderbilt University, Nashville, Tennessee

Shaké G. Toukmanian, PhD, Department of Psychology, York University, North York, Ontario, Canada

Daniel S. Weiss, PhD, Langley Porter Psychiatric Institute, University of California, San Francisco, California

Joseph Weiss, MD, The San Francisco Psychoanalytic Institute, San Francisco, California

Contents

III. THE METHODOLOGY OF PROCESS RESEARCH

Research Programs

Strategies and Methods

Foreword

This book reviews measurement systems for study of the psychotherapeutic process. It comprehensively summarizes major coding, rating, or inventory systems constructed to measure within-session processes from the perspectives either of the patient and therapist participants, or of external observers who rate transcriptions of the therapy sessions. Almost all the systems contained in this volume were designed for analysis of individual psychotherapy; two seminal and important systems, for the marital-family and group psychotherapy modalities respectively, are also included.

Appropriately, this volume is the updated successor of my 1973 book which comprised the first encyclopedic summary of individual psychotherapy process research. Suitably also, the present book offers an updated definition of process research as "the study of the interaction between the patient and therapist systems. The goal of process research is to identify the patterns and mechanisms of change in the interaction between these systems. Process research covers all of the behaviors and experiences of these systems, within and outside of the treatment sessions, which pertain to the process of change" (Greenberg and Pinsof, p. 18).

My comments that follow address what I consider to be important shifts, apparent in the present volume, in the study of psychotherapy process over the thirteen years since my earlier summary. I find these shifts fascinating, encouraging, and promising in their motion towards attainment of our goal to understand the essential ingredients of individual psychotherapy. While reading these chapters I also experienced a quiet personal realization that my own work played a catalytic role in the accomplishments depicted.

A glance at the table of contents will reveal immediately some familiar "faces," most notably the Experiencing Scale, Measures of Client and Therapist Vocal Quality, and the Relationship Inventory—measures that are among the oldest and most established in the field. All the other listed systems have appeared since 1973. Included are three additional systems, for measuring the helping (working or therapeutic) alliance. Recent applications of these alliance measures have produced a series of robust correlations with outcome across a variety of treatment approaches. One also finds three comprehensive coding systems designed to measure patient or therapist verbal responses in the speech-by-speech interchange of therapy. These wide-band systems represent sophisticated developments that are helping us to understand the most detailed level of therapeutic transaction and to chart similarities and differences among interventions from different therapeutic approaches. The table of contents also reveals that the predominance of Rogerian process measures has diminished, although four prominent systems continue that tradition. Balancing them, however, is an array of new systems based on such divergent frameworks as behaviorism, cognitive psychology, contemporary psychoanalysis, interpersonal psychology, marital-family systems, and small-group development.

In my view, the most important effect of this volume is that the field of psychotherapy research now has easily available for general use an array of methodologically so-phisticated and valid process measures. As Greenberg observes later in this book, ''the development of coding systems of varying complexity to describe and categorize dif-ferent phenomena that therapists pay attention to in therapy . . . represents an impor-tant step in transforming psychotherapy into a descriptive science'' (p. 713). We still have much to learn about each measure in this volume, but already we know quite a bit about each. We still have new measures to develop, but already important sections of the terrain have been sampled.

In the Preface to my 1973 book I lamented that ''psychotherapy process research has to rank near the forefront of research disciplines characterized as chaotic, prolific, un-connected, and disjointed, with researchers unaware of much of the work that has pre-ceded and the individual investigator tending to start anew completely ignorant of close-ly related previous work'' (p. svii). What the present volume demonstrates is that this statement is no longer accurate. Happily, the investigators found in this volume are *program* researchers who develop, apply, modify, re-apply, and iteratively validate their respective measures within long-term empirical projects. In some cases these program commitments have already encompassed several decades of the investigator's career. Hence, it is no random or uncorrelated fact that our yield of replicated process find-ings has increased markedly since 1973.

Even more remarkable is the extent to which present-day process investigators ap-ply in their studies, not only their own measures, but also those developed by others. Similarly impressive is the frequency with which researchers in one center make their therapy transcriptions and data easily available to researchers in other centers. These previously unheard-of collaborations and cross-fertilizations are markedly affecting the replicability, generalizability, and construct-validity findings of the entire process area.

Another significant shift evident in this volume redresses a misguided emphasis per-vasive in my earlier book. Partly as an arbitrary distinction, but also partly as an un-stated bias, I divided the process systems of that time into ''direct'' versus ''indirect'' measures. The former subsumed coding and rating systems that were applied by ob-server judges to live or transcribed therapy sessions. The latter referred to inventory measures designed to tap the self-report perspectives of the patient and therapist par-ticipants themselves. My labeling of the former as ''direct'' reflected an implicit value that the perspective of observers who rated the actual behaviors of the participants (the objective environment) was more valid than the subjective environments represented by the experience of the participants. As commented on several times in this volume, this bias is indeed unfair, has led to some design paradoxes for phenomenologically oriented researchers and, as empirical findings have demonstrated, is clearly invalid. As Orlinsky and Howard observe in their chapter,

> ''Participants' perspectives are necessary data for the study of social relationships. In psy-chotherapy, the patients' and therapists' construals of their reciprocal involvement are con-stitutive elements of the therapeutic process. We do not argue that the behaviors of pa-tients and therapists, as perceived by outside observers, are irrelevant; these, too, are con-stitutive elements of therapeutic process. But we do not think that research which is limited to externally scrutinized behaviors can provide an essential or a practical understanding of psychotherapy. (p. 498)

From this perspective it is quite gratifying to discover both process and outcome re-searchers now routinely incorporating measures from multiple measurement perspectives including both therapy participants, observer judges, and significant others in the patient's environment.

Perhaps the most noticeable continuity with my earlier book is found in the present volume's routine emphasis on the methodological issues of psychotherapy process research. I discussed these issues in detail in 1973 and organized my summary of major process measures around these methodological themes. Again and again throughout the following pages the reader will encounter sections which systematically address the following themes: definition of scoring, contextual, and summary units; reliability of the unitizing versus actual coding tasks; sampling issues of size and location within a session and across the therapy course; data-form issues; participant context and dimensionality issues; level of clinical sophistication required of judges; training procedures for judges; and interjudge and intrajudge reliabilties. The upshot is that sophisticated examination of methodological issues has become a routine part of contemporary process research,.

In 1973 only 5 of the 17 major systems reviewed offered comprehensive training manuals that systematically addressed these methodological issues and that provided standardized procedures for training of raters. In contrast, the rating and coding systems appearing in this volume all have a comprehensive manual either available or in preparation. It's clear that the age of manuals has arrived in psychotherapy research, not only for specification of treatment approaches in outcome studies (DeRubeis, Hollon, Evans, and Bernis, 1982; Luborsky, Woody, McLellan, O'Brian and Rosenzweig, 1982), but also for operationalization and rater training in process research. However, as Greenberg further clarifies in his closing chapter, although treatment manuals have markedly improved outcome research, "the real task, of describing what is actually occurring in a particular therapy, remains unaddressed" by them. "Although the manuals specify the component, they do not sequence or prioritize these components. Nor do they provide adequate descriptions of the complex, multidimensional variables involved in the therapist behaviors which are needed to describe not only the type but also the manner and quality of the behaviors" (p. 727).

In my judgment, the most important new methodological criterion appearing in this volume is the construct of "reconstructivity" (Pinsof, 1981). This refers to "the ability of a coding system to permit clinically meaningful reconstruction of therapeutic process and events from the specific code data" (Pinsof, p. 219 of this volume). Reconstructivity addresses the question whether the numbers provided by our measures permit us to retrace in clinically meaningful ways what patients or therapists were actually doing, thinking, feeling, and so on at the moments characterized. The distinctive contribution is that to the extent that a given measure is reconstructive the boundaries between research and practice/training are removed. With reconstructivity, our process measures are not only for research instruments, but also serve as standardized tools for training and therapy. Many of the process measures in this volume provide substantial reconstructivity, which makes them highly relevant for practitioner applications.

Before closing, I would like to leave the reader with an important perspective on process research that is developed in detail in the first and last chapters of this book. On those pages Greenberg and Pinsof discuss what I have called the "paradigm shift" in psychotherapy research (Kiesler, 1983). Another recent volume (Rice and Greenberg, 1984) has documented an important segment of this new research, and the trends have been comprehensively specified during a recent NIMH sponsored workshop on psychotherapy process research (Elkin, 1983; Elkin and Kiesler, 1986).

Two central conclusions set the stage for this emerging new approach. The first is that any study of psychotherapy process must directly target patient change if mean-ingful and heuristic findings are to emerge. No longer does it make any sense to per-petuate an artificial and spurious distinction between process and outcome research. If psychotherapy research is to build in any cumulative fashion, outcome-oriented re-searchers must integrate process measures into their investigations and process-oriented researchers must include measures of outcome. Regardless, then, of our particular em-phasis, we need to target important patient-change events occurring either in the ses-sion or concurrently outside the session. In this volume Stiles makes this point as fol-lows: ''An understanding of how psychotherapy works in the long term must rest on an understanding of how each encounter affects (or fails to affect) the client. There can be no long-term effects without short-term effects, even if the short-term effects are covert, requiring incubation or cumulation to some critical mass before appearing as major life changes'' (p. 184). The second conclusion is that our available theories of psy-chotherapy are too global or abstract to provide much guidance for identifying or dis-covering the significant change-process events occurring within or without the session. The result is that we need to develop, discover, or derive new ''miniature'' theories that elucidate smaller chunks of the change-process over the course of therapy.

In sum, the new ''process-change'' paradigm (Kiesler, 1983) for psychotherapy re-search involves study of patient-change events over the entire course of therapy and follow-up periods.

> Heuristic process research attempts to identify the more proximal patient-change events that occur in the therapy sessions themselves as well as the therapist activity and other transactional events that are contributory to these specific behavioral/experiential shifts. It further attempts to conceptualize and measure the hookups of specific in-session patient shifts (a) to concurrent extra-therapy patient shifts and (b) to later both in-session and extra-therapy patient changes. The cumulative empirical charting of these successive stages of events and their network of interrelationships throughout the entire therapy course and follow-up periods represents a comprehensive explanation of the process-outcome of a par-ticular therapy case. (Kiesler, 1983, p. 4)

Within this new process perspective, the long range significance of the present volume is that it makes an armamentarium of well-developed measures of the psychotherapy change-process available to us all as we pursue the goal of a more meaningful and com-prehensive understanding of psychotherapy. Our studies will require measurement of process variables at various levels of abstraction; employing different size units of trans-action; using sequential analyses as well as data-aggregate procedures; applying ex-perimental, quasi-experimental, and yet to be discovered methodologies; using group and single-case designs; applying both discovery oriented and hypothesis testing ap-proaches—at all times keeping in mind the transactional context in which therapy events occur wherein any factor may influence and be influenced by all other factors. Unques-tionably such a pursuit entails a quixotic journey towards a grandiose goal! Nonetheless, it's the only journey that offers any real excitement. One realization that can sustain our pursuit is that we have made definite progress, as this volume amply documents.

Donald J. Kiesler

References

DeRubeis, R., Hollon, S., Evans, M., & Bemis,K. Can psychotherapies for depression be discriminated? A systematic investigation of cognitive therapy and interpersonal therapy. *Journal of Consulting and Clinical Psychology*, 1982, *50*, 744–756.

Elkin, I. E. (Chair). NIMH workshop on psychotherapy process research. Bethesda, MD: National Institute of Mental Health, September 1983.

Elkin, I. E., & Kiesler, D. J. New directions in psychotherapy process research: Report of the 1983 NIMH workshop. Unpublished manuscript, National Institute of Mental Health.

Kiesler, D. J. *The process of psychotherapy: Empirical foundations and systems of analysis*. Chicago: Aldine, 1973.

Kiesler, D. J. The paradigm shift in psychotherapy process research. Summary discussant paper, NIMH workshop on psychotherapy process research. Bethesda, MD: National Institute of Mental Health, 1983.

Luborsky, L., Woody, G., McLellan, A., O'Brian, C., & Rosenzweig, J. Can independent judges recognize different psychotherapies? An experience with manual guided therapies. *Journal of Consulting and Clinical Psychology*, 1982, *50*, 49–62.

Pinsof, W. M. Family therapy process research. In A. Gurman & D. Kniskern (Eds.), *Handbook of family therapy*. New York: Brunner/Mazel, 1981.

Rice, L., & Greenberg, L. S. *Patterns of change: Intensive analysis of psychotherapy process*. New York: Guilford Press, 1984.

Preface

This book has three related goals. The first and primary goal is to stimulate research on the process of psychotherapy. The second goal is to expose the reader to innovative developments in the field of psychotherapy process research. The third and last goal is to consolidate methodological information on process research so that current and future investigators have a methodological base from which to proceed. We believe that this base must consist not only of the finished products of researchers' labors—instrument manuals and published reports—but also of a sense of the "process" of process research. Process research is arduous and frustrating, it is also challenging, exciting, creative, and fun. In addition to the final products, we want to give the reader a feeling of adventure of trying to unravel the mystery of psychotherapy.

Research on the process of therapy is designed to explore and determine how psychotherapy succeeds or fails. The major problem in conducting quantitative research is the tremendous complexity of psychotherapy. The methodological problems involved just in trying to describe psychotherapy scientifically are formidable. Foremost among them is the issue of instrumentation. To conduct process research we must have instruments or process analysis systems that reliably describe and analyze different aspects of the psychotherapeutic process.

This book is intended as a handbook on process research. In the first introductory chapter we attempt to describe the current "state of the art" and identify future directions for process research. The book is then divided into two major sections. The first, the substantive section, is a series of chapters each presenting a different process analysis system. The second section consists of three chapters dealing primarily with methodological issues or problems in process research. In essence, the first section presents the instruments and the second section illustrates and examines different ways in which they can be used to illuminate how psychotherapy works.

Over the last 30 years the field of process research has seen the development of a host of instruments designed to study the therapeutic process. In the first book devoted exclusively to process research, Kiesler (1973) summarized in encyclopedic fashion most of the existing individual therapy coding systems. Although a very significant advance, that book did not directly address the process of group and family therapy and, with the exception of the first chapter on research methodology, failed to give the reader a sense of the process of process research.

Since the publication of Kiesler's book, several things have happened. First, many of the process systems abstracted in Kiesler's book have fallen into disuse. A major problem in the area of process research is that each researcher or research team develops its own process analysis system, uses it once or twice, and then moves on to another system or abandons process research altogether. This makes it very difficult for knowledge to accumulate in any consistent fashion. Findings from one study with one system cannot easily be compared with findings from other studies with other systems.

Secondly, some new process analysis systems have come into existence since the publication of Kiesler's book. Some of these systems focus on group and family therapy, a major area of neglect in the early stages of the field, and some of them focus on individual treatment. In creating this book, we wanted to expose young (and old) researchers to what we consider to be some of the best process analysis systems for studying individual, family, and group therapy. "Best" in this context means three things: that the system is currently being used to study psychotherapy process; that the system has a high likelihood of continuing to be used; and lastly, that the system meets certain methodological criteria.

In planning this book we hoped to build on Kiesler's initial effort by including process analysis systems dealing with family and group therapy research, and by presenting them in a more accessible and personal fashion. Rather than summarizing coding systems, we decided to ask the authors of the systems we wanted to include in the book to present their systems themselves. To provide structure and to increase ease of system comparison, we gave each author (system creator) a detailed chapter outline to use as a guide (see page xvii), as well as stylistic guidelines. We wanted authors to present personal histories of their coding systems. These would provide the reader with a developmental understanding of both the process of process research and the process of the particular system being presented.

Each of the chapters in the first section of the book presents a biography of a process analysis system and a mini-manual on how to use the system. For those chapters dealing with observational coding systems, we also asked the authors to present at least one transcribed and coded segment of an actual therapy session to illustrate the way in which the coding system works. The personal, developmental style of the system chapters and the use of coded and transcribed segments of actual therapy sessions were both intended to make the system chapters as "user friendly" as possible.

In designing the book we wanted to include chapters covering different therapeutic modalities and orientations as well as chapters illustrating different research strategies and perspectives. For instance, the section on process analysis systems is divided into what Orlinsky and Howard (1978) call *nonparticipant* and *participant* observation systems, corresponding respectively to what have historically been called *observational* and *self-report* systems. We present 10 nonparticipant observation systems and 5 participant observation systems. We believe that both participant and nonparticipant measurement perspectives are essential to an adequate and comprehensive understanding of therapy process, and that neither perspective is inherently more epistemologically desirable or scientifically rigorous.

The field of process research is still focused primarily on the process of individual psychotherapy. However, we have attempted to include process analysis systems that can be applied to or have been designed to study group and family therapy process. The chapters by Stiles, Pinsof, and Benjamin and her colleagues examine the process of family therapy (which also includes marital therapy). The chapter by Beck and her colleagues examines the process of group therapy. Hopefully, the work presented in these chapters will stimulate others to pursue the scientifically neglected areas of family and group therapy process.

Nonparticipant process research, in addition to focusing primarily on individual psychotherapy, has also focused almost exclusively on verbal behavior. Fortunately, the chapter by Rice and Kerr, which studies vocal or paralinguistic aspects of therapy process, represents an important exception to the rule. We hope that in the future their excellent work will be joined by the work of others on additional nonverbal aspects of the therapeutic process.

Historically, the concept of process research has been limited primarily to the analysis of within-session variables; it is fortunately being expanded to include out-of-therapy process. The chapter by Phillips represents one of the first attempts to apply a process or *repeated measures* approach to the outcome of therapy. By including this chapter in the book, we hope to follow Kiesler's lead (1971) in calling for an end to the arbitrary *process* (in-therapy)/*outcome* (out-of-therapy) distinction. All of therapy is process, and process research encompasses the relationship between what goes on inside *and* outside the spatiotemporal limits of the psychotherapy sessions.

We have also attempted to include work coming out of various psychotherapy orientations. For instance, the chapters and systems by Klein and her colleagues, Rice and Kerr, Toukmanian, and Barrett-Lennard derive primarily from a client-centered orientation. The chapters by Suh and her colleagues at Vanderbilt, Alexander and Luborsky, Marmar and his colleagues at Langley Porter, and Sampson and Weiss, all come out of a psychodynamic or psychoanalytic tradition. The chapters and systems by Pinsof and Benjamin and her colleagues at Wisconsin are rooted in a systems or family orientation, although both can be applied to individual treatment and incorporate major components from a psychodynamic perspective. The chapters by Hill, Stiles, Orlinsky and Howard, Elliott, and Horvath and Greenberg are not strongly linked to any particular theoretical tradition and can be applied across different orientations.

Of the three chapters on methodology, the first two (Sampson and Weiss, and Beck and her colleagues) present research programs which are not linked to any particular process system, but which use a variety of systems to capture the overall process of treatment. We wanted to include these chapters because we believe that these two research programs represent very innovative and coordinated attempts to elucidate psychotherapy process. In addition to being one of the first programs to focus on group therapy process, the work of Beck's group represents a pioneering attempt to identify phases of treatment empirically. In the last chapter, Greenberg delineates various new strategies for process research, these, in conjunction with our recommendations in the first chapter, provide a number of guidelines and suggestions that will, we hope, facilitate future investigations of psychotherapy process.

The Society for Psychotherapy Research (SPR) has had a major influence on the development of this book. Most if not all of the contributors to the book have been active members of SPR and have spent numerous hours presenting and discussing process research at SPR meetings over the years. SPR has provided a wonderful forum for sharing our work with each other and for facilitating the establishment of a methodological base for the field.

We must acknowledge the limitations of this book. Unfortunately, due to the restrictions of time, energy, and space, we were not able to include all of the important work that is being done within the area of process research. The fact that a system or program is not included should by no means be taken as a reflection of the esteem with which we regard that system or program. We have included in the book only a sampling of what is important and worthwhile in the area of process research. There is much that we could not include in the population from which we sampled that is also significant and commendable.

A notable omission from this book that requires comment is a system for rating empathy from tape recordings of the interaction between the patient and the therapist. This omission does not reflect our selective bias against this type of procedure, but more the current state of the art in the measurement of tape-rated empathy. After a very active early life (Truax and Mitchell, 1971), tape-rated empathy did not hold up as a core condition, and a number of measurement and construct validity problems emerged with the predominant measures. Consequently, measures of tape-rated empathy have fallen into disuse. A new, more adequate measure has not emerged to date. We believe that rather than discarding this crucial area of inquiry, a systematic reinspection of the concept of empathy (and other similar interpersonal variables) and the issues involved in rating it from an observational perspective are required.

We would like to acknowlege the contributions of various people in the creation of this book. We thank Laura Rice and Andy Beck for suggesting that such a book needed to be done and encouraging us to do it. Irene Waskow at the National Institute of Mental Health has been a vocal and energetic supporter of this book from its inception; her support for process research has been and will continue to be invaluable. Don Kiesler's warmth, guidance, and support are deeply appreciated. Seymour Weingarten at the Guilford Press has been a wonderfully patient and helpful publisher. Lastly, we thank all of the contributors. Their time, energy, and thought will find its greatest reward in the research stimulated and guided by this book.

Leslie S. Greenberg   William M. Pinsof
North York, Ontario   Chicago, Illinois

References

Kiesler, D. J. Experimental designs in psychotherapy research. In A. Bergin & S. Garfield (Eds.), *Handbook of psychotherapy and behavior change: An empirical analysis.* New York: Wiley, 1971.

Kiesler, D. J. *The process of psychotherapy: Empirical foundations and systems of analysis.* Chicago: Aldine Publishing Co., 1973.

Orlinsky, D. E., and Howard, K. I. The relation of process to outcome in psychotherapy. In S. Garfield and A. Bergin (Eds.), *Handbook of psychotherapy and behavior change: An empirical analysis.* Second Edition. New York: Wiley, 1978.

Truax, C. R., and Mitchell, K. M. Research on certain therapist interpersonal skills in relation to process and outcome. In A. Bergin and S. Garfield (Eds.), *Handbook of psychotherapy and behavior change: An empirical analysis.* New York: Wiley, 1971.

Recommended Chapter Outline

This outline should be used as a guide for describing your system and research. Please feel free to ignore any questions that do not pertain to your work and/or add more information that might be helpful to the reader in understanding your work.

A. Present a brief summary and overview of your system specifying its purpose and how it functions.
B. Technical Aspects of the System
   Attempt to touch on most if not all of the following points. They do not necessarily have to be dealt with in the specified order.
   1. Coding system title:
      What do you call your system?
      What are the names of your scales?
   2. What variables are you trying to study with your system?
   3. From what theoretical orientation(s) does your system derive (psychoanalysis, client-centered, your own, etc.)? Briefly describe and provide references if available.
   4. What treatment modality or modalities (individual, group, family, etc.) and what orientations within that modality is your system designed to study? To date, to which modalities and orientations has it actually been applied?
   5. What access strategy or strategies does your system use (self-report, observational, mixed)?
   6. What communication channel or channels does your system target (verbal, paralinguistic, kinesic, mixed)?
   7. What data format does your system use (audiotape, videotape, transcripts, live coding, etc.)?
   8. Can your system be applied to any point in the process or do you select particular events for analysis?
   9. If you select events, what type are they and what criteria do you use to select them?
   10. Whose behavior is rated by your system (therapist, client, both, etc.)?
   11. How many scales does your system contain and what type are they (ordinal, nominal, interval, mixed)?
   12. What units does your system use? (see Kiesler, 1973, pp. 38–42).
       a. Scoring unit;
       b. Contextual unit (describe participant context);
       c. Summarizing unit (describe the unit to which statistical procedures are applied).
   13. Do you sample? If so, what, and how do you select your samples?
   14. Have you directly evaluated the representativeness of your samples (for instance, does a five minute sample accurately reflect behavior for the whole session?)?
   15. Coders—describe criteria for coder selection.
       a. Level of sophistication required to use your system;
       b. Clinical orientation (group, family, etc.);
       c. Training required to use your system.
   16. Do you have reliability data on your system? If so, how do you compute reliability? What statistic(s) do you use and do you train your coders to criterion and/or evaluate the actual reliability with which the data in each study are coded.
   17. Has any attempt been made to evaluate the dimensionality of your system (scales)? If so, please describe.
   18. What data analysis procedures have you used and/or are you planning to use (aggregate, sequential, statistics used, etc.)?
   19. If you have validity results from your system, please describe them.
C. Development and Application
   1. If you have an observational system, please apply it to two data segments that will highlight the assets of your system. Provide the segments and ratings.
   2. Discuss the origins and the process of development of the system with a potential system developer in mind. Offer suggestions and advice on system development and reflect on your personal creative process. Feel free to use the first person singular or plural (''I'' or ''we'') throughout your chapter.

INTRODUCTION

Process Research: Current Trends and Future Perspectives

Leslie S. Greenberg
York University
North York, Ontario

William M. Pinsof
Center for Family Studies/The Family Institute of Chicago
Northwestern University
Chicago, Illinois

Introduction

The process of psychotherapy has been an object of scientific study for approximately the last 30 years. By any standards, psychotherapy process research is a very young area of scientific inquiry. As with most new sciences, the first developmental phase has focused on the creation of instruments and methodology. Kiesler's (1973) book, the first devoted exclusively to process research, encyclopedically pulled together most of the methods and methodological expertise that had developed in the first two decades of the field's existence.

Within the last 10 years a number of new trends have begun to emerge in the area of process research which herald a new stage. Some clear processes are at work which give the field a greater sense of coherence and maturity. The field is moving out of its infancy into toddlerhood. The purpose of this chapter is to identify these trends and speculate about future developments in the field. This chapter sets the stage for the rest of the chapters in the book which we believe grow out of and will continue to shape these trends.

This chapter also represents our attempt to delineate the broad outlines of what we believe constitutes a new approach to psychotherapy research in general. This approach comes out of process research, but incorporates outcome research as well. We loosely refer to this emerging approach as "the new process perspective in psychotherapy research."

The New Conception of Process Research

The word "process" is a broad term. Dictionary definitions emphasize three related aspects of process: activity over time, directional change, and movement toward completion. Within the field of psychotherapy research, various definitions of process research have been proposed. Kiesler (1973), acknowledging the ambiguity and confusion around the definition of process research, defined it for his volume on process research, as:

> . . . any research investigation that, totally or in part, contains as its data some direct or indirect measurement of patient, therapist or dyadic (patient–therapist interaction) behavior in the therapy interview. (p. 2)

On the one hand, this definition emphasized a broad or generic sense of process research in contrast to emphasizing specific aspects of "behavior in the therapy interview," such as change or activity over time (sequential analysis). On the other hand, Kiesler's definition reflected a narrow sense of process research as pertaining solely to the domain of within-session behavior as opposed to behavior (typically of the patient) occurring outside of the interview. Historically, this latter domain has been defined as the realm of outcome research.

Kiesler's definition may have been more a heuristic device for delineating and thereby understandably limiting the scope of his book rather than an attempt to define the epistemological boundaries of process research. This conclusion emerges in the face of Kiesler's (1971, 1973) extensive comments on the problems inherent in making a strict distinction between process and outcome in psychotherapy research. He lamented the fact that the process–outcome distinction had perpetuated the use of pre- and posttreatment outcome designs which overlooked the form of the change function between the two points. Such designs precluded understanding the process or nature of change. Additionally, the process–outcome distinction created a false dichotomy in which in-therapy improvement or change was not seen as legitimate.

Over the last decade a shift has occurred in process research toward emphasizing the study of change. As psychotherapy began to be more extensively investigated and brought under all types of observation (video and audio), the process of change became more salient as an important target of investigation. With the greater availability of session recordings providing greater access to the inner workings of therapy, researchers, previously restricted to theoretical writings about change or to global therapist and patient recollections about therapy, began to feel more hopeful about tracking actual change processes.

The effect of recording therapy was complemented by the shift in the way in which young psychiatrists, psychologists, and social workers (the psychotherapy researchers of today) were trained in the 1960s and 1970s. During this period, clinicians were trained in a more open atmosphere in which they were frequently observed in the actual practice of psychotherapy (via tape and/or live supervision) and often had the opportunity to observe each other as well as master clinicians. As trainees in graduate school and subsequently as colleagues, we (the authors of this chapter) have spent many hours observing our work as therapists, consulting with each other, and discussing the vicissitudes of our practice. Theories, end goals, and the final outcomes of therapy were interesting, but it was the process of change which we ended up focusing upon and trying to facilitate in each other's work.

The opening up of therapy with recordings, one-way mirrors, and new training techniques began to shift the field's implicit definition of process research beyond a basic emphasis on the stream of behavior toward a greater concern with change and how it occurs. This trend was also encouraged by the growing social and political concern with demonstrating the efficacy of therapy. Process *per se* was not terribly relevant. It had to be linked to change.

Focusing process research on the process of change also had the serendipitous consequence of reducing the process–outcome dichotomy. Change inherently links process to some kind of outcome. Study of change integrates the essential strengths of both the process and outcome research traditions. It focuses the researcher on both the beginning and end points of treatment (or a treatment episode) and also attempts to identify the nature of the processes that lead to the change between the end points. Thus, process research ultimately becomes the study of mechanisms of change. This new emphasis on the description, explanation, and prediction of change is probably the most dramatic shift that has occurred since the publication of Kiesler's (1973) book.

We will return to the issue of the definition of process research after discussing below the specific trends in the field over the last decade and some of the new directions that are just beginning to emerge. We will conclude this chapter by offering a formal definition of psychotherapy process research that incorporates the theoretical and methodological conclusions manifested by these trends and new directions. This definition will be explicitly linked to the new process perspective mentioned above.

Major Trends in Process Research

The preceding section on the new conception of process research represents a summary condensation of the major trends in the field which have been emerging within the last decade. This section distinguishes and explores each of the major trends that lead to the new understanding of process research. As will be evident, these trends overlap considerably and emerge, to a significant extent, from the same underlying perspective—the new process "zeitgeist."

Integration of Process and Outcome Traditions

As mentioned above, historically the areas of process and outcome research were seen as separate domains. Process research pertained to what occurred within the spatiotemporal confines of the therapy session and outcome research pertained to patient change outside of the session. According to convention, outcome research was defined as research attempting to determine whether patients improved significantly (in the statistical sense) from the beginning to the end of therapy. A number of trends have converged to reduce if not eradicate the distinction between process and outcome research that Kiesler initially criticized. Interestingly, the trend has been bidirectional—outcome researchers and process researchers almost simultaneously have come to realize the necessity and value of integrating their two traditions.

From the outcome research perspective this integrative shift derives from the inevitable realization by outcome researchers that in order to develop a science of psychotherapy it was crucial to specify both *what* it was in psychotherapy that worked and *how* it worked (Bergin & Lambert, 1978). To say that something worked (or failed) without being able to specify what it was that worked undermines the replicability criterion of scientific research. A treatment or intervention that is allegedly effective cannot be reproduced if its essential characteristics cannot be determined and evaluated. To know that psychoanalytic treatment helped more patients in a study of anhedonia (inability to experience pleasure) than client-centered therapy is of minimal value if the researcher cannot specify what actually occurred in the respective therapies.

Basing outcome research on ascribed or alleged orientations without actual verification is equivalent to giving blue and green pills to patients in a drug study without knowing the contents of the pills. This realization led to recognizing the importance, in studies of therapeutic effects, of rigorous specification and control of treatment interventions delivered by the therapist in order to be able to make claims about what was bringing about the change in psychotherapy.

Along with the need to specify the treatment interventions delivered by the therapist, outcome researchers were further confronted with what drug therapy researchers call the "absorption problem"—did the patient receive and absorb the treatment that the therapist offered? Thus, it also became essential to look not only at the therapist's behavior, but also at the patient's experience of the therapy. More specifically, researchers needed to understand the patient processes that were induced by the therapist's interventions and associated with change. These realizations shifted outcome (and process) researchers' attention on to the specification of the in-session processes of the therapist and the patient.

As outcome researchers were coming to realize that outcome research without process or in-therapy measures could never illuminate the basic mechanisms of psychotherapy, process researchers were realizing that process research that is not eventually linked to some kind of outcome is ultimately irrelevant. For instance, to know that certain behavior therapists convey high levels of warmth and support to their patients during desensitization is interesting, particularly in regard to most behavior therapists' disregard of relationship issues, but ultimately such a finding is irrelevant unless it is linked to some kind of patient outcome. The critical question is did their high levels of warmth and support make any kind of meaningful difference? If process researchers were going to demonstrate the relevance of their work, they had to begin linking process or in-therapy variables to outcome or out-of-therapy variables.

As process and outcome research traditions began to converge the search began for process and outcome links. This initial quest led to some very distressing findings—in general, few studies found any significant relationship between any specific within-session process variable and any specific outcome variable (measured at termination and follow-up) which would hold up across more than one study or which could be replicated outside of a particular research group (Orlinsky & Howard, 1978; Parloff, Waskow, & Wolfe, 1978). Process researchers committed to the concept of specific effects for specific variables (typically and not coincidentally these researchers were also active clinicians and clinical teachers) offered various arguments to account for the lack of specific process–outcome findings. A major argument focused on the methodological shortcomings of the process–outcome research literature and argued for more sophisticated (specific) instruments, sampling procedures, and statistical methods. We will return to this methodological argument below.

The Conceptual Argument—Smaller is Better

Another major argument, implicit in much of the recent work in the process area, is primarily conceptual. It asserts that the conventional research strategies for studying process–outcome links are too demanding, if not altogether inappropriate for the examination of most therapeutic effects. Conventional research strategies for accessing process–outcome relationships usually involve relating some aspect of the in-session process at some point in treatment to the amount of pre–post change in the patient as measured at termination or follow-up. This strategy results in two types of research designs.

The first attempts to link some process variable, measured at some point in treatment, to outcome at termination or follow-up. This design is based on the expectation that a single event, or group of events, or the behavior of any particular variable, at a specific point in treatment (e.g., the 8th or 12th session) will be consistently related to the outcome of therapy after the full course of treatment (e.g., 40 or 50 sessions). This expectation is both extremely ambitious and somewhat naive. The possibility of other intervening events (within and outside of the therapy) affecting the outcome at termination is too great, unless the original events in question were so beneficial or traumatic that their effects could overwhelm subsequent experience.

Few psychotherapeutic experiences seems to be so potent for better or worse. The complexity and multiplicity of events over time will almost always weaken, if not negate the long-term impact of time-linked specific processes on termination-based outcome indices. Most psychotherapeutic effects that will be significant at termination are the result of the cumulative impact of a complex of events and factors that play out and accumulate over time. This is particularly true of long-term psychotherapeutic experiences.

The second design for linking process and outcome involves averaging process measures over the course of therapy and attempting to relate these averages to outcome at termination. Gurman's (1973) early research on the instability of certain therapeutic conditions and a considerable body of work on the Experiencing Scale (see Klein, Mathieu-Coughlin, & Kiesler, this volume) suggest that most therapeutic processes vary significantly both within single sessions and over the entire course of therapy, and that mean measures may obscure the variation that may be most related to outcome. For instance, with the Experiencing Scale, peak rather than mean indices seem to be most predictive of outcome.

Beyond the abovementioned problems, both of these research designs typically involve a variety of what Kiesler (1971) has referred to as "homogeneity myths," which critically oversimplify complex aspects of the psychotherapeutic situation and reduce the likelihood of elucidating psychotherapy. The primary myth that they embody from our perspective is the myth of the final, definitive outcome. Colloquially among process researchers, this has come to be referred to as the "Big O." Conventional designs for studying process and outcome have been based on the assumption or myth that outcome is a simple, static phenomenon that is best measured in some definitive sense at the conclusion of treatment or at follow-up.

Kiesler and others more recently (Rice & Greenberg, 1984) have argued for a "process approach" that views outcome as a fluid and continuous process that is not "best measured" at termination or any other single point. As the conventional process–outcome dichotomy disappears, outcome can be measured meaningfully at many points in treatment and follow-up. Outcome becomes a series of "little o's." From this perspective, psychotherapy research becomes the analysis of the processes that occur outside of the therapy sessions and processes that occur within the sessions and the interaction between them.

Replacing the process–outcome distinction with a within/outside session distinction also allows within-session variables to be conceptualized as outcome or effect variables. Outcome does not have to be confined to what occurs outside of the spatiotemporal confines of the therapy sessions. Ultimately, the process–outcome distinction is a matter of what Watzlawick, Beavin, and Jackson (1967) refer to as "the punctuation of the sequence of events" (p. 54). What is defined as a "process" and an "outcome" is arbitrary and relative. An intervention (a "process") can have various outcomes ranging from its immediate impact within the session (a "process–outcome"), to its longer-term impact after the session (a "little o"), to its even longer-term impact after termination (a "big O").

The abovementioned conceptual problems with conventional process–outcome designs call for the development of new strategies for accessing process–outcome links. Specifically, they suggest that we have been too ambitious and simplistic in our thinking about psychotherapy research. They lead to a new research strategy predicated upon a statement borrowed from the environmental movement of the 1970s—"smaller is better." This can also be referred to as the "small chunk" or "episode theory" of psychotherapy research.

This strategy attempts to elucidate the relationship between process and outcome variables that are more closely linked in time by focusing on smaller research units. It diminishes the likelihood of other events and experiences diluting or negating the process–outcome link. It involves a focus on what Pinsof (1981) referred to a "proximal" in contrast to "distal" outcome (p. 735).

Smaller units can be selected because of their theoretical relevance or because of their methodological utility and viability. Rice and Greenberg's (1984) recent book on process approaches focusing on particular classes of events or types of therapeutic episodes represents one manifestation of this "smaller is better" trend. The approaches presented in that book generally select their smaller units by virtue of their theoretical/clinical relevance. They particularly emphasize smaller units or episodes that contain patient behaviors that function as "markers" for specific therapeutic tasks and operations.

Pinsof and Lebow's (1986) research at the Family Institute of Chicago on the process and outcome of individual, couple, and family therapy represents a smaller unit approach based primarily on the methodological criterion of viability. It focuses on eight-session or unit chunks of therapy. Each case undergoes a major outcome evaluation every eight units (a unit is a week in which therapy has occurred, regardless of the number of sessions in that week). The eight-unit chunk seemed to be the smallest outcome unit, the evaluation of which would not place too great a research burden on the patients. Process data are collected during and after each session. The eight-unit chunk approach permits analysis of the process determinants of outcome within each chunk, as well as an additive analysis of multiple chunks that can be related to termination outcome.

Pinsof and Lebow's eight-unit or chunk model approximates a phase-guided process–outcome research strategy. Focusing specifically on phases, the work of Beck and her colleagues (this volume) on group therapy process examines the process patterns that are directly linked to specific, theoretically determined phases of therapy. Each phase has a process–outcome (within-therapy process) that indicates its successful completion and the group's readiness to proceed to the next phase. Combining Beck's emphasis on phase-linked process patterns with Pinsof and Lebow's focus on smaller process–outcome chunks, raises the possibility of using theoretically derived phases as smaller chunks of therapy that could be used as the building blocks of a cumulative, process–outcome analysis.

Focusing on short-term, smaller process–outcome units fits the current developmental stage of psychotherapy research far more than a focus on long-term links. The long-term findings may eventually be found, but they will have emerged out of the accumulation of evidence about the short-term links. In some ways, the "smaller is better" approach implicitly admits that we have been too grandiose in our expectations about process–outcome research. However, it must be remembered that it is no mean achievement to demonstrate a significant relationship between certain in-therapy processes and certain patient changes at certain points or during certain phases of therapy, even if those changes do not necessarily hold up at termination. Such knowledge lays the foundation for a scientific body of knowledge about how psychotherapy works.

In closing this section, it would be remiss not to mention an element of the "smaller is better" approach which has existed for many years and which has recently reemerged with greater prominence—the single-case or $N=1$ approach. Undoubtedly, Chassan (1967; 1981) has been the prime mover over the years in this area, articulating with considerable eloquence the shortcomings of the nomothetic or group approach and the virtues of the idiographic or single-case approach. The "smaller is better" approach is not identical to and should not be confused with the idiographic approach in that it can be realized with an idiographic or nomothetic methodology. However, researchers in the idiographic area have in fact been operating for years on the basis of many of the principles involved in the "smaller" approach. Recently researchers in the process area have used the idiographic method (case studies) to productively explore change events (Elliott, 1984; Greenberg, 1984; Rice & Saperia, 1984) and process–outcome links (Hill, Carter, & O'Farrel, 1983).

Micro, Context Specific Psychotherapy Theory

A major problem in the psychotherapy field which has retarded the development of psychotherapy research is that lack of clear, specific microtherapy theory that specifies what shoud occur when and the relationship between in-therapy and out-of-therapy processes at specific points in therapy (Pinsof, 1981). In order to continue refining and expanding the "smaller is better" research strategy, researchers need clinical theory more and more as a basis for determining where and when and what to look for in the course of therapy. Without good microtheory, research increasingly resembles a fishing expedition with a relatively low likelihood of discovering significant process–outcome links.

Clinical researchers have recently begun to develop more context specific microtheory. Rice and Greenberg's (1984) book presents various research programs that have effectively used clinical theory as a guide to the selection of moments and episodes (the "when") for empirical investigation. These programs also use clinical theory as a guide to select the process and outcome variables (the "what") to be examined in the episodes. Beck's research on group therapy (this volume) is an excellent example of how the elaboration of clinical theory can be used to guide sampling, the identification of variables, and the creation or selection of measures. The success of these programs in identifying change patterns may well derive from their theoretical specificity. The clinical theory clearly indicates where the researcher should look and what they should look for.

An interesting aspect of this issue is the potential impact of the small chunk research approach on the development of psychotherapy theory. Already, with the pressure to develop treatment manuals and compliance or adherence rating systems, the demands of research have forced clinicians or at least clinical researchers to refine and specify their theory. Now the emergence of the small chunk research strategy puts even more pressure on clinicians and clinical researchers to develop more specific microtheory about the mechanisms and process of change. This pressure represents an evolutionary or "naturally selective" force for the refinement and specification of psychotherapy theory which can only benefit therapists, trainees, and ultimately, patients.

The Therapeutic Alliance

Most, if not all psychotherapies and psychotherapists, acknowledge the importance of the relationship between the therapist and the patient. This relationship has been a major focus of psychotherapy research since Carl Rogers and his colleagues began exploring what Roger's (1957) called the core or "necessary and sufficient" conditions for change. Attempts to measure the core conditions from an observational perspective, particularly accurate empathy, initially looked very promising (Truax & Carkhuff, 1967), but eventually foundered on a number of conceptual and methodological problems (Lambert, Dejulio, & Stein, 1978; Mitchell, Bozarth, & Krauft, 1977). Barret-Lennard's work (this volume) on measuring the Rogerian conditions from a self-report perspective has been considerably more successful, but has not been widely employed outside of a client-centered framework.

After a temporary hiatus on relationship-oriented work in the process area, a number of research groups in North America simultaneously began to explore the concept of the Therapeutic Alliance as a, if not the, critical component of the relationship between the therapist and patient. The concept of the Therapeutic or Working Alliance emerged relatively early in the psychoanalytic literature (Bibring, 1937; Sterba, 1934) as a key component of the therapeutic process. However, only within the last decade has it begun to emerge as a research target in the process area.

That emergence was particularly facilitated by Bordin's (1975; 1979) integrative conceptualization in which both the relational bond and the tasks and goals of therapy are conceived as highly related components which combine synergistically to produce the Therapeutic Alliance. This conceptualization does not rigidly dichotomize general relationship factors and specific technical factors, but rather views the specific technical factors as requiring a particular type of relational bond; it is their correct combination which constitutes a good overall Alliance. This conceptualization holds great promise for combining "general" (relationship) and "specific" (technical) factors in a single overarching construct that does justice to the complexity of the processes involved in therapeutic change.

The general concept of the Therapeutic Alliance and particularly Bordin's integrative conceptualization offered psychotherapy researchers a new framework for examining the relationship between the therapist and the patient. Various North American research groups in the last decade developed instruments to measure the Alliance and have pursued the relationship between the Alliance as a process variable and a variety of outcome variables. A number of these instruments are presented in this volume.

The research from these groups supports the idea that the Alliance seems to be positively related to various outcome indices. The earliest empirical work was done by Luborsky and his colleagues at the University of Pennsylvania on the Penn Helping Alliance Scales (Alexander and Luborsky, this volume). They found that ratings of the *perceived helpfulness of the therapist* (Helping Alliance Type 1) and the *patient's collaboration or bonding with the therapist* (Helping Alliance Type 2) were fairly highly correlated with each other. Early session measures of the Helping Alliance based on the method of counting signs (observational) of the occurrence of Type I and II Alliances correlated between .57 and .59 with four outcome measures.

The work of Marmar, Marziali, Horowitz, and Weiss on the Therapeutic Alliance Rating System (Marmar *et al.*, this volume) focused on four theoretically defined subdimensions of the Alliance, termed *patient and therapist positive and negative contributions*. Their research revealed two consistent positive patient factors—*satisfaction with therapy* and *working capacity and commitment*. Results of predictive validity studies on this instrument are complex, with one study showing that an interaction between patient motivation for therapy and positive patient contribution correlated somewhat with general symptom change. Another study showed significant correlations with outcome for positive patient contribution (.25–.59) and negative therapist contribution (.27–.48).

Although not focused as explicitly on the Alliance, the work of Strupp and his colleagues on the Vanderbilt Psychotherapy Process Scale (Suh *et al.*, this volume), offers some indirect support for an Alliance–Outcome link. Their research has revealed a significant relationship between *patient involvement*, which consists of two subdimensions—*patient participation* and *patient hostility*, and outcome. They believe that patient involvement is an indicator of the alliance.

Along with these predominantly observational approaches to exploring the alliance, several research groups have taken a primarily self-report approach to the alliance. Two of these groups have based their instruments at least in part on Bordin's conceptualization of the Alliance as consisting of Task (perceived relevance of therapeutic tasks and techniques), Goal, (agreement on therapeutic goals and objectives), and Bond (relationship) subdimensions. At the University of British Columbia, Horvath and Greenberg (this volume) found significant correlations between their overall measure of the client's perception of the Working Alliance and self-reported measures of client change (.42–.49). The Task dimension components of the Working Alliance Inventory consistently showed the highest correlations with outcome (.50–.68) across different studies.

Pinsof and Catherall (1986) have developed the Integrative Psychotherapy Alliance Scales for measuring the Alliance in individual, couple and family therapy. They devised three scales, one for each context/modality. The Couple and Family Therapy Scales represent the first attempt to empirically assess the Alliance outside of the context of individual therapy. The Individual Therapy Alliance Scale goes beyond previous attempts to study the alliance in individual therapy by introducing a "systems approach" that also assesses the alliance between the therapist and the broader interpersonal system of which the patient is a part. Preliminary data support the reliability of the three Integrative Psychotherapy Alliance Scales and one study (Catherall, 1984) found that overall scores on each of the scales correlated positively and significantly with outcome (therapist ratings of progress to date) in each respective context.

The results on the patient and therapist rating system of the Therapeutic Alliance Rating System (Marmar *et al.*, this volume), showed that self-reported patient and therapist positive contributions were associated with improvements as rated posttherapy by patients, therapists, and clinical judges. Correlations ranged from .34 to .57 for patient contributions and from .37 to .52 for therapist contributions.

All of the abovementioned research on the Alliance, as well as other research in the area, demonstrates that the Alliance seems to have great potential as a potent predictor of outcome in a fairly wide variety of settings and contexts. What is particularly impressive is the capacity for the Alliance to be related to outcome when it is being measured in so many different ways at different research centers on different types of therapy. The robustness of the findings are unusual in the area of psychotherapy research.

However, a variety of cautions are necessary at this point. Before more measures of the Alliance are constructed and before more substantive tests of the Alliance are conducted, various conceptual and methodological problems need to be addressed. A major question concerning the construct validity of the measures is, are they measuring the same thing? On a more theoretical level, are the different research groups pursuing the

Alliance or even defining the Alliance in the same way? The titles of the scales (Psychotherapy Alliance, Working Alliance, Therapeutic Alliance, Helping Alliance, etc.) suggest that different constructs may be under investigation.

Another important and related question concerns the subdimensions of the Alliance. What are they and can they be empirically distinguished? Each research group and instrument conceptualizes the Alliance subdimensions differently. Do the subdimensions make any kind of meaningful difference or is it the overall Alliance measure or index which is most critical and valid? All of these conceptual and methodological questions need to be addressed before we become enmeshed in a confusing dialogue, believing we know what we are talking about and that we are all referring to the same phenomenon when possibly we are studying, measuring, and ultimately discussing different constructs.

As alluded to above, reconceptualizing the role of relationship variables in psychotherapy in the form of the working or therapeutic Alliance integrates the dichotomy between general and specific factors in the process of change. The integration occurs by taking a hierarchically structured view of change processes in which specific variables are nested within general variables. The specific variables shape and are involved in constituting the general variable, which in turn shapes the specific, more technical variables. Thus, the Alliance is not a factor unto itself, independent of technical factors, but rather is constituted in part by the doing of specific things in therapy that seem to make a difference. For instance, the Alliance in family and couple therapy may well be determined in the early stages of therapy by the therapist's activity level. Some research(Gurman, Kniskern, & Pinsof, 1986; Pinsof, 1981) evidence suggests that low therapist activity level is associated with premature terminations in family therapy.

Similarly, the particular quality of the alliance at particular points in therapy may or may not permit the successful implementation of certain techniques. For instance, to be successful, genetic transference interpretations probably require a somewhat different type of Alliance than is required by desensitization techniques. Stated differently, exploratory therapies may need a different type of Alliance than supportive and more behaviorally directive therapies. Specifically, the Bond subdimension of the Alliance may be more critical in exploratory therapies than in more behaviorally oriented treatments.

As indicated by the preceding review, the concept of the Alliance in psychotherapy process seems to hold great promise both theoretically and empirically. Research to date on the Alliance has been very encouraging, but the area has reached a stage where greater methodological and conceptual rigour are essential. The Alliance may well constitute a generic variable that can function as an integrating construct for relating general (relationship) and specific (technical) factors across different types of therapy and research settings. In this way, it might become a common thread or dimension providing greater coherence and intelligibility to the entire field of psychotherapy research.

Patient Involvement

Along with and closely related to the Alliance, the dimension of *degree of patient involvement* seems to have potential as a predictor of outcome and as an integrative construct for general and specific variables. Work on this dimension is just beginning to emerge and the area is not nearly as developed as the Alliance area. The conceptualization of Patient Involvement offered here as a generic variable is based on empirical findings and is a more empirically derived construct than the Alliance.

Findings from Alliance-related work show that patient participation, optimism, perceived task relevance, and responsibility are related to change. Similarly, research on the Experiencing Scale (Klein *et al.*, this volume) suggests that depth of Experiencing, a measure of a particular type of involvement important in experientially oriented therapies, is related to change. Taken together, all of these findings suggest a general patient variable—Involvement. Although similar to the Patient Involvement dimension identified by the Vanderbilt group, the Involvement construct we are discussing encompasses more subdimensions and targets a broader clinical phenomenon.

Although related to the concept of the Alliance, Patient Involvement differs enough to warrant separate consideration. The Alliance is a transactional variable that pertains to the system of interactional link created by the patient and the therapist. In contrast, Involvement is primarily a patient variable. It may well be that Involvement will emerge as the most critical patient subdimension and indicator of the Alliance. From this perspective, the Alliance occurs at a higher level of abstraction and ultimately subsumes the concept of Involvement.

Convergent research from different orientations supports the centrality of the Involvement dimension. Prior research has shown that depth of Experiencing and client-perceived empathy are important processes and are related to outcome in client-centered therapy. Additional support comes from research on the prognostic efficacy in client-centered therapy of a particular Client Vocal Quality which indicates involvement in internal processing (Rice & Kerr, this volume). When these client-centered measures are used in different therapeutic approaches the findings, however, are more complex, suggesting that different types of involvement are required in different types of therapy.

Research has also emerged supporting the relevance of Patient Involvement in psychoanalytic treatment. Bordin (1966) has shown that the ability to free associate is associated with productive psychotherapy. Sampson and Weiss (this volume) have found evidence that boldness of exploration is associated with progress in psychoanalytic psychotherapy.

These treatment specific findings suggest that appropriate involvement in different therapeutic tasks is related to change. More differentiated research is needed to unravel the issues involved in discriminating the different types of patient involvement that are productive in different tasks and treatments. In terms of future research possibilities, a general or pan-theoretical measure of Involvement, such as the Participation Scale of the Vanderbilt Psychotherapy Process Scale, could be complemented by orientation specific measures of Involvement. Different measures of Involvement could be developed for different approaches to therapy. For instance, in cognitive therapy, the concept of "inspection of evidence" could be operationalized as an orientation specific measure of Involvement. In behaviorally oriented family therapy, "completion of homework assignments" could be used as a indicator of Involvement. The development and application of such orientation specific measures, along with the use of more general measures of Involvement and the Alliance, would contribute significantly to our understanding of how patients engage in and change in psychotherapy.

Self-Report or Participant Observation Measures

Historically the area of psychotherapy research has been afflicted with a bias in favor of observational or what Orlinsky and Howard (1978) call nonparticipant methods of process analysis. Events or experiences observed by external observers or judges were accorded greater scientific validity than events or experiences reported or observed by participants. This bias led to the depreciation of self-report or what Orlinsky and Howard call participant observation measures and the overvaluation of observational methods.

Fortunately, this bias has begun to diminish, if not disappear within the last decade. Two major factors behind this shift have been the emergence of top quality instruments such as Orlinsky and Howard's *Therapy Session Report* (TSR) and Barret-Lennard's Relationship Inventory (both in this volume) and top quality theory to support the use of the these instruments (Orlinsky & Howard, 1978; also this volume). A third, and possibly the most critical factor has been the success of these self-report instruments (and the self-report instruments tapping the Alliance) in predicting outcome. Typically, the self-report measures have shown greater predictive validity (to outcome) than the observational measures.

This emergence of self-report measures hopefully will not lead to a flip-flop depreciation of observational instruments. Both approaches are necessary and ultimately complementary (Pinsof, 1981). They represent different access strategies and each strategy fits particular variables better than the other. Specifically, observational measures fit behavioral phenomena better and self-report instruments suit experiential phenomena better. A comprehensive process approach requires the use of both perspectives and the analysis of both types of phenomena (Elliott, 1983).

The same argument also fits the analysis of outcome data. It too requires both "inner" (patient report) and "outer" (therapist and observer report) perspectives, particularly as the process of change becomes a more focal research target. To understand the process and mechanisms of change what was "sent" and what was "received" must be examined.

Data Analysis: Context, Pattern and Sequence

Another critical shift in the process area over the last decade has been occurring in the area of data analysis. Historically, the predominant way of understanding process was to examine the frequency of some event at some point or points in time. Increasingly researchers became dissatisfied with this approach for a variety of reasons, foremost among them being the failure of the aggregate, frequency approach to reveal process–outcome links. Additionally, a frequency approach just did not seem to fit therapists' experience of therapy (Hertel, 1972). Advanced therapists do not operate in terms of frequencies; they perform acts in specific contexts and in specific sequences.

To remedy the problems inherent in frequency or aggregate data analysis strategies, researchers increasing turned to the techniques of sequential and contextual analysis. At this point we are referring to sequential and contextual approaches as essentially identical by virtue of the fact that they both examine events in context. This *event-in-context* approach is a generic methodology that can be realized with various research designs and statistical procedures. It is rooted in an epistemology that asserts that nothing can be known or ultimately even exists independently of the context in which it occurs.

This approach has been realized on a design level in the work of many of the research programs presented in Rice and Greenberg's (1984) book, *Patterns of Change*. Basically, these approaches examine what happens before and/or after some kind of critical event in therapy. The whole concept of change involves a shift in some variable from one state to another. At the minimum, the study of any change process requires the examination of a sequence of at least two events. In essence, the study of change requires comparing frequencies from at least two related time periods.

On the statistical level, this shift has been promoted through the development and/or application of sequential analysis procedures that go beyond the simple comparison of frequencies from related time periods. The simplest sequential statistic that has been widely used by behaviorists is the conditional probability that identifies, for a given set of data, the likelihood that event or state B will follow event or state A. Perhaps the most sophisticated statistic currently in use in the process area is lag sequential analysis (Sackett, 1978), a technique for identifying naturally occurring sequences of events or states. Lag sequential analysis can theoretically accommodate fairly long chains of events (e.g., four to eight events or states), indicating their frequency in a given set of data and the point at which the sequence approaches randomness.

Currently there is some dispute within the field as to the extent to which some of the more sophisticated sequential analysis techniques can ever truly elucidate the process of change. However, what is not in dispute is the emphasis on *patterns of processes in particular contexts* (Greenberg, this volume). The experience of the Vanderbilt group is particularly illuminating in this regard. Suh *et al.* (this volume) found that when they examined frequencies of process variables in the first three sessions they found no relationship to outcome, but when they examined the pattern of change in the variables over the first three sessions, process–outcome links began to emerge. Increases in therapist warmth and exploration, and in patient participation over the initial sessions were highly correlated with outcome.

As this research indicates, the specification of *when* in therapy particular processes are taking place and *how* they change over time is more likely to reveal process–outcome links than is a simple aggregate/frequency approach. This shift to a more complex view of *patterns of process in context* should greatly enhance the search for scientifically and clinically meaningful relationships between processes and outcomes.

The Development of Quality Methods

The last formal trend we will discuss concerns the emergence, within the last 10 to 15 years, of a variety of high-quality instruments for measuring the process of therapy. In many ways, this trend is the primary *raison d'être* of this book. A major effect of Kiesler's (1973) book was the dissemination of a set of methodological criteria for constructing and evaluating process systems. These criteria have been elaborated subsequently (Pinsof, 1981), but their initial presentation critically influenced the current generation of emerging process researchers.

The emphasis on process research as the study of change is not meant to minimize the importance of methodological research evaluating process instruments. Research that focuses on the construction of new instruments and the evaluation of their reliability and validity is essential. Most of the instruments presented in this volume need greater methodological evaluation. This statement is not meant to diminish their quality, but rather to make clear that the field is still very young and methodological concerns should not be set aside as we apply our measures to the study of change. In many cases, and particularly as we have discussed in regard to the Alliance research, it is still not clear exactly what our instruments are measuring and even in certain situations what they are intended to measure.

Although progress has been made over the last decades in the development of general measures of patient and therapist process variables, our ability to describe and reconstruct specific processes of change is still weak. The development and/or refinement of measures to capture specific change processes would greatly enhance our ability to explain and predict therapeutic change.

Future Developments

In discussing the major emerging trends in the field over the last decade we have more or less explicitly presented various recommendations for the field. In this section we move more explicitly into the exhortative position, identifying theoretical, empirical, and practical issues that we believe warrant serious consideration and future development.

Toward a Systemic View of the Psychotherapeutic Process

Historically, the field of psychotherapy research has been rooted in an individually oriented paradigm, in which the modal form of treatment is individual psychotherapy. When researchers and theorists working within this paradigm speak of psychotherapy research, they mean research on individual psychotherapy. With the emerging emphasis on family and marital psychotherapies, the individual paradigm no longer seems to fit the increasingly interpersonal and integrative nature of most psychotherapeutic practice. Although modern definitions of process research have attempted to include a "communications perspective" (Kiesler, 1973, p. 20) and to accommodate the pragmatic realities of group and family therapy (Orlinsky & Howard, 1978, pp. 284–285), they have not really incorporated the theoretical reality of what has been called *the systemic or systems perspective*.

A systems model of psychotherapy process views the interaction between the therapist(s) and patient(s) as occurring at the interface between two larger systems—the therapist system and the patient system. The therapeutic contract identifies the patient system as the system to be changed through the intervention of the therapist system. The therapist system consists of the therapist and all of the attendant systems that participate in providing treatment to the patient system. "The patient system consists of all the human systems . . . that are or may be involved in the maintenance or resolution of the presenting problem" (Pinsof, 1983, p. 20).

The concept of the patient system does not dictate which members of the system should be involved in what way at what point in treatment, but rather who gets onto the map of the relevant therapeutic terrain. It determines who must be considered in planning and ultimately understanding the process of treatment. In individual therapy, only one member of the patient system is involved directly in the treatment. In conjoint treatments, more than one member of the patient system is directly involved. Integrative treatment approaches directly involve different patient system members at different points in treatment. The central psychotherapeutic question in regard to the patient system is which members of the patient system should be involved in what way at which points in treatment to accomplish particular types of change.

The primary implication of a systems perspective is that the interaction between the patient system and the therapist system is a feedback loop or circle. The process of that loop is the process of therapy. The therapist system intervenes into the patient system, which in turn reacts to the therapist system, which in turn reacts to the patient system, which in turn reacts to the therapist system, and so on. Each major intervention reverberates throughout the patient system before it impacts the therapist system. For instance, encouraging a depressed man to be more assertive may lead him to confront his wife at home after the session. Her negative reaction to his new assertiveness may lead him to become more passive, which in turn may effect his capacity to engage in the treatment. As this example demonstrates, a systemic approach to psychotherapy process incorporates outcome or out-of-session variables into the process loop.

Methodologically, to complement our in-therapy process measures, we need to develop more instruments that are capable of describing and measuring out-of-therapy process. Along with such measures we need to continue developing data analysis strategies that permit us to identify process loops that lead to productive, desired endpoints as well as those that lead to destructive endpoints. To be comprehensive, such loops need to contain in-and-out-of-session measurements.

In terms of measures being developed, Pinsof's *Intersession Report* (1982), and Stiles' (1980) session evaluation questionnaire, administered before or after each session, hold promise for tapping patient changes that occur during or between sessions. Used as repeated measures, these instruments provide a profile of out-of-season changes during the course of therapy. Pinsof and Catherall's (1986) Individual Therapy Alliance Scale not only assesses the Alliance between the therapist and the individual patient, but also taps the patient's perception of the Alliance between the therapist and members of the patient system not directly involved in treatment. Phillips' (this volume) use of the Shapiro Personal Questionnaire and related techniques also demonstrates a very intriguing methodology for assessing the process of out-of-session change.

These instruments and methodologies begin to point the way toward a more systemic understanding of psychotherapy process. Hopefully, future investigations will build on this work, incorporating a systemic perspective into the study of psychotherapy process and psychotherapeutic change.

Toward a Multilevel Perspective

A comprehensive process analysis (Elliott, 1983) should attend to the different levels of action in psychotherapeutic systems. Greenberg (this volume) has proposed considering at least three hierarchically organized levels in any comprehensive process analysis—speech/action, episodes, and relationships. The interaction between the various levels occurs in the form of a circular, bidirectional feedback loop. For instance, the Alliance (relationship) in part determines the effect of specific techniques (speech/action) which in part determines the outcome of an episode which in part determines the Alliance, and so on. The causal process can also flow in the opposite direction.

A comprehensive battery of process instruments needs to be developed to assess these levels in such a way that activity on one can be related to activities on the others. Ideally, such a process battery would include instruments that would tap specific and general aspects of any particular treatment. Such a battery would facilitate the development of a common, multilevel process language that is capable of comparing and contrasting different treatments and change processes.

A multilevel perspective should not only include the three levels mentioned above, but should also consider at least the following levels of communication—kinesic, paralinguistic, and verbal. To date, the bulk of research in psychotherapy process has focused on the verbal level of communication. Psychotherapists of all persuasions agree that voice quality, facial expressions, and body posture are important aspects of psychotherapeutic communication, both for the therapist and the patient. Although the methodological problems in studying these nonverbal levels and types of communication are formidable, they desperately need to be addressed for the field to develop comprehensive theories of psychotherapeutic change. Hopefully, the work of Rice on voice quality in psychotherapy (Rice and Kerr, this volume) and Ekman in the area of facial expression (Ekman & Friesen, 1975) can serve to encourage process researchers to tackle these critical and virtually untapped dimensions of psychotherapy process.

Coordinated Research Programs

Psychotherapy research, and particularly the type of process-oriented research we have been discussing in this chapter, is very hard, time consuming, and expensive. The field is littered with one shot attempts to study process. We do not need more isolated process studies at this time. What we need are more concerted and sustained research programs pursuing, over extended periods of time, a series of leads. These leads are questions that grow out of research, that lead to more refined questions and research until finally some answers begin to emerge. By and large, the chapters in this book represent such programs. Their efforts need to be supported and sustained. Progressive programs of research (Lakatos, 1970) which build progressively from study to study are essential. It is only out of research programs of this sort that cumulative findings concerning a particular domain of change process will grow. It seems at this stage that rather than being able to evaluate grand or general theories in total, the task of psychotherapy research will be to build a network of findings that support or refute specific models derived concerning particular change processes. Such mini theories may eventually be connected by a general theory framework but it would suffice at present to be able to establish some hard facts concerning specific change processes of importance in psychotherapy.

Conclusion

At the beginning of this chapter we discussed the problems in previous definitions of psychotherapy process research and suggested some alternative conceptualizations. We will now present a definition of process research that incorporates many of the concepts and issues highlighted in this chapter. *Process research is the study of the interaction between the patient and therapist systems. The goal of process research is to identify the change processes in the interaction between these systems. Process research covers all of the behaviors and experiences of these systems, within and outside of the treatment sessions, which pertain to the process of change.*

We believe that the gap between conventionally defined psychotherapy research and the practice of psychotherapy (Luborsky, 1972) will be closed as research on the process of change develops. Process research, as defined above, speaks to clinicians because it ultimately is dedicated to informing them about how to become more effective change agents. The field of psychotherapy research will increase its relevance and impact by incorporating the new process perspective. In doing so, it gets to the heart of the psychotherapeutic endeavor.

References

Bergin, A., & Lambert, M. The evaluation of therapeutic outcomes. In S. Garfield & L. A. Bergin (Eds.), *Handbook of psychotherapy and behavior change*. New York: Wiley, 1978.

Bibring, E. Therapeutic results of psychoanalysis. *International Journal of Psychoanalysis*, 1937, *18*, 170–189.

Bordin, E. Free association: An experimental analogue of the psychoanalytic situation. In Gottschalk & Auerback (Eds.), *Methods of research in psychotherapy*. New York: Appleton Century Crofts, 1966.

Bordin, E. S. *The generalizability of the psychoanalytic concept of the working alliance.* Paper presented at the Society for Psychotherapy Research, Denver, Colorado, 1975.

Bordin, E. S. The generalizability of the psychoanalytic concept of the working alliance. *Psychotherapy: Theory, Research, and Practice*, 1979, *16*, 252–260.

Catherall, D. R. The psychotherapeutic alliance in family, marital and individual psychotherapy. Unpublished Doctoral Dissertation, Psychology Program, Department of Psychiatry and Behavioral Sciences, Northwestern University, 1984.

Chassan, J. *Research design in clinical psychology & psychiatry*. New York: Appleton Century Crofts, 1967.

Chassan, J. Some notes on the foundations and scope of intensive design. *The Journal of Psychiatry*, 1981, *44*, 34–38.

Ekman, P., & Friesen, W. *Unmasking the face*. Englewood Cliffs, N.J.: Prentice-Hall, 1975.

Elliott, R. Fitting process research to the practicing psychotherapist. *Psychotherapy: Theory Research & Practice*, 1983, *20*, 47–55.

Elliott, R. A discovery-oriented approach to significant events in psychotherapy: Interpersonal Process Recall and Comprehensive Process Analysis. In L. Rice & L. Greenberg (Eds.), *Patterns of change*. New York: Guilford, 1984.

Greenberg, L. A task analysis of intrapersonal conflict resolution. In L. Rice & L. Greenberg (Eds.), *Patterns of change*. New York: Guilford, 1984.

Greenberg, L. & Webster, M. Resolving decisional conflict by means of two-chair dialogue: Relating process to outcome. *Journal of Counseling Psychology*, 1982, *29*, 468–477.

Gurman, A. S. Instability of therapeutic conditions in psychotherapy. *Journal of Counseling Psychology*, 1973, *20*(1), 16–24.

Gurman, A. S., Kniskern, D. P., & Pinsof, W. Research on the process and outcome of marital and family therapy. In A. Bergin & S. Garfield (Eds.), *Handbook of psychotherapy and behavior change: An empirical analysis* (3rd ed.). New York: Wiley, 1986.

Hertel, R. Application of stochustic process analyses to the study of psychotherapeutic process. *Psychological Bulletin*, 1972, *77*, 421–430.

Hill, C., Carter, J., & O'Farrel, M. A case study of the process and outcome of time limited counseling. *Journal of Counseling Psychology*, 30, 1983, 26–30.

Kiesler, D. J. Experimental designs in psychotherapy research. In A. Bergin & S. Garfield (Eds.), *Handbook of psychotherapy and behavior change: An empirical analysis*. New York: Wiley, 1971.

Kiesler, D. J. *The process of psychotherapy*. Chicago: Aldine, 1973.

Lakatos, I. Falsification and the methodology of scientific research programmes. In I. Lakatos & A. Musgrove (Eds.), *Criticism and the growth of knowledge*. Cambridge: Cambridge University, 1970.

Lambert, M., Dejulio, S., & Stein, D. Therapist interpersonal skills: Process, outcome, methodological considreations and recommendations for future research. *Psychological Bulletin*, 1978, *85*, 467–489.

Luborsky, L. Research cannot yet influence clinical practice. In A. Bergin & H. Strupp (Eds.), *Changing frontiers in the science of psychotherapy*. Hawthorne, N.Y.: Aldine, 1972.

Mitchell, K., Bozarth, J., & Krauft, C. Reappraisal of the therapeutic effectiveness of accurate empathy, non-possessive warmth, and genuineness. In A. Gurman & A. Razin (Eds.), *Effective psychotherapy*. Elmsford, N.Y.: Pergamon Press, 1977.

Orlinsky, D. & Howard, K. The relation of process to outcome in psychotherapy. In S. Garfield and A. Bergin (Eds.), *Handbook of psychotherapy and behavior change: An empirical analysis* (2nd ed.). New York: Wiley, 1978.

Parloff, M., Waskow, I., & Wolfe, B. Research on therapist variables in relation to process and outcome. In S. Garfield & A. Bergin (Eds.), *Handbook of Psychotherapy and Behavior Change: An empirical analysis*. New York: Wiley, 1978.

Pinsof, W. M. Family therapy process research. In S. Gurman & D. Kniskern (Eds.), *The handbook of family therapy*. New York: Brunner/Mazel, 1981.

Pinsof, W. M. *The intersession report*. Unpublished instrument, Center for Family Studies/The Family Institute of Chicago, Institute of Psychiatry, Northwestern Memorial Hospital, 1982.

Pinsof, W. M. Integrative problem centered therapy: Toward the synthesis of family and individual psychotherapies. *Journal of Marital and Family Therapy*, 1983, *9*(1), 19–36.

Pinsof, W. M., & Catherall, D. R. The integrative psychotherapy alliance: Family, couple and individual therapy scales. *Journal of Marital and Family Therapy*, 1986, *12*(2).

Rice, L., & Saperia, E. Task analysis of the resolution of problematic reactions. In L. Rice & L. Greenberg (Eds.), *Patterns of change*. New York: Guilford, 1984.

Rice, L., & Greenberg, L. (Eds.), *Patterns of change*. New York: Guilford, 1984.

Sackett, A. (Ed.). *Observing behavior (Vol. II), data collection & analysis methods*. Baltimore, Md.: University Park Press, 1978.

Sterba, R. The fate of the ego in analytic therapy. *International Journal of Psychoanalysis*, 1934, *15*, 117–126.

Strupp, H., Hadley, S., & Gomes-Schwartz, B. *Psychotherapy for better or worse: An analysis of the problem of negative effects*. New York: Jason Aronson, 1977.

Truax, C. B., & Carkhuff, R. R. *Toward effective counseling and psychotherapy: Training and practice*. Chicago: Aldine, 1967.

Watzlawick, P., Beavin, J., & Jackson, D. *Pragmatics of human communication*. New York: Norton, 1967.

PROCESS ANALYSIS SYSTEMS

Nonparticipant Observation Systems

2

The Experiencing Scales

Marjorie H. Klein
University of Wisconsin
Madison, Wisconsin

Philippa Mathieu-Coughlan
Wesleyan University
Middletown, Connecticut

Donald J. Kiesler
Virginia Commonwealth University
Richmond, Virginia

Summary and Overview

The Experiencing Scale was developed from Gendlin's experiential and Rogers' client-centered theories to capture the essential quality of a client's involvement in psychotherapy. The concept of "experiencing" refers to the quality of a person's participation in therapy; by which we mean the extent to which inner referents become the felt data of attention, and the degree to which efforts are made to focus on, expand, and probe those data. The scale itself attempts to measure the way that these theoretically important levels of experiencing appear and are referred to in the client's speech during the therapy sessions.

The scale originated from a series of therapy process and outcome studies as a promising measure that related to client outcome in one of two ways: (1) as a quality or behavior that increased over time in more successful therapy, or (2) as present from the beginning and continuing throughout successful therapy (e.g., Gendlin, Beebe, Cassens, Klein, & Oberlander, 1968). Subsequent research, especially studies using more detailed ratings of longer segments of therapy, suggested that the Patient Experiencing Scale varies and goes through cycles within and across therapy sessions, and that both the level across therapy and the occurrence of particular patterns or peaks are related to successful outcome (e.g., Kiesler, 1971; Rogers, Gendlin, Kiesler, & Truax, 1967; Ryan, 1966).

The scale was designed for use with tape recordings and transcripts of individual therapy sessions, for units of 2–8 minutes in length. A number of methodological studies have addressed issues of unit length, sampling, data format, and methods of rater selection and training. A training manual presents the scale in detail, outlines rater training procedures, and includes practice materials (Klein, Mathieu, Gendlin & Kiesler, 1969). Excellent rater reliabilities have been obtained using this manual.

Aside from individual therapy, the scale has been applied to other interactional formats such as monologues, structured interviews, group therapy, and Gestalt two-chair exercises; and to therapy from different theoretical orientations, for example, dynamic, psychoanalytic, Gestalt, and cognitive. The scale has also been successfully used for written materials such as personal documents and responses to open-ended questions.

In addition to the basic Patient Experiencing Scale, we have recently made efforts to adapt the rating method to group interactions, therapist behavior, and standardized assessment interviews. These adaptations will be described later in this chapter.

Technical Description of the Experiencing Scale

The Patient Experiencing (EXP) Scale consists of one 7-point scale designed to be applied to tape recordings or transcripts of psychotherapy (Klein *et al.*, 1969; Kiesler, 1973). The seven scale "stages" or steps define the progression of client involvement in inner referents from impersonal (1) or superficial (2), through externalized or limited references to feelings (3), to direct inner referents (4), to questioning an unclear inner referent (5), to focusing with a step of resolution (6), and finally to the point where focusing comes easily and provides the connections for inner discourse (7).

Scale Stages

These general descriptions of each of the seven scale stages are amplified considerably in the manual (Klein *et al.*, 1969) and also outlined in Table 2-1. Examples of ratings can be found on pages 61–66. (We do not recommend that the scale be used without this additional detail and the standard training procedures.)

Stage 1   The chief characteristic of this stage is that the content or manner of expression is impersonal. In some cases the content is intrinsically impersonal, being a very abstract, general, superficial, or journalistic account of events or ideas with no personal referent established. In other cases, despite the personal nature of the content, the speaker's involvement is impersonal, so that he or she reveals nothing important about the self and the remarks could as well be about a stranger or an object. As a result feelings are avoided and personal involvement is absent from communication.

Table 2-1   Short Form of Experiencing Scale (Patient)

Stage	Content	Treatment
1	External events; refusal to participate	Impersonal, detached
2	External events; behavioral or intellectual self-description	Interested, personal, self-participation
3	Personal reactions to external events; limited self-descriptions; behavioral descriptions of feelings	Reactive, emotionally involved
4	Descriptions of feelings and personal experiences	Self-descriptive; associative
5	Problems or propositions about feelings and personal experiences	Exploratory, elaborative, hypothetical
6	Felt sense of an inner referent	Focused on there being more about "it"
7	A series of felt senses connecting the content	Evolving, emergent

Note. Copyright 1970 by The Regents of the University of Wisconsin. Revised, 1983.

Stage 2   The association between the speaker and the content is explicit. Either the speaker is the central character in the narrative or his or her interest is clear. The speaker's involvement, however, does not go beyond the specific situation or content. All comments, associations, reactions, and remarks serve to get the story or idea across but do not refer to or define the speaker's feelings. Thus the personal perspective emerges somewhat to indicate an intellectual interest or general, but superficial, involvement.

Stage 3   The content is a narrative or a description of the speaker in external or behavioral terms with added comments on feelings or private experiences. These remarks are limited to the events or situations described, giving the narrative a personal touch without describing the speaker more generally.

Self-descriptions restricted to specific situations or roles are also part of Stage 3. Thus feelings and personal reactions come into clear but limited perspective. They are "owned" but bypassed or rooted in external circumstances.

Stage 4   At Stage 4 the quality of involvement or "set" shifts to the speaker's attention to the subjective felt flow of experience as referent, rather than to events or abstractions. The content is a clear presentation of the speaker's feelings, giving a personal, internal perspective or account of feelings about the self. Feelings or the experience of events, rather than the events themselves, are the subject of the discourse, requiring the speaker to attempt to hold on to inner referents. By attending to and presenting this experiencing, the speaker communicates what it is like to be him or her. These interior views are presented, listed, or described, but are not the focus for purposeful self-examination or elaboration.

Stage 5   The content is a purposeful elaboration or exploration of the speaker's feelings and experiencing. There are two necessary components: First, the speaker must pose or define a problem, proposition, or question about the self explicitly in terms of feelings. The problem or proposition may involve the origin, sequence, or implications of feelings or relate feelings to other private processes. Second, the speaker must explore or work with the problem in a personal way. The exploration or elaboration must be clearly related to the initial proposition and must contain inner references that have the potential to expand the speaker's awareness of experiencing. These may also be evidence of and/or references to the process of groping or exploration itself.

Stage 6   At Stage 6 the way the person senses the inner referent is different. There is a *felt sense* of the there-and-yet-to-be-fully-discovered, that is, of an unclear inner referent that has a life of its own. It is a sense of potentially more than can be immediately thought or named. This felt sense is more than recognizable feelings such as anger, joy, fear, sadness, or "that feeling of helplessness." If familiar or known feelings are present, there is also a sense of "more" that comes along with the identified feelings.

Stage 7   The content reveals the speaker's steady and expanding awareness of immediately present feelings and internal processes. He or she clearly demonstrates the ability to move from one inner referent to another, linking and integrating each immediately felt nuance as it occurs in the present experiential moment, so that each new sensing functions as a springboard for further exploration and elaboration.

Variables

The scale is multidimensional and complex in that definitions and rating criteria for each stage include a range of domains (see Table 2-2). Grammatical criteria, especially the use of first-person pronouns, are important in the distinction between Stages 1 and 2. Questions and the subjunctive mood are important at Stage 5. Expressive–stylistic indicators of remoteness versus immediacy and freshness of feeling are relevant throughout the scale, but are especially germane to Stage 6, where evidence of direct sensing and fresh, changing experience is important. Paralinguistic indicators such as speech fluency versus disruption are also considered; for example, pauses and other indicators of dysfluency, when coupled with other criteria, are important for Stages 5, 6, and 7.

Throughout the scale content may also vary, not in the sense that the stages are about different topics, but in the sense that the speaker's perspective or point of view toward them changes: Stage 2 discourse is most likely to be a narrative of events or an abstract–intellectual presentation of ideas. Stage 3 involves brief references to feelings with limited situational or behavioral elaboration. At Stage 4 and beyond, there is an important shift in focus; the ideas, situations, or specific feelings described may be similar to lower stages, but the focus is now *on* the speaker's subjective account, so that the "story" is about personal associations and feelings rather than about events or actions. At Stage 5 questions are posed about this inner referent to be explored and elaborated. Focusing or direct sensing of the unclear "edges" of the referent with a new awareness

Table 2-2   Additional Stage Criteria

Scale Stage	Grammatical	Expressive	Paralinguistic	Content
1	No first-person pronouns; past or present tense	Remote, impersonal	Fluent	Impersonal, others' activities or events
2	Personal pronouns; past or present tense	Interested, intellectual	Usually fluent	Ideas, events, actions
3	Personal pronouns; past or present tense	Limited reactions	Some affect indicators, e.g., laughs, sighs	Parenthetical or limited references to feelings
4	Present or past tense	Immediate, expressive	Focused voice, expressions of affect	Subjective experiences and associations
5	Present tense, but past can be included; Subjunctive, tense questions	Immediate, groping, tense, tentative	Dysfluency	Questions about unclarity in own awareness
6	Present tense or vivid representation of past	Declarative, fresh, real	Exclamation, alternations of dysfluency and fluency, pauses	Directly sensed and emergent feeling
7	Present tense primarily	Affirmative	More fluency than dysfluency	What one "knows" for oneself

defines Stage 6. At Stage 7 the process of focusing comes easily, so that inner referents become a comfortable basis for discourse.

All of these criteria are meant to tap what is assumed to be an important general quality of a patient's working engagement in psychotherapy. While derived from phenomenological and client-centered therapy, the general construct—experiencing—is assumed to be important for a wide range of therapy and/or change situations. The concept of experiencing has been described and elaborated in great detail by Gendlin. It can be most simply stated as an individual's direct feel of "the whole complexity of one's living" (Gendlin, 1979, p. 323). Experiencing is always a composite of what one distinctly "senses" and the feel that there is more that, with effort, could be sensed. Experiencing may involve, but will never be just equal to, emotions, words, concepts, and muscle movements.

It is also important to state considerations and criteria that we have tried to eliminate or avoid in defining the scale so that it would be independent of these factors. We have tried to keep the scale definitions and rating instructions free of details of diagnosis, the patient's specific complaint or problem, personality, the style (largely), rate, and tone of speech, specific affective state, specific topic, or topic sequence. In training, we have particularly tried to discourage raters from confusing stage judgments with judgments about the clinical or dynamic importance of topics, the appropriateness of therapists' remarks, the techniques or goals of the therapy, aspects of the patient–therapist interaction, or liking for the patient or therapist. Aside from its concentration on feelings and personal meanings as core content, the scale makes no stipulations about what is presented or discussed, about the specific affective coloration of feelings, or even, to some degree, about the intensity of the feelings described. Topics such as dreams, hallucinations, and altered states of consciousness are not automatically rated high unless they are told experientially. Similarly, defensive states are not automatically downgraded unless they result in avoidance, isolation, intellectualization, or the like.

The deliberate exclusion of these considerations from the rating task should not be taken to mean that the scale is entirely independent of them. It is certainly not inconsistent theoretically to find EXP ratings related to diagnosis, severity of disturbance, expressiveness versus defensiveness, comfort with the therapist, et cetera. Indeed such relationships have contributed to the validity of the scale (see Dimensionality section). At the same time, it is critical that the rating technique be maximally freed of these variables if the scale is to serve as a general research tool.

Theoretical Base

Client-centered theory provided the context within which experiencing became defined and recognized as a factor related to successful therapy. Rogers and Gendlin contributed in discrete and complementary ways toward an understanding of what experiencing is and in what ways it contributes to the process of psychotherapy. As early as 1950 Rogers had labeled "experiencing" as the client's sense of exploring his or her perceptual field (Rogers, 1950). While client-centered theory with Rogers as its architect had "discovered" experiencing through the material gathered via direct observations of therapy hours, Gendlin was approaching the same phenomenon from the perspective of the phenomenological philosophers. It was primarily the writings of Merleau-Ponty and Husserl that led Gendlin in the direction of psychotherapy as a possible source of *in vivo* phenomenological processes (Gendlin, 1958). In this association Rogers and

Gendlin had separately arrived at a concept of a process that is central to authentic and in-depth self-understanding.

At about this time (the early and mid-1950s) Rogers was also launching what was to become a historic contribution to the field of psychotherapy theory and research—the pioneer empirical study involving, for the first time, the use of tape-recorded therapy hours (Rogers & Dymond, 1954). As a part of Rogers' research team at Chicago, Gendlin collaboratively (Gendlin & Zimring, 1955; Gendlin, Jenney, & Shlein, 1960) sought to identify the experiencing process, first inferentially via characteristics of the client's verbal expression and behavior such as richness of detail; and subsequently by devising a scale that would allow the counselor to estimate the level of the client's immediate experiencing.

By 1959 Rogers had set forth a new concept in the client-centered model, which until then had dealt with methods for doing psychotherapy. The new concept was that of optimal personality functioning, which he termed the fully functioning person (Rogers, 1959a). This addition to the theory was the logical but enlightened outgrowth of what Rogers had seen to be the ''process'' of therapy, whereby the goal of successful therapy would be for the person to be able to be open to his or her feelings, feelings that may constantly change as the person is fully engaged in the process of living. Thus the goal of successful psychotherapy became a definition of an optimal level of personality functioning. The process focused on as the means by which the person in therapy moves from rigidity to fluidity, from closed to open, and thence to awareness, Rogers defined movement involving seven strands, five of which refer to the therapy setting and two of which concentrate on feelings and experience (Rogers, 1958; Walker, Rablen, & Rogers, 1960): (1) *Communication of self* involves the person's willingness to talk about self freely. (2) *Personal constructs* focuses on the person's sense of being able to change aspects of the self—that is, how autonomous the person feels in bringing about change in the self. (3) *Relationship to problem* is concerned with how problems are defined and experienced. (4) *Manner of relating* measures the person's openness to feelings in an interpersonal (e.g., therapeutic) context. (5) *Incongruence* relates to the degree of similarity or dissimilarity between the person's objective experiences (as an outsider would perceive them) and the person's private representation of those experiences (e.g., in therapy). The remaining two strands are concerned with the quality of the person's awareness, acceptance of inner feelings, and the extent to which those inner feelings are used for further thought, self-exploration, and action, that is, (6) *relationship to feelings and personal meanings* and (7) *manner of experiencing*.

The seventh, experiencing strand clearly bore the influence of Gendlin's theoretical and empirical efforts, which had defined experiencing as the basic felt referent of awareness that can progress from elusive to clear. Thus defined, experiencing was dynamic and not static. This allowed Rogers to reconcile his concepts of pathology and personality change so that pathology is anchored at the lower end of the experiencing dimension and personality change and growth emerge at the higher end. Experiencing thereby became the critical vehicle by which that movement from rigidity to fluidity was verbally manifested in the therapy interactions. Thus, by 1959, coming from different orientations, theoretical and empirical, Gendlin and Rogers had collaboratively developed the experiencing construct, a critical element in the client-centered model for both the practice of psychotherapy and the measurement of personality change.

From 1960 to 1969 continuous efforts were made to instrumentalize the experiencing construct (Gendlin & Tomlinson, 1962; Gendlin & Tomlinson, 1967; Tomlinson, 1962a; Tomlinson, 1962b; Tomlinson & Hart, 1962; Rogers, 1958; Rogers, 1959b; Walker *et al.*,

1960; Rogers *et al.*, 1967). This work culminated in the present form of the scale (Klein *et al.*, 1969).

In his original work in 1962 Gendlin used the term "experiencing" to describe the "concrete . . . ongoing functioning [in us] of what is usually called experience" (Gendlin, 1962b, p. 11); it is the basic felt datum of our inwardly directed attention. It involves our preverbal, preconceptual, bodily sense of being in interaction with the environment, a guts-level sense of the felt meaning of things. This includes the feeling of having experience and the continuous stream of sensations, impressions, somatic events, feelings, reflexive awareness, and cognitive meanings that make up one's phenomenological field. Experiencing is not a reenactment of events, but includes their personally felt significance. It is not a set of concepts or logical operations; rather it is the inner referent used to anchor concepts. Also, experiencing is not simply the experience of affect, self-consciousness, or self-management. The term includes the broader band of implicit meanings that structure sensations and feelings and articulate one's sense of continuity by supplying the personal coloring of events and the personal significance of one's reaction to them.

Experiencing, as the basic referent of inwardly focused attention, can exist or be symbolized in different modes. Although it is essentially complex, changeable, and even irreducible, it can be structured indefinitely, carried forward, used as the basis for action, and provide feedback to produce an experiential effect or shift. In his more recent work Gendlin has increasingly specified steps of experiential unfolding or change, including felt referent, focusing on unclear edges of the referent, felt shifts in which new experiencing is released, and carrying forward where experiencing provides continuity and direction from the past-through-present to future and gives rise to a quality of wholeness and authenticity (Gendlin, 1964; 1967; 1969; 1974a; 1974b; 1979; 1981; 1982).

This construct is relevant to psychotherapy because it specifies alterations in a person's functioning which are essential for personality change. In this sense the experiencing conception is theoretically relevant to any therapeutic or personal growth situation. Gendlin's assumption is that experiencing defines the basic and essential processes that lead to change and health (i.e., the "how" of change). Thus the variable should be important for and measurable in all therapeutic contexts, that is, independent from the details or theoretical focus of specific schools or techniques (which provide the "what" or the "who"). While the construct spells out the means by which personality change and growth occur, it cannot be considered as an end in itself, that is, it is related, but not equivalent, to a conception of health or outcome.

Treatment Modalities

The Experiencing Scale was originally designed to be applied to the material of individual psychotherapy in units of from 2 to 8 minutes in length. However, there are no theoretical or instrumentational limitations that would confine the use of the scale to individual therapy or to brief segments. In fact, wherever an individual's speech can be isolated to be rated, the scale can be applied. Consequently, groups, couples, Gestalt two-chair exercises, and monologues have all been reliably rated (see Reliability section). The scale has also been able to accommodate therapy from different theoretical orientations, including dynamic, psychoanalytic, Gestalt, and cognitive. While the scale can be applied to a variety of formats and orientations, it is the basic responsibility of the researcher to determine how the construct and the data generated by the scale relate to the theoretical questions being asked in any particular study. (Some of the more detailed aspects of this issue are discussed in the Selection of Events and Sampling and Whose Behavior Is Rated—Patient sections of this chapter.)

The fact that the scale is topic free and can be applied to many instances of verbal behavior opens an array of potential applications and comparisons outside the traditional dyadic and group models. For example, comparisons could be made of EXP levels within and outside of therapy for different patient types or different therapeutic modalities, thus relating in-therapy achievement to more generalized behavior.

Access Strategy

The Experiencing Scale uses an observational rather than a self-report access strategy. The instrument was designed to be used by raters who have been thoroughly trained in applying the various scale stage judgments to typescripts and recordings of patient speech during actual psychotherapy. It is presumed that the raters will have achieved an acceptable level of interrater reliability before embarking on any data-collection task. It is also assumed that the raters are not the therapist (or the client) and that they are blind to important information about the research design.

Communication Channels—Mixed

It is important to distinguish among three levels of abstraction: (1) the underlying construct, (2) the way that the scale is meant to reflect or incorporate that construct, and (3) the operational criteria that raters are directed to consider in making their ratings. An awareness of the differences among these three levels is important both for rater training and for data interpretation.

The experiencing *construct*, as described above, refers to an individual's phenomenology. The scale, as developed, was specifically designed to measure or reflect the status of a client's *engagement in* and *manifest communication from* that experiencing in a therapy session. While it was assumed that the scale ratings would reflect the patient's phenomenological status, it was further assumed that for a therapy scale, it was essential that the patient be able and willing to manifest his or her experiencing in words in the presence of the therapist. Thus the scale is specifically directed at communication about experiencing since it assumes that people do not communicate about that which they do not experience, while leaving open the possibility that people may not always tell all that they do experience. The *stage criteria* and channels of communication that raters must actually consider in making ratings are complex and mixed, but more specific still. As laid out in the Scale Stages section and in Table 2-2, ratings incorporate judgments about grammatical, stylistic, paralinguistic, and content or topical issues simultaneously.

This transformation or translation of the construct into more concrete indicators was done deliberately to increase the reliability of the rating task. Rather than ask raters to make complex inferences about subtle or unobservable phenomenological events or to second guess the patient's motivation and communication, we request a more straightforward judgment. From these judgments, which have proved reliable, we can take the inferential steps about communication in therapy or about experiential state as we choose.

Data Format

Experiencing Scale ratings can be made from a variety of data formats. While originally and still most often used with either tape recordings and/or transcripts (less often with videotapes) of therapy dyads, the scale can and has been used with such first-person data as monologues, biographical essays, personal statements, responses to interviews, and open-ended questionnaires.

In an effort to determine what, if any, relationship existed between EXP ratings and the form in which the data were presented to the raters, Klein (1971) compared tape and transcript materials for 48 segments representing a range of patient types and therapy orientations. The 48 segments were divided into three blocks of 16 segments each, and three raters rated the three blocks under three different "formats": audio only, transcript only, and both audio and transcript (with the sequence of the methods varied for each rater according to a Latin square design). The findings indicated that peak ratings of the transcripts only were higher than for audio only segments of the same data. Just why this should be is not clear, but this study does suggest that the way the data are presented to the raters should be consistent in format within any one study.

In vivo ratings are also possible but are more suited to clinical than to research uses. Since the rater-training process is essentially an exercise in attending to what is being said by the patient, we and others (e.g., Hinterkopf & Brunswick, 1981) have found it to be of value in cultivating good "listening skills" on the part of therapists-in-training.

Selection of Events and Sampling

The scale can be applied to any point in the therapy sequence where there is appropriate material, that is, verbalizations of the person to be rated. While the system does not especially restrict the scale's use, the real decision as to where in the overall process it should be applied (as well as decisions as to location and length of segments) should be carefully considered by the researcher if meaningful data are to be generated. For example, if the scale is to be used as a prognostic index, then events from early in therapy are more relevant; if the questions posed have to do with change, then clearly both early and late points are necessary for comparison, and the more the better. Estimates of optimal EXP level (i.e., health) can be made from a single designated unit, provided the patient or subject is in a setting where there is opportunity, even encouragement, for high-level functioning (e.g., where an interviewer attempts to maximize EXP).

Neither we, the scale, nor the theory dictate any particular events for analysis. However, there is no reason why particular events should not be chosen as part of a research rationale, for example: (1) moments thought to relate to events that are personally important for either the patient or the therapist (e.g., the therapist's absence, a family crisis); or (2) theoretically relevant points where the experiencing level of the patient might be thought to change or to reach a specified level as a function of a particular therapeutic technique or intervention (i.e., the incorporation of family members in the session).

As a general rule, it is important to sample from *at least* two time periods in therapy, especially if EXP is to be considered in relation to outcome criteria. Some of the past studies suggest that it is also desirable to include samples from the midpoint or working phase of therapy (e.g., Ryan, 1966). Sampling only initial and terminal hours risks missing the patient's actual work and progress and getting instead early routine arrangements, goal setting and history taking, or termination material involving future plans, external details, a review of progress, or a period when defenses are deliberately reinstituted. Also, since some studies have shown that we cannot expect a strictly linear trend for EXP, the more samples that are taken from each case, the greater is the likelihood of getting reliable estimates of the variability, range, and trend of EXP.

The question of where within the therapy hour to draw samples for EXP ratings was addressed specifically by Kiesler, Klein, and Mathieu (1965) and more generally by Mintz (1969). In Mintz's study, EXP and other process ratings of 4-minute segments were found to be highly correlated with ratings of the hour as a whole, indicating the adequacy of a brief sampling. Some of the results of our 1965 study suggest complexities. In that study we found that EXP varied across the hour and yielded different profiles for different diagnostic groups, suggesting that different sampling methods had different informational value. To check on this, two random samples were drawn from the same data and the results were compared with those obtained for the five systematically obtained time blocks. Different profiles of significance were obtained: One of the random samples and the later time blocks reflected differences among groups; the other random sample and the earlier time blocks did not.

There are two concerns here. The first is that sampling randomly from a small number of cases to make comparisons among groups may miss the very data that would differentiate the groups. The second concern is that the apparent relationship between time within the hour and process may bias or confound data. In our 1965 study the group differences emerged most noticeably toward the end of the hour, suggesting that time within the hour is a potentially powerful basis for sampling. But if time is not chosen as a basis for sampling, its potentially confounding effect must be controlled or at least considered. In studies where the focus is on the characterization of a fairly homogeneous patient group, sampling a single time period within the hour may well control for the effect of time, but may not reflect the highest levels or full range of EXP operative in that group. In studies where a number of groups are considered, standardized sampling may maximize or obscure differences; it may favor one group over another, or in some other way distort the pattern that exists. Other criteria for systematic sampling—for example, around certain patient–therapist interactions, behaviors, feelings, or content—may be more appropriate for specific research interests. Sampling decisions must be tailored to hypotheses, and are best based on previous data for all groups included in the study or on pilot analyses of EXP trends over a few complete hours for a few cases.

In sum, random sampling may provide data more representative of the range of process in a given group and may afford more equitable coverage of several groups, provided the number of observations is sufficiently large that the bias from unequal representation of certain interview points is minimized. Sampling of standard time periods may have more precision and offer better control of the time factor in small samples, but it may not always yield representative data or data that can be readily interpreted without supporting information regarding the specific nature of intrainterview process trends. Thus it is important to bear in mind that the precision of any systematic sampling is strictly contingent upon the amount of reliable information available to the researcher regarding trends in the population as a whole.

Another problem arises when a researcher wishes to sample uniformly from periods that vary in length. To draw from the 36th to the 42nd minute of three therapy periods lasting 40, 50, and 80 minutes, respectively, would yield vastly different samples, breaking into the early half of the longest session or running through the end of the shortest session. Where the periods to be sampled differ in length, it is wiser to sample proportionately; that is, from the same relative point in each. Consistent with a segment from the 36th to the 42nd minute in a 50-minute session would be a sample taken two-thirds of the way into other sessions, that is, the 26th to the 32nd minute of a 40-minute period and the 54th to the 60th minute of an 80-minute hour. This adjustment is preferable to the alternative of varying segment length.

Whose Behavior Is Rated—Patient

In the patient form of the Experiencing Scale it is the patient's verbal behavior exclusively that is rated. Therapist speech is not filtered out, but raters are explicitly taught to ignore or discount the therapist's verbalizations except where necessary to provide topical anchorage and continuity. In a study in which segments with therapist speech deleted were compared with ratings of unedited segments, it was determined that EXP ratings were not affected by the presence or absence of therapist speech cues, and were of equal reliability (Schoeninger, Klein, & Mathieu, 1967).

Scale Type and Rating Procedures

The experiencing construct has been operationalized into a single ordinal scale. The strength of any ordinal scale rests with its ability to categorize data according to mutually exclusive, consecutively "greater than" stages. While only one basic scale is used to measure the experiencing process, the discriminant value of the ratings is enhanced by having raters make ongoing judgments of the material in each sample. Raters are encouraged to make "running ratings" as they listen to (or read) each patient speech "turn" or thought, listening carefully for peaks and/or changes in the scale stage. When the rater determines that a change in EXP is taking place, then a different scale level is assigned. Thus in sequential patient statements the EXP rating may remain constant or may fluctuate.

Mode and Peak Ratings   In the training manual (Klein *et al.*, 1969) raters are trained to summarize their running ratings by two scores: modal ratings and peak ratings. A modal rating characterizes the overall or average scale level of the segment or unit; that is, it is representative of the most general or frequently occurring experiencing level in the segment. A peak rating is given to any point where a higher level is reached even momentarily in the segment or unit. There are no length or location requirements for a statement to receive a peak rating. Often a peak is found only in one brief portion of the material. In some segments there may be no clear peak, so mode and peak ratings will be identical. Other segments may be expected to vary and cover a wide range of the scale. When this is the case, the following guidelines are used to make the distinctions between mode and peak:

1. If a segment is more or less equally divided between two stages of the scale, the higher stage should be the peak and the lower the mode.
2. If more than half of the segment is at the higher stage, then the mode and the peak should be the same.
3. If the statements at the higher stage occur so frequently and so regularly throughout the segment that they seem to encompass and upgrade any lower portion, the mode and peak can also be the same. For example, a patient may illustrate an idea or point at a high stage with examples that by themselves are concrete and at a lower stage. Such segments usually have an intrinsic, thematic unity.
4. If the segment covers a range of the scale (e.g., starting at Stage 1, moving to Stage 2, and ending at Stage 3), make the highest stage the peak and the predominant lower stage the mode. It is not usual for the modal rating to be two stages lower than the peak, especially in longer segments and/or when higher stages of the scale are found.

Running Ratings   Although we have generally used the process of "running ratings" (i.e., ratings of each patient speech turn or topic in long speeches, in sequence) simply as a device for helping raters attend to and track segments for the purpose of making decisions about mode and peak ratings, we have more recently used running ratings to provide more detailed profiles of EXP in longer segments and in whole sessions. We think this level of detail is possible, but will require more study and development of the training, scoring, and data analysis procedures. At present we would suggest this procedure only for experienced raters with access to transcripts.

One important difference between ratings of segments-as-wholes and running ratings is that each patient speech turn, particularly in highly interactive segments, must be considered in context—that is, in terms of previous statements—for if each turn is judged in isolation, ratings may be artificially lowered. In effect, the process of making running ratings involves a rater's establishing a stage level for a given speech and then carrying that rating on until clear changes up or down are noted. In this fashion continuing discussion of any given idea or topic can be treated as one unit; changes are most likely to occur when the subject changes or there is a clear change in the speaker's perspective on a subject (e.g., a change from narrative of an event to include mention of feelings about the event). To illustrate this process we have made running ratings of the sample material included at the end of this chapter.

Scoring and Contextual Units

The scoring and contextual units for the Experiencing Scale are one and the same, but while most often the summarizing unit is also the same, it may encompass more units in data analysis if the researcher so desires (e.g., the average for a whole session that has been rated in smaller segments). The unit scored by the raters is of a duration determined by the researcher, but thus far has most often been in the 2–8-minute range. These units are excerpted from the therapy hours at a location chosen to meet the needs of the particular study.

The units may be presented as physically separate units (each on an individual tape), but it is more economical to first order the segments in the sequence to be rated and then record them in that sequence, being sure to clearly demarcate the segments. This ordering forces raters to judge the material in each segment without any additional information. (To preserve confidentiality, all identifying remarks such as names and unique events are also presumed to have been edited from the segments before presenting them to the raters.)

The researcher is free to summarize ratings on the basis of each scoring unit or to average ratings over particular hours or even over the entire case if the object is to get an approximation of an overall level of experiencing. It is our impression that positive correlations of EXP and either outcome or global condition variables are most likely to be found when large summarizing units (e.g., blocks of 5 or more sessions, blocks of 30 sessions) are used. In contrast, hypotheses about the effect of specific therapist operations (e.g., certain kinds of interpretive statements) are best made by limiting sampling to points where the operations actually occur.

In order to determine ideal segment length, scale ratings were made for 2-, 4-, 8-, and 16-minute segments drawn from each of two therapy hours with eight normal, eight neurotic, and eight schizophrenic subjects (Kiesler, Mathieu, & Klein, 1964). Only the absolute EXP level proved to be influenced by segment length. Longer segments were scored higher, presumably because they provided more information. However, the reliabilities, range, and discriminatory power of the ratings were independent of the length of the segment. While it would not be recommended to mix segment lengths in a study, our experience indicates that segment lengths of 5 to 8 minutes provide the rater with enough information to identify high levels of EXP without becoming unwieldy or tedious.

Rater Selection and Training

Rater Selection   Time spent in training and work by raters can constitute one of the largest expenses in a research project. It is therefore important to identify any variables that may be related to good rating performance.

An accepted opinion is that psychologically sophisticated raters can introduce confounding material in the form of subtle theoretical frames of reference or more specific biases. Sophistication can develop either from intensive formal clinical training or extensive use of one or more process or process-type scales. This background can make it difficult for a rater to master the EXP scale because of a conflicting frame of reference. It may cause the rater to impose extrascalar evaluations that may distort the EXP criteria; for example, "I knew from my own experience that what the patient really meant was . . . " or "When one thinks of the broad goals of therapy, that statement can't be significant . . . " The result is that vital time and money may be lost before the biasing influence of prior experience can be identified or overcome. Thus a researcher must decide whether an individual who has been trained extensively, either in one of the mental health professions or in the specific application of another process instrument, should be used as an EXP rater. It is impossible to make hard-and-fast rules that would cover every contingency; however, some guidelines for evaluating individual situations are possible.

The researcher should know if the potential rater is well grounded in the field of psychology. If so, does his or her theoretical training conflict with the concept of experiencing? Does the potential rater think that experiencing is invalid or inadequate to describe patient process? In other words, are there indications that the rater-in-training has personal reservations about this particular scale that would make it very difficult to learn or to use?

If the potential rater's expertise is not in the field of mental health but rather has arisen from extensive application of another scale to process data, there are other concerns. For example, was the previous scale one that would tend to make the rater read extraneous factors into what is said, either interpreting or focusing on voice quality, innuendo, or other nonverbal elements? Such practices can be troublesome and make it difficult for someone to apply the EXP scale. This concern should not be restricted to prior use of patient process scales but should include therapist scales as well, since practice in applying these may well lead to the expectation that how the patient is doing is likely to be a function of what the therapist is doing or not doing.

We have also found that personal therapy or acute personal crisis can make it difficult for some raters to maintain objectivity about the material. Because of the ethical responsibility involved in rating, both maturity and discretion are essential in a rater-in-training; and because the research tasks can be lengthy and repetitive, some evidence of "staying power" and appreciation for detail is desirable.

Finally, the requirement that raters be blind to design conditions, hypotheses, and so on may exclude some raters altogether. Raters-in-training must have a cooperative attitude and a tolerance for ambiguity if they are to maintain interest where the structure is minimal and the feedback is limited over lengthy rating tasks. Raters sometimes find important prohibitions against sharing ratings or impressions of material with others frustrating methodologically.

To temper any sweeping generalizations that might result from these cautions, it is well to look at the results of an empirical study of these issues. Kiesler (1970) compared the EXP ratings of four PhDs, three of whom were clinical psychologists and one of whom was a counseling psychologist, with ratings by clinically naive raters used in an earlier study. The reliabilities were extremely high for both groups, with the inexperienced raters attaining only slightly higher reliability levels for modal ratings (.94 vs. .91) and equivalent reliability on peak ratings (.92).

The EXP scale is an assessment of verbal expression, and therefore it is important that the raters applying the instrument have good language skills. In our experience persons with a background in the humanities and social sciences are better able to grasp the concepts of the scale and the specific intent of the patient's verbal expressions than are persons from less verbally oriented fields, such as engineering, mathematics, and the physical sciences. Specific individuals may, of course, prove to be exceptions.

Rater Training   *The Experiencing Scale: A Research and Training Manual* details the theoretical and research background for the patient form of the scale and makes a number of procedural suggestions (Klein *et al.*, 1969). Explicit procedures and materials for rater training are given, including introduction of the concept, description of the scale, and instructions for the rating task. The formal training program for raters is divided into eight 2-hour sessions, each involving rating practice segments (10 for each session). Practice ratings are then compared with criterion ratings and justifications–explanations provided by the authors. Final assessments of rater reliabilities at the end of training are done on a block of 20 segments. The manual also includes suggestions for maintaining rater reliability over lengthy research periods, and for adapting training to different data for the situation format.

The procedure was designed for a situation in which several raters train together, alternating individual practice sessions with group meetings where problematic segments are played and discussed. Raters have also been trained successfully working alone.

Group versus individual training methods were directly compared and found to yield similar reliabilities after training and for ratings of research data (Schoeninger, Klein, & Mathieu, 1968). High correlations among raters and equivalent means for the two methods were also found for the two training groups ($r = .82$ and $.86$ for mode and $r = .86$ for peak ratings).

Reliability

Table 2-3 summarizes posttraining reliabilities obtained by a number of investigators using the EXP manual. Where possible, we have indicated the rater's level of professionalism. On the whole, reliabilities after training have been extremely high, with no differences apparent between professional and nonprofessional judges. The lowest reliabilities reported were for brief units from an experimental study in which subjects were asked to respond to standardized prerecorded "therapist" statements (Joyce, 1980). Raters in this study were also required to unitize the transcripts as they rated.

Table 2-4–2-8 summarize reliabilities for a number of studies, subdivided by type of material rated. First, reliabilities for psychotherapy session data were uniformly high

Table 2-3   Reliabilities after Training with EXP Manual

	N raters	rkk		r with manual
		Mode	Peak	
Undergraduate Raters				
Barrileaux and Bauer (1976)	3	.97	.94	
Greenberg (1983)	2	.86	.89	
Klein (1970)	2	.75	.88	
Professional Raters				
Jennen et al. (1978)	4	.98	.93	
Pattyn et al. (1975)	4	.88	.90	
Tarule (1978)	2	.99		
Level of Raters Unknown				
Elliott et al. (1981)	3	.82[a]	.84[a]	.80–.85
Lansford and Bordin (1983)	2	—	—	.89–.96
Fontana et al. (1980)	2	.88	.91	.86–.93
Gruver (1971)	3	.92	.91	
Joyce (1980)	2	.36 to .78[b]		
Mueller (1981)	3	.88	.92	

[a]Alpha. [b]Reliabilities were calculated separately for each of four sets of training materials.

across the 15 studies in Table 2-4. Despite variations in therapist orientation and client problem, coefficients were in the 80s or 90s for 12 of the 15 studies. No variations due to segment length or data form (tape vs. transcript) were apparent. This is consistent with the results of several studies in which issues of segment length and data form were specifically considered. In Kiesler et al. (1964), where 2-, 4-, 8-, and 16-minute segments of schizophrenics, neurotics, and normals were rated by independent groups of four raters each, identical reliabilities (all rkk's in the high 80s and 90s) were obtained. Very similar reliabilities were also found for a second study in which 4- and 8-minute segments were compared (Klein, 1971).

Reliabilities were not as independent of data form in a third study (Klein, 1971), where ratings made from audiotapes, transcripts, and both tape and transcripts were presented to three raters in a Latin square design. Coefficients (rkk) computed among the three judges across the three data forms ranged from .58 to .67; these were considerably lower than those generally reported, and also lower than the posttraining coefficients that were in the 80s for the same raters. The result suggests that reliabilities may be lowered if data forms are mixed.

Single-case studies, where raters rated a number of different segments from the same patient–therapist dyad, also present a special challenge to reliability. The results of the four n = 1 studies (three based on psychodynamic therapy) summarized in Table 2-5 are

Table 2-4   Reliabilities of Ratings of Individual Therapy Segments

Study	Segment Type and Length	N Raters	r_{kk} Mode	Peak
Rubenstein (1970)	Audio, $n=247$ ½ to 2 minutes	5	.91	.93
Rogers et al. (1967)	Audio, $n=592$ 4 minutes	4	.76	.79
Kiesler et al. (1964)	Audio, $n=21$ 4 minutes	4	.91 .89	.92[a] .89[b]
Kiesler (1971)	Audio, $n=780$ 4 minutes	4	.79	NR
Gruver (1971)	Audio, $n=90$ 4 minutes	3	.78	.87
Schaeffer & Ables (1977)	Audio, $n=80$ 4 minutes	2	.92	.88
Yalom et al. (1977)	Transcript, $n=807$ 5 minutes	3	.65	.61
Fontana et al. (1980)	Transcript, $n=120$ 5 minutes	2	.80	.91
Jachim (1978)	Audio, $n=46$ 5 minutes	2	.93	.91
Schoeninger (1965)	Audio, $n=30$ 6 minutes	4	.76	.91
Fishman (1971)	Audio, $n=287$ 6 minutes	3	.92	.90
Kiesler et al. (1965)	Audio, $n=120$ 8 minutes	4	.85	.87
Ryan (1965)	Audio, $n=96$ 8 minutes	4	.76	.77
Jennen et al. (1978)	Transcript, $n=176$ length unknown	4	.87	.86
Lietaer (1971)	Transcript, $n=36$ length unknown	4	.85	.84

[a]Early

[b]Late

lower than those for the multicase studies described above, but are still acceptable. The lowest coefficients were for the two studies that used variable-length segments, suggesting that mixing segment length may lower reliability just as does mixing data form. Our own experience with single-case ratings, and the comments of others, indicate other potential problems: The range of ratings may be restricted, particularly if all of the segments are from one phase of therapy. After repeated exposure to one patient, raters may develop biases, halo effects, and various judgmental reactions because of

Table 2-5   Reliabilities of Ratings From Single-Case Studies of Psychotherapy

Study	Segment Type and Length	N Raters	rkk	
			Mode	Peak
Pollack (1973)	$n = 50$ 8 minutes	2	.79	.87
Klein & Gill (1967)	$n = 82$ Variable length	2	.71	.73
Elliott *et al.* (1981)	Variable length	3	.61[a]	.64[a]
Silberschatz (1977)	$n = 92$ 6 minutes	4	.83	.84

[a]Alpha.

unavoidable familiarity with patient (or therapist) style, idiosyncrasies of expression, themes, or dynamics. Special practice materials and/or periodic review sessions may be needed to counteract these problems in single-case studies.

Although the EXP Scale was explicitly designed for therapy material, it has also been used in other research contexts, primarily for therapy analogue and/or nontherapy interview situations, as well as for studies using material from journals, monologues, and the like for assessment purposes. Generally good reliabilities have been obtained for a range of interview situations (Table 2-6), but have been lower and more variable for other kinds of assessments (Table 2-7). We suspect that the restricted range of ratings (usually between Stages 2, 3, and 4) characteristic of standardized assessments may account for this difference. It may be helpful also to include appropriate practice materials in training sessions for raters.

Table 2-6   Reliabilities of Ratings of Nontherapy Interviews

Study	Segment Type and Length	N Raters	rkk	
			Mode	Peak
Moulthrop (1973)	Character interpretations of patients	4	.64	.80
Greenberg & Rice (1981)	18 examples of 3 patients before and after empathic response	2	.72 to .81[a]	
Stern & Bierman (1973)	20 normal role playing "helping"	2	.70[a]	
Mueller (1981)	105 normals in therapy analog interview	3	.78	.76
Lansford & Bordin (1983)	30 analog interviews of college students	2	.83 to .83[a]	
McIntire (1973)	50 feedback sessions by teacher supervisors	3	.62	.64
Beckman (1978)	144 practicum critique sessions	2	.87	.96

[a]Pearson = r.

Table 2-7   Reliabilities of Ratings of Nontherapy Assessments

Study	Segment Type and Length	N Raters	rkk Mode	Peak
Barrileaux & Bauer (1976)	26 college students in structured interview about feelings	3	.97	.95
Kiesler (1969)	312 5-minute self-interviews	4	.58	.75
Luria (1970)	36 LSD monologues	2	.52	.53
Wexler (1974)	122 descriptions of specific emotions	4	.88	Not rated
Joyce (1980)	34 undergraduates in monologue on concerns	2	.79[a]	
Slack & Slack (1977)	Undergraduates monologue on feelings	3	.58	.74
Klein (1970)	28 undergraduates personal logs and autobiographies	2	.70	.77
Tetran (1981)	28 undergraduates personal logs	3	.59, .64, .81[a]	

[a]r. [b]Pairwise r's.

All of the above reliabilities have been obtained for studies where raters have been trained according to the training manual and used the full form of the scale. These generally high figures stand in contrast to the more variable coefficients presented in Table 2-8, which are drawn from five studies where variant or short forms of the scale were used. Hendricks and Cartwright (1978) used a special adaptation of EXP for dream reports, with explicit training; Custers' (1973) study training was centered around the

Table 2-8   Reliabilities of Variant and Short Forms without Training

Study	Segment Type and Length	N Raters	rkk Mode	Peak
Hendricks & Cartwright (1978)	66 dream reports, Dream Scale	2	.80	
Custers (1973)	31 therapy segments, short form of EXP	4	.85	.84
Mintz & Luborsky (1970)	60 therapy segments from 1 case, short form	3	.66	
Auerbach & Luborsky (1968)	60 therapy segments from 30 cases, short form	3	.60 .22[a] .48	.42[a]
Mintz (1969)	180 therapy segments from 30 cases, short form	3	.53	

[a]Correlation (r) of nonprofessional rater with each of the two professional raters.

short form; in the Penn studies (Auerbach & Luborsky, 1968; Mintz, 1969; Mintz & Luborsky, 1970) there was no mention of training, the professional backgrounds of raters varied widely, and—most important—many other variables were rated by the raters at the same time. While it may be necessary in some cases to adapt the scale (e.g., in the Hendricks & Cartwright, 1978, dream study), we do not recommend that systematic training be eliminated. Raters should first become proficient with the basic technique before attempting to master a variant version.

Dimensionality

While the EXP scale is theoretically anchored to a single process dimension, it is defined by the related strands and rating cues described in Table 2-2. Thus it is likely that EXP ratings are related to other dimensions of process and speech. The basic dimension of the scale is concerned with a gradual increase of inner referents. The progression from each stage to the next also involves a shift of frame of reference or perspective on the part of the speaker. Stages 1–3 define the progressive ownership of affective reactions. Stage 4 marks a transition that is especially important for most psychotherapy, that is, the point where content and focus shift from outside to inside, where the speaker's purpose is to describe phenomenology. Beyond this crucial transition, Stages 5–7 define the progressive expansion and integration of this perspective.

Studies in which EXP has been correlated with other process variables for the same segments are germane to the issue of dimensionality and also to the issue of scale validity. Originally the dimensionality of EXP was investigated within the context of Rogers' Wisconsin Project in a series of comparisons with other process variables. In Rogers *et al.* (1967) EXP, both alone and in relation to accurate empathy and congruence, proved to be associated with several measures of high patient expressive capacity and low affective distress, namely, amount of initial interview speech, TAT expressiveness, and Wittenborn Scale symptom severity ratings. These and other relationships to patient characteristics seemed to support an interactive view of therapist conditions–patient process relationships and to suggest that the experiencing variable should be interpreted as a reflection, not only of the patient's actual talking about feelings, but also of the patient's capacity for and commitment to self-exploration.

The results of more recent studies of EXP with other process measures are summarized in Table 2-9, with the other process variables grouped under headings: speech, focus or purpose of discourse, affect level, cognitive variables, and productivity. In general, it would seem desirable that EXP be independent of variables that might be interpreted as confounds (e.g, sheet amount of speech), while its relationship to conceptually related variables such as self-disclosure would serve as evidence of construct validity.

Speech Fluency and EXP   In an attempt to further understand the association of EXP to amount, pattern, and fluency of patient and therapist speech, samples of the data from the Wisconsin Project were later subjected to a more detailed analysis using Interaction Chronograph (IC) procedures (Saslow, Mattarazzo, & Guze, 1955) for both patient and therapist speech (Kiesler, Mathieu, & Klein, 1967). EXP was not consistently correlated with any of the 10 patient or therapist speech pattern variables examined, and previously observed differences between EXP in normals, neurotics, and schizophrenics were not in any way altered when these structural speech variables were statistically controlled. Only within the neurotics were there enough significant EXP-IC

Table 2-9   Correlations of EXP and Other Process Variables

Variable Rated (Study)	n	r with EXP
Amount and Fluency of Speech		
Patient activity (Kiesler *et al.*, 1967)	24	−.19 to .37
Statement length (Mintz and Luborsky, 1970)	60	.67[a]
Segment length (Klein and Gill, 1967)	82	.00
Verbal productivity (Fontana *et al.*, 1980)	30	.47*
Speech disturbance (Mintz and Luborsky, 1970)	60	−.30
Type or Intent of Discourse		
Problem expression (Mintz and Luborsky, 1970)	60	.45[a]
Disclosure form (Stiles *et al.*, 1979)	90	.63**
Free Association (Lansford & Bordin, 1983)	30	.31 to .54**
Communication of Unknown Self (Pattyn *et al.*, 1975)	39, 44	.36** to .57**
Concreteness (Pollack, 1973)	50	−.10
Request for specific information (Fontana *et al.*, 1980)	30	−.45*

(continued)

correlations to warrant attention, and these contradicted the previous results: EXP was higher as neurotic patients and therapists talked *less*. These results as a whole were taken as evidence that EXP is not systematically confounded by speech pattern or rate.

This conclusion is also confirmed by the pattern of correlations between EXP and speech variables in the other studies summarized in rows 2–5 of Table 2-9. The positive relationships for segment length reported by Mintz and Luborsky (1970) and for verbal productivity by Fontana, Dowds, and Eisenstadt (1980) are consistent with our earlier findings that EXP levels are to a much more significant degree a function of the amount of material available to a rater.

Type or Intent of Discourse   Results for six studies where evaluations were made of the type or intent of the patient's discourse suggest that EXP has been most consistently associated with ratings of self-disclosure, problem expression, and free association, but not with measures of concreteness. Perceptual concreteness was defined by Pollack (1973) to reflect the occurrence of detailed and sensorially specific descriptions of events (e.g., what actually happened). Descriptions of emotion were explicitly *not* to be scored concrete *unless* they included details of the physical manifestations of emotion (e.g., ''my face got red''). Given this definition, the lack of relationship with EXP is no surprise, for the concreteness variable was defined so as to guarantee lower EXP stage ratings (particularly Stages 2 and 3) and preclude high ratings. Indeed the perspective

Table 2-9   *(Continued)*

Variable Rated (Study)	*n*	*r* with EXP
Affect Variables		
Affect (Pollack, 1973)	50	.18, .17
Anxiety (Mintz and Luborsky, 1970)	60	.12[a]
Anxiety (Mintz et al., 1971)	60	.02[b]
Anxiety (Fishman, 1971)	36	.50*, .41*
Depression (Mintz et al., 1971)	60	.17[b]
Depression (Fishman, 1971)	36	.29*, .63*
Hostility (Fishman, 1971)	36	NS
Hostility (Mintz et al., 1971)	60	.31[b]
Cognitive Variables		
Internal causality (Fishman, 1971)	36	.32*
Differentiation—integration (Wexler, 1974)	122	.55*
Productivity		
Productivity vs. resistance (Pollack, 1973)	25	−.12, −.13
Productivity (Klein and Gill, 1967)	80	.09, .20
Patienthood (Fishman, 1971)	36	NS

[a]Loading on factor of Patient Involvement also containing EXP (.66). [b]Loading on factor called Integrative Therapy with Receptive Patient in which EXP also loaded.

*p < .05
**p < .01

shift that defines Stage 4 (from the events themselves to the more experiential) would have tended to lessen time devoted to concreteness. The significant negative relationship reported by Fontana et al. (1980) for EXP and the therapist's request for specific information are even more consistent with this view.

In contrast, several measures of self-disclosure or problem expression were positively related to EXP. Pattyn, Rombauts, and Lietaer (1975) reported high correlations of EXP with Moxnes' (1974) Communication Level Scale, which is very similar in content to EXP. This involvement quality has also been reflected in the results reported by Stiles, McDaniel, and McGaughey (1979), where EXP was particularly related to the two (of eight) verbal response modes that shared the dimension of intended self-disclosure. The strongest relationship was found for statements with both disclosure focus and intent (i.e., first-person self-disclosure). Self-disclosures with third-person focus (e.g., "it scared me") were also related to EXP. Both self-disclosure statement types together accounted for 40% of the EXP variance. However, while this association was striking for Stages 1–4, it did not hold for discriminations between Stages 4 and 6. In effect, levels of both kinds of disclosure were the same for segments with Stage 4, 5, and 6 ratings, suggesting a need in the Stiles *et al.* system for some finer discriminations about the disclosure at this point. This result was quite consistent with our view that the EXP scale involves and important turning point at Stage 4.

EXP was also found to load on a factor labeled Patient Involvement that included problem expression ratings in 60 segments drawn from a single therapy case (Mintz & Luborsky, 1970). And finally, Lansford and Bordin (1983) reported significant correlations for mode and peak EXP with general Free Association Scale scores ($r = .45$, $p < .05$; $r = .52$, $p < .01$) and with subscales for Involvement ($r = .54$, $p < .01$; $r = .54$, $p < .01$) and Freedom ($r = .41$, $p < .05$; $r = .44$, $p < .05$); while correlations for the Spontaneity subscale were positive but nonsignificant ($r = .31$ and $.35$).

Expressive versus Cognitive Process   The question whether EXP is related to affective and/or cognitive processes is very important for both dimensionality and construct validity. Results of several studies where EXP and affect-expression or cognitive-processing measures were examined suggest that both dimensions are involved, but that the cognitive dimensions have been the more consistently related. Only in one study by Fishman (1971) was there any relationship between EXP and affect as measured by Gottschalk–Gleser Scale ratings (Gottschalk, Winget, & Gleser, 1969). Other assessments have all yielded negative results (Fontana et al., 1980; Mintz & Luborsky, 1970), Mintz, Luborsky, & Auerbach, 1971; Pollack, 1973).

In contrast, both cognitive variables studied were associated with EXP. In Fishman's study (1971) the internal causality measure, which was derived from the patient's self-reported attribution of difficulties to emotional and internal causes, was significantly related to EXP. This is very consistent with the progressive ownership of feelings that is captured in the Stage 1–4 EXP scale progression.

A more conceptually grounded elaboration of a cognitive correlate of experiencing was provided by Wexler's (1974) definition of a person's differentiation and integration of meaning as a cognitive (as distinct from an expressive) component of experiencing. EXP and Wexler's much more formal and detailed procedure for scoring differentiation and integration were positively correlated for two segments of 61 undergraduates' monologues about their emotional states, with no differences for specific affective state (joy, anger, sadness).

Patient Productivity   Contrasting results have emerged from three attempts to relate EXP to more theoretically based evaluations of patient productivity, all made from a psychoanalytic perspective. Similar nonsignificant correlations for two independent studies of the same case are reported by Pollack (1973) and Klein and Gill (1967). In Pollack's study productivity ratings were based on Dahl's (1972) empirically derived method, which considered both resistance and content; nonsignificant negative correlations were found for two 8-minute segments taken from each of 25 hours. In the Klein and Gill study nonsignificant correlations emerged for segments from all 10 sessions of a single case, using the productivity rating method developed by Simon, Fink, and Endicott (1967), with the ratings done by three clinicians, one of which was the analyst. Finally, Fishman (1971) also found nonsignificant correlations in his multicase study using Merrifield's Patienthood Scale (Merrifield & Fishman, 1967). This rating involved an experienced clinician's judgment of how well the patient role was performed, with stress on the establishment and maintenance of a therapeutic alliance and the patient's manifest effort to explore his or her inner life combined with the therapist's ability to keep the patient on track. The fact that EXP does not relate to any one of these three psychodynamically derived measures is understandable given the different theoretical perspectives. Study of a wider range of patients and therapists is warranted before a final conclusion is drawn that EXP cannot be meaningfully applied in psychodynamic therapy.

Taken together, these studies suggest that the EXP scale is more closely related to conceptually similar measures of disclosure, problem expression, and internal focus than it is to measures of concreteness, speech fluency, affective distress, or psychodynamically formulated judgments of productivity. These results are not surprising and are consistent with the scale's focus on the progressive ownership of feelings, self-revelation, and problematic focus. The modest relationships for affect and negative relationships for concreteness are consistent with the fact that intense affective expression and situational detail are associated with lower stages of the scale. The negative relationships for the psychodynamic productivity scales no doubt reflect differences in theoretical perspectives and clinical priorities.

Data Analysis

The choice of data-reduction and analysis procedures for EXP ratings will depend on the purpose, hypotheses, and sampling strategies of each study. Scoring and summarizing procedures in use have ranged from (1) scores from selected segments or sessions averaged over the total course of, or large blocks of, therapy (e.g., the first thirty interviews), to (2) scores for all or part of specific sessions, to (3) scores for isolated segments within sessions, to (4) scores for specific "speech turns" made in sequence within segments or sessions (i.e., the running rating). In general, aggregate scores have been used for questions involving global process–conditions or process–outcome relationships or group comparisons (e.g., by therapy type or by diagnosis). Session or segment scores have been appropriate for considering EXP changes either over the therapy course or in association with therapist interventions or other events (e.g., EXP measured before and after some intervention such as focusing training). More detailed and specific EXP scores are necessary for more basic questions about therapy processes. The detail afforded by ratings of segments or speech turns in sequence is essential for understanding and describing the complex relationships of EXP and other process variables that must be explicated in the development of a taxonomy of significant therapy events (e.g., in studies where changes in EXP within a session are mapped in relation to therapist intervention ratings and/or other patient process variables such as voice quality). Complex descriptive techniques (e.g., curve fitting) and sequential analysis techniques (e.g., autocorrelations, Markov chains) are required to deal with the large amount of data generated by sequential ratings (Benjamin, 1979; and see chapters in this book by Benjamin & Elliott).

Validity

The theory from which the EXP scale was derived indicates several different tests of the scale's validity. Most importantly, EXP should be associated with successful therapy outcomes and/or with personality variables indicative of expressive and self-reflective capacity. To the extent that EXP may also reflect openness to and motivation for therapy, it may also be associated to some degree with distress at the beginning of therapy. Finally, to the degree that EXP represents a problem-solving skill that can be mastered, encouraged, or even taught, we would predict the EXP would be responsive both to therapeutic conditions in general and to very direct facilitation efforts (e.g., focusing instructions). The challenge here is to identify therapeutic variables that can be reasonably expected to enhance EXP, since all therapeutic interventions cannot be expected to influence it, and some may well lower it.

Here we have attempted to review research using the EXP scale since the publication of the training manual (Klein *et al.*, 1969). Work already reviewed in the manual is cited but not described in detail. First we consider studies in which EXP was related to measures of therapy prognosis, health, or personality. Next we consider studies, some of therapy sessions but more in analogue contexts, of efforts to facilitate or manipulate EXP either directly or as an index of self-exploration. We then take up the two most crucial areas of validity research: research on therapist conditions or interventions, and therapy outcome in relation to EXP. Finally, we present descriptions of how EXP has been used in group therapy research separately because of the different methodological and conceptual issues raised.

Experiencing and Personality   Early research suggested that EXP was to some degree a measure of health as well as an index of productive therapeutic involvement (Kiesler *et al.*, 1965; Kiesler, 1971; Rogers *et al.*, 1967). In addition, EXP was related to various indicators of verbal and expressive capacity that have, in turn, been consistently associated with good motivation and prognosis for therapy (Rogers *et al.*, 1967). On the other hand, in studies of focusing ability, which is theoretically a key activity at Stage 4 and above, this behavior has been associated with an introspective style (Gendlin *et al.*, 1968).

More recent studies have confirmed some of these trends. Considering the demographic and social adjustment variables usually associated with good prognosis for therapy, Fontana *et al.* (1980) reported first-session EXP to be significantly associated with verbal IQ and socio-economic status in a sample of 30 psychiatric outpatients with mixed diagnoses. Results for more specific measures of functioning versus distress have been more equivocal. Fishman (1971) found no relationship between initial-session EXP and either interview, patient self-report, or therapist ratings of overall work and social adjustment in 45 neurotic outpatients. In a more "normal" sample of test anxious undergraduate volunteers, EXP in brief analogue interviews was also not related to objective performance tests (Dealy, 1978). In nonsymptomatic student teachers McIntire (1973) also reported no relationship of EXP, assessed during supervisor feedback sessions, to seven dimensions of supervisor ratings of teacher effectiveness; however, there was a significant negative correlation for EXP and a teacher self-report inventory assessment of work.

Turning to relationships between EXP and various indices of health and distress, facets of the theory would support, and prior research has suggested, some contradictory predictions: The general trend for "healthier" people to have higher EXP levels (e.g., Kiesler *et al.*, 1965; Kiesler, 1971) must be qualified by the tendency for EXP to be somewhat elevated in conjunction with psychological distress and/or help seeking. Thus neurotic patients have higher EXP levels than schizophrenics, while non-help-seeking normal people often have low levels. Results of recent research can be found to support either possibility. Also, some analyses of EXP theory, such as that by Joyce (1980), suggest that EXP relationships with either pathology or distress may be complex and curvilinear.

In a diagnostically mixed outpatient sample, EXP in therapy was significantly associated with neurosis, as opposed to character disorder or psychosis (Fontana *et al.*, 1980). Within neurotic outpatient samples, however, seven studies have shown that early in therapy EXP was not straightforwardly associated with levels of general distress, neuroticism, or specific affective disturbances. Fishman (1971) reported nonsignificant correlations for EXP and patient self-ratings of anxiety, depression, and hostility, and no correlation for corresponding therapist ratings (the only exception was a negative relationship for EXP and therapist ratings of patient manifest hostility). Schaeffer and Ables (1977) found a complex interaction for EXP, a Minnesota Multiphasic Personality Inventory index of distress, and a projective test measure of attraction to therapy: Distressed clients (independent of attraction level) had moderate EXP levels in the second therapy session; the highest EXP level occurred among the nondistressed–attracted clients, and the lowest among the nondistressed–nonattracted. Finally, while there was no relationship for EXP and either patient expectations of change or patient attitudes toward therapy in Richert's (1976) study of 26 counseling center clients, Fontana *et al.* (1980) did find a significant positive correlation between EXP and a more objective measure of therapy attraction (session attendance).

Relationships of EXP to either neuroticism or distress are less clear in non-help-seeking samples. Dealy (1978) reported no correlation between EXP and Anxiety Scale scores in her sample of undergraduates selected as being high in test anxiety. Kiesler (1969) also failed to find significant main effects for either emotionality or introversion–extraversion in undergraduates, but did find a significant interaction of these variables with sex. Further, females were high in EXP regardless of personality type; while among males EXP was highest for obsessive neurotics, intermediate for hysterics, and lowest for (less distressed) extraverts and introverts, respectively. When Kiesler directly compared EXP in help-seeking versus non-help-seeking neurotics (defined as neurotic by high scores in Bendig's Emotionality Score), he again found a complex interaction suggesting high levels in all non–help seekers (regardless of sex or type of neurosis). Within help seekers (counseling center clients) sex and neurotic type were important: Females were higher in EXP than males; obsessive females were highest, while obsessive males were lowest. Consistent with this, Marlowe (1980) also found EXP correlated with self-rating measures of self-consciousness and EXP measured in videotape feedback (therapy analogue sessions) with normal undergraduates and with *low* self-esteem on the Rosenberg Self-Esteem Scale. This led him to conclude that both introspection and distress associated with low self-esteem may motivate nonclients to self-observation.

Attempts to anchor EXP to other qualitative measures of functioning are quite equivocal. In various patient samples EXP has been positively associated with measures of conceptual complexity and psychological differentiation (Fontana *et al.*, 1980), but not with therapist ratings of ego assets, or with a Rorschach measure of the patient's capacity for adaptive regression in Fishman's (1971) study, or with repression–sensitization scores (Barrileaux & Bauer, 1967). For nonpatients, the highest EXP was found among student teachers with moderate scores on measures of ego resilience and weakness (Mueller, 1981). This curvilinear relationship led Mueller to conclude that EXP is best interpreted not as a simple measure of conflict reporting that is adaptive or healthy when done in moderation in appropriate contexts (e.g., in therapy), but not indiscriminantly in all interactions. There was also evidence in Mueller's study that those who were moderate in EXP were best able to increase their EXP when encouraged to do so. Finally, in a study of counseling graduate students who were observed both as helpers and helpees, Stern and Bierman (1973) found that high EXP in the helpee (patient) role was associated with scores in the Type A group on the Whitehorn and Betz AB Scale, suggesting the greater accessibility of the A therapist to his or her own feelings.

Other studies have been concerned with EXP in relation to various imaginal and developmental processes. Hendricks and Cartwright (1978) looked at EXP in dream reports, using their adaptation of the scale. Dream EXP was found to be highly stable within individuals and positively related to a measure of psychological differentiation but unrelated to either extraversion–introversion or defensiveness. In an extension of this work, however, dream EXP in the same subjects was not associated with therapy outcome (Melstrom & Cartwright, 1983). When relating EXP from analogue interviews to dimensions of a self-report measure of daydream style, Joyce (1980) failed to find the predicted association of EXP with positive–vivid style, but did find positive relationships for mentation rate, boredom, and frightened reaction. He interpreted these results in terms of the mental effort involved in experiential processing. Other researchers have also investigated EXP in reflections made by midlife adults and elderly people about their lives and/or their development. When Tarule (1978) classified her sample by relative developmental stage, she found higher EXP levels for higher-stage subjects; within stages, higher EXP was characteristic of greater disequilibrium (i.e., with proximity to a transition point from one stage to another). Within a much older sample, Lieberman and Coplan (1970) and Gorney (1968) found EXP to be positively associated with the elders' capacity to adapt to the transition from independent to nursing-home living, but also found that EXP decreased both with age and with nearness to death, a finding they interpreted in terms of an adaptive avoidance process.

In sum, relationships of EXP to measures of health, personality, and cognitive style have not been altogether consistent. In help seekers (i.e., patients) EXP was more uniformly associated with neuroticism as a general factor than it was with any specific neurotic subtype or category of affective distress. There is some additional evidence of EXP having been higher in concert with introspectiveness, obsessiveness, or self-consciousness in both help-seeking and non-help-seeking samples. Finally, EXP has also been associated with measures of cognitive style—that is, complexity and differentiation—as well as with other indicators of reflectiveness, expressive capacity, or attraction to psychotherapy.

Facilitation of Experiencing   EXP has been used as a dependent variable in nine studies where patients or normal subjects were given direct training or exercises in self-expression, focusing, or other therapy-role behaviors. In four of these studies the facilitation was done by having subjects participate in brief Gestalt awareness training or encounter groups. The two studies with positive results used normal subjects' personal logs or journals to measure EXP (Klein, 1970; Tetran, 1981). Of the two studies with negative results, one (Yalom, Bond, Bloch, Zimmerman, & Friedman, 1977) used individual long-term therapy patients as subjects and measured EXP in their individual therapy sessions before and after training, while the other (Barrileaux & Bauer, 1976) used structured interviews and normal subjects to tap the effect of similar workshop experiences.

Results for five studies of more direct role-induction techniques are somewhat less equivocal. Experiencing was clearly facilitated in two studies using normal undergraduates in therapy-analogue interviews. Schoeninger (1965) found that the general trend for EXP to be higher in the early part of each of three "therapy" interviews was more pronounced when subjects had first been given an explicit orientation to the basic concept of experiencing—that is, had practiced the process of "looking inward . . . to find feelings and thoughts," had focused on emergent feelings, and had heard tapes modeling high experiencing. Similar results have been reported in a study of variations within a single analogue session with 10 subjects (McMullin, 1972). Experiencing levels rose significantly (from 2.97 and 2.89 to 5.02) in response to the presentation of Gendlin's focusing instructions, and dropped (to 3.18 and 3.53) when these instructions were discontinued.

Three studies have looked at the impact of focusing instructions on EXP in patient samples. Olsen (1975) administered an adaptation of Gendlin's focusing procedure that included visual imagery and relaxation to 23 nonpsychotic outpatients who were typical of private practice clients. She found that EXP during training sessions was significantly improved over pretraining therapy sessions, and that most clients reached Stage 4 or above with focusing instructions. Ability to focus and reach these higher stages of EXP were also significantly correlated with the clients' reports of mastery and insight on the Therapy Session Report. However, when focusing instructions were not given in regular therapy sessions after training, changes in EXP were not maintained. Hinterkopf and Brunswick (1981) also reported marked improvement in EXP (as measured by Hinterkoff's variant scale, the "Talker Rating Scale") in a very different population—acute and chronic schizophrenics. Here EXP facilitation consisted of eight sessions in which a "trainer" worked with patients in pairs to teach both "talker skills" (focusing and revealing bodily feelings, emotions, and reasons for emotions) and "helper skills" (empathic listening and reflection). The patients' use of affect and physical feeling words as measured in separate test sessions was 21% and 26% in two parts of the test after eight training sessions (a test after the first training session yielded no effect). However, patients did not increase in their ability to correct inaccurate "helper" reflections. Low SES Community Mental Health Center patients were also used in Jachim's (1978) comparison of a role induction interview versus filmed modeling. Neither intervention had any effect on EXP, self-disclosure, or attraction to therapy, but it must be noted that the induction attempt touched upon many issues.

Very consistent and positive effects on EXP are reported by Bierman and colleagues (Bierman, Davidson, Finkleman, Leonidas, Lumly, & Simister, 1976; Bierman & Lumly, 1973) from their large-scale, multiphase program to establish a "Humanizing Community." Basic to each step of their program was a 16-session communication workshop held over 12 weeks in which participants were instructed and given practice in (1) sharing experiencing, (2) empathic communication, (3) expressing respect, and (4) constructive authenticity. After community volunteers received training they, in turn, trained others. In each case EXP (assessed in three segments from pre- and postassessment sessions in which each person took both helper and helpee roles) was significantly increased (from 2.58 to 3.92; from 2.39 to 4.02; from 2.59 to 4.00) for three different samples. There were no differences in the outcomes of workshops led by professional or lay leaders, and no differences in the responses of professional and laypeople as participants. Similar significant differences were also found for EXP changes in more specialized workshop experiences: training of significant other pairs (EXP change from 3.11 to 4.19), self-realization training focused on work motivation (from 3.34 to 3.96), supervision–consultation sessions for workshop leaders (from 3.76 to 4.52), one-to-one tutoring (from 3.46 to 4.47 and 3.65 to 3.55 for each participant), and finally, job readiness training for college students (from 3.50 to 3.55). In each case pre–post t tests were highly significant, and in no instance did the workshop experience fail to significantly change EXP.

These studies confirm that experiencing skills can be taught, even to severely disturbed patients. The more directly the teaching is targeted to the experiential process itself, the more effective the training is likely to be. It is also apparent that the circumstances in which EXP is tested are important. Journals and analogue interviews with responsive listeners seem to be somewhat more consistently sensitive indicators of facilitation effects than are therapy interviews (where therapist effects and session agendas may be more controlling).

Experiencing and Therapist Conditions or Interventions   The original purpose for which the patient scale was developed was to test the relationship of EXP to the three therapist "conditions" variables: Positive Regard, Empathy, and Congruence, as defined by Rogers (1957; 1959). Strong associations of EXP with these therapist variables (measured from the perspective of both patients and raters) carried over from preliminary studies to the final analyses of the Wisconsin Project (Rogers et al., 1967). Overall, the most consistent relationships were found between EXP and (1) Accurate Empathy rated from tapes and (2) Congruence as perceived by the patient on the Barrett–Lennard Relationship Inventory.

Since the Wisconsin Project, this line of research has taken several directions. Truax, Carkuff, and various colleagues continued to test conditions—process linkages in a number of settings, using variant scales (Truax & Mitchell, 1971). Other researchers continued using the EXP scale and also gradually broadened the range of therapist conditions or interventions considered. As this research has proliferated, results have become more complex (e.g., Mitchell, Bozarth, & Krauft, 1976; Lambert, DeJulio, & Stein, 1978; Parloff, Waskow, & Wolfe, 1978).

Two "naturalistic" studies of EXP in relation to therapist conditions variables have yielded somewhat contradictory results. When Jennen, Lietaer, and Rombauts (1978) did an in-depth study of 176 segments from the beginning, middle, and end of therapy for 13 patients, they found no overall correlation of rated Accurate Empathy and EXP. But they did find EXP to be significantly higher in high Accurate Empathy (AE) segments (high AE is defined as Level 5 and above; low AE as Level 4 and below). Within cases, AE and EXP were significantly correlated for only 4 of the 13 patients. Turning to patient- and therapist-perceived conditions (specifically to the relationship between EXP averaged over all of therapy and Relationship Inventory Scores from Sessions 3 and 8), they found significant correlations for mode and peak patient ratings. Consistent with previous work, correlations were nonsignificant (and negative) for therapist-perceived conditions.

A more cross-sectional study of EXP in relation to a number of therapist variables by Rubenstein (1970) yielded negative results using more cases but much smaller samples per case. In this study Rubenstein had 16 experienced therapists submit tapes of their work with three to four clients each, from which he randomly selected nine 4-minute segments as a "behavior sample" of each therapist from which Accurate Empathy, Nonpossessive Warmth, and Congruence ratings were made. On the basis of these ratings, therapists were then classified as either high or low facilitators. At this point Rubenstein located examples of eight different categories of therapist behavior and extracted patient speech segments (which varied in length from ½ to 2 minutes) from points before and after each type of therapist intervention. For EXP ratings of these segments, there were no significant main effects or interactions for facilitation level (high vs. low), for response class (question, restatement interpretation, self-disclosure), or for response directionality (affectively vs. nonaffectively directed). The only interaction that approached significance ($p < .08$) suggested that high facilitative therapists *responded* at points when client EXP was higher more often than did low facilitators, but that these responses then *lowered* client EXP. It is possible that the small sample size and Rubenstein's decision to calculate EXP scores by averaging mode and peak ratings suppressed the expected effects, a possibility supported by the generally low level of his EXP ratings (average 2.63, range from 1.00 to 4.80).

Five other more intensive analyses of single cases employed a range of therapist interventions and other variables in relation to EXP, with greater specificity as to the hypothesized linkages between therapist operations and client response. Proceeding from an "eclectic–psychodynamic" framework, but also using a range of client-centered, Gestalt, and experiential techniques, Elliott and colleagues (Elliott, Cline, & Shulman, 1982; Elliott, Klein, & Mathiew-Coughlan, 1983) used EXP as one of many process variables in their comparison of four different evaluative paradigms in 10 therapy sessions. The paradigms compared were (1) sequential process, based on the effect of a number of therapist and patient variables on ratings of client EXP, working, and impact; (2) global process–outcome, where the same variables averaged over the 10 sessions were correlated with overall Therapy Session Report ratings of session effectiveness; (3) immediate perceptions of therapist helpfulness based on a client-and-therapist postsession interpersonal recall procedure; and (4) retrospective perceptions of therapist helpfulness from the same procedure taken at the end of the 10-session block. As one of the 44 process measures in this study, the EXP scale was applied to patient segments before and after key therapist interventions. In addition, the new therapist EXP scale was applied to therapist interventions. Results from each perspective support the conclusion that EXP is sensitive to important dimensions of therapist behavior: (1) Patient EXP is an important context for helpful therapist interventions; peak EXP levels in segments prior to therapist interventions were significantly correlated with helpfulness ratings made by client and therapist. (2) Therapist EXP is an important component of therapist helpfulness; therapist EXP ratings for both referent and manner loaded on a factor called "helpful experiencing," which also contained high levels of therapist helpfulness, positive state, and nonverbal expressiveness. (3) EXP was an important result of helpful therapist interventions; there was greater residual gain in EXP following therapist interventions rated as high in scales for helpful experiencing, depth, and empathy. (4) Finally, EXP was an important contributor to good outcome; client overall session effectiveness ratings were highly correlated with average patient EXP ratings for the same 10 sessions ($r = 73$, $p < .05$). In another analysis of the same case Elliott (1983) used EXP as one process variable to characterize one especially significant moment of client change. Here a Stage 6 rating on the patient scale closely followed the client's "felt shift," which occurred in response to a series of highly evocative and empathic therapist interventions.

Greenberg's studies of the Gestalt therapy "two-chair" technique in three clients have also yielded significant findings for EXP. According to the study design, therapists responded to a theoretically selected class of client conflict statements ("splits") with a predetermined random schedule of accurate empathy responses or "two-chair" operations (Greenberg, 1980). Higher levels of EXP, and specifically more peak EXP ratings at Stage 5 and above, were found after the two-chair operations than after empathic responding, suggesting the more direct and striking impact of the specifically targeted Gestalt technique. A more detailed process analysis of the course of EXP and CVQ ratings in the same set of two-chair segments revealed a very consistent pattern of split resolution (Greenberg & Rice, 1981). The "experiencing" (or self) chair first reached EXP Level 4; then the "other" chair, after having proceeded at low EXP levels, increased ("merged") also to Level 4; and finally, both chairs moved above 4 to Stages 5 or 6, where the conflict was resolved. Another interesting finding was that a shift to focused from externalized voice quality in the "other" chair was also characteristic of the moment when EXP was heightened. Essentially similar results were found when Greenberg (1983) later compared 14 instances of two-chair conflict resolution with 14 instances of nonresolution. While there were no group differences for either chair in the initial or "opposition" phase of the exercise, in the "other" chair during the "merging" phase (defined by the point when the "other" chair expressed affiliation toward the "experiencing" chair) EXP was significantly higher for the resolution group. EXP was also higher for the "experiencing" chair, and Focused voice was high in both chairs for resolution segments. Thus EXP in conjunction with several other process variables has served to demarcate a theoretically important process shift in Gestalt therapy.

Turning to more psychodynamic therapy, we find that EXP has also been associated with variables of therapist behavior defined from that frame of reference. When Silberschatz (1977; 1981) studied the impact of therapist interventions in the case of "Mrs. C" according to whether they passed or failed "key tests," significant increases in patient EXP were found in segments where a test was passed (e.g., where the therapist correctly handled a transference issue). Klein & Gill (1967) also used EXP as a process variable in a study of 10 psychoanalytic sessions from the case of "Mrs. A," where therapist interventions were also rated for "quality" on the basis of the researchers' independent judgments of how well the intervention advanced the therapeutic task in a particular session. While EXP within specific segments was not a function of intervention quality, Klein and Gill did find different patterns of EXP change when whole sessions were subdivided according to the overall (i.e., average) therapist intervention quality rating. In the five "better" hours both mode and peak EXP were highest in the middle of the sessions (and peak EXP was high again at the end), while in the five "less good" sessions EXP dropped at the midpoint and was lowest at the session end.

The sensitivity of EXP to therapist conditions and/or other variables of therapist behavior has also been the subject of several analogue studies. Joyce (1980) assessed the responses of 34 normal undergraduates (chosen as high in expressiveness) to an array of tape-recorded therapist responses from actual therapy sessions, which had been previously classified on several dimensions of facilitation. The taped statements were presented in random order to subjects who were instructed to "be themselves and hopefully become involved in being yourself" as they reacted to each statement. As predicted, mode EXP scores were significantly higher after high facilitative statements (with no difference for peaks). Less direct support of the same relationship can be drawn from one facet of the results of another study of the experiential effect of focusing instructions on 50 female undergraduates (McMullin, 1972). In "baseline" or control periods of the session (i.e., when focusing instructions were not given) the interviewer was directed to offer low conditions, and subject EXP levels were clearly not as high in that baseline period as in the focusing trial.

Finally, the specific content of therapist interpretations was systematically varied in Moulthrop's (1973) study in which patients, classified as either hysteric or obsessive, were asked to react to personality congruent and incongruent interpretive statements. When EXP was rated from the patient reactions to each statement (5 minutes of association to each interpretation), no differences were found.

While EXP has been associated with high-quality therapist interventions as measured from a variety of perspectives, this association has been stronger and more consistently found in finer-grained sequential analyses and single-case studies focused on a few sessions. The original finding of global and pervasive EXP–therapist conditions ratings in client-centered therapy have not been widely or consistently replicated.

Experiencing and Therapy Outcome   The early developmental work with EXP provided consistent evidence of relationships between EXP level, either averaged over all of therapy or at the end of therapy, with various measures of patient outcome (Klein *et al.*, 1969; Kiesler, 1971; Karon & VandenBos, 1970; Rogers *et al.*, 1967). At the same time, efforts to determine the course of change in EXP over therapy and to link EXP change to outcome, as measured either by end-of-therapy evaluations or by personality change measures, yielded more complex and inconsistent results. In both the original Wisconsin Project (Rogers *et al.*, 1967) and in Ryan's (1966) study of counseling center neurotics, it was the consistency of EXP improvement or the lack of backsliding that was related to good outcomes. In Kiesler's (1971) reanalysis of these data, in which he included additional counseling center neurotics for comparison purposes, EXP averaged over Interviews 1–20 and 1–30, but not 1–5, were positively related to outcome; however, there was no evidence in support of any consistent pattern of EXP change regardless of whether data from the first 5, 20, or 30 interviews were considered. From this, Kiesler concluded—correctly, we think—that while studies that use few data points may occasionally elicit dramatic EXP changes, these results are not likely to be widely generalizable or replicable when aggregate data from larger blocks of segments are considered.

More recent studies continued to find relationships between EXP levels measured at different points in therapy and outcome. First, when EXP was considered very early in therapy, EXP predicted outcome in two of six studies. Jennen *et al.* (1978) found early EXP correlated with outcome scores on the inner support subscale of the Personal Orientation Inventory. Nixon (1982), who studied the outcome of primal therapy, found a significant correlation between EXP measured in early "consultation sessions" and outcome. Within the "intensive" primal therapy sessions, only peak EXP was related to outcome as measured by patient self-report. Considering studies where relationships of early EXP to therapy outcome did not clearly emerge, in their review of 26 client-centered therapy cases Bommert and Dahlhoff (1978), using the German translation of the EXP Scale, did not find a significant difference between second-session EXP levels of more and less successful clients. For EXP early in psychodynamic therapy (first two sessions), Luborsky (1982) failed to find any overall relationships for EXP with either raw, rated, or residual patient improvement scores. The one exception was for male outpatients where there was a positive correlation with composite residual gain scores and early peak EXP. Custers (1973) found no relationship between EXP (either modes or peaks) rated from two early client-centered therapy sessions and a number of personality change indicators. This was also true for Fishman's (1971) study of outpatients in psychodynamic therapy.

When EXP has been considered at the therapy midpoint, there have also been mixed results. Bommert and Dahlhoff (1978) found a clear relationship of EXP to outcome in their middle-session segments: More successful patients were significantly higher (mean of 4.18) than less successful patients (mean of 3.51), and there was also a trend for a positive correlation of middle-session EXP and a self-report measure of well-being. In addition, EXP was significantly correlated with their self-report measure of relaxation. In contrast, Richert (1976) found ratings of EXP in eight middle sessions to be unrelated to cognitive change measures and to be negatively related to self-satisfaction at the end of therapy. Custers (1973) found no association for EXP and either MMPI or Butler-Haigh Q-sort outcomes with two segments sampled from the middle of therapy.

Positive results have emerged more consistently when EXP late in therapy or EXP change scores over therapy (which also reflect high late-therapy levels) are considered. Thus Fishman found late EXP associated with his measure of patient success, and Jennen *et al.* (1978) found both early and late EXP correlated with outcome scores on the Inner Support Subscale of the Personal Orientation Inventory. Both of the studies that examined outcome in relation to EXP *change* scores also found positive results. Fishman (1971) reported significant correlations for EXP change and both patient and therapist success ratings. Custers (1973) found EXP change over all of therapy and from mid- to end of therapy to be correlated with both MMPI and Q-sort success measures. Bommert and Dahlhoff (1978) did not find a significant difference for next-to-last-session EXP between more and less successful outcomes, but did find a significant rank-order correlation between EXP and their measure of well-being.

These patterns support the view that EXP reflects a process of productive engagement in the work of therapy that is related to the ultimate outcome of therapy.

Experiencing in Groups   Although the scale was not designed to rate the more complex interactions that take place in group psychotherapy, it has been used with increasing success, particularly as it has been adapted to group versus individual interactions. Gruver (1971) was the first to attempt to apply EXP to group interaction, and he found excellent reliabilities for both individual and group ratings. This was followed by studies carried out by Nichols and Taylor (1974) and Pattyn *et al.* (1975). All reported excellent reliabilities (*rkk*'s ranging from .73 to .97 for individuals rated in group settings) with comparable reliabilities for Gruver's attempt to rate the group as a whole (*rkk* .89 and .94). Substantive results for these studies, however, are not consistent. When Gruver compared the EXP levels of the same individuals in dyadic interviews and in group settings with overall group EXP ratings, he found no correlation across settings. This, combined with the failure of group EXP to relate to other group satisfaction measures, led him to question the appropriateness of the EXP scale for group data.

Several categories of therapist intervention were studied in more detail by Nichols and Taylor (1974) in relation to both EXP and a Group Immediacy Scale. They found no relationship for therapist interventions classified by the method of Howe and Pope (1961) and either EXP or group immediacy ratings. The focus and directness of interventions, however, were clearly important—that is, both interventions directed toward individuals and confrontation interventions were found to be correlated with higher EXP ratings for individuals and with a higher proportion of self- versus other responses on the Group Immediacy Scale.

Both of these studies, then, seem to suggest that while EXP can be validly used to reflect individual process in groups, it may not be as sensitive to group process without some scale modification. More recent applications of EXP to group process have been most directly and productively addressed by Beck, Lewis, and colleagues in the context of their efforts to operationalize a number of group process measures to identify phases and changes in group development (Lewis & Beck, 1983; Beck, Dugo, Eng, Lewis, & Peters, 1983). For this work, we collaborated with Beck and Lewis to adapt the EXP rating methodology to groups (see chapter in this book for a detailed description of these procedures). One particular concern was to discriminate individual from group material and to develop appropriate rating procedures for each. The result was that decision rules developed by Lewis were first applied to distinguish statements where individuals were focused on self from statements where the focus was on other group members or on the group as a whole. Individual (i.e., self-focused) statements were then rated on the Patient EXP Scale; all therapist statements and all non-self-focused statements made by group members were rated using the Patient Referent strand of the Therapist EXP Scale. Good reliabilities were found for all steps of this process.

To summarize the results described in detail in their chapter in this book, Beck and

Lewis found that EXP was significantly associated with several different perspectives on the group process. Composite group EXP scores (averaged across all members and leaders) were found to peak at important group process transition points ("phase shifts"). The EXP levels of group leaders closely followed the pattern of the composite ratings, thus reflecting the important role played by leaders in moving the group along. And finally, during the third "cooperative work" phase of group process, when members disclose themselves and further define personal goals, EXP profiles for individual group members showed a pattern of "turn taking" in that peaks in EXP reflected members' involvement in intense self-exploration.

Conclusion   In general, the validity studies reviewed above suggest the following:

1. As a personality characteristic, EXP has been more closely related to neuroticism, introspectiveness, and cognitive complexity than to affective distress. This suggests that the scale is more a measure of reflective or self-observational style than expressiveness.
2. While experiencing may come easily to some individuals, it can also be taught or encouraged. The more specifically the intervention was targeted at experiencing, the stronger this association has been.
3. While there has been some evidence of higher experiencing in relation to global measures of therapist skill and therapeutic climate, its relationship to therapist process variables has been considerably stronger and clearer in finer-grained sequential analyses. Higher levels of EXP were found in conjunction with "helpful" or dynamically apt therapist interventions in different kinds of individual therapy, and with an explicit experiential exercise in Gestalt therapy. When applied in modified form to group therapy, EXP peaks served to demarcate important points in the group's developmental process.
4. Finally, the association of experiencing to therapeutic outcome has been shown for EXP levels at various points in therapy, most consistently at points after the first few sessions. This suggests that the scale is a reflection of a mode of productive functioning rather than a stable personality trait. Thus the original view of experiencing as a process variable and of the scale as a reflection of this essential quality of self-involvement and participation in the therapy process still holds.

Later expansions of the construct and measure as reflections of personality traits, prognostic indicators, or stable aspects of personality change have been less consistently supported by research results. Thus the process facility that the scale captures, as reflected in a patient's verbal behavior, cannot always be expected to be present. It is more likely to vary as a function of setting and expectations—for example, as guided by patient goals or therapist techniques—so that when high-level experiencing is employed, it can lead to a productive personal experience. This view supports our current opinion that the most promising direction for future research with the scale is toward its application in finer-grained, sequential process studies where EXP can be examined in relation to other patient and therapist process measures. This is consistent with our conviction that at this point the field of therapy process research is better served by multidimensional and multivariate efforts to identify operations across different treatment modalities than by reductionistic attempts to explain all aspects of therapy from one conceptual perspective. While we think that the experiencing conception and rating methodology can be meaningfully applied to therapist and patient verbal behavior in different types of therapy, we also agree that many other concepts and measures are necessary for a rich and useful theoretical understanding of the complex therapeutic process.

Other Applications

In this section we introduce two new applications of the EXP scale. The Therapist EXP Scale was developed to complement the Patient EXP Scale. It has been especially powerful in relation to other process variables in detailed sequential ratings (e.g., Elliott *et al.*, 1983). The Experiencing Interview was developed specifically for the assessment of EXP capacity in brief, nontherapy interview situations. Neither method is validated at this point. As training procedures are not yet available, thorough training and background in the patient scale is essential for their application.

The Therapist Experiencing (EXP) Scale

The Therapist EXP Scale comes from our conviction that therapist conditions variables (e.g., Accurate Empathy) are most parsimoniously defined in experiential terms. This focus reflects our experiences listening to therapist interventions as we have rated EXP (and heard therapists either impede or enhance patient EXP), and also dovetails with Gendlin's progressive delineation of the therapist's task in experiential therapy (e.g., Gendlin, 1962; 1974a; 1974b; 1979; 1981; 1982). We offer this scale below as only tentative, with the caution that much testing and refinement will be necessary before it can be widely used. Examples of ratings on this scale are given along with the patient sample segments.

This scale is meant to assess the extent to which the therapist (or speaker) is engaged in the patient's (or another speaker's) experiencing. It has two components: referent and manner. Referent is that aspect or level of the patient's experiential process that is pointed to by the therapist's words. Manner is the level of the therapist's own experiential involvement in the interchange. Ideally both aspects of the therapist's level of experiential involvement are appropriate to the patient's level—that is, appropriate to sustain it or carry it forward to a higher level.

At the lowest level of therapist EXP, the therapist is impersonal, detached, and not referring to the patient. Moving up the scale, the therapist progresses from intellectual interest, to references to feelings and the patient's experiencing, to a point where a shared or common process develops. At higher levels, this shared, communicated process becomes for both the patient and the therapist the focus for exploration and the emergence of new experiencing.

Referent can be directly related to the Patient EXP Scale, that is, to the level of the patient's process, actual or potential, that the therapist's words refer: (1) the therapist's words underscore or affirm something the patient has actually said, or (2) the therapist's words refer to the experiential level implicit but not (yet) explicit in the patient.

Manner refers to the level of the therapist's own engagement—moving from detachment, through interest, to full and shared expression. At Stage 4 therapist and patient awareness merge, that is, the therapist makes the patient's process his or her own and thereby creates a common, shared experiencing. It is at this point that the dimensions of referent and manner are most likely to be related, but this is not always the case. Sessions can be high in referent and lower in manner, especially if the therapy is not done from a client-centered or experiential perspective.

Table 2-10   Therapist Experiencing Scale of Marjorie H. Klein and Philippa Mathieu-Coughlan

Stage	Patient (P) Content Referent	Therapists (T) Manner
1	External events not including P	Impersonal, detached
2	External events including P; behavioral or intellectual elaboration of P's thoughts or activities	Interested, intellectual self-referents
3	P's reactions to external events; limited or behavioral description of P's feelings	Reactive, T clearly expresses or refers to T's feelings
4	Description of P's feelings and personal experiences	Empathically involved, T elaborates or intensifies feelings and/or associations in this context
5	P's problems or propositions about feelings and personal experiences	T uses own feelings to explore P's feelings
6	Focus on P's emergent feelings and their impact	Uses own emergent feelings to affirm P's feelings
7	P's facility to move from one inner referent to another with authenticity	Expansive, with integration of all elements of the interaction, including P's feelings, T's feelings and the explicit content

Stage 1

Referent: The therapist is referring to events that are external to or not about the patient.

These may be either of two types:

1. Events that clearly do not include the patient.
2. Events in which the patient's involvement is minimal and/or impersonal so that the focus is more on the external event than on the patient. The patient is viewed as an object, spectator, reporter, or incidental participant.

Examples: The therapist talks about abstract ideas with no clear relation to the patient's situation (e.g., "Ego strength involves the ability to delay gratification").

The therapist talks about his or her own experience with no mention of relevance to patient: (e.g., "I went on vacation last week").

The therapist talks about objects or situations that the patient has mentioned, but excludes or passes over the patient's involvement other than as a reporter (e.g., "What kind of TV set was that?"; "You say it rained on Sunday—how much?").

Manner: The therapist is detached, remote, impersonal, barely there, minimally interested in the interchange, or withdraws from it. This may include:

1. The therapist withdraws his or her attention (e.g., therapist answers phone, falls asleep).

2. The therapist speaks to someone other than the patient; changes the subject to something not involving the patient (e.g., "Excuse me, was that a knock I heard?").
3. The therapist terminates the interaction.
4. The therapist is "there," but conveys noninvolvement by manner or tone of voice (e.g., yawning, displaying boredom or disinterest).

Disinterested withdrawal does not include acknowledged, felt withdrawal: "I'm sorry but our time is up," or "I hate to end this session," or "(sigh) I guess we have to stop."

Stage 2

Referent: The therapist refers to events including or involving the patient, with behavioral or intellectual elaboration of the patient's activities or thoughts, but these references do not refer to or define the patient's feelings.

1. The referent is to events in which the patient is personally involved, either as an active participant or as an interested bystander, that is, as an observer or as one affected by the events. References are to external or intellectual aspects of the patient's involvement in these events, but they do not identify the patient's inner feelings or perspective in any detail. Thoughts, opinions, wishes, attitudes, or evaluations may be referred to without explicit reference to associated feelings.
2. The word "feeling" may be used, but if terms like "you think" or "you wish" could be substituted, the remark is at Stage 2.
3. If the events referred to have not personally involved the patient, their importance to the patient is made explicit.
4. If the content is meant to be a description of the patient, it only serves to present ideas, attitudes, opinions, moral judgments, wishes, preferences, aspirations, or evaluations of capacities that describe the patient from an external, peripheral, or behavioral perspective.
5. If the content is an account of a dream, fantasy, hallucination, or free association, it should be treated in the same fashion as a narrative of events: for example, it would be at Stage 2 if the referent were to the patient's behavior or involvement.

Feelings and personal perspectives that may be apparent are still implicit, but not explicit. If the patient's feelings are mentioned, they are treated abstractly or impersonally as objects or are attributed to others. Third-person pronouns—for example, "one feels"— indicate this distancing.

Manner: The therapist's interest in or intellectual grasp of the interchange is explicit. Remarks indicate his or her ongoing attention and suggest that he or she has heard and is interested in what the patient says. Self-references do not disclose more personal feelings or immediate reactions but simply identify the therapist's role as an interested participant.

1. From his or her manner, the therapist seems interested in the content of the dialogue. The therapist's tone of voice, words of encouragement (e.g., "I see," "Uh huh"), or gestures provide contact on a superficial level.
2. When the therapist actively expresses his or her involvement (e.g., "I hear you," "I want to talk about this," "I understand that," "I want to know—tell me"), this

interest is clearly *content* oriented—that is, it is expressed for the purpose of continuing the patient's discourse and/or gaining clarity. Reactions are couched intellectually (e.g., ''I think . . . ,'' ''I know . . . '') and function to affirm that the therapist is still following the proceedings (e.g., ''That's right''). More personal or affective involvement, however, is passed over; or, if apparent, is very limited.

The therapist's intent and function is to get information or to keep the narrative going, but personal involvement is minimally expressed and feelings are not apparent.

Stage 3

Referent: The therapist refers to the patient's reaction to external events with some reference to feelings, but these are brief or limited to behavioral or descriptive comments. The result is a recognition of the patient's personal involvement without any detailed elaboration of the extent or quality of involvement. The patient's feelings are almost parenthetical; an event or idea is described, with the reference to the patient's feelings merely added.

1. Feelings are mentioned but not described or elaborated (''You were angry,'' or ''Your anger . . . '') except in situational, behavioral, or superficial terms.
2. The therapist refers to the patient's inner life or awareness, but in a limited fashion. Remarks recognize this perspective but do not elaborate it.
3. The content may be description of the patient as a person but the elaboration is limited to behavior or to certain roles or situations (e.g., patient as a parent) where the more personal perspective is assumed.

Manner: The therapist is involved, responsive, that is, personally and affectively involved in the interchange. The therapist is in the situation as a potential respondent and personal participant, as more than an interested observer.

1. The therapist clearly expresses or refers to his or her feelings or personal perspective.
2. If feelings are not explicitly mentioned, the therapist's reactive involvement or investment in the interchange is apparent from his or her expressive style, comments, immediacy of tone, spontaneity, and so on.
3. The therapist's expressed intent to become actively involved in the interchange or transaction is clearly communicated (e.g., ''I'm sitting here . . . waiting to react,'' or ''I hear the tremor in your voice'').
4. The therapist makes confrontive or provocative comments that do not explicitly state feelings, but clearly function to elicit or highlight the patient's feelings of the moment.

Stage 4

Referent: The therapist refers to the patient's feelings and/or internal, personal perspective. When events or situations are mentioned, it is only to provide context for the description of the patient's feelings and experiencing. Thus the elaboration at this stage provides a clearer picture of what the patient is like as a person through a description of his or her feelings and phenomenology.

The patient's feelings, motives, prior perceptions, goals, and so on are an integral part of the therapist's concern. They may be presented in several different temporal contexts:

1. Immediately felt emotions, perceptions, et cetera—as experienced by the patient at this moment in the interaction.
2. Vivid reliving or refeeling of past experiences, feelings, perceptions, motivations, et cetera.
3. Specifically directing the patient to speak about immediate experiencing (i.e., "What are you feeling now?").

Manner: The therapist clearly expresses being "with" the patient in an immediate, ongoing way.

1. The therapist takes over, continues, fills in, or reworks the patient's frame of reference as his or her own. This may include elaborations from the patient's content. The therapist speaks from and for the patient's perspective.
2. The therapist introduces his or her own feelings into the patient's situation (e.g., "If I were you, I would experience it as follows . . . ").
3. The therapist expresses, in style or tone, a clear intent to be an active sharing partner in the exchange.

Stage 5

Referent: The therapist invites the patient to explore and expand feelings and inner referents by stating a problem or proposition about them.

1. A feeling, reaction, or inner process (even a behavior pattern) is suggested by the therapist as a problem to be immediately explored (e.g., "Why are you so depressed?").
2. The therapist may ask a question to clarify or expand a patient's feeling or perspective (e.g., "Do you feel just anger or is there more?").
3. The therapist may offer bridging associations so that a problem or proposition is developed out of previous material the patient has provided ("That sounds as if you get angry when you feel put upon").
4. The therapist may simply refer to the patient's struggle to explore (e.g., "You're struggling with that").

The questions and formulations are not simply intellectual; rather, they encourage the patient to actively struggle to explore and expand his or her experience.

Manner: The therapist may use his or her own sense of struggle to expand the patient's search. While the therapist may say less than at earlier stages, there is little doubt about his or her full engagement in the process—the therapist communicates a sense of personal interest and commitment as well as his or her own struggle to know more.

1. The therapist's tone and style indicates his or her active struggle to go beyond what has been said. The therapist's grasp is no firmer than the patient's, however.
2. The therapist may simply continue to support the patient's exploration by revealing his or her own struggle and response (e.g., "I feel your frustration").

Stage 6

Patient Referent: The therapist focuses on the patient's directly sensed, emergent, newly recognized, or more fully realized feelings and/or experiences:

1. The therapist points to a vivid immediate sense of the patient's feelings emerging or changing. While the feelings and referents may still be unclear, the focus is clearly on the patient's direct and immediate sensing of them.
2. The therapist refers to the impact of the patient's emergent and/or shifting feelings, that is, to there being a more articulated and integrated sense of self and a clearer sense of personally significant issues (e.g., "If you could let go and feel needy, you'd find out it wasn't so awful").
3. If the therapist is referring to past shifts, this is done vividly and immediately.

As in Stage 5, the changes or the impact of changes must not just be recounted intellectually or abstractly; they must clearly be lived in the present moment.

Therapist Manner: Here the therapist is almost an extension of the patient, freely using his or her directly sensed feelings to confirm and extend the patient's shifting and expanding awareness. The therapist conveys that what is new and meaningful to the patient is equally new and meaningful to the therapist.

Stage 7

Patient Referent: The therapist's focus is on the patient's potential or present facility to move from one inner referent to another. The patient's capacity to build upon, link, and integrate each new realization on the former is noted or elaborated and fully shared.

Manner: Therapist and patient feelings and associations are dovetailed so that each flows from and builds on the other. There is an affirmative, illuminating quality to the dialogue and an integration of content and feeling in total support of the patient's steady and expanding awareness of immediately present feelings and internal processes.

Experiencing Interview

Another new direction involves the development of the Experiencing (EXP) interview as a means of directly assessing capacity for experiencing according to a standardized format. The proposed interview draws on features of both patient and therapist scales.

In light of the consistent relationships found between patient EXP and personality variables, we suspect that there may be considerable interest in and need for a more standardized way of assessing patient EXP apart from the effect of the therapy setting or the therapist's interventions. This is important, first, because an optimal personal experiencing capacity cannot be fairly judged unless the setting explicitly provides the appropriate opportunity; and second, because the therapy session itself, with its complex expectations, goals, and stresses, may not be the best place to gather a standardized picture of what a person can do. This interest in EXP assessment outside of therapy has origins in the original "sampling interview" method of the Wisconsin Project, where an independent clinician met occasionally with the patients for process and outcome assessments (Rogers *et al.*, 1967), and is also consistent with other attempts to design standardized assessment settings.

What is important about the EXP interview procedure we propose below is that, in contrast to more "open-ended" approaches, it is expressly designed to tap both baseline and "achievement" states, the latter being based on probes that are consistent with the scale stages. Like the therapist scale, the EXP interview is tentative and in need of considerable development. It is currently being used in somewhat altered form in a study of patients with alexithymia and/or a range of psychosomatic disorders. The two sample responses given below come from that study.

The EXP interview assumes that what is to be assessed is a person's typical or modal experiencing level (baseline phase) and the highest or peak level to which he or she can be led by an interviewer (response phase). Both scores would be of use in predicting response to therapy or other personality variables.

We assume that an individual's experiencing level at any one time is a result of:

1. the person's most comfortable or "operating" level
2. the content of discourse
3. the situation in which the discourse is taking place
4. the level of the experiencing directed and expressed by the interviewer (as described in the Therapist EXP Scale).

Thus a stepwise standard interview procedure would seem most appropriate, as follows.

Baseline Phase: The first purpose is to get a reading of the respondent's baseline experiencing and to establish a topic that is potentially important as subject matter for the subsequent response phase. The following instructions are first given:

- "Talk about yourself and what your life has been like for the past week."
- "Now talk about the most personally involving or significant experience in that time. If nothing seems relevant, then go back until one occurs to you." (Probes: "What was it like for you?" "What does/has it meant for you?" "How does this experience relate to other experiences you have had?")

The purpose of the probes is to see if the respondent makes experiential versus situational or intellectual connections with minimal direction on the part of the interviewer.

Response Phase: Next the interviewer attempts to raise the respondent's level of experiencing. In general, the interviewer should follow the outline in the referent portion of the Therapist EXP Scale.

If at Stage 1—Attempt to Raise to 2

- "What did you do?"
- "How did you participate?"
- "How or why was this of interest to you?"
- "Tell me more about what happened?"

If at Stage 2—Attempt to Raise to 3

- "How did you feel or react then?"
- "What was the impact on you?"
- "What was significant for you in that?"

If at Stage 3—Attempt to Raise to 4

- "What is/was (*feeling*) like?"
- "What was it like for you . . . what was it like for you to feel or to be that way?"
- "Focus on you at that time—what was it like for you?"
- "What is it like for you to be living this here, now, with me?"
- "Can you give a more personal account of that?"

If the respondent does not respond to these probes, stop and try the focusing instructions as outlined by Gendlin (1969; 1981). This may provide a more significant topic for the next set of probes.

If at Stage 4—Attempt to Raise to 5

- "What about (*that feeling*)?"
- "How can you use this, what can you make of it—what could it mean to you?"
- "Does this relate to anything that is a problem for you? Is there pain? Is it at all unclear or vague to you? If so, concentrate on that."
- "Is there anything that might surprise you if you stayed with the feeling? What does this say about you—does it relate to anything more about you that you know or could discover?"

If at Stage 5—Attempt to Raise to 6

- "Work now on that issue (the whole thing; feeling, connection, problem) or that feeling of wanting to learn more or resolve something important."
- "How does it feel now? Can you sense the crux of it?"
- "Is the feeling changing—do you feel a shift? What is coming out?"
- "Stay with it and see if something more comes."
- "Is there something new? Try to follow it."

If at Stage 6—Attempt to Raise to 7

- "Now that you've got it, can you say more about it?"
- "What does the whole picture feel like for you?"
- "Is it expanding? Does it link to other parts?"

Sample Segments of Patient and Therapist Ratings

The following two excerpts from therapy sessions are rated on Patient (P) and the two dimensions of Therapist EXP: Referent (TR) and Manner (TM). In the first segment from experiential therapy the therapist reflects the two phrases the patient uses to refer to the problem with school ("jittery" and "pull back") and clearly presses the patient to directly sense it (T9, T13) and focus on its unclear edges (T14). As the patient finds a new sense ("scared") she also vividly describes a complex and shifting perspective (feeling it, talking, withdrawn). When the therapist encourages a new perspective (being friendly with the fear) the patient then experiences a fuller sense of the problem.

C1: I was thinking about . . . on my way over . . . I don't seem to   P2
     think a hell of a lot of myself.
T1: So . . . you're asking . . . why do you have such a low esti-   TR5
     mate of yourself.   TM4

C2: Well, uh . . .

T2: Or, maybe not asking, exactly.   (See T1 above.)

C3: I had a dream . . . I was alone with this guy, ah (*silence*) . . .   P3
and the dream was real nice, it was a real nice relationship.
When I thought about it next day I thought, why don't I have
a real one! I don't think he could really see anything wrong
with me. I was also thinking why I was absent in school so
much. When it comes to the end of the line I don't have a
paper, I hold back. I get jittery and then I pull away from it.

T3: You're saying there is something similar about those two   TR5
things.   TM4

C4: Yeah. I have all these excuses about why I never do my best,   P3
uh . . .

T4: You come right up to the line and then something holds back.   TR4
                                                           TM4

C5: Yeah.

T5: And "jittery" is the best word for it.   (See T4 above.)

C6: Yeah, yeah. Uh . . . I pull back.   P3

T6: Pull back is it.   TR4
                                                           TM3

C7: The jittery is more a surface than the pull back. The jittery   P4
comes when part of me says well, you know, you really have
to do it now.

T7: So we don't know what pulls back, it's not the jittery that   TR5
pulls.   TM4

C8: No, the jittery is a result.   P4

T8: So we don't really know what the pull back feels like, what it   TR5
is that wants to pull back.   TM4

C9: Well I think it's . . . ah . . . that I don't want to test myself.   P5
And I'm afraid, ah, the bad things will be confirmed.

T9: Can you feel the pull back if you imagine yourself going ahead?   TR5
                                                       TM5

C10: Yeah, I can feel the pull back now. . . . . The pull back is into   P4
weed, that's what it does.

T10: Into weed.   TR3
                                                           TM2

C11: Marijuana, that's the perfect place to pull back.   P3

T11: That's a perfect place to pull back to.   TR3
                                                             TM3

C12: Yeah. But if I don't go to the line, then I don't have to pull   P5
back.

T12: As long as you don't really go across the line, there is no testing   TR5
of it, there is no proof, good, bad, and you're suspecting that   TM4
you're afraid of actually finding out.

C13: Right!

T13: I was interested also in just the feel quality of it, for a minute   TR6
you could feel the pull back.   TM4

C14: Yeah, I could feel it.   P4

T14: Let's just tap it lightly, and see what it turns up.   TR5
                                                            TM3

C15: (*Silence*) Scared . . . it's like the world is going to bite me or   P6
something (*laughs*).

T15: Umhum. Yeah, yeah.   TR5
                                                            TM4

C16: (*more silence*) It's very strange. Feeling this feeling underneath it, and trying to talk, right now.

T16: Sensing the feeling directly and trying to say what it is. And it's scared.   TR6 TM4

C17: It's very interesting, the fear is right underneath it. Now I'm content to just sit there with the withdrawn, and feel apathy until I . . . end up with the feeling, then I withdraw into the nice apathy again (*laughs*).   P6

T17: Mhm, the apathy is more comfortable and the fear is right under it, so you just push down and ah . . . there it is. (*silence*)   TR6 TM4

T18: Well, let's be friendly with the fear, and sort of say, that's all right, right now, we're not doing anything. We'd just like to hear from it. What it's so scared about. (*long silence, 3 minutes*)   TR6 TM5

C19: This is an all-good part of me but it would rather be dead than come out to . . . um . . . being tromped on.   P6

T19: It's all-good, but if it's going to get tromped on, it would rather be dead, or stay pulled back. (*silence*)   TR6 TM5

T20: Now, can you really be glad that part came out and that it's speaking to us, can you welcome it?   TR6 TM5

C21: It's like . . . when you're just being nice to a person, and someone watching later tells you that you were just trying to buy that person.   P6

T21: Inside you it's good and then they make something bad out of it?   TR6 TM5

C22: Yes. (*silence*)

C23: Well, that sure is different.   P6

The second sample is from eclectic–dynamic therapy. Here the therapist starts from a more interpretive stance to help the patient explore her feelings about her mother. When the therapist introduces a powerful image of the relationship ("suck you dry"), the patient also vividly encounters her feelings of fear.

T1: What would your grandmother say?   TR2 TM3

C1: I don't think she would have appreciated it too much. I think she would have condemned it. I think—   P2

T2: What would you have liked your grandmother to s—to have said?   TR3 TM3

C2: My mom just is right there in the middle of that—I just can't—   P2

T3: Hm. That's interesting. You mean you keep trying to think of your grandmother and your mom is standing there somehow in between you?   TR4 TM3

C3: It's like she's me, you know like she [T: Oh] like she's needing from my grandmother the same thing that I'm needing.   P3

T4: From your grandmother. You're both out in the cold then. Hmm. Both of you. Neither of you getting—   TR4 TM4

C4: And I don't —I don't want—I don't want her to be—forgiven or anything—you know I don't—   P3

T5: You don't want your mom to be forgiven?   TR4 TM4

C5:   No.   P4

T6:   Then how can you for—how can you be forgiven?—of the two   TR4
      of you competing for your grandmother's love like children.   TM4
      And you'd rather that neither of you got it—[C: Hm?]—than
      she—that she got it and you didn't.

C6:   No, I don't think she ever got it. [T: Hm.]   P2

T7:   But somehow it must have made you feel good that you were   TR4
      gettin' what your mom couldn't.   TM4

C7:   I just thought maybe the only reason I got it was because I   P2
      wasn't like her then.

T8:   Hhm. But that must have felt good to you.   TR4
                                                                           TM4

C8:   Not at the time because [T: Mhm]—I didn't care for her at the   P3
      time—you know.

T9:   For your grandmother?   TR2
                                                                           TM2

C9:   Yeah, I mean I really loved her and I felt I deserved that love—I   P4
      mean I never [T: Mhm] knew any different at that time an' my
      mom had nothing to do with it then [T: Mhm] but then later
      on 'hh I just really hated my mom an' I—for what she did to
      me an' the kind of person she is an' [T: Mhm] but I can see
      that she was really lacking things in her life—you know like
      maybe that love an' that attention from her mother. 'h

T10: You can see now maybe your mom got left—let down by your   TR4
      grandmother the same way you got let down by your mother.   TM4

C10: Yeah, a lot, a lot.   P4

T11: The same kind of rejection that you got from your mother.   TR4
                                                                           TM4

C11: Oh year [T: Mhm] yeah.   P4

T12: It keeps coming down that you and your mom are really equals   TR5
      though in a lot of ways, equally deprived—[C: Mhm] now   TM4
      equally rejected equally bad.

C12: How do I separate myself from her?   P5

T13: You've tried all your life to make yourself different from your   TR5
      mom. You tried to be good where she was bad, right? You tried   TM5
      to make her go away by going into your fantasies. Even the
      way you've talked about your mom it's always felt like there
      was a—I never a—knew s—had the right words to describe this
      to people but it's like a maelstrom, something pulling you
      down or pulling you into-it's like a suction or something an'
      she's trying to suck you into her an' you've put up walls and
      defended yourself and I think that was very scary—that that
      pull of hers trying to make you merge with her—into her—and
      you've always tried to make yourself different. To say I'm a
      person, I'm different from you.

C13: I still feel that—you know that's draining energy comes from—I   P6
      mean she can just drain me—you know?

T14: Mhm. Like—suck you dry.   TR6
                                                                           P6
C14: Yeah. 'hhh hh   P6

T15: So she's a very scary person also.   TR5
                                                                           TM4

C15: She's the only scary person. 'hh hhh   P6

T16: You mean everyone else is scary to the extent to which they're   TR5

like your mom.	TM4
C16: hhh Who do you mean?	P4
T17: You said she was the only scary person, she's the most scary person in your life really. But you're scared of other people— you're scared of me—you're scared of—you're scared of—you're scared of the psychologist—you're scared of a lot of people— that must be because in some ways you're afraid they're like your mom—like the day you saw me as your mom in some ways—trying to get—to you. You (?)	TR5 TM4
C17: I feel like—like I want to be a good person like that [T: Mhm] I don't feel like that's very much—like that that's really 'h very fragile—or very easily shattered—	P6
T18: Uhhuh, like you're afraid there's not really too much to you.	TR6 TM4
C18: Right, an' like [T: Uhmh] with all the defenses down—	P6
T19: You'd just be blown away.	TR6 TM4
C19: Yeah, an' that that's a real fear with—with anybody that I would do that with. 'hh	P6
T20: What are you afraid—that's a fantasy right? That's—that's p— fantasies practice is important, is the fantas—the nice fantasy— a fantasy that if you let down your defenses th—you might be completely—what? What is that fantasy about?	TR6 TM5
C20: It's like I just feel that—mostly with my mom—I just kind of feel like I'm gonna be annihilated, you know—I mean just like, 'h I don't know—I just—ugh—'h—like you said, just sucked— you know—hhhh.	P6

The following two examples of the EXP interview are from an ongoing study that uses a somewhat more standardized outline. Here the subject was asked to recall any recent instances of having had a strong feeling. The interviewer (*E*) was instructed to let the subject (*S*) talk for about 1 minute without probes before attempts to raise the EXP level (there were no probes for Stage 5 and above). After about 2 minutes of speech the subject was asked to rate the intensity of the feeling. In both examples the subjects responded to the instructions to describe feelings. The description of feeling pressured in Example 1 is external and cognitive (Stage 2 with a peak of 3) than the somewhat richer description of happiness (Stage 3 with a peak of 4) in the second example.

Example 1

E: Okay, good. Okay now, what I'd like you to do is I'd like you to think back to any recent or fairly recent situation which evoked a strong feeling in you of some sort. It doesn't matter to me what the feeling is—positive, negative, you know, good, bad, whatever—but any situation that you can recall that evoked some strong feeling. And once you've thought of a situation like that, I'd like you to describe that feeling to me.

S: Oh, I can tell you, it was a, there's a, it was very unusual as a matter of fact, it was yesterday and I was, I hadn't gotten much sleep and I'd just gotten back from my trip, and I was having problems with my motorcycle, and I had to be somewhere, and I just felt, I was thinking about all this stuff I had to do, and I felt very pressured, and I don't usually feel this way but I just felt extremely—um—frustrated and just like, ah, just frustrated and just gun it. When I got back to where I live I just unloaded my cycle and just threw it all down in the middle of my room, had to change real quick to make it to a doctor's appointment, and then I got there and the bike wasn't working properly and I didn't have money for the meter, and then I, they gave me 15 free minutes and I had to kinda race the doctor, he was kinda slow, and he didn't really say what I wanted to hear him say and I was just, it was just one thing after another, I was just totally, just, just about up to here, up to my neck with things and I just finally went and took a nap and that took care of everything.

E: Tell me more about the feeling of frustration as you were experiencing it.

S: When I get frustrated I feel a distinct lack of control over some things that are going on, that's what really frustrates me, and things pile up to cause that feeling and, um, I just feel so desperately unable to do anything, to, you know, even think rationally about, work myself out of that, and it doesn't happen that often, but when it happens it's very noticeable to me because I do, I just feel unable to cope and I just kind of know, and I try to figure out what my problem is and try and correct it, whether things are just lots coming down on me or what and then I just try and think that if I can I'll do something, and in this case the solution was I was very tired so I took a nap.

E: Take that feeling as you experienced it and put that to a scale of 1 to 10, 10 being the most frustrated, you know, and 1 being hardly at all frustrated. How would you rank that feeling?

S: Probably put that at 9. I was pretty frustrated.

Example 2

E: Okay. Now what I'd like you to do is to think back into the recent past to any situation that caused a strong emotion in you. A positive emotion, negative, could be pleasant, unpleasant, whatever, just any situation recently that you can recall.

S: Oh, wow, I have that every day.

E: Well, pick one and then tell me about that feeling.

S: How about, let's see, um, two weeks ago I went into my coach's office and he said to me, "How'd you like to run the race?" and I had been totally expecting not to go, had prepared myself not to be able to go because I had a good time last year, but this year I had hardly any meets and I didn't have a good enough time really to get in, and I thought he, at first I thought "Well, that creep, you know, he's just rubbing it in that I don't get to go," and I said, "Of course I'd like to go," and he said, "Well, you got invited," and I thought you're kidding, and I was just really excited and really happy. And I thought "Yaa for me." Everything like that, so that's what, I was really, really happy.

E: Okay. Tell me more about really excited and really happy.

S: I couldn't even, like how, how I get?

E: Well, ya, ya.

S: I just get really happy, um, smiling and just, it's like, I think it starts from like my toes and works its way up, you know, it's just my whole, I get, I think I'm—when I laugh, right?—really get involved and I'm just not oh ya, smile, I just yaa, you know, and I want to jump up and down in the air and, I think I hugged him, yaa, look it, I did this, I got invited, yaa for me.

E: Sounds pretty exciting to me too. Okay, put that feeling as you experience it also on a scale of 1 to 10 and tell me how strong that happy feeling was.

S: That was probably about a 9, 9 or a 10.

References

Auerbach, A. H., & Luborsky, L. Accuracy of judgments of psychotherapy and the nature of the "Good Hour." In J. Schlein, H. F. Hunt, J. P. Matarazzo, & C. Savage (Eds.), *Research in Psychotherapy* (Vol. 3). Washington, D.C.: American Psychological Association, 1968, pp. 155–168.

Barrileaux, S. P., & Bauer, R. The effects of Gestalt awareness training on experiencing level. *International Journal of Group Psychotherapy*, 1976, *26*, 431–440.

Beck, A. T., Dugo, J. M., Eng, A. M., Lewis, C. M., & Peters, L. N. The participation of leaders in the structural development of therapy groups. In R. R. Dies & K. R. MacKenzie (Eds.), *Advances in Group Psychotherapy*. New York: International Universities Press, 1983, pp. 137–158.

Beckman, J. F. Personal communication, California State College, Bakersfield, 1978.

Benjamin, L. S. Use of Structural Analysis of Social Behavior (SASB) and Markov chains to study dyadic interactions. *Journal of Abnormal Psychology*, 1979, *88*, 303–319.

Bierman, R., Davidson, B., Finkleman, L. Leonidas, J., Lumly, C., & Simister, S. *Toward meeting fundamental human needs: Preventive effects of the Human Service Community*. Unpublished report. Guelph (Ontario), 1976.

Bierman, R., & Lumly, C. Toward the humanizing community. *Ontario Psychologist*, 1973, *5*, 10–19.

Bommert, H., & Dahlhoff, H-D. *Das Selbsterleben (Experiencing) in der Psychotherapie*. Munchen: Urban & Schwarzenberg, 1978.

Custers, A. De manier van ervaren in het terapeuitisch proces. *Psychologica Belgica*, 1973, *13*, 125–138.

Dahl, H. A quantitative study of psychoanalysis. In R. R. Holt & E. Peterfreund (Eds.), *Psychoanalysis and Contemporary Science* (Vol. 1), New York: Van Nostrand Reinhold, 1972, pp. 237–257.

Dealy, M. T. An exploratory study of level of experiencing in test-anxious students exposed to "coping" and "mastery" modeling. Unpublished Doctoral Dissertation, New School for Social Research, 1978.

Elliott, R. "That in your hands": A comprehensive process analysis of a significant event in psychotherapy. *Psychiatry*, 1983, *46*, 113–129.

Elliott, R., Janus, E., Shulman, R., & Cline, J. *Significant events in psychotherapy: A systematic case study*. Paper presented at the meeting of the Society for Psychotherapy Research, Aspen, Colorado, June 1981.

Elliott, R., Cline, J., & Shulman, R. *Effective processes in psychotherapy: A single case study using four evaluative paradigms*. Unpublished manuscript, University of Toledo, 1982.

Elliott, R., Klein, M. H., & Mathieu-Coughlan, P. L. *A sequential analysis of empathy and experiencing: A case study*. Paper presented at the meeting of the Society for Psychotherapy Research, Sheffield (England), July, 1983.

Fishman, D. *Empirical correlates of the Experiencing Scale*. Paper presented at the meeting of the American Psychological Association, Washington, D.C., September, 1971.

Fontana, A. F., Dowds, B. N., & Eisenstadt, R. L., Social class and suitability for psychodynamic psychotherapy: A causal model. *Journal of Nervous and Mental Disease*, 1980, *168*, 658–665.

Gendlin, E. T. The function of experiencing in symbolization. Unpublished Doctoral Dissertation, University of Chicago, 1958.

Gendlin, E. T. Client-centered developments and work with schizophrenics. *Journal of Counseling Psychology*, 1962, *9*, 205–211. (a)

Gendlin, E. T. *Experiencing and the Creation of Meaning*. New York: The Free Press of Glencoe, 1962. (b)

Gendlin, E. T. A theory of personality change. In P. Worchel & D. Byrne (Eds.), *Personality Change*. New York: Wiley, 1964, pp. 100–148.

Gendlin, E. T. Values and the process of experiencing. In A. R. Mahrer (Ed.), *The Goals of Psychotherapy*. New York: Appleton-Century-Crofts, 1967, pp. 180–205.

Gendlin, E. T. The experiential response. In E. F. Hammer (Ed.), *Use of Interpretation in Treatment: Technique and Art*. New York: Grune & Stratton, 1968, pp. 208–227.

Gendlin, E. T. Focusing, *Psychotherapy: Theory, Research and Practice*, 1969, *6*, 4–15.

Gendlin, E. T. Client-centered and experiential psychotherapy. In D. Wexler & L. N. Rice (Eds.), *Innovations in Client-Centered Therapy*. New York: Wiley, 1974, pp. 211–246. (a)

Gendlin, E. T. The role of knowledge in practice. In G. F. Farwell, N. R. Gamsky, & P. Mathieu-Coughlan (Eds.), *The Counselor's Handbook*. New York: Intext Educational Publishers, 1974, pp. 269–294. (b)

Gendlin, E. T. Experiential psychotherapy. In R. Corsini (Ed.), *Current Psychotherapies* (rev. ed.). Itasca, Illinois: F. E. Peacock, 1979, pp. 317–352.

Gendlin, E. T. *Focusing*. New York: Bantam Books, 1981.

Gendlin, E. T. *Experiential psychotherapy*. Unpublished manuscript draft, 1982.

Gendlin, E. T., Beebe, J., Cassens, J., Klein, M., & Oberlander, M. Focusing ability in psychotherapy, personality, and creativity. In J. M. Shlein (Ed.), *Research in Psychotherapy* (Vol. 3). Washington, D.C.: American Psychological Association, 1968, pp. 217–238.

Gendlin, E. T., Jenney, R., & Shlein, J. M. Counselor ratings of process and outcome in client-centered therapy. *Journal of Clinical Psychology*, 1960, *16*, 210–213.

Gendlin, E. T., & Tomlinson, T. M. *Experiencing Scale*. Unpublished manuscript, University of Wisconsin Psychiatric Institute, 1962.

Gendlin, E. T., & Tomlinson, T. M. The process conception and its measurement. In C. R. Rogers, E. T. Gendlin, D. J. Kiesler, & C. B. Truax (Eds.), *The therapeutic relationship and its impact: A study of psychotherapy with schizophrenics*. Madison: University of Wisconsin Press, 1967, pp. 109–131.

Gendlin, E. T., & Zimring, F. M. The qualities or dimensions of experiencing and their change. *Counseling Center Discussion Papers*, 1955, *1* (Whole No. 3). University of Chicago Library.

Gorney, J. E. Experiencing and age: Patterns of reminiscence among the elderly. Unpublished Doctoral Dissertation, University of Chicago, 1968.

Gottschalk, L. A., Winget, C. N., & Gleser, G. C. *Manual of instructions for using the Gottschalk-Gleser content analysis scales*. Berkeley: University of California Press, 1969.

Greenberg, L. S. The intensive analysis of recurring events from the practice of Gestalt therapy. *Psychotherapy: Theory, Research and Practice*, 1980, *17*, 143–152.

Greenberg, L. S. Toward a task analysis of conflict resolution in Gestalt therapy. *Psychotherapy: Theory, Research and Practice*, 1983, *20*, 190–201.

Greenberg, L. S., & Rice, L. N. The specific effects of a Gestalt intervention. *Psychotherapy: Theory, Research and Practice*, 1981, *18*, 31–37.

Gruver, G. G. The use of a process research measure in student development groups. Unpublished Doctoral Dissertation, University of Arizona, 1971.

Hendricks, M., & Cartwright, R. D. Experiencing level in dreams: An individual difference variable. *Psychotherapy: Theory, Research and Practice*, 1978, *15*, 292–298.

Hinterkopf, E., & Brunswick, L. Teaching mental patients to use client-centered and experiential therapeutic skills with each other. *Psychotherapy: Theory, Research and Practice*, 1981, *18*, 394–402.

Howe, E. S., & Pope, B. An empirical scale of therapist verbal activity level in the initial interview. *Journal of Consulting Psychology*, 1961, *25*, 296–303.

Jachim, D. P. Comparative effects of pretherapy training on experiencing and self disclosure. Unpublished Doctoral Dissertation, Illinois Institute of Technology, 1978.

Jennen, M. G., Lietaer, G., & Rombauts, J. *Relationship and interaction between therapist conditions (as perceived by client, therapist and outside judges), client depth of experiencing during therapy and constructive personality change in individual psychotherapy*. Unpublished manuscript, University of Leuven (Belgium), 1978.

Joyce, A. S. Experiencing and the empathic response: A laboratory test and correlates from an inventory of imaginal processes. Unpublished Master's Thesis, University of Guelf, Ontario, 1980.

Karon, B. P., & VandenBos, G. R. Experience, medication, and the effectiveness of psychotherapy with schizophrenics. *British Journal of Psychiatry*, 1970, *116*, 427–428.

Kiesler, D. J. Comparison of Experiencing Scale ratings of naive versus clinically sophisticated judges. *Journal of Consulting and Clinical Psychology*, 1970, *35*, 134.

Kiesler, D. J. *Refinement of the Experiencing Scale as a counseling tool*. (Contract No. OEC 3-7-061329-2835) Report to U.S. Department of Health, Education and Welfare, Office of Education, Bureau of Research, 1969.

Kiesler, D. J. Patient experiencing level and successful outcome in individual psychotherapy of schizophrenics and psychoneurotics. *Journal of Consulting and Clinical Psychology*, 1971, *37*, 370–385.

Kiesler, D. J. *The Process of Psychotherapy*, Chicago: Aldine, 1973.

Kiesler, D. J., Klein, M. H., & Mathieu, P. L. Sampling from the recorded therapy interview: The problem of segment location. *Journal of Consulting Psychology*, 1965, *29*, 337–344.

Kiesler, D. J., Mathieu, P. L., & Klein, M. H. Sampling from the recorded therapy interview: A comparative study of different segment lengths. *Journal of Consulting Psychology*, 1964, *28*, 349–357.

Kiesler, D. J., Mathieu, P. L., & Klein, M. H. Patient experiencing level and interaction-chronograph variables in therapy interview segments. *Journal of Consulting Psychology*, 1967, *31*, 224.

Klein, J. M. *The application of process measurement to journal material from student development laboratories and autobiographical material*. Unpublished manuscript, University of Arizona, 1970.

Klein, M. H. *Overview of rating methodology*. Paper presented at the meeting of the American Psychological Association, Washington, D.C., September 1971.

Klein, M. H., & Gill, M. *Experiencing and patient productivity in ten psychoanalytic sessions*. Unpublished manuscript, University of Wisconsin, 1967.

Klein, M. H., Mathieu, P. L., Gendlin, E. T., & Kiesler, D. J. *The Experiencing Scale: A Research and Training Manual* (Vol. 1). Madison: University of Wisconsin Extension Bureau of Audiovisual Instruction, 1969 (copyright 1970).

Lambert, M. J., DeJulio, S. J., & Stein, D. M. Therapist interpersonal skills: Process, outcome, methodological considerations, and recommendations for future research. *Psychological Bulletin*, 1978, *85*, 467–489.

Lansford, E., & Bordin, E. S. A research note on the relation between the Free Association and Experiencing Scales. *Journal of Consulting and Clinical Psychology*, 1983, *51*, 367–369.

Lietaer, G. Personal communication, University of Leuven (Belgium), 1971.

Lewis, C. M., & Beck, A. T. Experiencing level in the process of group development. *Group*, 1983, *7*, 18–26.

Lieberman, M. A., & Coplan, A. S. Distance from death as a variable in the study of aging. *Developmental Psychology*, 1970, *2*, 71–84.

Luborsky, L. Personal Communication, University of Pennsylvania, 1982.

Luria, J. Personal communication, William Alanson White Institute, New York, New York, 1970.

Marlowe, J. L. The impact of videotape feedback on the observing ego functions in a psychoanalytic psychotherapy study. Unpublished Doctoral Dissertation, University of Wisconsin-Milwaukee, 1980.

Melstrom, M. A., & Cartwright, R. D. Effects of successful vs. unsuccessful psychotherapy outcome on some dream dimensions. *Psychiatry*, 1983, *46*, 51–65.

Merrifield, J., & Fishman, D. B. *Conceptual categories for assessing therapist–patient interaction in terms of how well the therapist contracts for and conducts psychotherapy*. Unpublished manuscript, Denver, Colorado, 1967.

Mintz, J. Dimensions of psychotherapy and their relation to outcome. Unpublished Doctoral Dissertation, New York University, 1969.

Mintz, J., & Luborsky, L. *P*-technique factor analysis in psychotherapy research: An illustration of a method. *Psychotherapy: Theory, Research and Practice*, 1970, *7*, 1–18.

Mintz, J., Luborsky, L., & Auerbach, A. N. Dimensions of psychotherapy: A factor-analytic study of ratings of psychotherapy sessions. *Journal of Consulting and Clinical Psychology*, 1971, *36*, 106–120.

Mitchell, K. M., Bozarth, J. D., & Krauft, C. D. A reappraisal of the therapeutic effectiveness of accurate empathy, nonpossessive warmth and genuineness. In A. S. Gurman & A. M. Razin (Eds.), *The Therapists Contribution to Effective Psychotherapy*. New York: Pergamon, 1976, pp. 482–502.

Moulthrop, M. A. Toward a differential psychotherapy technique: The experiencing reactions of obsessive and hysteric personalities to character interpretations. Unpublished Doctoral Dissertation, Emory University, 1973.

Moxnes, P. Verbal communication level and anxiety in psychotherapeutic groups. *Journal of Counseling Psychology*, 1974, *21*, 399–401.

Mueller, M. J. Conflict-reporting in social desirability contexts: Change in level of experiencing as a function of a social learning treatment, ego resilience, and self-actualization. Unpublished Doctoral Dissertation, University of Texas, Austin, 1981.

McIntire, J. W. The relationship of self-report and level of experiencing to teacher effectiveness. Unpublished Doctoral Dissertation, University of Texas, Austin, 1973.

McMullin, R. E. Effects of counselor focusing on client self-experiencing under low attitudinal conditions. *Journal of Counseling Psychology*, 1972, *19*, 282–285.

Nichols, M. P., & Taylor, T. Y. *Influence of style of therapist interventions on the process of group psychotherapy*. Paper presented at the meeting of the Society for Psychotherapy research, Denver, Colorado, June 1974.

Nixon, D. The relationships of primal therapy outcome with experiencing, voice quality and transference. Unpublished Doctoral Dissertation, York University, Ontario, 1982.

Olsen, L. E. The use of visual imagery and experiential focusing in psychotherapy. Unpublished Doctoral Dissertation, University of Chicago, 1975.

Parloff, M. B., Waskow, I. E., & Wolfe, B. E. Research on therapist variables in relation to process and outcome. In S. L. Garfield & A. E. Bergin (Eds.), *Handbook of Psychotherapy and Behavior Change: An Empirical Analysis* (2nd ed.). New York: Wiley, 1978, pp. 233–282.

Pattyn, M. R., Rombauts, J., & Lietaer, G. *Experiencing level in encounter groups*. Unpublished manuscript, University of Leuven (Belgium), 1975.

Pollack, M. The function of perceptual conreteness, affect and experiencing in a psychoanalysis. Unpublished Doctoral Dissertation, New York University, 1973.

Richert, A. J. Expectations, experiencing and change in psychotherapy. *Journal of Clinical Psychology*, 1976, *32*, 438–444.

Rogers, C. R. A current formulation of client-centered therapy. *Social Science Review*, 1950, *24* (Whole No. 4).

Rogers, C. R. The necessary and sufficient conditions of therapeutic personality change. *Journal of Consulting Psychology*, 1957, *21*, 95–103.

Rogers, C. R. A process conception of psychotherapy. *American Psychologist*, 1958, *13*, 142–149.

Rogers, C. R. A theory of therapy, personality, and interpersonal relationships, as developed by the client-centered framework. In S. Koch (Ed.), *Psychology: A Study of a Science: Volume III Formulations of the Person and the Social Context*. New York: McGraw-Hill, 1959, pp. 184–256. (a)

Rogers, C. R. A tentative scale for the measurement of process in psychotherapy. In E. A. Rubinstein & M. B. Parloff (Eds.), *Research in Psychotherapy* (Vol 1). Washington, D.C.: American Psychological Association, 1959, pp. 96–107. (b)

Rogers, C. R., & Dymond, R. F. (Eds.). *Psychotherapy and Personality Change*. Chicago: University of Chicago Press, 1954.

Rogers, C. R., Gendlin, E. T., Kiesler, D. J., & Truax, C. B. (Eds.). *The Therapeutic Relationship and its Impact: A Study of Psychotherapy with Schizophrenics*. Madison: University of Wisconsin Press, 1967.

Rubenstein, S. Changes in levels of client experiencing as a result of therapist responses made within the context of high and low levels of facilitation. Unpublished Doctoral Dissertation, University of Wisconsin-Madison, 1970.

Ryan, R. The role of the experiencing variable in the psychotherapeutic process. Unpublished Doctoral Dissertation, University of Illinois, 1966.

Saslow, G., Mattarazzo, J. D., & Guze, S. B. The stability of interaction chronograph patterns in psychiatric interviews. *Journal of Consulting Psychology*, 1955, *19*, 417–430.

Schaeffer, N. D., & Ables, N. Client attraction and distress: Unexpected impact on psychotherapeutic process. *Psychotherapy: Theory, Research and Practice*, 1977, *14*, 134–138.

Schoeninger, D. W. Client experiencing as a function of therapist self-disclosure and pre-therapy training in experiencing. Unpublished Doctoral Dissertation, University of Wisconsin-Madison, 1965.

Schoeninger, D. W., Klein, M. H., & Mathieu, P. L. Sampling from the recorded therapy interview: Patient experiencing ratings made with and without therapist speech cues. *Psychological Reports*, 1967, *20*, 250.

Schoeninger, D. W., Klein, M. H., & Mathieu, P. L. Comparison of two methods for training judges to rate psychotherapy recordings. *Journal of Consulting and Clinical Psychology*, 1968, *32*, 499.

Silberschatz, G. The effects of the analysts neutrality on the patient feelings and behavior in the psychoanalytic situation. Unpublished Doctoral Dissertation, New York University, 1977.

Silberschatz, G. Personal communication, Mount Zion Hospital and Medical Center, San Francisco, 1981.

Simon, J., Fink, G., & Endicott, N. A study of silence in recorded analysis. *Journal of the Hillside Hospital*, 1967, *16*, 224–233.

Slack, W. V., & Slack, C. W. Talking to a computer about emotional problems: A comparative study. *Psychotherapy: Theory, Research and Practice*, 1977, *14*, 156–164.

Stern, M. I., & Bierman, R. Facilitative functioning of A-B therapist types. *Psychotherapy: Theory, Research and Practice*, 1973, *10*, 44–47.

Stiles, W. B., McDaniel, S. H., & McGaughey, K. Verbal response mode correlates of "Experiencing." *Journal of Consulting and Clinical Psychology*, 1979, *47*, 795–797.

Tarule, J. M. Patterns of developmental transition in adulthood. Unpublished Doctoral Dissertation, Harvard University, 1978.

Tetran, B. Personal communication, University of Montreal, 1981.

Tomlinson, T. M. A validation study of a scale for the measurement of the process of personality change in psychotherapy. Unpublished Master's Thesis, University of Wisconsin-Madison, 1962. (a)

Tomlinson, T. M. Three approaches to the study of psychotherapy: Process, outcome, and change. Unpublished Doctoral Dissertation, University of Wisconsin-Madison, 1962. (b)

Tomlinson, T. M., & Hart, J. T. A validation of the process scale. *Journal of Consulting Psychology*, 1962, *26*, 74–78.

Truax, C. B., & Mitchell, K. M., Research on certain therapist interpersonal skills in relation to process and outcome. In A. E. Bergin & S. L. Garfield (Eds.), *Handbook of Psychotherapy and Behavior Change*. New York: Wiley, 1971, pp. 299–344.

Walker, A., Rablen, R. A., & Rogers, C. R. Development of a scale to measure process change in psychotherapy. *Journal of Clinical Psychology*, 1960, *16*, 79–85.

Wexler, D. A. *Depth of experiencing of emotion and the elaboration of meaning*. Paper presented at the meeting of the Western Psychological Association, San Francisco, April, 1974.

Yalom, I. D., Bond, G., Bloch, S., Zimmerman, E., & Friedman, L. The impact of a weekend group experience on individual therapy. *Archives of General Psychiatry*, 1977, *34*, 399–415.

3

Measures of Client and Therapist Vocal Quality

Laura N. Rice
Gillian P. Kerr
York University
North York, Ontario

The two process systems discussed in this chapter were originally constructed for use in the Quantitative–Naturalistic Research Program at the University of Chicago Counselling and Psychotherapy Research Center (Butler, Rice, & Wagstaff, 1962). The purpose of the program was to carry out rigorous naturalistic observation and research in order to identify significant patterns of client and therapist process in client-centered therapy. The patterns thus identified would then be linked with pretherapy prognostic measures and posttherapy outcome measures.

A number of client and therapist process systems, some verbal and others vocal, were constructed for the project by Rice and Wagstaff. The purpose was to provide an objective, multidimensional record of the actual moment-to-moment process engaged in by the two participants. It was intended that the client and therapist classification systems should reduce the complexity of the observations and permit quantification, while still making distinctions that promised to be clinically interesting. A basic assumption underlying this research program was that in successful client-centered psychotherapy the client participates in a way that leads to the generation of new inner experience, and that the expressiveness of the therapist influences and is influenced by the expressiveness of the client's style of participation (Butler, Rice, & Wagstaff, 1962). Of the different process systems constructed, the ones that yielded the most interesting patterns, as well as being the most different from existing process systems were the Client and Therapist Voice Quality Systems.

Strategy Decisions

Based on the goals and assumptions discussed above, a number of initial strategy decisions were made concerning the form that the process systems were to take. In the first place the measures were to be nominal not ordinal, with each class containing qualitatively different behaviors, rather than building in any assumptions about their order on some therapeutic dimension. The classes within each measure were to be mutually exclusive and exhaustive. Every segment in an audiotaped interview was to be placed in one and only one category and no remainder category was included. This has the advantage of forcing the rater to make a choice, which increases the power of the system in making discriminations, but it builds in some unreliability. There will always be indeterminate responses that have some features of two or more different classes. Thus even the most experienced pair of raters may place them in different categories.

A second decision, closely related to the first, was that the systems were to be descriptive of the actual behavior of the participants, involving low levels of inference on the part of the raters. Each category was to include behaviors (client statements) that were similar *as* behavior, rather than grouping together behaviors that were assumed to have similar conceptual meanings. Rather than building complex relationships into the system our goal was to *discover* relationships by means of the detailed analyses to be carried out.

The third decision, an especially important one, was to focus on *style* of participation rather than on content. For instance, in the Client Vocal Quality System we were not trying to specify the vocal cues for particular affects such as anxiety or depression as has often been done in psycholinguistic studies (Mahl, 1956; Siegman, 1978; Scherer, 1981). Our approach was to attempt to isolate a limited number of styles of engagement in the therapy process. One of the most basic beliefs of client-centered therapists is that it is the manner in which the client engages in the process of exploration, rather than the focus on some particular content that is decisive for therapeutic change.

A fourth decision that was made almost automatically proved to have important consequences. Inasmuch as we were clinical psychologists rather than psycholinguists by training, we looked for meaningful *patterns* of vocal features rather than the more usual practice of studying individual aspects such as pauses or pitch contours, for instance. Studies of single features have in general yielded rather ambiguous findings. It seems clear in retrospect that much of the power of the system lies in the fact that the significance of a given feature is judged only in relation to other features.

The fifth strategy decision was to make use of expert clinical judgment at the very beginning of system construction in order to locate meaningful stylistic patterns, and then attempt to specify these patterns in terms of objectively discernable aspects. Our goal was to minimize clinical judgment during the actual rating and in the interpretation of the ratings, but to maximize clinical judgment in the construction of the system. The opposite strategy is used in many psycholinguistic studies, which begin with detailed linguistic and paralinguistic transcriptions, and from them draw highly inferential conclusions (cf. Pittenger, Hockett, & Danehy, 1960).

In spite of their complexity, vocal measures seem to have some real advantages. In the first place the vocal channel seems to be perhaps the most sensitive indicator of key elements in client and therapist participation. Secondly vocal measures are flexible enough to reflect moment-to-moment shifts in participation as well as more enduring styles. A third, more practical advantage is that one can work from audiotapes without the expense of having tapes transcribed. Transcripts are helpful but not necessary provided that the first rater notes down the first few words of each response rated to make sure that both raters are including the same responses.

Construction and Development of Process Systems—A Suggested Outline

The experience of constructing these process measures and of developing them over the years, has suggested that distinguishing five general phases in the construction and development of process systems provides a useful structure for thinking about new process systems. The development of the present measures did not follow this orderly pattern, but in retrospect it seems like an illuminating structure within which to view process research. The five phases are discussed briefly below, and the discussion of the Client Vocal Quality System (CVQ) will follow this organization. Inasmuch as the

Therapist Vocal System is still in the process of development, only the first four steps are reported, with emphasis placed on the problems involved in developing such a process system.

1. The first step involves the clinical–theoretical base for the construction of categories within the chosen domain. Our experience suggests that it is valuable to begin with extensive clinical observation, involving intensive listening to tapes and/or videotapes and, if possible, tapping the clinical judgment of the therapists involved. Theory provides useful input, of course, but the categories as they are developed should be repeatedly checked against clinical observation. When this is disregarded, one may come out with a category system which is theoretically satisfying and logically arranged, but which will not make distinctions that are clinically interesting.

2. The second phase involves specifying in detail the aspects by which the behaviors in each class may be recognized. This is not only important for objective rating, but it has the value of yielding a fine-grained description of the behaviors that characterize each class.

Process systems that are too enmeshed in the theoretical constructs of a particular theoretical system are often misleading or meaningless in another orientation. A process system needs to be relevant to theory, but the closer we can stay to a truly descriptive system, while still reducing the complexity of our observations, the more we will be able to use our process languages in a variety of different orientations. That is, the different categories may not have the *same* meaning in different orientations, but they should have meaning. The concrete product of this second phase is a detailed manual for training raters.

3. The third step involves ensuring adequate interrater reliability. This is closely tied to the second step, since one moves back and forth between them. As we began to train raters we became aware of distinctions that needed to be clarified, or became aware of assumptions of our own that had not been made explicit.

4. The fourth phase involves establishing the predictive validity of the category system by investigating relationships with therapy outcome. This presents problems because final outcomes are remote in time and complexly determined. It is becoming more and more apparent that the usual approach of rating interview samples and summing ratings without regard to the context in which the behavior occurs may conceal more interesting relationships than it reveals (Rice & Greenberg, 1984). The relationships found are likely to be only moderately strong, and often somewhat ambiguous in meaning. Nevertheless it is an important step to find out if any of the categories in the system are systematically related to therapeutic change. Other categories may not relate significantly to outcome, but may prove to make useful distinctions in more detailed studies, and are therefore worth retaining.

5. The fifth phase involves investigating the construct validity of the categories. Although we are not usually trying to assess traits with process measures, we *are* using observable external process indicators to infer the internal processes taking place in the client at a given moment. Assumptions about internal processes are usually built into the construction of the system, and its ultimate productivity in yielding understanding of the mechanisms of therapeutic change will depend on the construct validity of its categories. The distinctions made by Cronbach & Meehl (1955) between predictive validity and construct validity of tests, and their methodological suggestions for establishing construct validity apply as well to therapy process measures as they do to psychological tests. Unfortunately in most studies using process systems we are of necessity testing the system as well as testing the stated hypothesis. If the construct

validity of a system has already been convincingly demonstrated, then one can use the instrument to test interesting and complex relationships. In empirically demonstrating construct validity one is explicitly placing the process measure into a theoretical network that other researchers can make use of in testing a variety of hypotheses. This step is not accomplished all at once, however, nor is it essential that it precede the broader use of the system. Examples of such uses are given in the final section of this chapter.

Client Vocal Quality

The Clinical–Theoretical Base for the Project

In constructing the client systems Rice and Wagstaff, functioning as clinician–investigators, began by listening intensively to interviews or sections of interviews that had been characterized by the therapists involved as "good" or "poor," and in which the client had been characterized as "really working," "difficult," "good client," and so on. Although the therapists were not given any criteria on which to classify the tapes, they were applying implicit criteria from their own experience and from the general client-centered point of view. Client-centered therapists have always been very much aware of the importance of a kind of inner awareness, differentiating out new aspects of it and attempting to symbolize them in words.

The client-centered therapist attempts to look through the client's eyes, responding in a way that will help the client to maintain or increase this inward focus, rather than relating in ways that would shift the client's focus to analyzing the material. This quality of turning inward, of groping along new paths, seemed to be the kind of process that would lead to generating new inner experience.

It became apparent as we listened to the tapes that the vocal rather than the verbal channel might be the clearest indicator of this inner concentration. We began to identify a particular pattern of vocal features at such moments, and began to call that pattern "Focused." Once we began to attend explicitly to the vocal channel, other patterns became apparent in client segments that had been characterized by the therapists involved as unfavorable process or as presenting particular kinds of difficulties.

As mentioned above the decision had been made initially to classify style variables rather than content variables. It was also decided, and here again this decision was consistent with client-centered thinking, to look for styles of engaging in exploration, rather than attending primarily to the interpersonal messages sent from client to therapist. It will become apparent that the categories probably do in fact reflect relationship messages as well as processing styles. The Externalizing pattern, for instance, seems to convey a deployment of attentional energy outward toward having an effect on the therapist, and some clinicians who have used the measure consider Externalizing voice to be an indication of defensiveness. Nevertheless, the most salient aspect of the Externalizing pattern in contrast with the inner exploring quality of the Focused style is the external rather than internal focus and the premonitored quality rather than the sense of new paths being explored.

From our initial list of possible patterns we eliminated overlapping or ambiguous classes. We also eliminated classes that seemed to remain invariant for a particular client over time and occasions, since we were trying to construct descriptors that would be sensitive to moment-to-moment shifts in involvement. We returned again and again to listening to the tapes and engaging in clinical discussions. Although client-centered theory was considered, each class to be included had to seem interesting clinically rather than simply completing some externally logical scheme. All this was extremely time consuming, but the people who served on the research teams all commented on the productivity of these discussions for their own clinical thinking. Construction of process systems is time consuming and at times frustrating, but it can also lead to new clinical thinking and may even be an interesting vehicle for training therapists.

The resulting classification system contained four mutually exclusive classes which formed a nominal measure. Although we had some hunches about the significance of the different classes, the important thing for us was to see each as a pattern in its own right rather than as a point on a scale, and then to let the significance of each class emerge from the research analyses. The fact that no indeterminate or mixed class was introduced probably led to some unreliability, since there are always some mixed types that yield little better than chance agreement, even with expert raters. Our judgment was that the loss in reliability would probably be compensated for by the gain in validity over the whole range of clients achieved by forcing raters to make a choice for every response. Any client response of more than a few syllables was placed in one and only one of these four classes.

One further theoretical point should be addressed here. This process system, like the others in the Chicago project, was designed to be a sensitive descriptor of moment-to-moment shifts in client process rather than a stable individual difference variable. And yet the predictive studies reported below suggest stability over time. The model of client vocal behavior that seems to make sense out of the findings from the different studies is that of "stylistic repertoire" (Rice & Koke, 1981). The assumption is that each person has a number of different processing styles available, but that the particular style deployed at any moment will depend on the person's judgment of the demands and possibilities of the particular situation. People seem to differ both in the styles that tend to be dominant and in the range of styles available to them. This seems to fit with a more general model of human beings as having capacities and tendencies that remain consistent over time, but as able to vary their behavior depending on their goals and construals of different situations.

Clinical Descriptions

Clinical descriptions of these four vocal patterns are given below. For the sake of clarity these are given in a more precise form than the ones we originally arrived at, and are based on continuing experiences with the system. These descriptions are based on clinical impression and are *not* used in training raters. Raters are trained to distinguish the patterns on the basis of the vocal aspects that will be discussed in the next section.

1. Focused. This vocal style involves a turning inward of attentional energy, deployed toward tracking inner experience and finding a way to symbolize it in words. There is a good deal of energy used in a concentrated way, rather than being discharged in overflow. The effort to symbolize seems to be as much for oneself as for the listener. The quality of groping and hesitation does not seem to be the nonfluency of thought disruption, but has the pondering quality of feeling one's way into new territory and generating new facets of experience.

2. Externalizing. This style seems to involve a deployment of attentional energy outward in an effort to produce some effect in the outside world. It has a premonitored quality, suggesting that the content being expressed is *not* being newly experienced and symbolized. Although the high energy and wide pitch range may initially give an impression of expressiveness, the rhythmic intonation pattern conveys a "talking at" quality.

3. *Limited*. This pattern seems to involve a holding back or withdrawal of energy. The effect of thinness is much more pronounced than an inward or outward focus. This pattern suggests a walking-on-eggs quality, distance from what is being said, and probably from what is being experienced.

4. *Emotional.* This class contains statements in which the speech pattern is disrupted or distorted to some extent by emotional overflow. It is this quality of overflow rather than the particular emotion being expressed that places the response in this class.

Descriptive Specification of Categories

The next step was to attempt to specify exactly the vocal aspects by which each of the four patterns could be recognized. We wanted to minimize clinical judgment and provide the raters with performance criteria for making judgments. This not only seemed important for training and for reliability, but also seemed to be an important step for eventually using the system in other therapeutic orientations. Each of these classes might have different meaning in different orientations, but at least we would be talking about the same performance patterns. We needed an objective, theory-neutral language with which to describe each of the vocal patterns. The most obvious source for this descriptive language was in the field of linguistics, especially the paralinguistic literature. This was not wholly successful since there is a surprising lack of agreement on terminology even within the field of linguistics, and there were often no good criteria for discriminating some of the aspects that had seemed most crucial in the clinical distinctions made. This whole issue will be discussed more fully in the therapist section.

We finally identified six discriminable aspects that seemed essential in making the necessary discriminations between classes. This was a complex process often involving juxtaposing two segments that shared some similar aspects but sounded different to us, and thus being able to pinpoint the feature that was making the difference. At other times we tried varying some aspect in our own speech to see if it made a difference to the listener. The six aspects listed below are not wholly independent, and not all are relevant to each one of the patterns.

1. *Production of Accentuations*. Raters are asked to note whether accentuation is produced primarily by pitch rise or by an increase in loudness together with some drawl.

2. *Accentuation Patterns*. Emphasis patterns may be more pronounced than is usual for English, giving the effect of a regular beat or even of a sing-song quality. On the other hand they may be even more irregular than is usual, with accentuation of two or more adjoining syllables in a single clause, followed by phrases with very little accentuation.

3. *Regularity of Pace*. The pace may be slow or fast, but in either case there may be a good deal of variation within a given utterance.

4. *Terminal Contours*. Raters are asked to note whether the pitch rises, drops, remains level, or slides on the last syllable of a clause. One is not making this analysis for each clause, but is noting whether the coutours are used in an accentuating, speech-making way, or whether they give the total intonation pattern a more ragged, unexpected sound.

5. *Perceived Energy*. Here the raters are essentially making two decisions. First they decide whether the voice sounds full or whether there is an impression of thinness.

Secondly they judge the "push" or force in the voice. An utterance that is above the natural voice platform of that person will sound limited when there is little push in the voice, but with more push the utterance will be placed in a different category.

6. Disruption of Speech Pattern. The decision to make here is whether or not the regular speech pattern is being disrupted or seriously distorted by emotional overflow.

The four vocal patterns are described below in terms of the vocal aspects by which they may be recognized. This information is summarized in brief form in Table 3.1 and is used as a kind of decision chart by the raters.

The Four Vocal Patterns

Focused

1. Accentuation. The accent on the syllables that receive the primary emphasis is achieved primarily by an increase in loudness rather than a pitch rise. There may also be some drawl on the stressed syllables.

2. Accentuation Pattern. The accentuation pattern is irregular even for English, and accents sometimes occur in unexpected places. For instance, adjoining syllables sometimes receive almost equal primary stresses.

3. Pace. The pace is irregular. It is usually slowed, with unfilled pauses in unexpected places, but there may be patches that are speeded up.

4. Terminal Contours. The contours at the ends of clauses may be somewhat unexpected in direction. It is difficult to specify what form this will take, but the question to ask yourself is whether the effect of the contour is unplanned and ragged or whether it sounds oratorical.

Table 3-1   The Four Vocal Patterns

Aspects	Focused	Externalizing	Limited	Emotional
Production of accents	Achieved with loudness and/or drawl more than pitch rise	Achieved with pitch more than loudness or drawl	Usual balance for English	Not applicable
Accentuation	Irregular	Extremely regular	Usual pattern for English	Usually irregular
Regularity of pace	Uneven; usually slowed but may be speeded patches	Even pace	Neither markedly even nor uneven	Usually uneven
Terminal contours	Ragged and unexpected	Highly expected in relation to the structure of what is said	Direction about as usual, but energy tends to peter out, yielding a breathy quality	Unexpected
Perceived energy	Moderate to high; voice may be soft but on platform	Moderate to high; may be a bit above platform but adequate push	Voice not resting on own platform; inadequate push	Not applicable
Disruption of speech pattern	No	No	No	Yes

5. *Perceived Energy*. The perceived energy is fairly high. This pitch is moderate to low, with appropriate push. The voice is full and resting firmly on its platform.

Externalizing

1. *Accentuation*. Accents are achieved primarily by means of pitch rise. There will probably be some increase in loudness, but the rise in pitch is primary.

2. *Accentuation Pattern*. The pattern of accents is unusually regular for English. The voice falls into a definite rhythm. At the lower energy levels this will give a slightly sing-song quality, and at the higher levels it will tend to give a slightly speech-making quality.

3. *Pace*. The pace is fairly even, though it may be slightly speeded as it approaches an accent point. The total effect is of an even pace.

4. *Terminal Contours*. These may go up, down, or remain level at times when this would not be quite the conversational pattern, thus sounding preplanned. The effect is oratorical rather than ragged.

5. *Perceived Energy*. The perceived energy is fairly high. The pitch is moderate to high, and the push is adequate for the pitch. The voice is fairly full and resting on its natural platform.

Limited

1. *Accentuation*. The primary accents are not very strong, and are achieved by a balance of pitch and loudness that is about normal for English.

2. *Accentuation Pattern*. The accentuation has about the usual degree of irregularity for English.

3. *Pace*. The pace may be somewhat slowed, but tends to be quite regular.

4. *Terminal Contours*. There is usually nothing notable about the contours, though sometimes the voice becomes even thinner as it comes to the ends of clauses.

5. *Perceived Energy*. The energy is low, and the push is not adequate for the pitch. The voice has a thinned quality, and the effect is that of a voice that is not resting on its own platform. This gives the voice a fragile, thin, or empty quality. This is one of the clearest distinguishing characteristics of Limited.

Emotional   This class is difficult to describe on the above features because a variety of different emotions are put in the same class. An utterance is *not* put in this class just because an emotion is being expressed. There has to be a clear overflow of the emotion into the speech pattern. The clearest indication of Emotional is a disruption of ordinary speech patterns. The voice may break, tremble, rise to a shriek, and so on. There may be breaks between words where the person is trying to speak but also clearly fighting to control the voice. Timbre and accentual patterns are changed in different ways for different emotions. It is difficult to describe all the possibilities, but in practice this is not a difficult pattern to recognize. In general laughter does not distort the speech pattern and therefore a segment would not be put in to Emotional because of the presence of laughter. In fact laughter is more likely to accompany the Externalizing pattern, although it can accompany any one of the patterns.

Raters are trained by means of a manual, which is accompanied by a cassette on which there are two illustrative segments from each class. (Rice, Koke, Greenberg, & Wagstaff, 1979). There are also 10 more extended examples which trainees are asked to rate one by one and then to check their ratings with the standard (experienced judge) ratings. It is very difficult to convey sound patterns in words, and listening to actual patterns is necessary.

The Unit

The scoring unit used is usually the "response," defined as anything said by the client between two therapist responses, or a client pause of over a minute separating utterance into separate responses. No formal comparisons of unit lengths have been made. Inasmuch as rhythm is an element in the ratings, a short response is difficult to rate reliably. On the other hand since each unit can be rated without knowledge of preceding or following units, it seems unlikely that the ratings obtained would be systematically related to the length of segment chosen. The *contextual unit*, to use Kiesler's (1973) term, is the same as the scoring unit. The rater does not need to listen to preceding or following client or therapist responses in making judgments.

Since vocal quality can change sharply even within a single response, it is necessary for raters to keep track of subunits as they listen to a response. These subunits are thought units, which usually consist of a simple sentence or independent clause. However, in spoken language the divisions imposed on the material by the intonations are a better guide than grammatical rules alone. With some preliminary training on thought units, raters can make these judgments in a somewhat impressionistic manner as they rate each response, and reliability seems to be approximately as high as for more precisely divided samples.

To arrive at a rating of a response the thought units are combined by means of a consistent set of rules. For instance, since the appearance of focused voice is considered to be important even in small quantities, the studies done with CVQ have used the rule that when there are at least half as many marks in the Focused category as in the category with the highest number of marks, the whole response is rated Focused. With the other three classes absolute number is used, but in cases of ties, the order of preference is Emotional, Externalizing, and then Limited. Correlations between thought unit scores and response scores for the same segments have been found to average between .60 and .80.

Reliability

Two different approaches to reliability are relevant here. If an aggregate score, based on number or proportion of responses in the total therapy is to be used, then an appropriate reliability figure would be the interrater correlation between aggregate scores. If the proposed study requires reliability of rating on a response-by-response basis, then agreement for each response must be considered. Using the aggregate approach on the sample used by Rice and Wagstaff (1967), rank order correlations (rho) between pairs of judges were .70 for Focused, .76 for Externalizing, and .79 for Limited. Wexler (1974), summarizing across his 4-minute, nontherapy segments, found a correlation of .88 between his two highly experienced raters. Inasmuch as the CVQ is a nominal rather than an ordinal measure the most suitable and most stringent measure of response-by-response interrater agreement is Cohen's kappa (1960). This represents the proportion of judgments in which there is agreement after chance agreement has been excluded. For the sample used by Rice & Wagstaff (1967), kappa was .49. This is highly significant, of course, but not as high as is typically found for such discrete aspects as length of pauses, or head nods (Duncan & Fiske, 1977). In using patterns rather than separate aspects there is probably a trade-off between decreasing reliability and increasing validity.

Predictive Validity

Two studies relating CVQ to psychotherapy outcome have confirmed the expected positive relationship between the amount of Focused voice in early interviews and the outcome of client-centered therapy. The process measures designed for use in the research program described above were first tried out on a sample of 20 clients in a client-centered therapy drawn from the population studied by Fiske, Cartwright, & Kirtner (1964). This subsample was drawn so as to cover a broad range of outcomes and a broad range of therapist experience levels. The original analysis related loadings on each of three factors to outcome judged from both therapist and client perspectives (Butler, Rice, & Wagstaff, 1962). The factors were computed using the CVQ system and two other lexical systems. Relationships with outcome have since been computed for vocal quality alone, using the number of responses (out of a possible 30) in each vocal class for second interviews. These are the findings that are discussed here.

The amount of Focused voice significantly differentiated between successful and unsuccessful clients, for both client and therapist outcome ratings. For Externalizing voice relationships with outcome were negative but did not quite reach significance for either the therapist or client success ratings. The amount of Limited voice was not significantly related to outcome from either perspective, though the trend was in the expected negative direction. The amount of Emotional voice was too small to make significant distinctions.

The CVQ system was then applied to the sample of 64 clients in the Quantitative–Naturalistic project described above (Butler, Rice, & Wagstaff, 1962). Clients in this study were seen twice a week for 10 weeks. At the end of that time there was a tentative termination, with the option of returning to the same therapist after a 10-week interval. The outcome measures reported are those taken after the first 20 sessions. The measures used here were the therapist success ratings and the pre-to-post change in the correlation between self and ideal Q-sorts.

The findings from this study, reported by Rice and Wagstaff (1965), involved factor loadings based on CVQ and a lexical measure. These have since been recomputed for Vocal Quality alone. The relationships with outcome were similar to the original findings, and for some interviews showed a clearer pattern because certain classes had in the original study been split between two factors. Inasmuch as there had been some hints from earlier studies that large, positive increases in the correlation between self and ideal Q-sorts from pre to post-therapy might for some clients represent a highly defensive reaction, the clients in the present study were divided into five subgroups as follows: (1) unequivocal success; (2) mixed group TH (high from therapist's perspective but low from client's); (3) mixed group CH (high from client's perspective but low from therapist's); (4) unsuccessful group (as seen from both perspectives); and (5) early attrition.

For the first interviews number of Focused responses (out of a possible 30) significantly differentiated the successful group from the mixed CH group, from the unsuccessful group, and from the attrition group. Neither Externalizing nor Limited made any significant discriminations in the first interview. For the second interviews Focused voice made these same discriminations. The only discrimination not made by Focused in the first and second interviews was between the successful group and the mixed TH group. This latter group was significantly higher on Focused than the mixed CH group or the attrition group.

The only discrimination made significantly by Externalizing voice was between the successes and the attritions, with the latter higher on Externalizing. There was a nearly significant trend toward higher Externalizing in the mixed CH group than in the success group. Many of the clients in both the mixed CH group and the attrition group showed extremely high concentrations of Externalizing voice. On Limited voice the unsuccessful group was significantly higher than the success group, the mixed TH group, and the mixed CH group. These findings suggest that Externalizing and Limited reflect relatively unproductive styles of therapy engagement, but in different ways. Most of the clients in the unsuccessful group used substantial amounts of Limited voice, while those in the mixed CH group and the attrition group tended to use substantial amounts of Externalizing voice. The clinical impression of the Limited voice is one of withdrawal of energy, of a rather passive and distanced quality, while the Externalizing style suggests high energy that is deployed outward rather than toward inner exploration. One might speculate that the high Externalizing clients are coping actively though often unproductively with the pressures of therapy, either by terminating early or by viewing themselves at the close of the 20 sessions in a much more favorable light, with the vulnerability that had led them into therapy being closed off. The clients using the Limited style remained in therapy but were not optimistic about its effect, and seemed to remain very vulnerable. It is interesting to note here that only one person in the mixed CH group returned to therapy after the 10-week vacation, significantly fewer than in the unsuccessful, mixed TH, or successful groups.

Use in Psychodynamically Oriented Psychotherapy

Although CVQ was constructed specifically for client-centered therapy, it seemed probable that some of the categories would be predictive in other therapeutic orientations. Sarnat (1976) studied 40 patients in psychodynamically oriented therapy for whom therapist ratings of outcome were available. Although Focused voice did not predict early attrition, she found a positive but nonsignificant correlation of .28 between Focused voice in the first interview and therapist ratings of outcome. Number of sessions had proved to be substantially correlated with therapist's rating of outcome. When number of sessions was held constant, the correlation between proportion of Focused voice and outcome was .34, significant beyond the .05 level. She concluded that Focused voice and number of sessions used together constituted one of the best predictors of outcome for her sample. The other three classes of vocal style were not analyzed in detail in her study.

A sample of tape-recorded segments from psychodynamically oriented psychotherapy from the Penn Psychotherapy Project was generously made available to us by Luborsky and his associates (Luborsky, Mintz, Auerbach, Christoph, Bachrach, Todd, Johnson, Cohen, & O'Brien, 1980). For each patient two 4-minute segments were available, one from the third interview, and one from the fifth. Length of therapy varied from 8 to 265 sessions. The two outcome measures available were Rated Benefit, which was a composite based on ratings by therapist and patient, and Residual Gain, a composite pre–post adjustment score, corrected for initial status. As Luborsky *et al.* (1980) have commented, these 4-minute segments proved to be inadequate in length and difficult to rate reliably. In some of the segments there was very little patient speech. Our reliabilities were somewhat below those found in Sarnat's study (1976) and considerably below those for client-centered samples. There were no significant relationships found with the Residual Gain outcome measure. For Rated Benefits there was a low but significant negative relationship with Externalizing, a nearly significant trend toward a positive relationship with Focused, and a trend toward a positive relationship with Emotional. Relationships between Limited and Rated Benefits were approximately zero. Although these findings are inconclusive, they suggest the interesting possibility that an Externalizing voice, with its high-energy, "talking-at" quality would be a negative predictor, while Limited voice, with its quiet passivity, would have more neutral implications, at least in the early stages of therapy. Although the frequency of Focused voice in this sample was rather low, there was some suggestion that it would be a mildly positive predictor.

The raters had commented that they had had difficulty rating a kind of vocal quality that did not have quite the rhythmic, premonitored quality of Externalizing but lacked the softened and irregular emphasis points of Focused voice. They described it as "serious" but without the "inner tracking" quality of Focused. It is possible that this style with some aspects of both Externalizing and Focused should be separated out, and its defining features specified. Not only might this improve the reliability of the ratings, but the new category might prove, either taken alone or summed with Focused, to be a positive predictor of outcome. The remaining "hard core" Externalizing style might well make sharper negative predictions. All this is highly speculative, but one of the advantages of a nominal system is that new classes of patterns can be identified and developed to make relevant distinctions in new situations.

Use in Gestalt Therapy

Thirty-six clients participated in a 6-week brief treatment program for resolving decisional conflicts in studies by Greenberg (1983). The Gestalt two-chair approach was used, and outcome was assessed 1 month after termination by means of a variety of measures from both client's and therapist's perspectives. The first 20 client statements made from the "experiencing" chair (as distinguishable from the criticisms made from the "other" chair) were rated on CVQ. The amount of Focused voice was significantly correlated with the residual gain score on the Vocational Indicision Scale (.37), with the client's Behavioral Self-report (.62), with the Goal Attainment Scale (.48), and the Target Complaint as viewed by the therapist (.53) and the client (.44). The relationship with residual gain for the State form of the State Trait Anxiety Inventory was in the predicted direction (−.29) but only reached the .08 level of significance.

These findings provide strong evidence for the predictive significance of Focused voice for outcome in at least one kind of application of Gestalt therapy. They also indicate very clearly the importance of the context in selecting client statements to be rated. If ratings had been summed with the ratings of statements made from the "Other" chair, in which a harsh, critical stance was encouraged by the therapist, the results might well have been inconclusive.

Use in Primal Therapy

Twenty-nine patients in a Wholistic Primal Therapy were studied by Nixon (1980). Four-minute samples, each containing a minimum of 2 minutes of patient speech, were rated. One was from the second interview and one was from the sixth interview in the first intensive series. Outcome was assessed 7½ months later, after a second intensive series and many group sessions. A variety of outcome measures from therapist, client, and psychiatric assessor perspectives were used.

Relationships between proportion of Focused voice and the outcome measures could not be adequately tested because the interrater agreement was not above the chance level for Focused, although it was satisfactory for the other categories. Poor audibility probably accounted for some of the difficulty, but in addition there was an extremely low rate of occurrence of Focused voice. This suggests that Focused voice is probably not a valued ingredient in this form of therapy. No significant correlations were found between the proportion of Externalizing voice and any of the outcome measures in spite of high interrater reliability. The trend of the relationships found was consistently negative and might have been significant with more cases.

Relationships between outcome measures and proportion of Limited voice in the second sessions were mixed and nonsignificant, but for the segment from the sixth session highly significant negative relationships were found with a number of the outcome measures, with a correlation of $-.54$ with the overall outcome measure that combined the three perspectives. The rater (Kerr) had commented at the time that for some clients Limited voice seemed to be a reflection of an attempt to control strong feelings, and that often Limited voice was followed by a breakthrough into Emotional. This observation fits well with some of the Rorschach findings discussed below. It is also interesting in relation to the finding that in the second interview the presence of Limited voice did not predict outcome but that by the sixth interview, Limited became a significant predictor of failure. One might speculate that if the client was not able to break through the control of affect by the sixth interview, then the control was at a deeper, less accessible level, and the prognosis would be unfavorable.

It had been anticipated that Emotional voice would be important in primal therapy, but it became apparent as soon as rater training began that there were two quite different kinds of Emotional voice in primal therapy. In both kinds the speech pattern was disrupted, but for some patients the disruption seemed to come from emotional overflow, while with others the emotion had a forced-out quality. A decision was made to split the original category into two parts, ''Emotional'' and ''Forced Emotional,'' and Kerr developed a description of the different vocal aspects that characterized the two categories. Interrater reliabilities were .68 for Emotional and .91 for Forced Emotional. The proportion of Emotional was significantly positively correlated with many of the outcome measures, with a significant correlation of .42 with the global outcome measure. In contrast, Forced Emotional had negative though nonsignificant correlations with all the criterion measures. Clearly if the category had not been split, the two relationships directions would have cancelled each other out and the conclusion would have been that Emotional vocal quality was not a good predictor for primal therapy. This was another example of a way in which the process system could be modified in order to make descriminations appropriate to the orientation being studied.

Further studies of relationships between vocal qualities and outcome in different therapeutic orientations should be carried out. Cognitive therapy populations would be especially interesting ones to study from the vocal perspective. Although there are probably some commonalities, different therapeutic approaches *do* seem to make rather different demands on the clients in terms of internal processing operations. In our opinion a really useful prognostic measure could not only predict which clients are likely to make constructive use of the therapy experience offered, but could tell us something about *why* the client is or is not able to cope with the demands of the particular therapy process. In other words the differences would be even more interesting than the commonalities.

Construct Validity of the Categories

An assumption underlying the construction of this process system was that the vocal channel might be one of the most sensitive indicators of the cognitive–affective processing of the client during the therapy hour. Focused voice was thought to indicate a deployment of attentional energy inward toward tracking and generating new inner experience. Externalizing voice seemed to suggest a deployment of attentional energy outward toward conveying to the therapist thoughts that followed well-worn tracks. In high concentrations this style seemed almost to preclude newness. Limited voice seemed to involve a withdrawal of energy from either direction, perhaps even a distancing from one's own experience. Emotional was thought to involve a spontaneous overflow of affect without much attempt at processing.

The first attempt to investigate the construct validity of the categories involved testing relationships between pretherapy Rorschach scores and the dominant in-therapy vocal style in first and second interviews (Rice & Gaylin, 1973). The Rorschach scores were ones originally chosen by Gaylin to be sensitive to the person's mode of functioning rather than the more structural Rorschach indexes that are often used. From the population of clients in client-centered therapy in the main project discussed above three relatively pure subgroups were formed, each with 11 clients with a majority of their responses in one of the three vocal patterns, and a stepwise multiple discriminant analysis was performed. Although the groups did not differ significantly on sex, age, or level of education, three of the Rorschach scores discriminated among all pairs of groups beyond the .01 level. The high Focused group showed a relatively high energy level, as indicated by number of Rorschach responses (R) and a substantial use of movement, color, and shading (non-F%), suggesting a high capacity for getting in touch with inner awareness. Their high number of nonroutine organizations (Z) suggested that they were able to organize this internal complexity in meaningful ways.

In contrast, the Externalizing group were lower on R, had fewer than 40% of their responses involving movement, color, or shading, and had fewer original organizations (Z). This seemed consistent with the clinical description of Externalizing voice as indicating little use of inner awareness and an emphasis on form rather than affect. The relatively low R might seem to contradict the high energy apparent in Externalizing voice, but it is important to remember that in the Externalizing style the energy is being deployed outward, and the Rorschach task does not make demands on this instrumental use of energy. In fact this is an interesting example of the importance of the task as well as the stylistic resources of the person in trying to understand the inner operations being assessed by observable process.

For the Limited group the clinically observed low energy is sharply confirmed by the low R, lower than either of the other groups. Their high percentage of nonform determinates (non-F%) suggested that they were more in touch affectively than were the Externalizing clients. This group had the lowest organizational ability (Z). The Rorschach diagnostician commented that his impression was one of almost too much affectivity and imagery compressed into too meagre an output, and without the organizational ability to handle it.

Vognsen (1969), using a therapy analogue, related the proportions of the different vocal qualities to a number of personality measures relevant to the hypothesized meanings of the vocal styles. He used the Similies Preference Inventory (Pearson & Maddi, 1966), and the various scales from the Activities Index (Stern, 1958). High Focused people seemed to form a somewhat internally consistent group, with significantly higher scores than low Focused people on need for new internal experience (Similies Preference

Inventory), high emotionality (Activities Index), and a marked lack of interest in structuring, manipulating, and understanding the outside environment (Activities Index). The Externalizing group did not form an internally consistent group. It was interesting to note that there was a negative though nonsignificant trend of relationship with the measures of interest in internal experience, and that, contrary to Vognsen's expectation, there was also a negative though nonsignificant trend of relationship with the three measures of interest in new experience from external sources (Activities Index). This is suggestive in relation to the idea that people whose dominant style is overwhelmingly Externalizing are not interested in new experience from either internal or external sources. The findings for the Limited group were clinically interesting but too complex to describe here.

One of the strongest pieces of evidence for the idea that Focused voice is an indicator of concentrated energy turned inward toward exploring and creating new experience is provided in a study by Wexler (1971). He constructed a measure to assess the degree to which an individual is currently engaged in "creating experience through the differentiation and integration of meaning structures." This measure was applied to the transcribed protocols (not the tapes) of 61 undergraduate volunteers who were asked to talk for 4 minutes about how they felt when experiencing each of three emotional states. Only the emotion of sadness was used in this study. The person spoke into a tape recorder without any feedback from the experimenter. CVQ ratings were made from the tapes by raters who were unaware of the other variables to be used.

The correlation between the proportion of Focused voice and Wexler's lexical measure of productivity in the creation of meaning structures was .84, while the correlation with proportion of Externalizing was $-.63$, both highly significant statistically. Proportion of Limited was not significantly related to his measure. These results also tend to confirm the idea that the Externalizing vocal style involves expression of content that is *not* being newly experienced or newly symbolized. Both of these findings are consistent with the findings from the Rorschach study. One further point that should be mentioned here is the extremely high relationship between Wexler's measure and proportion of Focused voice, suggesting as Wexler points out, that they may be two different measures of the same thing. Our own view is that such a high relationship with the differentiation–integration measure would not be found when the content discussed was not affective and did not involve getting in touch with inner experience, since F involves a turning inward as well as the creation of newness. As we suggested in relation to the Rorschach study, the nature of the demands of the task as well as the available processing styles must be considered in thinking about the meaning of process measures and the obtained relationships between them.

Inasmuch as each of the three studies above was based on a single sample of each person's processing style, we are not entirely justified in inferring that moment-to-moment shifts in vocal style do reflect parallel shifts in the internal processing operations. Two bits of evidence can be cited to support this inference. Spray (1978), using an adaptation of Wexler's design, found that varying the experimental conditions led to systematic differences in proportion of Focused voice. The second bit of suggestive evidence comes from the studies of speech planning and production done in the field of psycholinguistics. For instance, Goldman-Eisler (1968), using the task of having subjects explain magazine cartoons, concluded that certain momentary paralinguistic features such as hesitation phenomena were associated with increased amounts of information and more creative output. Several of the features she mentions are characteristic of the Focused speech pattern described in this chapter.

In summary, the evidence for the internal processing operations represented by Focused voice seems quite clear. For Externalizing the evidence shows rather clearly what is *not* happening, although there is less evidence concerning what *is* actually happening. From some of the studies discussed above one might conclude that Limited was a kind of half-way point between Focused and Externalizing, but that is probably not the case. Of the three Rorschach groups the Limited group had the least usable energy (R) but the highest percentage of movement, color, and shading responses (non-$F\%$). In client-centered therapy and in the study on primal therapy, Limited was one of the best predictors of failure. The meaning of the Limited style seems to be clinically interesting but needs further investigation before one could claim any construct validity.

Therapist Vocal Quality (TVQ)

The Clinical–Theoretical Base

Like the client version, the construction of the TVQ depended heavily on listening to tapes, but there was more emphasis on the theoretical base. Although no attempt was made to translate the three Rogerian conditions directly into vocal quality classes, it was assumed that unconditional positive regard, empathy, and congruence would be important constructs to consider in constructing the measure. It seemed probable that the voice might be the primary vehicle for conveying conditional or unconditional regard and an important aspect of the expression of empathy. Relationships with congruence would almost certainly be highly complex. Inasmuch as these three conditions are attitudinal ones that are seldom expressed explicitly but must come through in a way that can be perceived by the client, vocal quality seemed likely to be one of the primary vehicles through which they are conveyed to the client. An additional part of the theoretical base was the assumption that was central to the Quantitative–Naturalistic project, that an expressive, high energy therapist would tend to stimulate involved client participation, and the generation of new inner experience, and that dull or shallow therapist responses would have the effect of dampening the client's involvement.

Once again a pool of tapes served as the starting point, tapes that had been characterized in different ways by the therapists themselves. For some the therapist had expressed satisfaction with his or her involvement and with the interview as a whole. For others the therapist had not been pleased with his or her own participation in the interview. Whenever possible one of each of these kinds was obtained from the same therapist. In addition a group of tapes was included, involving as therapists interns who were at different levels in their training.

Here again Rice and Wagstaff, functioning as clinician–investigators, listened for patterns that sounded like good therapy, noting segments in which the therapist and client had seemed to be functioning well together, but always trying to weigh the impact of the voice rather than the content in making these judgments. Sections were also identified which seemed to be going badly, or in which the vocal quality in some way felt wrong to us.

Then we began to ask ourselves about the clinical implications of the patterns we were hearing. The questions we were asking ourselves here were more complex than those for the client system, because here there were at least three dimensions to be considered: (1) the interpersonal message to the client, (2) the therapist's own involvement in processing the client's explorations, and (3) the therapist's own feelings, sense of confidence, and so on. For instance, some of the therapist responses judged good by the therapists and sounding good to us had a quality of bringing to life the feeling being expressed by the client. These clearly seemed to have an expressive, stimulating quality, but we quickly realized that they also needed to have energy and centeredness coming from the therapist. If just anxiety was coming through, for instance, the effect seemed to be a negative one, of two anxious people in a room together. There seemed to be another kind of therapist response in which there was energy, but also a softened quality, a message of positive regard coming from the therapist. Another pattern sounded rather like the Focused quality in the client system, with a pondering, new paths quality, in which the therapist was trying to feel his or her way into what was being expressed by the client. Here there was energy being deployed toward sensing empathically the client's inner world, but with interest as the only interpersonal message.

Of the segments that sounded poor to us, there were very few with really negative reactions like dislike or boredom coming from the therapist. Instead there seemed to be three unfavorable patterns that occurred with some frequency. Two of the patterns sounded like subtler forms of client Externalizing, with the emphasis pattern for effect rather than reflecting spontaneous inner processing. The difference between them seemed to be one of energy, with the first kind having a good deal of energy output. The clinical impression of both of them was one of the therapist trying to express an interest and involvement he or she was not really feeling. The third negative pattern sounded somewhat like the client Limited, giving an effect of low energy and little involvement. The appearance of these kinds of negative categories rather than blatantly negative interpersonal messages, seemed to be consistent with the client-centered philosophy and training. Therapists were trying to enter the client's world in an empathic, caring way, but in some cases deficiencies in involvement, interest, and respect were coming through in subtle alterations of vocal patterns. We recognized that this might or might not be as true for other orientations.

One further category was added, which we labeled "usual." We had been reluctant to include a neutral category because of the possibility of its being used by raters as a "dumping ground" for therapist responses about which they were not sure. This seems to be a common dilemma in constructing process systems. In the case of the client system, we felt that sharper distinctions could be made without such a category. In the case of the therapist system, the absence of such a category seemed to present difficult validity problems.

Descriptive Specification of Categories

The next step was to spell out the patterns of vocal aspects by which each of these categories could be recognized. This step was not completed as successfuly as was the case for the client system. Although reasonable interjudge agreement was attained, there was almost certainly too large an element of clinical judgment involved. The descriptions of the eight categories are given below.

1. Here the therapist response brings to life the feelings of the client—fear, anger, pleasure, and so on. There is a high energy present. The inflection is that of genuine feeling, though with control rather than overflow. The therapist does not lose himself in the feeling. Listen for a high energy level, a fairly wide pitch fluctuation, and a good deal of emphasis. There will often be a high degree of "color" in the voice.

2a. The word that describes a response placed here is "caring." The voice has a good deal of energy and color. The pitch fluctuation is usually not great, but the voice is full, with plentiful overtones. The voice tends to stay in the lower part of its range, resting on its "platform." The quality that best distinguishes these responses from 2b is the "softening" of the voice, together with extra color.

2b. The word that best describes this class is "interest." Both 2a and 2b show "involvement" on the part of the therapist, but here it is shown as interest in the client and his or her message. These responses do not have the "softening" of a 2a, and there is usually less "color" in the voice at any given moment. However, there will be fully as much pitch fluctuation, and the intensity may be even more noticeable.

3. Here the therapist's voice has the "new path," exploring quality that characterizes a "Client Focused." It is a pondering, problem solving quality, accompanied by a high level of controlled energy. Listen for unevenness of inflection, with syllables lengthened or inflected in unexpected places, but with no suggestion of a regular beat.

4. The voice carries a note of newness of closure just arrived at. There is the interest of something newly understood or seen in a different way. There is usually a rise in pitch and a rising energy level. The pace is more fluent than in a 3.

5. In these responses the therapist is "present and accounted for." That is, the energy is appropriate to the situation and adequate to carry the message. However, the involvement of categories 1–4 is missing. The inflection is natural, though with more seriousness and less animation than a conversational tone.

6. The sound that seems to characterize this class is emphasis for affect rather than for spontaneous meaning. There is high energy present, but it is used for emphasis in a way that is quite different from categories 1–4. The most striking characteristic is the heavy emphasis that is given to certain syllables, usually accompanied by a pitch rise on the same syllable. The heavy emphasis point tends to recur regularly, often shifting the accent away from the point of natural meaning, and giving an effect of cadence.

7. The main difference between a 7 and a 6 is the comparatively low energy in a 7. Here again, one finds the regular accent points, but the comparatively low energy gives it a sing-song quality. Often a syllable at the end of a phrase, on which pitch would normally go down, has a rising or level pitch.

8. Comparatively little energy is present here. It is not just that the voice is soft; it is more that there does not seem to be enough energy to go around. This may take several different forms. It may simply sound as if the therapist might run out of energy before he or she got to the end of the response. At the extreme this sounds wispy or breathless. It may take the form of flatness, with complete lack of color in the voice, and an even, uninflected quality. The therapist has gone off and left his voice behind.

Rating Method and Reliability

Raters were clinical psychology interns at the University of Chicago Counseling and Psychotherapy Research Center. Training proceeded until raters could achieve at least 75% statement-by-statement agreement with the expert raters on three successive training tapes. They were asked also to rate at intervals a tape containing a standard set of segments, in order to control for rater drift over time. Formal reliability measures were not used but attempts were made to ensure quality control throughout the study.

Predictive Validity

The first test of the predictive validity of the system was conducted on the pilot sample of 20 clients described above for the client system (Butler, Rice, & Wagstaff, 1962). Although all of the eight categories had been used in making the ratings, the first four categories, all considered favorable, were combined into a class called "expressive."

The three categories considered unfavorable were combined to yield a class called "distorted." The "usual" category was left as a separate class. There were two reasons for combining categories. One was the rather low frequency in some of the categories. The second was the inevitable problem in using a nominal measure with a large number of categories in aggregate designs. Several categories may be alternative ways of engaging in positive process, therefore the amount of any *one* of them may not correlate with outcome measures. Combining categories has the disadvantage that one lacks evidence for the significance of the individual classes.

Although this study was originally reported in terms of factors that involved two lexical systems as well as the vocal system (Rice, 1965), the results were later recomputed for TVQ alone. For second interviews the number of Expressive responses (out of a possible 30) did not significantly differentiate successful from unsuccessful outcomes as assessed from either therapist or client perspective, although there was a strong trend in the predicted direction. The number of Distorted therapist responses (out of a possible 30) did significantly differentiate the successes from the failures as assessed from both therapist and client perspectives. It is important to note here that there was a significant relationship between level of experience of the therapist and rated vocal quality, with the less experienced therapists producing a higher proportion of Distorted voice and a lower proportion of Expressive voice than did the experienced therapists.

The TVQ was then slightly revised and applied to the sample of therapists from the Quantitative–Naturalistic project described above (Rice, 1973). All of the therapists in this sample were fairly experienced, with a minimum of two years experience. Probably for that reason there were very few responses falling in the Distorted class. Thus any discriminations to be made had to be between the amount of Expressive voice and amount of Usual voice.

The amount of Expressive voice in first or second interviews did not relate significantly to outcome from either client or therapist perspective, although the trend was in the predicted direction. By the 10th interview (the next ones rated) Expressive voice did not discriminate outcome over the whole range of outcome, but did discriminate significantly between the unequivocally successful and unsuccessful groups.

Our conclusion from the results of these two studies was that Expressive vocal qualities seem to form a weak predictor of therapy outcome, although promising enough to warrant further investigation and revision. The Distorted category formed a stronger predictor of outcome, but in the client-centered samples, the appearance of these categories seemed to be a phenomenon linked to lack of experience. It seemed possible that some of the vocal aspects that characterized these classes might occur in a less pronounced form with more experienced therapists but could still be distinguishable with more precise descriptions of the vocal features distinguishing the classes. The decision was that the system should be revised, before any further predictive studies were undertaken.

Revisions of the TVQ

Revisions and further testing of a TVQ measure were undertaken by Kerr (1980), building on the measure described above, as well as an illuminating study done by Duncan (1965) (Duncan, Rice, & Butler, 1968). Duncan investigated therapist vocal quality in therapist-chosen "peak" or "poor" therapy sessions, rating each session on intensity level and variation, vocal lip control, filled and unfilled pauses, and repeats. Factor analysis produced six different categories for the therapist, of which three differentiated peak from poor interviews. The factor correlated with peak interviews contained (1) normal stress with open voice, or (2) normal stress with oversoft intensity and overlow pitch, or (3) nonfluencies, except for filled pauses. The other two factors were associated with poor interviews, and included (1) flat stress, (2) normal stress with oversoft intensity and normal pitch, (3) inappropriate stress, and (4) filled pauses. The fact that oversoft intensity in conjunction with low pitch was associated with peak interviews, but oversoft intensity in conjunction with normal pitch accompanied poor interviews, strengthened our conviction that patterns, not isolated vocal behaviors, were the units to look for.

Revision of the TVQ followed the strategy decisions and general format of the original, but aimed to define each category using Duncan's paralinguistic descriptions as a model. Our aim was to increase the predictive validity of the system as well as to decrease the necessity for clinical judgment in rating.

First the psychological and linguistic literature were searched for hints on promising vocal characteristics to attend to. Then therapist responses taken from dozens of interviews from a number of orientations were collected on tape, providing hours of examples of TVQ. At the same time, Kerr began learning paralinguistic terminology from linguists, tapes, and written descriptions of voice. For the moment, the original TVQ was put aside, and the example tape was listened to intensively with an attempt to describe, in paralinguistic terms, each unique pattern that surfaced, with minimal regard to clinical relevance. Twenty-five categories were eventually labeled. In the development of the original TVQ, and in the process of revision, it was clear that a rater could not attend to more than eight or nine categories at once; either some were frequently left out, with raters choosing a few favorites to rate, or the complex cues for each category were ignored and only one or two vocal features attended to. Furthermore, more than eight or nine categories pose problems for data analysis in terms of degrees of freedom and reliability. The next step, therefore, was to weed through the 25 categories to eliminate those with a purely regional or idiosyncratic basis, and to keep those which seemed, in our opinion, to have clinical relevance.

At this point the literature was briefly checked again, and the original TVQ was used to point out omissions and gaps in the revised version. Thus, the revised TVQ had input from a variety of sources, and was based on therapist voice quality from many orientations besides client centered. We suspected that therapists using different techniques tended to use other vocal patterns than did client-centered therapists, or in different proportions. Therefore, some of the categories corresponded to ones in the original system and others were expanded or changed to fit an increased variation in vocal quality. There were nine nominal categories listed, for the rater's convenience, in order of energy level from low to high.

The strategy for revision was to concentrate on devising categories which could be described almost entirely in terms of paralinguistic elements. This attempt could not be entirely successful because of the relative poverty of standardized paralinguistic terminology; some vocal qualities discernable to the ear are not described clearly in paralinguistic terms yet, or standardized so that researchers can understand each other. Steps have recently been made to remedy the situation by publishing voice quality manuals with accompanying audiotapes (Laver, 1980).

The revised measure was tested on two samples; a psychoanalytically oriented group from the Penn Psychotherapy Project (Luborsky et al. 1980), and a client-centered group from the University of Chicago (Butler, Rice, & Wagstaff, 1962), which was also used in the development of the CVQ. Each of these groups had extensive outcome measures.

Segments from 30 client–therapist pairs from each orientation were rated and correlated with outcome. This study (Kerr, 1980) was intended to clarify the relationships of each category to outcome, as well as to point out problems with the category system. As such, it was a pilot study to hone the system, and the results were treated as feedback to help in the next stage. This is a valuable way of developing a process system, in the sense that it incorporates qualitative and quantitative research methods in a progression of studying clinical data intensively, then testing hypotheses statistically, and then using the results to go back to the data. In this case, the study showed clearly that another revision was needed, and provided insights and directions for the next effort.

The most theoretically interesting finding was that the results differed markedly with therapeutic orientation, both in the frequency of each category and the relationship of vocal quality to outcome. This could be due to sampling effects, since the two groups differed systematically in the length of each therapy segment, its position in the interview, and the position of the interview in therapy. However, there were striking differences in the use of vocal quality between the groups in a direction consistent with what one would expect. The client-centered therapists, on the whole, exhibited a higher proportion of exploring, hesitant voices than did the psychoanalytically oriented therapists, and less of an assured, definite voice. Because outcome measures were not the same for the two orientations, results could not be compared directly, but there were interesting trends that suggested that the meaning of vocal quality (in terms of client outcome) may vary with therapeutic orientation. For example, one vocal quality characterized by very wide register, normal or high pitch, high energy and unpredictable emphases (sounding involved and excited) was significantly correlated with good outcome for the psychoanalytic group but not at all in the client-centered group. It may have been that this category is more valuable in earlier sessions (where the psychoanalytic tapes were sampled), or that it has a different meaning in that orientation.

The major yield of this study was an awareness that in our attempt to make the TVQ more linguistically sound we had inadvertently made it less clinically valid. Upon analyzing the data we realized that in our preoccupation with definable linguistic features, some difficult to define but clinically important features had been dropped. Other categories were distorted in an effort to describe them without terms like ''soft'' and ''caring''—although we could *hear* the differences, our best efforts to define them either left out some important qualities or encouraged the kind of subjectivity and clinical judgments in the raters that we were trying to avoid. In a measure like this there must be a certain amount of swinging back and forth between the two disciplines of psychology and linguistics, each step synthesizing what has been learned before. The original TVQ had leaned too much on clinical impressions, to the detriment of objectively observable vocal behaviors, and the first revision had gone the other way, defining discrete behaviors with not as much regard to clinical impressions. For the second revision we could use what had been learned in the first two approaches, and integrate the linguistic with the clinical information.

The other important finding involved the relative frequency of categories in the pilot study. It was found that three categories each accounted for less than 3% of the total responses. A fourth category, hypothesized to be neutral and described as ''standard English,'' accounted for over half. To make the TVQ more efficient and discriminating, we decided that categories had to be redefined so as to include a large enough proportion of responses to be meaningful (at least 5–10%), without being too general (not over 35–40%).

The Second Revision

This time the approach was changed somewhat. We went back to clinical data and concentrated more on discriminable and clinically relevant categories than on producing descriptions free from clinical terminology. Although we used linguistic terms whenever possible, we were not restricted to them. We assume that if two people hear something, it must eventually be describable, and hope that investigations like these may help in pushing the limits of the available terminology.

For the second revision, Rice and Kerr had access to an analogue therapy study using Interpersonal Process Recall ratings. Each therapist response in the study had been rated for helpfulness, therapist empathy, and therapist discomfort by the client, as well as helpfulness ratings by a trained judge (Elliott, 1979). We could refine the system by having direct client feedback on perceptions of therapist understanding, helpfulness, and discomfort on each of approximately 500 responses with 28 different client–helper pairs. This was far preferable to the overall outcome measures used in most studies, since vocal quality shifts constantly from session to session and even from phase to phase.

Interpersonal Process Recall (IPR) ratings are ideal for studying therapist process, since the value of therapist vocal quality rests solely on its effect on the client. In this study we have access to 500 "miniature outcomes"; each therapist response can be analyzed in terms of the client's perception of it. The more usual method of taking outcome measures at the end of therapy has little relevance to a variable which changes so much from moment to moment. (For testing the new revision Elliott has provided tapes of actual therapy sessions, with even more detailed IPR ratings which are described in the Results section.)

In refining the system we went back to a primarily clinical stance, but in a broader, eclectic theoretical framework. Instead of being restricted to one orientation, we asked ourselves what functions are carried on in good therapy. In other words, what effect must a therapist have on a client in order to induce (or encourage or create the right conditions for) change? We already knew that some categories were useful as they stood, and reasonably predictive of outcome in at least one sample, and knew the categories that had to be broadened, narrowed, or redefined. Every new sample of therapist speech presents an opportunity to expand or refine the system on a larger population. In theory, this process never stops, since new orientations and therapeutic "schools" may be characterized by different patterns. However, additions or changes to the system should become fewer and rarer with use. In this new revision, some categories were retained with no changes. All of these, when used in the previous study, had shown definite trends with regard to outcome, were well-defined and easy to distinguish, had good interrater reliabilities, and were patterns used in therapy with some frequency. Those that did not fill these requirements were either dropped or redefined. In good therapy, we supposed, the therapist plays a number of roles. As stated above, he or she can affect the client through (1) communication of the therapist's state (emotions, attitudes, etc.), (2) by modeling a cognitive set and process by which internal material can be explored, and (3) through the interpersonal messages contained in the interaction. In the CVQ, the researcher is interested primarily in the client's stance toward new experience and exploration; one is interested in tracking the process of change *within the client*. In studying the therapist's process in an interview, too, one is interested basically in the *client's* change. Tracking the therapist's inner process is secondary to ascertaining his or her effect on the client. Therefore, the behavior to be analyzed is much more complex, taking in factors ranging from the therapist's like or dislike of the client to the client's prejudices against certain voice qualities. (It is well known that listeners attribute personality characteristics to speakers on the basis of their voice qualities alone—Addington, 1968, 1971.)

Revised TVQ

1. Softened. Adequate energy, standard English emphasis patterns, with a "lax voice"—that is, the vocal muscles are relaxed, and the voice sounds softened, with a lower pitch and amplitude than the speaker's baseline. It is often slower than standard English. A lax voice is sometimes described as "muffled or fuzzy." The effect is that of intimacy and involvement.

2. Irregular. The emphasis pattern is characterized by irregular intensity stresses with some pitch variation. The tempo is slow in places, then will speed up suddenly. There are variations in loudness and unfilled juncture pauses. Syllables are lengthened or inflected in unexpected places, and there is adequate energy. This pattern must have at least two of the following characteristics: unusual terminal pitch contours, unfilled nonjuncture pauses, and irregular emphases.

3. Natural. Here there is adequate energy, fairly full, standard English emphasis patterns and tempo, with neither an overly tense nor relaxed voice. The voice is unstrained and natural; the effect is one of interest. If the pattern seems close to Irregular, mentally remove the one greatest dysfluency and see if it still seems to belong in the Irregular category. If a response is too short to distinguish between Natural and Irregular, rate it as Natural.

4. Definite. Full, measured, assured, generally on the speaker's pitch platform. Stresses may be patterned, but they use intensity and not pitch rises for emphases. The tempo is slow or normal, there are filled or unfilled pauses, and the voice has a wide register, which contributes to its fullness. Stresses are usually downpitched, though they can rise in pitch if accompanied with high energy and an irregular pattern. Phrase endings are definite, with "heavy," strong emphases. This category includes "confrontational voice;" for example, "Well, what *are* you going to do?" This category can occasionally sound somewhat overbearing. It must have at least medium energy, and usually has fairly high energy.

5. Restricted. Adequate to carry the content, but strained. There is sufficient energy and variation, but the effect is unsatisfying, distanced, and seems uninvolved. Something is being held back; sometimes literally, when the breathing is shallow. The voice can be slightly tremulous, whiny, droning, or sounding as though the air is escaping before the word is formed. There is not enough color in the voice. Emphasis pattern is irrelevant except that there is more variation than in the Limited category. This voice is often tense, harsh, or distorted, in contrast to the Softened category.

6. Patterned. This category is patterned for emphasis, especially using pitch. Often a syllable at the end of a phrase, on which pitch would normally go down, has a rising or level pitch. The tempo is normal or fast, and the rhythm of the words is distorted to fit into the pattern. The category as a whole sounds "sing-song."

7. Limited. Low energy or flat stresses. This pattern may be just too soft—so whispery, breathy, or creaky that it fades away—or high-pitched, ending in a kind of squeak. It can also have adequate energy, but with no stresses or emphases in the voice; a monotone. There is just not enough life in this voice.

Function of TVQ in Therapy

The categories hypothesized to accompany good therapy are the Softened, Irregular, and Natural patterns. Each represents a different function in the process of psychotherapy. The first can be described as a "relationship" component; the therapist communicating to the client that the situation is safe, that the therapist can be trusted, and that the client is prized. This corresponds to the traditional client-centered view of necessary preconditions of therapy, and is especially important for insecure clients, for times in therapy when sensitive issues are being brought up, and often for the first few interviews when the relationship is being established. The vocal aspects expressing these characteristics are described in the Softened category.

Another component in therapy is exploration, and the finding of new paths. Here the emphasis is not on bolstering and strengthening the relationship, it is on work—both client and therapist are absorbed in discovery. The therapist's voice, engaged in the Irregular pattern, is much like the client's Focused—while it may have plenty of energy, it contains irregular, sometimes ragged emphases with pauses and dysfluencies as the therapist gropes for meaning. This in particular is a good "modeling" voice. If a therapist can slow a client's pace to match this voice quality, it may in itself facilitate exploration by breaking up habitual cognitive patterns and introducing gaps in the client's rush of externalizing verbiage.

The third component, also a "working factor" as opposed to a "relationship factor," involves working through what has already been discovered. The therapist uses normal stresses in an almost conversational tone (the Natural category), but with a softness and sensitivity that goes beyond the ordinary conversation. The emphasis is on the topic, not the relationship or even on the process of exploration, but in a non-threatening, relaxed way. In all of the first three TVQ categories the therapist is a partner with the client, not a judge or seer. Even interpretations are made in a way that leaves room for disagreement.

The Definite vocal quality belongs to another style of interaction, quite common in therapy, but which may have either positive or negative effects; the "therapist as expert." Here the therapist sounds confident, assured, and definite, with stresses of intensity and strong endings to phrases, usually down-pitched. Implicit is an expectation that the client will not disagree, or in extreme cases, that the client has no right to disagree. This is an example of a style that may be appropriate in some contexts and very inappropriate in others. Used in a direct answer to a question that has been troubling the client, it can be very reassuring ("I think you did very well last week, considering the circumstances"). In another situation it can be perceived as an attack ("You don't want to marry her because you're afraid of women"). It is possible that this category is perceived as helpful when the therapist is speaking in response to a client's need for support, and unhelpful when the therapist uses it to bolster a position of authority at the expense of a client's autonomy. Incidentally, this raises the familiar issue about the client ratings of outcome; a client may delight in reinforcement of feelings of dependency, and rate a response in this category helpful, but may leave the therapy with rather poor outcome just *because* of the fostered dependency. In the previous study of TVQ (Kerr, 1980), this category showed a positive relationship with client rating of outcome in the client-centered group, but a negative trend with regard to residual gain in both groups. The psychoanalytic group did not separate client and therapist ratings.

Other categories in the system describe process which is hypothesized to be negative in almost every context. The Limited category expresses lack of energy or interest. The Patterned category possesses adequate energy and pitch fluctuation, but deploys it much in the style of a CVQ Externalizing; somewhat sing-song, with regular emphasis patterns overriding the meaning of the utterance. Occasionally this is used to good effect when a therapist mimics an attitude or a person in this way: ''So you *know* you're supposed to do it and they keep *telling* you to do it and you'll be in *trouble* if you don't do it, but there's just *no way*.'' When used as more than infrequent comic relief it probably tends to block expressiveness and exploration. Interestingly, in the previous study this category was correlated with *therapist*-perceived good outcome in the client-centered group. while the residual gain showed a negative trend in both groups. Perhaps the habitual use of this voice quality is associated with a certain lack of sensitivity in the therapist. (As mentioned above, the psychoanalytic group did not have a separate therapist rating.) It may also be more common with lack of experience. In the first study using this measure (Butler *et al.*, 1962), a similar category was found quite frequently among therapists in training, while a similar category was almost never found among experienced therapists.

The final vocal pattern, Restricted, is adequate to carry a linguistic message but seems to lack an involvement with the client or the situation. It is somewhat distanced and may be strained, though not enough to distort the content. We suspected that it interacts more strongly with the content than most of the other categories, and that it is perceived as neutral in isolation.

Preliminary Results

Analyses of the data have not yet been completed. However, there are some interesting results that support the value of the TVQ in investigating therapy process. As mentioned above in the section on the second revision of the TVQ, data from an Interpersonal Process Recall (IPR) study (Elliott, 1979) was used for testing the category system. These data, unlike those used for the revision, were drawn from actual therapy sessions and consisted of a total of 216 responses from 16 sessions, each involving a different therapist–client pair. The IPR measures for each therapist response included separate client and therapist ratings of Therapist Empathy, Therapist Helpfulness, Cognitive Impact, and Affective Impact. In addition, there were observers' ratings of Therapeutic Alliance for each session as a whole.

Using Pearson correlations with an N of 16 five of the seven TVQ categories correlated significantly with one or more of the IPR measures, with a sixth showing a marked trend against the predicted direction for one of the therapist ratings.

The correlations of each TVQ category with the IPR ratings are summarized below, in order of their significance.

- *Irregular*—This pattern was strongly and significantly associated with positive ratings from all three viewpoints: client, therapist, and objective observer. The highest correlation was .62, for observer-rated General Helpfulness. The correlation for Therapeutic Alliance was fifth in descending order of significance, at .50.
- *Restricted*—Also strongly significant in the predicted direction, this pattern was associated with poor ratings from each of the client, therapist, and observer viewpoints. The highest correlation was − .57 for Therapist-perceived Affective Impact, with Therapeutic Alliance being sixth in significance, at − .42.
- *Natural*—Although this pattern was thought to be valuable in therapy, it was hy-

pothesized to have a neutral or at most mildly positive effect. From the clients' perceptions it was neutral, but was rated negatively by therapists ($r = -.53$ for Therapist-perceived Empathy).

- *Definite*—This pattern had a mildly negative nonsignificant trend with client and observer ratings on empathy and helpfulness but was strongly associated with therapist ratings of helpfulness and cognitive impact ($r = .62$ and $.53$, respectively).
- *Patterned*—The only IPR measure which showed any significant relationship to this category was observer-rated General Helpfulness, with which it was negatively correlated. This was probably due to chance, given the high number of correlations.
- *Limited*—There was no relation between this category and client ratings of helpfulness, empathy, and affective impact, but there was a nonsignificant trend in a positive direction for Therapist-perceived Empathy.
- *Softened*—There were no significant relationships with any of the IPR ratings for this vocal pattern, though there was a slight negative trend, opposite to the expected direction, for the client ratings.

The most exciting results have to do with the Irregular and Restricted categories, both of which seem to be important in psychotherapy process as seen by the three major viewpoints; both of the participants and the objective observer. It is especially interesting for future research to have one vocal pattern representing good process and one representing poor process. Many of the other TVQ categories appear to have relevance in therapy, and their importance may become clearer in further analysis.

Use of the System

Sampling

There are no built-in requirements for sampling therapist responses, but it is important that sampling be consistent with the purposes of the study and the outcome or concurrent measures used. It is not appropriate to take a 5- or 10-minute segment from 20 hours of therapy and correlate it with a global outcome measure, though it makes more sense to correlate it with a one-session rating of "outcome." In the present study investigating the second revision of the TVQ, each of approximately 200 therapist responses within 16 different client–therapist pairs has client and therapist ratings of helpfulness, therapist empathy, affective impact, and cognitive impact (Elliott, 1979). The therapist responses are sampled in segments of four or five responses taken from the beginning, middle, and end of each session. Each response will be given one and only one voice quality rating.

Rater Selection and Training

Raters need not have any prior training in psychotherapy or linguistics. Apart from the requirements of confidentiality, a rater must possess an "ear" for listening to voices: we have found that people differ in their sensitivity to voice quality, and that a few never manage to learn the fine discriminations of the system. This seems to have no relation to their competence in other areas, including therapy.

Raters are trained with a detailed written description of each category, a shortened table of features for quick reference, and a cassette tape of examples and practice segments, as described in the CVQ. The time required for training is approximately

10 hours, spread out over several days. A manual for distribution will be written for the second TVQ revision if the results of the study warrant it.

The criterion measure for finishing training (75% agreement with an experienced rater) and the precautions for drift are the same as for the original TVQ. However, after all responses have been scored by three raters, reliabilities can be calculated in four different ways, as described in the CVQ section on reliability. It is advisable to have three raters analyze the data in order to use the third as a tie breaker.

Interrater Reliability

Since there are seven categories in the TVQ as opposed to the four in the CVQ, with a concomitant increase in the difficulty of rating, interrater agreement was expected to be lower in the TVQ. This was borne out by the results. The response-by-response interrater agreements as calculated by Cohen's kappa for the seven nominal TVQ categories were .33, .31, and .31 for the combinations of the three raters. These values are highly significant but rather low for process measures. (In comparison, kappa for the CVQ was .49 in Rice and Wagstaff, 1967.) An estimate of the pooled Cohen's kappa for all three raters was calculated using the Spearman–Brown formula (equivalent to the standardized alpha), resulting in a respectable kappa of .58. Average Pearson r's for session-by-session agreement using proportions of TVQ (a more common level of analysis for process measures in psychotherapy research) were .68, .72, and .73. Since there were "borderline" areas between each TVQ category in which either of two different ratings may have been equally appropriate, each rater would vary slightly no matter how well trained. Most responses (201 out of 230; 87%) had agreement by at least two of the three raters. Of the 29 responses with three different ratings, 21 had spontaneous comments by at least one rater stating that the response was especially difficult and suggesting an alternative rating which agreed with one of the others. Using the Spearman–Brown formula for pooling the Pearson correlations of all three raters resulted in a session-by-session reliability of .89.

The problem of low reliability is unavoidable in this area, because of the complexity of voice quality and of the patterns that describe it. Although reliabilities do set an upper limit on validity, simpler approaches may yield better reliabilities with little or no validity. Unfortunately, low reliabilities may be one of the prices one must pay in investigating patterns of vocal quality in therapy.

Other Possible Categories

Because of the limitations in using a system like this in research, quite a few interesting and potentially valuable vocal patterns had to be ignored for their rarity. In other contexts they might have merited a closer look, but they took up too little variance to be included. One such pattern involved an interested or surprised quality, described as "very wide register, normal or high pitch, a mixture of normal and patterned stresses that involve a good deal of emphasis using pitch rises, but not predictably or in a sing-song manner. There are variations in tempo, and plenty of energy." Although this pattern, when rated by the main rater, had a significant positive relationship with outcome in the psychoanalytic sample, there were so few examples in the data that the interrater reliability was very low and the pattern was judged not sufficiently frequent to retain. Another example is a pattern we dubbed "combative." Once in a while we came across a voice that aroused feelings of hostility or combativeness in us, and we assumed a client would feel the same. These voices were difficult to describe; sometimes a whole phrase or sentence was said on a suspended, level pitch somewhat above the speaker's platform. This gave the impression of being accusing, as in "So what were you doing there?" Another characteristic that aroused these feelings was a distorted emphasis on the last syllable of each phrase; often starting out like the "definite, assured" voice described above, it ended in a sharp pitch fluctuation ("Are you *sure*?") or in an abrupt flattening ("What do you *Mean*?"). They did not have to be questions, but questions seemed to accentuate the offensiveness, coming across like a direct attack. There was an attempt to include this category in the previous system, but the reliability and rate of occurrence was, fortunately for the clients but regrettably for the system, too low.

Issues in Using Vocal Quality in Psychotherapy Research

There are a number of issues that arose in this investigation that have relevance to research using vocal qualities in psychotherapy. Two of the major ones are discussed briefly below.

   One of the most difficult problems plaguing psychotherapy research is the extent to which variables interact. It is obvious that therapy involves not only voice quality but also verbal content and body language, and that these elements must be used appropriately in the situation. It is not enough that a therapist have "a good vocal quality." A thorough analysis of a therapist vocal measure should include at least CVQ and linguistic content from both client and therapist. A step in this direction is being made with the current study using the second revision of the TVQ and Elliott's IPR therapy tapes. Each therapist response is rated by therapist and client on helpfulness, empathy, and so on, and also rated by external judges on "therapist action" (e.g., interpretation, open or closed question, reassurance, disagreement). We hypothesize that TVQ will interact with therapist action in relation to client ratings of helpfulness. For example, a Definite vocal pattern may be rated as unhelpful in the context of interpretation, but helpful in reassurance, while Irregular may be seen as helpful in interpretation and less helpful in reassurance.

   A great advantage of studying TVQ is its flexibility in application. It measures both individual consistency and variability, so it can be used as a moment-to-moment process indicator as well as a global predictor. The model behind TVQ, as well as CVQ, is the "stylistic repertoire"—the assumption that each speaker has a range of vocal patterns that is available for use in any given situation. The TVQ and CVQ are designed to tap into the speaker's variability around a baseline and provide a way of evaluating the speaker's responsiveness to situations requiring a shift in stance as expressed in vocal patterns. We assume that a therapist's vocal quality is consistent, in that he or she typically uses a certain range of expression, and that, properly sampled, this baseline or consistency can predict the quality of interaction with a client, to a degree. We also assume that the therapist constantly varies voice quality as the situation changes, and that this variation can be studied to track the therapy process. The TVQ can be used as a standard against which to measure all therapists' voices, or slightly redefined, as an individualized measure rating slight deviations from a speaker's baseline. For example, a therapist who, rated against other therapists on a set standard, may operate almost entirely in one category, may, when analyzed separately, be seen to shift slightly in the direction of other patterns throughout the session. These shifts are interesting and worthy of study in themselves.

Future Directions

From the preliminary results cited here, it appears that the TVQ holds real promise as a tool for psychotherapy research. The next step will be to establish predictive validity to client outcome (Step 4 in the development of process systems) in a variety of research designs and therapeutic orientations. At the same time we will need to clarify and expand our theoretical model of the role of TVQ in a move toward construct validity.

The field of psychotherapy research is now beginning to focus intensively on what the participants *do* within the session, as opposed to various theoretical techniques and personality traits which may or may not be related to actual behavior. To understand what makes therapy good or bad, we must be able to follow all of the important elements in the interaction. As one of the most important channels of paralinguistic communication, vocal quality must be studied along with the more accessible elements of verbal content. The development of a good TVQ is very difficult, partly because of the interactions between the different variables in psychotherapy, and it may require many attempts before it is completed. However, in light of the growing emphasis on client and therapist styles of interaction in therapy, it is especially important to continue work in this area. One approach is to examine its role in the therapeutic alliance, in particular its relation to the three components of working alliance as suggested by Bordin—bonds, tasks, and goals (1979; also see Horvath and Greenberg, this volume). There is evidence in the study reported here (Kerr, in preparation) that TVQ is indeed associated with therapeutic alliance, as well as several other process measures, and could be very valuable in the context of some of the new research directions discussed in the next section.

Exploring Mechanisms of Change—
New Uses of Process Systems

The dream of process researchers is to be able to *understand* the therapy process. We hope eventually to find out why some clients are able to engage in a productive process in some orientations but not in others. We want to understand which therapist interventions facilitate this productive process; which are the active ingredients of therapy and which are the inert elements that are carried in the folklore. This is what would make the extra effort involved in process research seem worthwhile. To some extent we have been able to bridge the gap between input variables and output variables, but the connections are fuzzy and the correlations are low. There is the continual frustration of catching glimpses of complex but extremely illuminating relationships that get lost in the correlations typical of our usual aggregate designs.

Probably the greatest obstacle to the kind of understanding for which we are searching has been the lack of research designs that are really appropriate for process research. The field now seems more ready to begin to move toward designs that are suited to the intensive analysis of process in the context of the event in which it is occurring (Barlow, 1981; Rice & Greenberg, 1984).

Another requirement for being able to study the key patterns in detail in a rigorous fashion is to have available a wide variety of process systems from different perspectives which are sensitive to moment-to-moment shifts and are descriptive in the sense of grouping together behavior that is similar as behavior. If we also have evidence for the kinds of internal operations which underlie these process descriptors, they can be used to explore the complex and interesting events of therapy.

Some recent examples of the use of process measures in making detailed studies of complex but important events in therapy will illustrate some of the possible interesting new applications of process systems. The examples all involve the CVQ since TVQ is not yet sufficiently developed in terms of either predictive or construct validity. If the study in progress and described above, relating the categories of the revised TVQ to IPR indexes of the effectiveness of therapist responses, yields interesting results, then CVQ and TVQ will be used together in a sequential analysis of selected classes of client–therapist interchanges.

As a result of engaging in a task analysis of the resolution of intrapersonal conflict splits through the use of a Gestalt two-chair dialogue, Greenberg (1983) advanced a three-stage model of conflict resolution. In order to test this model he compared the performance of two groups of clients in ongoing therapy. One group was made up of clients for whom conflict resolution was judged by client, therapist, and observer to have taken place successfully while the second group was composed of clients for whom resolution was not judged to have taken place. The proposed model contained three phases: (1) a phase of opposition between the experiencing chair and the harsh, critical ''other'' chair; (2) a merging phase in which the harsh critic softened, and became more understanding and more in touch with its own fears and concerns, and (3) an integration phase involving resolution. Taped segments from these three phases were rated on CVQ, the Experiencing Scale (Klein, Mathieu-Coughlan, & Gendlin, this volume), and the Structural Analysis of Social Behavior (Benjamin, this volume). The two groups were *not* significantly different from each other in CVQ in the opposition phase but in the merging phase the successful and unsuccessful groups *were* significantly different beyond the .01 level. For the successful group the proportion of Focused and Emotional voice in the merging phase was significantly higher than in the opposition phase. For the unsuccessful group the proportions did not change. These results, together with the findings from the other two process systems used, provided confirmation for the three-stage model proposed. Greenberg commented that the change to a Focused voice by the ''other chair'' seemed to be a valuable clinical cue that the client might be ready for an integration of the two sides.

This same kind of observation, that Focused voice often immediately precedes significant changes in other process systems, was noted at a workshop in which some taped segments of ''key transactions'' from a variety of orientations were blindly rated on a number of different process systems. On most of the key transactions there was a shift to Focused voice which often immediately preceded a shift on the lexical measures used (Rice, Klein, Greenberg, Elliott, Whiteside, Benjamin, & Hill, 1978).

Using a task analytic method, Rice & Saperia (1984) studied a class of change events involving the resolution of ''problematic reactions.'' The ''marker'' that signals a readiness to engage in the task of unfolding and exploring is the client's statement of an incident in which his or her own reaction was felt to be exaggerated, incomprehensible, or otherwise problematic. Detailed analyses were made of some successful performances in order to identify the client steps necessary for unfolding the experience in a way that leads to affective resolution and broader self-understanding. A coding system was constructed to describe the key client steps specified in the emerging model, as well as the client operations that seemed to lead up to the key steps. Since this coding system was both inferential and untried, two other, more descriptive process systems, CVQ and Levels of Perceptual Processing (Toukmanian, this volume), were used to test whether or not the new codes were correctly identifying the client's assumed internal operations. The segments that had been assigned codes that were assumed to involve some internal tracking were found to contain significantly higher levels of Focused voice than the segments characterized by codes assumed to involve external analysis. Inasmuch as the coding was done from transcripts and the CVQ ratings were done from tapes by an experienced rater who knew nothing about the new codes, these results, together with significant findings from Levels of Perceptual Processing, provided some confirmation for the assumptions underlying the new coding system.

Elliott (1984) made intensive analyses of four "insight events" identified by means of IPR. Using a wide variety of process systems as well as the reported reactions of the client and therapist, he attempted to explore and understand the nature of a developing insight. The occurrence of Focused voice in the first postintervention phase, together with the appearance of a number of other process indicators, led him to designate this as the initial "processing" phase, which was then followed by "insight" and further "unfolding." His study is a good illustration of the use of a whole range of process systems, not to test a model, but to explore and attempt to understand a key class of therapy phenomena.

The above examples of new uses of process systems, especially those utilizing a variety of different systems from different perspectives, seem to represent a very promising development. In these studies the systems are used to explore different classes of therapy events and to test performance models as they emerge. The focus is not on the correlation between the different systems but on the degree to which they are jointly able to describe different classes of therapeutic change events. The intersection of a variety of process systems, each with some evidence of construct validity, can broaden and enrich our understanding of the mechanisms of change.

References

Addington, D. W. The effect of vocal variation on ratings of source credibility. *Speech Monographs*, 1971, *38*, 242–247.

Addington, D. W. The relationship of selected vocal characteristics to personality perception. *Speech Monographs*, 1968, *35*, 492–503.

Barlow, D. On the relation of clinical research to clinical practice: Current issues, new directions. *Journal of Consulting and Clinical Psychology*, 1981, *49*, 147–155.

Bordin, E. The generalizability of the psychoanalytic concept of the working alliance. *Psychotherapy: Theory, Research and Practice*, 1979, *16*, 252–260.

Butler, J. M., Rice, L. N., & Wagstaff, A. K. On the naturalistic definition of variables: An analogue of clinical analysis. In H. Strupp & L. Luborsky (Eds.), *Research in Psychotherapy* (Vol. 2.). Washington, D.C.: American Psychological Association, 1962.

Cohen, J. A system of agreement for nominal scales. *Journal of Educational and Psychological Measurement*, 1960, *20*, 37–46.

Cronbach, L. J., & Meehl, P. E. Construct validity in psychological tests. *Psychological Bulletin*, 1955, *52*, 281–302.

Duncan, S. Paralinguistic behaviours in client-therapist communication in psychotherapy. Unpublished Doctoral Dissertation, University of Chicago, 1965.

Duncan, S., & Fiske, D. W. *Face-to-face interaction: Research, methods, and theory.* Hillsdale, N.Y.: Lawrence Earlbaum, 1977.

Duncan, S., Rice, L. N., & Butler, J. M. Therapists' paralanguage in peak and poor psychotherapy hours. *Journal of Abnormal Psychology*, 1968, *73*, 566–570.

Elliott, R. How clients perceive helper behaviours. *Journal of Counseling Psychology*, 1979, *26*, 285–294.

Elliott, R. A discovery-oriented approach to significant change events in psychotherapy: Interpersonal process recall and comprehensive process analysis. In L. N. Rice & L. S. Greenberg (Eds.), *Patterns of change: Intensive analysis of psychotherapy process*. New York: Guilford Press, 1984.

Fiske, D. W., Cartwright, D. S., & Kirtner, W. L. Are psychotherapeutic changes predictable? *Journal of Abnormal and Social Psychology*, 1964, *69*, 418–426.

Goldman-Eisler, F. Psycholinguistics: *Experiments in spontaneous speech*. New York: Academic Press, 1968.

Greenberg, L. S. Toward a task analysis of conflict resolution in gestalt therapy. *Psychotherapy: Theory, Research, & Practice*, 1983, *20*, 190–201.

Kerr, G. The relation of therapists vocal quality to client outcome: A pilot study. Unpublished Master's Thesis, York University, Toronto, 1980.

Kerr, G. P. Therapist vocal quality and psychotherapeutic effectiveness. Doctoral Dissertation, York University, Toronto, 1984.

Kiesler, D. L. *The process of psychotherapy: Empirical foundations and methods of analysis*. Chicago: Aldine, 1973.

Laver, J. *The phonetic description of voice quality*. Cambridge: Cambridge University Press, 1980. Published with accompanying audiotape.

Luborsky, L. Helping alliances in psychotherapy: The groundwork for a study of their relationship to its outcome. In J. L. Claghorn (Ed.), *Successful Psychotherapy*. New York: Brunner/Mazel, 1976, 92–116.

Luborsky, L., Mintz, J., Auerbach, A., Christoph, P., Bachrach, H., Todd, T., Johnson, M., Cohen, M., & O'Brien, C. P. Predicting the outcome of psychotherapy: Findings of the Penn Psychotherapy Project. *Archives of General Psychiatry*, 1980, *37*, 471–481.

Mahl, G. F. Disturbances and silences in the patient's speech in psychotherapy. *Journal of Abnormal and Social Psychology*, 1956, *53*, 1–15.

Nixon, D. S. The relationship of primal therapy outcome with experiencing, voice quality, and transference. Unpublished Doctoral Dissertation, York University, 1980.

Pearson, P. H., & Maddi, S. R. The similies preference inventory: development of a structured measure of the tendency toward variety. *Journal of Consulting Psychology*, 1966, *30*, 310–318.

Pittinger, R. E., Hockett, C. F., & Danehy, J. J. *The first five minutes*. Ithaca, N.Y.: Martineau, 1960.

Rice, L. N. Therapist's style of participation and case outcome. *Journal of Consulting Psychology*, 1965, *29*, 155–160.

Rice, L. N. Client behaviour as a function of therapist style and client resources. *Journal of Counseling Psychology*, 1973, *20*, 306–311.

Rice, L. N., & Gaylin, N. L. Personality processes reflected in client vocal style and Rorschach performance. *Journal of Consulting and Clinical Psychology*, 1973, *40*, 133–138.

Rice, L. N., & Greenberg, L. S. The new research paradigm. In L. N. Rice and L. S. Greenberg (Eds.), *Patterns of change: Intensive analysis of psychotherapy process*. New York: Guilford Press, 1984.

Rice, L. N., Klein, M. K., Greenberg, L. S., Elliott, R., Whiteside, J., Benjamin, L. S., & Hill, C. *Comparison of process systems as descriptors of productive psychotherapy*. Paper presented at the meeting of the Society for Psychotherapy Research, Toronto, June, 1978.

Rice, L. N., Koke, C. J., Greenberg, L. S., & Wagstaff, A. K. *Manual for the client vocal quality classification system*. York University Counselling and Development Centre, 1979.

Rice, L. N., & Koke, C. J. Vocal style and the process of psychotherapy. In J. K. Darby (Ed.), *Speech evaluation in psychiatry*. New York: Grune & Stratton, 1981.

Rice, L. N., & Saperia, E. P. Task analysis of the resolution of problematic reactions. In L. N. Rice & L. S. Greenberg (Eds.), *Patterns of Change: Intensive analysis of psychotherapy process*. New York: Guilford Press, 1984.

Rice. L. N., & Wagstaff, A. K. Client voice quality and expressive style as indexes of productive psychotherapy. *Journal of Consulting Psychology*, 1967, *31*, 557–563.

Sarnat, J. E. *A comparison of psychoanalytic and client-centered measures of initial in-therapy patient participation*. (Doctoral Dissertation, University of Michigan) Ann Arbor, Michigan University Microfilms, 1976, No. 76-9504.

Scherer, K. R. Speech and emotional states. In J. K. Darby (Ed.), *Speech evaluation in psychiatry*. New York: Grune & Stratton, 1981.

Siegman, A. W. The telltale voice: Nonverbal messages of verbal communication. In A. W. Siegman & S. Feldstein (Eds.), *Nonverbal behaviour and communication*. Hillsdale, N.J.: Lawrence Earlbaum, 1978.

Spray, M. B. The effects of instructional variation on self-disclosing behaviour. Unpublished Doctoral Dissertation, Waterloo University, 1978.

Stern, G. G. *Preliminary record: activities index—college characteristics index*. Syracuse, N.Y.: Syracuse University Research Center, 1958.

Vognsen, J. Need for new experience: An explanatory bridge between client vocal style and outcome of psychotherapy. Unpublished Doctoral Dissertation, University of Chicago, 1969.

Wexler, D. A. Self-actualization and cognitive processes. *Journal of Consulting and Clinical Psychology*, 1974, 42, 47–53.

4

A Measure of Client Perceptual Processing

Shaké G. Toukmanian
York University
North York, Ontario

The prevailing view in contemporary psychology is that a comprehensive perspective on human behavior is not possible without seriously considering how individuals perceive and attribute meaning to situations and events (e.g., Endler, 1983; Mischel, 1981). This viewpoint suggests a trend away from trait psychology and from the strict learning theory based operant and classical conditioning paradigms and toward a "structural" approach to the study of human behavior. The emphasis within this orientation is on the active and constructive nature of mental activity and on the conception that, as goal-directed organisms, individuals are capable of organizing, patterning, and reformulating information in ways that will help them achieve greater effectiveness in developing flexible and more functional life perspectives. Although the view that cognitions are important mediators in human functioning is not new in psychology, its resurgence in recent theoretical advances in cognitive (e.g., Broadbent, 1977; Neisser, 1976; Norman, 1976) and personality psychology (e.g., Cantor & Kihlstrom, 1981) has exciting implications for both theory and research in psychotherapy.

Client or patient cognitions (i.e., perceptions, experiences, insights, associations, thoughts, belief-systems, etc.) have generally played an important role in most traditional theories of counseling and psychotherapy. However, with the possible exception of Kelly's (1955) theory of personal constructs, these orientations have neither been clear about nor explicit in delineating the specific nature of client mental operations involved in the development and/or the modification of dysfunctional behaviors. This lack of systematic conceptual focus on client internal events and processes has, in the past, been problematic for psychotherapy researchers and practitioners alike. Although it has been demonstrated that all forms of psychotherapy are equally effective (e.g., Sloane, Staples, Cristol, Yorkstan, & Whipple, 1975; Smith & Glass, 1977), the fundamental question of what makes or fails to make psychotherapy therapeutic still remains unanswered. In other words, we still lack a basic understanding of how individual therapists and particular types of therapeutic interventions impact ongoing client internal events which occur, on a moment-to-moment basis, in therapy.

It is my contention, therefore, that if we, as psychotherapy researchers, are to strive for the ultimate goal of identifying therapeutically relevant process dimensions that are specific to types of treatments, therapists, and clients we first need to understand the nature of the mental operations and the mechanisms involved in client change. This perspective requires conceptualization of psychotherapy and research measures that focus specifically on client perceptual–cognitive functioning. Although a number of cognitively based models of therapy have recently appeared in the literature (e.g, Beck, Rush, Shaw, & Emery, 1979; Meichenbaum, 1977; Wexler, 1974), to date, very little attention has been paid to the development of process measures that would tap the essential components of client in therapy mental operations.[1] Thus, in constructing the *Levels of Client Perceptual Processing (LCPP)* my primary goal was to design a classification system that would delineate the qualitatively different modes with which clients perceive and process information when formulating their experiences of events in therapy.

Developing the System

As a therapist working with non-hospitalized and predominantly self-referred clients, I've often felt that (1) understanding the content of clients' communications is important to the extent that it reflects or is an expression of how they construe life situations generally, and that (2) the manner in which clients perceive self, others, and events, i.e., the kind of information that they detect and the way in which they organize this information to form their unique impressions of events, often changes dramatically over the course of productive therapy. To test the validity of these clinically based observations I needed to find a method of analyzing therapy sessions that in some way would tease out the characteristic nature of client mental operations and their functions in the process of therapy. This exercise, I thought, would also help me develop a functional perspective on the role of client mediational processes in the treatment of dysfunctional behaviors; for although my approach to psychotherapy has been anchored in the phenomenological-perceptual tradition of client-centered theory, my thinking has been influenced by a number of recently advanced models of information processing that focus on the constructive and integrating functions of mental activity (e.g., Neisser, 1976). It was with this particular perceptual-cognitive bias that I approached the task of constructing the LCPP.

---

1. Rogers' (1959) scale for evaluating process changes in psychotherapy takes into account seven closely related strands or elements of client process: communication of self, manner of experiencing, relationship to feelings, degree of incongruence, manner in which experience is construed, relationship to problems, and manner of relating. While distinct at first, these strands converge over the course of therapy and together they form Rogers' continuum of client experiencing (i.e., the activity of attending to and symbolizing subjective feelings in awareness) that "reaches from rigidity and fixity of psychological functioning on the one hand, to psychological flow and changingness on the other" (p. 96).

The Klein, Mathieu, Gendlin, and Kiesler's (1970) modification of the original Gendlin and Tomlinson's (1961) Experiencing (EXP) Scale is a global measure of the extent of client self-involvement in therapy. By definition the experiencing construct is an integrated composite of a variety of client internal events (i.e., feelings, attitudes, thoughts, and cognitions). These, however, are implicit to the process conception of experiencing and are subsumed within a single 7-point annotated rating scale. Each scale point on the continuum is viewed as an index of the quality of client experiencing and is assumed to represent the level of client process at any particular time in therapy. Derived from the client-centered framework, the EXP scale also focuses on the affective component in client's experiencing.

As it will be seen below, LCPP is a taxonomy of varying modes of client perceptual activity. Each of the categories of the measure depicts a particular way of information processing regardless whether perceptions relate to self, others, or to external situations or events. A basic assumption underlying LCPP is that all these cognitive operations are necessary aspects of a person's mental activity but that a functional perceptual system is one that involves more of certain kinds of these operations than others.

Deriving the Categories

When I first set out to develop the system I decided to systematize my observations by embarking on an intensive study of several complete sets of recorded therapeutic interviews. My initial intent was to describe, in as much detail as possible, my impressions of how clients expressed themselves when talking about distressful internal states or external situations, and to determine whether or not the quality of their discourse changed over the course of therapy.

As I examined the recordings, I became increasingly aware of several discernable patterns in the quality of clients' participation that were different at different points in therapy. In other words, although clients differed extensively in the complexity and amount of their verbal output, the pace, intensity, and level of energy with which they talked, and in the form and content of their verbalizations, there appeared to me to be a common core of identifiable features in the way clients went about presenting, exploring, and resolving some of their concerns across therapy sessions.

At first, I was able to extract six qualitatively different clusters of client communications that appeared in almost all therapeutic interviews but in varying frequencies. The first cluster consisted of client responses that were formulated in terms of simple, stereotypic, and evaluative types of statements. For example: "He is *so* inconsiderate. . . . his attitude drives me up the wall. . . . I just can't understand him. . . . ", or "I'm very critical of myself . . . of my friends . . . almost everybody. . . . I'm a very harsh judge of human character." In listening to these and similar kinds of expressions, I often had the impression that clients were aware of and recognized the "existence of a problem"; yet the manner in which they formulated and presented their view of the issue was simplistic and superficial in the sense that it represented a condensed version of the situation. In other words, in trying to make sense of the diversity of information surrounding complex intra- and interpersonal events, these individuals characteristically tended to use abstractions or generalities as a means of capturing and objectifying such events.

A second cluster of client responses that I was able to identify involved client expressions that relied heavily on factual information as a means of sorting out seemingly different aspects of an event. These communications were essentially elaborations or detailed accounts of the who, what, where, and when of an experience and appeared particularly in relation to clients' attempts at exploring different aspects of a problematic situation. For example, when encouraged by their therapists to examine an issue more closely I often noticed that clients would resort to scanning different contexts as if trying to produce "evidence" that would support or validate a particular thinking or feeling state. Their statements would usually take the form of: "what do I mean by inconsiderate? . . . well . . . like yesterday, for example, we were supposed to go to the movies . . . and what does he do? . . . he doesn't show up . . . and he doesn't call . . . and . . . ", or "I have tended to be critical of people all my life . . . for as long as I can remember . . . even when I was a kid. . . . I remember one day in school . . . I think I was in grade three. . . . " My sense of these clients was that while seemingly active in dealing with their concerns they essentially were making the same formulations of events and did not add much to what they had already said before. In other words, the quality of their discourse reflected a static manner of perceiving, one that helped them sustain rather than broaden their existing outlook on the event.

The main feature in the third cluster of responses was clients' use of external referents as a means of differentiating the elements contained in their experiences of events. In some cases, clients appeared to formulate their thoughts on the basis of an implicitly held convention or standard, like when a client remarked: "we're engaged . . . that should mean something to him . . . if he loves me and cares for me as he says he does . . . then . . . well . . . he shouldn't take me for granted." In other cases, I noticed that clients would utilize commonly held descriptors to deploy their own view or construction of self, others, and events; like "well . . . the term homosexuality . . . it is a loaded word . . . because when you say it they automatically set you apart as a queer . . . you lose your individuality immediately . . . and you become one of the horrible group." In either case the way in which these individuals approached the exploration of an issue was by adopting an external frame of reference, that is, they depended on external sources of information and other generated perspectives as a means of constructing their own experiences of an event.

A qualitatively different pattern of client responses emerged usually (but not always) around the mid- and late therapy interviews. The two most compelling characteristics of this pattern were: the specificity of clients' focus of explorations and the idiosyncratic nature of their communications. When relating their thoughts and feelings I found that clients would often tend to be more reflective, less general, and more focused in the manner in which they dealt with issues. In other words, they often tended to examine an event more closely and notice aspects of it that seemed to have never been part of their perceptual field before. Equally important, perhaps, was the unique personal quality of the clients' discourse. Their explorations and differentiations made of various facets of an experience were almost always made on the basis of internally generated descriptors that often (but not always) were rich in imagery and connotative language in the sense described by Rice (1974). For example, in attempting to characterize her "sense of detachment" a client made the following comment: "I feel uninvolved . . . kind of like . . . others have placed their hands on the handlebars of life and I'm still looking at the bicycle"; another client offered this perspective when exploring the issue of his sexuality: "I have difficulty conceiving of myself as a male in a male–female context . . . relationship . . . I don't see myself fitting in naturally as being really a . . . relevant partner. . . . " In short, my impressions of this category of responses was that more often than not clients used internal referents or sources of information for the formulation of their perceptions of events and that the manner in which they went about identifying and organizing this information was in some way instrumental in helping them make highly personalized interpretations of events.

The tentative manner in which clients attempted to deal with (i.e., interrelate and appraise) the differentiated aspects of their experience of an event constituted the main feature of the fifth cluster of client responses. The uncertainty with which clients expressed their thoughts and feelings about self and situations was reflected in the use of terms like "may be . . . ," "I'm not sure . . . but it would seem that . . . ," "I guess it is possible . . . ," and so on. In listening to clients' communications in this category my general impression was that they were actively involved in reorganizing previously evoked information to modify an existing perception and as a result were considering the possibility of construing the same event differently; for example " . . . it is possible . . . uh . . . it may be a show of acceptance . . . or . . . may be just a little bit of love from his part." The quality of discourse in this category suggested to me that clients were capable of suspending judgment and engaging in a propositional mode of information processing wherein there was considerable degree of latitude for several alternative interpretations of an event to coexist. Thus, my sense was that, in being able to accommodate alternative viewpoints on an issue, clients were in a position to weigh their "options" in a manner that potentially could lead them to "a resolution" or to the development of a new and personally more meaningful construction of the situation.

Finally, there was a discernable group of few responses that essentially did not fit in any of the previously identified categories. At first glance these responses "looked" or "sounded" like those in the first subclass in that they were statements that essentially conveyed an existing perspective on an experience. However, in examining them more closely, I found that the communications did not have the static and stereotypic quality of a categorical type of perceptual activity. On the contrary, my general impression was that these responses represented a synthesis of previously differentiated and recognized aspects of an experience that were now being expressed as an integrated new perspective. The quality of the discourse suggested to me that, having followed through a chain of thoughts, clients were inferring a relationship among seemingly dissonant information and in the process were moving from an extended and nonprecise to a more individualized and focused perception of an event. In other words, by virtue that these responses were almost always made in direct reference to internally discerned and evaluated aspects of an experience, clients appeared to me to have adopted a more complex view of a situation that was uniquely their own. As one client put it: " . . . it is like . . . I realize that . . . there is room enough for me in this world just as I am . . . I accept myself . . . they can be and I can be . . . I'm not alone. . . . " It was as though the client had arrived at a "flexible closure" that was to be used as a new perceptual base to further explore her constructions of self and the nature of the relationships between herself and others.

To summarize, my initial analysis of therapy interviews yielded six client response categories, reflecting six qualitatively different modes of client perceptual activity. Furthermore, my examination suggested that the differential quality of these clusters was the function of the kind of information that clients detected and the manner with which they processed this information to formulate their experiences of self, others, and external events. I also had the impression that there was a pattern in the frequency with which these types of verbalizations occurred over the course of therapy. In early therapy sessions clients characteristically tended to use responses depicting the first three categories; and although the latter three classes appeared across all sessions, they were generally better represented in the middle or late therapy interviews.

In the second phase of the system's development the six response categories were defined and several examples were provided for each. To obtain a measure of face validity, two experienced counseling psychologists were given this first version of LCPP and were asked to comment on the clarity of the definitions and the appropriateness of the examples in each category. The revised version of the system was then used by two trained judges to categorize randomly selected client communications that were transcribed, on a master audiotape, from different therapy interviews of different clients. Discussion of the discrepancies suggested two major difficulties. First, judges felt that often a single client response would contain several discernable response categories and that when faced with such a situation they relied on their subjective judgment for the choice of a category that best characterized the quality of the whole response. These comments led to the idea that, when deemed necessary, judges would break a client communication into "transitions" and assign an evaluation to each of its identifiable components. I thought the use of such a procedure would allow for a more complete description of the variability of clients' perceptual activity within a single response. However, there was still the problem of subjectivity. To minimize inferential judgments as to what constitutes a "transition" and to keep the number of scorable units constant across judges it was decided that assessments would be made by using both audiotapes and transcriptions that would be marked for changes in the manner of client respond-ing within a single communication (the procedure will be discussed more fully in a later section).

The second problem related to the judges' difficulty in discriminating between the third (differentiations of information using external referents) and fourth (differentia-tions of information using internally generated referents) categories. Judges felt that there was a subclass of differentiating responses that could not be assigned to either of these existing groups. An examiniation of these responses indicated that when discussing an event that was either internal or external to themselves, clients appeared to make discriminations of aspects of the event through the application of systematic logic. In other words, I noticed that although clients brought a variety of information to bear on their constructions of an experience and even though they often did not use external or other generated perspectives, the discriminations that they made reflected a distinctly logical (inductive or deductive) "if–then" mode of cognitive activity. The objective and intellectual quality of this manner of communicating is illustrated in the following example: " . . . on the other hand, there is another element there . . . which may also be true . . . and in some sense which is autonomous . . . the feeling that's not the way to go for having a relationship . . . being manipulative that is . . . assum-ing a relationship with a woman for . . . purely for reasons of sexual gratification . . . but it almost seems that it would be a corollary that one not really care about that person's feelings other than perhaps gratifying them." These observations resulted in the creation of a new category which was subsequently defined and incorporated into the previous version of the system.

Thus, the third and final form of LCPP consisted of seven mutually exclusive client response categories. An eighth category, labeled "other," was also added for responses that could not be legitimately placed into any other class, such as salutations, short af-firmations or negations, bids for clarification of a therapist intervention and so on. Brief definitions of these eight categories are presented in Table 4-1. When this final form was used by the same two judges to evaluate an independent set of randomly selected responses, a satisfactory percentage (i.e., 75%) of interjudge agreement was obtained.

A Tentative Model

As I listened, examined, and attempted to fit my observations into a conceptual frame-work, it became increasingly clear to me that the nature of processes and mechanisms involved in clients' behavior in therapy could best be described from a schematic-developmental view of perceptual activity. Within this context, my search for a model led me to consider several existing conceptualizations from cognitive and therapeutic psychology and resulted in the formulation of an integrated perspective on the nature of mental operations involved in client change over the course of therapy. This model, which has been elaborated upon elsewhere (Toukmanian, 1983), draws on Neisser's (1976) cyclic model of perceptual or schematic development, Craik and Lockhart's (1972) notion of "depth of processing," Shiffrin and Schneider's (1977) concept of "auto-mated" and "controlled" processing, and on several key tenets from Kelly's (1955) theory of personal constructs.

Briefly, these perspectives suggest that (1) human behavior is the manifestation of an integrated chain of cognitive processes; (2) the mental activity that assumes this critical integrative function is perception; (3) the act of perceiving is a dynamic and in-

Table 4-1   Categories of the LCPP Classification System

Category I:
Undifferentiated Statements. The main characteristic of this category is that the client's response conveys a condensed or packaged view of a complex inter- or intrapersonal event. When discussing self, others, or situations the client uses abstract, superficial, and glib statements to label his or her recognition of a "problem." The manner of communicating is nonreflective, categorical, and static.

Category II:
Elaborations. Responses placed in this category are detailed accounts of events. They represent a series of descriptive statements that serve to provide extended and often factual information about seemingly related incidents. The client talks as if he or she is an observer reporting on the who, what, where, and when of an experience.

Category III:
Differentiation with External Focus. The client describes a thought or a feeling about self, others, or situations using external referents. Other generated standards, rules, guidelines, etc., and external sources of information form the basis of the explorations and interpretations of his or her experience of an event.

Category IV:
Differentiation with Analytic Focus. The client explores and discriminates among various aspects of an experience in an objective and intellectual manner. He or she attends to internal as well as external sources of information and uses systematic logic to explain his or her perspective of an experience. The manner of communicating is reflective but tight and analytical.

Category V:
Differentiation with Internal Focus. Statements placed in this category are characterized by the idiosyncratic manner with which the client expresses himself or herself. He or she focuses on and explores the implied meanings of an event and uses uniquely personal descriptors to delineate differentiated aspects of an experience.

Category VI:
Reevaluation. Here the client is actively involved in exploring several interpretations of an experience in a focused and differentiated fashion. However, there is a quality of uncertainty or tentativeness in the client's manner of communicating. The general impression is that the client is engaged in weighing and appraising alternate constructions of an experience as if he or she is on the verge of "resolving" or coming to grips with a potentially more meaningful perspective.

Category VII:
Integration. Responses placed in this category reflect a synthesis of previously differentiated and alternately constructed aspects of an experience. The client conveys a newly emerged perspective. He or she generates a broader but a more personal perceptual base to further explore and modify his or her view of self, and the world.

Category VIII:
Other. Responses that cannot be classified in one of the above categories.

---

ferential process in that it is the construction of reality not as it actually is but as it is subjectively represented as "meaningful" by the individual; (4) the basic structure or unit of perceptual activity is the schema or construct; (5) perceptual development proceeds from rudimentary to more complex structures, and from superficial or categorical modes of cognitive activity to deeper and more comprehensive levels of processing, that is, from simpler to more complex or propositional mental operations that involve semantic associative analyses and the extraction of meaning; (6) at any given moment in time perceptual activity involves both same-level or automated as well as cross-level or controlled modes of information processing; and that (7) while both modes are inherent to cognitive functioning, it is the controlled or cross-level mode that is instrumental in enhancing a person's perceptual development. It is further contended that perceptual activity starts with the activation of the basic anticipatory units (i.e., the constructs or schemata) that serve to direct exploration and information gathering through multiple sensory modalities. Information thus obtained feeds into and modifies the original schemata. These altered anticipatory structures carry on the process in a continuous and cyclic fashion. Within this framework, several embedded perceptual cycles may be simultaneously activated by a variety of related schemata associated with a particular event. Each cycle, representing an aspect of the event, supports the others with the more extensive one often determining the direction of the course of exploration and information pickup to be realized.

Operating within this broad conceptual framework, the proposed model holds that, at any given moment in time, an individual's level of perceptual development, with respect to an internally or externally occurring event, is the interactive function of the nature of information that the person is capable of detecting (i.e., his or her schema availability) and the particular mode of processing that he or she brings to bear on the information for the construction of that event. From this vantage point, a client in therapy is seen as an individual whose manner of perceptual processing is deficient in the sense that it is not helping him or her to formulate alternative constructions of the environment to function adequately in it. A deficiency in a client's perceptual activity with respect to an event may entail a dysfunction at any point in the perceptual cycle. It may, for example, be a deficiency in the *kind* and *scope* of information that the client is capable of gathering and integrating (i.e., schematic deficits). He or she may lack well-developed schemata for a given event to adequately engage in its anticipation and hence, in the perception or experience of that event (e.g., a young person's experience of a first date).

Perceptual deficiencies may also be associated with the client's manner of information processing. This aspect relates to the temporal element in cognitive activity. Perceiving, like any other phenomenon, occurs within a time frame. As such, it requires a minimal interval of time for information pickup and for its integration into a single unitary experience. Most perceptual acts are deliberate and slow at first. However, with repeated exposures to the same invariant experience of an event, perceptual activity becomes habitual. In other words, the individual engages in the activity ''as if'' automatically. Automated perceptual processes (Shiffrin & Schneider, 1977) are highly functional in that they provide cognitive economy. They free time and cognitive resources for the person to process other simultaneously occurring perceptual cycles. However, while perceptual ''short cuts'' are necessary aspects of perceptual activity and render it more efficient, in and of themselves, they are not sufficient for *perceptual development*. A relatively well-functioning individual will have the schematic preparedness to simultaneously activate a variety of perceptual cycles (including habitual or ''automated'' ones) associated with different aspects of a particular event. Thus, while perceptual ''short cuts'' may, by necessity, be part of the person's perceptual activity they would play a *supportive* rather than a dominant role in the construction of the event. When faced with the demands of a particular situation such an individual would have the anticipatory readiness which characteristically would allow him or her to operate within a broad enough time frame and to engage in, what Shiffrin & Schneider (1977) call ''controlled processing,'' that is, a fuller exploration, pickup, and integration of information, that leads to schematic development.

In short, both modes of processing are seen to be essential to perceptual activity and both may be operative at any level of schematic development. Thus, the issue with respect to perceptual inadequacies is not one of controlled versus automated process-ing; rather, it is the extent to which perceptual cycles associated with a given event are automatized and the level of schematic development at which automatization has set in. The onset of automatization early on in a person's history of perceptual develop-ment *vis-à-vis* an event (i.e., schemata that are repeatedly exposed to limited infor-mation) arrests the development of these structures on simple and undifferentiated levels. This is because the same information is circulated through the perceptual cycles. In other words, repeated exposures to the same information would improve the per-son's perceptual efficiency but would offer very little to stretch his or her construals of this kind of event as it occurs on subsequent occasions. Consequently, the behaviors associated with such limited constructions would be highly routinized and predictable; and even though the environment may provide the person with varied information on subsequent occasions, because of the onset of automatization at simple schematic levels, most of the information surrounding the event will be beyond the person's perceptual sphere. The individual's construction of that event, by necessity, will only be partial, superficial, and vague.

Automatization may also occur on relatively deeper levels of processing, that is, with more complex schemata directing the perceptual activity. Here the schemata are capable of instigating several perceptual cycles for exploration and information pickup from a number of relatively broad environmental cues. However, when automatization occurs on such levels the same information is recirculated on repeated occasions, resulting in invariant schemata and hence in highly structured and predictable constructions of the event. Thus, while the individual appears to have the perceptual skills to scan the field reasonably well, the automatization of cycles precludes the introduction of new elements and arrests the flexibility with which the scanned information is reorganized in ways that will allow the individual to broaden his or her outlook on an event.

A therapist working from such a perceptual–cognitive perspective would first need to gain an understanding of the characteristic mode of client mental operations. Second, having identified the target, the therapist would function as a catalyst to help the client generate, on a moment-to-moment basis, information that potentially can be incor-porated into the client's system of cognitive operations. This is achieved through in-terventions that would "slow down" or deautomatize perceptual activity.[2] To the extent that the therapist is successful in holding a client in a sufficiently lengthy time frame to explore information surrounding a particular problematic event, the probability would increase that the client would "see" and "integrate" information that was previously ignored. Adding relevant elements to the perceptual system would contribute to the modification of schemata resulting in explorations of a wider range of elements in the client's perceptual field. This in turn would facilitate making finer discriminations of available cues and developing more complex internal representations of events. In other words, by focusing on the client's internal mental operations, the therapist would be able to engage the client in a controlled mode of processing which would involve careful scanning, sampling, and reorganizing elements for differential construals of events. The client's own production or creation of alternative perspectives would thus serve as a new and potentially more precise pool of information to carry on perceptual activity, leading the client to an alternative way of seeing things that would foster greater flexi-bility and adjustment.

---

2. A similar conceptualization emphasizing the importance of client reallocation of attentional resources in therapeutic activity has recently been advanced by Greenberg and Safran (1980; 1981).

The link between the LCPP categories and the conceptualized levels or stages of client perceptual activity is presented in Table 4-2. As can be seen, client statements classified in Categories V, VI, and VII reflect the availability of complex structures and the utilization of a predominantly controlled mode of processing which allow for the detection, reorganization, and integration of a wide array of information for the construction of an event. In other words, client responses in these categories represent more productive levels of perceptual functioning than those judged to be in the other categories.

At the present time, the value of the system is in its utility as a research instrument for the measurement of client perceptual functioning within a client-centered approach to therapy. Further work and experimentation would be needed to refine the model and establish its usefulness and generalizability to other therapeutic modalities.

Technical Aspects of the System

The LCPP can be applied to transcriptions and/or audiotape recordings of individual psychotherapy sessions. It can be used to evaluate client verbalizations at any point within or across several therapeutic encounters. Both random and systematic sampling of standard time periods in a given session or across sessions may be employed for data collection.

Unit of Analysis

The "summarizing unit . . . or the unit in terms of which quantification is performed" (Kiesler, 1973, p. 39) may be the sample itself, the session (i.e., two or more samples from a given session), or the entire series of therapeutic encounters (i.e., samples across several sessions), depending upon the purposes and aims of the researcher. Within this system, the global or "contextual" unit is the client's response or communication that intervenes between two counselor statements when a counselor statement is more than just a minimal expression of agreement (e.g., "mm-hm," a rapid "yes," "right," etc.) or an encouragement to talk (e.g., "go on," "continue," "then . . . ," "you were saying . . . ," etc.). In other words, the global unit is the patient in a therapist–patient–therapist communication sequence and represents "the largest body of content that may be examined in characterizing a scoring unit" (Kiesler, 1973, p. 38).

The "scoring unit" or the basic unit of analysis of the measure is that portion of client verbalization in a contextual (global) unit that can actually be coded by placing it in any one of the eight categories. In other words, scoring units are identifiable shifts or transitions in the manner of client processing. Thus, a contextual or global unit may have several or no transitions. In the latter case, the scoring unit becomes the global or contextual unit. Should the researcher be interested in the overall quality of a global unit, consisting of more than one transition, the modal scoring category is assigned to the segment for analysis. Table 4-3 provides an example of a coded 5-minute segment from a counseling interview to demonstrate this classification procedure.

Coders and Coding Procedures

To date, the system has been used by coders or judges who have had graduate level theoretical exposure to and training in client-centered therapy and who have had a minimum of 1 year (or 300 hours) of practical experience under supervision.

LCPP requires three trained judges. Prior to undertaking training, judges are exposed

Table 4-2   LCPP Categories Associated with Factors Involved in Perceptual Activity

LCPP Categories	Nature of Available Information		Processing Mode		Schemata in Operation
	Restricted and/or Invariant	Broad and/or Diverse	Automated (Same Level Processing)	Controlled (Across Level Processing)	
I (Undifferentiated Statement)	Predominantly	None	Predominantly	None	Simple
II (Elaboration)	Predominantly	None	Predominantly	None	
III (Differentiation with External Focus)	Largely	Some	Largely	Some	More Complex
IV (Differentiation with Analytic Focus)	Some	Largely	Largely	Some	
V (Differentiation with Internal Focus)	Some	Largely	Some	Largely	Complex associative structures
VI (Reevaluation)	Some	Largely	Some	Largely	
VII (Integration)	Some	Largely	Some	Largely	

to the theoretical rationale of the measure. The definition of each category is presented and discussed and clarification is provided through examples from actual therapy audiotapes. An explanation is also provided as to what constitutes a global unit and a transition.

The second phase of training involves the use of transcripts to train judges in the identification of scoring units. The aim of this phase is to develop an awareness of the qualitatively different aspects of client verbalizations found in global or contextual units. The actual word or place in a sentence that marks a transition is not important as long as judges agree on the general vicinity of transitions or shifts involved in a contextual unit. Judges are trained to identify transitions for an average of 75% absolute interrater agreement or better before proceeding with the training of assigning scoring units to particular categories.

In the third phase, judges are provided with training tapes (i.e., segments of actual therapy transactions). Transcripts of these segments, where scoring units or transitions are marked, are also provided. Discrimination training in the differential assignment of scoring units to different categories of the system continues until judges reach a

Table 4-3 An Example of a Coded 5-Minute Segment from a Counseling Interview

	Transcript	Transition or Scoring Unit[a]	Code	Global or Contextual Unit[b]	Code
T:	So you feel maybe that you've been creating some of . . .				
C1:	I may have. I mean that would get me off the hook kind of . . . if I embraced that approach, and that rationale.			C1	Differentiation with analytic focus; client is engaged in a logical analysis of an internal state.
T:	It would get you off the hook?				
C2:	Yeah. And uh, it . . . would reaffirm to myself that . . . there hasn't been a breakdown, there hasn't been a loss of receptors.			C2	Differentiation with analytic focus; client is engaged in a logical analysis of an internal state.
T:	So those real receptors are still there, that somehow its the imaginary ones that have disappeared.				
C3:	Its a nice way of thinking about it, if its, you know, if one can accept that interpretation . . . Its probably true. . . .			C3	Differentiation with analytic focus; client is engaged in a logical analysis of an internal state.
T:	Would that be a positive thing?				
C4:	Yes it would be. (long silence) . . . . It changes the direction of the feeling, maybe . . . before it was very . . . self-centered and maybe now . . . if I can be so presumptuous to say so, maybe if . . . when you're calmer, maybe you can redirect that feeling outward, to others, because then you're . . .			C4	Reevaluation; client is weighing alternative perspectives.

maybe it's the redirection of the flow.

T: Instead of those energies being caught up in yourself, there's energy for other people?

C5: (1) You're less engaged with . . . an internal battle . . . (*silence*)/

C5(1) — Differentiation with internal focus; client provides a personal characterization of an internal state.

(2) I, I think, I'm just sort of comparing, I, I had a conversation with a friend, and . . . well, I asked him to not, I mean, what I'm saying, I'm kind of comparing before and afterwards. Earlier, a month ago, in my past history, I think maybe . . . when people spoke to me like on the telephone, I have one friend, she's always telling me all her problems, I guess it's just like myself and she's telling me how much work she has to do and all of this and that, and stuff, and I listened/

C5(2) — Elaboration

C5 — Elaboration; client gives an account of an incident.

(3) but I didn't listen, in a sense. Now I, I can listen and . . . like before when she told me that, that would get me down kind of but now I can listen, but it doesn't upset me or I can (*long silence*) . . . I've got more time, more listening time perhaps.

C5(3) — Reevaluation; client evaluates and generates an alternative interpretation of past behavior.

(*continued*)

Table 4-3 (Continued)

Transcript	Transition or Scoring Unit[a]	Code	Global or Contextual Unit[b]	Code
T: That makes you . . .				
C6: (1) Yeah, one shouldn't concentrate on what type of . . . before I was very worried . . . (inaudible) . . . I had chances to do things and canceled because I was so worried about studying for a test, or studying, doing research or something and I . . . /	C6(1)	Elaboration		
(2) it was all me, like I was doing it all for me . . . because those tests meant so much and I had to do well and . . . I didn't have time, I didn't have time, you know, /	C6(2)	Differentiation with external focus; emphasis is on an externalized standard of performance.	C6	Elaboration; the overall quality of the response is one of giving factual information.
(3) but . . . its crazy to do that.	C6(3)	Undifferentiated statement		
T: And now?				
C7: (1) It's not, I still like to study for tests and I suppose, well I don't like to but I feel that I must, I should, so I do/	C7(1)	Differentiation with external focus; emphasis is on "musts" and "shoulds."		
(2) but it's not such a life and death matter really . . . I don't think as much as it used to be . . . I try to make time for things more . . . (inaudible) . . . to get away from doing for me and . . . (silence)/	C7(2)	Differentiation with internal focus.	C7	Differentiation with internal focus; client provides an internally generated interpretation.
(3) I need a mix . . . I think . . . (long silence) I am finding that I . . . I can enjoy people more . . .	C7(3)	Integration; a new perspective emerges.		

	Dialogue	Code	Category
	Finding out they are not these horrible, vile creatures . . .		
T:	What was so threatening about those people?		
C8:	(*silence*) The gates were locked in a sense, kind of . . .	C8	Differentiation with internal focus; client describes an internal state using idiosyncratic language.
T:	You felt closed into yourself . . . and you didn't have the key.		
C9:	And that was me there shutting the gate, and locking the lock is rejection. Maybe, how a smile instantly locks the key, I mean unlocks the, the lock of the door . . .	C9	Integration; client generates a new self perspective.
T:	Yeah that is the key . . .		
C:	Seeing their smiling eyes . . . and seeing their smiling face/		
C10:	(*silence*) Everybody's trying to get ahead, and so busy stomping on everybody else trying to get up to the top and . . . a lot of problems staying there.	C10	Differentiate with external focus; client uses other generated standards to describe an experience.
T:	You're saying its a kind of dog eat dog world?		
C:	Yeah.		
T:	Where does that place you?		
C11:	Umm, I missed that, no that last comment.	C11	Other

(*continued*)

Table 4-3 (*Continued*)

Transcript	Transition or Scoring Unit[a]	Code	Global or Contextual Unit[b]	Code
T: I just wondered where that places you, I mean in the dog eat dog world?				
C12: On the perimeter . . . yeah . . .Not part of the bunch . . . not part of that mechanism. And I saw them all, as them all clustered, and they grew up, but probably in reality they're very separate from each other and they're all, you know but I always saw them as being . . . all clumped together. . . .			C12	Reevaluation; client is engaged in the reappraisal of past perceptions.
T: And now?				
C13: There's more . . . there's still a great clump, but there's also . . . more . . . more people on the perimeter too. . . . I'm not the only one on the perimeter.			C13	Integration; client generates a new perspective on self in relation to others.
T: There have been a few people who have dared to break away from that clump?				
C: It's comforting that . . . (*inaudible*)				

T:	Perhaps you were never alone to begin with?		
C14:	There are other ways. . . . It's true that you don't have to be a part . . . of that huge machine. . . .	C14	Differentiation with internal focus; client uses newly emerged perspective to further define and confirm view of self.
T:	Are you saying that you don't have to be a part of the machine?		
C:	Umhmm.		
T:	So		
C15:	And I guess feeling a sense of value would reduce that, that . . . that antogonism between them and myself.	C15	Reevaluation; client arrives at a tentative realization of a potentially more meaningful stance.
T:	That antogonism?		
C16:	(1) Before I think I mentioned that, for example, the kind of thoughts that would be, that I would feel, kind of experiences that I would be experiencing, say if I was in a bus and there was a group of young people . . . and with the young teachers . . . umm/	C16(1)	Elaboration; client gives examples to put a thought across.

(continued)

Table 4-3 *(Continued)*

Transcript	Transition or Scoring Unit[a]	Code	Global or Contextual Unit[b]	Code
(2) . . . I'm clearly experiencing a different kind of life than I was. I'd . . . there'd be, I'd . . . feel some kind of hostility . . . and maybe I did feel threatened for some reason/	C16(2)	Reevaluation	C16	Reevaluation; client is attempting to come to grips with an alternate interpretation of an experience.
(3) . . . But now it's not as much but, I think I can . . . there's no . . . they can be and I can be, and it's fine. . . . I don't have to, I don't experience a lot that I did, the feelings that I did feel, I don't . . . so much anymore. . . .	C16(3)	Integration; client arrives at a more flexible and personally more satisfying self perspective.		

[a]The smallest scorable portion of a client's response. [b]A client response that intervenes between two counselor statements.

criterion of .05 level of significance using Cohen's (1960) coefficient of interrater agreement procedure. One of the three raters acts as the "marker" of transitions and the tie breaker.

Transcripts of the actual audiotaped segments to be rated are prepared. Working with both transcriptions and audiotapes, the "marker" denotes the global units and transitions to be rated by the other two judges who then code each unit independently from one another to provide the data. At intervals the level of interrater agreement is checked and, if deemed necessary, training is reintroduced.

Reliability

Initially, LCPP was used in an exploratory study to analyze segments of psychotherapy tapes of six individuals who were among 73 outpatients participating in the Penn Psychotherapy Project (Mintz, Luborsky, & Christoph, 1979). On the basis of extensive pre- and posttreatment evaluations obtained from therapists, patients, and observers, as well as residual gain scores, three of these patients were identified as highly improved and three as low in improvement. All patients in the project had undergone psychoanalytically oriented psychotherapy for differing lengths of time. Treatments for this group of two male and four female patients ranged from 28 to 123 sessions (mdn=46). The mean treatment period for the group was 68 weeks. Three audiotape recordings (from the early, middle, and late therapy sessions) for each participant were obtained and three 5-minute segments (from the early, middle, and late part) of each session were selected for analysis. The 54 psychotherapy segments thus obtained were coded and randomly transcribed onto a master tape. Transcripts for these segments, marked for transitions or shifts in level of client processing, were also prepared.

Two advanced graduate student judges, using both transcripts and audiotapes, rated a total of 350 global units and 542 transitions. The interrater agreement on both sets of data using Cohen's kappa was .37. Interrater reliability estimates for the same data using the intraclass method (Ebel, 1951) were .74 and .72, respectively. Raters agreed on 51% of the classifications across the system's eight categories. When the third trained judge was used as a tie breaker, it was possible to obtain 89% agreement between any two of the three raters.

Comparable estimates of interrater agreement have also been reported in a more recent study (Brown, 1984) in which LCPP was used to rate client responses from an early, middle, and late segment of two psychotherapy sessions from 29 university counseling center clients. Using the coding procedures described above, 785 global units and 1200 transitions or scoring units were extracted. The percentage of interrater agreements across the system's eight categories were found to be 64% and 62% and the corresponding kappa coefficients .38 and .42, respectively.

Validity

The value of a psychological measure and its usefulness as a tool in providing meaningful information concerning the nature of the behavioral domain of interest hinges upon the instrument's ability to capture essential aspects of the hypothetical construct (trait or quality) that it is designed to tap. Cronbach and Meehl (1955) have suggested that the logic and method involved in establishing the construct validity of an instrument are essentially those of the scientific method and that the process, by its very nature, is integral to efforts at validating the conceptual model underlying the measure. The construct validation paradigm, according to these authors, requires the clarification of the meaning of a construct as it is measured by a given instrument, through testing predictions about possible relationships between the construct and other relevant variables (i.e., establishing a "nomological network"); or alternatively, through advancing hypotheses about expected behaviors of individuals receiving different evaluations on the instrument in question, and then confirming or refuting these hypotheses empirically. Knowledge accumulated through these procedures would subsequently contribute to revisions in the model for more precise definitions of the construct and/or to reformulations and refinements of the instrument in question.

Within the present context, LCPP purports to tap seven modes of mental operations that have been formulated to depict differential aspects of a client's moment-by-moment perceptual activity in therapy. As indicated earlier, the model underlying the instrument proposes that the aim of psychotherapy is to help clients develop a more functional or flexible perceptual system, that is, to help them acquire skills in constructing more complex and precise propositional representations of events so that they can generate alternative perspectives of problematic life situations. Thus, one would expect that client "movement" in therapy would proceed from predominantly simple, less differentiated, and categorical modes of processing to more complex mental operations that involve deeper levels of semantic associative analyses and the extraction of meaning in the act of perceiving an event. Furthermore, it would also be expected that those cognitive operations that are conceptualized within the model to be desirable for client change would relate to other similarly conceptualized process variables depicted by other instruments and methods of investigation. At the present time, there are only preliminary data concerning both predictions with respect to LCPP.

In the exploratory study that used six patients from the Penn Psychotherapy Project described earlier in this chapter, an attempt was made to test the system's sensitivity or power to detect changes in the manner of processing by the three most improved and three least improved patients along the instrument's seven dimensions. The proportion of scoring units (transitions) of each patient falling within each of the eight categories of the instrument for each of the early, middle, and late therapy sessions was calculated. Units falling in the "other" category were excluded from the analyses. It was expected that relative to the early therapy session, the middle and late therapy encounters of most improved patients would show a higher proportion of Category IV, V, VI, and VII responses and that the proportion of units in these four classes for each of the least improved patients in their two later sessions would be either the same or lower than those in the early session. Considering the exploratory nature of this investigation and the low frequencies involved in some of the categories no statistical analyses were performed. Instead, data were examined descriptively and summarized in terms of high and low processing categories (Figures 4-1 and 4-2). Since the major interest of the study was to examine patient perceptual skills acquisition in the high processing categories the discussion that follows will focus primarily on Figure 4-1.

It can be seen from Figure 4-1 that, in general, the data are in the predicted direction. In the improved group this trend was most clearly delineated by Patient B who interestingly was also the highest ranked patient from the 10 who made most improvement among the 73 patients in the Penn Psychotherapy Project (Luborsky, 1982). Less dramatic but in the predicted direction is the trend seen in Patient C, followed by Patient A, who shows considerable improvement in processing skills at the midmark but fails to maintain the same levels at the end of therapy. All three of these patients are reported to have terminated therapy mostly at their own initiative.

In general, the trend in the least improved group of patients is also in the predicted

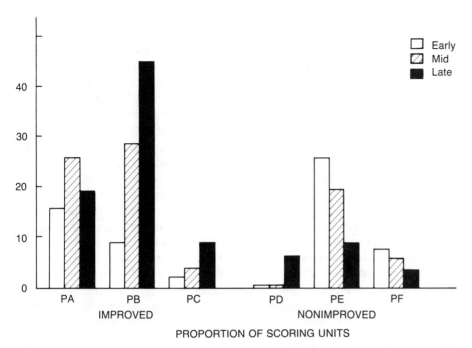

Figure 4-1   Proportion of scoring units in high processing categories for improved and nonimproved patients.

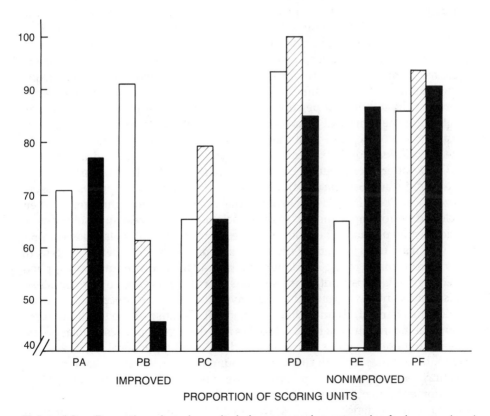

Figure 4-2   Proportion of scoring units in low processing categories for improved and nonimproved patients.

direction. Patients E and F demonstrate a progressive deterioration in high-level processing skills across sessions. The pattern for Patient D is not as clear. This patient starts therapy with a minimal level of the more advanced perceptual skills. Although she shows some gains by the end of therapy, she is reported to have terminated therapy against advice (Luborsky, 1982), suggesting that her gains may not have been significant enough to make an impact on her therapeutic experience. Of particular interest in this group is the pattern demonstrated by Patient E. This patient appears to have started therapy with relatively high levels of perceptual functioning but, for reasons that are largely unknown, has "lost ground" over the course of therapy and is reported to have terminated therapy to go to a different therapist (Luborsky, 1982). One possible reason for this progressive deterioration could be the nature of the patient's therapeutic experience which, from a perceptual skills development standpoint, could be seen as having offered very little to "stretch" the initial level of the patient's system of perceptual activity. In short, the picture that emerges from these trends suggests that LCPP is tapping some important process dimensions that are related to client change over the course of therapy. More fine-grained empirical investigations would be needed to provide further support for the efficacy of this process measure in delineating the differential relationships between varying patterns of client perceptual operations and therapeutic outcome.

Recently, Shirley (1983) and Rice and Saperia (1984) reported data that bear upon the construct validity of the instrument. In the first study, the relationship between LCPP and other measures of client process was investigated. When the Experiencing Scale (Klein, Mathieu, Gendlin & Kiesler, 1970), the Client Vocal Quality (CVQ) classification system (Rice, Koke, Greenberg & Wagstaff, 1979), and the LCPP were used to analyze the same segments of 40 analogue counseling interviews, it was found that LCPP categories relate well to conceptually relevant dimensions of the other two client process systems. More specifically, results from this study indicated that the mean Experiencing Scale rating for the combined LCPP Categories V, VI, and VII, which depict the most complex client modes of perceptual processing, was significantly higher than the mean rating for the other LCPP categories. As well, it was found that while these combined categories co-occurred with the Focused CVQ pattern, Categories I, II, III, and IV, reflecting the less complex client modes of processing, co-occurred with the Externalizing CVQ pattern consistently more often than expected by chance.

In the study by Rice and Saperia (1984), LCPP was used as an adjunct process measure to test the presence of certain kinds of client internal operations conceptualized, in their newly developed performance model, to be associated with successful resolutions of "problematic reaction points." The model specifies 24 task-relevant molar codes or process criteria which are used to identify the process steps involved in clients' successful resolutions of problematic tasks. This intensive task analysis procedure was applied to transcribed segments of psychotherapy sessions of two clients. The authors classified the 24 process criteria into five groups that were hypothesized to be conceptually related to LCPP Categories I and II, III and IV, V, VI, and VII. Because of the small numbers of observations falling into the last three categories and their corresponding molar codes, the frequencies in these categories were combined to permit a statistical test of association. The chi square values for both clients were found to be significant beyond the .001 level, indicating a strong relationship between these two methods of analyzing client moment-by-moment perceptual activity.

There is also some evidence to suggest that LCPP Category VI (Reevaluation) can reliably identify conflict resolution performances in the two-chair dialogue method of

Gestalt therapy (Greenberg, 1982). Category VI purports to depict client perceptual–cognitive processes involved in the reexamination of previously held perspectives, the weighing of alternative ways of organizing information, and the recognition by the client of the possibility that he or she can look at and interpret an event differently. In his analysis of a set of two-chair dialogues of "resolvers" and "nonresolvers," Greenberg reports to have found that in successful resolution performances Category VI co-occurs consistently with relevant dimensions of other process systems (e.g., Experiencing Scale, CVQ) in identifying the change instance by the "critic" and concludes that the measure is particularly useful in describing the mental processes of clients engaged in this method of Gestalt therapy.

These preliminary data indicate that LCPP is a viable research instrument for investigators interested in gaining an understanding of client moment-by-moment processing operations during therapeutic encounters. Needless to say, more empirical work will be needed to provide further evidence for the validity of the measure and its underlying constructs. Continued use of the system in investigations of therapeutic transactions of clients from different clinical populations with therapists from different orientations using different styles of intervention will help to establish whether or not LCPP can identify varying modes of client perceptual activity across diverse therapeutic contexts. Ultimately, however, the utility of this measure will depend upon future research that will demonstrate how well its process dimensions relate to immediate- and long-range consequences of therapy. While the available evidence is encouraging in this regard, more extensive investigations of the relationship between client in therapy mental operations and various psychotherapy outcome criteria will be needed to determine the potential of LCPP as a predictor of therapeutic outcome.

Acknowledgments

The author wishes to thank Dr. Lester Luborsky for providing the psychotherapy tapes used in the pilot study reported in this chapter and Dr. Sandra W. Pyke and Dr. David L. Rennie for their useful comments.

References

Beck, A., Rush, J., Shaw, B., & Emery, G. *Cognitive therapy of depression*. New York: The Guilford Press, 1979.

Broadbent, D. The hidden preattentive processes. *American Psychologist*, 1977, *32*, 109–118.

Brown, H. D. Counsellor and client in-therapy verbal behaviour. Unpublished Master's Thesis, York University, Downsview, Ontario, 1984.

Cantor, N., & Kihlstrom, J. F. (Eds.) *Personality, cognition and social interaction*. Hillsdale, N.J.: Lawrence Erlbaum, 1981.

Cohen, J. A coefficient of agreement for nominal scales. *Educational and Psychological Measurement*, 1960, *20*, 37–46.

Craik, F. I. M., & Lockhart, R. S. Levels of processing: A framework for memory research. *Journal of Verbal Learning and Verbal Behavior*, 1972, *11*, 671–684.

Cronbach, L. J., & Meehl, P. E. Construct validity in psychological tests. *Psychological Bulletin*, 1955, *52*, 281–302.

Ebel, R. L. Estimation of the reliability of ratings. *Psychometrika*, 1951, *16*, 407–424.

Endler, N. S. Interactionism: A personality model, but not yet a theory. In M. M. Page (Ed.), *Nebraska Symposium on Motivation 1982: Personality—Current Theory and Research*. Lincoln, Nebraska: University of Nebraska Press, 1983.

Gendlin, E. T., & Tomlinson, T. M. *Psychotherapy process rating scale: Experiencing (EXP) Scale.* Unpublished manuscript, Wisconsin Psychiatric Institute, 1961.

Greenberg, L. S. Personal communication, March 1982.

Greenberg, L. S., & Safran, J. D. Encoding, information processing and the cognitive behavioural therapies. *Canadian Psychology,* 1980, *21,* 59–66.

Greenberg, L. S., & Safran, J. D. Encoding and cognitive therapy: Changing what clients attend to. *Psychotherapy: Theory, Research and Practice,* 1981, *18,* 163–169.

Kelly, G. *The psychology of personal constructs.* New York: Norton, 1955.

Kiesler, D. *The process of psychotherapy.* Chicago: Aldine, 1973.

Klein, M. H., Mathieu, P. L., Gendlin, E. T., & Kiesler, D. J. *The Experiencing Scale: A research and training manual.* Madison: Wisconsin Psychiatric Institute, Bureau of Audio Visual Instruction, 1970.

Luborsky, L. S. Personal communication, February 1982.

Mintz, J., Luborsky, L., & Christoph, P. Measuring the outcomes of psychotherapy: Findings of the Penn Psychotherapy Project. *Journal of Consulting and Clinical Psychology,* 1979, *47,* 319–334.

Meichenbaum, D. *Cognitive-behavior modification: An integrative approach.* New York: Plenum Press, 1977.

Mischel, W. Personality and cognition: Something borrowed, something new? In N. Cantor & J. F. Kihlstrom (Eds.), *Personality, Cognition, and Social Interaction.* Hillsdale, N.J.: Lawrence Erlbaum, 1981.

Neisser, U. *Cognition and reality: Principles and implications of cognitive psychology.* San Francisco: W. H. Freeman, 1976.

Norman, D. A. *Memory and attention: An introduction to human information processing.* New York: Wiley, 1976.

Rice, L. N. The evocative function of the therapist. In D. Wexler & L. Rice (Eds.), *Innovations in Client Centered Therapy.* New York: Wiley, 1974.

Rice, L. N., Koke, C. J., Greenberg, L. S., & Wagstaff, A. K. *Manual for Client Vocal Quality, Vol. 1: Information for the investigator.* Toronto: Counselling and Development Centre, York University, 1979.

Rice, L., & Saperia, E. P. Task analysis of the resolution of problematic reactions. In L. Rice & L. Greenberg (Eds.), *Change Episodes in Psychotherapy,* New York: Guilford Press, 1984.

Rogers, C. R. A tentative scale for the measurement of process in psychotherapy. In E. A. Rubinstein & M. B. Parloff (eds.), *Research in Psychotherapy* (Vol 1). Washington, D.C.: American Psychological Association, 1959, pp. 96–107.

Shiffrin, R. M., & Schneider, W. Controlled and automatic human information processing: II. Perceptual learning, automatic attending, and a general theory. *Psychological Review,* 1977, *84,* 127–150.

Shirley, M. K. Three measures of client experiential process: Their relationship to each other and client cognitive differentiation. Unpublished Master's Thesis, York University, Downsview, Ontario, 1983.

Sloane, R., Staples, F., Cristol, F., Yorkstan, N., & Whipple, K. *Short term analytically oriented psychotherapy vs. behavior therapy.* Cambridge, Mass.: Harvard University Press, 1975.

Smith, M., & Glass, G. Meta-analysis of psychotherapy outcome studies. *American Psychologist,* 1977, *32,* 752–760.

Toukmanian, S. G. *A perceptual-cognitive model for counselling and psychotherapy* (Tech. Rep. No. 138). Downsview, Ontario: York University, Department of Psychology, 1983.

Wexler, D. A. Cognitive theory of experiencing, self actualization, and therapeutic process. In D. Wexler & L. Rice (Eds.), *Innovations in Client Centered Therapy.* New York: Wiley, 1974.

5

An Overview of the Hill Counselor and Client Verbal Response Modes Category Systems

Clara E. Hill
University of Maryland
College Park, Maryland

The study of verbal response modes in counseling/psychotherapy has a long history and many systems have been developed to measure this level of the interaction between counselor and client[1] (e.g., Aronson, 1953; Danish and D'Augelli, 1976; Goodman and Dooley, 1976; Hackney & Nye, 1973; Ivey, 1971; Robinson, 1950; Snyder, 1945; 1963; Spooner & Stone, 1977; Strupp, 1960; Whalen & Flowers, 1977). Obviously, many researchers have felt that counselor and client response modes capture an important dimension of the therapeutic communication process.

Verbal response modes are important because they reflect communication styles or patterns. In other words, the specific choice of what type of response to make indicates the relationship between two persons. For example, one person might communicate mostly by asking the other person questions, whereas another person might tell his/her own story (description) and never ask questions or express interest in the other person. These different response styles undoubtedly have different impacts on the receiver.

For counselors, the use of specific response modes seems to be related to their theoretical orientation and training (Hill, Thames, & Rardin, 1979). In other words, a counselor who wants to be passive and supportive but force the client to take the initiative might rely primarily on silence, minimal encouragers, and restatements. On the other hand, a counselor who is more directive and action oriented might use more direct guidance, information, and confrontation.

For a client, response modes describe the client's style of involvement in the interaction and predict the ability to participate in a verbal therapy interaction. A client who engages mostly in silence or description of the problem will probably have a more difficult time in insight-oriented therapy than would a client who more readily engages in experiencing and insight.

Within a counseling/psychotherapy interaction, the counselor and client use different response modes which relate to their different roles. The role of the client is to discuss and change him/herself, whereas the counselor's role is to facilitate the client's change. Because of these role differences, two different sets of response modes were deemed necessary to describe adequately the unique roles of each participant. For example, a

---

1. The terms counselor/psychotherapist and client/patient are used interchangeably in this chapter.

question or self-disclosure has different characteristics or functions for a counselor and client and therefore we have used more descriptive labels for each.

To place my response modes category systems within a context, let me refer to Russell & Stiles' (1979) classification schema for categorizing language analysis systems. They proposed a 2×3 framework of coding strategies by type of categories for classifying systems. Coding strategies can be either classical or pragmatic, depending on the amount of inference required to do the coding. In the classical coding, terms are highly operationalized and judgments can be made easily and reliably directly from the text with little or no inference by judges, for example, counts of words. In the pragmatic strategy, judges make inferences about psychological processes (e.g., transference) which may not have specific behavioral referents. The three types of categories are content (the semantic meaning of language, e.g., discussion of mother), intersubjective (the syntactic or grammatical structure of language, which implies a relationship between communication and recipient, e.g., a question), and extralinguistic (includes vocal noises, tonal qualities, and temporal patterning of speech, e.g., speech disfluencies or pauses).

On Russell and Stiles' (1979) dimension of type of categories, my response modes systems would be classified as intersubjective. The definitions rely primarily on grammatical structures as indicators of the specific response modes. Further, the type of behavior is reflective of an interaction between individuals, for example, a question is directed to another person. However, the response modes do not give information regarding the content or topic under discussion nor do they provide detail about all the other extralinguistic behaviors which occur concurrently with the verbal behaviors. Regarding the Russell and Stiles' dimension of coding strategy, my system falls between the classical and pragmatic strategies. The definitions are operationalized as much as possible but they do require more inference than simply counting the number of words. Some of the categories (e.g., minimal encourager, questions) rely more on a grammatical structure or form and are thereby more highly operationalized and easier to judge. Others (e.g., interpretation, confrontation) require more inference by judges and are more difficult to categorize. Further, many communications are not clear-cut and require judgment as to which category they fit in. For example, some communication may be phrased in one way but the intent is clearly different. For example, ''Tell me more'' is phrased like a direct guidance but the intent is an open question. Our guideline has always been to go with the intent more than the form in such a clear-cut case, because the intent seems to be more therapeutically meaningful.

Another framework for understanding where response modes fit into the larger counseling/psychotherapy picture was provided by me in a recent review of the process area (Hill, 1982). In this paper, I proposed that one can analyze counseling/psychotherapy at six levels, ranging from the most observable, easily rated, highly operationalized behaviors to the more abstract, inferential categories of behaviors. The six levels are: (1) ancillary behaviors (extralinguistic, linguistic, nonverbal, and physiological); (2) response modes; (3) content (topic of discussion); (4) ratings of behavior (attitudes, involvement); (5) covert behaviors (thoughts, perceptions, feelings, attitudes); and (6) clinical strategies (interventions, techniques). Overriding all of these six levels would be the philosophical or theoretical approach that a therapist espouses. Thus, a therapist's philosophical approach is composed of clinical strategies which are implemented by specific response modes in the presence of ancillary behaviors and overall attitudes. For example, a psychodynamic counselor might analyze resistance (intervention) by interpretations and confrontations (response modes), while sitting forward and maintaining eye contact (ancillary behaviors) and exuding empathy (rating of behaviors). Further, the counselor's reasons for his/her behavior at all levels might be determined by eliciting the covert behaviors and knowing the content. Obviously, all of these levels are important to get a complete overview of the psychotherapy process.

Description of Systems

The counselor system has 14 categories: minimal encourager, silence, approval–reassurance, information, direct guidance, closed question, open question, restatement, reflection, interpretation, confrontation, nonverbal referent, self-disclosure, and other. The client system has nine categories: simple response, request, description, experiencing, exploration of client–counselor relationship, insight, discussion of plans, and other.

To use these systems, three trained judges are required. Prior to categorizing, typed transcripts of sessions must be divided into response units by trained unitizers. Each of these response units is then assigned by judges to one and only one of the categories. Judges work independently to avoid influencing each other but later meet and discuss any categorizations on which all three disagree and eventually come to agreement on one category. For all other categorizations, the classifications of two of the three judges are used for the final analysis. In determining agreement levels between judges, a kappa statistic is used.

The categories in each system can be described as nominal, in that the judgment is made simply of presence or absence. No ratings of quality of response type are made, nor is it assumed that any response mode is better than any other; for example, interpretations are not deemed ''better'' than questions. The categories are mutually exclusive, such that each response unit gets classified in only one category. The mutually exclusive nature is desirable to simplify analysis and also to have categories conceptually distinct. The definitions of the categories specify observable behavior as criteria although a moderate amount of inference is required. Further, the categories in each system exhaust the range of possible behaviors at this level of analysis and cover behaviors observed in all theoretical orientations; that is, they are pantheoretical. The systems have face validity and demonstrated agreement level among judges and can be used for both training and practice. Finally, there are standardized training materials and techniques in a published manual (Hill, Greenwald, Reed, Charles, O'Farrell, & Carter, 1981) so that any new researcher can easily use the systems. These above criteria have all been proposed for evaluation of response modes systems (Butler, Rice, & Wagstaff, 1962; Goodman & Dooley, 1976; Kiesler, 1973; Russell & Stiles, 1979).

The counselor and client systems are presented below. For each category, the definition is followed by two examples.

Counselor Verbal Response Category System

1. Minimal Encourager: A *short* phrase that indicates simple agreement, acknowledgement, or understanding. It encourages but does not request that the client continue talking; also, it does not imply approval or disapproval. It may be a repetition of a key word, but does *not* include responses to questions (see Information).

CL: There's so much I need to do that I don't know where to begin.
CO: MmHmm.

CL: A year ago I decided to change my major from microbiology to physical education.
CO: Go on.

2. *Silence*: A pause of 5 seconds is considered the counselor's pause if it occurs between a client's statement and a counselor's statement or within the client's statement (except after a simple acceptance of the client's statement, e.g., "Yes" pause).

CL: I'm not sure what to do.
CO: (*Pause = 5 seconds*)

CL: I'm not sure what to do.
CO: [MmHmm.] (*Pause = 5 seconds*)

3. *Approval–reassurance*: Provides emotional support, approval, or reinforcement. It may imply sympathy or tend to alleviate anxiety by minimizing client's problems.

CL: I didn't know if I should come here.
CO: I think you did the right thing.

CL: I get so uptight before exams.
CO: Everyone feels that way from time to time.

4. *Information*: Supplies information in the form of data, facts, resources, theory, and so on. It may be information specifically related to the counseling process, counselor's behavior, or arrangements (time, place, fee, etc.). It may answer questions, but does not include directions for what the client should do (see Direct Guidance).

CL: What were the results of the test?
CO: The SCII indicates that your interests are forestry.

CL: How about Horney? Did she agree with that theory?
CO: I don't know the answer to that question.

5. *Direct Guidance*: Directions or advice that the counselor suggests for the client or for the client and counselor together, either within or outside the counseling session. It is not aimed at soliciting verbal material from the client (see Closed or Open Question).

CL: Do you have a solution for my tension right now?
CO: Practice this relaxation exercise 15 minutes a night.

CL: Last night the president was in my dream.
CO: Play the part of the man in your dream.

6. *Closed Question*: Data-gathering inquiry that requests a one- or two-word answer, a "yes" or "no," or a confirmation of the counselor's previous statement. The possible client responses to this type of inquiry are typically *limited* and *specific*. If statements are phrased in the form of a closed question but meet the criteria for another category, put in the *other* category.

CL: I'm still procrastinating.
CO: Did you read the book I suggested?

CL: My husband thinks I'm too fat.
CO: How much do you weigh?

7. *Open Question*: A probe that requests a clarification of feelings or an exploration of the situation *without purposely limiting* the nature of the response to a "yes" or "no" or a one- or two-word response. If statements are phrased in the form of an open ques-

tion but meet the intent or criteria for another category, put in the more appropriate category.

CL: I've had a backache for days.
CO: What's making you tense?

CL: My sister got all the attention in the family.
CO: How do you feel about that?

8. Restatement: A simple repeating or rephrasing of the client's statement(s) (not necessarily just the immediately preceding statements). It typically contains fewer but *similar words and is more concrete and clear* than the client's message. It may be phrased either tentatively or as a statement.

CL: I'm on probation and just got F's on tests.
CO: You say you're flunking out of school this semester.

CL: Since I got into trouble, no one will talk to me.
CO: So it seems that everyone is ignoring you.

9. Reflection: A repeating or rephrasing of the client's statement (not necessarily just the immediately preceding statements). It *must* contain reference to stated or *implied* feelings. It may be based on previous statements, nonverbal behavior, or knowledge of the total situation, and may be phrased either tentatively or as a statement.

CL: My best friend went out with a guy I had been dating.
CO: You feel hurt that she did that.

CL: I did better than I've ever done before.
CO: You're pleased and satisfied with your performance on the exam.

10. Interpretation: *Goes beyond* what the client has overtly recognized. It might take one of several forms: it might establish connections between seemingly isolated statements or events; interpret defenses, feelings, resistance, or transference (the interpersonal relationship between counselor and client); or indicate themes, patterns, or causal relationships in the client's behavior or personality. It usually gives alternative meanings for old behaviors or issues. If a statement also meets the criteria for a confrontation, put it in under confrontation.

CL: It makes me extremely mad when you bring that up.
CO: You may be hostile because I remind you of your mother.

CL: Nothing seems to be going well. School is really rough and my husband and I have been arguing constantly.
CO: Maybe your difficulties in school are related to your difficulties with your husband.

11. Confrontation: Contains two parts: The first part may be implied rather than stated and refers to some aspect of the client's message or behavior (this will usually be rated as a restatement). The second part usually begins with a "but" and presents a discrepancy. This contradiction or discrepancy may be between words and behavior, between two things the client has stated, between behavior and action, between real and ideal self, between verbal and nonverbal behavior, between fantasy and reality, or between the counselor's and the client's perception.

CL: Susan asked me how I felt about it, but I knew she didn't really care what I said. Nobody really listens to me; they're too concerned with themselves.

CO: You said nobody ever listens to you, but you didn't say anything to Susan when she asked how you were feeling.

CL: I'm just feeling great today.
CO: You say you're happy but you look sad.

12. Nonverbal Referent: Points out or inquires about aspects of the client's nonverbal behavior, for example, body posture, voice tone or level, facial expressions, gestures and so on. It does not interpret the meaning of these behaviors.

CL: I don't feel much of anything.
CO: You're fidgeting a lot with your hands.

CL: I guess you're right about that.
CO: Your voice was very soft just then.

13. Self-Disclosure: Usually begins with an "I." The counselor shares his or her own personal experiences and feelings with the client. Note: Not all statements that begin with an "I" are self-disclosure; it must have a quality of sharing or disclosing.

CL: I want to socialize but when I get to a party I get so uptight I can't make conversation with anyone. Everyone else always seems to be having a good time.
CO: I have a hard time at parties too.

CL: I'd like to have you as my father.
CO: I'd like you for a daughter.

14. Other: Statements that are unrelated to client's problems, such as small talk or salutations, comments about the weather or events; disapproval or criticism of the client; or a statement that does not fit into any other category.

CL: I spent yesterday watching football.
CO: Wasn't the game terrific?

CL: See you next week?
CO: Bye now.

Client Verbal Response Category System

1. Simple Response: A short and limited phrase (typically one or two words) which is usually of three types: (1) indicates agreement, acknowledgement, understanding, or approval of what the counselor has said; (2) indicates disagreement or disapproval with what the counselor has said; or (3) responds briefly to a counselor's question with specific information or facts. (Note: Just because the counselor asks a question, do *not* automatically put the client's response here. In fact, tend to put it in another category unless it is just a very simple response.) Generally, responses in this category do not indicate feelings, description, or exploration of the problem.

CO: As I said before, you seem angry.
CL: You're right.

CO: You would like to be more positive.
CL: I'm not sure.

2. Request: An attempt to obtain information or advice or to place the burden or responsibility for solution of the problem on the counselor.

CO: You're not sure what to do.
CL: What do you think I ought to do?

CO: (*Pause = 10 seconds*)
CL: Where do you want me to begin?

3. Description: Discusses history, events, or incidents related to the problem in a story-telling or narrative style. The person seems more interested in describing *what* happened than in communicating affective responses, understanding, or resolving the problem.

CO: What would you like to talk about today?
CL: My mother pulled a really dirty trick on me of telling my sister something I told her in complete confidence.

CO: Describe more about your problems with men.
CL: Like yesterday when I saw this really attractive man in the elevator, he didn't even look at me or notice that I existed.

4. Experiencing: Affectively explores feelings, behaviors, or reactions about self or problems, but does not convey an understanding of causality. It may indicate a growing awareness of behaviors or problems without necessarily understanding why they have occurred, but does *not* refer to feelings toward counselor/counseling situation. (Note: Sometimes listening to the audiotape is helpful to differentiate this category from Description.)

CO: You sound very angry right now.
CL: All I could do was withdraw and feel sad, but maybe I'm angry too.

CO: You've gotten very quiet.
CL: I feel blocked right now and am not sure what to say.

5. Exploration of Client–Counselor Relationship: Indicates feelings, reactions, attitudes, or behaviors related to the counselor or the counseling situation, but does *not* refer to feelings that are *not* directed toward the counselor.

CO: How did you feel about my not remembering your name when I saw you in the hall?
CL: I felt hurt that I was not important to you.

CO: Could you tell me how you're feeling right now?
CL: I'm scared that if I tell you, you'll get angry.

6. Insight: Indicates that a client understands or is able to see themes, patterns, or causal relationships in his or her behavior or personality, or in another's behavior or personality, and often has an "aha" quality. Insight statements usually have an appropriate internalization quality; that is, the client takes the appropriate responsibility rather than assuming too much responsibility, blaming the other person, or using "shoulds" imposed from outside rather than inside. Statements explaining the "why" of behavior should indicate a logical and reasoned explanation rather than a rationalization. (Note: This may be hard to determine; give the client the benefit of the doubt that he or she is not rationalizing unless it is an obvious distortion.)

CO: Why do you get so hostile to your mother?
CL: I just realized that I think it's because I didn't feel like she took care of me very well.

CO: You seem to have trouble organizing your time.

CL: I think I waste a lot of time and don't organize well because I'm afraid of having free time and not knowing how or who to spend it with.

7. *Discussion of Plans*: Refers to action-oriented plans, decisions, future goals, and possible outcomes of plans. The client seems to have a problem-solving attitude here. Discussion of past plans are *not* included here. Discussion should be about actual plans rather than hypothetical ruminations about the various possibilities open to the client in the future (these would fit under Description).

CO: What could you do about feeling overwhelmed by your commitments?
CL: I've decided to discontinue one of my projects and to cut some hours at my part-time job.

CO: I think it would be worth talking to him.
CL: I'll go home and tell him how frightened I am.

8. *Silence*: A pause of 5 seconds (4 seconds is close enough) is considered the client's pause if it occurs between the counselor's statement and the client's statement, within the counselor's statement, or immediately after a client's simple response.

CO: You look angry.
CL: No. (*Pause = 5 seconds*)

CO: What do you want to do?
CL: (*Pause = 5 seconds*)
CO: Would you like to come in again?

9. *Other*: Statements that are unrelated to the client's problem, such as small talk or salutations, comments about weather or events, or any statements that do not seem to fit into other categories due to difficulties in transcription, comprehensibility, or incompleteness.

CO: Bye.
CL: See you next week.

CO: Hello.
CL: It's really beautiful outside today.

Technical Aspects

Theoretical Base

I originally assumed that response modes commonly occur across all theoretical modes and thus strove to make the systems responsive to all theories. The counselor system was originally based on several other systems which were derived from a variety of theoretical orientations, primarily client-centered and psychodynamic (Aronson, 1953; Goodman & Dooley, 1976; Danish & D'Augelli, 1976; Hackney & Nye, 1973; Ivey, 1971; Robinson, 1950; Snyder, 1945; Spooner & Stone, 1977; Strupp, 1960; Whalen & Flowers, 1977). The client system was based on Snyder's (1945) client-centered system. Categories were added to both systems to reflect additional response modes from other orientations.

Experts from several orientations who were used to establish face validity indicated that both counselor and client systems covered the range of behaviors they would expect to occur within sessions. Studies by Hill (1978) and Hill, Thames, & Rardin (1979) indicated that the verbal behaviors of gestalt, psychoanalytic, phenomenological, and rational–emotive therapists could all be classified within the counselor system. Thus, these systems can be considered pantheoretical or atheoretical.

Treatment Modality

These systems were developed on and have been applied most often to individual counseling/psychotherapy sessions. Recently, Ziemelis (1980) also used the counselor system to characterize counselors' responses in a group counseling setting. Since the response modes are general to all situations, they could also be used to measure behaviors in other treatment modalities, such as couples and family counseling.

Access Strategy, Communication Channel, and Data Format

These systems employ trained judges who categorize responses based on reading transcripts of counseling/psychotherapy sessions. The access strategy is naturalistic and observational rather than self-report. The communication channel is verbal rather than nonverbal. The data format is generally transcripts rather than live coding or audiotape or videotape. However, the addition of tapes would probably enhance reliability.

Selection of Segments

In my past studies, I have coded all behavior rather than selecting certain segments. Because behavior varies both within sessions and across sessions, I have felt that selecting excerpts or segments would bias the data. Of course, I have always worked with a limited amount of data, for example, initial sessions or a 12-session case study. If an extremely large number of sessions (e.g., 100) from an individual client were available, the point of diminishing returns would be reached quickly. In this case, choosing two or three adjacent sessions from each phase of treatment would probably be adequate. I think that it would be important, however, to analyze the entire session rather than portions, because certain response modes, for example, restatement, are difficult to judge without knowing what has gone before. For specific research questions, it would be appropriate to select a segment or critical event, for example, looking at termination, discussions about the relationship (these only occur at certain times), and so on. Nevertheless, one must always be concerned about looking at any behaviors out of context of the entire treatment and be aware of possible distortions of meaning.

Units of Analysis

The scoring unit is the response unit, which is essentially a grammatical sentence. Rules and procedures for unitizing were adapted from Auld & White (1956) and are reprinted in the manual (Hill, Greenwald, Reed, Charles, O'Farrell, & Carter, 1981).

The contextual unit is all of the preceding verbal interaction between counselor and client within the interview. In other words, the judges begin coding at the start of a transcript and code each counselor *or* client response as they read it. In making the categorization, the judges should not read ahead to see how the other person responds but should rely on the preceding materials. Both the client's and counselor's verbalizations are present in the transcript and separate teams of judges are required to rate each participant's behavior. It is necessary to have both person's responses because these systems are based on interactions between them. For example, it is not possible to determine whether a counselor statement is a restatement or an interpretation (i.e., whether the response ''goes beyond'' what the client has said) unless the judge has read the client's previous statements.

The summarizing unit used in the past has been thirds of a session, the entire session, or stages of treatment. These summarizing units were chosen based on careful analysis of the data which indicated that behavior within such units was relatively similar but different from other units, for example, the first third of sessions was different than the last two-thirds (Hill, Carter, & O'Farrell, 1983).

Judges: Selection and Training

For computing agreement levels and resolving disputes over categorizations, three judges (rather than two) are required to use each of the systems when judging transcripts. My selection criteria for judges have been a high-grade point average (above 3.3 on a 4.0 scale), motivation, and ability to do the task. The latter two variables can be assessed by having persons categorize statements from a practice transcript (such as the one included in this chapter and the manual; Hill *et al*, 1981). Doing a practice transcript gives the person a sample of the type of work involved and also gives the researcher a chance to select those who score the highest. Either upper-level undergraduate or graduate students are suitable, with preference given to persons who have had some type of helping skills training. Such previous training is very beneficial in reducing the amount of time spent in familiarizing the judges with what happens in the counseling setting. Prospective judges should be made aware of the necessary attentiveness to detail and of the tediousness of the task. The judges I have selected in the past have enjoyed the task because they have an opportunity to learn about the counseling process.

Training essentially entails familiarization with the system and then practice and discussion on transcripts until judges are able to reach consensus with each other and with master judgments. (Transcripts and master judgments are in the manual; Hill *et al*, 1981.) It is important that judges not only agree with one another but also with master judgments so that the system remains consistent across various sets of judges. We have always continued training until at least two of the three judges agree on 75–80% of all categorizations, which usually requires about 20 hours.

When the counselor system was originally being developed, White (1977) did a study testing whether sex of judge and use of audiotape versus transcript affected the agreement levels between judges. Judges were given no training but simply read through the preliminary definitions of the 17-category system (See Hill, 1978). Kappas were quite low (.34 to .55; $X = .41$). Agreement levels were no different for female pairs versus male pairs nor were they different for pairs who used the audiotape in addition to the transcript versus those who only used the transcript. This study, however, emphasized the need for more detailed definitions and examples for each category as well as having practice transcripts with master judgments for use in training. Training of judges is also clearly necessary, although greater specification within the system itself is necessary to reduce bias among judges. No further studies have been done on characteristics of judges or on the training procedure.

Rating Procedures

Judges categorize statements on transcripts independently, preferably at home so that they avoid influencing each other. I have found it best to assign a prescribed amount per week (e.g., rating a 1-hour session) and then have a group meeting each week. The meetings serve several purposes: (1) to correct for judge drift; (2) to provide affiliation for an otherwise lonely job; and (3) most importantly, to give judges an opportunity to reconcile disagreements. Intermittently, it can also be helpful for the three judges to categorize a practice transcript together so that they can talk through each coding and verify that judges are not developing idiosyncratic criteria.

The judgment of two of the three judges is almost always accepted without discussion. When all three judges disagree, they discuss their decisions until they reach a consensus. (I prefer this approach to throwing all these disagreements into an additional unclassifiable category because less data are lost.) In discussions among the three judges, no one judge should dominate and sway the group. We have followed a procedure of alternating which person talks first. We try to ensure that each person gets equal time and respect when discussing his or her reasons for judgments. If any one judge is consistently different from the other two, that person's responses should be studied to determine if some systematic bias or misunderstanding is operating. Such checks should be done relatively often to ensure that the system is being used accurately.

Agreement Levels

Because the category system utilizes nominal data, agreement levels are computed by a kappa statistic (Cohen, 1960; Tinsley & Weiss, 1975). Kappa is percent agreement corrected for chance agreement. Simple agreement level is not appropriate because judges get a certain number of agreements by chance. Kappas are computed for each pair of three judges, yielding three kappas. I have always computed kappas on all the data, although a large, representative, randomly selected sample would be adequate. Further, I have always used a simple kappa, but a weighted kappa could be used based on the groupings of categories presented later for the counselor category system. A weighted kappa basically assumes that all errors are not equally serious and accommodates for errors between similar versus dissimilar categories. (See Tinsley & Weiss, 1975.) Thus, a disagreement between judges on restatement versus reflection is not as serious as a disagreement between restatement and direct guidance. It would probably be wise to report both the simple and the weighted kappa.

For the counselor system, past agreement levels have been quite high (e.g., over .65). Average kappas for judges were: Hill (1978) = .79; Hill, Thames, & Rardin (1979) = .71; Hill, Charles, & Reed (1981) = .79; Hill, Carter, & O'Farrell (1983) = .68; Patton (1981) = .77; Edwards, Boulet, Mahrer, Chagnon, & Meek (1982) = .73. I served as a judge in the first three studies, but I was not a judge nor did I train the judges in the last three studies. This indicates that the information in the manual (Hill et al, 1981) was sufficient to train judges, other than the originator, to the same agreement level.

The client system is relatively new and has only been used three times. In Hill, Carter, & O'Farrell (1983), average kappas were quite high (.92), but they were lower for Patton (1981) = .77 and for O'Farrell, Hill, & Patton (1986) = .71.

Determining agreement levels between judges for individual categories within each system is useful to see which categories are easy to rate versus those which are more difficult. The kappa statistic is not appropriate since it depends on at least two categories. I have used a simple method of charting the number of judges who agree on judgments within each category—three judges, two judges, or the response is put in the category only after discussion. The greater the percentage of responses within a category that all three judges agree upon, the more reliable that category is. Conversely, the greater the percentage of responses placed in a category only after discussion, the less reliable or more poorly operationalized the category is. Agreement levels for individual categories of the counselor system were computed for 9,652 judgments of a series of different judges in the Hill (1978), Hill, Thames, & Rardin (1979), and Hill, Charles, & Reed (1981) studies. High agreement levels were found for minimal encourager, silence, direct guidance, closed question, open question, and nonverbal referent, all of which appeared to be highly operationalized and easy to categorize. Low agreement levels were found for approval–reassurance, restatement, reflection, interpretation, and confrontation, indicating that these categories are more difficult to judge. These categories are more difficult to define operationally, require more inference by judges, and have a less standard grammatical structure.

No analyses of the individual categories of the client system have been done. Based on judges' reports, however, the categories of description, experiencing, and insight are the most difficult to differentiate.

Groupings of Categories

In developing the counselor system, we arranged the categories in a progression from simple to directive to reflective to interpretive responses, based on the ordering of categories in other systems (e.g., Snyder, 1945; Strupp, 1960). Initially, however, we were reluctant to collapse any of the categories into smaller groupings until there was some empirical evidence for similarity of categories.

Based on cluster analyses of counselor responses in the three studies reported in the last section, we suggested in the manual (Hill et al, 1981) that researchers subdivide the counselor system into five groupings: I. Minimal Responses = minimal encourager, silence; II. Directives = approval–reassurance, information, direct guidance; III. Questions = closed question, open question; IV. Complex Responses = restatement, reflection, interpretation, confrontation; V. Strange Bedfellows = nonverbal reference, self-disclosure, other. These groupings were used to analyze the data in the Hill, Charles, & Reed (1981) study, except that silence was not included in Minimal Responses and the Strange Bedfellows grouping was not analyzed (due to low frequency of occurrence). In this 1981 study, the groupings were useful from a statistical viewpoint because they provided fewer categories to analyze, particularly since the sample size was so small.

However, my further work with the counselor system suggests a better grouping that more adequately represents the separate phenomena yet reduces the number of categories:

    I.   Minimal Encourager
    II. Silence
   III. Directives: approval–reassurance, information, direct guidance
   IV. Questions: closed question, open question
    V. Paraphrases: restatement, reflection, nonverbal referent
   VI. Interpretives: interpretation, confrontation
  VII. Self-disclosure
 VIII. Other

As mentioned earlier under the agreement levels section, I would recommend using these eight groupings for a weighted kappa figure. In trying to determine whether to use the 14 categories or the eight groupings to represent the data, a researcher must consider the trade-offs. Fewer categories are better for statistical purposes, but the larger number gives more detailed information about the counselor's behavior.

No similar analysis to create a grouping for the nine categories has been done for the client system because not enough data have been collected.

Validity

Obtaining validity on a category system is not as straightforward as for a paper-and-pencil test. The systems are applied by judges to interaction behavior rather than having a person responding to standard items on a test. In trying to measure validity, I approached the problem from a number of different angles.

The response modes systems were based on existing category systems, thus assuring a type of content validity. Since the previous systems used a variety of labels, definitions, and examples, all of these were carefully studied for overlap and fit into the new scheme. This preliminary scheme was then piloted on actual data to ensure that all behavior could be described within the categories. Revisions continued until the systems were adequate and judges could reach high agreement levels. At that point, expert psychologists from several theoretical orientations were asked to match all examples with definitions to determine face validity. They also gave feedback about whether the categories were comprehensive of the range of behaviors expected within sessions.

The next step in validating the systems was to see whether they could be used to describe data in a way that made good clinical sense. In the first study (Hill, 1978) the counselor system was used to describe behavior of six counselors of differing therapeutic orientations (phenomenological, gestalt, psychoanalytic, ecclectic), each doing intake sessions at a university counseling center. The total sessions were characterized mostly by minimal encourager (35%), information (18%), and closed question (13%). The first two-thirds of sessions had more minimal encouragers, closed questions, and restatements. During the final third, the emphasis shifted to more information, direct guidance and interpretation with fewer questions, minimal encouragers, and restatements. These changes within sessions fit our clinical sense of the progress of intakes from setting the client at ease and gathering information to making a referral. Further, one would not have expected a large number of interpretations or confrontations in an intake session, particularly since the counselor typically did not see the client again.

Patton (1981) reanalyzed the 12 intake sessions, using a completely different set of judges. Similar results were obtained for most of the counselor systems, except that Patton's raters put more responses in information (25% vs. 18%) and reflection (6% vs. 2%) and fewer responses in interpretation (0% vs. 6%), indicating a probable lack of clarity in these categories. For client behavior, Patton found that the intake sessions were characterized by description of problem (52%), simple response (20%), experiencing (18%), other (6%), request (3%), silence (2%), insight (0%), discussion of plans (0%), and discussion of relationship (0%). This client profile again makes sense for an initial session in which the client is more often detailing his or her problem than actually engaging in change.

Another study (Hill, Thames, & Rardin, 1979) was done to determine whether the counselor system was pantheoretical, that is, applicable to therapists from divergent orientations. Indeed, Rogers, Perls, and Ellis proved to have very different profiles and these differences fit with the theoretical viewpoints. Rogers used mainly minimal encourager (53%), restatement (11%), interpretation (7%), reflection (7%), and information (7%). This profile fits with Rogers' encouraging, nonevaluative, client-centered stance. Perls used mainly direct guidance (19%), information (12%), interpretation (12%), open question (10%), minimal encourager (8%), closed question (6%), confrontation (6%), approval–reassurance (5%), and nonverbal referent (5%). The profile fits the gestalt emphasis on an awareness of here-and-now experiencing and confrontation. Ellis used primarily information (30%), direct guidance (21%), minimal encourager (14%), interpretation (12%), closed question (6%), and restatement (5%). This profile fits the rational–emotive emphasis on reeducating clients. Thus, the counselor system proved to be pantheoretical and useful in discriminating these three theoretical orientations.

Hill, Charles, & Reed (1981) examined the response modes used by 12 counseling psychology graduate students in brief counseling sessions. Their response modes consisted mostly of minimal encourager (35%), restatement (12%), information (10%), closed question (9%), open question (9%), reflection (6%), and silence (5%). Across the course of three years of graduate training, students increased minimal encouragers and decreased both closed and open questions during sessions.

Hill, Carter, & O'Farrell (1983) charted counselor and client behavior across the course of 12 sessions of time-limited counseling. For counselor behavior, the first four sessions were mainly characterized by minimal encourager (50%), interpretation (10%), information (8%), confrontation (6%), restatement (6%), and closed question (5%). The final eight sessions had fewer minimal encouragers (37%) and more interpretation (17%) and information (12%), with the other response modes remaining approximately stable across stages of counseling. Changes within sessions (first thirds compared to the last two-thirds of all 12 sessions) indicated that the first thirds were characterized by minimal encourager (56%), interpretation (9%), information (9%), and restatement (6%). The final two-thirds had fewer minimal encouragers (34%) and more interpretation (17%) and silence (5% vs. 1%). Based on these results, the treatment was described as highly supportive, experiential, and interpretive, with more support at the beginning and more interpretive behavior later both within and across sessions.

Across the 12 sessions of the same study, the client primarily used the response modes of description (54%), simple response (25%), experiencing (12%), and silence (7%). Over the course of the 12 sessions, client description dropped (session 1 = 90%, 12 = 47%) and experiencing increased (session 1 = 0%, 12 = 12%). Insight and discussion of plans occurred only in the second half of treatment, although both were infrequent. Changes within sessions indicated that during the first third, the client used mostly description (70%), simple response (21%), and experiencing (6%). In the final two-thirds, there was decreased description (40%) and increased simple response (28%), experiencing (16%), insight (1%), and silence (11%). These results indicated that the client became more experientially involved both as each session progressed and as counseling continued.

Ziemelis (1980) studied the counselor response modes for 24 hours of individual counseling or group counseling. The counseling was done mostly by masters level counselors with out-of-school youth (16–21 years) participating in an intensive residential 4-week CETA program. Individual versus group counselors engaged primarily in minimal encourager (23%, 17%), closed question (23%, 24%), information (14%, 12%), open question (9%, 14%), approval–reassurance (9%, 7%), and restatement (5%, 6%). The interesting comparison to data for the other studies reported above is the greater use of both closed and open questions. One might speculate that with a young, difficult population, more questions are needed to encourage clients to talk. Examining the clients' responses might indicate whether they differed markedly from those of the college students used in our studies.

Edwards, Boulet, Mahrer, Chagnon, & Meek (1982) examined Rogers' behavior in two initial sessions and found that Rogers' response modes were stable and consistent both within quarters of each session and between the two sessions. Further, his behavior in these two sessions was very similar to his behavior with Gloria in the Hill, Thames, & Rardin (1979) study. The main categories he used with these two clients were minimal encourager (62%, 21%), reflection (15%, 10%), restatement (14%, 44%), and information (2%, 12%).

Summary of Descriptive Research   The results of all of the studies that have used the category systems are summarized in Tables 5-1 and 5-2, with the addition of a study (O'Farrell *et al*, 1986) which just became available as this chapter went to press. For ease in visually comparing the usage of response modes by different counselors and clients, the earlier data are presented in Figures 5-1 and 5-2. In Figure 1, the categories are grouped as suggested earlier in this chapter, facilitating comparison of the major categories. For both figures, only those categories are presented which account for the greatest frequency.

This compilation of data is the beginning of a normative data bank on the usage of response modes. Thus far, we know most about what counselors do in initial sessions. Only two studies have examined response modes across the course of treatment (Hill, Carter, & O'Farrell, 1983; Ziemelis, 1980). This normative data will be useful as a means of comparing results from future studies; for example, if a counselor claims to be client centered, his or her profile ought to be similar to Rogers' profile.

Process to Outcome

The next step in developing the systems was to determine the impact of response modes. Testing proximal (also called immediate or moment-by-moment) outcome consists of evaluating whether specific counselor response modes lead to specific client response modes and vice versa. Testing distal or long-range outcome consists of seeing which response modes are associated with success or failure of a session or of the total treatment.

Moment-by-Moment or Proximal Outcome

Hill & Gormally (1977) did an analog study to test the effects of counselor reflection, restatement, and open question (labeled probe in this study) on client affective self-referent. All three response modes were standardized so that they focused on the content of the client's discussion but varied according to whether the counselor reflected the client's feelings (reflection), asked what the client was feeling (open question), or omitted any mention of feeling (restatement). Only open questions led to more client discussion of feeling over baseline. The increase may have been because of the demand inherent in the open question, for example, "How do you feel about your father not supporting you anymore?" Restatement and reflection do not request that the client say anything specific. However, it should be noted that clients did not discuss feelings very often in any of the conditions, perhaps because of the artificial nature of the analogue counseling, the brevity of the session (30 minutes), or the clients' lack of awareness of the importance of expressing feelings. The importance of this study for me was to emphasize the need to study these variables within a more naturalistic setting to provide a more realistic test for the impact of counselor behavior.

Patton (1981) in her reanalysis of the original 12 intake sessions (Hill, 1978) did a Markovian chain analysis between counselor and client response modes. This type of

Table 5-1   Proportions of Response Modes of Counselors

Response Modes	1 Intake X	1 Intake SD	2 Rogers	3 Perls	4 Ellis	5 Grad. Stu. X	5 Grad. Stu. SD	6 Rogers
Minimal encourager	19	35	53	8	14	35	13	62
Silence	4	2	2	1	0	5	5	0
Approval-reassurance	5	6	1	5	1	4	3	0
Information	18	18	7	12	30	10	6	2
Direct guidance	6	4	0	19	21	1	1	0
Closed question	7	13	2	6	6	9	5	2
Open question	4	5	1	10	3	9	4	1
Restatement	5	7	11	5	5	12	5	14
Reflection	2	2	7	1	2	6	4	15
Interpretation	5	6	7	12	12	4	3	1
Confrontation	2	1	2	6	1	2	3	1
Nonverbal referent	1	0	0	5	0	0	0	0
Self-disclosure	2	1	1	1	0	0	1	0
Other	2	1	1	1	2	2	1	0

Note. 1 = 12 intake sessions (Hill, 1978); 2 = Rogers in an initial 30-minute session (Hill et al., 1979); 3 = Perls in an initial 20-minute session (Hill et al., 1979); 4 = Ellis in an initial 15-minute session (Hill et al., 1979); 5 = 72 15-minute interviews by graduate students (Hill et al., 1981); 6 = Rogers with Cathy in an initial interview (Edwards et al., 1982); 7 = Rogers with Mike in an initial interview (Edwards et al., 1982); 8 = Master's level counselors across 24 hours of individual counseling with CETA youth (Ziemelis, 1980); 9 = Master's level counselors across 24 hours of group counseling with CETA youth (Ziemelis, 1980); 10 = First four sessions of Case I (Hill et al., 1983); 11 = last 8 sessions of Case I (Hill et al., 1983); 12 = 20 sessions of a case (O'Farrell et al., 1986).

analysis examines both the probabilities of behavioral events and how these probabilities change over time. She looked at the final response unit within the speaking turn for one participant to see if there was a greater than chance relationship with the first response unit of the next participant's speaking turn. In general, counselor minimal encourager was followed by more client description than experiencing (70% vs. 25%); information was succeeded by more simple response than description and experiencing (80% vs. 10% and 10%); approval–reassurance was succeeded by more description than experiencing (60% vs. 25%); closed question was followed by more simple response than description and experiencing (60% vs. 33% and 6%); open question was followed by more description than simple response and experiencing (50% vs. 27% and 17%); restatement was succeeded by more simple response than description and experiencing (60% vs. 28% and 12%). The clearest result here is that the client's first response unit is almost always a simple response or description, regardless of counselor behavior.

For client behavior leading to counselor behavior, simple response was followed by more information than closed question and minimal encourager (50% vs. 15% and 3%); description was succeeded by more minimal encourager than closed question or information (70% vs. 12% and 7%). Experiencing was associated with more minimal encourager than information and closed question (66% vs. 15% and 10%).

Table 5-1   (*Continued*)

7 Rogers	8 CETA-I		9 CETA-G		10 Hill I—First Stage		11 Hill I—Second Stage		12 Hill II	
	X	SD	X	SD	X	SD	X	SD	X	SD
21	23	12	17	8	50	20	37	15	35	11
0	2	4	0	0	4	5	3	4	1	1
0	9	17	7	6	2	1	4	2	2	2
12	14	12	12	7	8	2	12	4	8	6
1	3	3	4	4	2	2	1	2	2	2
4	23	12	24	9	5	1	4	2	2	1
1	9	7	14	9	3	1	3	1	3	1
44	5	5	6	6	6	1	7	2	4	2
10	0	1	0	0	4	2	6	2	2	1
2	2	0	4	4	10	8	17	6	25	9
0	1	1	0	1	6	4	5	4	16	7
0	0	4	0	0	0	0	0	0	0	0
3	2	3	4	4	1	0	0	0	1	1
0	7	10	7	5	0	0	0	0	0	0

In terms of change of probabilities across sessions, differences were found between the first and middle versus the final third of sessions. The probability of client description following counselor minimal encourager decreased (75% vs. 56%), whereas the probability of client experiencing increased (20% vs. 38%). The probability of client simple response following counselor information increased (60% vs. 86%), whereas description decreased (26% vs. 4%). The probability of counselor information following client simple response increased (35% vs. 68%).

Hill, Carter, & O'Farrell (1983), in our case study, did a sequential analysis of the immediate effects of counselor response modes on client response modes. To get a clearer analysis, we eliminated some categories (counselor: minimal encourager, self-disclosure, nonverbal referent, other; client: simple response, silence, exploration of counselor–client relationship, insight, discussion of plans, other), selected the "predominant" counselor response in each turn, and looked at the first two client units in the next turn to see if any client behavior occurred more often than chance. The results indicated that description was most likely to occur after closed question and least likely to occur after direct guidance and interpretation. Experiencing was most likely to occur after silence and least likely to occur after closed question. Insight occurred only rarely, but when it did, it was in the first unit after silence or the second unit after open question or confrontation. A more qualitative analysis of the same data indicated the importance of support (e.g., minimal encourager) followed by interpretation to enable the client to shift from description to experiencing.

Direct comparison of the Patton (1981) and Hill *et al* (1983) studies is not possible because different selection rules were used for choosing what data to analyze.

Table 5-2   Proportions of Response Modes of Clients

Response Modes	1 Intake		2 Case I—First Stage		3 Case I—Second Stage		Case II	
	X	SD	X	SD	X	SD	X	SD
Simple responses	20	21	18	8	29	7	17	6
Requests	3	2	1	0	0	0	1	1
Description	52	54	63	25	49	10	64	7
Experiencing	18	20	8	8	13	6	15	4
Insight	0	0	0	0	1	1	2	2
Plans	0	0	0	0	0	0	1	0
Relationship	0	0	0	0	0	0	2	1
Silence	2	2	8	9	7	6	2	0
Other	6	3	0	1	0	0	61	9

Note: 1 = 12 intake sessions (Patton, 1981); 2 = first four sessions of Case I (Hill et al., 1983); 3 = Last eight sessions of Case I (Hill et al., 1983); 4 = 20 sessions of a case (O'Farrell et al., 1986).

Distal or Long-Range Outcome

The link between response modes and session outcome was examined in the Hill, Carter, & O'Farrell (1983) case study by comparing the "best" and "worst" sessions as determined by the counselor's and client's postsession ratings. In the "best" session, the counselor did fewer minimal encouragers and closed questions but more interpretations and silences; the client did more simple responses, experiencing, and silences but less description. However, the "worst" sessions were still relatively good so these results must be viewed tentatively.

Further work needs to be done in this area relating response modes to ratings of individual sessions as well as to overall ratings of treatment.

Methodological Issues in Linking Process to Outcome

We have made preliminary attempts to link verbal response modes to both immediate and longer-range outcomes, but several methodological problems remain. First of all, no effort has been made as of yet to do quality ratings on the response modes. For example, a good interpretation would lead to a different client response than a bad interpretation. Thus, knowledge of both response modes and quality would be necessary to test the impact on client behavior. Secondly, the events leading up to a specific response have not been established. For example, Strupp (1980) noted that it is the entire relationship as it evolves from the first encounter which enables a particular therapist communication to help the client, who must in turn be in a state of "readiness." Thus, just knowing that a confrontation was done is not adequate. We must know what the building blocks were leading up to it. In our basic training, we were told to do 10 or so reflections before an interpretation. While this formula is probably not always correct, it does point up the need to know what has to happen before certain responses can be effective. Such relationships are particularly difficult to formulate because they may be idiosyncratic of a specific counselor–client dyad. For example, one client may need confrontation immediately, whereas another client may need a lot of support first. Third, particularly for the more complex responses (e.g., interpretations and confrontations), the effects on the client may not be evidenced until much later. The initial response might be denial, but three sessions later the client might return saying what the counselor said as if it were his or her own discovery. These issues make the process/outcome question very murky. Devising new ways to measure the process/outcome links is a great challenge for our future research.

Future Directions with the Systems

Recommendations for Use

In refining the implementation of the category systems, I would recommend that in addition to following all the procedures outlined in this chapter for assigning a category to each response unit, researchers might consider making two additional judgments concurrently. First, for counselors, add a 5-point quality rating to each judgment on

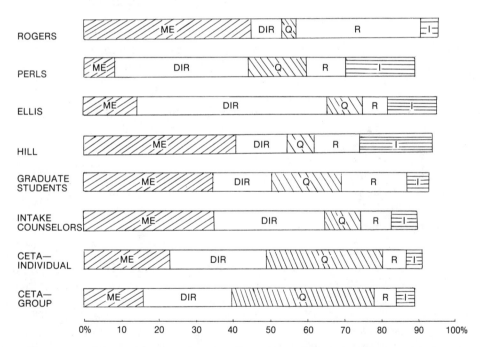

Figure 5-1   Proportions of response modes of counselors. ME = minimal encourager; DIR = directive; Q = question; R = reflective; I = interpretive. Data for Rogers is averaged for three initial sessions (Edwards *et al.*, 1982; Hill *et al.*, 1979); Perls and Ellis did initial sessions (Hill *et al.*, 1979); Hill is averaged from a 12-session case study (Hill *et al.*, 1983); graduate students did brief interviews (Hill *et al.*, 1981); intake sessions were with six experienced counselors (Hill, 1978); CETA—individual and CETA—group represent excerpts from 24 hours of counseling (Ziemelis, 1980).

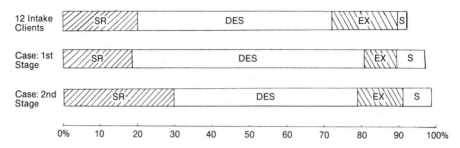

Figure 5-2   Proportions of response modes for clients. SR = simple response; DES = description; EX = experiencing; S = silence. Data for intake clients is from Patton (1981); data for case study is from Hill *et al.* (1983).

a response unit. The quality rating would consist of a judgment of correctness of timing, appropriateness, accuracy, and client receptivity (e.g., 1 = inappropriate; 5 = excellent). In the past, with just knowing what a counselor said, we did not have adequate information to determine therapeutic effectiveness. A quality rating alone has all the problems for which the empathy scale has been criticized (Chinsky and Rappaport, 1970; Gormally & Hill, 1974; Lambert, DeJulio, & Stein, 1978). The combination of the response mode with the global quality rating would provide information about both the type and effectiveness of the response.

A second type of judgment that would be helpful in summarizing the data is the judges' determination of the "predominant" or most impactful response within each speaking turn for both counselor and client. This judgment would be helpful for determining sequential analysis of responses, that is, the immediate impact of one person's statements on the other. It might also prove to be a better summarizing unit (in combination with the quality ratings) than simple proportion scores. In other words, predominant responses might indicate one interpretation (quality = 5) that was impactful, whereas a simple analysis as in the past would have simply shown two restatements, an interpretation, and a closed question. The latter does not indicate as clearly the impact of the counselor's statements. At this point, however, I would recommend reporting both figures—simple proportion scores and predominant responses.

Refining the Counselor Category System

As mentioned earlier, some categories have high agreement levels and seem very satisfactory (minimal encourager, silence, direct guidance, closed and open question, nonverbal referent). The other categories have lower agreement levels, indicating that the definitions are less clear and perhaps the responses are more variable and idiosyncratic. These categories thus need further development to increase their specificity. The most problematic categories are the cluster of restatement, reflection, interpretation, and confrontation. Conceptually, these response modes differ in that restatement and reflection paraphrase, summarize, and concretize the content and/or feelings that the client is expressing. Interpretation and confrontation, on the other hand, "go beyond" what the client is aware of and/or is expressing. This judgment, of course, requires some inference by judges as to whether the counselor has "gone beyond" and added substantially to the client's awareness. Also, counselor style in phrasing an interpretation or confrontation is typically highly variable. For example, a question can often be asked in service of an interpretation, or a confrontation might be a simple "Oh yeah!" Further, there are several different types of interpretation and confrontation. Interpretations can make connections between two statements or events, point out themes, connect present difficulties with past events, hypothesize reasons for behaviors, reframe the situation into a new explanation, or focus on the client–counselor relationship. Some confrontations might stress strengths, whereas others focus on weaknesses; further, the discrepancy might be between or among words, behavior, feelings, fantasy, or perception. Given the importance of these response modes for most types of treatment, further research on these categories would be highly useful.

Postscript. Since this chapter was originally written in 1982, a group of researchers who developed response modes systems (Robert Elliott, Bill Stiles, Alvin Mahrer, Myrna Friedlander, Frank Margison, and myself) have collaborated to rate the same seven sessions on our respective systems. An analysis of this data should lead to suggestions for further revisions of the Counselor Category System.

Refining the Client System

The major problematic area for this system is the overlap between description, experiencing, and insight. We noted that use of the audiotape was helpful to differentiate description and experiencing, which suggests that paralinguistic cues are involved in determining the experiencing category. Conceptually, the description category is similar to the lower levels of the Experiencing Scale and the experiencing category is very similar to the upper levels of the Experiencing Scale (Klein, Mathieu, Gendlin, & Kiesler, 1970). As with the counselor system, we felt that it was more descriptive to separate the response type from level of involvement, although this is a fuzzy area. Insight has many of the same problems noted above.

A further issue is that future researchers may choose to subdivide simple responses into agreement versus disagreement. We choose to leave them together but further research could determine whether this is the best possible way.

A further concern I have for the client system is whether it is truly representative of behaviors that behaviorists and cognitively oriented therapists would look for in clients. Perhaps new categories need to be added to make the system truly pantheoretical.

Research on Procedures

The use of several transcripts with master judgments (see manual; Hill *et al*, 1981) should make the training procedures more standard. However, further research is needed on the training procedures so that brainwashing of judges is minimized and reliability across sets of judges is maximized. Characteristics of judges (sex, intelligence, level of expertise, empathy level, score on practice transcripts), amount of training, and use of audiotape and/or transcript all need to be tested further.

Further Research Areas

I think it would be very beneficial to begin to collect a data bank of response modes. I would like to see data on all the various theoretical orientations, levels of experience, stages of treatment, and types of clients. The response modes, as moderated by these other variables, should also be correlated with success of each session and of total treatment. The development of such norms would perhaps enable us to begin to describe competency levels of practitioners.

Another area of research that I believe crucial is to link response modes with other behaviors within the counseling interaction. For example, we have recently developed a list of intentions (see Hill & O' Grady, 1985). These intentions focus on the reasons the counselor has for using a particular response unit at a given point in the session. This examination of the counselor's rationale can provide valuable explanations of how the therapeutic process works. Another type of analysis would be to measure how counselor response modes are related to the larger clinical strategies or interventions, such as analysis of transference or cognitive restructuring (see Goldfried, 1980). Such interventions are difficult to measure and have not been codified as of yet, but are important for conceptualization of the therapeutic process.

Another area is to examine and evaluate the effectiveness of each of the individual response modes. For example, one could examine interpretations and look at what most typically leads up to an effective interpretation, how it is best phrased, and under what conditions the client is most likely to accept it.

I would appreciate it if anyone who does any type of research using these category systems would send me a copy of the results.

Reflections on Developing the Systems

My training in graduate school at Southern Illinois University in the early seventies emphasized skills training. Bill Anthony, who was a student of Robert Carkhuff's, is a firm believer in the potential of training to teach persons to be good counselors. Human relations skills are distinct from empathy as discussed by Rogers (1957) which is more of a condition or attitude that the counselor possessed. Skills training consisted of teaching specific techniques (i.e., the response modes) that the counselor could use to promote self-exploration, understanding, and action in the client. Even though the emphasis was on specific skills or response modes of the counselor, the methodological means of testing the counselor's competency in using the skills remained the empathy scale (Carkhuff, 1969). This scale is a 5-point rating made by two judges listening to brief excerpts of the counseling interaction. Interestingly, in training to use the empathy scale, we came to rely increasingly on anchor points which were response modes themselves, for example, closed question or inaccurate or poorly timed interpretation = 1.5, open question = 2.0, good restatement or inaccurate reflection = 2.5, accurate reflection of feeling = 3.0, accurate interpretation or confrontation = 3.5, or more. These ratings have received a great amount of criticism (Gormally & Hill, 1974; Kagan, 1972; Chinsky & Rappaport, 1970). I felt that new ways of measuring counselor skills were needed. From my Carkhuffian training, I carried with me the convictions that counselor skills were crucial to facilitate client change and that these skills could be taught to prospective counselors.

In the later portions of my graduate training, I was exposed to behavioral techniques under David Rimm. The behavioral method again reinforced my belief that counselor skills and techniques served as change agents. Further, these methods emphasized the notion that they could be operationalized. Although I did not become behavioral in my orientation, I do maintain that counseling/psychotherapy is a science which can be articulated, measured, and taught.

During my internship at the University of Florida, Paul Schauble, who trained under Norman Kagan, was my primary influence. From him I learned Interpersonal Process Recall (Kagan, 1975), a technique whereby a counselor and/or client watch a videotape of a session and recall their thoughts, feelings, and perceptions of what was occurring at the time. These techniques have proven invaluable for finding out what is happening in counseling which does not show up in transcripts. The recall provides access to the reasoning process of the counselor and the impact of interventions on the client. The other thing I learned from Paul, who could probably be labeled humanistic and nontraditional in approach, was an appreciation of the variety of techniques that can work in counseling. For example, hypnosis, writing letters to a bright but withdrawn person, bringing significant others into sessions, and doing counseling in a couple's home were but a few of the spectrum of techniques he used to work with clients.

From there, I went to my present position on the psychology faculty at the University of Maryland. Like many places in the East, there is a strong psychoanalytic influence at the university. Consequently, what I often heard at case conferences was an emphasis on client dynamics to the exclusion of recognizing the impact of the counselor's behavior on the client. From this influence, I have gained a healthy appreciation of client dynamics and of unconscious processes. I have now shifted to more of an interactive perspective of looking at the reciprocal relationship between counselor and client. Another factor that has influenced me tremendously during my years at Maryland is teaching the theories of personality and counseling courses. In trying to help my students have an open mind and look for the positive aspects of each theory, I have come to believe that each theory has a tremendous amount to offer. Further, the research showing no differences in effects of treatments of therapists from varying theoretical orientations (e.g., Bergin & Lambert, 1978; Sloane, Staples, Cristol, Yorkston, & Whipple, 1975) has convinced me that there is no one right way to do treatment. Rather, I have tended to be atheoretical in my stance to research, preferring to find those commonalities which go across all treatments or to look at the varying theoretical explanations for the same observed behavior.

My ideas as to which skills are the critical ones went through a great deal of change over the years. Whereas the Carkhuff model implies that certain responses are good (e.g., reflection, interpretation) while others are bad (e.g., question, direct guidance), I came to believe that any of the response modes may be appropriate at some particular time in the process. For example, it became clear that sometimes a closed question is absolutely necessary to obtain a piece of information. This suggested that the response modes need to be considered in the context of client dynamics, quality of response, appropriateness, timing, and so on. The implication of this for measurement was that all of these variables need to be separated to provide a better description of the process than is possible with a simple 5-point scale. Further, by separating response modes and quality, one could determine whether a response was a bad reflection or a good restatement, for instance, rather than just knowing that the rating was 2.5. A simple number was not adequate enough for me in portraying what was happening in the session.

My style of teaching counseling skills also began to change during this period of time. Rather than teaching a standard set of basic skills, I tried to teach more of a personal scientist approach. The class would discuss the probable effects of the different response modes and then the students would experiment and see what effects the different modes had on the client. In this way, students were better able to choose the best response for the context and use the responses that fit their style.

These changes in my development have been reflected in my research. Based on my initial dissatisfaction using Carkhuff's empathy scale, a review article (Gormally & Hill, 1974) contained the beginning ideas of a response modes category system. For my dissertation (Hill, 1975), I developed a preliminary system. Most of the categories were there but the system was not psychometrically sound nor was it based on previous category systems in the literature.

One of my early studies in the area was a laboratory study designed to determine which counselor responses had the most impact on client behavior. While seemingly experimentally clean and impressive to my more hardcore psychology department colleagues, I found the analogue laboratory experiments woefully inadequate for describing the counseling process. There were two main issues: By isolating counselor behavior and manipulating it in an artificial setting, we seemed to create an artificial product very different from the counseling phenomena I was used to in my clinical practice. As the counselor in the study (Hill & Gormally, 1977), I used a reflection, restatement, or probe after a light signaled me and the client paused. I tried to make the statement as pertinent to the client's content as possible, but I was certainly restrained by the use of a particular strategy. The results indicated that clients responded in a particular way to a statement from the counselor which was not really tailored to their needs. Clearly, I was not going to find out what made counselor responses effective unless I studied them in a natural setting. However, in a natural setting, responses do not occur as clearly and operationally as they did in this study. Further, the whole range of counselor responses occur, so I felt the need to have a comprehensive counselor system for my future research. The second main conflict I had with my analogue work and the work that had preceded mine was the exclusive reliance on client affect as the dependent variable. This choice rose out of the client-centered research which viewed affect as the main point of intervention. And yet, other orientations value changes in behavior, cognitions, and insight. The implication of this was that eventually I would need to develop a client system also if I wanted to pursue my question of the impact of counselor responses on client behavior.

I decided to develop a counselor response modes system first. Why did I not just look at previous systems and choose the best one, for example, Snyder (1945)? There were probably a multitude of reasons. Most obvious was the notion that no one else's system fit my conceptualization of all the counselor skills. In each system, some categories were missing (e.g., confrontation, nonverbal referent). Also, as I began to look closely at the other systems, they seemed increasingly difficult to use—the definitions of categories were vague and unoperationalized. My corater (Carole Greenwald) and I could not reach any agreement on how to use the categories. Further, none of the category systems had impressive validity or reliability estimates nor had they been used often enough to establish credibility.

The development of the counselor system is recorded in Hill (1978). What is missing is the human element of the trial and tribulations it required to develop the system. I could find no "rules" for developing a category system, so I had to do a lot of consulting with my department colleagues (Jim Gormally, Jack Crites, and Phil Bobko were particularly helpful) and I kept trying new things. The most frustrating aspect was that just as I would think I had the system down right, something else would come up (low agreement between judges, comments from expert counselors) and I would have to begin all over again. Eventually, I went through six revisions until agreement levels and validity checks appeared satisfactory. Many times I wanted to give up—was it worth it, who cared anyway, maybe I was after the entirely wrong thing. I had never considered myself a compulsive person before and all of a sudden I was in the middle of a research area that required incredible painstaking attention to detail. Fortunately, I am persistent and task-oriented, so once started in this line of research, I developed a dedication to uncovering the impact of the counselor on the client and to finding out what makes counseling effective. Nevertheless, I still have my doubts as to how best to do research in the area, that is, as to whether response modes have anything to do with effectiveness. Undoubtedly an ability to question is the hallmark of a scientist, but it does have to be tempered with a willingness to go ahead even when everything is not perfect. For the most part, I would say this characterizes my style: First I question everything and try to come up with a new way of doing it. Then I commit myself to it and do it enough to understand what I am looking at in the research. Then, once a project is completed, I step back and question again. Strong (1981) has described researchers as either inchworms or hoptoads. In this program of research, I have definitely been an inchworm. Accordingly, it feels like I progress infinitely slowly and painfully and often want to hop away from it to another area. But since I feel that this type of research is crucial to our profession and I have a glimmer that I can add something, I keep coming back to process research.

Somehow on paper, however, this all sounds very different from the highs and lows I have experienced in doing process research. I have felt both excited by the research and conversely have felt despair about the value of all research and specifically my own ability to contribute anything.

Research in counseling/psychotherapy is particularly difficult because of the complexity of variables involved. Further, process research is itself in a relatively infant stage. As I discussed in a recent chapter on methodological issues in process research (Hill, 1982), probably the major advances in our field are increasing methodological sophistication (e.g., development of measures) and the discovery of what methodologies do not work well (e.g., simple frequency counts of isolated behaviors do not describe the complexity of the counseling process). What we still do not know is how to capture the process better. Case studies and examining qualitative methodologies look promising. Also, some of the new statistical techniques may be helpful. In conclusion, I find the process area both exciting and overwhelming. I think process researchers will be called upon increasingly to provide evidence for the efficacy of counseling/psychotherapy and I hope we will be able to meet the challenge.

Sample Transcript

Note of Explanation: Each response unit is demarcated with a slash mark. When judging, raters should assign each response unit to one and only one category. Numbers to the left of the transcript are classifications by trained judges as to the appropriate category for each response unit.

For the counselor, numbers to the left refer to the following categories: 1 = minimal encourager, 2 = silence, 3 = approval–reassurance, 4 = information, 5 = direct guidance, 6 = closed question, 7 = open question, 8 = restatement, 9 = reflection, 10 = interpretation, 11 = confrontation, 12 = nonverbal referent, 13 = self-disclosure, 14 = other.

For the client, numbers to the left refer to the following categories: 1 = simple response, 2 = request, 3 = description, 4 = experiencing, 5 = exploration of counselor–client relationship, 6 = insight, 7 = discussion of plans, 8 = silence, 9 = other.

Master
Judgments
14,7   CO: Hello./ Why don't you start out by telling me what is on your mind?/

4, 4, 4 4	CL:	I've just been feeling down lately./ I'm having a lot of trouble getting motivated and getting stuff done./ I haven't felt like going to class./ Nothing really interests me./
6	CO:	What is your major?/
3	CL:	I haven't really decided on a major because I haven't found anything that turns me on./
6	CO:	Are you living on campus?/
3, 4, 3 3, 3	CL:	I'm living at home/ and I feel a lot of pressure on me./ I would like to live in the dorm/ but my parents won't pay for it/ and I don't have the money myself./
1	CO:	MmHmm/
3, 3, 3 4	CL:	I mean, I live right near campus/ and they say why should you live in a dorm?/ You might as well live at home and save us money./ It is kind of a stifling feeling just being there./
8	CO:	You would rather live in a dorm than at home right now./
4, 4, 4 3, 3	CL:	I think I would feel more free in a dorm./ I just feel so restricted at home, like they're watching my every move/ and I don't feel free to come and go as I please./ For example, if you want to go out, they always tell me to stay out as late as I want and do what I want, but then the next day they're always asking and checking up on me./ I shouldn't have to put up with that any more at my age./
9	CO:	You're angry because they treat you like a little kid./
1, 4, 3 3	CL:	Yeah./ I'm not sure how to deal with that./ They're providing me with a place to sleep and helping me out a little with school/ so I feel like I can't say anything to them./
8	CO:	It sounds like you think that you have to stay home and do what they want./
1, 3, 3, 3	CL:	Yeah,/ but it's killing my social life./ It's not really what I want to do./ It's even having a bad effect on my schoolwork./
9	CO:	I hear you saying that you would feel freer to live your own life if you weren't living at home./
1, 3, 3, 3, 4	CL:	That's true./ But the problem with that is money./ I'm going to school part-time and working part-time and don't have enough money for a dorm or an apartment./ My parents won't give me any more money either./ What really burns me up is that my younger brother is not in school and works and they don't give him any of this crap./
1	CO:	I see./
8, 3, 3, 6, 6, 6, 6	CL:	(pause = 8 seconds)/ He can do anything he wants, you know, in terms of living at home./ They don't bug him at all about what he's doing and where he's going./ I guess they think that because I'm the oldest and more responsible, I can handle more than he can./ They both had a hard time as kids and they really want me to have what they didn't have./ I guess they think I've got a better chance than my brother does to succeed/ and so they're tougher on me./
12, 9	CO:	Your voice is very loud right now./ You must be very resentful./
4, 4	CL:	Well I just don't want to live their lives for them./ I want to have some fun on my own./
2, 8, 11	CO:	(silence = 5 seconds)/ You say you want to move out/ yet you don't./
6, 3	CL:	I guess I don't want to disappoint them./ Um, they'd feel real bad if if I left/ and
10	CO:	(pause = 3 seconds) I wonder if you're afraid of making the big step of growing up by moving out?/

1, 1, 3	CL:	I hadn't thought of it that way./ I don't know if that's exactly it./ I think I'm pretty independent./
4, 8, 11	CO:	Well, let's look at that for a minute./ You say you're independent/ but when your parents tell you to do all these things, you do them./
2, 2, 3, 3, 3	CL:	What else can I do?/ What choice do you think I have?/ I'm living there/ and the rule is that I should do what they say as long as I live under their roof./ They might kick me out if I didn't./
13, 13, 13, 10	CO:	You know, when I was your age I had a very difficult time leaving home./ My father had died and my mother was all alone./ I felt guilty for a long time about leaving her./ I wonder if you're feeling some guilt about growing up and leaving them!/
4, 2	CL:	Well, I do feel guilty about leaving but also angry at them for making me feel this way and for treating my brother differently./ What do you think I ought to do to resolve this?/
5	CO:	Maybe it would be a good idea to drop out of school for awhile, get a job, and make enough money to move into your own apartment./
4, 6	CL:	I've thought about that but feel anxious that I'd never go back to school./ But you know, as I think about it, maybe the reason I have so much trouble about motivation in school is because of these conflicts with my parents./
7	CO:	What do you mean?/
6	CL:	Well if I feel like I'm doing everything for them instead of because I want to do it and if there's always this battle over my future, it's pretty hard for me to figure out what I want./
12	CO:	When you said that, your forehead wrinkled up and you began to look tearful./
8, 8	CL:	(silence = 10 seconds)/
4, 7	CO:	We only have a couple of minutes left./ Where would you like to go from here with this problem?/
2	CL:	Do you think it would be worthwhile to talk to someone again?/
7	CO:	What do you think?/
5, 4, 5, 5, 5	CL:	You've made me think about some things./ I'm feeling really confused right now./ I wasn't sure before this about seeing you because I didn't know what to expect from this counseling/ but you seem to understand me./ Maybe you can help me figure out some of this mess with my parents and school./
1, 10, 3, 3	CO:	Yeah./ It sounds like you have trouble figuring out who you are and what you want out of your life, separate from what your parents want./ That certainly seems like something appropriate to talk about here in counseling./ I think it would be a good idea for you to continue to see me./
5	CL:	I do feel a bit anxious talking to you because it feels like you can see right through me./
13, 13, 3, 3	CO:	I feel somewhat anxious right now too./ I usually feel a little tense until I get to know a person and decide whether we can work together./ I think you did the right thing by coming in at this point in your life./ You'll probably feel better after talking about your concerns./
1, 7, 7, 7, 2	CL:	I hope so./ I think I'll go home and think about some of these things./ Maybe I'll think about my options about moving out and where I could afford to live./ Maybe I'll talk some to my parents about moving out./ Does that sound like a good idea to you?/
5, 4, 4	CO:	Why don't we talk through that at your next session./ We need to

		stop now./ I'll see you next week at the same time./
1, 9, 9	CL:	Great./ Thank you so much./ Have a nice day./
14, 14, 14	CO:	You too./ It's really beautiful weather out./ Feels like spring./
9, 9	CL:	It sure does./ Bye now./

Acknowledgments

I would like to express my appreciation to William Hopkins, Susan Humphrey, Pauline Price, and Mary K. O'Farrell for their help in the preparation of this chapter.

References

Aronson, M. A study of the relationships between certain counselor and client characteristics in client-centered therapy. In W. U. Snyder (Ed.), *Pennsylvania State College Psychotherapy Research Groups Group Report of a Program of Research in Psychotherapy*, 1953.

Auld, F., & White, A. M. Rules for dividing interviews into sentences. *Journal of Psychology*, 1956, 42, 273–281.

Bergin, A. E., & Lambert, M. J. The evaluation of therapeutic outcomes. In S. L. Garfield and A. E. Bergin (Eds.), *Handbook of Psychotherapy and Behavior Change*. New York: Wiley, 1978.

Butler, J. M., Rice, L. N., & Wagstaff, A. K. On the naturalistic definition of variables: An analogue of clinical analysis. In H. H. Strupp & L. Luborsky (Eds.), *Research in psychotherapy* (Vol. 2). Washington, D.C.: American Psychological Association, 1962.

Carkhuff, R. R. *Helping and human relations: A primer for lay and professional helpers* (Vols. 1 and 2). New York: Holt, Rinehart, & Winston, 1969.

Chinsky, J. M. & Rappaport, J. Brief critique of meaning and reliability of "accurate empathy" ratings. *Psychological Bulletin*, 1970, 73, 328–332.

Cohen, J. A coefficient of agreement for nominal scales. *Educational and Psychological Measurement*, 1960, 20, 37–46.

Danish, S. J., & D'Augelli, A. R. Rationale and implementation of a training program for paraprofessionals. *Professional Psychology*, 1976, 7, 38–46.

Edwards, H. P., Boulet, D. B., Mahrer, A. R., Chagnon, G. J., & Mook, B. Carl Rogers during initial interviews: A moderate and consistent therapist. *Journal of Counseling Psychology*, 1982, 29, 14–18.

Goldfried, M. R. Toward the delineation of therapeutic change principles. *American Psychologist*, 1980, 35, 991–999.

Goodman, G., & Dooley, D. A framework for help-intended interpersonal communication. *Psychotherapy: Theory, Research, and Practice*, 1976, 13, 106–117.

Gormally, J., & Hill, C. E. Guidelines for research on Carkhuff's training model. *Journal of Counseling Psychology*, 1974, 21, 539–547.

Hackney, H., & Nye, S. *Counseling strategies and outcomes.* Englewood Cliffs, N.J.: Prentice-Hall, 1973.

Hill, C. E. Sex of client and sex and experience level of counselor. *Journal of Counseling Psychology*, 1975, 22, 6–11.

Hill, C. E. Development of a counselor verbal category system. *Journal of Counseling Psychology*, 1978, 25, 461–468.

Hill, C. E. Counseling process research: philosophical and methodological implications. *Counseling Psychologist*, 1982, 10(4), 7–19.

Hill, C. E., & Gormally, J. Effects of reflection, restatement, probe, and nonverbal behaviors on client affect. *Journal of Counseling Psychology*, 1977, 24, 92–97.

Hill, C. E., & O'Grady, K. E. List of therapist intentions illustrated in a case study and with therapists of varying theoretical orientations. *Journal of Counseling Psychology*, 1985, 32, 3–22.

Hill, C. E., Carter, J. A., & O'Farrell, M. K. A case study of the process and outcome of time-limited counseling. *Journal of Counseling Psychology*, 1983, *30*, 3–18.

Hill, C. E., Charles, D., & Reed, K. R. A longitudinal analysis of changes in counseling skills during doctoral training in counseling psychology. *Journal of Counseling Psychology*, 1981, *28*, 428–436.

Hill, C. E., Thames, T. B., & Rardin, D. K. Comparison of Rogers, Perls, and Ellis on The Hill Counselor Verbal Response Category System. *Journal of Counseling Psychology*, 1979, *26*, 198–203.

Hill, C. E., Greenwald, C., Reed, K. R., Charles, D., O'Farrell, M., & Carter, J. *Manual for Counselor and Client Verbal Response Category Systems*. Columbus, Ohio: Marathon Consulting and Press (575 Enfield Rd.), 1981.

Ivey, A. E. *Microcounseling: Innovations in interviewing training*. Springfield, Ill.: Charles C. Thomas, 1971.

Kagan, N. Observations and suggestions. *Counseling Psychologist*, 1972, *3*(3), 42–45.

Kagan, N. *Interpersonal process recall: A method of influencing human interaction*. Unpublished manuscript, 1975. (Available from N. Kagan, 434 Erikson Hall, College of Education, Michigan State University, East Lansing, MI 48824.)

Kiesler, D. J. *The process of psychotherapy*. Chicago: Aldine, 1973.

Klein, M. H., Mathieu, P. L., Gendlin, E. T., & Kiesler, D. J. *The experiencing scale: A research training manual* (2 vols.). Madison Wisconsin Psychiatric Institute, Bureau of Audio Visual Instruction, 1970.

Lambert, M. J., DeJulio, S. S., & Stein, D. M. Therapist interpersonal skills: process outcome, methodological considerations, and recommendations for future research. *Psychological Bulletin*, 1978, *85*, 467–489.

O'Farrell, M. K., Hill, C. E., & Patton, S. M. A comparison of two cases of counseling with the same counselor. *Journal of Counseling and Development*, 1986, in press.

Patton, S. The verbal interaction between counselor and client in an initial interview. Unpublished Master's Thesis, University of Maryland, 1981.

Robinson, F. R. *Principles and procedures in student counseling*. New York: Harper, 1950.

Rogers, C. R. The necessary and sufficient conditions of therapeutic personality change. *Journal of Counseling Psychology*, 1957, *22*, 95–103.

Russell, R. L., & Stiles, W. B. Categories for classifying language in psychotherapy. *Psychological Bulletin*, 1979, *86*, 404–419.

Sloane, R. B., Staples, F. R., Cristol, A. H., Yorkston, N. J., & Whipple, K. *Psychotherapy vs. Behavior Therapy*. Cambridge, Mass.: Harvard University Press, 1975.

Snyder, W. U. An investigation of the nature of nondirective psychotherapy. *Journal of General Psychology*, 1945, *33*, 193–223.

Snyder, W. U. *Dependency in psychotherapy: A casebook*. New York: Macmillan, 1963.

Spooner, S. E., & Stone, S. C. Maintenance of specific counseling skills over time. *Journal of Counseling Psychology*, 1977, *24*, 66–71.

Strong, S. R. *Research training for counseling psychologists: A personal perspective*. Colloquium given at The University of Maryland, 1981.

Strupp, H. H. *Psychotherapists in action: Explorations of the therapist's contribution to the treatment process*. New York: Grune & Stratton, 1960.

Strupp, H. H. Success and failure in time-limited psychotherapy. A systematic comparison of two cases: Comparison 1. *Archives of General Psychiatry*, 1980, *37*, 595–603.

Tinsley, H. E. A., & Weiss, D. J. Interrater reliability and agreement of subjective judgments. *Journal of Counseling Psychology*, 1975, *22*, 358–376.

Whalen, C. K., & Flowers, J. V. Effects of role and gender mix on verbal communication modes. *Journal of Counseling Psychology*, 1977, *24*, 281–287.

White, W. P. Interrater agreement of the Hill Counselor Response System. Unpublished Master's Thesis, University of Maryland, 1977.

Ziemelis, A. *Residential career development program for out-of-school youth: Final report of research and evaluation findings*. Unpublished manuscript, Western Wisconsin Technical Institute, 1980.

6

Development of a Taxonomy of Verbal Response Modes

William B. Stiles
Miami University
Oxford, Ohio

Developing the System

Early Development

Jerry Goodman introduced me to response modes in the spring of 1969, while I was a graduate student in clinical psychology at UCLA. Through naturalistic observation of interacting dyads (Goodman, 1972), he had developed a framework of six modes—Question, Advisement, Silence, Interpretation, Reflection, and Disclosure—which he used for psychotherapy supervision (such as that he gave me and my cosupervisee, Judy Todd) and for teaching other helpers to listen. The framework was later published (Goodman & Dooley, 1976), and it has stimulated a good deal of research and thought (see Elliott, Stiles, Shiffman, Barker, Burstein, & Goodman, 1982). It has also been incorporated in a series of tape-led group sessions for teaching helping responses (Goodman, 1978).

I think it was the therapeutic power of Reflections that attracted me to response modes. I had read about client-centered therapy (Rogers, 1951), but I had not previously experienced the effect of "simply" repeating someone's communication. In tapes of therapy, in my own work as a therapist, and in my own experience of being listened to, the process-facilitating effect of Reflections (in contrast to, for example, the process-stopping effect of Questions) made a lasting impression, although its influence on my style of therapy and my research was delayed a few years by other interests.

By late 1973, however, I had reread Rogers, and I was beginning to use a very non-directive style of psychotherapy, therapy supervision, and classroom teaching. The axe I tried to grind in my first response modes research was the virtue of Reflection. I hypothesized that "high spots" in therapeutic hours, as perceived by the client, would be associated more with therapist Reflections than with other therapist responses. The data were tape-recorded therapy hours by graduate student therapists in various field placements; clients completed postsession questionnaires describing their experience. This project eventually foundered on the difficulty of identifying high spots (see Elliott, this volume, for a more successful procedure), but it provided a data base and focused my attention on classification of therapist responses.

From the outset, the Goodman framework seemed to me to carve nature at the joints. I assumed that each therapist response should be codable in one, and only one, of the six modes. I expected to find "litmus tests" to discriminate between modes in difficult cases. For example, I knew that Interpretation and Reflection are distinguished by the frame of reference, or viewpoint, that the therapist adopts in making the response; responses that take the therapists' viewpoint, such as "You are inhibited from expressing anger by your castration fears," are Interpretations, whereas responses that take the client's internal viewpoint, such as "You wish you could just tell him off instead of automatically clamming up," are Reflections. Confronted with a difficult discrimination between Interpretation and Reflection, I could ask, "Whose frame of reference is used?" and solve the puzzle. With this in mind, I set about coding and, more importantly, explaining coding to students.

A breakthrough came unexpectedly in October 1974. While trying, with Brian Premo, then a first-year graduate student, to decide whether a particular therapist response was Interpretation or Advisement, I realized both of these modes use the therapist's frame of reference but they differ in whether the central topic of the response comes from the client (Interpretation) or from the therapist (Advisement). To illustrate, "You did it wrong" (Interpretation) concerns what the client did (i.e., it explains, judges, or labels the client's behavior), whereas "Do it this way" (Advisement) suggests a new behavior, which is derived from the therapist's experience.

The central insight, which followed close on this realization, was that both *frame of reference* and *source of experience* (the new principle) could be used to describe all of the modes, not just Interpretation and Advisement. That is, each therapist mode is about either the therapist's or the client's experience (where "experience" is understood broadly to include knowledge, ideas, feelings, memories, and voluntary behaviors), and it views that experience from either the therapist's or the client's frame of reference.

Questions use the therapist's frame of reference but seek information from the client. "What did you think when she told you that?" has the client's thoughts as a topic, but seeks to place that "experience" in the context of the therapist's understanding. In effect, a Question reveals a hole in the therapist's frame of reference, to be filled in by the client.

Reflections use the client's experience as well as the client's frame of reference. "You feel proud of your promotion" seeks to express the client's feeling as the client views it, not necessarily as the therapist views it.

Disclosures reveal the therapist's own experience in the therapist's frame of reference. "I'm feeling distracted today" obviously concerns the therapist's feelings as viewed by the therapist.

Classifying Silence, the sixth mode, was problematic; however, as seen in the Goodman framework, Silence often has a receptive, facilitative function in helping relationships. At least this sort of therapist Silence appeared to concern the client's experience, as viewed in the client's frame of reference (and passively received by the therapist).

This cross-classification of the six modes by the two principles could be represented as a 2×2 matrix, shown as Table 6-1. Two features were strikingly apparent:

1. There was a blank cell, reminiscent to me of missing elements in a periodic table.
2. Each filled cell contained two modes; however, the pairings were of surprisingly dissimilar modes, whereas intuitively more similar pairs (e.g., Interpretation and Reflection) were in different cells. This suggested that a third dichotomous principle might distinguish between the modes in each pair.

The third principle was identified before the seventh and eighth modes. Called *focus*

Table 6-1   Therapist Response Modes Classified
by Source of Experience and Frame of Reference

Source of Experience	Frame of Reference	
	Therapist	Client
Therapist	Advisement	
	Disclosure	
Client	Question	Silence
	Interpretation	Reflection

after much discussion, it distinguishes Advisement, Interpretation, and Reflection (focus on client) from Disclosure, Question, and Silence (focus on therapist). The name of the principle conveys only part of its meaning. Modes that focus on the client entail a specific presumption by the therapist as to what the client's experience is, was, will be, or should be. Modes that focus on the therapist entail no such presumption. For example, the Interpretation, "You are exaggerating its importance" presumes knowledge of the client's experience, whereas the Question, "How important is it?" does not. The Advisement, "Tell her how frightened you are," presumes knowledge of what the client should do, whereas the Disclosure, "I was frightened," does not. The three principles are summarized in Table 6-2.

The cross-classification by three principles left two blank cells in the 2×2×2 (source of experience × focus × frame of reference) periodic table. Both concerned the therapist's experience and used the client's frame of reference, but they differed in focus, that is, in whether or not they entailed specific presumptions about the client's experience. We (Brian Premo collaborated in this effort) spent several months identifying and refining our concepts of these missing modes, but in the end they seemed as distinct as the others.

Therapist *Edifications* concern the therapist's experience and use the client's frame of reference, but make no specific presumptions about the client (focus on therapist). There is a paradox in using the other's frame of reference while presuming no knowledge of the other. The resolution is that the frame of reference is "objective reality," that is, a general, neutral viewpoint shared by *any* other person. Thus Edifications are representations of fact (though not necessarily true), such as "He visited me yesterday" or "The men's room is the first door on the left."

Table 6-2   Principles of Classification

1. *Source of experience* refers to whether the utterance's central topic derives from the speaker's experience (thoughts, feelings, knowledge, intentions, volitional behavior) or the other's experience.

2. *Focus* refers to whether the utterance relies only on the speaker's experience (focus on speaker) or additionally presumes knowledge of what the other's experience is, was, will be, or should be (focus on other).

3. *Frame of reference* refers to whether the utterance takes the speaker's viewpoint or takes a viewpoint that is shared with the other.

Therapist *Confirmations* concern the therapist's experience, use the client's frame of reference and *do* presume specific knowledge of the client's experience (focus on client). These are expressions of agreement, disagreement, or shared experience, such as "We both believe in being open" or "We've been over this a hundred times before." The topic of such responses is the therapist's idea or opinion, but in comparing that opinion to the client's, the therapist must presume to understand the client's viewpoint. In other words, therapist Confirmations presume a frame of reference that is shared with a particular client.

The name "Confirmation" was selected for its connotation of existential connection; one confirms another by using his or her viewpoint. "Confirmation," as used here, does not imply positivity or agreement; "We disagree" is just as much a Confirmation as "We agree." Both disagreement and agreement entail presuming knowledge of what the other person thinks.

Generalizing the Taxonomy

I had initially construed the response mode system as a classification of therapist responses—or, as Goodman and Dooley (1976) put it, of "help-intended communication." I had begun by referring to the categories as Listener Response Modes, following Goodman's original identification of the modes in the speech of individuals whose assigned task was to listen helpfully while a "discloser" revealed a personal concern (cf. Goodman, 1972).

It gradually became clear that this construction was far too limited, that the "values" taken by the three principles could be generalized from "therapist" and "client" (or as we had, confusingly, been calling them, "listener" and "discloser") to "speaker" and "other," and that the taxonomy was equally applicable to any verbal response by a communicator to an intended recipient, including cases in which the communicator and/or recipient was a collectivity. We thus began calling the categories Verbal Response Modes (VRMs). The categories are theoretically universal insofar as any verbal communication must be from one center of experience ("speaker") to another ("other").

The advantages of a general-purpose system seemed considerable to me. Chief among the practical advantages is the possibility of direct, quantitative comparisons across roles (therapist vs. client), across types of therapy, and across verbal communication generally (Stiles, 1978b). The same categories can be used for any verbal communication; the VRM system has already been used to study verbal communication in medicine, law, politics, education, and social and family relations, as well as psychotherapy (references cited in Research section, below), and many other applications are possible. Thus psychotherapy process can be placed in the general context of human verbal communication.

"Silence" Versus "Acknowledgment"

The change from Listener Response Modes to Verbal Response Modes emphasized the continuing problem of the Silence category. Although Silence is arguably a listener response (the argument concerns whether no response constitutes a response), it is clearly not a verbal response. After much discussion—and with considerable reluctance —I became convinced that Silence belongs to a different realm of phenomena than VRMs (i.e., Silence is a nonverbal or paralinguistic response; cf. Russell & Stiles, 1979). The category of responses that concern the other's experience and use the other's frame of reference but presume knowledge of neither is better called Acknowledgment.

Acknowledgments are brief, contentless responses such as "mm-hm" and "oh." We had had to confront such responses early in our work, since they are very common among psychotherapists. We had reasoned that the topic of a therapist's "mm-hm" was whatever the client had just said, that the frame of reference adopted was the client's (i.e., the "mm-hm" merely signaled receipt of the client's expressed view), and that no specific presumption of knowledge was entailed—in fact, therapists often said "mm-hm" before the client had completed a thought, so that no coherent presumption was possible. We had concluded that "mm-hm" and other nonlexical utterances were a kind of vocalized Silence, and we had coded them accordingly. Thus the initial practical effect of the change from Silence to Acknowledgment was only that we stopped scoring conversational pauses to a taxonomic category. Scoring pauses had been problematic anyway, since it had been difficult to decide, for example, when a Silence response had taken place (how long a pause is necessary?), how many Silences had occurred (should a long pause be scored more than once?), and who should receive credit (when is a pause coded as a therapist Silence and when as a client Silence?).

The Completed Taxonomy

With the addition of Edification and Confirmation and the change from Silence to Acknowledgment, the taxonomy took on its final (i.e., present) outline. It is summarized in Table 6-3 and detailed in a published manual (Stiles, 1978a).

Table 6-3 also represents a shift to *defining* the modes by the principles of classification. That is, coders can classify each utterance by asking: Whose experience is the topic? On whom is it focused? Whose frame of reference is used? Originally the modes were defined by verbal descriptions and examples. The principles began as coding aids, intended to articulate lines of cleavage between modes. However, with the $2 \times 2 \times 2$ tax-

Table 6-3   Taxonomy of Verbal Response Modes

Source of Experience	Focus	Frame of Reference	
		Speaker	Other
Speaker	Speaker	Disclosure (D) Reveals thoughts, feelings, perceptions, intentions	Edification (E) States objective information
	Other	Advisement (A) Attempts to guide the other's behavior; suggestions, commands, advice, permission, prohibition	Confirmation (C) Compares speaker's experience with other's; agreement, disagreement, shared beliefs
Other	Speaker	Question (Q) Requests information or guidance	Acknowledgment (K) Conveys receipt or receptiveness to other's communication
	Other	Interpretation (I) Explains or labels the other; judgments, evaluations of other	Reflection (R) Puts other's experience into words; repetitions, restatements, clarifications

onomy complete, it became possible to define modes by the principles, as if the system pulled itself up by its own bootstraps.

This changeover necessitated surprisingly little adjustment of category constituents. The original Goodman categories were natural ones—built on common intuition and extensive observation, and they approximated categories that had been widely used in theory, research, and training (Goodman & Dooley, 1976). I think that the principles of classification help explain why these particular categories seem natural and hence why the principle-defined categories are essentially the same as the intuitively defined ones. Each principle takes the values of "speaker" and "other," reflecting the most obvious line of demarcation in any interpersonal communication (there are no plausible intermediate values). The distinctness and coherence of the modes thus reflect the separateness of the people who are communicating.

The three taxonomic principles are theoretically distinct, but, in a way analogous to quarks in particle physics, they cannot be isolated. Each utterance embodies an experience, a focus, *and* a frame of reference, and hence displays their interactive effects. These interactive effects help to explain the unique character of each mode. For example, the "empty" or "seeking" character of Questions (Goody, 1978) may be explained by noting that the source of experience is the other, but no knowledge of the other is presumed (focus on speaker). Thus Questions ("Where is the cat?") seek information *from* the other, to be understood from the speaker's frame of reference. By contrast, Interpretations ("You goofed again") which also concern the other's experience as viewed from the speaker's frame of reference, *do* presume knowledge of the other (focus on other), so their character is "full," imposing the speaker's view (judgment, evaluation, explanation) on the other's thoughts, feelings, or behaviors. Disclosures ("I wish I had his energy") do not presume knowledge of the other, but neither do they concern the other's experience, so they also feel "full"; they reveal epistemologically private information—the speaker's experience in the speaker's frame of reference. The seeming abstractness of the principles is traceable to these interactive effects.

The taxonomic principles make the VRM categories mutually exclusive and exhaustive, standard desiderata for classificatory schemes (Holsti, 1969; Russell & Stiles, 1979). The modes are mutually exclusive insofar as each represents a unique combination of "speaker" and "other" values. The taxonomy is exhaustive insofar as all possible combinations of "speaker" and "other" are accounted for. Answering "speaker" or "other" to the three forced choices yields one and only one mode (Table 6-3).

After several years of work on the response modes, I belatedly discovered (through the proddings of several colleagues and students) that the behaviors I was studying had been known to philosophers and linguists for many years as *speech acts*, or more precisely as *illocutionary acts*. An illocutionary act is the act that is performed in making an utterance, to be distinguished from the content and from the external effect of the utterance (Austin, 1975; Searle, 1969; Stiles, 1981a). Speech act coding classifies what is *done* when a speaker says something, rather than what is *said*. Categories such as Disclosure or Question describe observable actions rather than ideational content.

An illocutionary act presupposes an intended receiver as well as a sender; the illocutionary force must be *on* some other person (Stiles, 1981a). A Disclosure presupposes someone to whom something is revealed; a Question presupposes someone who is asked something; and so forth. The VRM Classification System focuses on this *intersubjective* aspect of illocutionary acts, as embodied in the "speaker" and "other" values of the three principles (Russell & Stiles, 1979; Stiles, 1981a, in press-b). To put this another way, each mode category represents a distinct type of *microrelationship*. Each specifies a particular type of connection from one center of experience to another, and hence describes the interpersonal relationship for that utterance. Thus *Disclosure* specifies a microrelationship in which the speaker reveals (epistemologically) private information to the other; *Question* specifies a microrelationship in which the speaker seeks information from the other, and so forth.

Grammatical Form and Mixed Modes

Goodman and Dooley (1976), like others, recognized an intimate connection between the modes and distinctive grammatical forms. For example, in English, Question is associated with interrogative words and an inverted subject–verb order. This form may be considered as indicating the utterance's *literal meaning*, as contrasted with its *occasion meaning*, or intent, that is, the meaning intended by the speaker on a particular occasion (Grice, 1957; Stiles, submitted). Grammatical form does more than indicate an utterance's intent, since the forms retain some of their illocutionary force when they are used to express a different mode intent. For example, "Would you slow down?" uses a Question form (inverted subject–verb order) to express an Advisement intent as defined by the principles of classification (speaker's experience, focus on other, speaker's frame of reference). The Question form (literal meaning) has psychological and linguistic force—it attenuates the Advisement (occasion meaning), making it less presumptuous, more attentive, and hence relatively polite. In Goodman's phrase, this mixed utterance may be described as a "Question in service of Advisement."

Very early in my work, I made an assumption that each mode has a corresponding set of grammatical features and, conversely, each grammatical utterance can be classified as one of the modes according to its form. Put another way, each grammatical form has a literal meaning that is classifiable as one of the eight modes. Thus, in the VRM system, each utterance is classified twice, once according to its grammatical features and once according to the speaker's intent, using the principles of classification. Utterances in which form and intent coincide are called *pure modes*; utterances in which form and intent differ are called *mixed modes*. As a notational convention, the form symbol is written first and intent second in parentheses (see Table 6-3 for mode abbreviations). For example:

> Slow down. A(A)
> Would you slow down? Q(A)
> I'd like you to slow down. D(A)

The process of identifying which grammatical forms correspond to which VRM intents has been long and difficult. The results rest on the collective linguistic intuitions of the coders and collaborators who have worked on VRM research, as well as my own. Our method has been to discuss problematic examples encountered in coding and gradually to collect a set of grammatical features that characteristically express each of the eight intents. In each instance we ask, "What is the literal meaning of a particular grammatical expression, when taken out of its context?" Because this process is based on intuition, with only indirect recourse to principles of classification, VRM form categories are in one sense more tentative than VRM intent categories (even though form is usually coded more reliably than intent). On the other hand, the present VRM form specifications derive from my discussions with approximately 200 coders and collaborators, who have coded over a million utterances in varied types of discourse, and I have considerable confidence in them.

The current VRM form specifications are summarized in Table 6-4 and detailed in the VRM manual (Stiles, 1978a). The combination of eight forms with the eight principle-defined intents yields a taxonomy of 64 possible classifications—eight pure modes and 56 mixed modes.

In discussing and deciding form specifications, I have had a repeated sense of "falling into place." An early example followed the decision to code "yes" and "no" as Acknowledgment forms. I had previously refused to admit any lexical words to "Silence form," although as noted above, we had been coding vocalizations like "mm-hm" as Silence. With the change to the name Acknowledgment, I felt free to include contentless lexical forms, including "yes" and "no" (N.B., but not "I see," which is Disclosure form, or terms of evaluation like "alright" or "okay," which are Interpretation form). The most immediate effect was to solve the problem of coding the numerous "yeahs" in therapists' speech, which obviously had the same intent as "mm-hm" K(K). The bonus (falling into place) was that yes/no answers to closed questions became Acknowledgment in form. It had long been obvious that the *intent* of such answers depends on the content of the Question.

> (Are you angry with me?) Yes. K(D)
>
> (Has it stopped raining?) Yes. K(E)
>
> (Should I slow down?) Yes. K(A)

Coding the *form* Acknowledgment seemed (to us) to capture the flavor—the psychological impact—of such utterances. As implied by the expression, "Acknowledgment in service of Disclosure," a "yes" that reveals anger uses the *other's* words (i.e., the word "angry" was spoken only by the other) to communicate the speaker's feelings.

Theoretically, form and intent correspond to two distinct levels of the interpersonal relationship, an explicit, surface, or *formal* level and an implicit, deeper, or *intentional*

Table 6-4   Verbal Response Mode Forms

Mode	Form
Disclosure	Declarative; first person singular ("I"), or plural ("we") where other is not a referent
Edification	Declarative; third person (e.g., "he," "she," "it")
Advisement	Imperative, or second person with verb of permission, prohibition, or obligation
Confirmation	First person plural ("we") where referent includes other
Question	Interrogative; inverted subject–verb order
Acknowledgment	Nonlexical or contentless forms ("mm-hm," "oh," "well," "yeah," "no"); terms of address or salutation
Interpretation	Second person ("you"); verb implies an attribute or ability; terms of evaluation
Reflection	Second person ("you"); verb implies internal experience or volitional action

level. (However, there are additional, still deeper levels which are not coded, as discussed below.) For example, the interpersonal microrelationship conveyed by the answer "yes" to the Question, "Are you angry?" includes attentiveness and acquiescence at a formal level, while revealing subjective information at an intentional level. (To gain an intuitive idea of this formal level effect, imagine a therapy session in which all client utterances were "yes" or "no" answers to questions about his feelings, in contrast to a session in which he used only first person sentences about his feelings.)

Form–intent discrepancies often signal conflicting pressures; for example, the conflicting pressures of directing someone to do something and of avoiding imposing or offending them yields a realm of form–intent discrepancies that can be called *politeness* (Brown & Levinson, 1978; Stiles, 1981a), for example, "Could you lower your voice?" Q(A), and "I'd like some more potatoes," D(A), rather than "Lower your voice," A(A), and "Give me some more potatoes," A(A).

Work by Dore (1979), based on observations of children's speech, suggests an explanation for the existence of form–intent correspondences. He suggests that *conversational competence*—that is, the ability to use conversational acts appropriately—develops somewhat independently of *linguistic competence*—that is, the ability to understand and use language. Primitive conversational acts used by children before they attain linguistic competence appear to be classifiable as VRM intents. (By this I mean that Advisements, Disclosures, Questions, and so forth, are discriminable in children's primitive speech.) Theoretically, the VRM categories are universal because the underlying distinction between speaker and other is universal in children's social experience. Dore suggests that conversational and linguistic competence are eventually combined, with each accommodating to the constraints of the other. Presumably this accommodation has been going on throughout the development of all languages. To me this suggests that there is a continuous formative pressure on language to offer distinctive ways to express each mode. It is therefore not surprising to find that grammatical markers for each mode (e.g., inverted subject–verb order in Questions) are firmly entrenched in language and that the markers carry some of the mode's force even when used to express a different conversational intent.

VRM Intent as "On Record" Communication

Distinguishing grammatical form from communicative intent raises the question, "What exactly is communicative intent?" The best answer I know of comes from Bach and Harnish's (1979) analysis of speech acts, which in turn draws on Grice's (1957) analysis of meaning (see Stiles, in press-b). VRM intent (i.e., speaker's occasion meaning) is that which is *intended to be recognized as intended to be recognized*.

It took me about 20 minutes to sort out what this definition means. It specifies that VRM intent is fundamentally communicative; it is not private or unknowable. To illustrate, for an utterance such as "Close the window" to be scored Advisement intent, the speaker must intend that the other recognize that it is *intended to be recognized* as an Advisement; it is not sufficient that the speaker merely intends the other to recognize the Advisement intent. For example, if I say, "I feel chilly," then I may intend you to recognize that I want you to close the window without feeling that I have *requested* you to close the window. Such an utterance is *not* scored Advisement intent in the VRM system.

This definition implies that a VRM coder judging "intent" is epistemologically in the same position as the communication's intended recipient. By definition, a speaker must intend his or her VRM intent to be recognized as such by the other. Thus coders do not need to read a speaker's mind any more than a conversation's participants do.

An intuitively appealing way to summarize this definition is Brown and Levinson's (1978) term, *on record*. For example, the Advisement in "I wish you would close the window" is on record, that is, it is codable as D(A), if I thereby intend you to recognize that a command has been given. However, if I say "I feel chilly" and do not intend you to recognize that I intend you to recognize the Advisement, then the Advisement is *off record*; on record I have given a pure Disclosure.

Of course, the same words may be used with different illocutionary intents. "I feel chilly" could be codable as D(A) if, for example, you were a servant whose duties included opening or closing the window to maintain my comfort. Ordinarily, clues from context make it clear which VRM intent is on record.

The sense of the formula, *intended to be recognized as intended to be recognized*, may be made clearer by successively paring away parts of it to define progressively deeper levels of intent. These deeper levels are all off record, and are not coded in the VRM system as it has been applied. (On the other hand, developing coding strategies for applying VRM classifications to these deeper intents is a possible future generalization.)

If an utterance is only *intended to be recognized as intended* (but not intended to be recognized as intended to be recognized), then it might be called a *hint*. For example, if, by saying "I feel chilly," I intend you to understand that I want you to close the window but do not intend you to feel you have been told to close it, then the Advisement is at the hint level; the code might be written D(D(A)). The same utterance might be called a *manipulation* if the Advisement is only intended to be recognized (but not intended to be recognized as intended), that is, if I want you to shut the window but not to see that I intended you to recognize my wish. This manipulation might be abbreviated D(D(D(A))). On the other hand, if an underlying Advisement is only intended (but not intended to be recognized), then it might be called a *secret* or a *deception*, for example, if "I feel chilly" expresses a private wish that the window be closed, but is not intended to suggest any action to you. This secret or deception could be abbreviated D(D(D(D(A)))). Finally, to carry this to its extreme, if saying "I feel chilly" is motivated by my subconscious wish that you close the window, but I am unaware of this motive in saying it, it might be called a *self-deception* and abbreviated D(D(D(D(D(A))))).

As a practical matter, it seems unlikely that these off record levels could be coded reliably. However, they may be of considerable theoretical interest and clinical importance. In the majority of utterances, the intent is probably the same at all levels. In cases of discrepancies, keeping in mind the possibility of a discrepant intent at the hint, manipulation, secret, or self-deception level can help clarify which intent is on record in a given utterance.

What the VRM System Does Not Measure

In addition to off record intents, the VRM system does not directly measure an utterance's content, affect, psychological depth, truth, likelihood, relevance, or eloquence. The VRM system does not directly code nonverbal or paralinguistic behavior, such as laughter, voice tone, or facial expression. The VRM system does not measure the valence (positive or negative) of utterances or the emotional impact of the interaction on participants. VRM indexes may be empirically associated with any of these characteristics, but establishing such an association requires separate measurements.

The VRM system can and should be used in conjunction with measures that assess other aspects of process. Using the VRM system in no way denies the importance of other aspects, levels, or measures of interpersonal communication. I am a little sensitive on this point because the system has occasionally been criticized for not measuring one or another of these other aspects. This has always seemed to me like criticizing a ruler for not measuring brightness or weight.

The VRM categories are designed to be a mutually exclusive and exhaustive classification of the formal and the intentional levels of illocutionary force of speech acts. However, within this realm it is possible to construct subdivisions of VRM categories. For example, *blame* could be an illocutionary, intersubjective category that would be a subcategory of Interpretation (applying the speaker's judgmental frame of reference to the other's volitional behavior). *Agreement* and *disagreement* are possible subdivisions of Confirmation. The number of possible subdivisions of illocutionary act categories is probably infinite. Many of them combine illocutionary force with other features. My own preference is to measure content, affective tone, and so forth separately. This helps keep conceptually different aspects distinct.

Description of the VRM System

Summary of Category Definitions

This section integrates the material in Tables 6-2, 6-3, and 6-4 to give a description of each of the eight basic VRM categories. I have also included some examples of pure modes. Additional examples, including mixed as well as pure modes, are given in the section on VRM Coding of Family Therapy Excerpt below. A complete presentation of VRM categories is available in the VRM manual (Stiles, 1978a).

Disclosure (D) concerns the speaker's experience, requires no specific presumptions about the other's experience (focus on speaker), and uses the speaker's internal frame of reference. Thus Disclosures reveal the speaker's private experience—thoughts, feelings, perception, intentions. To know the truth (or more precisely, the sincerity) of a Disclosure, one would need to be "in the speaker's head." Disclosure form is declarative and first person singular ("I"), or first person plural ("we"), where the other is not a referent.

> I'm afraid of the dark.
> We wish you were here.
> I hear a clock ticking. (perception)
> I'm going to fix some coffee. (intention)

Edification (E) concerns the speaker's experience, requires no specific presumptions about the other (focus on speaker), and uses an objective or neutral frame of reference that is shared with *any* other. Thus Edifications state objective information, which, however, need not be true or emotionally neutral. An Edification's truth could, *in principle*, be determined by an observer in the right place at the right time with the right skills and equipment—or at least, such an observer could do as well as the speaker in determining its truth. Edification form is declarative and third person.

> A clock is ticking.
> She loves me. (third party's experience)

He asked, ''Why are you following me?'' (report of conversation)
The FBI is following me.

Advisement (A) concerns the speaker's experience (i.e., the content is the speaker's idea), it presumes specific knowledge of what the other should do (focus on other), and uses the speaker's frame of reference. Thus Advisements attempt to guide the other's behavior, to impose an experience on the other by suggestions, commands, advice, permission, prohibition, and so on. Advisement form is imperative (with a second person subject understood) or second person (''you'') with a verb of permission, prohibition, or obligation (e.g., ''may,'' ''must,'' ''should,'' ''have to'').

Please wash your hands.
You may leave now.
Help!
You ought to try it at least once.

Confirmation (C) concerns the speaker's experience but presumes knowledge of the other's experience (focus on other), and uses a shared frame of reference. Thus Confirmations compare the speaker's experience with the other's, by agreeing, disagreeing, or expressing shared ideas, memories, or beliefs. That is, a Confirmation uses specific knowledge of *both* speaker's and other's experience. Confirmation form is declarative and first person plural (''we,'' ''you and I'') where the other is a referent.

We seem to like the same restaurants.
We can't seem to agree on anything.
You and I don't know each other very well.
We've had a full session today.

Question (Q) concerns the other's experience, does not presume specific knowledge of the other (focus on speaker), and uses the speaker's frame of reference. Thus Questions seek information or guidance from the other. Question form is interrogative, with inverted subject–verb order or interrogative words such as ''who,'' ''what,'' ''where,'' ''why,'' ''when,'' or ''how.'' Note that a question mark—which usually signals a rising inflection in English—is *not* sufficient to code Question form, although it often signals Question intent.

Why did you say that?
Does your mother approve?
What?
Shall I call you back?

Acknowledgment (K) concerns the other's experience and uses the other's frame of reference but presumes no specific knowledge of the other. Thus Acknowledgment expresses no content—it conveys only receipt of or receptiveness to communication from the other. Acknowledgment forms are nonlexical utterances, such as ''oh'' or ''ah-hah,'' contentless lexical utterances such as ''no'' or ''well,'' and terms of address and salutation (including names and titles). Coding the intent of Acknowledgment forms depends almost entirely on context, since they are essentially ''empty'' forms.

Mm-hm.
Yeah.
Hello.
Dr. Greenberg!

Interpretation (I) concerns the other's experience and presumes knowledge of it but places it in the speaker's frame of reference. Thus Interpretations explain or label the other; they include psychological (e.g., psychoanalytic) interpretations, but also every-day judgments or evaluations of the other, since these presume to view the other's experience (including the other's voluntary behavior) from the speaker's perspective. However, judgments or evaluations of third parties or of other objects or events (for instance, works of art) are *not* VRM Interpretations, even though they might be colloquially described as "his interpretation." (These do not presume specific knowledge of the other.) Interpretation form is second person ("you"), with a verb that implies an attribute or ability of the other; terms of evaluation used alone such as "good," "fine," "all right," and "okay" are also coded Interpretation form.

You are identifying with your mother's hostility.
You say the nicest things.
Right!
You can do anything you set your mind to.

Reflection (R) concerns the other's experience, presumes knowledge of it, and uses the other's internal frame of reference. Thus Reflections put the other's experience into words, including repetitions, restatements, and clarifications. A Reflection may go well beyond what the other has literally said, providing its intent is to express the other's experience as viewed by the other. Thus the *other* is the arbiter of a Reflection's truth or accuracy. Reflection form is second person ("you") with a verb that implies internal experience (thoughts, feelings, perceptions, intentions) or volitional action. Note that Reflection and Interpretation forms are sometimes not clearly distinct in English.

You took the daddy doll out of the house.
You drove home afterwards.
You must have had a bad day.
You were very frightened.

Unscorable (*) is coded only for utterances that are incomprehensible or inaudible. Occasionally, the form of an utterance may be clear but the intent unscorable, or vice versa. The Unscorable category is *not* used for utterances that are merely difficult to code; coders are instructed to narrow their options and then choose the most likely code. Usually such choices are between two modes that differ only in one of the principles (e.g., Disclosure vs. Edification, which differ only in frame of reference, or Advisement vs. Interpretation, which differ only in source of experience). Consequently, *either* choice preserves much of the relevant information about the utterance. Most coding difficulties arise because natural speech is often fragmented, telegraphic, or ungrammatical. The VRM manual (Stiles, 1978a) discusses how to code such utterances. (See also examples in the section VRM Coding of Family Therapy Excerpt below.)

Technical Aspects of the VRM System

Applicability   The VRM system may be applied to any discourse. In particular, it can be used at any point in any type of psychotherapy to code the verbal behavior of any or all participants. Selection of how much or what parts or which participants can be made to fit the research question being addressed.

Access Strategy   VRM coding uses an observational access strategy, not self-report. The system codes what people *do* in verbal interaction—their speech acts—not what they think.

Communication Channel   The VRM system codes verbal behavior. Other channels, including paralinguistic and kinetic communication, may occasionally be useful for identifying the mode of an utterance, but they are not coded directly.

Data Format   VRM coding can be done from transcripts, audiotapes, videotapes, or live interactions. Most utterances can be coded accurately from verbatim transcripts; however, the patterns of emphasis, timing, and inflection evident on audiotape can clarify the intent of some utterances. (Form codes are less affected.) The additional (visual) information available from videotape or live interactions seems to add little that is necessary for VRM coding. Live coding of complex or rapidly moving interaction is likely to be inaccurate; it is frequently necessary to rewind and replay tape recordings to catch speakers' meanings.

Coding directly from audiotapes requires somewhat more skill than coding from transcripts. However, several VRM studies have now demonstrated adequate intercoder reliability from audiotapes (Stiles, Au, Martello, & Perlmutter, 1983; McDaniel, Stiles, & McGaughey, 1981; Stiles, 1981b).

Level of Measurement   VRM categories are nominal measures. However, some VRM indexes used to characterize an encounter are ordinal, interval, or ratio scales. For example, the frequency of Interpretations in a psychotherapy session is a ratio scale; a score of 20 is twice as high as a score of 10.

Scoring Unit   The VRM scoring unit is the *utterance*, defined as an independent clause, a nonrestrictive dependent clause, an element of a compound predicate, or a term of address, acknowledgment, or evaluation. This definition has been developed to give a grammatical specification of a unit for which there is one and only one VRM code.

Over the first year or two of using the VRM system, the scoring unit shrank from the speech (everything a speaker said without being interrupted) to the sentence (everything between one capital letter and the next on our transcripts) to the utterance, as we discovered instances of the larger units whose sense demanded two or more different VRM codes. To illustrate, independent clauses must be scored separately because of sentences like "He left me, but I didn't mind," E(E), D(D). Nonrestrictive dependent clauses must be scored separately because of sentences like "He left me, which didn't bother me," E(E), E(D). ("Which" is the third person subject of the second utterance.) Compound predicates must be scored separately because of sentences like, "He left me and made me feel worthless," E(E), E(D). ("He" is the subject of both utterances.) Terms of acknowledgment must be scored separately because of sentences like, "Yeah, it hurt you very badly," K(K), E(R).

Restrictive dependent clauses and subject and object clauses are not scored separately because they do not carry separate elocutionary force. For example, "Drop by the next time you're in town," A(A), requires only one code, for the main clause, "Drop by." (The subject "You" is understood.) The subordinate clause does not require a code because it does not assert (or Reflect) that "you're in town."

Contextual Unit VRM coders are instructed to score *form* based strictly on grammatical features of the utterance, and to use all available sources of information to judge intent.

In practice, form judgments are sometimes made difficult by fragmentary, incomplete, and ungrammatical utterances which do require reference to context. For coding the form of fragments, we have come to make a distinction between *telegraphic utterances* and *false starts*. In telegraphic utterances, the speaker says everything he or she intended to say, but the result is abbreviated, with the rest meant to be understood in context. In such cases, coders are instructed to code the full utterance, as it was meant to be understood. Frequently codes are based on parallelism with surrounding utterances. A particularly clear example of telegraphic speech is answers to questions.

A: Where do you live? Q(Q)
B: On Withrow Avenue. D(E)
A: Where is your house? Q(Q)
B: On Withrow Avenue. E(E)

The first answer is understood, "I live on Withrow Avenue"; the second is understood, "My house is on Withrow Avenue." False starts are utterances which the speaker initially intended to complete, but did not. These are coded if the main verb was said. Thus "My only worry . . . " is not coded, but "My only worry is . . . ," E(D), is coded.

VRM intent must always be considered in context. For virtually any utterance it is possible to imagine some other context in which its VRM intent would be different. To illustrate, "It's starting to rain" would be E(E) in most contexts, but it could be E(R) if it repeated something the other had just said, or E(A) if it was understood that the other was supposed to close the windows when it rained, or perhaps E(Q) if it was spoken with an upward inflection at the end.

In practice, VRM intent can usually be identified within a context of the one or two preceding utterances. However, occasional utterances may be understandable only in the context of much earlier events. Probably this is more common (though still a small minority of utterances) in longstanding relationships, as among family members. Like any outsider, VRM coders may miss meanings that are clear to participants. However, since the VRM system codes only the "on record" level of intent, based on grammatical features and the three principles, coders' ignorance of the more subtle, off record meanings of some utterances need not impair the validity of VRM codes.

Summarizing Unit The VRM system allows any size of summarizing unit from a single utterance to a whole class of relationships. For most VRM studies, the summarizing unit has been the encounter or a segment of the encounter (e.g., the medical history-taking segment of a medical interview). Utterances have typically been aggregated separately for each speaker (e.g., the percentage of the client's utterances that were Disclosure). However, it is also possible to aggregate by dyads or larger groups.

Sampling The VRM system can be applied to samples of encounters or to whole encounters or series of encounters. Of course, a VRM index of a sample of discourse can be only as representative as the sample is.

A discourse sample's representativeness depends on what it is designed to represent, and hence on the size of the differences between the samples being compared. Research so far (cited below) suggests that VRM use differs greatly across roles and tasks (e.g., therapist vs. client; psychotherapy vs. casual conversation), so relatively small samples are representative for comparisons across roles or tasks. Similarly, therapist VRM use differs greatly between schools of therapy (Stiles, 1979b). On the other hand, within a given role and task, individual differences may be minor. In one study of client VRM use, correlations across sessions of clients' percentages of particular modes averaged only .40 (McDaniel, Stiles, & McGaugey, 1981). Thus fairly large samples of discourse are needed to accurately represent one client as compared with other psychotherapy clients.

Coder Selection and Training   Most coders in past VRM studies have been undergraduate college students. Applying the VRM system reliably requires high verbal aptitude, interest in interpersonal communication, patience with detailed work, and intensive training and practice, but it does not require an extensive background in psychology. Competence in basic grammar is essential; I have the impression that people who enjoyed diagramming sentences in high school English classes tend to make good coders. Experience doing counseling or psychotherapy is not necessary, although I think it is helpful in understanding the concept of frame of reference.

Coder training has consisted of reading the manual, practice coding, utterance-by-utterance feedback on agreement with keys or other coders, and extended discussion. The VRM manual (Stiles, 1978a) documents computer programs for comparing coders' work and preparing feedback and descriptive statistics. Most coders become reasonably competent after 20 to 40 hours of training and practice. I have found it essential to continue periodic feedback and discussion to prevent "coder drift," the development of idiosyncratic ways of coding problematic types of utterances.

Reliability   VRM coding reliability is greatly affected by the coders' talent and experience, and by the difficulty and variability of the material being coded. Some categories are more easily identified in certain material, whereas other categories are easier in other material. In general, more common categories tend to be identified more reliably.

The mean percentage of utterances on which a *pair* of coders agree has ranged from 95.3% for form and 84.6% for intent in a study of courtroom interrogations of rape victims (McGaughey & Stiles, 1983) to only 80.9% for form and 65.8% for intent in a study of parent–child interactions (Stiles & White, 1981). The parent–child interactions were fragmented and hard to understand, and they used a very wide range of modes. The courtroom interrogations were highly structured, with a narrow range of modes, and with most responses clearly and fully articulated.

In many transcript-based VRM studies, three coders have independently coded each transcript, and their work has been combined, utterance by utterance, on a two-out-of-three basis. Utterances on which all three disagree have been coded *disagreement*. By this method, fewer than 5% of the utterances have been coded disagreement in most studies. Even the unusually unreliable coding of the parent–child study (Stiles & White, 1981) yielded two-out-of-three agreement of 96.9% for form and 92.2% for intent.

For estimating the reliability of particular modes the most appropriate measures are Cohen's kappa (Cohen, 1960; Fleiss, 1975) and the intraclass correlation coefficient (Ebel,

1951; Shrout & Fleiss, 1979). Kappa is a chance-corrected measure of agreement on nominal scales, which can be used where utterance-by-utterance comparisons are possible. The intraclass correlation coefficient gives an estimate of the reliability of the mean of n coders' results, (e.g., of the two-coder mean percentage of Disclosures in each encounter), and can be used when only summary data for each encounter are available. Table 6-5 gives some illustrative reliabilities. The kappa values are from a study of interactions of college students and professors (Cansler & Stiles, 1981); the intraclass correlation coefficients are from a study of political campaign oratory (Stiles *et al.*, 1983). As Table 6-5 illustrates, form codes are generally more reliable than intent codes, and reliability varies substantially across modes. The variability seems to reflect each mode's prevalence in each type of discourse, and hence probably coders' differential vigilance. For example, Confirmation was relatively less reliable in the student–professor study, where it was rare, than in the campaign oratory study, where it was relatively common. Interpretation was rare and unreliable in both of these studies, but more common and reliable in studies of psychotherapists' speech (Stiles, 1979b; Stiles & Sultan, 1979).

Aggregating VRM Codes   The VRM system offers a wide array of aggregate measures for characterizing an encounter. These include the frequency or percentage of each pure or mixed mode [e.g., the frequency of K(K); the percentage of D(E)] and the frequency or percentage of each form or intent (e.g., the frequency of Acknowledgment form, across intents; the percentage of Edification intent, across forms).

VRM categories can be aggregated on an empirical basis. To illustrate, in studies of the verbal exchange structure of medical interviews (Stiles, Orth, Scherwitz, Hennrikus, & Vallbona, 1984; Stiles, Putnam, & Jacob, 1982; Stiles, Putnam, Wolf, & James, 1979a)

Table 6-5   Illustrative Category-by-Category VRM Reliabilities

Mode	Cohen's Kappa[a]		Interclass Correlation for Two-Coder Mean Percentages[b]	
	Form	Intent	Form	Intent
Disclosure	.95	.74	.98	.87
Edification	.91	.79	.98	.87
Advisement	.71	.58	.94	.76
Confirmation	.66	.33	.93	.86
Question	.93	.93	.98	.91
Acknowledgment	.98	.88	.91	.91
Interpretation	.62	.45	.52	.35
Reflection	.60	.63	.94	.81

[a]Chance-corrected pairwise intercoder agreement (Cohen, 1960), based on a study of laboratory interactions of college students and professors (Cansler & Stiles, 1981).

[b]Reliability of mean of two coders' percentages—ICC (1, 2) in Shrout and Fleiss's (1979) notation—based on a study of political campaign speeches (Stiles *et al.*, 1983). This measure, ICC (1, 2), is conservative for purposes of discriminating among groups or conditions, since individual coder's constant biases are treated as error, but it is appropriate for estimating actual VRM use.

we used factor-based indexes that reflected both participants' verbal behavior. For example, an index of the *closed question* exchange included physician Q(Q) and patient K(E) and K(D) (yes/no answers); this index thus represented the extent to which a *dyad* engaged in a particular type of exchange.

Role Dimensions   The principles of classification are another, theoretical basis for aggregating VRM data. Elsewhere (Stiles, 1978b) I have described three *role dimensions*, informativeness versus attentiveness, unassumingness versus presumptuousness, and directiveness versus acquiescence, which correspond to the proportion of speaker versus other values on source of experience, focus, and frame of reference, respectively (cf. Table 6-3). For example, Disclosure, Edification, Advisement, and Confirmation (all speaker's experience) are considered informative, and the proportion of a speaker's utterances in these four modes is an index of informativeness. Attentiveness is measured as the proportion of utterances in the other four modes (other's experience), or equivalently as one minus informativeness. (In constructing these indexes, uncodable, i.e., inaudible or incomprehensible, utterances are ignored.) Indexes of the other role dimensions are constructed analogously, each as a proportion of utterances in four of the modes, as indicated in Table 6-6. The indexes may be calculated for form and intent separately or averaged across form and intent. The construct validity of these indexes has been supported by research in a variety of settings (Cansler & Stiles, 1981; McGaughey & Stiles, 1983; Premo & Stiles, 1983; Stiles, 1979b; Stiles, Putnam, James, & Wolf, 1979; Stiles, Waszak, & Barton, 1979; Stiles & White, 1981).

Each mode can be described using the role dimensions as well as by the principles. For example, Questions are considered attentive, unassuming, and directive, whereas Advisements are considered informative, presumptuous, and directive.

It is important to keep in mind that the role dimensions are generated from theoretical constructs rather than from intuitive impressions. For example, *attentiveness* refers to the proportion of utterances that concern the other's experience, not to a rater's impression of how attentive a speaker was. The role dimension names were chosen to approximate the interpersonal impact of using the designated modes, but the names do not *denote* that impact. It is an empirical question whether speakers with high VRM attentiveness indexes would be described colloquially as "attentive."

Table 6-6   VRM Role Dimensions

Role Dimension	Constituent Modes
Informativeness	Disclosure, Edification, Advisement, Confirmation
Attentiveness	Question, Acknowledgment, Interpretation, Reflection
Unassumingness	Disclosure, Edification, Question, Acknowledgment
Presumptuousness	Advisement, Confirmation, Interpretation, Reflection
Directiveness	Disclosure, Advisement, Question, Interpretation
Acquiescence	Edification, Confirmation, Acknowledgment, Reflection

Note. Each dimension index is the proportion of a speaker's utterances in the constituent modes.

Naming VRM Constructs   In general, in using and developing the VRM system, I have chosen to use familiar English terms rather than to invent neutral terms, such as ''characteristic x'' or ''response type 1.'' The strategy I have followed is problematic because the terms often have surplus meaning that can mislead some readers. However, invented neutral terms are virtually impossible to remember without constant reference to their definitions, and therefore represent a greater impediment to communication, in my opinion.

In the VRM system, the names are fitted to the measures, rather than vice versa. I and my collaborators have *not* set out to measure certain abstract concepts and then constructed indexes. Instead, we have developed indexes based on systematic combinations of modes (which rest on the three taxonomic principles), and then attempted to give each index an appropriate and useful label.

Data Analysis   VRM categories and indexes can be used as a correlative, dependent, or independent variable in a wide variety of statistical analyses. Most VRM studies have been descriptive or correlational, reflecting my interest in the naturalistic study of discourse. However, the system is well adapted to yield dependent measures of verbal interaction in studies which experimentally manipulate social or contextual conditions (e.g., Cansler & Stiles, 1981; Solomon, 1981).

The VRM system lends itself well to sequential analyses, using Markov or lag-correlational approaches (see Gottman & Krokoff, this volume). Its advantages include its exhaustiveness, so it leaves no gaps in the sequence, and its ability to be collapsed in various ways to reduce the number of categories. Small numbers of categories are necessary because sequential analyses require high frequencies of cooccurrences to estimate transitional probabilities. By collapsing across form, for example, the 64 modes are reduced to eight distinct intents. McLaughlin and Cody (1982) used this approach in their study of which VRMs preceded and succeeded ''awkward silences'' in conversations between college students. Or, modes can be collapsed across the principles of classification, for example, dividing all utterances according to whose frame of reference was used. By collapsing a set of VRM data in several different ways and performing sequential analyses on each version, a multidimensional picture can be drawn.

Research Using the VRM System

The VRM system has been used to study not only psychotherapy (Cromwell, 1981; McDaniel, 1980; McDaniel, Stiles, & McGaughey, 1981; Stiles, 1979b, 1981b, 1982, 1984; Stiles, McDaniel, & McGaughey, 1979; Stiles & Sultan, 1979), but also medical interviews (Carter & Inui, 1982; Inui & Carter, 1981; Putnam, Stiles, Jacob, & James, 1985; Stiles *et al.*, 1984; Stiles, Putnam, & Jacob, 1982; Stiles, Putnam, James, & Wolf, 1979; Stiles *et al.*, 1979a, 1979b), courtroom interrogations (McGaughey & Stiles, 1983), parent–child interactions (Stiles & White, 1981), husband–wife interactions (Fitzpatrick, Vance, & Witteman, 1984; Premo, 1979; Premo & Stiles, 1983), student–student and student–professor interactions (Cansler, 1979; Cansler & Stiles, 1981; McLaughlin & Cody, 1982; Sloan & Solano, 1984; Stiles, Waszak, & Barton, 1979), simulated job interviews (Solomon, 1981), and political oratory (Miller & Stiles, in press; Stiles *et al.*, 1983). The psychotherapy results are most germane to this volume.

VRM Psychotherapy Research

My first successful VRM psychotherapy study (completed by 1976, but not published until 1979) was a demonstration that psychotherapists of different theoretical orientations systematically use different modes for their verbal interventions. In transcripts of psychotherapy by prominent practitioners representing major schools of therapy, client-centered therapists used the client's frame of reference (mostly Acknowledgment and Reflection), Gestalt therapists used their own frame of reference (Disclosure, Advisement, Question, and Interpretation), and psychoanalytic therapists used the client's experience (Question, Acknowledgment, Interpretation, and Reflection) for over 90% of their utterances (Stiles, 1979b). The differences between schools were so large and so systematic that it seems implausible that any common success of the different approaches could be attributed to overlap in therapist mode use. Thus it seems unlikely that any one mode or combination of modes will be found to be best or most therapeutic in any general way (contrary to my original hypothesis that Reflection was best).

This basic phenomenon—that therapists of different schools use different modes—has been repeatedly demonstrated using different process coding systems (Auerbach, 1963; Brunink & Schroeder, 1979; Cartwright, 1966; Hill, Thames, & Rardin, 1979; Snyder, 1945; Strupp, 1955, 1957). Nevertheless, there has been a tenacious misconception that experienced therapists converge on some common core of techniques, which may arise from the work of such authors as Fiedler (1950a, 1950b, 1951) and Frank (1961), who have argued for common processes across schools. However, the commonalities they see are at a much higher level of abstraction—for example, the common tendency for therapists to have higher relative status or social power than clients, or the common feeling that good therapists are warm and concerned.

The VRM system adds to previous findings by showing that the technical differences among schools are systematic with respect to the principles of classification. The principles form a bridge between psychotherapeutic theory and technique; each theory's recommendations, recast in terms of the principles, can be seen as prescribing and proscribing particular modes. Client-centered theory (Rogers, 1951) holds that change comes from a client's exploring his or her own frame of reference and articulating unsymbolized experiences; the therapist is instructed to respond using the client's internal frame of reference exclusively, in order to communicate empathy and acceptance. Gestalt therapy theory (Perls, 1969; Perls, Hefferline, & Goodman, 1951) holds that change comes from recasting experience into the "now," which may be understood as the therapist's own existential frame of reference. A good therapist "stays absolutely in the now" (the therapist's frame of reference) and "doesn't listen to the content of the bullshit the patient produces" (the client's frame of reference; Perls, 1969, p. 53). Classical psychoanalytic therapy theory (e.g., Freud, 1912/1958) holds that change comes from making unconscious experience conscious, and by modifying the patient's understanding in light of the therapist's interpretations. "The doctor should be opaque to his patients and, like a mirror, should show them nothing but what is shown to him" (Freud, 1912/1958, p. 118). In VRM terms, the therapist should be concerned only with the patient's experience while revealing nothing of his or her own experience.

Typology of Psychotherapies

The VRM taxonomy's success at systematically discriminating therapist behavior across schools of therapy emboldens me to advance a fourfold typology of therapies, which appears here for the first time in print. The typology is parallel to the principles of classification and thus, like the role dimensions (above), presents another perspective on the principles' meaning in interaction.

1. In *nondirective* therapies, therapists use mainly the client's frame of reference (Edification, Confirmation, Acknowledgment, Reflection) while avoiding their own frames of reference; client-centered therapy is an example.
2. In *directive* therapies, therapists use mainly their own frame of reference (Disclosure, Advisement, Question, Interpretation) while avoiding the client's frame of reference; Gestalt therapy is an example.
3. In *analytic* therapies, therapists use mainly the client's experience (Question, Acknowledgment, Interpretation, Reflection) while avoiding their own experience; psychoanalytic therapy is an example.
4. In *hortatory* therapies, therapists use mainly their own experience (Disclosure, Edification, Advisement, Confirmation) while avoiding the client's experience. I have not yet studied explicit examples of hortatory therapies; presumably sermons and moral lectures would qualify. VRM profiles of college lectures and political speeches (Stiles *et al.*, 1983) conform to the hortatory specifications as closely as client-centered, Gestalt, and psychoanalytic therapies conform to the nondirective, directive, and analytic specifications, respectively (Stiles, 1979b), that is, for about 90% of the utterances. (The general—though by no means universal—phenomenon of therapy theories' restrictions on mode use is puzzling. Perhaps there is some value in a therapist's offering a highly predictable relationship, regardless of what that relationship is.)

For some reason, types of therapy seem equally tolerant or intolerant of modes that differ only in focus. Therapies that prescribe Reflections also permit Acknowledgments; therapies that prescribe Advisements also permit Disclosures; and so forth (cf. Table 6-3). Perhaps presuming knowledge of a client's experience depends more on the stage of the relationship or acquaintance with the problem at hand than on which theory is employed.

Client VRM Use

In contrast to therapists' diversity in mode use, clients tend to use roughly the same VRM profile regardless of their therapist's theoretical orientation or therapeutic technique (McDaniel *et al.*, 1981; Stiles & Sultan, 1979). Most (60–80%) of client utterances are in the four *exposition* modes, D(D), D(E), E(D), and E(E). Typically another 10% to 15% are brief, Acknowledgment forms, with the remainder spread over a wide variety of other modes. The common core of exposition modes suggested that if there is a common "active ingredient" in the psychotherapeutic process, then it is more likely to be found in the client's verbal behavior than in the therapist's.

Clients do vary in their relative proportions of the four exposition modes. This variation is correlated with raters' judgments of the quality of the psychotherapeutic process, as measured by the *experiencing* scale (Klein, Mathieu, Gendlin, & Kiesler, 1969; Klein, Mathieu-Coughlin, & Kiesler, this volume) and by scales for *client exploration* and *therapist exploration* based on the Vanderbilt Psychotherapy Process Scale (Strupp, Hartley, & Blackwood, 1974; O'Malley, Suh, & Strupp, 1983) as used by Gomes-Schwartz (1978). Clients' percentages of D(D) were correlated .58 with *experiencing* (Stiles, McDaniel, & McGaughey, 1979), .66 with *client exploration*, and .65 with *therapist explora-*

tion (McDaniel *et al.*, 1981). Clients' percentages of E(E) were correlated – .48 with *experiencing*, – .53 with *client exploration*, and – .56 with *therapist exploration* (all *p*'s < .01). Correlations of the mixed modes, E(D) and D(E), with these "good process" ratings were intermediate.

These findings suggest that good process, as judged by sophisticated raters, corresponds in part to clients' use of Disclosure as opposed to Edification. In terms of the principles, when clients convey information as seen from their own internal frame of reference rather than information seen from an external, objective perspective, they are judged as experiencing and exploring more deeply (a highly plausible result).

If client D(D) is a component of good process, then clients' use of D(D) in sessions should be correlated with clients' and therapists' judgments of the value of sessions and with measures of psychotherapy outcome. Two studies have been addressed to these implications.

In the first (McDaniel *et al.*, 1981), three sessions each from the brief (*M* = 17 sessions) psychotherapy of 31 anxious, depressed male college students were coded, and the percentage of D(D) (as well as other modes) was compared with measures of psychopathology and psychological distress taken at intake, termination, and follow-up, and with ratings of change in therapy. The interviews and outcome measures were collected in the Vanderbilt Psychotherapy Project (Strupp & Hadley, 1979). Results showed no consistent relationship of D(D) to improvement in therapy, as measured by change scores on psychological tests, interviews, and direct ratings. However, as Strupp and Hadley (1979) report, the measured improvement was only very modestly greater in the treated group than in wait-list controls, so there may have been little therapy-produced improvement to predict with any process measure. Client D(D) was positively correlated with measures of psychological distress, including the MMPI Depression scale and therapist ratings of overall severity of disturbance (*r*'s were about .5). Similar correlations were found with measures taken at intake and at termination. This finding is consistent with other researchers' observations of high levels of self-disclosures among depressed persons (e.g., Coyne, 1976a, 1976b).

In the other study (Stiles, 1981b, 1984), client D(D) was compared with clients' and therapists' postsession ratings of their encounters on the Session Evaluation Questionnaire (SEQ; Stiles, 1980; Stiles & Snow, 1984a, 1984b). The SEQ is a brief, bipolar adjective checklist, administered immediately after sessions. It yields two factor-based measures of sessions—*depth/value*, which discriminates sessions described as deep, valuable, full, special, and powerful from sessions described as shallow, worthless, empty, ordinary, and weak, and *smoothness/comfort*, which discriminates sessions described as smooth, comfortable, easy, pleasant, and safe from sessions described as rough, uncomfortable, difficult, unpleasant, and dangerous. Two types of VRM–SEQ correlations were calculated, the "between dyad" correlations, based on each dyad's average across its sessions and the "within dyad" correlations, calculated as the residual correlation of session VRMs with session SEQ ratings after variance due to mean dyad differences had been removed. Results showed that clients' percentage of D(D) was uncorrelated with either therapists' or clients' SEQ *depth/value*, either between dyads or within dyads. If postsession ratings of *depth/value* are taken as equivalents of *experiencing* (Klein *et al.*, 1969) or of *client exploration* (Gomes-Schwartz, 1978), then it appears that session participants do not agree with external expert raters about what constitutes good process.

SEQ *smoothness/comfort* showed different relationships with client D(D) depending on whether within-dyad or between-dyad correlations were considered. Within dyads, the relationship was significantly negative, both for clients and for therapists. That is, both tended to feel that sessions with relatively high levels of client D(D) were relatively rough, difficult, and dangerous. Between dyads there was a nonsignificant trend in the other direction; thus clients who typically used a high percentage of D(D)s were no more likely than others to have rough sessions, and may have even had slightly smoother ones according to participants' ratings. In other words, it appears to be deviations from a client's normal level of D(D)s, rather than his or her absolute level, that are associated with a session's seeming smooth and comfortable or rough and uncomfortable.

The association of client D(D) (across sessions) with relatively rough, uncomfortable sessions and (across clients) with depression and psychic distress is not necessarily inconsistent with its being a component of psychotherapeutic good process. Client Disclosure might function in psychological disruption analogously to a fever or an elevated white blood cell count in physical infection—primarily as part of an effective response to the disorder and secondarily as an index of the disorder (Stiles, in press-a). That is, Disclosure might be part of a "homeostatic" response to psychological discomfort or distress, which tends to promote psychological recovery. One would then expect correlations with indexes of distress as well as experts' judgments of good process, as we have found.

To stretch the analogy one more notch, if a high level of client Disclosures does reflect a healing process, it does not necessarily follow that forcing an even higher level would increase the benefit, just as artificially increasing an already above-normal body temperature might not aid in the fight against the infection. Obviously this point requires careful research.

Process and Outcome of Psychotherapy: Research Prospects

A natural question to ask about any process measured in psychotherapy is, "What good is it?" That is, how does it contribute to positive outcomes? The VRM system is a general-purpose descriptive system, and, so far as I know, it does not embody any position about which psychotherapeutic processes are best. In principle, the VRM system measures good and bad processes equally well; it does not concentrate on processes deemed by some theory to be most effective. Nevertheless, I have a few comments on the issue of process–outcome research.

1. Like all of the coding systems described in this volume, the VRM system is appropriate for correlational process–outcome studies. That is, the VRM system can quantify certain aspects of verbal interaction, and these numbers can be correlated with measures of outcome.
2. Because VRMs are, for the most part, voluntary acts, they may be especially appropriate as independent variables in *experimental* studies of outcome. That is, therapists can (with training) systematically vary their use of modes, whereas varying paralinguistic behaviors may be more difficult.
3. VRMs can be used as a manipulation check to demonstrate systematic differences between experimental treatments in comparative studies of outcome. As noted above, the VRM level of analysis corresponds to the level of therapeutic techniques as prescribed by theories of psychotherapy, and therapist VRM profiles vary systematically with type of therapy. Consequently, VRM coding could be used to

verify that the treatments under comparison were different and were in accord with theoretical prescriptions.

4. As described above, I have in several contexts (Stiles, 1979a, 1981b, 1982; Stiles, McDaniel, & McGaughey, 1979; Stiles & Sultan, 1979) advanced the hypothesis that the ''active ingredient'' in psychotherapeutic process lies in the client's behavior rather than the therapist's. This hypothesis is testable using VRM coding, but it is not a necessary consequence of the VRM approach.

5. Despite the foregoing, I have some doubts about whether traditional process–outcome research is asking the right questions. Asking ''What good is it?'' or ''Does it work?'' may presume a shared set of *values*, when in fact these values are not shared. Psychotherapeutic ''effectiveness'' may be partly a matter of taste. Different interpersonal processes (as measured by VRMs or other systems) may have systematically different psychological effects, but these effects may be valued differently by different people. (See Stiles, 1983, for a discussion of this possibility.)

Future Research Suggestions

In line with point 5 above, I see a need for research on the psychological effects of particular types of interpersonal encounters. The VRM system (and others described in this volume) offers a rich array of descriptive indexes, but little is known about the psychological consequences of types of encounters on participants. There is some progress in measuring the short-term impact of psychotherapeutic encounters (see especially chapters in this volume by Elliott by Phillips, by Barrett-Lennard, by Horvath and Greenberg, and by Orlinsky and Howard, as well as the above-cited work on the SEQ); however, this complex area is less developed than measuring process itself, in my judgment.

To illustrate, one might ask: What are the consequences of a 50-minute encounter with a purely directive, nondirective, analytic, or hortatory therapist (see above) over the succeeding 24 hours (or the succeeding 7 days)? Are there systematic effects of such an encounter on aspects of a client's cognition or affect? On interpersonal relations? On self-concept? Are there interaction effects with the client's expectations or personality? On an even more molecular level, one can ask: What are the effects of particular classes of therapist (or client) utterances on the psychological state of the client? What happens when the therapist makes a personal Disclosure? Or an accurate Interpretation?

In advocating descriptive research on the effects of encounters, I want especially to avoid asking which kinds of responses or encounters are best. Developing a (relatively) value-free vocabulary to describe effects of particular kinds of process is a challenge which is perhaps most likely to be met by novices (read: graduate students in search of dissertation topics), who have less investment and practice in conventional thinking.

The research I am suggesting differs from traditional process–outcome research not only in its focus on description rather than evaluation, but also in its attention to short-term rather than long-term effects. It seems to me that an understanding of how psychotherapy works in the long term must rest on an understanding of how each encounter affects (or fails to affect) the client. There can be no long-term effects without short-term effects, even if the short-term effects are covert, requiring incubation or cumulation to some critical mass before appearing as major life changes (cf. Rice & Greenberg, 1984).

VRM Analysis of Family Therapy Excerpt

Coding of Excerpt

The following excerpt was taken from Ackerman's (1966, pp. 3–7) book, *Treating the Troubled Family*. It illustrates many of the issues that typically arise in applying the VRM system. In my commentary, I have tried to articulate the rationale for the codes (particularly applying the taxonomic principles) and to indicate where and why alternative codes might be given. The excerpt is far too short to give an accurate characterization of this family's therapy. However, in a subsequent section, I have calculated some summary indexes to illustrate how VRM data may be aggregated. Examples of VRM-coded dialogue in individual psychotherapy and in segments of medical interviews are available elsewhere (Stiles, in press-b; Stiles *et al.*, 1979a).

Dr. A: *Bill,*   K(K)
        This is a term of address, so the form is Acknowledgment. I judged
        that the intent was to establish communication with Father—to in-
        dicate awareness of Father's experience without presuming any spe-
        cific knowledge of it.
        you heaved a sigh as you sat down tonight.   R(R)
        Heaving a sigh is a quasivolitional action, something that Father was
        probably more-or-less aware of; thus the other is the source of ex-
        perience. Dr. A presumes specific knowledge of that action, so the
        focus is on the other. I judged that the viewpoint taken was one
        shared with Father (other's frame of reference). Thus the intent is
        Reflection (see Table 6-3). Note that if the action was assumed (by
        the speaker) to be totally out of the other's awareness, the utterance
        would be scored differently. For example, ''You dropped your wallet
        as you sat down tonight'' would be scored R(E) if it merely commu-
        nicated a fact (speaker's experience), without presuming knowledge
        of the other's volition.
Father: *Just physical, not mental.*   E(D)
        This fragment has no subject or verb; however, it is a complete ut-
        terance (telegraphic speech, not a false start). In my judgment, some
        beginning like ''It's'' or ''The sigh was'' is clearly intended to be
        understood. All of the plausible beginnings that I could think of were
        third person, so I coded it Edification form. The intent is to commu-
        nicate the speaker's experience, as viewed by the speaker, without
        necessarily presuming knowledge of the other (focus on speaker),
        that is, Disclosure (see Table 6-3). This utterance reveals private infor-
        mation—the reasons or motives behind the sigh.
Dr. A: *Who are you kidding?*   Q(I)
        Either the interrogative word (''Who'') or the inverted subject–verb
        order would be sufficient for coding Question form. However, the
        intent is not Question; Dr. A is not really seeking information about
        who is being kidded. The topic is the other's experience (Father's
        motives), and Dr. A is presuming to understand that experience
        (focus on other) and to render a judgment about it (using his own
        frame of reference), that is, to suggest ''you are kidding,'' coded In-
        terpretation intent (see Table 6-3).
Father: *I'm kidding no one.*   D(D)

The subject is first person, so the form is Disclosure. The utterance communicates Father's private motives—the speaker's experience, from the speaker's frame of reference, focused on the speaker. Note that Father here responds primarily to the Question form, rather than the Interpretation intent of Dr. A's utterance. A disagreement with the therapist is probably present at deeper levels of intent—perhaps this could be scored D(D(C))—but in my judgment, Father is "on record" only as revealing motives.

Dr. A:	*Hmmm . . .*	K(K)

This counts as an utterance because it is clearly a verbal communicative act—not merely an autistic noise. The form is Acknowledgment—a nonlexical utterance. The topic is the other's preceding utterance, and the "Hmmm" merely indicates receipt (no presumption of knowledge of the other), at least on record, in my judgment. Possibly at deeper levels there is an Interpretation intent—K(K(I))—an off record repetition of the suggestion, "you're kidding."

Father:	*Really not . . .*	D(D)

Here the understood form seems to be "Really I'm not" or "I'm really not." The adverb "really" does not affect the code.

	Really physical.	E(D)

Again, scored as "It's really physical."

	I'm tired	D(D)
	because I put in a full day today.	D(D)

The form is Disclosure (first person). The intent concerns the speaker's experience and is focused on the speaker (no presumptions about the other). The frame of reference is somewhat problematic because of the phrase "full day." If this were taken to refer to objective information—the amount of time spent, number of activities engaged in, and so on—then the intent would be Edification. I judged that "full day" was also meant to convey the subjective experience of expending effort and feeling pressure—information that is knowable only through access to the speaker's private experience (coded as speaker's frame of reference).

Dr. A:	*Well,*	K(K)

The form is Acknowledgment, a contentless term. The topic is the other's previous utterance; however, no specific presumption of knowledge was necessary. In effect, Dr. A conveys simple receipt of Father's rationalization.

	I'm tired every day,	D(D)

Straightforward Disclosure by the therapist.

	and when I sigh, it's never purely physical.	E(D)

The main clause's subject is "it," so the form is Edification. The intent purports to reveal the private feelings that underlie Dr. A's sighs. The restrictive dependent clause, "when I sigh," is not coded; Dr. A does *not* actually assert "I sigh."

Father:	*Really?*	Q(Q)

This fragment appears to be a complete (telegraphic) communicative act, so it must be coded. I judged the understood sentence to be "Is that really so?" or "Is it really never physical?" I judged that, in a minimal way, Father here seeks information from Dr. A (topic is other's experience; no necessary presumption of knowledge; answer to be interpreted from speaker's viewpoint). An alternative code, Q(K), would imply that there is an understood sentence of

Question form, but that the speaker is merely indicating receipt of communication rather than seeking further information.

Dr. A:	*What's the matter?*	Q(Q)
Father:	*Nothing.*	E(D)

Understood as "Nothing is the matter," a subjective experience reported in a third person form.

Really!   E(D)

Understood as an emphatic repetition, "Really nothing is the matter."

Dr. A: *Well,*   K(K)

Acknowledges receipt.

your own son doesn't believe that.   E(E)

The subject is third person ("son"), so the form is Edification. The topic is Dr. A's observation (speaker's experience), no specific knowledge of the other's (Father's) experience is necessary (focus on speaker), although knowledge of a third party's (son's) experience is presumed. (Ackerman's commentary indicates that son had grinned knowingly.) The frame of reference is neutral, or objective, in relation to the speaker and the other; the assertion's truth or falsity could, in principle, be determined without access to either's private experience. Thus the intent is Edification. In general, descriptions of third parties' private experience are equivalent to descriptions of any other aspect of the external world, for VRM coding.

Father:	*Well,*	K(K)
	I mean,	D(D)

This empty clause is coded as a *filler* (see Stiles, 1978a), that is, an utterance with a recognizable grammatical form that takes its intent from the parent clause, in this case the next utterance.

nothing . . . nothing could cause me to sigh especially today or tonight.   E(D)

A third person subject ("nothing") in an utterance that reveals private experience.

Dr. A:	*Well,*	K(K)
	maybe it isn't so special,	E(R)

The form is Edification (third person pronoun). The intent is problematic because Dr. A never completes his train of thought. I judged that this communicates Dr. A's understanding of the nuance, "especially," in Father's preceding utterance, preparatory to a more direct interpretative attack (never launched) on Father's rationalization.

but . . .   not coded

False starts are coded only if the main verb is uttered.

How about it,   Q(Q)

Interrogative word, seeking information from the other. This is the first utterance directed to Son.

John?   K(K)

The term of address is an Acknowledgment form. I have coded this Acknowledgment intent, like the first utterance in the episode. Arguably this one (or perhaps both) could be treated as a filler, coded K(Q).

Son: *I wouldn't know.*   D(D)

First person; reveals speaker's private experience.

Dr. A: *You wouldn't know?*   R(Q)

The form is second person and the verb implies private experience, so the form is Reflection. There is no inversion of subject and verb, so the form is not Question. The rising inflection recorded by the question mark indicates that Dr. A is seeking information: verification of the preceding utterance. That is, in this utterance, Dr. A is not presuming to understand the Son's not knowing (so the intent is not Reflection); he is checking on whether the Son knows.

How come all of a sudden you put on a poker face?   Q(Q)

There is an Interpretation buried off record in this utterance.

A moment ago you were grinning very knowingly.   R(R)

This is second person with a verb that implies a volitional action (Reflection form). The topic is the other's behavior, and the speaker presumes knowledge of it.

Son: *I really wouldn't know.*   D(D)

Note that the insincerity of the utterance does not affect its VRM code.

Dr. A: *You . . .*   not coded

Since there is no verb, this false start does not count as an utterance.

Do you know anything about your pop?   Q(Q)

Son: *Yeah.*   K(D)

The contentless term "yeah" is Acknowledgment form. The utterance reveals private information—whether or not Son knows anything about his pop.

Dr. A: *What do you know about him?*   Q(Q)
Son: *Well,*   K(K)
I don't know,   D(D)
except that I know some stuff.   D(D)
Dr. A: *Well,*   K(K)
let's hear.   A(A)

The form "let's" is imperative—"you let us,"—coded Advisement. The intent imposes the speaker's idea on the other, by directing him to say something.

Son: *My . . .*   not coded
well,   K(K)
I . . . (laughs)   not coded

Laughter is not a speech act.

Father: *He's nailed down.*   E(E)

This third person statement (Edification form) concerns Son's internal experience, but it is addressed to Dr. A, so it concerns matters external to the speaker–other dyad (i.e., it uses an external frame of reference, shared with the other but requiring no specific presumptions of the other).

Dr. A: *He's a man?*   E(Q)

The subject is third person, so the form is Edification. The Question intent is signaled by a rising inflection transcribed as a question mark.

Son: *Yeah.*   K(E)

This answer to a (trivial) Question conveys the objective knowledge that Father is a man.

Father: *Come on,*   A(A)
come on,   A(A)
come on.   A(A)

These are imperative in form—with "you" as the understood subject—coded Advisement. Father presumes to impose an experience (i.e., answering Dr. A) on his Son. Thus the source of experience and frame of reference are the speaker's, but the focus is on the other, that is, Advisement intent. The verb is repeated three times, and each repetition is coded.

    Dr. A wants information from you.   E(E)

In this usage, ''Dr. A'' is a third person subject, not a term of address. Again, this utterance reports the private experience of a third party, which is coded Edification.

Son: *Eh,*   K(K)

I have coded this as an Acknowledgement to Father, indicating receipt of the preceding utterances. Possibly this was not intended to be communicative—merely a time-filling noise—in which case it should not have been coded.

    all right,   I(C)

This is a term of evaluation, like ''fine'' or ''okay,'' which is coded Interpretation form. In a formal or literal sense, Son is judging that something about the preceding utterances is ''all right.'' In intent, however, this is not a judgment but an agreement to comply with Father's directive to ''come on.'' In my judgment, this is addressed to Dr. A as well, and is an agreement to comply with his earlier directive, ''let's hear.'' That is, the ''other'' includes both Father and Dr. A for this utterance. Agreement concerns the speaker's experience but also presumes specific understanding of the other's experience (in this case, knowledge of what action is desired), and thus uses a shared frame of reference, coded Confirmation intent (Table 6-3).

    I'll tell you,   D(D)

In intent, this reveals Son's (private) intentions to say something. Unlike the previous utterance, this one seems addressed exclusively to Dr. A.

    Dr. A.   K(K)

Dr. A: *Your father uses his hand,*   E(E)

    you know,   R(E)

    not like your mother.   already coded

The first utterance gives objective information to Son, in a third person form, coded pure Edification. The phrase ''not like your mother'' is included as part of this first utterance. The ''you know'' is a filler (like ''I mean'' above, a grammatically separate utterance whose intent is taken from the parent clause). The second person subject with a verb denoting private experience makes the form Reflection. The intent is scored Edification, in effect a repetition or intensification of the parent clause.

Father: *Give,*   A(A)

    give,   A(A)

    give.   A(A)

Again, these repeated imperatives are addressed to Son.

Dr. A: *Mother's gesture is this,*   E(E)

    and Pop's gesture is give.   E(E)

These third person statements transmit objective information, scored Edification intent. They appear to be addressed to the whole family.

Son: *Ah,*   not coded

I judged that this is merely a time-filling noise, without communicative intent. If it was used to convey receipt of any of the preceding communication, it should have been coded K(K).

    I don't have much to say, to tell the truth.   D(D)

Son reveals contents of his private experience.

I can't . . .   not coded

For a false start to be coded in the VRM system, it must include the *main* verb. This includes only the auxiliary verb, so it does not count as an utterance.

He's just a normal man,   E(D)

Coding this intent rests on the intended meaning of "normal." Guided in part by the subsequent statement, "He's a good guy," which seems to be a clarification of this utterance, I took this one to be a value judgment, revealing Son's private attitudes. If "normal" is purely descriptive, the utterance should be coded E(E).

I mean,   D(E)

Again, this is a filler; the intent of the parent clause (the next utterance) is Edification.

he's my father.   E(E)

On record, this is merely a statement of fact, coded pure Edification. At deeper levels, there may be other intents.

He's a good guy.   E(D)

This third person statement clearly reports Son's private evaluations (albeit possibly not fully sincere).

Mother: *May I make a suggestion?*   Q(Q)

Subject and verb are inverted (Question) form, as Mother asks for permission. I judged that she was specifically asking permission from Dr. A; however, alternatively she may have been speaking to the whole group or to some subgroup.

Dr. A: *What's your suggestion?*   Q(Q)

Directed to Mother.

Mother: *Well,*   K(K)

uh,   not coded

I have been keeping an anecdotal record of the time that has elapsed since we were here. Not every minute of the time, but anything that I think is important enough to relate.   D(E)

I coded all of this as one utterance; the operative clause is "I have been keeping an anecdotal record," which uses first person to convey objective information, coded D(E). The rest of the utterance is a prepositional phrase—the object of "of"—and not coded separately. Thus I treated the period after "here" as if it were a comma. Alternatively, the portion beginning "Not every minute" could be treated as a separate utterance, with an initial understood repetition of "I have been keeping an anecdotal record of." In this case, two D(E)s should be coded.

Dr. A: *Um-hum.*   K(K)
Mother: *Now, I think this is good for many reasons.*   D(D)

When you read it, you sort of get a better view of things,   R(D)

This second person utterance describes the *speaker's* internal experience. Given that Mother intends to read the record herself, her phrasing "when you read it" suggests that "you" means "I."

and, uh, if you'd like me to read it, I will.   D(D)

This is a statement of private intentions. Note that "if" clauses do not affect form codes.

If you feel you'd rather ask questions, you can.   A(A)

This second person statement gives Dr. A permission to ask questions.

But that's my suggestion.	E(D)
Dr. A: *Well,*	K(K)
I'm glad you called my attention to that notebook in your lap there.	D(D)
You come armed with a notebook . . .	R(R)

This is a difficult call. I coded it Reflection rather than Interpretation because I judged that, on record, Dr. A was putting Mother's own experience (volitional behavior) into words, rather than explaining Mother to herself or evaluating her (i.e., I judged that the frame of reference was Mother's). However, as Ackerman's commentary indicates, the term ''armed'' hints at an Interpretation that the notebook is a weapon.

Mother: *. . . and I've been keeping this record since last week,*	D(E)
because I think it's very important.	D(D)
You forget very quickly what people say and how they say it unless you write it down right away.	R(D)

I coded this intent as understood ''I forget . . . ''

| *Now this is something that I do for children in my class,* | E(E) |

I coded this as a description of an observable activity. Note that the main clause is ''this is something,'' and that the restrictive dependent clause, ''that I do,'' is not coded.

| *that I have to for case histories,* | E(D) |

I coded this as separate from the preceding utterance because it seemed to express a different thought—the felt need for a mnemonic for case histories. The form was coded by parallelism with the preceding utterance (i.e., ''This is something'' is understood).

and I think it's a wonderful idea.	D(D)
Dr. A: *Well now,*	K(K)
what have you there?	Q(Q)
A ''case history'' on your whole family?	Q(Q)

The intent of this last utterance is clearly Question, but there is no subject or verb, and the parallelism with the preceding utterance is flawed. As a general rule in VRM coding, I advocate coding a pure mode by default when the intent code is clear and there is insufficient evidence to make a form judgment. The alternative, *(Q), where ''*'' means unscorable, seems to me to do violence to the clarity of this utterance. From a colloquial viewpoint, nothing is missing and the communication is unobstructed (the utterance is telegraphic rather than incomplete).

Mother: *Yes.*	K(E)
Dr. A: *Marvelous!*	I(I)

This is a term of evaluation, which is sufficient to code Interpretation form. In intent, this utterance evaluates Mother's volitional behavior (bringing the book) from Dr. A's frame of reference. The irony is not coded.

How long is it?	Q(Q)
Mother: *It's not that long.*	E(E)

Note that the imprecision of this statement is irrelevant to VRM coding. It purports to describe an objective characteristic of the ''case history,'' however vaguely.

| *I just started it.* | D(E) |

Describes observable behavior.

| *There's some here you didn't see last night.* | E(E) |

This is addressed to Father. The restrictive dependent clause, ''[that] you didn't see last night'' is not coded separately.

Father:	*Oh,*	K(K)
	you cheated.	I(I)
	This evaluates Mother's volitional behavior from Father's frame of reference.	
Mother:	*I didn't cheat.*	D(C)
	In intent, Mother disagrees—she conveys her own experience but also presumes knowledge of Father's viewpoint, in order to contradict him, coded Confirmation intent.	
	I just didn't tell you there was more to it,	D(E)
	that's all.	E(E)
	You read the front of the book . . .	R(R)
	This describes Father's experience from Father's viewpoint.	
Father:	*That's cheating,*	E(I)
	A repetition of the earlier Interpretation, this time in third person form.	
	isn't it?	Q(I)
	I judged that Father here repeats his Interpretation, rather than asking about it—that is, he continues to presume to understand Mother's behavior (focus on other).	
Mother:	*Oh,*	K(K)
	This Acknowledges receipt of Father's utterance.	
	no,	K(C)
	This disagrees with it. In my judgment, this is not merely an answer to a Question; both parties presume knowledge of each other's experience in this matter.	
	it isn't.	E(C)
	This repeats the disagreement.	
	So if you would like me to read it . . .	not coded
	I treated this as a false start, in which the main clause was never uttered.	
	It's sort of a little resumé of my thinking in the last week.	E(E)
	I coded this as a description of the document rather than as a revealing of Mother's thoughts.	
Dr. A:	*Fire away!*	A(A)
	Directs Mother to read.	

Procedures and Results of Coding

In applying the VRM system to group interaction, such as family therapy, it is essential to record who the speaker and other are for each utterance, since a speaker may behave systematically differently toward different others. The other may be one person, several persons, or the whole group. A sample coding form to keep track of these is illustrated in Table 6-7 (cf. Stiles *et al.*, 1983; Stiles, Waszak, & Barton, 1979; in these studies the "other" was an audience made up of many people).

The other includes only people directly addressed by the speaker; onlookers are excluded. Speaker–onlooker communications are treated as "off record" (e.g., hints or manipulations) for VRM purposes. For example, Dr. A's comment, "Your own son doesn't believe you," was addressed to Father, in my judgment, and was coded E(E) in the Dr. A–Father relationship. This utterance seemed also to serve as an off record Reflection in the Dr. A–Son relationship, but this hint is not coded. (On the other hand, it could be a fruitful future line of inquiry to explore the speaker–onlooker relationship by coding response modes at the hint level.)

Table 6-7   Excerpt of Sample VRM Coding Form for Family Therapy

Utterance Number	Speaker	Other 1	2	3	4	5	Form	Intent
21.11	1	0	0	1	0	0	K	K
21.12	1	0	0	1	0	0	A	A
22.11	3	1	0	0	0	0	K	K
23.11	2	1	0	0	0	0	E	E
24.11	1	0	0	1	0	0	E	Q
25.11	3	1	0	0	0	0	K	E
26.11	2	0	0	1	0	0	A	A
26.12	2	0	0	1	0	0	A	A
26.13	2	0	0	1	0	0	A	A
26.21	2	0	0	1	0	0	E	E
27.11	3	0	1	0	0	0	K	K
27.12	3	1	1	0	0	0	I	C
27.21	3	1	0	0	0	0	D	D
27.22	3	1	0	0	0	0	K	K
28.11	1	0	0	1	0	0	E	E
28.12	1	0	0	1	0	0	R	E
29.11	2	0	0	1	0	0	A	A
29.12	2	0	0	1	0	0	A	A
29.13	2	0	0	1	0	0	A	A
30.11	1	0	1	1	1	1	E	E
30.12	1	0	1	1	1	1	E	E

Note. Speaker numbers: 1 = Therapist; 2 = Father; 3 = Son; 4 = Mother; 5 = Daughter.

The utterance numbering system illustrated in Table 6-7 is as follows: each speech is numbered with an integer, sentences within speeches are numbered in the first decimal place, and utterances (e.g., independent clauses) within sentences are numbered in the second decimal place. The coding in Table 6-7 begins with Dr. A's speech, "Well, let's hear" (p. 188 above), which was numbered 21. Thus the speech's two utterances are 21.11 "Well," and 21.12 "let's hear." (Many other numbering systems are possible, of course; this one needs adjustments if speeches are more than nine sentences long.)

Utterance 27.12 by Son and utterances 30.11 and 30.12 by Dr. A are the only utterances in this excerpt that were addressed to more than one person, in my judgment. Each utterance's intended recipients are indicated by ones (rather than zeros) in the "other" columns. This format facilitates entering data for aggregation by computer.

As described above, the VRM system offers a variety of indexes, including (1) the frequency or percentage of each form–intent combination (pure and mixed modes), (2) the frequency and percentage of each form (aggregated across intents) and intent (aggregated across forms), and (3) the role dimensions (utterances aggregated across taxonomic principles; cf. Table 6-6). In describing group interaction, such as the family therapy excerpt, each index can be calculated across a variety of speaker–other combinations, for example, all therapist responses to the family, all family members' responses to the therapist, or all family members' responses to each other, as well as each separate speaker–other dyad. From this large array of possible indexes, a researcher can choose those that most directly address each study's questions or purposes.

The excerpt coded above is obviously too short to use for inferences about this family's typical relations with each other or this therapist's typical style. The following selection of VRM indexes is intended only to illustrate how the system can generate meaningful quantitative descriptors.

Table 6-8 presents two sorts of indexes, the raw frequencies of pure and mixed modes, and the role dimensions (each calculated as the proportion of utterances in four designated modes, averaged across form and intent, based on the taxonomic principles; see Table 6-6). The indexes in Table 6-8 were aggregated separately for each speaker–other relationship. Utterances addressed to more than one person were counted in each pertinent relationship. (This decision was somewhat arbitrary; alternatively utterances addressed to the group could have been aggregated separately, ignored, given fractional weights, etc.) The Dr. A–Daughter relationship, which consisted only of the two Edifications addressed to the whole family, is not shown.

Consistent with previous VRM results (McDaniel *et al.*, 1981; Stiles & Sultan, 1979), all family members used the exposition modes—D(D), D(E), E(D), and E(E)—for a substantial majority of their responses to the therapist. In all, 68% of family members' utterances to Dr. A were in the exposition modes, whereas only 19% of their utterances to each other and only 19% of Dr. A's utterances to the family were in these modes. (In these percentages, each utterance is counted only once, regardless of who or how many of the others it is addressed to.) The theoretically crucial category of Disclosure intent (including all forms) accounted for 77% of Father's, 63% of Son's, and 44% of Mother's utterances to Dr. A, whereas no family member used any Disclosure intents in utterances to each other. Mother's relatively greater use of Edification intent to Dr. A (39%, versus 13% by Son and 8% by Father) appears to index her tendency to retreat into external facts in this episode. (Of course, much more dialogue would be needed to conclude that this tendency is characteristic.)

Dr. A's principal modes in this excerpt were Question and Acknowledgment; 51% of his utterances were Q(Q) or K(K). His mode use was similar toward each of the family members, as he sought to gather information and facilitate exposition. Dr. A was thus relatively attentive; his attentiveness (cf. Table 6-6) was .612 toward Father, .643 toward Son, and .692 toward Mother. By contrast, their attentiveness toward Dr. A was .154, .282, and .195, respectively.

The presumptuousness dimension is of interest because previous VRM work has shown that it reflects relative status and intimacy (Cansler & Stiles, 1981; Premo & Stiles, 1983; Stiles *et al.*, 1979; Stiles, Waszak, & Barton, 1979). Replicating this previous work, the (higher status) professional, Dr. A, was more presumptuous to each of the family members than vice versa: .143 versus .000 for Father, .215 versus .063 for Son, and .231 versus .112 for Mother (Table 6-8). As in the previous work, the consistent direction of the differences reflected very low presumptuousness by the lower status person rather than high presumptuousness by the higher status person. Use of the presumptuous modes, Advisement, Confirmation, Interpretation, and Reflection, may be construed as excessively familiar and therefore impolite in addressing social superiors (Cansler & Stiles, 1981; Premo & Stiles, 1983; Stiles, 1981). In comparison to their behavior

Table 6-8 Summary of Family Therapy Excerpt Codes: Mode Use Frequencies and Role Dimensions

Mode[a]	Doctor A to: Father	Doctor A to: Son	Doctor A to: Mother	Father to: Doctor	Father to: Son	Father to: Mother	Son to: Doctor	Son to: Father	Mother to: Doctor	Mother to: Father
D(D)	1	0	1	5	0	0	7	0	4	0
D(E)	0	0	0	0	0	0	0	0	3	1
E(D)	1	0	0	5	0	0	2	0	2	0
E(E)	3*	3*	2*	1	1	1	1	0	3	2
A(A)	0	1	1	0	6	0	0	0	1	0
Q(Q)	1	4	4	1	0	0	0	0	1	0
K(K)	5	2	3	1	0	1	3	1	1	1
R(D)	0	0	0	0	0	0	0	0	2	0
R(R)	1	1	1	0	0	0	0	0	0	1
Other modes (used once)	E(R), Q(I)	E(Q), R(E), R(Q)	I(I)			E(I), Q(I), I(I)	K(D), K(E), I(C)*	I(C)*	K(E)	D(C), E(C), K(C)
Total	14	14	13	13	7	4	16	2	18	8

Role Dimension (Averaged Across Form and Intent)

Attentiveness	.612	.643	.692	.154	.000	.857	.282	.750	.195	.313
Presumptuousness	.143	.215	.231	.000	.857	.143	.063	.500	.112	.438
Acquiescence	.750	.572	.463	.346	.143	.500	.438	.500	.472	.875

[a]Mode abbreviations: D = Disclosure, E = Edification, A = Advisement, C = Confirmation, Q = Question, K = Acknowledgment, I = Interpretation, R = Reflection. Form is written first, intent second in parentheses.

*Includes utterances addressed to more than one person.

toward the therapist, all family members were much more presumptuous in their interactions with each other (Table 6-8). Note that the role dimension presumptuousness gathers Father's Advisements to Son, Father's Interpretations to Mother, and Mother's Confirmations to Father into the same broad concept. All of these modes require presuming knowledge of the other, and all reflect familiarity in the interpersonal relationship.

Even this short excerpt illustrates how the VRM taxonomy can characterize tasks, roles, and relationships (e.g., the consistent use of the exposition by clients to their psychotherapists; the attentive–informative polarization of therapist and client in this type of therapy; greater presumptuousness associated with higher relative status or greater familiarity). It also illustrates how an individual's speech acts may change across the roles that he or she assumes. For example, Father's VRM use varied drastically when he addressed people with whom he had different relationships. Dr. A, whose role was similar toward each family member, used a similar mixture of modes to each.

Conclusion

In this chapter I have tried to explain how the VRM system was developed. I have tried to say what VRMs are (illocutionary acts), to describe some of the system's technical features, to review some of the research results the system has produced, and to illustrate how the system can be applied. I have tried to indicate the system's versatility; it can be used to measure any discourse, and the resulting indexes can be used as independent, dependent, descriptive, or mediating variables. I have also tried to indicate the system's limited scope; it concerns only one of many facets of human interaction. Some of the other facets are dealt with in the other systems described in this volume. Investigators who prefer a more comprehensive description of psychotherapeutic process would do well to apply several systems to their data.

The VRM system's foundation is the principles of classification, which (however abstract they may seem at first) rest on the fundamental dichotomy of speaker versus other as separate centers of experience. The modes are universal because this dichotomy is central to every communicator's experience. The principles are also what distinguish this system from other classifications of speech acts.

References

Ackerman, N. *Treating the troubled family*. New York: Basic Books, 1966.

Auerbach, A. H. An application of Strupp's method of content analysis to psychotherapy. *Psychiatry*, 1963, 26, 137–148.

Austin, J. L. *How to do things with words* (2nd ed.). Oxford: Clarendon Press, 1975. [First edition, 1962. Based on 1955 William James Lectures, Harvard University.]

Bach, K., & Harnish, R. M. *Linguistic communication and speech acts*. Cambridge, Mass.: MIT Press, 1979.

Brown, P., & Levinson, S. Universals in language usage: Politeness phenomena. In E. N. Goody (Ed.), *Questions and politeness: Strategies in social interaction*. Cambridge, England: Cambridge University Press, 1978.

Brunink, S. A., & Schroeder, H. E. Verbal therapeutic behavior of expert psychoanalytically oriented, gestalt, and behavior therapists. *Journal of Consulting and Clinical Psychology*, 1979, 47, 567–574.

Cansler, D. C. Effects of status on verbal behavior (Doctoral Dissertation, University of North Carolina at Chapel Hill, 1979). *Dissertation Abstracts International*, 1979, 40, 2355B. (University Microfilms No. 7925895)

Cansler, D. C., & Stiles, W. B. Relative status and interpersonal presumptuousness. *Journal of Experimental Social Psychology*, 1981, *17*, 459–471.

Carter, W. B., & Inui, T. S., with Kukull, W. A., & Haigh, V. H. Outcome-based doctor-patient interaction analysis: II. Identifying effective provider and patient behavior. *Medical Care*, 1982, *10*, 550–566.

Cartwright, R. D. A comparison of the response to psychoanalytic and client-centered psychotherapy. In L. A. Gottschalk & A. H. Auerbach (Eds.), *Methods of research in psychotherapy*. New York: Appleton-Century-Crofts, 1966.

Cohen, J. A coefficient of agreement for nominal scales. *Educational and Psychological Measurement*, 1960, *20*, 37–46.

Coyne, J. C. Depression and the response of others. *Journal of Abnormal Psychology*, 1976, *85*, 186–193. (a)

Coyne, J. C. Toward an interactional description of depression. *Psychiatry*, 1976, *39*, 28–40. (b)

Cromwell, D. Therapists' responses to confrontation: An analogue study comparing theoretical orientation, level of self-actualization, and experience level (Doctoral dissertation, Boston University, 1981). *Dissertation Abstracts International*, 1981, *42*, 2522B. (University Microfilms No. 8125621)

Dore, J. Conversational acts and the acquisition of language. In E. Ochs & B. B. Schiefflin (Eds.), *Developmental pragmatics*. New York: Academic Press, 1979.

Ebel, R. L. Estimation of the reliability of ratings. *Psychometrika*, 1951, *16*, 407–424.

Elliott, R., Stiles, W. B., Shiffman, S., Barker, C. B., Burstein, B., & Goodman, G. The empirical analysis of help-intended communications: Conceptual framework and recent research. In T. A. Wills (Ed.), *Basic processes in helping relationships*. New York: Academic Press, 1982.

Fiedler, F. E. A comparison of therapeutic relationships in psychoanalytic, nondirective, and Adlerian therapy. *Journal of Consulting Psychology*, 1950, *14*, 436–445. (a)

Fiedler, F. E. The concept of an ideal therapeutic relationship. *Journal of Consulting Psychology*, 1950, *14*, 239–245. (b)

Fiedler, F. E. Factor analysis of psychoanalytic, nondirective, and Adlerian therapeutic relationships. *Journal of Consulting Psychology*, 1951, *15*, 32–38.

Fitzpatrick, M. A., Vance, L., & Witteman, H. Interpersonal communication in the casual interaction of married partners. *Journal of Language and Social Psychology*, 1984, *3*, 81–95.

Fleiss, J. L. Measuring agreement between two judges on the presence or absence of a trait. *Biometrics*, 1975, *31*, 651–659.

Frank, J. D. *Persuasion and healing: A comparative study of psychotherapy*. Baltimore: The Johns Hopkins Press, 1961.

Freud, S. Recommendations to physicians practicing psycho-analysis. In J. Strachey (Ed. and trans.), *The standard edition of the complete psychological works of Sigmund Freud Vol. 12*. London: Hogarth Press, 1958. (Originally published 1912.)

Gomes-Schwartz, B. Effective ingredients in psychotherapy: Prediction of outcome from process variables. *Journal of Consulting and Clinical Psychology*, 1978, *46*, 1023–1035.

Goodman, G. *Companionship therapy: Studies in structured intimacy*. San Francisco: Jossey-Bass, 1972.

Goodman, G. *SASHATapes: Self-led automated series on helping alternatives*. Los Angeles, Calif.: UCLA Extension, 1978.

Goodman, G., & Dooley, D. A framework for help-intended communication. *Psychotherapy: Theory, Research, and Practice*, 1976, *13*, 106–117.

Goody, E. N. Towards a theory of questions. In E. N. Goody (Ed.), *Questions and politeness: Strategies in social interaction*. Cambridge, England: Cambridge University Press, 1978.

Grice, H. P. Meaning. *Philosophical Review*, 1957, *66*, 377–388.

Hill, C. E., Thames, T. B., & Rardin, D. K. Comparison of Rogers, Perls, and Ellis on the Hill Counselor Verbal Response Category System. *Journal of Counseling Psychology*, 1979, *26*, 198–203.

Holsti, O. R. *Content analysis for the social sciences and humanities*. Reading, Mass.: Addison-Wesley, 1969.

Inui, T. S., & Carter, W. B., with Kukull, W. A., & Haigh, V. H. Outcome-based doctor-patient interaction analysis: I. Comparison of techniques. *Medical Care*, 1982, 20, 535–549.

Klein, M. H., Mathieu, P. L., Gendlin, E. T., & Kiesler, D. J. *The experiencing scale: A research and training manual, Volume I.* Madison, Wisc.: Wisconsin Psychiatric Institute, 1969.

McDaniel, S. H. Clients' verbal response mode use and its relationship to measures of psychopathology and change in brief psychotherapy (Doctoral Dissertation, University of North Carolina at Chapel Hill, 1979). *Dissertation Abstracts International*, 1980, 41, 359B. (University Microfilms No. 8013966)

McDaniel, S. H., Stiles, W. B., & McGaughey, K. J. Correlations of male college students' verbal response mode use in psychotherapy with measures of psychological disturbance and psychotherapy outcome. *Journal of Consulting and Clinical Psychology*, 1981, 49, 571–582.

McGaughey, K. J., & Stiles, W. B. Courtroom interrogation of rape victims: Verbal response mode use by attorneys and witnesses during direct examination versus cross-examination. *Journal of Applied Social Psychology*, 1983, 13, 78–87.

McLaughlin, M. L., & Cody, M. J. Awkward silences: Behavioral antecedents and consequences of the conversational lapse. *Human Communication Research*, 1982, 8, 299–316.

Miller, N. L., & Stiles, W. B. Verbal familiarity in American presidential nomination acceptance speeches and inaugural addresses (1920–1981). *Social Psychology Quarterly*, in press.

O'Malley, S. S., Suh, C. S., & Strupp, H. H. The Vanderbilt Psychotherapy Process Scale: A report of the scale development and a process-outcome study. *Journal of Consulting and Clinical Psychology*, 1983, 51, 581–586.

Perls, F. S. *Gestalt therapy verbatim.* Lafayette, Calif.: Real People Press, 1969.

Perls, F. S., Hefferline, R. F., & Goodman, P. *Gestalt therapy.* New York: Julian Press, 1951.

Premo, B. E. Verbal response mode use in married couples versus stranger dyads: Acquaintance and familiarity (Doctoral Dissertation, University of North Carolina at Chapel Hill, 1978). *Dissertation Abstracts International*, 1979, 40, 498B. (University Microfilms No. 7914395)

Premo, B. E., & Stiles, W. B. Familiarity in verbal interactions of married couples versus strangers. *Journal of Social and Clinical Psychology*, 1983, 1, 209–230.

Putnam, S. M., Stiles, W. B., Jacob, M. C., & James, S. A. Patient exposition and physician explanation in initial medical interviews and outcomes of clinic visits. *Medical Care*, 1985, 23, 74–83.

Rice, L. N. & Greenberg, L. S. (Eds.) *Patterns of change.* New York: Guilford, 1984.

Rogers, C. R. *Client-centered therapy.* Boston: Houghton-Mifflin, 1951.

Russell, R. L., & Stiles, W. B. Categories for classifying language in psychotherapy. *Psychological Bulletin*, 1979, 86, 404–419.

Searle, J. R. *Speech acts: An essay in the philosophy of language.* Cambridge, England: Cambridge University Press, 1969.

Shrout, P. E., & Fleiss, J. L. Intraclass correlations: Uses in assessing rater reliability. *Psychological Bulletin*, 1979, 86, 420–428.

Sloan, W. W., Jr., & Solano, C. H. The conversational styles of lonely males with strangers and roommates. *Personality and Social Psychology Bulletin*, 1984, 10, 293–301.

Snyder, W. U. An investigation of the nature of non-directive psychotherapy. *Journal of General Psychology*, 1945, 33, 193–223.

Solomon, M. R. Dress for success: Clothing appropriateness and the efficacy of role behavior (Doctoral Dissertation, University of North Carolina at Chapel Hill, 1981). *Dissertation Abstracts International*, 1981, 42, 2026B. (University Microfilms No. 8125621)

Stiles, W. B. *Manual for a taxonomy of verbal response modes.* Chapel Hill: Institute for Research in Social Science, University of North Carolina at Chapel Hill, 1978. (a)

Stiles, W. B. Verbal response modes and dimensions of interpersonal roles: A method of discourse analysis. *Journal of Personality and Social Psychology*, 1978, 36, 693–703. (b)

Stiles, W. B. Psychotherapy recapitulates ontogeny: The epigenesis of intensive interpersonal relationships. *Psychotherapy: Theory, Research, and Practice*, 1979, 16, 391–404. (a)

Stiles, W. B. Verbal response modes and psychotherapeutic technique. *Psychiatry*, 1979, 42, 49–62. (b)

Stiles, W. B. Measurement of the impact of psychotherapy sessions. *Journal of Consulting and Clinical Psychology*, 1980, *48*, 176–185.

Stiles, W. B. Classification of intersubjective illocutionary acts. *Language in Society*, 1981, *10*, 227–249. (a)

Stiles, W. B. *Verbal response mode correlates of session impact*. Symposium presentation, American Psychological Association Convention, Los Angeles, California, 1981. (b)

Stiles, W. B. Psychotherapeutic process: Is there a common core? In L. E. Abt & I. R. Stuart (Eds.), *The newer therapies: A sourcebook*. New York: Van Nostrand Reinhold, 1982.

Stiles, W. B. Normality, diversity, and psychotherapy. *Psychotherapy: Theory, Research, and Practice*, 1983, *20*, 183–189.

Stiles, W. B. Client disclosure and psychotherapy session evaluations. *British Journal of Clinical Psychology*, 1984, *23*, 311–312.

Stiles, W. B. "I have to talk to somebody": A fever model of disclosure. In V. Derlega & J. Berg (Eds.) *Self-disclosure: Theory, research, and therapy*. New York: Plenum Press, in press. (a)

Stiles, W. B. Levels of intended meaning. *British Journal of Clinical Psychology*, in press. (b)

Stiles, W. B. Verbal response modes as intersubjective categories. In R. L. Russell (Ed.), *Language in psychotherapy: Strategies of discovery*. New York: Plenum Press, in press. (c)

Stiles, W. B., Au, M. L., Martello, M. A., & Perlmutter, J. A. American campaign oratory: Verbal response mode use by candidates in the 1980 Presidential primaries. *Social Behavior and Personality*, 1983, *11*, 39–43.

Stiles, W. B., McDaniel, S. H., & McGaughey, K. Verbal response mode correlates of experiencing. *Journal of Consulting and Clinical Psychology*, 1979, *47*, 795–797.

Stiles, W. B., Orth, J. E., Scherwitz, L., Hennrikus, D., & Vallbona, C. Role behaviors in routine medical interviews with hypertensive patients: A repertoire of verbal exchanges. *Social Psychology Quarterly*, 1984, *47*, 244–254.

Stiles, W. B., Putnam, S. M., & Jacob, M. C. Verbal exchange structure of initial medical interviews. *Health Psychology*, 1982, *1*, 315–336.

Stiles, W. B., Putnam, S. M., James, S. A., & Wolf, M. H. Dimensions of patient and physician roles in medical screening interviews. *Social Science & Medicine*, 1979, *13A*, 335–341.

Stiles, W. B., Putnam, S. M., Wolf, M. H., & James, S. A. Interaction exchange structure and patient satisfaction with medical interviews, *Medical Care*, 1979, *17*, 667–681. (a)

Stiles, W. B., Putnam, S. M., Wolf, M. H., & James, S. A. Verbal response mode profiles of patients and physicians in medical screening interviews. *Journal of Medical Education*, 1979, *54*, 81–89. (b)

Stiles, W. B., & Snow, J. S. Counseling session impact as viewed by novice counselors and their clients. *Journal of Counseling Psychology*, 1984, *31*, 3–12. (a)

Stiles, W. B., & Snow, J. S. Dimensions of psychotherapy session impact across sessions and across clients. *British Journal of Clinical Psychology*, 1984, *23*, 59–63. (b)

Stiles, W. B., & Sultan, F. E. Verbal response mode use by clients in psychotherapy. *Journal of Consulting and Clinical Psychology*, 1979, *47*, 611–613.

Stiles, W. B., Waszak, C. S., & Barton, L. R. Professorial presumptuousness in verbal interactions with university students. *Journal of Experimental Social Psychology*, 1979, *15*, 158–169.

Stiles, W. B., & White, M. L. Parent-child interaction in the laboratory: Effects of role, task and child behavior pathology on verbal response mode use. *Journal of Abnormal Child Psychology*, 1981, *9*, 229–241.

Strupp, H. H. An objective comparison of Rogerian and psychoanalytic techniques. *Journal of Consulting Psychology*, 1955, *19*, 1–7.

Strupp, H. H. A multidimensional analysis of therapist activity in analytic and client-centered therapy. *Journal of Consulting Psychology*, 1957, *21*, 301–308.

Strupp, H. H., & Hadley, S. W. Specific versus nonspecific factors in psychotherapy: A controlled study of outcome. *Archives of General Psychiatry*, 1979, *36*, 1125–1136.

Strupp, H. H., Hartley, D., & Blackwood, G. L., Jr. *Vanderbilt Psychotherapy Process Scale*. Unpublished manuscript, Vanderbilt University, 1974.

7

The Process of Family Therapy: The Development of the Family Therapist Coding System

William M. Pinsof
Center for Family Studies/Family Institute of Chicago
Northwestern Memorial Hospital
Northwestern University
Chicago, Illinois

Introduction

Relatively little scientific attention has been paid to the process of family and marital psychotherapy (Gurman, Kniskern, and Pinsof, in press; Pinsof, 1981). This lack of attention derives, at least in part, from the tremendous complexity of studying the simultaneous interaction of one or two therapists and at least two patients. The context of family therapy presents the process researcher with all of the very difficult conceptual and methodological problems involved in the study of individual therapy process as well as its own unique problems. This chapter details the evolution of my efforts over the last 15 years to grapple with these problems in order to describe and analyze the process of family and marital therapy. (Hereafter "family and marital therapy" will be referred to generically as "family therapy".)

The evolutionary history of my research can be organized around the three research instruments that I and my colleagues have developed to study the family therapy process. The first instrument, The Family Therapist Behavior Scale (FTBS) (Pinsof, 1977, 1979), culminated the early phase of my research and functioned as a transitional evaluation point in the process that led to the development of the second instrument, The Family Therapist Coding System (FTCS) (Pinsof, 1980). Currently, the FTCS is the core process instrument in our research program and provides the major focus for this chapter. Both the FTBS and the FTCS are observational coding systems applied by trained raters to tapes and/or transcripts of family therapy sessions.

The third and newest instrument in the research program, The Integrative Psychotherapy Alliance Scales (IPAS) (Pinsof and Catherall, 1986), is a series of three self-report measures that use the same dimensions to study the patient's experience of the therapist–patient alliance in family, couple, and individual psychotherapy, respectively. The IPAS will be discussed briefly toward the end of the chapter. The FTCS and IPAS can be applied to individual as well as family therapy process, and both reflect my belief that the field of psychotherapy and psychotherapy research needs to move beyond "modality thinking" to a systemic framework that incorporates individual and interpersonal variables (Pinsof, 1983).

The evolutionary history presented in this chapter touches upon many of the problems and dilemmas that every process researcher must address. Each of the systems I have developed resolved some of the problems and created others. In this chapter I hope to provide the reader not only with "the facts," but with a sense of the struggle and the process of my research.

The Early Phase

Initial Explorations—The Truax and Carkhuff Scales

My interest in the study of the process of psychotherapy began in 1971, during my first year in graduate school at York University in Toronto. At that time I was exposed to the Truax and Carkhuff (1967) ordinal-process scales. I found these scales, particularly the Accurate Empathy (AE) Scale, to be very useful in guiding my own behavior as a novice therapist, and I became very interested in Truax and Carkhuff's theory, research, and training procedures.

In the fall of the 1972, I began a three-year practicum as a clinical fellow in the Department of Psychiatry at McMaster University in Hamilton, Ontario. At that time, McMaster was the primary center for family therapy training in Canada. In an effort to make sense out of what I was trying to learn as a therapist at McMaster, and as a young doctoral student thinking about a dissertation, I decided to conduct an informal experiment: I applied the Truax and Carkhuff scales to therapy tapes of expert supervisors and beginners at McMaster. To my surprise and consternation I found that the Truax and Carkhuff scales did not discriminate at all between the two therapist groups. Some of the experts, who were renowned family therapists with more than 15 years of experience, received very low scores on the short tape segments of their work we coded with the scales. In contrast, some beginners received very high scores.

At that time I also began a three-year training program at the Gestalt Institute of Toronto. To test the results of my initial informal research outside of the McMaster context, I decided to code transcribed vignettes of Fritz Perls's work as well as directly observed episodes of my Gestalt supervisors' work. They, too, received surprisingly low scores on the Truax and Carkhuff scales. These results presented me with a dilemma: Either my supervisors at McMaster, my Gestalt therapy supervisors in Toronto, and the premier Gestalt therapist (Perls) were poor therapists or something was wrong with the Truax and Carkhuff scales.

In the early 1970s, a number of studies and papers began to emerge questioning various aspects of the Truax and Carkhuff scales as well as the variables they were trying to measure. Bergin and Jasper (1969) and Garfield and Bergin (1971) found no relationship between the AE scale and outcome with non-client-centered therapists. Kurtz and Grummon (1972) and Caracena and Vicory (1969) questioned the construct validity of the AE scale. Chinsky and Rappoport (1970) raised issues about the reliability and meaning of the AE scale, and Gurman (1973) showed that the variables the scales attempted to measure were not stable within the same session.

On the basis of these articles and my own increasing experience as a therapist and young researcher, I decided that the Truax and Carkhuff scales, and particularly the

AE scale, were plagued with a number of insoluble problems. Several additional problems with the scales became apparent to me that went beyond those already identified in the literature. A primary problem was that these scales, like most ordinal scales, confounded evaluation and description. For instance, with the AE scale, a higher score meant that the therapist was more accurately empathic and therefore a better therapist. What my own experience as a therapist and researcher seemed to suggest (as well as the experience of others) was that in certain contexts, behavior that would be characterized as unempathic on the AE scale, might in fact be more "therapeutic" than high AE behavior. For this and other reasons, the separation of evaluation and description became a guiding principle in my subsequent process research.

The second critical problem with the Truax and Carkhuff scales was that they were not very revealing when applied to family therapist behavior and family therapy interaction. They did not seem to fit family therapy. The scales, and particularly the AE scale, were predicated upon individual therapy assumptions. For instance, the AE scale assumes that the therapist's intervention will follow the client's or patient's utterance, whereas in family therapy, a patient's utterance frequently will be followed by the utterances of other patients. Eventually, the therapist's intervention may only pick up on what one of the patients was saying or on what they were saying to each other as a group. In such situations, it is impossible to identify the "empathic target" of the therapist's intervention. It thus became apparent that one could not just transplant individual therapy process instruments to the context of family therapy.

Toward a Family Therapist Coding System

This realization led me to search for a suitable family therapy process measure that could help me understand the process of family therapy as well as the skills that I was trying to acquire as a family therapy trainee at McMaster. The only family therapist coding system that had been mentioned in the published literature at that time was a two-category system (Drive and Interpretation) that had been used by the research group at Jewish General Hospital in Montreal (Postner, Guttman, Sigal, Epstein, and Rakoff, 1971). That system was derived from Dollard and Auld's (1959) individual therapy coding system and was very global and nonspecific. Additionally, the Montreal research group was unable to find any link between its process measure and the outcome of treatment.

It soon became apparent that if I wanted to use a system that would delineate specific family therapist skills and interventions, I would have to develop it myself. At that time (1973), several senior staff at McMaster had just finished a project delineating the instructional objectives of their family therapy training program. Cleghorn and Levin (1973) identified three types of therapist skills: perceptual, conceptual, and executive. The last one concerned specific intervention skills, such as "confronting in the context of support" and "relinquishing control in the presence of adaptive behavior." Since a major personal goal of my research was (and still is) to understand the skills that I was trying to learn and master as a therapist, I began my attempt to build a family therapist coding system by examining the executive skills identified by Cleghorn and Levin. To my displeasure I found that their executive skills, although very useful for training, did not operate at a level of abstraction that would permit reliable coding. There were just too many ways to confront in the context of support, to interrupt maladaptive interaction patterns, and to relate symptomatic behavior to maladaptive transactions. As nominal categories in a therapist coding system, the executive skills were too global, they were not mutually exclusive, and they emerged in "units" of different sizes.

Attempting to operationalize these skills made me aware of the extent to which most, if not all, of the extant family therapy theory functioned at a level of abstraction that made it very difficult, if not impossible, to identify codable interventions. The theory was just too molar and nonspecific. My next step would have to involve breaking the executive skills (the intervention theory of the McMaster model) into smaller, mutually exclusive, and potentially reliable intervention categories.

An additional realization was beginning to dawn on me at that time. As my observational and clinical skills were developing, I became aware that advanced therapists seldom "work" or think in terms of an isolated intervention. Instead, they think in terms of a series of interventions with particular goals or objectives. In observing advanced therapists working at McMaster, it was clear to me that their behavior had a sense of momentum or purpose that conveyed to the observer (and probably to the family) that the therapist was "going somewhere" and that "they knew where they were going." In contrast, beginners' behavior typically lacked such momentum and purpose and frequently seemed to convey a "lost" or "treading-water" feeling.

Fortunately, the work of a professor of mine at York (Laura Rice) and a fellow graduate student (Les Greenberg) gave me a term to describe the way advanced therapists work—"operations." Laura Rice (1974) identified the "evocative" function or operation in client-centered therapy and Les Greenberg (1979) described the "two-chair" operation in Gestalt therapy. Basically, an operation consists of a series of planned therapist interventions designed to accomplish a particular task in the face of a particular type of patient behavior (a "marker"). The evocative operation helps the patient reprocess experience, whereas the two-chair operation helps the patient resolve internal or intrapsychic conflict.

Family Therapist Operation Scales

Taking off on the idea that Cleghorn and Levin's executive skills actually represented condensed labels for therapist operations, I decided to develop a set of operation scales that could be used to measure the extent to which the therapist performed the complete operation or executive skill. I developed seven, seven-point ordinal scales to tap the major executive skills. Two of these scales are presented in Table 7-1 (The Transaction–Control Process Scale) and Table 7-2 (The Focus–Process Scale).

These operation scales appeared to resolve a number of methodological problems. First, they were macroscopic enough to capture the major executive skills identified by Cleghorn and Levin. Second, by incorporating the concept of a therapeutic operation, the scales permitted identification of the specific (and potentially reliably codable) behaviors or interventions that comprised the operations. Thus, it appeared that the operation scales simultaneously allowed us to break up *and* capture the entirety or gestalt of the major executive skills. The scales seemed to permit scientific precision as well as clinical richness.

Each of the seven, seven-point ordinal scales presented the specific therapist behaviors in a specific sequence. Each of the behaviors or interventions were considered to be essential components of the operation. The therapist's score on a particular scale was based on the extent to which the specific behaviors were performed in the "ideal" sequence. The more interventions performed in the correct order, the higher the score. The scales were intended to be applied to six-minute scoring units sampled from videotaped family therapy sessions.

Table 7-1   Transaction–Control Process Scale

Therapist Behaviors (or Interventions)

(7)   T effectively stops a maladaptive transaction and gets family's attention (1). T then asks fs if they know what just happened (2). If necessary, T will query each family member. If fs cannot label the pattern, T will label it clearly and accurately for them (3). T then effectively relates the labeled pattern to relevant syptomatic behavior in the family (4). T continually emphasizes family responsibility by getting fs to do as much of the work as possible (5). As quickly as possible, ''T'' attempts to shift the responsibility for controlling the maladaptive patterns from himself to the family.

(6)

(5)   T stops a maladaptive transaction and gets family's attention (1). T then asks fs if they know what just happened (can they label the process?) (2). If fs cannot label the pattern, T labels it for them (3). T attempts to relate the transactional pattern to the symptomatic behavior, but his interpretation is not convincing or particularly effective (4). Either ''T'' timing or ''T'' mode of presentation is ineffective. During initial labeling and when the pattern recurs, T does not get the family to do the work but tends to do it himself (5). ''T'' does not push family to take control of their own behavior.

(4)

(3)   T stops maladaptive transaction and gets family's attention (1). T asks fs if they know what just happened, but is not persistent in his inquiry (2). T's effort to label the transactional pattern is not clear and/or convincing to the family (3). T does not even get to the point of attempting to relate the transactional pattern to symptomatic behavior (4). T does not attempt to shift responsibility to the family but, instead, either gets caught up in defending his transaction labeling or lets the family control the session and loses his focus on the transaction in question (5).

(2)

(1)   T does not stop maladaptive transactions (1) and makes no attempt to perform components (2), (3), (4) and (5). T does not control the session and symptomatic behavior proliferates and is not dealt with at all.

(0)   Not applicable. Maladaptive transactional patterns and symptomatic behavior did not appear in this segment.

Components: (1) Stop maladaptive transaction.
(2) Transaction query.
(3) Transaction label.
(4) Relate transaction to symptomatic behavior.
(5) Family responsibility.

To illustrate, the Transaction–Control Process Scale consisted of five component interventions designed to functionally relate maladaptive family transactions and symptomatic behaviors. If the therapist (1) stopped the maladaptive family transaction, (2) then queried the family members about their awareness of the transaction, (3) then labeled the maladaptive transaction if the family members did not do so in response to step 2, (4) then related the transaction to the symptomatic behavior, and (5) finally assigned responsibility to the family members for monitoring and controlling the transaction in the future, the therapist would receive a maximum score of 7. In contrast, if the therapist performed the first three steps, but did not do the second (query) and third (label) steps persistently or clearly, the therapist would receive a scale score of 3. If none

Table 7-2   Focus–Process Scale

Therapist Behaviors (or Interventions)

---

(7) T consistently, but not rigidly, focuses on a problem (1). When F defocuses, "T" makes a defocus query (2). His query is persistent and may involve querying individual f's. If an f does not label the defocusing process, T labels it clearly and accurately (3). If F does not refocus on the original issue, T refocuses them (4).

(6)

(5) T focuses on a problem (1) and effectively sustains focus. When F defocuses, T consistently refocuses (4). Frequently, but not always, T labels the defocusing process (3) but, if F refocuses, T does not have to (4). T seldom if ever queries the defocusing process (2). Conscious training of F to become aware of their defocusing process, that is, the educational component, is minimal. T does not push F to become aware of and change their own behavior. He does it himself.

(4)

(3) T focuses on a problem (1), but cannot sustain focus for extended periods of time (8 or more "speeches"). When F defocuses T might try to refocus (4), but does not refocus effectively or consistently. "T" seldom, if ever, queries defocusing (2) or labels the defocusing process (3). The educational component is totally lacking at this level. It also appears as if the T and F are in a power struggle, and F is winning (controlling the attentional process).

(2)

(1) T does not focus on a problem for more than 2 or 3 speeches (1). When F defocuses, T does not query the defocusing process (2); T does not label the defocusing process (3); and T does not refocus on the original issue (4). At this level there is no power struggle between F and T. F is clearly in control of the therapy attentional process.

(0) Not applicable. F focuses on a problem and consistently and appropriately maintains problem focus. "F" refocuses themselves.

Components: (1) Focus on a problem.
                      (2) Defocus query.
                      (3) Defocus labeling.
                      (4) Refocus.

of the steps were performed in an appropriate context, the therapist would receive a score of 1. A score of 0 meant that the operation embodied in the scale was not appropriate in the six-minute scoring unit: Maladaptive transactions and symptomatic behaviors did not occur.

A number of methodological problems emerged when we began applying these scales to videotapes of expert-level family therapists at McMaster. These problems revolved around the ordinal nature of the scales. The first problem was the scales' lack of specificity. The therapist received a single score on each scale on a six-minute behavior sample that did not specify the actual behaviors the therapist performed. For instance, a score of 3 on the Transaction–Control Process Scale might mean that the therapist either did component one very well and component two slightly, or did the first three components poorly. The score would also not identify the point within the sample when the therapist performed the various scale or operation components. A scale score could never reflect the actual, specific behaviors of the therapist. Concomitantly, it was impossible to know exactly what cues the raters used to make their scale score decisions.

The scales' lack of specificity, combined with the fact that, like most ordinal scales, they combined evaluation and description, rendered them subject to considerable coder bias. The operation scales required the coder to make an evaluative (good–bad) judgment, rather than to categorize nonevaluatively or describe the actual therapist behaviors within the behavior sample. If coders liked or were impressed with certain therapists, they would be more likely to rate them higher than therapists they disliked.

The major problem that emerged with the scales was that they did not seem to be able to meet what was emerging as a basic developmental criterion for an adequate coding system: They could not consistently differentiate beginning and advanced family therapists. In pilot testing, the same problem that plagued the Truax and Carkhuff scales emerged. With certain families, at certain points in therapy, low-level therapist behavior (that would receive a low scale score) seemed to be more appropriate than higher-level behavior. For instance, with the Focus–Process Scale, it might be more appropriate for the therapist to focus on an issue (step 1) and then simply to refocus on that issue when the family changed the topic (step 4), without querying (step 2), or labeling (step 3) the defocusing process. Deleting the middle steps of the operation in this way would be most appropriate with highly resistant or defensive families early in treatment. Querying and labeling the behavior of resistant/defensive families, particularly during the early phases of treatment when the therapeutic alliance is just beginning to emerge, is more likely to increase their defensiveness and jeopardize proper alliance development.

The operation scales were constructed on the basis of additive (more components equals better) and sequential (right order equals better) principles. Thus, in the Focus–Process Scale example mentioned above, a beginner, who only performed certain components (steps 1 and 4) because he was incapable of performing others, would receive the same score as an advanced, expert therapist who flexibly adjusted his behavior to meet important clinical contingencies. The scales' additive and sequential rigidity precluded their ability to differentiate consistently advanced and beginning therapist behavior. Most importantly, the scales did not seem to fit or reflect accurately the complex, contingent, and improvisational nature of the psychotherapeutic process.

Before abandoning the ordinal operation scales altogether, I developed a five-point ordinal Appropriateness Scale that would accompany each of the operation scales. My hope was that the Appropriateness Scale would permit the operation scales to differentiate beginning and advanced therapists. Thus, an Appropriateness-Scale score would be combined with each operation-scale score to yield a "better" index of the therapist's behavior.

Unfortunately, in pilot testing with various expert family therapists as coders, we were unable to establish adequate reliability with the Appropriateness Scale. Surprisingly, expert therapists, trained and supervising within the same theoretical orientation, were unable to agree consistently about the appropriateness of different therapists' (advanced and beginner) behavior. In fact, there seemed to be such wide divergence among the therapist-coders about what constituted appropriate therapeutic behavior in specific contexts, that I decided it may well be altogether impossible to code reliably the appropriateness of therapists' verbal behavior.

This decision also coincided with the decision to abandon the ordinal therapist-operation scales as research instruments to study family therapist verbal behavior. About four years later (1978), I returned to these scales and started to use them non-quantitatively as training tools in the context of clinical simulations. Subsequently, we have even developed additional therapist operations. Although these scales did not work out as research instruments, their additive and sequential properties have made them very useful tools for teaching novice family therapists to think and work in terms of operations rather than isolated interventions.

Our experience with the operation scales highlighted the fact that research and training tools may have to be designed to fit different criteria and may well be of very limited utility outside of their respective domains. A major problem with the Truax and Carkhuff scales may well have been that they were designed to fit both research and teaching needs, when, in fact, they were most useful as training tools for teaching novice psychotherapists to listen attentively and reflect feelings accurately. Psychotherapy researchers interested in teaching and in research should probably consider developing different versions of similar instruments to teach and scientifically investigate similar therapeutic skills.

The Family Therapist Behavior Scale (FTBS)

After abandoning the operation scales as research instruments, a decision was made to build a coding system around the behavioral components (interventions) that comprised the operations. This entailed a shift from an ordinal scaling system to a straight categorization system (nominal scale). This change remedied the additive and sequential rigidity problems with the ordinal scales and increased specificity and resistance to coder bias.

Shifting to a nominal scale that coded the therapist's behavior at the discrete intervention or act level (as opposed to the operation level) removed the pattern or "sequence-of-acts" component from the coding process. This "loss" presented a major problem since it deleted the scale's capacity to identify what seemed to be critical characteristics of family therapist behavior—timing and sequence. Fortunately, a potential solution to this problem appeared when I became aware of the literature that was starting to emerge in the area of sequential analysis (Hertel, 1972; Mishler and Waxler, 1975; Raush, 1972). The patterns did not have to be identified during coding; they could be identified during the statistical analysis phase of the research. The statistical analysis could be focused to identify the actual (vs. ideal) patterns that existed within the therapist's behavior stream and possibly could even be used to discover and specify other therapist operations.

The new nominal scale was entitled The Family Therapist Behavior Scale (FTBS). It was constructed by going through the operation scales and culling out the different, specific therapist interventions that comprised the operations. Many of the operations used similar, if not identical, steps at various points (e.g., process queries and labels), which reduced the number of categories or interventions that needed to be included in the new scale. The first version of the FTBS consisted of 26 mutually exclusive code categories that targeted the therapist's verbal behavior.

Because of low reliability during pilot testing, seven code categories were dropped (collapsed into other codes) from the original FTBS. Additionally, to facilitate coding, the individual code categories were organized into theoretically related groups (Affect codes, Behavior codes, etc.). Coding became a two-step procedure. Initially, the coder placed a therapist's statement in a particular group or code family (e.g., Affect); subsequently the coder assigned the statement to a particular code category within that group (Affect-Now). The final FTBS consisted of 19 mutually exclusive code categories that targeted the structure and/or function of the therapist's verbal behavior in family therapy. In order to be included in the final version of the scale, a code category had to meet two criteria: It had to be able to generate a relevant clinical/experimental hypothesis that could be tested, and the category had to have a reliability coefficient (proportion of agreement) of at least .60. The FTBS codes are briefly defined in Table 7-3.

At 19 cateogries, the FTBS still seemed capable of greater refinement and specification. However, in order to get my research into a structure that would allow me to complete my dissertation, I decided (somewhat arbitrarily) to "freeze" the FTBS at 19 categories and to test formally the reliability and validity of the scale. The feedback from this evaluation would then be used to shape the subsequent "system" development process.

Methodological Characteristics of the FTBS

Exhaustiveness   The FTBS was exhaustive. It coded every intelligible therapist's utterance into one of the 19 mutually exclusive code categories. The scale did not contain a "dump" category for "unratable" or "borderline" interventions. Exhaustiveness was built into the FTBS in order to keep the coders "on their toes"; every choice had to be an active discrimination in which an utterance was placed (as opposed to dumped) into a code category. Exhaustiveness also reflected my desire to create a "comprehensive" coding system that could code and actively describe the entire "stream" of intelligible therapist verbal behavior. This is particularly important in looking at formal variables like therapist activity level and intervention or speech complexity (the number of different interventions attempted within one "speech"). Finally, exhaustiveness is a necessary characteristic of coded data that can be used in a sequential, statistical analysis. It leaves no gaps.

Scoring Unit   Most, if not all, observational psychotherapy process research systems, until the last few years, employed "fixed" or rigid scoring units (Dollard and Auld, 1959; Kiesler, 1973). The size of the unit in these systems does not vary, at least during a study. In contrast, the FTBS used a "sliding" or flexible scoring unit—the *therapist statement*. It is defined functionally and structurally: It performs at least one function (labeling, supporting, interpreting, etc.) and may have distinctive structural features. The size of the therapist's statement varies according to the code category to which it is assigned. For instance, "You're looking pretty angry," by itself, would be coded as Affect-Now (AN); whereas the statement "You're looking pretty angry since your wife started expressing her doubts about the relationship" would be coded as Sequence-Now (SN). A therapist's speech (everything said by one person between the intelligible utterances of one or more other people) or utterance can contain one or more codable statements.

Most methodological innovations, like the flexible scoring unit, simultaneously solve or ameliorate certain problems and create or exacerbate others. Its primary advantage is its clinical sensitivity and verisimilitude: it recognizes the fact that different interventions come in different sizes. Even the same type of intervention will be sized differently by different therapists or even by the same therapist at different times. It accommodates the grammatical to the functional dimensions of the scoring unit.

The major shortcoming of a flexible unit is that it requires the coder to unitize and categorize simultaneously. It complicates the coding procedure and thereby introduces potential coding errors that can reduce interrater and intrarater reliability. A fixed unit would be more likely to increase reliability, but it would severely diminish the clinical sensitivity and relevance of the FTBS. Our hope was that the loss of reliability would not be disastrous in the trade-off for clinical richness.

Table 7-3   The 19 Code Categories of the Family Therapist Behavior Scale (FTBS) Briefly Defined and Exemplified

1. **Support (S).** Statements in which the therapist validates experience and/or identifies or praises assets or strengths: "It must have been a terrible period in your life."

2. **Intention-Desire (ID).** Statements in which the therapist deals with intentions and/or desires: "What are you going to do about it?"

3. **Therapist Experience Label (TEL).** Statements in which the therapist deals with his own affective or cognitive experience: "I'm a little confused by what you're saying."

4. **Control-Structure (CS).** Statements in which the therapist explicitly structures or directs behavior or discussion content: "Why don't you move over there."

5. **Direct Interaction Task (DIT).** Statements in which the therapist directs one person to interact with another: "Why don't you tell her what she just did."

6. **Refocus (R).** Statements in which the therapist explicitly returns the conversation to a topic that was previously identified and temporarily lost: "Let's get back to what your wife was saying about your not following through on the discipline."

7. **Block-Expectation (BE).** Statements in which the therapist deals with expectations about what would happen if someone performed a blocked behavior or experienced a blocked feeling or thought: "What do you think will happen if you tell how you feel?"

8. **Functional Relationship (FR).** Statements in which the therapist deals with a functional relationship between at least two sets of events: "You know, I think your fighting keeps the two of you from getting too close."

9. **Other Affect Statement (OAS).** Statements in which the therapist deals with how one person thinks another person feels: "Did you know she was sad?"

10. **Affect-Now (AN).** Statements in which the therapist deals with feelings that occur during the current interview: "How do you feel about what she just said?"

11. **Affect-Then (AT).** Statements in which the therapist deals with feelings that occur outside of the current interview: "It must have made you very sad."

12. **Affect-Communication (AC).** Statements in which the therapist deals with the communication of feelings: "Do you ever get angry at him?"

13. **Sequence-Now (SN).** Statements in which the therapist deals with two or more temporally linked events or an event and its context that occur within the current interview: "When we started to talk about you and your husband, Timmy began to bother Suzy and you quickly got on their case."

14. **Sequence-Then (ST).** Statements in which the therapist deals with two or more temporally linked events or an event and its context that occur outside of the current interview: "When she gets angry at you, you just give up and back off."

15. **Behavior-Now (BN).** Statements in which the therapist deals with nonsequential and noncontextual behaviors or events that occur within the current interview: "You just looked out the window."

16. **Behavior-Then (BT).** Statements in which the therapist deals with nonsequential and noncontextual behaviors or events that occur outside of the current interview: "So you threw him out?"

17. **Other Cognition-Opinion (OCO).** Statements in which the therapist deals with what one person thinks another person thinks about something or someone: "What does he mean by 'less arguments'?"

18. **Individual Cognition-Opinion (ICO).** Statements in which the therapist deals with one person's cognitions and/or opinions about something or someone: "What do you think about that?"

19. **Relational Cognition-Opinion (RCO).** Statements in which the therapist deals with the separate cognitions and opinions of more than one person and/or disagreement/agreement between people. "Do you agree with your daughter?"

Code Conflicts   The idea that code categories within the FTBS would conflict with each other was implicit in the use of a flexible scoring unit. In pilot testing the FTBS, two kinds of code conflicts emerged—supersession and ambiguity conflicts. The former refer to situations in which a statement or series of statements could be clearly coded within one or more of the FTBS categories. The AN–SN statements presented above exemplify a *supersession conflict*.

To deal with the fact that the FTBS uses a single, mutually exclusive coding procedure (a statement can be coded into only one code category), we created a hierarchy in which certain FTBS code categories predominate over others in supersession conflict situations. The FTBS supersession hierarchy is presented in Table 7-4. It consists of seven levels, with higher-level codes taking priority over lower-level ones in conflict situations. The hierarchy uses two priority principles—structural and/or functional complexity and sophistication. More complex and sophisticated (special family therapy interventions) intervention categories predominate over less complex and sophisticated ones.

The supersession hierarchy priorities were based on a series of clinical–experimental hypotheses concerning differences in the behaviors of advanced-versus-beginning family therapists at McMaster. The guiding theory was that advanced therapists would be more likely to perform more complex and sophisticated behaviors. Conversely, a larger part of the beginners' repertoire would fall into lower-level (simpler and less clinically sophisticated) code categories in the hierarchy.

Ambiguity conflicts occur when a therapist's statement does not clearly fit within the definitional boundaries of competing code categories. In such situations, the coder, after consulting the coding manual, still cannot clearly decide between competing codes. To deal with ambiguity conflicts and borderline statements, we created a priority structure that reversed the supersession rules in Table 4. In conflict situations, lower-level codes predominate over higher-level ones.

The decision to reverse the supersession hierarchy for ambiguity conflicts was based on the desire to make the ambiguity rules work against the experimental hypotheses that were implicit in the supersession hierarchy. Thus, when a coder could not decide where to put an ambiguous statement, regardless of whether it was uttered by an advanced or beginning therapist, it would be assigned to a lower-level category. This rule meant ambiguity conflicts would make it more difficult for the coding system to dis-

Table 7-4   The Conceptual Structure of the 19 Category System
Presented as a Supersession* Hierarchy

Level	
I:	Other Affect Statement (OAS); Direct Interaction Task (DIT); Other Cognition-Opinion (OCO)
II:	Block-Expectation (BE); Functional Relationship (FR); Refocus (R)
III:	Relational Cognition-Opinion (RCO); Affect Communication (AC)
IV:	Support (S); Intention-Desire (ID)
V:	Sequence-Now (SN); Sequence-Then (ST)
VI:	Affect-Now (AN); Affect-Then (AT); Behavior-Now (BN); Behavior-Then (BT); Individual Cognition-Opinion (ICO)
VII:	Control-Structure (CS); Therapist Experience Label (TEL)

*Supersession Rule: Higher codes supersede or take priority over lower codes in clear conflict situations.

criminate between advanced and beginning therapists. It thereby penalized the FTBS for ambiguity conflicts.

Ironically, when we started to use the supersession and ambiguity rules in pilot coding, we realized very quickly that they actually created more problems than they solved. The coders did not differentiate ambiguity and supersession conflicts consistently. When confronted with a supersession conflict that was resolved in the FTBS Manual, coders frequently treated it like an ambiguity conflict and only referred to the ambiguity priority table (reverse of the Table 4). Basically, the coders got lazy, stopped using the coding manual to resolve conflicts, and leaned inordinately on the priority table. We remedied this problem by deleting the supersession and ambiguity rule table from the final FTBS Manual, which effectively meant that when a code conflict emerged, the coder would be more likely to consult the manual. This was one of those not-infrequent incidents in process research where methodological and conceptual refinements backfired and created a more serious problem than the one they were intended to resolve.

Statement and Location Specification   Due to the unitization problems inherent in the use of a flexible unit, as well as the redundancy and complexity of therapist speech, the FTBS coders were required to write out every statement they coded in a box on the coding sheet. The appropriate code category abbreviation (symbol) was written next to the statement. The coders also indicated the location of the statement with the beginning and ending videotape counter numbers. Statement and location specification permitted computation of an extremely accurate reliability index by allowing for exact identification of ''hits'' (agreements) and ''misses'' (disagreements). This procedure specified the scoring unit—exactly what material the coder considered in making the code assignment.

The McMaster FTBS Study

The McMaster Study formally tested the validity and reliability of the the FTBS. The validity test focused on the discriminant validity of the scale—its capacity to make a meaningful and predicted distinction between two or more groups known to differ on certain dimensions. The discriminant validity question functioned as an informal development criterion for the FTBS and its predecessors by requiring the instrument to be capable at least of consistently differentiating the verbal behavior of advanced and beginning therapists. The McMaster Study (Pinsof, 1977, 1979) is reported here in some detail because it also provided the raw data for the first test of the Family Therapist Coding System (FTCS), which is discussed below.

Procedure and Design   The design of the McMaster Study combined the known group's (beginner vs. advanced) distinction with an extreme condition distinction. The study tested the capacity of the FTBS to find significant and predicted differences between a trainee condition-group and a supervisior condition-group. In the trainee condition-group, eight novice therapists conducted a standard (50- to 55-minute) initial (first- or second) family therapy interview with a normally assigned new case. In the supervisor condition-group, eight advanced family therapists conducted a supervisory family interview. In this condition-group the advanced therapist observed, behind a one-way mirror, the first 20 minutes of a supervisee's initial session with a new family case. After 20 minutes, the advanced therapist–supervisor was sent, by the experimenter, into the trainee's session and took over the rest of the interview. All 16 sessions were videotaped.

The supervisory interview, commonly referred to as "live supervision" (a normal supervisory practice at McMaster), was used in this study to magnify the differences between the beginning and advanced therapists. Beyond being more experienced and expert than the trainees, the advanced therapists' 20-minute observation period before entering the session allowed them time to gather their thoughts and plan their interventions. This advantage made it even more likely that the advanced therapists' behavior, in contrast to the trainees', would be closer to the ideal articulated in Cleghorn and Levin's instructional objectives (1973).

The extreme condition-group design offered the FTBS a minimal validity criterion. If the scale was valid, it should at least be able to discriminate significant, predicted differences between such extreme condition-groups. The design maximized the likelihood of finding differences. Failure to find an adequate number of predicted differences would bode poorly for the future development of the FTBS and the kind of thinking it embodied.

Subjects   The 16 subjects were family therapists at the Chedoke Child and Family Centre at McMaster. Therapists were assigned to condition-groups in terms of two criteria: number of families treated and colleague ratings of expertise. These ratings were collected as part of the McMaster Outcome Study (Santa-Barbara, Woodward, Levin, Goodman, Streiner, and Epstein, 1979) and involved a card-sorting procedure derived from Cleghorn and Levin's (1973) instructional objectives. Each trainee had seen less than 20 families and had been rated by his/her supervisor as a beginner. The eight therapists in the supervisor condition-group had each seen over 100 families and some had been rated by their colleagues as advanced. Those without ratings did not participate in the outcome study and were among the most senior family therapists at McMaster. Each had treated over 250 cases. The groups were composed of approximately half psychiatrists (or residents) and half masters-level social workers or therapists. The therapists in the trainee condition-group were by and large supervised by therapists in the supervisor condition-group. Participation of all therapists in the study was voluntary. The 16 therapists in the study comprised over half of the clinical staff at the Clinic.

The 16 cases were intact Caucasian families with a nonpsychotic child as the identified patient. Most were referred with some kind of "behavior problem." At least both parents and the identified patient were present for the interview.

Coding and Sampling   In this study, three five-minute excerpts were selected from each therapist's one-hour-long videotape. At the time of this study (1974–75) there was virtually no scientific evidence to guide us in our search for the proper amount of material to sample from a session in order to get a representative picture of the therapist's behavior throughout that session. The decision to sample 15 minutes was a compromise between the desire to sample as much as possible and the realities of coder time, energy, and experimenter resources.

To get as representative a picture as possible, samples were selected from fixed points in the first, second, and third, thirds of each tape. The coders coded from videotape, attending primarily to the audio portion and using video to clarify linguistic meaning.

The two coders were intermediate-level family therapists and full-time staff members at the Chedoke Centre. They had participated in the development of the FTBS and had piloted all of the prior systems and versions of the FTBS. Although they knew many of the therapist subjects, they were blind to the specific research hypotheses and the subjects' experience/expertise ratings.

Unfortunately, it is impossible to say how much training a coder needs to use the FTBS, because the two coders from the McMaster Study were trained on the prior versions. They spent over a year working in weekly and biweekly meetings (1–3 hours) learning and applying the FTBS and its predecessors. On the final FTBS, the coders were trained on videotapes in the McMaster library, until they attained an interrater reliability of at least .75 (unadjusted proportion of agreement) on three consecutive samples from three different tapes of different therapists.

In the study, to reduce the likelihood of one coder's response bias inordinately influencing the results, each coder rated approximately half the data (which totalled 48 five-minute segments) and coded at least one segment from each therapist–subject's tape. Each coder rated the same number of first, second, and third segments and the same number of segments from each condition-group.

FTBS Reliability Procedures and Findings Out of the 48 segments, the two coders rated six in common for the interrater reliability check. Three were taken from each condition-group and two were taken from each segment location. Coding assignments were given independently to each coder, and both coders were blind about which segments they coded in common. For the intrarater check, each coder rated two additional segments twice, one from each condition-group.

The mean interrater percentage of agreement (POA) was .58, with a range of .41 to .90. Using a more conservative and sophisticated statistic (Cohen's 1960 k), the mean interrater k was .50, with a range of .29 to .80. It differed from chance at less than the .001 level. As expected, the intrarater reliabilities were higher: mean POA was .69 and the overall k was .635. These results indicated that the FTBS had at least adequate coder reliability.

Another very interesting finding emerged in the reliability analysis. To compute Cohen's k, a 19×19 reliability matrix must be constructed that indicates the exact "location" of each coder hit and miss. We added a twentieth category to this matrix that covered *unitization errors*—situations in which one coder coded a statement that the other coder did not code or treat as a distinct scoring unit. This matrix revealed that about a third of the coder misses involved unitization errors. When these were deleted from the reliability index, k increased from .50 to .60.

Differentiating unitization from straight categorization errors allowed us to evaluate the cost of the flexible scoring unit—one third more errors and a significant drop in reliability. This finding was to have a substantial impact on the development of the scoring procedure for the FTCS.

FTBS Validity Findings The validity analysis involved one independent variable (trainee vs. supervisor condition-group) and 21 dependent variables. Nineteen of the dependent variables were the code categories from the FTBS, whereas the other two were formal variables—therapist Activity Level (number of statements per five-minute summarizing unit) and Intervention Range (number of code categories used per unit). Despite the fact that there were 21 dependent variables, only 16 of them were "active." An active variable carried a directional research hypothesis that predicted a significant difference between the condition-groups. The five "passive" code categories did not carry any research hypotheses in this study, but were included in the data analysis due to the exploratory nature of the research.

The validity results are presented in Table 7-5. The findings supported over 40% of

Table 7-5   FTBS Validity Results

Variables	Hypothesis	Mean Trainee (T) Proportion	Mean Supervisor (S) Proportion	t
Support (S)	S > T	.021	.035	1.59*
Refocus (R)	S > T	.002	.018	2.01†
Functional Relationship (FR)	S > T	.000	.04	3.26‡
Affect-Communication (AC)	S > T	.026	.045	1.66*
Sequence-Now (SN)	S > T	.009	.036	2.173†
Behavior-Now (BN)	S > T	.041	.10	3.09‡
Individual Cognition-Opinion (ICO)	T > S	.29	.196	2.55†

*$p < .10$(df14).
†$p < .05$ (df14).
‡$p < .01$(df14).

the 16 research hypotheses (at least at the .05 level of significance). The supervisor–therapists, in comparison to the trainees,

> were more active, used a wider range of interventions, were more interpretive (FR) and supportive (S), maintained a greater explicit topic focus (R), dealt more with behaviors that occurred in the here-and-now (BN and SN), focused more on sequences of behavior (SN) and dealt more with the communication of feelings between family members (AC). In contrast, the trainee–therapists dealt more with the nonrelational thoughts and opinions of the individual family members (ICO). (Pinsof, 1979, p. 459)

The relative behavioral profiles of the two condition groups are in accord with the profiles delineated by Cleghorn and Levin's (1973) instructional objectives. Overall, the results of the McMaster Study strongly supported the discriminant validity of the FTBS. The scale was able to discriminate various predicted and clinically relevant differences in therapist verbal behavior between two extreme condition-groups within one school of family therapy (the McMaster Model).

The Family Therapist Coding System (FTCS)

The FTBS and the McMaster Study (1974–75) were transitional evaluation points in the system development process. They revealed that the coding system suffered from a number of methodological and substantive problems. After the McMaster Study, the system development process continued and pursued these problems, eventually culminating five years later in the creation of the Family Therapist Coding System (FTCS) (Pinsof, 1980).

The FTCS was the first coding system explicitly designed to describe and differentiate specific, clinically relevant verbal behaviors of family therapists from various theoretical orientations. It consists of nine nominal scales (see Table 7-6 for scale and code category headings); each tap a distinct aspect or dimension of the therapist's verbal

Table 7-6 Family Therapist Coding System (FTCS) Scale and Code Category Headings

Topic—1

1. Conation (CON)

2. Emotion
   a. Positive (PE)
   b. Negative (NE)
   c. Nonspecific (NSE)

3. Behavior
   a. Positive (PB)
   b. Negative (NB)
   c. Spatial (SB)
   d. Nonverbal (NVB)
   e. Verbal (VB)
   f. Nonspecific (NSB)

4. Cognition
   a. Positive (PC)
   b. Negative (NVC)
   c. Neutral (NLC)

5. Somatic–Physical (SP)

6. Experience (EX)

7. Fact (F)

Intervention—2

1. Disagree/Disapprove (DD)

2. Self-Disclosure (SD)

3. Refocus (R)

4. Direction (DN)

5. Interpretation
   a. Transposition (TR)
   b. Etiology–Motivation (EM)

6. Support (S)

7. Identification
   a. Boundary–Rules (BR)
   b. Expectation (EN)
   c. Process (PR)
   d. Communication (C)
   e. Problem (PM)
   f. Status (ST)

Temporal Orientation—3

1. Now (N)

2. Current (CR)

3. Future (F)

4. Past (P)

5. Atemporal (AT)

To Whom—4

1. Cotherapist (CT)

2. Family (FM)

3. Parent–Child (PC)

4. Couple–Parents (CP)

5. Wife–Mother (WM)

6. Husband–Father (HF)

7. Children (C+)

8. Child 1 (C1)

9. Child 1 (C2)

10. Nonspecific (NS)

Interpersonal Structure—5

1. Group (G)

2. Triadic (TC)

3. Dyadic (DC)

4. Monadic (MC)

5. Topic (T)

System Membership—6

1. Inclusive (INC)

2. Therapy (TY)

3. Cross-Generational (CG)

4. Family of Origin
   a. Therapist (TFO)
   b. Cross-Generational (CFO)
   c. Marital (MFO)
   d. Parental (PFO)
   e. Sibling (SFO)
   f. Extended (EFO)
   g. Nonspecific (NFO)

5. Nuclear Family
   a. Therapist (TNF)
   b. Cross-Generational (CNF)
   c. Marital (MNF)
   d. Parental (PNF)
   e. Sibling (SNF)
   f. Extended (ENF)
   g. Nonspecific (NNF)

6. Other
   a. Therapist-Family (OTF)
   b. Therapist (OT)
   c. Family (OF)
   d. Other (O)

7. Topic (T)

Route—7

1. Indirect Target (IT)

2. Direct–Indirect (DI)

3. Indirect (I)

4. Direct (D)

Table 7-6   (*Continued*)

Grammatical Form—8	Event Relationship—9
1. Command (CD)	1. Cyclical (CY)
2. Question	2. Functional (FN)
a. Open (QO)	3. Incongruous (IN)
b. Closed (QC)	4. Temporal (T)
3. Label (L)	5. Multiple (M)
	6. Isolate (IS)

behavior. The scales can be used collectively, individually, or in various combinations to test a wide variety of clinical hypotheses about the verbal behavior of family and individual psychotherapists. However, the information derived from each scale is most meaningful in the context of the information derived from the other scales. Thus, the FTCS constitutes a *system*. The scales function synergistically: The information from them as a group exceeds the sum of the information from them individually. The complete system—all nine scales—was designed explicitly to provide a highly specific and clinically meaningful gestalt or picture of therapist verbal behavior.

FTCS Scales—Resolving the Multidimensionality Problem

One of the major methodological and theoretical problems with the FTBS was that the scale was inconsistently and ambiguously multidimensional. Some of the code categories, like Support (S) (e.g., "The two of you are really working very hard in therapy") captured a single dimension or aspect of the therapist's behavior. Other FTBS codes like Affect-Now (AN) (e.g., "How are you feeling right now?") captured two dimensions: the topic area addressed in the intervention (Affect) and its temporal orientation (Now). Some codes, like Other-Affect Statement (OAS) (e.g., "How do you think your wife felt about what you just said?") even addressed three dimensions: topic area (Affect), the interpersonal structure of the intervention (dyadic), and the way in which the therapist routed the intervention (talking to one person, the *other*, about another person, the *target*).

In working with the FTBS, it became apparent that at least each of the dimensions addressed by the scale could be applied to every intervention. In other words, every intervention had a temporal orientation, a topic focus, a route, etc. It also became apparent that a single-scale coding system could never adequately and consistently account for multiple dimensions of therapist interventions. Thus, we decided to shift from a single- to a multiple-scale coding system. Each of the nine FTCS scales targets a different, theoretically relevant aspect or dimension of (family) therapist verbal behavior. The scales are briefly defined below. More extensive definitions are available in the *FTCS Coding Manual* (Pinsof, 1980).

1. The Topic Scale involves 16 nominal code categories that deal with the topic or content areas addressed by the therapist's intervention. Topics addressed include Positive Emotion (PE), Negative Cognition (NC) (disagreement), and Spatial Behavior (SB).

2. The Intervention Scale includes 13 nominal code categories that target the intention, purpose, or function of the therapist's intervention. Typical Intervention code categories are Self-Disclosure (SD), Direction (DN), and Transposition–Interpretation (TR).

3. The Temporal Orientation Scale consists of five nominal code categories that concern the "tense" or time period within which the principle action addressed in the intervention takes place. Code category examples are Now (N), Past (P), and Future (F).

4. The To Whom Scale consists of ten nominal code categories that identify the target or person(s) to whom the therapist is talking. Typical codes are Cotherapist (CT), Couple–Parents (CP), and Husband–Father (HF).

5. The Interpersonal Structure Scale includes five nominal code categories that deal with the structure of the relational or personal system targeted by the therapist's intervention. Common code categories are Triadic (TC), Monadic (MC), and Group (G).

6. The System Membership Scale consists of 22 nominal code categories that identify the primary interpersonal systems to which the people mentioned in the therapist's intervention belong. Exemplary code categories are Family-of-Origin–Parental (PFO), Nuclear-Family–Marital (MNF), and Nuclear-Family–Sibling (SNF).

7. The Route Scale involves four nominal code categories that identify the "routing" (or manner of approach) of the therapist's intervention. This refers to the distinction between *to whom* the therapist is talking (the target) and *about whom* the therapist is talking (the subject). Typical Route codes are Direct (D), Indirect (I), and Indirect-Target (IT).

8. The Grammatical Form Scale includes four nominal code categories that identify the grammatical form of the therapist's intervention. Code category examples include Question–Open (QO), Question–Closed (QC), and Command (CD).

9. The Event Relationship Scale consists of six nominal code categories in an ordinal (highest to lowest) relationship that define the nature and level of complexity of the relationship between the events mentioned in the therapist's intervention. Typical code categories are Cyclical (CY), Temporal (T), and Isolate (IS).

Development Process and Criteria

Five criteria were used explicitly to shape the development of the FTCS. They were applied throughout the development process to evaluate each new version of the FTCS. This process primarily occurred within a small group (three to six people at any one time) that met on a biweekly basis for about four years (1976–80). The composition of the group changed at several points during that time period and consisted of various colleagues and graduate students interested in family therapy and process research.

Typically, a new version of the FTCS would be typed and applied to several different transcripts of well-known family therapists. Insofar as that version failed to meet the development criteria, the group would modify it. When a number of significant changes had occurred, the manual would be retyped and the new version of the coding system would be applied to expert transcripts. We went through at least five different versions of the system until the final version emerged. Scales and code categories were added, modified, and occasionally deleted from the system. The development process stopped once we felt that the system basically (more often than not) satisfied the five criteria described below.

Specificity   The first and most basic criterion that permeated all aspects of the development of the FTCS was specificity. Perhaps more than any other term, specificity has become the primary watchword of the field of psychotherapy research since the late 1960s. It refers to the need for researchers to specify and pinpoint the exact variables they are attempting to investigate. The predominant generic issue in psychotherapy research has come to be known as the specificity question—"What are the specific effects of specific interventions by specified therapists upon specific symptoms or patient types?" (Bergin, 1971, p. 246).

As a development criterion for the FTCS, specificity functioned in two ways. The first, *coder specificity*, concerns the researcher's need to know exactly what *cues* the raters used to make their code category decision. Many coding systems require a high-level rater decision that involves abstracting out of a complex of variables a subset that pertains to the particular variables or dimensions tapped by the scale in question. For instance, deciding whether telling a couple to avoid intimacy between now and the next session is a paradoxical directive or a genuine recommendation, is a very complex decision that requires the coder to use many contextual cues. A coding system that requires this type of coding decision makes it very hard to determine the exact cues the coders used.

Initially, I became aware of this problem when I was learning to use the Truax and Carkhuff scales. Therapists were more likely to receive a higher score on the Accurate Empathy (AE) Scale if they used emotion words and mild profanity (e.g., damn, darn, etc.). Feeling and profane words seemed to be among the primary cues that raters used to make their AE ratings. "Seemed to be" is the key phrase in this regard, because with systems that require such high-level decisions, it is impossible to know with adequate specificity exactly what cues the raters actually used to make their ratings. The higher the level of coder inference required by a scale, the lower the degree of coder specificity. In the service of knowing what our coders were actually rating, we attempted to make the FTCS scales as specific and noninferential as possible.

The second function is *consumer specificity*. This refers to the research consumer's ability to know what actually occurred in the process of therapy. We wanted the FTCS to be able to provide the research consumer with a very specific image or sense of the therapist's verbal behavior. For instance, the original Dollard and Auld (1959) coding system used by Postner *et al*. (1971) to study family therapy broke therapist behavior into two categories: Drive and Interpretation. One of the key problems with such molar, nonspecific categories is that it is virtually impossible to know what any specific Drive or Interpretation code assignment refers to. The categories cover so much verbal territory that it is impossible to get a clear picture of any specific piece of the terrain. We wanted the FTCS to provide the research consumer with a specific sense of the therapist's verbal behavior.

The problem created by attempting to maximize coder and consumer specificity with the FTCS is that once behavior gets broken down into small, specific bits, it is very hard to recreate a meaningful picture of what actually occurred in the therapy. It is very difficult to put humpty-dumpty back together again after having broken him into very specific pieces. The critical methodological question is: "Can the parts be reassembled to create a clinically meaningful whole?" This problem forced us to consider the next development criterion—reconstructivity.

Reconstructivity   The second criterion, new to the field of psychotherapy process research, is reconstructivity. It refers to the ability of a coding system to permit clinically meaningful reconstruction of therapeutic processes and events from the specific code data. Most process research systems yield simple numbers or codes that do not provide the researcher and/or research consumer with a veridical sense or picture of what actually occurred within the therapy session. Reconstructivity is designed to increase the meaningfulness and relevance of process research and process data.

In terms of the FTCS, reconstructivity was used throughout the system development process to determine the final number of scales or dimensions necessary to capture meaningfully the therapist's intervention. Reconstructivity is ultimately an intuitive criterion. In developing the FTCS, we continually applied the system in its various incarnations to transcripts of renowned family and marital therapists from a wide variety of theoretical orientations. Eventually, the nine scales were sufficient to satisfy our sense of clinical meaning and relevance. The coded data reflected what seemed to be the relevant aspects of the transcripts we analyzed. Through this process, the nine scales came to represent what we considered to be the relevant dimensions of family therapist verbal behavior.

The FTCS permits clinically meaningful reconstruction of many, if not most, therapist interventions with the nine scales that comprise the final system. For example, the therapist intervention, ''Why don't you express your anger to your wife right now?'' would be coded NE/DN/N/HF/DC/MNF/D/QO/IS. From these codes we can reconstruct that the therapist directly (D=Direct from the Route Scale) used an open question (QO from the Grammatical Form Scale) to direct (DN=Direction from the Intervention Scale) the husband (HF=Husband–Father from the To Whom Scale) in regard to angry or negative feelings (NE=Negative Emotion from the Topic Scale) between he and his wife (MNF=Marital-Nuclear Family from the System Membership Scale and DC=Dyadic from the Interpersonal Structure Scale) within the current session (N=Now from the Temporal Orientation Scale). These code data also show that the therapist was dealing with an isolated event (IS=Isolate from the Event Relationship Scale) as opposed to multiple events related in various ways.

Reconstructivity is designed to operationalize the systemic or synergistic quality of the FTCS by creating a clinically meaningful gestalt from distinct bits of coded information. However, reconstructivity is always partial. Certain therapist styles and interventions seem to be more amenable to reconstruction with the FTCS than others. No feasible coding system will ever permit complete reconstruction of all possible interventions. However, maximizing the reconstructivity of a coding system can only increase its utility and the meaningfulness of the data it generates.

Universality   The FTBS was designed to identify clinically relevant verbal behaviors of short-term problem-oriented family therapists at McMaster. After the McMaster FTBS study it became apparent that the field of family therapy research needed a process instrument that would permit within- and across-school studies and that the FTBS was too parochial for that task. This conclusion was predicated upon the awareness that however sophisticated a within-school process instrument, it would never provide for across-school comparisons and the necessary development of a scientific data base. If the field of process research and particularly family therapy process research is to proceed, results of one study must be able to be compared with the results of another study from a different orientation. For this to occur, the field required a common language process system that would permit identification of the unique and common features of the various family therapy schools.

To meet this need, the FTCS was universalized. It was created to identify and differentiate clinically relevant verbal behaviors of a wide variety of family therapists with theoretically divergent orientations. The FTCS was designed to delineate the distinct and common features of the various schools of family therapy.

Universality was incorporated into the FTCS theoretically and pragmatically. During system development, scales and code categories were created to reflect the major clinical theories and theorists within the family therapy field (Ackerman, 1958, 1966; Alexander and Barton, 1976; Alexander and Parsons, 1982; Bowen, 1978; Haley, 1971, 1976; Minuchin, 1974; Minuchin, Rosman, and Baker, 1978; Patterson, 1976; Paul and Paul, 1975; Satir, 1967; Stierlin, 1977; Watzlawick, Weakland, and Fisch, 1974). Most of the code categories from the FTBS, based on the McMaster model of short-term, problem-oriented family therapy (Cleghorn and Levin, 1973; Epstein and Bishop, 1973, 1981) were also integrated into the FTCS.

Universality was incorporated pragmatically by "pushing" the FTCS during pilot coding sessions. This involved refining and extending the FTCS to identify characteristic interventions of a number of well-known family therapists. Code categories and scales were created or modified to accommodate and differentiate the unique intervention characteristics (styles) of the various expert therapists. For instance, the Therapist–Nuclear Family (TNF) category of the System Membership Scale deals with statements in which the therapist explicitly mentions himself ("I" or "me") and any subsystem of the nuclear family ("You" or "he/she"). It was created to identify the personal, "I/you" quality of many advanced therapists' style, apparent in interventions like: "Don't tell me you aren't mad" (Minuchin, 1974, p. 177).

Most distinctive interventions of particular family therapy orientations are not captured with single code categories, but rather with various combinations of codes from several FTCS scales. For instance, no single scale or code category deals with interventions such as prescribing or predicting the symptom (Haley, 1976; Weeks and L'Abate, 1982). Prescribing the symptom (e.g., "This week, I think the two of you should probably have at least one fight") would generally be captured with the following code configuration: NB = Negative Behavior from the Topic Scale; DN = Direction from the Intervention Scale; and F = Future from the Temporal Orientation Scale. Most behavioral symptom prescriptions like this would be picked up with the NB/DN/F combination, which indicates directions for negative behavior in the future. In contrast, predicting the symptom, a less directive intervention (e.g., "The two of you may have to get into a fight this week"), would be picked up with a slightly different code combination: NB from the Topic Scale; ST = Status from the Identification subscale of the Intervention Scale; and F from the Temporal Orientation Scale, which indicates the identification of negative or maladaptive behavior in the future.

The full range of family therapist verbal behavior across all the schools of family therapy incorporates most interventions that occur within the primary schools of individual therapist verbal behavior. Thus, the attempt to universalize the FTCS in regard to the full spectrum of family therapist verbal behavior automatically made the system capable of describing many distinctive individual therapist verbal behaviors. For instance, a psychoanalytic intervention like the negative transference interpretation, "You feel I'm blaming you for your problems the way your father did," would be captured with the following code combination: NB = Negative Behavior from the Topic Scale; TR = Transposition from the Interpretation subscale of the Intervention Scale; TC = Triadic from the Interpersonal Structure Scale; and TFO = Therapist from the Family of Origin subscale of the System Membership Scale. This code combination indicates a triadic transferential interpretation involving at least the therapist and the patient's family of origin that deals with some type of maladaptive behavior.

Exhaustiveness The fourth criterion used to develop the FTCS was exhaustiveness. This criterion, which ensures that every intelligible intervention is coded into a meaningful category on each scale, was also used in the development of the FTBS and has been described above.

Novice–Expert Discrimination The fifth and last explicit criterion that shaped the development of the FTCS was also central to the development of the FTBS. It concerns the coding system's ability to differentiate predicted differences in the verbal behavior of expert and novice family therapists. In the development of the FTBS and the FTCS, the novice–expert discrimination functioned as the minimal validity criterion. If the coding system was unable to differentiate the behavior of beginners and advanced therapists, it is unlikely that the system would be capable of performing the more subtle tasks involved in discriminating therapists from different orientations or in linking process to outcome variables.

In creating the FTCS, this criterion was operationalized in the following way. As a scale, subscale, or specific code category was created, it was included in the final version of the FTCS if it, alone or in conjunction with other categories or scales, appeared likely to discriminate predicted differences in the in-therapy verbal behavior of expert and novice family therapists. Not all of the categories were intended to discriminate differences in an aggregate (frequency or proportion) analysis dealing with the "what" or "how much" of therapist verbal behavior. Many of the code categories in the FTCS are only likely to pick up novice–expert differences in a sequential analysis that deals both with the "what" and "when" of family therapist behavior.

Specifically, a scale or category remained in the FTCS if the system development group could develop at least one plausible and relevant hypothesis about the behavioral characteristic in question. That hypothesis could be an aggregate or sequential hypothesis, but it had to pertain to the expert–novice distinction. For instance, we included the Therapist–Nuclear Family (TNF) category in the System Membership Scale because we thought that the use of self implicit in the more personal style tapped by that category would characterize advanced, but not beginning, family therapists.

The novice–expert distinction actually came to represent over time a "good therapist/ bad therapist" distinction. What we came to attribute to beginners inevitably represented what we thought was poor therapy. In contrast, what we attributed to advanced expert therapists was clearly what we considered to be good therapy. Thus, the FTCS was not only developed to differentiate beginning and advanced therapists, but also to differentiate good or successful and poor or unsuccessful therapists. A code category was included if we thought the behavior or behavioral characteristic it targeted was likely at some point in therapy to affect the progress or outcome of therapy.

A related point is that the coding system was clearly the product of our theory of therapy. In essence, the coding system represented our delineation of the factors in the therapist's verbal behavior that we thought were likely to affect the progress or outcome of treatment. The problem with this situation is that our micro process–outcome theory was and still is largely implicit. This problem characterizes not only the work of our group, but also the work of all family therapists and most psychotherapists in general. By and large the field of psychotherapy, and the family therapy field in particular, lacks an explicit, specific, and behaviorally focused micro-theory (Greenberg and Pinsof, this volume; Pinsof, 1981).

The result of this situation is not necessarily negative. It means that the FTCS was designed to test a very wide variety of clinical hypotheses about effective family therapist verbal behavior. These hypotheses are based on a largely implicit theoretical base that was tied empirically, in the development process, to published transcripts of renowned family therapists in action. Each code category in the FTCS can be used individually or in conjunction with other categories to test one or more clinically relevant hypotheses about family therapist verbal behaviors. The hypotheses are not built into the code category as is the case with most ordinal scales that merge description and evaluation. Rather, each code category can be used to test one or more hypotheses without deciding in advance the direction or nature of results. For instance, the Disagree/Disapprove (DD) code category of the Intervention Scale was designed to test hypotheses about the effect of therapist disagreement and disapproval. The category in itself is neutral as to the value of disagreement/disapproval. It is designed solely to identify its occurrence and is based, in fact, on a theory that asserts that disagreement/disapproval can be beneficial in certain contexts and disastrous in others.

Criteria Summary   The five abovementioned criteria have been presented independently. In developing the FTCS, they were not used independently, but functioned as a group to create a partially explicit image of the type of coding system we wanted to create. The FTCS approximates that image and is a compromise between the ideal and the practical. It represents our best effort to create a highly specific coding system that can meaningfully depict and test a wide variety of aggregate and sequential hypotheses about the verbal behavior of family (and individual) therapists from various theoretical orientations.

Coding Procedure

Following Kiesler's (1973) tripartite distinction, the FTCS uses three hierarchically integrated process units: the scoring unit, the contextual unit, and the summarizing unit.

The Scoring Units   The scoring unit "is the entity that is actually coded and counted" (Kiesler, 1973, p. 38). The McMaster FTBS Study taught us that the use of the flexible scoring unit that combined unitization and categorization had an appreciable impact on the reliability of the coding system—one third more errors and a considerable drop in reliability. Therefore, we decided to separate unitization and categorization with the FTCS. This resulted in a two-step coding process and the use of a fixed scoring unit. Initially, the data are unitized into the fixed scoring units. Subsequently, the fixed scoring units are categorized with the FTCS. The decision to move to a fixed scoring unit had a variety of methodological implications.

The first implication was that we would have to shift from videotape, which the FTBS used, to typed *transcripts* as the basic data format. In coding verbal behavior, the researcher can choose one of three data formats: videotape, audiotape, or transcripts. It is much more time-consuming and costly to break tape into fixed units, particularly when dealing with thousands of scoring units. Once the initial costs of transcription are encompassed, transcripts permit rapid and easy identification of fixed units.

Additionally, as I have pointed out elsewhere (Pinsof, 1981), transcripts permit the greatest degree of channel isolation when the coding system targets verbal behavior. The transcript presents only the therapist's words and deletes the potentially informative *and* confounding data from kinesic and/or paralinguistic channels present in video and audiotape data formats. This means that the researcher can be sure that the coder is only using verbal cues. When coding verbal behavior from video or audiotape, the coder may base particular ratings on the kinesic or paralinguistic cues as well on the primary verbal cues. Channel isolation increases coder specificity at the same time that it decreases the coder's access to information that might help the coder make a more veridical rating. This decision exemplifies the methodological trade-offs that researchers continually confront in process research.

The second implication of the fixed unit decision was that it forced us to use multiple, hierarchically integrated scoring units of different sizes. The flexible FTBS scoring unit was predicated upon the awareness that all interventions do not come in the same-size package. It also implicitly recognized the fact that different process variables are tapped ideally by scoring units of different sizes. When we started working with the first, multiscale versions of the FTCS, we very quickly realized that there was no single scoring unit that did proper justice to each and every FTCS scale.

For instance, the Topic Scale seemed to focus on the smallest scoring unit. We found that the therapist could deal with multiple topic areas (emotion, facts, cognitions, behaviors, etc.) in a single sentence. If we wanted to identify the topic areas addressed by the therapist, we needed to find a scoring unit smaller than the sentence that fit that scale. In contrast, the Event Relationship Scale seemed to deal with the largest scoring unit. Therapists typically had to use more than one sentence to make an intervention that would fall into the Cyclical (CY) category. Relating multiple events in a cyclical pattern usually requires, at the very least, a compound sentence.

In working with the early versions of the FTCS, three different, hierarchically integrated scoring units emerged that appeared to be capable of appropriately capturing the variables tapped by the different scales. The smallest, which we called the *Verb Unit*, fits the first scale in the FTCS, the Topic Scale. Working with the Topic Scale, the coder assigns a code to each and every verb unit in the therapist's speech. A verb unit "expresses or indicates an action, condition–state or process, and refers to a verb, a verb phrase . . . and verbals" (Pinsof, 1980, p. 9).

On the transcript, therapist speeches are broken into verb units by underlining. When a verb and its auxiliary words are separated, each part of the verb unit is underlined and connected with a line. The unitizing procedure for delineating verb units is illustrated in the two transcripted examples in the Appendix to this chapter. When the verb unit does not clearly tap a Topic Scale category, as is usually the case with verbs like "to be" ("is," "am," etc.), the associated subject, object, or complement is used to clarify the topic referent. For instance, "You *are* very angry at your husband," would be coded as Negative Emotion (NE) on the Topic Scale.

The next seven scales on the FTCS—Intervention, Temporal Orientation, To Whom, Interpersonal Structure, System Membership, Route, and Grammatical Form—code the intermediate-size scoring unit of the FTCS—the *Main Clause Unit*. This unit contains a main clause and its attendant subordinate clauses. We found that the main clause, which consists of a subject and at least one verb, constituted the smallest meaningful linguistic unit that can stand alone. This unit also covers condensed or elliptical clauses or phrases in which the subject and/or the verb are not explicit (e.g., "Stop," "Impossible," etc.). On the transcript, main clause units are delineated with beginning and ending slashes (/). A main clause contains one or more verb units. Main clauses are demarcated throughout the transcripts in the Appendix.

The ninth and last scale in the FTCS, Event Relationship, uses the most molar scoring unit, the *Speech Unit*—everything that the therapist says between two successive utterances by other participants (family members of co-therapists). The speech consists of at least one main-clause unit and one verb unit. Of the three scoring units, the speech is the most easily identified. In most cases, the transcriber identifies the speech in the transcription process, although we found that speech identification is not always such a hard-and-fast process. Occasionally, it is even difficult for coders to determine whether two speeches, punctuated by a brief or simultaneous patient speech, constitute the same or separate speeches, particularly, when the patient speech interrupts an ongoing therapist speech (or main clause unit).

The transcript is broken into these three scoring units by the unitizer. As well as marking the transcript appropriately, the unitizer numbers each of the speeches within the sample to be coded. Thus, the FTCS coder receives a preunitized transcript that removes the necessity for any decisions relating to unitization. The coder's sole task is categorization.

The Contextual Unit   The contextual unit refers to that portion of transcript that can be considered in rating any particular therapist intervention (Kiesler, 1973, p. 38). For the FTCS, the contextual unit consists of the entire sample that the coder rates at any one time. The size of this sample is determined by the needs of the particular study. Typical sample sizes range from five to twenty minutes of audiotape time, which generate varying numbers of transcript pages depending on the amount of verbal activity in the sample. The transcript includes all intelligible therapist and patient statements. All statements within the sample can be considered in making any particular rating.

The contextual unit is equivalent to what might be called the *sampling unit*. The sampling unit is sampled or selected from the unit about which conclusions will be drawn. For instance, if the experimenter is interested in testing hypotheses about the first, middle, and last thirds of therapy sessions, the sampling unit might be five minutes from each third of the interview.

The Summarizing Unit   The summarizing unit, the unit to which summarizing statistics are applied and about which conclusions can be drawn, is not determined by the FTCS. It is a function completely of the goals of the particular study. If the experimenter wants to test hypotheses about portions of an interview, then the summarizing unit will most likely be a quarter or a third of an interview. In contrast, if the experimenter is primarily testing hypotheses about entire interviews, then the summarizing unit will be the whole interview.

It is important to distinguish between the sampling/contextual unit and summarizing units. In certain studies, they may be identical, whereas in others they will differ. For instance, in one study, the experimenter may sample five minutes from each third of an interview, but make conclusions about each third. In another study, the experimenter might sample (code) the whole third and draw conclusions about each third. In the former situation, the sampling and summarizing units are distinct, whereas in the latter they are identical. Once again, the FTCS does not dictate the size of either the sampling or summarizing units. They are determined by the goals of the particular study and the resources (money, time, available coders, etc.) of the experimenter.

Code Assignment Rule and Priorities   The FTCS code-assignment rule specifies that a scoring unit receives only one code from each appropriate scale. The code categories on each scale are mutually exclusive. However, frequently a particular scoring unit may be codable in more than one category on a scale. For instance, the therapist statement, "You're just avoiding really dealing with your sadness by yelling at your wife," could be coded in the Disagree–Disapprove (DD) and Interpretation–Transposition (TR) categories of the Intervention Scale. If the contextual unit does not indicate clearly that the intervention is either a DD or a TR, the coder needs some framework for selecting one code category.

To resolve dilemmas like this, which we also encountered and attempted to address with the FTBS (see the sections on Code Conflicts and Ambiguity Conflicts above), we created a priority structure. That structure is reflected in the layout and order of presentation of the code categories of each scale (see Table 6). A category takes priority over all subsequently presented codes on a scale. In terms of layout, all categories with a lower number or letter (a=lowest; z=highest) predominate over all categories with higher ones. Thus, the example presented above would be coded into the DD category if the context did not clearly indicate otherwise, because DD comes before and predominates over TR.

This priority structure is based on two related criteria: conceptual complexity and specificity. More specific, descriptive and informative categories (interventions) take priority over lesser ones. Similarly, more conceptually sophisticated and complex interventions predominate over simpler, more mundane interventions. A third criterion, hard to distinguish from the first two, might be termed "salience" or "unusualness." For instance, DD and TR probably do not differ appreciably in terms of descriptiveness and complexity, but we felt that from the patient's perspective disagreement and disapproval would be more salient (stand out more) than the interpretation embedded in the intervention. We also felt that with most therapists, DD would be an unusual, low frequency intervention and we wanted to "skew" the coding system to pick it up whenever it occurred.

These criteria were used intuitively, in much the same way as the development criteria. They clearly reflect a variety of clinical/theoretical hypotheses about the importance and salience of different therapist interventions that may or may not be true. We have articulated the criteria, which are implicit in the priority structure, to make clear the biases of the coding system, not necessarily because we believe they are "right" or reflect "reality" more accurately.

Coding Process, Coder Status, and Training

In comparison to coders for other social-interaction or content-analysis systems, FTCS coders generally need to be very bright and clinically sophisticated. In terms of general intelligence, they need to be able to discriminate various, subtle differences between distinct types of verbal behaviors. More specifically, they need to be able to apply simultaneously all nine FTCS scales to the same transcript segment. This involves mentally jumping from one scale to another until each entire speech is coded on all nine scales. The scales are applied to the speech and the proper scoring units in the order in which they are presented in Table 6.

Coders can also code a transcript segment with just one scale at a time. This entails going over the same segment nine different times. We consider this single scale coding procedure to be unnecessarily time-consuming and in pilot testing also found it to be boring for the coders. Using all nine scales at the same time challenges the coder and seems to be more aesthetically satisfying—it gives the coder a greater sense of reconstructing or capturing a whole intervention, rather than abstracting a single, isolated dimension.

The FTCS also requires a clinically sophisticated coder. Coders do not need to be expert-level family therapists, but they definitely need some degree of basic familiarity with the key theories and theorists in the family therapy field. They also need to have a high degree of perceptual sensitivity in order to notice and properly code a wide variety of therapist styles and behaviors. Although not essential, being a native English speaker also seems to be helpful. Some of the coders we have worked with at various points, who were not native English speakers (Hispanics and Israelis), had difficulty making certain discriminations and understanding certain subtle behaviors. Extensive training as a family therapist can help to overcome this linguistic deficit.

In the various projects that we have done with the FTCS, we have used, typically, second and third year doctoral students in clinical and counseling psychology who were interested in process research and family therapy. All of them had some experience doing family therapy and were interested in the process of family therapy from an intellectual, scientific perspective as well as from a more clinical viewpoint.

Different coders require different amounts of training. We typically train to a criterion of interrater agreement between two raters of .75 (percentage of agreement). On the average this requires about 12 to 15 two-hour training sessions (once or twice a week) with approximately two to three hours of practice coding (homework) between sessions. During the first nine training sessions, a new scale is presented each week. Homework involves applying the scale presented at the previous session, as well as all the other scales that have been presented, to the practice transcript(s) for that week. Typically, the Interpersonal Structure Scale would be presented at the fifth or sixth session; for homework it would be applied to the practice transcript along with the Topic, Intervention, Temporal Orientation, and To Whom Scales. Transcripts are selected for homework from the published family therapy literature and should cover a wide variety of schools, styles within schools, presenting problems, and interpersonal configurations (dyads, triads, etc.).

Each practice session, after the first, begins with the trainer and coders going over part of a practice transcript. They should compare their codings and decide at each point of disagreement on a mutually acceptable code assignment. It usually is not feasible to try to go over all the homework; thus, selecting key segments is important. The second part of the training session usually involves discussion of the new scale and some preliminary practice coding with it. The last part entails handing out the practice transcripts for homework and discussing any conceptual or methodological problems with the system and scales. Ideally, to save time, the trainer or one of the coders should unitize the practice transcripts prior to the training session.

As training progresses, particularly during the last five or six training sessions, it is helpful to use the reliability matrix necessary to compute Cohen's k to help the coders identify the exact nature of their disagreements. Computation of k is probably not necessary during the practice sessions, although a formal reliability index helps the coders have an objective indicator of their progress. The simpler percentage of agreement statistic is sufficient for such feedback. The tremendous value of the matrix is that it lets everyone know exactly where the major coder disagreements are occurring and thereby permits the training session to focus on those disagreements. For instance, one coder may code certain interventions consistently as Now (N) on the Temporal Orientation Scale that another coder codes as Current (CR). The matrix will identify how often this occurs and will allow the trainer to focus the session on clarifying the disagreement.

Groups of coders can be trained together, but we have found that it is best to team them up in pairs that work together throughout training. The pairs need to be compared at points with each other and, of course, with the trainer in order to minimize the likelihood of a pair establishing their own *folie à deux*—a shared, reliable, and idiosyncratic understanding of the coding system. Competitiveness within and between pairs, up to a point, makes training fun and facilitates learning. Training is most effective the more it approximates serious play.

Research on the FTCS

We have used the complete FTCS in three studies. The first and primary methodological study applied it to the data from the McMaster FTBS Study. This will be referred to as the McMaster FTCS Study. The results of the second and third studies will be reported briefly. They used the same subjects and examined the training program at the Center for Family Studies/Family Institute of Chicago. They are referred to as the Training I and II Studies. The studies involved reliability and validity components. Additional research with the FTCS is beginning to be conducted by researchers outside of our research group at the Family Institute and will be discussed briefly below.

The McMaster FTCS Study

This study applied the FTCS to the 16 interviews from the McMaster FTBS Study as a basic test of the discriminant validity of the FTCS. It used the McMaster data in order to provide some sense of how the findings from the two coding systems—the FTBS and FTCS—related to each other. The use of new data would have been a discontinuous jump in the system development process.

The basic procedures, design, and subjects for this study were described above for the FTBS study. The primary differences between the two studies were that the FTCS study used the FTCS rather than the FTBS, the FTCS was applied to the entire interview (50–55 minutes) rather than three five-minute segments, and the data format was transcripts rather than videotape. Transcripts were necessary because they are the basic FTCS data format. The rationale for studying and coding whole sessions is discussed below.

Sampling and Coding Procedures   The first concern that led to the use of whole sessions was the low frequency of certain key process events—a perennial problem in process research. Certain interventions that are of great theoretical/clinical significance do not occur very often. For instance, most family therapists will not disapprove of family behavior or interpret the systemic function of symptomatic behavior more than once or twice during most sessions. Furthermore, such behaviors are less likely to occur during initial interviews. The research problem with these events is how to get a sufficient number to provide an adequate N for statistical analysis. For the discriminant validity analysis, our solution to this problem was to code all of the available data—all 16 complete interviews.

Although we wanted to focus on the whole session, we realized that it would be impossible for coders to code a whole interview in a reasonable period of time. Thus, we decided to break each interview into thirds, making the third the basic summarizing and contextual unit (the largest amount of data that could be considered in rating any particular intervention). A third covered about 18 to 20 minutes of real time and averaged 15 to 18 prepared transcript pages (see the transcript format in the Appendix). There were 48 (3×16) contextual or sampling units for the FTCS study.

Breaking the session into thirds, and coding each entire third, also meant that we could look at the way in which the therapist's verbal behavior changed over the course of the session. We could attempt to look at process patterns (changes over time) within initial sessions and test the capacity of the FTCS to make more subtle pattern distinctions.

The second concern that led to the decision to use whole sessions and segments was to provide an adequate statistical base for the reliability analysis. In the reliability analysis for the FTBS study, the low frequency problem was critically apparent. In that study, six five-minute segments (12.5%) of the total study data were coded in common for the interrater reliability check. Certain key code categories of the FTBS, like Refocus (statements in which the therapist explicitly refocuses the discussion on a previously identified topic) occurred only once in the reliability segments. Without a much larger reliability sample, it is impossible to even begin to evaluate the reliability of categories that target such low frequency events.

To minimize the effects of the low frequency problem in the FTCS reliability analysis, we overlapped a third of the data—sixteen 18- to 20-minute contextual units were coded in common by the two coders. In relation to the FTBS study, the FTCS study not only used ten more segments for the reliability analysis, but the use of whole sessions permitted the use of segments that were three to four times longer.

The last factor leading to the whole session/segment decision was the desire to determine the smallest amount of data to sample in order to obtain a representative picture of the whole interview. Process researchers have not addressed empirically the crucial question of how much to sample in order to obtain a representative picture of a session. Virtually all contextual and sampling units are selected on the basis of theoretical and pragmatic (time, personnel, and money) considerations. Sampling whole interviews meant that we could compare the data derived from progressively smaller segments with the data from the whole session in order to determine the exact point at which sample size changed the data profile. Additionally, whole sessions allowed us to examine samples from different points in the session to determine their relationship to each other and to the data from the complete interview. Such methodological research could help us identify the smallest (least expensive) representative contextual/sampling unit for future studies. Unfortunately, time and fiscal constraints have not yet allowed us to pursue this minimum sample size issue.

Coders and Coding Assignments   The two coders for the McMaster FTCS Study were advanced doctoral students in clinical (male) and counseling (female) psychology at Northwestern University. They were beginning-level family therapists and had worked as my research assistants for several years prior to coding the study data. Both had relatively extensive backgrounds in psychological research and were very interested in family therapy.

Coding assignments were done to reduce, if not eradicate, the likelihood of coder bias affecting the results. Each coder coded two-thirds (32) of the 48 segments (thirds) in the total data base. Each coder coded half of the data (24 segments) for the validity analysis plus eight additional segments that were part of the other coder's assignment for the reliability analysis. For the validity analysis, each coder coded at least one segment from each of the 16 tapes. Assignments for the validity and reliability analyses ensured that the coders coded equal numbers of first, second, and third segments, as well as equal numbers of segments from the beginner and advanced interviews. The coders were blind about the status of the therapist (advanced or beginner) they were coding.

The data were coded in four equal batches over a six-month period. Each batch contained four reliability segments so that the reliability index actually reflected the reliability with which the data were coded. The coders were blind as to which segments were for the validity and reliability analyses. The four batches contained equal numbers of first, second, and third segments from beginner and advanced sessions. Because the coding took place over such an extended period, when the coders handed in a batch of segments, I would meet with and show them the results of the analysis of the reliability segments in that batch. Using the k matrices, we would identify the exact nature of their disagreements and resolve them. These recalibration sessions were used to counteract what Patterson, Cobb, and Ray (1972) refer to as "coder drift." They brought the coders back together and also made sure their agreement corresponded with my understanding of the scales and code categories in question.

Reliability Results

The reliability index for the FTCS was Cohen's k, the most sophisticated and conservative statistic for computing the reliability of nominal scales. It adjusts for marginal (chance) rates of agreement and permits determination of the significance level of any k statistic. The interrater reliabilities of the nine FTCS scales are listed in Table 7-7.

The average (of the 16 reliability segments) k values of the nine scales ranged from a high of .92 for Grammatical Form to a low of .49 for Intervention. These two scales, respectively, also had the highest (.99) and lowest (.33) scores in the total sample of 144 (9 scales $\times$ 16 segments). All but one of the 144 scores was significant at $p < .001$. The mean k score for all the FTCS scales was .70.

The segment score that was not even significant at $p < .05$ was the .38 score for Event Relationship. A problem with that segment was that there were only 28 scoring units—the smallest number of speech units in any of the 16 segments. According to Cohen (1960), the assumption that k is normally distributed is questionable with such a small N, which makes the validity of the reliability index for that segment somewhat problematic.

Schwartz (1983) examined the effect of several factors on the reliability data from this study. He found no main or interactive effects for segment location. There were no significant differences in the reliability scores from first, second, and third segments on any of the FTCS scales. No main or interactive effects were found for the type of condition-group (advanced vs. beginner) for eight of the scales; however, a main effect was found for Temporal Orientation. Interrater agreement was greater ($p < .05$) for advanced therapists than beginners on Temporal Orientation.

Examination of the k reliability matrices revealed that the coders had an unusually large number of disagreements with a particular subset of Temporal Orientation code categories on the beginner segments. Eighty-nine percent of the disagreements involved interventions that one coder assigned to the Atemporal (AT) category that the other coder assigned to the Current (CR) category. When the data in these two categories were removed from the analysis, the differences between beginning and advanced condition-groups disappeared.

Of all the specific time categories in the Temporal Orientation Scale (Past, Now, Future, and Current), Current (CR) is the least specific. As such, it is the closest category to Atemporal. The level-of-experience results on the Temporal Orientation Scale suggest that there is a greater degree of ambiguity about time, particularly in terms of the delineation of activity within the current time period (recent past and future), in the

Table 7-7   Interrater Reliabilities (Cohen's *k*) of the FTCS Scales
(McMaster FTCS Study)

Scale	Average Index (*k*) from 16 Reliability Segments	*k* Range*
1. Topic	.70	.62–.82
2. Intervention	.49	.33–.71
3. Temporal Orientation	.64	.24–.86
4. To Whom	.74	.56–.89
5. Interpersonal Structure	.82	.72–.89
6. System Membership	.75	.65–.85
7. Route	.63	.53–.75
8. Grammatical Form	.92	.72–.99
9. Event Relationship	.64	.38–.87

*With one exception, all *k* values for the 144 (9×16) segments differed from chance at less that the .001 level of significance. The exception was the .38 score for the Event Relationship Scale on one segment, which was not even significant at the .05 level.

verbal behavior of beginners. It may well be that when advanced therapists target activity in the current time period, they add more explicit qualifiers (e.g., "recently," "these days") or specify the context (e.g., "The two of you are making a lot of progress in setting fair limits with Tom") in greater detail.

Schwartz (1983) also examined the effect of the level of scale inference on FTCS reliability. Two experienced FTCS raters, blind to the purposes of the study, rank ordered the nine FTCS scales in terms of the level of inference required to use each scale. Level of inference was defined as

> the extent to which coding decisions involve a process of reasoning about the therapist's verbal behavior in order to categorize it. The level of inference may be thought of as synonymous with the depth of cognitive processing. (Schwartz, 1983, p. 13).

The two raters' rank orderings of the scales on level of inference were compared with the scales' reliability rank order with Kendall's coefficient of concordance, *W*. The rankings were concordant at the .02 level of significance; the higher the rated level of inference, the lower the level of reliability. Both raters ranked Scale 2, Intervention, as requiring the highest level of inference.

The reliability results of the McMaster FTCS Study were encouraging and informative. The fact that virtually all of the reliability indices differed from chance levels at the .001 level, with a conservative statistic like *k*, demonstrates that the FTCS exceeds what Cohen considers the minimal reliability requirement for nominal scales. The location of the sampled reliability segment within the interview did not affect the reliability of any FTCS scale. With the exception of Temporal Orientation, the type of condition-group also did not affect scale reliability. The level of inference required to use an FTCS scale appeared to be inversely related to the reliability of that scale.

Validity Results

The discriminant validity analysis attempted two tasks: (1) to differentiate significant, clinically expected differences in the verbal behavior of the therapists in the two condition-groups, and (2) to identify, for the group of therapists as a whole (all 16) as well as for each of the subgroups, clinically meaningful patterns of behavior within the sessions. The first task pertains to the condition-group factor or variable, and the second task concerns the segment location (first third, second third, third third) or pattern factor. A third task looked at the interaction between the two major factors.

The discriminant validity analysis involved the use of log linear statistics on the frequencies with which the advanced and beginner condition-groups used each code category on each FTCS scale. For each code category there were six scores—the frequency of the category in each third of the interview for each of the two condition-groups. These six scores permitted the equivalent of a two-factor ANOVA with repeated measures on one factor. One factor was the condition-group (advanced vs. beginner); the other, the repeated measure factor, was segment–location (first, second, and third). The log linear analysis produces a main effect chi-square score (the equivalent of a main effect F ratio) for each factor as well as a chi-square for the interaction of the factors. The significant findings from the log linear analysis as well as the mean code category frequencies for each condition-group on each segment are presented in Table 7-8 and are discussed below separately for each scale.

As indicated in Table 8, there were many significant results. They must all be understood in light of the fact that the advanced therapists were significantly more active than the beginners and tended to have higher frequencies in most of the code categories. There has been an ongoing debate within process research as to the appropriateness of frequencies or proportions as the basic datum. Frequencies reveal how often a particular category of behavior occurred, whereas proportions reveal how much of the entire behavioral repertoire fell into that category. Frequencies are absolute; proportions are relative.

In analyzing these data, I wanted to conduct a backup to the primary log linear frequency analysis that examined proportions as well as frequencies. This analysis would wash out of the data the effects of the advanced therapists' higher activity level. Unfortunately, log linear statistics cannot be applied to proportional data. Thus, we decided to also analyze the data with the more conservative, conventional two-factor analysis of variance with repeated measures on one factor with proportions as the basic datum. The results of the proportion ANOVA are discussed in the presentation of the data for each scale.

Topic Scale No. 1 In terms of the condition-group factor in the log linear frequency analysis, the advanced therapists were significantly higher on every code category except Positive Behavior, Spatial Behavior, and Fact. In the proportion ANOVA, the only significant finding was that the advanced therapists attended more to Nonverbal Behavior. The relative picture that emerges from the major findings is that the therapists in the advanced condition-group, in contrast to the beginners, focused much more on negative emotions and behaviors, nonverbal behaviors, and disagreements (Negative Cognition) between family members.

The log linear analysis on the segment location factor revealed many significant findings. For the sake of simplicity and brevity, I will focus solely on Topic results that were significant at $p < .001$. In terms of Negative Emotion, the beginners addressed negative emotions most in the middle segment of the interview, whereas the advanced therapists focused on negative emotions most in the first third and decreased over the course of the interview. Not only did the advanced therapists address painful and distressing affects much more than beginners, they did so soon after they entered the interview.

In terms of the behavior categories on the Topic Scale, advanced and beginners focused on Positive Behavior primarily in the last third of the interview. The advanced therapists focused increasingly over the course of the interview on Negative Behavior, whereas the beginners maintained a fairly consistent focus over the whole session. Both beginners and advanced therapists focused primarily on Nonverbal Behavior in the first third and decreased over the course of the interview. Both beginning and advanced therapists focused most on Nonspecific Behavior in the last third of the interview. This finding is hard to interpret because the Nonspecific Behavior category is probably the broadest and most frequently used in the entire FTCS. It covers such a wide variety of behaviors that its specific meaning is difficult to determine.

For both condition-groups, the data reveal an increasing emphasis on behavior (positive, nonverbal, and nonspecific) as such over the course of the interview. For the advanced therapists, there is an additional emphasis on negative and maladaptive behaviors. A major condition-group difference that consistently emerges from the data is the advanced therapist's willingness to address negative effects and behaviors during the initial session. They do not hesitate to engage painful feelings and disagreements or shrink from labeling and working with maladaptive behaviors.

The Neutral Cognition category, which revealed a dipping and ascending pattern (lowest in the middle segment, highest in the last), is also hard to interpret. Like the Nonspecific Behavior category, Neutral Cognition is broadly defined, frequently used, and hard to interpret. These two categories come as close to "dump" categories as any in the entire system. They cover scoring units that do not fall in the more specific categories on the scale. Frequently coders would "dump" an intervention into one of these two categories when they could not find any other category in which to place it.

The last significant segment location finding on the Topic Scale concerns the Fact category. Both beginning and advanced therapists focused most on factual information during the last third of the session. This factual closing may reflect the establishing of contractual arrangements at the end of the initial session.

In terms of the ANOVA proportion analysis on the segment location factor, we found basic confirmation ($p < .05$) of the log linear findings on Negative Emotion, Nonspecific Emotion (which was only significant at the .004 level in the log linear analysis: middle segment high for both groups), Nonverbal Behavior, Nonspecific Behavior, and Fact.

Intervention Scale No. 2   The log linear analysis revealed that the advanced therapists disagreed/disapproved more (Disagree/Disapprove), explicitly refocused the discussion more (Refocus), interpreted the meaning and causes of behavior/experience more (Etiology–Motivation), identified the boundaries and rules about who does what and when more (Boundary–Rules), focused more on the process and sequence of behavior/experience (Process), explicitly focused on communication per se more (Communication), and spent more time identifying the status of various phenomena in regard to the categories of the Topic Scale (Status). The ANOVA revealed no significant findings on the Intervention Scale.

In terms of the segment location log linear analysis, the advanced condition-group was three times more disapproving/disagreeable (Disapprove/Disagree) in the middle of the interview than in either of the other thirds. In contrast, the beginners decreased

Table 7-8   McMaster Data (Log Linear on Frequencies)

Topic Scale

Category	Time	Means		Therapist Group		Time		Interaction	
		Beginning	Advanced	Chi Square	Probability	Chi Square	Probability	Chi Square	Probability
Conation	1	6.875	9.625	6.30	.012*	26.19	.000**	.89	.641
	2	6.125	8.250						
	3	11.625	13.375						
	mean	8.208	10.417						
Positive Emotion	1	2.875	5.875	9.43	.002**	.60	.741	2.20	.332
	2	4.000	5.625						
	3	4.375	5.500						
	mean	3.750	5.667						
Negative Emotion	1	5.125	19.875	30.57	.000**	20.79	.000**	44.67	.000**
	2	10.125	11.375						
	3	7.875	7.125						
	mean	7.708	12.792						
Nonspecific Emotion	1	3.250	5.500	16.30	.000**	11.03	.004**	1.37	.504
	2	5.625	8.125						
	3	3.000	6.250						
	mean	3.958	6.625						
Positive Behavior	1	7.125	7.375	1.97	.160	45.14	.000**	9.66	.008**
	2	8.500	4.250						
	3	12.875	13.250						
	mean	9.500	8.292						
Negative Behavior	1	8.000	9.000	30.58	.000**	17.51	.000**	7.43	.024*
	2	7.375	12.625						
	3	8.625	17.875						
	mean	8.000	13.167						

				F	p	F	p	F	p
Spatial Behavior	1	4.250	4.000	3.78	.052	1.26	.533	4.01	.135
	2	3.375	6.250						
	3	3.625	4.500						
	mean	3.750	4.917						
Nonverbal Behavior	1	1.250	4.875	30.07	.000**	22.81	.000**	.05	.976
	2	.625	2.125						
	3	.375	1.375						
	mean	.750	2.797						
Verbal Behavior	1	29.500	42.875	65.95	.000**	7.85	.020*	3.54	.170
	2	29.500	48.250						
	3	36.500	48.250						
	mean	31.833	46.458						
Nonspecific Behavior	1	55.500	58.875	31.50	.000**	115.77	.000**	21.07	.000**
	2	31.750	53.250						
	3	65.125	76.875						
	mean	50.792	63.000						
Positive Cognition	1	3.000	5.500	14.23	.000**	7.96	.019*	.59	.744
	2	3.500	6.000						
	3	5.250	7.625						
	mean	3.917	6.375						
Negative Cognition	1	.625	2.375	17.26	.000**	2.10	.351	.77	.679
	2	.750	2.000						
	3	1.250	2.750						
	mean	.875	2.375						
Neutral Cognition	1	54.250	72.750	58.21	.000**	16.40	.000**	.84	.658
	2	48.625	66.500						
	3	60.875	77.000						
	mean	54.583	72.083						
Somatic-Physical	1	.500	1.125	6.30	.012*	25.41	.000**	33.01	.000**
	2	5.500	.750						
	3	.750	2.000						
	mean	2.250	1.292						

(continued)

235

Table 7-8 (*Continued*)

Topic Scale (*Continued*)

Category	Time	Means Beginning	Means Advanced	Therapist Group Chi Square	Therapist Group Probability	Time Chi Square	Time Probability	Interaction Chi Square	Interaction Probability
Experience	1	2.625	7.125	5.89	.015*	6.43	.040*	15.72	.000**
	2	3.375	5.125						
	3	7.000	5.500						
	mean	4.333	5.917						
Fact	1	.750	1.375	.76	.384	63.61	.000**	4.42	.110
	2	.750	1.000						
	3	5.750	3.750						
	mean	2.417	2.042						

Intervention Scale

Category	Time	Means Beginning	Means Advanced	Therapist Group Chi Square	Therapist Group Probability	Time Chi Square	Time Probability	Interaction Chi Square	Interaction Probability
Disagree/Disapprove	1	.625	.750	7.58	.006**	3.93	.140	8.41	.015*
	2	.250	2.375						
	3	.750	.750						
	mean	.542	1.292						
Self-disclosure	1	2.250	1.625	.78	.377	7.87	.020*	.58	.747
	2	1.375	1.000						
	3	.750	.875						
	mean	1.458	1.667						
Refocus	1	.375	1.625	11.65	.001**	10.68	.005**	3.46	.177
	2	1.000	3.000						
	3	.750	.750						
	mean	.708	1.792						
Direction	1	6.875	5.875	.44	.506	7.10	.029*	5.38	.068
	2	4.875	6.750						
	3	9.375	7.000						
	mean	7.042	6.542						

Transposition	1	.000	.125	2.91	.088	7.78	.051	.40	.526
	2	.000	.000						
	3	.125	.500						
	mean	.042	.208						
Etiology–Motivation	1	7.000	10.500	19.13	.000**	6.42	.040*	2.58	.276
	2	6.875	9.375						
	3	4.125	8.625						
	mean	6.000	9.500						
Support	1	1.750	2.875	1.22	.270	11.89	.003**	1.44	.487
	2	2.000	2.500						
	3	4.125	4.125						
	mean	2.625	3.167						
Boundary Rules	1	6.375	2.375	8.19	.004**	3.46	.177	7.78	.020*
	2	4.500	4.000						
	3	6.000	5.125						
	mean	5.625	3.833						
Expectation	1	2.625	2.625	1.33	.248	.58	.748	.71	.702
	2	2.375	3.375						
	3	2.125	2.750						
	mean	2.375	2.917						
Process	1	10.000	23.000	97.22	.000**	.43	.807	4.22	.121
	2	13.125	21.750						
	3	10.500	23.750						
	mean	11.208	22.833						
Communication	1	14.125	24.625	53.67	.000**	2.08	.354	6.53	.038
	2	15.750	20.125						
	3	13.750	26.500						
	mean	15.542	23.750						
Problem	1	10.500	8.750	1.54	.215	4.45	.108	2.17	.338
	2	10.000	7.750						
	3	10.875	11.500						
	mean	10.458	9.333						

(continued)

Table 7-8 (*Continued*)

Intervention Scale (*Continued*)

Category	Time	Means		Therapist Group		Time		Interaction	
		Beginning	Advanced	Chi Square	Proba-bility	Chi Square	Proba-bility	Chi Square	Proba-bility
Status	1	36.250	52.500	42.00	.000**	33.97	.000**	5.28	.071
	2	30.375	43.375						
	3	46.500	54.375						
	mean	37.708	50.083						

Temporal Orientation Scale

Category	Time	Means		Therapist Group		Time		Interaction	
		Beginning	Advanced	Chi Square	Proba-bility	Chi Square	Proba-bility	Chi Square	Proba-bility
Now	1	28.625	40.750	71.08	.000**	5.76	.056	.96	.618
	2	24.750	39.750						
	3	29.375	45.125						
	mean	27.583	41.875						
Current	1	13.375	6.875	77.66	.000**	14.26	.001**	4.01	.135
	2	9.375	3.500						
	3	14.000	4.375						
	mean	12.250	4.917						
Future	1	2.625	.875	2.96	.086	127.62	.000**	23.83	.000**
	2	2.500	7.250						
	3	10.875	11.500						
	mean	5.333	6.542						
Past	1	19.125	15.500	13.70	.000**	106.75	.000**	2.31	.315
	2	10.625	6.375						
	3	7.000	4.500						
	mean	12.250	8.792						

Scale				To Whom Scale					
Atemporal	1	34.875	72.625	206.35	.000**	7.38	.025*	10.66	.005**
	2	45.375	68.375						
	3	44.625	77.375						
	mean	41.625	72.792						
Cotherapist	1	.0000	.0000	1.39	.239	2.20	.333	0.00	1.00
	2	.0000	.0000						
	3	.0000	.125						
	mean	.0000	.042						
Family	1	1.000	.625	.93	.336	5.61	.061	3.43	.180
	2	2.125	1.125						
	3	.625	1.125						
	mean	1.250	.958						
Parent–Child	1	.0000	.0000	—	—	—	—	—	—
	2	.0000	.0000						
	3	.0000	.0000						
	mean	.0000	.0000						
Couple–Parents	1	5.750	8.250	7.95	.005**	16.58	.000**	2.66	.264
	2	4.500	7.625						
	3	9.375	10.500						
	mean	6.542	8.792						
Wife–Mother	1	31.125	38.000	18.60	.000**	23.33	.000**	8.80	.012*
	2	44.125	46.000						
	3	34.375	49.375						
	mean	36.542	44.458						
Husband–Father	1	27.875	35.250	52.90	.000**	4.27	.118	6.22	.045*
	2	20.000	35.250						
	3	24.250	35.875						
	mean	24.042	35.458						

(continued)

239

Table 7-8 (*Continued*)

To Whom Scale (*Continued*)

Category	Time	Means		Therapist Group		Time		Interaction	
		Beginning	Advanced	Chi Square	Proba-bility	Chi Square	Proba-bility	Chi Square	Proba-bility
Children	1	.375	.500	.40	.526	5.94	.051	3.90	.142
	2	.250	.000						
	3	.125	.000						
	mean	.250	.167						
Child 1	1	19.625	31.500	26.46	.000**	32.29	.000**	4.91	.086
	2	14.500	20.375						
	3	16.625	18.875						
	mean	16.917	23.583						
Child 2	1	.250	1.750	17.65	.000**	7.29	.026*	9.56	.008**
	2	1.250	2.125						
	3	0.000	1.375						
	mean	.500	1.750						
Child 3	1	0.000	0.000	—	—	—	—	—	—
	2	0.000	0.000						
	3	0.000	0.000						
	mean	0.000	0.000						
Child 4	1	0.000	0.000	2.77	.096	4.39	.111	0.00	1.00
	2	0.000	0.000						
	3	0.000	.250						
	mean	0.000	.083						
Nonspecific	1	11.625	20.125	31.81	.000**	145.16	.000**	12.58	.002**
	2	4.875	11.625						
	3	23.000	27.500						
	mean	13.167	19.750						

Interpersonal Structure Scale

Group	1	5.500	10.250					
	2	6.750	7.500					
	3	9.125	14.750					
	mean	7.125	10.833	18.51	.000**	22.98	.000**	4.15	.126
Triadic	1	6.375	10.250					
	2	5.375	8.250					
	3	10.250	11.125					
	mean	7.333	9.875	9.04	.003**	14.08	.001**	3.43	.180
Dyadic	1	38.375	46.000					
	2	34.750	39.375					
	3	39.500	51.625					
	mean	37.542	45.667	19.07	.000**	14.21	.001**	1.70	.427
Monadic	1	44.375	70.500					
	2	42.750	66.625					
	3	46.375	65.125					
	mean	44.500	67.417	113.42	.000**	1.10	.578	1.90	.386
Topic	1	2.500	.625					
	2	2.000	2.875					
	3	3.500	1.625					
	mean	2.667	1.708	5.08	.024*	4.59	.101	11.44	.003**

System Membership Scale

Inclusive	1	3.000	5.375					
	2	1.500	5.875					
	3	6.500	10.500					
	mean	3.667	7.250	28.76	.000**	38.68	.000**	6.50	.039*
Therapy	1	1.625	5.750					
	2	1.875	2.875					
	3	4.000	6.500					
	mean	2.500	5.042	20.97	.000**	17.82	.000**	5.10	.078

(continued)

Table 7-8 (*Continued*)

System Membership Scale (*Continued*)

Category	Time	Means		Therapist Group		Time		Interaction	
		Beginning	Advanced	Chi Square	Probability	Chi Square	Probability	Chi Square	Probability
Cross-generational	1	0.000	0.000	—	—	—	—	—	—
	2	0.000	0.000						
	3	0.000	0.000						
	mean	0.000	0.000						
Therapist (FOO)	1	0.000	0.000	—	—	—	—	—	—
	2	0.000	0.000						
	3	0.000	0.000						
	mean	0.000	0.000						
Cross-generational (FOO)	1	0.000	0.000	—	—	—	—	—	—
	2	0.000	0.000						
	3	0.000	0.000						
	mean	0.000	0.000						
Marital (FOO)	1	.250	0.000	2.77	.096	4.39	.111	0.00	1.00
	2	0.000	0.000						
	3	0.000	0.000						
	mean	.083	0.000						
Parental (FOO)	1	.125	.250	.00	1.00	4.87	.182	.68	.410
	2	0.000	0.000						
	3	.250	.125						
	mean	.125	.125						
Sibling (FOO)	1	0.000	0.000	2.09	.148	6.49	.090	3.45	.063
	2	.250	.250						
	3	0.000	.500						
	mean	.083	.250						

Extended (FOO)	1	0.000	0.000	—	—	—	—	—	—
	2	0.000	0.000						
	3	0.000	0.000						
	mean	0.000	0.000						
Nonspecific (FOO)	1	0.000	0.000	8.32	.004**	13.18	.001**	.00	1.00
	2	0.000	0.000						
	3	0.000	.750						
	mean	0.000	.250						
Therapist–Nuclear Family	1	8.625	18.250	50.57	.000**	31.74	.000**	4.06	.131
	2	7.500	14.000						
	3	14.750	21.625						
	mean	10.292	17.958						
Cross-generational Nuclear Family	1	.375	0.000	.14	.705	1.32	.516	9.56	.008**
	2	0.000	.375						
	3	0.000	.125						
	mean	.125	.167						
Marital–Nuclear Family	1	7.875	19.625	68.27	.000**	9.68	.008**	8.34	.016*
	2	12.625	17.875						
	3	12.500	23.625						
	mean	11.000	20.375						
Parental–Nuclear Family	1	22.000	16.750	18.74	.000**	22.00	.000**	.57	.752
	2	16.125	10.750						
	3	15.875	11.750						
	mean	18.000	13.083						
Sibling–Nuclear Family	1	.875	0.000	7.71	.006**	.72	.696	4.43	.109
	2	.500	.125						
	3	.625	.375						
	mean	.667	.167						
Extended Nuclear Family	1	0.000	0.000	9.70	.002**	15.38	.000**	0.00	1.00
	2	0.000	.875						
	3	0.000	0.000						
	mean	0.000	.292						

(continued)

Table 7-8 (Continued)

System Membership Scale (Continued)

Category	Time	Means Beginning	Means Advanced	Therapist Group Chi Square	Therapist Group Probability	Time Chi Square	Time Probability	Interaction Chi Square	Interaction Probability
Nonspecific Nuclear Family	1	44.625	65.625	96.37	.000**	.02	.992	.37	.830
	2	44.125	66.750						
	3	45.500	64.875						
	mean	44.750	65.750						
Other Therapist Family	1	.375	0.000	9.75	.002**	1.41	.493	1.48	.478
	2	.375	0.000						
	3	.625	.125						
	mean	.458	.042						
Other Therapist	1	.250	.250	.40	.526	.87	.646	.64	.725
	2	.125	.125						
	3	.375	.125						
	mean	.250	.167						
Other Family	1	2.750	2.000	8.18	.004**	5.46	.065	2.25	.324
	2	2.375	.750						
	3	1.750	.875						
	mean	2.292	1.208						
Other	1	1.250	1.000	11.05	.001	-.00	1.00	5.25	.072
	2	2.000	.250						
	3	1.625	.625						
	mean	1.625	.625						
Topic	1	2.500	.625	5.08	.024*	4.59	.101	11.44	.003**
	2	2.000	2.875						
	3	3.500	1.625						
	mean	2.667	1.708						

Route Scale

Indirect Target	1	10.875	14.000					
	2	11.125	11.125					
	3	7.750	10.125					
	mean	9.917	11.750	3.73	.054	9.40	.009**	1.95	.376
Direct–Indirect	1	11.500	18.125					
	2	12.250	18.375					
	3	14.375	20.250					
	mean	12.708	18.917	29.44	.000**	3.50	.174	.39	.822
Indirect	1	22.375	28.625					
	2	17.875	28.125					
	3	31.875	34.875					
	mean	24.000	30.542	18.88	.000**	33.18	.000**	6.87	.032*
Direct	1	51.875	74.875					
	2	50.000	66.125					
	3	54.750	78.625					
	mean	52.208	73.208	84.79	.000**	9.72	.008**	1.13	.568

Grammatical Form Scale

Command	1	3.375	3.625					
	2	2.625	4.625					
	3	4.875	3.250					
	mean	3.625	3.833	.14	.709	.74	.691	7.02	.030*
Question-open	1	23.875	37.250					
	2	22.625	31.500					
	3	18.000	23.500					
	mean	21.500	30.750	39.51	.000**	31.01	.000**	1.64	.441

(continued)

245

Table 7-8   (Continued)

Grammatical Form Scale (Continued)

Question-closed	1	34.750	40.875						
	2	36.000	38.125						
	3	32.125	35.625						
	mean	34.292	38.208	5.08	.024*	3.90	.142	.83	.661
Label	1	34.125	52.875						
	2	29.750	49.000						
	3	52.875	80.500						
	mean	38.917	60.792	116.12	.000**	133.70	.000**	.60	.742

Event Relationship Scale

Cyclical	1	0.000	0.000						
	2	0.000	0.000						
	3	.125	.500						
	mean	.042	.167	1.93	.165	10.99	.027*	.00	1.00
Functional	1	0.000	.250						
	2	.375	.875						
	3	.250	.250						
	mean	.208	.458	2.31	.129	6.35	.042*	2.11	.348
Incongruence	1	.375	1.500						
	2	1.500	1.250						
	3	1.000	1.750						
	mean	.958	1.500	2.89	.089	1.74	.419	4.73	.094

246

Temporal	1	13.875	24.250	61.86	.000**	3.77	.152	.73	.696
	2	12.875	20.750						
	3	11.375	21.375						
	mean	12.708	22.125						
Multiple	1	11.125	14.375	3.88	.049*	4.34	.114	.74	.689
	2	9.500	11.125						
	3	10.625	11.500						
	mean	10.417	12.333						
Isolate	1	31.000	38.875	8.86	.003**	14.10	.001**	1.38	.501
	2	35.375	38.750						
	3	27.750	31.500						
	mean	31.375	36.375						

*$p < .05$
**$p < .01$

by almost half the level of this behavior in the middle segment. During the middle third, the advanced therapists were almost ten times more disapproving/disagreeable than the beginners. The advanced therapists' behavior on this dimension is almost identical to the beginners' during the first and last thirds. The picture that emerges is that the advanced therapists "join" the family in the same way as the beginners for the first 20 minutes, but shortly thereafter they move into a more judgmental posture. As the session ends, they return to the less critical position of the beginners and the first third.

Both condition-groups begin with relatively high levels of Self-Disclosure, which decrease as the interview progresses. As would be expected, both groups also do most of their explicit refocusing (Refocus) in the middle segment. Both condition-groups also become most directive (Direction) in the last third of the session, which probably reflects the shift at the end of the session toward recommendations and specific plans. Although barely significant ($p < .04$), both groups appear to reduce the level of interpretations pertaining to motivation and meaning (Etiology–Motivation) over the course of the interview. A strong finding is that both groups become increasingly supportive (Support) as the session progresses. For both groups there is a curvilinear midsession dip around interventions identifying the states targeted by the Topic Scale categories (Status). The ANOVA proportion segment location findings for the Intervention Scale revealed a midsession peak for Refocus ($p < .03$) and a last third peak for Transposition ($p < .04$) and Support ($p < .05$) for both condition-groups.

In terms of the session as a whole, the Intervention Scale portrayed the therapists in the supervisor condition-group as relatively more critical or challenging (Disagree/Disapprove), as more controlling of the discussion content (Refocus), as more interpretive (Etiology–Motivation), and as more explicitly concerned with identifying the psychosocial boundaries (Boundary–Rules), activity sequences (Process), and communication patterns (Communication) in the family system. These findings basically corroborate the earlier McMaster FTBS findings.

In terms of the within-session patterning of therapist behavior, the Intervention Scale revealed that the therapists in both condition-groups disclosed personal information primarily in the first third of the session (Self-Disclosure), explicitly controlled discussion content primarily during the middle phase, and were most directive (Direction) and supportive during the last third. In contrast to the beginners, advanced therapists were most critical (Disagree/Disapprove) in the middle of the session, which gave the family time to warm up before and come down after they challenge the system.

Temporal Orientation Scale No. 3   The log linear analysis on the condition-group factor for this scale found that the advanced therapists were higher on two of the five code categories—Now and Atemporal. In contrast, the beginners were higher on Current and Past. The ANOVA proportion analysis only found the beginners to be significantly higher on Current. The picture provided by the Temporal Orientation Scale portrays the advanced therapists as more explicitly concerned with behavior/experience occurring within the spatiotemporal confines of the therapy session (Now). They focused much more on the here and now. When not focusing on the immediate present, the advanced therapists were more likely to not anchor their interventions in any specific time frame (Atemporal). This may well reflect a greater emphasis on "trait" or enduring as opposed to "state" or transitory characteristics of the family. In contrast, the beginners focused more on activity within the current time period outside of the therapy session (Current) and events from the past.

In terms of within-session patterning, the log linear analysis demonstrated that both condition-groups decreased concern with current functioning (Current) in the middle third and understandably focused most on the past (Past) during the first third or data-gathering phase of the session. Both groups also understandably focused most on the future (Future) during the last phase of the session; however, the advanced therapists in comparison to the beginners hardly focused on the future during the first phase and jumped almost to the third-phase level in the middle phase. In other words they focused explicitly on the future during the last two-thirds of the session. On Atemporal, the beginners jumped to and sustained a higher level after the first phase, whereas the advanced therapists dipped slightly in the middle third. The ANOVA proportion analysis confirmed the increasing emphasis on Future and decreasing emphasis on Past for both condition-groups.

The Temporal Orientation findings clearly reveal that the therapists in the supervisor condition-group focus more than the beginners on the here and now, which confirms the earlier FTBS findings. Additionally, the phase-pattern findings about the early focus on the past and the late focus on the future support the scale's ability to capture expected and logical patterns of therapist verbal behavior.

To Whom Scale No. 4   Log linear analysis on the data from this scale show that the therapists in the supervisor condition-group addressed more interventions (main clause units) to the parental couple (Couple–Parents), the Wife–Mother, the Husband–Father, the only or oldest child (Child 1) and the second child (Child 2) in the family. They also made more Nonspecific interventions that were not directed toward any specific target. The condition-group data for this scale are clearly affected by the increased activity rates of the advanced therapists. They directed more interventions to each specific family member as well as the parental couple. The ANOVA proportion data, which control for activity level, found no significant condition-group differences in the To Whom data.

The segment location data from the log linear analysis show several within-session patterns. Both groups increased the number of interventions directed to the parents as a unit (Couple–Parents) and decreased the number directed to the oldest child (Child 1) over the course of the session. The oldest child was usually the identified patient. This pattern reflects a relative shift away from the identified patient toward the parents as a focal subsystem.

When a second child was present, both groups of therapists directed most of their interventions to that child during the middle segment. Surprisingly, the beginners did not address the second child at all during the third segment. Both groups had U-shaped distributions (low middle segments) for the frequency of Nonspecific interventions. However, the beginners had almost three times fewer Nonspecific interventions than the advanced therapists in the middle segment.

The therapists in the advanced condition-group increased interventions directed to the wife over the course of the session and held phenomenally constant the number of interventions directed to the father. The beginners spoke most to the mother (normal distribution) and least to the father (U-shaped distribution) during the middle segment.

These data clearly indicate that the therapists in the advanced condition-group directly addressed each individual in the session as well as the parental unit within and throughout the first session. The advanced therapists' shift in relative emphasis from the identified patient to the parental couple over the course of the session fits the short term, problem-oriented therapy model taught at McMaster (Cleghorn and Levin, 1973) during the time the data were collected. Within that theory, the parental–marital dyad is the key family subsystem.

Interestingly, the number of advanced therapists' interventions explicitly directed to the mother, father, and oldest child (identified patient) during the first segment were fairly similar (38, 35, 31, respectively). During the remaining segments the frequency of interventions directed to mother went up (49), the frequency to father stayed the same (35), and the frequency to the child decreased (19). These shifting patterns suggest that the advanced therapists initially join the family by equally addressing all of the key members (identified patient, mother, and father). Gradually, they shift their interaction rates in favor of the parents in an effort to engage them as the central actors in the treatment. The rate shifts suggest that engaging mother becomes the focal task.

Interpersonal Structure Scale No. 5   On this scale, the log linear analysis revealed that the therapists in the advanced condition-group were higher ($p < .003$) on four of the five categories—Group, Triadic, Dyadic, and Monadic. The beginners were higher ($p < .03$) on the remaining category—Topic. These differences mean that the advanced therapists dealt more with personal systems. Most of the advanced (and beginner) interventions dealt with or focused on individuals (Monadic, 67) and dyads (Dyadic, 45), with roughly equal numbers of interventions dealing with triads or the whole group. The two condition-groups did not differ on any of the code categories in the proportional ANOVA.

Four segment location findings emerged from the log linear analysis. Both groups of therapists peaked on Group, Triadic, and Dyadic in the last segment. Since these constitute the interpersonal categories on the Interpersonal Structure Scale, these data show that the therapists were most interpersonally oriented during the concluding phase of the session.

On Topic, the category that covered interventions in which the therapists did not deal with personal systems (e.g., "It sure is hot out today"), the beginners had a U-shaped distribution that peaked in the last segment, whereas the advanced therapists' distribution peaked in the middle and was almost four times less than the beginners in the first segment. Also, during the first segment, the advanced therapists made twice as many interventions that dealt with the entire family system (Group) as the beginners. This means that the advanced therapists dealt almost exclusively with personal and interpersonal systems in the first segment of the session.

The primary finding from the Interpersonal Structure Scale data is that the advanced therapists attended more to personal and interpersonal systems in their interventions than beginners. Furthermore, this difference was most extreme early in the interview. Both condition groups were most interpersonally oriented during the last segment.

System Membership Scale No. 6   The log linear analysis on this scale identified numerous significant differences between the two condition-groups. The advanced therapists made more interventions in which they explicitly dealt with everyone in the room, including themselves, as members of one group (Inclusive; e.g., "We're getting off track here"). They made more interventions in which they explicitly mentioned the therapist system (Therapy; e.g., "We're going to try to help you solve your problems with Timmy"). This finding may well be a result of the context of the interviews. The advanced therapists were in the room with the beginning, student therapist; whereas the beginners were alone in the room during their interviews. In essence, the advance therapists were in a co-therapy context in which comments dealing with the therapist or co-therapist system would be more appropriate.

In contrast to the beginners, the advanced therapists also made some interventions that dealt with the parents' families of origin (Nonspecific Family of Origin). The advanced therapists, as we had anticipated in developing the personally oriented Therapist–Nuclear Family category, made more interventions in which they mentioned themselves and one or more family members (e.g., "Your wife is getting mad at me"). They also explicitly focused about twice as often as the beginners on the marital system (Marital–Nuclear Family; e.g., "You don't share those feelings with your wife?"). In contrast, the beginners focused more on the parental (Parental–Nuclear Family; e.g., "The two of you have trouble setting limits on Tim") and sibling (Sibling–Nuclear Family; e.g., "Do you agree with your sister about that?") subsystems within the family.

The therapists in the advanced condition-group dealt with some members of the extended family (grandparents, cousins, etc.), whereas the beginners never did (Extended Nuclear Family). The advanced therapists focused more interventions than beginners on family members without specifying their system membership (Nonspecific Nuclear Family; e.g., "You look sad right now").

In regard to the categories of the System Membership Scale that dealt with "other" systems like school and work, the findings were intriguing and somewhat contrary to expectation. The beginners made more interventions that simultaneously focused upon the therapist, the family, and an "other" system like school or work (Other–Therapist–Family; e.g., "I think Susie may not want to go to school, because she is afraid to leave you alone"). They also made more interventions that simultaneously addressed the family and an "other" system without mentioning the therapist (Other–Family; e.g., "Losing your job put the whole family into a tailspin").

As expected, particularly in light of the findings from the Interpersonal Structure Scale, the therapists in the beginner condition-group were higher on Topic—the category on the System Membership (and Topic) Scale that covers statements that do not deal with any personal or human system. The only significant proportion ANOVA finding showed the advanced therapists to be higher on Therapist–Nuclear Family.

The segment location findings from the log linear analysis of the System Membership data reveal that both groups made more Inclusive and Therapy interventions in the last segment of the session. More "we" comments and statements dealing with the therapist system and conduct of therapy (rules, expected behaviors, etc.,) are likely to occur during the final stages of the initial session as the session is brought to a close and as plans are made about the structure and content of subsequent meetings.

Both condition-groups also peaked in the last segment on Therapist–Nuclear Family, although the advanced therapists were almost as high during the first segment. Both groups also peaked on Parental–Nuclear Family during the first segment. The advanced therapists focused most on the marital system (Marital–Nuclear Family) during the last segment, whereas the beginners increased their emphasis on the marital dyad by about 50% in the second and third segments (from 7.8 to 12.6 and 12.5). The advanced therapists hardly made any Topic or impersonal interventions during the first segment, whereas the beginners were highest in the first and third segments. The proportion ANOVA supported the segment location findings on Inclusive (increasing over the session) and Parental–Nuclear Family (decreasing over the session).

The key significant findings from the System Membership Scale basically reveal a variety of predictable differences between the condition-groups. The primary finding cluster that is clinically relevant concerns the advanced therapist's greater focus on the marital system and the beginner's greater concern with the parental, sibling, and "other" nonfamilial systems. These findings are very congruent with the McMaster Model of family therapy, in which the therapist attempts to shift the focus from the identified patient to the marital system.

Typically, within the McMaster Model and most of the other early family therapy models, the symptomatic child is seen as the homeostatic regulator of the marriage. As quickly as possible, the therapist ideally shifts the focus to the marital system in order to identify the marital issues and help the parents learn to regulate themselves without using their child. The advanced therapist clearly is engaged in this process during these initial, supervisory sessions, whereas the beginner's behavior reflects a relative over-emphasis on the parent–child system, siblings and "other" systems, and an underemphasis on the marital dyad. The segment location findings suggest that the advanced therapist's emphasis on the marital system pervades the session, but peaks slightly in the last segment.

The other significant finding-cluster concerns the personal quality of the advanced therapists' behavior. The Therapist–Nuclear Family finding, coupled with the Inclusive finding, reveal that the advanced therapists more often linked themselves personally ("I" or "me") to the family and defined themselves more often as part of the same system as the family ("we" or "us"). Both of these behaviors diminish psychological distance between the therapist and the family, add a more personal quality to the therapy, and may well function to create a better therapeutic alliance. The presence of these behaviors along with the reduced use of the Topic category by advanced therapists further emphasizes the personal quality of the advanced therapists' work.

In summary, the Interpersonal System data suggest that the advanced therapists differ from the beginners in that they go directly for the core of the family—the marital system—and they do so in a more personal, "I–you" fashion.

Route Scale No. 7   The log linear findings on this scale reveal that the therapists in the advanced condition-group were higher on three of the four categories, although the differences were not as dramatic (never more than 50% higher) as some of the difference findings on the other FTCS scales. Specifically, the advanced therapists made more Direct–Indirect interventions (e.g., "You don't like it when your wife interrupts you") in which they speak about the person they are talking to (the target) as well as the person they are talking about. They also made more Indirect interventions (e.g., "Joey is sad") in which they talk about someone other than the person they are talking to, and more Direct interventions (e.g., "You avoid dealing with your pain by drinking") in which they speak directly to the person they are talking about. The proportion ANOVA did not find any significant condition-group differences on the Route Scale.

The log linear segment location analysis found that both groups decreased the frequency of Indirect Target (e.g., "You think that Timmy resents his father") interventions over the course of the session. These are the most complicated Route interventions, in that they involve the therapist in asking the person they are talking to (the target) what they think another person (the indirect target) thinks or feels about something or someone. It seems appropriate that these interventions would be most frequent during the initial, exploratory phases of the interview when the therapist assesses and enters the family system.

The mean frequency of Indirect interventions generally increased over the course of the session for both condition-groups. Their respective patterns, however, differed slightly. The advanced therapists stayed at the same level for the first two segments of the session and jumped to their peak in the third. In contrast, the beginners were at a moderate level initially, dipped in the middle segment, and peaked in the third. Both group's Direct interventions dipped slightly in the middle segment and peaked moderately in the third. The proportion ANOVA did not reveal any significant segment location patterns.

The Route Scale data show that over three quarters of therapist interventions fell in the simpler Direct and Indirect categories. The Indirect Target findings indicate that the therapists decreased the extent to which they assessed how well one family member understood and could articulate the thoughts and feelings of another family member over the course of the session. Concomitantly, they increased the frequency of their Direct and Indirect interventions.

Grammatical Form Scale No. 8   The strongest condition-group findings from the log linear analysis revealed that the advanced therapists asked more open questions (Question–Open; e.g., "How do you feel about that?") and did more labeling (Label; e.g., "She felt abandoned when you became depressed"). The advanced therapists also asked slightly ($p < .03$) more closed questions (Question–Closed; e.g., "Are you irritated with him?"). The proportion ANOVA showed that the therapists in the beginner condition-group asked proportionally (36% to 28%) more closed questions and did less labeling than the advanced therapists.

The log linear segment location findings revealed that the advanced therapists were most directive (Commands) during the middle segment, whereas the beginners peaked in the last segment. Their respective distributions were bell and U shaped. Understandably, both groups decreased the frequency of open questions and increased the frequency of labeling over the course of the interview. The proportion ANOVA findings on segment location supported the open question and label findings (decrease/increase) from the log linear analysis, and also demonstrated that the proportion of closed questions decreased over the course of the session.

The most expected condition-group difference finding that emerged on this scale was that the advanced therapists asked more open questions. Naturally, open questions, which require more than a "yes" or "no" answer, elicit more information than closed questions. Frequently, novice therapists need to be taught to use more open questions; thus, one would expect advanced therapists to be higher. Also, it was not surprising that a significantly higher proportion of the beginner's repertoire was devoted to closed questions. The open question decrease and label increase over the course of the session suggest a natural progression from information collecting to labeling and identifying different aspects of the family's behavior/experience.

The Command pattern findings show that the novice therapists were most explicitly directive (Commands are explicit directives in contrast to other types of directives using a question format) during the final segment when it is most appropriate to make recommendations for subsequent treatment. The advanced peak in the middle segment suggests that the advanced therapists may have used commands less as a future prescription and more as behavioral stimulus within the session. They may well have been stimulating more interaction or prescribing "enactments."

Event Relationship Scale No. 9   The log linear findings on the condition-group factor showed that the advanced therapists made more speeches in which they dealt with events in time (Temporal; e.g., "You moved closer as she began to withdraw"), multiple events outside of a temporal context (Multiple; e.g., "He steals from the kids at school and he's also having academic problems"), and isolated events (Isolate; e.g., "He's depressed"). The ANOVA proportion results supported the Temporal finding, which was the strongest log linear result.

The log linear segment location analysis revealed that both groups of therapists made all their Cyclical (e.g., "You attack him. He withdraws. Then you sulk and he re-engages until you feel crowded and attack again") interventions in the last segment and had bell-shaped Functional (e.g., "You provoke Mom and Dad to keep the heat on you and off of their marriage") distributions with mid-session peaks. There were no significant proportion ANOVA results on segment location.

The Event Relationship results fit the expectation that the advanced therapists would deal more with events in time (Temporal) or sequences of behavior than beginners. The Process findings from the Intervention Scale also support this finding. Although the advanced therapists had much higher frequencies on the more complex Cyclical and Functional categories (4 to 1, and 2 to 1, respectively), the very low N's in those categories made attaining significance extremely difficult. The results support the conclusion that the advanced therapists used more complex interventions than the beginners, although the low frequencies of certain categories weakened the statistical base of the analysis.

The segment findings fit the expectation that the therapists would make more all-encompassing, circular interventions and analyses in the last phase of the session. They would almost have to wait that long to get enough information to delineate cycles and circular patterns. Also, more Functional interpretations would logically occur in the middle segment when the therapist is testing hypotheses about the systemic function of various behaviors and symptoms.

Summary and Discussion of McMaster FTCS Findings

Overall, the results of the McMaster FTCS Study support the reliability and discriminant validity of the FTCS. The system proved to be adequately reliable and was able to make a host of distinctions between the two condition-groups. With few, if any, exceptions, the distinctions were in the expected direction and fit the theory of the McMaster model of family therapy. Additionally, the FTCS was able to identify a number of significant and expected patterns of therapist behavior within the sessions.

Although primarily conceived as a reliability and validity test, the FTCS McMaster Study also revealed a considerable amount of information about the verbal behavior of family therapists in one particular setting. Before summarizing that information, it is important to restate and clarify the context of the findings. All of the therapists were videotaped during initial (first or second) interviews with intact families presenting with a child as the identified patient. The eight therapists in the beginner condition-group conducted normal initial sessions in which they were only observed by the experimenter-cameraman (Pinsof) and in which they were the only therapists.

In contrast, the eight therapists in the supervisor condition-group were actually conducting live supervision interviews. These sessions began with the supervisor behind a one-way mirror with the experimenter observing a beginner conduct the first 20 minutes of an initial session. After 20 minutes, the supervisor–therapist entered and took over the session. The beginner stayed in the room, but by and large did not participate after the supervisor joined the session.

This contextual information is presented to highlight once again the fact that this study cannot be interpreted as a comparison of beginning and advanced therapists at McMaster. It is actually a study of these two groups under different conditions—hence the term condition-group. It may well be that the findings would have been different had the advanced therapists conducted normal (nonsupervisory) initial interviews or the beginners conducted live supervision sessions. From my own experience as a beginner and supervisor at McMaster, during live sessions as opposed to normal sessions in which they were working alone with their own cases, supervisors tended to be more active, stuck closer to the model, and felt freer to challenge and confront the family. To use a surgical metaphor, it was as if they opened the patient up and showed the beginner how to do some of the most difficult work that they would have to do during the rest of the operation. They then withdrew from active involvement in the operation (therapy), unless their expertise was necessary at particularly critical points. Thus, the supervisors' work had a pedagogic, demonstration component that typically would be lacking in normal, nonsupervisory sessions. The supervisors also tended to work faster than they would have in normal sessions with their own cases.

To summarize the results in light of this contextual information, the advanced therapists differed from the beginners in a variety of expected ways. First of all, the data from the Topic Scale clearly revealed that the advanced therapists focused much more on painful, distressing affects, maladaptive behaviors, and disagreements within the family. The focus on distressing affects was most intense right after the supervisor entered the session and decreased over the course of the session as the emphasis on maladaptive behaviors increased. The Intervention Scale showed that the advanced therapists were more disapproving of the family, controlling of the family's verbal behavior, interpretive, concerned with the family's boundaries and rules, and much more attentive to sequences and processes of behavior and communication. Patternwise, the advanced therapists were most disapproving/disagreeable and controlling during the middle of the session.

The Temporal Orientation Scale demonstrated that the advanced therapists focused much more on activity within the session, and the To Whom Scale showed that after initially touching base with each family member, the advanced therapists (and the beginners as well) focused increasingly on the marital couple. Both the Interpersonal Structure and the System Membership Scales depicted the advanced therapists as being more personal and focused on personal systems than beginners. The personal quality of their behavior was most apparent soon after they entered the session. The latter scale also revealed that the advanced therapists focused much more on the marital couple as husband and wife, whereas the beginners focused on them more as mother and father.

The Grammatical Form Scale showed that the advanced therapists used the more revealing open-question format more than beginners and were most explicitly directive during the middle phase of the session. The Event Relationship Scale confirmed the Process findings from the Intervention Scale, depicting the advanced therapists as more concerned with sequences of events or events in time. The Route scale findings were not particularly illuminating, but did show an expected decrease in the assessment of empathic interpersonal perception (how one family member understands the thoughts and feelings of another member) over the course of the session.

Overall, these results reveal that the advanced therapists attempted to penetrate much more deeply and rapidly into the painful and maladaptive aspects of the family's life. They focused much more on what went on in the session and did not shy away from dealing with the marital system. They did all of the above with a more personal "I-you" style and with a greater concern for sequences and patterns of behavior. Interestingly, they dared to be disagreeable or challenging, but typically waited until they had done some preliminary joining before they "lowered the boom." As they moved into a more challenging position during the middle of the session, they also became explicitly directive. The general picture shows the advanced therapists as personally and actively engaging the core aspects of the family and attempting to bring about change within the family in a short, intense encounter.

Before concluding this section, it must be remembered that this presentation of the data has focused primarily on differences between the two condition-groups and patterns within the sessions. What has not been emphasized are the background characteristics of all the therapists' behavior. For instance, all of the therapists become more supportive, directive, and concerned with positive behavior over the course of the session. Thus, the advanced therapists' emphasis on negative or painful affects and maladaptive behavior must ultimately be understood in light of these more general patterns. To illustrate: As the advanced therapists were becoming more supportive and concerned with positive behavior, they increased the extent to which they challenged the system (Disagree/Disapprove) and focused on maladaptive behaviors. Before leaving the family, they reduced the level of confrontation and continued increasing the level of support and concern with positive, adaptive behavior. To simply say that the advanced therapists were more concerned with negative affect and behavior is to distinguish them from the beginners, but not to describe properly the complete "gestalt" of their verbal behavior during the sessions.

In conclusion, the advanced therapists, as well as engaging in most of the verbal behaviors displayed by the beginners, were more active, bolder, more interpretive, more personal, and more penetrating. They went directly to the core of the family and were not afraid to challenge the family system directly. They joined the family when they entered by focusing on painful affects and being more personal. This picture of their behavior is consistent with what might be expected of McMaster supervisors in a live supervision context.

The Training Studies

Two studies with the FTCS were conducted by myself and my colleague, Sherry Tucker, at the Center for Family Studies/The Family Institute of Chicago. The first study, Training I, which constituted part of Tucker's dissertation, involved a single group, pre–post design applied to the first year of the two–year family therapy training program at the Family Institute. This study attempted to determine the extent to which the in-therapy verbal behavior of 19 family therapy trainees changed in predicted directions after one year of training. The Training II study used a pre–mid–post design to evaluate the extent to which the in-therapy verbal behavior of nine of the nineteen trainees changed over the entire two-year program. The two-year program is an eclectically oriented family and marital therapy training program, that involves didactic and supervisory components. The basic procedures and some of the results of the Training I study have been published by Tucker and Pinsof (1984).

Procedure   In order to evaluate the in-therapy verbal behavior of the family therapy trainees with a reasonably standard stimulus, we devised a procedure called the "live family simulation." This procedure involved training four professional actors to simulate a real family (mother, father, son, and daughter) that had been referred for treatment because the son had committed a petty crime. The actors were trained to resemble a "united front" or "pseudo-mutual" family. The two training studies involved the use of three separate actor families at the pre-, mid-, and post-training evaluation points. The families were trained to resemble each other, but minor details were changed to provide variation and to challenge the trainees. The procedure for training the actors and establishing family equivalence has been described elsewhere (Tucker, 1981; Tucker and Pinsof, 1984).

The trainees were instructed to conduct an initial family therapy interview with the actor families at the beginning of the two-year training program (August, 1978), at the midpoint after one year (July–August, 1979), and at the conclusion of the two-year program (July, 1980). The trainee therapists knew that they were interviewing an actor family, but they were told by the experimenter or research assistant to proceed as they would with a real family. The actors remained in role throughout the entire session. Therapists were briefed before the session on family membership, family history, and presenting problems (which differed slightly at each testing).

Subjects   Nineteen mental-health professionals (10 females and 9 males), who entered the two-year training program in the fall of 1978, were the subjects in the Training I study. They are described in detail by Tucker and Pisnof (1984). They were tested at the beginning of training and at the end of the first year. Four of these subjects dropped out of training before the end of the two-year program. For the Training II study, we had the 15 remaining subjects participate in the final testing at the end of the program. Unfortunately, due to a tape recorder malfunction, the tapes of six of the subjects were erased during data collection, which left us with only nine subjects for the Training II study. Although we considered this N barely sufficient for a proper data analysis, we viewed the Training II study as an opportunity to collect more information about the sensitivity and capability of the FTCS.

Sampling, Coding, and Data Analysis   The sampling and contextual unit for the training studies was the five-minute segment. In order to get a representative sample of the therapists' behavior, three five-minute segments were taken from fixed points in the first, second, and third, thirds of each session. These segments were transcribed and unitized prior to coding. The data from both training studies were coded by two coders who did not participate in the McMaster FTCS Study. They were both advanced graduate students at Northwestern who participated in the development of the FTCS. All coding assignments were counterbalanced and equalized as they were in the McMaster Study.

The summarizing or data-analysis unit for the training studies was the full 15-minute sample (the sum of the three five-minute samples). Like the McMaster FTCS Study, the training studies used log linear analyses with the frequency for each code category for each session as the basic datum. The Training I analysis tested for significant differences on each code category between the two test points (pre- and mid-) for all 19 subjects. The Training II study tested for significant differences over the three test points (pre–mid–post) for the nine remaining subjects. Like the McMaster data, both of these can be viewed as reliability and discriminant validity studies of the FTCS. The small size of the segment samples (five minutes) did not provide an adequate statistical base for the type of segment location pattern analyses that we did with the McMaster data.

The validity results reported below differ somewhat from those reported in our previous publication (Tucker and Pinsof, 1984). At the time we originally analyzed the training data, we were not familiar with log linear statistics, which are ideally suited to low-frequency process data. In our 1984 paper, therefore, we used a standard proportion ANOVA, which requires extremely large low frequency differences in order to attain statistical significance. The additional findings reported below for the Training I study derive from our more recent reliance on log linear statistical procedures.

Training Results: Reliability   For the Training I study we not only attempted to determine the interrater reliability of the FTCS scales, but also attempted to determine the reliability of the unitization process. The raw Training I data consisted of 114 five-minute segments (57 pre- and 57 post-). We overlapped 20% of the data (19 segments) for the interrater reliability check. First we had both coders unitize the reliability segments. Their interrater unitization (percentage of exact agreement) reliabilities for the three FTCS scoring units were: .92 for verb units; .87 for main clause units; and .96 for speech units.

Using Cohen's k, the interrater categorization reliabilities for the nine FTCS scales ranged from a low of .41 for the Event Relationship Scale to a high of .76 for the To Whom Scale. All k values differed from chance at $p < .001$, thereby meeting Cohen's minimal criterion for nominal scale reliability.

Training I Results: Discriminant Validity   The discriminant validity log linear analysis produced a wide variety of significant differences between the pre- and midtesting points. Consistent with both the FTBS and FTCS McMaster Studies, the therapists became significantly more active (used more verb, main clause, and speech units) and used a wider range of interventions on the Topic, Temporal Orientation, and Grammatical Form Scales after one year of training.

On the *Topic* Scale, after one year, the therapists increased on Positive Emotion ($p < .02$), Negative Emotion (.001), Negative Behavior (.02), Nonspecific Behavior (.001), Neutral Cognition (.0001), and Fact (.01). The Intervention Scale revealed increases on Interpretation–Transposition (.004), Interpretation–Etiology–Motivation (.006), Support (.02), and Status (.0001). On Temporal Orientation the therapists increased on Now (.0001), Future (.01), and Past (.0001).

These findings reveal that the therapists dealt more with specific types of emotion, maladaptive behaviors, and factual information. Although not as widespread, these findings basically corroborate the McMaster differences. The Family Institute trainees also became more interpretive and supportive. These changes partially support the McMaster data, but clearly lack the confrontive quality reflected in the McMaster Disagreement/Disapproval results. The 19 therapists increasingly focused their interventions on specific time periods—the here and now, the past, and the future. The focus on the Now supports the McMaster results and was particularly impressive—a total frequency of 887 compared to 79 for Future and 469 for Past.

On the To Whom Scale, the therapists increased the number of interventions directed to the Couple–Parents ($p < .0001$), to the Wife–Mother (.0001), and to Child 2 (.0001), the identified patient. The Interpersonal Structure Scale revaled increases on Triadic (.004), Dyadic (.0001), Monadic (.0001), and Topic (.02). On System Membership the therapists increased on Cross-Generational (.03), Parental–Family of Origin (.001), Nonspecific-Family of Origin (.02), Parental–Nuclear Family (.0001), Extended-Nuclear Family (.001), Nonspecific-Nuclear Family (.0001), and Topic (.01).

The shifts on the To Whom Scale in the direction of the parental couple, the mother, and the identified patient parallel the shifts on that scale in the McMaster Study. The increases on the Interpersonal Structure Scale were extensive and not fundamentally dissimilar from the changes in the McMaster Study. In contrast, the increases on the System Membership Scale differed from the McMaster data, reflecting a much greater emphasis on family of origin, cross-generational patterns, and the parental–couple. The Training I data lack the McMaster emphasis on the marital system. Interestingly, the training program at the Family Institute involves a much greater emphasis than the McMaster program on cross-generational patterns and the current impact of unresolved family-of-origin issues. Additionally, the general style of the Family Institute program is not as confrontive of and intrusive into the marital system.

On the Route Scale the only significant finding was an increase in Indirect ($p < .0001$) interventions, which was consistent with the McMaster Indirect results. Significant increases occurred on all of the code categories on the Grammatical Form Scale. The strongest findings were on Label (.0001). The Query–Closed or yes–no question findings did not parallel the McMaster data—the Family Institute therapists increased (.006). The Family Institute findings completely corroborated the McMaster data on the Event Relationship Scale—increases on Temporal (.01), Multiple (.0001), and Isolate (.001).

Overall, the Training I results support the discriminant validity of the FTCS. The system was capable of making many significant distinctions in the verbal behavior of the therapists after one year of training. The results confirm over 60% (16) of the 25 predictions made by Tucker and Pinsof (1984). Overall, they revealed that as the trainees became more active, interpretive, and supportive, they focused increasingly on specific effects, maladaptive behaviors, and the here and now. They directed more of their interventions to the parents as a unit, to the mother, and to the identified patient. They also increased their focus on cross-generational patterns linking the current nuclear family and its families of origin. The data portray these therapists as probing (not confronting) more deeply into the affective system with an increasingly historical perspective that links the past and the present.

Training II Results: Discriminant Validity   The log linear analysis of the data from the nine subjects involved in the pre-, mid-, and posttests revealed various linear and curvilinear patterns. For these nine subjects, activity level did not continue to increase from the mid- to the posttest. On the Topic Scale, the therapists continued increasing their focus on Negative Emotion ($p < .0001$) and Nonspecific Behavior (.0001). New findings were increases on Positive (.05) and Spatial Behavior (.03) and a decrease on Negative Cognitions (.05) or disagreements within the family.

On the Intervention Scale a number of new findings emerged. Over the two years, the nine therapists increased on Refocus ($p < .02$), Direction (.001), Process (.0001), and Problem (.02). With the exception of Interpretation–Transposition, which decreased significantly (.001), most of the gains that all 19 therapists manifested at midtest were sustained by this subgroup at posttest on the Intervention Scale. This was also the case with Temporal Orientation, with the exception of Current and Atemporal, which decreased (.01) and increased (.001), respectively, at posttest.

On the To Whom Scale, most of the midtest changes were sustained at posttest. New findings were that Family (talking to the whole group) decreased from mid- to posttest (.001), interventions directed to the Husband–Father increased (.0001), interventions to the children as a group increased (.001), and Nonspecific interventions, with no specific target group or person, increased (.001). In addition to sustaining the midtest changes, on Interpersonal Structure the therapists decreased on Group (.02) and continued to increase on Triadic (.001).

The System Membership Scale continued to reflect most of the midtest shifts, but also showed a major increase in the therapists' focus on the marital system (Marital–Nuclear Family, $p < .0001$). On Route, the therapists continued to increase on Indirect (.0001) and showed a new jump on Direct interventions (.0001) from mid- to posttest. Grammatical Form revealed a major decline in closed questions (Query Closed, $p < .0001$) as well as a major increase in open questions (Query Open, .0001) and Commands (.002). The pre- to midtest changes on Event Relationship were sustained at posttest and no new findings emerged.

The Training II findings are intriguing. First of all, they suggest that certain changes occur in the first year of training, and that other changes occur in the second year. Some of the changes are additive over the course of the whole program, whereas others delete or subtract (increase at midtest and decrease at posttest). These findings have obvious implications for training programs, particularly in terms of whether certain types of changes are epigenetic and must necessarily precede or follow others. Of course, it must be remembered that the findings from this study and the Training I study are very preliminary, and that before any firm conclusions or implications can be drawn far more work needs to be done.

The picture of the nine therapists at posttest more closely resembles the advanced McMaster therapists than the picture painted by the FTCS of the nineteen therapists at midtest. At posttest, the Family Institute therapists were less interpretive, more directive, controlling, problem oriented, and concerned with process. They respectively reduced and increased the amount of closed and open questions, and focused much more on the marital system within the nuclear family. Of course, it must be remembered that these changes can only be attributed to the nine therapists in the Training II study. It is not clear as to whether these changes would also characterize all nineteen therapists or the 15 therapists who were actually evaluated at posttest.

FTCS Results Summary

The research that has been reviewed above supports the reliability and discriminant validity of the FTCS. The system achieved adequate reliability and was able to make many expected and clinically meaningful discriminations in several studies with different therapist populations. Particularly intriguing was the system's capacity to identify clinically relevant patterns of therapist behavior within sessions as well as the system's ability to capture changes in verbal behavior over the course of family therapy training.

Various limitations of the research to date must also be identified. The FTCS has only just begun to be used by researchers outside of our group at the Family Institute of Chicago. At the State University of New York at Albany, Friedlander, Highlen, and Lassiter (1985) used four of the FTCS scales (Temporal Orientation, Interpersonal Structure, System Membership, and Route) to descriptively analyze the verbal behavior of the therapist *and* family members in four sessions with famous family therapists. More work by other researchers needs to be done in order to determine the extent to which the FTCS "works" outside of the context in which it was developed.

Another major limitation concerns the predictive validity of the FTCS—its capacity to predict the outcome of treatment. The FTCS has been able to make some clinically meaningful distinctions. We currently have no good empirical evidence to support the hypothesis that these distinctions are related to treatment outcome. The next major area of research with the FTCS involves testing the system's ability to tap processes that are related to the outcome of treatment. In terms of the system's overall validity, the initial task of establishing its discriminant validity has been achieved. The next task is to investigate its predictive validity. Once that task has been accomplished, the methodological soundness of the instrument and its utility for the field of psychotherapy and family therapy research will be established.

Future Directions

The FTCS is a research tool that can be used within family therapy research to test a multiplicity of hypotheses about the verbal behavior of therapists and family members. We believe it can also be used to study the behavior of individual therapists, in that it encompasses many significant individual therapy dimensions. Beyond the obvious and immediate goal of using the FTCS to look at the relationship between process and outcome variables, we are particularly interested in FTCS research in three areas.

The first concerns the relationship between the processes tapped by the FTCS and the therapeutic alliance. As mentioned at the beginning of this chapter, Don Catherall and I (Pinsof and Catherall, 1986) have developed three scales to measure the therapeutic alliance in individual, couple, and family therapy. We view the alliance as an experiential (as opposed to observable) variable that both affects and is affected by specific therapist behaviors. Currently, in our research we are attempting to determine the relationship between the variables targeted by our self-report alliance measures and the observer-report FTCS measures. We view the alliance as a primary mediator of the efficacy of therapist interventions. It is equivalent to the vessel or container in which the specific interventions occur. It sets the context.

The second major area of future research goes back to the issue of reconstructivity. To use the FTCS as a reconstructive measure, we must be able to analyze combinations of codes. To date we have only focused on analyzing the data from each scale separately. We recently attempted to examine combinations of codes from the McMaster data. Looking at all nine scales, there were over 5000 different combinations of codes that occurred within the 16 McMaster sessions. The most frequent combination of codes from all nine scales (NSB/PR/AT/WM/MC/NNF/D/QO/T) occurred just 18 times. Over 95% of all the actual combinations occurred less than four times in the entire data base. Such low frequencies virtually preclude standard statistical analysis. We have just begun to look at other, smaller chain combinations that we believe might capture certain types of interventions like symptom prescriptions (NB/DN/N/. . . .), genetic interpretations (__ __/TR/CR/__ __/__ __/CG/__ __/__ __/T), etc.

The third area of investigation concerns data reduction. We have just begun to explore data reduction strategies. For instance, we used log linear statistics to examine whether there were differences within the McMaster data with regard to the affective orientation of the therapists. Using the PE+NE+NSE code combination (collapsing these codes into one Affect category) from the Topic Scale, we found that the advanced therapists were significantly more (.03) affectively oriented. The related areas of reconstruction analysis and data reduction have only just begun to be examined and require much further work.

Conclusion

As well as presenting the FTCS and research pertaining to its methodological characteristics, this chapter has attempted to give the reader a sense of the research process. In all likelihood, the FTCS, like the FTBS and its other precursors, will be modified and probably replaced in our subsequent work. The FTCS represents a condensation of my thinking and the thoughts of my colleagues at a particular time concerning certain aspects of the process of family therapy. It resolves certain problems, overlooks others, and even creates some. As we learn more about process research, undoubtedly our solutions to these myriad problems will evolve in new directions.

I hope that the perspective on the research process provided by this chapter conveys a sense of the pleasure, challenge, frustration, and excitement of process research. Ultimately, my hope is that this saga about the productive and blind alleys I have explored as a process researcher will encourage and facilitate the research of others, leading eventually to a greater understanding of how psychotherapy works.

References

Ackerman, N. W. *The psychodynamics of family life*. New York: Basic Books, 1958.

_____. *Treating the troubled family*. New York: Basic Books, 1966.

Alexander, J. F., & Barton, C. Behavioral systems therapy with delinquent families. In D. Olson (Ed.). *Treating relationships*. Lake Mills, Iowa: Graphic, 1976.

Alexander, J. F., & Parsons, B. *Functional family therapy*. Monterey, California: Brooks/Cole, 1982.

Bergin, A. The evaluation of therapeutic outcomes. In A. Bergin, & S. Garfield, (Eds.). *Handbook of psychotherapy and behavior change: An empirical analysis*. New York: John Wiley, 1971.

Bergin, A., & Jasper, L. Correlates of empathy in psychotherapy: A replication. *Journal of Abnormal Psychology*, 1969, 74, 447–481.

Bowen, M. *Family therapy in clinical practice*. New York: Jason Aronson, 1978.

Caracena, P., & Vicory, J. Correlates of phenomenological and judged empathy. *Journal of Counseling Psychology*, 1969, 16(6), 510–515.

Chinsky, J., & Rappoport, J. Brief critique of the meaning and reliability of "accurate empathy" ratings. *Psychological Bulletin*, 1970, 73, 379–382.

Cleghorn, J., & Levin, S. Training family therapists by setting instructional objectives. *American Journal of Orthopsychiatry*, 1973, 43(3), 439–446.

Cohen, J. A coefficient of agreement for nominal scales. *Educational and Psychological Measurement*, 1960, 20(1), 37–46.

Dollard, J., & Auld, F. *Scoring human motives: A manual*. New Haven, Conn.: Yale University Press, 1959.

Epstein, N., & Bishop, D. Position paper—family therapy: State of the art—1973. *Canadian Psychiatric Association Journal*, 1973, 18, 175–183.

_____. Problem-centered systems therapy of the family. In A. Gurman, & D. Kniskern (Eds.). *Handbook of family therapy*. New York: Brunner/Mazel, 1981.

Friedlander, M., Highlen, P., & Lassiter, W. Content analytic comparison of four expert counselors' approaches to family treatment: Ackerman, Bowen, Jackson, and Whitaker. *Journal of Counseling Psychology*, 1985, 32(2), 171–180.

Greenberg, L. Resolving splits: The use of the two chair technique. *Psychotherapy Theory Research and Practice*, 1979, 16, 310–318.

Gurman, A. S. Instability of therapeutic conditions in psychotherapy. *Journal of Counseling Psychology*, 1973, 20, 16–24.

Gurman, A. S., Kniskern, D. P., & Pinsof, W. M. Research on the process and outcome of marital and family therapy. In S. Garfield and A. Bergin (Eds.). *Handbook of psychotherapy and behavior change* (3rd ed.). New York: Wiley, in press.

Haley, J. Family therapy: A radical change. In J. Haley (Ed.). *Changing families: A family therapy reader*. New York: Grune & Stratton, 1971, 272–284.

_____. *Problem solving therapy*. San Francisco: Jossey-Bass, 1976.

Kiesler, D. J. *The process of psychotherapy: Empirical foundations and systems of analysis*. Chicago: Aldine, 1973.

Kurtz, R. R., & Grummon, D. L. Different approaches to the measurement of therapist empathy and their relationship to therapy outcomes. *Journal of Consulting and Clinical Psychology*, 1972, *39*, 106–115.

Minuchin, S. *Families and family therapy*. Cambridge, Mass.: Harvard University Press, 1974.

Minuchin, S., Rosman, B. L., & Baker, L. *Psychosomatic families: Anorexia nervosa in context*. Cambridge, Mass.: Harvard University Press, 1978.

Patterson, G. R. The aggressive child: Victim and architect of a coercive system, In L. Mash, A. Hamerlynk, & L. Handy (Eds.). *Behavior modification and families*. New York: Burnner/Mazel, 1976, 267–316.

Patterson, G. R., Cobb, J. A., & Ray, R. A social engineering technology for retraining the families of aggressive boys. In H. Adams, & L. Unikel (Eds.). *Georgia symposium in experimental clinical psychology, Vol. II*. Springfield, Ill.: Charles Thomas, 1972.

Paul, N. L., & Paul, B. B. *A marital puzzle: Transgenerational analysis in marital counseling*. New York: W. W. Norton and Co., 1975.

Pinsof, W. M. *Family therapist verbal behavior: Development of a coding system*. Unpublished doctoral dissertation, Dept. of psychology, York University, Toronto, 1977.

_____. The family therapist behavior scale (FTBS): Development and evaluation of a coding system. *Family Process*, 1979, *18*(4), 451–461.

_____. *The family therapist coding system (FTCS) Coding Manual*. Chicago: Family Institute of Chicago Monograph Series, 1980.

_____. Family therapy process research. In A. Gurman, & D. Kniskern (Eds.). *Handbook of family therapy*. New York: Brunner/Mazel, 1981, 699–741.

_____. Integrative problem centered therapy (IPCT): Toward the synthesis of family and individual psychotherapies. *Journal of Marital and Family Therapy*, 1983, *9*(1), 19–35.

Pinsof, W. M., & Catherall, D. R. The integrative psychotherapy alliance: Family, couple and individual therapy scales. *Journal of Marital and Family Therapy*, 1986, *12*(2).

Postner, R. S., Guttman, H., Sigal, J., Epstein, N., & Rakoff, V. Process and outcome in conjoint family therapy. *Family Process*, 1971, *10*, 451–474.

Rice, L. N. The evocative function of the therapist. In D. Wexler, & L. Rice (Eds.). *Innovations in client centered therapy*. New York: Wiley, 1974, 289–312.

Santa-Barbara, J., Woodward, C., Levin, S., Goodman, J. Streiner, D., & Epstein, N. The McMaster family therapy outcome study: An overview of methods and results. *International Journal of Family Therapy*, 1979, winter, 304–323.

Satir, V. *Conjoint family therapy* (rev. ed.). Palo Alto: Science and Behavior Books, 1967.

Schwartz, D. An examination of the determinants of the reliability of the family therapist coding system. Unpublished pilot research project paper, Clinical Psychology Program, Dept. of Psychiatry and Behavioral Sciences, Northwestern University, Chicago, 1983.

Stierlin, H. *Psychoanalysis and family therapy: Selected papers*. New York: Jason Aronson, 1977.

Truax, C. B., & Carkhuff, R. R. *Toward effective counseling and psychotherapy: Training and practice*. Chicago: Aldine, 1967.

Tucker, S. J. Evaluation of family therapy training. Unpublished doctoral dissertation. Department of Psychology, Northwestern University, Evanston, Ill., 1981.

Tucker, S., & Pinsof, W. The empirical evaluation of family therapy training. *Family Process*, 1984, *23*, 437–456.

Watzlawick, P., Beavin, J. & Jackson, D. *Pragmatics of human communication: A study of interactional patterns, pathologies and paradoxes*. New York: W. W. Norton, 1967.

Watzlawick, P., Weakland, J. & Fisch, R. *Change: Principles of problem formation and problem resolution*. New York: W. W. Norton, 1974.

Weeks, G. & L'Abate, L. *Paradoxical Psychotherapy: Theory and practice with individuals, couples and families*. New York: Brunner/Mazel, 1982.

Appendix

This appendix to Chapter 7 presents two examples of how the FTCS can be applied to actual transcripts of family therapy sessions. To illustrate the range of interventions that the FTCS is capable of capturing, I selected two vignettes from two different renowned family therapists that illustrate very different types of interventions. The first vignette presents the work of Salvador Minuchin and is taken from his book, *Families and family therapy* (1974, pp. 165–174). It captures many basic structural interventions and highlights the personal, here and now quality of Minuchin's family work. The second vignette presents the work of Norman Paul and is taken from a book that he co-authored, *A marital puzzle: Transgenerational analysis in marital counseling* (Paul and Paul, 1975, pp. 179–187). Paul's vignette captures the confrontive, historical, and interpretive quality of his marital treatment.

The Minuchin Vignette

This vignette is from a transcript of a consultation session that Minuchin conducted with a psychiatrist (Dr. Farrell) and a family he was treating—the Smiths. Mr. Smith had been a psychiatric patient for ten years and had been hospitalized several times for depression. Recently, he has become symptomatic (agitated, anxious) and has requested hospitalization. Mr. Smith (age 49), his wife (age 42), their only son Matthew (age 12), Mr. Brown (Mrs. Smith's father, who has lived with the couple since marriage), and Dr. Farrell are present at the consultation session. The vignette begins in the middle of an exchange between Minuchin and Mr. Smith about the latter's job.

V1–F M1–ST/P/HF/MC/ NNF/D/QO S1–IS	1	Minuchin:	/How long have you been working
			there?/
		Mr. Smith:	Thirty years.
V1–F M1–S/P/HF/MC/ NNF/D/L S2–IS	2	Minuchin:	/Thirty years! My goodness!/
		Mr. Smith:	Yeah. With the company. But not in this job thirty years. Just about seven years on this job.
V1–NLC M1–SD/AT/HF/MC NNF/I/L	3	Minuchin:	/I don't know./ I never worked
V2–NSB M2–SD/P/HF/MC/ NNF/I/L			any place more than seven years./
V3–F–NSB M3–SD/AT/HF/MC/ NNF/I/L			This is the longest time I have
V4–NB M4–SD/AT/HF/DC/ TNF/I/L			worked./ I am much more restless
V5–NB M5–SD/AT/HF/MC/ NNF/I/L			than you, clearly./

S3–M

I <u>am</u> a very <u>restless</u> kind of

person./

Mr. Smith: Mm.

V1–PB
M1–S/AT/HF/MC/
  NNF/D/L
S4–IS

4 Minuchin: /You <u>are</u> not, evidently./

Mr. Smith: No, I wouldn't say I'm restless. I mean, I sleep. But I don't—

V1–PB
M1–S/AT/HF/MC/
  NNF/D/L
S5–IS

way

5 Minuchin: /But you <u>are steady</u> in one —/

Mr. Smith: As far as the job's concerned, yeah. Well, I went there at nineteen, and I've stayed down there.

V1–F
M1–ST/CR/HF/MC/
  NNF/D/QC
S6–IS

6 Minuchin: /You <u>are</u> now forty-nine?/

Mr. Smith: Forty-nine.

V1–F
M1–SD/CR/HF/G/
  INC/DI/L
S7–IS

7 Minuchin: /We <u>are</u> the same age./

Mr. Smith: Are we?

V1–NSB–NE
M1–PM/P/HF/MC/
  NNF/D/QO
S8–IS

8 Minuchin: /And when <u>did you begin</u> to kind of

<u>worry</u> about things?/

Mr. Smith: Ten years ago.

been worrying

V1–NE
M1–PM/P/HF/MC/
  NNF/D/L
V2–VB–F
M2–ST/AT/HF/DC/
  TNF/D/QC
S9–M

9 Minuchin: /Ten years./ <u>Tell</u> me, maybe your

is

son— your only son?/

Mr. Smith: Yeah.

V1–VB–NLC
M1–PM/N/C1/MC/
  PNF/I/L
V2–PC–NLC
M2–PM/AT/C1/DC/
  MNF/I/L
V3–NSB–NE–NB–NE
M3–PR/AT/C1/MC/
  NNF/I/QO
S10–T

10 Minuchin: /Your father <u>said</u> he <u>is</u> the problem,/

and your mother <u>agrees</u> that he <u>is</u>

the problem in the family./ But

rpt

what <u>are</u> the things that m̸ake

your father—that <u>irritate</u> him,

that <u>make</u> him <u>upset</u>, so he <u>gets</u>

			<u>pissed</u> off?/
		Matthew:	I don't know. I don't think it's like—anybody that puts it on him. It's just—I don't know.
V1–NVC–NLC	11	Minuchin:	/I just <u>can't believe</u> that, you
M1–DD/AT/C1/DC/			
TNF/DI/L			
V2–NSB–NB–NLC			<u>know</u>./ People <u>are</u> always part of—/ *inc*
M2–PR/AT/C1/G/			
NNF/I/L			
V3–NLC–NB			when people <u>live together</u>, then
M3–ST/AT/C1/TC/			
TNF/I/L			
V4–NLC–NB			they <u>irritate</u> each other, you <u>know</u>./
M4–ST/AT/C1/TC/			
TNF/DI/L			
V5–NB			I <u>am sure</u> your father <u>irritates</u> you
M5–PR/AT/C1/TC/			
PNF/D/L			
V6–NLC			sometimes./ And I <u>am sure</u> that your
M6–ST/AT/C1/MC/			
TY/I/L			
V7–PC			grandfather <u>irritates</u> you sometimes./
M7–ST/AT/C1/DC/			
TNF/I/QC			
S11–CY			And you in turn <u>irritate</u> your
			grandfather and your mother and
			father./I <u>am sure</u> of that./ <u>Am</u> I <u>right</u>?/
		Matthew:	Yeah. But I don't irritate him that much, like really nervous. I might, you know, be bad sometimes. But I don't think I really irritate him that much.
V1–NB	12	Minuchin:	/What about your grandpa? <u>Does</u> he
M1–ST/AT/C1/DC/			
PFO/IT/QC			
S12–IS			<u>irritate</u> your father?/
		Matthew:	No. He don't say much.
V1–VB	13	Minuchin:	/Grandpa <u>doesn't say</u> much./ How
M1–C/AT/NS/MC/			
ENF/I/L			
V2–F			old <u>are</u> you, Mr. Brown?/
M2–ST/CR/GP/MC/			

NNF/D/QO
S13–M

                    Mr. Brown: I don't know. Sometimes I think I say too much.

V1–F
M1–R/CR/GP/MC/
   NNF/D/QO
S14–IS

     14 Minuchin: /How old <u>are</u> you?/

                    Mr. Brown: How much do you think?

V1–F
M1–ST/CR/GP/MC/
   NNF/D/L
S15–IS

     15 Minuchin: /Oh, *I think* like fifty-three./

                    Mr. Brown: Seventy-eight.

V1–F
M1–ST/CR/GP/MC/
   NNF/D/L

     16 Minuchin: /Seventy-eight *are*./ You <u>look</u> fine./

V2–PC
M2–S/CR/GP/MC/
   NNF/D/L
S16–IS

                    Mr. Brown: No, I'll tell you now what I think. What brings it on is Bob himself. He's always worried about me. He wants everything done just certain ways, see? He's particular, in other words, see? And he sees something ain't done, and right away, he's got to go and do it. And someone says, "I'll do it." "No, I'll do it. I'll do it," he says. That's one thing, now. Now, another—

V1–VB–PE–PB
M1–EM/AT/GP/DC/
   NNF/DI/QC
S17–IS

     17 Minuchin: /You <u>are saying</u> he <u>likes</u> to do

                    things instead—for other people?/

                    Mr. Smith: I think he missed the point.

                    Mr. Brown: No, no, no. For himself. Now, suppose there's dirt on the carpet or something like that. He'd say, "Well, there's dirt on the carpet." She'd say, "I'll clean it up." "Never mind, I'll do it." And he'd go right away and clean it up. Now I don't think he should do that.

V1–PB
M1–S/AT/GP/MC/
   NNF/I/L
S18–IS

     18 Minuchin: /He's <u>helpful</u> that way./

                    Mr. Brown: I don't think it's good. I don't think he should do that. There's lots of things that he does that he shouldn't do. He should let someone else do something too.

                    should he let

V1–NSB
M1–PM/AT/GP/DC/
   NNF/I/QO
S19–IS

     19 Minuchin: /Like who?/

                    Mr. Brown: Any one of the three of us.

V1–NSB

     20 Minuchin: /He <u>takes everything on</u> his

M1–PM/AT/GP/MC/
   NNF/I/QC
S20–IS

                                             shoulders?/

Mr. Brown: Almost everything. I—pretty near everything.

V1–F–VB   **21 Minuchin:** /You—what's your name, you said?/
M1–ST/AT/C1/MC/
   NNF/D/QO
S21–IS   **Matthew:** Matthew.
V1–NVC   **22 Minuchin:** /Matthew. You disagreed with
M1–R/N/C1/DC/
   ENF/DI/L
S22–M   that—with your grandfather's
                                statement./

Matthew: I think he's partly right. I don't think
he takes that—you know. He does try to
do a lot of things. Like, somebody will
offer. He'll say, "No I can do it myself."
I don't feel like he takes everything on.
He'll do a lot of that. Not really too
much. But he tells me to take out the
trash and all, still. Stuff like that, I still
got to do most of.

Mrs. Smith: But then when you don't do it, he ends
up doing it.

Mr. Smith: I don't think that's what's wrong, because I don't—I could help my wife
more as far as cleaning is concerned.

Matthew: Yeah, like he'll come home and, like,
run the carpet sweeper.

Mr. Smith: Just fast stuff.

Matthew: Yeah.

Mrs. Smith: But it's a big help.

Mr. Smith: Heavy cleaning, I don't do for her, and
dishes, I don't do for her. Yeah, I do
help her with the dishes ever since I've
been married, but not all the time. Most
of the time.

Matthew: I think he means like if something's,
like, broken in the house, or—

V1–VB   **23 Minuchin:** /Wait a moment,/wait a moment./
M1–DN/N/C1/MC/
   NNF/D/CD
V2–VB
M2–DN/N/C1/MC/
   NNF/D/CD   Who means?/
V3–NLC
M3–ST/AT/C1/MC   **Matthew:** My grandfather.
   NNF/I/QO
S23–M   *means*
V1–NLC   **24 Minuchin:** /Your grandfather./ You are ____

M1–ST/N/C1/MC/
   ENF/I/L
V2–VB
M2–EM/N/C1/DC/
   ENF/D/L
S24–M

		explaining your grandfather./

Matthew: Yeah. Like if something's broken in the house or something, he'll want to do it himself, or something.

Mr. Smith: No, I'm not too handy a person that way. I want it done right away, probably, and characteristic—

Matthew: Yeah, like you want it done right away.

Mrs. Smith: He hasn't enough patience to wait. But I don't think that's bad. A lot of people are that way.

V1–VB–PB
M1–BR/N/C1/TC/
   PNF/DI/L
S25–IS

25 **Minuchin:** /Mom was saying, ''Don't be critical

of Dad.''/

Matthew: She what?

V1–VB–PB–VB–NB
M1–R/N/C1/TC/
   PNF/DI/L

26 **Minuchin:** /She just said, ''Don't be critical

of Daddy.'' Because you were saying,

V2–VB–NLC–NSB
M2–R/N/C1/DC/
   OF/I/L
V3–PB
M3–EM/AT/C1/DC/
   MNF/I/QC
S26–T

''He's impatient,''/ and Mom says,

''Well, you know, a lot of people

are like that.''/ Is she protective

of Father?/

Matthew: I don't think so.

V1–PB
M1–S/AT/C1/DC/
   MNF/I/L
V2–NLC–PB
M2–S/AT/C1/TC/
   TNF/I/L
S27–M

27 **Minuchin:** /There is nothing wrong with that./

I think it is rather nice./

Matthew: She is a little bit, I guess. I don't think she's really overprotective.

V1–NLC–PB
M1–S/AT/C1/TC/
   TNF/I/L
V2–PC
M2–ST/AT/WM/DC/
   TNF/D/QC
V3–NSB–NSB–NSB–NSB
M3–BR/AT/WM/DC/
   MNF/I/QC
S28–M

28 **Minuchin:** /I just mean protective, in a nice

way. In the same way in which

Daddy apparently is protective of

everybody else, according to

	Grandpa./ Is that true?/ Is
	your husband trying to do things,
	trying to do your job?/
	Mrs. Smith: Well, he worries about me excessively.

V1–NE
M1–PM/AT/WM/DC/
   MNF/I/L
V2–NE
M2–BR/AT/WM/DC/MNF/DI/QC
S29–M

29 Minuchin: /He worries about you./ That you

don't like?/

Mrs. Smith: Yes. I don't think he should, because I feel I'm an individual, and he shouldn't worry so much. Because he has a lot of his own problems he should take care of.

V1–NLC–NE
M1–ST/AT/WM/DC/
   MNF/DI/L
V2–NE
M2–PR/AT/WM/DC/
   MNF/DI/L
V3–NSB
M3–ST/N/HF/DC/
   TNF/D/QC
S30–T

30 Minuchin: /You mean he worries about you,/

sometimes it bothers you./ Can

I have a cigarette, Mr. Smith?/

Mr. Smith: Sure.

V1–NSB–NLC
M1–SD/AT/NS/MC/
   TY/I/L
V2–NLC–NE
M2–SD/N/NS/MC/
   TY/I/L
V3–NSB
M3–SD/N/NS/MC/
   TY/I/L
V4–F
M4–ST/AT/HF/MC/
   MNF/I/QO
S31–T

31 Minuchin: /I smoke only when I just don't

know what to do,/ but by this

time I don't know what to do, so

I am worried./ I am smoking./

What's your wife's name?/
Mr. Smith: Rosemary.

V1–F
M1–ST/AT/HF/MC/
   MNF/I/L
V2–F
M2–ST/AT/HF/MC/NNF/D/QO
S32–M

32 Minuchin: /Rosemary./ And yours?/
         is   *is*

Mr. Smith: Bob. Robert.

V1–VB–NE
M1–BR/AT/HF/DC/
   MNF/DI/L
V2–NLC
M2–C/N/HF/MC/
   MNF/IT/QO

33 Minuchin: /Bob. Rosemary says that sometimes

you worry too much about her./

S33–M		What <u>does</u> she <u>mean?</u>/
	Mr. Smith:	Well, I'm—I don't really know what she means by that. I'm concerned over her, and I'm very much in love with her, and I don't think I worry too much.
V1–VB M1–DN/N/HF/G/ INC/D/CD	34 Minuchin:	/Let's find out./ Let's find out./
V2–VB M2–DN/N/HF/G/ INC/D/CD	Mr. Smith:	I don't know what you mean by—
S32–IS	Mrs. Smith:	Well, sometimes actually, like when I come home from work or something, for instance Saturday. Well, maybe not Saturday. Any day.
	Mr. Smith:	M—hm.
V1–NLC M1–ST/N/NS/G/ MNF/D/QC	35 Minuchin:	/You <u>know</u> something?/ You <u>have</u>
V2–SB M2–ST/N/CP/DC/ MNF/D/L		that chair, that one, in the
S35–IS		middle, kind of between you./
	Mr. Smith:	Started being more, uh—
	Minuchin:	Yeah.
	Mrs. Smith:	He questions, like, all my movements, and it's nothing that—
		inc.
V1–SB M1–DN/N/HF/MC/ MNF/D/QC	36 Minuchin:	/Can you <u>look</u> at—can you <u>turn</u>
S36–IS		your chair?/
	Mr. Smith:	Turn my chair?
V1–SB M1–DN/N/HF/DC/ MNF/D/L	37 Minuchin:	/Yeah. Just so that you <u>can look</u>
S37–IS		at her./
	Mr. Smith:	Yeah.
V1–VB M1–EM/N/HF/DC/ MNF/D/L	38 Minuchin:	/Because maybe you don't—you
S38–IS		<u>miss</u> some of the messages./
	Mr. Smith:	The last twenty-three years.
	Mrs. Smith:	No, but like, he'll always—it's very hard to explain. I really don't know how to explain it.
	Mr. Smith:	I think that she means—
		stop
V1–VB M1–DD/N/CP/G MNF/D/CD	39 Minuchin:	/No, no, no./
S39–IS	Mrs. Smith:	No, but he's always—
V1–VB	40 Minuchin:	/<u>Tell</u> him./ <u>Tell</u> him./ <u>Tell</u> him./

M1–DN/N/WM/DC/
　　MNF/D/CD
V2–VB
M2–DN/N/WM/DC/
　　MNF/D/CD
V3–VB
M3–DN/N/WM/DC/
　　MNF/D/CD
S40–IS

Mrs. Smith: All right. Like when I come home,
"What did this one say, what did that
one say?" That's when I go to the hair-
dresser's. When you go somewhere and
see somebody and see Mary, or somebody, and I'll say, "What did Mary
say,"—which is nothing wrong when
you ask me. But yet, at the same time,
he don't tell me. But yet in another aspect, like if I'm sick, he'll come home
from work and I'll be laying up in bed,
and I'll be waiting, waiting for you to
come up and see how I am. And you
don't come up. You'll sit down and
have a beer and a cigarette, and then
decide to come up. And I—remember
when I was in the hospital? What a
hard time you gave me in the hospital?
You—you vary. I just don't know how
to explain it, really.

Mr. Smith: Yeah.

Mrs. Smith: And yet, I know he—you love me, and I
love you. But—maybe that's the prob-
lem. Maybe you don't know how to
show love. You think that could be it?

Mr. Smith: All right to answer?

V1–VB
M1–DN/N/HF/DC/
　　MNF/D/CD
V2–VB
M2–C/N/HF/DC/
　　MNF/I/L
S41–T

41 Minuchin: /Yeah. Yeah, please. <u>Answer</u> to

her./ She <u>asked</u> you a question./

Mr. Smith: M—hm. I don't think that's good reasoning there. I don't think that's not a
problem. But I don't think that's my
problem. I know I get concerned a lot of
times about your personal things, which
I don't think you like, and which I
shouldn't be concerned about. But,
well, I mean, she—it is true. I've come
home and I knew she was sick, and I
didn't go right up but—

V1–VB
M1–R/N/NF/DC/
　　MNF/I/L
V2–NSB–VB–VB
M2–DD/N/HF/TC/
　　TNF/DI/L
V3–VB
M3–DN/N/HF/DC/

42 Minuchin: /Bob, Rosemary <u>asked</u> you a question./

You <u>don't need</u> to <u>answer</u> me, because

she <u>asked</u> you a question./ So you

MNF/D/CD
S42–T   <u>answer</u>./

The Paul Vignette

This vignette is taken from the fifth session in a series of seven marital counseling sessions that Norman Paul conducted with a couple experiencing a variety of marital problems—Van (age 32) and Cindy (age 31) Hoops. The vignette begins in the middle of an exchange between Paul and Van in which they are discussing Van's fears of loss of control, particularly in regard to his own and his wife's sexuality. Paul has just interpreted Van's sexual withholding as a way of protecting Cindy from going insane.

	Van:	Hmmm. (sighs) Yeah. I'm trying to think of the messages that I got about sex. And I come up with a blank. The messages I got from my parents were that they didn't have sex. I remember one occasion which was particularly guilt-producing for me. I don't think I've ever said this before, but uh, my father had a lot of financial difficulties at one point, and this was right after, I guess, he went into business, maybe it was right before, I can't remember. I think it was right after. But we lived in a very small place, and uh, there were only two bedrooms. I slept in the same bedroom with my mother and father.	

V1–F
M1–ST/P/HF/TC/   1 Paul: /At what age?/
  PFO/D/QO

S1–IS   Van: Oh, this is when I was a sophomore, freshman in high school.

V1–SB
M1–ST/P/HF/G/   2 Paul: /And what <u>was</u> the bed arrangement?/
  PFO/D/QO

S2–IS   Van: Ummmmmmmm. I'm trying to . . . I'm sure this is true. Part of my memory says no, that isn't true; I slept down on the couch. But uh . . .
                                Cindy: Uh-uh. (meaning no)

V1–SB   3 Paul: /You <u>were</u> there?/
M1–ST/P/WM/TC/
  PFO/D/QC

S3–IS   Van: No, you weren't there.
                                Cindy: No, but I know what . . . I remember your mother was telling me about her feelings about that arrangement.

V1–VB   4 Paul: /What'd she say?/
M1–C/P/WM/DC/
  PFO/I/QO

S4–IS   Cindy: She said she's . . . this goes to a lot of stuff about Van's sister who is eleven months younger than Van, and how Dorothy always got everything and his mother said, one time, "I always feel so bad that poor Vanny had to sleep in the same room with Daddy and me."

V1–NSB   5 Paul: /For how long?/
M1–ST/P/WM/TC/

PFO/I/QO
S5-IS

Cindy: I don't know, but she says, "We felt it was important that Dorothy have her own room, and poor Vanny was just left to have to do the best he could." And she said, "It always bothered me that he had to sleep with his mom and dad."

Van: I have foggy memories of it. I can remember when my sister went away to school, then I took over her bedroom. So I had a bedroom of my own when I was a senior. But it must have been in the sophomore and junior years of high school that I either slept on the couch in sort of living room–kitchen combined.
Hell, there were only three rooms in the whole stupid place. But I . . . whew, boy, that's a . . . thinking about that sometimes, I don't think about it because of sort of a horrible situation it was. But at any rate, I do remember walking . . . this was my senior year at high school, because I remember walking from my bedroom through the bathroom into my parent's bedroom . . .

Paul: Yeah.

Van: . . . And they were making love.

V1–PB   6   Paul: /So they did make love./
M1–ST/P/HF/DC/
   MFO/I/L

S6-IS

Van: Well, that was the only time I ever saw it. But . . . when I walked into the room, I can remember my father rolled off of my mother, and he was on top.

Paul: Yeah.

Van: And I remember he rolled over and sort of rolled over to his side of the bed with his face away from my mother, and she was absolutely bullshit at me.

Cindy: Oh.

Van: She . . . she said later, I think it was either that evening or it was the next day, she said, "That's the first time your father has ever treated me as a woman in a long time," and to the effect, "You ruined it."

Cindy: Oh.

Van: And I can remember feeling horrible. Just absolutely horrible, because I had walked in on them without announcing myself. Or anything like that.

V1–NB   7   Paul: /Why would you do that?/
M1–EM/P/HF/DC/
   PFO/D/QO

S7-IS

Van: I went to get a drink of water in the kitchen.

V1–NLC–PB–PB   8   Paul: Well, you know, it's just a matter
M1–BR/AT/HF/DC/
   PFO/D/L

S8-IS

of courtesy to knock on the door./

Van: Oh, but maybe you don't understand the arrangement of the, the . . . it was sort of . . . it wasn't done, it wasn't anything unusual for me to walk through that bedroom.

V1–NLC–VB–NSB   9   Paul: /No, but it gets involved with what
M1–EM/P/HF/MC/

NNF/D/L
S9–M

you're <u>talking about</u> when you first

came in . . . <u>space</u>./ It <u>was</u> as if that
                                inc
<u>was</u> part of . . .

| | | Van: | <u>Boundaries</u>. |

V1–NB   10   Paul: /Their boundaries, and your boundaries
M1–BR/P/HF/DC/
PFO/DI/L

V2–NB   <u>were</u> interchangeable./ Their space
M2–BR/P/HF/DC/
PFO/DI/L

S10–IS   and your space <u>were</u> the same./
                     Van: Yeah. Well, it certainly was true for a couple of years. I
                              can't really . . .

V1–NVB–SB   11   Paul: /<u>Did</u> you <u>see</u> them when you <u>were</u> in
M1–BR/P/HF/DC/
PFO/DI/QC

S11–IS   their bedroom changing dress, or . . . /
                     Van: No, I don't remember.

V1–NLC   12   Paul: /You <u>don't remember</u>./ That <u>sounds</u>
M1–DD/N/HF/DC/
PFO/D/L

V2–NLC   like a very loaded scene./
M2–BR/P/HF/G/
PFO/D/L

S12–IN   Van: It is. Oh, it was. Very powerful.
V1–NLC–NSB–VB– 13 Paul: /You <u>know</u>, you <u>had</u> an option of
  NSB–SB–NSB
M1–BR/P/HF/DC/
PFO/D/L

V2–NLC–PB–NLC   requesting that you <u>could've gotten</u>
M2–BR/AT/HF/DC/
  O/I/L

S13–T   a sleeping bag, and <u>slept</u> in the

                              kitchen, if it<u>'s</u> that tight./ You

                              <u>know</u>, kids <u>have</u> options, whether

                              they <u>think</u> about them or not./
                     Van: That<u>'s</u> why I say it's fuzzy to me, because there are times
                              I remember sleeping on the couch in the living room. But
                              there are other times that I remember sleeping in their
                              bedroom.

V1–NLC–NB   14   Paul: /<u>Did</u> you ever <u>think</u> of <u>screwing</u> your
M1–EM/P/HF/DC/
  CFO/D/QC

S14–IS   mother?/
                     Van: Well . . .

V1–NLC–NLC–VB
M1–EM/P/HF/DC/
   TFO/D/L
S15–T

15 Paul: /That <u>would follow</u>. I <u>mean</u>, in

                  terms of what you're <u>describing</u>./

Van: I remember very negative feelings, negative feelings about any eroticism toward her. And it must . . . I'm sure it has something to do with defending against some feelings. Because I remember my . . . it was almost a reaction formation.

Paul: Un—huh.

Van: That is, my mother was very heavy, and I never . . .

V1–F
M1–ST/P/HF/MC/
   PFO/I/QO
S16–IS

16 Paul: /What color hair <u>did she have</u>?/

Cindy: Blonde. She was blonde and had blue eyes. But I can remember that her weight was offensive to me. I never saw her as an attractive woman. I saw her as heavy. Her legs were very large. I can remember . . .

V1–SP
M1–ST/P/HF/MC/
   PFO/I/QC
S17–IS

17 Paul: /She <u>was</u> always heavy?

Van: No, earlier when I was a little kid . . .

Paul: Yeah.

Van: She . . . earlier when I was a little kid, she probably weighed between 130 and 140.
      was

V1–F
M1–ST/P/HF/MC/
   PFO/I/QO
S18–IS

18 Paul: /What height about?/

Van: She was about 5′6″. But through most of my preadolescence she was about 230. So she was very obese.

V1–SP–PB
M1–EM/P/HF/DC/
   CFO/I/L
S19–FN

19 Paul: /Maybe she <u>put on weight</u> so she

                  wouldn't attract you./

Van: No, she had lots of weight long before that. I think she put on weight for other reasons earlier as a little kid. She had no relationship whatsoever to her father and mother. Shoved around, lived with an aunt here and there, and her father was off searching for rainbows, and . . .

Cindy: Pictures of her show her as a real fat little kid.

Van: She was a fat little chubby kid too. Well, I'm trying to hear what you're saying too. I would have said that she had difficulty with that in terms of other relationships outside of the marriage, and after my father died. That her weight protected her from her femininity. Or protected her from having to deal with that.

V1–EX
M1–ST/P/HF/DC/
   PFO/D/QO
S20–IS

20 Paul: /What was your relationship with her?/

Van: Ahhh. (sighs)

V1–NVB
M1–C/N/HF/MC/

21 Paul: /How loaded <u>was</u> that?/

NNF/D/QO
S21–IS

Van: I get bits and pieces of things that come to mind. I get pictures of being a momma's boy. Terrible time. I had school phobia, more or less, in the first grade. I screamed and yelled when she left. I was very, very attached to her. I spent most of my early childhood being very dependent on her.

V1–NB–NB 22 Paul: /You <u>didn't have</u> much of your father,
M1–TR/P/HF/TC/
CFO/D/L
S22–T

so there <u>was</u> a relational imbalance there./

Van: No, that's true. I rarely remember doing anything with my father by himself. In fact, I don't remember anything, except I remember one time when they fought, my father took my sister and I for a car ride, and we were panicked. I was panicked at least. Both my sister and I were crying because we thought he was leaving my mother. She threw her rings in the sink in a big scene, and he took us off in the car and rode around for a couple of hours. Not a word was said; he never said a word the whole time. So it <u>was</u> loaded. I was very close to her.

V1–NB 23 Paul: /He <u>was gonna kidnap</u> you from Momma./
M1–EM/P/HF/TC/
CFO/I/L
S23–FN

Van: Yeah. I think that's the fear that didn't get verbalized, but I think it's the fear that we had.

inc

V1–VB–NSE 24 Paul: /I <u>don't know</u> what she had . . . /Did she
M1–C/P/HF/TC/
SFO/I/QC
S24–M

ever <u>tell</u> you about how she <u>felt</u>

about those scenes?/

Van: On that occasion, I think . . . on that occasion it seems to me she spent some time talking to my sister and I, maybe the next day, about the fact that she was angry at Dad.

V1–NLC–VB 25 Paul: /I <u>mean have you talked</u> to your sister
M1–C/P/HF/TC/
SFO/D/QC
S25–M

about these things?/

Van: Oh, my sister was uh . . . she dealt with the home situation much different than I did. She dealt with it by being angry, by exiting . . . any change or opportunity, she went, zip!

went zip

V1–NB 26 Paul: /Your sister?/
M1–ST/P/HF/DC/
SFO/I/QC
S26–IS

Van: Yeah.

V1–NLC–VB–EX 27 Paul: /But I <u>mean</u>, you still <u>talk</u> to her
M1–C/CR/HF/TC/
SFO/D/QC
S28–M

about what she <u>experienced</u>?/

Van: Yeah. So her experience was anger at all that stuff. My experience was feeling sorry for my parents, as best as I can recall it. I felt badly about it . . . I felt guilty for it, maybe at some level I felt responsible for whatever troubles they might be having. Where she was always kind of out of the door, never really involved.

V1–NSE–NB
M1–EM/P/HF/TC/
  SFO/I/L

S28–T

28 Paul: /Involved *was* but not <u>letting it appear</u>./

Van: Yeah, I became my mother's confidant. She would tell me about all the problems and troubles. In many ways I sort of was a substitute for a nonverbal, noncommunicative father or husband, who . . . jeepers, most of his life he just sat around on the couch and watched TV and read . . . and worked. He spent his whole life working.

V1–NSB–NB
M1–EM/P/HF/DC/
  CG/D/QC

S29–T

29 Paul: /<u>Is</u> that what you've been doing?/

Van: I used to, a hell of a lot more than I do now. You can report better than I can about that. I sure used to.

V1–PE
M1–ST/CR/HF/DC/
  PFO/D/QC

S30–IS

30 Paul: //*do*<u>Miss</u> your mother?/

Van: Hmmm?

V1–PE
M1–ST/CR/HF/DC/
  PFO/D/QC

31 Paul: /Do you <u>miss</u> your mother?/

S31–IS

Van: I can't get in touch with that. There are times when I do.

V1–PB
M1–EM/P/HF/DC/
  PFO/I/L

32 Paul: /Cause she <u>was</u> a lifeline as a kid./

S32–T

Van: Yeah. (sighs) I miss both my parents. Yes. And on some occasions I run from those feelings. There are times when Cindy says, "I know you must be thinking about your mother now . . . "

Paul: Um—hm.

Van: Or, "You must be thinking about your parents because it's a holiday," and so on, and I'll generally say, "Yes, but," or, "I'm not sure." I do run from those feelings.

V1–NLC–EX
M1–ST/CR/WM/DC/
  MNF/D/QO

S33–M

33 Paul: /Cindy, how <u>do you feel</u> things are

____ going between the two of you, within

yourself?/

Cindy: Really great. I really feel I've had a turn-on experience lately, with uh, with my husband and with my marriage.

V1–PE
M1–ST/AT/WM/DC/
  MNF/D/QO

34 Paul: / *had* In what sense?/

S34–IS

Cindy: And with myself. Well, it just . . . we're just relating differently, we're . . . I mean, I'm always having good feelings, I'm not having any more tight gut feelings in situations, and I, I'm just feeling things differently, reacting differently, I . . . we've had three kinds of settings where the old Cindy would have gotten a tight, gutty-reaction feeling, and I'm on top of those feelings. And I really see Van coming on. We're doing some uh . . . I don't know. I can't describe it, but I'm feeling it's . . . we're having some new behavior modifications (laughing) or something . . . we're really in an ex . . . kind of, I guess, in experimental stages, but I can really see that . . .

V1–NSB   35 Paul: /We are all the time, experimental./
M1–S/AT/WM/G/
  INC/DI/L

S35–IS

Cindy: I'm really feeling that we're trying to practice what some of our insights are.

V1–NLC   36 Paul: /What do you feel about the tapes?/
M1–ST/CR/WM/MC/
  NNF/D/QO

V2–NLC–PC   Do you feel they're useful?/
M2–ST/CR/WM/MC/
  NNF/D/QC

S36–IS

Cindy: Oh, yes. In fact . . .
Van: It's amazing how much you forget.
                        Right

V1–PC   37 Paul: /Yeah./
M1–S/N/HF/MC/
  TNF/D/L

S37–IS

Cindy: And the way I sound when I'm talking to you . . . when I think I'm just talking . . .
Van: We decided that Cindy comes on, as a castrating bitch or shrew, and I come on as little professor, uh . . .
Cindy: Yeah.
                      come on as

V1–NB   38 Paul: /Milquetoast./
M1–PR/AT/HF/DC/
  MNF/D/L

S38–IS

Van: Yeah. Oh, sure! (All laugh) Ecch! It's terrible.
Cindy: Caspar.
Van: Oh, God, Yeah, it's been uh . . . I find there's less threat about things when we talk about things, that I can raise issues or try to talk about things and Cindy can respond to them without personalizing them to the point that I feel like she's being destroyed if I say them.
Paul: Uh—huh.
Cindy: Yeah. Well, for the first time my gut doesn't react that way, and I don't know why. But it's not my gut that's sending messages any more.
Van: Yeah, and I don't know either. But it's a hell of a lot more comfortable feeling than the tension that was around our relationship before.
Cindy: Well, one thing for sure, I've been able to see that the

way Van has always dealt with me, it was nothing I ever did . . . well, I'm assuming this, but anyway . . . nothing I ever did or would say to Van would ever threaten him. He would just be able to take the information and deal with it and stay cool, calm, and collected. And then he would . . .

Van: On the surface anyway.

Cindy: Well, see this is it. But . . .

V1–NB–NLC
M1–EM/P/WM/DC/
  MNF/I/L
S39–IS

39 Paul: /He <u>was</u> like a computer <u>processing</u>

it, a data processor./

Van: Yeah.

Cindy: But just hearing just now, with him talking, I realize how emotional I am and how unemotional he is, because I'm very sensitive on Mother's Day, when I really get to missing my mother . . . I immediately feel the loss, for his mother. And I want to deal . . . and I say, ''Gee, I'm feeling depressed for you today for you're missing your mother,'' and . . .

Van: I've always had to protect myself from that.

Cindy: And I just realize . . .

Van: My whole life I've spent holding everybody else together. My father I had to hold together, my <u>mother</u> I had to support because my father was falling apart, my sister I had to, to uh . . . I became the mediator, the savior, the therapist, the shrink in the family.

Cindy: Yeah.

Van: . . . The negotiator . . . all those roles were mine.

Cindy: Yeah.

Van: And I . . . so I guess I run from those feelings. I don't deal with them because they were always something I didn't have the luxury of dealing with.

Cindy: Yeah. I know.

Van: I couldn't get sad. My mother was . . . my . . . or, and my father were <u>so</u> damned sad all the time.

Cindy: And then you <u>got</u> this wife who overreacts . . .

Van: Why in the hell do you think I picked you, I guess? Because you could do things I couldn't. Maybe in my unconscious I knew that kind of spontaneity was . . . could help <i>me</i> grow.

Cindy: Yeah. And I . . .

Van: And you needed my control.

Cindy: Yeah.

Van: I think, anyway . . .

Cindy: I know, like, Van said the other day . . . I mean I'm not exactly sure how he worded it, but the other day he said . . . this makes you angry, when I try to recall . . . anyway, in dealing about Jennifer, he said, ''I was hoping,'' or something, ''that when I told you about it, that you would've been able to say, 'We have a crisis, now what are we gonna do about it?' instead of falling apart.'' You know, I went berserk . . . And I thought, just now, he has always dealt calm, cool, collected; "Let's talk." And I have always overreacted; I do want to cry and scream and throw things and that's how I've always reacted. And he was disappointed in me that I didn't take this news and channel it and then make the best of it instead of falling apart.

V1–NLC–NSB   40 Paul: /Like what? What <u>did you expect</u> she
M1–EN/P/HF/DC/
   MNF/IT/QO
S40–IS   <u>would do?</u>/

Transcript Analysis

Appendix Table 1 presents the proportions and frequencies for all of the FTCS code categories that Paul and Minuchin used in their vignettes. The code categories are rank ordered for each therapist on each scale ranging from the most frequently used to the

Appendix Table 1   Family Therapist Coding System (FTCS): Comparison between Norman Paul and Salvador Minuchin

Norman Paul			Salvador Minuchin		
Code Category	(%)	Frequency	Code Category	(%)	Frequency
TOPIC					
NLC	23	(16)	VB	23	(26)
NB	17	(12)	NLC	16	(18)
VB	10	(7)	NSB	13	(15)
NSB	10	(7)	F	12	(14)
PB	9	(6)	NB	9	(10)
SB	8	(5)	PB	9	(10)
F	4	(3)	NE	9	(10)
PE	4	(3)	PC	4	(4)
EX	4	(3)	SB	3	(3)
NVB	3	(2)	NVC	2	(2)
SP	3	(2)	PE	1	(1)
NSE	3	(2)			
PC	1	(1)			
INTERVENTION					
ST	36	(16)	ST	28	(22)
EM	23	(10)	DN	14	(11)
BR	16	(7)	SD	11	(9)
C	11	(5)	S	10	(8)
S	4	(2)	PM	9	(7)
DD	2	(1)	R	6	(5)

(continued)

Appendix Table 1   *(Continued)*

Norman Paul			Salvador Minuchin		
Code Category	(%)	Frequency	Code Category	(%)	Frequency
TR	2	(1)	EM	5	(4)
PR	2	(1)	PR	5	(4)
EN	2	(1)	BR	5	(4)
			DD	4	(3)
			C	4	(3)

TEMPORAL ORIENTATION

P	68	(30)	AT	49	(39)
CR	14	(6)	N	36	(29)
AT	11	(5)	CR	9	(7)
N	7	(3)	P	6	(5)

TO WHOM

HF	80	(35)	HF	38	(30)
WM	20	(9)	CI	31	(25)
			GP	11	(9)
			WM	11	(9)
			NS	6	(5)
			CP	2	(2)

INTERPERSONAL STRUCTURE

DC	55	(24)	MC	44	(35)
TC	20	(9)	DC	39	(31)
MC	18	(8)	TC	10	(8)
G	7	(3)	G	8	(6)

SYSTEM MEMBERSHIP

PFO	45	(20)	NNF	34	(27)
SFO	11	(5)	MNF	31	(25)
MNF	11	(5)	TNF	14	(11)
CFO	9	(4)	ENF	5	(4)
NNF	9	(4)	PNF	5	(4)
MFO	2	(1)	TY	5	(4)
INC	2	(1)	INC	4	(3)
O	2	(1)	PFO	1	(1)

Appendix Table 1   *(Continued)*

Norman Paul			Salvador Minuchin		
Code Category	(%)	Frequency	Code Category	(%)	Frequency
TFO	2	(1)	OF	1	(1)
TNF	2	(1)			
CG	2	(1)			
ROUTE					
D	57	(25)	D	42	(34)
I	32	(14)	I	40	(32)
DI	9	(4)	DI	15	(12)
IT	2	(1)	IT	2	(2)
GRAMMATICAL FORM					
L	43	(19)	L	58	(46)
QO	30	(13)	QC	16	(13)
QC	27	(12)	QO	14	(11)
			CD	12	(10)
EVENT RELATIONSHIP					
IS	65	(26)	IS	57	(24)
T	15	(6)	M	26	(11)
M	12	(5)	T	14	(6)
FN	5	(2)	CY	2	(1)
IN	2	(1)			

least frequent. Various differences between the two sessions are apparent: Many of them have to do with the fact that one is an initial family consultation (more than two patients) and the other is a marital session in the midst of ongoing treatment.

However, there are also many differences that reflect the fact that the therapists are focusing on very different issues in very different ways in the sessions. Clearly, some of the major differences concern: Minuchin's directiveness in contrast to Paul's interpretive style; Minuchin's personal, self-disclosing style as opposed to Paul's focus on the patients; Paul's focus on the Past and Current time periods versus Minuchin's emphasis on Now and Atemporal interventions; and Minuchin's emphasis on the nuclear family in contrast to Paul's focus on family-of-origin issues. Also intriguing are the similarities in their styles: similar topic concerns; the preponderance of interventions directed to one member (the husband–father); and similar routings. An unexpected difference is Paul's greater explicit emphasis on family-system boundaries and rules.

Once again, these vignettes were selected to highlight different aspects of the FTCS. The differences between the therapists may well have more to do with the way in which the vignettes were selected than in basic differences between them. Minuchin may have worked very differently with a sophisticated couple like the Hoops, and Paul could well have resembled Minuchin had he worked with the Smiths. Hopefully, future process research can help us to obtain a better sense of the real (as opposed to alleged) differences and similarities between the major schools and theorists within the family field as well as some sense of how those differences and similarities relate to outcome with specific types of cases.

8

The Vanderbilt
Process Measures:
The Psychotherapy
Process Scale (VPPS)
and the Negative
Indicators Scale (VNIS)

Chong S. Suh
Hans H. Strupp
Vanderbilt University
Nashville, Tennessee

Stephanie Samples O'Malley
Yale University School of Medicine
New Haven, Connecticut

When psychotherapy research began to gather momentum in the 1940s and 1950s, investigators were faced with the necessity of forging tools for the objective study of the phenomena considered in need of scientific scrutiny. Essential were techniques for quantifying the verbal—and to a lesser extent—the nonverbal messages exchanged between patients and therapists. Among the initial purposes of these techniques—to name but a few—were objective comparisons between therapists adhering to the same or different theoretical orientations, and the patients' responses to different therapeutic techniques and many others. Readers interested in the history of process measures will find comprehensive accounts in Kiesler (1973), Marsden (1971), and Auld & Murray (1955).

All researchers in the area have been impressed with the enormous conceptual and technical difficulties in capturing the essence of the fluid and elusive phenomena that constitute the complex interpersonal processes we call psychotherapy. Thus it is small wonder that there have been many false starts and few of the early systems are even remembered. It is also noteworthy that most originators of process–analysis systems have eventually abandoned their brainchildren and turned to (presumably) more rewarding pursuits. (The third author who entered this field with a system for quantifying therapist communications [Strupp, 1957a, 1957b] regards himself a battle-scarred veteran.) The challenge, however, has remained, and the study of psychotherapy—considerably more sophisticated today than, say, around 1950—demands continued and sustained efforts if we are to make progress in understanding how therapeutic change comes about, how process relates to outcome, and how patient–therapist interactions may be tracked over time.

In this chapter we have set ourselves the task of describing the development of two major process measures which have occupied the attention of the Vanderbilt research team for the last decade.[1] They serve somewhat different purposes and have divergent origins, which we shall try to make explicit.

The Vanderbilt Psychotherapy Process Scale (VPPS) was dictated by the practical needs of the Vanderbilt Psychotherapy Project, a long-range process and outcome study of time-limited psychotherapy (to be described more fully below). The overriding objective was to evolve a general-purpose instrument to assess (what we hypothesized to be) salient aspects of the patient–therapist interaction. As will be seen, this instrument has undergone extensive field testing, statistical analysis, and general refinement. At this time, its utility has been well documented, and it promises to be a useful methodological tool in future investigations.

The Vanderbilt Negative Indicators Scale (VNIS) grew from explorations into the problem of negative effects in psychotherapy. This research was stimulated by Morris B. Parloff, then Chief of the Psychotherapy and Behavioral Intervention Section of the Clinical Research Branch at NIMH. The work of the Vanderbilt Psychotherapy Research Team in this area has been summarized by Strupp, Hadley, and Gomes-Schwartz (1977). While the VPPS and the VNIS, as will be seen, share certain common elements, a major difference lies in the fact that the VNIS is a specialized methodological tool (in contrast to the VPPS which is a "general-purpose" instrument). The VNIS focuses more specifically on aspects of the therapeutic interaction that are hypothesized to be related to negative treatment outcomes. Furthermore, it makes more stringent demands on the clinical raters' technical expertise; that is, not only must raters have a good grasp of principles and techniques of dynamic psychotherapy but they must undergo more intensive training than is true of raters employing the VPPS. Finally, less developmental and empirical work has been conducted with the VNIS to date.

Since Strupp (1957a) developed a multidimensional system for quantifying therapists' communications, the reader may wonder why it was considered necessary to evolve new systems. The most compelling reason was the need for techniques with which to study therapist *and* patient variables (the 1957 system was restricted to the measurement of therapist communications) and, to the greatest extent possible, to focus on qualitative aspects of the *interaction* between the patient and the therapist. These efforts were aided by progress that had resulted in a clearer understanding of the patient–therapist relationship as a dynamic system. Furthermore, forceful attention had been drawn, particularly by clinicians, to the importance of the *therapeutic alliance*. The VPPS, whose conception owes much to the pioneering research of Orlinsky & Howard (1967, 1975), was our first attempt to develop a practical and robust method for quantifying salient aspects of the therapeutic dyad. The VNIS, on the other hand, was intended as a magnifying glass of *adverse* characteristics and events in the therapeutic interaction.

In this chapter we shall trace the evolution and development of the Vanderbilt Psychotherapy Process Scale and the Vanderbilt Negative Indicators Scale. The presentation is more detailed for the VPPS because this instrument has been more extensively investigated and many of the issues discussed for the VPPS are relevant to the VNIS.

---

1. Numerous members of the Vanderbilt research team have contributed to the development and refinement of the VPPS and the VNIS, some to both. The names include, in alphabetical order: Stephen Armstrong, Grady L. Blackwood, Jr., Beverly Gomes-Schwartz, Suzanne W. Hadley, Dianna E. Hartley, Lois J. Keithly, Karla Moras, Janet Sandell Sachs, and Gloria Waterhouse.

Following these descriptions, we shall refer to substantive studies in which these instruments have been applied. In a concluding section we shall briefly identify unfinished tasks and sketch future directions. A clinical example will illustrate the use of the VPPS; because of the greater complexity of the VNIS a parallel example has been omitted for that instrument.

The Vanderbilt Psychotherapy Process Scale

The Vanderbilt Psychotherapy Process Scale (VPPS) is a general-purpose instrument designed to assess both positive and negative aspects of the patient's and the therapist's behavior and attitudes that are expected to facilitate or impede progress in therapy. While built on general assumptions of psychotherapy as an interpersonal process, it is intended to be largely "neutral" with respect to any particular theory of psychotherapy, and to be applicable to a wide range of therapeutic interventions. Specific subscales of the instrument tap characteristics such as level of exploration occurring during the session as well as the patient's active engagement in the process of therapy, his emotional stance, and the level of negativism displayed by the patient. Assessments are also provided of the therapist's warmth and emotional involvement, and negative attitudes manifested during the session.

As is true of other systems of content–analysis, the VPPS is designed to reduce complex interactions to manageable proportions and to achieve research economy by providing maximally useful information on a given therapeutic interaction with a minimum of effort. Ratings are typically made on the basis of selected segments of therapy. The quantitative measures derived from these ratings are seen as a compromise between global clinical impressions of an entire therapeutic hour and atomistic assessments of single patient or therapist communications. The former are viewed as too broad, the latter as too narrow.

In this section we shall review the development and current status of the VPPS. Since its conception, the scale has been used in several studies with revisions being dictated by increasing experience with the instrument. First, we shall describe the background, original construction, and subsequent revisions of the instrument. In addition, two initial studies are discussed which used earlier versions of the scale and were closely tied to the revision process. There follows a description of the item composition, subscale structure, and psychometric properties of the final version of the VPPS. Next, the different procedures that have been used when applying the VPPS are reviewed and contrasted. We shall then focus on two recent studies that investigated the predictive validity of the latest version of the instrument. The last part of the section is devoted to a discussion of directions for future research and of the potential utility of the scale in clinical practice and training. To illustrate the use of the VPPS, segments of rated therapy sessions are presented in the Appendix.

Development of the Scale and Initial Investigations

Background

The VPPS was developed in the course of the Vanderbilt Psychotherapy Project, which began in 1973 following a 2-year period of pilot work. The project was designed as a systematic comparison of treatment outcomes for a group of patients treated by highly experienced psychotherapists and a comparable group treated by college professors who had been selected for their ability to form warm and empathic relationships with college students. Using a comprehensive assessment battery, systematic evaluations were made of each patient's status prior to therapy, at termination, and at follow-up conducted 1 year after intake. All assessment interviews and selected therapy sessions were recorded on videotape, and sound recordings were made of all therapy sessions. The initial analyses of this study found no difference in outcome for the two treatment groups (Strupp and Hadley, 1979). A more recent reappraisal of the data (Suh & Strupp, 1982), however, has provided evidence suggesting that professional therapists were more effective than untrained college professors.

In addition to the original objectives of comparing treatment outcomes, the availability of the rich data base created by this project provided an excellent opportunity to study various factors influencing outcome. In particular, the availability of the recorded therapy sessions stimulated investigations of the ongoing process characteristics of psychotherapy. Given the voluminous nature of these data, however, the first task was to abstract and quantify meaningful dimensions of the process of psychotherapy from the recorded transactions. In particular, the goal was to develop an instrument that would systematically assess theoretically and clinically important aspects of the patient, the therapist, and their interaction which might be related to the subsequent outcome of therapy.

Original Construction of the VPPS

The first version of the VPPS was constructed by Strupp, Hartley, and Blackwood (1974). The Therapy Session Report (Orlinsky & Howard, 1967; 1975) served as a point of departure because some of its items seemed to tap outcome-related dimensions of the psychotherapy process. While the VPPS adopted some of these items, many items were also added. In addition, there are major differences between the two instruments that are noteworthy. The Therapy Session Report (TSR) is a self-report measure to be completed by the patient and the therapist immediately after each therapy hour. In contrast, the VPPS is designed to be rated by uninvolved clinical observers, either from the actual therapy sessions or from video- or audiotapes of therapy. Therefore, while the TSR was intended to measure subjective reactions and perceptions of each member of the dyad regarding the feelings and behaviors of his own as well as the other partner, the purpose of the VPPS was to obtain objective assessments of the characteristics of the participants and of their transactions. For this reason, the rating of the VPPS involves multiple clinical raters to evaluate and ensure the reliability of these objective ratings.

In developing the specific items, several criteria were used as guidelines: (1) Therapist items were designed to cover a broad spectrum of theoretical orientations and techniques; (2) items were designed to be primarily descriptive rather than evaluative; (3) unidimensionality of items was stressed; and (4) the level of inference required for ratings was minimized for the purpose of enhancing interrater reliability (e.g., Kiesler, 1973; Strupp, 1960). The resulting instrument consisted of 84 Likert-type items to be scored on an ordinal scale ranging from 1 to 5 indicating the extent to which the characteristic is present.

Initial Application of the VPPS

This first version of the VPPS was used by Gomes-Schwartz and Schwartz (1978) in an investigation of the instrument's ability to distinguish between therapists of different theoretical orientations. Two judges used the VPPS to rate videotapes of the entire third session of therapy for 25 college males who were treated in the Vanderbilt project by either nonprofessional therapists, analytically oriented therapists, or experiential therapists. For the purpose of this study, the items of the VPPS were subdivided into eight subscales on the basis of an *a priori* content analysis. Two subscales tapped therapist dimensions, Therapist Exploration and Therapist Directiveness. Three subscales measured patient factors: Patient Exploration, Patient Psychic Distress, and Patient Negativism. The remaining three scales gauged dimensions to which both the patient and the therapist contributed: Feeling Attention, Task Orientation, and Therapeutic Relationship. These scales were internally consistent (average coefficient alpha = .82) and interrater reliability was satisfactory (average interrater r = .82).

As demonstrated by differences on six of the eight subscales, therapists of varying orientations could be distinguished on the basis of the VPPS. Furthermore, the differences observed were consistent with predictions made on the basis of earlier studies (D'Augelli, Danish, & Brock, 1976; Pope, Nudler, Vonkorff, & McGee, 1974; Strupp, 1960; Sundland & Barker, 1962). In this regard, analytically oriented therapists were less directive and tended to explore the psychodynamics of their patients. Compared to patients treated by experiential and nonprofessional therapists, their patients exhibited greater anxiety during the session. Gomes-Schwartz and Schwartz speculated that this may have been due to the analytic therapists' exploration of sensitive intrapsychic and interpersonal issues. While experiential therapists made less use of exploratory techniques, they tended to focus on establishing warm therapeutic relationships with their patients. Both groups of professional therapists were task oriented, dealing with significant therapeutic issues. They also attended to the feeling state of their patients. In contrast, nonprofessional therapists tended to engage in informal conversation and advice giving. As with experiential therapists, alternative therapists offered a positive therapeutic atmosphere.

First Revision of the VPPS

The first revision of the scale was undertaken by Gomes-Schwartz (1978a) in the course of investigating the relationship between the process of therapy and outcome. Although the eight subscales derived from the first version of the instrument were found to be internally consistent and to discriminate among therapists of different theoretical orientations, Gomes-Schwartz felt that the original groupings did not adequately tap the process dimensions that were hypothesized as predictors of outcome. Thus, in an attempt to obtain a different perspective on how the individual items might be related, Gomes-Schwartz performed a principal components factor analysis with Varimax rotation on the VPPS item scores using the data obtained in her first study (Gomes-Schwartz & Schwartz, 1978). Although factor analysis is generally of questionable value with small samples, it was felt that this technique might generate some meaningful combinations that had not been apparent in the *a priori* content analysis. Rotated factors with eigenvalues > 1 were defined by items loading > .50.

Six factors were identified from the factor analysis. Items comprising these factors were examined and only those items which tended to discriminate among therapists' orientations or between different outcome categories were retained. From the factor structure, Gomes-Schwartz derived seven scales, six of which were hypothesized to tap outcome-related dimensions. This revised version of the VPPS consisted of 60 items and was used by Gomes-Schwartz (1978a) in an initial investigation of the relationship between process and outcome.

First Investigation of the Relationship
of Process and Outcome

Using this revised version of the VPPS, Gomes-Schwartz (1978a) investigated the role of three factors, exploratory processes, the therapist-offered relationship, and patient involvement, that are postulated as major determinants of therapy outcome by different schools of psychotherapy. Exploratory processes are considered instrumental to therapeutic change by psychodynamic therapists (e.g., Bibring, 1954; Glover, 1955; Langs, 1973; Malan, 1976). In contrast, Rogers (1957), and Rogers, Gendlin, Kiesler, and Truax (1967) asserted that the effective ingredients of therapeutic change lie in the attitude of the therapist that is conveyed to the patient—the therapist-offered relationship. Similarly, Frank (1973) stressed the importance of "nonspecific factors" rather than the technical aspects of therapy. Finally, the attributes of patients, such as their willingness and capacity to become involved in the therapeutic process, have been emphasized by both psychodynamic theorists and by Frank.

In order to examine the relative impact of these three process dimensions on outcome, the VPPS was used to rate 10-minute audiotaped segments selected from four sessions of therapy for each of 35 cases. Ratings made for the third session, the middle session, the session three-quarters of the way through treatment, and the next-to-last interview were summed for analyses. The six scales of the VPPS were grouped into three broader categories. Exploratory Processes were assessed by the scales of Patient Exploration and Therapist Exploration. The dimension of Therapist-Offered Relationship was tapped by the scales of Therapist Warmth and Friendliness and Negative Therapist Attitude. Finally, Patient Involvement was gauged by the VPPS scales Patient Participation and Patient Hostility.

Multiple regression analysis was performed for each of the three dimensions with constituent scales as multiple predictors of outcome. The results of these analyses showed that positive Patient Involvement in therapy consistently predicted various outcome measures, whereas only weak relationships were found for Exploratory Processes and Therapist-Offered Relationship.

Second Revision and the Development
of a Rating Manual

The results of the initial investigations appeared promising, suggesting that the VPPS was an instrument that could be reliably rated and used to quantify clinically meaningful dimensions of the therapeutic process. In assessing the utility of the instrument, however, the Vanderbilt research team felt that the absence of a rating manual would make it difficult for other investigators to use the scale. Furthermore, explicit guidelines would help raters in making judgments and thus increase the reliability of ratings. These considerations led to the development of a rating manual in which each item was defined. While carrying out this task, the research team rated samples of therapy using the VPPS and modified those items on which there was poor interrater agreement. Generally, modifications involved reducing the ambiguity of items and the level of inference required in making judgments. In addition, new items were added which seemed to tap clinically important aspects of the therapeutic interaction.

A description of this final version of the VPPS is presented in the next section. The reported scale properties were assessed in a recent investigation by O'Malley, Suh, and Strupp (1983). The substantive findings of the study relating process characteristics of early sessions to outcome are presented in the Concluding Remarks section.

Description of the Current Version of the VPPS

Items

The VPPS presently consists of 80 Likert-type items which are rated on an ordinal scale from 1 ("not at all") to 5 ("a great deal"). The first three items on the scale are used to obtain global impressions regarding the quality of the therapeutic relationship, the overall productivity of the session, and the patient's current level of functioning. The remaining items are divided into two sections, patient and therapist items (40 and 37 items, respectively). Each section comprises two parts, one dealing with characteristics of each participant's "behavior" during the session and the second consisting of adjectives which describe each participant's "demeanor."

Procedures for Developing Subscales

Eight subscales have been derived from among the items on the basis of a principal components factor analysis with Varimax rotation (O'Malley et al., 1983). Initially 12 factors with eigenvalues greater than 1 were obtained and were defined by items loading greater than .50. Since five of the factors comprised so few items (less than four) as to be unreliable, they were not retained as scales. One of the seven remaining factors contained both therapist and patient items. In an attempt to develop separate scales for patient and therapist characteristics, this factor was divided into two subscales which were subsequently named Patient Exploration and Therapist Exploration.

Generally, items that fell on more than one factor were not included in the subscales. One exception, however, was a subset of items that fell both on the Patient Exploration Scale and an additional factor. Because these items seemed to relate to the patient's attempts to deal with his or her feelings and problems, they were retained on the Patient Exploration Scale. The same items, however, were deleted from the second factor of which the remaining items primarily referred to the patient's feelings. This subscale was named Patient Psychic Distress. Scales corresponding to the remaining five factors are Patient Participation, Patient Hostility, Patient Dependency, Therapist Warmth and Friendliness, and Negative Therapist Attitude. Scale scores are computed by summing scores on the constituent items.

Description of the Subscales

The first factor that emerged from the factor analysis was called *Patient Participation*. This factor appeared to tap the extent to which the patient is positively engaged in the therapeutic interaction. Low scores on this subscale characterize patients whose behavior is restrained and tentative. In contrast, high scores portray patients who are actively involved and relate freely with their therapists. Examples of the eight items comprising the scale include: withdrawn ($-$); inhibited ($-$); actively participated in the interaction; took the initiative in bringing up the subjects that were talked about.

While Patient Participation represents a continuum from low involvement to high involvement, the next subscale, *Patient Hostility*, seems to tap the negative end of this continuum. Furthermore, in contrast to the more subtle evidence of disengagement tapped by low ratings on Patient Participation, Patient Hostility reflects more blatantly negative aspects of the patient's behaviors and attitudes. The six items in this scale include: hostile; impatient; frustrated; intellectualizing; reacted negatively to the therapist's comments; defensive.

Patient Psychic Distress gauges the feeling state of the patient, particularly feelings of discouragement. Relatively high correlations between this subscale and Patient Exploration and Therapist Exploration suggest that these feelings are associated with the exploratory processes of therapy. Examples of the nine items making up the scale are: self-critical; ashamed; depressed; defeated; portrayed self as overwhelmed by personal problems.

The scale of *Patient Exploration* taps the level of examination of feelings and experiences on the part of the patient. This scale comprised seven items including: tried to understand the reasons behind problematic feelings or behavior; concern was with how to deal more effectively with self and others; seemed to be motivated for therapy; was struggling to achieve better control over feelings or impulses.

The final patient subscale, *Patient Dependency*, measures the patient's reliance and dependency on the therapist. Although the predictive validity of this subscale has not been pursued in our investigations to date, it has been retained as a measure of potential research and clinical value. Representative of the six items are: relied upon the therapist to solve problems; asked for advice on how to deal more effectively with self or others; tried to elicit approval, sympathy, or reassurance from the therapist; dependent; deferential.

The *Therapist Exploration* Scale is the counterpart to Patient Exploration and is moderately correlated with it. The scale measures therapist's attempts to examine the patient's feelings and behaviors and the reasons behind them. This scale consists of 13 items that are positively toned. Examples of these items include the following: tried to help the patient recognize his or her feelings; tried to help the patient understand the reasons behind his or her reactions; placed the patient's report in a new perspective or reorganized the patient's experience; conveyed expertise.

The remaining therapist scales, *Therapist Warmth and Friendliness* and *Negative Therapist Attitude*, assess the therapist's attitudes and behaviors toward the patient. *Therapist Warmth and Friendliness* measures the therapist's display of warmth and emotional involvement with the patient. Scores on Therapist Warmth and Friendliness represent a continuum of the quality of the relationship offered to patients. For example, for the item "involved," high ratings are given if the therapist seemed engaged in the patient's experience, whereas, a low rating would be merited if the therapist was detached from the patient's experience or inattentive to the patient's concerns. Other representative items are: helped the patient feel accepted in the relationship; showed warmth and friendliness toward the patient; supported the patient's self-esteem, confidence, and building hope; involved.

In contrast to Therapist Warmth and Friendliness, the subscale of *Negative Therapist Attitude* is composed of items tapping therapist's attitudes which might intimidate or threaten the patient. The following items are included on the scale: judgmental; authoritarian; lecturing; defensive; intimidating; confronted the patient in a negative manner.

Psychometric Properties of the Subscales

The psychometric properties of the subscales are presented in Table 8-1. As can be seen, both internal consistency and interrater reliability are high for all subscales. Internal consistency as measured by coefficient alpha ranged from .81 for Patient Dependency to .96 for Patient Exploration and for Therapist Exploration. For all eight subscales, the two judges' scores were highly consistent, as evidenced by high interrater reliabilities ranging from .79 to .94. Although the divergent procedures used in different investigations make direct comparisons difficult (see the Procedures for Application of the VPPS section), we feel that the provision of item definitions in the rating manual contributed significantly toward improving the psychometric properties of the VPPS.

Procedures for Application of the VPPS

The VPPS has been used to assess therapy process in three studies (Gomes-Schwartz, 1978a; Gomes-Schwartz & Schwartz, 1978; O'Malley, Suh, & Strupp, 1983). Each study, however, used a different version of the instrument and varied in the methods used for data collection. In this section on methodological issues we shall review the different procedures that have been employed and offer recommendations when possible. Because of the diversity of the procedures used, the information is summarized in Table 8-2.

Data Collection Context

To date, the VPPS has been applied exclusively to therapy cases treated in the Vanderbilt Psychotherapy Research Project (Strupp & Hadley, 1979).[2] The patient sample in the project consisted of 38 male college students who were treated by either highly experienced professional therapists (analytic or experiential) or untrained college professors. The initial criteria for patient selection were elevated scores ($T \geq 60$) on the Depression (2), Psychasthenia (7), and Social Introversion (0) Scales of the Minnesota Multiphasic Personality Inventory. The patients were further screened on the basis of clinical interviews. These patients were given up to 25 sessions of therapy on a once or twice a week basis.

Data Form

The data forms which have been used in VPPS process studies are videotape (Gomes-Schwartz & Schwartz, 1978) and audiotape (Gomes-Schwartz, 1978a; O'Malley *et al.*, 1983). With regard to the appropriateness of the various data forms, we recently conducted a methodological study that directly examined the influence of the presentation medium on the reliability of VPPS ratings (O'Malley & Gomes-Schwartz, 1983). In this study, five media forms were evaluated: (1) transcript; (2) audiotape; (3) videotape; (4) audiotape supplemented with a transcript; and (5) videotape plus transcript. Twenty-five graduate students with varying amounts of clinical experience served as judges and received a minimum amount of training in using the VPPS. These judges were assigned to one of five groups, each of which rated therapy segments presented in one of the five media forms. Ratings were made for 10-minute segments randomly selected from the third session of therapy for four patient–therapist dyads. These dyads were chosen from among the patients treated in the Vanderbilt project to represent divergent treatment outcomes with different therapists.

For each presentation medium, interrater reliability for the subscales was estimated by using intraclass correlation for composite ratings (Guilford & Frutcher, 1978; Tinsley & Weiss, 1975). These coefficients are presented in Table 8-3. As can be seen in the table, ratings made from transcripts were generally less reliable than ratings made from the

---

2. Several investigators have applied the VPPS to their own data but the results are as yet unpublished.

Table 8-1   Psychometric Properties of VPPS Subscales

Scale and Description	Internal Consistency[a]	Interrater Reliability[b]
Patient Participation [PP]: 8 items Patient's active involvement in the therapy interaction	.93	.91
Patient Hostility [PH]: 6 items Level of negativism, hostility or distrust displayed by the patient	.83	.92
Patient Psychic Distress [PPD]: 9 items Level of emotional distress and feelings of discouragement expressed by the patient	.92	.92
Patient Exploration [PE]: 7 items Patient's level of self-examination and exploration of feelings and experiences	.96	.94
Patient Dependency [PD]: 6 items Patient's reliance and dependency on the therapist	.81	.88
Therapist Exploration [TE]: 13 items Therapist's attempts to examine the psychodynamics underlying the patient's problems	.96	.94
Therapist Warmth and Friendliness [TW]: 9 items Therapist's display of warmth and emotional involvement with the patient	.91	.86
Negative Therapist Attitude [NTA]: 6 items Therapist's attitudes which might intimidate or threaten the patient	.82	.79

[a]Coefficient alpha. [b]Pearson correlation coefficients are based on ratings made for the three sessions ($n = 110$).

other data forms. More interestingly, the discrepancy was quite substantial for three of the subscales, Therapist Warmth and Friendliness, Negative Therapist Attitude, and Patient Hostility. An examination of the items falling on these scales suggests that vocal and visual cues that are unavailable in transcripts may be important in rating these items. In contrast, the subscales of Patient Participation, Patient Exploration, and Therapist Exploration depend primarily on content cues and the reliability of ratings made on these factors are less affected by the presentation medium. It is also noted that supplementing audiotapes and videotapes with transcripts generally did not enhance the reliability of ratings beyond that obtained from audiotapes or videotapes alone.

On the basis of this study, we feel that transcripts are generally inadequate for making VPPS ratings, particularly if minimal training is provided or raters with low levels of clinical experience are used. Audio or videotapes are preferable given the higher level of interrater reliability that was obtained under these conditions. This is especially true if the researcher is interested in studying those factors that seem to depend on vocal and visual cues in addition to content such as Therapist Warmth and Friendliness, Negative Therapist Attitude, and Patient Hostility.

Table 8-2 Summary of Three Investigations Using Different Versions of the VPPS

	Gomes-Schwartz & Schwartz (1978)	Gomes-Schwartz (1978a)	O'Malley, Suh, & Strupp (1983)
Characteristics			
VPPS version	Original scale	First revision	Current version
Number of subscales	8	7	8
Internal consistency (coefficient alpha)	.62–.90 Average = .82	.65–95 Median = .84	.81–.96 Median = .92
Interrater reliability (Pearson r)	.79–.90 Average = .82	.60–.93 Median = .83	.79–.94 Median = .92
Procedures			
Number of patients	25	35	38
Data form	Videotape	Audiotape	Audiotape
Unit length	Entire hour	10-minute segment	15-minute composite
Sampling within sessions	—	Random sampling method	Systematic sampling method (5 minutes from the beginning, middle, and end of hour)
Sampling of sessions	Third session	Representative sessions (session 3, sessions one-half and three-quarters way, and the next-to-last session)	Early sessions (first three sessions)
Raters	Advanced clinical students	Advanced clinical students	Recent PhD clinical psychologists

295

Table 8-3   Interrater Reliability for VPPS Subscales as a Function of Presentation Mode

Subscales	Transcript	Audiotape	Videotape	Audiotape + Transcript	Videotape + Transcript
Patient Participation	.97	.98	.99	.98	.99
Patient Hostility	.56	.88	.93	.72	.90
Patient Psychic Distress	.79	.52	.82	.80	.89
Patient Exploration	.95	.96	.97	.99	.98
Therapist Exploration	.73	.93	.77	.92	.80
Therapist Warmth	.13	.65	.54	.68	.73
Negative Therapist Attitude	.31	.73	.85	.91	.84

Note. Intraclass correlation for composite ratings was used to assess interrater reliability.

Unit Length

The three investigations utilized different unit lengths: 10-minute segments (Gomes-Schwartz, 1978a), 15-minute segments (O'Malley *et al.*, 1983), and the entire therapy hour (Gomes-Schwartz & Schwartz, 1978). Although the psychometric properties were satisfactory for all three unit lengths (see Table 8-2), the comparability of the different units has not been investigated. Therefore, whether segments are representative of the total hour remains unknown. However, the results of the validity studies (presented in the Predictive Validity of the VPPS section) which demonstrated the relationship of VPPS ratings to outcome may be regarded as providing indirect support for the representativeness of segments. Based on these findings, we feel that 15-minute segments may be adequate for capturing the process characteristics that the VPPS is designed to assess.

Sampling Within Sessions

Different sampling procedures have been used for selecting segments within sessions. Gomes-Schwartz (1978a) employed a random sampling method. In her study, a segment was selected from a randomly determined point for each case, and the succeeding 10-minute segment served as the unit for ratings. O'Malley *et al.* (1983), on the other hand, used a systematic sampling procedure. Each segment consisted of a composite of the first, middle, and last 5 minutes of a therapy session. This method was adopted in order to provide the raters with an overview of the entire course of a given therapy hour.

Sampling of Therapy Sessions

The third therapy hour was studied by Gomes-Schwartz and Schwartz (1978) primarily because of the availability of the videotapes of this session. In her second investigation, Gomes-Schwartz (1978a) selected four sessions across the course of therapy in order to provide a broad representative sample of the therapeutic process. These included the third session, the sessions half-way and three-fourths of the way through treatment, and the next-to-last interview. Finally, the recent study by O'Malley et al. (1983) was specifically designed to investigate the process of psychotherapy in the early phase of treatment. For this reason, the first three sessions were selected for study.

From the substantive findings of the two validity studies (presented in the Predictive Validity of the VPPS section), two recommendations may be made regarding the selection of therapy sessions. While research questions dictate which sessions should be investigated, early sessions appear to be critically important for the subsequent course of therapy. Furthermore, even if ratings from later sessions demonstrate stronger associations with outcome, they may not elucidate the actual processes responsible for the development of qualities manifested in the later sessions. For this reason, we suggest that early sessions be included in future investigations. Secondly, as the validity study by Suh and O'Malley (1982) demonstrates, changes in both the patient's and the therapist's behavior across sessions are strongly related to outcome. These findings suggest that it is essential to include multiple sessions and to investigate sequential aspects of process characteristics in using the VPPS.

Raters

Multiple raters are used to evaluate and ensure the reliability of observations made using the VPPS. To date, raters have been chosen from among advanced clinical students and recent Ph.D. clinical psychologists. While raters are expected to have some knowledge of the therapy process, preliminary evidence suggests that graduate students with minimal clinical experience can also use the instrument reliably (O'Malley & Gomes-Schwartz, 1983). The relatively low level of clinical experience required is a strength of the system, which may be attributed to the minimum level of inference involved in making judgments.

Training of Raters

In order to enhance the reliability of ratings, judges undergo training to a criterion level. The procedure used in the most recent study (O'Malley et al., 1983) consisted of two parts. Initially, the judges rated segments of therapy for which ratings by the Vanderbilt research team are available. This process was designed to provide the raters with information regarding the research group's conceptualization of items on the scale. The second step was designed to enhance the agreement level between the raters themselves. Thus, the judges continued to rate additional tapes until they reached the criterion level of interrater reliability ($r = .90$). In order to achieve this rigorous standard, judges rated a total of 19 therapy segments.

Predictive Validity of the VPPS

We have recently completed two studies which investigated the predictive relationship of the current version of the VPPS to therapy outcome. The first of these investigations by O'Malley, Suh, and Strupp (1983) studied the process of therapy using a methodology similar to that used by Gomes-Schwartz (1978a). This study, however, focused on the first three sessions of therapy. The critical importance of early sessions was suggested from our informal clinical observations as well as from intensive analyses comparing "successful" patients and "unsuccessful" patients treated by the same therapist (Strupp, 1980a, 1980b, 1980c, 1980d). The second study, which used the data base obtained by O'Malley *et al.*, was specifically designed to identify therapist characteristics associated with differential outcomes (Suh & O'Malley, 1982). Because these two studies utilized the final version of the VPPS, their findings are described in detail. A brief discussion is also included at the end regarding in-therapy patient changes as outcome.

Initial Investigation Using Early Sessions

As in the Gomes-Schwartz (1978a) study, O'Malley, Suh, & Strupp (1983) investigated the relationship between process and outcome by grouping the VPPS subscales into three broader dimensions: Patient Involvement (Patient Participation, Patient Hostility), Therapist-Offered Relationship (Therapist Warmth and Friendliness, Negative Therapist Attitude), and Exploratory Processes (Therapist Exploration, Patient Exploration, Patient Psychic Distress). Six outcome measures were employed. They represented two sets of indices, overall improvement and improvement in target complaints, assessed from three perspectives, the patient, the therapist, and the independent clinician who interviewed the patient at intake and termination. The process dimensions were related to these outcome measures by using multiple regression analyses. Separate analyses were performed for each session.

Two major findings emerged from these analyses. First, consonant with the results of the Gomes-Schwartz (1978a) study, the process dimension of Patient Involvement showed the most consistent relationship to outcome. The results from the third session are summarized in Table 8-4. Of more direct clinical relevance, however, was the pattern of increased association between process and outcome across the three sessions, from virtually no relationship in the first session to moderate correlations in the third session. The predictive relationship demonstrated in the third session suggests that the course of therapy was, to a certain extent, set in this early phase of therapy. Similar findings have been reported by other investigators (e.g., Luborsky, 1976; Saltzman, Luetgert, Roth, Creaser, & Howard, 1976). However, the absence of such a relationship in the first session and the relatively weak relationship in the second session suggest that the characteristics measured by the dimension of Patient Involvement are not necessarily the antecedent qualities of the patient. Rather, these characteristics that were associated with positive outcome appear to develop in the course of therapy.

Although this initial investigation did not identify therapist characteristics that may have facilitated the development of these positive patient qualities, the pattern of correlations across the sessions suggests that therapists may have exerted a marked influence on the patients. These considerations led to further exploration of the data in a subsequent investigation by Suh and O'Malley (1982).

Table 8-4   Summary of Multiple Regression Analyses Predicting Outcome from the Third Session VPPS Scores

Outcome Measures	Exploratory Processes			Patient Involvement			Therapist-Offered Relationship		
	R	R^2	F	R	R^2	F	R	R^2	F
Overall ratings									
Therapist	.58	.33	5.35**	.45	.20	4.24*	.46	.21	4.36*
Clinician	.34	.12	1.43	.41	.17	3.34*	.22	.05	<1
Patient	.42	.17	2.20	.53	.28	6.35**	.35	.13	2.37
Target complaints									
Therapist	.47	.22	3.07*	.44	.20	4.01*	.35	.12	2.29
Clinician	.31	.09	1.11	.42	.18	3.51*	.34	.12	2.19
Patient	.34	.12	1.41	.44	.19	3.85*	.26	.07	1.23

Note. Degress of freedom for F tests for Exploratory Processes = 3,32; Degrees of freedom for other F tests = 2,33.
  *$p < .05$.
  **$p < .01$.
  ***$p < .001$.

Investigation of Therapist Characteristics Associated with Differential Outcome

Although both the Gomes-Schwartz (1978a) and the O'Malley *et al.* (1983) study demonstrated the predictive validity of the VPPS, these findings predominantly pertained to patient characteristics and not to therapist factors. In this regard, our results paralleled the frequent observations in the psychotherapy research literature regarding the relative magnitudes of the relationship of patient and therapist variables to outcome (e.g., Luborsky, Chandler, Auerbach, Cohen, & Bachrach, 1971; Parloff, Waskow, & Wolfe, 1978). In view of the lack of success in demonstrating the unique contribution of therapists to the patients' treatment outcomes in our study, Suh and O'Malley (1982) proceeded to reexamine the data obtained by O'Malley *et al.* Based on the speculation that conventional methods of data analyses may be inadequate and thereby may have contributed to our inability to identify effective therapist characteristics, this study attempted to explore alternative research strategies for the purpose of studying therapist variables. Specifically, it was speculated that our exclusive emphasis on statistical significance (e.g., correlation coefficient) may be at variance with the clinical meaningfulness of research findings. For example, if only a small subset of therapists in a given sample were particularly effective or harmful, their differential impact would not show up in statistical analyses. From a clinical perspective, however, it would be profitable to study the characteristics of these therapists.

The foregoing considerations regarding the nature of therapy outcome data led to the development of an alternative research strategy. Instead of demonstrating the overall relationship between a given variable and outcome for the entire sample of therapy cases, this approach focuses on "prediction failure" cases. The essence of this strategy involves grouping the patient sample on two dimensions: predicted outcome ("prognosis" for therapeutic change) and actual outcome. The rationale for this categorical method was that the study of those cases with significant discrepancies between their expected outcome and their eventual outcome would elucidate therapist characteristics associated with these unexpected results. For example, for patients who achieved high outcome despite an unfavorable prognosis, one may ask what the therapist did to potentiate such therapeutic change in these patients. Conversely, if some of the patients with a potential for positive outcome eventually achieved poor outcomes, we may attribute the incongruous results to adverse therapist characteristics.

In this study, the ratings on the Patient Participation Scale from the *first* session served to group the patients into high and low prognostic categories. This process variable was selected as the prognostic index because it consistently predicted outcome from the *third* session. The same scale, however, showed no relationship to outcome in the *first* session. This discrepancy led us to hypothesize that therapists might have been responsible for facilitating the development of this desirable quality. Next, patients were classified into high and low outcome groups based on a composite of multiple outcome indices.

When the VPPS therapist scale scores were examined according to the resulting four prognosis–outcome categories, striking differences in therapist characteristics emerged that were not evident in our previous study. The discriminating features involved different *patterns of change* in the therapist's behavior across the first three sessions and *not the absolute level, per se*, of the therapist quality measured in a given session. In an attempt to quantify the pattern of each therapist's behavior, a change score was computed for each of the therapist scales by first subtracting the first session scores from the second and the third session scores and then summing the two resulting difference scores.

A case-by-case summary of the therapist characteristics associated with each prognosis–outcome category is presented in Table 8-5. Substantial change across sessions 1 through 3 is indicated in the table with either a "+" or a "−" sign, depending on whether the change was desirable (+) or negative (−).[3] Similarly, high scores on Negative Therapist Attitude assessed in the first session are noted with a "−" sign. This table also includes significant changes on Patient Participation across early sessions. When the characteristic measured (e.g., change or initial level) was not notably positive or negative, no entry was made. In reading the entries for Patient 9, for example, the table headings indicate that he was a low prognosis–high outcome case. His therapist showed substantial increases in Therapist Warmth and Friendliness and Therapist Exploration. Furthermore, the patient became more engaged in the therapy process in this early phase of therapy which is indicated by the "+" sign in the Patient Participation entry in the table. (The therapy segments presented at the end of the chapter were taken from this case.)

Different entries in the table for the four groups may be summarized as follows: For patients who had a high prognosis and a high outcome, therapist behavior was characterized by initially positive reactions as well as increases in Therapist Warmth and

---

3. These decisions were made on an informal basis. Statistical results presented later in Table 8-6, however, support these informal observations, suggesting the usefulness of this strategy.

Table 8-5   Summary of Prominent Patient and Therapist Qualities on the VPPS for Individual Cases Classified Into Prognosis-Outcome Categories

Measures Associated with Outcome	High Prognosis							Low Prognosis								
	High Outcome					Low Outcome		High Outcome				Low Outcome				
	1	2	3	4	5	6	7	8	9	10	11	12	13	14	15	16
Change[a] in Negative Therapist Attitude						−										−
Change[a] in Therapist Warmth	+		+			−	−	+	+	+		+	−	−	−	−
Change[a] in Therapist Exploration	+	+	+		−	−	−		+	+						
Negative Therapist Attitude in the First Session						−						−	−		−	
Change[a] in Patient Participation				−		−		+	+	+				−	−	

Note. ''+'' indicates positive qualities and ''−'' indicates negative qualities.
[a]Change refers to increases or decreases in the level of the quality measured across the first three sessions.

Therapist Exploration across sessions. Next, as Suh and O'Malley (1982) hypothesized, only a small proportion of the high prognosis patients achieved a low outcome (two out of seven patients). Their therapists were characterized by initially high levels of Negative Therapist Attitude which increased across sessions with a concomitant decrease in Therapist Warmth and Therapist Exploration. Therapist behavior was markedly different for the group of four patients who achieved a high outcome despite an initially low prognosis. Their positive outcome appears to be a function of increases in Therapist Warmth and Therapist Exploration. Although Patient Participation was initially low for these patients, three out of four showed large increases in Patient Participation across sessions. Finally, therapists for low prognosis–low outcome cases not only exhibited high initial levels of Negative Therapist Attitude but there was a decrease in Therapist Warmth over sessions.

This informal inspection of the data served to elucidate differential therapist characteristics contributing to varying outcomes. In order to further corroborate the importance of the change in the therapist's behavior across sessions, correlation analyses were performd between various outcome measures and the amount of change in the VPPS therapist factors. The large magnitudes of the correlation coefficients shown in Table 8-6 substantiate the foregoing observations. These finding stand in contrast to the weak relationship between the session scores on the VPPS therapist factors and outcome. For Sessions 1 and 2, no therapist factor was correlated with outcome. Although the third session scores did show some relationship to outcome, the association was found only for therapist measures of outcome (see Table 8-6).

Table 8-6   Correlation Coefficients Illustrating the Greater Predictive Power of Change Scores Compared to Session Scores on VPPS Therapist Scales

	Change Scores[a]		Third Session Scores	
Outcome Measures	Therapist Warmth	Therapist Exploration	Negative Therapist Attitude	Therapist Warmth
Overall ratings				
MMPI change	.47*	.58**	—	—
Therapists	.70***	.58**	− .51*	—
Clinicians	.58**	.54*	—	—
Target complaints				
Patients	—	—	—	—
Therapists	.72***	.58**	− .43*	.44*
Clinicians	.64**	.43*	—	—

[a]Change across the first three sessions of therapy.
*$p < .05$.
**$p < .01$.
***$p < .001$.

Patient Process Change as a Measure of Outcome

Kiesler (1966, 1973, 1981) has repeatedly stressed the importance of studying patient change within therapy. He asserts that any meaningful therapeutic changes must first be evident within therapy sessions. Therefore, in-therapy patient changes should be regarded as legitimate outcomes. In the Suh and O'Malley (1982) study, this issue was addressed by examining the relationship between change scores on Patient Participation and outcome. As shown in Table 8-7, the correlation coefficients are high, suggesting that the amount of change in patient qualities tapped by this scale can be viewed as a meaningful index of outcome. As would be expected, these coefficients were generally greater than those for session scores on Patient Participation. For purposes of comparison, the correlation coefficients between the third session scores and outcome measures are also presented in the table. Further evidence for the validity of changes in the Patient Participation as outcome was provided by the high correlation ($r = .75$) between these change scores and the amount of change from intake to termination on the Social Introversion Scale of the MMPI. These findings lend strong support to Kiesler's argument that therapeutic change can be and should be assessed by patient process characteristics in therapy. Furthermore, it is noteworthy that this outcome-related patient process change took place as early as in the first three sessions of therapy.

Concluding Remarks

In this section we have described a series of studies aimed at quantifying clinically meaningful dimensions of psychotherapy process. This work has resulted in the current version of the VPPS. The instrument is accompanied by a rating manual in which each item is explicitly defined. Concrete instructions provide raters with standards for rating each item. The high magnitudes of the psychometric properties attest to the reliability of the instrument. Moreover, the procedural methodology of applying this instrument in research has become refined in successive investigations. As a result of progress in these two areas, we feel that the scale is ready for use by other investigators.

Finally, the substantive findings of our studies point to the potential utility of this instrument for clinical practice and training. First, the scale may be used as an assessment instrument for therapy patients. Patient qualities may be assessed either from the intake interview or the initial therapy session. This assessment information could be useful to the therapist, particularly when the patient manifests negative qualities. Once therapy is under way, the therapist could be provided with feedback from the VPPS therapist scales. The finding that it was a pattern of change across sessions and not the absolute level of therapist characteristics that predicted outcome makes the clinical application of the scale easier because there is no need for concern regarding the constant error associated with raters (rater bias) and thus no need for normative data. For cases in which the assessment reveals negative reactions on the part of the therapist, the therapist may be well advised to seek consultation in order to better understand the source of antitherapeutic reactions toward the patient.

Although the findings obtained with the VPPS appear promising, it is noted that their generalizability is as yet limited because the scale has been applied to only one data base (see, however, the earlier footnote). For future investigations, an important question that needs to be addressed is the extent to which patient characteristics exhibited in the first therapy session represent the patient's stable characteristics versus his or her unique reaction to the particular therapist with whom he or she is interacting. This question may be studied by comparing VPPS ratings on the patient scales made from intake and those obtained from the first therapy hour. Finally, it would be useful to

Table 8-7   Correlation Coefficients Showing the Relationship of Change Scores and Third Session Scores on the VPPS Patient Participation Scale with Outcome

	Patient Participation	
Outcome Measures	Change Scores[a]	Third Session Scores
Overall ratings		
MMPI change	.57**	—
Therapists	.49*	.50*
Clinicians	.63**	.46*
Target complaints		
Patients	.77***	.64**
Therapists	.53*	.50*
Clinicians	.68**	.47*

[a]Change across the first three sessions of therapy.
$*p < .05$
$**p < .01$
$***p < .001$

investigate whether feedback and consultation provided to the therapist after the second or third therapy hour regarding the negative characteristics of the therapy interaction might serve to alter the course of therapy.

The Vanderbilt Negative Indicators Scale

Development of the Scale

The development of the Vanderbilt Negative Indicators Scale (VNIS) was stimulated by the growing concern that psychotherapy may produce harmful as well as beneficial results (e.g., Bergin, 1971). In an initial attempt to explore the problem of negative effects in psychotherapy, Hadley and Strupp (1976) surveyed expert clinicians, theoreticians, and researchers in the field concerning their views on this issue (also, see Strupp, Hadley, & Gomes-Schwartz, 1977). Of particular interest were the factors considered by respondents to be associated with or held responsible for negative effects. Based on Hadley and Strupp's analysis of these data, Gomes-Schwartz (1978b) made an initial effort to construct an instrument that would measure characteristics of the patient, the therapist, and their interaction that might lead to negative change. This original scale consisted of 25 items: 8 of these tapped patient characteristics, 9 dealt with therapist attitudes and personal characteristics, and the remaining 8 items gauged nonfacilitative interactions that primarily involved therapists' errors in technique.

Gomes-Schwartz (1978b) conducted a preliminary investigation of this instrument. Five experienced clinicians were asked to rate audiotapes of seven complete sessions for each of two cases treated in the Vanderbilt project (Strupp & Hadley, 1979), a positive changer who achieved substantial improvements and a negative changer who either showed minimal gain or deteriorated following therapy. The results of this investigation were promising: Most of the items on the instrument could be reliably rated, and eight items differentiated the positive and negative outcome cases at a statistically significant level. The negative changer was characterized as more self-derogatory as well as less psychological minded than the positive changer. His therapist was assessed to be colder, more insensitive, and more rigid compared to the therapist of the patient with positive outcome. The therapy of the poor outcome case was more often marked by superficiality, therapists' errors in goal setting, and failure to take responsibility for the session. Although these findings were at best tentative (largely because of the small sample size), the results nevertheless were promising, and further work was undertaken to make the instrument more systematic and comprehensive.

The second phase in the development of the instrument, which came to be known as the Vanderbilt Negative Indicators Scale (VNIS), involved extensive effort to transform the original process scale into the current version. Each item was defined in an accompanying rating manual (Strupp, Moras, Sandell, Waterhouse, O'Malley, Keithly, & Gomes-Schwartz, 1981). The Vanderbilt research team pursued this task of major revision in two stages. First, actual therapy sessions from the files of the Vanderbilt project were studied in an effort to detect and conceptualize differential characteristics of the patient, the therapist, and their interaction which were associated with positive and negative outcomes. Secondly, the team endeavored to create items that could be reliably rated while preserving the clinical relevance of the instrument. Accordingly, item definitions were made as specific and concrete as possible in order to translate common clinical concepts into observable behaviors.

Description of the Current Version of the VNIS

The current version of the VNIS consists of 42 items, grouped into five subscales. Four of these subscales reflect current conceptions of the major outcome-related dimensions of psychotherapy: Patient Qualities, Therapist Personal Qualities, Errors in Technique, and Patient–Therapist Interaction. The fifth subscale, Global Factors, includes items designed to tap general clinical impressions of the session. The items within each subscale are further divided into conceptually distinct categories. For example, the 17 items in the Patient Qualities subscale are grouped into eight categories such as Lack of Motivation, Insufficient Self-Disclosure, and Negative Attitudes. Table 8-8 presents the VNIS subscales, categories, and selected items. Compared to the VPPS subscales which were derived from a factor–analytic procedure, the items in the VNIS subscales are grouped together on a conceptual basis.

As mentioned earlier, the VNIS items are accompanied by explicit definitions that are intended to aid clinical raters. Because the VNIS specifically refers to negative characteristics of the therapeutic transaction that are not expected to occur frequently, raters use a two-stage decision process. The first judgment involves a simple dichotomous decision as to whether a given characteristic is present or absent. The guiding principle for this decision is whether or not a classifiable event or quality exceeds "normal limits," that is, whether there is evidence that it exceeds "expectable limits" of an "average" therapy session. Following this initial decision, those items judged "present" are assigned numerical ratings on a 1–5 scale reflecting the frequency or intensity of the negative indicator.

Investigations Using the Current
Version of the VNIS

The revised VNIS has been applied to the Vanderbilt project data in two investigations. In the first study (Strupp, Keithly, Moras, Samples, Sandell, & Waterhouse, 1980), two experienced clinicians rated videotapes of the third therapy session in its entirety for 10 cases from the Vanderbilt project. These cases consisted of one high change and one low change patient for each of five therapists. Interrater reliabilities for subscales were moderate to high, except for the subscale of Errors in Technique which, unaccountably, produced a negative correlation coefficient. The comparison of VNIS total scores between high and low outcome cases were found to be statistically significant, suggesting the predictive validity of the instrument. Similar comparisons based on the subscale scores, however, failed to discriminate between high and low outcome groups, which might be attributed to the small samples and large variabilities.

Building upon the initial study by Strupp *et al.* (1980), Sandell (1981) examined the relationship between VNIS ratings and outcomes in a larger sample. In this study, the VNIS was applied to the first three sessions of therapy for the 18 Vanderbilt project patients who were treated by professional therapists. Two clinically sophisticated judges who were psychodynamicaly oriented received 20 hours of training in using the VNIS. During training, judges were instructed to adhere to item definitions, to avoid highly inferential judgments, to ignore minor flaws, and to select only one item to describe a given negative occurrence. Raters acquired experience in using the scale by rating segments of therapy sessions from other projects. In order to develop a perspective on the range of behaviors in the Vanderbilt sample, the judges also listened to 5 minutes

Table 8-8 VNIS Subscales, Categories, and Representative Items

Subscale	Category	Representative Items
Patient Personal Qualities (17 items)	1. Lack of motivation	Failure to take responsibility for problems
		Passivity in the therapeutic interaction
	2. Insufficient self-disclosure	Evasiveness
		Apparent dissimulation
	3. Verbal communication problems	Problems with verbal self-expression
	4. Problems with affect	Problems with affect
	5. Self-derogation	Self-rejection tendencies
	6. Unrealistic expectations	Inappropriate expectations
	7. Negative attitudes	Negative attitudes toward therapist or therapy
	8. Deficient ego resources	Deficient sense of self and/or reality
		Disordered thought, language, and communication
Therapist Personal Qualities (9 items)	1. Deficiencies in therapeutic commitment	Exploitative tendencies
		Lack of warmth
	2. Rejecting attitudes	Lack of respect for the patient
		Critical tendencies

3. Controlling tendencies	Moralistic tendencies
	Tendency to dominate the patient
4. Deficient enactment of therapist's role	Lacks confidence
	Defensive behavior
Errors in Technique (10 items)	
1. Failure to make necessary interventions	Failure to structure or focus the session
	Failure to address signs of resistance
2. Inappropriate or inadequate interventions	Superficial interventions
	Poorly timed interpretations
3. Potentially harmful interventions	Destructive interventions
	Inappropriate use of silence
4. Inflexible use of therapeutic techniques	Inflexible use of therapeutic techniques
Patient–Therapist Interaction (2 items)	
1. Poor therapeutic relationship	Problems in the therapeutic relationship
2. Poor collaboration	Inadequate therapeutic collaboration
Global Session Ratings (4 items)	
1. Poor match	Poor match between patient and therapeutic approach
2. Dull interaction	Dull interaction
3. Negative impact of therapy session	Destructiveness of the therapy session
	Ineffectiveness of the therapy session

from one session for each patient–therapist dyad in the project without making ratings. For the actual study, audiotapes of 15 minutes from the middle of each of the first three sessions were presented in random order. For each segment, the tape was stopped after 7½ minutes and judges independently checked those negative indicators considered present. Final ratings of presence and intensity were made after raters had listened to the remaining 7½ minutes. As with the VPPS, judges discussed their ratings periodically in order to prevent rater drift.

In assessing the psychometric properties of the VNIS subscales, only those items that were rated greater than 0 at least once were considered ($n = 32$). Furthermore, for an item to be included in the analyses, a minimum level of interrater reliability had to be reached ($r \geq .60$) (Kraemer, 1980). Twenty-five of the 42 items met these two criteria. Measures of internal consistency and interrater reliability for the subscales are presented in Table 8-9. The alpha coefficients for the subscales ranged from .26 for Patient-Therapist Interaction to .81 for Therapist Personal Qualities, suggesting that some of the subscales do not tap unified dimensions. This might be expected as the subscales were derived on a conceptual rather than an empirical basis. As also shown in Table 8-9, interrater reliability was generally good for the subscales, although the reliability coefficients were somewhat lower for Errors in Technique ($r = .58$) and Patient-Therapist Interaction ($r = .63$). In both the study by Strupp et al. (1980) and Sandell (1981), Errors in Technique achieved the lowest level of interrater reliability, suggesting that it is difficult for judges to agree on this important facet of therapy.

As a reasonable level of interrater reliability was achieved, judges' ratings were summed for further analyses examining the relationship between the VNIS scores and outcome. Although multiple outcome indices were used in the study, only the findings based on a composite measure of outcome are presented here. This outcome measure called Overall Improvement was obtained by summing assessments of global improvement that were made, at termination, by the patient, the therapist, and the independent clinician. Table 8-10 presents the correlation coefficients between the VNIS subscale scores and this composite measure for each of the first three sessions. As can be seen, all the subscales except Therapist Personal Qualities demonstrated at least one significant correlation with outcome, with the Errors in Technique subscale showing the strongest and most consistent relationship to outcome. Partial correlations were computed in an attempt to explore the specific contribution of each subscale although the sample size

Table 8-9 Psychometric Properties of VNIS Subscales

Scales	Reliable Items	Internal Consistency[a]	Interrater Reliability[b]
Patient Qualities	9	.60	.88
Therapist Personal Qualities	4	.81	.74
Errors in Technique	7	.46	.58
Patient–Therapist Interaction	2	.26	.63
Global Session Ratings	3	.52	.79

Note. $N = 18$. Measures of interrater reliability and internal consistency are based on those items that were reliably rated, i.e., with $r \geq .60$.
[a]Coefficient alpha. [b]Pearson correlation coefficients are based on the sum of the three session scores. The coefficients were slightly lower for individual sessions.

Table 8-10   Pearson Correlations Between VNIS Ratings and
Overall Improvement

	Session		
VNIS Subscales	1	2	3
Patient Qualities	−.27	−.13	−.53*
Therapist Personal Qualities	−.22	−.31	−.16
Errors in Technique	−.57**	−.46*	−.48*
Patient–Therapist Interaction	−.34	−.31	−.49*
Global Session Ratings	−.45*	−.24	−.52*
Total VNIS Ratings	−.55**	−.36	−.52*

Note. Negative correlations represent an inverse relationship between
VNIS ratings and therapeutic outcome.
    *$p < .05$.
    **$p < .01$.

was rather small for such procedures. Only Errors in Technique produced significant
partial correlation coefficients. These findings provided preliminary evidence for the
role of therapist technique as a determinant of outcome in psychotherapy. In subsequent analyses Sandell examined the relationship between the subscales and outcome
separately for psychodynamic therapists and for experiential therapists. Consistent with
the perspective taken in developing the instrument, Errors in Technique was found to
be related to outcome only for psychodynamic therapists, suggesting that the instrument may be most appropriate for evaluating psychodynamically oriented therapists.

Concluding Remarks

Unlike most process measures of psychotherapy which can be readily applied by relatively inexperienced judges, the VNIS demands a fairly high degree of sophistication.
This is so because before making evaluations of a therapist's personal qualities, the adequacy of his or her techniques, and so on, one must have a clear frame of references.
Thus, raters should ideally be well-trained therapists who, on the basis of their own clinical experience and observation, are familiar both with the range of therapeutic practices
and quality of performance. To a greater extent than is true of other instruments, the
VNIS calls for *value* judgments. Therein may lie its greatest strength as well as its greatest
potential weakness: On the one hand, it is deliberately sensitive to deficiencies and errors in the therapist's performance; on the other, there is, except in glaring cases, considerable room for disagreement on what constitutes good as well as poor practice. We
should also repeat that the VNIS is anchored in psychodynamic conceptions and may
therefore be less applicable to therapies based on divergent theoretical assumptions.

The VNIS, probably in part for the reasons mentioned above, has as yet undergone
less testing and application than the VPPS. Our own experience, however, has been
quite encouraging. In particular, we have been pleased by the demonstration of a reasonable consensus on seemingly fluid and elusive phenomena and the statistical associations between VNIS measures and therapeutic outcomes. These are promising begin-

nings, and the leads, especially those obtained by Sandell (1981), should be pursued.

In our sanguine moments we have foreseen a time when the VNIS might become a regular component of licensing or competence examinations. It would seem quite feasible for applicants to submit samples of their therapeutic work (as they are already required to do by ABPP and by some licensing boards) which would then be evaluated by clinical judges using the VNIS or a similar instrument. To our knowledge, the VNIS is the first attempt to systematize judgments of a therapist's performance by pinpointing deficiencies. These might then be eliminated by further training, supervision, personal therapy, and the like.

Concluding Comments

In this chapter we have described two major systems of process–analysis developed by the Vanderbilt Psychotherapy Research Team as part of its ongoing research effort. Process–analysis, for most investigators, is a means to an end, not an end itself. The ultimate goal is to understand the "active ingredients" in the therapeutic process that give rise to particular therapeutic outcomes. How do the events of therapy session 1, 2, . . . , k account for therapeutic success or failure? What actions by the therapist lead to differential outcomes? If we were able to answer these questions with greater specificity and assurance we would be farther ahead in our understanding of what psychotherapy "is."

The foregoing formulation harks back to a static (treatment) model of psychotherapy which is gradually being superseded. Researchers, however, are barely on the threshold of developing methodological tools that would allow them to catch up with more advanced clinical thinking. To restate the problem: Traditionally, it has been assumed that therapist behaviors A, B, . . . , K will lead to good outcomes, whereas the absence of these behaviors or the presence of therapist behaviors L, M, . . . , Q would lead to poor outcomes. To test this hypothesis, one would then identify these behaviors, count them, and relate them statistically to a more or less arbitrary criterion ("outcome"). Even if, as is true in more recent process systems, the patient's behavior is taken into account, we still have no measures that would permit us to deal more adequately with the *dynamics* of the patient–therapist interaction. It is now generally recognized that the patient and the therapist continually influence each other, and that we must account for the feedback as well as the patient's (or therapist's) input. While there exist certain statistical techniques (e.g., autocorrelation, time-series analysis, etc.) that might help to deal with these complexities, they are exceedingly cumbersome to apply and, perhaps for this reason alone, have not found great favor with the rank and file of psychotherapy process researchers. We shall soon return to this problem.

Outcome itself is, of course, a rather slippery criterion. At what point in the ongoing patient–therapist interaction does process become "outcome"? Further, unless one defines an outcome in narrow behavioral terms (e.g., cessation of smoking, or disappearance of a troublesome symptom), outcome becomes a shorthand label for complex and multifaceted aspects of an individual's feelings, cognition, and behavior. As Strupp and Hadley (1977) have pointed out, assessments of the meaning and adaptational significance of human behaviors that often depend on situational contexts require *value* judgments by the patient, the therapist, significant others, and/or society at large. For practical purposes it may not be too difficult to decide whether a patient, following therapy, is "improved," "deteriorated," or "unchanged," but it should occasion no surprise if, depending on the judge's perspective, there is a lack of consensus. By the same token, any predictors, singly or in combination, can account only for relatively small portions of the variance, no matter how refined the measurements may become. In short, lack of precision is only in part a measurement problem.

But what are the predictors, that is, the patient or therapist "behaviors" we have spoken of before? Does it make sense to treat them in linear fashion? If a certain therapist behavior, say, empathy is "good," is a greater amount "better"? Can we simply sum behaviors in which we are interested? Can we legitimately omit the context in which a given therapist behavior occurs? To illustrate: At what point does the therapist's human concern for a patient's misfortune become an antitherapeutic form of pampering? When is a therapist's silence productive and when is it counterproductive? The meaning (and therapeutic value) of a given therapist behavior may be different early in therapy and later in therapy, when the patient is "resistant" or collaborating, and so on. Thus, when assessed against the clinician's refined understanding of therapeutic phenomena (let us forget for the moment that clinicians frequently disagree on the meaning and significance of these phenomena), the indices yielded by existing systems of process-analysis emerge as rather primitive and crude attempts at objectifying human events that are elusive in the extreme. Even more serious is the criticism that those aspects of the patient–therapist interaction that lend themselves to objectification and quantification may not be the ones that ultimately lead to a better understanding of the psychotherapeutic process. (We are reminded of the oft-told anecdote of the drunk who looks under a lamp post for the keys he has lost in a dark alley because the light is better).

Nonetheless, at some point quality shades into quantity and it becomes possible to characterize a therapist as "empathic" or "unempathic," "constructive" or "destructive," and so on. The history of psychology (e.g., intelligence measurement) attests to the pragmatic correctness of E. L. Thorndike's dictum that whatever exists, exists in some amount and can thus be measured. Therefore, we may reaffirm our faith in the ultimate value of process-analysis in psychotherapy. Future systems will undoubtedly look very different from existing ones. However, if we can master the challenge of translating salient therapeutic phenomena (e.g., transference, resistance, therapeutic alliance) into meaningful quantifications, process-analysis will have a bright future. To us, this suggests that there is no substitute for incisive thinking which must precede the creation of scales and measures. No doubt, the limits of human ingenuity have not been reached in this arena. It is also predictable that the advent of the computer age may open undreamt of vistas to the process researcher in the years to come. In the meantime, systems like the ones described in this chapter (and other contemporary attempts) can clearly contribute to improved understanding of therapeutic outcomes and their process antecedents. Comparisons of patients with sharply divergent treatment outcomes, exemplified by Strupp (1980a, 1980b, 1980c, 1980d), embodied one strategy for casting light on the challenging problem of why two seemingly similar patients treated by the same therapist had very different experiences in therapy. Although the foregoing comparisons were done *post hoc*, they yielded promising hypotheses which we plan to test in research now being planned. As in other areas of experimental science, the investigator must create conditions which force Nature to reveal her secrets in the sense of providing meaningful answers to specific questions. In this quest, systems of process-analysis can play a crucial role.

References

Auld, F., Jr., & Murray, E. J. Content-analysis studies of psychotherapy. *Psychological Bulletin*, 1955, *52*, 377–395.

Bergin, A. E. The evaluation of therapeutic outcomes. In A. E. Bergin and S. L. Garfield (Eds.), *Handbook of psychotherapy and behavior change*. New York: Wiley, 1971.

Bibring, E. Psychoanalysis and the dynamic psychotherapies. *Journal of American Psychoanalytic Association*, 1954, *2*, 745–770.

D'Augelli, A. R., Danish, S. J., & Brock, G. W. Untrained paraprofessionals' verbal helping behavior: Description and implications for training. *American Journal of Community Psychology*, 1976, *4*, 275–282.

Frank, J. D. *Persuasion and healing*. Baltimore, MD.: Johns Hopkins University Press, 1973.

Glover, E. *The techniques of psychoanalysis*. New York: International Universities Press, 1955.

Gomes-Schwartz, B. Effective ingredients in psychotherapy: Prediction of outcome from process variables. *Journal of Consulting and Clinical Psychology*, 1978, *46*, 1023–1035. (a)

Gomes-Schwartz, B. *Development of a scale to predict negative change in psychotherapy*. Paper presented at the annual meeting of the Society for Psychotherapy Research, Toronto, June 1978. (b)

Gomes-Schwartz, B., & Schwartz, J. M. Psychotherapy process variables distinguishing the "inherently helpful" person from the professional psychotherapist. *Journal of Consulting and Clinical Psychology*, 1978, *46*, 196–197.

Guilford, J. P., & Fruchter, B. *Fundamental statistics in psychology and education* (6th ed.). New York: McGraw-Hill, 1978.

Hadley, S. W., & Strupp, H. H. Contemporary views of negative effects in psychotherapy. *Archives of General Psychiatry*, 1976, *33*, 1291–1302.

Kiesler, D. J. Some myths of psychotherapy research and the search for a paradigm. *Psychological Bulletin*, 1966, *65*, 110–136.

Kiesler, D. J. *The process of psychotherapy*. Chicago: Aldine, 1973.

Kiesler, D. J. *Process analysis: A necessary ingredient of psychotherapy outcome research*. Invited paper presented at the annual conference of the Society for Psychotherapy Research, Aspen, Colorado, June, 1981.

Kraemer, H. Statistical coping strategies for clinical research. *Journal of Consulting and Clinical Psychology*, 1981, *49*, 309–319.

Langs, R. *The technique of psychoanalytic psychotherapy*. New York: Aronson, 1973.

Luborsky, L. Helping alliances in psychotherapy. In J. Claghorn (Ed.), *Successful psychotherapy*. New York: Brunner/Mazel, 1976.

Luborsky, L., Chandler, M., Auerbach, A. H., Cohen, J., & Bachrach, H. M. Factors influencing the outcome of psychotherapy: A review of quantitative research. *Psychological Bulletin*, 1971, *75*, 145–185.

Malan, D. H. *Towards the validation of dynamic psychotherapy: A replication*. New York: Plenum Medical Books, 1976.

Marsden, G. Content-analysis studies of psychotherapy: 1954 through 1968. In A. E. Bergin & S. L. Garfield (Eds.), *Handbook of psychotherapy and behavior change*. New York: Wiley, 1971.

O'Malley, S. S., Suh, C. S., & Strupp, H. H. The Vanderbilt Psychotherapy Process Scale: A report on the scale development and a process-outcome study. *Journal of Consulting and Clinical Psychology*, 1983, *51*, 581–586.

O'Malley, S. S., & Gomes-Schwartz, B. *The reliability of psychotherapy process ratings as a function of presentation mode*. Unpublished manuscript, Vanderbilt University, 1983.

Orlinsky, D. E., & Howard, K. I. The good therapy hour. *Archives of General Psychiatry*, 1967, *16*, 621–632.

Orlinsky, D. E., & Howard, K. I. *Varieties of psychotherapeutic experience*. New York: Teachers College Press, 1975.

Parloff, M. B., Waskow, I. E., & Wolfe, B. E. Research on therapist variables in relation to process and outcome. In S. L. Garfield & A. E. Bergin (Eds.), *Handbook of psychotherapy and behavior change* (2nd ed.). New York: Wiley, 1978.

Pope, B., Nudler, S., VonKorff, M. R., & McGee, J. P. The experienced professional interviewer vs. the complete novice. *Journal of Consulting and Clinical Psychology*, 1974, 42, 680–690.

Rogers, C. R. The necessary and sufficient conditions of therapeutic personality change. *Journal of Consulting Psychology*, 1957, 21, 95–103.

Rogers, C. R., Gendlin, G. T., Kiesler, D. J., & Truax, C. B. *The therapeutic relationship and its impact: A study of psychotherapy with schizophrenics.* Madison: University of Wisconsin Press, 1967.

Saltzman, C., Luetgert, M. J., Roth, C. H., Creaser, J., & Howard, L. Formation of a therapeutic relationship: Experiences during the initial phase of psychotherapy as predictors of treatment duration and outcome. *Journal of Consulting and Clinical Psychology*, 1976, 44, 546–555.

Sachs, J. S. Negative factors in brief psychotherapy: An empirical assessment. *Journal of Consulting and Clinical Psychology*, 1983, 51(4), 557–564.

Strupp, H. H. A multidimensional system for analyzing psychotherapeutic techniques. *Psychiatry*, 1957, 20, 293–306. (a)

Strupp, H. H. A multidimensional analysis of techniques in brief psychotherapy. *Psychiatry*, 1957, 20, 387–397. (b)

Strupp, H. H. *Psychotherapists in action: Explorations of the therapist's contribution to the treatment process.* New York: Grune & Stratton, 1960.

Strupp, H. H. Success and failure in time-limited psychotherapy: A systematic comparison of two cases (Comparison 1). *Archives of General Psychiatry*, 1980, 37, 595–603. (a)

Strupp, H. H. Success and failure in time-limited psychotherapy: A systematic comparison of two cases (Comparison 2). *Archives of General Psychiatry*, 1980, 37, 708–716. (b)

Strupp, H. H. Success and failure in time-limited psychotherapy: With special reference to the performance of a lay counselor (Comparison 3). *Archives of General Psychiatry*, 1980, 37, 831–841.(c)

Strupp, H. H. Success and failure in time-limited psychotherapy. Further evidence (Comparison 4). *Archives of General Psychiatry*, 1980, 37, 947–954. (d)

Strupp, H. H., & Hadley, S. W. A tripartite model of mental health and therapeutic outcomes. *American Psychologist*, 1977, 32, 187–196.

Strupp, H. H., & Hadley, S. Specific vs nonspecific factors in psychotherapy: A controlled study of outcome. *Archives of General Psychiatry*, 1979, 36, 1125–1136.

Strupp, H. H., Hadley, S. W., & Gomes-Schwartz, B. *Psychotherapy for better or worse: An analysis of the problem of negative effects.* New York: Jason Aronson, 1977.

Strupp, H. H., Hartley, D., & Blackwood, G. L., Jr. *Vanderbilt Psychotherapy Process Scale.* Unpublished manuscript, Vanderbilt University, 1974.

Strupp, H. H., Keithly, L., Moras, K., Samples, S., Sandell, J., & Waterhouse, G. *Toward the measurement of negative effects in psychotherapy.* Paper presented at the annual meeting of the Society of Psychotherapy Research, Pacific Grove, California, June, 1980.

Strupp, H. H., Moras, K., Sandell, J., Waterhouse, G., O'Malley, S., Keithly, L., & Gomes-Schwartz, B. *Vanderbilt Negative Indicators Scale: An instrument for the identification of deterrents to progress in time-limited dynamic psychotherapy.* Unpublished manuscript, Vanderbilt University, 1981.

Suh, C. S., & O'Malley, S. S. *The identification of facilitative therapist factors: Methodological considerations and research findings of a study.* Paper presented at the annual meeting of the Society for Psychotherapy Research, Smuggler's Notch, Vermont, June, 1982.

Suh, C. S., & Strupp, H. H. *Appropriateness of residual gain scores in psychotherapy research: An analysis with special reference to the Vanderbilt Psychotherapy Project.* Paper presented at the annual meeting of the Society for Psychotherapy Research, Smuggler's Notch, Vermont, June, 1982.

Sundland, D., & Barker, E. N. The orientations of psychotherapists. *Journal of Consulting Psychology*, 1962, 26, 201–212.

Tinsley, H. E. A., & Weiss, D. J. Interrater reliability and agreement of subjective judgments. *Journal of Counseling Psychology*, 1975, 22, 358–376.

Appendix

In order to illustrate the VPPS, we have selected for presentation transcripts of segments from the first three sessions of therapy for a 20-year-old male college student who was treated by a male psychiatrist in the Vanderbilt project. Our decision to focus on a single case rather than on comparing ratings for two patients with divergent outcomes was based on the finding of Suh and O'Malley (1982) that it was the *pattern of change* over sessions and not the level of the characteristics tapped by the various VPPS factors which was highly correlated with outcome. The case presented was chosen because he was a low prognosis case who achieved high outcome in the classification system used by Suh and O'Malley (Patient 9 in Table 5). According to this approach, patients with low scores at Session 1 on the VPPS scale of Patient Participation were classified as having a low prognosis for change. Several observations gleaned from the clinical records of the case support the validity of his classification as a low prognosis patient: The therapist requested comprehensive psychological assessments for this patient after the second therapy hour because he was concerned about the seriousness of the disturbance. In this regard, the assessment information suggested an extremely shy and introverted person with a schizoid tendency as well as very low self-concept, depression, and anger. It is interesting to note that the therapist conducted 30-minute sessions after the third hour because the patient was "so inhibited" that the therapist did not think they could tolerate 45 minutes each session. Furthermore, in an interview following termination, the therapist remarked that the patient did better than he had anticipated.

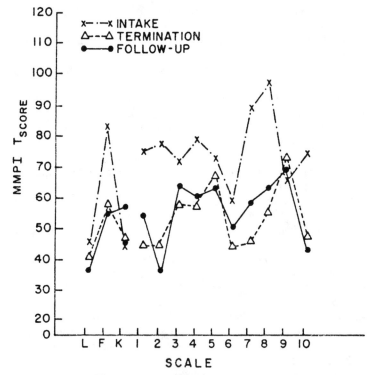

Figure 8-1   MMPI profile obtained at intake, termination, and follow-up, illustrating the initial disturbance and therapeutic changes of the patient presented in the Appendix.

Despite his apparently limited potential for change, however, this patient clearly achieved a high outcome. His ratings posttherapy indicated impressive improvements in the areas of concern that he had specified at intake ("lack of self-confidence," "shyness," "unable to talk to girls or people in general"). Ratings made by the therapist and the independent clinician were consistent with his assessment. For purposes of illustrating the patient's initial disturbance and the therapeutic changes that took place, his MMPI profile obtained at intake, termination, and follow-up is shown in Figure 8-1.

The VPPS scores that accompany the transcripts were rated as part of the study by O'Malley *et al.* according to the procedures described earlier. Although the judges made ratings on the basis of the first, middle, and last 5 minutes of each session in this study, only a subsample of these segments is presented here. We hope that it will convey the flavor of the qualities assessed without being unnecessarily lengthy. In addition to the scores on the VPPS subscales for the three sessions, scores on items that characterized the subscale or changes in the subscale scores across the three sessions are also presented. It is noted that, although many of the items did not show substantial changes, the changes were nevertheless consistent in their direction and thus contributed to more reliable changes in subscale scores.

Patient Participation

The patient's initial PP score of 45.0 was far lower than any in our sample of 16 patients, but increased in the second session (sixth rank order). The items listed in Table 8-11 showed notable changes across sessions.

Table 8-11

	Session		
	1	2	3
Scale score	45.0	55.0	48.5
Took the initiative	2.25	3.5	2.75
Inhibited	3.0	1.75	2.5
Spontaneous	1.5	2.5	2.5
Passive	2.75	1.75	2.25

Patient Hostility

The first and second session score on this subscale were near the average of the sample. We speculate that the increase in the third session might be related to the patient's reaction to the psychological evaluation he had received before this session. Although only one item showed significant increase, the remaining items showed small but consistent changes (Table 8-12).

Table 8-12

	Session		
	1	2	3
Scale score	14.0	14.0	20.5
Intellectualizing	1.25	1.25	2.25

Patient Exploration

The scores on this subscale appear to be consistent with those on PP. Again, the first session score was one of the lowest observed in the sample with an increase in the second session which is followed by a drop in the third session score. Notable changes were observed on two items (Table 8-13).

Table 8-13

	Session		
	1	2	3
Scale score	41.5	50.0	46.5
How productive was this hour?	3.0	3.5	4.0
Talked about his feelings	2.5	3.5	3.0

Patient Psychic Distress

Several items on this subscale (Table 8-14) showed increases over the three sessions which might be related to the increases in Patient Exploration.

Table 8-14

	Session		
	1	2	3
Scale score	45.5	56.0	55.5
Guilty	1.75	2.75	3.25
Self-critical	2.0	3.25	4.0
Depressed	2.25	3.5	2.25
Ashamed	2.0	2.75	3.0

Patient Dependency

Because we have not investigated this subscale, we do not have adequate understanding to interpret the ratings at this point. Only one item showed noticeable changes (Table 8-15).

Table 8-15

	Session		
	1	2	3
Scale score	13.5	14.5	21.0
Tried to learn more about what to do in therapy and what to expect from it	1.0	1.25	2.5

Therapist Warmth and Friendliness

This therapist's scores on the Therapist Warmth and Friendliness Scale were generally low. We speculate that the lack of correlations between the absolute level of therapist warmth and outcome is because this scale taps more of stylistic differences among therapists. On the other hand, compared to other therapists who reacted antitherapeutically to the patients' negative qualities, this therapist maintained and, in fact showed some increases, in therapist warmth. This is the reason we feel that change scores on this scale are so strongly related to outcome. Although no item showed notable amount of changes, most of the changes were in the expected direction (Table 8-16).

Table 8-16

	Session		
	1	2	3
Scale score	50.0	49.5	54.5

Therapist Exploration

Substantial increases were observed across the session on this scale. The changes were noted in the items given in Table 8-17.

Table 8-17

	Session		
	1	2	3
Scale score	79.5	92.5	95.0
Tried to help the patient evaluate his reactions and feelings	2.25	3.75	3.75
Placed the patient's report in a new perspective or reorganized the patient's experience	2.25	3.5	3.5
Identified themes in the patient's experience or behavior	2.0	3.0	2.75

Some of the items did not show changes but instead were consistently high, for example:

- Tried to get a better understanding of the patient of what was really going on.
- Tried to help the patient recognize his feelings.
- Tried to help the patient understand the reasons behind his reactions.
- Encouraged depth rather than shallowness.
    (All of these items were given a score of ''4'' in all three sessions.)

Negative Therapist Attitude

The variability of scores on this subscale was quite small in our sample with most therapists scoring low. No item showed noticeable changes in this scale (Table 8-18).

Table 8-18

	Session		
	1	2	3
Scale score	13.0	13.0	15.0

A Sample Transcript

First Session

Beginning

T: Do I understand that—uh—you went to the Counseling Service originally, is that correct? or . . .

P: No.

T: No? Can you fill me in on that?

P: Well, first off I went to—uh—"a mental health" center.

T: Uh-huh.

P: Drug Treatment Center. And since I didn't have any particular problem with drugs, they thought it'd be best if I came over here. And I kinda put it off til—uh—they sent out a questionnaire about whoever, who wanted to get into counseling.

T: Oh, I see.

P: And that's how I got into it.

T: Uh-huh. Right. And how much has been explained to you about this—uh—what's your understanding?

P: Nothing. I don't—well—nothing in particular has been explained, so . . .

T: Did they give you some idea of how often you'd be seen . . . or?

P: No.

T: Uh—how many times you'd be seen and so forth?

P: No.

T: They—they did not explain to you that—anything about that?

P: No.

T: Uh-huh.

P: They—uh—he said he did want me to meet with you about—uh—10 or 12 sessions, I believe, and that's all that was said.

T: Yup. There's a maximum of 25, I believe, sessions.

P: Mm-hm.

T: But, uh, it could be fewer if that seems to be in order, it depends upon what does seem to be in order. Now, did they also explain anything to you about a study project or anything of that sort?

P: No.

T: Well, let me, uh, see if I can understand from you your reason for being interested in getting some help and if you would explain to me your interest in deriving help.

P: Well, I—I'm basically shy with people, uh, it's not—I don't—it doesn't seem to me like it's, uh, just the shyness that everybody has—I'm—I'm, uh, I have more trouble meeting people it seems like than everybody else does, and then, uh, getting in conversations with them, things like that.

T: Mm-hm.

P: And . . . (*pause*) . . . well, I guess that's about it right there.

T: Uh-huh. Are there other things?

P: No . . . It all seems to fall around that.

T: Can you amplify what you told me about it—about the shyness?

P: Well . . . (*very long pause*) . . . It's just any strange situation, uh, any situation, uh, . . . where I'm going to meet somebody or anything like that, I'm always shook up and put it off 'til—put if off and if it's something that I don't feel is very important I won't even get around to doing it.

T: Mm-hm.

P: And, uh, things like that and then in the case of girls, I can't even talk to them you know, and it's just hard for me to even start, uh, start a conversation with them.

T: Mm-hm. Is it more difficult with girls than with—or, women, than with men?

P: It seems to be.

T: Mh-hm. How long have you been aware of this kind of problem?

P: About 2 years, I guess.

T: Mm-hm.

P: But it - really, it hadn't really bothered me that much, uhh, I guess I kept thinking it'd blow over or something (T: Uh-huh) that I'd grow out of it, something like that. Up until about the last 6 months, it hadn't really bothered me that much.

T: I see. Now, prior to 2 years ago, was it that the problem didn't exist or that you were simply not aware of it, or didn't pay any attention to it?

P: It existed, I just didn't pay any attention to it.

T: Uh-huh . . . (*pause*) . . . And then, in the past 6 months it's become more marked.

P: Mh-hm.

T: Any explanation for this?

P: Nm-mnh, no. Not that I know of.

T: Is it that it troubles you more, or that you're actually more shy?

P: It troubles me more, I'm not any more shy, in fact it seems that I'm a little less (T: Mm-hm) in certain situations, but—it still bothers me more.

T: Mm-hm. Do you have any ideas yourself about why it bothers you more?

Second Session

Middle

P: . . . I don't really know. Uh . . . (*long pause*) . . . uh . . . having more dates than I've had, for one thing (T: Mm-hm) And, uh, not developing as many friends . . . things of that nature.

T: Mm-hm. . . . (*pause*) . . . So that in other words, it has interfered . . . really with the formation of friendships and the going on dates.

P: Mm-hm.
   (*pause*)

T: What—what was it that, uh . . . made it possible for you, for example, to line up that date with . . . the young woman that, you had a date with recently.

P: Well . . .

T: How'd you manage that?

P: Took me about a week really . . . before I got around to calling . . . Uhh, I called a mutual friend . . . I—I was s—scared as hell, anyway, of asking her to start with, so I called a mutual friend of ours and, uh, I asked her if she would, try to set it up, you know.

T: Mm-hm.

P: And so, she called me back and said that, uh, Vicki wanted to talk to me about it. So I put if off for a day or two and then finally called her . . . before . . . I got things set up.

T: I see. Practically sounds a little bit like, uh, uhh, Miles Standish and, uh, John Alden.

P: Uh-huh. . . . (*pause*) . . . And, in fact that's the way I've gotten most of the dates that I've had, is through friends (T: Mm-hm) setting them up.

T: What is it, the fear that (*clearing throat*) someone will rebuff you, someone will . . . say no (P: Yeah) to you, and that you'll feel so hurt, (P: Mm-hm)—that it would be too painful? (P: Mm-hm.) So that you're kind of protecting yourself against the possibility of that kind of pain?

P: Yeah.

T: Mm-hm. Can you talk some more about that?

P: Well it seems like, uh . . . back when I was first . . . trying to date, asking girls out, seems like I picked . . . ones—the wrong ones, and, uh . . . everytime I asked one of them out they'd—I'd get turned down, you know. That happened about 5 or 6 times in a row, and I started wondering if it was, not necessarily that they had something else planned, but if it was something with me, you know.

T: Mm-hm.

P: And, uh, that's how it all got started.

T: Yeah, so that you would feel rejected.

P: Uh-huh.

T: And hurt.

P: Uh-huh.

T: And I take it you're sensitive on that score.

P: Mm-hm.

T: So that since that time you've, done things to protect yourself. First you make an inquiry to find out whether it . . . (P: Mm-hm) it'll be possible.

P: Yeah.

T: And once you're—you've gotten enough encouragement, as a result of the indirect approach . . .

P: Well, sometimes I don't even make the direct approach, it—just—a friend will set it up for me.

T: I see.

P: And I'll go meet the girl the day of the date, you know . . . if I've never met her before (T: Mm-hm), if that's the case.
    (*pause*)

T: Mm-hm. That's on blind dates.

P: Mm-hm.
    (*pause*)

T: Any other thoughts about why you—you may be so sensitive to being . . . rebuffed or rejected.

P: No.

T: Now that accounts for, uhh, dates, but what about, you know, uh, friendships?

P: It's, uh, probably the same feeling of rejection, I . . . I'm . . . guess I'm a sensitive person.

T: Mm-hm.

P: And I like to be accepted. . . . And, on top of that I'm, a little bit of a perfectionist. . . . It's uh, see other people . . . that get along well, think . . . well I ought to be able to, too. (T: Mm-hm) and uh, (T: *clearing throat*) . . . but, uh, for some reason, it's uh . . . feeling that somebody's not going to like me. And, uh . . . that keeps me away from them.

T: Mm-hm. Well, it's not difficult to understand that you would want people to like you but, it is more difficult to understand why you're concerned that people won't . . . or you—why you *anticipate* that they're not going to like you.

P: Well, I don't really know that. . . . I can't think of any reason why . . . why I should be like that.

End

P: Uh . . . she lived up the street from me I think; I don't remember very much about it. In fact I hadn't thought about it since, since it happened. (T: um-hum) But she lived up the street from me and we were pretty good friends I guess at the time and I used to go to her house all the time, and uh . . . I don't know what happened, just for some reason . . .uh . . . that uh . . . I quit going over there and uh, we quit playing together, things like that.

T: Um-hum. . . . (*pause*) . . . You were around 6 or 7?

P: Um-hum. I believe so.

T: Anything else happen when you were around 6 or 7?

P: Not that I remember. . . . Except a bicycle wreck, and that's the only other think I can remember. . . . I was coming down a hill where, near where I live and uh didn't turn sharp enough and caught some gravel. The bicycle slid out from under me. It uh . . . messed up this side of my face a little bit; you know, just tore the skin off, didn't hurt it or anything. But, other than that, there wasn't anything. I do remember everybody laughing about it and everything, thinking how funny it was. And I'd have done the same thing too, uh. . . . (*pause*) . . .

T: Is one of your concerns, or one of the reasons that you hold back, a concern about people laughing at you or being embarrassed?

P: I think so. . . . Like, I don't like to do things unless it's something I know what I'm doing. I don't like to do things in front of others.

T: I see. So you have to really be sure of yourself?

P: Um-hum.

T: Nothing is going to happen that will cause people to laugh?

P: Um-hum.

T: Even if it is at your expense.

P: Well, even at that, in the situation where I do know what I'm doing, I'm still a little concerned about people looking over my shoulder.

T: Um-hum. So it's not only your concern about being rebuffed that kind of holds you back (P: Uh-huh), but it's also a concern about being embarrassed (P: Um-hum). . . . (*pause*) . . . How strong is this concern about being embarrassed?

P: Pretty strong. It, it gets to the point where I get so nervous that I can't continue sometimes. If it's, I'm doing something with my hands my nerves get so bad that I have to stop (T: I see) for a few minutes.

T: Mm-hum. . . . (*long pause*) . . . Well, we're going to have to stop in just a moment or two. Let me uh, uh suggest this at this point. As part of our procedure for what we're going to have you do is have, uh, some psychological tests at the, uh, probably at the Counseling Center, and then I will meet with you after the tests and then next time I will talk with you definitely about exactly how we will proceed (P: OK) from here on out. Are there any questions that you have at this point?

P: Uh, no.

(The session ends with a brief discussion concerning the evaluation and the next appointment.)

Third Session

Middle

P: It all builds up and I get down on myself because I think I should have done it before, before I waited—before I did and not have waited so long—gets, uh, it gets me down sometimes.

T: Mm-hm.

P: But I guess everything is practically over now, so, I'm feeling all right today.

T: Mm-hm. School finishing up?

P: Mm-hm . . . (*pause*) . . . Today was the last day of classes. And so, I made—and so, uh, as far as I'm concerned it's over, except for finals.

T: When are those?

P: Uh, next week and the week after. They start next Wednesday for me.

T: Mm-hm.

(*pause*)

P: And it doesn't seem like I have as much trouble getting myself up to study for the finals as I do the rest of the year in the course.

T: Mm-hm.

P: It's just something easier for me to do.

(*very long pause*)

P: I can't think of anything else to say.

T: Well, suppose you just talk about whatever you think of as you sit here.

(*long pause*)

P: One thing that is bothering me. I—I don't think I should ask it though. I'll ask it anyway. How did the test come out?

T: In what way?

P: Uh, I don't know . . . Did they, uh—were they generally what you were expecting?

T: I would say so . . . (*pause*) . . . Do you have any thoughts about them?

P: No, not really. It was a new experience for me. I never had taken anything like that.

T: Mm-hm.

P: I didn't really know what to think about it.

(*long pause*)

T: Any thoughts about why you were hesitant to ask?

P: No, not really. I just didn't feel like it was something I ought to know . . . (*pause*) . . . I don't know why—it's just something I felt.

T: Mm-hm.

P: That's another thing I put a lot of belief in is feelings. How you feel about a situation. (T: Mm-hm) And that's . . .

T: In asking about the test, do you think, basically, your question was what do I think about you?

End

P: I don't know . . . it's a conflict in values it seems like to me. Because on the one hand, one part of me tells me that don't worry about the grades, everything's gonna be all right regardless. And then, the other side of me that I don't listen to—he's always telling me that I ought to be doing this and I ought to be doing that to get better grades in school and to do my best at everything. But, uh, it's just a conflict there.

T: Mm-hm. Well, it seems that you listen to it—you don't always follow it, perhaps.

P: Well, I listen to it—I don't—I hardly ever follow it. But, uh, the other part's the one I usually end up following. Like I say, I put everything off to the last minute.

T: Well it sounds to me like you operate with a lot of pressure in yourself but at various times you just try to push it aside and say, you know, I—I won't respond to it.

P: I guess I do, uh, I . . .

T: So that you kind of, at times, go the exact opposite direction.

P: Mm-hm. I tend to put more pressure on myself than I should, I guess.

T: Mm-hm. Well, it's uh, evidently not just a matter of pressure but it's a matter of expectations.

P: Mm-hm.

T: And it's not only that you expect so much of yourself but you assume that others are going to, as well. You're more tolerant with other people than you are with yourself.

P: Seems like it's easier to be, though. Because you—you're looking at them from a different perspective and you can see, (T: Exactly) uh, that they are doing the best they can with what they've got.

T: Yea, but the question still would be why you can't have that same perspective with yourself?

P: I don't know.

T: We'll have to see what we can understand about that. We're going to have to stop now. (P: O.K.) We're set up, uh, times for this coming week. Uh, will you be able to come in this coming week?

(Patient and therapist proceed to set up an appointment time.)

9

The Penn Helping
Alliance Scales

Leslie B. Alexander
Graduate School of Social Work and Social Research
Bryn Mawr College
Bryn Mawr, Pennsylvania

Lester Luborsky
University of Pennsylvania School of Medicine
Department of Psychiatry
Philadelphia, Pennsylvania

The Penn Helping Alliance Scales

The fact that most forms of psychotherapy produce positive changes in a substantial proportion of patients has been established in recent years (see Luborsky, Singer, & Luborsky, 1975; and Smith, Glass, & Miller, 1980, for extensive reviews). However, the nature of the curative factors is only sketchily understood and provides an ongoing challenge for psychotherapy researchers.

Within the last decade, a number of variables, each at one time or another considered pivotal, have been shown to account for far less of the outcome variance than previously believed. These include pretherapy patient and therapist factors, as well as technique and type of treatment variables (Luborsky *et al.*, 1975; Sloane, Staples, Cristol, Yorkston, & Whipple, 1975; Strupp & Hadley, 1979; Smith *et al.*, 1980; Luborsky, Mintz, Auerbach, Christoph, Bachrach, Todd, Johnson, Cohen, & O'Brien, 1980; and Luborsky and McLellan, 1981). Of these, patient factors have contributed the most toward explaining the variance in outcome. Most recently, however, positive relationship factors have been shown to be even more predictive than pre-treatment patient factors (Luborsky and Auerbach, 1985a).

At the same time that the size of the contribution of these variables has been questioned, some psychotherapy researchers have begun to cast their net wider in search of the general factors common to all effective psychotherapeutic efforts (see, for example, Frank, 1971, 1974; Raimy, 1975; Luborsky, 1976; Strupp & Hadley, 1979; Goldfried, 1980; and Garfield, 1984). This, in turn, has led to the revival of an interest in an old and established concept in the clinical and theoretical literature of psychoanalysis, referred to variously as "the therapeutic alliance" (Zetzel, 1958), the "working alliance" (Greenson, 1965, 1967; Greenson & Wexler, 1969), or Luborsky's term for it, "the helping alliance" (Luborsky, 1976).[1]

---

1. For excellent, thorough reviews about the history and theoretical development of, empirical evidence for, and controversies surrounding the therapeutic alliance concept, see the following: Lester Luborsky and Arthur

The concept of the helping alliance, broadly defined as the patient's experience of the treatment or relationship with the therapist as helpful or potentially helpful, is ultimately traceable to two important relationship factors between patient and analyst, articulated by Freud early in this century. The first is the concept of transference. The helping alliance concept derives from the cooperation–inducing part of the transference; the "conscious," "unobjectionable," positive feelings of the patient to his analyst. Although not stressed to the same degree as transference and resistance, Freud also underlined the importance of a second factor, typified by affection, friendliness, and sympathetic understanding. He stated in 1913:

> It remains the first aim of the treatment to attach (the patient) to it and to the person of the doctor. . . . If one exhibits a serious interest in him, carefully clears away the resistances that crop up at the beginning and avoids making certain mistakes, he will of himself form such an attachment. . . . It is certainly possible to forfeit this first success if from the start one takes up any standpoint other than one of sympathetic understanding. . . . . pp. 139–140

This chapter will describe and analyze the Penn Helping Alliance Scales, which represent the first attempt in psychotherapy research to quantify the concept of the helping alliance by a method applied directly to the therapy session. The following areas will be addressed: (1) description and technical details; (2) application of the scales to two data segments which highlight its strengths; (3) discussion of the origins and the process of development of the scales; (4) the similarities and differences of these scales with other existing measures of the helping alliance; (5) plans for future research; and (6) summary and conclusions.

Technical Aspects of the Scales

Scale Description, Scoring

The Penn Helping Alliance Scales, which measure the complex variable, the helping alliance, derive from the psychoanalytic perspective described above. (See the Memoir of the Development of the Scales section for additional sources of developmental influences.)

The scales consist of three major instruments: the Penn Helping Alliance Counting Signs Method (HA_{cs}) (Luborsky, 1976; Luborsky, Crits-Christoph, Alexander, Margolis, & Cohen, 1983); the Penn Helping Alliance Rating Method (HA_r) (Morgan, Luborsky, Crits-Christoph, Curtis, & Solomon, 1982); and the Penn Helping Alliance Questionnaire Method (HA_q) (Luborsky, 1984; Luborsky et al., 1985).

H. Auerbach. The therapeutic relationship in psychodynamic psychotherapy: The research evidence and its meaning for practice. In R. Hales & A. Frances (Eds.). Psychiatry Update: American Psychiatric Association. Annual Review, Vol. 4, pp. 550–561. S. H. Frieswyk, J. G. Allen, D. B. Colson, L. Coyne & G. O. Gabbard, L. Horwitz, and G. Newsom. The therapeutic alliance: its place as a process and outcome variable in dynamic psychotherapy. Journal of Consulting and Clinical Psychiatry, in press; Dianna E. Hartley. Research on the therapeutic alliance in psychotherapy. In R. Hales and A. Frances (Eds.) Psychiatry Update. American Psychiatric Association Annual Review, Vol. 4, 1985, 532–549; and Dianna E. Hartley and Hans H. Strupp, The therapeutic alliance: its relationship to outcome in brief psychotherapy. In J. Masling (Ed.) Empirical Studies of Analytic Concepts, vol. 1, Hillsdale, N.J.: Lawrence Erlbaum, 1983.

HA$_{cs}$ Method

The first developed of the scales, the HA$_{cs}$ method, entails the identification and counting of literal or almost literal "signs" of the patient's experience of a helping alliance, these signs are divided into two broad types of helping alliances: Helping Alliance Type 1 (HA Type 1), defined as the patient's experience of the therapist as providing, or being capable of providing the help that is needed; and Helping Alliance Type 2 (HA Type 2), defined as the patient's experience of treatment as a process of working together with the therapist toward the goals of treatment. HA Type 1, or *perceived helpfulness of the therapist*, and HA Type 2, *patient's collaboration or bonding with the therapist*, are therefore the two major components of the helping alliance variable. HA Type 1 and HA Type 2 are each composed of several subscales. The four subscales of HA Type 1 are: (1) The patient believes the therapist or therapy is helping; (2) the patient feels changed since the beginning of treatment; (3) the patient feels a rapport with the therapist; and (4) the patient feels optimism and confidence that the therapist and treatment can help. HA Type 2 contains three subscales: (1) The patient experiences himself or herself as working together with the therapist in a joint effort; (2) the patient shares with the therapist similar conceptions about the sources of his or her problems; and (3) the patient demonstrates qualities that are similar to those of the therapist, especially those connected with the tools for understanding.

Each of these seven subscales may appear in positive or negative form. The positive form is the one listed above and the negative form is its opposite. First, the judge is required to locate all relevant patient statements, that is, "signs," in the transcript which fit each helping alliance subtype, to classify them as positive or negative, and then to rate their intensity on a 5-point scale (from 1 = very low to 5 = very high). A score, therefore, includes the following components: whether it is positive or negative, Type 1 or 2, subtype a, b, and so on, and the degree of its intensity. A score such as HA + 1a5 would mean a Type 1 helping alliance, where the patient indicates that he or she feels the therapist is helping him or her (subscale a) to a very great extent (+5 intensity). A score such as HA + 2b2 would refer to a Type 2 helping alliance, where the patient indicates that he or she shares, to a mild degree (+2 intensity), similar conceptions about the sources of his or her problems (subscale b). (See Appendix I for the HA$_{cs}$ Manual.)

In the HA$_{cs}$ method, each patient's score is the sum of the number of signs in each session, weighted by the intensity ratings. Three different sums of scores can be used: positive scores, negative scores, and difference scores, that is, the difference between positive and negative scores. The HA$_{cs}$ method is therefore comprised of seven nominal subscales, whose intensity is rated on 5-point Likert-type, interval scales.

HA$_r$ Method

The HA$_r$ method is conceptually identical to the HA$_{cs}$ method, representing the conversion of each of the seven HA$_{cs}$ subscales into 10-point Likert-type rating scales. All subscales in the HA$_r$ method are measured at the interval level. The HA$_r$ method contains a total of 10 subscale items, three of which are not found in the HA$_{cs}$ method. Two of these new items are included under HA Type 1: (1) The patient feels that the therapist is warm and supportive and (2) the patient feels that the therapist respects and values him or her. The third new item is included under HA Type 2: (3) The patient expresses his or her belief that he or she is increasingly able to cooperate with the therapist in terms of understanding his or her own behavior. (See Appendix II for the HA$_r$ Method Manual.)

A patient's score equals the sum of the subscale ratings.

HA$_q$ Method

The HA$_q$ method is conceptually identical to the HA$_{cs}$ and HA$_r$ methods. Unlike the latter two, which are observer-rated, the HA$_q$ method is rated by the patient. This method consists of 11 items, which roughly parallel those in the HA$_r$ method. There are eight HA Type 1 items and three HA Type 2 items. Each item is rated on a 6-point Likert scale, with a range from +3 ("Yes, I strongly feel that it is true") to +2 ("Yes, I feel it is true") to +1 ("Yes, I feel that it is probably true, or more true than untrue") to −1 ("No, I feel that it is probably untrue, or more untrue than true"); to −2 ("No, I feel it is not true") to −3 ("No, I strongly feel that it is not true") (See Appendix V for the HA$_q$ method manual)

A patient's score equals the sum of the subscale ratings.

Treatment Modalities, Therapy Orientations

To date, the HA$_{cs}$ and HA$_r$ methods have only been applied to individual, supportive-expressive (SE) psychoanalytically-oriented psychotherapy. However, there is no reason to restrict these two methods to that particular treatment orientation. In fact, the HA$_q$ method, which is conceptually identical to the other two methods, has been used quite successfully with cognitive-behavioral therapy, drug counseling, as well as supportive-expressive psychotherapy (Luborsky et al., 1985). All three methods, then, would seem well suited to any psychotherapeutic or counseling method.

Likewise, with some modification in the wording of the items, the instruments would seem applicable to group and family treatment modalities which are themselves conceptually compatible with the basic assumption of the helping alliance concept, that is, that the major locus of change in treatment lies in the interaction between patient and therapist.

Access Strategies, Communication Channels, Data Format

The HA$_{cs}$ and HA$_r$ methods involve an observer's assessment of the patient's experience of treatment and his or her relationship with the therapist, based on transcripts of selected therapy sessions. Because the use of the instruments has been limited to transcripts, only the verbal channel of communication has been tapped.

Since the HA$_{cs}$ method requires the observer first to locate and then to classify and rate specific "signs," defined by each of the subscale items and consisting of a sentence or group of sentences, transcripts seem more suitable than tape recordings as a basis for applying that method. However, the HA$_r$ method, which consists of a global judgment of each of the subscale items, using whatever length segment of the therapy session that has been decided upon, is suitable for use with either videotapes or live coding as well. In fact, a convincing argument can be made that either of these data formats would permit a more vivid and complete assessment of the HA$_r$ subscale items than do transcripts alone. If either of the former data formats were used, then a mixed group of communication channels, including verbal, paralinguistic, and kinesic, could be targeted.

As a patient self-report measure, the HA_q method assesses the extent to which the patient experiences the therapist and the therapy as helpful.

Sampling Issues, Units Rated, Data Analysis Techniques

The normative sample to which the HA_{cs} and HA_r methods have been applied, are identical sessions from 20 patients, the 10 most and the 10 least improved among the 73 patients in the Penn Psychotherapy Project (Luborsky et al., 1980; Morgan et al., 1982; Luborsky et al., 1983). These two subgroups were used to avoid the huge expense of transcribing sessions from all 73 cases and as a way to get an initial estimate of the value of the methods. Improvement was based on two moderately highly correlated ($r = .76$) composite outcome measures: rated benefits, a composite of ratings of improvement, and residual gains, a composite of residualized differences between initial and termination measures.

Eighteen therapists treated these 20 patients in supportive–expressive (SE) psycho-analytically oriented psychotherapy, recently described in a manual (Luborsky, 1984). Sixteen of the therapists had one case each; two of the therapists had two cases each. Ten of the therapists were second or third-year residents under supervision, and eight were more experienced. The demographic characteristics of the 10 more versus the 10 less improved patients were similar: All were nonpsychotic patients, most of whom came for treatment at the outpatient clinic of the Hospital of the University of Pennsylvania, Philadelphia. Thirteen were female; the mean age was 26. All patients had at least 25 therapy sessions, with the median length of treatment for the more improved patients being 61 weeks, while the median length for the less improved was 43 weeks.

Regarding the portion of the therapy session to be examined, or the *contextual unit*, the first 20 minutes of selected sessions were chosen and transcribed. In the HA_{cs} method, the *scoring unit* is usually a sentence, although sometimes a group of sentences can represent one scorable unit if they reiterate the same theme. If the patient says the same thing more than once on the same page of typescript, only one score is given for each type of sign. In the HA_r method, the scoring unit and contextual unit are the same: the first 20-minute segment of a therapy session.

The choice of the 20-minute segment is based on theoretical and empirical evidence. The beginning rather than the middle or end of the session was chosen because it was felt that the judge needed to know all that had happened in the session thus far in order to adequately assess evidence of the patient's experience of a helping alliance. The 20-minute segment was chosen as a compromise between the whole session, which, though desirable, would have been too costly and time consuming to transcribe, and the more typical 5-minute unit in psychotherapy process research, which would have been too short for judging a relationship variable such as the helping alliance (Mintz and Luborsky, 1971).

Regarding sampling across sessions, the first 20 minutes from four therapy sessions for each of the 20 patients were chosen. Two segments were from the initial stage of treatment (Sessions 3 and 5) and two were from the final stage: the session at which 90% of the treatment had been completed and the prior session. A total of 80 segments were rated. The representativeness of these 20-minute segments of the whole therapy session has not yet been directly evaluated.

At the time the research was begun, there were no precedents to guide the sampling procedure for assessing the helping alliance. The fifth session was chosen, following the work of Barrett-Lennard (1962), whose relationship questionnaire is administered to the patient (and therapist) at that point and which appears to estimate, in part, facets of helping relationships. The third session was added to learn how early in treatment the helping alliance appeared and also to enlarge the sample of scorable data. The two sessions near the close of treatment were chosen to learn the degree to which helping alliance manifestations might vary over the course of treatment. There were many different temporal possibilities.

With the 20 patients in the Penn Psychotherapy Project, it was found that the HA scores of the two early sessions were moderately consistent with the HA scores of the two late sessions for both the HA_{cs} method (positive items, $r=.58**$, and for the HA_r method, $r=.53*$. For the more improved patients, the consistency of scores between early and late sessions was more evident than for the less improved patients. Within the more improved group, the correlations were: by the HA_r method, $r=.59$ ns; by the HA_{cs} method, positive, $r=.54$ ns; negative, $r=.47$ ns; difference, $r=.47*$.[2]

The contextual and scoring units for both methods have already been discussed. Several different *summarizing units* have been used, some of which are common to both methods. One such important summarizing unit was the summation of the HA scores (Types 1 and 2) for Sessions 3 and 5, yielding an early treatment score, and the summation of the same scores for the session at which 90% of the treatment was completed and the prior session, yielding a late-treatment score. Then all of the HA1 and HA2 subscales for each method across all four sessions were summed and correlated, first separately, and then in combination with the major composite outcome measures, described previously. It should be noted that, in the HA_{cs} method, each of the above calculations was performed separately for positive helping alliance scores, negative helping alliance scores, and for the difference in positive and negative helping alliance scores.

The normative sample to which the HA_q method has been applied consists of 110 male, veteran, methodone hydrochloride-maintained drug dependent patients in the VA-Penn Project (Woody et al., 1983). All participants were between the ages of 18 and 55 and were non-psychotic. The major psychiatric diagnoses indicated that the group of patients had much in common with patients who are typically given psychotherapy.

In this study patients were randomly assigned to one of three, six-month treatment conditions: drug counseling (N=39); supportive-expressive psychoanalytically-oriented treatment plus drug counseling (N=32); or cognitive-behavioral treatment plus drug counseling (N=39). Attendance ranged from 3 to 24 sessions, with a mean of about 12 sessions for patients undergoing psychotherapy and 16 sessions for patients having counseling. Treatments were carried out by well-trained therapists, all of whom were guided by treatment manuals for their respective therapies. There were 27 therapists in all, 18 of whom were drug counselors and 9 of whom were psychotherapists (five expressive-supportive and four cognitive-behavioral therapists). All psychotherapists except two had either MD or PhD degrees and at least two years of clinical experience post training. All also had had some experience with alcoholics or addicts. The drug counselors had worked in the treatment program for an average of five years.

Subsequent discussions in this chapter of the HA_q method will be based on the results of 77 patients of the nine therapists (three from each treatment group), who had the largest patient caseloads in this study. (Luborsky et al., 1985)

---

2. Throughout this chapter, one asterisk (*)=$p<.05$, two asterisks (**)=$p<.01$, and three asterisks (***)= $p<.001$.

The Helping Alliance Questionnaire was administered to patients at the end of the third treatment session. The choice of the third session was guided by earlier work on the HA_{cs} and HA_r methods (Luborsky, 1976) and by the findings of Marziali et al. (1981), Gomes-Schwartz, 1978; and Hartley and Strupp, 1983). All of these studies indicated that ratings of the therapeutic alliance from the patient's perspective early in therapy (from roughly the third to the sixth session) correlated significantly with outcome. The Helping Alliance Questionnaire scores were then correlated with seventh-month outcome scores. The latter were based on assessments of drug use, employment and legal status, and psychological functioning (Luborsky et al., 1985, Table 5) as measured by the Addiction Severity Index (McLellan et al., 1980).

Judges: Level of Clinical Sophistication and Training

Although the clinical orientation of the judges can vary among the range of psychotherapeutic and counseling methods, it is essential that raters be clinically experienced to use the HA methods. There are manuals for each of the two methods, which contain the scales and directions for scoring the items. In the HA_{cs} Manual, there are also examples of each of the subscale items (see Appendixes I and II).

To date, two pairs of independent clinically experienced judges have applied the manuals to the 80 sessions. For the HA_{cs} method, one judge was experienced in clinical psychology (Rater 1) and one in social work (Rater 2). They were affiliated with different teaching institutions and did not know each other. They were trained separately by the second author of this chapter, using transcripts that were not part of the study itself. Training continued until the subscale items were appropriately understood and applied.

For the HA_r method, the two independent judges (Raters 3 and 4) were experienced psychoanalysts who had worked together clinically. They were given a session of training in the use of the manual by a collaborator (Dr. Rose Morgan), applying it to sample transcripts which were, as above, not part of the study itself. After the training session, these judges rated the transcripts. Interrater reliability estimates were made after the first 10 20-minute segments were rated. All four segments were rated by each judge before proceeding to any of the transcripts of another patient. Once another transcript had been read, no previous ratings were changed. Since the HA_q method involves the patient's self-report, the level of clinical sophistication and training of the judges is not an issue.

Reliability of Methods

For the HA_r method, the correlations (Pearson's r) for the 10 subscales, using a pair of raters, ranged from .75 to .88, with most in the .80's. Interrater reliability was, therefore, quite adequate. The estimate of internal reliability for all the subscales (coefficient α) was .96, also quite satisfactory.

The reliability assessment for the HA_{cs} method is more complex and the results more mixed. Determining agreement in scoring is harder for the HA_{cs} method because each judge must first locate in the lengthy transcripts those examples which fit the subscales in the manual. Therefore there are two kinds of unreliability in the HA_{cs} approach. (1) The first occurs when one judge does not score a unit of the transcript which another judge has located and indicated as fitting a subtype of the HA_{cs} method. This "locational unreliability" can result from a lack of attention by one judge to the particular statement which another judge rates. (2) If two judges assign different "signs" to the same portion of the transcript, this might be considered "true unreliability." Of the two kinds of unreliability, the second seems more serious.

In examining the results of the HA_{cs} scoring by the two judges, many of their "errors" were of the first type and did not involve "true unreliability." As anticipated, the judges did not score the same number of "signs." In the identical four 20-minute segments of sessions of the 20-patient sample, Rater 1 scored a total of 120 "signs" while Rater 2 scored a total of 173 "signs." This difference seems due in part to differences in scorer style and in part to missing some examples during the reading of the long transcripts. Counting signs types of content analysis systems are typically vulnerable to the latter kind of error, unless a separate judge is first assigned to locate the sets of scorable data, thereby highlighting and circumscribing what is to be rated (see Johnston & Holzman, 1979, for an example).

Although they were not always identical signs, there was moderate agreement in the number of signs scored by each judge across patients. In correlational terms, the positive items were agreed upon especially well (for early sessions, .69***; for late sessions, .82***; for early and late sessions, .81***). The correlations for the negative items were as follows: for early sessions, .53*; for late sessions, .47*; for early and late sessions, .47*. The higher correlations for the positive item may be due partially to their greater number (total number of positive items = 168 vs. total number of negative items = 125).

On the other hand, only 74 signs among all those scored by both judges were exactly the same statements. For these 74 signs, only 33 (i.e., 45%) were scored exactly the same for all four scoring components: (1) the value, that is, positive or negative; (2) the type, that is HA Type 1 or HA Type 2; (3) the subtype or subscale, that is, a, b, c, d; and (4) the intensity, that is, a rating on a scale of a low of 1 to a high of 5. Although simultaneous agreement on all components was not obtained, very high agreement was obtained for each component alone: for value (100%), for type (97%), for subtype (82%), and for intensity (61%). Hence, once the scores on the *same* components are compared, the agreement between judges is satisfactory. While we would also conclude that the inference process is simpler in the HA_{cs} method than in the HA_r method, this conclusion only applies to the scoring of the same statements. Formal reliability study is underway for the HA_q method.

Validity

HA_{cs} and HA_r Methods   Although the dimensionality of the HA_{cs} and the HA_r methods has not yet been directly evaluated by means of factor analysis, other validation efforts have been undertaken for each of the instruments.

1. For both methods, HA Type 1 scores were highly correlated with HA Type 2 scores. For the HA_r method, the correlation was .91; for the HA_{cs} method, it was .68. Although collaboration with the therapist (HA Type 2) is conceptually separate from the patient's experience of the therapist as warm, helpful, and supportive (HA Type 1), they are highly related empirically. Perhaps, as suggested for the Menninger Helping Alliance Scales (Allen, Newsom, Gabbard, & Coyne, 1982), the patient's experience of HA Type 1 sets the stage for the experience of HA Type 2.

2. Since both the HA_{cs} and HA_r methods are intended to measure the same concept, they should be highly intercorrelated. In fact, the HA_{cs} and HA_r were significantly correlated for both early and late session ratings. Agreement was higher for late positive (.83***) rather than early positive sessions (.57**), possibly because the prob-

Table 9-1   Agreement (Correlations) Between
HA_{cs} and HA_r[a]

HA_{cs}	r
Early Sessions' Ratings	
Positive	.57**
Negative	−.21
Difference	.58**
Late Sessions' Ratings	
Positive	.83***
Negative	−.19
Difference	.80***
Early + Late Sessions' Ratings	
Positive	.86***
Negative	−.14
Difference	.81***

[a]The three HA_{cs} scores are each correlated with the single score for HA_r.

**p < .01

***p < .001

From: Luborsky, L., Crits-Christoph, P., Alexander, L., Margolis, M., and Cohen, M. Two helping alliance methods for predicting outcomes of psychotherapy: A counting signs vs. a global rating method. *Journal of Nervous and Mental Diseases*, 1983, *171*, 484.

able outcome of treatment was sometimes evident in the interaction between patient and therapist in the late sessions. The fact that there are fewer negative than positive signs might account for the greater agreement for HA_{cs} positive signs. The fact, then, that the HA_{cs} method is moderately correlated with the HA_r method implies some validity for the two instruments.

3. Even more important is the fact that both methods have the power to predict the outcomes of psychotherapy with moderate success. Predictive success was determined in two ways: by a two-factor mixed model analysis of variance and by correlations.

For the analysis of variance, the between-groups factor was based on dividing the subjects into two groups, more improved (MI) and less improved (LI), and the within-group factor was the early versus late sessions. In the analysis for both methods, the scores of the two sets of judges were summed. For the HA_{cs} method, there were significant F ratios for the outcomes for positive (16.3***) and difference scores (7.1*), meaning that the MI had more HA_{cs} signs than the LI. The stage-by-outcome interaction was only significant for the difference score measure (F ratio = 7.1*). Looking more closely, it is evident that within the MI patients, the positive scores go up over time while the negative scores do not change. For the LI patients, on the other hand, the negative scores go up with little change in the positive ones (see Luborsky *et al.*, 1983, Tables 4 and 5).

Using the HA_r method, for HA Type 1 scores the test for treatment (more vs. less improved) was significant ($F=5.9$, $df=1$, 1, 18, $p<.05$). The test for treatment stage (early vs. late) and the test for the treatment outcome-by-treatment stage interaction were not significant (F ratios >1). Analyses of HA Type 2 scores showed similar results. In addition, the early sessions' ratings alone (HA1+HA2) correlated at .44 ($p<.05$) with the mean outcome measure (more vs. less improved). When the HA1 and HA2 ratings for early and late sessions were summed, the HA1 score was .47 and for HA2 scores alone, .46 ($p<.05$).

Expressed correlationally, both methods, although different, attained moderately successful predictions, with correlations of around .5 on four major outcome measures: rated benefits; residual gain; a summary measure of the therapist's view of the patient's degree of success, satisfaction, and improvement (SSI) during treatment; and change in target complaints, that is, the specific symptoms for which the patient came to treatment. Overall, the HA_{cs} method had slightly more success as a predictive measure. Looking at the HA_{cs} results more specifically, although the correlations of the late

Table 9-2   Correlations of Helping Alliance with Outcome Measures

		Rated[a] Benefits	Residual[a] Gain	SSI[b]	Target Complaints
HA_{cs}					
	Positive				
	Early sessions	.57**	.58**	.59**	.59*
	Late sessions	.58**	.60**	.69***	
	Early+late	.64**	.65**	.73***	
	Negative				
	Early	.29	.23	.29	
	Late	−.08	−.10	−.21	
	Early+late	.08	.04	−.02	
	Difference				
	Early	.31	.34	.32	
	Late	.53*	.55*	.69***	
	Early+late	.52*	.55*	.64**	
HA_r					
	Early sessions	.46*	.44*	.49*	.44*
	Late sessions	.33	.37	.44*	
	Early+late	.45*	.46*	.53*	

[a]From the Penn Psychotherapy Study (Mintz *et al.*, 1979). [b]SSI=Sum of success, satisfaction, and improvement outcome ratings.

  *$p<.05$
 **$p<.01$
***$p<.001$

From: Luborsky, L., Crits-Christoph, P., Alexander, L., Margolis, M., and Cohen, M. Two helping alliance methods for predicting outcomes of psychotherapy: A counting signs vs. a global rating method. *Journal of Nervous and Mental Diseases*, 1983, *171*, 485.

sessions were generally higher, the earlier sessions are of more interest predictively because they are assessed earlier and are less subject to overlap with the outcome measures. Using the early sessions, then, the highest correlations were for early positive HA_{cs} scores: They correlated .57** with rated benefits, .58** with residual gain, .59** with SSI, and .59* with changes in target complaints.

Although not quite as high, the results for the HA_r method on the same measures were also impressive: .46* with rated benefits, .44* with residual gain, .49* with SSI, and .44* with target complaints.

4. Support for the concurrent validity of the scales comes from examining a number of correlations derived both from during-treatment and pretreatment measures.

Looking at *during-treatment* measures first, results from two measures will be examined: the Therapist Facilitative Behaviors' Counting Signs Method (TFB_{cs}) and its counterpart, the Therapist Facilitative Behaviors' Rating Method (TFB_r). (See Appendixes III and IV.) The scales were constructed to see the extent to which the therapist's facilitative behaviors set the stage for the development of the helping alliance. The items in the TFB_{cs} method generally parallel those of the HA_{cs} method, representing therapist behaviors which either facilitate or inhibit the development of the helping alliance. The scoring components are identical to those in the HA_{cs} method. Similarly, the items in the TFB_r method generally parallel those of the HA_r method, and like the HA_r method, represent the conversion of the TFB_{cs} items into 10-point, Likert-type scales. Scoring for the TFB_r method is identical to scoring for the HA_r method.

Reliability estimates for both measures were equally good. For the TFB_r method, interrater reliability levels, using a pair of judges, were mostly in the .80's. Coefficient alpha for the subscale items was .94. For the TFB_{cs} method, interrater reliabilities were as follows: early positive signs = .85***; late positive signs = .80***.

Concerning the validity of these measures, a sample of correlations of the HA measures with the TFB measures reveals some significant results. For example, early HA_r correlated .85*** with early TFB_r; .76*** with late TFB_r. Early HA_{cs} positive signs were not significantly correlated with early TBF_{cs} positive signs. However, late HA_{cs} positive signs were correlated .80*** with late TFB_{cs} positive signs. These correlations suggest that the therapist's attempts to facilitate HA behavior were successful. The correlations for HA_{cs} positive with TFB_{cs} positive may indicate that the therapist's attempts (i.e., late) became successful eventually. At the same time, it should be noted that neither the TFB_r or TFB_{cs} methods tended to predict therapy outcome significantly.

Regarding the correlates of helping alliance measures with *pretreatment* measures, the significant correlations should be taken with some skepticism, since there were 82 pretreatment variables in the Penn Psychotherapy Project (Luborsky *et al.*, 1980). The four helping alliance measures were correlated with 82 pretreatment measures for a total of 328 correlations. By chance, the number of significant ($p < .05$) correlations would be 16; 13 were found. Thus, any of these significant correlations have to be considered with some caution. Using a conservative selection of significant correlations, the ones presented subsequently had to have significant correlations with both HA_r and HA_{cs}. If the correlation was significant with only one of the methods, it had to be approaching significance with the other.

a. Similarities of Patient and Therapist: The similarity score, which significantly correlated with both HA_r and HA_{cs}, was based on 10 mainly demographic, similarities chosen on an *a priori* basis: age, marital status, children, religion, religious activity, foreign-born parents, institutional affiliation, cognitive style (scores on Rod-and-Frame, and Embedded Figures Test, standardized and combined), education, and occupation. Allowing one point for each item on which patient and therapist were similar, the sum of these similarities correlated .60** with positive HA_{cs} and .62** with the difference between positive and negative signs, and .53* with HA_r. Not all similarities contributed equally, for example, age match and religious activity match contributed the most.

   b. *Random Assignment of Patients to Therapists*: This correlated negatively with both HA_r and HA_{cs} measures of helping alliances. The HA_{cs}, for example, correlated − .60** and the HA_r, − .56** with random assignment.

   c. *Somatic Problems*: The Klein Somatic Scale, a rating by a clinical observer of the patient's physical complaints, correlated negatively with the helping alliance measures, particularly HA_r, for example, − .58* with total helping alliance, and − .58* with total therapist facilitating behaviors.

   d. *Amount of Life Change*: A measure based upon the Holmes and Rahe Life Change Scale correlated − .52* with HA_r and − .48* with TFB_r.

   e. *Cognitive Style*: While the comparable correlation for the HA_r method was .29, therapists' Embedded Figures Test correlated with early positive HA_{cs} .62***, with HA_{cs} difference score, .51*.

   f. *Competence as a Psychiatrist*: The mean of ratings by other staff members who had known the therapist's work over the years was used. This was significantly correlated with the HA_{cs} difference score, .47*, and with HA_{cs} negative signs, − .61**. The correlation with the HA_r, however, was only .24. (With TFB_r the correlations were somewhat higher: .50* and .33 for the TFB_{cs} difference score.)

   g. *Psychological Health–Sickness*: Measures of this variable were inconsistently correlated with the HA measures; for example, with positive HA_{cs}, the Health–Sickness Rating Scale (HSRS) correlated .44*, but was not significant with HA_r. (See Luborsky et al., 1980, for references to the specific measures cited.)

   5. Finally, multiple correlations of the most promising pretreatment with the most promising during-treatment predictors were examined. The Health–Sickness Rating Scale (HSRS) was one of the best pretreatment predictors (Luborsky et al., 1980), and the helping alliance (HA) was the best during-treatment predictor. Standard multiple regression analyses using these two predictor variables (HA and HSRS) were performed with each of the two outcome criteria. A sample of these multiple correlations includes the following: (1) HSRS and early positive HA_{cs} as predictors of Rated Benefits produced a multiple R of .61*. While the two predictors did not both independently contribute significantly to the multiple, HA_{cs} contributed the most, with a F value of 4.1, which is nearly significant at the .05 level. The HA negative scores and the HA difference scores, used in separate multiple regressions in combination with the HSRS, were not as strong predictors as the HA positive scores. (2) HSRS and early HA_r as predictors produced a multiple R with Rated Benefits of .62*, and with Residual Gain of .58*. Both predictors contributed significant individual variance to the multiple. (3) The HA typically contributed most in multiple regressions with three types of measures, HSRS, HA, and TFB. TFB added very little to the multiple.

   These correlates, then, can also be understood as representing facilitating or impeding conditions which may influence the development of a helping alliance. These conditions include the following: (1) Certain basic similarities between patient and therapist seem to facilitate the formation of the patient's experience of a helping alliance with the therapist. Although patients may not be aware of all of these similarities, they may sense their existence. Work on the helping alliance appears to fit with the research field sometimes referred to as "human attraction." One finding in that research is that human attraction is partly mediated by perceived similarity (Byrne, 1971). (2) Somatic problems are an impending condition: the more the patient is beset by somatic problems, the less he or she is likely to form a helping alliance. In addition, the therapist is less likely to facilitate the development of the helping alliance. (3) The amount of life change is an impending condition. When the patient is absorbed in adapting to life change demands, he or she may be less able to be self-involved in the treatment relationship. This limits his or her ability to form a positive helping alliance. (4) Random assignment is another impediment, since it tends to militate against the formation of a positive helping alliance. This is probably because the patient and therapist may experience the random assignment as a forced assignment. This is consistent with the negative correlation of random assignment (i.e., no choice given to the therapist) with outcome of treatment (Luborsky *et al.*, 1980). Presumably, its counterpart, giving the patient a choice, would be facilitating (Luborsky and McLellan, 1981). (5) The therapist's competence as a psychiatrist facilitates the development of the helping alliance. (6) Relatively field-dependent therapists, who may be more responsive to their patients and form a closer bond with them, also provide a facilitating condition. This would be reflected in more positive helping alliance scores. (Field-dependent is modified by the word "relatively" since the therapists as a group had a mean score on the field-independent side [i.e., Embedded Figures Test score 309]). Similar trends have been reported elsewhere; for example, (a) therapists and patients who were relatively more field dependent had a shorter interval between each others' utterances, implying that field dependence is related to greater social responsiveness; (b) dyads that included one or two field-dependent persons more often reconciled their differences than dyads with two field-independent persons (Oltman, Goodenough, Witkin, Freedman, and Friedman, 1975).

HA_q Method   The HA_q method predicted seventh-month outcomes in the VA-Penn Study with impressive success at the high end of the range of correlations found in previous studies. The correlations which were all statistically significant ($p < .01$) ranged from .51 in legal status, to .58 in psychological status, to .70 in employment status, and to .72 in drug use (Luborsky *et al.*, 1985).

In answer to the possible objection that the correlations of the HA_q with the outcome measures reflect only the overlap in the two measures, and hence are not true predictions, two strong arguments can be made. First, while the outcome measures cover a wide range of benefits received, the items in the HA_q tap only a limited segment of the patient's attitude toward therapy. Second the benefits measured by the HA_q at the end of the third treatment session are typically quite minimal in contrast to the benefits measured by the outcome criteria after six months of treatment.

Just as the HA_{cs} and HA_r methods have parallel observer-rated methods that tap the therapist's perspective, the TFB_{cs} and the TFB_r methods, so, too, does the HA_q method. This is called the Penn Therapist Facilitating Behaviors Questionnaire Method (TFB_q), which is completed by the therapist at the end of the third treatment session and assesses the degree to which the therapist feels that he or she is helping the patient. The TFB_q method contains 11 items, parallel to those in the HA_q method, and is scored similarily: (See Appendix VI). As was true with the TFB_{cs} and TFB_r methods, an important aim of the TFB_q is to better understand the origins of the helping alliance—that is, what the therapist does to inhibit or facilitate its development.

In the VA-Penn Study, the HA_q and TFB_q methods predicted outcome about equally well (Luborsky *et al.*, 1985).

Application of the Scales to Two Data Segments

This section will provide transcripts and scoring from the first 20 minutes of two therapy sessions of Patient 27 (Mr. B. N.), who participated in the Penn Psychotherapy Project and whose data were included in the studies of the HA_r method (Morgan *et al.*, 1982) and the HA_{cs} method (Luborsky *et al.*, 1983), described previously. Following the sampling plan in each of those studies, one early session (3) and one late session (89) are provided. Following each transcript is the scoring, using the HA_{cs}, then the HA_r method, provided by the two pairs of independent judges described in the previous section.

Transcript of First 20 Minutes of
Third Therapy Session, Patient 27, 8/19/68

P: Hi!

T: How have you been?

P: I've been feeling a little bit, uh, more alive lately, y'know, but I've had—I've had a lot of, uh, anxiety and nervousness connected with it. I haven't been sleeping too well, like, uh, y'know, with just—with talking to people I—I feel better, things like that, uh. One thing that, uh, sorta just hit me, and I guess it's one of these delayed action things that seems to happen to me quite a bit. There's this guy I was—lived with—lived with us for about a month during July and he's, uh, I mean, we didn't get along too well, and, uh, whenever he got into a conversation or any-thing, y'know, he, uh—he'd immediately try to dominate it and things like that. He did a lot of things that irritated me and at the time I guess I just, y'know, I repressed everything, and just sunk back. And lately I've been sort of brooding about it, and y'know, I've been getting really worked up and pissed off over it, y'know, and then, uh, uh, y'know, it's as I said, I said, it's a delayed action thing, I guess. It's like he was stepping on my toes a lot when I was there, you know, yet I didn't even have the guts to say "Ouch!" And that now that's—that's what all these fantasies were, y'know. It comes back and I—I put *him* down, and things like that.

T: What do you mean, "fantasies?"

P: Uh, just thinking about it, and y'know, brooding on it and, uh, waking, y'know, daydreams.

T: What are you doing to, uh, daydream?

P: Uh, y'know, it's usually in conversation, like, uh, I remember one time there were—there were four of us and we were talking. And, and I remember there, there was a pause in the thing and he was doing all the talking and, uh, I had said something, and he turns to me and says, "Excuse me for interrupting," and then he, y'know, continues like that. It's this type of thing I was getting from him like the whole time he was there. And, uh, in the end of the fantasies I was, uh, the positions were reversed and I was stepping on *him* like that.

T: Um—huh.

P: *(pause 10 seconds)* It's, uh, I guess I—y'know I can't really—that's a type of situa-tion where I run into a person like that who—who, y'know, it's, it's one thing that I can't handle too well—I don't know how to cope with, uh, y'know, I usually have one of two types of reactions, either I, y'know, crawl back into a hole or, or I really snap out, y'know, bluntly, crudely and, uh, y'know I think there ought to be a better way to handle it but I'm not quite sure, y'know, how it's gonna work.

T: By "snap out," you mean what?

P: Uh, y'know, really, uh, come out with the hostilities that he arouses and things.

He prob- in, uh, disproportionate to, uh, to what, what should grip, y'know, the reality of the situation, like, uh, in, in one of the fantasies, uh, y'know, as I was reliving this thing where he, uh—that, that incident I just described when he said, uh, "Excuse me for interrupting"—at the time I was dri- I was drinking a glass of water or something. And in this fantasy I threw the water in his face, or something like that. (*pause 10 seconds*) (*clears throat*) I think I—I tend to get abnormally worked up and, you know, frightened and—and angry at—at people who—who do things like this. (*pause 10 seconds*)

T: We were talking quite a bit about that last time.

P: In fact I think, y'know, anybody who comes on as an—as an authority figure, y'know, tends to, uh, y'know, when they're stepping on somebody it tends—it tends to really scare me. When I was—I was out in the park, Rittenhouse Square, the other day and, uh, some guy and his wife who, uh, I—who I had just met them, they were—they were sitting together on the bench and I guess the guy's wife had her leg draped over one of his legs, like this, and this cop comes up and he was talking like John Wayne and tells her to sit right. And well they stood up to him and, uh, you know, he finally carted them off and charged them with lewd and suggestive conduct or something like that, but while he was over there talking to them, I was just sitting, they were sitting on the bench and I was sitting on the wall behind them, and I—y'know, my heart started really beating fast and I got really anxious about it, y'know, I just sort of imagined what—what I would do in a situation like that, and I think what I would do was automatically (*snaps fingers*) obey the first thing he said. (*long pause 35 seconds*)

T: Could I bum a light off you, too?

P: Oh, excuse me, sure. (*exhales*) Another thing I've—I've been running into lately is like getting involved with people and getting friendly with people whom I—I guess tol—ultimately I really don't want to be friends with. Uh, there's this, uh, weird, uh, guy that's been hanging around campus for some years now. He's a big colored guy, six-four, three-ten or something like that. And I just met him and like, uh, he comes around all the time and I really don't want him around and, uh, you know, it comes down to do I have a choice between being mean and being a hypocrite. Y'know, when I first met him I—he's a—y'know, I guess he's insanely insecure or something but he, uh, uh, goes out, y'know, goes out of his way to be outgoing and friendly and he's, he's witty, sometimes charming, like I can't—I can't, you know, I'm never gonna have any type of really but relationship with this guy because he doesn't get serious about anything and he's really a—well he's 29 years old and he's just bumming around and smoking pot, and things like that. But like, uh, I—I have this girl, uh, I know, uh, been cooking dinners for me lately and like, y'know, there's a—I really don't want to get involved with her sexually because I heard some bad rumors about her like she has the clap or something like that which—and, uh—I, y'know, I just can't talk to her that well either although, y'know, maybe if I saw her once a month I could, y'know, carry on a piece of conversation or something like that but I get too close to these people that I can't really get close to and I keep doing things like this, not too close but too, uh, involved, I guess.

T: Well, what do you think you're seeking when you're—

P: Well, y'know, I guess, uh, I'm just sort of a (*pause*) a—hungry to have people around that I can talk to, things like that.

T: What do you need them for?

P: I don't know, it's, uh—usually pretty hard, hard for me to just, to just be alone. And, uh, well this has been sort of a pattern that developed in the, y'know, past couple of years, y'know, just to be alone or—or to, uh, to really get into, uh, something that does interest me, and I apparently haven't found out, uh, y'know, what

I can do and what I like to do, really like to do yet.

T: What happens when you're alone?

P: Uh, usually I get, I get really bored, I can't, I can't, I don't know what to do with myself.

T: And then what happens?

P: Usually I sort of, uh, just lay back and accept it, lethargically. (*pause 5 seconds*) I, y'know, I think I probably tend to withdraw, y'know, but, uh, I, y'know, I don't think I, uh, uh, y'know, y'know given a specific situation where I'm alone and I don't necessarily go out and then look for it, y'know, other people or anybody to, to talk to, uh, usually.

T: Well, you seem to dislike being alone, and I'm just wondering what's bad about it.

P: The same thing, uh, that, y'know, that happens to me when I'm—I'm alone and as when I get into a, a situation where there's a group, group of people talking and—I'm not really saying that much. I feel very—uncomfortable and like I'm, y'know, I'm not really sure I exist for, for other people, for some reason. Y'know, maybe it's because I'm not really too aware of, uh, myself. (*pause*)

T: There is, I gather, a feeling of quite a lot of anxiety in being alone.

P: Yeah. (*pause*) Like, like I used to be able to, uh, to read a lot, and do things like that but like, uh, now I find that, y'know, when I'm reading or something like I feel like I should be out doing something else, like, like relating to people. Y'know, I have this—y'know, it's, it's, uh, not quite, I guess, a—well, maybe it is a compulsion to, uh, y'know, go out there and, and, uh, y'know, because I seem to think that's where it's really, really at, or something.

T: Yeah, but you seem to have carried it to the point that you know that you don't really count for anything unless you do relate to people.

P: Uh, yeah.

T: Or something. (*pause*) And you can't seem to be satisfied just being alone—

P: Yeah—

T: —yourself—

P: Yeah, I feel like I, I have to go out and prove myself or something like that. I have to go out and come across to people and, and impress them. (*long pause 35 seconds*) I think what's, uh, happening to me right now in here is, uh, typical of a situation when I start feeling better, when I start feeling more, y'know, aware, more alive, more interested in things. And that's at, uh, y'know, I get to a point where I want to, I want to, I want to go back—I want to close up again.

T: Are you feeling that way now?

P: Yeah, well, y'know, I think, you know, that's why I'm, I'm probably having trouble talking and discussing things.

T: I'm not sure you're having that much trouble talking unless you interpret the silences we've had—

P: Well—

T: —as voids that need to be filled.

P: Yeah, yeah, I tend to do that a lot.

T: Do you think that's true necessarily?—

P: Uh—I guess, I guess it really—

T: —Do we have to fill every space with something?

P: No. I guess I should play it cooler, be able to be a little cooler about it, I mean, rather than getting worked up about it, y'know, silence, or something like that. (*pause*) I don't know what—what I just said about, y'know, withdrawing, is really true right now. But like that's what's—that's what's happened in the past. Whenever I get so I am feeling more alive and more stronger, uh, I—I tend to have—have tendencies to retreat, uh, and, uh, like, uh, the sessions that I had with Dr. T, there were a couple of them where, you know, when I was feeling pretty good where I didn't—I didn't really—they weren't really that productive, or I didn't really talk about that much or—or anything like that. And like, uh, I guess, uh, I didn't see him for about a—about a month, towards the end of, uh, of last—last fall semester, I guess, uh, December, and then part of November I didn't see him at all. And, uh, I was feeling better then, y'know, stronger and more alive than I had in a long time. (*long pause 15 seconds*)

T: Dr. T's come up in our conversations a few times. Do you think you miss him?

P: Um (*pauses 5 seconds*), well not really—um (*long pause 10 seconds*), I mean right now I don't really feel that I do.

T: Do you think you have some feelings about his leaving?

P: Uh, I don't know.

T: You had—you had worked with him for a year.

P: I hadn't, y'know, I guess I do, but, uh, like, like the last session was really, was really pretty good and y'know it was sort of a fitting in, I think. (*pause 5 seconds*) I didn't—I didn't feel really, y'know, at least immediately I didn't feel that, uh, anxious about it, or—or up—upset about it at all. Y'know, right now I really can't see that there's, y'know, there's much, much to that.

T: Well, I was just wondering.

P: (*10-second pause*) Y'know, I think I took the, y'know, the change, y'know, the—sanely, uh, sanely as I, as I've taken any, any change. (*35-second pause*) I've been wondering about, uh, I guess, uh, the future a little bit more now. And like, uh, next semester I'm going to be carrying a heavy load, and a lot of things. I'm going to be taking six courses and, uh, one of the courses I want to take is like, uh, a dry course and it's, it's more hours than a normal course, and it's also a lot of work outside of class, and then I'm gonna have to have a job, and I hope to have a—a cycle, which is gonna take some—some of my time. And it's probably as—as heavy a load as I've, I've ever carried in a semester. It's m—it's heavier. And—and I think like my sophomore year, the second semester of my sophomore year when I was working in this hospital as an orderly, I sort of loaded myself up with a lot of things to do, and I just—towards the end of it, uh, I, y'know, I quit, y'know, I got—I got into all these things and then all, y'know, I suddenly, suddenly withdrew, and, uh, sort of, uh, wondering about, y'know, since something like that is going to happen in the next semester.

T: The question is why are you taking on so many things, if you find them hard to carry?

P: Well, I think I haven't, y'know, I'm—I'm capable of it, y'know, I have the stuff in me to do it, uh, I have to take six courses I—and also—

T: How about the job? Why are you—

P: Well, I'm gonna need the job. I need the money. Like the cycle is sort of, I guess I don't really need that, like I want to—

T: You mean you need the job because you're going to spend the money on the cycle—

P: Probably— (*laughing*)

T: —Is that correct?

P: Well, uh—well, it's, uh—I'm gonna need the job partly because of that but like the money I was going to use to buy the cycle is not money that I really needed. It was money that I was going to keep in the bank and let it collect interest and then having that backing me up, uh-. I guess I want to—I want to fill up my life a little bit more. I've been sort of a—the boredom has been really getting to me, this summer. And I just want to get into these, these things, like, uh, uh, the cycle. It's something I'm going to have to get into. I'm going to have to learn—learn how to take care of it, and things like that, because I know nothing, mechanically. And, uh, right now, y'know, I sort of, uh, pleasurably anticipate, uh, learning something about things like this. And, uh, y'know, the same thing with that drawing course,

I'd like to get into, fool around with something like that. It's, uh, the course, I guess, the teacher I hear is pretty good. Like he doesn't really care about your, uh, technical ability to render so much as he cares about getting you to learn how to *see*, y'know, to be aware of, uh, space, architectural space and perspective, and things like that. And I'm, uh, kind of excited over—over getting, y'know, getting into something like that. (*15-second pause*)

T: Well, what, what I'm wondering is, whether you're going to have enough time to do as well in all these things as you would like to do.

P: I don't know.

T: Whether you're going to be so busy you won't be able to do any of them well and then you'll drop it all. Well that's what you're wondering, I guess.

P: Yeah. But I was also thinking of—of—of something else sort of that, uh, y'know, I'm—I'm almost, you know, anxious about getting into something that I really like, and a lot of these things appeal to me. (*15-second pause*) Because I think I'm gonna have enough time because I'm really not that, uh, concerned at all about, uh, grades.

T: Well, um, what?

P: Uh, uh, one semester, uh, one thing I don't think I'm gonna do badly, and, uh, another thing is that, uh, I'm not—I don't feel any particular pressure to do excellently, y'know, even though I think I might have some capabilities to do pretty well because like one semester is not going to make, uh, that much difference in my *cum*, which is, uh, just a little bit above average right now. (*15-second pause*) I mean like if I got C's in everything it wouldn't particularly bother me, y'know, depending on how much work I have to do in, uh—. (*20-second pause*) I guess it's sort of basically right now I sorta feel like I'm on the verge of something, y'know, uh, that I'm anticipating, uh, getting into things that are gonna be, uh, rewarding, exciting. (*10-second pause*) I, uh, called home last night and I talked to my mother about, uh, y'know, the money for the cycle. Originally when I first thought of the idea of getting it, y'know, I thought of doing it, was sort of behind their back and just waiting till the money came then, uh, y'know, buying it, sort of as a shock and a surprise to them but, y'know, as, as I said, I think I said once before I think I have a genuine interest in, uh, in getting a motorcycle on—and it's, you know, so I called and I—and I didn't run into any problems at all. She said that she thought I was old enough to make a decision like this for myself, etcetera, etcetera. And, uh, there's also sort of a technical matter that I want to get the bike before school starts, so I had to ask to sen—for the money to be sent cause I wouldn't have gotten it till later. (*15-second pause*) I think I still have sort of an ulterior motive in buying a cycle, y'know, and—and—and this is, uh—I don't know if it's totally ulterior, but like it's along lines of impressing people.

(End of 20 minutes)

Scoring of the Transcript, Using HA$_{cs}$ Method
Patient 27, Session 3

	Rater 1	Rater 2
1. Page 338, line 3:		
"I've been feeling a little bit, uh, more alive lately"	+ 1b3	+ 1b1
2. Page 338, line 4–5:		
"I haven't been sleeping too well"	– 1b3	( )
3. Page 340, line 32–33:		
"I think what's, uh, happening to me right now in here is, uh, typical of a situation when I start feeling better,		

when I start feeling more, y'know, aware, more alive'' (   )   +1b3
4. Page 341, lines 16–17:
     '' . . . right now I really can't see that there's, y'know,
     there's much, much to that''   −1a1 ?

Note that in this early session there are relatively few scores, all of them are HA Type 1 (either subtype a or b), and all are rated a low to moderate intensity level. Note, as well, that there is definite locational unreliability, since the two judges picked the same sign only once. The parentheses indicate that, in rereading the transcripts and scores, the second author and Rater 2 judged that that item listed by one of the raters was indeed scorable. The last rating by Rater 1 was one whose scorability was questionable.

Scoring of the Transcript, Using HA$_r$ Method, Patient 27, Session 3

Scale Items	Ratings for Each Subscale	
	Rater 3	Rater 4
1. Patient feels the therapist is warm and supportive.	4	3
2. Patient believes the therapist is helping him or her.	3	2
3. Patient feels changed by the treatment.	3	2
4. Patient feels a rapport with the therapist.	6	5
5. Patient feels the therapist respects and values him or her.	6	5
6. Patient feels treatment is valuable in helping to overcome his or her problems.	5	4
7. Patient sees him or herself as working together in a joint effort with the therapist.	7	6
8. Patient shares similar concepts about the etiology of his or her problems.	5	3
9. Patient believes he or she is increasingly able to cooperate with the therapist to understand own behavior.	5	5
10. Patient demonstrates abilities similar to the therapist, especially regarding tools for understanding.	6	7
Totals =	50	42

Although only discrepant by more than one step for the one subscale, 8, the two raters were discrepant by one step most of the time (80%) in this particular segment. These small discrepancies reflect the overall high reliabilities of the individual subscales across the 80 segments. Note that the means of 5 (Rater 3) and 4.2 (Rater 4) signify a somewhat-to-moderate overall helping alliance score which is reasonably comparable to the results obtained using the HA$_{cs}$ method.

Transcript of First 20 Minutes of Session 89 (90% in-treatment Point), Patient 27, 2/27/70

P: —Certainly ultimately. Yeah, please. (*pause*) I've, uh, finally got my GRE scores; Graduate Record scores in the mail.
T: Uh-huh.
P: And I took them around to some professors and got the, um, recommendations

in the—either sent out or in the process of being sent out. And I have to write a—a 1,000-word, uh, autobiography, then I'm all applied to the, uh—

T: Is that at Cooperstown?

P: Yes. That's a—the only program that I think of that I'm really—that interested in right now. It has everything I want. It's a terminal Master's program. It's supposed to be a very good little program, and, uh, I—I'm not that sure what my chances are of—of even getting in, uh. My teachers thought it was quite obvious from my board scores that I was an underachiever in the—the things but they didn't know if that was going to be that big a help, although they said they'd write good recommendations. So I've got to, uh, two out of three anyway, but (*pause 1 minute, 10 seconds*) I frankly feel sort of at a loss for things to talk about. I don't know if that's uh, good or bad, but it just seems to me that, uh, you know, the general trend of—of at least me being in therapy, you know, with you here has been sort of negative reinforcement, I guess they call it, and I think that, uh, um, well, I mean, in—in a sense like when I was going through something, uh, I don't know—maybe I've used the term wrong. Now that I've been going through something, um, that's been bad for me that it, you know, this has helped me really get it—get it straightened out. But that, when I—you know, since I've been feeling good, I don't—I don't know if that, uh, you know, if this is the type of thing I want, you know, I—I, that I'm going to be able to use, or even that I should think of using as, uh, something to—to grow in a more positive sense with.

T: Well, it's something worth discussing, that's true, when we're going to phase out and how to do that. We've brought that up before.

P: Uh-huh. Uh-huh. I mentioned some time ago that, that I—I was going to see you four more times, and I've seen you one time since then, and I've skipped a thing, so I—but I'd still like to—to keep the—the sequence, so—

T: No, I tol—I don't know if I told you or not that I would be away for two weeks.

P: Ooh, uh (*surprise*), you probably did and I ha—ha—had forgotten it, 'cause I realize there's a vacation coming up.

T: Yes. It'll be the next two Fridays.

P: Uh-huh. You mean this next week, the sixth, and the week after?

T: And the thirteenth.

P: Uh-huh. Yeah. Everybody's going away, I know that, now that I think that, uh, the school has a vacation too. Well, I think that, uh, that that would almost be a good thing to have, sort of a break in there. (*pause 25 seconds*)

T: Well, is there any difference, you know, say lately in the way you look at coming here than you did six months ago, or so?

P: Well, for one thing I think I've been looking at it and just a few thoughts that I've had about, uh, uh, this being part of, on my part, part of in—in a way, it's sort of a way of me using, uh, uh, uh, trying to exploit, uh, a feeling of weakness, or illness or something to—to gain a relationship, and, uh, I thought that that's, you know, partially how this—this has worked. It's certainly how I got into it. I don't think that that's so true now.

T: But in the sense of saying and looking forward to coming with feeling is important to come.

P: I—I've been feeling since, ah, uh, we've brought up this thing about stopping that it—it—it—it's, uh, it's something that I'm beginning to think about less.

T: Are you de-cathecting, as they say?

P: (*laughs*) That's quite possible. Yeah. Like I—I, you know, like I haven't tha—felt that in, uh, you know, it's, uh, there's been a lot of anxiety or pressure for me to—to cause like I think it can work as a thing to—to bring things out of me, you know, like I think it could do that. That type of situation tends to, like when I've got a limited amount of time to write a paper, say, or a limited amount of time, say, to see you, then I think it would induce me to bring up things that are—that are bothering me, but I think now that I've just sort of been fading a little bit. Now I—I find that, uh, it—it's more of a deliberate thing when I do think about this—by actually coming here or—or what's been going on between us and things like that. Although I—and one of the things I do tend to—to slip into is like whenever I—and I run into a situation that I want to sort out in my mind now, I have like a sort of another part of my mind that's sort of a fantasy of you, and I'm talking to you in my mind and that just sort of (*heh*), ha-ha, happens like that and so I—I started to work things out.

T: What would he say about it, you mean?

P: (*laughs*) Yes. Yeah. Only, you know, maybe even a little more of a dramatized fantasy than that.

T: That's not at all uncommon, by the way.

P: I—I didn't—I didn't—I thought it might—it might not be, but, you know, it's just sort of a, you know, there's a—a degree, a dimension of objectivity.

T: Uh-huh.

P: And, uh, it wasn't there. (*pause*)

T: You know, I think that that's a useful way to gain objectivity sometimes.

P: I—I just—I just sort of noticed it that beginnings—that type of thing really beginning about last summer. I didn't have that other, you know.

T: Uh-huh. (*sound of puffing pipe*) (*clears throat*) And I think people who've been in treatment for a while, what they do eventually is just take that on as part of themselves. I mean, it ceases to become a separate thing.

P: Uh-huh.

T: Just develop sort of a different kind of critical faculty than they used to have.

P: That—that's—

T: Incorporate some of the ideas of—

P: That's certainly true of me, 'cause like I've even—when I—I tend to find myself sinking into fantasies that aren't structured or all that they're not on top of. Like I find much more inclined to get out on top of it this way.

T: (*puffing on pipe*) (*pause*)

P: Ah, I can say that therapy has definitely been a good thing for me. Now I think I've got a—a lot more things to do with myself, you know, from now—from now on. I know like I—I feel like I'm leading sort of a pretty circumscribed existence, like I've got my personal life going, you know, in a very personal sense, I've got my personal life going fairly well now. But, you know, I'm not—I don't really know anything about, uh, the social interaction, you know, like say with institutions or something like that. I'm not—not—I don't really know what's going on in—in that sphere.

T: One thing you might consider at some time later is, um, several people I know have found it useful to join a group, to develop those kinds of skills.

P: Uh-huh.

T: It's often very hard to, um, I don't know, get sort of a social sense in a one-to-one relationship.

P: Right.

T: You get to relate better one-to-one (P: uh, huh), but often—but it doesn't help as much with—as it would if you had and experience in relating, say, to six people or eight people.

P: N—I—I don't understand that much about groups, like I'm not sure what (the point? of it is.) (T: interrupts)

T: Nobody does.

P: (*laugh*)

T: But my experience has been, uh, in running several, that in some very intangible way, people who have sort of a social anxiety or feel clumsy socially—

P: Uh-huh. Uh-huh. Well, that's not exactly specifically what I was—I was referring to—

T: No—Well, or, I don't know, have some kind of reticence in—

P: Eh, well, that—

T: Opening groups, they—

P: You know, I gu—

T: It helps them.

P: I guess I do because when I'm in groups I—I'm, you know, I—I do—I feel comfortable if, you know, the thing that's going on is going on along intellectual lines, I feel very comfortable in a situation like that, but I, if it, uh, if it involves something else, something maybe more personal (T: You—), or—I—I'm inclined to—to still stay detached from it.

T: It seems to me one of the concerns you have from time to time is how others see you.

P: Uh-huh.

T: And this is something you can get—

P: No, that's (covered by T's remarks)

T: Direct confirmation on in groups.

P: Uh-huh.

T: If the group is running well, people will tell how they see you.

P: Uh-huh.

T: And often do so in a very blunt way.

P: Uh-huh. I think I'm more able to—to, uh, withstand something like that. I think a year ago I would have been, uh, frightened, not—well, maybe a little bit more than a year ago, now that I think about it, but I would have been a bit frightened about getting into a group, just—that I would have felt too sensitive.

T: I'm not saying that for any immediate thing, but it's something to (P: Uh-huh) consider if—if you want to continue an exploration on a different level.

P: Uh-huh.

T: It's (voice fades). But you ought to do it somewhere where you're going to be for awhile—

P: Uh-huh.

T: Since you don't know where you're going to be right now.

P: That's, um, an understatement. I don't even know if this—this place, Cooperstown, New York, has—has such things as psychiatry and—and medicine. (laugh) I'm not—I'm not sure. (laugh)

T: You could talk to me in your mind. (pause—approximately 35 seconds)

P: (clears throat) I really feel sort of un—uncertain about in this—when I'm saying social aspect, I—I guess I'm, you know, I mean my relationship with institutions maybe, and, uh, that's—that's very, very uncertain to me right now. Like I—

T: Just which institutions?

P: Um, draft, colleges.

T: At least you're not alone there, baby.

P: (laugh)

T: Little solace as that may be.

P: Yes.

T: There's always Canada.

P: Yes, I know. Not—a lot of my—in fact most of my friends that are in the city now are—are thinking of leaving it in one way or another.

T: So I have a feeling things are going to probably improve quite a bit in the next couple of years.

P: Yeah, I think so too. (pause) I don't know. Tho' every—everybody's got their own, uh, their own vision of doom, at least the people that I know do.

T: Well, think of it this way. Laos at least has mountains. (*P laughs*) It's not as messy.

P: (*laugh*) Laos is a—I real—I really was unhappy with that situation.

T: Hm?

P: I really don't know what's going to happen with that situation. That could really mess up the whole possibility of Vietnam—getting out of that. (*15-second pause*) (*noise of moving things about*)

T: I think I've—my quips have distracted you.

P: Yes, they have.

T: Go on with what you were gonna say. I'm sorry.

P: Oh, I was just, uh, I—I even forgot what I was, what I was thinking on at the time. What occurs to me now is this, uh, a lot of my friends are just very—very unsure of their relationship also to—to institutions, not only to the draft. But it seems that I know too many people that are just drifting that I—I don't know anybody that is that—that balanced yet. I feel pretty well balanced, you know, in a very personal way.

T: uh-huh.

P: (*pause*) But, I, you know, I don't feel balanced in external ways yet or especially in unbalanced for that matter.

T: (*clears throat; pause 10 seconds*) Well, you know, we've talked about from time to time on your difficulty in relating to authority figures, and it seems to me the institutions just represent an extension of that.

P: Well, in—in some cases that might be true, like, like with the draft, but I think, like with colleges, uh, maybe that has been true in—in the past, but I don't know if that's—so sure that that's true any more. I mean, for some reason I was really defeating myself with the college all, you know, through the last four—four years. And I only came out of it, uh, only began to come out of it that last—last semester. (*pause*) I found it like it was, um, it's always been a lot easier when I've been able to have some connection with the teacher, and this, you know, I guess takes effort on my part, and I've made it in some cases, but, you know, just enough to get me the required amount of recommendations to grad school, and I guess that wasn't really my—my only motivation. The people that I did talk to were people that, uh, whose courses I happened to like, whom I happened to like as teachers. (*pause 15 seconds*)

T: Have you given any thought why, uh, you might become close to one or two teachers, why that might help you do better, apart from the fact that the courses might be interesting?

P: U-huh. Oh, I know with this, um, um, Doctor L.

T: Doctor L.

P: Yes, that, uh, some of the things that he had to talk about intellectually, struck me personally, and it's this whole notion of, of, um, you know, an identity, and there's this like a style in American Letters, the tough-guy tradition in American Letters, you know, heading for PhD thesis, um, Hemingway, O'Hara, even latter day people like Norman Mailer, whose prose style is different, but who's still cultivating this sense of a—of a personal style. And—and it's just your particularity, gestures, uh, use of words, um, how you order a drink, how you come across to a chick, you know, that's your identity, you know, the uses of personal ritual. And this— this seemed to really—to really strike me because I—I don't think I—I really thought of ever defining myself in very specific terms, but for a while I started to really start thinking in these—in this way.

T: And what conclusion did you come to (P: Well) in this event?

P: It wasn't even a conclusion. I was—I know—actually trying to live this way (*laugh*) you know, I was buying, you know, a certain style of clothes, and that was the only period in my life when I was doing that, and this was like when I was still going with P (*girl*), it was my first semester, junior year, and, uh, (*clears throat*) I remember after I broke up with her, I was still pushing myself, you know, to get into it, and I was trying to, you know. At that time I was, you know, I was wearing turtleneck, uh, those turtleneck shirts with, uh, coats, and I was very conscious of this, these styles and stuff like that, and, and then, uh, you know, all of a sudden I just quit, you know. And this was the summer when I—I went to live, uh on R. Street with a couple friends of mine, A (*boy*) and J (*boy*), and, uh, I got into, uh, a lot of drugs that summer, I really got into a lot of drugs, and that just helped me, uh, retreat from things, it helped me fall apart. But the whole notion of, uh, being that sensitive to detail and in—in your identity or how you present yourself to, to others. Uh, I guess that's—that's that concept of it.

T: I would think whatever sense of identity you've developed now, which seems not to depend on that—

P: Right.

T: It does have a much stronger base.

(End of 20 minutes)

Scoring of the Transcript, Using HA$_{cs}$ Method, Patient 27, Session 89

		Rater 1	*Rater 2*
1.	Page 344, lines 12–14: " . . . the general trend of—of at least me being in therapy, you know, with you here has been sort of negative reinforcement."		+1b3
2.	Page 344, lines 17–18: " . . . this has helped me really get it—get it straightened out."	+1a4	
3.	Page 344, lines 18–21: "I don't know if that, uh, you know, if this is the type of thing I want, you know, I-I, that I'm going to be able to use or even that I should think of using as, uh, something to—to grow in a more positive sense with."	−1a3	
4.	Page 344, lines 40–43: " . . . trying to exploit, uh, a feeling of weakness or illness or something to—to gain a relationship, and, uh, I thought that that's, you know, partially how this—this has worked. It's certainly how I got into it. I don't think that that's so true now."	+1b2	+1b2
5.	Page 345, lines 6–7: "I have like a sort of another part of my mind that's sort of a fantasy of you, and I'm talking to you in my mind."	+2c4	+2c3
6.	Page 345, line 32: "Ah, I can say that therapy has definitely been a good thing for me."	+1b5	+1b4
7.	Page 345, lines 36–39: "I don't really know anything about, uh, the social interaction, you know, like say with institutions or something like that. I'm not—not—I don't really		

		Rater 1	Rater 2

know what's going on in that sphere.'' $-1a4$

8. Page 346, lines 2–3:
  "Uh-huh. Uh-huh. Well, that's not exactly specifically what I was—I was referring to— $-1c2$

Rater 1   *Rater 2*

9. Page 346, lines 11–13:
  " . . . if it involves something else, something maybe more personal . . . I—I'm inclined to—to still stay detached from it. $-1b3$?

10. Page 346, line 24:
  "I think I'm more able to—to, uh, withstand something like that." $+1b3$ $+1b2$

11. Page 347, lines 15–16:
  "I feel pretty well balanced, you know, in a very personal way." $+1b3$ ( )

12. Page 347, line 27:
  "And I only came out of it, uh, only began to come out of it that last—last semester." $+1b3$ ( )

In this session, which is near the end of treatment, there are more ratings and more common agreement among the two judges, using this method (perfect agreement in four instances for value, type, and subtype, with intensity ratings never diverging more than one step). Interestingly, Rater 2, who across all 80 segments identified fewer "signs" than Rater 1, identified seven more than Rater 1 in this particular segment. In rereading the segments, the second author and Rater 2 judged that two of these (noted by parentheses) were clearly scorable and one, noted by a question mark, was a possibility. Locational unreliability was still a problem here.

There are two other points of interest. Note that signs 1, 2, and 3 were rated differently. Rater 2 rated all three as 1, with a rating of $+1b3$. Rater 1 rated two of the three items, and in a different direction. After rereading the session after the scoring was completed, the second author and Rater 2 judged that the three signs would best be scored as 1, with a rating of HA-1d$_2$. Note also that one HA Type 2 rating occurred (sign 5), which both raters saw as a clear example of internalization on the part of the patient.

Scoring of the Transcript, Using HA$_r$ Method
Patient 27, Session 89

	Ratings for Each Subscale	
	Rater 3	*Rater 4*
1. Patient feels the therapist is warm and supportive.	8	7
2. Patient believes the therapist is helping him or her.	8	7
3. Patient feels changed by the treatment.	6	8
4. Patient feels a rapport with the therapist.	8	7
5. Patient feels the therapist respects and values him or her.	8	6
6. Patient feels treatment is valuable in helping to overcome his or her problems.	8	7
7. Patient sees him or herself as working together in a joint effort with the therapist.	8	8
8. Patient shares similar concepts about the etiology of his or her problems.	8	7

9. Patient believes he or she is increasingly able to cooperate with the therapist to understand own behavior.	8	6
10. Patient demonstrates abilities similar to the therapist, especially regarding tools for understanding.	7	5
Totals =	77	68

Although the raters were discrepant by two steps more frequently in this segment than the prior one, in 60% of the ratings, there was a one-or-less discrepancy, again reflective of overall good reliability. It should be noted that overall sums for all of the subscale ratings are much higher for this segment than for the previous segment (for Rater 3, 77 vs. 50; for Rater 4, 68 vs. 42). As one of the 10 most improved cases examined in the Penn Psychotherapy Study, this case supports empirically the theoretical underpinnings of the helping alliance concept. As the patient nears termination, one would expect, as demonstrated here, higher helping alliance scores for some improved patients.

Memoir of the Development of the Scales
(by Luborsky)

After the first analysis of the data of the Penn Psychotherapy Project in 1974, with the discovery that, at best, only modest levels of pretreatment prediction of the outcomes of psychotherapy were achieved (Luborsky et al., 1980), I tried to get my bearings on why these predictions did not do better. It seemed natural to suppose that prediction would be easier from the early sessions after the patient–therapist interaction got under way rather than from the patient or therapist as they are evaluated pretreatment. While trying to orient myself to the predictive aspects of the early sessions, a serendipitous invitation came from Ed Bordin to take part in a panel on the helping alliance at the next SPR meeting (in 1975). The helping alliance seemed like just the kind of early relationship variable which might be predictive. I reviewed the large clinical literature and then searched through the studies to find any on this topic that were clinical–quantitative in style, but could find none.

I decided then to sample some early sessions of the 73 patients in psychotherapy in the Penn Psychotherapy Project. Since transcription time is so expensive, I chose to use only Sessions 3 and 5 and at that, only the first 20 minutes of these sessions for the 10 most improved and the 10 least improved patients. Only if these produced a significant prediction would I be encouraged to sample the entire 73 treatments and to try the same analyses on other samples.

I am aware of four types of quantitative studies that had an impact on my approach to scoring the helping alliance. The first was Rosenzweig (1936) who reviewed the common elements in different forms of psychotherapy and pointed out the most obvious commonality: in all of them, a helping relationship is set up. Secondly, Barrett-Lennard's (1962) successful prediction of the outcomes of psychotherapy by his self-report relationship inventory suggested that some of his items might be measuring a helping alliance. Thirdly, Ryan (1973) had shown that a pretreatment interview could predict what appeared to be helping alliance relationship qualities in the first psychotherapy session. Fourth, some of the research in social psychology on mutual attraction (Byrne, 1971; Huston, 1974) played a part, principally the well-known studies on the attribution of warmth as a basis for positive evaluation and wishing to get to know a person.

The clinical studies suggested at least two kinds of helping alliances, which I have called "Type 1" and "Type 2." As described previously, in the first part of the treatment, the patient sees the help as being provided by the therapist and in the last part, the patient sees him or herself as part of the positive working relationship with the therapist. Type 2 probably fits more closely to the usual clinical definition of a therapeutic alliance.

These clinical ideas drew me to immerse myself in reviewing the transcripts to learn to recognize examples of these types. I was able to discriminate four subtypes of Type 1 and three subtypes of Type 2. Then I fashioned a scoring manual that would enable any judge who was trained in the use of the manual to classify examples, that is, signs of those subtypes, in the transcript. The resulting manual, since it was based on counting these signs, was called the Penn Helping Alliance Counting Signs Method Manual (Luborsky, 1976).

Another instrument, the HA_r method, was constructed, based on a different scoring principle: that of allowing judges more freedom to use their clinical acumen by permitting them to examine the entire segment to be scored and rating it as a unit. As described previously, the HA_r method represents the conversion of the HA_{cs} subscales into 10-point, Likert-type scales. Part of the development of this work was based on Dr. Rose Morgan's PhD dissertation (1977) at the University of Miami.

Because both the HA_{cs} and HA_r methods are time consuming and expensive to use—the former requiring typescripts and the latter, either typescripts, audiotapes, or videotapes—I developed two questionnaires to help tap helping alliance phenomena. These two questionnaires described previously, are the Penn Helping Alliance Questionnaire (HA_q) and the Penn Therapist Facilitating Behaviors' Questionnaire (TFB_q). The questionnaire method is simpler and much more economical to use than the observer–rated method. It also provides different, perhaps more direct assessments of the therapeutic alliance, since the patient and therapist, not independent observers, do the assessments. Both the work of Barrett-Lennard (1962) and Orlinsky and Howard (1968) indicate that when questionnaires administered to the patient which measure something akin to the helping alliance are used, they have some value in predicting the outcome of psychotherapy.

Both questionnaires have been used in two studies at the Department of Psychiatry, University of Pennsylvania. For each, the capability of the questionnaire method to predict outcome will be examined. As described previously, this has already been done in the VA-Penn Study (Luborsky et al., 1985, Woody et al., 1983). The second study is the Penn "Re-Pairing" Study, a study of patient–therapist matching which is ongoing at the Outpatient Psychiatric Department, University of Pennsylvania (Alexander, Luborsky, Auerbach, Ratner, Schreiber, and Cohen, 1982). In this study, patients have the opportunity to try treatment with two different therapists for two sessions each and then choose the therapist of the two that he or she wishes to "re-pair" with for continuing therapy after the fourth session. The questionnaires are completed by the patient and each therapist after the patient has seen each therapist twice. We anticipate that there will be more evidence of the experience of a helping alliance with the chosen as compared to the nonchosen therapist.

Comparison of the Penn Scales with Other Helping Alliance Measures

Since the inaugural presentation of the Penn HA_{cs} method at the 1975 Society for Psychotherapy Research (SPR) meeting, a number of other empirical helping alliance methods have been introduced. These include: the Vanderbilt Psychotherapy Process Scale (Gomes-Schwartz, 1978; Moras and Strupp, 1982; O'Malley *et al.*, 1983); the Vanderbilt Therapeutic Alliance Scale (Hartley and Strupp, 1983); the Therapeutic Alliance Rating System (Marziali *et al.*, 1981; Horowitz *et al.*, 1984; Marmar *et al.*, this volume) from the Center for the Study of Neuroses at the Langley Porter Institute; the Working Alliance Inventory (Horvath and Greenberg, this volume); the Menninger Therapeutic Alliance Scales (Allen *et al.*, 1984); and the Marziali Alliance Scales (Marziali, 1984). The latter is comprised of three scales: the original judge-rated scale (Marziali *et al.*), plus a patient-rated and a therapist-rated scale, each developed to parallel the dimensions included in the original judge-rated scale.

In briefly comparing the Penn scales to other existing helping alliance measures, the HA_r method rather than the HA_{cs} method will generally be used, since the former is more comparable in format to most of the other existing helping alliance methods. To our knowledge, the HA_{cs} method is unique in using a counting signs approach to capture helping alliance phenomena. Although more time-consuming to use, the HA_{cs} method does have the beneficial quality of a precise location for the content scored.

In comparing all of the measures, each consists of Likert-type scales which are applied to varying predetermined therapy segments, spanning the course of the therapy. The scoring units range in length from 5-minute segments (Vanderbilt Therapeutic Alliance Scale), to 20 to 25-minute segments (Penn HA_r method and the Therapeutic Alliance Rating System), to the entire therapy session (Menninger Therapeutic Alliance Scales.) Except for the Penn HA_q method, the Working Alliance Inventory, and the Marziali Alliance Scales, all are observer-rated methods. All of the methods can be rated from audio or video tapes except for the Penn HA_{cs} method and the Menninger Scales, which require transcripts. All of the observer-rated methods require clinically sophisticated judges who have received considerable training in the use of the instrument and their accompanying manuals. To date, all methods have been used with relatively small patient samples ($N < 40$) and have generally been used with nonpsychotic patients, in outpatient settings, in planned short-term treatment (25 sessions or less). It should be noted, however, that the length of treatment of the normative sample for the Penn HA_{cs} and HA_r methods were longer: the median length for the more improved patients was 61 weeks, for the less improved, 43 weeks.

A significant amount of reliability and validity study has been undertaken for all of the measures. Reliabilities (both interrater and internal consistency measures) have generally been high (.70–.90 range), although no reliability studies have yet been published, using judges outside of the groups from which the scales were developed (Hartley, 1985). With acceptable reliabilities having been achieved, the current trend has been to further understand the nature of the helping alliance concept. Although the scales vary in terms of the number of items, from a low of 10 in the Penn HA_r method to 60 in the Vanderbilt Psychotherapy Process Scale, there is significant overlap both conceptually and in the actual wording of many of the items. Most of the measures are dyadic, examining both patient and therapist contributions to the alliance. The Penn HA_r method and the Menninger scales, however, focus primarily on the patient's perception and/or contribution to the alliance. All but the Menninger scales contain, at a minimum, items analogous to HA Type 1 (patient's experience of the therapist as warm, supportive, and helpful) and HA Type 2 (patient collaboration with the therapist) alliances. The Menninger scales more narrowly confine the helping alliance to collaborative behavior with the therapist, analogous to the HA Type 2 alliance. Finally, the Marziali Alliance scales and the Penn Scales permit the comparison of three different perspectives on the therapeutic alliance: that of the patient, the therapist, and an independent observer.

Considerable recent attention has been focused on two other facets of validity: the ability of the scales to predict outcome of psychotherapy and those factors that predispose a patient to form a helping alliance. Regarding the prediction of outcome, Gomes-Schwartz (1978), Morgan et al. (1982), Luborsky et al. (1983), Marziali et al. (1981), Horvath and Greenberg (this volume), Moras and Strupp (1982) and O'Malley et al. (1983) have all reported that the patient's early development of a positive helping alliance is predictive. Hartley and Strupp (1983) also reported a significant difference on their helping alliance measure in favor of the high outcome group at the point at which 25% of the treatment had been completed.

While Horowitz et al. (1984) did not find the patient's positive contribution to the alliance directly predictive of outcome, they did find an association between the interaction of the mean patient positive contribution to the alliance and motivation. The relationship between patient positive contribution and outcome was positive for lower values of motivation, but as motivation increased, shifted from positive to negative. This suggests that in patients with lower motivation, greater emphasis on the development of a positive view toward the therapeutic alliance is associated with better outcomes, while with far more highly motivated patients, more patient emphasis on the establishment of the alliance is associated with poorer results. There was also a significant relationship between the interaction of patient negative contribution and motivation, such that patients with lower motivation who made more negative contributions to the alliance had poorer outcomes while more motivated patients, higher on negative contributions, had more favorable outcomes.

Findings from the Horowitz et al. study (1984) suggest that there is not a simple line between either process or patient variables and outcome. Rather process and dispositional factors must be examined in interaction with outcome. Like all of the studies reported above, this study also concluded that the patient's positive contribution to the alliance is a better predictor of outcome than the therapist's contribution to the alliance. Beyond this general finding, however, both Marziali (1984) and Luborsky et al. (1985), using patient and therapist self-report measures of the alliance, found that both patient and therapists' positive contributions to the alliance were predictive of favorable outcomes.

Work on the second issue, on what potentiates the alliance, is currently underway and will certainly receive more attention in future research. As mentioned above, the work of Horowitz et al. (1984) and Luborsky et al. is suggestive. Examination of this issue involves both patient and therapist variables, taken singly as well as in interaction with each other to potentiate or impede alliance development. Among the more promising pretherapy patient variables are psychological health and adaptive functioning (Luborsky et al., 1983; Moras and Strupp, 1982), patient's adequate interpersonal relations (Moras and Strupp, 1982), and certain patient–therapist similarities, both demographic (Luborsky et al., 1983) as well as affective and attitudinal (Alexander et al., 1982). The focus on therapist factors has been directed both to positive aspects, such as commitment, skill, acceptance, and enlisting the patient as a partner (see, for example,

Morgan *et al.*, 1982; Luborsky *et al.*, 1983; Hartley & Strupp, 1983; and Allen *et al.*, 1984) as well as the research on negative indicators, most notably therapist errors in technique (Sachs, 1983). As suggested by Luborsky *et al.* (1985), the therapists' personal qualities seem to mainly influence his (or her) ability to form helping alliances.

Future Directions for Research

Several lines of research are already under way. First, the predictive power of the helping alliance, using the questionnaire method, is being examined in two studies at the University of Pennsylvania School of Medicine, described in the Memoir of the Development of the Scales section. The first is the VA-Penn study of 110 drug-abusing patients (Luborsky *et al.*, 1985), whose results have already been described. The second is the "re-pairing" study (Alexander *et al.*, 1982). In the "re-pairing" study, the overall comparability of the three different measurement techniques—the counting signs, the rating, and the questionnaire methods—will be examined. Because of its relative simplicity, if the questionnaire method is comparable to the others predictively, it would become the future method of choice in terms of efficiency and economy of time for measuring helping alliance phenomena.

Third, even though the analysis of helping alliance signs and ratings from the third and fifth sessions significantly predicted outcome, we suspect that the predictions would be improved even more, were more early sessions used. We plan to carry this out with the Penn Psychotherapy Project data. If it proves fruitful, we will do the same with the re-pairing study data. Fourth, following the same plan as above, we will compare the results of the HA_r method, using the typescripts versus the audiotapes, first in the Penn Psychotherapy Project and in the re-pairing study. Fifth, since both scales have only been used with extreme groups, we would like to use both methods on some of the cases with middle-range outcomes. In this regard it is of interest to note, however, that the large significant correlations between the HA_q method and outcome in the VA-Penn Study were based on using the whole sample, not just extreme groups.

Sixth, the scoring unit will be expanded from the first 20 to the first 30 minutes of the early and late sessions for the 10 most improved and 10 least improved patients in the Penn Psychotherapy Project (Luborsky *et al.*, 1980). If, as we anticipate, the 30-minute segment produces more robust predictability for the helping alliance measures with outcome, the 30-minute segment will also be used to analyze helping alliance data in the re-pairing study. Seventh, the relationship of the patient's preferences for therapists with the therapist's skill, as measured by the Vanderbilt Negative Indicators Scale, will be examined in collaboration with Dr. Janet Sachs. Eighth, using the re-pairing study, we will respond to the concern about what factors facilitate the formation of the helping alliance by examining the relationship between a series of patient–therapist similarities, which have been so promising to date, and the development of the alliance.

Last, collaboration will be sought with developers of other helping alliance systems so that several different alliance measures can be applied to a common data set. If helping alliance research as a whole is to advance further, this is a critical step.

Summary and Conclusions

This chapter has provided a summary of the following information for the Penn Helping Alliance Scales: (1) description and technical details; (2) application of the scales to two data segments; (3) a comparison of the Penn scales to other existing helping alliance measures; and (4) a description of ongoing and further research efforts, using these scales.

The following important points have been demonstrated. (1) The HA_{cs} and HA_r methods can be rated with moderate-to-high reliability, respectively. (2) In terms of validity, several results are pertinent. First, scores from the HA_{cs} method showed moderate agreement with scores from the HA_r method. Second, for both methods, scores were fairly to moderately consistent from early to late in treatment. Third, and perhaps most exciting and promising, is the fact that both the HA_{cs} and the HA_r methods significantly predicted the outcomes of psychotherapy. Their level of predictive success is as good as, or better than most of the best pretreatment measures examined in the Penn Psychotherapy Project (Luborsky *et al.*, 1980). In fact, the helping alliance proved to be the best during-treatment predictor of outcome. When the most promising *pretreatment* predictor, the Health–Sickness Rating Scale, a measure of the degree of psychological severity, was combined in a multiple regression with early positive HA_{cs} and early HA_r scores, the following multiple R's were obtained with rated benefits: .61* for early positive HA_{cs} and .62* for early HA_r. What this implies is that favorable outcomes of treatment are particularly likely for patients who come to therapy without significant pathology, or are well endowed psychologically, and who, early in the course of therapy, form a positive helping alliance with the therapist.

These measures, taken together, account for about 25% to 35% of the variance in treatment outcome. This is a significant finding for psychotherapy research in general, and provides support for the development of a helping alliance as one important curative factor in successful therapy.

Basic background similarities between patient and therapist, such as age and religious activity, attained high correlations with both helping alliance measures. The sum of 10 similarities correlated .60** with early positive HA_{cs} and .53* with HA_r. These background similarities can be understood, then, as facilitators of the development of a helping alliance. Although neither the TFB_{cs} nor the TFB_r Methods added much to the multiple R, there was evidence suggesting that therapist-facilitating behaviors served as a potentiator of helping alliance behavior. On the other hand, such factors as the presence of somatic problems, significant life changes, and random assignment of patients to treatment were clear inhibitors of the development of a helping alliance. Finally, it is of considerable interest that the HA_q method—a brief questionnaire assessing early in treatment the patient's view of the helpfulness of the therapist and the therapy —could have such predictive power.

In light of all of these findings, the helping alliance concept and measures of it have demonstrated their usefulness and merit ongoing study and refinement. It is heartening to see how much work has been accomplished in this area, since the publication of the first empirical study on the subject in 1976 (Luborsky, 1976).

Appendix I

Penn Helping Alliance Counting Signs
Method Manual (HA$_{cs}$)

1. Read through the transcripts of the sessions and score every example (i.e., sign) of each of the seven positive or negative subtypes listed in this manual. Give a

score for each explicit, or nearly explicit, example. The example must clearly fit one of the seven subtypes in this manual.

It is important for the judge to keep in mind that what is being scored is the patient's indication of his or her perception of the treatment or the relationship with the therapist as helpful or potentially helpful. Usually these are explicit indications given by the patient that he or she is getting better or getting worse. Occasionally, a self-description which is not explicit is clear and scorable, nevertheless, from the context; for example, "I am not depressed" in a patient who has been depressed.

2. The scoring unit is usually a single sentence, although sometimes a group of sentences can represent one scorable unit if they reiterate the same theme. If the patient says the same thing more than once around the same place, only one score is given for each type of sign.

3. A score includes these components: whether it is positive or negative, Type 1 or 2, subtype 2, b, and so on, and intensity, for example: HA + 1a5, HA = helping alliance; +1 = positive, Type 1; a = P says he believes T is helping him; 5 = 5 on a 1–5 scale of intensity where 1 = "very low" and 5 = "very high."

Positive Type 1	*Negative Type 1*
A helping relationship which depends upon the patient's experiencing the therapist as helpful, supportive, and facilitating achievement of the treatment goals:	A hindering relationship in which the patient experiences the therapist as unhelpful, nonsupportive, or impeding achievement of the treatment goals:
a. The patient believes the therapist (or therapy) is helping him or her and gives evidences of the benefits. (It is Type 1 since the benefits are seen as given by T and not that a joint effort has gone into the change.) *Example*: "I was pleased with the new understanding you gave me in the last session."	a. The patient believes the therapist (or therapy) is not helping him or her. *Example*: "Treatment is not helping me." "The problem I came to treatment for is still with me."
b. The patient feels changed since beginning the treatment in ways he or she considers to be better. (Evidence does not have to be presented that it directly has to do with the therapist's efforts or the treatment.) *Example*: "I am feeling better recently."	b. The patient feels changed in ways he considers to be worse. *Example*: "I am feeling worse recently."
c. The patient feels understood and accepted. (To receive a score the patient's response has to clearly show feeling understood and not just be based on saying "yes" to what the therapist says.) *Example*: "I feel you understand me."	c. The patient feels *not* understood and *not* accepted by the therapist. (Minor differences about the accuracy of T's clarifications are not rated as evidence of the P's not feeling understood.) *Example*: "I feel you do not understand me."
d. The patient expresses feelings of op-	d. The patient feels pessimistic and un-

timism and confidence that the treatment can help.
Example: ''I feel you can help me.''

sure that the therapist and treatment can help. *Example*: ''You expect things of me which I can't do so I don't feel that the treatment is helping.''

Positive Type 2

A helping relationship based on the sense of working together in a joint struggle against what is impeding the patient. The emphasis is upon shared responsibility for working out the treatment goals, and on the patient's ability to do what the therapist does.

a. The patient experiences him or herself as working together with the therapist in a joint effort, as part of the same team.
   Example: ''We are doing the work of the treatment together.'' (Use of ''we'' *may* imply an alliance.)

b. The patient shares similar conceptions about the source of his or her problems. (In order to score this, it is necessary to know the therapists's conceptions.)
   Example: ''I know it is through understanding of my symptoms that I will get relief.''

c. The patient demonstrates qualities which are similar to those of the therapist, especially those having to do with tools for understanding.
   Example: ''I feel I can analyze myself now, much as we have done here.'' (This last sign begins to show the development of a capacity to perform autonomously the functions the patient and therapist did together.)

Negative Type 2

A hindering relationship based on a sense of not working together in a joint struggle against what is impeding the patient, a sense that the responsibility for working out the patient's goals is not being shared, and patient is not able to do what the therapist does.

a. The patient experiences him or herself as *not* working together with the therapist in a joint effort, as not part of the same team.
   Example: ''I am the patient and you are the doctor and that puts me in an inferior position.''

b. The patient has different conceptions about the etiology of his or her problems.
   Example: ''I think I need medication and that my depressions are physical and that you think they are psychologically based.''

c. The patient sees him or herself as *not* having the tools for self-understanding.
   Example: ''As soon as I am away from here (the treatment) I find I can't function.''

Appendix II

Penn Helping Alliance Rating Method (HA₁) Manual

Read through the transcript of the therapy session and rate these 10 helping alliance scales. Each scale has the low or negative pole on the left and the high or positive pole on the right, as follows:

1	2	3	4	5	6	7	8	9	10
Very little or none		Some		Moderate amount		Much		Very much	

Type 1

Type 1 is a helping alliance that depends on the patient's experiencing the therapist as warm, helpful, and supportive with him or herself as the recipient.

1. The patient feels that the therapist is warm and supportive.
2. The patient believes the therapist is helping him or her (without indicating that his or her own efforts and abilities have gone into his or her own change). Example: "I was pleased with the new understanding you gave me in the last session."
3. The patient feels changed by the treatment. Example: "I am improving," or "I am less anxious."
4. The patient feels a rapport with the therapist; he or she feels understood and accepted.
5. The patient feels that the therapist respects and values him or her.
6. The patient conveys a belief in the value of the treatment process in helping him or her to overcome problems.

Type 2

Type 2 is working alliance based on the sense of working together in a joint struggle against what is impeding the patient. The emphasis is on shared responsibility for working out the treatment goals and on the patient's ability to do what the therapist does.

1. The patient experiences him or herself as working together with the therapist in a joint effort, as part of the same team.
2. The patient shares similar conceptions about the etiology of his or her problems. (To score this it is necessary to know the therapist's conceptions.)
3. The patient expresses his or her belief that he or she is increasingly able to cooperate with the therapist in terms of understanding his or her own behavior.
4. The patient actually demonstrates abilities similar to those of the therapist, espe-

cially with regard to tools for understanding. (This sign begins to show the development of a capacity to do for him or herself without the therapist, i.e., autonomously, what they did together.)

Addendum to Rating Directions for HA$_r$ Manual

1. A way to deal with the absence of complete information on a specific category is to make an additional rating of certainty on a similar 1 to 10-point, Likert-type scale. The rating would provide information about which categories tend to be rated with high or low levels of certainty.

Appendix III

Penn Therapist Facilitating Behaviors
Counting Signs Method Manual (TFB$_{cs}$)

1. These therapist behavior subtypes are mostly the counterpart of those in the Helping Alliance Counting Signs Manual—they are the therapist behaviors which facilitate or inhibit the helping alliance. Every example in the transcript is to be scored.
2. The scoring is usually a single sentence although sometimes a group of sentences can represent one scorable unit if they reiterate the same theme. If the therapist says the same thing more than once around the same place, only one score is given for each type of sign.
3. A score includes these components: whether it is positive or negative, Type 1 or 2, subtypes a, b, and so on, and intensity. For example, "TFB + 1a5": TFB = Therapist Facilitating Behaviors; +1 = positive Type 1; a = therapist conveys wanting the patient to achieve the patient's goals; 5 = a rating on a 1–5 scale of intensity where 1 = "very low" and 5 = "very high."

Positive Type 1	*Negative Type 1*

Giving Helping Behaviors

a. The therapist conveys a sense of wanting the patient to achieve the patient's goals.

b. The therapist conveys that he or she feels that he or she understands and accepts and respects the patient.

c. The therapist is warm and receptive.

a. The therapist conveys a sense of disinterest in whether the patient achieves the patient's goals.

b. The therapist conveys a sense of *lack* of understanding, acceptance, and respect.
Example: "I do not understand you" (meant in a general sense, not just informationally). (Behaviors in which the patient is put down, e.g., jokes at the patient's expense.)

c. The therapist is cold and unreceptive.

d. The therapist conveys a sense of hopefulness that the patient's treatment goals can be achieved.

e. The therapist gives recognition where appropriate that the patient has in some way made some progress toward the patient's goals.
Example: "You wanted to do well in your work. It must please you that you do now."

d. The therapist conveys a sense of lack of hopefulness that the patient's goals can be achieved.

e. The therapist believes the patient has *not* made progress toward the patient's goals.
Example: "You have not achieved what you wanted out of the treatment."

Positive Type 2   *Negative Type 2*

Facilitating "We" Behaviors

a. The therapist says things which show that he or she feels a "we" bond with the patient, that he or she feels a sense of alliance with the patient in the joint struggle against what is impeding the patient.
(Just scoring all "we's" is insufficient); the usage must convey presence of a bond or team.)
Example: "We have worked well together in trying to get you to your goals."

a. The therapist says things which show that he or she does not feel a "we" bond with the patient.

b. The therapist conveys that he or she accepts the patient's growing sense of being able to do what the therapist does in terms of using the basic tools of the treatment. The therapist can accept the fact that the patient also can reflect on what the patient is saying and come up with valid observations.
Example: "You came up with that understanding yourself."

b. The therapist conveys that he or she does not accept the patient as someone who can use the basic tools of the treatment.

c. The therapist refers to experiences that he or she and the patient have been through together, building up, as it were, a joint backlog of common experiences. (Score here any references by the therapist to some past event they have been through together in the treatment.)
Example: "Yes, you and I are familiar with that kind of problem; we discussed it on other occasions."

c. The therapist does not refer to experiences he or she and the patient have been through together.

d.[1] The therapist is effectively supportive, in the sense of assisting the patient to maintain helpful defenses or
helping to maintain activities which
are supportive.
Example: "I see you are finding ways
of managing your job (or school)
which are helpful to you."

d.[1] The therapist is unsupportive. The
therapist undermines or does not
support necessary defenses or necessary activities.

Appendix IV

Penn Therapist Facilitating Behaviors' Rating Method Manual (TFB_r)

These scales are the counterpart of the Helping Alliance Rating Method Manual. Read
through the transcript and rate these 10 therapist facilitative behaviors' scales. Each scale
has the low or negative pole on the left and the high or positive pole on the right, as
follows:

1	2	3	4	5	6	7	8	9	10
Very little or none		Some		Moderate amount		Much		Very much	

Type 1

1. The therapist is warm and supportive.
2. The therapist conveys a sense of wanting the patient to achieve treatment goals.
3. The therapist conveys a sense of hopefulness that treatment goals can be achieved.
4. The therapist conveys a sense that he or she feels a rapport with the patient, that
   he or she understands the patient.
5. The therapist conveys feelings of acceptance and respect for the patient as opposed
   to behavior in which the patient is put down (e.g., by jokes at the patient's expense).

Type 2

1. The therapist says things that show that he or she feels a "we" bond with the patient, that he or she feels a sense of alliance with the patient in the joint struggle
   against what is impeding the patient.

---

1. This subcategory was not in the original manual but may be useful for further research.

2. The therapist conveys recognition of the patient's growing sense of being able to do what the therapist (indicates does needs to be done) in terms of the basic tools of the treatment (e.g., ability to introspect and analyze his or her own behavior).
3. The therapist shows acceptance of the patient's increased ability to understand his or her own (the patient's) experiences.
4. The therapist acknowledges and confirms the patient's accurate perceptions of him or her (the therapist).
5. The therapist can accept the fact that the patient also can reflect on what the patient and he or she have been through together, building up, as it were, a joint backlog of common experiences. (References by the therapist to past patient–therapist exchanges sometimes may fit here.)

Note that the same addendum to the HA_r manual applies equally to the TFB_r method.

Appendix V

Penn Helping Alliance
Questionnaire Method (HA_q)

I.D. _____   Date _____

Below are listed a variety of ways that one person may feel or behave in relation to another person.

Please consider each statement with reference to your present relationship with your therapist.

- - - - - - - - - - - - -

Mark each statement according to how strongly you feel that it is true, or not true, in this relationship. *Please mark every one.* Write in +3, +2, +1, or −1, −2, −3, to stand for the following answers:

+3: Yes, I strongly feel that it is true.   −1: No, I feel that it is probably untrue,
+2: Yes, I feel it is true.   or more untrue than true.
+1: Yes, I feel that it is probably   −2: No, I feel it is not true.
    true, or more true than untrue.   −3: No, I strongly feel that it is not true.

- - - - - - - - - - - - -

_____ 1. I believe that my therapist is helping me.
_____ 2. I believe that the treatment is helping me.
_____ 3. I have obtained some new understanding.
_____ 4. I have been feeling better recently.
_____ 5. I can already see that I will eventually work out the problems I came to treatment for.
_____ 6. I feel I can depend upon the therapist.

_____ 7. I feel the therapist understands me.
_____ 8. I feel the therapist wants me to achieve my goals.
_____ 9. I feel I am working together with the therapist in a joint effort.
_____ 10. I believe we have similar ideas about the nature of my problems.
_____ 11. I feel now that I can understand myself and deal with myself on my own (that is, even if the therapist and I were no longer meeting for treatment appointments).

- - - - - - - - - - - - -

KINDS OF CHANGE:
I feel improved in the following ways: _____

_____

_____

I feel worse in the following ways: _____

_____

_____

ESTIMATE OF IMPROVEMENT SO FAR:

| | | | | |
Not at all   Slightly   Moderately   Much   Very much

Appendix VI

Penn Therapist Facilitating Behaviors' Questionnaire Method (TFB$_q$)

I.D. _____   Date _____

Below are listed a variety of ways that one person may feel or behave in relation to another person.

Please consider each statement with reference to your present relationship with your patient.

- - - - - - - - - - - - -

Mark each statement in the left margin, according to how strongly you feel that it is true, or not true, in this relationship. *Please mark every one.* Write in +3, +2, +1, or −1, −2, −3, to stand for the following answers:

+3: Yes, I strongly feel that it is true.
+2: Yes, I feel it is true.
+1: Yes, I feel that it is probably true, or more true than untrue.

−1: No, I feel that it is probably untrue, or more untrue than true.
−2: No, I feel it is not true.
−3: No, I strongly feel that it is not true.

- - - - - - - - - - - - -

_____ 1. I believe I am helping my patient.

_____ 2. The patient believes that he or she is getting help from me.

_____ 3. I believe I convey a sense of wanting my patient to achieve his or her goals.

_____ 4. The patient has obtained some new understanding.

_____ 5. I believe the patient has been feeling better than when he or she began.

_____ 6. I believe the patient will eventually work out the problems he or she came to treatment for.

_____ 7. I feel I understand the patient.

_____ 8. The patient feels I understand him or her.

_____ 9. I feel that I am working together with the patient in a joint effort; we are on the same team.

_____ 10. I feel that the patient feels a growing sense of being able to do by him or herself what we do together.

_____ 11. I believe we have similar ideas about the nature of the patient's problems.

References

Alexander, L. B., Luborsky, L., Auerbach, A., Ratner, H. K., Schreiber, P., & Cohen, M. *The Effect of the Match Between Patient and Therapist: Findings from the Penn Re-Pairing Study*. Paper presented at the annual meeting, Society for Psychotherapy Research, Smuggler's Notch Village, Vermont, June 16, 1982.

Allen, J. G., Newsom, G. E., Gabbard, G. O., & Coyne, L. *Assessment of the Therapeutic Alliance from a Psychoanalytic Perspective*. Paper presented at workshop on "The Therapeutic Alliance: Controversies in Definition and Measurement," annual meeting, Society for Psychotherapy Research, Smuggler's Notch Village, Vermont, June 19, 1982.

Allen, J., Newsom, G., Gabbard, G., & Coyne, L. Scales to assess the therapeutic alliance from a psychoanalytic perspective. *Bulletin of the Menninger Clinic*, 1984, *48*, 383–400.

Barrett-Lennard, G. T. Dimensions of therapist response as causal factors in therapeutic change. *Psychological Monographs*, 1962, *76* (43, Whole No. 562).

Bordin, E. The generalizability of the psychoanalytic concept of the working alliance. *Psychotherapy: Theory, Research, and Practice*, 1979, *16*, 252–260.

Byrne, D. *The Attraction Paradigm*. New York: Academic Press, 1971.

Frank, J. D. Therapeutic factors in psychotherapy. *American Journal of Psychotherapy*, 1971, *25*, 350–361.

Frank, J. D. Therapeutic components of psychotherapy. *Journal of Nervous and Mental Disease*, 1974, *159*, 325–343.

Freud, S. (1913). On beginning the treatment: Further recommendations on the technique of psychoanalysis. In J. Strachey (Ed), *Standard Edition* (Vol. 12). London: Hogarth Press and Institute of Psychoanalysis, 1958.

Frieswyk, S. H., Alter, J. G., Colson, D. B., Coyne, L., Gabbard, G. O., Horwitz, L., Newsom, G. The therapeutic alliance: it's place as a Process and Outcome Variable in dynamic psychotherapy. *Journal of Consulting and Clinical Psychiatry*, in press.

Garfield, S. L. Psychotherapy: Efficacy, Generality, and Specificity. In J. B. W. Williams & R. L. Spitzer (Eds.). *Psychotherapy Research: Where Are We and Where Should We Go?* New York: Guilford Press, 1984.

Goldfried, M. R. Toward the delineation of therapeutic change principles. *American Psychologist*, 1980, *35*, 991–999.

Gomes-Schwartz, B. Effective ingredients in psychotherapy: Prediction of outcome from process variables. *Journal of Consulting and Clinical Psychology*, 1978, *46*, 1023–1035.

Greenson, R. R. The working alliance and the transference neurosis. *The Psychoanalytic Quarterly*, 1965, *34*, 151–181.

Greenson, R. R. *The Technique and Practice of Psychoanalysis*. New York: International Universities Press, 1967.

Greenson, R. R., & Wexler, M. The non-transference relationship in the psychoanalytic situation. *International Journal of Psychoanalysis*, 1969, *50*, 27–40.

Greenspan, S., & Cullander, C. A systematic metapsychological assessment of the course of an analysis. *Journal of the American Psychoanalytic Association*, 1975, *23*, 107–138.

Hartley, Dianna E., Research on the therapeutic alliance in psychotherapy. In R. Hales & A. Frances (Eds.). *Psychiatry Update*. American Psychiatric Assoc. Annual Review. Vol. 4. 1985, 532–549.

Hartley, Dianna E., & Strupp, H. H. The therapeutic alliance: Its relationship to outcome in brief psychotherapy. In J. Masling (Ed.), *Empirical Studies of Analytic Concepts* (Vol. 1). Hillsdale, N.J.: Lawrence Erlbaum, 1983.

Horvath, A. O. and Greenberg, L. The development of the working alliance inventory, this volume.

Horwitz, M. J., Marmar, C., Weiss, D., Dewitt, K. N. & Rosenbaum, R. Brief psychotherapy of bereavement reaction: The relationship of process to outcome. *Archives of General Psychiatry*, 1984, *41*, 438–448.

Huston, T. (Ed.). *Foundations of Interpersonal Attraction*. New York: Academic Press, 1974.

Johnston, M., & Holzman, P. *Assessing Schizophrenic Thinking*. San Francisco, California: Jossey-Bass, 1979.

Luborsky, L. Helping alliances in psychotherapy: The groundwork for a study of their relationship to its outcome. In J. L. Claghorn (Ed.), *Successful psychotherapy*. New York: Brunner/Mazel, 1976.

Luborsky, L. *Principles of Psychoanalytic Psychotherapy: A Manual for Supportive-Expressive Treatment*. New York: Basic Books, 1984.

Luborsky, L. and Auerbach, A. The therapeutic relationship in Psychodynamic Psychotherapy: The research evidence and its meaning for practice. In R. Hales & A. Frances (Eds.). *Psychiatry Update*. American Psychiatric Assoc. Annual Review. Vol. 4, 1985.

Luborsky, L., Crits-Christoph, P., Alexander, L., Margolis, M., & Cohen, M. Two helping alliance methods for predicting outcomes of psychotherapy: A counting signs vs. a global rating method. *Journal of Nervous and Mental Diseases*, 1983, *171*, 480–492.

Luborsky, L., and McLellan, A. T. Optimal matching of patients with types of psychotherapy: What is known and some designs for knowing more. In E. Gottheil *et al.* (Eds.), *Matching Patient Needs and Treatment Methods for Alcohol and Drug Abuse*. Chicago: Charles Thomas, 1981.

Luborsky, L., McLellan, T., Woody, G., O'Brien, C., & Auerbach, A. Therapist success and its determinants. *Archives of General Psychiatry*, 1985, *42*, 602–611.

Luborsky, L., Mintz, J., Auerbach, A., Christoph, P., Bachrach, H., Todd, T., Johnson, M., Cohen, M., & O'Brien, C. P. Predicting the outcomes of psychotherapy: Findings of the Penn Psychotherapy Project. *Archives of General Psychiatry*, 1980, *37*, 471–481.

Luborsky, L., Singer, B., & Luborsky, L. Comparative studies of psychotherapies: Is it true that "everybody has won and all must have prizes?" *Archives of General Psychiatry*, 1975, *32*, 995–1008.

Marmar, C. R., Marziali, E., Horwitz, M. T. & Weiss, D. S. Development of the therapeutic alliance rating system. This volume.

Marziali, E. Three viewpoints on the therapeutic alliance: Similarities, differences, and associations with psychotherapy outcomes. *Journal of Nervous and Mental Disease*, 1984, *172*, 417–423.

Marziali, E., Marmar, C., & Krupnick, J. Therapeutic alliance scales: Their development and relationship to psychotherapy outcome. *American Journal of Psychiatry*, 1981, *138*, 361–364.

McLellan, A. T., Luborsky, L., O'Brien, C. P., and Woody, G. E. Improved diagnostic instrument for substance abuse patients: The Addiction Severity Index. *Journal of Nervous and Mental Diseases*, 1980, *168*, 26–33.

Mintz, J., & Luborsky, L. Segments vs. whole sessions: Which is the better unit for psychotherapy process research? *Journal of Abnormal and Social Psychology*, 1971, *78*, 180–191.

Moras, Karlas, & Strupp, H. Pretherapy interpersonal relations, patients' alliance, and outcome in brief therapy. *Archives of General Psychiatry*, 1982, *39*, 405–409.

Morgan, R. W. The relationships among therapeutic alliance, therapists' facilitative behaviors, patient insight, patient resistance, and treatment outcome in psychoanalytically oriented psychotherapy. Doctoral Dissertation, University of Miami, 1977.

Morgan, R., Luborsky, L., Crits-Christop, P., Curtis, H., & Solomon, J. Predicting the outcomes of psychotherapy by the Penn Helping Alliance Rating Method. *Archives of General Psychiatry*, 1982, *39*, 397–402.

Oltman, P., Goodenough, D., Witkin, H., Freedman, N., & Friedman, F. The psychological differentiation as a factor in conflict resolution. *Journal of Personality and Social Psychology*, 1975, *32*, 730–736.

Orlinsky, D. T., & Howard, K. I. Communication, rapport, and patient "progress." *Psychotherapy: Theory, Research and Practice*, 1968, *5*, 131–136.

Raimy, V. *Misunderstanding of the self*. San Francisco: Jossey-Bass, 1975.

Rosenzweig, S. Some implicit common factors in diverse methods of psychotherapy. *American Journal of Orthopsychiatry*, 1936, *6*, 412–415.

Ryan, E. R. The capacity of the patient to enter an elementary therapeutic relationship in the initial psychotherapy interview. Unpublished Doctoral Dissertation, University of Michigan, 1973.

Sachs, J. S. Negative Factors in brief psychotherapy: an empirical assessment. *Journal of Consulting and Clinical Psychology*, 1983, *51*, 557–564.

Sloane, R. B., Staples, F. R., Cristol, A. H., Yorkston, N. J., & Whipple, K. *Psychotherapy versus behavior therapy*. Cambridge, Mass.: Harvard University Press, 1975.

Smith, M. L., Glass, G. V., & Miller, T. I. *The benefits of psychotherapy*. Baltimore: Johns Hopkins Press, 1980.

Strupp, H. H., & Hadley, S. Specific versus nonspecific factors in psychotherapy: A controlled study of outcome. *Archives of General Psychiatry*, 1979, *36*, 1125–1136.

Strupp, H. H., Hartley, D., & Blackwood, G. L., Jr. *The Vanderbilt Psychotherapy Process Scale*. Unpublished manuscript, Vanderbilt University, 1974.

Woody, G. E., Luborsky, L., McLellan, A. T., O'Brien, C. P., Beck, A. T., Blaine, J., Herman, J. and Hole, A. Psychotherapy for opiate addicts: Does it help? *Archives of General Psychiatry*, 1983, *40*, 639–645.

10

The Development of the Therapeutic Alliance Rating System

Charles R. Marmar
Mardi J. Horowitz
Daniel S. Weiss
Langley Porter Psychiatric Institute
University of California
San Francisco, California

Elsa Marziali
Clarke Institute of Psychiatry
University of Toronto
Toronto, Ontario

Overview of the System

The intention of this research is to develop, through a series of applications and revisions, a reliable and valid measure of the therapeutic alliance. The initial focus of the work has been on the development of an observer-based rating system to be utilized by independent clinical judges reviewing recordings of psychotherapy sessions. This instrument is designed for ratings of audiotapes or videotapes rather than transcripts or process notes, with the specific rationale of including along with verbal content, important nonverbal communicative signals in the patient–therapist interaction as a data base for judgments.

Heavy emphasis has been given to the development of a system that uses external raters in order to advance beyond reliance on patient ratings of the therapeutic relationship. Much past research has focused on the patient's perception of the therapist and therapeutic setting as a predictor of outcome. However, reliance on patient's ratings of both process and outcome carries with it the danger of circularity. The patient's in-treatment reports of the "therapeutic relationship" or "therapeutic alliance" may reflect a dimension of global satisfaction with therapy. This rating then might well be highly correlated with patient's ratings of outcome because of this redundancy of perspective. We wished, therefore, to avoid this potential confound in process and outcome measurement by having nonparticipant judges rate aspects of the therapeutic alliance. These independent ratings could then be related to outcome judged from the perspectives of patients, therapists, and independent evaluators.

The strategy behind our approach to the measurement of the therapeutic alliance was to stress the affective and attitudinal aspects of the therapeutic climate while excluding specific classes of therapist actions, such as interpretation of the transference, encouraging the expression of affect, or working on termination in order not to confound technique with the status of the alliance. Those therapist efforts assessed on this instrument are general in character, and reflect attempts on the part of the therapist to encourage and sustain a working alliance with the patient. An illustrative item is the following: "The therapist conveys a working bond with the patient, a sense that they are in a joint struggle against what is impeding the patient."

Items were selected to assess separately the therapist's positive and negative contributions, as well as the patient's positive and negative contributions, rather than to assess patient–therapist interaction as a dyadic unit. In separating the two contributions, we were guided by the earlier studies which demonstrated a lack of convergence of therapist and patient contributions. As will be described in detail in the discussion of the dimensional properties of this measure, the four separate scales were defined on theoretical grounds and later supported by factor analytic findings. These scales are the Therapist Positive Contribution (TPC), the Therapist Negative Contribution (TNC), the Patient Positive Contribution (PPC), and the Patient Negative Contribution (PNC).

Theoretical Basis for the Therapeutic Alliance Rating System

Understanding the meaning, quality, and function of the therapeutic alliance has been a topic of interest since Freud's first attempts to describe the treatment relationship. Beginning with his earliest papers, Freud clearly demonstrated his interest in various aspects of the analytic relationship which accounted for a positive and productive therapeutic process. His concern with overcoming resistances (Freud, 1913), maintaining a positive transference (Freud, 1912) and the development of the "analytic pact" (Freud, 1937) led him to delineate the neurotic, irrational aspects of the relationship, in contrast to the collaborative and realistic aspects. These were viewed to function in tandem, each essential in promoting the progress of the analysis.

Zetzel (1956) was probably the first to use the term "alliance" and used the terms "working alliance" and "therapeutic alliance" interchangeably. She saw the phases of analysis as paralleling stages of psychological development. That is, the patient, early in the analysis, projected infantile fantasies onto the analyst. According to Zetzel the analyst needed to employ phase-specific clarifying responses to counter the patient's distorted perceptions of the therapist in order to ensure the formation and maintenance of a therapeutic alliance.

In a similar vein, Greenson (1965), in his definition of the "working alliance," drew attention to the realistic (nontransference) aspects of the patient–therapist relationship. He recommended that the analyst actively differentiate the patient's realistic reactions to the analyst (external reality) from internal misperceptions.

These authors maintain that positive and productive treatment alliances do not occur by accident. They require the persistent, informed, and sensitive attention of the therapist. Technically, behaviorally, and affectively the therapist needs to be constantly attuned to the meanings of the dyadic communications that occur. Also, a mutually positive regard of the therapist and patient for each other, while a valuable component of the alliance, is in itself insufficient to achieve the aims of therapy. Only when the therapist and patient become collaborative partners in taking up the tasks of treatment (the working alliance) does the therapy achieve its aims.

The quality of the relationship between the patient and therapist depends upon a complex interplay of factors. Although there are theoretical discussions of the different roots of the patient's feelings about the therapist (Greenson, 1965; Horowitz, 1979), to date there has not been an empirical study which differentiates the social, working, and transferential aspects of the alliance. This remains an unsolved problem in measurement in this area.

Technical Aspects of Our Rating System

The initial version of the Therapeutic Alliance Rating System consisted of 41 items, of which 21 were therapist items (12 TPC items and 9 TNC items) and 20 were patient items (11 positive and 10 negative contributions to the alliance). The positive or negative dimensionality of each item was based on the consensus of four clinical judges (later supported by factor analysis). The rationale for separately scaling the therapist and patient contributions follows from the need to address certain disparities in earlier findings. Clinical reports have focused on the interactive contribution of the two parties in individual psychotherapy sessions. For conceptual and methodological reasons more recent psychotherapy research studies on the therapeutic alliance have tended to focus separately on the contributions of the therapist and patient toward the establishment of a therapeutic relationship. Early research studies, predominantly within the client-centered tradition, focused on the therapist-offered relationship as an important process variable. Gomes-Schwartz (1978) pointed out that although a number of early efforts demonstrated that high levels of the therapist-offered relationship of warmth, understanding, empathy, and respect predicted a good outcome in treatment, more recent efforts to replicate these findings both within and outside of the client-centered school have not yielded consistent results. Gomes-Schwartz concluded that a good therapist-offered relationship sometimes, but not invariably, contributes to a good outcome, and that the patient's contribution to the therapeutic alliance must be taken into account. Similar controversies are raised by Gurman (Gurman & Razin, 1979) who indicates that while the patient's perception of the therapist-offered relationship has been a consistent predictor of therapeutic gains, objective ratings of the therapist-offered relationship by external judges and by the therapists themselves has not been a powerful predictor. While our long-term strategy, therefore, is to address this disparity by developing scales which will separately measure the therapist's and patient's contribution to the alliance, from the unique perspectives of independent clinical judges, the therapist, and the patient, we focused our initial efforts on the rater's version.

Treatment Modalities and Orientations

This system has been primarily developed in the study of time-limited dynamic psychotherapies of persons having neurotic level reactions to stressful situations. Targeted populations have included individuals suffering posttraumatic stress disorders after serious life events, as well as those with adjustment disorders following a variety of less traumatic stressors. The measure is not intended for exclusive use on time-limited dynamic psychotherapies in the context of stress, and pilot studies on cognitive therapies and behavioral therapies appear promising in terms of the more broad applicability of the instrument. While drawing heavily for its theoretical underpinning on psychoanalytic conceptions of the therapeutic alliance, the therapeutic alliance scales are intended to assess the collaborative relationship between the therapist and patient in a more generic sense, and should have relevance in any dyadic therapeutic relationship. The measure is not directly applicable to family or group settings.

Criteria for Selection of Clinical Judges

Clinicians with a psychodynamic orientation have served as judges on therapeutic alliance rating scale tasks. In prior studies we have utilized both experienced clinicians as well as advanced trainees in psychiatry, psychology, and psychiatric social work. As will be reported below, adequate reliabilities can be achieved using advanced trainee raters following intensive calibration training. However, it is our impression that more experienced clinicians can be more readily trained to a criterion of reliability. At this stage of the instrument development we would recommend against the use of a heterogeneous group of raters with disparate levels of experience.

Targeted Clinical Materials and Sampling Procedures

The independent rater version of this scale is designed for scoring of audiorecordings and videorecordings of psychotherapy sessions. Experience to date has been predominantly with the scoring of audiotapes. However, pilot efforts suggest that videotape would be a preferable scoring medium. While we believe that audiotapes represent an advance over process notes and transcripts as a data base, as they permit raters to cue on voice quality as well as verbal content, videotape permits richer access to nonverbal communication, including facial expression, body posture, gestures, and mannerisms. Judgments based on integrative communication patterns with particular attention to incongruencies between verbal comments and nonverbal behavior should permit more fine-grained assessments of the therapeutic alliance. Future studies comparing the reliability and validity of ratings on transcripts, audiotapes, and videotapes would empirically address these distinctions.

Our sampling strategies have focused on relatively lengthy segments selected from the early, middle, and later phases of the therapies. In the case of a 12-session time-limited dynamic psychotherapy, we sampled the second, fifth, eighth, and eleventh sessions, with ratings on selected segments of varying length (25 minutes in some studies, 20 minutes in others). In one study, ratings of the first half of the 50-minute sessions were highly correlated with ratings on the second half, suggesting that the beginning segment may be representative of the whole hour. However, these ratings were done sequentially by the same raters, introducing the possibility of a halo effect accounting for this high correlation, and will be repeated with independent raters, separately assessing the early and late segments. This scoring system is not designed to isolate particular events in the therapeutic interaction, but rather to sample an adequate continuous segment of therapist and patient behavior in an effort to determine the nature of the working relationship.

Scoring, Contextual, and Summarizing Units Used by the System

As is the case with certain other psychotherapy process rating scales, for example, the Experiencing Scale of Klein, Mathieu, Gendlin, and Kiesler (1970) the scoring unit and the contextual unit are identical for the Therapeutic Alliance Rating System. The audio or video contents of particular 20- or 25-minute segments represent the scoring unit, that is, the specific segment of content that is actually rated. In addition, these segments represent the contextual unit, since the rater is not provided with knowledge of any other materials in addition to these segments.

The summarizing unit, defined as the group of scoring units about which some summary statement is made, is variable for the purposes of rating the therapeutic alliance scales. In some instances the ratings of the early, middle, and later hours are pooled to form mean judgments for a whole treatment; in other instances, the rating from an individual half or whole hour segment is used as a more particular unit of rating for subsequent analysis. As an example, alliance ratings on an isolated early treatment hour can be used as a predictor of therapeutic change.

Psychometric Properties of the Therapeutic Alliance Scales: Reliability, Dimensionality, and Validity

Pilot Study of Selected Good and Poor Outcome Cases

In a pilot application of this 41-item scale, Marziali, Marmar, and Krupnick (1981) studied five good outcome and five poor outcome cases. The sample was drawn from a group of 25 patients treated in brief, dynamic psychotherapy at the Center for the Study of Neuroses, Langley Porter Institute, University of California, San Francisco. Nine psychodynamically oriented therapists (two staff psychiatrists, six senior psychiatric residents, and one psychiatric social worker) conducted the 12-session psychotherapies with these patients. Each session was audiorecorded with the informed consent of the participants.

The 10 patients included in the study had all experienced neurotic level reactions to traumatic life events, meeting diagnostic criteria for posttraumatic stress disorder. Eight of the patients were women and two were men, with a mean age of 33.9 years.

The outcome of treatment of these patients was defined as good or bad on the basis of several self-report and rater instruments. These included the Impact of Event Scale (10), a patient self-report of stress specific symptomatology, the Hopkins Symptom Checklist-90 (11), a patient self-report of general symptomatology, and two patient global change ratings.

Two raters (a psychiatric social worker with doctoral training and 18 years clinical experience, and a psychiatric social worker trained at the master's level with 5 years of experience) underwent 12 hours of training prior to rating the sample. In the study proper, each rater judged 40 therapy hours, specifically 4 hours from each of the five good outcome and five poor outcome cases. The 2nd, 5th, 8th, and 11th sessions of each psychotherapy were selected as representative of the phases of the time-limited dynamic treatment. Twenty-minute segments were chosen on a random basis from the first, middle, or last portion of audiorecordings of the hours for rating. In total, then, 40 segments were coded and presented in random fashion to the two raters. Raters were kept blind to the outcomes of treatment as well as to the particular hour being rated.

Results

Good interjudge reliability was achieved on the alliance ratings. The item level reliabilities, calculated using Finn's r (1973), showed an average mean for the therapist items of .82 with a median of .85. For the patient items, the mean Finn's r was .76, with a median of .78.

The intercorrelations of the four theoretically defined dimensions (TPC, TNC, PPC, and PNC) were low across patient–therapist perspectives (example: $r = .03$, ns for patient negative with TNC), and high within patient or therapist perspectives (example: $r = -.88$, $p < .001$ for patient positive with PNC). This led us to collapse the two dimensions in analyzing these data into a Therapist Total Contribution Scale and a Patient Total Contribution Scale. These two newly defined scales had high internal consistencies (alpha = .88 and .94, respectively), and a low intercorrelation ($r = .21$, ns).

In this pilot study we also assessed the relationship bwtween ratings on the therapeutic alliance scales with outcome, employing the Mann–Whitney U Test. It was the statistic of choice for the study because our sample selection purposely violated the assumptions of normality, as it was our strategy to sample from the extremes of the outcome distribution. We found that the patient total contribution to the alliance was predictive of outcome (Mann–Whitney U Test, $U = 0$, $p < .01$), while the therapist total contribution did not differentiate the outcomes. The direction of the relationship of the finding for the patient total contribution was as hypothesized; more positive patient contributions to the alliance were related to favorable symptomatic outcome and more negative patient contributions to the alliance were related to persistent symptomatic disturbance as assessed 4 months after the termination of treatment.

These results were encouraging, both in terms of preliminary reliability and dimensionality properties, as well as predictive capacities. The strategy of sampling good and poor outcome cases increases the power to find an effect if it is there in a small sample. However, in order to be able to generalize the results, we wanted next to rate an entire spectrum of outcomes within a relatively homogeneous cohort of patients. Following the initial study, systematic application of the Therapeutic Alliance Rating System to samples was initiated, both at Langley Porter Psychiatric Institute in San Francisco and the Clarke Institute of Psychiatry in Toronto.

Reliability Studies

Our general procedures for training raters on the observer form of the instrument involves a period of approximately 12 hours of training on calibrated cases. Raters thoroughly familiarize themselves with all extended item definitions as provided in the rating manual. Raters are then trained to a criterion of reliability prior to embarking on the specific rating task. We aimed for an intraclass correlation greater than or equal to .70, based on the appropriate pooled rater estimate form of the statistic. It is our eventual aim to achieve single rater estimates of the intraclass correlation greater than or equal to .70. This magnitude of reliability would permit the economy of having individual raters, rather than teams, to generate observer data. Our present approach is to use a team of raters to generate independent ratings on each targeted data segment in order to continually assess if our data have achieved that threshold of reliability.

Following the initial pilot study, the 41-item version of the measure was scored on 15 selected time-limited dynamic psychotherapies of persons suffering posttraumatic stress disorders. These treatments were done by eight experienced psychotherapists of varied disciplines, averaging 10 years of postlicensure experience. The third and ninth treatment sessions were chosen for scoring in order to sample an early and late session from the therapy. The exception was a single 20-session psychotherapy, in which the 5th and 16th sessions were selected for phase comparability. Two clinical judges independently reviewed the audiotapes of the selected hours, making separate ratings for the first half and second half of the hours.

Interrater reliabilities for each of the scales were calculated using the intraclass coefficient. Because both raters assigned ratings for all segments, we employed the two-way analysis of variance (ANOVA) layout form of the ICC. The coefficients we obtained for the pooled ratings ranged from .50 to .72. It should be noted that these figures include differences in level as well as differences in ordering between the judges' ratings. We next examined the internal consistency or homogeneity of each of the items comprising the four scales. The data used for these calculations were the means of the two judges' ratings for the items. The homogeneity, expressed in terms of coefficient alpha, ranged from .82 to .85.

A third sample, studied for issues of reliability in observer ratings of the therapeutic alliance, involved 52 time-limited dynamic psychotherapies of persons suffering pathological grief reactions, meeting diagnostic criteria for either posttraumatic stress disorder or severe adjustment reactions. The treatments were 12 sessions in length. Thirty-two of the subjects were treated following the death of their parent, and the remaining 20 were women treated following the death of their husband. There were 50 female subjects and two male subjects, both men being a part of the death of a parent group. The mean age of the sample was 39.3 years, with a standard deviation of 14.8 years, and a range of 21 to 72. The mean educational level (using the Hollingshead and Redlich system) was 5.3, with a standard deviation of 1.1 (5 is some college). The mean time elapsed from the date of the bereavement to the date of the initial evaluation was 34.71 weeks, with a standard deviation of 29.13 weeks.

Nine therapists conducted the treatment of these 52 cases. In terms of professional disciplines, five were clinical psychologists, three were psychiatrists, and one was a psychiatric social worker. The male-to-female ratio of therapists was five to four. The average level of postdoctoral clinical experience was 8.8 years. One therapist treated nine cases, two contributed eight, two contributed seven, one contributed six, one contributed four, one treated two cases, and one therapist treated only a single case.

Over this $N = 52$ sample, alliance scale ratings were made by a set of seven raters, all of whom were at one time paired with all the other raters. Pairings were not, however, systematic, and were constructed for logistic purposes. Because of this format, interrater reliabilities were calculated using the one-way ANOVA layout of the ICC. Judges were randomly assigned to position 1 and position 2 before the coefficients were calculated. The pooled individual hour level reliabilities on the sample were marginal for the PNC (.62) and TNC (.51) Scales. In addition lower hour level reliabilities for the Patient Positive Contribution and TPC Scales necessitated a different pooling strategy. We computed the mean rating for each of the hours. Reliability was then assessed using the ICC two-way layout that eliminates the level differences from the denominator (coefficient alpha is equivalent to this form of the ICC). If the mean hour level ratings were not consistent, then the alpha coefficient would have been low when calculated across the 2nd, 5th, 8th, and 11th hours. The analysis produced the following coefficients: .75, .69, .76, and .65 for the TPC, TNC, PPC, and PNC scales, respectively.

Dimensionality Studies

A central question in this line of research concerns the exploration of the dimensions that underlie the alliance construct. As prior theoretical and empirical findings pointed to separate contributions to the alliance by the patient and therapist, we predicted that the factor structure of the alliance ratings in our sample would reflect these separate dimensions. However, the delineation of "patient contributions" or "therapist contributions" is global in character, and we hoped that factor analysis would shed light on meaningful facets of these more broadly defined components. If such factors emerged in a first study, we would attempt to replicate the results in a separately generated sample.

Toward this end, we undertook dimensionality studies in two successive samples. The first was a sample of 15 therapies of posttraumatic stress disorders (the sample described above which produced 60 rated segments). In addition, the structure of the total item pool was investigated. All the coefficients for the four scales were significant; they ranged from .46 to .81. For these nonselected cases, with a more representative range of outcomes, the covariation of the scales was greater than that seen in the Marziali, Marmar, and Krupnick (1981) study of extreme outcome cases. Next, we generated the intercorrelation matrix of the items.

We then subjected this 41×41 matrix to a principal components analysis followed by a varimax rotation. This analysis produced six factors with eigenvalues greater than or equal to 1.0. An examination of the items having strong loadings on the six components indicated a therapist positive factor, a therapist negative factor, two patient positive factors, and two patient negative factors. The two therapist factors were strongly defined by items that corresponded to our theoretical scale designations. This was less obvious for the patient dimensions. The first patient positive factor was interpreted as a dimension assessing patient satisfaction with therapy. This factor was defined by items such as "the patient is hopeful," "the patient is confident about therapy," and "the patient indicates that therapy is helpful." The second patient positive factor appeared to be a working capacity and commitment dimension. This is reflected by the loadings of these items: "The patient is willing to explore own contribution to his troubles," "the patient is willing to self-reflect," and "the patient identifies with the therapist's style of working." There is a similar separation in the two patient negative factors, the first being a patient dissatisfaction with therapy, and the second a negative capacity or lack of commitment to working in treatment. The emergence of separate patient satisfaction and patient working capacity factors points toward a clearer conceptualization of the theoretical constructs, and a revised approach we will discuss later.

Cross-Validation of Factor Structure

In an effort to cross-validate the initial factor structure, audiorecordings of 32 time-limited dynamic psychotherapies of adults treated for neurotic level reactions to the death of a parent were rated on the alliance system. The 2nd, 5th, 8th, and 11th hours of the 12-hour treatments were chosen as representative of the phases of the brief psychotherapy. In cases where mechanical, technical, or contextual factors made use of these hours impossible, a neighboring hour was randomly selected for replacement. This occurred very infrequently, in approximately 3% of the set of ratings. The total data set comprised 128 rated segments.

The sample consisted of 30 women and 2 men, each of whom sought psychotherapy because of difficulty in coping with their response to the death of a parent. The mean age of the sample was 27.1 years, with a range of 21–53 years. Fourteen subjects experienced the death of their father and 17 the death of their mother. One subject had lost both parents. Eight therapists conducted these 32 treatments, one therapist contributing seven cases, three contributing five cases each, and one each contributing four, three, two, and one case, respectively. These eight faculty level therapists included four clinical psychologists, three psychiatrists, and one psychiatric social worker, with a mean of 8.3 years of posttraining clinical experience.

The mean rating from two raters on each of the 128 hours was investigated using a principal components analysis with a varimax rotation. Five factors with eigenvalues greater than 1.0 were extracted. This five-factor solution is similar to the six-factor solution which emerged from the analysis reported above. The exception is that only a single patient negative dimension emerged with an eigenvalue greater than 1.0 in this sample. The two-patient positive factors, patient satisfaction with therapy, and patient working capacity and commitment were confirmed in this solution, replicating the findings for these dimensions.

Studies Assessing the Validity of the Therapeutic Alliance Rating System

Examination of Convergent and Discriminant Validity

Using the $N=52$ sample, mean ratings of hours 2, 5, 8, and 11 on the four alliance scales were correlated with other patient characteristics to assess issues of convergent and discriminant validity. Table 10-1 shows the interrelationships among these variables. None of the four alliance scales was significantly correlated with initial symptomatic distress as determined by the pretherapy levels based on the patient's self-report on the total pathology score on the symptom checklist-90 (SCL-90). That is, scores on the alliance scales are not measures of symptomatic distress. This is consistent with our expectations as there was no theoretical reason to assume that initial distress variables would be significantly related to in-therapy ratings of the therapeutic alliance.

Two pretherapy estimates of relationship stability and maturity, pretreatment social and work functioning as assessed by a composite variable based on ratings using the Patterns of Individual Change Scales (Kaltreider, DeWitt, Weiss, & Horowitz, 1981), and ratings on a measure of developmental level of the self-concept (Horowitz, 1979) were predicted to show some association with subsequent therapeutic alliance ratings. Of these eight correlations, only one showed a significant relationship. Pretherapy estimates of developmental level were associated with the PPC scale ($r=.40$, $p<.01$). This relationship is in the expected direction; patients who were rated at the pretherapy evaluation as having greater stability of self-concept and better differentiation of self and other were scored as making a stronger contribution to the alliance. The judgments of developmental level were made by clinicians who had no knowledge of the ratings made on the alliance system. Similarly, the alliance judges did not have knowledge of

Table 10-1   Pearson Correlations of Alliance Scale Scores with Other Patient Characteristics

Alliance Scale	Pretherapy General Symptoms SCL Total	Developmental Level	Relationship Composite (PICS)	Motivation	Educational Level	Age
Patient Positive Contribution	− .096	.403**	.284	.357*	.016	.426**
Patient Negative Contribution	.228	− .128	− .014	− .266	− .134	.279
Therapist Positive Contribution	.090	.150	.202	.050	− .368**	.295
Therapist Negative Contribution	.132	.074	− .061	− .020	.020	.173

Note: N's vary from 52 to 44.
*$p < .05$
**$p < .01$

the patient's pretreatment ratings on any of the variables used in these analyses.

It was also expected that patients rated as being more motivated for psychotherapy would be subsequently seen as bringing a stronger positive contribution to the therapeutic alliance. This expectation was supported by the positive relationship between motivation and the patient's positive contribution to therapeutic alliance ($r = .36$, $p < .05$). We did not anticipate strong associations among demographic variables with the Therapeutic Alliance Rating System Scales. The results showed no relationship between educational level and both patient's contributions scales. There is an unexpected association between age and the PPC Scale, with older patients rated as having a stronger positive contribution to the alliance ($r = .43$, $p < .01$). There is in addition a negative relationship between educational level and the TPC scale ($r = −.37$, $p < .01$). One possible interpretation of this unexpected finding is that the therapist makes a greater effort to form an alliance with less well-educated patients.

In summary, the relationships among the alliance scales and other patient characteristics lend empirical support toward the validation of the system. Evidence for convergent validity was seen in the meaningful associations between patient motivation and patient developmental level with the PPC Scale. In addition, the lack of correspondence between alliance ratings and general symptomatic distress is an important result supportive of the discriminant validity of the Therapeutic Alliance Rating System. The two results involving demographics and alliance scales were unanticipated and will be further investigated in subsequent studies.

Predictive Validity

We assessed the relationship between the therapeutic alliance scales and outcome in the $N = 52$ sample of time-limited dynamic psychotherapies of persons with either posttraumatic stress disorders or severe adjustment disorders following the death of a loved one. We predicted that the positive scales would be correlated significantly and positively with outcome, and that the negative scales would be negatively correlated with outcome. In our primary data analysis, we computed the partial correlation between each alliance scale and two outcome variables, adjusting outcome for initial level. The outcome variables, selected on the basis of a set of factor analyses of a larger group of variables, were (1) a measure of change over time on the total pathology score of the SCL-90, and (2) a measure of relationship functioning derived from the Patterns of Individual Change Scales (Kaltreider *et al.*, 1981). The alliance scale scores were the mean values pooled over the ratings of hours 2, 5, 8, and 11.

In this primary analysis one of the eight partial correlation coefficients was significant. The mean PNC score was negatively related to the rate of decline in general symptoms, as determined by the SCL-90 change score. This finding was in the predicted direction; patients with a less strong alliance showed less symptomatic relief.

The finding of only one partial correlation of alliance variables with outcome in eight tests of this relationship raised a serious question concerning the predictive capacity of this rating system in explaining therapeutic outcomes. We wondered if certain patient characteristics might differentially interact with alliance ratings, obscuring direct alliance–outcome correlations. To test this hypothesis, we additionally assessed the predictive power of the alliance scores in combination with important characteristics of the patient. In particular, we were interested in the interaction between patient motivation as well as developmental level of the self-concept with therapeutic alliance scale ratings. Motivation scores were generated by independent clinical judges using the Motivation for Psychotherapy Rating Scale (Rosenbaum & Horowitz, in press). The judges reviewed the entire videotaped pretherapy evaluation session and generated reliable ratings on this measure. The other dispositional variable of interest was the patient's developmental level (Horowitz, 1979), as rated by the independent clinician evaluator at the time of the pretherapy interview and described briefly above. It yields an estimate of the patient's stability and coherence of self-concept, also taking into account the character of differentiation of self from other.

We used a hierarchical multiple regression approach to assess the effect on outcomes of the interaction between the alliance variables and the dispositional variables.

The order of entry of the variables in the hierarchical regression was as follows:

Step 1. Initial level of outcome variable.

Step 2. Dispositional variable.

Step 3. Process variable.

Step 4. Dispositional by process interaction-bearing product.

Step 5. (for test of homogeneity of regression of initial level)
   a. Initial level of outcome variable by dispositional interaction-bearing product.
   b. Initial level of outcome variable by process interaction-bearing product.
   c. Initial level of outcome variable by dispositional times process interaction-bearing product.

With motivation entered as the dispositional variable, there were eight possible results (four therapeutic alliance scores and two outcome variables). The preliminary steps of the hierarchical regression showed that the initial value of SCL-90 accounted for 19% of the variance in the SCL-90 change variable ($R^2 = .189$, $p = .002$). Motivation, entered as the next variable, accounted for only an additional 2% of the variance, which was not significant. In the tests of the alliance by motivation interactions, two of the four analyses showed significant increments in variance accounted for by the interaction term. The result that accounted for the greater proportion of variance (increment in $R^2 = .20$, $p < .01$, 26% of the adjusted variance) was the association of the interaction between the PPC Scale and motivation to general symptom change. The relationship between PPC and outcome was positive for lower values of motivation, and shifted from positive to negative as motivation increased.

The second significant result was the relationship of the interaction between motivation and PNC to general symptom change. This term accounted for an additional 10% of the variance of outcome (increment in $R^2 = .10$, $p < .05$; 13% of adjusted variance). These results are the negative parallel of those presented above, that is, PNC was negatively related to outcome at low levels of motivation, but changed direction and became positive as motivation increased.

The tests of the motivation by alliance interactions using the work and social functioning outcome variable all yielded nonsignificant results. In that set, the initial level accounted for 30% of the variance in the final level of relationship status ($R^2 = .297$, $p = .001$), and motivation by itself accounted for another 6% ($p = .005$). Eight similar regression analyses were conducted using developmental level as the dispositional variable. They did not provide significant findings as none of the interaction terms added a significant increment over and above the contribution of the initial symptom level, the dispositional variable, and the process variable by itself.

What is the meaning of these results? As with other studies, including an earlier pilot finding in our own center (Marziali, Marmar, & Krupnick, 1981) the clinical judges' ratings of the patient's contribution to the therapeutic alliance were significantly associated with outcome. The multiple regression analysis indicated that motivation interacted with scales of the therapeutic alliance as a predictor of outcome in a meaningful way. The data suggest that especially in patients with low motivation, attention to establishment of a positive attitude toward the therapeutic alliance may be associated with better therapeutic results. The TPC and TNC Scales, as determined by clinical judges' ratings of tape recordings of selected psychotherapy sessions, did not correlate with outcome, either alone or in interaction with dispositional characteristics.

Of interest is the fact that the effect size for significant interactions of alliance by disposition which were found was substantial, considering the statistical approach used. It can be compared with the effect size of initial level as a predictor of final outcome level, one of the most robust predictors of outcome in psychotherapy research. For both the SCL-90 change and the work and relationship variables, the initial level value was significantly and substantially correlated with outcome, accounting for 20% in SCL-90 outcome and nearly 30% in the work and relationship variable. When an interaction of alliance by disposition term was significant, the size of the effect was about the same as that for initial symptom level. This is so even though the interaction is accounting for variance over and above that of initial level, disposition, and process.

Therapist- and Patient-Rated Versions of the Alliance Scale

Another phase of the development of the alliance measurement system was carried out at the Clarke Institute of Psychiatry, Toronto, Canada. The thrust of this work involved the assessment of the similarities and differences between three evaluative perspectives of the therapeutic alliance; that is, patient, therapist, and external judge alliance ratings of the same sessions. The only other example of scales that elicit both patient and therapist perceptions of the therapeutic relationship are Orlinsky and Howard's Session Reports (Orlinsky & Howard, 1975), and Saltzman's Session Ratings (Saltzman, Leutgert, Roth, Creaser, & Howard, 1976). However, in both of these methods the items used for the patient-rated scale did not duplicate those used for the therapist-rated scale. No studies were found which used the same scales to rate the alliance from the separate perspectives of the patient, the therapist, and an external judge. It was assumed that each perspective would provide unique information about the relationship and in particular that patient responses could not be fully understood until parallel rating schemes were used to determine the patient, therapist, and external rater evaluations of the therapeutic alliance at the same points across the entire course of treatment.

Development of the Scales

The original external rater scale described earlier was in part reorganized. Some items were reformulated to ensure unidimensionality, uniformity of language, and a balance of positive and negative items. Each item is represented in each of the three rating systems in the same order, but is addressed differently to suit the perspective of each of three groups of raters—the patients, the therapists, and the external judges. An example follows:

Patient-Completed Scale
   Item 6: To what extent did your therapist's comments help you to feel good about yourself?

Therapist-Completed Scale
   Item 6: To what extent did your comments help your patient to feel good about him or herself?

External Rater Scale
   Item 6: To what extent did the therapist's comments help the patient to feel good about him or herself?

The final form of the scales in each of the rating systems consists of 21 therapist contribution items (11 positive and 10 negative) and 21 patient contribution items (11 positive and 10 negative).

Psychometric Properties

The alliance was rated from the three perspectives in a study of brief psychotherapy. The sample consisted of 42 patients, selected on specific criteria from the general pool of patients referred to a psychiatric outpatient service. The selection criteria were generated from Malan's indications and contraindications for brief psychotherapy. The criteria for patient inclusion comprised a history of sustaining some satisfactory relationships, motivation for exploring the meaning of symptoms and behavior, and evidence that a circumscribed treatment focus could be maintained during the course of a brief therapeutic contact. Criteria for exclusion included indications of psychotic disturbance, evidence of complex, deep-seated psychological issues which there seemed no hope of working through in a short time, and indications that prolonged work would be necessary in order to develop a productive therapeutic alliance. Three experienced clinicians independently rated videotapes of the patient assessment interviews. For inclusion, two of the three judges needed to agree fully on the presence of all criteria of inclusion and on the absence of all criteria of exclusion. Approximately one-third of all patients referred qualified for the study. Once selected, each patient was randomly assigned for treatment to one of 15 experienced psychodynamically oriented therapists.[1] The 20-session treatments were audiorecorded.

All study patients were given DSM III, Axis I and Axis II diagnoses by the assessing clinician. On Axis I, 52% were diagnosed as having dysthymic disorders or adjustment disorders with depressed mood, and 24% had anxiety disorders or adjustment disorders with mixed disturbance of emotion. The remaining 24% had Code V, phase of life problems. On Axis II the majority of patients were classified as having compulsive, histrionic, or narcissistic personality disorders. Seven more severely disturbed patients were diagnosed as schizoid or borderline personality disorders.

Demographically, the study sample consisted of 11 men and 31 women; their mean age was 30.5; 20 were single, 12 were married or living common-law, 9 were separated or divorced, and 1 was widowed. Seven of the patients had completed some high school education and 35 had postsecondary education ranging from 2 years at a community college to 4 years postgraduate training. In terms of occupation, 21 were professionally employed, 8 were employed in clerical positions, 2 were employed in skilled areas of work, 6 were unemployed, and 5 were students. Fifteen of the 42 patients had had some previous psychotherapy, but not within the year prior to beginning the 20-session therapy. Thirty-five patients completed therapy (20 sessions), five terminated by mutual agreement, at sessions 10, 13, 14, 16, and 17, and two patients prematurely terminated at session 5.

Alliance Ratings

After providing written consent, patients and therapists completed the alliance measures immediately following sessions 1, 3, 5, 10, 15, and 20. Most studies have assessed the alliance at some point following the second to the sixth session, following on Barrett-Lennard's suggestion that five therapy sessions allows for "a safe minimum period of association between client and therapist that would provide the participants with a meaningful basis from which to answer the relationship inventory items" (Barrett-Lennard, 1962). In this study the earlier and later sessions were included in order to examine the variability, if any, across the entire therapy.

For the external rater scale, two judges, both social workers with a minimum of 5 years posttraining clinical experience, were trained using a revised manual which paralleled the second version of the scale. The same sessions that were rated by the patient and the therapist were also rated by the external judges. For each patient the first, middle, or last 20 minutes of each of the six sessions was chosen on a random basis for rating. The segments were coded and randomly presented to the two judges who were blind to the outcomes. Interrater reliability was calculated using the standard one-way ANOVA in which the between-judges variance was included in the error term (Tinsley & Weiss, 1975). The intraclass correlation coefficients for ratings of the patient contribution positive and negative item subscales ranged between .60 and .83, and for ratings of the therapist contribution positive and negative item subscales ranged between .61 and .77.

---

1. Distribution of patients per therapist was as follows: One treated one patient, eight therapists treated two patients each, three treated three patients each, one treated four patients, and two treated six patients each.

Outcome Measures

Treatment effects were measured from three perspectives; the patient, the therapist, and clinician judges. The patients completed Derogatis' Behavior Symptom Index (Derogatis, Lipman, & Covi, 1973), Beck's Mood Scale (Beck, Ward, Mendelson, Mock, & Erbough, 1961), and Weissman's Social Adjustment Scale (Weissman & Bothwell, 1976), pretherapy and again 3 months following the termination of therapy. The patients and therapists completed Therapy Evaluation Forms which measured the patient's overall change following treatment termination. Dynamic outcome was measured on five scales which were derived from Malan's Method for Evaluating Global Outcome (Malan, 1976) and Kaltreider's Patterns of Individual Change Scales (PICS) (Kaltreider et al. 1981). Five scales were selected from the PICS measure on the basis of the general criteria which Malan included in his estimates of global outcome. However, unlike Malan's method, individual change criteria for each patient were not generated for the ratings. Raters observed in succession videotapes of the assessment and 3-month follow-up interviews, and assigned a change score on each of the scales. The scales included measurements of (1) Friendship, (2) Intimacy, (3) Capacity to Use Support, (4) Self-Esteem, and (5) Assertiveness. Each scale was rated on an 11-point Lickert-type scale ranging from -5 (substantially worse) to $+5$ (substantially better). A manual was developed to describe behavioral changes and score equivalents in each category. Two experienced clinician judges were trained to apply uniformly the operational definition for each scale. Interrater reliability was calculated using the one-way ANOVA of the ICC (Tinsley & Weiss, 1975). The coefficients for the five scales ranged from .83 to .95. The mean score of the five scales was computed to yield a dynamic total score.

Alliance Scale Analysis

In an initial analysis of the scales, a principal component factor analysis with varimax rotations was carried out on each of the alliance measurement systems: patient rated, therapist rated, and external judge rated. These exploratory analyses were carried out even though there was a less than optimal number of subjects in proportion to the number of scale items.

The purpose of the analyses was to examine the consistency of the factor structure both within and between the three measurement systems. For all analyses the scores on the negatively polarized items were reversed, so that high scores indicated positivity for all items. The factor analyses were carried out on each of the six rated sessions using all the scale items. The analyses were repeated for each session using each of the subscales; that is, the patient's ratings of him or herself (positive and negative items) and the patient's ratings of the therapist (positive and negative items). The same analyses were repeated for each of the three measurement systems. The factor structure was consistent for all three measurement systems across all six sessions and for each of the subscales within each measurement system. Two factors emerged: Factor I, consisting of all positive items; Factor II, consisting of all negative items. The criteria used for item inclusion in each of the factors were coefficients of .50 or better and item loading on the same factor for all three measurement systems. Factor I consisted of 14 positive items: six item ratings of the patient and eight item ratings of the therapist. Factor II consisted of 11 negative items: six item ratings of the patient and five item ratings of the therapist.

Items that loaded on the positive factor included the following: (1) The therapist conveyed that he or she liked the patient, felt hopeful about therapy, was committed to help, encouraged and supported the patient, and conveyed a feeling of mutually working together; and (2) the patient felt helped, hopeful, liked the therapist, and was willing to examine his or her behavior and understand his or her problems. Items that loaded on the negative factor included the following: (1) The therapist was judgmental, criticized the patient, ignored the patient's wishes, and communicated annoyance about the patient's slow progress, and (2) the patient expressed anger, avoidance, resistance, and argued with the therapist. The findings of these analyses (the positive and negative item-loadings on separate factors) paralleled the findings of the California group's work; however, the number of factors differed.

The analyses of the factor structure corroborate the clinical reasoning used when the original scales were constructed. That is, unlike the development of most psychological measurement schemes, in the construction of these scales the negative items were not intended to be viewed as inverse equivalents of the positive items. Rather, scale items were selected to reflect clinical judgment as to what constituted either positive or negative behaviors in either the patient or the therapist. Thus the negative item subscales are intended to reflect separate and different dimensions than those represented in the positive item subscales.

All subsequent analyses of the three alliance measurement systems were conducted using the original 42 items.

Internal Reliability

The internal consistency of the positive and negative contribution subscales for each of the three measurement systems was evaluated using Cronback's Alpha Statistic. The results of the patient ratings are as follows: the patient rating him or herself on positive items, alpha = .85, the patient rating him or herself on negative items, alpha = .81; the patient rating the therapist on positive items, alpha = .88; the patient rating the therapist on negative items, alpha = .89. For the therapist ratings of the alliance, the results are as follows: the therapist rating the patient on positive items, alpha = .89; the therapist rating the patient on negative items, alpha = .86; the therapist rating him or herself on positive items, alpha = .89; and the therapist rating him or herself on negative items, alpha = .82. For the external judge ratings of the alliance the results of the reliability analysis were similar: the judge ratings of the patient positive items, alpha = .93; the external judge ratings of the patient negative items, alpha = .88; the external judge ratings of the therapist positive items, alpha = .86; the external judge ratings of the therapist negative items, alpha = .87.

Within Rating System Correlations

For each of the three rating systems, the mean scores of the six session alliance ratings of the patients' separate positive and negative contributions and the therapists' separate positive and negative contributions were computed. Within each of the three rating systems, the separate patient positive and negative contributions were correlated with the separate therapist positive and negative contributions. The patients' ratings of their own positive contributions correlated significantly with their positive ratings of the therapist ($r = .79$). Similarly, the patients' negative self-ratings correlated with negative perceptions of the therapist ($r = .82$). This pattern was replicated in the other two measurement systems. The therapists' positive ratings of the patient were correlated with their positive self-ratings and yielded an r value of .70, and for the correlations between the therapists' negative ratings of the patients and their negative self-ratings, the r value was .71. For the external judges' ratings, correlations of the positive ratings of the patient and positive ratings of the therapist resulted in an r value of .51, and correlations of the negative ratings of both the therapist and the patient resulted in an r value of .51.

The consistency of the patients' and therapists' ratings of self and of the other partner in the relationship probably indicates that interactive factors influence these ratings. For example, when the patient rates him or herself, ratings are influenced by perceptions of the therapist and similarly when he or she rates the therapist, these ratings are influenced by self-perceptions. The same argument applies to the therapist's ratings. These results are expected, since neither the patient nor the therapist can be expected to provide objective ratings of each other or of themselves when the perceptions necessary for making these judgments draw on an interpersonal process which, by its very nature, is subjective.

Between Rating System Correlations

The mean scores of the patients' ratings of their own positive and negative contributions and the therapists' positive and negative contributions were correlated with the mean scores of the therapists' and external judges' ratings of the same subscales. The results of the 12 sets of correlations are as follows: the patients' ratings of their own positive contributions correlated significantly with both the therapists' ($r = .65$) and the external judges' ($r = .56$) positive item ratings of the patients. Also the therapists and external judges rated the patients' positive contributions in a similar direction ($r = .59$). The intercorrelations of the three system ratings of the therapists' positive contributions were significantly lower (r range .32 to .41). There was agreement between the three rating systems in ratings of the patients' negative contributions (patients and therapists $r = .43$; patients and external judges $r = .44$; and therapists and external judges $r = .51$). However, there was little agreement between the three measurement systems in their ratings of the therapists' negative contributions. All three coefficients from this latter intercorrelational matrix were nonsignificant.

These results indicate that the patients, therapists, and external judges were in significant agreement in their ratings of the patients' positive and negative contributions. There was somewhat less agreement between the three rating systems in their judgment of the therapists' positive contributions, and no agreement in their estimation of the therapists' negative contributions. Clearly, in making their ratings, the patients, the therapists, and the external judges drew on different perceptions of negative aspects of the therapists' behaviors. Possibly the therapists and clinical judges experienced conflict in making negative judgments about professional performance. Alternately, professional envy or competitiveness may have determined the external judges' ratings of the therapists. It may be also true that the therapists either underestimated or overestimated their own negative contributions because of the difficulty in maintaining objectivity while immersed in a subjective process. The patients may have been cautious in rating the therapists negatively, fearing that the results of the ratings would be shown to their therapists, even though they were assured from the onset of therapy that this would not be the case.

Between and Within System Variations of Ratings
Across All Six Sessions

A multivariate analysis of variance was computed to assess between and within system of measurement effects across the six measurement times. The averaged rater responses (mean of patient, therapist, and external ratings) on the patient positive alliance contributions were significantly lower in the first and third sessions in contrast with the

20th session (Scheffe Averaged $F=5.6$, $p<.001$). Similarly, across raters, the therapists' positive contributions were significantly lower in the first session as compared with the 20th session (Scheffe Averaged $F=9.5$, $p<.001$). The three rater groups did not significantly vary in their estimates of the patients' and therapists' negative contributions across the six measurement times.

The between rater group differences were as follows: Overall, the therapists rated the patients' positive alliance behaviors significantly lower than either the patients or external judges (Wilks Lambda Averaged $F=5.4$, $p<.01$). The therapists rated themselves less negatively than the averaged patients' and external judges' ratings (Wilks Lambda Averaged $F=11.7$, $p<.001$). Similarly, the patients rated themselves less negatively than either the therapists or external judges (Wilks Lambda Averaged $F=5.1$, $p<.01$). The patients viewed their therapists less positively than either the therapists or the external judges. Also, the averaged patients' and judges' ratings of the therapists' positive contributions were significantly lower than the therapists' self-ratings (Wilks Lambda Averaged $F=8.9$, $p<.001$).

The assessment of the between session and between measurement system estimates of the alliance supports clinical expectations. During the initial phase of therapy (Sessions 1 and 3) the positive components of the treatment relationship are not well established. Thus, the lower ratings of the patients' and therapists' positive contributions in these early sessions in contrast to the final session illustrate the progression of the development of the therapeutic encounter. Typically, patients and therapists use the first three to five sessions to explore compatible modes for relating to each other. If, following this early tentative interaction, the relationship achieves a positive stance, then the work of therapy is carried through to a positive outcome, reflected in the higher ratings in the final session. For the between measurement system differences it is interesting to note that, in the overall ratings, the patients rated themselves less negatively than the other two sets of raters, whereas the therapists rated themselves more negatively than either the patients or external judges. Also, the patients and therapists rated the other less positively than either the external judges or their treatment partner. Several explanations of these results may apply. The patients possibly are less aware of the negativeness which they communicate in the therapeutic encounter, whereas the therapists' negative self-ratings may reflect awarenesses of counterreactions which are perceived to be adversely influencing the therapeutic relationship. The fact that the treatment partners rate the other less positively than they rate themselves suggests that the more positive self-ratings may reflect a sense of hopefulness about the worth of their own therapeutic efforts. Also, the less positive perception of the treatment partner may provide an ongoing threat to the therapeutic relationship; that is, it may characterize the anxiety which mobilizes motivation and commitment to continue the work of therapy.

Convergent and Discriminant Validity

The total mean scores of the six session alliance ratings of the patients' positive and negative contributions within each of the three systems of measurement were correlated with three pretherapy measures of the patient's social adjustment and symptomatic status. The patients' pretherapy ratings of social adjustment correlated significantly with (1) their negative self-ratings and ratings of the therapists' negative contributions; (2) the therapists' ratings of the patients' positive and negative contributions; and (3) the external judges' ratings of the patients' negative contributions (r range .34 to .51). All correlations were in the expected direction. These were expected relationships. Patients who experience themselves, pretherapy, as having more stable and satisfying networks of social relationships will more readily establish a positive relationship with the therapist and view the therapist positively. Conversely, patients who view themselves as having problematic social relationships will view themselves and their therapists more negatively. The mean scores of both the therapist and external judge ratings systems did not correlate with either the pretherapy symptom index scores or the pretherapy mood scores. For the patient rating system, the patients' judgment of the therapists' negativeness was significantly correlated with both the pretherapy symptom index and mood scores; however, the r values, in each case, were of a low magnitude (.26 and .25).

Predictive Validity

The associations between the mean scores of the subscales of each of the three alliance rating systems and outcome were assessed. A partial correlation between each of the subscales within each rating system and six outcome variables, in each instance adjusting outcome for initial level, was computed. The outcome measures consisted of the Derogatis Symptom Index, the Beck Mood Scale, the Weissman Social Adjustment Scale, both Patient and Therapist Post Therapy Evaluations, and an Estimate of Dynamic Outcome. Three outcome measures (patient and therapist evaluations, and clinician judges' estimates of dynamic outcome) were completed only at follow-up. The patients' evaluation of outcome correlated significantly with the patients' pretherapy ratings of social adjustment, and the therapists' and clinician judges' estimates of outcome correlated significantly with initial symptomatic level. Consequently, in all partial correlations with the patients' evaluations of outcome the effects of initial level social adjustment was controlled; and for the partial correlations with the therapists' and clinician judges' evaluations of outcome initial symptomatic level was controlled.

For each of the three rating systems, the mean scores of the separate patients' and therapists' positive and negative contributions were used in all the computations. Seventy-two partial correlations were computed. Of these, 27 coefficients were significant (see Table 10-2). Consistently the patients' positive and negative contributions estimated in each of the three rating systems were the best predictors of outcome. All coefficients were in the expected direction; that is, positive patient contributions were positively associated with greater improvement as rated posttherapy by the patients, the therapists, and the clinical judges. These findings were consistent across all three rating systems. Similarly, the therapists' positive contributions rated in each of the three systems were correlated, in the expected direction, with the patients' and therapists' posttherapy evaluations of outcome, and with dynamic outcome. In addition, the patients' and therapists' ratings of their own positive contributions were positively associated with a decrease in general symptoms posttherapy.

In the next set of analyses, partial correlations with outcome were computed using the mean scores of the patients' and therapists' positive and negative contributions, computed from the first and third sessions. The analyses were repeated for all three rating systems. The purpose of this analyses was to explore whether or not the early ratings of the alliance might be equally predictive of outcome as the six session ratings of the alliance. The findings paralleled those obtained when the mean scores of the alliance ratings of the six sessions were used. In general, the coefficients were of a lower magnitude (see Table 10-3).

These findings indicate that regardless of which alliance rating system is used, esti-

Table 10-2   Partial Correlations of Subscales of Three Alliance Rating Systems with Outcome (Using Means Scores of Ratings of Six Sessions)

	General Symptoms	Depressive Mood	Social Adjustment	Patient Evaluation	Therapist Evaluation	Clinician Evaluation (Dynamic Outcome)
Patient Rating System						
Patient positive items	− .34*	− .18	− .14	.57***	.43**	.38**
Patient negative items	− .11	− .07	.22	.31*	.27*	.01
Therapist positive items	− .30*	− .16	− .07	.45**	.29*	.47**
Therapist negative items	.02	.01	.28	.07	.23	− .16
Therapist Rating System						
Patient positive items	− .37**	− .17	.04	.52**	.51***	.14
Patient negative items	− .23	− .21	.18	.35*	.38**	.13
Therapist positive items	− .30**	− .22	.02	.32*	.32*	.13
Therapist negative items	.04	.06	.11	.23	.29*	.03
External Judges Rating System						
Patient positive items	− .14	− .08	.11	.59***	.48**	.25*
Patient negative items	− .03	.01	.27	.43**	.48**	.27*
Therapist positive items	− .11	− .21	− .16	.30*	.08	.19
Therapist negative items	− .15	.11	.21	− .01	− .03	− .02

Note: (1) Scores on negatively polarized items were reversed so that high scores indicate positivity for all items, and (2) due to missing data, the N's vary from 42 to 26.

*$p < .05$
**$p < .01$
***$p < .001$

mates of both the patients' and therapists' positive contributions to the therapeutic alliance are the best predictors of outcome following a course of brief psychotherapy. Of particular interest is the fact that early estimates of the positivity of the alliance are associated with outcome. These beginning trends in the therapeutic encounter can be determined as early as the first and third sessions.

The analyses of three measurement systems of the therapeutic alliance expand clinical understanding of the impact of this factor in the process of psychotherapy. One of the more interesting findings was the uniform agreement between each measurement system on estimates of the patients' and therapists' positive contributions. That is, the therapists and external judges agreed with each other and with the patients' ratings of the patients and therapists positive alliance behaviors. The consistency across the three measurement systems is supported in the findings of the partial correlations be-

Table 10-3   Partial Correlations of Subscales of Three Alliance Rating Systems with Outcome (Using Mean Scores of Sessions I and III)

	General Symptoms	Depressive Mood	Social Adjustment	Patient Evaluation	Therapist Evaluation	Clinician Evaluation (Dynamic Outcome)
Patient Rating System						
Patient positive items	−.22	−.16	−.19	.47**	.30*	.34*
Patient negative items	−.15	−.06	−.18	.23	.25*	−.06
Therapist positive items	−.23	−.17	−.21	.39**	.18	.46**
Therapist negative items	−.01	−.05	−.19	−.01	.28	−.24
Therapist Rating System						
Patient positive items	−.29*	−.17	−.04	.33*	.34**	.12
Patient negative items	−.23	−.21	.29	.23	.12	−.01
Therapist positive items	−.30*	−.22	−.04	.33*	.21	.14
Therapist negative items	.04	.06	.22	.19	.18	−.16
External Judges Rating System						
Patient positive items	−.09	−.09	.04	.31	.33*	.14
Patient negative items	−.03	−.12	.07	.20	.35**	.04
Therapist positive items	−.19	−.27*	−.23	.20	.10	.29*
Therapist negative items	.24	.11	.13	−.22	.12	−.21

Note: (1) Scores on negatively polarized items were reversed so that high scores indicate positivity for all items, and (2) due to missing data, the N's vary from 42 to 26.
   *p<.05
  **p<.01
***p<.001

tween the patients' and therapists' positive contributions and four of the six measurements of outcome.

Integration of Results Across Studies

As noted in Table 10-2, 27 of 72 partial correlations of alliance variables (from the three perspectives of patient, therapist and external judge) with outcome were found to reach significance in the Toronto study. At first glance, these results seem to be at variance with the findings reported in the "N=52" California bereavement sample as reported on page 373. In that bereavement sample, only one out of eight partial correlations of alliance with outcome reached significance. However, if one were to exclusively examine those findings in Table 10-2 for comparable alliance and outcome variables to the earlier California bereavement sample, then only two of eight partial correlations are significant (external judge ratings of the alliance with general symptomatic and dynamic outcome variables). Further, in this subset of findings in the Toronto sample, it is the external judges' ratings of the patient's, rather than the therapist's, contribution to the alliance that is predictive in these two restrictive domains of outcome. This finding replicates both the pilot study sample and the "N=52" bereavement sample findings of the California group.

It is of interest that the strongest and most prevalent findings reported in Table 10-2 are for alliance ratings with " patient evaluation" and "therapist evaluation" outcomes (18 of 24 tests yielded significant correlations). These two outcome variables, which represent posttreatment global ratings of change by either the patient or therapist, were not employed in the California studies. By contrast, in the Toronto findings reported in Table 10-2, 4 of 12 tests of alliance variables with general symptomatic outcome were significant, 0 of 12 tests of alliance with depressive symptoms were significant, 0 of 12 tests of alliance with social adjustment outcome were significant, and 4 of 12 tests of alliance with dynamic outcome were significant. The findings that alliance ratings were consistently and strongly predictive of global change determinations of outcome, but were inconsistent and of lower magnitude in the prediction of symptomatic, social functioning, and dynamic outcomes, has important implications. It raises questions concerning the nature of the underlying issues tapped by alliance ratings systems, as well as the profound effect different approaches to the measurement of change in psychotherapy can have on process–outcome relationships.

Of further interest is the finding in the Toronto sample, reported in Table 10-2, of a number of significant correlations of both therapist positive and therapist negative contributions to the alliance with outcome. This is an important finding since, in our own prior research and that of other investigators (for example, the findings of Gomes-Schwartz in the Vanderbilt study), it has been exclusively the patient's contribution to the alliance which has consistently predicted outcome. Of the total of 36 tests of therapist contribution to the alliance with outcome (two therapist contribution variables × three ratings systems × six outcomes), nine reached significance. These findings for therapist contributions as predictors of outcome suggest a strategy of further systematic investigation of those therapist actions which might contribute to the alliance, especially when the patient is initially reluctant to enter into a working collaboration with the therapist. Both the California and Toronto groups are presently pursuing such a line of investigation. Initial findings reported by Foreman and Marmar (1985) support the importance of therapist interventions that address the patient's problematic feelings towards the therapist, as well as the patient's defensive avoidance of communicating these negative reactions to the therapist in the immediate "here and now" of the treatment situation, as strategies countering an initially poor therapeutic alliance.

Summary

Generation of the initial item pool for the rating system drew upon three separate conceptual sources. The first was the theoretical writings of authors predominantly from the psychoanalytic tradition including Alexander (1946), Zetzel (1956), Greenson (1965), Langs (1975), and Dickes (1975). In addition, the important contribution of Frank (1971) which addressed the "nonspecific" aspects of the healing therapeutic climate was influential in the generation of the initial item pool. The second major influence was the prior empirical work on the therapeutic alliance including studies by Bordin (1975), Luborsky (1976; Morgan, Luborsky, & Crits-Christoph, 1982), Strupp (1958; Moras & Strupp, 1982), and Hartley (1978), as well as colleagues working within these psychotherapy research centers. Finally, results of intensive case studies applying the method of configurational analysis (Horowitz, 1979) provided novel items for the original pool.

At the next step of development, the initial item pool was circulated to a group of experienced practitioners working within the psychodynamic tradition for suggestions and revision. Pilot applications involved experienced clinicians using tape recorded psychotherapy sessions. Their efforts led to useful modifications of the original items pool. At that stage of development of the system, the items along with their theoretical rationale and organization were sent to a number of professional experts on the subject of the therapeutic alliance, and detailed feedback was provided guiding further modification.

The subsequent steps involved the psychometric evaluation of the external judge rating system as well as the development and psychometric evaluation of parallel patient and therapist ratings systems.

Results of work to date demonstrate some of the consistencies and discrepancies between rating systems as well as possible problems with dimensions within systems. There is a need to reconsider the optimal number of dimensions required to encompass the domain of the therapeutic alliance. At the same time, these results suggest that there may be a need to separately assess some dimensions within rating systems that have, up to this point, been combined into single variables.

References

Alexander, F. *Psychoanalytic therapy*. Chicago: University of Chicago Press, 1946.

Barrett-Lennard, G. T. Dimensions of therapist response as causal factors in therapeutic change. *Psychological Monographs, 76* (43, whole No. 562), 1962.

Beck, A. T., Ward, C. H., Mendelson, M., Mock, J., & Erbough, J. An inventory for measuring depression. *Archives of General Psychiatry*, 1961, 4, 561–571.

Bordin, E. S. *The generalizibility of the psychoanalytic concepts of the working alliance*. Paper presented to annual meeting of the Society of Psychotherapy Research, Boston, 1975.

Derogatis, L. R., Lipman, R. S., & Covi, L. SCL-90: An outpatient psychiatric rating scale— preliminary report. *Psychopharmocological Bulletin*, 1973, 9, 13-28.

Dickes, R. Technical consideration of the therapeutic and working alliance. *International Journal of Psychoanalytic Psychotherapy*, 1975, 4, 1–24.

Finn, R. H. A note on estimating the reliability of categorical data. *Educational and Psychological Measurement,* 1973, *3,* 71–76.

Foreman, S. A., & Marmar, C. R. Therapist actions that address initially poor therapeutic alliances in psychotherapy. *American Journal of Psychiatry,* 1985, *142,* 922–926.

Frank, J. D. Therapeutic factors in psychotherapy. *American Journal of Psychiatry,* 1971, *25,* 350–361.

Freud, S. The dynamics of transference. *Standard Edition,* 1912, *12,* 97–108.

Freud, S. On the beginning of treatment. *Standard Edition,* 1913, *12,* 121–144.

Freud, S. Analysis terminable and interminable. *Standard Edition,* 1937, *23,* 209–253.

Gomes-Schwartz, B. Effective ingredients in psychotherapy: Prediction of outcome from process variables. *Journal of Consulting and Clinical Psychology,* 1978, *46,* 1023–1035.

Greenson, R. The working alliance and the transference neuroses. *Psychoanalytic Quarterly,* 1965, *34,* 155–181.

Gurman, A. S. & Razin, A. M. *Effective psychotherapy: A handbook of research.* New York: Pergamon Press, 1977.

Hartley, D. Therapeutic alliance and the success of brief individual psychotherapy. Unpublished Doctoral Dissertation, Vanderbilt University, 1978.

Horowitz, M. J. *States of mind.* New York: Plenum Press, 1979.

Horowitz, M. J., Wilner, N., & Alvarez, W. Impact of Event Scale: A measure of subjective stress. *Psychosomatic Medicine,* 1979, *41,* 209–218.

Kaltreider, N. B., DeWitt, K. N., Weiss, D. S., & Horowitz, M. J. Patterns of Individual Change Scales. *Archives of General Psychiatry,* 1981, *38,* 1263–1269.

Klein, M., Mathieu, P. L., Gendlin, E. T., & Kiersler, O. J. *The Experiencing Scale: A research and training manual.* (2 vols.). Madison: Wisconsin Psychiatric Institute, Bureau of Audio-visual Instruction, 1970.

Langs, R. Therapeutic misalliances. *International Journal of Psychoanalytic Psychotherapy,* 1975, *4,* 77–105.

Luborsky, L. Helping alliance in psychotherapy. In J. L. Cleghorn, (Ed.), *Successful psychotherapy.* New York: Brunner/Mazel, 1976.

Malan, D. H. *Toward the validation of dynamic psychotherapy.* New York: Plenum, 1976.

Marziali, E., Marmar, C., & Krupnick, J. Therapeutic alliance scales: Development and outcome. *American Journal of Psychiatry,* 1981, *138,* 361–364.

Moras, K., & Strupp, H. H. Pretherapy interpersonal relations, patients' alliance, and outcome in brief therapy. *Archives of General Psychiatry,* 1982, *39.*

Morgan, R., Luborsky, L., & Crits-Cristoph, P. Predicting the outcomes of psychotherapy by the Penn Helping Alliance Rating Method. *Archives of General Psychiatry,* 1982, *39,* 397–402.

Orlinsky, D., & Howard, K. *Varieties of psychotherapeutic experience.* New York: Teachers College Press, 1975.

Rosenbaum, R. R., & Horowitz, M. J. Motivation for psychotherapy: A factorial and conceptual analysis. *Psychotherapy: Theory, Research, and Practice,* in press.

Saltzman, C., Leutgert, M. J., Roth, C. H., Creaser, J., & Howard, L. Formation of a therapeutic relationship: Experiences during the initial phase of psychotherapy as predictors of treatment duration and outcome. *Journal of Consulting and Clinical Psychology,* 1976, *44,* 546–555.

Strupp, H. H. The psychotherapist's contribution to the treatment process. *Behavioral Science,* 1958, *3,* 34–67.

Tinsley, H. E., & Weiss, D. J. Interrater reliability and agreement of subjective judgements. *Journal of Counselling Psychology,* 1975, *22,* 358–376.

Weissman, M., & Bothwell, S. Assessment of social adjustment by patient self-report. *Archives of General Psychiatry,* 1976, *33,* 1111–1115.

Zetzel, E. Current concepts of transference. *International Journal of Psychoanalysis,* 1956, *37,* 369–376.

11

Breaking the Family Code: Analysis of Videotapes of Family Interactions by Structural Analysis of Social Behavior (SASB)

Lorna Smith Benjamin
Sharon W. Foster
Laura Giat Roberto
Sue E. Estroff
Department of Psychiatry, University of Wisconsin
and Wisconsin Psychiatric Research Institute
Madison, Wisconsin

Decades of debate have failed to soften the false dichotomy between biological and social-interpersonal formulations of mental illness. The greatest current momentum is in the direction of remedicalization (Zola, 1978) of mental illness by health care providers, researchers, third party payers, legislators, and other important lay persons. The belief that mental illness is a genetically transmitted, neurochemically expressed disorder of the body is accompanied by the philosophy that drugs and other somatic therapies offer the best choice for treatment. Even though it is quite clear from research that pharmacologic treatment alone is insufficient (e.g., Hogarty *et al.*, 1979; Schooler *et al.*, 1980) even for psychotic disorders, psychosocial therapies are given inadequate attention in training and research. Presently, most resident psychiatrists are taught that if there are family difficulties relating obviously to the hospitalized patient's problem, then the illness probably is not "biological"; usually these cases should be classified on Axis II of DSM-III as a personality disorder. For those cases where family difficulties are obvious and in addition there are "objective" symptoms of illness such as weight loss, sleep disturbance, or thought disorder, then the problem is "biological" and can be classified on Axis I; the part of the patient's pain relating to interpersonal difficulties represents an Axis II "overlay." One gets the impression that biological practitioners believe that behaviors related to family troubles, as distinguished from symptoms, are secondary to the underlying biological disorder.

Psychosocial therapies have been devalued from a scientific point of view in part because the time frame for results, derived from psychopharmacological treatment, has been inappropriately applied (Mosher & Keith, 1980). Recent long-term research with persons who are mentally ill suggests that if the research period is sufficiently extended, more positive results from psychosocial treatment can be achieved. Psychotherapy also has lagged in its potential development toward scientific respectability because for their part, many social–behavioral scientists and humanists have persisted in their unorganized, nonscientific, largely experience-oriented approach to psychotherapy. The idea of a real science of psychotherapy is hopeless, they claim; there is no way all the subtle complexities of effective clinical practice can be accounted for by scientific method. They have viewed laboratory and biological scientists as opponents, whose research behaviors are interpreted as symptoms of characterological disturbance. Unfortunately, this return volley of reductionism in the troublesome biological–social dichotomy has not been helpful.

Except for the efforts of a small group of psychotherapy researchers and some social scientists, the dichotomy between the scientists and the humanists widens. The challenge is mighty for those who believe that psychotherapy can be scientific too. It is difficult to find scientific procedures to operationalize and account for concepts such as double-bind, ambivalence, conflict, coalition, overinvolvement, enmeshment, negation, disqualification, and the like. Mere construction of rating scales to gather a clinician rating for a complicated concept like "degree of differentiation" seems like a bootstrap operation. Such scales may do no more than substitute a number for a word. The meaning of the number from such a scale is not at all comparable to the chemist's number which reflects atomic weight or atomic number when describing hydrogen. The chemist's numbers relate very specifically to testable constructs given validity by corroborative laboratory experiments whereas the clinician's rating scale merely summarizes the clinician's opinion.

In recognition of such deficiencies in the relatively young science of psychotherapy, the editors of this volume are trying to stimulate and facilitate efforts to meet the challenge of furthering the science of psychotherapy.

Some Basic Requirements for Developing a Science of Psychotherapy

While reaching toward the goal of making a science of psychotherapy without losing touch with humanism and while engaging with complicated clinical realities, there comes a moment of truth which has not yet been faced fully. There is a tendency to create models and "systems" of psychotherapy that can be understood quickly and easily. Taking one workshop and/or reading one book appears to suffice for presenting oneself as a provider qualified in some of the new approaches to psychotherapy and/or psychotherapy research. The current norm is that a system not only can, but must be mastered in a relatively short period of time. If a system cannot be mastered quickly, it is criticized and dismissed as too complex and unusable. Yet no one would dream of insisting on the same self-evident qualities for a major theory and measurement system in physics or chemistry. It would be audacious indeed to present oneself as a research chemist after a few months training. Likewise, it may turn out that if a science of psychotherapy is truly to be applicable to the clinical realities, it may not be possible to master it with just a few months training. In requiring such simplicity, perhaps we underestimate the magnitude and difficulty of the task. These observations should not be taken to suggest that complexity is a virtue in itself. Parsimony is and should be a high scientific value. But it may be that there is no short cut for a science of psychotherapy. We may have to proceed as slowly and as tortuously as the laboratory sciences.

If it is granted that a viable scientific system for psychotherapy will require substantial mental energy to develop, master, and apply to research, it may follow that the user–researcher also will have to have a high level of technical skill. Basic scientists (e.g., chemists, physicists, engineers) assume that they must develop mastery of mathematics, computer science, and other related technical fields in depth. Although as a senior investigator, a physicist will have technical assistants, he or she usually is able to actually do what the assistants are doing. This assures quality supervision and quality control. Yet, some social scientists, including psychotherapy researchers, appear to believe that mastery of statistics and a working knowledge of computers including programming is "not their field." Such activities are reviewed as technical lower level and appropriately "hired out." Unfortunately, there are many potential pitfalls in defining variables, measuring them, getting them in the right order in the computer files, and having the computer process them correctly. In addition, what sounds good hypothetically may fall apart when operationalized in a computer program. It was once suggested to the senior author that it would be beneficial to do time series analyses on family therapy sessions. Having programmed time series analyses in a psychophysiological context, and having programmed analyses of family sessions, it was immediately apparent that the idea was close to nonsense. Lagging from unit to unit would completely overlook the fact that in a family session there are different speakers and as "auto" correlations basic to time analysis would not be "auto" at all. The only way the suggestion would make sense would be if one accepted the family as an undifferentiated, amorphous, homogeneous mass. But clinically speaking, such a failure to identify different speakers would endorse pathology in the extreme. Would one want to base a family analysis on an assumption that is applicable only to a certain type of pathology, namely the undifferentiated family mass? This sort of technical–clinical problem can be recognized only if the investigator knows both the clinical and the technical aspects of the problem. In conclusion, future theorists and researchers probably should plan on mastering technical skills themselves and not count on big budgets and hired hands to do basic analyses only dimly understood by the principal investigator.

Not only should the investigator master technical skills, but he or she also should become an experienced clinician. Formal training followed by two or preferably more years of direct clinical experience are required to develop skills requisite for creating a meaningful system for researching psychotherapy. Without such knowledge, the investigator is more likely to misinterpret what is happening between patient and therapist and produce irrelevant superficial and/or artifactual concepts and results. This need for combining technical and clinical skill is known as the Boulder Model (Garfield, 1982).

The clinician-scientist can measure the success of his/her efforts by a test of whether the proposed system meets the criteria for an hypothetical construct detailed so well by MacCorquodale and Meehl in their classic paper "On Hypothetical Constructs and Intervening Variables" (1951). A sound hypothetical construct generates an infinitude of testable ideas. It is concrete enough to be proven wrong, and abstract enough to relate meaningfully to nearly everything of interest in the domain to be studied.

A Biography of Structural Analysis of Social Behavior (SASB)

This chapter will present an hypothetical construct called Structural Analysis of Social Behavior (SASB). The model presumes to be biologically based in the sense that it is built on primate behaviors thought to be basic to the evolutionary process. Being based on behaviors common to higher primates, SASB theory cuts across species and across many different "schools" of psychotherapy. The common biosocial core for different therapies can be identified: most therapies and systems relate to one degree or another to basic concepts such as power, aggression, affiliation, and separate territory. In this ethological framework, the word "biological" includes behaviors as well as structure; behavior and structure are presumed to have evolved together and in direct relation to one another because they both were subject to principles of natural selection. Such an integrated view of behavior and structure breaks down the needless dichotomy between "behavioral" and "biochemical" or physical. *Both* are derived from a biological base and subject to principles of evolution. It is appropriate to refer to the behavioral aspect of biology as biosocial, and the chemical aspect as biochemical.

SASB theory has adequate complexity to encompass many complicated clinical phenomena including differentiation, double-bind, ambivalence, conflict, and the like. The model has been developed continually since 1968 with several major revisions occurring in response to an iterative interaction between data and theory. The spirit of the data gathering is to seek reality and keep changing theory to approximate truth, rather than to prove oneself to have been right. The value is on operationalizing to the point that results can be reliably replicated by others, while not simplifying to the point of becoming trivial.

Presently the SASB theory and technology is being used in a large-scale Interpersonal Diagnosis Project with the purposes of (1) building self-concept and social milieu into the DSM-III and/or (2) suggesting an alternative interpersonal nosology. To date, it appears that the first goal will be possible; there are clear operationally defined differences among DSM-III categories in terms of self-concept and social behavior.

In sum, the SASB model and its associated technology have undergone a lengthy series of tests involving gathering of data, revising theory, gathering more data, and so on. Speaking more personally, from the point of view of the senior author, the development of SASB has required freedom from everyday distractions, ability to delay gratification, and an inner directedness sufficient to withstand many discouraging experiences. It is, after all, somewhat audacious to put forward a model which presumes to apply to many different schools of psychotherapy and to operationalize many different difficult clinical concepts. Future developers of systems and theories should know that the grander the aspirations, and the more different the proposal from establishment views, the more vigorous the criticisms will be. Many rejections of proposals for research, of presentations for meetings, and of papers for journals can be expected. But perhaps the knowledge that such difficulties are the norm will help the responsible but ambitious theorist to persist. For concrete illustration, let the energetic graduate student contemplate the following anonymous, gratuitous, patronizing, and somewhat inaccurate remarks received in an early review of SASB conducted on behalf of a major and distinguished publishing house in the behavioral sciences.

Models are very individual things in psychology, as in other disciplines. Models do not present facts, and, unlike theories, they cannot be proved right or wrong. Models are abstractions, and they represent ways of looking at or describing phenomena. Consequently models can be judged only with respect to whether they are useful or helpful. Most behavioral scientists have their own preferred models for organizing their ways of thinking or practicing. Very few writers, no matter how creative, have successfully generated models that have achieved broad currency. Exceptions tend to be giants in the field, such as Erickson, whose life-cycle model has received broad acceptance as a way of conceptualizing human development. There are very few people who have been successful in developing an elaborate model that has subsequently been used or written about by many people other than themselves and their students. The remainder shelves are packed with books that explicate models that seem to their originators a beautiful way of looking at things.

Structural Analysis of Social Behavior (SASB)

There are three aspects to the SASB approach: (1) the model itself, (2) questionnaires for rating individuals in terms of the model, accompanied by a variety of computer programs for generating parameters useful in clinical and research analyses, and (3) methodology for coding observed interactions informally as when doing psychotherapy or formally as when researching psychotherapy. Several different computer programs are available for analysing the research codings of observed and recorded interactions.

Because of limitations on space, the present review of (1) the model itself and of (2) the questionnaires will be brief. A major purpose of this chapter is to emphasize aspect (3) by presenting a "minimanual" for coding therapy sessions with SASB, and for using the associated computer software.

The SASB Model and the Literature

Because of the similarity of names, it is appropriate to consider first the relation of SASB to Structural Family Therapy. These two approaches developed independently and SASB is different from Structural Family Therapy (Aponte & Van Deusen, 1981; Minuchin, 1974; Stanton, 1981) in its particular detail, its degree of operationalization, its specificity, its attention to psychometric principles, and its highly developed software. SASB shares with Structural Family Therapy the belief that there are basic structures that regulate and organize human behavior. Codes can be identified which organize observations about social behavior, and, since families are a major source of social learning, families are considered vital to the understanding of the individual. Major concepts in Structural Family Therapy are boundary, alignment, and power; Structural Family Therapy research measures have been of communication patterns, affective relations, executive behaviors, enmeshment, rigidity, overprotectiveness, conflict, physiological stress, and interpersonal perception. SASB theory and technology is capable of operationalizing and measuring many of these constructs as will be illustrated in subsequent sections. SASB also shares with the interactional views from the Mental Research Institute (Lederer & Jackson, 1968; Watzlawick, Beavin, & Jackson, 1967) an emphasis on the relation of specific interpersonal behaviors to the interactional *sequences* in which they are embedded.

The SASB model is more directly related to the work of Murray (1938), Leary (1957), Schaefer (1965), Lorr, Bishop, and McNair (1965), and other investigators using Murray-based needs arranged by circumplex models for social behavior. Murray's list of needs was heavily influenced by the clinical theories of Sullivan (1953, 1962). A very rich and meaningful application of Leary's circumplex version of Murray's list of needs to psychotherapy research was offered by Mueller and Dilling (1969). A comprehensive review of the relation between SASB and the circumplex literature appeared in Benjamin (1974) along with a discussion of how its validity has been tested using methods of circumplex analysis, autocorrelation, and factor analysis. In more recent years, validity has also been tested by a dimensional ratings procedure (Benjamin, 1980a; draft, 1986).

Structure of the SASB Model   The first version of SASB appeared in Benjamin (1973) and the current version of the SASB model (Benjamin, 1979) is presented in Figure 11-1.

Focus

The model consists of three diamond-shaped surfaces distinguished by *focus*. The first, or top surface, describes focus on other and involves a transitive action directed toward the other person. The second, or middle surface, describes focus on self and refers to an intransitive state, a reaction to another person. The third, or bottom surface, describes introjected focus on other, or what the subject is actively doing to him or herself. Focus on other reflects prototypically parent-like, active, transitive behaviors, coming from one person to affect the other. Focus on self reflects prototypically child-like, reactive, intransitive behaviors or states which emerge in one person in reaction to the other. Parent-like or active behaviors are not necessarily temporally prior to child-like or reactive behaviors. One type of focus should not be regarded as more "primary," important, or responsible than the other.

Focus on self is distinguished from an introject in that the introject surface describes intrapsychic events resulting from actions turned inward upon the self, whereas focus on the self represents interpersonal events involving reaction to another person. The concept of introjection has not been included in previous Murray-based models of interpersonal behavior, but it is the key to linking self-concept to social milieu. The concept of focus defines three different surfaces and much of the predictive power of the SASB model comes from theoretical statements about relations among the three surfaces.

The Axes

The horizontal axes of all three surfaces SASB model represents affiliation. All points on the right-hand side of Figure 11-1 show varying degrees of friendliness, and those on the left-hand side show varying degrees of unfriendliness.

The vertical axis for each type of focus describes interdependence. Behaviors involving varying degrees of enmeshment are shown in the lower halves of the surfaces and behaviors involving varying degrees of independence or differentiation are shown on the upper halves of each surface.

Behaviors at the poles of the axes reflect "primitive basic" issues. For example, on the focus on other surface, the poles are, informally speaking, sexuality, power, murder, and allowing the other person separate territory. Points in between the poles are made up of proportions of the two underlying dimensions of affiliation and interdependence. For example, the point 117, "You can do it fine," has coordinates $(+2, +7)$ where the X coordinate represents 2 units on the affiliation axis and the Y coordinate represents 7 units in the independence or differentiation direction on the interdependence axis.

Tracks

Points with coordinates having the same absolute values for affiliation and interdependence reflect similar interpersonal issues, topics, or tracks. The opposite of "You can do it fine," is 137, intrude, restrict $(-2, -7)$ and both relate to the topic: "intimacy-distance." On the focus on other surface, other points relating to "intimacy-distance" are the opposite pairs: 147, benevolent monitor $(+2, -7)$, and 127, forget $(-2, +7)$. In general, tracks include all points on the model having the same $(\pm X, \pm Y)$ values on the axes; they all relate to the same interpersonal "topic." Model points on a given track

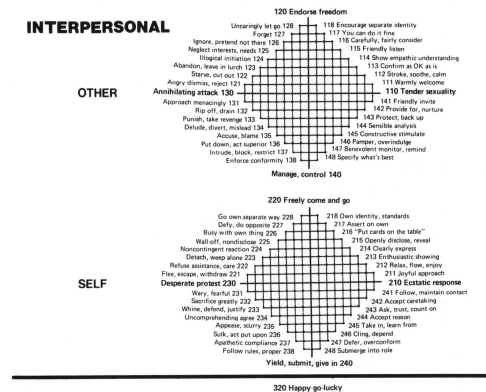

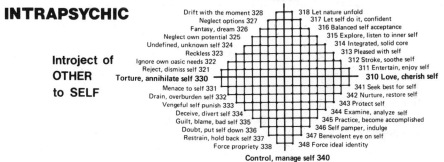

Figure 11-1 Full model for Structural Analysis of Social Behavior (SASB). The three diamonds or surfaces reflect focus on other, focus on self, and focus on other turned inward, or introjected upon the self, respectively. All points on the right-hand side of the model are friendly, and all points on the left-hand side, unfriendly. All points in the upper halves of the model represent independence, and points on the lower halves represent interdependence or varying degrees of enmeshment. SASB theory describes a broad array of social behaviors in terms of these basic dimensions: focus, friendliness, and interdependence. The theory is explicit about what behaviors are associated with each other, about what facilitates constructive change, and about the connection between social milieu and self-concept. From L. S. Benjamin, Structural analysis of differentiation failure, *Psychiatry*, 1979, 42, 1–23. Copyright 1979 by the William Alanson White Psychiatric Foundation. Reprinted by permission.

can be identified by the fact that their code numbers all end in the same last digit. The examples just cited were 117, 137; 127, 147 and belong to track 7. The respective tracks are named 0=primitive basics, 1=approach–avoidance, 2=need fulfillment, contact, nurturance, 3=attachment, 4=logic and communications, 5=attention, to self-development, 6=balance in relationship, 7=intimacy–distance, and 8=identity.

In summary, the SASB model classified interpersonal transactions in terms of focus (other, self, introject), affiliation (love to hate), interdependence (enmeshed to differentiated), and topic or track.

Three Levels of Complexity:
Full, Cluster, Quadrant Versions of SASB

The SASB model presented in full version in Figure 11-1 can be used at varying levels of complexity. The simplest version appears in the center of Figure 11-2 and is called the quadrant version. There each surface of the model is divided into four quadrants successively numbered 1, 2, 3, 4 starting with a 1 in the upper right-hand corner and proceeding counterclockwise as is the Cartesian convention.

A knowledge of the structure of the *code numbers* for each point in the full version of the SASB model shown in Figure 11-1 makes it easier to follow the SASB predictions of relations among social behaviors. The first or hundreds digit describes focus with 100=focus on other, 200=focus on self, and 300=introject. The second or 10's digit describes quadrant and ranges from 1 to 4 to seriate the four respective quadrants shown in the middle of Figure 11-2. The third, or units digit describes the subdivision of the quadrant or track and ranges from 0 (=axes) to 8.

The cluster version of the SASB model is created by grouping points into eight clusters per surface. In Figure 11-2, clusters are shown by boxes with each SASB questionnaire item in a box corresponding to a point on the full version of the model shown in Figure 11-1. The correspondence can be traced exactly by using the code numbers appearing in both Figures 11-1 and 11-2. In the full model, there are 36 points per surface for a total of 108 points. The boxes defining the cluster version in Figure 11-2 divide each surface into eight sections. In sum, the quadrant version divides each surface into four parts; the cluster version divides each surface into eight parts, and the full version divides each surface into 36 points. The cluster version is intermediate in complexity between the quadrant version and the full model. Names for the clusters were developed by the senior author in collaboration with Clinton W. McLemore. The cluster version of SASB is the basis of the behavioral coding system to be described subsequently. When referring to the cluster version, O=other surface, S=self surface, and I=introject surface. Clusters are identified by numbers 1 to 8 as shown in Figure 11-2. The current 1983 questionnaire items for each point appear within the boxes, but citations in the text are of the 1980 items.

Complementarity

The SASB method codes interpersonal transactions in terms of focus, affiliation, and interdependence. In addition, the internal logic of the model includes several structural features which allow the generation of hypotheses about etiology of social malfunctioning and to generate ideas for prescribing treatment interventions. Structural features making such predictions possible include the concepts of complementarity, opposition, introjection, antithesis, and the Shaurette principle.

If two people show the same amounts of affiliation and interdependence, they are *complementary* if one is focusing on the other, and the second is focusing on him or herself. For example, suppose one person shows behaviors described in Figure 11-2, cluster 6, point 135: "Accuses and blames person, tries to get person to admit wrong-doing." In this case, there is hostile and controlling focus on other, classified in the cluster model as O-6. The complementary focus in this region of hostile interdependence is S-6 on the focus on self surface, cluster 6. The exact full model point is 235: "Buries rage, resentment, and scurries to appease person to avoid disapproval." The combination: blame–appease or O-6: S-6 is a stable *complementary* relation. You can predict if one person adopts one of these postures, there will be stability if the other person complements that posture as specified by the SASB model. Maximal instability occurs when the dyad is at comparable points but each member maintains the *same* focus. Two blamers, two appeasers, two ignorers, for example, are in a maximally unstable or "unmatched" interactions.

Opposition

Opposite behaviors appear on the same surface at 180 degree angles. Using the cluster version defined by the boxes in Figure 11-2, the opposite of cluster O-6 would be cluster O-2. For the focus on other surface, this means the opposite of Belittling and Blaming is Affirming and Understanding. On the full model, opposites of specific points are found in their opposing clusters. For example, within clusters 6 and 2, the exact single-point opposites are 135, "Accuses and blames and tries to get person to admit wrong-doing" and 115, "Actively listens, accepts, and affirms person even with disagreement." For the full model, opposite points end in the same units digit shown by the code numbering of Figure 11-1.

Double-Binding, Ambivalence, Conflict

Double-bind is operationally defined by SASB as opposite communications coded on the focus on other surface, whereas ambivalence is operationally defined as opposite codes on the focus on self surface. A conflict-laden self-concept involves opposite codes on the Introject surface. Formal parameters for defining statistically significant opposition in a single rating are discussed in Benjamin (1984).

Antitheses

A third structural principle of the SASB model is antithesis. Antithesis can be invoked to try to elicit a behavior in someone which is opposite from the one being shown. For example, the opposite of Belittle and Blame (other surface, cluster 6=O-6) is Affirm and Understand (other surface, cluster 2=O-2). The complement of O-2 is S-2, Disclose and Express. Therefore, S-2 is the antithesis of O-6. Speaking clinically, a blamer is optimally handled by feedback about the impact of the blaming. Consider point 215 in cluster S-2: "Freely and openly discloses innermost self so person can truly know who s/he is." Such self-disclosure teaches empathy and inhibits abuse by normal and mildly disturbed persons. In general, more normal and younger people are more likely to exhibit affiliative complementarity and therefore respond to positive antitheses. Many pathological persons are more disaffiliative and rigid; for them, other types of interactions are necessary to stimulate constructive change toward affiliation.

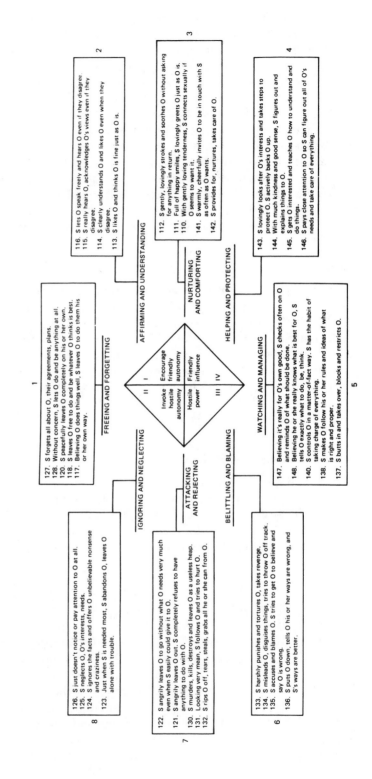

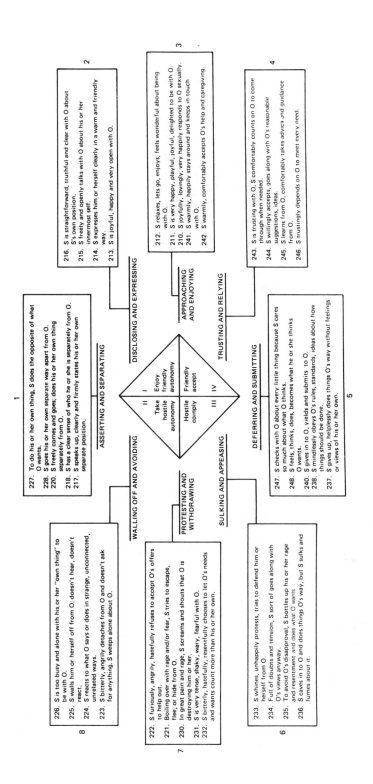

Figure 11-2 The SASB model at levels of increasing complexity. (1) The quadrant version appears at the center of the figure. (2) The middle section provides names for 8 subdivisions or *clusters*. (3) The outer ring shows boxes corresponding to each of the clusters and containing specific model points from Figure 11-1. Model points in this figure present text from the INTREX questionnaires, to give coders a highly specific description of each model point in each cluster. Clusters are numbered from 1 to 8, clockwise from 12 o'clock. Quadrant version copyright 1979 by William Alanson White Psychiatric Foundation. Cluster version and questionnaire items copyright 1982 and 1983, respectively, by INTREX Interpersonal Institute. From L. S. Benjamin, Principles of prediction using structural analysis of social behavior (SASB), in R. A. Zucker, J. Aronoff, & A. J. Rabin (Eds.), *Personality and the prediction of behavior* (New York: Academic Press, 1984. Reprinted by permission.

401

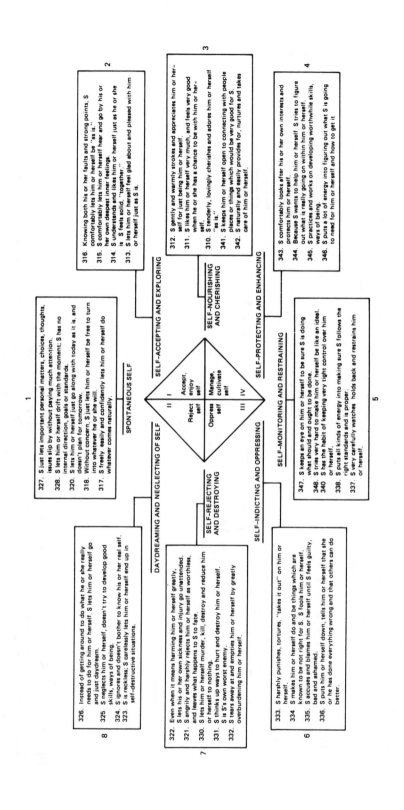

402

Figure 11-2 (Continued)

The Shaurette Principle

One powerful alternate approach for more disturbed individuals has been named the Shaurette principle after Glen Shaurette who runs an inpatient milieu treatment program using the SASB model to describe patients and prescribe social treatment interventions (Benjamin, 1982). Briefly, the Shaurette principle involves a progression of interpersonal moves starting with complementing the undesirable disaffiliative posture, switching focus as needed, and moving stepwise around the SASB model in a *counterclockwise* (i.e., through dominance and warmth) direction. The Shaurette principle is orderly, rational, and done with the knowledge and consent of the patient. The technique has aspects in common with some of the so-called "paradoxical" interventions of Structural Family Therapy. For example:

> Patient: Nobody has been able to do a thing about my manic attacks and you can't either (O-6: Belittle and Blame).
> Therapist: You're probably right. There isn't much I can do (S-6). The "paradoxical" remark is classified as the complementary posture, Sulk and Appease.
> Therapist: What can we do to be helpful? (S-5: Defer and Submit—the therapist is moving counterclockwise by adding warmth).
> Patient: You can have somebody watch me and let me know when I'm getting manic and insist I stop what I'm doing and take my Lithium (patient O-5 = Watch and Manage the therapist, plus S-4, Trust and Rely—showing the patient has become warmer and switched focus).
> Therapist: Well, you might be likely to get pretty mad at me if I did that, wouldn't you? (O-4: Helping and Protecting—therapist complements S-4 trust and now the focus is successfully switched to the patient).
> Patient: Yeah, I might (S-4: Trust and Rely).
> Therapist: Well, what would help you remember you don't want to get out of control? A note from yourself to yourself which I could keep to give to you when necessary? (O-4: Helping and Protecting).
> Patient: Maybe that would work. I'll write one to myself (S-2, patient Discloses and Expresses in an autonomous fashion. He writes a candid note about the signs of his manic attack and what he wishes to do about it; he addresses the note to himself—Introject-4 = Self-Protective).

The therapist now leaves (O-2) the patient to be his own monitor (I-4) of impending manic attacks.

In this oversimplified sequence, the blaming, controlling manic has been moved progressively through therapist's complementary and orderly stepwise progression toward a position of friendly autonomy. The therapist's "paradoxical stance" ("You're right, there isn't much I can do") was brief and had a very explicit, concrete well-planned rationale backed up by a specific positive follow-up plan.

Preparation of Material for SASB Coding

Readers interested in the technology associated with the SASB questionnaires, named the INTREX questionnaires, are referred to Benjamin (1974, 1977, 1980, 1982, 1984). Questionnaires can be administered to the same persons whose behavior is to be coded so that perceptions of self and family as measured by questionnaire can be compared with coder judgments of actual behavior.

Behavior must be video- or audiorecorded for SASB research because the coding process is so microscopic it could not be accomplished in real time. We have experimented with having coders use a field recorder to make quick judgments in real time about focus, affiliation, and interdependence, but these have been unsuccessful. Possibly someone with several years experience would be able to use a field recorder for coding in real time, but no one has mastered this yet. Videotapes are preferred to audiotapes because the nonverbal information on them is helpful in classifying focus, affiliation, interdependence, and topic.

Typescripts are prepared to define units of speech and to remind coders of what was on the tape. The typescript is broken into separate speeches or *units*. Each unit is broken into an *element*, defined as "a complete thought" or "psychologically meaningful interaction." Complete thoughts usually are brief, so a given unit may have several elements. Then an element may be described by one cluster on the SASB model in which case there is one *entry* in the computer file for that element. If the element is a multiple communication, it will require more than one entry.

The purpose of elementizing is to divide speeches so that independent coders are focusing on the same psychologically meaningful interaction. If the elements are too large, coders might be more likely to code differing parts of the interaction, causing spurious lack of reliability. On the other hand, if the elements are too small, there may not be sufficient information to code. A new speaker always creates a new unit. A unit can contain only two elements by the same speaker. One speech (an uninterrupted verbalization from one speaker) may, if too long, be presented as more than one unit. When a speaker is assigned more than one unit, then the computer program sequential count uses the last unit as a leading unit to the next speaker.

Because the SASB coding process is so microscopic and expensive, it is recommended that intense but relatively brief (e.g., 20-minute) highly relevant samples be selected. The sequential analyses require long strings of units so short spot sampling is inappropriate. The task of selecting a "loaded" 20-minute sample is difficult but a structured task which has the family interact intensively over an issue of specific, everyday concern to them is recommended. For example, Foster obtained rich material for her dissertation by asking families to discuss a recent disagreement. A Family Consensus Task from the Interpersonal Diagnosis Project forced families to concentrate on their relations with the identified patient (IP) by rating themselves on selected SASB questionnaire items. A study comparing families with anorexics to families with bulimics provides a "loaded" vignette for families to react to (Humphrey, 1983).

In the typescript, each speech appears on a separate line and is preceded by number designating who was the speaker. Up to seven referents can be identified. These include all participants plus absent persons or concepts that are important. For example, it is possible to define coalitions or family alignments as referents. A special referent for "family as a group" can be useful in coding family conferences and another for the coalition "mother plus father" allows descriptions of messages sent to the parents as an undifferentiated pair in instances where no distinction between them is made by the speaker. In general, it is recommended that these coalition codes be used conservatively and be restricted to combinations which occur frequently and where identification of the specific recipient of the message (e.g., mother *or* father) truly is not possible. For example, if daughter says "you guys" meaning parents, but posture and context mean "mother," it is better to code the message as being from daughter to mother rather than from daughter to parents. Having too many referents can dilute the sample size for some of the statistical procedures to be described subsequently.

Process and content are coded independently. Process is defined as the here and now transaction and content is defined as what the participants are talking about. Frequently coders (and therapists) focus exclusively on content and overlook process. For example, the patient may be discussing an unfaithful lover (content = abandonment) in a context where the therapist is being manipulated (process is hostile control). It cannot be overemphasized how frequently coding of both process and content sharpens the perception of what is going on whether the analysis is being used for research or therapeutic purposes.

Steps in SASB Coding

Coders watch the videotape once to get the "feel" of the session. Then they code the typescript. Finally, they review the tape again, to be sure that the coding they have recorded really fits what is on the tape. Naturally the final review is completed *before* coders learn of the computer's analysis. The steps in the SASB coding process will be reviewed in chronological order:

XY For each unit, the first coding decision is who is speaking (X) to whom (Y). X is easy to determine because speaker is indicated by the transcript. The Y referent may be indicated explicitly ("Mike, you never do what I ask you to"), nonverbally (by eye contact, orientation of the body, a wave of the hand), or may be sometimes inferred from the context (e.g., when the parents are arguing back and forth and the husband turns away to address someone else, but the "parting shot" is obviously addressed to the wife). At other times, specification of the Y referent may not be so readily determined, in which case the referent is designated as "9" which means uncodable. Any unit for which both X and Y cannot be identified is ignored by the computer programs. Again, X and Y have names ranging from 1 to 7 and can represent specific individuals (1 = daughter), coalitions (5 = mother plus father) or concepts (7 = family).

Focus Focus is the next decision, chosen from three possibilities: focus on other (transitive action affecting another person, coded "O" or "1"), focus on self (intransitive state arising from reaction to another, coded "S" or "2"), and intrapsychic (transitive action directed inward upon the self, coded "I" or "3").

Affiliation and Interdependence

The next step uses the 5-point scales shown in Figure 11-3 describing affiliation–disaffiliation (horizontal dimension) and interdependence (vertical dimension). For the affiliation rating a "5" indicates maximal affiliation, "3" indicates "neutral," and "1" indicates maximal disaffiliation. "2" and "4" provide appropriate midpoints. Examples of "5," on the affiliative dimension would be sexual bonding with warm affection or intense love; of "4," friendly and appreciating interaction with a friend; "3," affectively neutral responses to a coworker or stranger; "2," berating or scolding a child; and "1," physical or psychological attack, torture, or in the extreme, murder.

Judgments on the second dimension, interdependence, are not quite so easy to make intuitively. A rating of "5" would exemplify autonomy giving to an indifferent passerby. At the other extreme, a "1" would include wholesale monitoring of the thoughts, feelings, and activities of a teenaged child (focus on other), or extreme submission as in

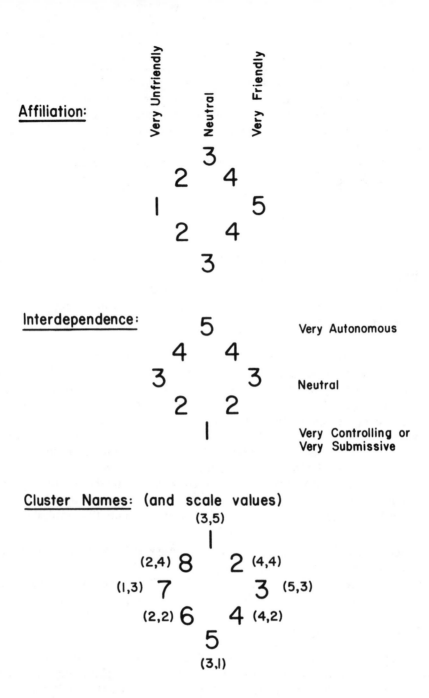

Figure 11-3 Five-point scales used to classify transactions in terms of the cluster version of the model shown in Figure 11-2. The top part of Figure 11-3 shows affiliative values assigned to each of the clusters on any of the diamond-shaped surfaces. The middle section of the figure shows the interdependence values assigned to each of the clusters on any of the diamond-shaped surfaces. The lower part of the figure shows how the eight clusters can be inferred using the 5-point judgments made about affiliation and interdependence. For example, cluster 1 at the top of the diamond is inferred if the judgment for the affiliation scale was a 3 and the judgment for the interdependence scale was a 5. Use of these scales and the internal logic of the model directs the coder's attention to the underlying dimensionality and minimizes the tendency impulsively to select a cluster which "sounds right."

following orders in the armed services under emergency conditions (focus on self). Moderate power and moderate submission are denoted by ''2,'' while moderate autonomy giving or taking are indicated by ''4.'' Coders must learn to recognize that behaviors can appear qualitatively different but actually be equivalent except for focus. For example, a ''sadist'' who punishes another is as hostile and as interdependent as the ''masochist'' who accepts the punishment.

Combining Judgments

After completing the ratings of focus, affiliation, and interdependence, the logic of the SASB model generates a cluster judgment. Figure 11-3 shows how to combine the affiliation–autonomy ratings to select an SASB cluster. In the figure, affiliation–autonomy ratings for the various clusters are presented in parentheses, and the logically associated clusters are shown in brackets. For example, the figure shows that an affiliation rating of ''3'' and an autonomy rating of ''5'' would yield cluster 1 as a good first approximation to the final cluster judgment.

To refine the classification suggested by the three judgments, focus, affiliation, and interdependence, the rater next codes the track. For example, ''You never tell me what you're feeling'' involves focus on other, is mildly unfriendly (horizontal scale, 2), and somewhat influencing (vertical scale, 2). The sequence of judgments showing the coordinates (2,2) for ''You never tell me what you're feeling'' would suggest cluster O-6, Belittling and Blaming, on the focus on other surface. The topic might be track 6 = Balance in Relationship. In Figure 11-2, cluster O-6, the item on track 6 is: 136, ''Puts person down, tells person she/he does it all wrong. Says own ways are superior.'' Here the track judgment identified a specific item within the cluster chosen by sequential judgments of focus, affiliation, and interdependence.

The Final Clinical Test

It is not always true that the track judgment confirms choice of the cluster which was identified by the sequential judgments. Contradiction between track and cluster judgments can be resolved by the next step which is ''the Final Clinical Test.'' Here, raters are asked to ''step back'' from their selected cluster and ask themselves the question, ''*If* this judgment were shown on a computer output as a description of this particular interaction and you knew no more than what the computer output says, would it accurately represent the clinical feel of the element?'' NOTE, *this is not a circular process*; coders *never* look at the actual computer printout itself and then go back and recode. This Final Clinical Test is an imaginary exercise on a unit-by-unit basis completed prior to the computer analysis.

Coders have been encouraged to learn to attend to such contextual cues as tone of voice, posture, eye contact, and role relationships among subject participants, as well as to the context known by the preceding units. Linguistically identical statements might be assigned different, even opposite codes. The statement ''Oh, so you're going to be out Thursday night'' for example, might be coded Freeing and Forgetting, Affirming and Understanding, or perhaps Belittling and Blaming, depending on additional contextual cues from a preceding interaction, paralinguistic information, or role demands.

Multiple and Complex Communications Coding

The SASB method identifies two types of complicated communication: *multiple* and *complex*.

A *multiple communication* is simply a speech or unit consisting of more than one discernible message from the speaker to any number of other participants. For example, suppose the father says to the mother, "Let's go out to dinner tonight," immediately after the daughter announces she would like him to accompany her for 2 hours on his bike as she goes on a training jog. In some contexts, the father's behavior toward the daughter might be coded Ignoring and Neglecting (O-8), but in a family where father–daughter enmeshment was an issue being corrected, it could be coded as a friendly invitation to mother, Nurturing and Comforting (O-3, point 141 on Figure 11-1), and, if accompanied by social tact, the message to the daughter could be coded as Asserting and Separating (S-1) rather than Ignoring and Neglecting (O-8). In either context, the multiple messages here are clear and distinct and the SASB system simply codes the different messages and to whom they are addressed. Multiple communications *per se* are not thought to be pathological and the SASB software treats them with the same logic as units with a single cluster coding.

Sometimes, however, it is necessary to use more than one cluster to describe a communication and clearly discernible messages cannot be extracted. These *complex messages* have inextricable elements which bend back upon themselves as in *Knots* (Laing, 1970). Complex communications can be the "mind benders" that make the normal person "feel crazy" even when just reading about them. For example:

> Mother: What's the matter? (Affirming and Understanding, O-2)
> Daughter: Nothing. (Asserting and Separating, S-1)
> Mother: Well I hope you don't let it bother you all day. (Watching and Managing, O-5 plus
> Ignoring and Neglecting, O-8)

Here the "negative hallucination" of the daughter's assertion (O-8) is combined inextricably with the presumptive control described by item 148 in cluster O-5 ("Believing it's for person's own good, tells person exactly what to do, be, think"). The sentence "Well, I hope you don't let it bother you all day" cannot be broken up into a part containing O-5 and O-8. They are inseparable. Such complex communications receive a special code in the coding unit to allow special study by the computer. If as Bateson *et al.* (1956) and Singer and Wynne (1965) and others suggest, complex recursive communication deviance is characteristic of some types of psychopathology (especially schizophrenia), then special study of units coded as complex is warranted.

The New Geometric Method for Coding on the Full SASB Model

The 5-point scales on the affiliation and interdependence axes and the logic specified by Figure 11-3 were used to train research coders to classify interpersonal events in terms of the cluster version of the SASB model. The computer analyses to follow are based on this 5-point digital method of coding. However, that method is now outdated. In 1983, after this chapter was sent to press, the senior author gave a series of workshops teaching SASB coding to practicing psychotherapists in a continuing education program, and found that 18-point scales corresponding to the full version of the SASB model (Figure 11-1) could be used reliably. If judgments on these 18-point scales (e.g., -9 to 0 represents decreasing degrees of attack, and 0 to $+9$ represents increasing degrees of friendliness) are plotted as a point on an 18×18 unit grid, and if a coding line is drawn from the origin through that point, then placement of a transparent copy of the SASB model over the grid and the coding line will yield an exact classification of the transaction in terms of the full SASB model. A complete exposition of this geometric analogue method for reliably classifying on the full SASB model appears elsewhere (Benjamin, 1986a; 1986b).

The future plan is for research coders also to use the 18-point scales and the analogue geometric method. The new method is preferred to the 5-point method described in this chapter because of the following: (1) The new method reliably, often astonishingly, yields very good classifications in terms of the full, not just the cluster version of the SASB model. (2) The new method always yields a classification; there is never a "miss" as there can be with the 5-point scales when, using the logic of Figure 11-3, the result fails to "land" in a box on the cluster model. (3) There is an automatic measure of intensity in terms of distance from the origin. For example, a judgment of $-2, -2$ describes a 45 degree bisection of quadrant III. If the focus is on other, the classification for a bisection of quadrant III would be SASB model point 135, accuse, blame. Judgments of $-9, -9$ would also yield the classification 135, accuse, blame. However, the first code $(-2, -2)$ would represent a mild, perhaps subtle blame (as in "that hurt my feelings"), but the second $(-9, -9)$ would represent an intense catastrophic blame as in a revengeful murder.

Training Coders in the Use of the SASB Coding System

Selection of Coders

It could be that the microscopic and highly complex character of the SASB coding process means that only highly experienced clinicians also familiar with the SASB model and coding rules would be capable of using this system. There has been good reliability using SASB on difficult material between experienced clinicians. It is desirable to determine whether less experienced persons can be trained to use SASB on difficult material with satisfactory reliability *and* validity. To answer this question, the Interpersonal Diagnostic Project has selected and trained masters level students from social work, counseling and guidance, and psychology for SASB training and for judging families having subtle if any pathological interactions. The coders' levels of clinical experience varied, but was not extensive in any case.

Some persons, in spite of clinical and/or research training, do not appear to "catch on" to the coding system. Those with strong backgrounds in psychoanalytic therapy, for example, may tend to code events largely in terms of intrapsychic events, while missing the interpersonal transactions. Others consistently misread every event in terms of one dimension, usually power. Still others cannot grasp the notion of focus. Another difficulty arises with coders who understand the dimensions, but who have little clinical acumen. Such coders may focus too concretely on the language in the transcript, overlooking the nonverbal information about focus, friendliness, and interdependence. In our experience with selection and training, the following criteria are useful for coder selections: (1) If not experienced clinicians, then coders should be graduate students or advanced undergraduate students in clinical or counseling psychology, social work, or a related discipline. (2) Coders should have had research experience or, minimally, coursework in research methods. (3) Coders should have some clinical interviewing experience, preferably in both individual and family therapy. (4) In the screening interview, candidates should show some evidence of being interpersonally sensitive and "cognitively complex." Persons are unsuitable who see the world in terms of all-or-nothing absolutes such as: right or wrong; good or bad. Coder trainees are given a trial period of approximately six training hours, after which their responsiveness to training is evaluated. Those who have demonstrated an ability to learn the system are retrained for further training.

Sequence of Coder Training

Basic coder training may be expected to require at least 60 to 80 hours, with training sessions of 2 hours each and approximately 2 hours of "homework" prior to each session. Coders begin by reading several articles about the SASB model. In the first formal training session, the model is introduced by discussion of the two fundamental axes presented as 5-point dimensional rating scales of Figure 11-3 and keyed to the cluster version of the SASB model in Figure 11-2. Brief, one-sentence illustrations are coded on the 5-point horizontal scale for affiliation and then on the 5-point vertical scale for interdependence. It is important that some time be spent practicing at this stage, and that after the initial demonstration by the instructor, coders have ample practice making dimensional ratings for homework. Although conceptually the two dimensions are simple enough, the impact of cultural confusion makes the task more difficult than it might seem. For example, "I love you" in an ideal context should be coded as maximally affiliative (+5) and as neutrally interdependent (0). This type of loving statement should be neither influencing nor submissive according to SASB theory, but culturally speaking, there is much "noise" in love messages. For example, "If you love me, you'd do what I want" is a manipulation, not pure love. Experience with this context may cause "I love you" to mean control and/or submission to some people. Attack and control are another example of dimensions theoretically orthogonal but culturally confused. For example, "Do it this way" is pure control, but many power-sensitive individuals experience such a statement as overt attack. They equate "Do it this way" with "I'm going to annihilate you." Prior experience biases coders to mix together statements about warmth with statements about power in idiosyncratic ways.

These exercises with making dimensional ratings are useful orientation for coders prior to presentation of the full model. Here (as throughout training) coders learn from each other's mistakes, and from feedback, while the group reaches consensus on the coding of a given problem. For efficiency, training should be conducted with a group of two or more coders.

In the second training session, the full SASB model is presented. Earlier interpersonal models are briefly described, and the theoretical, psychometric, and historical contexts of the SASB model are explained. There is an introduction to the concept of a circumplex: Behavior can be ordered serially around a circle with adjacent behavior correlating positively and behavior at 180 degree angles correlating negatively. SASB items in the three circumplexes (surfaces) are reviewed and the relation of items to the clusters shown in Figure 11-2 are detailed.

The next training session is devoted to focus. Coders generally require some time and practice before accurately and reliably being able to code focus. One useful exercise is for coders to generate a series of statements to illustrate various types of focus for each cluster. Focus is coded both for process and content in the illustrative statements. Most coders have found that the concept of focus seems to "click" at approximately four to six training hours after the concept is introduced and the write-your-own-examples exercise is completed. It is also true that many family interactions are characterized precisely by complexity in focus. For example consider, "I really liked you until I got to know you better." In process, the speaker is focusing on the other person (O-6, Belittling and Blaming) but at the same time is reacting (S-1, Asserting and Separating). The knowledge that focus is confused by speakers and listeners appears to free coders from self-doubt and permits them to attend more openly to the range of cues available, and to the possibility of coding an interaction in terms of multiple types of focus rather than just giving up and calling the unit uncodable.

In subsequent training sessions, there is a review of affiliation, interdependence, and track. There is practice with difficult examples involving multiple coding. Details of entering judgments on the coding sheets so that they are computer-ready are introduced (see Benjamin, Giat, & Estroff, 1981).

In earlier phases of training, the emphasis is on the sequence of independent decisions about focus, affiliation, interdependence, and topic. The logical classification derived from this sequence is stressed to counteract the tendencies of many raters to "leap" to a final focus and cluster judgment just on the basis of intuition. The systematic dissection of the transaction into its independent components often leads to a different judgment than one might have selected at first glance. The sequential rule following improves reliability enormously. Including the Final Clinical Test, which causes the coder to review the entire sequence if the judgment doesn't meet the Final Clinical Test, adds to the validity as well as the reliability.

Threshold is another concept that has been useful in coder teaching. Sequence has been argued to be a crucial feature in the study of pathological interactions. In family sessions, coders may sense that one is slowly building up to a conclusion, that is, that there is a hidden agenda. To preserve a pure-culture sample for sequential analysis, coders are urged not to read in or anticipate such agendas. Once coders have mastered the concept of multiple meaning and have coded enough transcripts to see that agendas can emerge, they can be introduced to the concept of "threshold." If a coder senses an agenda unfolding, he or she may code it only at the point where the threshold is crossed by the emergence of enough specific information to justify the code. Sometimes the gradual move toward the culmination can be tracked by noticing that each successive speech involves a stepwise increase in, for example, control or in hostility until the final "nailing" transaction emerges in full. At this point the blaming message, O-6 is coded. The coder's "urge" to have recorded the agenda earlier is satisfied by noting there had in fact been a progressive increase in the amount of control or hostility in the preceding judgments.

Boundary

A boundary problem can occur because of the arbitrary nature of the cutoff points between clusters in Figure 11-2. A specific item within a cluster may describe a transaction very well, but the cluster to which the item belongs may not summarize the transaction as well as the adjacent cluster. In this case, coders should pick the adjacent cluster which summarizes better. Consider, for example, "No, that's wrong—here let me show you the right way." This message is well described by item 136: "Puts person down, tells person s/he does it all wrong, says own ways are superior." Item 136 belongs to cluster O-6, Belittling and Blaming, but the "feel" of the transaction is better "rounded off" as cluster O-5, Watching and Managing. The Final Clinical Test permits coding O-5 rather than O-6 because O-6 on the average is more hostile than O-5; this particular context provided a message which was more purely controlling, not blatantly hostile.

If the put-down message had more attack and less pure control in it, then coding O-6 would be proper as in "No—you idiot—that's wrong—here let me show you the right way." Here, adding "you idiot" puts the message clearly into O-6, and there would be no boundary problems.

General Observations on the Reliability of Coding

Reliability is measured by Cohen's weighted kappa (Cohen, 1968) if data are to be analyzed by Markov chaining logic. In other words, kappa measures the agreement between coders on an event by event basis. The weights in kappa are determined rationally by SASB theory. If coders disagree by just one cluster on the same surface there is a high positive weight; if they code opposite clusters on different surfaces there is a heavy negative weight or penalty. The weights range from $+1$ (exact agreement) to -1 (maximal disagreement in every dimension: affiliation, interdependence, and focus) with weights for steps inbetween being determined by linear interpolation. Details for computing kappa appear in Benjamin, Giat, and Estroff (1981).

Kappas between independent experienced clinicians familiar with SASB logic range between .70 and .85 on difficult material with multiple and complex messages.

The second author, Foster, trained graduate students to code family arguments videotaped for her dissertation to reach kappas (using marginal entries for estimates of chance) ranging between .65 to .78 for process, and from .62 to .86 for content. These same students coding the more bland FCT task of the Interpersonal Diagnostic Project did not perform so well. Kappas for process were unacceptable and ranged from .45 to .61 and the worst example, the one with kappa = .45, is presented subsequently. The disagreement was clinically important as will be shown below. It appears that training coders on material involving explicit fighting does not prepare them reliably to handle the subtle and complicated "fighting" in families with pseudofriendliness (Wynne, Ryckoff, & Hirsch, 1958). In the Interpersonal Diagnostic Project, seemingly friendly, but subtly hostile multiple messaging is characteristic of many of the families with hospitalized inpatients.

However Humphrey (1983) was able to train advanced undergraduate and graduate students in clinical psychology reliably to code the pseudofriendly interactions in families with a hospitalized anorexic and a hospitalized bulimic. Training required nearly 100 hours, and involved having judges code independently at home, and then go over their codes in a group to yield a group consensus code. "The Kappas for Process codes ranged from .61 to .79 with a mean of .69 between independent coders, and from .80 to .84 with a mean of .81 between coders and consensual judgments (i.e., ratings made by consensus of all four raters following discussion). Content codes had kappas ranging from .68 to .81 with a mean of .74 between independent coders, and from .77 to .89 with a mean of .82 between coders and the group consensus codes" (Humphrey, 1983, p. 7). Humphrey's results are very encouraging. It would seem that to get reliable kappas for coding complex, subtle, multiple messaging, there has to be explicit training on coding these particular types of interactions. It does appear that with specific training, clinically inexperienced coders can learn to code difficult material reliably. Incidentally, Humphrey's coders reported that they felt their clinical skills were greatly improved by this research training experience.

Kappa for an event by event test is a very stringent measure of coder agrement. Such a strict measure is necessary only if a statistical test that requires event-by-event precision is to be used. Sequential analyses demand such agreement. On the other hand, if there only is to be an analysis of profiles or a cross-sectional summary of each participant's action during a session, then a statistic that compares coding summary scores for the session is perfectly adequate. If, for example, one wishes to compare parents' relative amounts of power, warmth, freedom-giving, and so on, then a comparison of their totals for the respective categories suffices. Product-moment r is good for comparing patterns in profiles (Skinner, 1978).

Product-moment r's between experienced clinician researchers using SASB have been as high as .97. In the case of Foster's dissertation coders, product-moment r's ranged from .82 to .95. The discrepancy in magnitude between kappas that attend to sequence, and product-moment r's that attend only to total profiles is major and is noteworthy.

Validity of SASB Coding

Even if agreement between coders is high, it can be that the results are not useful. For example, it is easy to get high reliability on who is speaking and this in turn can yield a measure of activity level. Although it certainly is relevant, the activity level of each family member is not a very valid measure of the process of psychotherapy itself. To be *valid* as well as *reliable*, a coding system must yield numbers that relate to concepts meaningful to the clinician. And here the challenge is monumental. If family interactions were obviously and blatantly related to psychopathology, we would not have developed the false dichotomy between biological and humanistic, or between biochemical and psychosocial approaches to treatment. Assume for the moment that family interactions *do* relate to psychopathology; since primary affective disorders and schizophrenias, to name two categories, are often observed in "nice" families with many sociocultural advantages, how can it be that the family has anything to do with these very severe illnesses? Obviously, if families do have anything to do with these disorders, then a coding system that identifies the role of the family will have to go far beneath "what meets the eye." Many eyes have already "missed it" after years of looking! Here we may have a case of "proving the null hypothesis." The conclusion has been that families don't have anything to do with illnesses like primary affective disorders and schizophrenia because scientists can't find anything to establish that they do. But then, as always is true when trying to prove the null hypothesis, maybe we have not looked in the right place at the right time in the right way.

To develop a coding system which could look in the right place in the right way at the right time, which could go beneath the obvious to find the "microscopic" psychonoxious agents, and which could be operationalized and reliable is difficult to say the least. Again, it seems patently apparent that a successful and *valid* psychosocial microscope cannot be learned quickly or used with little effort. SASB potentially is that microscope.

Illustrative Data from the Family Consensus Task

To give SASB a testable (replicable) and highly meaningful challenge, a family participating in the Family Consensus Task (FCT) of the Interpersonal Diagnostic Project was selected at random for this presentation without knowing the results ahead of time. The family had an identified patient (IP) representing a diagnostic category believed by many "biological" type psychiatrists to have little or no relation to family interaction, namely schizophrenia (paranoid type).

The primary SASB coder was a student hourly worker with a master's degree in social work who had had 2½ years clinical experience working as a family therapist on an inpatient service supervised by an Ackerman-trained psychiatrist. The alternate SASB coder was a student hourly with a master's degree in social work who had no clinical experience. The primary coder was trained by Foster, and the alternate, by Giat Roberto. Benjamin had never met either coder prior to the generation of the data, and coders were kept blind to the diagnoses and to any current results or hypotheses from the Interpersonal Diagnostic Project.

The selection of a family at random plus the use of coders not trained by the principle investigator were intended to test the general applicability and communicability of the admittedly difficult SASB coding system. There was no assumption that the $N = 1$ shown here necessarily will characterize the families of paranoid schizophrenics. What was assumed was that the SASB coding scheme might generate scientifically useful and meaningful quantitative descriptions which also are seen as valid by psychosocially inclined clinicians, but have heretofore eluded many research methodologies. The analyses that follow demonstrate how the available SASB software can analyse codings in a way which makes sense clinically, and which shows scientific promise as a means of learning more about pathological and normal family interactions.

The FCT is a highly structured family interaction requiring the family to reach agreement on a number ranging from 0 to 100 which best describes how well-selected items from the INTREX questionnaire apply to the mother, the father, and the significant other when interacting with the IP. The experimental design provides that the mother, the father, and the significant other each be the target person for an equal number of items, and the order or presentation of target person is determined by a Latin square design. The actual rating developed by the family is irrelevant, but the *process* of reaching agreement is videotaped, transcribed, and segmented.

The FCT meets all the requirements of providing a concentrated brief sample of family interactions. However, on ordinary reading, the transcripts seem bland and even boring. Families usually are polite and agreeable as they reach their decisions; little affect is displayed and one might conclude on scanning the tapes and transcripts that these seriously ill psychiatric inpatients have ordinary families and the major inpatient psychiatric presentation could have little to do with family interaction.

To follow the SASB analysis of this difficult transcript, the reader will need to refer frequently back to Figure 11-2 because data are reported in terms of cluster names, and names alone do not adequately convey the meaning of SASB classifications. For example, the cluster Helping and Protecting (O-4) is often used to describe the experimenter's instructions to the family, and yet those words do not convey what is going on. Cluster O-4 involves Friendly Influence; it is easier to accept the judgment that the experimenter instructions are influencing and friendly than it is to accept the label "Helping and Protecting." Even if the cluster name does not adequately convey the nature of the transaction, specific items within the cluster usually do. Within cluster 4, item 145 does exactly describe the experimenter "Helping and Protecting." Item 145 reads: "Stimulates and teaches person, shows him or her how to understand, do." If there were no discernible warmth in the experimenter's manner, then the structuring of the task would be coded in cluster 1-5, Watching and Managing and specific items selected within that cluster might be: 140, "Manages, controls person, takes charge of everything," or maybe 138, "Insists person follows norms, rules, does things 'properly'."

A Detailed Consideration of the Process Coding
of the Transcript for Family 045

In all FCTs, Referent 1 = the identified patient, Referent 2 = the mother, Referent 3 = the father, Referent 4 = the significant other, Referent 5 = the mother + father combination, Referent 6 = the experimenter, and Referent 7 = the family in general. The transcript for Family 045 began:

1. Experimenter (E): The first sentence is, Actively listens, accepts and affirms D. as a person, even if their views disagree. First agree together on how to rate mother with D.

The process coding of the first element of this use was X,Y = 6,7, meaning the communication was from the experimenter (6) to the family in general (7). Cluster O-4, Helping and Protecting, was selected to describe the experimenter's process. It represents friendly influence and is best described by the particular point 145: "Stimulates and teaches person; shows how to understand, do." The coder saw more power in the second element, and so it was coded X,Y = 6,7, cluster O-5.

2. Father (F): I didn't hear what we're supposed to do.

Process is X,Y = 3,1, cluster S-4. The videotape suggested the communication was from father (3) to the daughter (1) and the coder judgment was that he was Trusting and Relying upon the daughter. Within cluster S-4, point number 243 summarizes the judgment: "Is trusting, asks for what s/he wants and counts on person to be kind and considerate."

3. Daughter (D): You didn't hear her? You didn't hear her?

Process in Unit 3 was X,Y = 1,3, cluster O-2, suggesting that the communication was from daughter to father and the mode was Affirming and Understanding. Here, the coder judged the daughter was focused on the father, friendly, and reacting to him as a separate person; the actual point selected in cluster O-2 probably was 115, "Actively listens, accepts and affirms person even with disagreement." If the coder had detected a hostile and coercive tone, the transaction might have been coded 0-6, Belittling and Blaming. However, the videotape suggested warmth and separateness and coding was identical for both elements.

4. F: No.

X,Y = 3,3, cluster = S-1. The communication was from father to daughter in the mode of Asserting and Separating himself. Perhaps the coder selected point 216 in cluster S-2: "Is straightforward, clearly expresses positions so person can give them due consideration."

5. D: I don't think he understood what you asked him.

X,Y = 1,6, cluster S-1 reflects the daughter's assertion to the experimenter and X,Y = 1,6, cluster O-4 adds a description of her focus on the experimenter in a friendly, influencing fashion. Again, if there had not been warmth in the communication, cluster O-5, Watching and Managing might have been selected to put more emphasis on the daughter's control here.

6. E: I'd like you to reach an agreement as to how much mother actively listens, accepts, and affirms D. as a person even if their views disagree.

Process was X,Y = 6,3, cluster O-4. The communication is from experimenter to father in the mode of friendly influence. Here, the coder missed the process of the experimenter being forced by context to comply with the daughter; this aspect would be coded X,Y = 6,1, cluster S-4 to reflect experimenter behavior described by point 244: "Willingly accepts, yields to person's reasonable suggestions, ideas." The father's uncertainty could have been worked out directly between the experimenter and the father but father had turned to the daughter, not the experimenter to clarify; the daughter responded by intruding herself into the process in a fairly powerful way here. No doubt the experimenter would have responded to the father anyway, had the daughter not intervened. The father's deference to daughter and the daughter's intervention on his behalf forces the experimenter to be in a compliant position and the coding system is capable of recording such multiple meanings. Probably the experimenter would report a degree of discomfort at being forced to show the simultaneous complements O-4 and S-4.

7. D: Do I agree with this one too?

Process is XY = 1,6, cluster O-2. At the first level, the daughter is asking the experimenter a question in a friendly, independent mode. The coder also recorded XY = 1,6, cluster S-4 to reflect the apparently compliant posture suggested by the peculiar use of the word "agree." In addition, the communication should have been called "complex" and could have had an additional coding of cluster S-8, Walling off and Avoiding, to include item 224, "Does strange, irrelevant, unrelated things with what person says or does, goes on 'own trip'." The schizophrenic daughter is seemingly compliant (after being so controlling), but simultaneously is retaining the opposite (ambivalent) posture of autistic hostile autonomy by peculiar word usage. The addition of cluster S-8 would be reflective of the schizophrenic-like concretism implied by the use of the word "agree" immediately after the experimenter used it while reading . . . "even if their views disagree."

8. E: Everyone can participate.

X,Y = 6,1, cluster O-4. The message from experimenter to daughter is friendly influence.

Units 9–75 are omitted to save space. During this segment daughter and father did most of the interacting and mother was asked occasionally what she thought; her responses were agreeable but she showed minimal self-disclosure. Starting with unit 60, the father became the target as required by the FCT task. The first several items related to father were treated in the usual family fashion of agreeability, but then, in unit 76:

76. E: Okay. Again, I'd like you to rate father with D. (Experimenter projects a new item which states that: father buries his rage, and resentment and scurries to appease the daughter to avoid her disapproval).

Process is XY = 6,7, cluster O-2 reflecting the "okay," followed by XY = 6,7, cluster O-4 reflecting the influence inherent in asking for the judgment.

77. D: Okay, it's talking about, dad burying his own rage and resentment about me? I would say no then, zero.

Process is XY = 1,6, cluster O-2. The daughter first addresses the experimenter in a questioning fashion. A second process coding for the daughter was XY, = 1,6, cluster S-2. The daughter discloses and expresses her opinion about the rating.

78. E: The sentence would be, how much might dad bury his own rage and resentment and scurry to appease you or to avoid your disapproval?

Process is XY = 6,1, cluster O-4. Experimenter shows friendly influence to the daughter.

79. D: Oh, I don't know. He wouldn't, so I'd say zero. What do you say?

Process is coded X,Y = 1,6, cluster S-8. The daughter first addresses the experimenter in a nondisclosing manner. Then she does disclose: X,Y = 1,6, cluster S-1. The third element, "What do you say?," is coded X,Y = 1,3, cluster O-2 to reflect the fact shown on videotape that the daughter has turned to the father and asked for his opinion.

80. F: What did you say?

Process is X,Y = 3,1, cluster O-2. Father openly questions daughter. The coder also added X,Y = 3,1, cluster S-8 to reflect the fact the father has so obviously "tuned out" the daughter's very clear message.

81. D: Zero.

Process is X,Y = 1,3, cluster S-1. The daughter's response to the father was coded as a clear assertion.

82. Sister (S): I don't know if you understand the question. I think you should explain it perhaps maybe so they'll understand what they're discussing.

Process is XY = 4,7, cluster O-4 as the sister addressed the IP plus father, approximated best by the family code "7." The sister tells father and daughter they do not understand the question. The second element is X,Y = 4,6, cluster O-5 as the sister turned to the experimenter and now, in a powerful manner, suggests that the experimenter should straighten the family out.

83. E: Sure. The idea here would be whether father might bury his own anger at times, his own rage or resentment over something, in order to appease D. and avoid her disapproval. How much is that true from a scale of 0 to 100?

Process is XY = 6,4, cluster S-1. The coder sees the experimenter assert, but it might better have been recorded as S-4 to show the experimenter complied with the sister's request. The next element is X,Y = 6,7, cluster O-4 to reflect the experimenter addressing the family in a friendly influencing fashion. The last element is coded X,Y = 6,7, cluster O-4 to reflect the request for a rating.

84. S: The word appease here meaning?

Process is XY = 4,6, cluster O-2. The sister turns to the experimenter and inquires to understand. The coder also identifies an agenda as above threshold and codes the sense of coercion with XY = 4,6, cluster O-5. The fact there are two very different messages in the same element defines this communication as complex.

85. E: Uh, so that she would approve, in other words do it her way so she would approve. How much might dad do that?

Process is XY = 6,4, cluster S-1 to reflect the experimenter's stating what the task is. Then XY = 6,7, cluster O-4 describes the message to the family in general that it should meet the requirements of the task.

86. Mother (M): Well, I think I'd give that about a 70.

Process is X,Y = 2,6, cluster S-1 to reflect mother responding to the experimenter in an assertive manner. This is mother's first assertion.

87. F: To avoid disapproval. What would that mean?

Process coded X,Y = 3,2, cluster S-8 (Walling off and Avoiding) reflects the father's "not understanding"; the lengthy inquiry about the meaning of the item seems inappropriate and is judged to mean more than just not hearing the question. X,Y = 3,4, cluster S-4 is added to reflect the fact father then turned to the sister in a dependent manner.

88. S: That you don't want D. to disapprove of, in other words, if you are angry about something, you wouldn't let it show necessarily because you wouldn't want D. to disapprove, as I understand it.

Process is X,Y = 4,3, cluster O-4. The sister relates to father in a friendly influencing fashion.

89. F: (to E.) Is that it? I see. I had this wrong. (*mumbles*) What does D. think?

Process is X,Y = 3,6, cluster S-4. The father relates to the experimenter in a manner described by item 245, "Learns from person, takes advice from person." His self-criticism would be recorded in content, not process. The coder added XY = 3,6, cluster S-8 to reflect his autistic-like mumbling. The coder flagged these two opposing messages of agreement and withdrawal as complex. Then XY = 3,1, cluster O-2 describes his turning to the daughter with an inquiry about her position.

90. D: Well, I would, I don't know. But as far as I know I don't feel that you bury your feelings, so I would give it a zero.

Process is X,Y = 1,3, cluster S-8 and suggests nondisclosure, best described by item 225, "Walls off from person, doesn't hear, doesn't react." In the second element, the coder recognizes the implied put-down of mother and records XY = 1,2, cluster O-6. The self-disclosure which then follows is recorded XY = 1,3, cluster S-1. Finally, the daughter makes a commanding statement coded XY = 1,3, cluster O-4.

91. F: Huh?

X,Y is 3,1, cluster O-2 to reflect father inquiring openly of daughter.

92. D: So I would rate it a zero. Because I don't feel . . .

Process X,Y = 1,3, cluster S-1 and reflects the daughter's assertion.

93. F: No, I never, I never . . .

Process is coded X,Y = 3,1, cluster S-5. Father is seen as giving in to the daughter here. Note the blatant contradiction between process and content here. Father's content is assertive (S-1), but his process is submissive (S-5).

94. D: That you try to please me.

X,Y is coded 1,3, cluster S-1. The daughter autonomously continues her assertion begun in unit 92.

95. F: No—I—no.

Process is X,Y = 3,1, cluster S-5. Father agrees completely with daughter's insistence the item does not apply.

96. D: So I don't, do you understand what I'm saying now?

Process is X,Y = 1,2, cluster O-6 to reflect the daughter turning to the mother in a patronizing, mildly hostile manner presented as open inquiry coded XY = 1,2, cluster O-2. The combination is coded as complex.

97. M: Um, hm.

Process is X,Y = 2,1, cluster S-4. Mother defers to the daughter.

98. D: I mean he doesn't.

Process is coded X = 1,2, cluster O-6 to reflect the continued diversion of mother as described by item 134: "Misleads, deceives, deludes, and diverts person," along with XY = 1,3, cluster O-4 to reflect the fact the daughter talks to mother, but is also clearly sending a message of influence to the father.

99. F: I . . . (*mumbles*)

This unit is uncodable.

100. M: No, I see what you mean, I see what you mean, a lot of these questions are kind of . . . um . . .

Process is X,Y = 2,1, cluster S-5 and represents the capitulation to the daughter. By now it's becoming clear that the family as a unit is having a great deal of trouble dealing with this particular item; if not understanding the item does not suffice to deal with the problem, they try criticizing the questions and perhaps this should have been coded XY = 1,6 cluster O-6. The experimenter persists:

101. E: The point here would be whether you feel dad might at times bury his anger so that D. wouldn't disapprove of him.

Process is coded X,Y = 6,7, cluster O-4. One might consider cluster O-5 to reflect the persistent control, but the videotape reveals steady, pleasant warmth from the Experimenter.

102. D: Did you hear that?

Process is XY = 1,2, cluster O-2. The daughter has turned to the father in an open manner of inquiry followed by an implied demand: XY = 1,2, cluster O-5. The tension in this "simple" message is called complex by the coder.

103. F: (*mumbles*)

X,Y = 1,3 is uncodable.

104. D: So what do you think?

Process is X,Y = 1,2, cluster O-2 to reflect the daughter's inquiry now directed toward the mother, in the context of a demand for compliance: XY = 1,2, cluster O-5. The coder calls this combination a complex communication. Whatever else is true, it can be seen from this sequence that the daughter is playing an extremely active role in eliciting and consolidating judgment about the father on the "appeasing" item. The mother stayed in the periphery until drawn in by the sister, when she made a short-lived attempt to express her own divergent opinion. The passage that follows shows what happens when mother more actively attempts to defy the father–daughter coalition:

105. M: Well, I'm just sort of stuck. I'm thinking that, could I give an example?

Process is XY=2,3, cluster S-2 to reflect her disclosure. Then X,Y=2,6, cluster S-4 reflects the mother addressing the experimenter in a deferential manner.

106. E: Please however you want to.

Process is coded X,Y=6,2, cluster O-1. The experimenter gives the mother complete freedom.

107. M: I was just thinking now when we learned D. smokes, which we didn't know, then we certainly didn't approve of it but we just went along with it and I say we, I too, we didn't approve of it.

Process is X,Y=2,6, cluster S-1 indicating that the mother has addressed the experimenter in a very assertive manner.

108. D: But you didn't go into a *rage* about it.

Process is coded XY=1,2, cluster O-6 plus XY=1,2, cluster S-8. This reflects the blatant manipulation (134: "Misleads, deceives, deludes, diverts") of mother plus autism (224: "Does strange, irrelevant, unrelated things with what person says or does; goes on 'own trip'"). Recall that the item being discussed was point 235, "The father buries rage and resentment and scurries to appease D. to avoid disapproval." The family has this item in clear, full view projected upon the wall so that blatant misunderstanding represents a forthright distortion of reality in order to avoid endorsing the item. In other words, the item reads that father suppresses rage. There is not any reference to father going into a rage, and yet the family is behaving as if the item describes the father going into a rage. Such a blatant distortion of reality is reflected by the S-8 code. The O-6 and S-8 combination was a complex communication, though the coder did not record it as such in this case. In retrospect this omission was found to be a proof-reading error.

109. F: (*simultaneously with mother*) No—we didn't—no . . .

Process is X,Y=3,1, cluster S-6 reflecting father deferring again to daughter.

110. M: No we didn't go into a rage or anything. No.

Process is X,Y=2,1, cluster S-6. Mother shows blatant submission to the daughter's control. Possibly the coder was using item 234: "Even though suspicious and distrustful of person, goes along with person's arguments, ideas."

111. E: That would be an example of this kind of thing, the idea would be he might bury his own feelings in order to appease D. or avoid her disapproval.

Process is X,Y=6,7, cluster O-4, again showing the experimenter addressing the family with a friendly instruction. If the experimenter had been in a therapist role, the discrepancy between what the item said and what the family was saying surely should have been discussed. The experimenter appropriately conformed exactly to the research protocol of only reading the items. If the family chose to continue to distort, it could.

112. M: He knows that she shouldn't, but he does it all the time too, and, so, that question is . . . right.

Process is X,Y=2,3, cluster O-6 reflecting the mother putting down the father. X,Y=2,6, cluster S-1 shows the mother asserting to the experimenter her opinion that the item does describe father. Mother now has taken a very separate position from the father–daughter coalition and that could have been coded XY=2,1, cluster S-1 and XY=2,3, cluster S-1.

113. F: But I didn't go into a rage or that sort of thing.

Process is X,Y=3,2, cluster S-6 reflecting the coder judgment that father is defending himself. Item 233 reads: ''Whines, protests, tries to explain, account for self.'' He is, however, as noted above still pretending that the item is describing him going into a rage rather than suppressing it and his distortion of reality should have been included XY=3,2, cluster S-8, complex.

114. M: No you didn't go into a rage or anything, you just accepted it. So we don't know just how to . . .

Process is XY=2,3, cluster S-1; XY=2,3, cluster O-4; XY=2,3, cluster S-6. The coder viewed the mother addressing father in an assertive, protective and yet compliant way. The mother continued ''So we don't know just how to . . . ,'' which the coder called XY=2,6, cluster S-2, a disclosure with substantial autonomy rather than dependence. The communication is multiple, but not complex.

115. D: Well that would be, that would indicated on the left then, 50% side then. See what I'm saying?

The scale projected for the family to use is marked false for ratings of less than 50 and true for ratings of 50 or more. In other words, the daughter was maintaining here that the description was not true; she held it was inappropriate when applied to the father even though the mother had clearly given an example showing that the statement was true. The coder recorded this process X,Y=1,2, cluster S-1 indicating the daughter asserted in relation to the mother. The second element, ''See what I'm saying?,'' was coded complex: XY=1,2, cluster S-5 to reflect deference; XY=1,2, cluster O-2 to reflect inquiry; and XY=1,2, cluster O-5 to reflect the implied demand. The father responded quickly:

116. F: On the low side.

Process is X,Y=3,1, cluster S-4. The coder recorded father's agreement with the daughter.

117. D: Yes. See.

Process is X,Y=1,3, cluster O-2 showing the daughter was listening to the father plus X,Y=1,2, cluster O-5 described the daughter turning to the mother with a demanding ''See.''

118. F: Well, I would think so too.

Process is coded X,Y=3,2, cluster O-5. The father turned to the mother and reinforced the daughter's controlling message.

119. M: Ya, I guess that would be.

Process is XY=2,3, cluster S-5. The mother ''cracked'' and gave in again.

120. E: Can you agree on a number?

Process XY = 6,7, cluster O-2. The experimenter asked for a response in a way which clearly left it "up to them."

121. F: 40? (*whispers*)

Process is X,Y = 3,7, cluster O-2 to reflect the father's listening to the developing consensus that the item is "untrue."

122. D: I guess 40's fine with me.

Process is X,Y = 1,3, cluster O-2, suggesting the daughter listens to father. She was not coded as compliant here probably because of father's "opinion" was her's in the first place. This is an example of how context often affects coding which would look different if done strictly on a unit-by-unit basis.

123. M: Okay.

Process is X,Y = 2,3, cluster S-5 reflecting the mother complying with father. The episode ends with mother agreeing to call the item not true, although she had tried for a while to establish otherwise.

The remainder of the task consisted of family trying to decide what to do with the $30 they were to be paid for participation in the task, and that was resolved by the daughter's making the decision ("I think we should go and have a treat"). She was backed up immediately by the father.

The unedited casual reading of the typescript without benefit of microscopic commentary suggested a friendly family not fighting at all, working out agreement about what number to give each item with a fair amount of "give and take." The alternate coder, who completed this assignment without knowing the content of the items being rated by the family, missed the distortions of reality manifest as the family contemplated the item that proposed father's possible appeasement of the daughter. The alternate coder's record was of affable give-and-take among family members, and clusters 2 and 4 on both interpersonal surfaces were used almost exclusively. These particular clusters, Affirming and Understanding, O-2, Disclosing and Expressing, S-2, Helping and Protecting, O-4, and Trusting and Relying, S-4, would suffice to summarize the observations of a casual observer. However, the close microscopic examination by the coder with clinical experience who had been instructed to attend carefully to the content of the items yielded a very different description of the family. There were some passages which suggested thought "disorder" or, at a minimum, that participants who did not agree with what was going on in the family might think they had poor reality testing. The item describing chart point 236, which actually suggested father's rage and resentment was buried and hidden so that he could avoid daughter's disapproval was transformed into an imaginary item which would have described father as going into a rage rather than burying it. The father and daughter then "disagreed with" this imaginary item and forced the mother to agree with the imaginary item as if it had been the real one. The interesting thing, of course, is that it is the daughter, not the mother, who was the person with the schizophrenic label here. Actually there is no diagnostic information on anyone in this family other than the daughter. The coding suggests an understudied phenomenon of "parent abuse" and underscores the need to look at the whole system to understand the presentation of one of its members. In much of the family literature, the mother is identified as a noxious agent (e.g., Fromm-Reichmann,

1950), and in many instances, she may be. This example shows the role of the IP must also be considered, and fathers must not be overlooked in the analysis of family interactions either. In the family research literature, frequently fathers are only assessed in terms of their dominance (=''normal'') or lack of it (=''abnormal'').

Analysis of SASB Coding

Program PROCESS—A Summary of Process

There are several computer programs available to analyze SASB codings. The most basic is the program PROCESS which simply counts process interactions. In PROCESS, the computer scans each unit to identify the speaker, the person to whom the speaker addressed a message, and then reports the number and the percentage of interpersonal clusters used by this speaker in relation to each of the family members present. For family 045, PROCESS first provided a report for the distribution of interpersonal postures exhibited by the daughter when addressing the mother, by the daughter when addressing the father, by the daughter when addressing the combination mother+father, and by the daughter addressing the experimenter. According to PROCESS, the daughter never directly addressed the sister. PROCESS repeated this type of analysis for each of the family members present.

Figure 11-4 presents cross-sectional profiles from PROCESS for the father, daughter, and mother in relation to each other. The top part of Figure 11-4 shows father–daughter interactions, the middle shows mother–daughter interactions, and the bottom, the marital interactions. Each horizontal line in Figure 11-4 adds up to 100%, so the profiles for each person show which behaviors were most characteristic in each relationship. These cross-sectional data show at least four interesting major trends: The daughter showed more pure control and more hostile control toward her mother than toward her father (compare clusters 5 and 6 on the left-hand side of the middle graph with clusters 5 and 6 on the top one). The mother complemented this control by showing far more submission to the daughter than vice versa (on the right-hand side of the middle figure, compare the mother and daughter curves for clusters 4, 5, and 6). Both parents complemented the daughter's tendency to focus on other by a tendency to focus on themselves and neither parent was very assertive or very controlling of the daughter (compare the daughter curves on the left-hand side of the top and middle figures with the corresponding parent curves on the right-hand side).

Since SASB theory suggests that focus on other is prototypically parent-like and focus on self is prototypically child-like, it is clear that there is a role reversal between the daughter and her parents. Ideally, by adulthood, a child ''grows'' up and equal amounts of focus on self and other are shown by both parent and child. In this family, the father–daughter combination approaches balance of focus better than does either the mother–daughter or the father–mother combination. (For each person compare percentage of responses on the left-hand side with the percentage of responses on the right-hand side. For the middle and lower graphs, a discrepancy or imbalance in the two types of focus is more apparent.) One therapeutic implication would be that the mother should be less submissive and reactive; more assertiveness and influencing behaviors from her in relation to the daughter and father would provide more equitable balance. Since complementarity is interactive, there is no ''blame'' assigned to the mother. The daughter's excessive control and inordinate focus on other is one part of this family's

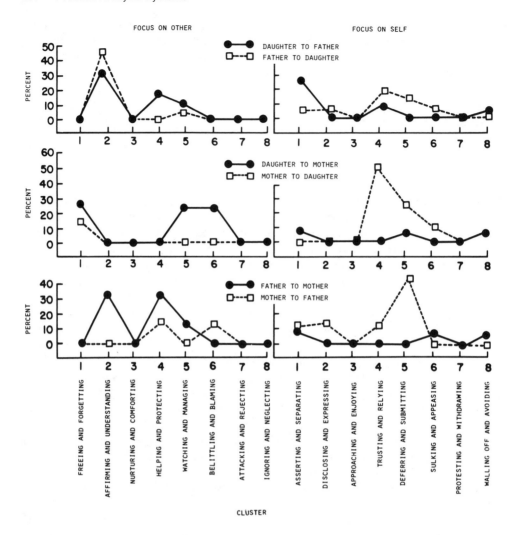

Figure 11-4   Cross-sectional summary of Family 045 generated by PROCESS. The top part of the figure shows behavioral profile for the daughter and father in relation to each other, the middle describes the mother–daughter relationship, and the bottom part describes the marital relationship. The text elaborates upon how this cross-sectional profile permits characterization of the interpersonal postures of family members in relation to each other.

equation. More about the dynamics of control in this family appears in a subsequent section presenting analysis of the complex communications.

In sum, the program PROCESS provides a cross-sectional view of the behavior of each family (or group) member in relation to every other. These profiles point to the predominant styles and could permit testing of various dynamic hypotheses such as who is generally dominant over whom and who generally complements whom. Therapeutic implications for the family system may be specified by SASB theory (using principles of complementarity, introjection, antithesis and the Shaurette Principle). Product-moment r would be an adequate measure of reliability for the cross-sectional profiles produced by PROCESS.

Did the Family See Itself
as the Behavioral Coders Did?

Family perceptions of interactions with the identified patient are measured in the Interpersonal Diagnostic Project by having family members rate each other on the INTREX questionnaires which have been described elsewhere (Benjamin, 1979, 1981, 1982). Briefly, a given family member (e.g., father) rates another (e.g., daughter) on a series of 72 items corresponding to the 72 interpersonal points on the SASB model using a scale from 0 to 100. Zero indicates the item never fits and is entirely inappropriate, whereas 100 indicates the item is extremely apt and also applies consistently. Fifty is the boundary between "true and false." There are several different computer programs available for processing the questionnaire data for clinical and for research purposes. Only the average cluster scores (one set of the many available parameters) are used here to compare the family perceptions measured by the questionnaire with actual behavior as recorded by the coder of the FCT. The average cluster scores from the questionnaire data correspond most directly to the percentage of codings recorded by the judges for each cluster in Figure 11-2. Average cluster scores generate a profile similar to those shown for the behavioral codings of Figure 11-4. With eight clusters per surface, there are 6 degrees of freedom for r and an $r > .71$ is significant at better than the .05 level when comparing questionnaires with behavioral ratings, or when comparing coders with each other.

Program COMP generates an infinite number of experimenter-defined r's between surfaces to test hypotheses about complementarity and similarity. COMP also provides a variety of distance measures (Mahalanobis') for situations where discrepancy is of more interest than similarity. In the case of FCT, COMP is convenient for generating correlations testing agreement between judges, among family members, and between judges and family members.

Product-moment correlations between family perceptions and the coder judgments of family behavior were much higher for the alternate coder having no clinical experience and not instructed explicitly to attend to the content of the items. In other words, the more casual and clinically untrained observations were more consistent with the family's self-descriptions on the questionnaires. The family agreement with the primary coder, who recorded manipulations (cluster O-6), autisms (clusters O-8 and S-8), and control (cluster O-5) along with friendliness (pseudomutuality), was, for the most part, not very high. Although correlations may not be averaged and then tested for statistical significance, they have been averaged here simply to give an impression of the degree of correspondence. Each of the correlations presented is an average of the following set of 4: Person A focuses on Person B; A reacts to B by focus on self; B focuses on A; B reacts to A by focus on self. "React" does not mean "follows in time" or "is not responsible." Focus on self can precede focus on other. The average r between the patient's view of her relationship with her father and the alternate coder's view was .60; for the primary coder, $r = .53$. For the father's view of his relationship with the patient, $r = .69$ in the alternate coder's judgment; with the primary coder, $r = .52$.

Ratings of correspondence between family view and coder view when the patient's interactions with the mother were the target were very poor for both judges: for the patient's view and the alternate coder's view, $r = .33$; for patient view and primary coder, $r = -.05$; for mother's view and the alternate coder, $r = .28$; and for mother's view compared to the primary coder's, $r = .11$. In sum, the family's generalized perception of each other in general showed some correspondence to the alternate coder's judgment of their behavior in the FCT task, especially when rating the patient with her father; when describing the patient with the mother, family agreement with both coders' views was poor.

Do Coders Agree with Each Other in Their Perceptions of the Family?

Coder agreement with each other was better when the father was the target; coder agreement was .71. However, when the mother was the target, coder agreement was only .39; when the patient with father was the target, agreement was .58; when patient with mother was judged, between coder agreement was .25. It was the transactions between the patient and her mother which were most complex.

Although many of the specific r's (not the average r's) did reach .71 or more, suggesting statistically significant agreement, the magnitude of correspondence was rarely impressive. Inspection of codings and of the transcript established that the discrepancy between coders often occurred when the alternate coder took the family at "face value," and the primary coder saw more messages in the transactions.

Program CONTENT—A Summary of Content

The SASB coding method allows what the family is talking about to be recorded and analyzed independently of the manner in which they talk (process). Program CONTENT functions as PROCESS except it uses content rather than process ratings. To save space, content analysis is not discussed here. In general, content analysis is more relevant and productive for individual hours in psychotherapies such as psychoanalysis where the content of patient's productions is emphasized. In family therapy where the process itself is believed to enhance the treatment effect, SASB process analysis is most appropriate. In individual psychotherapies where the patient–therapist interaction is considered major, then process rather than content analysis should be emphasized. Of course, both may be included for research as well as clinical purposes.

Program FOLLOW—A One-Step Sequential Analysis

There may be more to be learned by adding a study of sequences to the cross-sectional survey provided by PROCESS. For example, most families punish children for "misbehavior" and so perhaps normal families cannot be distinguished from clinical families on the basis of frequency of punishment. It is possible however, that a sequential analysis of contexts for punishment would provide critically important additional information. One clinical belief is that punishment follows dependent behavior (especially for males) in normal families, whereas punishment follows independent behaviors in pathological families (e.g., Benjamin, 1979b). In some types of pathological families (e.g., those with major depression), maybe parental hostile control follows the child's assertion and independence. According to SASB theory, assertiveness would then be less likely while spineless conformity and dependency, the complements of hostile control, would be more likely.

For sequential analyses, kappa is the proper measure of reliability, because it measures coder agreement on an event-by-event basis. The basic method currently used for sequential analysis of SASB codings is called Markov chain analysis and was reviewed in Benjamin (1979b) when analyzing two-person interactions between patient and therapist. Program FOLLOW creates a transition matrix for each family member in relation to each other family member. For the Markov chain dyadic analysis of family interactions, it was necessary to identify as the basic unit instances where Speaker A *addressed Person B*, Person B was the next speaker, and *B directed his/her communications back to A*. The conditions underlined were not included in the original version of FOLLOW written for studying patient–therapist interactions. When more than two people are present, there can be instances of process wherein Person B follows Person A, but A was not talking to B and/or B then speaks to someone else. To illustrate these problems, consider units 117 and 118:

117: Daughter: Yes. See.
118: Father: Well, I would think so too.

In the context provided previously, these "simple" exchanges received significant codings. Process for 117 was $X,Y = 1,3$, cluster S-4 to show the "Yes" represented daughter's agreement with what father had said in 116. The "See" was coded $X,Y = 1,2$, cluster O-5 to reflect the control then directed toward the mother. Unit 118 was coded $X,Y = 3,2$, cluster O-5 to describe the control from father to mother, and $X,Y = 3,1$, cluster O-2 to capture the open listening position from father to daughter. Note that even though these short statements received more than one process code, they were not called "complex." There was more than one message in them, but the messages did not involve the inextricable recursiveness required for a complex code. The multiple messages here were quite clear, distinct, and sent to different family members.

If the dyadic analysis of the father–daughter relationship is to be studied by looking at this segment where the father spoke immediately after the daughter, it is clear that the codings having to do with the mother should not be counted in the study of the father–daughter relationship. Without the underlined restrictions, units 117 and 118 would contribute to the generation of output looking as if the daughter was directing control toward the father, and vice versa when in fact here they were collaborating with each other to convince the mother of the daughter's point of view.

Program FOLLOW provides a one-step count of the percentage of times each cluster was coded when a given family member followed another under the restrictions underlined above. Illustrative units 117 and 118 were included in the study of all instances wherein the father spoke immediately after the daughter. The underlined restrictions provide that the messages to the mother would be ignored here; they only would show up in the cross-sectional report from PROCESS. Since so many of the communications from daughter to mother, like this one, were in the context of other speakers' interactions with the daughter, there was almost no data on direct mother–daughter interaction recorded by FOLLOW. However, the rare direct mother–daughter interaction which was detected was very informative: When there were direct mother–daughter communications, FOLLOW reported the mother always complied (S-4) no matter what the daughter had done (O-2 or O-6). And when the daughter spoke immediately after the mother directly addressing the communication to the mother, it was to put the mother down (mother S-4, daughter O-6).

Program FOLLOW also provides an activity report of the percentage of instances wherein A addressed a message to B, and B followed, but spoke to someone else. For this family, the activity report showed that the father spoke back to the daughter frequently when he was addressed by her (70%), whereas the mother did not (33%). By contrast, 71% of the time, the mother spoke directly back to the father when addressed by him. With these numbers, the activity report suggests that another problem in the mother–daughter relationship in addition to the daughter's extraordinary influence and the mother's unusual deference, is that the mother did not respond directly back to the daughter.

Occasionally, there is a unit wherein more than one process code is needed to describe a message from A to B. In this case, the multiple event provides more than one count so that the total number of events reported by FOLLOW can be greater than the total number reported by PROCESS. For example, as Family 045 discussed the $30 payment for participation in the research:

127: Father: Well, we don't need the money terrible bad (X,Y=father to experimenter, S-2), is there a real good charity we could give it to? (father to experimenter, S-5).

128: Experimenter: Well, why don't you discuss this among yourselves, what you'd like to do (experimenter to father, O-4).

In the study of father–experimenter communication, there would be one count of father S-2, to experimenter O-4, and another count of father S-5 to experimenter O-4. Program PROCESS, by contrast, would count the instance of the experimenter O-4 only once. FOLLOW had to count the experimenter O-4 twice because it did follow father's two different postures: S-2 and S-5. It would not be appropriate to maintain that the experimenter was responding just to one or the other of the father's leads in unit 127.

Selected data from FOLLOW can be punched for subsequent use by MARKOV. Printed reports from FOLLOW typically are quite long and show a variety of responses from one family member to another. For example, consider the report on daughter leads, father follows: $N=8$ for daughter leading with O-2; father followed with O-2=33%, S-1=25%; S-5=13% and S-8=25%. $N=2$ for daughter leading with O-4; father followed with O-2=100%. $N=2$ for daughter leading with O-5; father returned O-5=50%, and S-4=50%. $N=6$ for daughter leading with S-1; father followed with O-2=33%, O-5=17%, S-4=17%, S-5=33%. $N=1$ for daughter leading with S-8; father followed with O-2=100%.

Program MARKOV—Projecting Ahead on the Basis of One-Step Sequential Analyses

It is hard to know what to do on an $N=1$ basis with the complicated reports from FOLLOW. Between group trends are expected to be found for a larger sample. It may be, for example, that in the group of paranoid schizophrenics, the IP will frequently show control over one parent as the daughter did here. The only completed analysis of the FCT of a major depressive disorder showed the expected emphasis on compliance by the IP. In addition, the mother of the major depressive did have a noticeable tendency to invoke hostile power on the rare occasion the IP tried to assert. Such trends toward complementarity may be identified on a group basis; lack of it may characterize some diagnostic groups.

On an individual basis, the complicated results from FOLLOW can be simplified and highlighted by MARKOV. On the left-hand side of Figure 11-5, the MARKOV chain analysis for daughter-initiated sequences are presented and father-initiated sequences appear on the right-hand side.

The mathematics used by MARKOV are from Isaacson and Madsen (1976) as summarized by Benjamin (1979b). Briefly, data for Figure 11-5 were started with the matrix: daughter led–father followed (call this matrix A) postmultiplied by the matrix-tabulating steps when father led and daughter followed (B). The result, $T = AB$, summarizes the sequence: daughter initiated, father responded, daughter reacted to that. On reflecting on the rules for matrix multiplication of a simple 2×2 matrix, one can observe that for any given cell in a matrix like T, there is input from all the cells in that given cell's row, and all the cells in the given cell's column. For example, the cell describing the daughter's transition from Affirming and Understanding her father (O-2) to Asserting and Separating from him (S-1) describes the likelihood that she will move from O-2 to S-1 when engaged in a direct exchange with father. That likelihood statement includes a consideration of all possible one-step transitions from and to both these clusters (O-2, S-1) by both the father and the daughter. Since the 16×16 matrixes A and B contain a large number of empty cells (unused clusters), there are a number of possibilities for a nonzero entry in A or B to get "zeroed" out when cross-multiplying to compute matrix $T = AB$ (see also Benjamin, 1986b).

The matrix T can be taken to higher powers, P, to represent what would happen if this one-step chain were to repeat itself $P + 1$ times. Program MARKOV takes AB to the third power, so it presents an estimate of daughter's transition probabilities from one state to another if the entire FCT sequence were to be repeated four times. Taking AB to higher powers subjects the surviving entries in T to further possibilities of zeroing out. Often, successive powers of T diminish toward the null matrix. However, sometimes, as in the case of the father–daughter interactions shown in Figure 11-5, strong stable trends become emphasized as others drop out. Figure 11-5 presents only probabilities from T^3 which are greater than .30. This number arbitrarily has been selected by appeal to the equally arbitrary convention of noticing (factor) loadings of .30 or more.

Inspection of Figure 11-5 suggests that the daughter had a stable and compelling tendency to move toward a state of assertiveness and separation from the father. SASB theory provides that assertiveness (S-1) is the antithesis of control (O-5), and so the pattern shown by the daughter in Figure 11-5 may represent a defense against being controlled. Resistance to being controlled via oppositional independence is consistent with the clinical presentation of paranoid schizophrenics. Perhaps such patterns in T^3 also will characterize a larger sample of paranoids.

The right-hand side of Figure 11-5 shows the father moving consistently toward cluster O-2, Affirming and Understanding (listening to) the daughter. This noninfluential autonomy-giving posture on the part of the father is nearly complementary to her strong position of separateness (S-1). Whether he has always given her so much "room" is not known; possibly her "illness" has served to give her the desired separate space. A prospective developmental study might be the only way to know if such extreme assertiveness is, in fact, a defense against (response to) overcontrol. The IP's retrospective ratings on the INTREX questionnaires of the parents during childhood did not suggest that control perceived from the parents was markedly off the norm.

In addition to providing a measure of transition probabilities, MARKOV yields an estimate of the probability the IP would be in any of the states (clusters) at the end of the hypothetical fourth FCT session. This prediction begins with a starting vector, $\mathbf{v}$, which represents the base rate for this individual. The base rate for each cluster is simply the frequency with which it occurred according to PROCESS, divided by the total number of clusters coded for this individual. The quantity $\mathbf{v}T^3$ represents the desired prediction, which psychologically speaking, the vector represents a joint venture consideration of (1) the overall base-rate likelihood of showing behavior coded in a given

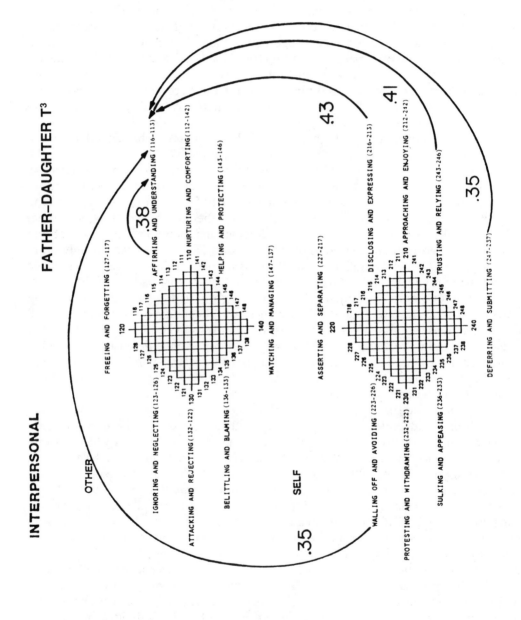

FATHER–DAUGHTER T³

INTERPERSONAL

430

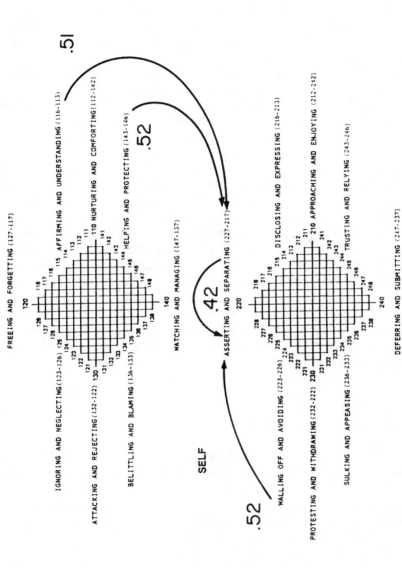

Figure 11-5 Markov chain analysis of the father–daughter relationship. The left-hand side of the figure suggests that when the daughter initiates transactions which are responded to by the father with a message directed back toward the daughter, there is a consistent sequential tendency for the daughter to move toward a state of absolute autonomy, the opposite of submitting to control. The right-hand side of the figure shows the Markov transition analysis for the father–daughter relationship when the father initiates an interaction with the daughter and the daughter responds directly back to the father. His movement is consistently in the direction of listening to and allowing the daughter autonomy in a friendly fashion. The transitional probabilities of father and daughter suggest they tend to move toward nearly complementary states, although the father is judged as showing slightly more warmth than is the daughter.

cluster and (2) the likelihood of moving from one cluster to another. The specific predictions for the daughter from $\mathbf{v}T^3$ were O-2 = .11; O-4 = .08; S-1 = .42; S-8 = .05; and zero for the unmentioned clusters. In other words, at the end of the hypothetical session, the daughter would be highly likely to be Asserting and Separating (S-1), and somewhat, but much less likely to show behaviors coded in the listed other nonzero clusters.

On the right-hand side of Figure 11-5, there is a presentation of father-initiated transitions, wherein $T = (BA)^3$. Father's final vector, $\mathbf{v}T^3 = O$-2 = .33; O-4 = .07; S-2 = .03; S-4 = .07; S-5 = .16; and zero for the balance. Again, the final vector summarizes what the transition matrix suggests: the father is most likely to end up in a position of listening to and affirming the daughter.

Analysis of mother–daughter interactions by T^3 showed the daughter relentlessly moving toward cluster O-6, reflecting her hostile manipulations. The daughter's final vector $\mathbf{v}T^3$ showed a probability of .56 for cluster O-6, Belittling and Blaming, and zero for the balance. The mother's final vector, by contrast, suggested she would rest in a state of friendly deference to the daughter (S-4 = .54) if this sequence were to be repeated four times.

The marital interactions for Family 045 zeroed out completely, showing that the interaction patterns for mother and father did not mesh in a way which would allow a prediction of how they would be coded if the FCT sequence were to continue. The mathematics of zeroing out seem complex and preclude simple psychological interpretation of what such a null finding means. However, qualitatively speaking, it is true that as one scans the typescript for Family 045, one can get a clear sense of the daughter very much holding her own (S-1), of the father being responsive to her in a nondeferential way (O-2), and of the mother "giving in" affably (S-4). These clinically discernible psychological trends were also shown by nonzero T^3. By contrast, it is not easy on reading the typescript to get a clear sense of how mother and father related, and this lack of palpability may in fact be the psychological meaning of the zeroed-out T^3.

Further exploration of correspondence between the ability to get a clinical sense of what is happening in a session, and nonzero T^3 is necessary.

Program COMPLEX and Its Derivatives—Analysis of the Rare but Clinically Significant Events

Programs PROCESS, FOLLOW, and MARKOV ignore whether the clusters reported were part of complex communication. To study complex coding and to see if the coding of communications as complex contributes to clinical understanding, three programs that analyze only complex communications have been prepared. For Family 045 there were only 8 units out of 139 which had entries coded as complex. This base rate for complex messages may itself be a meaningful descriptive parameter. It could be, for example, that complex messages are more likely in families of schizophrenics than in others. Even where there is an IP with schizophrenia, Family 045 demonstrates that the base rate for complex communications can be relatively low. These special programs, then, are working with the researcher's nightmare, the clinically significant but rare event. Among other things, the low base rate means that any trends observed must be very consistent when they are detected. With small N, there is little room for "normal" variability.

Program COMPLEX is like PROCESS except it records only elements coded as complex. The analysis of Family 045 showed that the daughter used complex communications *only when addressing the mother*. The father and the sister each used complex communications when addressing the experimenter. No complex communications were recorded from the mother or the experimenter. All clusters involved in a complex communication were on or adjacent to the vertical axis. Those on the axis were O-5, O-1, S-5, S-1 and those adjacent to the axis were O-6, S-2, O-2, S-4, S-8. If confirmed on a larger sample, this alignment would suggest complex communications occur in a context of and relate importantly to sequences involving control–give autonomy–submit–differentiate.

A second program, FOLLOWCOMPLEX1, is like FOLLOW except that it is not required that the speaker in Unit I actually addresses the speaker in Unit I + 1. Such a restriction would nearly wipe out the already small sample of complex communications. Removal of the restriction means MARKOV should not be used on this output. FOLLOWCOMPLEX1 does, however, make a separate record for what happens if the speaker in unit I + 1 speaks to someone other than the speaker in unit I. In sum, FOLLOWCOMPLEX1 keys in when a speaker addresses anyone with a complex message, and studies what happens specifically in relation to everyone present after a complex message has been sent.

In Family 045, both the mother and the father showed instances of speaking immediately after the daughter had sent a complex message. *In 100% of those instances (N = 3) wherein the parent spoke directly back to the daughter*, the parent submitted affably (S-4) to the daughter.

Once, when the mother followed the daughter's complex communication, she spoke to the experimenter (with compliance), and once, she spoke to the father. When speaking to the father following a complex communication from the daughter, the mother was assertive (S-2).

Program FOLLOWCOMPLEX2 is a sequential study of what triggers a complex message. It keys into the unit preceding a unit where a complex message is identified, and again the speaker in the leading unit can be addressing anyone, not necessarily the person who follows with a complex message.

The father gave only one complex communication (unit 89); it followed the daughter, and was addressed to the experimenter. The sister's complex communication (unit 84) followed the father and also was addressed to the experimenter. Both these instances involved simultaneous compliance plus assertiveness and occurred when the sister appeared to be trying to enlist the experimenter's help in getting endorsement of the item which would describe the father as appeasing the daughter.

By far most of the events (N = 6) identitifed by FOLLOWCOMPLEX2 involved the daughter following the mother and sending a complex message back to the mother. In 100% of these instances, *what triggered the daughter's complex communication was the mother's (S-1, S-2) assertion and/or attempts to influence (O-4). This is remarkable because PROCESS showed that most of the mother's communications were compliant.* The only times the mother was noncompliant were *all* the times the daughter followed with a complex message aligned on the vertical axis!

In sum, results for the three programs analyzing complex coding for Family 045 confirm the clinical impression that the daughter "worked on" the mother to get her to give up the idea of endorsing the item that suggested father appeases the daughter. Results are consistent with the clinical belief that complex communication is important in schizophrenia. In addition, the analyses suggest that complex message sending can be successful at achieving uncomplaining compliance and the squashing of assertiveness and other manifestations of differentiation. Complex communications here had the function of generating nonhostile compliance to the speaker. Inordinate control was implemented in a context of pseudomutuality.

SASB Coding and the Clinical Evaluation

The primary coder's record of the brief, seemingly friendly FCT session showed pseudomutual behavior, defined as a presence of affiliative clusters accompanied by a palpable number of complex codings which included some form of hostile behavior. There was a cross-generational coalition between the IP and her father shown by their warm listening and deference to each other without complex exchanges along with a lack of mutual responsivity to the mother. The IP sent controlling and complex communications to the mother, always in response to the mother's attempts at assertion. The IP's sequential patterns with the father suggested relentless progression toward Asserting and Separating (S-1), the antithesis of control. Marital modeling was stereotyped normal in that the father was influential, the mother, compliant. Role reversal occurred between the daughter and both parents; she focused mostly on them, and had more influence than they did.

Some Clinical Detail About the IP in Family 045

The inpatient chart indicated that the family regarded the patient as a "loner." She had been living and working independently several years prior to this hospitalization. The patient's stated opinion about family dynamics was that the father bossed the mother, and the mother always gave in to him. She felt the family did not permit conflict and she recalls feeling guilty frequently. The reason she was hospitalized was that her voices gave her commands that caused her to act out in annoying but not dangerous ways. She agreed to be hospitalized because she felt she would be safe there from some people she believed were trying to harm her. She showed a good response to antipsychotic medications and was clear at the time of the Family Consensus Task. Her MMPI showed $T > 80$ for Hy (Hysteria), > 70 for D (Depression) and Pt (Psychasthenia). Pa (Paranoia) and Sc (Schizophrenia) were well within normal limits.

In sum, the MMPI showed acting-out tendencies, depression, and anxiety, but no hints of paranoid schizophrenia. The INTREX forms measuring family perceptions showed the patient had weak bonding to the family, and in some relationships, strong autonomy; the questionnaires also showed a poor self-concept when the patient was at her worst, and they did identify the interpersonal attributes of her voices. The clinical chart reported no remarkable trauma or stress and the family seemed affable in the FCT. The analyses of SASB codings of family behavior overwhelmingly confirmed the family perception of the daughter as autonomous. Surprising new information gained from the research codings was that the patient had much control over the mother, the confirmation of the clinical hypothesis that complex communications do exist in families of schizophrenics, and that they can serve the purpose of gaining control in contexts where anger and conflict are forbidden. Another surprise was that several members of the family used complex communications, and users of these techniques did not include in this case the "usual" villain, namely the mother.

These trends may or may not be confirmed with a larger sample of SASB coding of FCT interactions of families having an IP with paranoid schizophrenia. In any event, it is clear that the SASB coding and software are a very promising combination for studying subtle but important family interactions known to skilled clinicians, but heretofore intractable to research methods.

Use of SASB to Measure
Outcome of Psychotherapy

In the overall developmental program for SASB questionnaires, behavioral coding methods, and software, there has been a desire to "begin at the beginning" and avoid getting the proverbial cart before the horse. The rationale has been that first there needs to be an effective system for describing and defining psychosocial problems and hence the decision to start with interpersonal diagnosis. There is no definitive scientific methodology for the diagnosis of persons or family systems in a manner that has direct relevance to the questions: (1) of psychosocial attributes of people appearing for treatment; (2) of how to decide on different psychosocial interventions specifically appropriate to each individual; (3) of how to implement these different approaches; and (4) of how to measure their effectiveness.

The present exposition has illustrated how the SASB coding system is being used at Step 1, a psychosocial description of the problem. From analyses of this "innocuous" 20-minute task, the implications for therapy for this family are many. Some of the more obvious ones are that the daughter's imbalance of focus, inordinate control, use of complex communications, lack of bonding, and excessive autonomy are part of her "illness." The family's complementary responses to her "ill" responses were demonstrated and, according to SASB theory can be viewed as reinforcing the "illness." Such complementarities that lock the family system in a fixed position need to be interrupted and alternative, more constructive interactive patterns must be substituted. The pseudomutuality and conflict avoidance that accompany the complex communications need to be acknowledged and replaced by more overt expressions of disagreement and more tolerance of differences. Less arbitrary control, more balanced functioning, and the absence of complex, "mind bending," pseudomutual communications would be expected in a normal family, and if absent after a period of treatment, could serve as limited measures of successful treatment of this family. Of course, the disappearance of the "voice" and the substitution of more affiliative social interactions also would be indications of successful treatment outcome. This patient's rating of her voices suggested that they functioned much like a child's imaginary playmate. The self-stimulation and extreme autonomy of having voices should be replaced by an increase in sociability. More affiliative ratings of her self-concept would also be a measure of successful treatment as would the formation of a lasting attachment to a peer.

Behavioral codings, questionnaire ratings, and software used here for diagnosis would be identical when applied to measurement of therapy process and treatment outcome. The SASB model presumes to apply to all possible types of social interaction, and so it should be applicable at any point in the sequence definition of problem, solving the problem, and measuring the effectiveness of the solution.

Conspicuously missing is mention of affect, and, of course many psychotherapies specialize in the facilitation of the expression of affect. At this point, only two considerations about affect will be mentioned.

1. There is a model for affect (SAAB) which parallels the model for social behavior (SASB) and the prediction is that SAAB affective codings would parallel the SASB social codings in meaningful ways. For example, the affective model suggests anger is an affect paralleling focus-on-other disaffiliation, whereas hate is an affect paralleling focus-on-self disaffiliation. Forcefulness or "power tripping" is an affect paralleling dominance. Arrogance, which parallels cluster O-6, is an affect made up of some power

tripping and some focused anger. As O-6 disappears in successful treatment, so would arrogance. A brief description of SAAB appears in Benjamin, (1981 and 1986a).

2. A second prediction about affect is that therapists whose interventions lead to more SASB-codable units would be the therapists having clients showing deeper levels of experiencing (Klein, Mathieu, Gendlin, and Kiesler, 1970). For example, "I'm upset" is a very general statement. The therapist should help the patient discover whether the upset is due to rejection, to imposition of control, to withdrawal, or what. Such an increase in specificity of discussion should lead to specificity and intensity of experiencing.

These are only some among many potential measures of outcome using SASB. Obviously social value systems can affect the choice. For example, members of traditional marriages might choose a baseline in quadrant IV as a more desirable outcome than would members of androgenous marriages; the latter probably would prefer quadrant I. A special advantage of the SASB concepts is that they are so broadly applicable. Whatever the therapeutic approach and outcome, the coding system should be able to describe its interpersonal aspects and there are accompanying implications for what affects would be present. Moreover, there are also predictions for parallel cognitive styles (SACB; see Benjamin, 1981 and 1986a). To date, the potential for discovering what SASB (and SAAB and SACB) might contribute to the understanding of psychotherapeutic process and outcome is essentially untapped.

Acknowledgments

This work was supported in part by a grant from NIMH, "Diagnosis Using Structural Analysis of Social Behavior" MH-33604 to Lorna Smith Benjamin. L. Roberto and S. Foster were successive associates on the project and had primary responsibility for selecting, training, and supervising the student hourly coders. S. Estroff had a major role in preparing the original 1978 SASB coding manual with the senior author. In the present chapter, Foster and Roberto provided major contributions to the sections Steps in SASB Coding and Training SASB Coders. Roberto was the experimenter for the FCT reported here. Thanks are expressed to Dee Jones, Sara Edwards, and Sandy Tetzloff for their patient and unfailingly accurate assistance in preparing FCT data files.

References

Aponte, H. J., & Van Deusen, J. M. Structural family therapy. In A. S. Gurman & D. P. Kniskern (Eds.), *Handbook of family therapy*. New York: Brunner/Mazel, 1981.

Bateson, G., Jackson, D. D., Haley, J., & Weakland, J. Toward a theory of schizophrenia. *Behavioral Science*, 1956, *1*, 251–264.

Benjamin, L. S. A biological model for the study of individual differences. In J. Westman (Ed.), *Individual differences in children*. New York: Wiley, 1973.

Benjamin, L. S. Structural analysis of social behavior. *Psychological Review*, 1974, *81*, 392–425.

Benjamin, L. S. Structural analysis of a family in therapy. *Journal of Consulting and Clinical Psychology*, 1977, *45*, 391–406.

Benjamin, L. S. Structural analysis of differentiation failure. *Psychiatry: Journal for the Study of Interpersonal Process*, 1979, *42*, 1–23. (a)

Benjamin, L. S. Use of structural analysis of social behavior (SASB) and Markov chains to study dyadic interactions. *Journal of Abnormal Psychology*, 1979, *88*, 303–319. (b)

Benjamin, L. S. *Internal validity of structural analysis of social behavior (SASB)*. Unpublished manuscript, 1980. (a)

Benjamin, L. S. A psychosocial competence classification system. In J. D. Wine & M. D. Smye (Eds.)., *Social competence*. New York: Guilford Press, 1981.

Benjamin, L. S. Use of structural analysis of social behavior (SASB) to guide interventions in psychotherapy. In J. Anchin & D. Kiesler (Eds.), *Handbook of interpersonal psychotherapy*. Pergamon Press, 1982.

Benjamin, L. S. Principles of prediction using Structural Analysis of Social Behavior (SASB). In R. A. Zucker, J. Aronoff, & A. J. Rabin (Eds.), *Personality and the prediction of behavior*. New York: Academic Press, 1984.

Benjamin, L. S. *Interpersonal Diagnosis and Treatment: The SASB Approach*. New York: Guilford Press. draft, 1986.

Benjamin, L. S., Adding social and intrapsychic descriptors to Axis I of DSM-III. In T. Millon and G. Klerman (Eds.) *Contemporary issues in psychopathology*. New York: The Guilford Press, 1986. (a)

Benjamin, L. S. Operational definition and measurement of dynamics shown in the stream of free associations. *Psychiatry*, May 1986. (b)

Benjamin, L. S., Giat, L., & Estroff, S. *Manual for coding social interactions in terms of structural analysis of social behavior (SASB)*. Unpublished manuscript, 1981.

Cohen, J. Weighted Kappa: Nominal scale agreement with provision for scaled disagreement or partial credit. *Psychological Bulletin*, 1968, 70, 213–220.

Fromm-Reichmann, F. *Principles of intensive psychotherapy*. Chicago: University of Chicago Press, 1950.

Garfield, S. L. The emergence of the scientist-practitioner model: Background and rationale. *The Clinical Psychologist*, 1982, 36, 4–6.

Hogarty, G. E., Schooler, N. R., Ulrich, R., Mussare, F., Ferro, P., & Herron, E. Fluphenazine and social therapy in the aftercare of schizophrenic patients. *Archives of General Psychiatry*, 36, 1283–1294.

Humphrey, L. L. A sequential analysis of family processes in anorexia and bulimia. In *New Directions in anorexia nervosa: Proceedings from the Fourth Ross Conference on Medical Research*. Columbus, Ohio: Ross Laboratories, 1983.

Isaacson, D. L., & Madsen, R. W. *Markov chains theory and applications*. New York: Wiley, 1976.

Klein, M. H., Mathieu, P. L., Gendlin, E. T., & Kiesler, D. J. *The Experiencing Scale: A research and training manual*. Madison, Wis.: Bureau of Audio-Visual Instruction, 1970.

Laing, R. D. *Knots*. New York: Vintage Books, 1970.

Lederer, W. J., & Jackson, D. D. *The mirages of marriage*. New York: Norton, 1968.

Leary, T. *Interpersonal diagnosis of personality: A functional theory and methodology for personality evaluation*. New York: Ronald Press, 1957.

Lorr, M., Bishop, P. F., & McNair, D. M. Interpersonal types among psychiatric patients. *Journal of Abnormal Psychology*, 1965, 70, 468–472.

MacCorquodale, K., & Meehl, P. Hypothetical constructs in intervening variables. In H. Feigl & M. Brodbeck (Eds.), *Readings in the philosophy of science*. New York: Basic Books, 1951.

Minuchin, S. *Families and family therapy*. Cambridge, Mass.: Harvard University Press, 1974.

Mosher, L. R., & Keith, S. J. Psychosocial treatment: Individual, group, family, and community support approaches. In *Schizophrenia*, 1980. Special Issue of *Schizophrenia Bulletin*, 6, 4, 127–158.

Mueller, W. J., & Dilling, C. A. Studying interpersonal themes in psychotherapy research. *Journal of Counseling and Psychology*, 1969, 16, 50–58.

Murray, H. A. *Explorations in personality*. New York: Oxford University Press, 1938.

Schaefer, E. S. A configurational analysis of children's reports of parent behavior. *Journal of Consulting Psychology*, 1965, 29, 552–557.

Schooler, N. R., Levine, J., Severe, J. B., Brauzer, B., DiMascio, A., Klerman, G. L., & Tuason, V. B. Prevention of relapse in schizophrenia: An evaluation of fluphenazine decanoate. *Archives of General Psychiatry*, 1980, 37, 16–24.

Singer, M., & Wynne, L. Thought disorder and family relations of schizophrenics: Methodology. *Archives of General Psychiatry*, 1965, *12*, 187–200.

Singer, M., & Wynne, L. Principles for scoring communication defects and deviances in parents of schizophrenics: Rorschach and TAT scoring manual. *Psychiatry*, 1966, *29*, 260–288.

Skinner, H. A. Differentiating the contribution of elevation scatter and shape in profile similarity. *Educational and Psychological Measurement*, 1978, *38*, 297–308.

Stanton, M. D. An integrated structural/strategic approach to family therapy. *Journal of Marital and Family Therapy*, 1981, *7*, 427–439.

Sullivan, H. S. *The interpersonal theory of psychiatry*. New York: Norton, 1953.

Sullivan, H. S. *Schizophrenia as a human process*. New York: Norton, 1962.

Watzlawick, P., Beavin, J. H., & Jackson, D. D. *Pragmatics of human communication*. New York: Norton, 1967.

Wynne, L. C., Ryckoff, I. M., Day, J., & Hirsch, S. I. Pseudomutuality in family relations of schizophrenics. *Psychiatry*, 1958, *21*, 205–220.

Zola, I. K. Medicine as an institution of social control. In J. Ehrenreich (Ed.), *The culture crisis of modern medicine*. New York: The Monthly Review Press, 1978.

Participant Observation Systems

12

The Relationship Inventory Now: Issues and Advances in Theory, Method, and Use

Godfrey T. Barrett-Lennard
The Centre for Studies in Human Relations
Perth, Western Australia

In form, the Relationship Inventory is a questionnaire research instrument. It also represents an approach to the study of interpersonal relationships generally, and of therapeutic or helping relationships in particular. By this time, with over a quarter-century history of development and manifold application, a large body of resulting literature, a far-reaching theoretical foundation, and a still-growing variety of specific forms, the term "system" is perhaps more indicative than "instrument." Any of several labels is useful, according to the context.

As the name implies, the Relationship Inventory (RI) does not tap or "count" discrete units of interaction, is not designed primarily for use by external raters or "judges" and, in general, does not imply rejection of "subject" experience as scientifically valid data. On the contrary, the approach pivots on systematic gathering of (preselected) facets of experience in particular relationships, and on cumulating these facets of experiential information such that they point, for example, to a level of received empathy-in-relationship and to relationship-specific positions on three other interpersonal response variables conceived as axial. The RI method thus presumes that some fundamental aspects of experience in a relationship *can* be measured or, more exactly, that they can be meaningfully and usefully represented on a scale of quantity, provided the the origins, procedures, and main presumptions of such measurement are held in view.

In its most used forms, the RI first of all *samples* the interperceptions of either participant in a dyadic relationship focusing on the response of one to the other, and relevant to the variables of empathic understanding, congruence, level of regard, and unconditionality of regard. Specifically, the respondent may attend to the other person in the setting of their relationship, using in this (usual) case an "other toward self," or OS form of the RI. Or, the focus may be on the reporting person's own response to the other; using a "myself to the other," or MO form of the instrument. Other kinds of set and focus, such as "How I think the other sees me as responding to him/her" will be considered later in this chapter, for example, under the heading New and Underused Applications of the RI. The sample of perceptions, in the basic English language forms in use since the mid-1960s, consists of answers to 16 items for each of the four variables. In each (dispersed) set, eight of the item statements are worded positively and eight negatively. (Barrett-Lennard, 1964, 1969, 1978a).

Each item statement is answered on a six-step anchored scale, with numerically coded answers ranging from +3 (yes, as strongly felt agreement) to −3 (no, as strongly felt disagreement). The rationale for and specific method of scoring the answer data on each scale is described later in this report. In the meantime, many issues involved in the content and methodology of the instrument would gain illumination from close-up consideration of the theoretical and operational underpinnings of the RI—centrally, what it is that the instrument is designed to measure, and how this design is implemented at the level of item statements.

A Current View of the Theoretical Structure of the RI

Carl Rogers' (1957) classic conception of the necessary conditions of therapy prompted original development of the RI and was the major source of the theory and constructs built into it. The conditions were revised and more tightly defined in the process of developing the instrument. These definitions and the course of their development at the time are rather fully presented in my *Psychological Monographs* report (Barrett-Lennard, 1962) and prior doctoral dissertation (Barrett-Lennard, 1959a). Further refinements are reflected in subsequent revisions of the RI and in the way its major forms may now be viewed. Experience and developments outside the context of formal therapy also have prompted new thought regarding applications in therapy research. My focus to start with is on the theoretical variable and its operational expression, in each of the separate scales.

Level of regard has been modified the least of any RI variable, since its separation from the operationally awkward concept of unconditional positive regard (Barrett-Lennard, 1957, 1959a, 1959b, 1962). In principle, and in original language, it is "the overall level or tendency of one person's affective response to another" (Barrett-Lennard, 1961); or "the affective aspect of one person's total response to another, projected into a single positive-to-negative continuum" (Barrett-Lennard, 1958). Level of regard does not refer to a generalized interpersonal trait but to a sphere and axis of experienced response in a particular relationship, at the present juncture (in most cases) but not with reference to the immediate moment or a very brief episode in that relationship.

The relevant elements of experience in relationship are "positive" feelings and affective attitudes, and "negative" feelings and attitudes, on the part of the person whose regard is being considered, toward the other person. (These feelings may be as apprehended from different positions within the relationship—particularly including the standpoint of the receiving person—or from outside it. The latter may include the perspective of a sensitive and/or involved observer). Combining elements of metaphor and of operational definition, level of regard is the composite "loading" of the distinguishable feeling reactions of one person toward another, positive and negative, on a single abstract dimension (Barrett-Lennard, 1958, 1959a, 1959b, 1961, 1962). Further, "the 'lower' extreme of this dimension represents predominance and intensity of negative type feeling, not merely a lack of positive feeling" (Barrett-Lennard, 1962, p. 4).

Implied in my original writing (especially Barrett-Lennard, 1958a), and more clearly seen now, Regard does not even in principle encompass all aspects of feeling response in a relationship. On the positive side, it is concerned in various ways with warmth, liking/caring, and "being drawn toward," all in the context of responsive feelings for the other as another self like oneself. It does not encompass very close, passionate feelings (as of romantic love), or attitudes which do not imply interactive relationships. Nor is it linked explicitly to particular liked or disliked features of the appearance or behavior of the recipient person; which might feed into regard, or to conditionality, but are limited in generality of application and theoretical directness. On the negative side, feelings of extreme aversion (except for contempt), or of anger to the point of rage, are not encompassed. No item points to possible feelings that allude to fear of the other. As it is, the RI is quite demanding and moderately stressful for some respondents[1]; *and* the lowest ranges of the regard scale are very rarely used. Following are illustrative Regard items from the principal OS form of the RI. (The examples are from Form OS-F-64. Form OS-M-64 is identical except for the gender of pronouns referring to the other person in the relationship.)

Positive Items

- She respects me as a person.
- I feel appreciated by her.
- She is friendly and warm toward me.
- She is truly interested in me.
- She cares for me.

Negative Items

- She feels that I am dull and uninteresting.
- I feel that she disapproves of me.
- She is impatient with me.
- At times she feels contempt for me.

Empathic understanding is conceived as a pivotal but not sufficient relationship condition in therapy and in other developmental or nutrient relationships. If it is focused on as though it were *the* critical condition, the evidence may tend to be self-confirming, partly because of its vital contribution, and partly because higher levels of empathy tend to accompany relatively high levels of regard and of congruence and are seldom associated with particularly low unconditionality. This view is consistent at least with a large quantity of evidence and with the theoretical underpinnings of the RI from the time of its first development.

The definition of empathy utilized in the original preparation and main revisions of the RI (Barrett-Lennard, 1959a, 1962, 1978a) follows. It has been slightly rearranged, in order to more sharply expose the components of meaning and process. Exactly quoted elements are reproduced in italics.

Qualitatively, empathic understanding is (A_1) an *active process* of *desiring to know* (B_1) *the full present and changing awareness of another person,* and (A_2) *of reaching out to receive* (B_2) *the other's communication and meaning.* This involves (C_1) *translating his words and signs into experienced meaning* which (C_2) *matches at least those aspects of his awareness that are most important to him at the moment.* All this (D) *is an experiencing of the consciousness "behind" another's outward communication* but (E) *with continuous awareness that this con-*

---

1. Particularly, including hospitalized subjects diagnosed as schizophrenic (Rogers, 1967).

sciousness is originating and proceeding in the other (Barrett-Lennard, 1962, 1981a, 1981b). Elements A_1 and A_2 imply that empathy is seen to involve active and purposeful engagement with the other. The region or focus of this engagement, as implied in B_1 and B_2, is the communication, experiencing, and (felt) meanings of the other. This engagement unfolds in a particular way, namely, one that entails an accurate experiential grasp of that which has priority or centrality for the other in his or her awareness—as indicated in C_1 and C_2. The process can go further, beyond "experiential grasp" to a kind of entry into and coexperiencing of features of the other's inner consciousness of which his or her outward communication is an expression (see element D). Effectively, the empathizing person sees, at least in glimpses, through the other's eyes, pulses with his or her feeling, shares the person's struggle, knows as from within how it is to be the other—at some special or critical moments in their journey (element D, expanded). This lived knowing, however, proceeds or happens within a frame of clear awareness that its touchstone and sphere of reference is the moving consciousness of the *other* person (E, expanded).[2]

Illustrative items from a main 64-item form of the RI (Barrett-Lennard, 1964, 1978a) are listed below. They are marked A, B, C, D, or E, to indicate their close relation with the components identified in the definition of empathy; and by a '+' or '−', to confirm their positive or negative wording.

A (+)   2. He wants to understand how I see things.

A (−) 58. His response to me is usually so fixed and automatic that I don't really get-through to him.

B (+) 34. He usually understands the whole of what I mean.

B (+) 30. He realizes what I mean even when I have difficulty in saying it.
D

C (−)   6. He may understand my words but he doesn't see the way I feel.

C (+) 42. He appreciates exactly how the things I experience feel to me.

D (−) 18. He does not realize how sensitive I am about some of the things we discuss.

E (−) 26. Sometimes he thinks *I* feel a certain way, because that's the way he feels.

E (+) 62. When I am hurt or upset, he can recognize my feelings exactly without becoming upset himself.

Unconditionality (of regard) originally centered on the aspect of "how little or how much variability there is in one person's affective response to another. It was defined as the degree of constancy of regard felt by one person for another who communicates self-experiences to the first" (Barrett-Lennard, 1962, p. 4). It was pointed out that in a very casual or superficial relationship, the concept would have no meaning. "Regard might

---

2. Such empathy is a form of midwifery in the sense that it aids the emergence of new discriminations, especially those which entail a coming into strongly apprehended view of new connections or wholes which otherwise may remain unborn—embryos of a sort, perhaps absorbing energy but providing no new life. In alternate metaphor, it is a form of knowledge in which the empathic knower is both instrument and musician, devoted at the time to hearing and illuminating (and, in so doing, to advancing) the *other's* music—albeit in a style influenced by his or her own distinctive qualities—but not to presenting melodies of separate origin, nor to externally "correcting" the other's score. (There is no loss of self-other differentiation in the interflow and experiential resonation of empathy.)

be constant but so shallow and unrelated to the other person that it would not be perceived as a feeling [-response] toward him" (Barrett-Lennard, 1962, p. 4). The cautionary relevance of the last point remains important. In most relationships which are fleeting or involve very little communicative information, respondent *expectations* of how others—or particular categories of other persons—will respond and be in a face-to-face relationship must play a very large part in answers to the RI. Where the focus of interest is on *qualities of the perceiver* rather than the relationship itself, or the partner, such data may have meaning—although of a different kind than in the usual case of data based on experience in a particular relationship. The role of expectancy in RI data, and the potential of a virtually unused "conditional" form of the RI (e.g., "S/he *would* respect me as a person") justify later attention in their own right.

In the principal revision of the RI, the unconditional/conditional continuum was interpreted literally; that is, with the focus being on *conditional* variation of regard or its absence (Barrett-Lennard, 1964, 1969, 1978a). More precisely, regard is conditional to the extent that it is contingent on, or triggered by, particular behaviors, attitudes, or (perceived) qualities of the regarded person and is experienced as referent to that *person or self*. "Thus the regarding person is said to be conditional to the extent that his/her response experientially implies that the recipient person is more or less pleasing, worthy, valued, trusted, liked or disliked if s/he manifests certain self-attributes than if or when s/he manifests others" (Barrett-Lennard, 1978a, p. 7). Regard (whether generally high or low in level) that is strongly unconditional is stable, in the sense that it is not experienced as varying with or otherwise dependently linked to particular attributes of the person being regarded.

A prerevision item from the MO (or "therapist") form of the RI, "Sometimes I feel quite warmly toward him and at other times I really feel indifferent" certainly points to variation in A's regard for B. A "yes" answer to the statement would not always imply however, that this variation was evoked by features of B's behavior, communicated feelings, or other self-expressions. In a given instance, "A may experience his varying warmth or interest in relation to B (and B *may* correctly perceive this) as resulting essentially from factors extraneous to their relationship"—which, for example, strongly affect A's mood (Barrett-Lennard, 1978a, p. 8).[3] Examples of positively worded (first four listed) and negatively worded (latter four) unconditionality items from a basic 64-item OS form of the RI follow:

39. How much he likes or dislikes me is not altered by anything that I tell him about myself.

23. I can (or could) be openly critical or appreciative of him without really making him feel any differently about me.

51. Whether the ideas and feelings I express are "good" or "bad" seems to make no difference to his feeling toward me.

59. I don't think that anything I say or do really changes the way he feels toward me.

11. Depending on my behavior, he has a better opinion of me sometimes than he has at other times.

27. He likes certain things about me, and there are other things he does not like.

---

3. In fact, a majority of the original items in this category did imply *contingency*, as discussed here. One of the most obvious exceptions (replaced in the revision) from the Client form of the RI was "His general feeling toward me varies considerably" (Barrett-Lennard, 1962, p. 35, item 59; Barrett-Lennard, 1978a, p. 42).

55. Sometimes I am more worthwhile in his eyes than I am at other times.

63. What other people think of me does (or would, if he knew) affect the way he feels toward me.

Congruence has from the start been considered a foundation variable—on which each of the others partially depend—among the quartet tapped and measured by the RI (Barrett-Lennard, 1962, p. 5). The core of the definition used and developed in constructing the RI follows:

> The degree to which one person is functionally integrated in the context of his relationship with another, such that there is absence of conflict or inconsistency between his total *experience*, his *awareness*, and his overt *communication*, is his congruence in this relationship. The concept is theoretically centered on consistency between total experience and awareness, which is considered to be the main determinant or condition for congruence between awareness and communication . . .
>
> In brief, optimum congruence means maximum unity, wholeness or integration of the total spectrum or organismic processes in the individual, from physiological to conscious symbolic levels. (Barrett-Lennard, 1962, pp. 4–5, italics added)

In the definition given, "experience" includes all ways in which the person is aroused and active at a given moment which *could*, in the nature of the human organism, register and be integrated in conscious awareness. Implied is the notion that persons may be more or less "open to experience" at a given time, as a function both of situational and personality determinants. Experience, in this meaning, that is not in or immediately available to the experiencing person's articulate awareness can be expressed indirectly in any of a variety of verbal and nonverbal ways. An interacting other person may sense or be struck by signs of unacknowledged experience, whether adding to or contradicting the overt messages of the first person.[4] On the other hand, the same kind of inferential process is not available to the experiencing person him or herself, who obviously cannot step outside his/her own awareness and see discrepancy between this awareness and aspects of functioning that are not in awareness. That is, it is not possible to perceive particular incongruence in oneself while this incongruence continues. One can at most be aware of it retrospectively, or in the moment of change. One may also discriminate indirect, theoretically cogent signs.

Thus, as between the OS (participant–observer) and MO (self-report) forms of the RI, the evidence respondents provide relevant to congruence differs in principle. In the case of the OS form, although respondents lack the primary datum of the other's inner experience, they are not confined to the self-awareness of the other, with its particular limitations in relation to appraisal of his or her immediate level of congruence. In the OS form of the RI, congruence items range from those that call for the respondent's inferential *sensing* of aspects of the other's underlying experience (for example, items 40, "At times I sense that she is not aware of what she is really feeling with me," and 56, "I have not felt that she tries to hide anything from herself that she feels with me") to those that tap direct observation on the respondent's part but where more inference is involved in the selection of items (for example, 4, "She is comfort-

---

4. I would grant the likelihood of a projective or attributional component entering into A's impressions implying incongruence/congruence in B; but argue that typically this would be a component and not the exclusive source of such impressions. And, in any event, it will be the perceiver's impressions that most directly influence his or her experience and behavior within and resulting from the relationship.

able and at ease in our relationship,'' and 16, ''It makes her uneasy when we ask or talk about certain things''). Other items fall in between, and in a variety of ways tap the extent to which the other person is seen as personally honest, open, and in touch with her or himself in the relationship.

In replying to the congruence items in the *self-report MO* forms of the RI, the respondent's report could be expected to provide a fairly good indication of level of comfort/discomfort with him or herself in the relationship, tapped, for example, by item 4, ''I feel at ease with her.'' It should also give as good or *better* indication of consistency or inconsistency between inner awareness and overt communication than an observer can give via the OS form. (Some ''yes'' answers are given in response to item 24, ''I would really prefer him to think that I like or understand him even when I don't,'' and probably more frequently to 52. ''There are times when my outward response to him is quite different from the way I feel underneath''). The respondent is looking back on processes in the referent relationship and quite possibly would discriminate his or her functioning in a different light—perhaps with more openness or wholeness in important ways—than would have been possible at the moment of interaction. Thus, while there is some ambiguity to the concept of congruence in a self-report context, in practice, RI responses are given from a reflective–contemplative focus of consciousness drawing upon but occurring outside interaction in the referent relationship. This may largely explain empirical observations that the (MO) congruence scale is both internally consistent and reliable and behaves in predictive studies like other scales in the same RI form.

As originally prepared, exactly parallel wording of corresponding items in the Client (now OS) and Therapist (now MO) RI forms was used throughout, with the *aim* of ensuring equivalence. In practice, this approach contributed to instances of forced or unnatural forms of expression, and to some items that it would be much more difficult to agree applied to one's own behavior in response to another person than to perceive in the response of the other to oneself. The 64-item revision grew in part from concern to achieve forms of statement that are closer than before to the language of subjective experience and, in the case of corresponding items, more nearly equivalent in meaning and strength of expression (Barrett-Lennard 1978a, pp. 11–12). The congruence scale yields convenient examples of how the wording was varied from the OS to the MO forms—as already indicated for item 4. (About 40% of all items remain in exactly parallel form.) The following statements extend the sample of congruence items and—via close inspection—illustrate the issues just mentioned.

Further OS Items (Congruence)	*Corresponding MO Items*
12. I feel that she is real and genuine with me.	12. I feel that I am genuinely myself with him.
20. I feel that what she says nearly always expresses exactly what she is feeling and thinking as she says it.	20. When I speak to him I nearly always can say freely just what I'm thinking or feeling at that moment.
40. At times I sense that she is not aware of what she is really feeling with me.	40. At times I just don't know, or don't realize until later, what my feelings are with him.
64. I believe that she has feelings she does not tell me about that are causing difficulty in our relationship.	64. I feel there are things we don't talk about that are causing difficulty in our relationship.

The original Client and Therapist forms of the RI encompassed a fifth construct and scale called "willingness to be known." Unlike the other four, this variable for the most part was not significantly predictive of therapy outcome, or of hypothesized differences between expert and nonexpert therapists (working with equivalent groups of clients). Both the research results and reconsideration of theory led to a decision to drop willingness to be known as a separate concept and measure. Refinement of its meaning took two directions: one, leading to preliminary elucidation of a broader concept called "availability" (Barrett-Lennard, 1963); and the other blending into the author's view of congruence (Barrett-Lennard, 1962, p. 28). The idea of availability in a helping relationship is reflected implicitly in the RI but was represented by a distinct sample of items only in an early exploratory "long form" of the instrument (Barrett-Lennard, 1958; Thornton, B. M., 1960; Thornton, F. C., 1960. Among congruence items in the 64-item OS form, the most direct legacy of willingness to be known is 44: "He is willing to express whatever is actually in his mind with me, including any feelings about himself or about me.

In the early 1970s, I began some fresh theoretical examination of the variables underlying the RI (Barrett-Lennard, 1972), particularly including empathy and congruence. Fruits of this work are partly reflected in my preceding discussion of the concepts here. Further discriminations regarding unconditionality are articulated more closely than before in my final report on the 64-item revision (Barrett-Lennard, 1978a) and I would like to be able to add thought that is beyond my purview in this chapter (Lietaer, 1984; Barrett-Lennard, 1984b). Most pivotal of all, in relation to the RI as an approach and method, is basic new work on empathy.

The new theoretical differentiation of the process of empathy in helping and other relationships (Barrett-Lennard, 1976) went beyond but was not at odds with the formational definition, as already represented here with further nuances of meaning. Essentially, the advance involved distinguishing a sequence or—particularly in therapy—repeating cycle of distinct steps or phases in the total interactive process of empathy. In a word, three main linked but distinct "semiautonomous" phases were discriminated. In therapy these are: empathic resonation by the therapist to particular expressed/implied experience of the client (Phase 1 empathy); communicative expression by the therapist of the essence of this inner responsive awareness or impression of the client's experience (Phase 2, expressed empathy); and the client's sense and perception of the degree to which the therapist is attuned and actually "with" him, or her, in immediate personal understanding (Phase 3, received empathy) (Barrett-Lennard, 1981a, 1981b). This phasic model amounts to refinement of the underlying perspective on human (helping) interaction involved in the RI *as a whole*, and thus leads directly to my next main topic.

Interaction Phases in the Client–Therapist Dyad, Corresponding to the Principal RI Forms

Phase 1 empathy, as implied, is the process of experiential resonation to the client's ongoing, felt, or lived experience—and may range (for example) *from* being distinctly and precisely attuned to the essence of this experience *to* involving little or no "gut" sense of the other's feeling and being quite off-target as far as the basic content of the client's messages and frame of reference are concerned. But, when empathy in this phase *is* high—when the therapist knows almost how it is to be the client, right then—this quality of knowing may or may not be expressed to the other; and, if expressed, it might or might not be "heard." And, when there is very little Phase 1 empathy, it is possible that highly polished communicative skills, or the thirst of the receiver for understanding, may yield relatively higher "readings" for Phase 3 empathy.

As in the case of Phase 1 empathy, regard in the first instance is an experiential process occurring in the regarding person. (A high or low level of felt regard may or may not be closely matched or portrayed in the regarding person's expression; and typically there is some slippage on reading the signals that are present.) Likewise, an unconditional or conditional quality of regard has reference in the first place to a quality or *pattern* of responsive/reactive experience in the regarding person. So too with congruence, which in definition is concerned centrally with quality of integration, including relative presence or absence of free flow between primary arousal experience and accompanying awareness, and of consistency or harmony between self-presentation and conscious awareness. Thus, one may speak not solely of Phase 1 empathy, but of Phase 1 of the relation conditions that are tapped by the RI. As in the case of the empathy scale in particular, this phase corresponds to the MO (myself-to-the-other) form of the RI.

In this extended perspective, the MO form takes on a new stronger significance and status than formerly in nearly all the literature, including my own research. When the respondent is seeking to give as faithful an account as possible—that is, under adequate conditions of administration—of his or her own experienced way of being with and toward the other (in this case, a therapist to his or her client/patient), the RI is tapping relationship conditions of therapy *at their source*. (I do not mean to imply that it is the sole or ultimate source—if there is such—but to point out that expression or communication of empathy, regard, and so on, have no relevant meaning without this prior phase; that unless such processes within the therapist are influencing or feeding into the client's perceptions in some degree *no* authentic interaction is taking place.)

By extension of the thought leading to distinction of Phase 2 empathy, the level of communicative expressions and signs (both intended and unrealized, by the therapist) is a basic recurring stage in the flow of the interactive–relational process, applicable to each theoretical construct embodied in the RI. It is not represented directly in the generally used forms of the inventory, which are answered by participants in the relationship. However, third-person observer (or judge) forms (Barrett-Lennard, 1981c), variably used in a number of studies (see Barrett-Lennard, 1978a, 1982a, 1985b), could be tailored to tap the degree to which the therapist is seen by the observer respondent to be communicatively *expressing* the relational elements represented item by item in the RI. Normal scoring procedures would yield measures of Phase 2 empathy, congruence, regard, and unconditionality. The precise instructions and set of the respondents would be crucial, as well as the nature and degree of their exposure to the client-therapist interaction. Considerable variation in observer judgments could be expected; and apt selection of observers would be called for, but should not as a rule be coupled with any special coaching-type training in responding to the RI.

The third phase, of received empathy, regard, and so on, corresponds directly to the (other's response to self) OS form of the RI (Barrett-Lennard, 1976, 1978a, 1981a, 1981b). The client's perceptions will be mediated by the Phase 2 level of process as discussed and also by role-related expectancies and personal qualities of functioning and outlook of the client. It is consistent with substantial filtering in these ways to view the perceptions of the client–receiver as deriving indirectly from the Phase 1 level of therapist experience and behavior.

Whether or not the phases of the therapy relationship conditions in action—given some further dilution, in the course of measurement, of the necessary but also limited connection revealed in theoretical analysis—will be significantly correlated in a given sample, and in the case of particular relational conditions and pairs of phases (for example, Phase 1 and Phase 3 empathy), is problematic. From the standpoint advanced, however, the *overall trend* of associations in data from client-therapist (C–T) pairs, on any of the four RI scales, should be positive, presuming generally able therapists *and* significant experience—a few interviews at least—in the particular C–T pairs, before the RI data are gathered. This chapter is not a research review, and the point just made warrants checking via a literature search for relevant results, *and* through fresh research.[5]

Measures from the OS form of the RI (based on client perceptions) should be most strongly related to client change, a proposition now clearly in keeping with evidence from numerous studies (Gurman, 1977). In seeming but not actual paradox, unless the more weakly outcome-related Phase 1 process step (measured by the MO form) did contribute through the next step to the Phase 3 level (client OS form measures), augmentation of the process–outcome link from step to step would not be expected to occur. The situation is somewhat analogous to the phenomenon of increasing concentration of DDT in certain plant–animal food chains (granted this progression has negative valence). Species B acquires the DDT through species A, its presence in A thus being a necessary condition for its increased presence in B, this in turn being critical for species C, for whom (say) the DDT condition–survival outcome link is very strong and of most direct interest.

In therapy, level of empathy (for example), derived from the client's experience of the therapist is strongly linked to outcome (see Kurtz & Grummon, 1972; Gurman, 1977). Empathy-relevant signs and signals visibly conveyed by the therapist are a partial but critical determinant of the "concentrated" client-perception measure, although less strongly related to client outcome. Level of empathy tapped at its source in the therapist's experience is more indirectly and weakly related to client outcome (Barrett-Lennard, 1962, 1981a) but its effects are critical and "magnified" via its contribution to the client's outcome-related perceptions.

Critical appreciation of the theoretical foundations of the RI in terms of the variables and constructs embodied, and at the level of broader strategy and rationale (inherent in the various forms and kinds of actual/possible application), has not always been evident in reported research. I hope that the preceding discussion will helpfully contribute on this level to the quality of future work. An articulating account of down-to-earth practice and procedures in the actual use of the instrument and method is my next focus, and is similar in its broad purpose.

Gathering, Scoring, and Analysing RI Data: Practice and Rationale

Administering the Inventory

In therapy research, where the purpose is to obtain significant measures of the relationship conditions that are experientially manifest and potentially influential in the process of therapy, it is of course vitally important that client or therapist (and/or other)

---

5. One of the few studies I have identified, using full-length forms of the 64-item RI answered by (experienced) therapists, observers and clients, was reported by La Crosse (1977). Although observers were much more conservative than clients, with therapists falling between, in respect to derived levels of empathy and on the other RI variables, the strongest and only significant correlations in scores from the differing vantage points were those from observer and client data—effectively, from adjacent phases 2 and 3.

respondents not only have a clear understanding of the task (normally conveyed by the instructions on the RI forms, supplemented as relevant) but of why it is they are being called to respond to the questionnaire returns, who will have access to them and, in general, how or with what attitude and care this rather demanding-to-give and sensitive information will be treated. There is virtually no intentionally hidden meaning in the RI. Taken item-by-item, the statements Ss are called on to consider and position themselves in regard to, in reference to a particular relationship, are mostly transparent and rather revealing in the respondent's view. Careful gradation of response, using the same anchored multipoint scale (not a broad, yes/no response) for each statement, is called for. It is important that subjects be as open as they can be to their experience, in responding to the instrument, and either encouraged in or not distracted from motivation to faithfully record what they experience. Any condition that would stimulate or encourage interest in slanting answers, to give a more (or less) favorable picture from the respondent's standpoint, would reduce the integrity of the primary data and all subsequent steps in its treatment and interpretation.

In general, then, at least three conditions (or groups of conditions) seem essential to ensuring adequate administration and data gathering for research purposes, with the RI.: (1) a felt attitude of informed confidence and trust by responding individuals in the persons requesting and gathering the relationship data and in the (broad) purpose for which it is being obtained; (2) data-gathering arrangements such that other parties to the relationships being described do not handle the questionnaire returns at any stage and would not be consulted during the answering process; and (3) avoidance of mass administration of the inventory, especially in settings directly associated in the respondents' experience with formal examinations, quizzes and the like, or with predominantly impersonal interactions.

The Issue of Timing in Gathering RI Data

In my original research with the RI five interviews in therapy were judged and chosen to provide a "safe minimum" amount of contact between client and therapist in order for subjects to respond to the full range of items in the RI on the basis of experience in, and with specific reference to, *this* relationship (Barrett-Lennard, 1962, p. 8). The first few subjects in my sample were tested after three interviews, and again after six, and in settling on five (rather, say, than three) I might have erred a little on the conservative side. In most counseling and therapy research by other investigators, using the RI, the inventory data have been gathered earlier, not infrequently, after only one interview or, *in analogue studies*, after 30, 20, 15 or even 6 to 10 minutes' contact or observation (Alvarado, 1976/77; Brauer, 1979/80; Brown, 1980/81; Brown & Calia, 1968; Feldstein, 1982; Fretz, Corn, Tuemmler, & Bellet, 1979; Goldfarb, 1978; Mann & Murphy, 1975; McKitrick & Gelso, 1978; Melchior, 1980/81; and Seay & Altekruse, 1979). Such "early" data gathering may not completely vitiate the validity of the RI but yields results that must have a fundamentally different meaning than those obtained after several full (actual) therapy interviews or longer, or within the context of life relationships with significant others.

In principle, and no doubt in practice, subjects *could* answer the RI in conditional form (e.g., "S/he would respect me as a person") to describe the way they *expected* a relationship to be, with a fictional or real other they had not met but were given some brief personal picture of. Answers to the RI in this case would be almost wholly a matter of expectancy; and variability among respondents presented with the same "portrait" would be entirely reflective of their own characteristics. After a very brief, prestructured interaction—as in most analogue studies—expectancy and respondent character-istics still would be the principal source of variability of response.[6] After a single in-terview in therapy, situation-related expectancy and subject characteristics, plausibly, still would play a major part in the perceptions of responding participants. As therapy continued, experience in this relationship in particular, including recurring instances of distinctive or relationship-specific responses by the other (or of self in response to the other) would tend to play an increasing part in the client's (or therapist's) percep-tions. In client-centered and related therapies, this increase may be quite rapid. And, even where transference was being cultivated, the therapist would—gradually or in periodic sudden shifts—stand out more in his or her own person and less in terms of "projected" characteristics (especially assumptive characteristics generalized to a broad class of others).

In summary, on the issue of how soon RI data are gathered, unless research interest is centered on individual or group differences in response to a "standard" relation-ship stimulus, or in some way is focused on respondent characteristics rather than the engagement itself, it is essential that there be substantial experience in the relationship considered (or adequate observation, in the case of observer RI usage). Only under this condition could subjects reliably be responding in large measure to the specific rela-tionship; focusing with discrimination from experience which, for example, speaks to OS form items or to (MO) statements concerned with their own reaction to the par-ticular other. My current judgment is that, in general, at least three interviews in ac-tual therapy or help-intended relationships are necessary to provide the experience from which the forming identity of that specific relationship can dependably begin to be revealed via the RI.[7]

Scoring Rationale and Procedure

In reference to scoring the RI data, once obtained, various indications, including con-sistently high reliability of the scales (Gurman, 1977, Table 1), support treating the answer codes (+3, +2, +1, −1, −2, and −3) as an interval scale, and continua-tion of the main scoring method used throughout the history of the RI. In its original development, the item answer system was seen literally as providing for "three grades of 'yes' and three grades of 'no' response" (Barrett-Lennard, 1962, p. 6), for which the numerical symbols used were convenient codes with a form and "logic" that helped to make them easy to remember, *and* which could (and did) turn out to facilitate scoring. Significant precedent both for the basic approach (the differentiation of a "yes/no" scheme) and the form (use of the same " + " and " − " answer codes, applied to a total of six categories in two symmetrical groups) was found in the California E Scale (see Ardorno, Frenkel-Brunswik, Levinson, & Sanford, 1950). Nothing in the origins of the scheme, or subsequent experience and thought, have prompted actual use of a neutral, midpoint category. Further, such a category could very easily be used for the "wrong" reasons; for example, to avoid the feeling of commitment or vulnerability in recording

---

6. A study with usefully suggestive bearing on this issue was conducted by McKitrick and Gelso (1978).

7. This is not to negate the potential importance and impact of the initial interview in therapy, which in my observation may constitute or complete the entry phase of therapy (Barrett-Lennard, 1984b, chap. 6). How-ever, more experience than is usually possible in a 1-hour or so contact is needed to furnish the store of ex-periential events and impressions indigenous to a particular relationship which the RI (in most applications) assumes and calls upon.

a reluctant (but real) "yes" or "no" perception or, simply, to dispose of the task more easily where a leaning toward "yes" or "no" was not immediately obvious.[8]

As indicated, the number codes have proven quite satisfactory to take and use literally, without any transformation, as a measuring scale.[9] *Given* this approach, an issue that arose at the beginning, and which might occur to the reader, is the existence and justification for what amounts to a 2-point difference between +1 and −1 answers. (Other adjacent answer categories are only 1 point apart.) In accord with the discussion above, it is plausible to infer an implicit, although unused, "equally true and untrue" middle category, for which a logical answer code would be "0," in the +3 to −3 scheme. If this implicit latent step was visibly incorporated—if in effect this "missing" element in the spectrum was included—no change in the *present* number codes would be required. A gap would be filled in so that *all* adjacent categories *were* equidistant, by literal interpretation of the codes. From a slightly different standpoint, it can be argued that there is a qualitative difference (with quantitative implication) between (1) discriminating something as either true or probably true, and (2) deciding that probably something *is* true or probably it is *not* true (or is untrue). These considerations, as well as the fact the procedure works well (in terms of psychometric indicators), converge in supportive accord with the six-step item scale form in prevailing use.

Both at the item and scale score levels, the fact that half of the possible range is negative sometimes creates awkwardness in statistical treatment of scored data. For this reason in part, other workers occasionally have substituted number codes of 1 (in place of −3) through 6 (in place of +3). Besides eliminating negative scores, this change influences the scoring range and distribution contour, by shrinking the distance between the +1 (now 4) and −1 (now 3) categories to a single point. This feature alone appears unlikely to have important effects on associations or group differences of interest, provided direct comparison of figures with those obtained through standard scoring is not involved. However, the "1-to-6" answer code system would be most compatible with a mental set toward varying shades of agreement, from low to high, rather than with choices running "up" to a strong yes and "down" to a strong no. The drop in intuitive correspondence between number codes and verbally formulated answers would tend to make the answer categories as given less easy to hold in view throughout, thus reducing the sharpness or reliability of discrimination, and may result in a shift in center of gravity and shape of answer distributions.

The main form designed for handscoring of the inventory is reproduced in Figure 12-1. It portrays in detail the standard scoring method, and also can be drawn on directly in setting up machine scorable systems or preparing programs for computer scoring. Desk-top computers or consoles arranged for respondent use with automatic storage

---

8. Even in instances where, on some items, respondents could most accurately represent their experience via an "equally true and untrue" alternative, elements of error arising either through forced choice of +1 and −1—applied to a rather even balance of positively and negatively worded items—would tend to cancel out and disappear in the scoring.

9. I do not believe or mean to imply that it would be plausible to think that each "point" contributed by item A toward its scale score regularly had the same theoretical or practical significance as each point for item B, or item C, D, and so on, or that there was literal equality in each given instance to the difference between, say, a +3 and +2 answer and a −1 and −2 answer to particular items. Treating the data as if such presumptions are sound demonstrates, however, that fine-grained variability or "error" must tend to cancel out, and at the least, that scale scores (in adequately constituted arrays and comparisons) approximate linear measurement.

Figure 12-1 Illustration of handscoring of an RI protocol.

RELATIONSHIP INVENTORY SCORING SHEET

Code _____   Date answered: _____

R.I. form: _____   *64 item forms*

Type or class of relationship _____

Respondent (e.g., husband, client) _____   Other person(s) _____

Level of Regard		*Empathy*		*Unconditionality*		*Congruence*	
Positive Items	Answer	Positive Items	Answer	Positive Items	Answer	Positive Items	Answer
1	3	2	2	7	1	4	3
5	1	10	2	15	2	12	2
13	2	18	2	23	2	20	1
25	1	30	2	31	3	28	3
37	3	34	2	39	2	36	1
41	2	42	2	47	−2	44	−1
57	2	54	2	51	2	48	3
61	−1	62	3	59	2	56	3
Sum: Subtotal 1	13		17		12		15

Negative Items	Answer	Negative Items	Answer	Negative Items	Answer	Negative Items	Answer
9	−3	6	−2	3	−2	8	−2
17	−2	14	−1	11	2	16	−3
21	−1	22	−3	19	−1	24	−3
29	−2	26	−2	27	−2	32	−2
33	−2	38	1	35	−2	40	−2
45	−1	46	−2	43	−1	52	1
49	−2	50	−3	55	2	60	−2
53	−2	58	−3	63	−3	64	−3
Sum (for negative items)	−15		−15		−3		−16
−1×Sum: Subtotal 2	15		15		3		16
Subtotal 1+2: *Scale Score*	28		32		15		31

Note: Plus (+) signs have been omitted, in transposing item answers from the RI protocol.

and subsequent scored printout of RI answers are likely soon to be a further alternative in many research contexts.

In the handscoring form, the numbers of each item (1 through 64) are arranged in four columns, according to the scale the item belongs to. Within each column the numbers are sorted into those representing positively worded items (in the upper half of the scoring sheet) and items in negatively stated form (in the lower half of the sheet). Entries taken directly from an actual protocol—except for omission of + signs—are given for all items, to fully illustrate the scoring procedure. Generally, the *majority* of answers to positively worded items involve some grade of yes and, therefore, are numerically positive. The opposite tends to be true for the negative items. The arithmetic total is obtained, and shown, for each block of eight items. For positive items, these totals correspond to "Subtotal 1," for each scale.

The sum of numerical answers to negative items have an opposite directional significance to those that are positively worded. (For example, a no answer to item 17, "He is indifferent to me," has the same direction as a yes answer to item 13, "I feel appreciated by him".) Thus, reversing its sign (multiplying by -1), transforms the negative item sum to the same direction as the sum for positive items, and is identified as "Subtotal 2." Addition of the two subtotals yields the scale score, in each case. Investigators should not be alarmed to find that one subtotal is positive and the other negative, particularly in the case of relatively low scores; *or* that there is quite wide variation in the scores generated on the four different scales, from the same respondent. Since a relationship is an emergent product of two (or more) unique individuals, and is "born" and lives in highly varied external conditions, its configuration of features can be expected to differ from the profile of another relationship. In addition, it would be a surprising rather than expected outcome, if each of the four RI scales happened to have very similar distribution characteristics—even in large random samples from relationship populations.

It is true that the majority of scale scores generated from individual respondents are in practice on the positive side of zero. A (generous) sprinkling of negative scores within a given sample is not unusual, nor is it rare even in data from C–T relationships. There is no absolute meaning to the zero point—in the middle of the theoretical range—and significance has not been attributed a priori to any scoring values. This said, a below zero score implies that more often than not a respondent is answering "no" to positive items and/or "yes" to negative ones, and this does suggest that the relationship is lacking substantially in the aspect in focus. Average scores in samples from most categories of relationship tend to be higher for Level of Regard than for other scales; and usually they are lowest on the Unconditionality scale. Means for Empathy and Congruence most often fall in between.

Norms for the RI: Issues, Problems, and an Approach

Official norms for the RI, which would indicate for example that in 5, or 10 or 20, and so on, percent of cases scores on a given scale exceed or fall below a specified value, do not exist. Although not ruled out in principle, the task in practice is particularly complex in the case of the RI. (Fortunately, such norms are not essential for most research.) Stemming from the original "client" and "therapist" RI forms, there now are at least 10 principal variants of the 64-item revision of the instrument, and as many further, significant adaptations and revisions. More than half of the current forms have been appropriately used in therapy research and there is room (and need) for important work with additional variations. The same norms would not apply across this spectrum.[10]

Variation of different origin also limits direct comparison. As mentioned, RI data have been gathered after a few minutes of highly structured, systematically varied contact (in a variety of analogue studies), after first interviews, and following several (or many) hours of experience in intensive therapy. Besides scoring method and range, the aspects of data–source, angle of view, and duration and kind of relationship would need to be the same or broadly similar in order to accumulate and organize data in meaningful normative form.

A possible starting point would be to focus on client/patient-generated scores derived from data gathered after (say) three to six interview hours in actual therapy, using the OS 64-item RI. Further choices would be called for in terms, for example, of whether to consider only clients coming voluntarily for therapy in outpatient and private treatment contexts, of selecting some (minimum) experience level and/or other criteria of therapist expertise, of choosing which psychotherapeutic orientations to encompass and combine results from, and so forth. The task of literally establishing satisfactory, empirically based norms for psychotherapy relationships would be formidable.

In light of all the issues mentioned, my own suggestion is to utilize a threefold approach to assembling comparison data and working standards—avoiding as far as possible slippage into a highly prescriptive–evaluational stance which often accompanies the language of "norms." It would not be taken for granted that more means better on all RI scales, in all cases. One "prong" of this approach would be to organize means and variance data (the latter perhaps in terms of z score–scale score equivalents) from 10 to 12 studies reporting such data from 64-item OS RI forms. Selection criteria would include regular scoring, carefully conducted and monitored data gathering after at least two or three therapy interviews (but without mixing in posttherapy RI data), and clearly described samples of actual clients and professional therapists. I would not advocate combining the data across all the studies, because the variation among them would be important to hold in view. However, a composite profile from sources having very relevant ingredients in common, may be useful in conjunction with the sample-by-sample data.

A second component would involve gathering data systematically from the clientele (and from their therapists, if possible) of a particular treatment center or setting, in order to build up a local data pool which would cumulate to give current RI scale specifications for that context. This would provide comparison data for further work and programs in the same setting, and make it possible to meaningfully view scores and scoring levels against the arrays from reported data, selected and organized as suggested above. If therapist and/or treatment program evaluation was one main purpose of this exercise, sophisticated consideration would need to be given to the populations of clients involved in the samples compared—bearing im mind (for example) (1) that better-functioning clients are likely to perceive their therapists more positively in respect to empathy, congruence, and

---

10. This discussion does not take into account the further complications, in terms of norm–creation, of the numerous categories of interpersonal relationship, besides formal therapy associations, now studied via use of the R.I. In a recent bibliography (Barrett-Lennard, 1982a) I distinguished about 20 such nominal classes, required to code reported research.

other RI variables (Barrett-Lennard, 1962) and (2) that clients who are quite impoverished in extent and quality of life relationships may gain from more modest in-therapy levels of received empathy, and other conditions than are required by clients whose interpersonal life environments are more favorable (Barrett-Lennard, 1978a, 1978b; Holland, 1976).

The third kind of entry to establishing comparison standards—suggested as a complementary framing to the approach thus far described—is to consider the significance of different scoring levels based on the ways that subjects must tend to be replying, item by item, in order to give rise to these scores. The meaning of below-zero scores, in light of item-level answers that would generate them, has been referred to. Any scale score can be linked to an average response to the constituent items, and vice versa. By the standard scoring method (with a scale range of -48 to $+48$) a scale score of 40 or above would require a mean response of at least 2.5 (produced, say, by $+3$ and $+2$ answers on all positive items and -3 and -2 on all negative ones, with as many 3's as 2's). Viewed item by item this degree of consistency and strength of "positive" response would seem about as high as one could plausibly expect in terms of honest, discriminating perception. In practice, scores above 40 occur but are infrequent, except on the level of regard scale where distributions tend to be negatively skewed and whose "ceiling" may be lower than optimal for some relationships and respondents.

A score of 32, which is not uncommon in most samples, represents an *average* item score of 2 (after conversion of answers to negative items). Such a case would almost always involve a sprinkling of 3's in a positive direction, and some 1's. Very few, if any, item answers would weigh in a negative direction. Thus, this score on the face of it would imply clear affirmation that the referent person was experienced as very *substantially* empathic or congruent, and so on. A similar analysis applied to a score of 24—at the boundary between the third and fourth quartile of the theoretical range—suggests that this level would tend to be adequate in helping relationships. On the other hand, scores of 16—resulting conceivably from answers of "probably yes" $(+1)$ and "probably no" (-1) to every item, and otherwise stemming from a mix of responses carrying positive and negative weight—would be expected to represent a less than adequate level in therapy relationships.

A synthesis of these approaches to systemic organization of comparison data is a project—or a species of project multiplied by principal, differing forms and application of the RI—waiting to be undertaken. A thorough combing of relevant, existing reports—including doctoral dissertations—could now provide most of the necessary data for the illustrated focus on client-generated RI measures in therapy. Another basic area in which reported research now provides very extensive information has to do with reliability and validity of the RI scales, especially in respect to the principal OS and MO forms applied in two-person helping relationships.

Reliability and Validity: Issues and Evidence

Reliability is centrally concerned with whether, in fact, measuring system yields the same result whenever it is applied to something that it is designed to measure which has itself remained constant from one occasion of measurement to another. In the case of assessing complex psychosocial variables (say), by addition or other combination of numerous nonidentical bits of information, if one subset of bits yields approximately the same result—on the same occasion—as another similarly representative subset, metric consistency is well on the way to being established. In this case what is being measured is quite unlikely to have changed, as it may in test–retest situations. Further, if *each bit* of information used in a particular scale contributes regularly in the expected direction the resulting homogeneity of elements makes for measurement constancy. Of course, if one subset of elements yields exactly the same result as another, or if each "bit" correlates very highly with the whole, the component information is duplicating itself and parts of it are redundant as they stand.

Steps relevant to attaining adequate reliability, in developing the RI originally, and the first direct evidence of achievement of this goal (from split-half analysis applied to Client and Therapist RI data; and test–retest correlations for a sample of friend and family relationships) are outlined in my initial monograph report (Barrett-Lennard, 1962, pp. 6–7, 11–12). In each analysis and on every scale, reliability coefficients exceeded .80, save in one instance involving the scale later omitted. In *each* sample, mean reliabilities across the five component scales were .85 or above. It should be noted that the data were gathered in keeping with conditions and precepts earlier mentioned.

The generally favorable results encouraged further refinement and length-reduction of the inventory, partly in order to expand its effective range of application. As summed up already: "In essence, the 64-item revision was directed toward enhancing the sampling and quality of items, relative to earlier versions . . . " Steps to this end included modifying the language of some more complex or abstract item statements, "ensuring that unconditionality (and congruence) items were in keeping with definitional requirements, making adjustments suggested by detailed analysis of the extent to which individual items were aligned and in step with their scale scores, and further offsetting certain response bias possibilities—particularly by balancing positively and negatively stated items." (Barrett-Lennard, 1978a, p. 4).

The "detailed analysis" referred to is closely reported in the same work as the above quotations, and I shall touch on it briefly. An original item-analysis procedure was separately applied to five data samples gathered with pre-(64-item) revision Client/OS and Therapist/MO forms of the RI, to track the extent to which each item was working to produce scores on the scale to which it belonged. Each item had a directly comparable Item Discrimination Index value, with a mean of unity (+ 1) for all items in any scale. Items that were weak or inconsistent contributors to their scale were modified, or omitted. Some items were altered for other reasons, but with a careful eye to their discrimination properthus-far-attained answer distributions (on the + 3 to − 3 scale). A small number of essentially new items were introduced in keeping with theoretical refinements and the positive/negative item balance. The procedure certainly should have maintained, and would be expected to have increased, the homogeneity of the item samples for each scale. In practice, it would also have tended to diminish any redundancy. (It would not have ruled out the possibility of some items correlating fairly strongly with scales additional to their own.) Ideally, (1) the procedure would have been repeated using fresh samples of data gathered with the 64-item revision in tentatively final form, and (2) this step would have been accompanied by or followed by alpha coefficient determination for both the OS and MO versions. Subsequent reliability evaluation by other investigators suggests that these possible further steps could not, in the event, have led to adjustments with much effect on internal consistency.

The review by Gurman (1977) includes the principal published cumulation of internal and test–retest reliability of RI scales, based on data from a substantial range of contexts and investigators. Fifteen respondent samples from the work of 12 investigators or collaborating pairs generated the data for internal reliability assessment using split-half and alpha coefficient methods. Results from differing RI revisions, from several groups additional to the therapy–relationship majority, and from naturalistic and analogue studies, are included together. Five of the samples used non-English translations/revisions of the RI. In 11 cases, separate reliabilities for all four of the primary scale variables are presented. The means of coefficients cumulated by Gurman are for regard .91, empathy .84, unconditionality .74, and congruence .88. Only one of the 50 coefficients listed is below .67. Sixty percent were .87 ($\equiv$ 75% "constant variance") or above.

The test–retest reliabilities listed (Gurman, 1977, Table 1) are based on 10 samples, yielding 45 scale and total score coefficients, which range from .61 to .95. There is more evenness across the four scales than in the case of internal consistency, with means of coefficients varying only from .80 (for unconditionality) to .85 (for congruence). The extremes in test–retest intervals were 12 days and 12 months. Taking all the relevant evidence, in view of the heterogeneity of sources, methodologies and specific RI forms, the consistency and levels of obtained reliability are striking. It can safely be said that, given sound administration/data-collection procedures, existence of a very adequate level of technical reliability of the primary forms of the RI is not in question.

The issue of *validation*, in all its ramifications, is exceedingly complex in psychosocial measurement. It hinges on clarity of concept and definition of what is intended (or thought) to be measured, on the meaningfulness of viewing the construct involved as varying on a high to low continuum or sequence, and on congruence between this conceptualized dimension and the variable produced in operation by a particular measuring scheme. The various types of validity often distinguished—content, concurrent or predictive, "factorial," construct, and so on—involve alternate/complementary strategies or levels of entry in dealing with these basic issues. At this stage in the life of the RI, I shall proceed directly to claim that providing the instrument is understood and applied appropriately, its scales may be presumed and treated as valid. Grounds for this claim—largely implied in information already advanced—are in summary as follows.

1. In original development of the instrument, and in the subsequent revisions, much care was taken to adequately sample each of the defined interpersonal variables which it is designed to measure. In practice, the total endeavor to do justice to the theory, in producing the RI scales, led to further refinement and sharpening of the constructs themselves. Direct checks on the effectiveness of the operational translations initially included appraisal of the items by five judges. The judges were asked to classify each statement as a positive or negative expression—with the option also of identifying it as neutral or nonrelevant—of the theoretically described variable. All items retained met the criterion of being classified in the same way by all judges, except for one item receiving a single neutral rating (Barrett-Lennard, 1962, pp. 6–7). In preparing the 64-item revision, each of three relevantly experienced colleagues were asked to review and comment on the draft selection and wording of items, given detailed item analysis information as well as the theoretical grounding and purposes of the revision. In this case, the feedback lent itself to qualitative use in finalizing the exact sampling and form of the items (Barrett-Lennard, 1978a, p. 14 and Appendix A). These steps, and others, have assisted or provided evidence of content validity.

2. The RI is deemed metrically sound (1) judging from the nature and described principles of its structure, (2) given the reported item analysis and data used in its refinement (Barrett-Lennard, 1978a, pp. 4–6, 12–13, and Appendix A), and (3) in view of the extensive evidence of high internal reliability and stability of measurement already referred to. (Implications of factor analytic studies are mentioned below.) These features and the careful theoretical grounding establish potential for valid measurement.

3. The positive results of a range of independent predictive studies concerned with association between the RI-assessed relationship conditions and outcome, *in actual therapy or help-intended situations*, cumulate to form extensive and strong evidence of (predictive) construct validation. From his searching review of research in this sphere, involving use of the RI in nearly all cases, Gurman (1977, p. 523) concluded that "it is clear from the findings presented . . . *that there exists substantial, if not overwhelming evidence in support of the hypothesized relationship between patient-perceived therapeutic conditions and outcome in individual psychotherapy and counselling*" (italics in original). It is compatible with this statement that the evidence is most clear-cut in respect to the OS (or Client) forms but is not unequivocal in regard to the lesser-used MO (Therapist) form measures when treated in identical fashion. However, in light of the perspective newly advanced in this chapter, the typically much lower outcome predictive power of the MO form scales is to be expected and is not evidence of invalidity.

4. The many studies in contexts other than therapy, which have examined cogently predicted intersection of RI measures with other relational and behavioral parameters, or with effects of change-intended experience, include examples in the marriage and family sphere, in education and in other areas not feasible to sample in this summary. The first such investigation was by B. M. Thornton (1960), using data from marriage partners, each of whom completed both OS and MO RI forms on their relationship. Either partner's perception of the other's response (OS RI scale and total scores) were very strongly correlated with the classical measure of marital adjustment—unlike the RI in content or scope—developed by Burgess and Cottrell (1939). Thornton also found, as anticipated and at levels of highly significant association, (1) that the greater the *discrepancy* between the husband's perception of his own response and the wife's perception of his response in their relationship (or correspondingly the wife's self-perception and husband's perception of her) the lower the level of marital adjustment; and (2) that for either partner the greater the difference between the way they perceived their own response to the other and the other's response to them, the lower the index of marital adjustment.

In an important later study, Quick and Jacob (1973) found that scores on each of the RI scales, from perceptions of the husbands or the wives of the other's response, were significantly lower where either or both partners were seeking counseling than for couples not evidencing distress. Further, the RI differences held up even where the influence of a correlated Marriage Role (conflict) Questionnaire (MRQ) was partialed out, but the MRQ difference did not survive partialing out the RI contribution. The investigators concluded that the RI process dimensions evidently were more basic in marital disturbances than the behavioral role conflict components. Wampler and Powell (1982) collated mean score data for each RI scale as reported by a number of investigators, for their samples of distressed and/or nondistressed couples. For three scales, the means without exception are much higher for the assorted, nondistressed groups. For unconditionality, the pattern is not totally consistent, although the overall separation is strongly in the same direction. (The figures Wampler and Powell report are per item, and may be multiplied by 16 to approximate results from the regular 64-item forms.)

A variety of other careful studies focusing on intervention (helping/communication-learning) strategies and their effects, with groups of couples, have used the RI *as a measure of change*. The evidence is that the most used scales (empathy, regard, and congruence) are as a rule especially sensitive to effects that have been carefully expected, or assessed in alternate ways, in the sphere of attitude and relationship quality (Wells, Figurel, & McNamee, 1975; Epstein & Jackson, 1978; Wampler & Sprenkle, 1980; VanSteenwegan, 1979 & 1982; see also Wampler & Powell, 1982, pp. 141–142).

Within the educational arena, there has been moderately extensive and (only) moderately adequate usage of the RI in the research measurement of teacher regard, empathy, and the other conditions. Much of this work involves studies of association between the teacher–student relationship and variously focused and assessed qualities of learning, gains in academic achievement, and/or other development. I see no basis for positing a direct relationship between the relational process conditions and gains in academic achievement—as though the latter were directly comparable with personal-emotional recuperation or development. Thus, a study by Griffin (1977/78) concerned with reading improvement, in which the pattern of results imply that level of the RI-measured conditions affected the learner's attitude toward reading, and that this attitude was associated with reading achievement gain, is in my view cogent in ways that tend to cross-validate the measures.

In research by Hall (1972/73), with younger-than-usual subjects—fourth graders—pupils who were above the median in RI-measured quality of relationship with their teacher scored significantly higher on later measures of reading achievement and self-esteem, and lower on anxiety, than those below the median. This meaningful interlocking of results has validation–relevance for the simplified form of the RI employed. In some studies (e.g., Ryan, 1973/74) the combination of proposed connections found and not found, carry as much or more weight than if all the predictions had been upheld. Other investigations with direct or indirect relevance in the present context, include those by Mason and Blumberg (1969), Libby (1974/75), and Smetko (1982/83).

5. Studies which have used RI variables as *de*pendent measures, often in quasiexperimental designs predicting effects of particular individual or group characteristics, or of training or other interventive procedures, have yielded mixed results. However, the more well-conceived and managed work of this broad kind, involving uncontrived data or well-crafted analogue situations and using the full RI, has usually upheld hypotheses in regard to factors which should convincingly influence relationship quality. Examples of early work include Emmerling's (1961/62) study, in which students of more "open" teachers—who felt primary responsibility for difficulties and remedial action in their work—saw these teachers in a significantly more positive light, on all RI scales, than the pupils who described teachers of a more closed, externalizing orientation; and research by Cahoon (1962), who found experiencing levels (Gendlin Experiencing Scale) *and* open-mindedness (Rokeach Dogmatism Scale) of practicum counselors were significantly related to client-perceived relationship quality. Tosi (1970) also used the Rokeach scale and RI, with results similar to Cahoon's.

Other research of related theme includes: Churukian's (1970/71) study, centering on types of interpersonal need compatibility between supervising and student teachers, with effect on their relationship; the work reported by Abramowitz and Abramowitz (1974), concerned with the differential relation of client "psychological mindedness" to relationship quality and outcome in insight-oriented group therapy versus non-insight-oriented therapy (see also Gurman, 1977, pp. 529–530); Brauer's investigation (1979/80) focusing on therapy relationship effects of high and low self-concept on the part of deaf students, and their relative perception of deaf and hearing interviewers; and a study, by Junek, Burra, and Leichner (1979) using a "half-length" observer adaptation of the RI applied with novel effectiveness to study effects on interview quality of a carefully portrayed practice-training seminar for psychiatric residents.

6. Factorial studies *that begin with item intercorrelations* (from full-length RI forms) have led the investigators involved to make adjustments in the exact selection and arrangement of items. (Factor analyses based on correlations between the four or five RI scales have been pointless, even misleading.) The interitem analyses have, however, yielded

factors—four or more in number—on the whole closely congruent with the theoretically based variables. (See reviews/discussion by Gurman, 1977 and by Barrett-Lennard, 1978a.) The brief outline following and adapted from the sources just mentioned to its context here, refers in part to work which is unpublished or not in English.

Walker and Little (1969), using a two-tier procedure, found 10 homogenous item clusters, including, for example, three "empathy dimensions." Second stage analysis proceeding from intercorrelation of the initial dimensions yielded three factors, in which unconditionally a composite of empathy and congruence, and level of regard, are principally reflected. In their Dutch language studies, Lietaer (1974) and VanSteenwegan began with a long RI (OS) form—adding earlier and new items to the basic 64 item set—applied to a large sample of parent–child (college student) relationships. The five emergent factor scales, each composed of 10 items, were identified as empathy (including seven out of eight of the regular $E+$ items), positive regard (a cluster *not* including any regular E, C or U items), unconditionality (including eight out of eight of the regular $U+$ items), transparency (made up of congruence and earlier willingness to be known items), and directivity (reflecting in part newly introduced items). Similar analysis later applied to data from 100 C–T pairs yielded 7 factor-based scales (Lietaer, 1976). Five of these warranted the same labels as before, although not identical in item composition. The "new" scales were negative regard (four items) and incongruity (with seven of the eight items drawn from previous congruence scales). Especially prominent in Lietaer's careful work is the extraction of factor scales largely composed either of positively worded *or* negatively worded items. Otherwise, apart from "directivity," they are in keeping with the original structure of the instrument.

An important factor study by Bebout (1971/72) has not been reported in detail. In the course of his large sample research on intensive groups, Bebout factor-analysed (with varimax rotation) two sets of OS 64-item RI data: group members' perceptions of leaders (Set 1) and outside friend perceptions of members (Set 2). Each data set yielded four factors congruent with the original RI scales. As well, five items loaded on a factor concerned with perceived imposition/nonimposition and related to Lietaer's directivity factor. (In the friend data only, a small sixth factor emerged.) The level of regard factor in Bebout's data included most of the $R+$ and $R-$ items (15 out of 16, in Set 1). Three-quarters of the congruence items loaded on an "open-genuine" factor, nine of the same items appearing also under the headings of "transparency" or "incongruity" in Lietaer's scales. Most items in the empathy and unconditionality scales were, respectively, from the $E+$ or $U+$ subgroups, also closely resembling Lietaer's scales. Only one item from either set of data turned up adequately loaded on the "wrong" factor among the principal four. In summary, and as appraised and carefully stated by another author (Gurman, 1977, p. 513): *"On the basis of the existing data deriving from properly conducted factor-analytic studies, it appears that the R.I. is tapping dimensions that are quite consistent with Barrett-Lennard's original work on the Inventory."*[11,12]

---

11. New factor-analytic studies in England by D. Cramer are producing the same pattern of results as the work referred to here. Initially, Cramer (1986/in press) used the pre-revision Client RI form (less the willingness to be known items) to gather data from 169 "closest friend" relationships. He concludes, in his abstract, that "The first four factors [after varimax rotation] reflected the postulated factors, thus supporting the construct validity of the original RI". This study is now being replicated using the current 64-item OS RI form. I have not yet seen any results, but would expect a lower attrition rate of items not adequately weighted on any main factor, from the revised RI data. (Attrition is bound to occur, as implied in my earlier-written remarks in footnote 12, following.)

12. While factor-analytic work, for example, of the kind cited here, is a useful *contributory* means of validation, or even of further refinement, it is not in my estimation optimal to restructure an instrument such as the

7. The reputation and usage of the instrument in hundreds of doctoral dissertations and other theses (see, for example, Barrett-Lennard, 1982a) and in major programatic studies,[13] while not in itself constituting formal evidence of validity, reflects positive appraisal by other investigators for whom much is riding on the feasibility and integrity of their own work or research which they are supervising. This situation has been evolving quietly for over 25 years. Usage has become more diversified within counseling and therapy research and includes wide application in other human service contexts and significant personal life relationships. The burden of proof has shifted such that to discount the instrument as gravely deficient, or invalid in well-considered application, would require extensive new evidence quite contrary in thrust from that which has accumulated.

While overall the validation evidence is perhaps as unequivocal as one could expect in the presumptuous sphere of *measuring* complex attitudinal–relationship variables, no claim is implied here that the RI is literally perfected, that it should not be tested in new ways, or that it should not be altered in any circumstance. Clearly, by now, it should *not be altered lightly*. One kind of development involves generating new adaptations (preserving the same structure, scoring and basic item content) which expand the scope and utility of the Inventory and which can or should involve an aspect of refinement. That is, an adaptation can draw on a growing pool of experience and knowledge, and should be at least as well conceived and tuned to the new purposes to which it is put as the basic forms are for their sphere of application. This issue leads to the next main section of this report, concerned with promising un- and under-used applications of the RI—applications that seem to me to be strongly beckoning or promising directions.

New and Underused Applications of the RI: A Glancing View of Further Potentiality

Full exploration of my present topic would be far beyond the feasible scope of this chapter and would as well risk infringing on the inventiveness of the reader. I will therefore focus on potentialities where at least initial studies or pilot work have been done or which have been suggested or in my own thought for some time. I will attend more to the nature or issue-value of these potentialities than to specific method, while including some suggestions here and there on the latter level. If my remarks prompt freshly differentiated work with the RI, in useful directions, their best purpose will be accomplished.

RI, theoretically founded and designed to measure subtle and complex interactional–attitudinal qualities, directly on the basis of factor–analytic data. The detailed results of factorial procedures from different samples and nominal classes of relationship obviously do not coincide and the factor–extraction methods themselves can legitimately differ. Further, there are inherent limitations to separating and clustering units of information on the basis of a single (essentially simple) concept of the meaning of being in our out of step. As an example, the emergence of factors in which all or most items are positively (or else negatively) stated is fully in keeping with a response bias toward saying "yes" (or "no") which the combination of positive and negative items in the regular RI scales is designed to offset. (See also Barrett-Lennard, 1978a, pp. 33–34.)

13. Relevant programmatic research 'began' with the Wisconsin study of psychotherapy with schizophrenic patients (Rogers, 1967) and, at present, includes the very extensive Psychotherapy of Depression Collaborative Research Program coordinated by Dr. Irene E. Waskow and others, through the U.S. National Institute of Mental Health.

Life Relational Environment: Helping Relationship Baseline?

One very underused adaptation of the inventory yields a profile of the respondent's experienced interpersonal world, in the range of the RI and encompassing the three main areas of family relationships, voluntary "friend" relationships, and work/public life relationships (Holland, 1976; Barrett-Lennard, 1978a, 1978b). Holland's (1976) validity study provides strong preliminary evidence that this adaptation—Form OS-S-42—*is* a means to effectively sample and appraise main areas and axes of the respondent's lived interpersonal world. Technical measurement characteristics approach those of the regular RI forms.

It seems to me of special interest that Form OS-S-42 offers a way of obtaining an empirical grip on whether or how clients entering therapy differ in their (experienced) interpersonal environments from control samples not entering therapy, or from themselves after therapy. Further, an implied assumption of conditions theory, which needs to and could be tested using this form, is that in therapeutic/helping contexts higher levels of empathy and of the other conditions exist in the C–T relationship than in any other currently active relationships in the client's life.

It further appears, from research to date, that even in client-centered and related therapies the qualities tapped by the RI via client perceptions account for a limited, although significant, *part* of the variance in outcome. Is this a result of differences among clients in the quality of their relationships outside therapy; such, for example, that the received empathy level in the therapy relationship for a particular client is close to the level he or she experiences in some other significant "nontherapy" relationship, while for another client a similar achieved level in therapy is totally outside and beyond the range of any experienced relationship outside therapy? More precisely and generally, is it the absolute received level of empathy (or congruence, etc.) in therapy which is most important, or is the degree to which this level exceeds the client's own baseline experience more critical? RI Form OS-S-42 is waiting to be used, to shed empirical light on this issue.

Family Relationships and Change

Various forms of the RI have, as implied earlier, been used over a long period in the study of couple and family relationships. Examples include reported work by B. M. Thornton (1960), Hollenbeck (1965), Griffin (1967/68), DeMers (1971), VanderVeen & Novak (1971), Quick & Jacob (1973), Lietaer (1974), Luber and Wells (1977), Epstein and Jackson (1978), Wampler and Sprenkle (1980), Gomes (1981), Schumm, Bollman & Jurich (1981), Carter (1981/82), and VanSteenwegen (1982). Given the burgeoning development of research on family process and relationships, and the varied demonstrations of utility and versatility of the RI in this sphere—leading to some spirited advocacy from within the field (Wampler & Powell, 1982)—a mean of only one or two studies a year since B. M. Thornton's (1960) original application suggests unwarranted oversight and neglect of this salient resource. Probably part of the explanation lies in the RI's origin in individual therapy and psychology, a context that is more restrictive by association than in substance.

Besides the more traditional focus on one person's response (A) to one other (B), as separately perceived by A and/or B—in a marital or parent–child dyad—powerful new forms of the RI which directly tap experienced relationship systems as such, are now available in experimental versions. These include a dyad–observer form (Form DO-64), in which representative items read "They respect one another" (R+), "Each nearly always knows what the other means" (E+), "It makes them uneasy to bring up or talk about certain things together" (C−), "They are openly themselves with one another" (C+), "They appreciate exactly how the other one's experiences feel *to the other*" (E+), and "Each wants the other to be a particular sort of person" (U−). Another form, used by Gomes (1981) in his thesis study with me, yields any family member's perception of the whole (nuclear) family system. Sample items are "We (the members of my family) respect one another" (R+), "The interest we feel in one another depends on the things each one says or does" (U−), "We may understand each other's words but we don't see and take in each other's feelings" (E−), "We are openly ourselves, as we really are, in the family" (C+), "Sometimes we regard or judge each other as more worthwhile than we do at other times" (U−), and "I don't think that what any of us say or do actually changes the way we feel toward each other" (U+).

Gomes (1981) and I also adapted Form OS-S-42 for application solely to family relations. This version maintains the multiple relationship feature, specifically including the response of single others and of family twosomes. An example of the latter from a child's position, is the instruction to describe the response of "your mother and father in the way they generally respond to you when they are involved together as a pair. In this case, you need to think of the two people as one 'you' or 'they' in the way they respond to 'me' when they also are occupied with each other." (Cited from "Family Adaptation #1," 1/1980, of Form OS-S-42, prepared by Barrett-Lennard and Gomes).

The newest RI adaptation in this cluster, benefitting in detail from work on the other forms mentioned, is answered by participants in a couple relationship to describe their "we" dyad as one unit. Instructions on this form indicate that it "points to features of the relationship *twosome* as seen by either member [and] It is understood that one member or partner would not give exactly the same picture as the other one, and that either person's view could change." The respondent is advised to "think of what actually goes on and of the atmosphere of feeling and attitude between you. If you can, bring to mind pictures of the two of you in usual or everyday situations with each other, and also perhaps at unusual times that have stayed in your memory." Assurance is given that "the 'right' answer in each case is how you truely see and feel this whole relationship we, as of now". Following is a sample of the wording of the 64 items— three from the empathy group, and one each from the other scales: "We each look at what the other does from our own individual point of view"; "We realize each other's meaning, even when something is hard to say—or find words for"; "We often don't realize (at the time) how sensitive or touchy the other one is about things that are said or done"; "We like and enjoy one another"; "Either of us can be 'up' or 'down' in our mood without it changing the other one's attitude toward us," and "Sometimes one or other of us is not at all comfortable but we go on, outwardly ignoring it" (cited from BLRI Form DW-64, as prepared late in 1984.)

These and other arrangements and refinements of relationship "systems" forms of the RI clearly have potential for new lines of research in the family process field, where established forms of the instrument also remain much underused. One main area of application is that of relationship change associated with family therapy. From evidence (e.g., B. M. Thornton, 1960) and theory, not only change as such but shifts in disparity or convergence between experience-derived measures of the "same" systems from different vantage points would also be pertinent to study. My own systematic "metatheory" of family relations offers in detail an original person-centered systems view, with implications and suggestions for research that could fruitfully entail new usages of the RI. Included, also, is an outline presentation of Gomes' work (Barrett-Lennard, 1982/84, 1984a).

Classroom and Child-Adult Relationships

Although a number of studies have been cited using the RI in educational research, including varied application to teacher–student relationships, as in the case of family research the level and range of application taps only a part of the evident and inviting potential. Younger children (prehigh school) are seldom heard from directly in terms, for example, of interpersonal educational environments which nurture or awaken their curiosity and potential to learn and to know. Even at high school level, students rarely are invited to candidly portray the basic interactive attitudes and response of their teachers. More broadly, working beliefs and arrangements regarding the promotion of learning have little or none of their anchorage in knowledge of the actual impact on learners of their teacher's empathy, regard, and other RI-measured qualities.

The Teacher–Pupil Relationship Inventory (TPRI) in particular, developed by Scheuer and myself in the late 1960s (see Scheuer, 1971; Barrett-Lennard, 1978a) has, as implied, received some modest further use but has for the most part lain in wait, its mission and potential left largely in abeyance. *One* element helping to limit obvious applications may have been the "experimental" quality of the TPRI itself. In any case, the adaptation has been further revised and refined with language experience and needs of children of about 10 to 14 years old—including grades 5 through 8, or equivalent—especially in mind.[14] Illustrative items from the revised TPRI are: "He (or she) deals with my behaviour but he (she) doesn't understand how *I feel* about things" (E−), "Whatever mood I'm in doesn't change the way he feels about me" (R−), "He doesn't pretend to be something he isn't" (C+), "He knows what I mean even when I have trouble saying it" (E+), "He wants me to be a particular kind of person" (U−), "He's truly interested in me" (R+), "At times he looks down on me—thinks I'm nothing" (scores R−, includes element of U−), and "There are times when I feel that what he says out loud is really different from the way he's feeling inside himself" (C−). School administrators and teachers may see an uncomfortable reversal of positions, or feel awkwardness on other grounds, about letting children answer these and related questions; and where such is permitted, I think it extremely important to treat the children's responses with sensitive and genuine consideration to all who are involved. (One expression of such consideration would be to offer teachers anonymous and group feedback in a form that invites exploration and, perhaps, discovery.) There is, it appears, a vast reservoir of awareness and discrimination among children to which the TPRI could give very illuminating partial access and expression, helping to open to founded view phenomena that may switch learning through teaching on or off.

New possibilities in a still broader arena would follow from (also) adapting the TPRI to a general child form, for application in research on child and family therapy, studies in parent–child and sibling relations, and systematic inquiry focusing on the interpersonal experience *of children* in hospitals, recreational and sport settings, and a great variety of other contexts. For too long, the RI has been used almost entirely with adult and near-adult respondents. The more formative interpersonal worlds of children constitute another strongly beckoning and potentially crucial sphere for its direct usage and contribution.

---

14. There has been occasional reported use of simpler, briefer forms with even younger children (for example, Hall, 1972/73), but until the TPRI is more widely tested and fully established in use (with further refinement if called for), I am not inclined, myself, to focus on developing and testing an adaptation for still younger children.

Predicting the Other's View: Metaperception Applications

What I have called metaperception applications of the RI, in which, for example, A's view of B's response in their relationship is compared with B's best judgment and prediction of how his or her response will be seen and described by A, are, to my knowledge quite rare. One instance is in my own work (Barrett-Lennard, 1967). Thought and evidence to date strongly suggests that the degree to which B correctly anticipates A's perception of his or her response is akin to empathy, and perhaps more open than the latter to the influence of learning and development. In usage, A and B answer the same RI form, except for an adjustment to the instructions for B. This adjustment indicates clearly that B's task is to answer as he or she thinks A will answer, that is, in a way that reflects his or her closest sense of the way A sees B being and responding in their relationship.

A's direct view of B's response yields, of course, a measure of empathy of primary import and influence so far as A is concerned. Using the symbols to stand for B's empathy toward A, as experienced or received by A, this may be coded B's $E \to A : A$. The metaperception procedure provides a secondary or alternative level of access to B's awareness of A's frame of reference, in the sensitive and nuclear sphere of their relationship. Taking the empathy items and scale in particular, this metalevel could be coded (B's $E \to A : A$) : B, the portion in parentheses having the same meaning as before, with the addition now of " . . . as viewed by B." The nearer the ratio (B's $E \to A : A$) : B $\div$ B's $E \to A : A$ approaches unity, the more closely B evidently is in touch with A's perspective on their relationship. Thus far, application of the OS form of the RI is implied. To also use the MO form ("I respect him/her") in the same way would be meaningful in complementary fashion. In code, B's $E \to A : B$ would refer to B's self-perceived response to A, scored on empathy, and the ratio (B's $E \to A : A$) : B $\div$ B's $E \to A : B$ would represent B's view of the way A experiences him (let us say B *is* male) as compared with B's direct experience of his own response to A. For this ratio to approach unity, particularly in the absence of equality in the first-mentioned comparison, would imply that B's self-experienced response to A was tending to govern his view or assumptions about the way A would see him responding. (In some circumstances, it might also imply that A's open and strongly expressed view in interactions with B, of B's response to her (say), had strongly influenced B's self-view.)

These examples only begin to illustrate potentially salient comparisons and patterns. I have not, for example, mentioned the metaview coded (B's $E \to A : B$) : A, (referring to A's predictions/assumptions regarding B's self-perceived response to A). Furthermore, it may well be the case that predictions usually are more on target with respect (say) to regard and congruence than to unconditionality or even empathy. More generally, there may be different profiles of accuracy of prediction among the RI variables that have distinctive implications and meaning. The largely-untapped potentials of metaperception applications of the RI appear to me to have special salience in the twin spheres of interpersonal learning and relationship change. In the present context, a setting for their application which stands out is marital and family therapy research. (Informal observation suggests also that the RI has practical value, as an aid in relationship-oriented counseling with couples.)

I hope that this total, illustrative discussion of new and underused applications of the RI, in addition to being directly useful, will trigger the readers' own fresh thought, thus contributing to work that carries or proceeds beyond the scope of possibilities explicitly referred to. Encouraged by the editors of this volume, my concluding comments are not by way of a literal and perhaps redundant summary, but observations of a more informal, personal kind relating to my own overall odyssey with the RI—now furthered by this chapter.

My "Affair" with the R.I.: An Informal R]sum]

Just 30 years before this publication, at the midpoint of my doctoral studies and internship experience at the University of Chicago, and with the planning of a dissertation as the next step, Carl Rogers first circulated his classic formulation of "the necessary and sufficient conditions of therapy" (Rogers, 1957). I don't remember struggling to find a suitable topic for my doctoral research. Rogers' presentation struck me as an exciting, daring propositional integration of experienced-based ideas, which I would love to put to empirical test. The problem, in a word, was how, since no means existed for measuring each of the posited relationship conditions, nor was it at all obvious what kind of design (if any) might be both feasible and effective. The worthwhileness and interest of this challenge were not in question, and the whole context encouraged me to presume that it could be met.

It soon was evident that further refinement or tighter casting of theory would be necessary for measurement; and that the potent Q-sort procedure, then strongly in vogue at Chicago (see, for example, Bown 1954; Butler & Haigh, 1954), might provide an approach to measurement of the relationship variables (Barrett-Lennard, 1957). My account of the original development of the RI, of the interplay between theory and operational expression and back again in the course of generating item statements, and of reasons for abandoning the Q-sort method and adopting and developing the type of questionnaire finally chosen, is on record (Barrett-Lennard, 1959a, 1961, 1962). Whether this writing reflects the enormous interest and satisfaction I experienced for the first time in conducting empirical research, whether our excitement as the long-gathered, hand-analysed data yielded its "secrets" has shown through, or the strong early (1958/59) encouragement to revise the instrument for immediate use in the Wisconsin Psychotherapy Project with hospitalized schizophrenic patients has been apparent, I do not know. I doubt that it has been clear that, from the very beginning of the research, applications outside therapy also were envisaged, given positive results in a therapeutic context (Barrett-Lennard, 1957, page 11. Also see Rogers, 1959). The panorama of meaningful possibilities kept unfolding, and continues to do so.

Completion of my dissertation (Barrett-Lennard, 1959a), which does not include any results for the data gathered from therapists, did not complete the original project. I feel singularly fortunate that the conditions of my doctoral work helped me to *want* to continue my research afterwards, that with an NIMH "small grant" was forthcoming, and that there was real encouragement from colleagues in Chicago, Wisconsin, Auburn (1/1959–1961), and then Australia. Its completion and publication, extending over 4 years, seemed then to take a long time. Readers of my *Psychological Monographs* report (Barrett-Lennard, 1962) usually noticed the University of New England affiliation, but not many would have known that this institution was then the smallest and most isolated university in Australia and that my report was largely written up in very modest physical conditions in the hot Australian summer (1961/62); that one or two very experienced readers who respected my work advised me that the manuscript was far too long (and I knew that it could have been divided and published "in bits") but that Norman Munn, as editor of *Psychological Monographs*, did accept the manuscript as submitted, without revision; that later the work was formally scheduled for republication in Hart and Tomlinson's (1970) *New Directions in Client-Centred Therapy* (and was mentioned in early advertizing) but dropped by late decision of the publishers to reduce the size of the volume; and that I still receive occasional requests for reprints although none are to be had from any source except, possibly, in microfilm/microfiche form.

The 1962 monograph is still the most frequently cited reference source in research using the RI, although in light of the instrument's evolution this tends to be misleading without mention of later sources as well (for example, Barrett-Lennard, 1978a). Many among generations of graduate students in counseling and clinical psychology and related fields came to know of the monograph in its own right or as a primary reference to the more visible RI. Although this prominence was gratifying, I worried a bit about the "classroom knowledge" hazard so eloquently portrayed by Rogers in his preface to *Client-Centred Therapy* (1951). Experience, however, with the students who have been individually and *directly* in touch with me (at the rate of 30 to 40 per year since the mid-1960s) has not reinforced this worry. Often members of this group have gone to considerable trouble to track me down. Usually they have been excited about their work and wished to be as well informed as possible about the RI. Mostly, they have struck me as resourcefully keen that their research actually contribute to thought or practice in its area.

The contact with students actively seeking me out is as much as anything at the heart of the personal and professional meanings to me of the long enterprise of my work on and connected with the inventory, including the dimension of continuing effort to produce resource materials and articles useful to other investigators. In retrospect, it is possible to distinguish several phases in my total involvement with the RI, externally including the work it has spawned or furthered and, more internally, as a major unfolding strand in my own professional-scholarly journey.

The *first phase* includes the most fruitful, culminating stage of my studentship at Chicago, continuing through early steps in my career academic/teaching activity, to the completion of my 1962 monograph. It includes having graduate student advisees working with me and choosing to make central use of the RI (B. M. Thornton, 1960; F. C. S. Thornton, 1960; Emmerling, 1961/62; Rosen, 1961) and students and associates in a variety of other settings calling on me and sharing their planning and/or findings with the RI (Barrington, 1961; Berlin, 1960; Cahoon, 1962; Hollenbeck, 1961, 1965; Kagan, Hungate, Hau, & Lewis, 1964; Snelbecker, 1961/1967; Van der Veen in 1961 and later reports). Also sandwiched between my dissertation and the monograph (and besides the NIMH-supported research), several conference presentations were eventful and affirming. (Barret-Lennard, 1959b, 1959c, 1961).

The overlapping *second phase* involved intensive work on and completion of the principal revision of the RI (Barrett-Lennard, 1964), a growing vision of its potentials in and beyond psychotherapy research, and my own first strong development of interdisciplinary interest and involvement. On the research side, this involvement included use of the RI in measurement of actual and ideal relationships, and its first metaperception application, focusing on workshop-related change in group members' awareness of an outside person's perception of relationship with the member (Barrett-Lennard, 1967). A descriptive paper for nonspecialist readers, stemming from my research and applied work, and titled "Significant aspects of a Helping Relationship," was published in *Mental Hygiene* (Barrett-Lennard, 1963) and (by request) in *Canada's Mental Health* (1965) and other contexts. Its wide circulation surprised and encouraged me. It is the main place in my writing where the concept of availability,[15] reflected in an exploratory long form of the RI in place of willingness to be known, is spelled out.

I regard this second phase as ending with a year on a visiting appointment at Southern Illinois University, where more than a dozen thesis/dissertation studies using the RI have been conducted. While there, I became much more aware of the (partly fortuitous) way in which the RI was providing encouragement and a vehicle for others in a variety of fields to focus on the crucial issue of how beneficial change or movement in help-intended relationships, and in enabling interpersonal processes in other life contexts, worked. The still-new 64-item forms were in fact lending themselves to widening use, each project adding to the spectrum. A student at SIU helped me to prepare (in 1966) the first substantial, cited compilation of studies using the inventory.

The *third phase* extended through the latter 1960s to 1972/73—my first seven years at Waterloo. Truax and Carkhuff (1967) and their associates were working with great energy and ambitious vigor on inquiry, training, and practice pivoting on "core conditions," in turn resting in primary origin on Rogers' conception, although in some basic respects on a different wavelength from his thought (see Carkhuff & Berenson, 1967, and later works by Carkhuff). On the surface, the variables were much the same as those tapped by the RI, although quite different in data source, specific discrimination, and approach to measurement. A basic difference with ramifying implication lay in the fact that each element of information is a nonparticipant judgment based on a small segment of interaction viewed through the lens of a single multistep rating scale, for any given variable. The method from the start was described as "objective" as opposed to procedures, notably the RI, drawing directly on the experience and observations of participants and thereby labeled "subjective."

My growing sense that there were not only fundamental differences between the approaches, but also, widely unrecognized difficulties with the Truax/Carkhuff scales and methodology, was a source of concern on more than one level. Careful, good work on empathy and the other relationship conditions within a spirit of inquiry and involving well-grounded thought were dear to my own heart. We were I felt, and feel, on the track of something extremely important but it would be misleading to imply conclusive knowledge, and vitally important to make strenuous effort to avoid self-confirming steps. It appeared to me that my influential colleagues did not share these and related concerns or values (or did not give them priority) and the possible consequences worried me. As the person centrally involved with the RI method, for me to find fault in print with Truax's and/or Carkhuff's work could very easily have been taken as special pleading for "my own" approach, and would have absorbed time and energy needed to further my own primary work and to encourage and assist others who draw on it. This at any rate seemed the most constructive pathway for me, and I had begun to feel that real difficulties would have to become apparent and be brought into substantive view by others.

Further (phase 3) steps in 1969 and the beginning 1970s, with the direct and indirect aid of a Canada Council research grant, included revising my "Technical Note on the 64-Item Relationship Inventory" (since responsively sent to at least 500 other investigators), preparing forms of the RI worded for a group "other" (they respect me . . . /I respect them), compiling new bibliographies with student assistants (Barrett-Lennard, Bond, & Taylor, 1972), drafting preliminary versions of a comprehensive

---

15. A version of availability was explicitly included in a French language study by Belpaire and Archambault (1969). If any important aspect of a helping relationship is "missing" from the RI, my sense and belief is that it relates to what I was driving at then, but did not focus and experiment with sufficiently to feel sure about adding to the tested features.

report on the 64-item revision of the RI and its main adaptations (which grew into the 1978 monograph), and taking the first concrete steps on fresh conceptual work (Barrett-Lennard, 1972) initially to try to clear up the confusion surrounding the conditions concepts and research. (These steps seem to me the threshold of the next phase.) By the time it appeared, Truax's chapter in the first edition of Bergin and Garfield's *Handbook of Psychotherapy and Behaviour Change* (1971), in which the reader is not alerted to the RI or to any body of work with it, did not strongly concern me. The very much lower-key advancement of work with the RI reached a level—judging from the evidence of others in contact with me and published records—of over 40 new English language studies being undertaken in one year. I also became aware that significant use of the inventory had begun in other languages.

The *fourth phase* began with a year of study leave, which was not primarily concerned with RI-related work but in particular included much more fleshing out of my mentioned new thinking on empathy—advanced at an Australian Psychological society conference during my leave, and first published in Australia (Barrett-Lennard, 1976). At the time the article appeared in print, Holland (1976) was completing his validity study, with me, of the relational life-space form (OS-S-42) of the RI. Deeply distressing and distracting administrative/program crises were occurring in my setting in Waterloo; and new writing or research—beyond attention to work by others—was stalled for a time. I succeeded in giving prepublication feedback on about the first half only of Gurman's (1977) excellent and heartening review, which centered on the RI in the context of therapy research. As soon as local matters improved somewhat, a priority task became completion and publication of my 1978 monograph. It had been periodically in the making for 7 or 8 years, and in draft versions for 6; and it was at first mistakenly rejected as involving too much duplication of Gurman's review! I regard phase 4 as ending with the initial edition in mid-1979 of my bibliography of the ''second decade'' of studies with the RI (Barrett-Lennard, 1982a).

The *current phase*, the *fifth* and last to date in this reckoning, coincided in birth with entry to the 1980s, and with a major turn in the settings of my work, away from the full-time shelter and support of established academic institutions and into a more uncertain, self-generating and open-ended path. I cannot see ahead to the next RI-relevant transition, but the last emerged during another year at SIU, and the moment of this writing—in the midst of settling again in Australia—may be the point of greatest challenge in this phase.[16]

Flowing most directly from another center of interest, in the small-group field (see especially Barrett-Lennard, 1979), during the SIU year I first spelled out some new ideas in the family relations sphere—further developed in Barrett-Lennard (1982/84, 1984a)—which interested a student working with me. As earlier implied, the new RI adaptations we developed were used with interesting, valuable effect in this research (Gomes, 1981). Quite independently, Wampler and Powell (1982) were preparing their vigorous advocacy of the RI for research on marital relationship quality, which I first saw in near-final form. Thus, my own now-focused interest in family relations, coupled with the

---

16. This chapter was initially completed late in 1983, shortly after returning to Australia; with some elements in the text and reference list being updated at the proof-reading stage, two years later. The challenge I mentioned has been to create an independent path on a *full-spectrum* basis: a path that combines—with priority to each—clinical and consulting services, scholarly writing and research, an educational and professional development component, and a wider involvement that grows from and feeds into all of these.

breaking of new ground (actual and prospective) in marital–family research using the RI, forms one main thrust or strand in phase 5.

Another strand involves the continuing evolution of my interest in empathy (Barrett-Lennard, 1981a, 1981b), and its broader effects and connections. One effect is the view advanced in this chapter of interaction phases for all RI variables corresponding to those for empathy. Another conjunction of ideas, of excitement to me, has been to consider empathy toward human system entities—that is, toward two or more persons as an interrelated unit with its own life or ''being'' (Barrett-Lennard, 1981b). This strand also embraces recent-to-present RI usage in which the empathy scale is the primary or sole focus (for example, Brown, 1980/81; Finneran, 1980/81; Kirk & Thomas, 1982).

A further current strand directly involves my experience and unfolding activity as a largely independent scholar, especially in relation to students and others using the RI and to first-hand research. It is not feasible to provide materials or much time *gratis*, and a research materials and consultation service is an explicit part of my work.[17] I expect that an again-adequate foundation for long-term research will evolve through The [new] Center for Studies in Human Relations (see Barrett-Lennard, 1985b) and other suitable affiliations.[18] Should this happen, in a way that substantially involves the RI, it may mark the transition to another professional/personal phase, in the vein of those shared here.

Coda

No formal summary conclusion seems necessary, or even congruent, in sequence with my just-finished discussion. I hope that the interested reader will not be deterred by geographical distance from seeking me out, offering feedback, sharing related work and interest, calling on me for resource materials, inviting me to be a consultant, or even, seeking my collaboration. I feel privileged to have been able to sustain a focus of interest for so long—with no end in sight—adding other substantial interests which in turn have drawn on, expanded, or deepened the first. At the risk of presumption, I can recommend such an anchorage and element of continuity.

As I write these concluding lines, a kind of personal interest and fellow-feeling for readers who have followed the course of this chapter wells up in me, and an awareness surfaces that there are ways in which you would know me pretty well. I hope that my ''company'' has been worthwhile and, if it has, I look forward to yours.

References

Abramowitz, S. I., & Abramowitz, C. V. Psychological mindedness and benefit from insight-oriented group therapy. *Archives of General Psychiatry*, 1974, *30*, 610–615.

Alvarado, V. I. Perception of counselors: A function of culture. *Dissertation Abstracts International*, 1976/77, *37-A*, 3407. (University Microfilms No. 76-28, 097).

---

17. Unpublished articles and other material reproduced by me (or issued through The Centre for Studies in Human Relations) may be obtained—at moderate cost—by writing to me at 6 Dover Crescent, Wembley Downs. Western Australia, Australia, 6019; or at Box 881, West Perth, Australia, 6005 (office postal address).

18. For example, a continuing (honorary) position as Visiting Fellow, in Social Inquiry—Psychology, at Murdoch University, Western Australia.

Adorno, T. W., Frenkel-Brunswik, E., Levinson, D. J., & Sanford, R. N. *The authoritarian personality*. New York: Harper, 1950.

Barrett-Lennard, G. T. An experimental study of certain theoretically basic dimensions of a therapeutic relationship: A research proposal. *Counseling Center Discussion Papers*, 1957, *3*, No. 7. University of Chicago Library.

Barrett-Lennard, G. T. Relationship study: Progress report 1, and 2. *Counseling Center Discussion Papers*, 1958, *4*, No. 1 and No. 19. University of Chicago Library.

Barrett-Lennard, G. T. *Dimensions of perceived therapist response related to therapeutic change*. Doctoral Dissertation (Psychology), University of Chicago, 1959. (a)

Barrett-Lennard, G. T. *The Relationship Inventory: A technique for measuring therapeutic dimensions of an interpersonal relationship*. Paper given at the annual meeting of the Southeastern Psychological Association, St. Augustine, Florida (Mimeo.), 1959. (b)

Barrett-Lennard, G. T. Therapeutic personality change as a function of perceived therapist response. *American Psychologist*, 1959, *14*, 376. (c)

Barrett-Lennard, G. T. *Dimensions of a therapeutic relationship*. Paper presented to the annual conference of the British Psychological Society, Australian Branch, held in Sydney (Mimeo.; circulated by author), 1961.

Barrett-Lennard, G. T. Dimensions of therapist response as causal factors in therapeutic personality change. *Psychological Monographs*, 1962, *76* (43, Whole No. 562).

Barrett-Lennard, G. T. Significant aspects of a helping relationship. *Mental Hygiene*, 1963, *47*, 223–227. (Republished in *Canada's Mental Health*, 1965, *13* (July/Aug.). Supplement No. 47.)

Barrett-Lennard, G. T. *The Relationship Inventory. Form OS-M-64 and OS-F-64 Form MO-M-64 and MO-F-64*. University of New England, Australia (First printing), 1964.

Barrett-Lennard, G. T. Experiential learning in small groups: The basic encounter process. *Proceedings of the Canadian Association of University Student Personnel Services*: The Ottawa Conference, 1967, pp. 2–12.

Barrett-Lennard, G. T. Technical note on the 64-item revision of the Relationship Inventory. University of Waterloo, 1969. (Paper in circulation, 1966–present. Amended and retyped 1982.)

Barrett-Lennard, G. T. *Relational variables in psychotherapy: Needed theoretical clarification and implications for measurement*. Presented at the annual meeting of the Society for Psychotherapy Research, Nashville, Kentucky; and arranged as two short working papers: "Notes on empathy" and "Notes on congruence" (Mimeo.), 1972.

Barrett-Lennard, G. T. Empathy in human relationships: Significance, nature and measurement. *Australian Psychologist*, 1976, *11*, 173–184.

Barrett-Lennard, G. T. The Relationship Inventory: Later development and applications. JSAS: *Catalog of Selected Documents in Psychology*, 1978, *8*, 68 (Ms. No. 1732. Pp. 55). (a)

Barrett-Lennard, G. T. *Methodology in process: New therapy-relevant adaptations of the Relationship Inventory*. Paper given at the annual conference of the American Psychological Association, Toronto, 1978. (b)

Barrett-Lennard, G. T. A new model of communicational-relational systems in intensive groups. *Human Relations*, 1979, *32*, 841–849.

Barrett-Lennard, G. T. The empathy cycle: Refinement of a nuclear concept. *Journal of Counseling Psychology*, 1981, *28*, 91–100. (a)

Barrett-Lennard, G. T. *The semi-autonomous phases of empathy*. Paper presented at the annual conference of the American Psychological Association, Los Angeles. Waterloo/Perth: The Centre for Studies in Human Relations (Mimeo.), 1981. (b)

Barrett-Lennard, G. T. *The Relationship Inventory: Observer forms 0-64F and 0-64M*. (Mimeo.) 1981.(c)

Barrett-Lennard, G. T. *Studies using the Relationship Inventory, 1970–79: A selective resource bibliography*. Waterloo/Perth: The Centre for Studies in Human Relations. (Mimeo.; 40 Kings Park Road, West Perth, W.A. Australia 6005), 1982. (a)

Barrett-Lennard, G. T. The topography of family relationships: A person-centered systems view. In A. S. Segrera (Ed.), *Proceedings of the First International Forum on the Person-Centered Approach*, held in Oaxtepec, Mexico, 1982. *Mexico D. F.: Universidad Iberoamericana (Centro di Difusion Y Extention)*. 1982–84.

Barrett-Lennard, G. T. The world of family relationships: A person-centered systems view. In R. F. Levant & J. M. Shlien (Eds.) *Client-Centered Therapy and the Person-Centered Approach: New Directions in Theory, Research and Practice*. New York: Praeger, 1984.(a)

Barrett-Lennard, G. T. *The Person-Centered Helping System: Birth, Journey and Substance*. Perth: The Centre for Studies in Human Relations, 1984. (b)

Barrett-Lennard, G. T. *Studies drawing on the B-L Relationship Inventory. A supplementary bibliography: Research in the 1980s*. Perth: The Centre for Studies in Human Relations, 1985.(a)

Barrett-Lennard, G. T. Directions—a first issue editorial [and other items. The *Ceshur Connection* (International newsletter of the The Centre for Studies in Human Relations), 1985, *1* (1).(b)

Barrett-Lennard, G. T., Bond, J. A., & Taylor, D. D. *Resource bibliography of reported studies using the Relationship Inventory. Part A* (List of Studies) and *Part B* (Abstracts). University of Waterloo (Mimeo), 1972.

Barrington, B. L. Prediction from counselor behavior of client perception and of case outcome. *Journal of Counseling Psychology*, 1961, *8*, 37–42.

Bebout, J. (1971/72). Personal communications, including detailed results from factor analyses of the RI. Berkeley, Talent in Interpersonal Exploration Project. (Related publication: Bebout, J., & Gordon, B. The value of encounter. In L. N. Solomon & B. Berzon (Eds.), *New Perspectives on Encounter Groups*. San Francisco: Jossey-Bass, 1972).

Belpaire, F., & Archambault, Y. Tentative de spécifier les éléments thérapeutics d'un milieu de rééducation pour jeunes délinquants. Centre D'Orientation, Section Recherches: Montreal (39 ouest, boulevard Gouin), 1969.

Bergin, A. E., & Garfield, S. L. (Eds.). *Handbook of psychotherapy and behaviour change*. New York: Wiley, 1971.

Berlin, J. I. Some autonomic correlates of therapeutic conditions in interpersonal relationships. Unpublished Doctoral Dissertation, University of Chicago, 1960.

Bown, O. H. An investigation of therapeutic relationship in client-centered therapy. Unpublished Doctoral Dissertation, University of Chicago, 1954.

Brauer, B. A. The dimensions of perceived interview relationship as influenced by deaf persons' self-concepts and interviewer attributes as deaf or non-deaf. *Dissertation Abstracts International*, 1979/80, *40*, 1352-B. University Microfilms No. 7918835.

Brown, J. T. S. Communication of empathy in individual psychotherapy: An analogue study of client perceived empathy. (Doctoral dissertation, University of Texas at Austin, 1980). *Dissertation Abstracts International*, 1981, *41*, 2748-B.

Brown, O. B., & Calia, V. F. Two methods of initiating student interviews: Self-initiated versus required. *Journal of Counseling Psychology*, 1968, *15*, 402–406.

Burgess, E. W., & Cottrell, L. S. *Predicting success or failure in marriage*. New York: Prentice-Hall, 1939.

Butler, J. M., & Haigh, G. V. Changes in the relation between self-concepts and ideal concepts consequent upon client-centered counseling. In C. R. Rogers & R. F. Dymond (Eds.), *Psychotherapy and personality change*. Chicago: University of Chicago Press, 1954.

Cahoon, R. A. *Some counselor attitudes and characteristics related to the counseling relationship*. Doctoral Dissertation, Ohio State University, 1962. University Microfilms No. 63-2480.

Carkhuff, R. R., & Berenson, B. G. *Beyond counseling and therapy*. New York: Holt, Rinehart & Winston, 1967.

Carter, J. A. Couple's perceptions of relationship variables, marital adjustment and change before and after treatment. *Dissertation Abstracts International*, 1981/82, *41*, 3172-B.

Churukian, G. A. An investigation of relationships between the compatibility of supervisor-supervisee interpersonal needs and the quality of their interpersonal relations and productivity of supervision. *Dissertation Abstracts International*, 1970/71, *31*-A, 5656–5657. University Microfilms No. 71-2045.

Cramer, D. An item factor analysis of the original Relationship Inventory. *British Journal of Medical Psychology*, 1986, *59* (in press).

De Mers, N. A. Predicting parental and marital empathic development. Master of Applied Science Thesis (psychology/human relations), University of Waterloo, 1971.

Emmerling, F. C. A study of the relationship between personality characteristics of classroom teachers and pupil perceptions of these teachers (Doctoral Dissertation, Auburn University, 1961). *Dissertation Abstracts*, 1961/1962, *22*, 1054–1055. University Microfilms No. 61-3002.

Epstein, N., & Jackson, E. An outcome study of short term communication training with married couples. *Journal of Consulting and Clinical Psychology*, 1978, *46*, 207–212.

Feldstein, J. C. Counselor and client sex pairing: The effects of counseling problem and counselor sex role orientation. *Journal of Counseling Psychology*, 1982, *29*, 418–420.

Finnernan, M. R. The relationship between therapists' and clients' assessments of therapists' level of empathy and views of women. *Dissertation Abstracts International*, 1980/81, *41*, 519-B.

Fretz, B. R., Corn, R., Tuemmler, J. M., & Bellet, W. Counselor nonverbal behaviors and client evaluation. *Journal of Counseling Psychology*, 1979, *26*, 304–311.

Goldfarb, N. Effectiveness of supervisory style on counselor effectiveness and facilitative responding. *Journal of Counseling Psychology*, 1978, *25*, 454–460.

Gomes, W. B. The communicational-relational system in two forms of family group composition. Unpublished Master's Thesis, Southern Illinois University, 1981.

Griffin, E. J. A study of effects of a curriculum-centered college reading course and an affectively oriented curriculum focused course on reading achievement and attitude toward reading. *Dissertation Abstracts International*, 1977/78, *38-A*, 6496. University Microfilms No. 71-24372.

Griffin, R. W. Change in perception of marital relationship as related to marital counseling. *Dissertation Abstracts International*, 1967/68, *27-A*, 3956. University Microfilms No. 67-6466.

Gurman, A. S. The patient's perception of the therapeutic relationship. In A. S. Gurman & A. M. Razin (Eds.), *Effective psychotherapy: A handbook of research*. New York: Pergamon, 1977.

Hall, K. E. The effects of a teacher-led guidance program on selected personal and inter-personal variables among fourth grade pupils. *Dissertation Abstracts International*, 1972/73, *33-A*, 1436. University Microfilms No. 72-27,194.

Hart, J. T. & Tomlinson, T. M. (Eds.), *New Directions in Client-Centered Therapy*. Boston: Houghton Mifflin, 1970.

Holland, D. A. The Relationship Inventory: Experimental Form OS-S-42. A validity study. Honours Bachelor Thesis, Psychology Department, University of Waterloo, 1976. (Summary available from present author.)

Hollenbeck, G. P. Conditions and outcomes in the student-parent relationship. *Journal of Consulting Psychology*, 1965, *29*, 237–241. (Based on the author's doctoral dissertation, University of Wisconsin, 1961.)

Junek, W., Burra, P., & Leichner, P. Teaching interviewing skills by encountering patients. *Journal of Medical Education*, (1979), *54*, 402–407.

Kagan, M., Hungate, J. I., Hau, C., & Lewis, B. An exploratory study of selected dimensions of the field instructor-student relationship during second year social field work practice. Part 2 of *The Field Instructor-Student Relationship in Social Work*. The Graduate School of Social Work, University of Texas, Austin, 1964.

Kirk, W. G., & Thomas, A. H. A brief in-service training strategy to increase levels of empathy of psychiatric nursing personnel. *Journal of Psychiatric Treatment and Evaluation*, 1982, *4*, 177–179.

Kurtz, R. R., & Grummon, D. L. Different approaches to the measurement of therapist empathy and their relationship to therapy outcomes. *Journal of Consulting and Clinical Psychology*, 1972, *37*, 106–115.

La Crosse, M. B. Comparative perceptions of counselor behaviour: A replication and extension. *Journal of Counseling Psychology*, 1977, *24*, 464–471.

Libby, G. W. Source of referral, type of program, and the initial teacher–pupil relationship in selected resource programs for the child with emotional difficulties. *Dissertation Abstracts International*, 1974/75, *35-A*, 5172.

Lietaer, G. Nederlandstalige revisie van Barrett-Lennard's Relationship Inventory: Een faktoranalytische benadeving, van de student-ouderrelatie. *Nederlands Tijdschrift voor de Psychologie*, 1974, *29*, 191–212.

Lietaer, G. Nederlandstalige revisie van Barrett-Lennard's Relationship Inventory voor individueelterapeutische relaties. *Psychologica Belgica*, 1976, *16*, 73–94.

Lietaer, G. Unconditional positive regard: A controversial basic attitude in client-centered therapy. In Levant, R. F. & Shlien, J. M. (Eds), *Client-Centered Therapy and the Person-Centered Approach: New Directions in Theory, Research and Practice*. New York: Praeger, 1984.

Luber, R. F., & Wells, R. A. Structured short-term multiple family therapy: An educational approach. *International Journal of Group Psychotherapy*, 1977, *27*, 43–58.

Mann, B., & Murphy, R. C. Timing of self-disclosure, reciprocity of self-disclosure, and reactions to an initial interview. *Journal of Counseling Psychology*, 1975, *22*, 304–308.

Mason, J., & Blumberg, A. Perceived educational value of the classroom and teacher-pupil interpersonal relationships. *Journal of Secondary Education*, 1969, *44*, 135–139.

McKitrick, D. S., & Gelso, C. J. Initial client expectancies in time-limited counseling. *Journal of Counseling Psychology*, 1978, *25*, 246–249.

Melchior, W. C. The effects of counselor and observer gender, empathy level and voice inflection upon observers' perceptions and evaluations of counselors' communication. *Dissertation Abstracts International*, 1981/82, *41*, 3013-A.

Quick, E., & Jacob, T. Marital disturbance in relation to role theory and relationship theory. *Journal of Abnormal Psychology*, 1973, *82*, 309–316.

Rogers, C. R. *Client-centered therapy*. Boston: Houghton Mifflin, 1951.

Rogers, C. R. The necessary and sufficient conditions of therapeutic personality change. *Journal of Consulting Psychology*, 1957, *21*, 95–103.

Rogers, C. R. A theory of therapy, personality and interpersonal relationships, as developed in the client-centered framework. In Koch, S. (Ed.), *Psychology: A study of a science* (Vol. 3). New York: McGraw-Hill, 1959.

Rogers, C. R. (Ed.) *The therapeutic relationship and its impact: A study of psychotherapy with schizophrenics*. Madison: University of Wisconsin Press, 1967.

Rosen, H. H. Dimensions of the perceived parent relationship as related to juvenile delinquency. Unpublished Master's Thesis, Auburn University, 1961.

Ryan, J. F. The association of teacher–student interpersonal relationships and classroom verbal interaction. *Dissertation Abstracts International*, 1973/74, *31*-A, 4089. University Microfilms No. 73-21, 820.

Scheuer, A. L. The relationship between personal attributes and effectiveness in teachers of the emotionally disturbed. *Exceptional Children*, 1971, *38*, 723–731.

Schumm, W. R., Bollman, S. R., & Jurich, A. P. Dimensionality of an abbreviated version of the Relationship Inventory. *Psychological Reports*, 1981, *48*, 51–56.

Seay, T. A., & Altekruse, M. K. Verbal and nonverbal behavior in judgments of facilitative conditions. *Journal of Counseling Psychology*, 1979, *26*, 108–119.

Smetko, J. A. Student perceived facilitation as a correlate of academic achievement, academic self-concept and self-concept among inner city seventh and eighth graders. *Dissertation Abstracts International*, 1982/83, *43*, 1902-A. University Microfilms No. DA8226021.

Snelbecker, G. E. Influence of therapeutic techniques on college students' perceptions of therapists. *Journal of Consulting Psychology*, 1967, *31*, 614–618. (Based on the author's doctoral dissertation, Cornell University, 1961.)

Thornton, B. M. Dimensions of perceived relationship as related to marital adjustment. Unpublished Master's Thesis, Auburn University, 1960. (On Microfilm, Auburn U. Library.)

Thornton, F. C. S. Mother perception and peer perception. Unpublished Master's Thesis, Auburn University, 1960.

Tosi, D. J. Dogmatism within the client–counselor dyad. *Journal of Counseling Psychology*, 1970, *17*, 284–288.

Truax, C. B., & Carkhuff, R. R. *Toward effective counseling and psychotherapy*. Chicago: Adline Press, 1967.

Van der Veen, F. The perception by clients and by judges of the conditions offered by the therapist in the therapy relationship (Psychiatric Institute Bulletin No. 10e). Madison: Wisconsin Psychiatric Institute, 1961.

Van der Veen, F., & Novak, A. L. Perceived parental attitudes and family concepts of disturbed adolescents, normal siblings and normal controls. *Family Process*, 1971, *10*, 327–343.

VanSteenwegan, A. Residentiele partnerrelatietherapie: Een evaluatieonderzoek. *Tijdschrift voor Psychiatrie*, 1979, *21*, 426–440.

VanSteenwegan, A. Intensive psycho-educational couple therapy: Therapeutic program and outcome research results. *Cahiers des Sciences Familiales et Sexologiques*, No. 5. De L'Universite Catholique de Louvain, 1982.

Walker, B. S., & Little, D. F. Factor analysis of the Barrett-Lennard Relationship Inventory. *Journal of Counseling Psychology*, 1969, *16*, 516–521.

Wampler, K. S., & Powell, G. S. The Barrett-Lennard Relationship Inventory as a measure of marital satisfaction. *Family Relations*, 1982, *31*, 139–145.

Wampler, K. S., & Sprenkle, D. H. The Minnesota Couple Communication Program: A follow-up study. *Journal of Marriage and the Family*, 1980, *42*, 577–584.

Wells, R. A., Figurel, J. A., & McNamee, P. Group facilitative training with married couples. In A. S. Gurman and D. G. Rice, *Couples in conflict: New directions in marital therapy*. New York: Jason Aronson, 1975.

13

The Psychological Interior of Psychotherapy: Explorations with the Therapy Session Reports

David E. Orlinsky
Department of
Behavioral Sciences
University of Chicago
Chicago, Illinois

Kenneth I. Howard
Department of Psychology
Northwestern University
Evanston, Illinois

Some good things start over soup, as the Campbell Company might want you to think. But it is hard to say how many bowls of soup it took, and how many conversations flowing intermittently across them, for the idea of the *Therapy Session Report* to take shape.

The Idea of the Therapy Session Report and How It Developed

In the dining room of an old hotel on South Michigan Avenue in Chicago (typically rather deserted at 5:30 in the afternoon), the two of us met each Tuesday and Thursday for a light supper before our evening's work as staff psychotherapists at the nearby Katharine Wright Mental Health Clinic. It was late 1963. John F. Kennedy was still alive. We were a few short years out of the 1950s and the doctoral program in clinical psychology where we had met and become friends. Since graduation we had each been engaged in teaching and research, and a bit of clinical practice, on the "Boulder model" of clinical psychology. The teaching and research activities separated us, but our common positions at the Katharine Wright Clinic—and especially the bowls of soup that we shared beforehand—gave us a chance to keep a good friendship growing.

For the historical record, let it be said that the soup was good, and that it came with a nice assortment of rolls. Sometimes the conversation that accompanied this fare was merely sociable. At other times we just sat in silent communion and stared into our bowls, contemplating life's way with us. But there were occasions when the talk became personal and we shared the concerns and feelings that were with us, whether these were about the patients we were about to see that evening or about happenings in other corners of our lives.

Gradually we began to notice and remark to one another that when we did talk in this personal way, beforehand, the therapy sessions of the evening went extremely well. We seemed better able to "tune in" (such were the expressions of the mid-60s), hearing what our patients said to us as persons with a minimum of the interference usually caused by the rattling and rumbling of background thoughts. We each felt that we did our best therapeutic work on these occasions.

Was it this two-man over-the-counter "encounter group" (another mid-60s excitement) that brought out the best in us as therapists? Could participation in a relatively brief personal encounter before seeing their patients produce the same results for other therapists? As we discussed the matter, it began to sound more and more like a researchable question. The experimental manipulation could be the assignment of therapists at the clinic to a "warm-up" encounter session on random evenings before seeing patients. The dependent variable would be the quality of therapeutic experience, comparing sessions that had been preceded by a therapist "warm-up" with sessions approached in the usual manner. We became excited about the idea. This was the "Boulder model" at work, combining scientific research and clinical practice in a fruitful way.

But what are the significant aspects of therapeutic experience? And how might they best be measured? We needed to delineate the specific dimensions on which our therapeutic experiences had been influenced. We needed to see if these dimensions were meaningful to other therapists. We also began to wonder whether the differences that we had noticed in our experiences as therapists made any difference at all to our patients. Who is therapy for, anyway?

The very business of studying experience in an acceptably scientific way posed no small problem. Research on psychotherapeutic process had been established, largely by Carl Rogers and his associates at the University of Chicago, through the audio recording of therapy sessions. Systematic ratings of these recordings, or of transcriptions made from them, by independent judges was the accepted *modus operandi* in process research (ironically so, since Rogers' theory stressed phenomenological rather than behavioral constructs). The main alternative, at the time, to this "objective" procedure was the subjective and largely impressionistic case history written by the therapist. Neither option offered a satisfactory approach to our principal interest, which in the first instance was the patient's experience of the therapy session.

Back in graduate school, one of our professors recalled to us that during World War II an elaborate study had been undertaken by Army psychologists to select troops who would be effective soldiers in the Arctic. After reviewing a variety of predictive tests and measures, the research team found that the single best predictor of Arctic effectiveness was asking the soldier, himself, how well he liked cold weather. We cannot vouch for the literal truth of the story, but the moral seemed worth remembering.

We had been educated in a properly but not narrowly positivistic spirit in the graduate psychology program at the University of Chicago. We learned our Hull, Tolman, Guthrie, and Skinner; but we were also exposed to Freud, Allport, Murray, and Lewin, and the phenomenological, client-centered concerns of Carl Rogers and his colleagues at the University's Counseling Center. The Rogerians provided the strong assumption that experience could and should be made the subject of psychological science, even if they did not furnish a fully appropriate research methodology. Our approach to the latter was undoubtedly influenced by the work of another eminent Chicago psychologist, L. L. Thurstone, whose pioneering accomplishments in the psychometric scaling of subjective qualities and attitudes provided the basis for attempting the same sort of thing with participants' experiences in psychotherapeutic sessions.

Although we were not directly students or disciples of either Rogers or Thurstone, the combination and cross-fertilization of their teachings in the psychology department at Chicago made it somehow natural for us to think of conducting a systematic, objectively scaled study of patients' and therapists' experiences of psychotherapy. Moreover, the best way to do this seemed to be that of the legendary Army psychologists: ask the subjects, themselves, to tell us what they experienced.

Content of the Therapy Session Reports

Starting out close to home, we began by reflecting on our own experiences in psychotherapy, as therapists and as patients. We drew, of course, on our theoretical understanding of psychotherapy as a special kind of relationship, and more generally on our broader understanding of personality and social relationships. However, what we wanted were questions that were as purely descriptive and noninferential—as close to the experienced "surface" of events—as possible. We wanted questions about the most obvious features of the experience of psychotherapy, questions that could be answered "None," "Some," or "A Lot" without lengthy reflection or calculation. Drawing inferences about the meaning of the experiences that were reported to us would be our responsibility as researchers, using the techniques of multivariate statistical analysis (e.g., factor-analysis, which was another Thurstone legacy).

In discussing our own experiences of psychotherapy, we found ourselves agreeing that psychotherapy could be conceptualized as a *dialogue* between patient and therapist; that this dialogue is in part pursuant to, and in part the medium for a certain kind of *exchange* of values; that given the particular nature of the service involved, the process of exchange will significantly tend to focus upon and to evoke *feelings* within the participants; and that the characteristics of dialogue, exchange, and feeling between patient and therapist determine, and are also qualified by, the overall pattern or manner of their interpersonal *relationship*. Finally, we thought that these four interrelated aspects of therapeutic experience—dialogue, exchange, feeling, and relationship—unfold in a *sequential development* through time in each therapy session, moving more or less effectively toward the realization of the participants' goals.

We thought that since the therapy session is (from one point of view) a dialogue or conversation between people, we should ask specific questions about the *topics* or subjects they discuss, and about the *concerns* they express in relation to those topics. Eventually, we arrived at a list of 19 topics, referring to diverse aspects of self (e.g., "bodily functions, symptoms, or appearance"), of interpersonal relations (e.g., "my mother"), and of institutional involvement (e.g., "religious feelings, activities or experiences"). Similarly, we defined a variety of problems or issues reflecting the sort of concerns that patients might express (e.g., "being assertive or competitive," or "who I am and what I want"), and developed a list of 12 concerns that reflected common areas of psychosocial and developmental conflict.

Turning to view the therapy session as a process of exchange in which certain outcomes are sought or avoided, offered or withheld, welcomed or suffered, we thought that we should ask specific questions about (1) what the patient wanted from the therapy session, (2) what the therapist sought to provide, and (3) what the patient got. This led to our formulating three more or less parallel lists: 14 things that patients might want, 14 goals that therapists might pursue, and 13 outcomes that patients might receive (actually, 12 plus "nothing"). Patients and therapists were both asked for their perceptions of the patient's wants or motives. However, to contract a rapidly expanding questionnaire, only therapists were asked about the therapist's specific intentions, and only patients were asked about the patient's specific satisfactions.

A third aspect of therapy that seemed to us to be very salient for most people is its affective quality. Patients come to therapy because of emotional disturbances, because they are upset or upsetting to others. In most forms of psychotherapy considerable attention is focused on the patient's feelings and emotions. Also, as therapy deals with sensitive and highly personal issues, feelings are apt to be evoked by it. Therefore, we prepared two parallel checklists describing feelings that the patient might experience in therapy sessions, one for patients and one for therapists, and a second set of parallel checklists describing feelings that the therapist might experience in psychotherapy. The former contained approximately 30 items and the latter about 25.

A fourth aspect of psychotherapy that has received much attention is the quality of relatedness between patient and therapist. By this we mean the formal aspect of the relationship, in contrast to the communicative, utilitarian, affective, or other contents of the relationship. Relatedness, in this sense, refers not so much to *what* people do when together but rather to *how* they act toward each other as they do it. This interpersonal facet of interaction process has been described in many studies of social behavior in terms of the two dimensions of reciprocal influence (e.g., dominance vs. submission) and mutual attraction (e.g., love vs. hate). Our belief that these complex behavioral dimensions could be conceptually simplified led us to make the following distinctions. We divided reciprocal influence into ratings of each participant's behavior with respect to *initiative* (being assertive and/or receptive) and with respect to *control* (being controlling and/or accommodating). Similarly, we divided mutual attraction into ratings of each participant's behavior with respect to *interpersonal attitude* (being accepting and/or rejecting) and with respect to overt *responsiveness* (motor activity and/or affective expressiveness). Scales for each of these eight conceptual dimensions were developed for the rating of patient behavior and of therapist behavior by both patients and therapists.

We reasoned that the same dimensions should apply as well in rating a person's relatedness to self. Many authors, such as the philosopher and social psychologist George Herbert Mead (1956), have recognized this dual or reflexive nature of self-experience as a compound structure consisting of self-as-subject ("I") and self-as-object ("Me"). Varying modes of relatedness between the "I" and the "Me," depicting different types and degrees of "centeredness" or self-estrangement, can be defined concisely in terms of the dimensions of *activation* (ideational activity and/or emotional arousal), *self-evaluation* (self-approval and/or self-criticism), *self-awareness* (self-definition and/or self-receptiveness), and *self-control* (self-discipline and/or self-indulgence). Since these dimensions of self-relatedness are significant concerns in most psychotherapies, they seemed worth including in our questionnaire.

Finally, we recognized that the four "systemic" aspects of therapy mentioned above —dialogue, exchange, feelings, and relatedness—occur together, interlaced in an unfolding complex of events that have a beginning, middle, and end in each therapy session.

From this last point of view, the experience of the therapy session is one of sequential development. Session development, however, is more than the mere passage of time; it is the realization of a more or less complete "social act" in that unit of time. For a general analysis of the social act, we drew again on the work of George Herbert Mead. Mead (1956) provided a conceptual framework of "stages in the act," which we interpreted with respect to the psychotherapeutic session to entail (1) the participants' respective *motivation* (eagerness or reluctance) in approaching the session, (2) their respective *understanding* of and (3) their instrumental *responses* to one another in the session, and (4) their sense of *goal attainment*. Thus we asked patients and therapists: how much they were looking forward to their sessions; how well the patient was able to focus on and express his or her real concerns; how well the therapist was able to understand and respond helpfully to the patient; and, how much progress the patient seemed to make in the session.

To all these specific questions we added two more because of their general relevance. We asked both participants to give us their evaluation of the quality of the session, and their sense of how well each thought the patient was currently "getting along, emotionally and psychologically."

Structure and Administration of the
Therapy Session Reports

The order of questions to be presented in the *Therapy Session Report* questionnaires was another matter for thought. We wanted the overall form to follow the model of a debriefing interview, and sought for a psychologically natural progression of items.

The first question posed concerned the participant's qualitative evaluation of the session: "How do you feel about the session which you have just completed?" After this, the questions for both the patients and the therapists focused first on the patient's involvement, and then on the therapist's participation.

Questions focusing on the patient were, in sequence: "What subjects did [the patient] talk about during this session?" "What did [the patient] want or hope to get out of this session?" "What problems or feelings [was the patient] concerned about this session?" "What were [the patient's] feelings during this session?" Following each of the foregoing was a checklist of items to be rated "No," "Some," or "A Lot." Then a set of 16 4-point scales was presented focused on the eight conceptual dimensions of the patient's self-relatedness and interpersonal relatedness *vis-à-vis* the therapist. This, in turn, was followed by a set of four questions on the patient's: motivation for coming to the session; sense of progress; emotional and psychological functioning; and, motivation for the next session (this question on the patient's form only). The last items concerning the patient consisted of a checklist responsive to the question (also on the patient's form only): "What do you feel that you got out of this session?"

Questions focusing on the therapist began (for therapists only, in place of the patients' list of possible satisfactions) with a checklist responding to the query, "What aims or goals were you working toward with your patient during this session?" After that came two questions for both patients and therapists focusing on how well the therapist understood the patient, and on how helpfully the therapist reacted toward the patient during the session. Following these were three questions (for therapists only) on motivation for the session, self-disclosure, and possible countertherapeutic personal reactions. Both the patients' and the therapists' questionnaires concluded with a set of eight scales focusing on the therapist's relatedness or interpersonal behavior toward the patient (based on the same conceptual dimensions discussed for the patient's interpersonal relatedness and self-relatedness), and then with a checklist responding to the question: "How did [the therapist] seem to feel during this session?"

The whole process of writing, pretesting, and revising the *Therapy Session Report* questionnaires (Orlinsky & Howard, 1966) for individual (i.e., dyadic) psychotherapy took about 1 year. (After another 6 months of formal data collection and analyses, reported at length in our book *Varieties of Psychotherapeutic Experience* (Orlinsky & Howard, 1975), a few minor modifications of the questionnaires were made. The description of the research instrument given above includes these further changes.)

The next step before attempting any experimental manipulations, such as we had first imagined, was to establish reliable baseline data on patients' and therapists' experiences in therapy as it occurred under normal clinical conditions. Our colleagues at the Katharine Wright Clinic made this possible by agreeing that we could solicit the cooperation of their patients in filling out the *Therapy Session Report* forms, and by participating themselves in this project.

We established a procedure by which patients routinely went to a specially designated "research room" after finishing each of their therapy sessions, where they were given the questionnaire booklet by our associate, James A. Hill. Patients were assured directly, as well as by this practical arrangement, that their individual answers to the questionnaire would not be known to their therapists or to other clinic staff, but would be used confidentially for research purposes only. Patients generally were quite faithful in this task, and would comment that they found it a meaningful adjunct to their therapy sessions. Therapists at the clinic were kept supplied with the therapists' version of the *Therapy Session Report*, and were asked to complete questionnaires on their sessions with patients as soon as possible after each session.

Data collection continued in this fashion for about 2 years, from 1965 to 1967, until approximately 2500 patient forms and 1500 therapist forms had been completed, many by patients and their therapists for the same sessions. Since data collection was begun and ended on certain dates, some of the participants started using the forms while therapy was already in progress, and others stopped using the forms before therapy was terminated. However, for many patients data collection encompassed the entire course of treatment.

Life's ways with a person are sometimes quite strange, as we reflected on some of those long-past evenings, staring into our bowls of soup in that old hotel dining room on South Michigan Avenue. One of the passing strange ways that life has taken with us is that we have never gotten around to doing the experiment that we first conceived. Nevertheless, the years that followed our design of the *Therapy Session Report* questionnaires have shown these instruments to be a rich source of information about the psychotherapeutic experiences of patients and therapists. Most of our work thus far has focused on individual psychotherapy, but we have also designed a parallel form for use with couples in marital therapy (developed with Michael O'Mahoney), as well as a form for use with patients in group psychotherapy (developed with the collaboration of Gary Bond, Jack Martin, and David Liebenthal and presented in Liebenthal, 1980). The empirical material that we shall discuss in the following sections draws upon this range of therapeutic modalities.

Some Questions About the Study of Experience

First, however, we would like to give some attention to questions concerning the assumptions on which our approach is founded. "How can experience be studied by means of a questionnaire?" Possibly, one who would ask this might be thinking that questionnaires are limited to verbal responses, while the full range of experience includes more than is verbal; or that questionnaires are limited to conscious responses, while the full range of experience includes what is nonconscious. Many therapists, for example, might feel that what is most important in a person's experience is characteristically nonverbal, characteristically nonconscious, or both; hence, a questionnaire would inevitably be too superficial to validly reflect anything of deeper significance about the experiences of patients and therapists in psychotherapy. Many researchers, on the other hand, might think that questionnaires are too superficial because they show only what the participants in therapy choose to report about the process rather than the process itself; hence, responses will be too subjective a basis from which to draw scientifically sound conclusions about the psychotherapeutic process.

What is basically at issue is our concept of experience, and the relationship of language to experience. In brief, our approach to the matter derives from cognitive psychology. We use the general term "experience" to refer inclusively to all contents of cognition, that is, to all information which individuals encode concerning their external and internal (somatic) environments. Language is not the only medium for encoding information that persons rely on, but it is the most powerful and distinctively human. Language may thus be viewed as integral to, and as very broadly constitutive of, a person's experience. Experiments guided by labeling theory have shown that even such apparently nonverbal experiences as emotions may be partially dependent on verbal categories for their formation (e.g., Schachter & Singer, 1962).

From this point of view, a questionnaire is not in principle an inappropriate means for studying people's experiences. Not all experiences take form in words, and individuals do differ in their ability to put their nonverbal experiences into words. But a well-designed questionnaire can provide most literate individuals with a suitable set of words and statements for reporting at least the most salient features of their experience in a predefined situation (such as the psychotherapy session), and a well-designed questionnaire provides a standardized set of descriptions that makes possible the comparison of reports from different individuals, or from the same individual on different occasions.

On these grounds, we hold that the verbal reports of persons' perceptions are neither too superficial nor too subjective to be made the basis for valid research on experience. We grant that there are often meaningful *patterns* in a person's experience of which he or she is not directly aware, and thus cannot directly report. But if the salient *elements* of the person's experience are reported in a form that can be quantified, statistical analyses may reveal those patterns that even the persons reporting, themselves, could not directly formulate. For example, a correlational analysis might show that a patient tends to report feeling sad in the same therapy sessions in which he or she also reports talking about mother, and in which the therapist is perceived as feeling withdrawn. The researcher (like the therapist) might recognize this as a psychodynamically meaningful finding, even if the patient were not able to make the connection.

There is a further question that affects the validity of our findings: "Will the participants report their perceptions of themselves, each other, and the events of therapy honestly?" We believe that people who participate in a study voluntarily will tend to be truthful in their statements unless they have some specific reason not to be. The reasons for dissimulation can be characterological or situational. If they are characterological—for example, if a person expects to be disadvantaged or harmed in almost all situations—then this dispositional trait should lend a rather distinctive and recognizable coloration to the individual's experience, and thus become a part of the data to be analyzed. As to the situational motives for dissimulation, we did all that we could to remove them: separation of the research procedures from contact with the therapeutic relationship; guarantee of confidentiality to the patients and the therapists; use of code numbers instead of names for identification; restriction of the time routinely needed to finish the questionnaire to not more than 10 or 15 minutes; administration of the research procedures by a likeable, clinically sensitive and tactful person. Under these circumstances, we think that most of the people who voluntarily seek outpatient psychotherapy would be inclined to respond honestly to the *Therapy Session Report*, and if not would probably choose not to participate in the study or to discontinue participation.

Another question that we have frequently heard is: "Doesn't the use of these questionnaires by patients and therapists alter the very phenomenon under study, that is, their experiences in psychotherapy?" The answer, of course, must be "Yes," but we believe that the real question in this connection should be whether the inevitable alterations that research procedures induce in the process of observing a phenomenon are compatible or incompatible, facilitative or disruptive, to the general form and tendency of the phenomenon. Psychotherapy clearly induces a self-reflective mode of experience in both the patient and the therapist. The *Therapy Session Report* draws on that same mode of experience, extending it for a brief time beyond the normal span of the therapy session. From the comments that they have sometimes made to us, personally or in the margins of the printed form, it appears that people who have used the questionnaires have generally found them to be a useful adjunct to the therapeutic experience. If the questionnaires change the participants' on-going experiences in therapy, it should be in the direction of clarifying and perhaps intensifying their recognition and awareness of their participation.

Dimensions of the Intersubjective Reality: What the Therapy Session Reports Have Shown About Relationships

We have come a long way since our first bowls of soup, and it is time to discuss some of the findings from research with the *Therapy Session Reports*. We shall focus on two levels of interpretation. In this section, we shall view therapy *generically* as a relationship between people, a relationship that is realized and sustained primarily through a series of direct face-to-face encounters. On this level of generality, the psychotherapeutic relationship shares much with other social relationships, especially those types of relationship in which "personal" conversation is a principal activity. For all the significant differences that one may expect to find among different types of social relationship, the study of any one type at an appropriate level should contribute something toward the understanding of their generic features.

Later, we shall view psychotherapy *specifically* as a solicited and intentional intervention by one type of person acting as a socially recognized "therapist," to help, repair, or otherwise beneficially influence the psychological affairs and well-being of another type of person who is identified as a "patient." The *Therapy Session Reports* were designed to reflect the specific features of psychotherapy sessions as these might be experienced by patients and therapists, without using technical terms or jargon derived from any one school or technique of therapeutic practice. After discussing psychotherapy as a relationship in general, we hope to show something of what our findings indicate about the specific nature and *modus operandi* of therapeutic treatment.

Psychotherapy as a Relationship in General

The unique contribution of the *Therapy Session Report* questionnaires to the study of social relationships in general is that the external or nonparticipant investigator is given a means for penetrating into the psychological "interior" of relationships. Through the usual nonparticipant methods of studying interaction process, the investigator observes only the overt actions and expressions of the participants—the frequencies of their speech, the content of their talk, their vocal tones and rhythms, their facial expressions, postural attitudes, and so on. Rich as such observations can be, they categorically fail to encompass the aspect of social relationships that is most distinctively human. We refer to the fact that persons consciously experience, react to, reflect upon, and seek to realize values in their relationships. There is a basic and inescapable aspect of subjectivity that makes every human social relationship an *intersubjective reality*—not in the sense of consensual observation, but in the broader sense of mutually conditioning and interpenetrating subjective perspectives (Berger & Luckmann, 1967).

Each participant in social contact constructs a subjective perspective on the relationship or the group in which he or she is involved—encompassing experiences of self and other(s), their shared situation, and their relations—simply by virtue of participation in it. The intersubjective reality of a dyadic relationship, for example, is determined by the two subjective perspectives of the participants taken together, that is, by the interrelations of their two perspectives. From this point of view, each person's subjective perspective is only one part of a larger structure, and is liable to misinterpretation if thought of as an isolated phenomenon.

As a general rule, there are as many subjective perspectives on a social relationship or group as there are persons who are party to it. To be more precise, one should say that there are at least as many perspectives as there are persons involved, to allow for the contingent presence of witnesses, uninvolved bystanders, or other nonparticipant observers. The intersubjective reality of the relationship or group is a multiplex structure of which the several subjective perspectives are the constituent parts.

Normally, of course, each participant–observer in a social situation is limited to the data apparent from his or her own perspective. Only one part of the individual's subjective perspective is comprised by a construal of the perspectives of others, and that is usually a sketchy and largely unverified interpretation, which need be only accurate enough to permit following some course of action *vis-à-vis* those others. In most relationships, the pragmatics of the individual's involvement tends to preclude extensive inquiry about the other person's experience. It also tends to preclude critical reflection on the other person's statements, actions, and expressions, which might be valid bases for inferences about the other's subjective perspective. (The professional negotiator, the diplomat, and the psychotherapist are probably among the exceptions in this regard, since the pragmatics of their respective involvements constrains them toward such an awareness.) However, even when the other person's subjective perspective is made the focus of conscious reflection, the participant–observer's interpretation of it is subject to distortion arising from his or her vested interests.

The methodology of the *Therapy Session Report* questionnaires permits the investigator to overcome some of the limitations that beset the individual participant–observer. This methodology draws on the personal observations of all participants, not just one or another, and it provides each with a means for reporting on the events of the relationship that have just been enacted. The questions are systematic in coverage, standardized in presentation, and quantified in response format. Because of this, the results can be treated objectively as research data, and can be subjected to statistical exploration. Most crucially in this immediate context, the subjective perspectives of the different participants in a relationship can be compared and analyzed systematically in relation to one another.

By using the *Therapy Session Reports* from participants in a relationship following a series of interactive encounters, the investigator is able to delineate the objective structure of its intersubjective reality. By accumulating such observations over a series of relationships of the same type, the investigator can explore the typical structure of intersubjective reality in a certain class of relationships. We have done something of the sort for relationships in individual psychotherapy to illustrate this research potential of the *Therapy Session Reports*.

In our book, *Varieties of Psychotherapeutic Experience* (Orlinsky & Howard, 1975), a series of statistical analyses was reported based on data collected on 890 therapy sessions from 60 patients, and on 470 sessions from 17 therapists. Each facet of experience (e.g., feelings) was factor analyzed separately for patients and therapists, and then the facet–factor scores were factor analyzed again to determine the overall dimensionality of psychotherapeutic experience for patients as a group and for therapists as a group.

Eleven dimensions of patient experience were found, and hence each session experienced by each patient could be characterized by a set of 11 factor scores. Similarly, as 11 dimensions of therapist experience were also found, each session experienced by each therapist could be described by another set of 11 factor scores. This enabled us to create and factor analyze a 22×22 matrix based on the patient–therapist pairs in our sample who had each completed *Therapy Session Reports* on a series of their common sessions. The results of this "conjoint" analysis were quite interesting, and merit retelling.

Seven dimensions were found in the patient–therapist matrix of conjoint experience, describing the structure of intersubjective reality in these relationships. One dimension was defined exclusively by therapist experiences and another dimension was defined exclusively by patient experiences. These each reflected alternative passive and active styles of approach to their respective roles in psychotherapy. The patients' experience of their help-taking role was called "Patient Agency Versus Patient Passivity." The therapists' experience of their help-giving role was called "Therapist Agency Versus Therapist Catalysis." Curiously, only the patients experienced their different styles of approach as a separately organized dimension, as did the therapists theirs. The fact that two of the seven dimensions in the conjoint experience matrix were defined exclusively by the experiences of only one set of participants is worth noting, since it was perfectly possible for scores from both sets of participants to define them. In the structure of intersubjective reality revealed here, these two dimensions were "outside" the bounds of an otherwise mutually determined experience.

The other five dimensions of conjoint experience were each defined by the experiences of both patients and therapists. These organized the shared realm of intersubjective reality in those particular relationships, and provide a unique stereoscopic glimpse into the psychological "interior" of the therapeutic process. There are various ways one might choose to characterize these dimensions. One that bears emphasis in the present context distinguishes the dimensions which demonstrate *convergence* between the two participants' perspectives from those in which the participants' subjective perspectives are *divergent*, or even contrary, but nonetheless meaningfully interrelated.

An example of the convergent patterning of conjoint experience is the recognizable structure of benign positive transference, which we called "*Healing Magic*." This dimension was defined, on the patients' side, by a factor that had been descriptively, if long-windedly, labeled "Therapeutic Satisfaction: Healing Progress and Good Relationship with a Therapist Seen as Pleased and Helpful." From the therapists' perspective, the dimension was defined by a factor called "Engagement with a Patient Perceived as Enthusiastically Accepting and Open." Clearly, both participants were experiencing their positive therapeutic involvement in congruent terms.

A less positive mode of involvement that was convergently experienced was the conjoint dimension titled "*Ambivalent Nurturance–Dependence.*" This was defined from the patients' viewpoint primarily by a factor named "Courting a Therapist Who is Seen as Rejecting," and secondarily by another patient factor named "Passive Dependence with a Therapist Seen as Directive." The same intersubjective dimension was experienced by therapists mainly in terms of two factors, "Unresponsive Activity with a Patient Seen as Passively Dependent" and "Felt Mutual Failure: Sense of Failure with a Patient Perceived as Feeling Inferior."

A third example of congruent patterning of intersubjectivity was a dimension of conjoint experience that we found it reasonable to label "*Therapeutic Alliance.*" This pattern was defined by three patient experience factors: "Therapist Perceived as Involved and Helpful," "Collaborative Exploration of Heterosexual Involvements," and "Painful Self-Exploration." From the therapists' viewpoint, this pattern was experienced in terms of a "Collaborative Relationship: Responsive Intervention with a Patient Perceived as Wanting Insight and Relating Collaboratively" and "Effective Movement: Sense of Progress with a Patient Seen as Responsive and Motivated."

However, the most surprising and informative patterns of conjoint experience were those in which the subjective perspectives of the two participants were divergent, or opposed as in a mirror image. Two examples nicely illustrate this intriguing and hard-to-recognize form of intersubjectivity, one showing the mutual projection of hostililty and another the mutual concealment of distressing sexual feelings.

"*Defensive Impasse*" was the opposite pole of the bipolar dimension containing "*Therapeutic Alliance.*" From the patients' side, "*Defensive Impasse*" was experienced mainly as "Therapist Perceived as Mean and Attacking," while from the therapists' viewpoint it was experienced as "Abiding a Patient Perceived as Assertively Narcissistic." The strange thing here is that each perceived the other as attacking, and the self as besieged. Although both participants perceived a state of hostility, each felt victimized by the other. Their subjective perspectives reversed the attribution of agency in a way that clinicians who do marital therapy will find familiar.

The second example of divergent intersubjectivity was a dimension of conjoint experience that we called "*Conflictual Erotization.*" What the patients in this pattern mainly experienced was "Erotic Transference Resistance: Blocking and Embarrassing Sexual Arousal with a Therapist Seen as Indulgent" and, as if to counter that, "Hostile Provocation Toward a Seemingly Noncommital Therapist." Secondary definitions of the patients' experience came from the factors "Painful Self-Exploration" and "Toying with the Therapist: Seductiveness with a Therapist Perceived as Feeling Ineffective and Withdrawn." The therapists' corner of this divergent pattern included the experience of "Uncaring Detachment: Passive–Aggressive Response to a Patient Felt to be Intellectualizing," and "Erotic Countertransference: Distressing Bodily Arousal with a Patient Perceived as Feeling Angry and Guilty." Also part of the therapists' experience was a marked *absence* of "Cheerful Warmth: Self-Confident Nurturant Warmth with a Patient Seen as Feeling Inferior." Neither person is aware of the other's plight. To dwell on this awkwardly human impasse seems almost indiscreet.

The Psychotherapist as Observer

A further indication of the oblique linkage of the participants' subjective perspectives in a relationship comes from a different line of inquiry that we pursued using the matched session data from patient–therapist dyads. The question that interested us was, "How good are therapists as observers of patients' experiences?"

As a preliminary, we distinguished conceptually between two modes of observation, "object perception" and "empathic induction." Object perception refers to the formation of a consciously articulated image of a specific "target" by focusing attention on the immediate sensory evidence about it, ratified more or less explicitly by an interpretive judgment on the evidence. (Example: "John is crying.") The criteria of good object perception are clarity and precision; the result is "objective" awareness. (Usually the "target" of object perception is external, such as another person or the things around one, but object perception can be directed reflexively upon self-experience, as in introspection.)

Empathic induction, on the other hand, involves the "feeling" that one gets in a situation—a feeling that may suggest itself in the form of a wish, a fantasy about the other person, a bodily sensation, or a mood free-floating in the social "atmosphere." (Example: "It feels gloomy in here.") Sometimes this mode of observation is called "intuitive" rather than "factual" because there is generally no direct sensory evidence that one can refer to—only one's "gut level" (i.e., sensorimotor) responsiveness to subtle cues that are given, and given off, in the situation. Reliable use of empathic induction as a source of information about others requires an awareness of one's idiosyncratic sensitivities and blind spots, and an understanding of one's own personal presence. This is one reason why therapists often need to undergo therapy themselves.

If therapists are good observers of their patients' experiences in the mode of object perception, their reports about their patients should match closely with what their patients report about themselves. If therapists are good observers in the mode of empathic induction, their reports about themselves and about the interactive ambiance of the therapy session should be correlated with significant aspects of their patients' experiences.

The data relevant to these propositions were subjected to detailed analysis in Chapter 13 of *Varieties of Psychotherapeutic Experience* (Orlinsky & Howard, 1975). From a naive viewpoint, the results were both disappointing and surprising. The main disappointment was that therapists' object perceptions of their patients' experiences, in general, were not very accurate, when judged in relation to what patients reported about themselves. Two aspects of patient participation that proved exceptions to this conclusion were *dialogue* and *session development*. Significant and substantial correlations between patients' and therapists' reports were found for 11 of the 18 topics of dialogue, and only 3 of the 18 showed negligible correlations. Similarly, four of the five questions pertaining to session development showed significant correlations between therapists and their patients. On the other hand, there were comparatively few significant correlations between patients' and therapists' reported perceptions of the patients' concerns, their aims in *exchange*, their behavior in terms of interpersonal *relatedness*, and their *feelings*. These findings leave us with the impression that object perception is relatively accurate for some of the external, but generally not for the internal facets of the *other's* involvement in a relationship.

By way of contrast, the main surprise in our findings was the degree of sensitivity shown by therapists in the mode of empathic induction. Not a few of the dimensions of therapist experience had numerous correlates among dimensions of patient experience. Among the most sensitive empathic indicators in the therapists' experience, judging by the number of significant correlates, were the therapists' view of their patients as "communicating effectively" and of themselves as "feeling good." Communicating effectively was a factor of the therapists' sense of session development that was defined by perceptions of the patients as able to focus well on the thoughts and feelings of real concern to them, as able to express themselves freely, and by the therapists' feeling of rapport or being in touch with what their patients were experiencing. The therapists' sense of communication rapport was especially valuable as an indicator of their patients' subjective sense of making progress in therapy (Orlinsky & Howard, 1968).

"Feeling good" was a dimension of therapists' affective experience defined by feeling cheerful, effective, optimistic, confident, pleased, and sympathetic. This dimension of therapist experience was significantly correlated with the patient's own experiences of wanting to win the therapist's respect, of relating collaboratively, of communicating effectively, and of not feeling bad. Similarly, another of the therapists' affective factors, "feeling resigned" (i.e., bored and discouraged), was significantly correlated with the patients' own experiences of not having a sense of doing well and making progress, of not getting insight and rapport, and of not looking forward to therapy sessions. These and other examples suggest that therapists can learn much of clinical value from their own feelings in therapy, if they can learn how their own feelings are empathically responsive to their patients' experiences.

These views into the psychological "interior" of the psychotherapeutic relationship are interesting in their own right, but they should also serve to suggest how much might be learned by adopting the methodology of the *Therapy Session Reports* more widely as an approach to research on the social psychology of relationships and groups. We can imagine parallel investigations, with relevant questionnaires, of recurrent encounters in marriages, friendships, work partnerships, tutorial relationships, and so on. We can also imagine investigations of group encounters such as school classes and social parties. Perhaps a few more bowls of soup will set us, or someone else for that matter, to exploring this new frontier. Thus far we have found collaborators willing to extend the *Therapy Session Reports* more modestly from individual psychotherapy to the related treatment modalities of marital therapy and group psychotherapy.

Feelings Resurrected in Tranquility: What the Therapy Session Reports Suggest About How Therapy Works

The reflections that follow have their point of origin in our uncontrollable desire to see results from our research project as quickly as possible. The very first thing that we did when we had data in hand was to calculate the frequencies of responses to the various items in the *Therapy Session Report* questionnaires. Using the questionnaire is something like taking a snapshot of therapeutic experience. By summing and averaging over a large number of session reports from patients, and from therapists, we developed a composite portrait of psychotherapy from the subjective perspectives of each group (see, for example, Chapter 5 in *Varieties of Psychotherapeutic Experience*, Orlinsky & Howard, 1975). Some items were endorsed in a surprisingly high percentage of sessions, others rather infrequently. Things that happen only rarely can, of course, be quite significant. But there is a fascination, too, in what is most common, and much to be learned from the obvious. What, then, is most obvious about psychotherapy?

When we had collected some data using the newly designed marital therapy and group psychotherapy versions of the *Therapy Session Report*, we were seized by the same old impulse to rush into the darkroom and develop the "negatives." That done, how could we keep ourselves from displaying the "rushes" side by side to get a comparative view of psychotherapeutic experience in different treatment modalities?

The results of this comparison hardly amount to a controlled study. The samples available to us were quite variable in size and heterogeneous in composition. The largest amount of data came from patients in individual psychotherapy: three sessions selected at random from 271 persons (813 reports) in outpatient treatment at the Katharine Wright Clinic, the Michael Reese Medical Center Clinic, and assorted clinics and private practitioners in the Chicago area, as well as the Lincoln Institute for Psychotherapy in New York City. Much smaller samples were available for the other modalities. A total of 212 reports, based on sessions with 23 different couples in marital therapy, came from the Northwestern University Institute of Psychiatry and from private practice sources in Chicago. For group psychotherapy, there was a total of 144 questionnaires based on four sessions from each of four patients drawn at random from each of nine different outpatient groups, some from the Northwestern Institute of Psychiatry and some from Evanston Hospital.

There were patients of both sexes and various ages, various social, ethnic and religious backgrounds, and various occupational, marital, and parental statuses. The therapists and the clinical settings involved were also different, adding to the heterogeneity. The case would be quite hopeless, if we were interested in examining the *differences* between therapeutic modalities. However, the situation is very different if we focus instead on the impressive *commonalities* across modalities—consistencies that are all the more remarkable because of the uncontrolled variability within and between the different groups of patients and therapists. Although there were also some differences in content between the individual, marital, and group therapy questionnaires, there were large areas of overlap that allowed us to compare patients' experiences.

Psychologically the most interesting of these comparisons concern the patients' perceptions of relatedness with their therapists, patients' perceptions of their own self-relatedness, and their perceptions of their own and of their therapists' feelings. The striking fact, as we shall show, is that psychotherapy in all modalities provides patients with a rather uniform and very specific type of intrapersonal and interpersonal experience.

The quality of *relatedness* with their therapists that patients experienced was determined from reports of their manner of relating to their therapists, and their perceptions of their therapists' style of relating to them. Manner or style of relating (as discussed in the first section) was conceived by us in terms of four facets of interaction—responsiveness, attitude, direction, and control—each of which was defined by two coordinate dimensions. The questionnaires contained eight scales for style of relating, one for each conceptual dimension, rated as follows: "slightly or not at all" (0); "some" (1); "pretty much" (2); "very much" (3).

What we want to present here are data on the *typical* or modal ratings by patients in individual, marital, and group psychotherapy on the eight scales describing patients' style of relating and the eight parallel scales describing their perceptions of their therapists' styles of relating. To verbally convey the degree of concentration of responses at certain parts of the scales, we shall cite the percentages of sessions from individual (I), marital (M), and group (G) therapy falling into the diverse segments of the scales using the following adjectives: "minimally" (0); "slightly" (0 or 1); "somewhat" (1); "moderately" (1 or 2); "pretty" (2); "strikingly" (2 or 3); "very" (3).

In terms of *responsiveness*, for example, *patients* typically saw themselves as *pretty talkative* (2: 50% I; 54% M; 44% G), if not *strikingly talkative* (2+3: 89% I; 74% M; 64% G). This means that in half of the individual therapy sessions that were observed, patients reported talking "pretty much," and in 9 out of 10 sessions patients reported talking either "pretty much" or "very much." Similar concentrations on this dimension of responsiveness can be observed for very high percentages of patients' reports from marital and group psychotherapy. That all this talk by patients was not merely idle chatter in their view is indicated by the fact that they also saw themselves as *pretty*, even *strikingly expressive of feeling* in their sessions (2: 38% I; 51% M; 41% G) (2+3: 62% I; 84% M; 68% G). Patients not only talked a lot; they typically talked about matters that seemed to have real emotional significance for them.

Patients reported too that they typically saw their *therapists* as at least *moderately talkative* (1+2: 77% I; 87% M; 75% G) and also as at least *moderately expressive of feeling* (1+2: 67% I; 71% M; 75% G). Thus, while not as intensely responsive as patients, therapists were typically seen as definitely responsive in both the dimensions of activity and affectivity—not as silent "blank screens," and not as emotionless technicians. Considering the broad responsiveness of both their therapists and themselves, patients generally experienced a vivid, lively quality of relatedness, in all modalities of psychotherapy.

In terms of interpersonal *attitude*, *patients* typically reported themselves as being *pretty* or *strikingly friendly and respectful* (2: 46% I; 51% M; 49% G) (2+3: 75% I; 82% M; 60% G), and for the most part as being *minimally* or at most *slightly critical* (0: 76% I; 82% M; 42% G) (0+1: 93% I; 98%M; 85% G). This degree of affirmation was matched by what patients perceived in their therapists' interpersonal attitudes toward them: *therapists* were seen as *strikingly friendly and supportive* (2+3: 74% I; 85% M; 76% G), and *minimally* or at most *slightly critical* (0: 72% I; 77% M; 39% G) (0+1: 94% I; 98% M; 85% G). Clearly, patients typically experienced a marked quality of mutual affirmation in relatedness in all treatment modalities.

In terms of *direction*, *patients* perceived themselves as at least *moderately taking initiative* in determining the course of their sessions (1+2: 66% I; 78% M; 69% G), while being *strikingly attentive and receptive* to initiatives taken by their therapists (2+3: 85% I; 91% M; 83% G). Moreover, in this facet of relatedness too, patients saw their therapists as relating to them in precisely the same way: *therapists* were perceived as at least *moderately exercising initiative* (1+2: 66% I; 78% M; 69% G), while being *strikingly* if not *very attentive and receptive* to their patients' initiatives (2+3: 92% I; 92% M; 76% G) (3: 53% I; 50% M; 38% G). The impression that this leaves of the typical quality of relatedness with regard to the direction of therapy, in the patients' experience, is one of mutually sensitive and considerate collaboration.

Finally, in terms of *control*, *patients* typically experienced themselves as only *slightly* to *moderately attempting to persuade or induce* their therapists to certain actions (0+1: 80% I; 62% M; 71% G) (1+2: 51% I; 76% M; 70% G). At the same time, patients saw themselves as at least *moderately* or even *strikingly agreeing or acceding* to the influence of their therapists (1+2: 70% I; 77% M; 71% G) (2+3: 69% I; 78% M; 68% G). The therapists too once again were seen by their patients typically, only somewhat less intensely, in practically the same manner: *therapists* were *slightly attempting to persuade or induce* the patient (0+1: 82% I; 86% M; 53% G), while at least *moderately agreeing or acceding* to the patients' influence (1+2: 80% I; 87% M; 72% G). What quality of relatedness do these respective manners define with regard to control? Very clearly, a mutual freedom from pressure or strong constraint, and a willingness to go along with one another. In other words, a liberal and open quality of relatedness was experienced by patients, in all therapeutic modalities.

Given all the variability in patients, in therapists, in settings, in orientations, and in modalities of treatment, the consistency of these *typical* experiences of relatedness is quite amazing. In anywhere from 2 in every 3 to 9 in every 10 sessions, on the average, *patients perceived the therapeutic relationship as vivid, as mutually receptive and sensitively collaborative, as liberal and open, and as warmly and mutually affirming.* This degree of regularity implies that the form of relatedness here described is a highly dependable (i.e., "structural") aspect of psychotherapy, an integral aspect of the environment that psychotherapy provides for most patients most of the time.

The form of relatedness itself, in its vivid affirmation and mutual receptivity, suggests some features of the symbiotic infant–mother dyad, the "holding environment" that D. W. Winnicott (1965), for one, conceives as the original and recurrent interpersonal basis for psychological growth. It is also possible, without stretching the point, to see how the conditions of empathy, authenticity, and nonjudgmental acceptance that Carl Rogers (1957) thought essential for therapy might be reflected and reciprocally augmented in these typical qualities of relatedness. Here, then, is a quite specific view of the so-called nonspecific factors at work in psychotherapy; the reason, perhaps, why patients on average derive a moderate but significant benefit from almost all the forms of psychotherapy that have been studied (Luborsky, Singer, & Luborsky, 1975; Bergin & Lambert, 1978; Smith, Glass, & Miller, 1980).

Supposing this line of inference to be plausible, the next question to arise is: What does the experience of such a relationship do for the patient psychologically? What psychological processes and activities are facilitated or made possible for the patient within the interpersonal environment of psychotherapy? The *Therapy Session Report* questionnaires provide us with information that may be relevant to these questions in two respects: patients' experiences of self-relatedness during therapy; and, their perceptions of their own and their therapists' feelings.

The facet of self-relatedness in the *Therapy Session Reports* was conceptualized in the same terms as interpersonal relatedness, but viewed from a reflexive perspective. Thus, interpersonal responsiveness was reflected intrapersonally as inner responsiveness (ideation and affective arousal); direction was conceived reflexively as self-awareness (self-definition and self-attunement); control was viewed as self-regulation (self-discipline and self-indulgence); interpersonal attitude was translated as self-evaluation (self-approval and self-rejection). When we examined the ratings made by patients in individual, marital, and group psychotherapy on the eight self-relatedness scales, we were again struck by the consistency of modal responses.

In terms of *inner responsiveness*, ideation was construed as the counterpart of overt activity, and affective arousal the inner correlate of emotional expressiveness. Patients in therapy typically perceived themselves as *very* or at least *strikingly fluent in ideation* (3: 64% I; 53% M; no data, G) (2 + 3: 90% I; 87% M; no data, G), and as at least *moderately stirred or aroused affectively* (1 + 2: 63% I; 72% M; 64% G). Thus, the reflexive correlative of the patients' vivid and lively interpersonal relatedness was a comparable state of inner stimulation and productivity.

In terms of *self-awareness*, the dimensions corresponding to receptivity and initiative were conceived of as self-attunement or the ability to focus on one's feelings and concerns, and as self-definition or the ability to articulate and organize what one means to express. The data showed that patients typically perceived themselves as *strikingly able to focus* on their inner concerns (2+3: 70% I; 77% M; 60% G), and as at least *moderately organized and coherent* in defining their emergent experiences (1+2: 80% I; 81% M; 89% G). This combination suggests a self-explorative state of mind, an openness and receptivity to what is current and forthcoming in the stream of consciousness.

In terms of *self-regulation*, the questions that we asked concerned the patient's sense of inner mastery or being "on top of" their feelings and impulses, and their sense of spontaneity or freedom from inner constraint. Patients typically perceived themselves as *moderately* to *strikingly in control* of their feelings and impulses (1+2: 70% I; 74% M; 76% G) (2+3: 63% I; 79% M; 72% G), but also as *moderately* to *strikingly inwardly free and spontaneous* (1+2: 68% I; 80% M; no data, G) (2+3: 69% I; 70% M; no data, G). The phrase that comes to mind to convey this blend of conditions is "self-possession." To be self-possessed is to be self-accommodating as well as self-disciplined, both flexible and balanced. Patients in all therapeutic modalities typically seem to experience a substantial measure of self-possession during their sessions.

Finally, how well did the patients seem to like what they found within them in their stimulated, self-explorative, self-possessed states of mind? In terms of *self-evaluation*, patients typically were at least *moderately self-approving* (1+2: 71% I; 87% M; 74% G), but were also *slightly* to *moderately self-critical* (0+1: 71% I; 80% M; 71% G) (1+2: 57% I; 74% M; 63% G). As might be expected, given the difficult and distressing issues that are probed in psychotherapy, the result for patients was a mixture of satisfaction and dissatisfaction with self. If satisfaction was on average somewhat more present than dissatisfaction, patients nevertheless seemed to find enough in themselves that they would wish to change.

It is impossible, of course, to assign a simple causal connection to the juxtaposition of the experienced qualities of relatedness between patient and therapist and the patient's state of self-relatedness within the therapy session. On the other hand, it is just as difficult to imagine that there is no significant causal connection, however complex it might be. No doubt the patient's readiness to participate in an effective therapeutic alliance is to some extent reflected in the experience of such self-relatedness. No doubt such a productive, self-explorative, self-possessed, and self-confronting state of mind facilitates the development of a good working relationship between patient and therapist. But it is also plausible to suppose that the sustained experience of a mutually involving, attentively collaborative, open and strongly affirming relationship creates a psychological environment in which such a state of mind can be conceived and nourished. The causal connection may very well be circular: state of mind developing within a relationship, in turn making further relationships of the same sort easier, which in turn further reinforces that state of mind, and so on. (Perhaps this is why patients tend to have more than one course of psychotherapy, and why patients who have had psychotherapy previously seem to do better in and to benefit more from their current treatment.)

Once more supposing this general line of inference to be plausible, a further question arises: What goes on in the patient and what does the patient do, in this "open" state of mind within this "holding" relationship, that produces beneficial change in psychological well-being? We think that we have found some clues to answering this question in the perceptions of their own and their therapists' feeling-states that patients recorded for us on the *Therapy Session Reports*.

Feelings are critically rich phenomena for psychological study because they spontaneously register one's immediate, prereflective sense of self-in-situation, one's sense of what is "going on" within and between oneself and others. By emphasizing feelings we do not mean to isolate them as a category that is separated from ideation or from action. We do not mean to repeat the ancient philosophical division between cognition, conation, and affect—between thought, behavior, and emotion. On the contrary, our conception of feelings includes several points that explicitly link feelings to cognitive and behavioral processes.

First, feelings reflect the convictions and assumptions, often not readily conscious, on the basis of which one orients one's operations in any particular situation. One's feelings follow from, and reflect, convictions and assumptions about oneself, about one's companions, and about the appropriate ends and means defining the social situation. These convictions and assumptions characteristically are not formulated in words, but they are cognitive constructs and their message contents are susceptible to transliteration. In this sense, the study of feelings offers access to a level of cognition that is not normally approachable directly through introspection.

Second, feelings also reflect the aims and energies through which one directs and sustains one's efforts of thought and courses of action. Feelings are sensations that stimulate us, moods that dispose us, sentiments that stir us, emotions that move us, passions that drive us. Put differently, how one feels about things (including oneself) defines one's motivation toward them, and as such constitutes a major determinant of how one is likely to act with respect to them. In this sense, feelings are predictors of behavior and, though imperfect, are often viewed as such.

Third, feelings communicate both intrapersonally and interpersonally. One's feelings are spontaneously articulated "inwardly" into concrete symbolic representations or fantasies, and are conveyed "outwardly" through involuntary facial, vocal, gestural, and postural signs that are "read" both for what they imply about one's operational beliefs and for what they predict about one's behavior. Inwardly, one's more vivid and persistent imaginings tend to command one's attention, making conscious and thereby available to reflective calculation one's own intentions in advance of their commitment to action. So it is that we come to know our own minds. Outwardly, one's more vivid and persistent feeling expressions serve to give others an impression of one's aims and disposition, either consciously or through evoking resonant feelings in them in accordance with their own active assumptions and strivings. So it is that we come to know each other's minds.

Thus, we think it is no accident that good clinicians in practice pay careful attention to their patients' (and to their own) feeling expressions, whatever their theoretical orientations may be; nor, we think, is it a perverse sensitivity that attributes great significance to the impact of therapists' feeling expressions on their clients. Good clinicians are careful about their own and their patients' feelings.

What, then, are patients' typical perceptions of their feelings and of their therapists' feelings in individual, marital, and group psychotherapy? How consistent are feelings across treatment modalities? How do patients' feelings and therapists' feelings interact? And, finally, what does all of this imply for our understanding of how therapy works?

The following *patient feelings* were reported as present to some degree in more than three-fifths of the sessions in individual psychotherapy, in marital psychotherapy, and in group psychotherapy: accepted, anxious, confident, confused, frustrated, hopeful, pleased, relaxed, relieved, and serious. (In marital and group therapy, patients also typically felt alert, calm, interested, optimistic, and affectionate—feelings not included in the individual questionnaire.)

These typical patient feelings are accounted for by three of the eight empirical dimensions that we found in a factor analysis of patient affect in individual therapy (Howard, Orlinsky, & Hill, 1970): *Feeling Anxious* (anxious, confused, frustrated, serious); *Feeling Confident* (accepted, confident, relaxed); *Feeling Relieved* (hopeful, pleased, relieved). Not included in the individual *Therapy Session Report*, and therefore not assignable to a factor, were the feelings: alert, calm, interested, and optimistic. However, we would hazard a guess that alert, calm, and interested might have been included in Feeling Confident, and optimistic in Feeling Relieved. In other words, there was a high likelihood that patients in any of the three treatment modalities would experience feelings of Confidence, Anxiety, and Relief in any one of their sessions.

Turning to patients' perceptions of their *therapists' feelings*, we found an even more impressive consistency of high endorsement across modalities. The following were reported by patients about their therapists' feelings in about four-fifths or more of their sessions: alert, confident, effective, interested, involved, relaxed, sympathetic, and thoughtful. In at least 70% of sessions therapists were also seen as feeling cheerful, optimistic, and pleased.

These typical feelings are accounted for by three of the six empirical dimensions that we found in a factor analysis of patients' perceptions of therapist affect in individual therapy (Howard, Orlinsky, & Hill, 1970): *Feeling Expansive* (cheerful, interested, optimistic, pleased, relaxed); *Feeling Effective* (alert, confident, effective, sympathetic, thoughtful); *Feeling Intimate* (involved). Again, this means that there was a very high likelihood that patients in any of the three treatment modalities would experience their therapists as having feelings of Expansiveness, Effectiveness, and Intimacy in any one of their sessions.

There is a basic complementarity discernible between the feelings that patients experience in themselves and those that they see in their therapists. First of all, patients typically feel accepted, relaxed, and confident (Feeling Confident) when they are with their therapists. These are all positive feelings which imply an underlying cognitive position that might be put into words like "At least when I'm here with you, I'm O.K." or "I'm safe here with you." Perhaps it is comparatively easy to experience oneself this way with someone important who is seen as feeling cheerful, interested, optimistic, pleased, and relaxed (Feeling Expansive) in one's presence. This impression of outgoing geniality is reinforced by the patients' sense that the therapist also feels involved. The message one is very likely to sense in such affective expressions is some variant of "I'm worthwhile, and I find you worthwhile" (Feeling Expansive) and "I care about what is going on with you" (Feeling Intimate). These messages do not need to be put into words, of course, and may well be all the more convincing if they are not put into words. After all, words can be used deliberately, with some ulterior purpose in mind. If a therapist said these words to a patient, the patient might discount them with the thought "You're just saying that to make me feel better; it's your job to say that." The same message conveyed affectively, that is, nonverbally, will seem more sincere (literally, "without thought" or calculation), more genuinely meant, and thus more believable.

Patients also typically encounter negative feelings in themselves during therapy sessions. Feelings of anxiety, confusion, and frustration are frequent companions as the patient explores painful and problematic personal issues. People, of course, do not enter psychotherapy as patients when they are feeling good about themselves and when their lives are proceeding satisfactorily. Serious distress, or the vivid memory of serious distress, is requisite motivation for seeking treatment. Patients carry feelings of anxiety, confusion, and frustration (the sensed conviction "I can't cope, I don't know what to do") into therapy with them, and may also on occasion have such feelings stirred up directly through interaction with the therapist. However, if things that the therapist says or does sometimes leads the patient to Feeling Anxious, this seems to occur by and large in a very supportive context.

The very sense of being valued by someone with a presumed reputation for discernment in judging character, and therefore of seeming worthwhile to oneself, probably enhances the patient's courage to explore and come to terms with those issues and life experiences which have been too painful or too debilitating to deal with alone. But in addition, when patients take that risk, or when they cannot keep their bad feelings at bay even within the sanctuary of the therapy session, they are very likely to perceive the therapist as feeling alert, confident, effective, sympathetic, and thoughtful (Feeling Effective). Somehow, in relation to these perceptions of their therapists, patients also very frequently feel relieved, pleased, and hopeful ("I guess it's really not so bad, I really can deal with it") during their sessions.

Perhaps it is enough at times that therapists simply do not get overwhelmed or upset by their patients' problems and bad feelings, that they manage to sustain and project a sense of mastery and control. But it seems more probable to us that therapists are regularly able to say and do things which their patients really do find helpful, which is the source both of their being seen as Feeling Effective and their patients Feeling Relieved. Moreover, we are prepared to believe that different therapeutic orientations each provide their adherents with some "interventions" or "techniques" that, if used intelligently, are effective ways of helping many patients.

What we imagine, then, as a result of these data on patients' reports of their own and of their therapists' feelings, is a cycle of Feeling Confident, Feeling Anxious, and Feeling Relieved in patients, aided and abetted by their perceptions of their therapists as reliably Feeling Expansive, Feeling Intimate, and Feeling Effective. The therapists' affective message, "I'm worthwhile and so are you," (Feeling Expansive) finds a response in the patients' affective message, "I'm safe and O.K. when I'm with you" (Feeling Confident). With courage enhanced, and with the additional support of the therapists' message "I care about you" (Feeling Intimate), patients can more readily tolerate and intelligently explore issues with which their experience has been "I can't cope, I don't know what to do" (Feeling Anxious). In response to this, therapists say or do things that convey the message "I understand and can handle what is bothering you" (Feeling Effective), and that leads their patients to sense "It may not be so bad, I really can deal with it" (Feeling Relieved).

Some evidence to support this line of inference can be found in a paper that we published more than 15 years ago (Howard, Krause, & Orlinsky, 1969). The study in question made a causal analysis of the direction of affective influence between patients and therapists in 45 pairs in individual psychotherapy, where both patient and therapist had completed *Therapy Session Reports* after from 5 to 58 joint sessions. Feelings were analyzed simply in terms of positive and negative dimensions of affect. Patients' perceptions of their own positive feelings (P+) included: affectionate, confident, grateful, hopeful, pleased, relaxed, and relieved (i.e., what we have treated more differentially here as Feeling Confident and Feeling Relieved). Negative patient feelings (P−) included: angry, anxious, cautious, depressed, embarrassed, frustrated, guilty, impatient, inadequate, inhibited, strange, and withdrawn. (These include Feeling Anxious, together with a number of less frequent dysphoric states that are probably associated with the specific issues with which patients sense themselves not able to cope.) Therapists' perceptions of their own positive feelings (T+) included: affectionate, cheerful, close, effective, optimistic, pleased, and sympathetic. Negative therapist feelings

(T−) included: apprehensive, demanding, perplexed, and unsure (none of these being frequent occurrences, as perceived by patients).

The question explored in the study was whether therapists' feelings (T+, T−) could be construed as causes of patients' feelings (P+, P−), and vice versa. The distribution of patient feelings against therapist feelings was used to define a fourfold table for each combination of feeling dimensions (e.g., P+, not P+ vs. T+, not T+) for each patient–therapist pair, fitting the coordinates to the data points so that one of the quadrants would essentially be empty. The location of the empty quadrant in each case determined whether the data were consistent or inconsistent with the hypotheses of patient influence or therapist influence (Howard & Krause, 1970).

The results indicated (1) that, overall, neither patients' nor therapists' positive feelings (P+, T+) were necessary nor, in themselves, sufficient to evoke positive feelings in the other. However, if therapists' level of experience was taken into account, then (2) patients' unusually positive feelings were sufficient for therapists to experience unusually positive feelings when the therapists had less that 6 years of experience, while (3) therapists' unusually positive feelings were sufficient for patients to experience unusually positive feelings when the therapist had 6 or more years of experience practicing psychotherapy. In other words, less experienced therapists were more likely to respond to their patients' good feelings, perhaps because they needed reassurance of their own competence or of their patients' good prognoses, and patients' good feelings provide such evidence. On the other hand, more experienced therapists probably have a more secure concept of their efficacy as therapists, and so are less affectively responsive to their patients in this way. It may also be that, being more secure, they could convey a clearer and more vivid sense of their positive affect to patients than could the less experienced therapists.

In the case of negative patient and therapist affects, the results indicated (4) that the presence of negative feelings in the therapist was usually sufficient to evoke negative feelings in the patient; or, in other words, that although patients could feel unusually badly in any particular session, they were considerably more likely to feel badly if their therapists felt badly. This seems quite understandable, since the patient, but not the therapist, is supposed to be feeling badly. Negative affects are part of what qualify and motivate a person to become a patient in psychotherapy. Bringing such feelings into therapy is part of the patient's task, and no reason for competent therapists to feel badly themselves (certainly no reason for feeling inadequate as a therapist). However, if the therapist does feel this way, that would seem reason enough for the patient to feel badly. Patients come preoccupied with their problems, expecting to receive help from an expert. If the expert feels badly, how can the patient hope to get help?

Comparisons of patients' negative feelings with therapists' positive feelings (P− vs. T+), and of patients' positive feelings with therapists' negative feelings ((P+ vs. T−), led to a further finding. In these cases it appeared (5) that the experience of a marked degree of one type of feeling by one participant (e.g., positive affect) precluded the experience of the opposite type of feeling (e.g., negative affect) by the other participant. These data are logically consistent with both of the following statements: (1) if the patient feels especially badly, the therapist cannot feel especially effective; (2) if the therapist feels especially effective, the patient will not feel especially badly. Both of these interpretations seem clinically plausible, and if both are true then the issue may hang in the balance of relative affective intensity and stability between the participants. That is, if the patient enters a session feeling especially badly and the therapist enters the same session feeling especially expansive, caring, and effective, it is a matter of which one projects the feeling more strongly, and which one is better able to sustain the feeling in the face of contrary influence from the other. A line from the old song, "Something's Got to Give," drifts through one's mind: "When an irresistible force such as you/Meets an old immovable object like me . . . " Perhaps most experienced therapists will recall one or two situations of the sort.

What do all these findings from the *Therapy Session Reports* on patients' perceptions of relatedness, self-relatedness, and affects suggest about how therapy works? The line of reasoning we have pursued leads us to this: Psychotherapy in all modalities typically provides an experience of relatedness with the therapist (and perhaps, in group therapy, with the group as a whole) that approximates what Winnicott has termed a "holding environment." This mode of relatedness facilitates an open, nondefensive frame of mind in which new learning (psychological restructuring, growth) is most probable. While in such a state of self-relatedness, patients are encouraged by the affective messages they sense from their therapists to explore painful and problematic areas of experience that they would otherwise avoid because they have been unable to cope tolerably with them in the past. With the aid of effective therapist interventions (of one sort or another) patients bring a fuller range of their present psychological resources to bear on these painful issues, find relief from them, and emerge with enhanced confidence. It seems highly plausible that a knowledgeable sense of the patient's Feeling Confident is the exportable product of experience in therapy sessions, remembering that this confidence has been tested and tempered by successful exposure to many of the patient's worst fears. That kind of confidence can be a stable, resilient foundation for one's self-esteem and morale (Frank, 1974), as it can also be a most favorable basis for engaging with others in the basic personal relationships out of which one builds one's life.

Why You Should Use The Therapy Session Reports in Your Research

We have described the *Therapy Session Report* questionnaires, and have discussed some findings that illuminate the psychological "interior" of social relationships in general, and of psychotherapy in particular. We hope that we have persuaded some of you of the utility of our method, and the clinical and scientific value of its results.

The *Therapy Session Reports* and our use of them in research have run counter to some traditional methodological biases of psychotherapy researchers. Many researchers have, we think, tended to confuse avoidance of experiential or "subjective" data with the need to develop explicit, systematic, and replicable—that is, "objective"—methods. They have recorded and analyzed the externally observable actions of patients and therapists, in the belief that in this way they could study the raw, "objective" process of psychotherapy, as if it could be approached the way it actually is "in nature," undistorted by the perceptions of the subjects. The fact that psychotherapy, like other human involvements, does not exist "in nature" seems not to have bothered these researchers, nor has their dependence on the subjective perceptions of "judges" for ratings of their recordings, films, and transcripts struck them as inconsistent. From our point of view, these researchers have sacrificed much in pursuit of a misleading concept of science.

Participants' perspectives are necessary data for the study of social relationships. In psychotherapy, the patients' and therapists' construals of their reciprocal involvement are constitutive elements of the therapeutic process. We do not argue that the behaviors of patients and therapists, as perceived by outside observers, are irrelevant; these, too, are constitutive elements of therapeutic process. But we do not think that research which is limited to externally scrutinized behaviors can provide an essential or a practical understanding of psychotherapy. From an external and strictly behavioral perspective, the therapeutic process must to some extent remain a psychological "black box." Research that does not include data on the patients' and therapists' experiences cannot penetrate the psychological "interior" of psychotherapy. And research findings based on variables that are not couched in terms of the therapist's experience of psychotherapy, or are not empirically translatable into such terms, cannot be clinically utilized by practitioners.

For these reasons we would argue that the *Therapy Session Reports*, or some version of them, ought to be included in all studies seeking data on psychotherapeutic process. Studies that are principally concerned with some aspect of process might include this instrument as one among several, to permit the analysis and interrelation of data from diverse observational perspectives. Studies that are focused primarily on outcome, or on other aspects of psychotherapy, should include at lease one process measure as an indicator that the phenomena observed are typical of therapy—and if only one such measure is used we would argue that it should be some version of the *Therapy Session Reports*. The instrument is standardized in form and is easily administered. It requires relatively little time from subjects, and—since it is precoded and quantitative in format— it requires far less time from research personnel than any other type of process measure. Finally, and crucially, though they deal with "subjective" experiences as data, the *Therapy Session Reports* provide a public, systematic, and repeatable method for doing so—and therefore meet the real criteria of scientific methodology.

Try it. You'll like it.

References

Berger, P. L., & Luckmann, T. *The social construction of reality*. Garden City, New York: Doubleday, 1967.

Bergin, A. E., & Lambert, M. J. The evaluation of therapeutic outcomes. In S. L. Garfield & A. E. Bergin (Eds.), *Handbook of psychotherapy and behavior change*, (2nd ed.). New York: Wiley, 1978.

Frank, J. D. Psychotherapy: The restoration of morale. *American Journal of Psychiatry*, 1974, *131*, 271–274.

Howard, K. I., & Krause, M. S. Some comments on "Techniques for estimating the source and direction of influence in panel data." *Psychological Bulletin*, 1970, *74*, 219–224.

Howard, K. I., Krause, M. S., & Orlinsky, D. E. Direction of affective influence in psychotherapy. *Journal of Consulting and Clinical Psychology*, 1969, *33*, 614–620.

Howard, K. I., Orlinsky, D. E., & Hill, J. A. Affective experience in psychotherapy. *Journal of Abnormal Psychology*, 1970, *75*, 267–275.

Liebenthal, D. M. *The experience of patients in group psychotherapy*. Unpublished Doctoral Dissertation, Northwestern University, 1980.

Luborsky, L., Singer, B., & Luborsky, L. Comparative studies of psychotherapies. *Archives of General Psychiatry*, 1975, *32*, 995–1008.

Mead, G. H. *The social psychology of George Herbert Mead* (A. Strauss, Ed.). Chicago: University of Chicago Press, 1956.

Orlinsky, D. E., & Howard, K. I. *Therapy session report*, Forms P and T. Chicago: Institute for Juvenile Research, 1966.

Orlinsky, D. E., & Howard, K. I. Communication rapport and patient "progress." *Psychotherapy: Theory, Research and Practice*, 1968, *5*, 131–136.

Orlinsky, D. E., & Howard, K. I. *Varieties of psychotherapeutic experience.* New York: Columbia Teachers College Press, 1975.

Rogers, C. R. The necessary and sufficient conditions of therapeutic personality change. *Journal of Consulting Psychology,* 1957, *21,* 95–103.

Schachter, S., & Singer, J. E. Cognitive, social and physiological determinants of emotional state. *Psychological Review,* 1962, *69,* 379–399.

Smith, M. L., Glass, G. V., & Miller, T. I. *The benefits of psychotherapy.* Baltimore: The Johns Hopkins Press, 1980.

Winnicott, D. W. *The maturational processes and the facilitating environment.* New York: International Universities Press, 1965.

Additional Selected Publications Using the *Therapy Session Reports*

Bottari, M. A. & Rappaport, H. The relationship of patient and therapist-reported experiences of the initial session to outcome: An initial investigation. *Psychotherapy: Theory, Research and Practice,* 1983, *20,* 355–358.

Brenner, D., & Howard, K. I. Clinical judgement as a function of experience and information. *Journal of Clinical Psychology,* 1976, *32,* 721–728.

Fiester, A. R. Clients' perceptions of therapists with high attrition rates. *Journal of Consulting and Clinical Psychology,* 1977, *45,* 954–955.

Genthner, R. W., & Saccuzzo, D. P. Accuracy of perception of psychotherapeutic content as a function of observers' level of facilitation. *Journal of Clinical Psychology,* 1977, *33,* 517–519.

Genthner, R. W., & Saccuzzo, D. P. Facilitation skills and perception of client wants. *Journal of Psychology,* 1978, *99,* 93–96.

Hill, J. A. Therapist goals, patient aims and patient satisfaction in psychotherapy. *Journal of Clinical Psychology,* 1969, *25,* 455–459.

Hill, J. A., Howard, K. I., & Orlinsky, D. E. The therapist's experience of psychotherapy: Some dimensions and determinants. *Multivariate Behavioral Research,* 1970, *5,* 435–451.

Howard, K. I., Orlinsky, D. E., & Hill, J. A. The patient's experience of psychotherapy: Some dimensions and determinants. *Multivariate Behavioral Research. Special Issue: Progress in Clinical Psychology Through Multivariate Experimental Designs,* 1968, 55–72.

Howard, K. I., Orlinsky, D. E., & Hill, J. A. The therapist's feelings in the therapeutic process. *Journal of Clinical Psychology,* 1969, *25,* 83–93.

Howard, K. I., Orlinsky, D. E., & Hill, J. A. Content of dialogue in pschotherapy. *Journal of Counseling Psychology,* 1969, *16,* 396–404.

Howard, K. I., Orlinsky, D. E., & Hill, J. A. Patients' satisfaction in psychotherapy as a function of patient–therapist pairing. *Psychotherapy: Theory, Research and Practice,* 1970, *1,* 130–134.

Howard, K. I., Orlinsky, D. E., & Perilstein, J. Contribution of therapists to patients' experiences in psychotherapy: A components of variance model for analyzing process data. *Journal of Clinical and Consulting Psychology,* 1976, *44,* 520–526.

Howard, K. I., Orlinsky, D. E., & Trattner, J. H. Therapist orientation and patient experience in psychotherapy. *Journal of Counseling Psychology,* 1970, *17,* 263–270.

Migdoll, J. *Therapists' ratings of the treatment process: A component of variance analysis.* Unpublished Master's Thesis, Northwestern University, 1983.

Mintz, J., Auerbach, A. H., Luborsky, L., & Johnson, M. Patients', therapists', and observers' views of psychotherapy: A "Rashomon" experience or a reasonable consensus? *British Journal of Medical Psychology,* 1973, *46,* 83–89.

O'Mahoney, M. *Therapist behavior and facilitative conditions in client experience.* Unpublished Doctoral Dissertation, Illinois Institute of Technology, 1972.

Orlinsky, D. E., & Howard, K. I. The good therapy hour: Experiental correlates of patients' and therapists' evaluations of therapy sessions. *Archives of General Psychology,* 1967, *12,* 621–632.

Orlinsky, D. E., & Howard, K. I. Dimensions of conjoint experiential process in psychotherapy relationships. *Proceedings, 75th Annual Convention, APA*, 1967, 251–252.

Orlinsky, D. E., & Howard, K. I. Inside psychotherapy. *Psychology Today*, 1968, 2, 50–53.

Orlinsky, D. E., & Howard, K. I. Varieties of patient experience in psychotherapy. *Voices*, 1975, 11, 68–71.

Orlinsky, D. E., & Howard, K. I. The effect of sex of therapist on the therapeutic experiences of women. *Psychotherapy: Theory, Research and Practice*, 1976, 13, 82–88.

Orlinsky, D. E., & Howard, K. I. The therapist's experiences in psychotherapy. In A. S. Gurman and A. M. Razin (Eds.), *Effective psychotherapy: A handbook of research*. Oxford: Pergamon, 1977.

Orlinsky, D. E., Howard, K. I., & Hill, J. A. The patient's concerns in psychotherapy. *Journal of Clinical Psychology*, 1970, 26, 104–111.

Orlinsky, D. E., Howard, K. I., & Hill, J. A. Conjoint psychotherapeutic experience: Some dimensions and determinants. *Multivariate Behavioral Research*, 1975, 10, 463–477.

Saccuzzo, D. P. Canonical correlation as a method of assessing the correlates of successful and unsuccessful therapy hours. *Psychotherapy: Theory, Research and Practice*, 1975, 12, 353–356.

Saccuzzo, D. P. Naturalistic analysis of verbal behavior in psychotherapy. *Psychological Reports*, 1975, 37, 911–919.

Saccuzzo, D. P. What patients want from counseling and psychotherapy. *Journal of Clinical Psychology*, 1975, 31, 471–475.

Saccuzzo, D. P. Feelings of inexperienced therapists in psychotherapy: A factor analytic study. *Perceptual and Motor Skills*, 1976, 43, 359–362.

Saccuzzo, D. P. Factor-analytic structure of patient internal states. *Journal of Clinical Psychology*, 1976, 32, 129–135.

Silverman, M. S. Perceptions of counseling following differential practicum experiences. *Journal of Counseling Psychology*, 1972, 19, 11–15.

Silverman, M. S. Practicum perceptions of initial interviews: Client–counselor divergence. *Counselor Education and Research*, 1973, 158–161.

Stein, M. L., & Stone, G. L. Effects of conceptual level and structure on initial interview behavior. *Journal of Counseling Psychology*, 1978, 25, 96–102.

Tovian, S. M. *Patient experiences and psychotherapy outcome*. Unpublished Doctoral Dissertation, Northwestern University, 1977.

Van Noord, R. W., & Kagan, N. Stimulated recall and affect simulation in counseling: client growth reexamined. *Journal of Counseling Psychology*, 1976, 23, 28–33.

14

Interpersonal Process Recall (IPR) as a Psychotherapy Process Research Method

Robert Elliott
University of Toledo
Toledo, Ohio

As we talk with people, we think of things which are quite different from the things we are talking about . . . If we ask you at this moment just when you felt the counselor understood or didn't understand your feelings, or when you were trying to say something and it came out quite differently from the way you wanted it to, it would probably be very difficult for you to remember. With this TV playback immediately after your interview, you will find it possible to recall these thoughts and feelings in detail. (Kagan, Krathwohl, *et al.*, 1967, p. 13)

Interpersonal Process Recall (IPR) is a special interview procedure in which a conversation is taped and immediately played back for the participants. The informant is asked to remember and describe the momentary experiences and perceptions associated with particular events in the conversation. IPR makes it possible for participants to recapture fleeting impressions and reactions which would ordinarily be forgotten or merged into more global perceptions. The idea is simple, and its results are fascinating; unsurprisingly, it has been "discovered" by a number of different researchers working independently of one another. These researchers have referred to it by various names, including: "the method of stimulated recall" (Bloom, 1954); "Playback" (Fanshel & Moss, 1971); videotape "inquiry" (Knudson, Sommers, & Golding, 1980); "Empathy Transaction Scale" (Brown, 1981); "the Retrospection Method" (Dole *et al.*, 1979, 1982); "videotape reconstruction" (Meichenbaum & Butler, 1979); and "Nachträglichen Lauten Denkens" ("Retrospective Thinking Aloud"; Wagner & Weidle, 1982; Kommer & Bastine, 1982).

A Brief History of
Interpersonal Process Recall (IPR)

The development of IPR was made possible by the introduction of inexpensive sound (and later video) recording technology. Its use as a method for studying psychotherapy was perhaps foreshadowed by the presentation of therapist-annotated transcripts of psychotherapy sessions (e.g., Evraiff, 1963; Rogers, 1942; Wolberg, 1967). However, IPR was first used as a systematic research method by B. S. Bloom and his colleagues in the late 1940s and early 1950s for the purpose of studying the thought processes of college students during discussion sections (Bloom, 1954; cf. Wagner, Maier, Utlendorfer-Marck, Weidle, & Barz, 1982). Subsequently, N. Kagan (1975) (see also Kagan, Krathwohl, & Miller, 1963) was the first to apply this method to psychological helping situations; he renamed it "Interpersonal Process Recall." Kagan was less interested in IPR as a data collection procedure and made the technique the center of a program for training counselors and other psychological helpers.

Nevertheless, psychotherapy researchers have long recognized the potential value of IPR. Over the years IPR has been recommended repeatedly in major statements on psychotherapy research methodology (e.g., Bergin & Strupp, 1972; Kiesler, 1973; Lambert, DeJulio, & Stein, 1978). However, the potential of this method for studying psychotherapy has only recently begun to be exploited, as psychotherapy researchers have adapted IPR as a research tool for the systematic study of interpersonal processes in psychotherapy and counseling (see review below). Finally, the most recent application of IPR can be found in its use as a cognitive assessment technique (referred to as "videotape reconstruction"; Meichenbaum & Butler, 1979).

How IPR Works

The vivid recall which IPR makes possible is due to a number of factors:

First, the recording acts as a *cue* to assist the participant in retrieving memory traces which would otherwise be lost in the welter of interfering information generated during any communication episode. In Bloom's original terminology, the recording allows "stimulated recall," which is much more powerful than ordinary free recall (Bloom, 1954).

Second, there is a *recency* effect for these memories: they can be much more readily activated and are noticeably more vivid when recall takes place as soon after the interaction as possible (i.e., less than 48 hours).

Third, the IPR process *slows down* the interaction by allowing the informant to stop the tape in order to describe what he or she was experiencing at particular moments. This allows the informant time to put inchoate experiences into words, a process similar to Gendlin's (1978) "Experiential Focusing" technique.

Fourth, in instructing the informant, the researcher (commonly referred to as "recall consultant" or "inquirer") attempts to induce in the informant a *psychological set* in which attention is focused on specific experiences and perceptions which were occurring at that particular instant in time. Thus, the informant is asked to do what he or she can in order to get back into the "there-and-then" of the interaction, to avoid making inferences or generalizations, and to distinguish clearly between what is being recalled and what he or she is seeing now during the recall.

Fifth, IPR is carried out so as to make the informant feel *safe*: The recall consultant is interested and permissive; the informant is given as much control as possible over the recall process. The result is that most informants are far more open with the recall consultant than they were during the session being reviewed. For example, therapists are much freer with diagnostic assessments and descriptions of strategy, while clients are generally much more willing to admit transference feelings and defensive maneuvers.

The Place of IPR in Psychotherapy Research

As a method for measuring the process of psychotherapy, IPR combines the advantages of the two major strands of therapy process research: the phenomenological approach using global questionnaires (e.g., Barrett-Lennard, 1962; Orlinsky & Howard,

1975; 1977); and the observer process rating approaches such as are described in the first section of this volume. That is to say, IPR combines the event-based specificity of the behavioral process rating scales with the clinical relevance and richness of client and therapist self-report data. Thus, IPR allows the researcher to gather information on the moment-to-moment perceptions, intentions, and reactions of clients and therapists during therapy sessions, subjective impressions which are missing from even the best transcriptions or recordings of therapy sessions (Spence, 1979).

Although Bloom's (1954) original use of IPR was highly structured (the researcher stopped the tape of a class discussion at predetermined points in order to ask the students what they were thinking), Kagan's (1975) adaptation of the method is much more loose. For Kagan, IPR approximates a clinical interview focused on the replaying of the conversation being recalled: virtually complete control of the recall process is given to the informant, who is allowed to stop the tape wherever he or she wishes, while the recall consultant's role is to ask exploratory questions and to make the informant feel comfortable. Interestingly, as IPR has been adapted for research purposes, researchers have returned to more structured formats reminiscent of Bloom's original use: The researcher generally controls the stopping of the tape and focuses the information gathering by means of rating scales or brief interview schedules.

It is important to keep in mind that IPR differs from the process measures described earlier in this volume in that it is *not* a rating scale or instrument. Instead, it is a specialized interview situation in which various structured information-gathering formats may be used (i.e., rating scales, nominal category systems, open-ended questions). However, this specialized interview situation has required the development of new phenomenological rating scales which can be used for characterizing specific therapy events (e.g., the Helpfulness Scale described below). Thus, this chapter will address both Interpersonal Process Recall as a general research procedure and the particular measures that have been developed for use with it.

The plan for this chapter is as follows: First, I will give an autobiographical account of how I came to use IPR as a process research tool and how those uses evolved. Second, I will summarize features of the various process measures which have been developed for use with IPR and the psychometric data and major substantive findings which are available regarding these measures. Third, there will be an overview of practical and validity issues involved in the use of IPR, including suggestions for maximizing the quality of IPR data. Fourth, I will present a segment of therapy illustrating the use of IPR for describing the process of psychotherapy. Finally, the chapter will conclude with a list of recommendations and implications for psychotherapy research, theory, and practice.

IPR as a Process Research Method:
A Personal Account

In 1974, when I was a second year graduate student, I was challenged by one of my professors (Kelyn Roberts) to come up with an alternative to traditional process analysis methods. Like Stiles (this volume), I had been working with Goodman's response modes (Goodman & Dooley, 1976). As I examined these therapy process variables, what struck me was that they assumed that the meaning of a particular type of helping process did not depend on the context in which it occurred. My readings in role theory (Sarbin & Allen, 1968) and social interactionism (Goffman, 1961) led me to believe that this assumption was unwarranted. Clearly, as a given client and therapist work together, they develop a unique set of shared understandings which shape the meaning of what is currently happening between them (Spence, 1982). However, this proposition raised several issues for me about conventional process research: First, it raised doubts about the validity of process measures. Second, it suggested the need for contextually sensitive process measures. Consideration of these issues led me to wonder what would happen if one asked the involved client and therapist, in effect administering a version of the process measure (e.g., the response modes) to client and therapist. Asking client and therapist after the session, as in Barrett-Lennard's Relationship Inventory (1962), would not do the trick, since the information could not be directly related to actual events in the session. The best way to do this, I reasoned, was to play a tape of the therapy session back for the participants and to ask each to describe particular events. For example, Goodman and Dooley (1976) assumed that advisements carry the intention of guiding the client's behavior; but what would the client and therapist say? More importantly, would not the perceptions of the participants be more relevant for the outcome of treatment than the narrowly trained perceptions of third party observers?

Another graduate student, David Rapkin, and I tried this method out on ourselves; we were amazed at being able to remember and put into words intricate and subtle details of the helping process. Next, we tried it out on several of our fellow students. Not long after that, quite by accident, I ran across Kagan, Krathwohl, and associates' (1967) report on IPR. Although we were at first dismayed by our lack of originality, it soon became clear that Kagan had not used IPR in the way we planned to, and that we could learn from his experience with it.

While I was carrying out further pilot studies, Chris Barker and Nancy Pistrang joined the project. I was interested in comparing client and trained observer perceptions of Goodman's response modes; as fellow Goodman students, they were interested in demonstrating the superiority of the reflection response (cf. Stiles, this volume). Thus, during 1976, we worked together to develop a structured version of IPR: The client viewed a videotape of particular therapist responses, described them in terms of the therapist's intention (we used a free response format to avoid biasing the client's perceptions), then rated the response for helpfulness and empathy on 6-point unipolar scales ("not at all" to "extremely"). This method was used in "Study 1," an analogue study involving undergraduate volunteers in half-hour helping interviews. It was further modified for "Study 2," which used actual therapy cases, additional rating scales, and therapist as well as client recall.

The results of these two studies comparing client and therapist perceptions of particular therapist responses with each other and with trained observers' ratings of response modes have been reported in a series of papers (Caskey, Barker, & Elliott, 1984; Elliott, 1979; Elliott, Barker, Caskey, & Pistrang, 1981, 1982). However, although the results were statistically significant, their modest size ($r = .10–.30$) meant that the results would not be particularly useful to therapists. In addition, we were left wondering whether the small correlations could be attributed to unreliable measures or to important discrepancies among the three perspectives.

As we studied the results, several methodological improvements were suggested or occurred to us: First, in measuring client and therapist perceptions of response modes, we had been relying on a free response format that required a messy subsequent process of transcription and content analysis. Accordingly, we devised a structured procedure for rating perceived therapist intentions (Elliott & Feinstein, 1978). Second, Les Greenberg suggested that we might do better to focus on significant therapeutic events.

It occurred to us that helpfulness ratings could be used to identify significantly helpful and hindering therapist interventions.

In 1978, using streamlined recall procedures and refined measures, Larry Feinstein and I carried out "Study 3," another analogue study (20-minute helping interviews with prescreened undergraduates as clients). Using audiotape recall, we had clients rate the helpfulness of all therapist interventions in the session; then, on the basis of these ratings, the client selected the four most and the four least helpful therapist responses in the session; a "second pass" recall was then conducted on these significant responses, with the client rating therapist intentions on a set of rating scales and giving an explanation of what made the response helpful or nonhelpful; subsequently, the therapist reviewed the tape and rated his or her intentions for a sample of responses, including those identified as significant by the client. Later, the therapist interventions were rated for response modes by trained observers.

The results of this study were more encouraging (Elliott, 1980; Elliott, 1985): For one thing, therapist intentions and client perceptions were found to correspond quite closely with observer response modes; in addition, clear evidence for the convergent and discriminant validity of response mode ratings was found (Elliott, 1980). Furthermore response modes and perceived intentions substantially predicted client helpfulness ratings. However, it also became clear that such associations, even though they accounted for 20–25% of the variance, were not specific enough to be useful to practicing therapists. This conclusion led us to the realization that, in general, response modes do not differ greatly in perceived helpfulness. Returning to our starting point, we concluded that contextual factors, including other facets of therapy process, must be at work. Consistent with this, we found that clients' qualitative descriptions of significant events (most and least helpful responses in a session) offered a rich source of information about the change process. These descriptions have subsequently provided the basis for a taxonomy of significantly helpful and hindering therapist responses (Elliott, Stiles, Shiffman, Barker, Burstein, & Goodman, 1982; Elliott & Feinstein, 1981; Elliott, 1985).

During this period, coinciding with my move from UCLA to the University of Toledo in 1978, my research began to focus more on significant psychotherapy change events. With the consultation and encouragement of Laura Rice and Les Greenberg, my students and I organized the Significant Events Project. We adapted the methods used in the previous analogue study (with Feinstein) to standard-length 50-minute sessions. To save time, we experimented with a speech compression device; unfortunately, it reduced audibility too much and had to be dropped. We had been using audiotape recall; however, at Don Kiesler's urging, we switched back to videotape recall, in order to be able to study kinesic behavior associated with significant events. In addition, we adapted the schedule of questions used during the second pass recall of selected significant events to make it consistent with Rice and Greenberg's (1984) work on task analysis.

The significant events project, which is still underway, involves a series of intensive case studies involving different types of therapy (e.g., Elliott, James, Shulman, & Cline, 1981). The goals of this project are as follows: (1) to develop and refine a taxonomy of significant change events; (2) to compare and cross-validate client and therapist helpfulness ratings with a variety of other methods of evaluating the effectiveness of therapist interventions; (3) to describe the nature and unfolding of particular types of significant change event.

Finally, we have recently developed a further adaptation of IPR: Retrospective Review (Elliott, Cline, & Reid, 1982), which involves making a composite videotape of significant events and replaying this tape for client and therapist after the conclusion of treatment. This is an exciting development, because it allows for two things: (1) a study of delayed and changing impacts of therapy events; and (2) measurement of the "test-retest" reliability of client and therapist helpfulness ratings.

A Survey of Process Research Using IPR

In this section, I will summarize the research to date which has used IPR to measure psychotherapy process. This research represents a variety of alternative methodological approaches, strategies, focuses, and uses of IPR. Thus, it seems reasonable to begin this survey by reviewing the methodological options taken by various researchers. This discussion will be followed by a summary of the psychometric and other information generated by IPR.

Methodological Options Used with IPR

IPR has been used to measure therapy in a surprising number of ways. Tables 14-1 through 14-4 summarize the major features of these uses. Examination of these tables suggests the following conclusions:

1. Researchers have used IPR to study four aspects of therapy process (see Tables 14-1 through 14-4): therapist response quality (e.g., helpfulness), therapist action or intention (e.g., explaining client), therapist or client state or content (e.g., annoyed), and significant events (e.g., insight). Therapist response quality is the most commonly studied kind of process.

2. IPR has generally been used to evaluate or describe therapist interventions rather than client participation in therapy.

3. Clients and therapists have both frequently been used as recall informants.

4. Most researchers have employed some sort of structured measurement format, most commonly rating scales; however, these have often been supplemented by free response formats.

5. Researchers have used a broad array of measurement units, most commonly either adopting some sort of linguistic unit (e.g., the speaking turn) or else allowing the informant to choose an "experiential unit" (i.e., corresponding to a subjective experience of the informant).

6. Researchers have usually asked informants to evaluate all units in a session ("complete sampling"); however, stratified sampling and sampling of significant events offer less time-consuming alternatives.

7. Researchers have used IPR to study a range of helping situations, including actual treatment, brief one-session helping interviews, and controlled experimental analogues.

Substantive Areas and Issues in the Use of IPR

Having reviewed the methodological options used in IPR research, I will now summarize the psychometric and substantive findings of these studies. This review will be organized into the four aspects of therapy process most commonly examined in this body of research.

IPR Measures of the Quality of Therapist Responses

IPR measures of therapist response quality (e.g., helpfulness, empathy; see Table 14-1) can be put to two major uses: First, IPR response quality measures constitute what have been referred to in the literature variously as measures of "suboutcome" (Rice & Greenberg, 1984) and "immediate criteria" for judging the effectiveness of therapist interventions (Robinson, 1950). Second, response quality measures can be used to identify significant change events in therapy, which can then be studied more thoroughly either with IPR or with more traditional process research measures.

Reliability   Although the n's are small, there are data on the internal (interitem) and temporal (rate–rerate) reliability of IPR response quality ratings. Internal reliabilities (assessed by comparing ratings of helpfulness, empathy, and cognitive and affective impact) were modest in the major study to examine them (Elliott, Barker, Caskey, & Pistrang, 1981: .50–.66). However, Dole and associates (1979) report data for their case study which indicate internal reliability (assessed by comparing helpfulness and empathy ratings) to be in the .90s. Elliott, Cline, and Reid (1982), in the only study to examine temporal reliability (by comparing original to retrospective helpfulness ratings), reported overall values in the .40 to .60 range, although there were considerable differences between cases. The safest conclusion is that IPR response quality measures are "noisy" measures of modest reliability and that more research is needed.

Convergent Validity   IPR measures of therapist response quality can be shown to be valid if they converge (correlate significantly) with measures of the same variable (e.g., helpfulness) taken from different measurement perspectives. Thus, comparisons of client, therapist, and observer ratings have generally produced r's in the .20–.40 range (Caskey, Barker, & Elliott, 1984; Elliott, 1985; Elliott, Cline, & Reid, 1982). That is, the measures possess statistically significant but modest degrees of convergent validity. It is likely that these values are attenuated by the modest reliability of the measures, and, in particular, by moment-to-moment idiosyncratic fluctuations in experienced response quality. Thus, client–therapist convergence on helpfulness and affective impact improved dramatically when ratings were averaged over entire sessions (Caskey, Barker, & Elliott, 1984); while client–observer convergence on empathy improved when ratings were averaged to the session level (Elliott, Filipovich, Harrigan, Gaynor, Reimschuesel, & Zapadka, 1982). Nevertheless, the response-level convergence is small enough to indicate strongly the need for using multiple perspectives to measure response quality.

Predictive Validity   The predictive validity of response quality ratings can be evaluated either by obtaining process ratings of what the client does next in the session ("sequential impact") or by collecting session outcome data (e.g., session helpfulness ratings) and then examining how well these scores relate to response quality ratings. With regard to sequential impact, we have found significant but small correlations ($r = .10$–$.24$) with client exploration (Elliott, Filipovich, Harrigan, Gaynor, Reimschuessel, & Zapadka, 1982; Elliott, Reimschuessel, Filipovich, Zapadka, Harrigan, & Gaynor, 1982) and significant moderate-sized correlations with client experiencing (Elliott, Klein, & Mathieu-Coughlan, 1983; $r = .35$ and $.45$ for client and therapist ratings, respectively). More impressively, IPR ratings have been found to be strong predictors ($r = .60$) of session outcome in three studies (Elliott, unpublished data, "Studies 1 & 2"; Brown, 1981).

Table 14-1 IPR Measures of Therapist Response Quality

Study	Person Measured	Perspective	Variable	Measurement Format	Unit	Sampling Strategy	Type and N of Interviews
Elliott et al., "Study 1"[a]	Therapist (T)	Client (C)	Helpfulness Empathy	6-point unipolar rating scales	Speaking turn[e]	Stratified	30-minute 1-shot (N=28)
Elliott et al., "Study 2"[b]	T	C, T	Helpfulness Empathy Affective impact Cognitive impact	7-point bipolar scales	Turn[e]	Stratified	Ongoing therapy (N=16)
Elliott, "Study 3"[c]	T	C	Helpfulness	9-point bipolar scale	Turn[e]	Complete	20-minute 1-shot (N=24)
Elliott et al., "Case Studies"[d]	T	C, T	Helpfulness[f]	9-point bipolar scale	Turn[e]	Complete	Short-term therapy (N=6 ×12 sessions)
Young, 1980[a]	T	C	Empathy	7-point scale	Predetermined points	Stratified	Experimental analogue (N=24)
Brown, 1980	T	C	Empathy	6-point unipolar mechanical scale	Experiential	Complete	20-minute 1-shot (N=15)
Dole et al., 1979, 1982	T	C	Helpfulness Empathy	5-point unipolar scales	Client–therapist turn pair	Complete	Ongoing counseling (N=20 sessions)
Barkham & Shapiro, in press	T	C	Empathy[g]	3-point bipolar mechanical scale	Experiential	Complete	Ongoing therapy (N=16)

[a]Elliott, Barker, Caskey, & Pistrang, 1981, 1982; Elliott, Filipovich, Harrigan, Gaynor, Reimschuessel, & Zapadka, 1982: unpublished data. [b]Elliott, Barker, Caskey & Pistrang, 1981, 1982; Caskey, Barker & Elliott, 1984; Elliott, Reimschuessel, Filipovich, Zapadka, Harrigan & Gaynor, 1982; unpublished data. [c]Elliott, 1985; unpublished data. [d]Elliott, James, Shulman, & Cline, 1981; Elliott, Cline, & Reid, 1982. [e]Client had option to divide turn into smaller or larger units. [f]Retrospective (posttherapy) ratings also obtained. [g]In vivo ratings also obtained.

Objective Correlates of Experienced Response Quality   In addition to psychometric considerations of reliability and validity, it is also important to consider what observable therapist behaviors are associated with client and therapist response quality ratings. A number of studies have addressed this question (Brown, 1981; Elliott, 1985; Elliott, Barker, Caskey, & Pistrang, 1981, 1982; Young, 1980a). These studies have identified a broad range of objective correlates of perceived response quality, most commonly, collaborative manner, interpretation, and nonquestions. They have also suggested a central role for more global factors in determining response quality; the most promising global factor is attitude toward therapist [e.g., Young's, 1980a, "warm–cold" manipulation, or evidence for the role of therapeutic alliance or collaboration in Elliott, Barker, Caskey, and Pistrang (1981)].

Thus, IPR measures of response quality are usable but "noisy" measures with moderate levels of convergent and predictive validity. The fact that stronger relationships with other variables are obtained when ratings are averaged across segments or sessions suggests that there is much unpredictable fluctuation in perceived helpfulness at the response level. In any case, it is recommended that quality ratings be obtained from both clients and therapist and for entire sessions (to facilitate averaging). Further psychometric study of these important measures is urgently needed.

IPR Measures of Therapist Intentions

Another promising application of IPR is its use for obtaining client and therapist perceptions of therapist interpersonal intentions or "response modes" (see Table 14-2; also Stiles, Hill, this volume; Elliott, Stiles, Shiffman, Barker, Burstein, & Goodman, 1982). Informants' self-reports obtained via IPR can then be compared to the more usual observer measures of response modes.

Construct Validity   Although there are no data on the reliability of client and therapist ratings of therapist intentions there is consistent evidence for their construct validity: First, in two studies using a free response format and content analysis approach to measuring therapist intentions (Elliott, "Studies 1 & 2") correlations among client, therapist, and observer ratings of the same therapist intention variables (e.g., gathering information) had average values in the .20s. In the one study (Elliott, 1985; "Study 3") to use a structured intention rating format (Elliott & Feinstein, 1978), larger values (mean $r =$ .30–.44) obtained. Second, in these studies, there was very little overlap among therapist intention variables (mean $r = .00$ to $-.10$). These two findings add up to a demonstration of classical construct validity (cf. Campbell & Fiske, 1959).

Predictive Validity   Two kinds of predictive validity criterion are available for IPR therapist intention measures: sequential impact (on client exploration immediately following the therapist response) and immediate perception of effectiveness (measured by response quality ratings by client or therapist).

With regard to sequential impact, client and therapist perceptions of gathering information and explaining have been found to be associated with increased client exploration (Elliott, "Studies 1, 2, & 3"). In these studies, the best predictors of response quality ratings were the intention ratings by the same person—that is, client perceptions of therapist intentions best predicted client helpfulness ratings, while therapist perceptions were the best predictors of therapist helpfulness ratings ($R = .30–.49$; Elliott,

Table 14-2 IPR Measures of Therapist Action

Study	Person Measured	Perspective	Variable	Measurement Format	Unit	Sampling Strategy	Type and N of Interviews
Elliott et al., "Study 1"[a]	T	C	Intention (6 dimensions)	Free response, w/content analysis	Turn	Stratified	30-minute 1-shot (N=28)
Elliott et al., "Study 2"[b]	T	C, T	Intention (6 dimensions)	Free response, w/content analysis	Turn	Stratified	Ongoing therapy (N=16)
Elliott, "Study 3"[c]	T	C, T	Intention (10 dimensions)	2- or 3-point scales	Turn	Complete	20-minute 1-shot (N=24)
Hill et al., 1979	T	T	Intention (10 or 12 categories)	Free response, w/content analysis, later, checklist	Sentence	Stratified	Ongoing counseling (N=7)
Santa-Barbara & Pinsof, 1976	T	T	Action	Free response	Experiential	Significant event	Family therapy (N=?)
Hill, 1983	T	T	Clinical intention (14 dimensions)	Checklist	Turn	Complete	Ongoing therapy (N=?)

[a]Elliott, Barker, Caskey & Pistrang, 1981, 1982; unpublished data. [b]Elliott, Barker, Caskey, & Pistrang, 1981, 1982; Caskey, Barker & Elliott, 1984; Elliott, Reimschuessel, Filipovich, Zapadka, Harrigan, & Gaynor, 1982; unpublished data. [c]Elliott, 1980, 1985; Elliott & Feinstein, 1978; unpublished data.

Elliott, Filipovich, Harrigan, Gaynor, Reimschuessel, & Zapadka, 1982; unpublished data.

Barker, Caskey, & Pistrang, 1981, 1982). In addition, in "Study 3" (Elliott, 1985) therapists rated their intentions using the improved, structured technique; these ratings also predicted client helpfulness $(R = .43)$.

Conclusions   IPR measures of therapist intentions using both free response and structured formats have been shown in these studies to have adequate construct (convergent and discriminant) and predictive validity. On the other hand, no direct evidence of the reliability of these measures is available, so that there is no way of knowing the degree to which the validity coefficients may be attenuated by measurement error. The available data, while not extensive, certainly justify the further use of these measures. The structured rating format (Elliott & Feinstein, 1978) is much easier to use and is therefore recommended for most purposes. Along this line, Hill (1983; Hill & O'Grady, 1985) has recently developed another structured IPR procedure for obtaining ratings of therapist clinical intentions (e.g., "encouraging a sense of self control"); this new measure warrants further use as well.

IPR Measures of State or Content

In contrast to the areas of IPR research just reviewed, IPR research on client or therapist state or content (see Table 14-3) is less developed, consisting for the most part of disparate studies which ask different questions and generally do not build on one another.

Katz and Resnikoff (1977) conducted a rate–rerate reliability study using a peer analogue situation in which client and therapist ratings of their own comfort were obtained both *in vivo* and immediately after the interview via IPR. The results suggest that while client ratings of own discomfort had adequate temporal reliability $(r = .63)$, the therapist role interferes with reporting or recalling comfort. Young (1980c) also addressed rate–rerate reliability, finding somewhat higher values.

Hill, Siegelman, Gronsky, Sturniolo, and Fretz (1981) carried out the best designed, most interesting, study using IPR measures of client or therapist state: Clients and therapists used a checklist format to rate their own affective state, the affective state they believed they communicated to the other, and their perception of the other's affective state. These ratings were obtained at 1-minute intervals throughout a brief helping interview. Proportion of agreement between actual and expressed affect yielded a measure of *intra*congruence, while proportion of agreement between actual affect and that perceived by the other yielded a measure of *inter*congruence.

High internal reliability was demonstrated for the intracongruence measures. Convergent validity, given by the intercongruence measure, was modest. Several of the IPR congruence measures also predicted session outcome: client intracongruence (really an index of self-perceived "openness") significantly predicted client evaluations, while therapist intercongruence (agreement between client and therapist on therapist affect) predicted scores on the Barrett-Lennard Relationship Inventory.

Dole and associates (1979, 1982) have carried out a number of case studies in which they measured the content of therapists' thoughts or "internal speech" during counseling sessions. In these case studies, they classified therapists' free response retrospections using a carefully developed content analysis system measuring six dimensions of attentional focus: time frame (past, present, future), location (in session vs. out of session), focus (client vs. therapist), locus (behavior vs. inference), orientation (professional vs. personal), and mode (cognition vs. negative or positive affect). Factor analy-

Table 14-3   IPR Measures of Therapist and Client State and Content

Study	Person Measured	Perspective	Variable	Measurement Format	Unit	Sampling Strategy	Type and N of Interviews
Katz & Resnikoff, 1977	C, T (self)	C, T	Comfort[a]	5-point bipolar mechanical scale	Experiential	Complete	15-minute peer analogue (N=10)
Young, 1980b	C	C	Comfort[b] Expressiveness[b]	7-point bipolar scales	Predetermined	Stratified	20-minute experimental analogue (N=12)
Hill et al., 1981	C, T	C, T	Congruence[c]; Own affect, Other's affect, Own communicated affect (13 categories)	Checklist	1-minute time samples	Complete	30-minute 1-shot (N=40)
Johnson, 1978	T	T	Immediate subjective feelings[d]	5-point unipolar scales; free response w/content analysis	Predetermined	Stratified	4-minute film analogue (N=4)
Dole et al., 1978, 1982	T	T	Content of internal speech (6 aspects)	Free response w/content analysis	Experiential	Complete	Ongoing counseling (N=20 sessions)

[a]In vivo ratings also obtained. [b]Repeated recall after 20 minutes. [c]Two kinds of congruence measured: intercongruence was agreement between own affect as perceived by self and other; intracongruence was agreement between self-perceived experienced and communicated affect. [d]Rating scales: liking for client, client attractiveness, empathy, own comfort; content analysis categories: sympathy, identification, defensiveness, anger.

ses of these ratings generated unique content factors for each therapist, each with apparently high internal reliability, but having little if any relationship to client response quality ratings or to therapist response modes. They concluded that therapist retrospections are largely independent of observable therapist behaviors and client satisfaction, and that each therapist has his or her own pattern of retrospections.

Finally, Johnson (1978), one of Dole's associates, used a film analogue in combination with IPR to study gender differences in therapists' reactions to angry and depressed clients (she found that female therapists reacted with more empathy and more anger). She used both free response and structured measurement formats, and reported that the free response format generated richer data.

Conclusions   IPR has great potential as a measure of client and therapist psychological state (cf. Horowitz, 1979); unfortunately, this potential has not yet been exploited. Much more research, especially of a programmatic kind, is needed. Hill and associates' (1981) checklist measure of affective state might be a useful starting place.

IPR Measures of Significant Therapy Events

As Johnson (1978) noted, using structured data collection formats may fail to exploit the richness of the information provided by IPR. Thus, as researchers have begun to apply IPR to the study of significant therapy events, they have adopted free response formats and qualitative data analysis procedures (cf. Bogdan & Taylor, 1975), in order to avoid the inherent restrictions and potential biases of rating scales and checklists (see Table 14-4).

Helpful and Hindering Events   As mentioned earlier, my colleagues and I have conducted several studies aimed at discovering types of significant therapy change event (Elliott, 1985; Elliott, James, Shulman, & Cline, 1981). In both studies, clients identified significant therapist responses using helpfulness ratings; they were then asked to describe what it was about the event which made it significantly helpful or hindering. In the first study (referred to in this chapter as "Study 3," Elliott, 1985), I found eight clusters of significantly helpful events: new perspective, understanding, problem solution, clarification of problem, reassurance, personal contact, focusing awareness, and client involvement. In addition, there were six clusters of hindering events: misperception, misdirection, negative therapist reaction, unwanted thoughts, unwanted responsibility, and repetition. Most of these clusters of significantly helpful events were then found to be associated with observer response mode ratings or perceived therapist intentions.

Next, Elliott, James, Shulman, and Cline (1981) applied the same approach in a systematic single case study. They found five clusters of helpful events: insight, painful awareness, painful opening, involvement, and personal contact. They also found three clusters of hindering events: misperception, unmet dependency, and feared hopelessness. Involvement events were associated with positive shifts in client experiencing, while unmet dependency events involved negative shifts in experiencing. Less helpful therapy sessions were characterized by insight and misperception events, while more helpful sessions were characterized by painful opening events. Finally, unmet dependency and feared hopelessness events switched from hindering to helpful, while misperception events became more negative by the end of treatment.

Table 14-4 IPR Measures of Significant Therapy Events

Study	Person Measured	Perspective	Variable	Measurement Format	Unit	Identification Strategy	Type and N of Interviews
Elliott, "Study 3"[a]	T, C	C	What made event significantly helpful/hindering?	Free response w/cluster analysis	Turn	Helpfulness ratings	20-minute 1-shot (N=24)
Elliott et al., "Case Studies"[b]	T, C	C, T	Context of event; T intention; What made it significant?; Impact on C; What changed?	Free response w/cluster, content analysis and verbatim	C–T–C sequence	Helpfulness ratings	Short-term therapy (N= 3×12 sessions)
Brown, 1980	T	C	What action led you to believe he understood you?	Free response, verbatim	Experiential	Empathy ratings	20-minute 1-shot (N=15)
Shonkoff & Jones, 1979[c]	C, T	T	Nature of interaction; T's feelings and thoughts; T's coping strategies	Free response w/content analysis	Experiential	Distress ratings by T, observer	Suicide hotline calls (N=35)
Wagner & Weidle, 1982	C	C	What was going through your mind?	Free response w/qualitative analysis	40-second time samples	Presence of cognitive "knots"	In progress
Kommer & Bastine, 1982	T	T	Verbalize everything that occupied you at the time.	Free response w/content analysis	Action sequence (15–30 seconds)	Most important episode	Gestalt therapy (N=1)

[a]Elliott, 1985; Elliott & Feinstein, 1978; unpublished data. [b]Elliott, James, Shulman, & Cline, 1981; Elliott, Cline, & Reid, 1982. [c]Used immediate free recall with aid of observer's notes but without use of recordings.

Empathic and Nonempathic Events   Brown (1981) examined the characteristics of therapist responses which made clients feel particularly understood or misunderstood. He asked clients to describe what it was that led them to believe the therapist understood them; he noted the repeated theme of therapist accuracy in these events. He also identified numerous behavioral correlates of the events.

Therapist Crisis Events   Shonkoff and Jones (1979) used a procedure very similar to IPR for examining suicide hot-line workers' "moments of distress." The worker was asked to describe (1) the nature of the stressor, (2) their initial subjective reaction to the stressor, and (3) how they coped with the situation. Five types of stressor event were found: suicide issues, anger–hostility, depression–loss, sex-related, and communication difficulties. Qualitative analyses of subjective reactions to the stressors suggested five types of negative reaction: frustration, feeling inadequate, anxiousness, feeling overwhelmed, and feeling uncertain. Next, qualitative analyses of successful worker coping strategies turned up two broad strategies: turning attention to caller (e.g., empathizing) and turning attention to self (e.g., telling self to "hang in there"). Lastly, the use of these successful coping strategies was associated with call outcome ratings by the worker and an observer.

European Research in Progress   Finally, several teams of German researchers are using IPR in ongoing studies of significant therapy events: Wagner and her associates (e.g., Wagner *et al.*, 1982) have used IPR to examine students' "cognitive knots" in learning situations. ("Cognitive knots" are defined as psychological paradoxes produced by imperative cognitions or "shoulds.") They have now begun studying similar client cognitive knots in psychotherapy, especially cognitive therapy (Wagner & Weidle, 1982). Kommer and Bastine (1982), on the other hand, are focusing on the structure of therapist cognitions (especially regarding clinical intentions) during significant change events in psychotherapy. The work of these two teams of researchers illustrates the potential of IPR for developing models of client and therapist problem-solving processes (cf. Rice & Greenberg, 1984).

Conclusion   The studies reviewed serve to illustrate the potential of open-ended approaches using IPR to study significant therapy events. Even though there is less research in this area than in the other three areas reviewed, it is my opinion that this is the area in which IPR has the greatest potential for contributing to our understanding of the psychotherapy process.

Practical and Validity Issues in the Use of IPR

What are the practical and methodological issues and problems involved in the use of IPR? How can these best be dealt with? In my discussion, I will first deal with preliminary practical considerations that may govern a researcher's decision to use IPR or not, then I will describe six critical methodological pitfalls or "validity threats" involved in the use of IPR, along with suggestions for minimizing them.

Resources Needed for Using IPR in Process Research

In order to use IPR as a therapy process research tool, a number of resources are required. These requirements make IPR a time-consuming, expensive data collection procedure:

1. *Researcher Time and Energy.* Largely because the procedure and equipment are relatively complex, using IPR in research requires a major commitment of time and energy on the part of the researcher.

2. *Facilities and Equipment.* In order to use IPR, the researcher also needs observation facilities (e.g., one-way mirror) and recording and playback equipment.

3. *Consent and Active Cooperation of Clients and Therapists.* Like all recording of therapy, IPR is moderately intrusive and potentially reactive. Clients should be carefully selected. IPR appears to work best with YAVIS-type clients, but is not restricted to them. Offsetting these limitations is the fact that the procedure often helps to uncover difficulties in the therapy process and may enhance the assimilation of therapeutic work. One problem which may affect the cooperation of clients and therapist is the time-consuming nature of IPR (2½ to 3 hours per session).

From all this, it should be clear that there are much easier ways to study psychological helping processes (e.g., traditional process ratings). This means that the use of IPR as a research method can only be justified by the fact that in some cases it is the *only* way to obtain otherwise unobtainable information about client and therapist perceptions and experiences of particular therapeutic events.

IPR Validity Threats and Suggestions for Dealing with Them

Measurement Assumptions and Validity Threats   Although there has been little actual investigation of the theoretical basis and validity of IPR, writers (e.g., Bloom, 1954; Dole & associates, 1982; Kagan, 1975; Meichenbaum & Cameron, 1980) are fairly consistent in describing both the factors which are theorized to make it possible and the limitations which may affect its validity or range of application. The factors described earlier as the theoretical basis of IPR suggest that IPR is itself a complex process. Thus, it is not surprising that, as is the case with all assessment methods, the validity of IPR depends on a network of assumptions. These assumptions include the following:

1. The informant was *aware* at the time of what he or she was experiencing or perceiving.
2. The informant *remembers* during recall what he or she was experiencing or perceiving at the time.
3. The informant has the *language* needed to describe the experience.
4. The informant is *willing* to reveal to the recall consultant what it was that she or he was experiencing.
5. The informant *avoids fabrication* of data; that is, he or she does not feel pressured to invent material when there is nothing to describe.
6. The aspect of subjective experience under study occurs at the *event level* that is, it is not a global, higher-order, meta-, or summative experience or impression.

Potential violations of these assumptions give rise to IPR's particular "validity threats" (cf. Cook & Campbell, 1979). The number and variety of these threats also attests to the fact that there is no simple answer to the question, "Is IPR valid?" Consequently, each threat should be examined carefully in order to make sure that it is being minimized and does not exceed acceptable levels in a given situation.

Unconscious Processes   IPR cannot be used to tap phenomena of which the informant is completely unaware, for example, the psychological processes associated with certain stylistic variables (e.g., vocal quality; Rice & Kerr, this volume). More problematic is the possibility that clients may be unaware of certain psychological states, perhaps because of warding off processes. However, my experience with IPR suggests that clients are much more aware of their subtle defensive processes and momentary psychological states than most observers or therapists believe.

Forgetting   IPR appears to be a powerful technique for stimulating memory; however, it seems to follow a standard memory decay curve (Bloom, 1954). In our experience, recall is easiest if done immediately after the session, and becomes increasingly difficult if delayed by more than two days. Thus, IPR should be carried out as soon as possible after the therapy session, in order to minimize memory limitations, particularly for clients.

Language Unavailable   In our first studies using IPR (Elliott, 1979; Elliott, Barker, Caskey, & Pistrang, 1982), my colleagues and I found that many clients had difficulty describing therapist intentions. When client perceptions did not correspond to those of trained observers, we were left to wonder if this was due in part to the clients' lack of adequate language for describing perceived intentions. Two remedies for this problem are to replace the free response format with a structured rating procedure (e.g., Elliott, Shapiro, & McGlenn, 1986) and to use a skilled recall consultant, who can use nonleading probes to help the informant give his or her experience some approximate expression.

Social Desirability   Perhaps the most worrisome threat to the validity of IPR data is the possibility that the informant will tell the recall consultant what he or she believes the recall consultant wants to hear (cf. Meichenbaum & Butler, 1979). Furthermore, this threat may be compounded by experimenter bias in the form of the recall consultant asking leading questions, or putting words in the informant's mouth. The problem of social desirability can best be minimized by screening clients with a social desirability measure, and by carefully training recall consultants to avoid leading responses.

Fabrication   The validity threat of fabrication works in combination with one of the previous threats, effectively disguising problems of awareness, memory, language, or social desirability. The fact that these other threats may be disguised by informant fabrication is especially disturbing. At issue is the possibility that the informant will not admit it when he or she has, for one reason or another, nothing to describe but will instead feel obligated to invent, "reconstruct," or fabricate something in order to please the recall consultant. Most commonly, informants will report how they are now interpreting what happened, rather than describing their recollections. This is particularly likely when subsequent events have altered the meaning of the original event.

The problem of fabrication or, to put it more kindly, "reconstruction," is a thorny one, touching on philosophical issues regarding the verification of personal experience. Some, such as Wittgenstein (1953) or Kagan (personal communication), would say that such questions are irrelevant or meaningless. Unfortunately, they will not go away. Some possible strategies for dealing with the possibility of fabrication include: encouraging the informant to adopt a "there-and-then" focus; asking the informant to distinguish "then" and "now" perceptions; and giving the informant permission not to say anything. In addition, the researcher should collect validating information from the other participant (e.g., therapist) and by using observer process ratings.

Inappropriate Unit of Analysis   The final validity threat comes from the fact that IPR focuses on particular events or responses within a therapy session. The problem is that some phenomena occur at a more general level of analysis, for example, global feelings about the therapist as a person. In particular, the therapist speaking turn may be too small a unit for measuring many process variables, including empathy (Elliott, Filipovich, Harrigan, Gaynor, Reimschuessel, & Zapadka, 1982). The implication is that researchers should limit their use of IPR to variables which occur meaningfully at the event level. Variables which show strong autocorrelations or much unpredictable variation at the response level are likely instances of this problem and would probably be more validly measured by using larger units of analysis such as the episode (cf. Rice & Greenberg, 1984) or the session.

IPR in the Analysis of a Segment of Therapy

In this section I will illustrate the use of IPR in analyzing therapy process. The intent will be to highlight the use of IPR; therefore, I will simply present a transcript of the segment, along with what the client and therapist said about it in IPR. More thorough examples of the use of IPR for identifying and analyzing significant therapy events can be found elsewhere (e.g., Elliott, 1983c, 1984). The segment presented here comes from the first of our case studies (cf. Elliott, James, Shulman, & Cline, 1981). The client, case ''300,'' was a female undergraduate in her early 20s who sought treatment for problems centering around interpersonal anxiety. The therapist was a male clinical psychologist (the author) with 6 years therapy experience. The approach taken with this client was eclectic and broadly psychodynamic. The segment comes from about 30 minutes into the first session and was selected because it contained interesting running commentary on the therapy process by both client and therapist. At the beginning of the segment, the client is discussing her application to take part in an experimental living situation and the fact that she will feel rejected if her application is turned down.

Segment 300-1-560[1]

C1:   . . mm . . mm . . but, you know, it's just like the oth— You know, I— It's not gonna be— I just know that's how I'm gonna feel and I don't know . .'h. It doesn't mean th(h)ey've rejected me and all, you know. I—it really (T: Mhm) just means that they— That's somethin' they can't do yet And this is talkin' about people in < place name > that this has (T: Mhm) never been done before an' h

T1.1:   That's the rational intellectual part of you sayin' that, right? (C: Yeah). But I think the feeling part is saying, "Oh my God, you know, (C: *laugh*) here's these people I trusted and I've op— made myself vulnerable. An'— (C: hh) an'— an' I've gone into therapy (*1.5 seconds*) partly cause of them (1.2) just when I— and made myself vulnerable and then just when that's goin' on, maybe they're gonna, close

---

[1]Transcription symbols:

h,'h: breaths

=: no gap between speaking turns

/: beginning of overlap with other speaker

>: end of overlap with other speaker

RC: Recall Consultant

the door." (1.8) (C: Mhm) An' that doesn't *feel* good. (C: Mm-mm mhm) Is— That's the feeling part, and then the rational part's saying, 'h "But really you know this <living situation> is just an experiment anyway and"

(Client recall: That was an 8¼ <on 9-point helpfulness scale>: That kind of summed up I think how I was feeling and it also— I kind of knew that I didn't have to worry about trying to analyze it myself or be intellectual about it. It was just OK to say how I felt about it, no explanations, no trying to put it in an intellectual perspective necessary.)
(Therapist recall: At the time it was a 5.5, but now it's a 6.5. It was too long, but basically it was good.)

C1.1: (laughs) uh— (1.2) Yeah— (2.3) So I— I— I don't know, Umm— (1.5) mm (1.5)

T1.2: I think I threw you off there. Did I? (.6)
(Client recall: Helpfulness: 4)
(Therapist recall: Helpfulness. 6: I thought I talked too long.)

C2: Mm-mm (T: OK) (7.5) mmm I don't— uh— I don't know if this makes— where it's going to go, but— 'hh I— I just know umm— (1.0) I don't know how in touch I (h) am with my feelings and all. = An that's another thing that really bothers (T: Mm) me, you know. Like I know 'h, you know, this is really important. Like I've had a lot of anxiety (T: Mhm) about doin' this (T: Mhm) and I would have liked to have just been able just to cry about it and get it out of my system / but I couldn't do that.

T2: Mhm. I think> you're in touch with some feelings right now. Or that you— they're right sort of, pretty close. An', you're scared by 'em. (C: Mm) Is that accurate? (2.9)
(Client recall: That was a 2 < =greatly hindering>, because I felt like there was something that he was saying I needed to look at then and I didn't know what it was.)
(Therapist recall: 3.5: I scared the shit out of her there. I think that frightened her; I don't think she was willing to get into that.)

C3: Hmm. I'm not— (h) I don't know. Hmm. (.5)

T3: And I guess the image I have is they're right, 'h *here* and you're not quite in touch but you know that they're *there* (C: h) and you're not sure you want to touch 'em right now. (5.6)
(Client recall: That's a 2 again, <although> I don't think it's the same response. I still felt in the dark. <RC: You weren't sure what he was talking about?> Yeah.)
(Therapist recall: 3: I should have given her more space.)

C4: Hm. (2.8) hh I'm— I'm not real sure. I'm uh— hm (.5) (T: Mm) (12.5; *T drinks from cup*) and I just— (1.4) see, I just think I'm lookin' for a (*laughs through:*) expectations <about what I'm supposed to do in therapy>. I don't know. (*laughs through*)

T4: Pardon? (.4)
(Client helpfulness: 4; therapist helpfulness: 5)

C5: I think I'm looking for expect— expectations. I don't know if I'm, you know, on the right— This is one of the things that I— I get afraid of is, goin' off the track or something', I know I can do that. I mean I don't know. (1.2)

T5: There's somethin' you're thinkin' about talkin' about. (C: Mm) (1.2) Is that it? (.6)
(Client recall: 3: I still don't think at that point I knew; I understood what he was saying, <but> I didn't understand what he was referring to at that point. (laugh).)
(Therapist recall: 3: Oh God, that was really painful.)

C6: I'm— I don't know (it) for sure. I— I just know that, you know, I was thinkin' about— Been thinking about this and what all it's gonna involve and things that I (T: Mhm) have to talk— You know, things that I know. 'h (1.2) And like I know, like the reje(h)ction thing was one thing. You know, like— like how I'm gonna feel if this community rejects me. (T: ?) 'h And I was just thinkin' in terms of the therapy, well it's just gonna— There's been other times in my life where

I'm sure I've felt— felt that but I don't know if I did or not even. But 'h I don't know if it's just sayin' that or not, you know. (T: Uhh uh.) Might just— <be> Significant— You know. I know, things and all.=

T6:   Let's see, I'm ha— I'm tryin' to put this together 'cause I think it's— it's sort of not quite put together for you, either. And I'm— (1.0) One thing I'm— one *feeling* I'm getting, I'm not sure it's true, is that I think you're having some doubts about whether you want to *do* this here, 'Cause of you're afraid it'll make you feel vulnerable an'— 'h an' you might get rejected and they're— I think you're thinking of them as like a safety net or something, 'h for your therapy. (.9) (C: Mm) If you fell off the rope or somethin' they'd catch ya with their love or something. An'— an' now you're sayin' "I don't know if they'll be there for me and I'm not sure I want to talk about this. = I'm not sure I want to get into this stuff." Or maybe part of you is saying that. (3.1) Is that accurate? (4.5) (*Client recall: 1.5: That wasn't right. What he said wasn't right. <RC: So it was hindering because it wasn't right?> Yeah. <Second pass recall:> Just that whole "safety net to catch" me that he said; I didn't like looking at it <the therapy> that way. I felt angry at the time; it was unpleasant to think of it that way.* (*Therapist recall: 3: That was where I was pushing her. It was wrong. I was checking to see if she wanted to be here.*)

C7:   Hm. (15.5) 'h I don't know. I feel— I don't know I— (T: Mhm) um— (6.3) I guess I really like where I'm at— at now because 'h with them, I mean, I *know* (1.3) as much— Like all things I told you about being independent and everything else, I've always wanted, so(h)mebody to be there, more or less. 'h And, (T: Uhh uh.) you know, that need for people has always been— has— has always been there in a real— (.8) (T: Real strong.)=real apparent to me. (T: Yeah). As much as— um— (1.5) As much as I've tried to (h) get—really get control of it and get— get away from it, and everything else, so that (T: Mhm) 'h (1.6) it's— This is just not somethin' that I would want to. (*Client recall: In terms of what I just said, that's really what I needed to say, so in a sense that previous <therapist> response put me on the track of what I really needed to get out, but I thought only because it was challenging to me to explain. I still felt hindered at that point, but it didn't prevent me from talking about it. <RC: So in retrospect you may rate it differently. At the time you felt this is really hindering but you also saw it had some benefit because it challenged.> Yep, and what I was saying there was really to the point, more than everything else had been, so it might be that that was at the other end of the scale. I don't know. <RC: Do you want to put a "now" rating?> That would be like an "8". <RC: Because it challenged you and pushed you into saying exactly what you wanted to say, which comes following his last response.> Yeah.*)

This segment, together with the ratings and descriptions collected via IPR, provides a portrait of a typical early therapy process. Through it, client and therapist are groping toward a common understanding of treatment content and tasks: T1.1 is significantly helpful for the client; it tells her she does not have to intellectualize in therapy. Thus unfettered, the client provides new material, which the therapist misunderstands (T2–T5). The therapist sees his responses at this point as introducing unwanted thoughts, but the client experiences them as mystifying references to hypothetical feelings which are out of her current frame of reference (this would probably come closest to being a misdirection event). The therapist's repeated confusing references lead the client to express out loud her questions about what is going to be expected of her in therapy (C4–C6). The therapist then (T6) mistakes the clients' questions for doubts about whether the client wants to be in therapy at all. This makes the client feel misunderstood; in addition, his reference to her needing the support of the people in her community during her therapy introduces an ideas which she finds unpleasant and which makes her angry. (Thus, from the therapist's point of view, T6 was a misperception event, while the client's initial reaction contains elements of both misperception and unwanted thoughts, although the latter is probably predominant.)

In C7, the client tries to clarify the misunderstanding by disclosing more new material about her dependence–independence conflict; in retrospect, she now sees T6 as significantly helpful in challenging her to disclose this essential information (it would probably be classified as an involvement event).

Thus, T6 and C7 are a turning point, because from this point on, the misunderstandings and confusions begin to clear up. While the misunderstandings and confusions of this segment were uncomfortable for client and therapist, the process of clarification begun here led to several other significantly helpful events during the remainder of this initial session, with the result that the client emerged from the session with insight, confidence, and trust in the therapist, and with an understanding of what she could expect from subsequent sessions. Furthermore, the IPR ratings and commentary provide a much more precise picture of the nature of this process.

Conclusions and Recommendations

In this chapter I have reviewed the historical and theoretical basis of IPR; the history of my own use of the method; the uses to which IPR has been put; the empirical results of those various uses; validity threats and practical suggestions for using IPR in psychotherapy research; and a segment of therapy illuminated by IPR. By way of summing up, I will now present the following recommendations and conclusions.

Methodological Conclusions and Recommendations

Psychometric Status of IPR Measures   IPR measures of several areas of therapy process (therapist response quality and intentions) are psychometrically adequate for wider research use. However, it is clear that these measures are not as "clean" as might be desired by methodological purists. In any case, further traditional psychometric work is needed, including research on the reliability (internal and temporal) and validity (convergent and predictive) of the measures.

Untapped Aspects of Therapy Process   IPR has natural potential for measuring client and therapist psychological states, client response quality, and client intentions. However, adequate IPR measures have not yet been developed for mesuring these aspects of therapy process. Hill et al. (1981) have made a good start at measuring client and therapist psychological states with their measure of actual, communicated, and perceived feelings, but more work is needed on this measure, which was actually developed to measure "congruence." No measures have yet been devised for client response quality (e.g., "working") and a draft content analysis measure of client intentions (e.g., exploring, avoiding) has only recently been piloted (Elliott, Reimschuessel, Sack, Cislo, James, & Hebert, 1983). Such measures should be developed and refined.[2] On the

---

[2]A briefer, more structured IPR procedure for significant therapy events has recently been developed (Elliott, Shapiro, & McGlenn, 1986); the procedure includes Hill & O'Grady's (1984) therapist intention measure, and new rating scales for therapeutic impact (cf. Elliott, 1985) and client intentions and feelings (cf. Elliott, Reimschuessel et al., 1983).

other hand, it will probably not be useful to develop IPR measures of style (a variable such as voice quality is likely to be out of informants' awareness).

Discovery-Oriented Nature of IPR   The research reviewed earlier suggests that it is important to continue to develop structured IPR measurement formats with good reliability and validity; however, it is also essential to exploit the power of open-ended uses of IPR for uncovering subtle and covert aspects of therapy process. Examples of such processes include complex chains of client or therapist inference and implicit and shared meanings (cf. Kommer & Bastine, 1982; Spence, 1982). The significant events schedule is an example of a format that exploits the richness possible with IPR. Unfortunately, a major stumbling block for such an approach is analysis of the qualitative data generated.[3] Methods such as cluster and content analysis need further development.

Theoretical Conclusions

IPR and Therapy Theories   IPR has untapped potential for testing therapy theories. Whereever theory is articulated to the point of specifying change mechanisms and precise therapist interventions (e.g., cognitive therapy of depression), IPR should be employed to provide a test of the theory (e.g., Cline & Elliott, 1985).

Indirect and Unexpected Change Processes   Using IPR to study therapy makes it apparent that many interventions have effects on clients which were not intended by their therapists. This is implicit in the relatively small correlations between client and therapist perceptions of response quality and therapist intentions. The role and nature of indirect and unexpected change processes has not been adequately addressed by theorists (but see Spence, 1979). Theoretical and empirical work on therapeutic paradox and client cognitive processes provide possibly relevant leads. Nevertheless, the existence of unexpected effects suggests that therapy may involve an element of basic unpredictability, a possibility that warrants further investigation.

Implications for Therapy Practice

Clinically Useful Therapy Research   It is common among clinical researchers to lament the lack of influence of their research on clinical practice, including their own (e.g., Barlow, 1981; Elliott, 1983a; Luborsky, 1972). However, I have found personally that my research with IPR has changed how I do therapy: In using IPR over the past few years I have seen that clients are much more aware of what is going on in the therapy process than most therapists are willing to give them credit for. For example, many are quite aware of their own defensive processes, even though they might never spontaneously admit this to the therapist. This understanding has helped me to discover the usefulness of carrying out IPR-like procedures during therapy sessions and has led me to be much freer in discussing the process of therapy with clients.

---

[3]Rennie (1984, 1985) has recently reported the use of IPR with a grounded theory approach (Glaser & Strauss, 1967) in a series of intriguing qualitative investigations of the structure of client experiences in psychotherapy.

References

Barkham, M. J., & Shapiro, D. Counselor verbal response modes and experienced empathy. *Journal of Counseling Psychology*, in press.

Barlow, D. H. (Ed.). Empirical practice and realistic research: New opportunities for clinicians. *Journal of Consulting and Clinical Psychology*, 1981, *49*, 147–219.

Barrett-Lennard, G. T. Dimensions of therapist response as causal factors in therapeutic change. *Psychological Monographs, 76* (43, Whole No. 562).

Bergin, A. E., & Strupp, H. H. *Changing frontiers in the science of psychotherapy*. Chicago: Aldine, 1972.

Bloom, B. S. The thought process of students in discussion. In S. J. French (Ed.), *Accent on teaching: experiments in general education*. New York: Harper & Brothers, 1954.

Bogdan, R., & Taylor, S. J. *Introduction to qualitative research methods*. New York: Wiley, 1975.

Brown, J. T. S. Communication of empathy in individual psychotherapy: An analogue study of client perceived empathy. (Doctoral dissertation, University of Texas at Austin, 1980). *Dissertation Abstracts International*, 1981, *41*, 2748-B. (University Microfilms No. 8100879.)

Campbell, D. T., & Fiske, D. Convergent and discriminant validation by the multitrait-multimethod matrix. *Psychological Bulletin*, 1959, *56*, 81–105.

Caskey, N., Barker, C., & Elliott, R. Dual perspectives: Clients' and therapists' perceptions of therapist responses. *British Journal of Clinical Psychology*, 1984, *23*, 281–290.

Cline, J., & Elliott, R. *Therapeutic ingredients in the cognitive therapy of depression*. Poster presented at meetings of Society for Psychotherapy Research, Evanston, IL, June, 1985.

Cook, T. D., & Campbell, D. T. *Quasi-experimentation*. Chicago: Rand-McNally, 1979.

Dole, A. A., & Associates. Six dimensions of retrospections by therapists and counselors—A manual for research. *Catalog of selected documents in psychology*, 1982, *12*, (2), 23 (JSAS Ms. 2454).

Dole, A. A., DiTomasso, R., & Young, J. *A penny for your thoughts! Counselor behaviors and client satisfaction as a function of counselor retrospections*. Paper presented at meeting of American Educational Research Association, San Francisco, 1979.

Elliott, R. How clients perceive helper behaviors. *Journal of Counseling Psychology*, 1979, *26*, 285–294.

Elliott, R. *Reliability and validity of a revised helper behavior rating system*. Unpublished manuscript, Department of Psychology, University of Toledo, 1980.

Elliott, R. Fitting process research to the practicing psychotherapist. *Psychotherapy: Theory, Research & Practice*, 1983, *20*, 47–55. (a)

Elliott, R. *Interpersonal Process Recall (IPR) as a research method for studying psychological helping processes: A research manual*. Unpublished manuscript, University of Toledo, Department of Psychology, 1983. (b)

Elliott, R. "That in your hands . . . ": A comprehensive process analysis of a significant event in psychotherapy. *Psychiatry*, 1983, *46*, 113–129. (c)

Elliott, R. A discovery-oriented approach to significant events in psychotherapy: Interpersonal Process Recall and Comprehensive Process Analysis. In L. Rice & L. Greenberg (Eds.), *Change episodes*. New York: Guilford, 1984.

Elliott, R. Helpful and nonhelpful events in brief counseling interviews: An empirical taxonomy. *Journal of Counseling Psychology*, 1985, *32*, 307–322.

Elliott, R., Barker, C., Caskey, N., & Pistrang, N. Measuring and predicting the effectiveness of helping responses: Correlates of client and therapist perceptions. *Resources in Education*, Feb. 1981. (ERIC/CAPS No. ED 192 229.)

Elliott, R., Barker, C. B., Caskey, N., & Pistrang, N. Differential helpfulness of counselor verbal response modes. *Journal of Counseling Psychology*, 1982, *29*, 354–361.

Elliott, R., Cline, J., & Reid, S. *Tape-assisted retrospective review: A method for assessing the changing effects of therapist interventions in psychotherapy*. Paper presented at meetings of Society for Psychotherapy Research, Jeffersonville, VT, June, 1982.

Elliott, R., & Feinstein, L. *Helping intention rating procedure*. Unpublished manuscript, University of Toledo, Department of Psychology, 1978.

Elliott, R., Filipovich, H., Harrigan, L., Gaynor, J., Reimschuessel, C., & Zapadka, J. K. Measuring response empathy: The development of a multi-component rating scale. *Journal of Counseling Psychology*, 1982, *29*, 379–387.

Elliott, R., James, E., Shulman, R., & Cline, J. *Significant events in psychotherapy: A systematic case study*. Presented at meetings of the Society for Psychotherapy Research, Aspen, Colorado, June, 1981.

Elliott, R., Klein, M., & Mathieu-Coughlan, P. *The sequential analysis of empathy and experiencing: A case study*. Paper presented at meetings of Society for Psychotherapy Research, Sheffield, England, July 1983.

Elliott, R., Reimschuessel, C., Filipovich, H., Zapadka, J. K., Harrigan, L., & Gaynor, J. *Validation of the Revised Response Empathy Scale: Comparison with client and therapist perceptions*. Paper presented at meeting of Society for Psychotherapy Research, Jeffersonville, Vermont, June 1982.

Elliott, R., Reimschuessel, C., Sack, N., Cislo, D., James, E., & Hebert, K. *Significant events content analysis rating system—1983 version*. Unpublished manuscript, University of Toledo, 1983.

Elliott, R., Shapiro, D. A., & McGlenn, M. *Brief Structured Recall: A more efficient method for identifying and describing significant therapy events*. Paper presented at meeting of Society for Psychotherapy Research, Wellesley, MA, June 1986.

Elliott, R., Stiles, W. B., Shiffman, S., Barker, C. B., Burstein, B., & Goodman, G. The empirical analysis of helping communication: Conceptual framework and recent research. In T. A. Wills (Ed.), *Basic processes in helping relationships*. New York: Academic Press, 1982.

Evraiff, W. *Helping counselors grow professionally*. Englewood Cliffs, NJ: Prentice-Hall, 1963.

Fanshel, D., & Moss, F. *Playback: A marriage in jeopardy examined*. New York: Columbia University Press, 1971.

Gendlin, E. T. *Focusing*. New York: Everest House, 1978.

Glaser, B. G., & Strauss, A. *The discovery of grounded theory: Strategies for qualitative research*. Chicago: Aldine, 1967.

Goffman, E. *Asylums: Essays on the social situation of mental patients and other inmates*. Anchor Books, Doubleday & Co. Inc., Garden City, New York, 1961.

Goodman, G., & Dooley, D. A framework for help-intended communication. *Psychotherapy: Theory, research and practice*, 1976, *13*, 106–117.

Hill, C. E. *Therapists' intentions in selecting interventions within psychotherapy sessions*. Paper presented at meetings of Society for Psychotherapy Research, Sheffield, England, July, 1983.

Hill, C. E., McKitrick, D. S., Thames, T. B., Varvil-Weld, D. C., & Birckhead, L. J. *Intentions for counselor verbal responses*. Unpublished manuscript, Department of Psychology, University of Maryland, 1979.

Hill, C. E. & O'Grady, K. E. List of therapist intentions illustrated in a case study and with therapists of varying theoretical orientations. *Journal of Counseling Psychology*, 1985, *32*, 3–22.

Hill, C. E., Siegelman, L., Gronsky, B. R., Sturniolo, F., & Fretz, B. R. Nonverbal communication and counseling outcome. *Journal of Counseling Psychology*, 1981, *28*, 203–212.

Horowitz, M. J. *States of Mind: Analysis of Change in Psychotherapy*. Plenum Medical Book Co., New York, 1979.

Ivey, A. E., & Gluckstern, N. B. *Basic attending skills: Participant manual*. North Amherst, Mass.: Microtraining Associates, 1974.

Johnson, M. Influence of counselor gender on reactivity to clients. *Journal of Counseling Psychology*, 1978, *25*, 359–365.

Kagan, N. *Interpersonal process recall: A method of influencing human interaction*. 1975. (Available from N. Kagan, 434 Erickson Hall, College of Education, MSU, East Lansing, Michigan 48824.)

Kagan, N., & Krathwohl, D. R., et al. *Studies in human interaction: Interpersonal Process Recall stimulated by videotape*. Educational Publications Services, College of Education, Michigan State University, East Lansing, Michigan, 1967. (ERIC Document Reproduction Service No. 017 946.)

Kagan, N., Krathwohl, D. R., & Miller, R. Stimulated recall in therapy using videotape—a case study. *Journal of Counseling Psychology*, 1963, *10*, 237–243.

Katz, D., & Resnikoff, A. Televised self-confrontation and recalled affect: A new look at video-tape recall. *Journal of Counseling Psychology*, 1977, *24*, 150–153.

Kiesler, D. J. *The process of psychotherapy*. Chicago: Aldine, 1973.

Knudson, R. M., Sommers, A. A., & Golding, S. L. Interpersonal perception and mode of resolution in marital conflict. *Journal of Personality and Social Psychology*, 1980, *38*, 751–763.

Kommer, D., & Bastine, R. Retrospective think aloud: A method of psychotherapy process research. In W.-R. Minsel & W. Herff (Eds.), *Proceedings of the First European Conference on Psychotherapy Research, Trier, 1981* (Vol. I). Frankfurt: Peter Lang, 1982.

Lambert, M. J., DeJulio, S. J., & Stein, D. M. Therapist interpersonal skills: Process, outcome, methodological considerations, and recommendations for future research. *Psychological Bulletin*, 1978, *85*, 467–489.

Meichenbaum, D., & Butler, L. Cognitive ethology: Assessing the streams of cognition and emotion. In K. Blankstein, P. Pliner, & J. Polivy (Eds.), *Advances in the study of communication and affect: Assessment and modification of emotional behavior* (Vol. 6). New York: Plenum, 1979.

Meichenbaum, D., & Cameron, R. Issues in cognitive assessment: An overview. In T. Merluzzi, C. Glass, & W. Genest (Eds.), *Cognitive assessment*. New York: Guilford, 1980.

Orlinsky, D. E., & Howard, K. I. *Varieties of psychotherapeutic experience*. New York: Teachers College Press, 1975.

Orlinsky, D. E., & Howard, K. I. The therapist's experience of psychotherapy. In A. S. Gurman & A. M. Razin (Eds.), *Effective psychotherapy: A handbook of research*. New York: Pergamon Press, 1977.

Perls, F. S. *Gestalt therapy verbatim*. Lafayette, Calif.: Real People Press, 1969.

Rice, L. N., & Greenberg, L. (Eds.) *Patterns of change*. New York: Guilford Press, 1984.

Rennie, D. *Clients' tape-assisted recall of psychotherapy: A qualitative analysis*. Paper presented at meeting of the Canadian Psychological Association, Ottawa, May, 1984.

Rennie, D. *Client deference in the psychotherapy relationship*. Paper presented at meeting of Society for Psychotherapy Research, Evanston, IL, June, 1985.

Robinson, F. P. *Principles and procedures in student counseling*. New York: Harper, 1950.

Rogers, C. R. *Counseling and psychotherapy*. Cambridge, Mass.: Houghton-Mifflin, 1942.

Santa-Barbara, J., & Pinsof, W. *Family therapy and therapist's skills*. Workshop presented at meeting of Society for Psychotherapy Research, San Diego, June 1976.

Sarbin, T. R., & Allen, V. L. Role theory. In G. Lindzey & E. Aronson (Eds.), *Handbook of social psychology* (Vol. 1). Reading, Mass.: Addison-Wesley, 1968.

Shonkoff, A. D., & Jones, E. E. *Hot-line volunteer response to moments of distress*. Paper presented at meeting of the American Psychological Association, New York, 1979.

Spence, D. P. Language in psychotherapy. In D. Aaronson & R. W. Rieber (Eds.), *Psycholinguistic research: Implications and applications*. Hillsdale, NJ: Erlbaum, 1979.

Spence, D. P. *Narrative truth and historical truth*. New York: Norton, 1982.

Wagner, A. C., Maier, S., Uttendorfer-Marek, I., Weidle, R., & Barz, M. *Knoten in Denkprozessen von Lehrern*. Munchen: 1982.

Wagner, A. C., & Weidle, R. Knots in cognitive processes: Some empirical results and implications for cognitive psychotherapy. In W.-R. Minsel & W. Herff (Eds.), *Proceedings of the First European Conference on Psychotherapy Research, Trier, 1981*, Vol. II. Frankfurt: Peter Lang, 1982.

Wittgenstein, L. *Philosophical investigations*. New York: Macmillan, 1953.

Wolberg, L. R. *The technique of psychotherapy* (2nd ed.). New York: Grune & Stratton, 1967.

Young, D. W. Meanings of counselor nonverbal gestures: Fixed or interpretive? *Journal of Counseling Psychology*, 1980, *27*, 447–452. (a)

Young, D. W. *The meanings of counselor nonverbal gestures: A function of perceiver personality and counselor verbal style*. Unpublished dissertation, University of Rochester, 1980. (b)

Young, D. W. *Reliability of videotape-assisted recall in counseling process research*. Unpublished manuscript, School of Education, University of Rochester, 1980. (c)

15

The Development of the Working Alliance Inventory

Adam O. Horvath
Simon Fraser University
Burnaby, B.C.

Leslie Greenberg
York University
North York, Ontario

Bordin (1975) proposed that the development of the Working Alliance, between the person who seeks change and the person who offers to be a change agent, is a key aspect of the change process. He suggested that the Working Alliance can be defined in terms of three features: an agreement on goals, the degree of concordance regarding tasks, and the development of personal bonds. The Working Alliance Inventory (WAI) (Horvath, 1981), referred to in this chapter, is a 36-item self-report instrument designed to assess the strength and dimensions of the alliance as conceptualized by Bordin. The instrument was primarily designed to sample therapeutic relationships in its early stages of development (between third and fifth sessions) although applications later in therapy should prove to be equally feasible.

In developing the inventory, three potential applications were considered: (1) predicting therapy outcome; (2) use as a clinical tool (to indicate weaknesses in the alliance and alert the therapist to remedial procedures); (3) as a research device to investigate the *qualitative* differences between alliances developed by therapists using different theoretical/conceptual approaches.

Our work, so far, has focused on the first of these three applications. We have plans to expand the investigation into the other two areas and hope that enough interest will be stimulated to involve other researchers who might find the WAI a useful instrument for investigating the Working Alliance.

The inventory was generated as a by-product of a project initially designed to explore the different Working Alliances that are typically developed by therapists of different theoretical orientation. As it often happens, it was discovered that no instrument was available to investigate the otherwise very simple research question. After debating the various exigencies involved, the decision was made to develop "the tool to do the job." In essence this "minor detour" has supplanted the initial objectives and now, 2 years later, we are once again considering the original problem of examining the different alliances developed by therapists of different orientations.

The motivation to develop the WAI came from the belief that recent conceptualizations of the working alliance (Bordin, 1975, 1976; Luborsky, 1976) represented a significant attempt at specifying a generic variable which might account for aspects of therapeutic success. It was apparent that a psychometrically sound instrument, which could capture aspects of the alliance, would greatly facilitate research relating general relationship variables to outcomes. In developing this measure of the alliance it was important, from the start, to construct an instrument that would not be governed by any specific theoretical approach but *would apply across orientations*. Safeguards were therefore taken to prevent the authors' theoretical biases creeping into the instrument firstly, by having items which were sufficiently general to cover diverse approaches to therapy and secondly, by having a large number of therapists from different orientations involved in judging item appropriateness.

Authors of assessment systems are often restricted to reporting the formal facts about the reliability and validity of their instruments. In contrast, the approach in this chapter will focus on some of the issues and choices involved in generating a system. (At least we will discuss the areas where we were aware of alternatives and disclose our own reasoning regarding these.) Besides arguing for the choices made we will explore at a conceptual level, issues that may be of value to the systems generator. Inherent in this method of presentation is the hope that psychotherapists as well as psychometricians will develop an interest in developing systems which capture variables that are significant in the clinical as well as the actuarial sense.

The Rationale Behind the System

Generic Versus Specific Variables

Our interest in the Working Alliance arose out of speculations about the relationship of the specific versus general factors in psychotherapy. Attempts to demonstrate differential treatment effectiveness have not been overly productive (Smith & Glass, 1977) and this has led to a renewed interest in investigating the effects of common factors in several forms of psychotherapy.

Frank (1972, 1973), Bordin (1975, 1976), and Rogers (1951, 1957), as well as others, have explored the nature of the factors in psychotherapy that are generalizable across a variety of theoretical frameworks. They made it clear that these generic factors were indeed treatment specific, concrete, definable, and legitimate objects for psychotherapy research. This has enabled investigators to separate nontherapy specific factors such as generalized expectations, the physical act of going to therapy on a regular basis, passage of time, or broad halo effects from those that are *specific* to the provision of some form of active psychotherapy but *generalizable* across all or many of the different forms of this endeavour (Kazdin, 1979).

Types of Generic Variables

The investigation of these general factors has, in the past, been based on two major theoretical views. The first, and certainly one that has generated the most research, grew out of the theoretical work of Rogers (Rogers, 1951, 1957; Rogers & Dymond, 1954; Truax, 1962; Truax & Carkhuff, 1967). Client-centered therapists identified the Therapist-Offered Conditions as both necessary and sufficient for the generation of therapeutic progress. These concepts have undergone progressive refinement over the years, and have resulted in the development of a number of instruments that measure these conditions. The most important of these instruments, from the point of view of frequency of use, the amount of data available on its psychometric properties, and its prognostic potential is the Barrett-Lennard Relationship Inventory (RI) (Barrett-Lennard, 1962, 1978, 1979).

More recent major investigative efforts directed toward the general factors in psychotherapy have come from social psychologists (Cartwright, 1965; Strong & Matross, 1973). Their work on the effects of Social Influence in psychotherapy was based on the work of Hovland, Janis, and Kelley (1953), Lewin (1948), Strong (1968), and Patton (1969). The general or generic variables postulated by this approach were the clients' perception of the therapist's Expertness, Attractiveness, and Trustworthiness (Barak & La-Crosse, 1975; Johnson & Matross, 1977; LaCrosse, 1977; Strong, 1978).

Therapist-Offered Conditions and Social Influence Conceptualizations

Before developing a new instrument, or indeed a new theoretical model, it is the investigator's responsibility to determine whether there is a genuine need for a new conceptualization, or whether there is an existing instrument or combination of instruments that can successfully account for the phenomenon at hand. We decided in favor of developing a new instrument to measure psychotherapy process because, in our view, both of the previous conceptualizations of generic factors had some problems which we believed could be remedied.

Firstly, with respect to the client-centered concept of Therapist-Offered Conditions, the examination of the research applications of this model by Rogers, Gendlin, Kiesler, and Truax (1967) indicated that the "necessary and sufficient condition" of therapeutic gains depended entirely on the provision of a therapeutic ambience by the *therapist*.

> The ability of the therapist (to) accurately and sensitively understand experiences and feelings and their meaning to the client during the moment to moment encounter of psychotherapy . . . (it) means that the therapist is completely at home in the universe of the patient . . . It is a sensing of the client's inner world . . . "as if" it were the therapist's own . . . The ability and sensitivity required to communicate these inner meanings back to the client in a way that allows these experiences to be "his" is the other major point . . . A high level (of empathy) will indicate not only a sensitive understanding of the apparent feelings but . . . by its communication clarify and expand the patient's awareness of these feelings or experiences (Rogers *et al.*, 1967, pp. 104–105).

From the point of view of psychotherapy process analysis, a model that posits the psychotherapist as the major variable influencing both the process and the outcome of such endeavour is inherently incomplete. It is both logically and clinically apparent that a conceptualization of the therapy process that includes the contributions of both the client and the therapist, potentially, could account for more of the process and outcome of therapy. The empirical investigations that have utilized factors based on both of the participants have in fact given indirect support to the above argument. At first the research results based on Therapist-Offered Conditions were highly optimistic, especially with regard to communicated Empathy as a generic psychotherapy process variable.

> Therapists or counsellors who are accurately empathic . . . are indeed effective . . . These findings seem to hold with a variety of therapists and counsellors regardless of their training or theoretic orientation and with a wide variety of clients . . . The evidence suggests that these findings hold in a variety of therapeutic contexts . . . (Truax & Mitchell, 1971, p. 310).

Subsequent investigations (Matarazzo, 1971; Meltzoff & Kornreich, 1970) however indicated that the relationship between communicated Empathy and psychotherapy outcome in a variety of therapy situations was not entirely predictable (Bergin & Lambert, 1978).

In addition to attempts to rate therapist-communicated Empathy, a measure of client-reported Empathy had been developed. Barrett-Lennard's (1962) RI represented a different approach, both methodologically and conceptually, to the early studies of tape-rated empathy. The RI was used to estimate the *client's perception* of the therapist along the dimensions originally postulated by Rogers (Barrett-Lennard, 1962, 1978). The RI directly tapped the participant's experience via a questionnaire. Using the client's perception of the therapist permits the investigator to glean more information than a measure of the therapist behavior alone, because a client report reflects the client's experience of therapy. Notwithstanding Truax and Carkhuff's (1967) original objection to the use of client perception of therapist behavior, empirical studies using participant's perceptions of client-centered dimensions have turned out to be more successful in terms of predicting outcome than those that used third party evaluations of these dimensions (Gurman, 1977; Lambert & DeJulio, 1977; Parloff, Waskow, & Wolfe, 1978).

The most powerful of the client perception variables was found to be perceived Empathy. Whereas, generally speaking, the importance of the other client-centered conditions of Positive Regard, Congruence, and Unconditionality tended to be susceptible to variation depending on the therapeutic milieu, Empathy remained more robust under these circumstances. Gurman (1977) in his review of 23 studies using the RI found substantial intercorrelations between the 4 subscales of the instrument. He also found that the range of correlations (r) between client's and therapist's assessment of Empathy was between .02 and .46, with only 3 out of 13 studies reviewed demonstrating significant relationships. The results indicate that the therapist's and client's version of RI measure different aspects of the therapeutic relationship.

Social Influence theorists, taking a rather different approach to the client-centered one, have suggested that the underlying mechanism responsible for therapeutic effectiveness is some form of cognitive dissonance (Cartwright, 1965). Within this framework, the client and the therapists are seen as having two different conceptual views of the rationale of the clients feelings and/or behavior, and that this discrepancy is resolved in favor of the therapist view if, and only if, the therapist has "power" to influence. This power in turn stems from the therapist's perceived Attractiveness, Trustworthiness, and Expertness. Once again some characteristics of the therapist seem to carry all the explanatory power.

We have found this conceptualization problematic on several accounts. First, at the practical level, even if these factors were to account for a large degree of variability in psychotherapy outcome, it is difficult to conceive of methods by which these therapist variables can be manipulated. Even if it is true that an attractive therapist is more successful than his or her homely counterpart, we would not suggest "a beauty contest" as part of the evaluation criteria for certification of therapists. In addition, beauty tends to be in the eyes of the beholder. That is, it would be just as logical to suggest that the client who experiences his or her therapist as helpful will find this person attractive, as to ascribe a person of greater attractiveness more power of influence. The other two dimensions, Trustworthiness and Expertness, are likely to be highly situation specific and can only be evaluated as such. Finally, the research on these variables tends to be on client's initial perception of the therapist (LaCrosse, 1977; LaCrosse & Barak, 1976). The important issue is however, probably one of how a therapist comes to be seen as attractive, expert, and trustworthy over the course of therapy rather than the client's initial view of the therapist.

The instrument developed to assess the Social Influence dimensions of psychotherapy process is the Counselor Rating Form (CRF) (Barak & LaCrosse, 1975; LaCrosse, 1977). The initial research substantiating these scales used analogue-type studies. In these studies the Social Influence dimensions were manipulated artificially and indeed appeared to produce differential outcome (Cash, Kehr, & Salzbach, 1978; LaCrosse & Barak, 1976; LaCrosse, 1977; Heppner & Dixon, 1978).

After reviewing both the theoretical and empirical research connected with these Social Influence and client-centred approaches, we felt convinced that an attempt to develop another psychotherapy process instrument was justified on the basis of potential improvement of the previous conceptualizations. Of particular importance was the fact that the Working Alliance conceptualization did not postulate the therapist as an autonomous provider of the key element of psychotherapy; neither did it suggest that the client's attributions were the sole factors of importance. Rather the construct attempted to capture the *interactive components* of an effective working relationship.

At the same time, it must be noted, that both the theoretical foundation and the methodology of the WAI owed a great deal to the body of knowledge that was generated via the use of the aforementioned instruments. For instance, we were aware that Barrett-Lennard's self-report instrument had proved a better predictor of outcome than third party ratings of Empathy. In addition, both the RI and CRF instruments pioneered the development of a terminology that was unbiased with respect to schools of psychotherapy.

Theoretical Basis of the WAI

The Working Alliance Inventory was based on theoretical formulations developed by Bordin (1975, 1976). Bordin's concept of a Working Alliance was developed as a generalization of the psychoanalytic construct of the same name, which in turn, was explicated from the more general construct of transference by Freud in 1912.

> I proposed that the psychoanalytically based ideas about the therapeutic working alliance could be defined in more general terms so as to encompass all approaches to change in which a person seeks change and a change agent offers to participate in that change process . . . I further identified three aspects of collaboration for change; namely, mutual agreements and understandings regarding the goals sought in the change process and the tasks of each of the partners, and, finally, the bonds required to sustain the enterprise. I went on to suggest that therapeutic collaborations embodying these qualities could be differentiated in kind and in strength, and that these differences would prove to be the keys to evaluations of the kinds and degrees of outcomes. (Bordin, 1980).

Our working definition of the Working Alliance, based on Bordin's original development of this construct, were as follows. In a strong working alliance:

1. The helper and the helpee will have a sense of agreement about the *goals* of the helping process. The helpee will have an awareness that these goals are relevant to him or her and feel a degree of identification with the explicit and implicit aims of the particular helping process he or she is engaged in. The helper will have some direct or indirect evidence that the goals established in the therapy relationship are explicitly or implicitly shared and accepted by the client.
2. The helper and the helpee will have a sense of mutuality (agreement) that the *tasks*

demanded of each of them in the helping process are reasonable and within their global capabilities (or expertise), and relevant in a direct or indirect way to the goals of the helping process to which they are mutually agreed.
3. The helper and the helpee will experience a sense of *bond* between them. Some of the bases on which such therapeutic partnerships will be built are a sense of mutual trust, liking, understanding, and caring.

Our efforts in building the WAI were to measure these three components of the Working Alliance effectively and to be able to relate these to the effectiveness of psychotherapy. Bordin's conceptualization suggested that different therapeutic orientations and strategies will make different demands on the participants of psychotherapy in terms of each of these components. These special demands will create a unique quality to each successful alliance. It was expected however, that all successful psychotherapies will have to attain a basic quantitative level in each of these three in order to produce beneficial results. Bordin's theoretical formulation, we believed, provided some unique advantages for measuring generic psychotherapy process components. These advantages can be summarized under three headings: validity, generalizability, and concreteness. Let us review each of these issues separately since they played a major role both in the selection of a theoretical model and the method by which the inventory was developed.

Validity

An investigator developing an instrument has to make a major commitment both in time and energy. Whether or not the effort will be worthwhile from the point of view of producing an end product depends on whether the construct has a clinical and empirical as well as a theoretical relevance to reality. Today, we have the technology to generate inventories or measuring instruments, of constructs that have little claim to relevance outside the originator's imagination, and no reality beyond that which is created by operationally defining the construct via the instrument itself. Working Alliance, however, had the promise of being a theoretically and clinically valid concept. We base this contention on the fact that this construct has been in constant and expanding use since it was originally generated by Freud in 1912 (in its original form—as a component of transference). It was refined by Freud (1913), Greenacre (1954), and Anna Freud (1954). Working Alliance as a major component in successful therapy as discussed in the literature by Sterba (1934), Loewenstein (1945), and Greenson (1965, 1967). The concept was further elaborated and used by the object relation therapist who saw the concept as a "new object relationship" formed between the client and the therapist which provides the model for realistic social functioning (Bibring, 1937; Gitelson, 1962; Horowitz, 1974; Zetzel, 1956). More recently several investigators (Bordin, 1975, 1976, 1980; Greenson, 1965; Horowitz, 1974; Luborsky, 1976; Strupp, 1974), have been discussing the importance of the Working Alliance as a generic concept possibly independent of the psychodynamic framework. In fact, Bordin's (1975, 1976) conceptualization clearly indicates that Working Alliance, and its strength, is an important process variable in a variety of interpersonal relationships, not only in the therapeutic process. In addition, over the last 10 years, there have been a number of empirical studies that used various versions of the Working Alliance conceptualization (Hartley, 1978; Luborsky, 1976; Morgan, 1977; Strupp, 1974). Although the fact that this construct has been actively in use since 1912 does not, in and of itself, guarantee its validity, nonetheless a concept that has survived the ideological changes in psychotherapy for the last 90 years must have, at least some clinical utility. Additionally, the evidence that in the last 10 years Working Alliance has captured the interest of empirical investigators, and has generated a number of important studies, further supports the notion that we are grappling with a concept of some inherent worth. In summary, it was felt that there was growing evidence that this construct is emerging from the psychodynamic background and is being generalized as a generic concept. This development indicated that this construct has a degree of utilitarian value.

Generalizability

Careful review of Bordin's explication of the Working Alliance (Bordin, 1975, 1976, 1980) suggested that it was conceptually and theoretically free of issues that would make it specific to a particular therapeutic environment or to therapies with particular philosophical orientation. This was a very important consideration for this project. Clearly, Working Alliance defined as a component of, or related to, transference or countertransference is not a *generic* process variable. It was important to define constructs in terminology that was universal and free from hypothetical events which depended conceptually on philosophic or theoretical framework in order to be able to measure it meaningfully across different therapists and therapies. In addition, it was important to define the results in conceptual terminology that was potentially useful across the gamut of therapist orientation. Bordin's conceptualization of the Working Alliance has met these criteria.

Concreteness

Lastly, it was important to define this generic construct in terms that were sufficiently specific for measuring purposes. This aspect is particularly important in relation to a concept that purports to sample a therapy process variable across different approaches. The issues at hand have to be defined in language that is concrete, so that presence or absence of the phenomena can be reasonably ascertained by respondents who are not only naive to the theory behind the terminology, but who may not be "psychologically minded." The terms and constructs constituting our definition of the three components of the Working Alliance appear to be reasonably concrete and close to the use of ordinary language so that, given proper presentation, the subject can be expected to introspect and determine if these events or experiences have taken place.

Technical Issues

Selection of Data Source

Perhaps the most fundamental issue on which a developer of a psychotherapy assessment system has to take a position is the choice of the source of his or her information; that is, whether he or she will collect information from the *client*, the *therapist*, or some *independent judge* and, following from this decision, the most appropriate methodology by which to collect this information.

Before delineating the alternatives and choices that were reviewed by us in creating the WAI, we should acknowledge that since each of these points of views will yield a unique source of data—the best of all possible worlds would be some kind of combination of all of these data sources (Waskow & Parloff, 1975). Without going into detail, we would suggest, that in this instance, both the conceptual and technical problems associated with a multiple perspective system are such that the complexities would have been overwhelming.

Given that the choice had to be made, the perspectives of these three different points of view were contrasted. The *therapist* is the "manager" of the therapeutic situation; it is his or her conceptual framework, expertise, and techniques that are presumably the most stable factors in any psychotherapy process. Also, it is safe to presume that the psychotherapist is capable of absorbing our conceptualization of the Working Alliance and, because of his or her training and experience, is capable of making "professional" judgment on the therapy events.

The *client* on the other hand is in a position to give first hand information on how therapy process is *experienced*. The very "naivete" of the client permits him or her to make judgments that are not biased by theoretical preconceptualizations and, unless one views psychotherapy as an entirely unconscious process, any therapy event that has reality must be available to the client in some experiential form.

The advantages associated with a *third party* evaluation of psychotherapy event usually relate to a perceived objectivity. That is to say, since both parties in a psychotherapeutic interaction (therapist and client) are presumably entwined in a powerful relationship, there is a danger of powerful unseen and uncontrollable variables effecting their judgments. A third party observer, however, can be presumed to be free of such biases. On the other hand, such observers, no matter how well trained, can only respond to the behavioral evidence available to them. Important affective and cognitive components of the psychotherapy process are entirely unavailable to such raters. On the positive side, usually these judgments are made on the basis of some sort of recorded material (transcript, videotape, or audiotape) and therefore it is technically feasible to repeat such ratings across several raters to gain a degree of "reliability" that is inherently not possible with data that are based on first hand information. It should be noted that the elevated reliability referred to above is interrater reliability. Unfortunately, the more a particular system restricts the input (e.g., length of sample), and the complexity of the output (e.g., number of categories), the more reliable it usually becomes. Furthermore, interrater reliability coefficients are a function of both system specific factors (which are presumably stable across different applications) and situations specific factors (similarities of rater's education, background, socioeconomic status, etc.). For these reasons reliability values of rating systems and paper-and-pencil applications are not directly comparable.

Each of these sources of data suggest specific data collection techniques. Third party observations can be implemented by a behavior analysis or content analysis, either global or based on some specific scales. Data based on therapists and/or clients involve some kind of self-report, once again, either global or via responses to a specific set of questions or stimuli.

The alternatives and the options implied by each of these are discussed in some detail because the authors believe that these issues represent an important point where theory and measurement considerations interact. For example, behaviorally oriented psychotherapies tend to be evaluated by third party evaluations using some kind of behavior analysis, whereas more dynamically oriented psychotherapists, if they elect to use a third party evaluation form, will use content analysis of some kind. It seems obvious to us that the data that are produced and consequently, the kind of information available regarding each of these approaches to psychotherapy, will be different *because* of the measurement strategy involved.

Our conceptual framework suggested that the important generic variables in psycho-therapy resided in the interpersonal events during therapy. These events were conceptualized as both cognitive (i.e., selection and agreement on goals, development of tasks) and affective (i.e., feelings toward one another). Consequently a methodology was chosen which would optimize the emergence of these components. Clearly, not all the cognitive nor all the affective processes in the therapeutic interaction are directly observable by third parties, and would have to be inferred from the observable evidence. We believed that the "observable" content of the psychotherapy session might not by itself yield sufficient information to decide on the quality of the Working Alliance. We therefore chose to go via the route of a self-report inventory. We were further influenced in this choice by the history of the research involving the construct of the Therapist-Offered Conditions. It appears clear from the reviews (Gurman, 1977; Mitchell, Bozarth, & Krauft, 1977; Parloff, Waskow, & Wolfe, 1978) that using client- and therapist-experienced process data to predict therapy outcome has been more successful than process rating based on third party evaluations.

The last important consideration entering into the decision-making process was that previous research on the Working Alliance has been based on third party evaluations, either content analytic (Luborsky, 1976; Strupp, 1974; Morgan, 1977) or based on a global rating scale (Hartley, 1978). These researchers have made important contributions to the knowledge about the Working Alliance; however all of the procedures appear to be time consuming and complex to the point of making them difficult to use in clinical applications. It was our goal to develop a measuring system that would not only be useful in research, but eventually would be of clinical value.

Sampling Techniques

Coincidental with decisions involving the choice of respondent, the system generator must confront the complex choices that will eventually determine when and how often the system must be applied in order to generate the information desired. In constructing the WAI, the question of "how often?" to take a measurement, involved a choice of conceptualizations.

The theoretical framework of the inventory had implications both for the ongoing nature of the alliance, and for its quantitative aspects. Specifically, certain patterns of the alliance over time (such as the weakening and rebuilding of its components) were seen as essential features of successful therapy (Bordin, 1975, 1976, 1980; Mann, 1973), as well as the moment-to-moment aspect of the alliance (Bordin, 1975, 1976; Frank, 1971, 1973). The difference between these two aspects roughly corresponds to the contrast between longitudinal and "cross-sectional" investigation. From the point of systematic data gathering, the implications of these contrasting research approaches are important, albeit relatively unexplored (Waskow & Parloff, 1975).

Typically, paper-and-pencil inventories or tests ignore "unit of time" that the respondent should be referencing. For example, the STAI (Spielberger, Gorsuch, & Lushene, 1970) asks: " . . . indicate how you *generally* feel." When a subject responds the unit of time referenced is unclear. Self-reported data, by its very nature, tends to be summative and the researcher should attempt to specify the unit or event that he or she wishes the rater to use as reference. The difficulties involved in asking a client to summarize experiences over time includes the problem that the causal relationship between the referent event (in this case, therapy) and the summative judgment becomes more and more tenuous due to the questions both of accuracy of recall as well as the impossibility of separating out the impact of nontherapy events. While the techniques of making moment-to-moment reports provides a closer link between the stimulus (therapy) and self-report, frequently repeated questions tend to be intrusive to the point that the quality of the therapeutic relationship can assume to be effected. Recognizing these issues, a compromise position was adopted; we chose to generate information on the accumulated experience of the Working Alliance after the third therapy session.

The choice of sampling the alliance at this particular time was based on practical considerations. Since our first objective was to predict outcome it was desirable to generate the information as early in therapy as it was feasible. The review of the literature suggested that the therapist–client relationship *between the third and fifth therapy sessions* may be a propitious time to sample the alliance for purposes of outcome predictions (Gurman, 1977; Orlinsky & Howard, 1978; Saltzman, Luetgert, Roth, Creaser, & Howard, 1976).

Besides the empirical evidence cited above, it seemed logical that clients and therapists should have developed some ideas about the short-to-medium term *goals* for the therapy. Similarly, the client after the third session should have engaged in the activities (tasks) typical of the sessions and have had a chance to reflect on these processes in terms of their appropriateness to their perceived needs. Lastly, we believe that the degree of liking and trust that is generated between the therapist and client (through not necessarily reflecting peak values throughout therapy) during the first three sessions is a good estimate of their later value.

It can be legitimately argued that in certain instances (e.g., psychoanalysis) the Working Alliance may not be fully established so early in the relationship. We considered this issue and chose not to be influenced by it for the following reasons: (1) We were primarily interested in short-term therapy and (2) some more behaviorally oriented therapies average approximately 8–10 sessions, dictating that process observations (if they are to be clinically useful) should be made during the first third (i.e., approximately third session) of the therapy. If the WAI is to be applied in medium- to long-term (20 + session) environments, the suggested sampling points should be chosen in relation to the expected duration of contact.

Development of the System

Goals and Objectives

The methodological sequence followed for the development of the WAI was very much influenced by its projected use. In particular, it was seen as evident that the generalized construct of the Working Alliance, although it has benefitted from logical development over the past 90 years, was the seminal work of one person's (Bordin's) conceptualization of the issues involved. Such being the case, there was a perceived danger that the generation of our system would be recursive, in the sense that we were now creating an instrument that in essence defined the construct that it purports to measure. In other words, in the first phases of generating our system, two of our main objectives were (1) to develop construct validity for the WAI in such a way that inputs outside of the systems generating the constructs and the theory behind the constructs were utilized and, (2) to develop an inventory which was, in terms of its constructs, a reasonably faithful representation of the theoretical concept as it was defined by Bordin (1975, 1976, 1980). The second one of these two objectives was important because we believed that, by and large, the generation of a theoretical construct and the development of instrumentation to measure a construct are two processes that have very different goals and objectives. It seemed to us that the separation of these two activities not only enhances the product but also the credibility of the procedures. In line with this reasoning we attempted to explicate a theoretical proposition and tried not to confound, at this stage, the system with alternative views of the alliance. Indeed, it seems logical to us, that the research generated by our system should (ideally) clarify and enhance our understanding of the Working Alliance. Based on these empirical findings the theory might be adjusted and, if indicated, the system can be then redesigned to generate the information needed to test the hypotheses suggested by the revised theory.

The building of the WAI proceeded through three rather distinct stages: logical analysis and item generation, construct validation procedures, and clinical testing. These three steps will be presented below with a particular emphasis on delineating those issues that involved choices or decisions that appeared to have generalizable significance for instrument building in this field.

Logical Analysis and Item Generation

Since the choice was made that the instrument, as far as it was practical, would reflect Bordin's articulation of the Working Alliance, the material generated by Bordin (1975, 1976) was scrutinized to determine the general structure of the inventory. The first decision we made was that, according to our understanding, the Working Alliance consisted of three components. These components we named Tasks, Goals, and Bond. Since the original work suggested that both the strength of the individual alliance and the kind of alliance that was typical of different methods of intervention were embedded in the relative strengths of these three components, it was felt that the quantitative information resulting from the inventory should be available in two forms: as a total "alliance score" and as a quantitative evaluation of each of these components. Because the theoretical development did not specify whether the "shape" of the alliance, (i.e., the relative strengths of the components) was the most important consideration or the total quantum of all of the alliance related experiences, feelings, thoughts, and behaviors, it was decided that initially the inventory should give equal weight to each of these three components, and that across a large number of individual alliances the overall alliance score would indicate the viability of the therapeutic relationship regardless of the relative strengths of the components. In practical terms this meant an inventory of three equal parts, with each of those parts hopefully sampling the alliance constituents, that is, Goal, Bond, and Task. The second decision that arose out of our theoretical stance on system generation was that we should seek consensual validation of our inventory as a means of verifying construct validity.

We believe that the choice of the method of construct validation is a crucial decision in the construction of any measuring instrument. The procedures used should logically follow from theoretical premises on which the instrument is based. As we noted above, one of our concerns was to avoid generating a self-referent system. Therefore, we chose a method of validation that maximized the weight of the "outside" input throughout the validation process.

Approximately 90 items for each of the three constituent components of the Working Alliance were generated. In the item generation phase we had three objectives: first, to produce items that adequately reflected the theoretical constructs behind each of our alliance components; second, to review items from the domain of generic psychotherapy process variables that were known to be related to outcome and to glean from this collection of items, phraseology, modes of presentation, and successful scaling techniques; and third, a review process was implemented to ensure that the wording of the items was "neutral" with respect to methods of psychotherapy. Clearly, we wanted to avoid words or phrases which would have idiosyncratic meaning within a particular theoretical framework, or which would have either very strong positive or negative connotation that was not uniform across the different therapeutic vocabularies. The items generated, therefore, were discussed at length with psychologists using behavioral, Gestalt, analytic, as well as client-centered interventions. This process was informal in order to allow the researcher to modify and experiment with item stems until what appeared to be an optimum compromise was reached, between item content, clarity, and neutrality with respect to theories. This task turned out to be challenging and at times quite frustrating, especially with respect to the Task scale. To our knowledge there has been little published about the question of the language of tests and its interaction with the language habits or meaning associations developed by therapists and clients. It appears to be a potentially exciting area of investigation. At the end of the item generation phase, 35 items were retained for the Bond dimension, 33 items referencing the Goal dimension, and 23 items relevant to the Task domain.

Initial Construct Validation

Support for the constructs represented by the WAI were sought from two different sources. Initially, consensual validity of the items representing the constructs in the instrument was established. To this end, the initial item pool was rated on two occasions. First, a group of experts were identified on the basis of recent (the last 10 years) publications related to the Working Alliance. We purposely chose to include investigators who were dealing with the notion of the Working Alliance from different theoretical bases, that is, individuals whose working definition of the alliance would differ from ours. The reasoning behind this choice was that, although we believed that individuals who were familiar with Bordin's concept of the Working Alliance would be perhaps more accurate in assessing how precisely we translated Bordin's concept into items for a questionnaire, we felt that there was a danger of developing a design that was circular and self-reinforcing. We therefore chose a more varied group of experts and supplied them with our own working definition of the alliance, and each of its three components.

These raters were asked to accomplish two tasks. First, we asked them to rate each item on a scale of 1 to 5 on the question: Is this item relevant to the Working Alliance? And second, we asked them to decide which of the three components (Task, Goal, Bond) of the Working Alliance this particular item was referencing.

As a result of the first set of ratings, information of two kinds were received on each of our 91 items: the degree of relevance to our construct, and whether or not they concurred with our original classification of the items as referencing a particular dimension. Each item had a mean rating (Xr), that is, the average value assigned to the item by our experts as an answer to the question "Is this item relevant to the Working Alliance?"; (on a scale of 1–5) and a percentage agreement (Pa) rating that indicated the percentage of raters that agreed with us with respect to this item referencing a particular dimension.

The criteria that we used for item selection were as follows: Any item that received a mean rating of 4 or above was retained. Items with Xr of less than 4 were discarded. In terms of an item being referenced to one of the three dimensions, the minimal criteria applied was 70% agreement with our original specification for that item.

Of the original 91 items rated by our experts, 70 met the criteria specified above. Out of these 70 items, 11 were "borderline," that is, had an Xr of 4 or Pa of 0.7. These items were reworded using suggestions by the raters. Table 15-1 shows the summary statistics for the retained items.

Further consensual validation was sought by rerating the remaining 70 items by a different group of "experts." The second rating was implemented by a group of clinical and/or counseling psychologists selected randomly from the membership of the local psychological association. We chose to rerate the items for the following reasons:

1. The second group of experts represented a population which, it was presumed, would evaluate the items from a somewhat different point of view: Our first group of raters were all committed to the notion of the importance of the Working Alliance (although their definition of the Working Alliance varied). Therefore, in a sense, these raters had to be considered members of an "in group" because they had devoted time and energy to development of the construct of the Working Alliance and its application to psychotherapy process. We felt that they could have a considerable conceptual expertise regarding the construct, but at the same time because of their interest in the area of the Working Alliance, their rating might be influenced in the direction of including issues under the umbrella of Working Alliance which could be more properly considered under different conceptual frameworks. Our second group of raters were more representative of psychotherapists in the field, and their attitude towards the Working Alliance presumably would be representative of the prevailing clinical attitudes.

2. The whole process of conceptual validation and particularly the second step of the rating procedure underlies the compromise that has to be achieved between developing a system of measurement that represents a very specific conceptualization of constructs, and therefore must be generated by the person or persons who share this unique perspective regarding the phenomena, and the notion of avoiding recursiveness by letting a diversity of opinions influence the construction of the system. It seemed to us that our system which was consensually validated would become more generalized as a result, and at the same time would benefit from the clinical experience of psychotherapists with a wide range of approaches to the therapy process and therefore would be appropriate for use as a truly generic psychotherapy variable.

The procedure followed for a second rating procedure was identical to the first rating. The evaluation of the items by the second group of judges according to the criteria mentioned above, resulted in the elimination of 15 items and the rephrasing of three. The remaining 55 items constituted the final item pool from which the actual items for the WAI were selected.

During the initial item generation it was our objective to include units with overlap-

Table 15-1   Item Rating Summary: Retained Items (n of Raters $= 7$)

Domain	Number of Items	Mean Rating	Standard Deviation	Percent Agreement
Goal	24	4.38	.30	76.1
Bond	26	4.50	.31	80.0
Task	20	4.45	.29	75.8
Total	70	4.44	.30	77.5

ping content, and allow the process of consensual validation to select from among these the most appropriate ones. The remaining items therefore were segregated into the three pools (Bonds, Tasks, and Goals) and within each of these pools, items with highly similar content were grouped together. Within each of this content pool, one item was selected to represent the construct. This procedure resulted in 13 items in the Bond dimension, 12 in the Task dimension, and 12 in the Goal dimension. The 13 items in the Bond dimension were reexamined and two of these with the most similar contents were pooled resulting in an equal number of items in each of the three subscales (12).

In choosing the "best" item from among those with similar content, a higher rate was given to the percentage agreement (*Pa*) values than to the mean agreement (*Xr*) figures. This approach was taken because, as the instrument construction proceeded, we became more and more convinced that the three dimensions of the Working Alliance that we were tapping were probably quite unique, and possibly somewhat independent of each other. Consequently we felt the percentage agreement value would indicate an item that was referenced to a construct that was *specific* to a particular scale. It was hoped thereby to reflect more accurately the unique conceptualization of the Working Alliance that was present in the theoretical material on which our work was based.

The final inventory consisted of 36 items, 12 items in each dimension. Table 15-2 presents the item rating summary of these 36 retained items based on our second group of raters.

The Preparation of the WAI

Prior to the actual development of the WAI, two additional tasks were undertaken: (1) The items referencing positive and negative alliances were counterbalanced and (2) an alternate form of WAI was generated suitable for use with therapists. (The original form was geared toward a client questionnaire). The therapist version of the inventory was developed to measure therapist perception of the alliance components of the psychotherapeutic relationship. The inclusion of the therapist's point of view of the alliance was important for several reasons:

1. To permit an examination of the similarities and differences between the therapist and a client's perception.
2. To facilitate the comparison of the relationship of the alliance components with other therapy process indicators that used the therapist's perception as a point of reference.

Table 15-2   Item Rating Summary: Retained Items (*n* of Raters = 21)

Domain	Number of Items	Mean Rating	Standard Deviation	Percent Agreement
Goal	12	4.38	.19	85.3
Bond	12	4.43	.14	94.8
Task	12	4.23	.16	86.2
Total	36	4.35	.18	88.7

The T (therapist) version of the WAI was developed from the original by rephrasing the individual items of the inventory. There were three possible points of reference that might have been used to reformulate the items:

1. The therapist's beliefs or experiences in therapy.
2. The therapist's impression of the client's belief or experiences.
3. The therapist's impression of the client's impression of the therapist's experience or beliefs.

Initially, the approach was to adopt *one* of the above three alternatives and use it exclusively throughout the instrument. However, attempts to use one of the three options outlined above exclusively resulted in some awkward items. Therefore, the therapist's beliefs or experiences in therapy were used whenever it was feasible to obtain direct, "first hand" evidence. However, the other two points of view were also used when the therapist's referenced statement would have resulted in awkward items, or would have altered the focus of the item. The final wording of the items was verified for clarity and parallelism with the source items from the WAI(C) by two experienced psychotherapists.

In developing the therapist's version, next to maintaining item parallelism, logical relevance to therapy outcome was given the highest priority. Empirical evidence has shown (Hill, 1974; Meltzoff & Kornreich, 1970; Mintz, 1977) that information supplied by the therapist will be based on a different conceptualization of therapy events, *regardless of the identity of the stimulus*, than the client's conceptualization of the same event. It appeared reasonable to sacrifice some consistency in favor of fine tuning the items of the instrument to obtain "best" information regarding a particular concept or construct.

The actual inventory contained the following: face sheet containing instruction for the subjects (including one sample statement), followed by the 36 items of the inventory. Each of the items was randomly drawn from the three item pools and each item was followed by a 5-point "Likert" scale on which the subjects were to indicate the degree to which a particular statement was accurately referencing their experience in the current therapy situation. The five options were specified on top of each of the inventories' pages: 1—never; 2—seldom; 3—sometimes; 4—often; 5—always.

Further Steps in Construct Validation

The second phase of construct validation for the WAI involved applying Campbell and Fiske's (1959) model of multitrait–multimethod analysis to the instrument. This step of the investigation was implemented in conjunction with a clinical field trial which was also aimed at evaluating the efficacy of the WAI to predict psychotherapy outcome.

We will present the design of these procedures, followed by the pertinent results. The ability of the WAI to predict psychotherapy outcome will be the topic of later sections.

The Design

The WAI (both forms) were initially pilot tested in an analogue environment involving 14 pairs of graduate students in counseling psychology acting as counselors and therapists. These protocols were examined for procedural difficulties and the completed

WAIs were item analyzed to determine the item homogeneity of the scales. We used Hoyt's (1941) procedure to evaluate subscale homogeneity, and Cronbach's (1951) alpha to evaluate the reliability of the full inventory. On the basis of the results, some conservative adjustments were made in the phrasing of three items.

The subjects of the clinical phase of the construct validation were 29 clients undergoing individual psychotherapy either in the United States or Canada. These subjects were recruited through agencies who were prepared to cooperate with the study. Participation involved voluntary consent on the part of both the therapist and the client. An attempt was made to include as wide a variety of therapy situations and approaches as it was feasible within the limitations of the study. On the basis of self-reported therapeutic orientation we established that we had client-Centered, behaviorally oriented, eclectic, Gestalt, psychodynamic, Jungian, and existential therapists. (These labels refer to the orientation used with the particular client, not necessarily the overall orientation of the therapists.)

After the third psychotherapy session, the subjects were asked to complete: (1) the appropriate version of the WAI; (2) a questionnaire asking for pertinent demographic data. After the 10th therapy session, the therapist and the client were asked to complete an evaluation form which was based on Strupp, Wallach, and Wogan's (1964) Client Posttherapy Questionnaire.

The results were analyzed from two points of view: First, the convergent and discriminant validity of the WAI using the three scales of the WAI and the Empathy scale of the RI as "traits" and clients' and therapists' reports as alternative methods of measurement in a multimethod–multitrait matrix was determined. Second, the results were evaluated to estimate the efficiency of each of the alliance scales to predict different aspects of therapy outcome based on the posttherapy questionnaire.

The rationale for using the multimethod–multitrait procedure was to examine the convergent–divergent validity of the three dimensions of the WAI. Since one of the reasons which attracted us to the theoretical framework we adopted was the degree of specifity offered by the model, it seemed reasonable to evaluate the degree to which the WAI could identify specific components and the extent to which the WAI could be differentiated from related constructs (i.e., empathy, etc.).

The Subjects

The study was based on 29 clients with a mean age of 34.6; the youngest client was 19 years of age, oldest was 65. There were 17 female clients and 12 male; 15 were married, 6 were single, 7 divorced, and 1 separated. The majority of clients have completed a university degree, 5 were in university, and 4 were high school graduates. Therapists identified themselves as; counselors ($n = 16$), psychologists ($n = 10$), or social workers ($n = 2$). Six therapists had doctorate level training, 8 were trained at the masters level, while the remaining were engaged in some form of postgraduate training. Ten of the therapists had between 1 and 5 years of experience; 11 had between 6 to 10 years of experience, and 3 had more than 15 years of experience. These data were not reported in five cases.

The Process–Outcome Dilemma

Before we discuss the results of the study we will present some of the theoretical issues we perceive as germain to the process–outcome dilemma. At first glance, the distinction and the relationship between process and outcome appear clear. On closer examination, however, this issue becomes challenging. Outcome or change can be conceptualized as immediate microscopic changes in the client's perception, cognition, affect *or*, as distant macro events representing a major alteration of the client's mood, performance, lifestyle, stress levels, or occupation. On a different dimension, some changes are short term in duration and expressed within a single incident or behavior, others are enduring and can be experienced over a long period of time, affecting many of the client's daily activities. Most importantly, in psychotherapy—as in all life sciences—the outcome of event A is part of the process resulting in B, and so on. Clearly it is not appropriate to pursue these issues to their logical conclusion here; it is important, however, to introduce the notion of scale and relativity and the concept of "process of outcome." This same issue is also embedded in the difficulty of developing a desirable outcome categorization for a given client problem as seen from the perspectives of different therapy orientations. Most typically, a behaviorally oriented therapist, for example, would define "outcome" in a very concise, circumscribed manner and the outcome criteria are simply the ability or frequency of performance of a specific behavior. More dynamically or existentially oriented therapists, on the other hand tend to define the desired outcomes in broader terms involving long-term experiential or personality changes. One of the ways of "reconciling" the differences in scales arising from these different orientations is to conceptualize the "behavioral" type outcomes as either process or short-term intermediate products. We are not suggesting that such schema would satisfy a behaviorist—or, for that matter, a psychoanalyst. The point we try to raise is that certain problematic elements in the process–outcome controversy can be reconciled if therapy is seen as a sequence of interdependent change events. In such linked sequence the researcher is free to select two temporarily separated events and call the earlier "process" and the later "outcome" as long as it can be reasonably demonstrated that the former is sufficient to elicit the later. The "value" attached to such "outcome" depends on (1) the intrinsic value attributed to the event by the client, (2) the importance of this event in the theoretical framework of the therapist, and (3) the utility of the event to promote other events that are valued.

Results

Multimethod–Multitrait Analyses

The results reported here used the source of evaluation (i.e., the therapist or client), as "method," and the three WAI dimensions and Empathy as "traits" (Table 15-3).

This table compares the main diagonal of a correlation matrix representing the multimethod–monotrait correlations with the off-diagonal elements representing the various combinations of monomethod–multitrait and multimethod–multitrait correlations.

The Goal scale meets the criterion that convergent validity (i.e., the value of the diagonal element 0.80) representing the correlation between clients' and therapists' rating on the Goal Scale, exceed the values of the corresponding horizontal and vertical off-diagonal elements.

The main diagonal value of Task (.76) is also greater than the corresponding off-diagonal elements of this scale (although very closely approximated by the correlation between client's Task and therapist's Goal). The value of $r = .53$ obtained as the diagonal element of the Bond dimension is exceeded by the correlation between the therapist's Bond and the client's Empathy scales, as well as the correlation between the client's Bond and the therapist's Goals scales. In addition, this diagonal value was matched

Table 15-3   Multitrait–Multimethod Matrix of the
Relationship Variables

		Client		
Therapist	Bond	Task	Goal	Empathy
Bond	.53	.43	.50	.55
Task	.46	.76	.66	.33
Goal	.55	.75	.80	.48
Empathy	.53	.32	.48	.50

in magnitude by the correlation between the therapist's Empathy and client's Bond scales.

In summary, the findings offer some support for the convergent validity of the WAI Goal and Task scales. Evidence regarding the convergent validity of the Bond scale is equivocal; while the elevated correlation between Bond and Empathy was explicable on the basis of the similarity of the underlining constructs, the strong relationship between the client's Bond and the therapist's Goal scale suggests the possibility that the concepts underlying these two scales were conceptually difficult to differentiate for our subjects.

Reliability

In addition to our evaluation of the convergent and discriminant validity of the WAI, we were able to item analyze the S's protocols to estimate the reliability of our system. Table 15-4 summarizes the results of these investigations. With the exception of the

Table 15-4   Reliability Estimates of the Working Alliance Inventory $n = 29$

Dimension	N of Items	Mean	SD	Hoyt[a]	Cronbach[b]
Client form WAI(C)					
Goal	12	45.21	9.14	.88	
Task	12	45.10	8.85	.88	
Bond	12	49.07	7.02	.85	
Composite	36	139.38	23.63		.93
Therapist form WAI(T)					
Goal	12	44.86	8.03	.87	
Task	12	45.03	6.83	.82	
Bond	12	47.59	5.10	.68	
Composite	36	137.48	18.05		.87

[a]Hoyt's estimate of reliability (Hoyt, 1941).
[b]Cronbach's alpha for composite (Cronbach, 1951).

WAI(T) Bond scale the subscale reliabilities are quite acceptable for a self-report instrument. The composite reliability indices (Cronbach's alphas) are also well within the range of values expected of this type of system.

Examination of the weakest scales (WAI(T) Bond) reveals that (1) the group mean is high, 80% of the maximum score, and (2) the reported variability is the lowest of all the subscales (SD = 5.10). It seems plausible that the "ceiling effect" of the therapists rating themselves highly on Bond and, particularly, the relatively lower variability of the scale is at least partly responsible for the lower Hoyt value obtained for this scale.

In validating the WAI, the best *source* of outcome data raised a number of issues. Theoretically, we were in agreement with Waskow and Parloff's (1975) view that, all three major sources (client, therapist, significant others) should be utilized as independent and cross-validating sources of data. We opted for collecting the participants retrospective evaluation of therapy outcome first because some of the applied considerations of the study prevented certain methods of data collection and secondly, the variety of therapeutic orientations and client problems in our sample made it difficult to obtain comparable outcome data across such a varied sample except on self-reports of change.

Although self-report data have been criticized on the ground of "lack of objectivity" and also because they might reflect general satisfaction, research has shown (Waskow & Parloff, 1975) that such evaluation consistently shows significant correlation with other sources of outcome evaluation. Furthermore it might be argued, self-reported data are logically more sensitive to inner changes that might not result in overt, observable changes for some period of time than other forms of assessment.

Although this type of outcome evaluation falls short of the ideal, the instrument that we chose, the Client Posttherapy Questionnaire (PTQ) (Strupp *et al.*, 1964), has proved its usefulness and has shown positive correlation with other sources of outcome measurement in several previous investigations (Cartwright, Kirtner, & Fiske, 1963; Klein, 1960; Nichols & Beck, 1960; Strupp *et al.*, 1964). If all of the possible perspectives (client, therapist, others) cannot be obtained, the client's view or level of satisfaction is a crucial source of evidence of therapeutic progress.

The Relationship Between the Outcome Criteria and the WAI

In order to gain a better perspective of the self-reported outcome measure, the 11 questions of the posttherapy questionnaire were subdivided into three groupings based on question content. The first subset of questions dealt with satisfaction with therapy, the second with perceived and observed change, and the third with the client's adjustment with respect to the presenting complaint.

Table 15-5 presents the correlations between PTQ and the predictor variables using client- and therapist-reported data. The findings suggest that the WAI predicted psychotherapy outcome more efficiently than did the other four scales monitored in our study. Additionally, it appears that of the three dimensions of the Working Alliance, the Task dimension seems to be the most useful predictor of all aspects of therapy outcome based on client self-report.

An overview of the results of the correlational data based on therapist report indicate that the Task domain was the most effective in predicting therapist-reported client satisfaction and adjustment. The therapist perception of client's changes, however, most strongly correlated with the therapist-reported Bond component.

Table 15-5   Zero Order Correlation Coefficients of the Relationship and Outcome Variables, $n = 29$

	Satisfaction	Change	Adjustment	Composite
Client Rating				
WAI(C)	.50[a]	.33[a]	.22	.42[a]
Task	.65[a]	.45[a]	.31	.57[a]
Bond	.32	.23	.21	.31
Goal	.40[a]	.24	.09	.30
Empathy	.11	.05	.26	.15
Attractiveness	− .07	− .06	.03	− .05
Trustworthiness	.02	− .10	.16	.01
Expertness	.15	.09	.14	.15
Therapist Rating				
WAI(T)	.66[a]	.38[a]	.27	.52[a]
Task	.68[a]	.37[a]	.32	.54[a]
Bond	.48[a]	.47[a]	.16	.48[a]
Goal	.60[a]	.22	.25	.39[a]
Empathy	.54[a]	.31	.03	.34[a]

[a] $p < .05$.

The data were further analyzed to investigate whether we could detect some pattern of complementarity among the predictor variables. In order to obtain this information a series of stepwise regression equations were generated using all of the process variables. A summary of this investigation is shown in Table 15-6. Because of our limited sample size the results of these analyses are highly tentative. Nonetheless, they appear to suggest that the Task dimension of the WAI captures a significant portion of the variability in outcome which is not captured by some of the generic process variable systems commonly used today.

Additional Research on the Working Alliance Using the WAI

Subsequent investigations have looked at the differential effectiveness of the Task scale predicting outcome on standardized outcome measures.

Relationship and outcome measures were obtained from 36 subjects involved in a program in which the Gestalt two-chair method was used to help resolve decisional conflicts. In this program, the goal was prespecified as being one of resolving a decisional conflict and so it was decided to use only the Task subscale of the WAI plus Barrett-Lennard's Empathy measure and the Social Influence variables. The instruments were used in that study for purposes of selecting good helping relationships for the further intensive study of processes of resolution of decisional conflict (Greenberg & Webster,

Table 15-6   Stepwise Regression Analyses (Client Data)

Dependent Variable: Composite Outcome $n = 29$	
p to Enter $= .05$ $R^2 = .56$ F Probability $= .000$	
Variables entered	**Increment in R^2**
Task	.33
Goal	.14
Attractiveness	.08
Variables remaining	**F probability**
Bond	.94
Empathy	.38
Trustworthiness	.95
Expertness	.25

Dependent Variable: Satisfaction $n = 29$	
p to Enter $= .05$ $R^2 = .57$ F Probability $= .000$	
Variables entered	**Increment in R^2**
Task	.43
Empathy	.15
Variables remaining	**F probability**
Bond	.64
Goal	.07
Attractiveness	.09
Trustworthiness	.21
Expertness	.49

Dependent Variable: Change $n = 29$	
p to Enter $= .05$ $R^2 = .20$ F Probability $= .013$	
Variables entered	**Increment in R^2**
Task	.20
Variables remaining	**F probability**
Bond	.25
Goal	.09
Empathy	.07
Attractiveness	.20
Trustworthiness	.24
Expertness	.59

1982). Data, however, were available for further validation of the Task scale of the WAI.

In the study, clients completed pre- and posttherapy plus 1-month follow-up measures on the Scale of Indecision (Osipow, Carney, & Barak, 1976), State-Trait Anxiety Inventory (STAI) (Spielberger *et al.*, 1970) and Target Complaint Improvement (TC) (Battle, Imber, Hoen-Saric, Stone, Nash, & Frank, 1966) reported by both client and therapist. Five clients dropped out of treatment by the end of the third session but completed all the forms. The remainder continued until they had resolved their conflict or the program terminated. All clients were urban adults, 31 women and 5 men, seeking counseling for their difficulties in making a decision, in response to a program advertised for that purpose. Acceptance into the program was based on Malan's (1976) criteria for brief dynamic psychotherapy. Six therapists with experience ranging from 2 to 7 years with the Gestalt method were assigned to clients on a random basis.

At the end of the second session with the therapist, the clients completed at home the Task scale of the WAI, the Empathy scale of Barrett Lennard's RI, and the Social Influence (CRF/scales), Expertness, Attractiveness, and Trustworthiness. In addition to these relationship report measures, a measure of Client Vocal Quality in the first session, which has been shown to relate to outcome in client-centered therapy (Rice, 1979), was taken. The proportion of focused voice quality from 20 statements of two-chair dialogue in the first session was used as the independent variable for voice quality.

Table 15-7 shows the zero order correlations between the different prognostic measures and the four outcome indices. The Task scale of the WAI can be seen to consistently relate to the outcome indices more highly than any of the other prognostic measures. On occasion Empathy or Client Voice Quality approaches magnitudes similar to that of the Task scale but the consistency and magnitude of the correlations between Task and outcome are quite striking. Task accounted for between 30 and 46% of the outcome variance. The correlations provided are on 1-month follow-up, but therapy termination scores showed a highly similar pattern with Task being clearly most predictive of therapy outcome. It is important to note that all the clients were engaged in a highly similar, active therapeutic task, that is, Gestalt two-chair dialogue, so that these results apply to a situation in which a directed therapeutic task is being used.

With regard to the correlations among the prognostic variables we see that Task and Empathy are most highly correlated. This is consistent with the relatively high correlation between these variables in the previous sample of 29 and suggests that utilization by the therapist of Tasks which were perceived by the client as relevant may lead the client to perceive the therapist as empathic. Task is possibly more highly related to outcome by virtue of it being a more specific and more interactional measure indicating that if clients perceived their therapists' in-session suggestions or requests as relevant to their goals, they may perceive the therapist as empathic even if the suggestions or requests are challenging or confronting.

Revision of the WAI Scale

Based on the studies reported in the previous sections, additional psychometric and clinical information emerged enabling us to refine the instrument (Horvath, 1982). The purpose of the revision was twofold, first, to increase the variability of the scales. The original 5-point scale was changed to a fully anchored 7-point Likert scale. Second, a number of items were revised in order to make the language clearer (based on feedback from the field studies) and to improve the conceptual distinction between the three subscales.

Table 15-7 Correlation Matrix

	Ind[a]	STAI	TC	TTC	Task	Expertness	Trustworthiness	Attractiveness	Empathy	Voice Quality
Task	-.68	-.55	.65	.60	1.00	.65	.44	.32	.73	.41
Expertness	.28	-.08	.26	.08	.65	1.00	.73	.51	.69	.10
Trustworthiness	-.17	-.11	.19	.00	.44	.73	1.00	.62	.55	.15
Attractiveness	-.08	-.08	-.02	-.18	.32	.51	.62	1.00	.35	-.07
Empathy	-.45	-.29	.34	.24	.73	.69	.55	.35	1.00	.32
Voice quality (focused)	-.37	-.30	.44	.62	.41	.11	.15	-.07	.32	1.00

[a]Ind. = Indecision
STAI = State-Trait Anxiety Inventory
TC = Target Complaint
TTC = Therapist Target Complaint

551

Research on the Revised WAI

Moseley (1983) investigated the relationship between the Working Alliance and short-term psychotherapy outcome on 25 clients in brief therapy (6–12 sessions) from a variety of orientations. Pre- and posttherapy measurements were taken on the STAI (Spielberger *et al.*, 1970) and the Tennessee Self-Concept Questionnaire (TSC) (Fitts, 1965). He also collected outcome measures using the Target Complaints measure (TC) (Battle *et al.*, 1966) and the PTQ (Strupp *et al.*, 1964). The reliability coefficents for the revised instrument were quite satisfactory (Table 15-8).

The intercorrelation between the WAI subscales, particularly the correlation between Goal and Task, were found to be high (Table 15-9).

This strong relationship, which persisted despite the recent revisions of the scale, raises the possibility that issues pertaining to therapy objective (goals) and therapy activities (tasks) are highly overlapping in the early phases of the alliance. The current version of the WAI scale does not appear to differentiate between these dimensions by the third therapy session.

The WAI in general, and the Task scale in particular, were found to be reliably correlated with therapy outcome as measured by the TC and the PTQ. No significant relationship was found between the alliance measure and the change in the state anxiety and self-concept measure (Table 15-10).

It seems that the personality variables, anxiety and self-concept, probably require a longer time span to respond to therapy-induced change, since they showed little change over the brief therapy.

Conclusions

The object of our development of the WAI was to devise a clinically useful instrument that measures the three dimensions of Working Alliance based on the theoretical work of Bordin. The methodology used to generate the inventory and validate the constructs

Table 15-8   Reliability Estimates of the Revised WAI, $N = 25$

Dimension	Items	Mean	SD	Hoyt	Cronbach
Bond	12	69.6	10.1	.92	
Task	12	68.6	9.8	.92	
Goal	12	67.3	11.1	.89	
Composite	36				.93

Table 15-9   Intercorrelation Among the Revised WAI Subscales, $N = 25$

	Goal	Task
Bond	.69	.78
Task	.92	1.00

Table 15-10   Relationship Between the WAI Scales and Outcome Indicators (Based on Mosley, 1981)

	Residual Gain Scores $N=25$		Posttherapy Scores	
	STAI (State)	TSC	TC $N=19$	PTQ $N=22$
Bond	−.16	.11	.51[a]	.46[a]
Task	−.13	.21	.53[b]	.50[b]
Goal	−.04	−.02	.33	.37
Composite	−.12	.10	.49[a]	.47[a]

[a]p .05. [b]p .01.

was based on both conceptual construct validation via consensual rating by two groups of experts, and on the examination of convergent and discriminant validity indices using the methodology established by Campbell and Fiske.

Based on our investigation there appears to be preliminary indications that the WAI system is useful for research and perhaps clinical applications. In addition, there appears to be suggestion that one of the three components (Task) conceptualized as part of the Working Alliance may be a critical component in psychotherapy process across a variety of intervention strategies.

References

Barak, A., & LaCrosse, M. B. Multidimensional perception of counselor behavior. *Journal of Education Psychology*, 1975, *16*, 202–208.

Barrett-Lennard, G. T. Dimensions of therapist response was causal factors in therapeutic change. *Psychological Monographs*, 1962, *76* (Whole No. 43).

Barrett-Lennard, G. T. The Relationship Inventory: Later development and adaptations. *JSAS Catalog of Selected Documents in Psychology*, 1978, *8*, 68.

Barrett-Lennard, G. T. *Relationship Inventory Form D-O 64*. Personal communication, 1979.

Battle, L. C., Imber, S. D., Hoen-Saric, R., Stone, A. R., Nash, E. H., & Frank, J. D. Target complaints as a criteria of improvement. *American Journal of Psychotherapy*, 1966, *20*, 184–192.

Bergin, A. E. & Lambert, M. J. The evaluation of therapeutic outcomes. In S. L. Garfield, & A. E. Bergin (Eds.), *Handbook of Psychotherapy and Behavior Change*. New York: Wiley, 1978.

Bibring, E. On the theory of the results of psychoanalysis. *International Journal of Psycho-analysis*, 1937, *18*, 170–189.

Bordin, E. S. *The generalizability of the psychoanalytic concept of the working alliance*. Paper presented at the annual meeting of the Society for Psychotherapy Research, Boston, June, 1975.

Bordin, E. S. *The working alliance: Basis for a general theory of psychotherapy*. Paper presented at a symposium of the American Psychological Association, Washington, D.C., September, 1976.

Bordin, E. S. *Of human bonds that bind or free*. Presidential address delivered at the meeting of the Society for Research in Psychotherapy, Pacific Grove, California, 1980.

Campbell, D. T., & Fiske, D. W. Convergent and discriminant validation by the multitrait-multimethod matrix. *Psychological Bulletin*, 1959, *56*, 81–105.

Cartwright, D. S. Influence, leadership, control. In J. G. March (Ed.), *Handbook of organizations*. Chicago: Rand McNally, 1965.

Cartwright, D., Kirtner, W., & Fiske, D. Method factors in change associated with psychotherapy. *Journal of Abnormal and Social Psychology*, 1963, *66*, 169–175.

Cash, T. F., Kehr, J., & Saltzbach, R. F. Help-seeking attitudes and perceptions of counselor behaviour. *Journal of Counseling Psychology*, 1978, *25* (4), 264–269.

Cronbach, L. J. Coefficient alpha and the internal structure of tests. *Psychometrika*, 1951, *16*, 297–334.

Fitts, W. H. *Tennessee Self Concept Scale*. Nashville, Tenn.: Counselor Recordings and Tests, 1965.

Frank, J. D. Therapeutic factors in psychotherapy. *American Journal of Psychotherapy*, 1971, *25*, 350–361.

Frank, J. D. Common features account for effectiveness. In A. E. Bergin & H. H. Strupp (Eds.), *Changing frontiers of psychotherapy*. Chicago: Aldine, 1972.

Frank, J. D. *Persuasion and healing*. Baltimore: John Hopkins Press, 1973.

Freud, A. The widening scope of indicators for psychoanalysis. Discussion. *Journal of American Psychoanalytical Association*, 1954, *2*, 607–620.

Freud, S. The dynamics of transference. *Standard edition of the complete works of Sigmund Freud* (12, 97–108). London: Hogarth Press, 1958. (Originally published, 1912.)

Freud, S. On beginning the treatment: Further recommendations on the technique of psychoanalysis. *Standard edition of the complete works of Sigmund Freud* (12, 122–144). London: Hogarth Press, 1958. (Originally published, 1913.)

Gitelson, M. The curative functions of psychotherapy. *International Journal of Psychoanalysis*, 1962, *43*, 194–205.

Greenacre, P. The role of transference: Practical considerations in relation to psychoanalytic therapy. *Journal of the American Psychoanalytic Association*, 1954, *2*, 671–685.

Greenberg, L. S., & Webster, M. C. Resolving decisional conflict by gestalt two-chair dialogue: Relating process to outcome. *Journal of Counseling Psychology*, 1982, *29*, 468–477.

Greenson, R. R. The working alliance and the transference neurosis. *The Psychoanalytic Quarterly*, 1965, *34* (2), 155–181.

Greenson, R. R. *Technique and practice of psychoanalysis*. New York: International University Press, 1967.

Gurman, A. S. The patient's perception of the therapeutic relationship. In A. S. Gurman & A. M. Razin (Eds.), *Effective psychotherapy*. New York: Pergamon Press, 1977.

Hartley, D. C. *Therapeutic alliance and the success of brief psychotherapy*. Unpublished Doctoral Dissertation, Vanderbilt University, 1978.

Heppner, P. P., & Dixon, D. N. Effects of client perceived need and counselor role on clients behaviors. *Journal of Counseling Psychology*, 1978, *25* (6), 514–519.

Hill, C. E. A comparison of the perceptions of a therapy session by clients, therapists, and objective judges. *JSAS Catalog of Selected Documents in Psychology*, 1974, *4*, 16 (Ms. No. 564).

Horwitz, L. *Clinical predictions in psychotherapy*. New York: Jason Aronson, 1974.

Horvath, A. O. An Exploratory Study of the Working Alliance: Its Measurement and Relationship to Outcome. Unpublished Doctoral Dissertation, University of British Columbia, 1981.

Horvath, A. O. *Working Alliance Inventory* (rev. ed.), 1982.

Hovland, C. I., Janis, I. L., & Kelley, H. H. *Communications and persuasion: Psychological studies of opinion change*. New Haven: Yale University Press, 1953.

Hoyt, C. L. Test reliability estimated by analysis of variance. *Psychometrics*, 1941, *6*, 153–160.

Johnson, D. W., & Matross, R. P. Interpersonal influence on therapy: A social psychological view. In A. S. Gurman & A. M. Razin (Eds.), *Effective therapy*. New York: Pergamon Press, 1977.

Kazdin, A. E. Nonspecific treatment factors in psychotherapy outcome research. *Journal of Consulting and Clinical Psychology*, 1979, *47* (5), 846–851.

Klein, H. A study of changes occurring in patients during and after psychoanalytic treatment. In I. P. Hoch & J. Zubin (Eds.), *Current approaches to psychoanalysis*. New York: Grune & Stratton, 1960.

LaCrosse, M. B. Comperative perceptions of counselor behavior: A replication and extention. *Journal of Counseling Psychology*, 1977, *29*, 464–471.

LaCrosse, M. B., & Barak, A. Differential perception of counselor behavior. *Journal of Counseling Psychology*, 1976, *23*, 170–172.

Lambert, M. J. & DeJulio, S. S. Outcome research in Carkhuff's human resource development training programs: Where is the donut. *Conseling Psychologist*, 1977, 6, 79–86.

Lewin, K. *Resolving social conflicts*. New York: Harper & Row, 1948.

Loewenstein, R. M. Some remarks on defenses, autonomous Ego, and psychoanalytic techniques. *International Journal of Psycho-Analysis*, 1954, 35, 158–193.

Luborsky, L. Helping alliance in psychotherapy. In J. C. Claghorn (Ed.), *Successful psychotherapy*. New York: Brunner/Mazel, 1976.

Malan, H. D. *Toward the validation of dynamic psychotherapy: A replication*. New York: Plenum Press, 1976.

Mann, J. *Time limited psychotherapy*. Cambridge: Harvard University Press, 1973.

Matarazzo, R. G. Research on the teaching and learning of psychotherapeutic skills. In A. E. Bergin & S. L. Garfield (Eds.), *Handbook of psychotherapy and behavior change: An empirical analysis*. New York: Wiley, 1971.

Meltzoff, J., & Kornreich, M. *Research in psychotherapy*. New York: Atherton Press, 1970.

Mintz, J. The role of the therapist in assessing psychotherapy outcome. In A. S. Gurman & A. M. Razin (Eds.), *Effective psychotherapy*. New York: Pergamon Press, 1977.

Mitchell, K. M., Bozarth, J. D., & Krauft, C. C. Reappraisal of the therapeutic effectiveness of accurate empathy, non-possessive warmth, and genuineness. In A. S. Gurman & A. M. Razin (Eds.), *Effective psychotherapy*. New York: Pergamon Press, 1977.

Morgan, R. The relationship among therapeutic alliance, therapists' facilitative behaviors, patient insight, patient resistance and treatment outcome in psychoanalytically oriented psychotherapy. Unpublished Doctoral Dissertation, University of Miami, 1977.

Moseley, D. The therapeutic relationship and its association with outcome. Unpublished Master's Thesis, University of British Columbia, 1983.

Nichols, R., & Beck, K. Factors in psychotherapy change. *Journal of Consulting and Clinical Psychology*, 1960, 24, 338–399.

Orlinsky, D. E., & Howard, K. I. Relation of process to outcome in psychotherapy. In S. L. Garfield & A. E. Bergin (Eds.), *Handbook of psychotherapy and behavior change*. Toronto: Wiley, 1978.

Osipow, S. H., Carney, C. G., & Barak, A. A scale of educational vocational undescidedness: A typologycal approach. *Journal of Vocational Behavior*, 1976, 9, 233–343.

Parloff, M. B., Waskow, I. E., & Wolfe, B. E. Research on therapist variables in relation to process and outcome. In S. L. Garfield & A. E. Bergin (Eds.), *Handbook of psychotherapy and behavior change*. New York: Wiley, 1978.

Patton, M. J. Attraction, discrepancy, and responses to psychological treatment. *Journal of Counseling Psychology*, 1969, 16, 317–324.

Rice, K., Koke, C., Greenberg, L., & Wagstaff, A. *Manual for client voice quality*. Toronto, Canada: York University Counselling and Development Centre, 1979.

Rogers, C. R. *Client centered therapy*. Cambridge, Mass.: Riverside Press, 1951.

Rogers, C. R. The necessary and sufficient conditions of therapeutic personality change. *Journal of Consulting Psychology*, 1957, 22, 95–103.

Rogers, C. R., & Dymond, R. T. *Psychotherapy and personality change*. Chicago: University of Chicago Press, 1954.

Rogers, C. R., Gendlin, G. T., Kiesler, D. V., & Truax, L. B. *The therapeutic relationship and its impact: A study of psychotherapy with schizophrenics*. Madison, Wisc.: University of Wisconsin Press, 1967.

Saltzman, C., Luetgert, M. J., Roth, C. H., Creaser, J., & Howard, L. Formation of a therapeutic relationship: Experiences during the initial phase of psychotherapy as predictors of treatment duration and outcome. *Journal of Consulting and Clinical Psychology*, 1976, 44 (4), 546–555.

Smith, M. L., & Glass, G. V. Meta-analysis of psychotherapy outcome studies. *American Psychologist*, 1977, 32 (9), 752–760.

Spielberger, C. D., Gorsuch, R. L., & Lushene, R. E. *Manual for the Stait-Trait Anxiety Inventory*. Palo Alto, Calif.: Consulting Psychologists Press, 1970.

Sterba, R. F. The fate of the ego in analytic therapy. *International Journal of Psychoanalysis*, 1934, 15, 117–126.

Strong, S. R. Counseling: An interpersonal influence process. *Journal of Counseling Psychology,* 1968, *15* (8), 215–224.

Strong, S. R. Social psychological approach to psychotherapy research. In S. L. Garfield & A. E. Bergin (Eds.), *Handbook of psychotherapy and behavior change.* Toronto: Wiley, 1978.

Strong, S. R. & Matross, R. P. Change processes in counseling and psychotherapy. *Journal of Counseling Psychology,* 1973, *20,* 25–37.

Strupp, H. H., Wallach, M. S., & Wogan, M. Psychotherapy experience in retrospect: Questionnaire survey of former patients and their therapists. *Psychological Monographs,* 1964, *78* (Whole No. 588).

Strupp, H. H. On the basic ingredients of psychotherapy. *Psychotherapy and Psychosomatics,* 1974, *24,* 249–260.

Sundland, D. M., & Barker, E. N. The orientations of psychotherapists. *Journal of Consulting Psychology,* 1962, *26,* 201–212.

Truax, C. B. Therapeutic conditions. *Psychiatric Institute Bulletin.* University of Wisconsin, 1962, *1* (10).

Truax, C. B., & Carkhuff, R. R. *Toward effective counseling and psychotherapy: Training and practice.* Chicago: Aldine, 1967.

Truax, C. B., & Mitchell, K. M. Research on certain therapist interpersonal skills in relation to process and outcome. In A. E. Bergin & S. L. Garfield (Eds.), *Handbook of psychotherapy and behavior change: An empirical analysis.* New York: Wiley, 1971.

Waskow, I. E., & Parloff, M. B. (Eds.), *Psychotherapy change measures.* Rockville, Md.: National Institute of Mental Health, 1975.

Zetzel, E. R. Current concepts of transference. *International Journal of Psychoanalysis,* 1956, *37,* 369–376.

16

Shapiro
Personal Questionnaire
and Generalized
Personal Questionnaire
Techniques:
A Repeated Measures
Individualized Outcome
Measurement

J. P. N. Phillips
Psychology Department
University of Hull
Hull, England

Introduction

A primary feature of most psychiatric patients is that they present with statements about themselves and their condition. These may be either symptom statements, that is complaints (e.g., of feeling depressed or anxious or compelled to do certain things, of irrational fears or obsessional thoughts or sexual problems) or signs (e.g., expressing delusions, or manic excitement). Their utterance of such statements is often the most (and almost always an) important fact about them, which affects, and frequently determines, their acceptance for treatment, the type of therapy they receive and the assessment of its success, and their discharge.

Surprisingly, however, such statements do not appear to have been very often used directly as tools in scientific experiments with psychiatric patients. Three reasons for this neglect suggest themselves. Firstly, from a strict (and outmoded) Watsonian behavioristic point of view, such statements are subjective, and therefore not acceptable as scientific evidence, so that objective tests (sometimes of doubtful clinical relevance) have usually been preferred. This, of course, ignores the facts that they are sometimes, in the present state of our knowledge, the only available evidence for the state of mind they describe, and that although they may be subjective evidence for such states of mind, the fact that a patient utters them is an objective fact. Perhaps, with the coming of the cognitive revolution in clinical psychology and psychiatry (Mahoney, 1974; Beck, 1976; Meichenbaum, 1978; Beck, Rush, Shaw, & Emery, 1979), this reason may come to be seen as less than compelling. Secondly, objective experimental workers in this field have tended on the whole to come down in favor of the nomothetic side of the idiopathic–nomothetic division, and thus used questionnaires standardized on large groups of patients, which are suitable for group experimental designs, rather than have anything to do with the unique statements of a unique psychiatric patient. Noteworthy exceptions have been Stephenson (1953), Kelly (1955) (although not some of his more enthusiastic than self-critical followers), and Osgood, Suci, and Tannenbaum (1957). Since there is now a growing literature (e.g., Sidman, 1960; Shapiro, 1961b, 1966; Chassan, 1967; Davidson & Costello, 1969; Hersen & Barlow, 1976; Kratochwill, 1978) on single-subject experiments, it is to be hoped that the balance may now shift. Thirdly, patients naturally describe changes in their condition by the use of everyday language qualifiers, such as "very" or "a little," and it is not immediately clear how these may be quantified, especially since appropriate quantification may differ from patient to patient.

Generalized Personal Questionnaire Techniques

A solution to this problem of quantification is given by generalized personal questionnaire techniques. These are methods of constructing a questionnaire which is tailor-made for an individual psychiatric patient, and which can be repeatedly administered to scale successive levels of intensity of his or her symptom- and sign-statements. They are characterized by two features. Firstly, the questionnaire items are constructed from statements elicited from the patient. Secondly, there is a common rationale for the form of the items (a rationale based on a general method of scaling, which will not be discussed here: cf. Phillips, 1963, 1977). They thus constitute an objective, idiopathic method of investigating the relationships between such statements and their response to attempts to modify experimentally or to cure the patient's condition.

The purpose of this chapter is to give an account, illustrated by a number of clinical examples, of these techniques and their development, with sufficient detail to enable the reader to make use of them.

An Adumbration

The first feature of generalized personal questionnaire techniques mentioned above, namely that they are constructed from statements elicited from the patient, is already found in a paper by Shapiro and Ravenette (1959), which foreshadowed the invention of the first type of personal questionnaire by Shapiro 2 years later.

Example 0

Shapiro and Ravenette carried out an experiment on the effects of discussions of guilt and paranoid beliefs with an individual male paranoid patient, using a guilt questionnaire constructed from statements given in an inventory by Sandler (1954) and a paranoid questionnaire constructed from statements made up on the basis of an interview with the patient [see Table 16-1(a), (b)]. The questionnaire was administered on a number of occasions, each time by asking the patient to sort the statements into five categories of agreement, scored 0–4, as shown in Table 16-1(c). The design and results

Table 16-1   Specimen Questionnaire Items from Shapiro and Ravenette (1959)

(a) Guilt (from Sandler, 1954)

    1   I feel that I am an unworthy man.

    5   People would despise me if they really knew me.

    9   I believe that my sins will find me out.

(b) Paranoid Beliefs (on the Basis of Interview with the Patient)

    4   I believe that "they" use microphones and electronic devices to keep a record of my every move.

    13   I believe that my wife has been unfaithful to me.

    20   I believe that dope has been put into my food to make me irritable.

(c) Scoring

Category	Score
This is definitely the case.	4
This may be the case.	3
I am not sure.	2
This may not be the case.	1
This is definitely not the case.	0

of the experiment are shown graphically in Figure 16-1. There was no significant change on the guilt scale, but a significant overall decrease on the paranoid scale. Further, it appeared that all changes in the paranoid scale occurred during weekends, the delusions becoming stronger over weekends following discussions of guilt and weaker over weekends following discussions of delusions.

Thus, clinically and scientifically meaningful results followed from the use of a questionnaire based on the patient's own statements. However, the form of the questionnaire was still conventional.

The Shapiro Personal Questionnaire

Example 1

The first true personal questionnaire was reported by Shapiro (1961a), and will here be illustrated by data from the 28-year-old depressive patient studied by Shapiro.

Construction

This consists of a number of stages.

Elicitation and Discussion of Statements   In a special standardized interview (Shapiro, 1961c, 1975) a list of statements describing his or her condition is elicited from the patient. If it is thought necessary, this list is discussed with the patient's psychiatrist, and then jointly with the patient, to ensure the clinical relevance of each statement on it. Each statement will be the basis of a separate item in the questionnaire: those for Shapiro's patient are shown in Table 16-2(a).

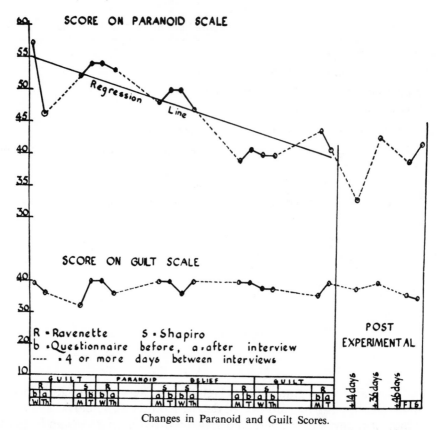

Changes in Paranoid and Guilt Scores.

Figure 16-1   Results of first Shapiro and Ravenette (1959) attempt at a generalized personal questionnaire.

Formulation of Symptom- or Sign-Levels   Each elicited statement is called the "illness," or "dysfunction" or no. (iii) statement. From it are constructed two further statements:

1. The "improvement," or no. (ii), statement, designed to indicate that the symptom is improving, but is still sufficiently unpleasant to require medical attention.
2. The "recovery" or no. (i), statement, to indicate that the symptom is no longer unpleasant enough to require medical attention.

This is illustrated, for two of the illness statements of Table 16-2(a), in Table 16-2(b).

Rules to help with the formulation of the improvement and recovery statements are given by Shapiro (1961c, 1975): The aim is that they should describe the degree of unpleasantness specified in the next stage.

Scaling Procedure   Each of the statements thus obtained is typed on a separate 3×5 inch index card, and the patient is asked to rate the unpleasantness of the state of mind it implies, in terms of a modification of the Singer–Young Affect Rating Scale (Singer & Young, 1941), Table 16-2(c). Any statement which is not rated as indicated in this table is immediately discussed with the patient so as to obtain an agreed reformulation which is so rated.

Table 16-2   Construction of a Shapiro PQ (from Shapiro, 1961)

(a) Statements

Thinking Difficulties

My mind is very unclear.

I can't put my mind to anything.

Hostility

I feel very much like hitting people.

I feel very much like throwing things.

I feel very much like screaming.

Hypochondriacal Delusion

I feel certain that I am going mad.

I feel certain that there is something eating away my brain.

Delusions of Reference

I feel certain that I look peculiar.

I feel certain that people laugh at me.

I cannot bear crowds.

Depression

I have not got any energy.

I cannot go out and enjoy myself.

I feel very depressed.

I feel very much like crying.

I have a miserable feeling in my eyes.

I feel that life is not worth living.

Somatic

I am unable to sleep at nights.

My appetite is very poor.

I have a terrible pain in my head.

I suffer very badly from constipation.

(b) Modified Statements

(iii) Illness: I feel certain that I look peculiar.   I have not got any energy.

(ii) Improvement: I feel it is possible I look peculiar.   I have a little energy.

(i) Recovery: On the whole I do not feel I look peculiar.   On the whole I have some energy.

(c) Modified Singer–Young Affect Rating Scale, with Desired Positions of Statements

Very great unpleasantness
Very unpleasant
} Illness statement

Moderately unpleasant
Slightly unpleasant
Undecided
} Improvement statement

Slightly pleasant
Moderately pleasant
Very pleasant
Very great pleasure
} Recovery statement

(d) Cards

| I feel certain that I look peculiar. |
| I feel it is possible I look peculiar. |

| I feel it is possible I look peculiar. |
| On the whole I do not feel I look peculiar. |

| On the whole I do not feel I look peculiar. |
| I feel certain that I look peculiar. |

Preparation of Questionnaire Material   From each set of three statements a questionnaire item is produced by typing each of the three possible pairs of statements on a separate 3×5 inch index card, one member of the pair above the other (which is the upper and which the lower being decided at random, subject to the requirement that the number of times a more severe statement appears above a less severe one is, as far as possible, equal to the number of times the reverse occurs). This is illustrated, for the first of the "Delusions of reference" statements of Table 16-2(a), in Table 16-2(d). For hand scoring, it is convenient to enter on the back of each card the number of the item to which it belongs, the number [(i), (ii), or (iii)] of the upper statement and the number of the lower statement.

Administration

On each occasion of administration, two further index cards, bearing the words "TOP" and "BOTTOM," respectively, in block capitals, are placed side by side in front of the patient. Then all the questionnaire cards (which have been shuffled together in random order) are presented in turn to the patient, who is asked to sort them into two piles according to whether the top or the bottom statement comes closer to describing his (or her) present state.

Scoring

Recording Responses   For each item, the responses to the three cards constituting it are entered in a "matrix" such as those in Figure 16-2(a), where a 1 in a cell indicates that the statement at the head of the column in which the cell lies has been judged by the patient to come closer to describing his current condition than the statement at the left of the row in which it lies, and a 0 indicates the reverse. For hand scoring, it is convenient to make use of a previously prepared record form containing at least as many empty matrices as there are questionnaire items: these are easily drawn up and duplicated. First, the pile of "TOP" cards is turned face down, and for each card in turn a 1 is entered in the cell whose column is that of the upper statement and whose row is that of the lower statement, of the matrix for the item. Then, the "BOTTOM" pile is treated similarly, except that now a 1 is entered in the cell whose row is that of the upper statement and whose column is that of the lower. (Although to read, and perhaps the first time one scores a Shapiro questionnaire, this procedure seems hideously complicated, with practice it rapidly becomes very easy.) Zeros are then entered in all empty off-diagonal cells: it will be noticed that the pattern in the bottom left-hand half of each matrix is a negative mirror image of that in the top right-hand half, a fact that is useful as a partial check against slips of recording.

Rationale of Scoring   Just how response patterns are to be scored requires a little careful consideration, and is illustrated in Figure 16-2.

All eight possible response patterns are shown in Figure 16-2(a). Four of them are, in fact, inconsistent, as shown in Figure 16-2(b). In each of pattern V and pattern VII the patient has indicated that the no. (i) statement better describes how he feels than the no. (iii) statement, which better describes how he feels than the no. (ii) statement, that is, that the severity of his symptom lies both below the midpoint of the no. (i) and no. (iii) statements, and above the midpoint of the no. (ii) and no. (iii) statements. As may be seen from the figure, this is impossible. Similarly, in each of patterns VI and VIII he has indicated that the no. (iii) statement better describes how he feels than the

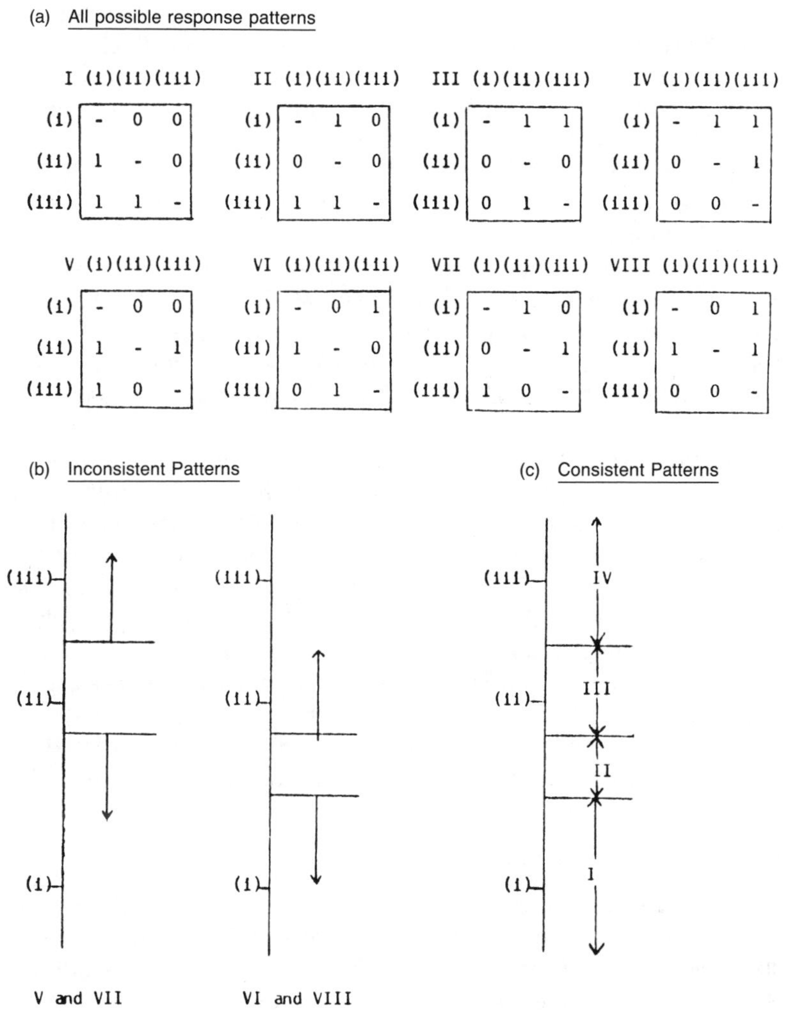

(a)   All possible response patterns

Figure 16-2   Example of the scoring of response patterns.

no. (i) statement, which better describes how he feels than the no. (ii) statement, so that there is a similar inconsistency involving the midpoints of the no. (i) and no. (ii) statements and of the no. (i) and no. (iii) statements, as may be seen from the figure. (Shapiro makes a distinction between "circular" and "noncircular" inconsistent response patterns, which will not be used here.)

Each of the remaining patterns is consistent, and assigns the current level of the symptom to one of the four regions shown in Figure 16-2(c). Thus pattern I places the current level below the midpoint of the no. (i) and no. (ii) statements, pattern II places it above that midpoint but below the midpoint of the no. (i) and no. (iii) statements, and so on. These four patterns were scored 1 to 4, respectively, by Shapiro; equivalently, they may (in accordance with the scoring of general ordered metric and ordinal personal questionnaires described below) be scored 0 to 3, respectively.

Each of the inconsistent patterns differs by just one response from a consistent pattern, and may be scored as the consistent pattern it least differs from or, when there is more than one such, as their average. Thus pattern V differs least from, and may be scored as, pattern I; pattern VI differs least from patterns I and III, and may be scored as their average, namely pattern II; similarly, pattern VII may be scored as pattern III and pattern VIII as pattern IV.

A Shapiro personal questionnaire thus provides two things. Firstly, it gives a scaling of the successive current levels of the patient's symptoms, which may be tabulated (with the inconsistent patterns being distinguished in some way, e.g., by being circled) and/or graphed as they are obtained, giving an ongoing picture of the fluctuations of the various aspects of the patient's symptomatology. This is illustrated, for the patient of Example 1, in Figure 16-3, which graphs the average score on each of the six classes of symptoms over nine successive occasions. Statistical analysis showed very highly significant differences between occasions in the overall level of illness, no significant differences between the various classes of symptoms, and a very highly significant interaction between classes and occasions, indicating that the illness changed its content and character from occasion to occasion, as is evident from the graph. Thus the personal questionnaire has revealed features of the patient's illness of which a clinician relying only on clinical interview data might very well have been only dimly, if at all, aware.

The second thing provided by a Shapiro personal questionnaire is a check on the internal consistency of the patient's responses. In the present example the patient produced just three inconsistent response patterns out of 180, and this high degree of consistency is quite typical of personal questionnaires (see also Examples 2, 3, 5, and 6).

Significance Tests for Consistency

In the event of a large number of inconsistent response patterns, either on a particular occasion, or on a particular item, or, indeed, over all occasions and items, the user may wish to know whether there is any evidence that the responses are not entirely random. Since, out of the eight possible response patterns, four are consistent and four inconsistent, the probability, on a null hypothesis of completely random responding, of a consistent response is ½. Thus the null hypothesis may be tested either, with a small number of items and occasions, exactly, by means of the binomial test, or, with a larger number of either, approximately, by the normal approximation to the binomial test.

For example, with 180 response patterns, the binomial probability of three (which is not a large number, but will serve as an illustration) or fewer being inconsistent is given by

$$6.34 \times 10^{-49}$$

Alternatively, since the binomial distribution with $n = 180$ is closely approximated by normal distribution, in the present example with mean 90.0 and variance 45.0 the standard score for three inconsistent items out of 180 is

$$-12.9691942$$

with a one-tail normal probability of approximately 2.7×10^{-10}. (Shapiro, 1975, suggests the use of χ^2 here: however, it seems to the present writer that this is one of those extremely rare situations where a one-tail test is appropriate.)

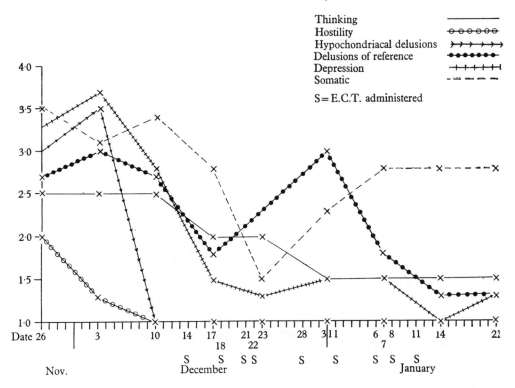

Figure 16-3   Results of a Shapiro (1961) personal questionnaire.

By either test, the hypothesis of random responding may be rejected at a high level of confidence. Analogous tests can similarly be carried out for a single occasion (over all items) or for a single item (over all occasions).

The provision of such a check, not requiring any repeated responses, of consistency, together with an associated significance test, is most unusual in questionnaires.

Random responding to the Shapiro personal questionnaire appears to be a rare phenomenon. Shapiro (1975) reports meeting it in only three cases after some 14 years experience. However, in each case further enquiry revealed clinically meaningful reasons for the inconsistency, so that it should not be ignored when it occurs.

The wide range of applications of Shapiro's technique may be illustrated by three further examples.

Example 2

The first, by McPherson and LeGassicke (1965), shows how a personal questionnaire may be used to monitor symptom relief in a therapeutic experiment. The drug Wy 3498 (a sedative analogous to chlordiazepoxide) and an indistinguishable placebo were administered on successive occasions to a woman of 26 showing a variety of anxiety and obsessional symptoms. The results are shown in Figure 16-4. (Just 2 out of 336 response patterns were inconsistent.) The only significant effects were a superiority of drug to placebo and differences between the symptoms ($p < .01$ in both cases).

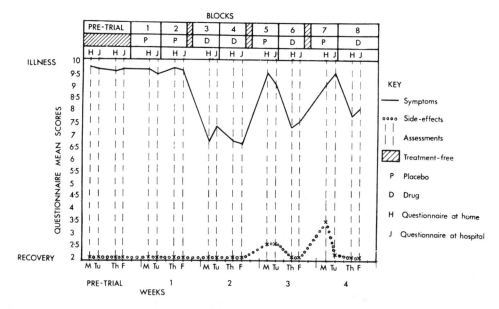

Figure 16-4   Results of a personal questionnaire used to monitor symptom relief in a thera-peutic experiment (McPherson & LeGassicke, 1965).

Example 3

The next example, by Shapiro, Marks, and Fox (1963), illustrates the use of a personal questionnaire in a therapeutic experiment with more complex design and results. A 38-year-old woman with incapacitating phobias was treated by means of both rational retraining (in fact real life systematic desensitization) and nondirective psychotherapy, a personal questionnaire being administered either immediately after, or 3 days after, the treatment, the occasions of treatment being classified as either midweek (Tuesday, Wednesday, and Thursday) or weekend (Monday and Friday), the whole experiment being divided into first and second halves. The average personal questionnaire scores are graphed in Figure 16-5 (just 2 out of 368 response patterns were inconsistent), which also shows the design of the experiment. The most salient results are as follows.

There was a highly significant difference between questionnaire items, six of the eight items with highest mean scores appearing phobic, the remaining two seeming to in-volve parental concern, nine of the eleven items with moderate mean score being describable as anxiety items, and the four items with lowest mean score being depressive in content. However there was no significant interaction of the items with any of the other variables.

The other significant main effects cannot be interpreted directly, since each is involved in significant interactions. An interaction between kinds of treatment and immediate versus delayed measures was a consequence of behavior therapy being always followed by an immediate improvement and a delayed relapse, whereas the psychotherapy was followed by an immediate improvement and various delayed effects giving an average improvement. An interaction between kinds of treatment and halves of the experiment might have been due to the withdrawal of Shapiro from the behavior therapy in the second half of the experiment or the change in its character from preparation to actual desensitization. An interaction between kinds of treatment and midweek versus weekend was difficult to interpret.

Example 4

The final example here, by Slater (1970, 1976) is of a more systematic investigation of the relationship between symptoms than either of the two preceding examples. It comprises a principal components analysis of the personal questionnaire responses in an experiment (briefly reported by Shapiro, 1969) with a 40-year-old male depressive patient. Of the principal components extracted, the first, interpreted as one of aggravation or relief of symptoms in general, accounted for 60% of the variation and the second, provisionally described as one of internal/external reference, accounted for 12%. The results of the analysis are shown graphically in Figure 16-6. There is a clear curvilinear relationship between the two components, which is interpreted by Slater (1976) as suggesting that "the externally referred symptoms were the ones most easily relieved." For further discussion of this analysis, see Rump (1974) and Slater (1974).

These examples can only give a brief indication of the research which has been carried out using Shapiro's personal questionnaire technique. The literature, which still only begins to tap the potential of the method, is reviewed by Phillips (1977). Since then, Reading and Newton (1978) have reported an adaptation of the McGill Pain Questionnaire (Melzack, 1975) into Shapiro personal questionnaire format.

Extensions of Shapiro's Technique

Nevertheless, Shapiro's method has certain restrictions, the removal of which leads to more general types of personal questionnaire techniques. The first restriction is an implicit limitation, through the scaling experiment in the construction of the questionnaire, to symptoms or signs whose most important characteristic is that the patient experiences them as unpleasant. There were good clinical reasons for this in the type of patients Shapiro was working with while developing his questionnaire. However, some symptoms or signs, for example, delusions of persecution, would almost certainly be considered pathological by a clinician even if the patient did not (although he probably does) find them unpleasant: the most appropriate scaling dimension here might be the

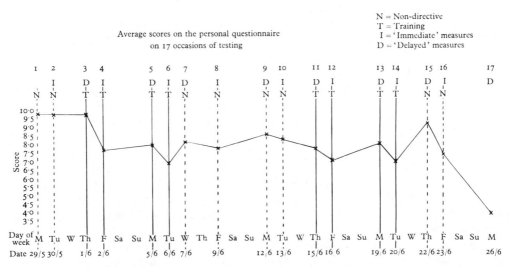

Figure 16-5   Average personal questionnaire scores for a woman with incapacitating phobias (Shapiro, Marks, & Fox, 1963).

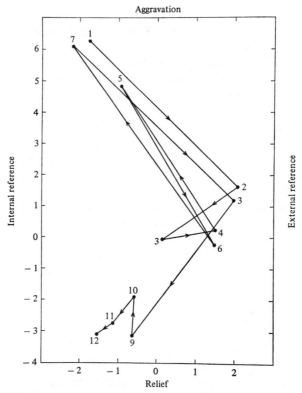

Figure 16-6   Example of a principal components analysis of the personal questionnaire responses in an experiment with a 40-year-old male depressive patient (Slater, 1970: a slip in the labeling of the axes [cf. Slater, 1974] has been corrected).

degree of subjective certainty with which the patient held these beliefs. Others, for example, hysterical symptoms in a patient displaying *belle indifférence*, might not be experienced as particularly unpleasant. Still others, for example, delusions of grandeur or socially unaccepted sexual behavior, gambling, alcoholism, and drug addiction, might be immediately pleasant but unpleasant in their long-term consequences. There would therefore seem to be advantages in allowing a scaling of symptoms along any clinically relevant dimension.

The second restriction, which is linked to the first, is the limitation that the number of statements in an item must be exactly three. Although here also there were good reasons for this, for some symptom- or sign-statements some other number might be more appropriate. For example, with paranoid delusions five statements, modeled on the five levels of agreement used by Shapiro and Ravenette (1959), seem more natural than three. Further, some symptoms or signs, for example, inability to concentrate or poor memory, might, even at their highest level of intensity, be less disturbing to a particular patient than others at an intermediate level, for example, a panic attack or depression. Again, if more statements were used, greater precision of measurement would, in principle, be obtainable. There would therefore seem to be advantages also in allowing this number to vary from item to item.

The removal of these two restrictions leads to the (general) ordered metric personal questionnaire technique. The method is also capable of a third, rather different, kind of extension, namely allowing types of patient-judgment other than that of which of two statements comes closer to describing the current level of severity of the symptom. Allowing also other types of judgment leads to other types of personal questionnaire technique. Thus in an ordinal personal questionnaire the patient-judgments are of whether the current level of severity of the symptom is higher or lower than that of a single statement, and in an interval personal questionnaire the patients make a quantified version of the same judgment, that is, whether the current level of severity is higher or lower than that of a statement, and by how much (in terms of a specified standard difference).

These three generalized types of personal questionnaire technique are described in turn below.

The General Ordered Metric Personal Questionnaire

Construction

Rationale for Item Construction   An ordered metric personal questionnaire is, as explained above, basically the same as a Shapiro personal questionnaire, and differs only in that the statements of an item may be scaled along any clinically relevant dimension, and there may be any appropriate number of them greater than one. (There must be at least two, since the patient's judgments involve pairs of statements: with more than about five, except for occasional items, the method, although in principle possible, tends to become unwieldy.) Now when the number of statements is thus allowed to increase above three, two problems arise. Firstly, the number of pairs of statements to be presented to the patient rapidly rises to an unmanageable size, and also, for certain response patterns, it is no longer possible to know (without further scaling information) whether they are consistent or not. The most practical solution of the first problem and approach to a solution of the second was suggested by Shapiro (personal communication), and consists of omitting some of the possible pairs. It then turns out (Phillips, 1966) that it is always possible to determine which patterns are consistent and which are not if and only if pairs are omitted in such a way that the cells corresponding to the remaining pairs in the top right-hand half of the response matrix form a path which always moves to the right or downward. This is illustrated, for the cases of four to seven statements, in Figure 16-7(a), where only the top right-hand half of each empty matrix is given (the information in the other half being redundant), and where the matrix for Shapiro's three-statement item is included for comparison. There are many ways in which pairs can be thus omitted: the writer prefers those in which each statement occurs as far as possible an equal number of times, and these are the ones shown in Figure 16-7(a) (note that there are two such for four statements), but others have been used by Ingham (1965), Mulhall (1976), and Singh and Bilsbury (1982).

Example 5

A female undergraduate was referred complaining of severe anxieties in unfamiliar social situations and approximately daily hour-long daydreams of having coped much better in some social situations than she actually did.

Elicitation and Discussion of Statements   Statements can be elicited by means of Shapiro's (1961c, 1975) standardized interview, or by any other method which the user considers suitable.

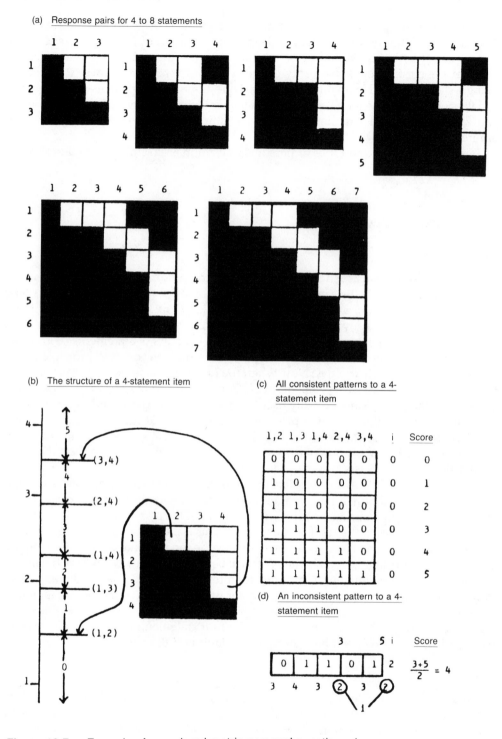

Figure 16-7　Example of an ordered metric personal questionnaire.

In the present case seven statements about her problems were elicited, for example,

I am always late for lectures.

My concentration is terrible.

I daydream a lot.

Formulation of Symptom- and Sign-Levels   Further statements expressing various levels of the symptom or sign should be formulated as considered clinically appropriate. Because the restriction on the number of statements per item has been relaxed to allow just this freedom, it does not seem possible to lay down any hard and fast rules here.

For example, from the statements above were derived the following three from the first, four from the second, and five from the third.

I am *always* (*sometimes, never*) late for lectures.

My concentration is *terrible, not very good, adequate, excellent*.

I daydream *to the exclusion of most other things* (*a lot, a fair amount, just a little*). I do *not* daydream *at all*.

and similarly for the other elicited statements.

Scaling Procedure   A scaling of the statements of each item may be carried out by any suitable means (e.g., ranking) along any dimension considered clinically appropriate. Here, also because the restrictions on the dimension of scaling and number of statements have been relaxed, Shapiro's scaling procedure will, in general, no longer be appropriate.

In the present case the rank ordering of the statements of each item was informally checked with the patient.

Preparation of Questionnaire Material   From each set of statements a questionnaire item is produced by typing each of the pairs of statements to be used (e.g., those in Figure 16-7(a), or some other set of pairs satisfying condition mentioned in the section Rationale for Item construction) on a separate 3×5 inch index card, one member of each pair above the other (which is the upper and which the lower being decided at random, subject to the restriction mentioned in the section The Shapiro Personal Questionnaire). For hand scoring it is convenient to enter items and statement numbers on the back of each card, as with a Shapiro questionnaire. The completed questionnaire consists of all the cards thus produced.

Administration

This is precisely as with a Shapiro questionnaire.

Scoring

Recording of Responses   This is as with a Shapiro questionnaire, making use of a previously prepared record form. Here it is convenient to prepare one master form (this will in general have to be done afresh for each new questionnaire) as illustrated in Table 16-3(a), for the patient of Example 5, and run off duplicate copies as required.

Rationale of Scoring   Although it is not here practicable, as it was with a Shapiro item, to list all possible response patterns (since the number of them rises very rapidly as the number of statements per item increases above three), scoring a response pattern is extremely simple, provided the item satisfies the condition mentioned in the section Rationale for Item Construction. For then, as illustrated in Figure 16-7(b) for a four-statement item, the midpoints of the pairs of statements (constituting the item) increase in value from the top left-hand cell of the response pattern matrix to the bottom right-hand cell, so that a consistent response pattern has the form of a string of nought or more 1s followed by a string of nought or more 0s. This is represented more clearly by arranging the cells corresponding to used pairs of the matrix in a row, as in Figure 16-7(c), which shows all possible consistent patterns for the four-statement item of Figure 16-7(b). Consistent patterns may be scored by the number of 1s they contain, and the regions corresponding to each of the consistent patterns in Figure 16-7(c) are indicated in Figure 16-7(b).

Inconsistent response patterns may (following the rationale developed by Slater, 1960, 1961) be scored as the consistent pattern from which they differ least, that is, by as few cells as possible (or as the average of such patterns if there are more than one). For example, the inconsistent pattern 01101 differs least (by two cells) from each of the consistent patterns 11100 and 11111, and therefore may be scored $(3+5)/2=4$. The minimum difference from a consistent pattern may be used as a measure of inconsistency (it is, in fact Slater's statistic i): in particular, consistent patterns have inconsistency $i=0$.

Confusion may occasionally arise in hand scoring an inconsistent pattern. The following very simple algorithm (which is illustrated in Figure 16-7(d) for the pattern 01101 mentioned above) should remove any problem, and is also adaptable for computer implementation. First, write the pattern in a row of cells, and write underneath the left-hand border of the left-hand cell the number of 1s in the pattern. Then work from left to right through all the right-hand borders of all the cells in turn, increasing the number last written down by one if the cell contains a 0, and decreasing it by one if the cell contains a 1: the smallest number thus written down is i. Each time it occurs, write above the cell border (below which it lies) the number of cells to the left of that border: the numbers thus written are the scores of the consistent patterns from which the given pattern differs least, and their average is the score assigned.

When response patterns are recorded, nonzero inconsistencies may be written as superscripts to the score, and the scores of consistent patterns written without superscript, as in Table 16-3(b). The results for the patient of Example 5 are shown in Table 16-3(b), the number of pairs of statements being indicated in brackets beside each item. (For the sole inconsistent item, i was equal to 1, as indicated by a superscript.)

Imaginal systematic desensitization of the social anxieties was begun on 10/2/71. (Treatment of the daydreaming by means of "thought-stopping" was offered, but declined on the grounds that she would like to retain the ability to daydream if she so chose.) At the end of the spring term some progress had been made, but when she was seen on the first day of the summer term she reported that during the vacation she had seen an endocrinologist who, after extensive tests, had advised her to stop taking her thyroid tablets. This she had done, and felt greatly improved in all phobic situations, so much so that she did not think it worthwhile to continue desensitization, particularly in the term of her final examinations. She summed up the situation by saying that the desensitization had caused some improvement, but that stopping her thyroid tablets had virtually cured her.

Table 16-3   An Ordered Metric Personal Questionnaire

(a) Specimen Record Form

(b) Results

		4/2/71	10/2/71	18/2/71	24/2/71	10/3/71	10/5/71
1 Frustrated about not doing things I want	(3)	3	3	1	1	1	0
2 Panicky with people known slightly	(5)	5	3	2	2	2	0
3 Not going to parties	(5)	3	5	2	2	2	0
4 Late for lectures	(3)	2	3	2	3	2	1
5 Concentration	(5)	5	5	3	1	2	1
6 Memory	(5)	5	5	4	4	3	1
7 Daydreaming	(7)	6^1	7	3	3	3	1
	Sum i	1	0	0	0	0	0

Significance Tests for Consistency   Essentially the same tests may be used here as with a Shapiro questionnaire, but now account has to be taken of the fact that with an item of more than three pairs of statements, i is not limited to the two possible values 0 and 1 each with probability ½. (The probability of i taking a specified value, together with the mean and variance of i, for a single ordered metric item of from three to seven pairs of statements, is shown in Table 16-4.)

Table 16-4   Distribution of Slater's i for 3–7 Boundaries

	Number of boundaries				
	3	4	5	6	7
0	$\frac{1}{2}$	$\frac{5}{16}$	$\frac{3}{16}$	$\frac{7}{64}$	$\frac{2}{32}$
1	$\frac{1}{2}$	$\frac{9}{16}$	$\frac{8}{16}$	$\frac{25}{64}$	$\frac{9}{32}$
2		$\frac{2}{16}$	$\frac{5}{16}$	$\frac{27}{64}$	$\frac{14}{32}$
3				$\frac{5}{64}$	$\frac{7}{32}$
Mean (i)	$\frac{1}{2}$	$\frac{13}{16}$	$\frac{9}{8}$	$\frac{47}{32}$	$\frac{29}{16}$
Variance (i)	$\frac{1}{4}$	$\frac{103}{256}$	$\frac{31}{64}$	$\frac{639}{1024}$	$\frac{183}{256}$

The exact test uses the method of generating functions to compute the probability of obtaining a value of the sum of i (either over all items on a single occasion, or over all occasions on a single item, or over both all occasions and all items) as small as, or smaller than, that observed. For example, the probability for the first occasion in Example 5 (when this was *not* a large number of inconsistent patterns) can easily be shown, using Table 16-4, to be

$$0.0003508$$

A simple computer program has been developed to carry out this test.

A normal approximation to the exact test may be illustrated with the same example. from Table 16-4 the mean and variance of sum i are $^{117}\!/_{16}$ and $^{807}\!/_{256}$, respectively, so that the z score for sum $i = 1$ is -3.5554, with a (one-tail) normal probability of approximately .0001887.

By either test, the hypothesis of random responding may be rejected at a high level of significance.

Two final remarks on general ordered metric personal questionnaires: firstly it can be seen that in construction, scoring, and significance test for consistency, a Shapiro personal questionnaire is simply a special case of a general ordered metric questionnaire; secondly, it is worth noting that their format has also been used in the construction of standard questionnaires, namely the modified Sexual Orientation Method (SOM) of Sambrooks and MacCulloch (1973) and the Sexual Interest Questionnaire (SIN) of Harbison, Graham, Quinn, McAllistar, and Woodward (1974).

The Ordinal Personal Questionnaire

Although the judgments required of the patient in an ordered metric personal questionnaire are formally pair comparisons, in that a preference between two statements is expressed, in fact this is really a preference between two distances, and the judgments involve three entities, namely the two statements and also the current level of the symptom. A simpler method would therefore be to require a comparison between just one statement and the level of the symptom. This is the procedure employed in the ordinal personal questionnaire technique (Phillips, 1970b).

Example 6

The technique may be illustrated by the case of a young married woman who was referred for treatment of frigidity and a number of phobias.

Elicitation and Discussion of Statements ⎫ These are precisely as with
Formulation of Symptom- or Sign-Levels ⎬ a general ordered metric
Scaling Procedure ⎭ questionnaire.

In the present case the nine statements

   I feel slightly disgusted with sex.
   I feel a little frightened of sex.
   I get very little pleasure from sex.
   I am frightened of spiders (wasps, bees, snakes, black clocks, thunder and lightening).

were elicited. ("Black clock" is a local term for a kind of beetle.) From the one concerning pleasure from sex, five statements were derived, namely

   I get *no* pleasure *at all* from sex. I get *very little* (*a fair amount, a great deal, a tremendous amount*) of pleasure from sex.

From each of the others, three statements were derived, on the pattern *very, a little* (*slightly* in the case of disgust with sex), *not at all*. It was informally checked that the patient ranked them in the obvious way.

Preparation of Questionnaire Material   From each set of statements a questionnaire item is produced by typing each individual statement on a separate 3×5 inch index card. For hand scoring it is convenient to enter the item and statement number on the back of each card. The completed questionnaire consists of all the cards thus produced.

Administration

On each occasion of administration, two further index cards, bearing the words "BETTER" and "WORSE," respectively, in block capitals, are placed side by side in front of the patient. Then all the questionnaire cards (which have been shuffled together into random order) are presented in turn to the patient, who is asked to sort them into two piles according to whether the present level of the symptom referred to is "better or worse than it says on the card." (Occasionally a patient may have difficulty with the words "better" and "worse," and prefer to say whether the symptom is MORE or LESS intense than the card indicates, or use some other paraphrase.)

Scoring

Recording of Responses   For each item, the responses to the cards constituting it are entered in a two-way table whose rows correspond to items and whose columns correspond to statements within items, a 1 indicating that the patient has judged the current level of his or her symptom to be worse than the statement at the head of the column, and a 0 that he or she has judged it to be better. For hand scoring, a special record form can be prepared in advance, but this is not really necessary: a sheet of ordinary squared paper will suffice. First, the pile of "BETTER" cards is turned face down, and for each card in turn a 0 is entered in the cell whose row is that of the item and whose column is that of the statement. Then the "WORSE" pile is treated similarly, except that 1s are now entered instead of 0s.

Rationale of Scoring   It turns out that the scoring of an ordinal item is formally identical to that of an ordered metric item, in the sense that, when the response patterns to each type of item are considered simply as sequences of 1s and 0s, the same patterns are consistent for each (and have the same scaling) and the same patterns are inconsistent. With an ordered metric item, because the patient is asked to say which of two statements comes closer to describing how he or she feels, the midpoints of pairs of statements form the boundaries of regions corresponding to consistent response patterns. With an ordinal item, this situation is simpler: because the patient is asked to say whether the intensity of his or her symptom is greater than or less than a statement, the statements themselves form the boundaries or regions corresponding to consistent response patterns. This is illustrated, for the case of a five-statement item, in Figure 16-8, which should be compared with Figure 16-7(b).

Thus precisely the same scoring procedure may be used with the response patterns to an ordinal item as with those to an ordered metric item (q.v.).

The results for the patient of Example 6 are shown in Table 16-5. Adapting an idea of Shapiro and Post (1974, personally communicated earlier by Shapiro), the first three items of the questionnaire, dealing with her feelings about sex, were also administered on every occasion (except 9/14/70, when she came alone) to her husband, using statements modified to allow him to express what he thought his wife's feelings were (e.g., "My wife feels *very* disgusted by sex."). (All response patterns to both questionnaires were consistent.) Training in relaxation, from which she reported deriving some general benefit, was begun before the questionnaire had been constructed. Imaginal systematic desensitization of sexual situations was begun on 7/13/70 and the first two items on the hierarchy ("My husband stroking my back when I am nude" and "My husband stroking my back under my nightgown") were presented without any anxiety being signalled: she and her husband were especially warned not to rush things or to attempt to force the pace. When they arrived for their next appointment, on 8/3/70, she wore the smile of a cat which has stolen the cream, and reported having had intercourse five times, each time reaching orgasm, indeed once a double orgasm. Over the next few sessions she reported continued sexual improvement, and on the principle of leaving well alone, no further treatment of her sexual feelings was attempted: instead, hierarchies were constructed in preparation for imaginal desensitization of her phobias.

However, on 10/19/70, she and her husband expressed a wish to discontinue treatment in view of great difficulties in finding a baby-sitter. At that time she was, sexually, going from strength to strength (although her husband was, almost certainly unrealistically, not completely satisfied), but her phobias, of which no specific treatment had yet been attempted, were completely unchanged.

Significance Tests for Consistency   These are precisely analogous to the corresponding tests for a general ordered metric questionnaire, using Table 16-4. The only difference is that here the number of *statements* per item is used where the number of *pairs of statements* per item was used for the ordered metric questionnaire. Thus for any occasion with the questionnaire of Example 6, the probability that sum $i=0$ is .007324. Since the mean and variance of sum i are $4\frac{1}{8}$ and $15\frac{9}{64}$, respectively, we have

$$z = -3.2515$$

with a (one-tail) normal probability of approximately .0005740, so that by either test, the hypothesis of random responding may be rejected at a high level of significance.

Schemes for Semiautomatic Construction and Scoring of Ordered Metric Ordinal Personal Questionnaires

Both the construction and the scoring of an ordered metric or an ordinal questionnaire involve a considerable amount of laborious unskilled routine work, and therefore a

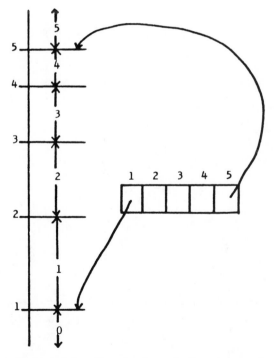

Figure 16-8   The structure of a five-statement item.

Table 16-5   Ordinal PQ

Wife		8/6/70	22/6/70	29/6/70	6/7/70	13/7/70	3/8/70	14/9/70	17/9/70	5/10/70	19/10/70
1 Disgust	(3)	1	1	2	1	1	1	0	0	0	0
Sex 2 Fear	(3)	2	1	1	1	0	0	0	0	0	0
3 Pleasure	(5)	4	3	3	2	2	2	1	0	0	0
4 Spiders	(3)	3	3	3	3	3	2	1	2	1	2
5 Wasps	(3)	3	3	3	3	3	3	1	3	3	3
Fears 6 Bees	(3)	3	3	3	3	3	3	3	3	3	3
7 Snakes	(3)	3	3	3	3	3	3	3	3	3	3
8 Black clocks	(3)	3	3	3	3	3	3	3	3	3	3
9 Thunder and lightning	(3)	3	3	3	3	1	1	1	1	2	3
Sum _i_		0	0	0	0	0	0	0	0	0	0

Husband		8/6/70	22/6/70	29/6/70	6/7/70	13/7/70	3/8/70	14/9/70	17/9/70	5/10/70	19/10/70
1 Disgust	(3)	3	1	2	1	2	1	2	2	0	2
Sex 2 Fear	(3)	3	2	2	1	2	1	1	1	1	1
3 Pleasure	(4)	4	3	2	2	2	2	1	1	2	1
Sum _i_		0	0	0	0	0	0	0	0	0	0

number of schemes have been developed for carrying out those phases of the methods partially or completely automatically.

A Computer-Card Scheme   Phillips (1968a) reported a scheme for computer scoring a Shapiro personal questionnaire, and this scheme has since been considerably extended (Phillips, 1979). The cards for an ordered metric or an ordinal questionnaire are computer cards with statements typewritten on the blank side, and punched in the first few columns with numbers identifying the item and statement(s), and in the last two columns with two digits which can be used, in conjunction with a card sorter or manually, to arrange the cards in a fresh (restrictedly) random order before each administration. (A computer program has been developed to punch such packs, but the typing of the statements on the cards has to be done manually.) At each administration the patient sorts the cards into two piles in the usual way, and these are then headed with marker cards and assembled, together with parameter cards and a terminator card, into a data pack for computer scoring. An example of a printout of such a scoring [the first administration of Table 16-3(b)] is shown in Figure 16-9. The numbers punched in the last two columns of each card make possible, in addition to the scoring of the questionnaire, a reconstruction of the complete sequence of responses, and hence offers the opportunity for tests of certain kinds of irrelevant response set (Phillips, 1979).

With an ordered metric questionnaire, there are three such. Firstly, *bias*, a tendency to favor "TOP" (or "BOTTOM") responses irrespective of the content of the card, may be assessed by means of a 2×2 contingency table. (It is necessary to distinguish here between two types of cards: those, called Type 1, on which the upper of the two statements indicates a lesser degree of illness than the lower, so that a "TOP" response is one of relative health and a "BOTTOM" response one of relative illness, and those called Type 2, in which the reverse holds.) The distribution here is the usual hypergeometric one, and Fisher's exact test, or its chi-square approximation, is appropriate. Secondly, *sequential dependency* of the implied health or illness responses may be assessed by the number *health–illness runs*, which has the usual runs distribution, and may be tested by the exact Wald–Wolfowitz test or its normal approximation (Siegel, 1956). Thirdly, *sequential dependency* of the "TOP" and "BOTTOM" responses may be assessed by the number of *top–bottom runs*, whose distribution depends on the sequence of Type 1 or Type 2 cards, but for moderate or large n is approximately normal. (There is also a large-sample overall chi-square test.) These three indices are inevitably correlated, although there are methods of ordering the Type 1 and Type 2 cards which minimize these correlations. (The possibility of such tests was suggested by Shapiro, personal communication.)

With an ordinal questionnaire, only one type of response set is tested for, namely sequential dependency of "BETTER" and "WORSE" responses, which may be assessed by the number of *better–worse runs*, with the usual runs distribution.

The Computer-Assisted Psychometric System (CAPS)   Sambrooks and MacCulloch (1973) reported a system in which the statement pairs of the SOM (a standard questionnaire in general ordered metric format: see above, immediately before section The Ordinal Personal Questionnaire) are projected from slides in a carousel on to a screen, and the subject responds by pressing one of two buttons, thereby causing the next statement pair to be projected and the response and its latency to be recorded on punched tape for computer scoring and analysis of latencies.

MISS X. X. XXXXXX
4/2/71
ORDERED METRIC P. Q.

ITEM	PATTERN	I	SCORE
1	111	0	3.
2	11111	0	5.
3	11100	0	3.
4	110	0	2.
5	11111	0	5.
6	11111	0	5.
7	1111101	1	5,7.
	SUM I =	1	

ANALYSIS OF IRRELEVANT RESPONSE SET

SEQUENCE OF RESPONSES

TYPE OF CARD	11112122111211212122221211121221
HEALTH OR ILLNESS	IIIIIHHIHIIIIIIIIIHIIIIIIIIIIII
TOP OR BOTTOM	BBBBTTBTTBBTBBTBTBTBTTBTBBBTBTTTB

BIAS

OBSERVED HEALTH ILLNESS   EXPECTED HEALTH ILLNESS

TYPE 1	2	16	18	TYPE 1	2.18	15.82	18.00
TYPE 2	2	13	15	TYPE 2	1.82	13.18	15.00
	4	29	33		4.00	29.00	33.00

EXACT P = 1.0000

SEQUENTIAL DEPENDENCY

7 HEALTH-ILLNESS RUNS (EXPECTED   8.03) EXACT P = 0.4996
21 TOP-BOTTOM RUNS   (EXPECTED 18.12) CHI-SQUARE = 1.3103 WITH 1 D.F. N.S.

CORRELATION BETWEEN INDICES

	......	BIAS	......	HI RUNS	TB RUNS
.	− 1.0000	− 1.0000	1.0000	− 0.0738	0.0878
BIAS .		− 1.0000	1.0000	0.0738	− 0.0878
.			− 1.0000	0.0738	− 0.0878
.				− 0.0738	0.0878
HI RUNS					− 0.0633

EXPECTED FREQUENCIES TOO SMALL FOR SOME SIGNIFICANCE TESTS

Figure 16-9   Computer scoring of a Shapiro personal questionnaire.

The Personal Questionnaire Rapid Scaling Technique (PQRST)   Mulhall (1976, 1978) reported a technique using a standard set of eight phrases (maximum possible, very considerable, considerable, moderate, little, very little, almost none, absolutely none) giving rise to eight-statement items or, by omission of the first and seventh phrases, six-statement items. Ingeniously devised answer sheets, on which each symptom is written by the patient, reusable booklets, and scoring stencils permit easy and rapid scoring.

The Computerized Ordered Metric Scales (COMETS)   Mulhall (1980) has also developed a computer program which prints out the items of a personal questionnaire on a lineprinter in the format of a conventional questionnaire, and an associated program for scoring the patient's responses.

Projected Desk-Top Minicomputer Scheme   Some preliminary work has been done on a scheme in which the questionnaire cards would be presented on the screen of a desk-top minicomputer, and the patient would answer by pressing one or other of two appropriate keys (T or B for an ordered metric questionnaire, B or W for an ordinal questionnaire). On completion of an administration, the results would be output on a lineprinter.

Such an approach would appear, in principle, to combine all the advantages, with few if any of the disadvantages, of each of the preceding schemes.

The Interval Personal Questionnaire

The judgments elicited from the patient in an ordered metric or an ordinal questionnaire are dichotomous. Although, as has been seen, a considerable amount of information can be obtained in this way, still more is made available if numerical judgments are elicited. This is the procedure employed in the interval personal questionnaire technique (Phillips, 1970a). Since it is usually most convenient with an interval personal questionnaire to administer each item separately (rather than by randomly shuffling together all the cards of all the items into a single questionnaire pack, as with the preceding types), the technique will be illustrated with just one item from such a questionnaire.

Example 7

A male postgraduate student self-referred for a disabling stammer was treated by Dr. D. C. Kendrick and the author, using both imaginal systematic desensitization of anxieties about speaking, and by shadowing. At each session his current status was scaled by means of an interval personal questionnaire consisting of five items, concerning:

1. Worry about the problem of speaking.
2. Depression about the problem of speaking.
3. Tension in speaking situations.
4. Frequency of speaking fluently.
5. Difficulty in speaking fluently.

Item 5 will be described in detail.

Construction   ⎫ These are precisely as with a
Elicitation and Discussion of Statements   ⎬ general ordered metric or an
Formulation of Symptom- and Sign-Levels ⎭ ordinal questionnaire.

In the present case the four statements of item 5 were:

5.4 At the worst I have *not* been able to pronounce *a single word*.

5.3 At the worst I have been speaking with *extreme difficulty*.

5.2 At the worst I have been speaking with *slight difficulty.*

5.1 I have been speaking with *fluency all the time.*

Scaling Procedure   There is an optional interval scaling procedure (Phillips, 1970a) which will not be described here. If that is omitted then it is adequate to scale the statements as for a general ordered metric or an ordinal questionnaire. In the present case the patient scaled the statements as above by rank ordering them.

Preparation of Questionnaire Material   Each statement is typed on a separate 3×5 inch index card. It is convenient to enter the item and statement number on the back of each card. Also, two statements are selected as a standard pair, and the difference between them is assigned an arbitrary value. In the present case the standard pair was "Fluency all the time" and "Not a single word," and the difference between them was assigned the value 100. A strip of card is prepared, with the statements at either end and the assigned difference indicated between them, as in Figure 16-10.

Administration

On each occasion of administration the strip is laid before the patient (who, if it is thought necessary, is reminded of the difference between the standard pair). Then each of the item cards (in random order) is presented to him in turn, and he is asked to say whether the present level of the symptom referred to is worse (greater) than or better (less) than it says on the card, and by how many points in terms of the standard difference.

Scoring

Recording of Responses   The patient's judgments are entered in the appropriate cell of a two-way table such as that shown in Table 16-6, "worse" judgments being recorded as positive and "better" judgments as negative.

Rationale of Scoring   The extra information provided by the numerical judgments elicited from the patient (as opposed to the judgments of greater or less with a general ordered metric or an ordinal questionnaire) makes available the apparatus of analysis of variance. The obvious model to be used is

$$d_{ij} = \mu + \omega_j - \theta_i + \epsilon_{ij} \qquad (i = 1, \ldots, r; \quad j = 1, \ldots, c)$$

where:

d_{ij} is the patient's response to the ith statement on the jth occasion,
μ is a constant,
θ_i is the scale value of the ith statement,
ω_j is the level of the symptom on the jth occasion,
ϵ_{ij} is a random normal deviate, and
ϵ_{ij} are independent with mean 0 and the same standard deviation.

This is, of course, the usual model for a two-way design, except for the negative sign of θ_i.

There are two stages in the scoring of an interval personal questionnaire item.

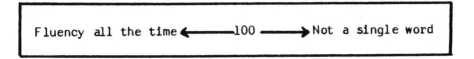

Figure 16-10   Example of a statement pair with assigned arbitrary value.

In the first, concurrent, stage, the questionnaire is scored after each administration (just as with the two preceding types of questionnaire) to obtain an estimate of the (unstandardized) level of the symptom on that occasion. Writing $\Omega_j = \mu + \omega_j$, it is clear that the least squares estimate of Ω_j is given by

$$\hat{\Omega}_j = \frac{1}{r}\sum_{i=1}^{r} d_{ij}$$

(which is the sum of the usual estimates for the mean and the column effect). Thus the score for an item on a particular occasion is simply the average of the patient's judgments on that occasion, as shown in the bottom row of Table 16-6. These scores can also be entered, as they are obtained, in an ongoing graph of the results, as shown in Figure 16-11. After the final administration, scale values for the statements can also be computed: the least squares estimate for θ_i is

$$\hat{\theta}_i = \frac{1}{c}\left[\sum_{j=1}^{c} d_{ij} - \frac{1}{r}\sum_{i=1}^{r}\sum_{j=1}^{c} d_{ij}\right]$$

(which is the usual estimate for the row effect, but with the sign reversed because in the model, the statement value is *subtracted* from the occasion value). For example, with the data of Table 16-6,

$$\hat{\theta}_1 = -\frac{1}{32}\left[(-28) - \frac{651}{4}\right] = -\frac{1}{32}\left[-190.75\right] = 5.9609375$$

These estimates can be entered on the ordinate of the completed graph, as shown in Figure 16-11.

In the second, final, stage of scoring, after all administrations of the questionnaire, a final analysis of variance of the data is carried out (replacing and greatly extending the significance tests for consistency with ordered metric and ordinal questionnaires). The results are shown in Table 16-7. This analysis is an ordinary two-way analysis of variance, with two additional features. Firstly, the sum of squares for the mean is not (as is usually the case) subtracted from the total sum of squares, but is included as a separate term (for reasons given below in the interpretation of the results): secondly, Tukey's sum of squares for nonadditivity (Winer, 1971) is extracted from the error sum of squares.

The interpretation of the analysis of variance is as follows. The significance of the *occasions* F ratio indicates that the patient's self-judged difficulty in speaking fluently was not static throughout the experiment: The standard error of estimate for an occasion score is .84, and this can be indicated on the graph.

The significance of the *statements* F ratio shows that the statements were not all indiscriminable: indeed, the standard error of a statement estimate, namely .30, which can also be indicated on the graph, shows that each statement is discriminable from each other.

Table 16-6   Concurrent Scoring of an Interval Item

Date	Day	25	30	2	7	9	6	7	12	19
	Month	6		7			10			
	Year	70								
Method		D	S	S	D	D	S	S	D	S
Experimenter		A	A	B	B	B	B	A	A	B
4. Not a single word		0	0	0	−2	−2	0	−8	−1	−2
3. Extreme difficulty		4	3	3	3	3	3	−3	1	0
2. Slight difficulty		10	8	8	10	8	15	2	7	12
1. Fluency all the time		18	8	7	15	12	20	5	12	6
Total		32	19	18	26	21	38	−4	19	16
Score		8.0	4.75	4.5	6.5	5.25	9.5	−1.0	4.75	4.0

Key: D = Systematic desensitisation. S = Shadowing.   (*continued*)

The significance of the *mean difference F* ratio indicates merely that the mean of the occasion scores was different from (in fact, greater than) zero, which is of no particular relevance here. Indeed, the corresponding sum of squares (which is simply the usual correction term) is, as noted above, most often subtracted from the total sum of squares in analyses of variance. It is, however, included in the analysis for an interval personal questionnaire item because it is sometimes psychologically meaningful. For example, with a patient undergoing aversion therapy for transvestism, the pleasantness for him of dressing up in his wife's clothes was scaled throughout by means of an interval item whose statements were based on the Singer–Young Affective Rating Scale [Singer & Young, 1941; cf. Table 16-2(c)], and thus symmetrically placed about a point of hedonic neutrality: the significance of the mean difference *F* ratio there indicated that his feelings about dressing up were on average different from zero (in fact, pleasant) throughout the course of the (unsuccessful) treatment, a fact of obvious clinical relevance.

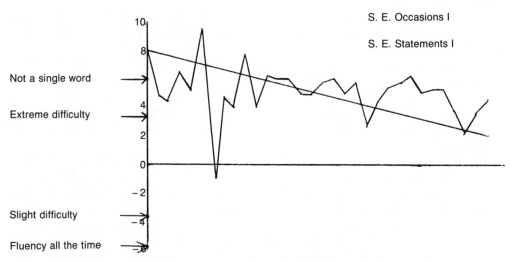

Figure 16-11   The significance of the linear component for trend.

Table 16-6   (*continued*)

20	21	26	2	3	4	9	10	17	18	23	25	1	2	7	15
			11									12			2
															71
D	D	S	S	D	D	S	D	S	S	D	D	S	S	D	S
A	B	A	A	B	A	B	B	B	A	A	A	A	B	B	A
−1	−2	0	0	0	0	0	0	0	−1	0	−2	0	0	0	0
0	0	3	2	2	2	2	2	2	1	2	0	1	2	2	3
12	8	12	10	10	8	8	9	9	8	9	7	7	9	9	10
20	10	10	12	12	10	10	12	13	12	12	5	10	11	12	12
31	16	25	24	24	20	20	23	24	20	23	10	18	22	23	25
7.75	4.0	6.25	6.0	6.0	5.0	5.0	5.75	6.0	5.0	5.75	2.5	4.5	5.5	5.75	6.25

(*continued*)

The significance of the *nonadditivity F* ratio shows that there was some systematic distortion in the patient's judgments, in that they were (in fact positively) related to the *product* of the statement and occasion values.

The final analysis of variance is most conveniently carried out by computer.

If the questionnaire has been administered as part of a (therapeutic or other) experiment, then the *between occasions* sum of squares can be partitioned into meaningful components, which can be tested against the item error variance estimate (thus making possible a more powerful test than if just the scores were observations). In the present example, the treatments (methods and experimenters) were applied in an order which was balanced for linear and quadratic trend (cf. Cox, 1951; Phillips, 1968b), so that the extended analysis shown in Table 16-8 can be carried out. The insignificance of the three components for *treatments* does not give any evidence that either of the two treatments or either of the two experimenters differed from one another in effectiveness, or that there was a significant interaction between their effectivenesses. The significance of the *linear* component for *trend* can be seen from Figure 16-11 to show that on this item the patient was improving linearly. (This result must be heavily qualified by the fact that items 1, 2, and 3 of the questionnaire showed no significant trend and item 4 showed a significant deterioration.) Finally, the significance of the *remaining between occasions* component indicates that there was further *between occasions* variation which was not accounted for by the above components.

Summary and Conclusions

Generalized personal questionnaire techniques are methods, the first of which was devised by Shapiro (1961a), for constructing a questionnaire for an individual psychiatric patient to scale the current level of his symptoms. They are characterized by two properties. Firstly, the items of the questionnaire are based on symptom-statements elicited from the patient. Secondly, they employ particular methods of item construction, which provide a check on the consistency of responses. Three such methods have been described: the ordered metric method, in which pairs of graded symptom-state-

Table 16-6   (*continued*)

Date		Day Month Year	18	23	25	5 3	8	11	17	Total	Estimate
Method			D	D	S	S	D	D	S		
Experimenter			B	A	B	B	A	B	A	Total	Estimate
4. Not a single word			0	−1	0	0	−4	−2	0	−28	5.9609375
3. Extreme difficulty			2	1	3	2	−2	0	2	51	3.4921875
2. Slight difficulty			8	9	8	7	7	6	10	280	−3.6640625
1. Fluency all the time			10	12	10	6	8	10	6	348	−5.7890625
Total			20	21	21	15	9	14	18	651	
Score			5.0	5.25	5.25	3.75	2.25	3.5	4.5		

ments are presented to the patient, who is asked to say which member of the pair comes closer to describing his or her current state; the ordinal method, in which single statements are presented and the patient is asked to say whether he or she feels better or worse than the statement would indicate; and the interval method, in which single statements are again presented, and the patient is asked to give numerical judgment of how much better or worse he or she feels than the statement would indicate.

There appears to be little to choose between the ordered metric and ordinal methods. They are both somewhat laborious to construct and score, and a number of schemes have been devised for doing so semiautomatically.

In contrast to the ordered metric and ordinal methods, both of which require relatively simple judgments of the patient, the interval method requires numerical judgments. Interval items are easier to construct and score than the other two types, and allow a powerful final analysis of data for which, however, a computer program is desirable.

The techniques have been illustrated by examples showing their use for routine monitoring of the progress of therapy and for therapeutic experiments and investigations both simple and complex.

Table 16-7   Analysis of Variance of Interval Item Results

Source	df	SS	VE	F	p
Occasions	31	414.30468750	13.36466734	4.73	<0.001
Statements	3	3029.33593750	1009.77864583	357.49	<0.001
Mean difference	1	3310.94531250	3310.94531250	1172.18	<0.001
Nonadditivity	1	64.55123477	64.55123477	22.85	<0.001
Error	92	259.86282773	2.82459595		
Total	128	7079.00000000			

Table 16-8   Extended Analysis of Variance of Internal Item Results

Source		df	SS	VE	F	p
Occasions		31	414.30468750	13.36466739	4.73	<.001
Treatments	Method	1	1.32031250	1.32031250	<1	NS
	Experimenter	1	7.50781250	7.50781250	2.66	NS
	M×E	1	5.69531250	5.69531250	2.02	NS
Trend	Linear	1	24.44760356	24.44760356	8.66	<.01
	Quadratic	1	2.66793304	2.66793304	<1	NS
	Remaining	26	372.66571340	14.33329667	5.07	<.01
Statements		3	3029.33593750	1009.77864583	357.49	<.001
Mean difference		1	3310.94531250	3310.94531250	1172.18	<.001
Nonaddivity		1	64.55123477	64.55123477	22.85	<.001
Error		92	259.86282773	2.82459595		
Total		128	7079.00000000			

Table 16-9   Methods×Experimenters Subtotals (from Table 16-6)

		Experimenter		
		A	B	
Method	D	165	167	332
	S	145	174	319
		310	341	651

References

Beck, A. T. *Cognitive therapy and the emotional disorders*. New York: International Universities Press, 1976.

Beck, A. T., Rush, A. J., Shaw, B. F., & Emery, G. *Cognitive therapy of depression*. New York: Wiley, 1979.

Chassan, J. B. *Research design in clinical psychology and psychiatry*. New York: Appleton-Century-Crofts, 1967.

Cox, D. R. Some systematic experimental designs. *Biometrika*, 1951, *38*, 312–323.

Davidson, P. O., & Costello, C. G. *N & 1: experimental studies of single cases*. New York: Van Nostrand Insight, 1969.

Harbison, J. J. M., Graham, P. J., Quinn, J. T., McAllister, H., & Woodward, R. A questionnaire measure of sexual interest. *Archives of Sexual Behavior*, 1974, *3*, 357–366.

Hersen, M., & Barlow, P. N. *Single-case experimental designs: strategies for studying behavior change*. New York: Pergamon, 1976.

Ingham, J. A method for observing symptoms and attitudes. *British Journal of Social and Clinical Psychology*, 1965, *4*, 131–140.

Kelly, G. A. *The psychology of personal constructs*. New York: Norton, 1955.

Kratochwill, T. R. (Ed.). *Single subject research: Strategies for evaluating change*. New York: Academic Press, 1978.

Mahoney, M. J. *Cognition and behavior modification*. Cambridge, Mass.: Ballinger, 1974.

Meichenbaum, D. B. *Cognitive-behavior modification: An integrative approach*. New York: Plenum, 1977.

Melzack, R. The McGill Pain Questionnaire: major properties and scoring methods. *Pain, 1*, 1975, 277–299.

McPherson, F. M., & LeGassicke, L. A single-patient self-controlled trial of Wy 3498. *British Journal of Psychiatry* , 1965, *111*, 149–154.

Mulhall, D. J. Systematic self-assessment by PQRST. *Psychological Medicine*, 1976, *6*, 591–597.

Mulhall, D. J. *Manual for the Personal Questionnaire Rapid Scaling Technique*. Windsor: NFER Publishing Co., 1978.

Mulhall, D. J. Computerised ordered metric scaling. *International Journal of Man-Machine Studies*, 1980, *12*, 25–33.

Osgood, C. E., Suci, G. J., & Tannenbaum, P. H. *The measurement of meaning*. Urbana: University of Illinois Press, 1957.

Phillips, J. P. N. Scaling and personal questionnaires. *Nature*, 1963, *200*, 1347–1348.

Phillips, J. P. N. On a certain type of partial higher-ordered metric scaling. *British Journal of Mathematical and Statistical Psychology*, 1966, *19*, 77–86.

Phillips, J. P. N. A scheme for computer scoring a Shapiro personal questionnaire. *British Journal of Social and Clinical Psychology*, 1968, *7*, 309–310. (a)

Phillips, J. P. N. Methods of constructing one-way and factorial designs balanced for trend. *Applied Statistics*, 1968, *17*, 162–170. (b)

Phillips, J. P. N. A new type of personal questionnaire technique. *British Journal of Social and Clinical Psychology*, 1970, *9*, 241–256. (a)

Phillips, J. P. N. A further type of personal questionnaire technique. *British Journal of Social and Clinical Psychology*, 1970, *9*, 338–346. (b)

Phillips, J. P. N. Generalized personal questionnaire techniques. In P. Slater (Ed.), *The Measurement of Intrapersonal Space by Grid Techniques, Vol. 2, Dimensions of Intrapersonal Space*. London: Wiley, 1977.

Phillips, J. P. N. A method for the investigation of irrelevant response set in ordered metric and ordinal questionnaires. *British Journal of Mathematical and Statistical Psychology*, 1979, *32*, 252–268.

Reading, A. R., & Newton, J. R. A card sort method of pain assessment. *Journal of Psychosomatic Research*, 1978, *22*, 503–512.

Rump, E. E. Cluster analysis of personal questionnaires, compared with principal component analysis. *British Journal of Social and Clinical Psychology*, 1974, *13*, 283–292.

Sambrooks, J. E., & MacCulloch, M. J. A modification of the Sexual Orientation Method and an automated technique for presentation and scoring. *British Journal of Social and Clinical Psychology*, 1973, *12*, 153–174.

Sandler, J. Studies in psychopathology using a self-assessment inventory: I. The development and construction of the inventory. *British Journal of Medical Psychology*, 1954, *27*, 142–145.

Shapiro, M. B. A method of measuring changes specific to the individual psychiatric patient. *British Journal of Medical Psychology*, 1961, *34*, 151–155. (a)

Shapiro, M. B. The single case in fundamental clinical psychological research. *British Journal of Medical Psychology*, 1961, *34*, 255–262. (b)

Shapiro, M. B. *Abbreviated manual. THE PERSONAL QUESTIONNAIRE*. Unpublished, 1961. (c)

Shapiro, M. B. The single case in clinical-psychological research. *Journal of General Psychology*, 1966, *74*, 3–23.

Shapiro, M. B. Short-term improvements in the symptoms of affective disorder. *British Journal of Social and Clinical Psychology*, 1969, *8*, 187–188.

Shapiro, M. B. *The assessment of self-reported dysfunctions: A manual with its rationale and applications*, Unpublished, 1975.

Shapiro, M. B., & Ravenette, A. T. A preliminary experiment on paranoid delusions. *Journal of Mental Science*, 1959, *105*, 295–312.

Shapiro, M. B., Marks, I. M., & Fox, B. A therapeutic experiment on phobic and affective symptoms in an individual psychiatric patient. *British Journal of Social and Clinical Psychology*, 1963, *2*, 81–93.

Shapiro, M. B., & Post, F. Comparison of self-ratings of psychiatric patients with ratings made by a psychiatrist. *British Journal of Psychiatry*, 1974, *125*, 36–41.

Sidman, M. *Tactics of scientific research: evaluating experimental data in psychology*. New York: Basic Books, 1960.

Siegel, S. *Nonparametric statistics for the behavioral sciences*. New York: McGraw-Hill, 1956.

Singer, W. B., & Young, P. T. Studies in affective reaction: I. A new affective rating scale. *Journal of General Psychiatry*, 1941, *24*, 281–301.

Singh, A. C., & Bilsbury, C. D. Scaling subjective variables by SPC (sequential pair comparisons). *Behavioural Psychotherapy*, 1982, *10*, 128–145.

Slater, P. The analysis of personal preferences. *British Journal of Statistical Psychology*, 1960, *13*, 119–135.

Slater, P. Inconsistencies in a schedule of paired comparisons. *Biometrika*, 1961, *48*, 303–312.

Slater, P. Personal questionnaire data treated as forming a repertory grid. *British Journal of Social and Clinical Psychology*, 1970, *9*, 357–370.

Slater, P. Cluster analysis versus principal component analysis: a reply to E. E. Rump. *British Journal of Social and Clinical Psychology*, 1974, *13*, 303–312.

Slater, P. Monitoring changes in the mental state of a patient undergoing psychiatric treatment. In P. Slater (Ed.), *The measurement of intrapersonal space by grid technique, Vol. 2, Explorations of intrapersonal space*. London: Wiley, 1976.

Stephenson, W. *The study of behavior. Q-technique and its methodology*. Chicago: University of Chicago Press, 1953.

Winer, B. J. *Statistical principles in experimental design* (2nd ed.). New York: McGraw-Hill, 1971.

THE METHODOLOGY OF PROCESS RESEARCH

Research Programs

17

Testing Hypotheses: The Approach of the Mount Zion Psychotherapy Research Group*

Harold Sampson
Mount Zion Hospital and Medical Center
Department of Psychiatry
San Francisco, California

Joseph Weiss
The San Francisco Psychoanalytic Institute
San Francisco, California

Introduction

In this chapter we shall describe our approach to research on the therapeutic process. We shall present our hypotheses about therapy and describe how we went about testing them. We shall, in addition, describe some of our studies in order to illustrate specific methods and findings.

Our hypotheses, as will be seen, were derived from psychoanalytic theory, and they were first tested on psychoanalyses. However, the hypotheses and the methods for testing them may be applied equally well to other kinds of therapy. Indeed, several members of our research group, including Saul Rosenberg, George Silberschatz, John Curtis, and Thomas Kelly, have been applying certain of our hypotheses and methods to a number of brief psychotherapies carried out on a variety of patients by a variety of therapists.[1] Moreover, our research strategy, while used by us to test our theoretical ideas, may be used by other investigators to test different theoretical ideas.

*Requests for reprints should be sent to Harold Sampson, Ph.D., Mount Zion Psychotherapy Research Group, Department of Psychiatry, Mount Zion Hospital and Medical Center, P.O. Box 7921, San Francisco, California 94120.

1. These studies are being carried out as part of two research projects. The first, titled "Role of the Therapist in Brief Psychotherapy," is codirected by Saul Rosenberg and George Silberschatz, and is supported in part by NIMH Grant No. MH34052. The second, titled "Process and Outcome of Psychotherapy with Older Adults," is codirected by George Silberschatz and John Curtis, and is supported in part by NIMH Grant No. MH35230.

Features of Our Research Approach

Our approach to psychotherapy research has the following distinctive features: First, we test fundamental propositions about the motivation and behavior of the patient in psychotherapy. Second, we study therapeutic processes which are immediately relevant to practice. Third, in investigating each individual case, we conduct a number of different studies (that is, studies of different processes) which, taken together, are designed to cast light on our hypotheses. Fourth, we use highly individualized (i.e., case-specific) measures of the variables pertinent to our hypotheses.

Our research follows a course which has been used successfully in other scientific fields (Kuhn, 1970), but which has seldom been used in investigations of psychotherapy (Sampson & Wallerstein, 1972). This course is to test hypotheses or theories which purport to account for significant data pertinent to the field. In our work, we test certain competing hypotheses (or theories) about therapy against each other.

In testing the explanatory power of two competing theories, we take the following steps. First, we infer, by reasoning from theory, those situations in which one theory predicts a particular finding and the competing theory predicts a different finding. Then we devise procedures to obtain reliable and objective findings by which we may determine which theory is in better accord with observation.

Because the hypotheses we are testing were devised to explain how the patient behaves and how the therapist may influence the patient, our research on these hypotheses is relevant to practice. Indeed, each of our studies is concerned with events which are familiar and meaningful to the therapist. These events take place in the everyday practice of psychodynamically oriented therapies, they are recurrent, and they are readily observable by the practitioner.

One of our studies, for example, is concerned with the familiar observation that the patient in therapy often makes a powerful implicit or explicit unconscious demand (pull) on the therapist to respond to him[†] in some particular way. The patient may, for example, demand that the therapist give affection, approval or praise, guidance or advice, scolding or punishment, an argument, rejection, special treatment, or condescending action. In studying such an event, we asked ourselves: What major theories have been offered to account for the patient making such a demand or pull on the therapist? What principles are contained in these theories to guide the therapist in his response? How, according to such theories, is the patient likely to respond if the therapist does accede (or does not accede) to the demand?

Psychoanalytic theory offers two explanations for the patient's making such a demand. According to one explanation, the patient, in making such a demand on the therapist, may be attempting to gratify an unconscious wish. The therapist, according to this theory, should not accede to the patient's demand. If the therapist does not accede, the unconscious wish will be frustrated, and hence intensified. Moreover, the patient's conflict with the wish will become intensified, and hence more interpretable.

According to the other explanation, the patient, in making a demand on the therapist to respond in a particular way, may be testing a frightening unconscious belief or expectation in relation to the therapist. The patient may, for example, demand guidance from the therapist in order to test the frightening belief that the therapist (like a parent

---

†Note: The pronoun he is used in a generic sense only; sexist language is not intended.—Editor.

in childhood) wishes to run his life. The patient, in this example, unconsciously will hope that the therapist will not accede to the demand, and so help the patient to disconfirm the frightening belief. The patient may then be reassured if the therapist does not accede to the demand, and he may become less anxious and more productive in the therapy.

From the above it is evident that the two explanations of the patient's making a demand, as described above, make different predictions about how the patient will react if the therapist does not accede to the patient's demand. According to the first explanation, the patient will become more tense; according to the second, the patient will become more relaxed. (We shall, later in this chapter, present research based on the fact that the two explanations make different predictions about how the patient will react to the same behavior on the part of the therapist.)

The therapy events we are studying are, as in the above example, observable and recurrent. They may be identified reliably by independent judges. Moreover, hypotheses about them may be investigated by replicable methods.

We test our hypotheses on one case at a time, and by use of case-specific measures of the variables which we are investigating. The use of case-specific measures is time consuming but, in our opinion, essential. Indeed, as will be seen, our testing our general propositions about therapy requires us to coordinate theoretical terms with measures specific to each individual case.

Data and Coding

Our primary data consists of both process notes and the verbatim transcripts of psychotherapies and psychoanalyses. In some of our researches, we carry out pilot studies using process notes, then conduct more definitive studies on verbatim transcripts. In others (for example, in studies tracing changes in a patient over an extended sweep of hours), we use process notes data to describe the changes, then verify these changes in samples of transcripts. In certain studies (such as those which use measures of nonverbal cues as, for example, clinical judgments of anxiety), we use audiotapes of segments of therapy sessions.

The primary data are transformed into measures of pertinent variables by procedures which require varying degrees and types of clinical inference. Correspondingly, three kinds of coders or judges have been used. Graduate students in psychology have been used to score or rate such measures as the Gottschalk–Gleser Anxiety Scales (Gottschalk, 1974a, 1974b; Gottschalk & Gleser, 1969), the Mahl measures of speech disruption (Kasl & Mahl, 1965; Mahl, 1956, 1959a, 1959b), and the Experiencing Scale (Gendlin, 1961; Klein, Mathieu, Gendlin, & Kiesler, 1970). Experienced clinicians of varying psychodynamic orientations have been used to judge segments of verbatim transcripts for such variables as the patient's boldness in tackling problems; the patient's relaxation, freedom, and flexibility; and the patient's degree of insight. Finally, we have used clinicians familiar with the application of particular concepts to the understanding of therapy to rate or judge clinical material in terms of these concepts. For example, clinicians familiar with the concept of unconscious testing of the therapist are used to identify instances of such testing, and to rate how effectively the therapist has responded to the patient's tests.

Alternative Theories

Our hypotheses about the therapeutic process were developed by Joseph Weiss. Weiss, in developing these hypotheses, was guided in a general way by concepts about mental functioning evolved by Freud in his late theorizing. Weiss elaborated these concepts, and made them into clinical hypotheses, by studying their application to case material. Because Weiss developed the hypotheses in relation to case material, the hypotheses are readily linked to observation, and therefore testable.

Clinical hypotheses derived from Freud's late theory provide different explanations of certain therapeutic processes than do clinical hypotheses derived from Freud's early theory. Moreover, they lead to different predictions about the behavior of the patient in certain situations. It is, therefore, possible to test one set of hypotheses against another. Indeed our research is designed to test the power and accuracy of certain hypotheses (derived by Weiss) from Freud's late theory against certain corresponding hypotheses derived from Freud's early theory.[2]

Freud's Early and His Late Theories

We shall introduce these alternative hypotheses by presenting a brief summary of certain contrasts between Freud's early and late theories.[3]

Freud's early theory presents a relatively simple view both of unconscious motivation and the unconscious regulation of mental life. According to the early theory, unconscious motivation consists of impulses and defenses. The impulses, which seek immediate gratification, interact dynamically with each other and with the defenses opposing them, and by these interactions determine behavior.

Unconscious mental life, according to the early theory, is regulated automatically by indications of pleasure and pain. Wishful impulses automatically seek gratification in accordance with the pleasure principle, uninfluenced by thoughts, anticipations, beliefs, or reality. The unconscious mind automatically turns away from unpleasure. Moreover, defenses, once instituted, are regulated automatically by indications of pleasure and pain.

Freud's late theory includes his early views both about unconscious motivation and about unconscious automatic regulation. However, his late theory adds significantly to the earlier conceptions. Freud's late theory assumes that a person unconsciously not only seeks certain immediate gratifications, but also is guided by certain motivations which serve purposes other than gratification. For example, a person may be motivated unconsciously to repeat a traumatic childhood experience in order to master it (Freud, 1920). A person may remain ill out of an unconscious sense of guilt and a need to suffer (Freud, 1923). He may pursue certain long-term goals, or develop and maintain cer-

---

2. Freud changed his ideas almost continuously throughout his life, and his work does not exist as a discrete early theory and late theory. Moreover, he retained most of his early concepts throughout his theorizing, and some of his important later concepts appear implicitly or peripherally or in weak form in his early writings. Nonetheless, the distinction made here between his early and late theories is a valid and useful one, for his late theories introduce and develop concepts which have significant new implications for a theory of the mind as well as for a theory of therapy.

3. A comprehensive account of the contrast between Freud's early and late theories is presented by Joseph Weiss in a book in preparation by Weiss, Sampson, and the Mount Zion Psychotherapy Research Group (to be published by The Guilford Press in 1986). A more abbreviated account is available to the reader in Bulletins #4 and #5 of the Mount Zion Psychotherapy Research Group, available through the authors.

tain attitudes or traits of character, on the basis of unconscious identifications with lost love objects (Freud, 1923). Moreover, as we shall discuss in the next section, a person may be guided unconsciously by certain beliefs acquired in the traumas of childhood, and by the feelings of fear, anxiety, and guilt which stem from such beliefs.

Freud's late theory assumes that unconscious mental life is regulated not merely by indications of pleasure and pain. Parts of unconscious mental life (in particular, parts of the unconscious ego, including the repressions) may be regulated, not automatically, but by the person's higher mental functions, and the person's assessments, by these functions, of danger and safety. Thus Freud wrote:

> The ego's constructive function consists in *interpolating* between the demand made by an instinct and the action that satisfies it, *the activity of thought* which, *after taking its bearings in the present and assessing earlier experiences, endeavors, by means of experimental actions to calculate the consequences of the course of action proposed.* In this way the ego *comes to a decision* on whether the attempt to obtain satisfaction is to be carried out or postponed or whether it may not be necessary for the demand by the instinct to be suppressed altogether as being dangerous.
>
> Just as the id is directed exclusively to obtaining pleasure, so *the ego is governed by considerations of safety* . . . The ego has set itself the task of self-preservation . . . *It makes use of the sensations of anxiety as a signal to give a warning of danger that threatens its integrity.* (1940, p. 199, italics ours)

Pathogenic Beliefs and Psychopathology

Freud's early theory assumes that the neurotic symptom is a gratification of an unconscious infantile wishful impulse which has been disguised and distorted by the ego. Freud's late theory, while including this view, assumes that infantile fears stemming from grim and frightening unconscious beliefs may play a crucial role in the development and maintenance of psychopathology. For example, the pathogenic belief in castration as a punishment for sexuality may, according to Freud, cause the person to institute repressions and indeed to develop symptoms. A person, in Freud's late theory, may develop a symptom in order to remove him from a situation of danger predicted by a pathogenic belief (Freud, 1926).

According to our concept about pathogenic beliefs (which is derived from Freud's late theory), such beliefs are acquired from traumatic experiences in childhood by normal processes of thought, albeit thought which necessarily reflects the child's limited perspective, and which may be distorted by infantile omnipotence or by projection. A patient may develop a grim, unconscious belief from an early pathogenic relationship with a parent, especially if, as is not unusual, the parent, by his behavior, encourages the development of such a belief. Such a belief (like the belief in castration) may be a reasonable intellectual achievement for a child, but nonetheless be inaccurate objectively.

> For example, a patient had observed, in early childhood, that when he offered his mother a chance to take care of him, she would become cheerful, and that when he was strong and challenging, she would become upset and on occasion would complain that he was "killing her." The patient's memory that his mother told him he was killing her was probably accurate, for during his analysis he observed that when his own son challenged his mother, she would complain to his son in such terms.
>
> The patient, as a result of his early experience with his mother, acquired the pathogenic belief that he was responsible for her happiness and unhappiness. He believed that if he

were to become independent of her, he would hurt her, and if he were to remain dependent on her, he would keep her happy. As a consequence of this belief, the patient became
intensely worried about his mother, especially when she complained that he was neglecting her. Indeed, he became so worried about her that he repressed his wish to become
independent. Moreover, he even repressed his image of his mother as weak and helpless.
At the beginning of his analysis he reported that during his childhood his mother had been
strong and resourceful, and that he had enjoyed letting her take care of him.

The patient in the example had inferred a connection between his struggle to become
independent of his mother and her becoming upset. Moreover, his inference was probably based on certain accurate observations. Nonetheless, the belief he acquired, though
a reasonable intellectual achievement for a child, was objectively inaccurate.

The patient had greatly exaggerated his effect on his mother. The patient, of course,
in his reasoning about his relationship to his mother, was severely handicapped by his
limited perspective. He had no prior relationships by which he could evaluate his relationship to his mother, nor did he, like the older child or adult, have access to knowledge about how one person is likely to affect another.

According to our views, which are derived from Freud's late theory, a patient's symptoms and inhibitions may stem either from the pathogenic belief that he will damage
a parent, by disobeying what he believes to be the parent's wish that he fail or suffer,
or from the pathogenic belief that he will damage the parent by not suffering or failing
like the parent had suffered and failed. A patient who is hampered by the first kind
of belief may attempt to remove himself from the danger of guilt by torturing himself,
as he believes unconsciously the parent wanted him to torture himself. A person who
is hampered by the second kind of pathogenic belief may attempt to remove himself
from the danger of guilt by handicapping himself, or torturing himself, as he unconsciously believes a parent handicapped himself, or tortured himself.

The patient in the example presented above remained dependent on his mother and
so attempted, by complying with what he believed were her wishes, to protect himself
from guilt.

Some Implications for Therapy

An important difference between Freud's early theory and his late theory concerns the
patient's attitudes toward his symptoms.

In Freud's early theory, the patient has no unconscious wish to overcome his symptoms. They are sources of unconscious gratification, so that the patient is strongly
motivated to maintain them. In his late theory, however, Freud assumes that a patient
may wish unconsciously to overcome his problems, and indeed that he may repeat
traumatic experiences in order to master them (1920). Freud, in certain later works, also
implied an unconscious wish for mastery by his concept that the ego may develop an
alliance with the analyst in order to subdue (master) certain uncontrolled parts of the
id (1937).

We, following Freud's later theorizing, assume that the patient has a strong unconscious wish to overcome his problems. Indeed, the idea that a patient would like to
master his problems follows from the assumption that his problems may arise from
grim, unconscious beliefs acquired in trauma. If (as the early theory assumes) a person's symptoms unconsciously are highly gratifying, he would presumably want,
unconsciously, to keep them. If, however (as in Freud's late theory and as we believe),

they are unconsciously distressing and if they stem from horrifying and constricting unconscious ideas, a patient would presumably wish, unconsciously, to overcome them.

According to our observations, the patient does wish to overcome his problems. Moreover, he may work to overcome them, by attempting, unconsciously, to change the pathogenic beliefs which underlie them. Indeed, he may work to change these beliefs by testing them, in his relationship to the therapist.

The patient described previously, who had remained dependent on his mother (and later other authorities) because he believed his independence would hurt her, tested this belief in relation to the therapist in a variety of ways and over an extended period of time. For example, he behaved independently with the therapist, not in order to hurt him by his independence but in order to assure himself that he would not hurt him by his independence as he believed he had hurt his mother. A patient, by such testing, hopes to overcome the contricting beliefs which impede him from pursuing certain important goals.

A patient's testing is ordinarily carried out unconsciously, for a patient who is attempting by his testing to disconfirm a particular pathogenic belief cannot be aware of his testing the belief if the belief is unconscious. For example, the patient just described did not remember that he had believed that his independence had been hurtful to his mother until he had assured himself, through repeated testing of the therapist, that his independence did not harm the therapist.

The Need for a Case-Specific Research Approach

The preceding clinical example illustrates why we test our hypotheses on one case at a time, with measures specific to the individual case. In order to investigate propositions about the patient's attempts, by testing the therapist, to disconfirm certain pathogenic beliefs, we must determine the specific beliefs the patient is attempting to disconfirm, the specific tests he is undertaking to disconfirm these beliefs, and the kinds of reactions to these tests by the therapist which will tend to support or disconfirm these beliefs. If we did not link theory to observation in a case-specific way as described above, we would fail to capture the essential features of the processes we are studying.

For example, the patient who believed his mother was hurt by his independence once tested the therapist by coming late to a session, and was relieved when the therapist remained neutral and thus did not seem to feel especially concerned about his coming late. The patient inferred that the therapist, unlike his mother, was not threatened by his independence, and did not wish to run his life. Another patient, who suffered from the pathogenic belief (based on certain childhood experiences) that his parents would permit him to be self-destructive, also tested his therapist by coming late to a session. This patient was troubled by the therapist's failure to refer to his lateness. He inferred that the therapist, like his parents, would permit him to be self-destructive. This patient then unconsciously tested his belief further by missing the next session, and he was relieved when the therapist began to investigate his behavior.

We should also note that in order for judges to make reliable and accurate judgments about such phenomena as a patient's testing of the therapist, the pathogenic beliefs which the patient is attempting to disconfirm by such testing, and the meaning to the patient of the therapist's responses, the judges must be conversant with the clinical application of the concepts of pathogenic beliefs and of testing.

Testing the Therapist Versus Seeking
Gratification: An Empirical Study of Two Theories

We shall now briefly report a study of the familiar event which we described earlier. It is the patient's making a powerful implicit or explicit demand (or pull) that the therapist respond to him in some particular way. For example, a patient, as described by Freud in his paper on transference love (1915), may declare his or her love for the analyst and demands some form of reciprocation from him. According to Freud's early theory, a patient, in making such a transference demand, is seeking to gratify an imperious unconscious wish without regard to reality. He or she is seeking "to put his passions into action without taking any account of the real situation . . . " (1912, p. 108). The patient's behavior is also a resistance, for the patient in demanding love is inevitably repeating rather than remembering an infantile experience with a parent.

The analyst, in response to the patient's demand, should, according to Freud's early theory, frustrate it by maintaining a neutral attitude of investigation. The analyst, by such an attitude, attempts to prevent the patient from succeeding "in acting out, in repeating in real life, what she ought only to have remembered . . . " (1915, p. 166).

How does a patient respond when the analyst does not reciprocate his transference demands? According to Freud's early theory, the patient's unconscious transference wishes are frustrated, his unconscious longings are intensified, and his unconscious conflicts between impulses and defenses are intensified. The patient may, therefore, appear to be in greater conflict, or he may appear to be much more defensive.

The investigators in the Menninger Psychotherapy Research Project (1968), apparently guided by the early theory, predicted that " . . . patients whose neurotic needs are not gratified within the transference respond to this frustration *with regressive and/or resistive reactions, and/or painful affects*" (Sargent, Horwitz, Wallerstein, & Appelbaum, 1968, p. 85, italics ours).

Concepts derived from Freud's late theory provide a different explanation of the patient's behavior, a different rationale for the therapist's response, and a different prediction of how the patient will respond when the analyst does not accede to a transference demand.

According to these concepts, a patient, in making a powerful pull or demand in the transference, may unconsciously be carrying out a trial action designed to test an unconscious pathogenic belief. For example, a patient may invite the analyst to reciprocate her professed love, in order to test, in relation to the analyst, a frightening unconscious belief that if she were affectionate or felt a sexual interest in a parental figure, she might seduce him. Such a patient does not want to seduce the analyst, and hopes therefore that the analyst does not give signs of reciprocating her affection. The therapist, in not acceding to a patient's demand for love, may be taking a step toward helping the patient to disconfirm her frightening unconscious belief that she will seduce him. The therapist, in not acceding, would then be reassuring the patient rather than frustrating her.

A patient, according to this theory, should feel unconsciously pleased rather than frustrated by the therapist's not yielding to his demand. He should feel more confident in the therapy and the therapist; he should feel more relaxed; and he should show reduced defensiveness and increased freedom and boldness in exploring his problems.

Because the two theories differ in their predictions about how a patient responds in a particular situation, it is possible to test empirically which theory better fits observation. We shall refer to the first theory, based on Freud's early concepts, as Theory A; and the second theory, derived from Freud's late concepts, as Theory B.

Silberschatz (1978) carried out a research study (on the first 100 sessions of a recorded analysis) to test the two theories. His research was carried out in three stages: (1) He identified a number of transference demands which the patient made on the therapist and which were conceptualized in one way by Theory A and in another way by Theory B. These transference demands were conceptualized by judges familiar with the clinical use of Theory A as behaviors in which the patient attempted unconsciously to gratify a key (important) wish in relation to the therapist. They were conceptualized by judges familiar with the clinical use of Theory B as behaviors in which the patient was unconsciously making a key test of the therapist. (2) Silberschatz then obtained ratings from Theory A judges about whether, and to what extent, the therapist, in each instance, frustrated the patient's demands, and from Theory B judges about whether, and to what extent, the therapist, in each instance, passed each of the patient's tests (i.e., responded in a way which would tend to disconfirm the patient's pathogenic belief). (3) Silberschatz then used a new group of judges to obtain measures of the patient's behavior before and after the analyst's responses. His purpose was to determine which theory best predicted the patient's reactions to the analyst's behaviors.

The first stage of Silberschatz's research (the identification of crucial transference demands which met the criteria of both Theory A and Theory B as described above) was carried out in three steps. The first step was the selection from the verbatim transcripts of the first 100 sessions (by nine judges who were graduate students in clinical psychology) of a pool of transference pulls or demands. (Each of the first 100 hours was read by two judges independently.) The result of this first step was a pool of 87 transference demands. Typescripts of the 87 segments containing the demands were then prepared. The segments included in each instance the patient's transference demands and the analyst's response (which in some instances was silence).

In the second step, five judges familiar with the clinical application of Theory A and four judges familiar with the clinical application of Theory B each independently rated the analyst's response to each of the patient's transference demands. Theory A judges, using a 7-point scale, rated the extent to which the analyst, in each instance, had frustrated the patient's demand. Interrater reliabilities were satisfactory: r_{11} was .35 and r_{kk} was .74.[4] Theory B judges, using a 7-point scale, rated the extent to which the analyst, for each instance, passed the test. Reliabilities were again satisfactory: r_{11} was .47; r_{kk} was .78.

A third step was used to select those instances which met the *stringent criteria of both theories*. A new group of three Theory A judges read a short case formulation which was in accord with Theory A and which had been prepared by the treating analyst and a senior colleague of his who was familiar with the case. The three new Theory A judges then identified which of the pool of 87 transference demands represented attempts by the patient to gratify a *central or key unconscious wish* (in contrast to a peripheral or unim-

---

4. Reliability data for these ratings—as well as for all of the other measures—are in terms of the intraclass correlation (Ebel, 1951; Guilford, 1954) using the residual mean square as the error term (i.e., mean differences in judges' ratings are not regarded as error). Two figures are reported: r_{11} = the estimated reliability of the average judges, and r_{kk} = the estimated reliability of the mean of K judges' ratings. For an overview of the various methods of computing interrater reliability, see Tinsley and Weiss (1975); or for a more comprehensive treatment of reliability theory, see Cronbach *et al.* (1972).

portant one). They identified reliably 59 such demands. Similarly, a new group of three Theory B judges read a short case formulation prepared by senior clinicians familiar with the case and with the clinical use of Theory B, including the concept of unconscious testing. The Theory B judges then identified (reliably) which of the pool of 87 demands represented attempts by the patient to carry out a *central or key test* (in contrast to a peripheral or unimportant one). They identified 49 such demands. There were 34 demands identified by *both* groups of judges as instances to which their respective theories applied. The 34 demands were used for further data analyses.

An example of such a demand, along with the rating of the therapist's intervention by each group of judges, follows:

Patient: (*3 minute silence*) Thinking back on your question just a little while ago, I think probably my, after initially reacting when I was talking in here, then I thought back on the remark about my stirring up things and I think probably my first inclination was to think, now which way did you mean it, did you mean it as something I shouldn't do or is it all right for me to do it? (*pause*) And perhaps one reason why I get feeling sort of panicked when I have nothing to say is that I feel you'll feel very impatient that I'm not saying anything, or even disapprove. (*silence*)

Analyst: When you think I'll be impatient or disapprove if you don't say anything, what do you imagine would happen then?

Rating the Analyst's Intervention

Theory A judges interpreted the patient's behavior as an implicit demand for the analyst's reassurance and approval. They considered this demand to be a derivative of the patient's unconscious wish for the analyst's love. They believed that the analyst's intervention was neutral and investigatory, and that it frustrated the patient's unconscious wish. Each of the five Theory A judges rated the analyst's intervention 6.0 on a scale ranging from 0 (the analyst gratifies the patient's wish) to 6 (the analyst frustrates the patient's wish). This scale is presented in Table 17-1.

Theory B judges interpreted the patient's behavior as an unconscious test of whether the analyst wished to tell her what to do, and to regulate her behavior by his approval or disapproval. They considered her behavior to be a test of her pathogenic belief that her parents wanted to control her, and that they would be threatened and upset if she were autonomous. The Theory B judges believed that the analyst's intervention was neutral and investigatory, and that it tended to disconfirm the patient's belief that the analyst, like her parents, would want to control her. The analyst's intervention, in their opinion, thus "passed" the patient's test. The four Theory B judges gave the analyst's intervention a mean rating of 5.8 on a scale ranging from 0 (clear-cut failing of patient's test) to 6 (clear-cut passing of patient's test). This scale is presented in Table 17-2.

Patient Measures

In order to compare the patient's behavior before and after the analyst's intervention, each pre- and postintervention segment of patient behavior was scored on several different measures. Moreover, each of the measures was scored by a different group of judges. These segments, which were approximately 6 minutes of patient speech, were each presented in *random order*, without any *context*, and with the judges unaware of whether the segment was a preintervention segment or a postintervention segment. In addition, all judges were unaware of the aims of the research.

Table 17-1   Rating of Analyst's Interventions: Theory A Judges

0	1	2	3	4	5	6
Analyst's response is clearly *non-neutral*; the analyst in effect gratifies the patient's wish. He may console the patient when she seeks consolation, reassure her, punish her, etc.	Analyst's response is *non-neutral*; he gratifies the patient's wish, albeit in a somewhat subtle fashion. His consolation, reproach, punishment, etc. is more subtle than in 0.	Analyst's response is *mildly non-neutral*; his gratification of the patient's wish is extremely subtle, but his response remains more non-neutral than neutral.	Analyst's response is *either ambiguous or falls midway between neutral and non-neutral*. The response may contain both neutral and non-neutral aspects, *but these are not explicit enough to warrant a higher or a lower rating*.	Analyst's response is *mildly neutral*: there are no non-neutral aspects to his response, but the neutral aspects are not sufficiently explicit or clear to warrant a higher rating.	Analyst's response is *neutral*; it contains the elements described in 6 but it is less clear.	Analyst's response is an *excellent, clear-cut example of a neutral intervention*; the patient's wish is in effect frustrated. The analyst may ask for clarification, or he may remain silent, interpret the patient's wish or demand, etc., but he does not gratify the patient's wish.

Table 17-2 Rating of Analyst's Interventions: Theory B Judges

0	1	2	3	4	5	6
Analyst's response is an explicit, clear-cut example of failing the patient's test.	Analyst's response is an example of a failed test; his failing the test is somewhat more subtle than in 0.	Analyst's response is an example of mildly failing the patient's test.	Analyst's response is either ambiguous or falls midway between passing and failing the test; the response may contain elements of both passing and failing the test but these are not explicit enough to warrant a higher or lower rating.	Analyst's response is an example of mildly passing the test; there are no aspects of failing the test in his response but it is not sufficiently explicit or clear to warrant a higher rating.	Analyst's response is an example of passing the test; it contains the elements described in 6 but less clear.	Analyst's response is an excellent, clear-cut example of passing the test.

The measures included the following:

The Experiencing Scale, a 7-point scale, is designed to evaluate the quality of a patient's involvement in psychotherapy. Four raters, after receiving standardized training, used this scale to score all of the pre- and posttransference–demand segments. The interjudge reliability was .88.

The Boldness Scale (see Table 17-3), developed by Joseph Caston, is a 5-point rating scale that assesses the degree to which the patient is able to confront or elaborate "nontrivial material"; that is, the extent to which the patient boldly tackles issues or retreats from them. Following a brief training period, two judges rated all of the segments with an interjudge reliability of .64.

The Relaxation Scale (see Table 17-4), designed by E. Mayer, F. Sampson, and A. Bronstein, measures the patient's degree of freedom and relaxation in the psychoanalytic session. At the high end of the scale, the patient is able to associate freely, easily, and flexibly; to be playful with ideas and to explore the connections between her thoughts in an uninhibited, spontaneous manner. At the low end of the scale, the patient is defensive, constricted, or narrow in her associations; she is halting, timid, or bothered by her train of thoughts; in general, she seems tense, rigid, tight, or grim. Three judges applied the scale to all of the segments with an interjudge reliability of .72.

The patient's emotions were categorized according to an affect classification system developed by Dahl (Dahl, 1978; Dahl & Stengel, 1978). We used four of his affect categories (love, satisfaction, anxiety, and fear). Two undergraduates who underwent extensive training with Dahl scored all of the segments with reliabilities ranging from .63 to .94.

The results of the Silberschatz study are summarized in TAble 17-5. All seven correlations are in the direction predicted by Theory B and opposite to the direction predicted by Theory A. Four of these seven correlations are statistically significant.

These results indicate that when the analyst did not accede to the patient's transference pull or demand, the patient tended to become more relaxed, free, more positive in her feelings toward others, less anxious, less fearful, and bolder in tackling her problems.

These results lend support to the Theory B hypotheses about testing the therapist. The patient, according to these hypotheses, may, by making a demand on the therapist, be unconsciously testing a frightening pathogenic belief. He may be tempting the therapist to accede to a demand to which the patient unconsciously does not want the therapist to accede. If the patient tests in this way, he would experience the therapist's acceding to the demand as tending to confirm the belief, and he would experience the therapist's not acceding to the demand as tending to disconfirm the belief. Moreover, to the extent that the patient experiences the therapist as helping him to disconfirm the pathogenic belief, he may feel reassured and he may work more productively on his problems.

The results of the study provide no support for the Theory A hypothesis that the patient, in making a transference demand, is almost invariably attempting to gratify an unconscious wish. These results, of course, cannot rule out the possible applicability of Theory A hypotheses to other cases, or to other parts of the case studied. The results, however, do rule out the hypothesis that all transference demands are explainable by Theory A, and they lend support to the Theory B hypothesis that such demands may be made by the patient in order to test the therapist.

Table 17-3 Boldness Scale

1	2	3	4	5
Patient manifests clear-cut anxious retreat or inhibition, or clear-cut dissatisfaction *about* her handling of the material.	Patient manifests a mild to moderate degree of anxious retreat or inhibition, or shows some indication of dissatisfaction *about* her own handling of the material.	Patient manifests ambiguous trends, or lukewarm attempts to deal with the issues.	Patient manifests moderate boldness or interest in tackling the material.	Patient manifests a bold or interested tackling of issues, or plunges ahead *even if* material is painful or distressing.

Table 17-4 The Relaxation–Constriction Rating Scale

1	2	3	4	5
Patient seems uncomfortable, beleaguered, driven, defensive, constricted, tense, tight.	Patient seems somewhat constricted, defensive, tense, etc. (relatively less so than in 1).	Patient is just about as constricted and tense as she is free and relaxed.	Patient is somewhat free, spontaneous, relaxed, undefensive.	Patient is relaxed, free, unconstricted, spontaneous (relatively more so than in 4).

Table 17-5   Correlations Between Ratings of the Therapist's Behavior and Changes in the Patient Measures for Segments Identified as Both Key Frustrations and Key Tests ($N = 34$)

	Results Obtained	Predicted by Theory A	Predicted by Theory B
Experiencing	+.23	−	+
Boldness	+.41[a]	−	+
Relaxation	+.35[a]	−	+
Love	+.36[a]	−	+
Satisfaction	+.15	−	+
Fear	−.31	+	−
Anxiety	−.34[a]	+	−

[a]$p < .05$, two-tailed test.

Process and Outcome

The Silberschatz study demonstrates a lawful relationship between a therapeutic process and an *immediate* outcome. The patient, according to this study, would, following a passed test, make immediate progress. She would become less anxious, more positive toward others, bolder in tackling her problems, and at the same time more relaxed, freer, and more flexible in working to solve her problems.

This finding suggests the possibility (which is consistent with our theoretical views) that if the therapist, in a given case, generally passes the patient's tests, the patient will be likely to have a successful outcome, and that if the therapist generally fails the patient's tests, the patient will likely have an unsuccessful outcome. Saul Rosenberg, George Silberschatz, and John Curtis have designed studies to test this hypothesis on a series of brief psychotherapies (Rosenberg & Silberschatz, 1982; Silberschatz & Curtis, 1982). They are determining, by reliable measures, whether the therapist in each case generally passes the patient's tests, generally fails the patient's tests, or is in between. They are also in each case studying the success of treatment at the end of therapy, at 3 months following termination, and at 1 year following termination. They are, in their studies of therapy outcome, using a variety of familiar measures, as well as some new measures. Their findings will cast light on the relation between a therapist's passing the patient's tests and the long-term outcome of the treatment.

Another Test of Alternative Theories

We shall now present in summary fashion another study we carried out on the first 100 sessions of the same case, Mrs. C. This study is intended to cast light on the conditions under which a patient becomes conscious of some mental content (attitude, wish, memory, belief, etc.) which had previously been warded off by defenses. Does he do so in accordance with hypotheses based on Freud's late theory (Theory B) or in accordance with hypotheses based on Freud's early theory (Theory A)?

This study may be introduced by a prototypical observation made by Weiss which he referred to as "crying at the happy ending":

> A person who was watching a movie about a love story experienced little or no emotion when the lovers quarreled and left each other. He was moved, however, when, at the happy ending, they resolved their difficulties. He became happy, then experienced a brief but not unpleasant sense of sadness, and wept. (1952, p. 338; 1971, p. 462)

Weiss, in discussing this common experience, asked: Why does the moviegoer experience sadness *at just the moment when he has become happy*?

The moviegoer did not (as Theory A would assume) experience his sadness because it had become intensified and thus thrust its way into consciousness. Indeed, according to the early (thrust) theory, the sadness should have been more intense when the lovers separated, and it should have been weakest when, at the happy ending, the occasion for the sadness was eliminated. Yet the moviegoer did not experience sadness at the separation, but only after the happy ending.

Moreover, if the sadness, in spite of the defenses against it, had pushed its way to consciousness, its emergence would have resulted in conflict. The moviegoer in this case should have felt tense or anxious before and during the coming forth of his sadness, and he should, after it came forth, have remained in conflict with it. Yet the moviegoer was not anxious as his sadness became conscious, nor was he in conflict with it after it emerged.

It is evident that the repressed sadness did not thrust forth in search of gratification, for sadness is not intrinsically gratifying. Indeed, the coming to consciousness of sadness in the "crying at the happy ending" phenomenon is an example of the kind of process which Freud stated in *Beyond the Pleasure Principle* (1920) contradicts his earlier assumption that unconscious processes are regulated exclusively by the search for pleasure. As you will recall, Freud stated in that work that people repeat, both in life and in analysis, *experiences which cannot at any time have been pleasurable*. These are experiences of trauma rather than of gratification.

Weiss offered the following explanation of why the moviegoer experienced his sadness at just the moment when he became happy: The moviegoer was saddened by the lovers quarreling and separating from each other. However, he had felt endangered by his sadness then (perhaps because it reminded him of his own sadness) and so repressed it (or suppressed it). Later, at the happy ending, he stopped being endangered by his sadness, and so could experience it safely. Since he no longer needed to repress the sadness, he lifted the repression opposing its emergence, made the sadness conscious, and gained relief from the effort he had been making to keep it repressed.

In summary, the crying at the happy ending phenomenon is most readily explained by concepts which assume: first, that a person has a capacity to lift his defenses and to experience a mental content such as sadness which had been warded off; second, that a person is likely to lift his defenses against a repressed content when he decides unconsciously that it is safe for him to experience the content; third, that he may bring forth the content not in order to gratify it, but rather to resolve his conflict with it.

Clinical Application of the Late Theory

In subsequent studies carried out on the process notes of analyses, Weiss sought to investigate how, and under what circumstances, the analytic patient becomes conscious of repressed mental contents, especially if such contents are not interpreted. He found that the analytic patient (and the patient in psychotherapy) behaves much as the moviegoer in the preceding example. The patient generally maintains the repression of a particular warded off mental content until he unconsciously decides that he may experience it safely, then he lifts his defenses and makes it conscious.

An example will illustrate this phenomenon:

> A woman patient had decided to terminate her analysis, which was then in its fourth year. She cited the progress she had made and stated that she was ready to work on her own. The analyst, after an initial futile investigation of her decision to terminate, told her that she did not understand her decision to stop and that she should continue treatment until she did understand it. After a few sessions of protest, the patient decided to continue. She then brought forth a new (and long forgotten) childhood memory in which she felt rejected by her mother. (Indeed, she had assumed, as the result of an experience with her mother, that her mother wanted her to die.) The memory made her intensely sad, and she wept freely while telling it.

This is a direct example, from an analysis, of crying at the happy ending. It shows that a deeply repressed sadness, a sadness repressed for many years, may become conscious in the same way as the moviegoer's sadness became conscious. The patient, according to Weiss, threatened to terminate in order to test the analyst. She wanted to find out whether the analyst would reject her as she had assumed (whether or not correctly) that her mother had rejected her. When the analyst did not do so, she was unconsciously pleased and reassured. She then brought forth a powerful new unconscious memory and the sadness associated with it.

Thus the patient brought forth her repressed sadness when the analyst, as she experienced it, did not reject her. She became, as a result of the analyst's acceptance, a little less sad. She began, moreover, to disconfirm her pathogenic belief that she was inherently rejectable. Then she brought forth the sadness when she unconsciously began to assume that it was not her fault that her mother rejected her. She could then safely experience it. Paradoxically, the intense sadness and feeling of rejection which the patient brought forth reflected a *reduced* fear of rejection and *reduced* feelings of sadness.

The clinical intuitions which have been associated with Freud's early theory are deeply ingrained in much clinical thinking, outside psychoanalysis as well as within it. Indeed it is commonly assumed that if a person begins to experience a mental content, or begins to express that content prominently in his behavior, it is because that content has become more powerful. If a person, according to this view, experiences intense, formerly repressed sadness—and especially if he does so without interpretation—it is because the sadness has become more intense relative to the strength of the defenses opposing its expression.

The hypothesis based on Freud's later theory, as illustrated by crying at the happy ending, modifies our understanding of such phenomena, and thereby modifies our clinical intuitions. It proposes that a person may experience repressed sadness (or other unconscious contents) with greater intensity not because the sadness or other content has become more powerful in relation to the person's defenses, but instead because the person has become less endangered by the sadness, has decided unconsciously that he may experience it safely, and has lifted his defenses and allowed himself to experience it.

The patient in therapy or analysis, according to Theory B (derived from Freud's late theory), behaves like the moviegoer. He generally maintains the repression of a particular warded-off mental content until he unconsciously decides that he may experience it safely, then lifts his defenses and makes it conscious. Moreover, he works unconsciously by testing the analyst to create conditions which make it safe for him to experience the content. If Theory B is correct, we should expect to find:

1. That patients in analyses (or in certain psychotherapies) regularly become aware of mental contents which they had previously warded off by defenses, even when these contents have not been interpreted.
2. That patients may become aware of such previously warded off contents *without much anxiety,* for they do not, in most circumstances, decide to lift their defenses and make the contents warded off by them conscious until they have to a considerable extent unconsciously overcome their fears of being endangered by the contents.
3. That patients may not come into powerful conflict with previously repressed contents when these contents become conscious—for patients generally do not make the contents conscious until they judge that it is safe to experience them.
4. That patients need not isolate the previously repressed contents once they emerge into consciousness (or otherwise defend against awareness of their meaning). This is because patients generally do not make repressed contents conscious until they decide that they may safely face them.

In contrast, in Freud's early theory (Theory A), a repressed mental content which is not interpreted ordinarily remains unconscious unless the content is intensified. According to Theory A, a repressed content which is intensified may push more powerfully toward consciousness, and evoke intensified defensive efforts. If it is intensified enough, it may emerge to consciousness in a relatively undisguised form, in which case the patient continues after its emergence to be in conflict with it, to feel anxious about it, and to attempt to rerepress it. If, however, the repressed content becomes conscious in a sufficiently disguised compromise formation, the patient may not experience further conflict with it, but, since its import is disguised, the patient does not understand the significance of the newly emerged content, and does not use the content to understand himself better until its significance has been interpreted.

The Research Study

Suzanne Gassner and her associates carried out a research study (Gassner, Sampson, Weiss, & Brumer, 1982) of how warded-off contents become conscious in the first 100 sessions of the Mrs. C. case. The method used by Gassner was originally devised by Professor Leonard Horowitz of Stanford University in conjunction with several other members of our research group (Horowitz, Sampson, Siegelman, Wolfson, & Weiss, 1975). In the present study, this method was improved, and was applied to a new case.

The purpose of Gassner's study was to determine, as our hypotheses would lead us to anticipate, (1) whether a patient during analysis may become conscious of previously unconscious contents which have not been interpreted, (2) whether he may become conscious of them without feeling anxious about them, and (3) whether he may use his knowledge of them to advance his understanding of himself.

The first step in this study was to identify a pool of *new* contents or themes within the 100 sessions; that is, contents which had not been described by the patient earlier. In carrying out this step, Gassner identified all of the new themes appearing in hours 41 to 100.

The second step required psychoanalytic clinicians to judge, on the basis of their own formulations of Mrs. C. (derived from reading the process notes of the first 10 sessions of her analysis), which of this pool of new themes had, at the beginning of her analysis, been unacceptable to the patient, and hence warded off. We used 19 psychoanalytic clinicians for this judgment. The judges rated each new theme on a 5-point scale. A rating of "5" reflected the judge's strong belief that the new theme had previously been unconscious.

In presenting the statements of the new themes to the judges (for judgment as to whether they had been previously warded off), we omitted any cues as to whether or not the patient was anxious or conflicted when the themes first emerged. Our purpose was to avoid biasing the judgment by such cues.

Findings and Discussion   Thirteen of the 100 statements received a mean scale score of "4" or greater—that is, there was substantial agreement between judges that these 13 statements had been previously unconscious. These statements were designated as "judged previously warded off."

Did our method *actually* yield *clinically meaningful* warded off contents? We believe so. The patient herself, the treating analyst and, finally, a research group working independently from the judges, all concluded from their own independent perspectives that the statements judged as warded off had indeed been previously warded off, and, moreover, that they were of central significance to the patient.

The evidence that the patient judged the statements to contain warded off themes is the following: Seven of the 100 new themes were introduced by the patient with phrases acknowledging her own awareness of facing a previously warded off content. Examples of such phrases are: "I've never let myself before think or feel such and such" or "I can't believe I'm saying that . . . " We did not provide the judges with these cues. That is, we *had deleted these prefatory comments*. Nonetheless, the judges gave these seven statements—which the patient herself identified as previously warded off—a mean rating of approximately "4."

The treating analyst also thought that the statements which our 19 judges identified as previously warded off had indeed been warded off earlier. The treating analyst independently completed the same judgment task as our 19 judges. He rated as highly warded off *11 of the 13* statements which the judges had identified as warded off. Moreover, he considered the statements to which our judges had given the highest ratings as so revealing that he asked us to disguise their contents for purposes of publication.

Finally, our research group, working independently of the judges, on the basis of its own case formulation, evaluated the statements identified by the 19 judges as previously unconscious. The research group agreed with the judges that these new themes expressed significant, previously unconscious impulses or previously unconscious painful childhood memories and ideas.

Thus, three converging lines of evidence gave us confidence that our method—which is, after all, a variant of the usual clinical method of identifying unconscious contents—*did identify clinically meaningful and significant previously unconscious contents.*

Our next finding (which required us to read every statement which the analyst made prior to the emergence of the new themes) was that the analyst had not made any interpretations, prior to their coming forth, which were in any way related to 12 of the 13 statements containing themes judged highly warded off.

Thus, we demonstrated that a number of clinically meaningful unconscious contents became conscious in the latter part of the first 100 hours of Mrs. C.'s analysis, *and they did so without prior interpretation.*

Did the patient experience much anxiety or conflict as these contents emerged? To determine this we used three different measurements of anxiety or conflict: Mahl's speech disturbance ratio; the Gottschalk–Gleser anxiety scale; and clinical ratings of anxiety by experienced clinicians.

The following example illustrates the application of these anxiety measures to a brief segment of patient speech:

> (*silence*) And I was just thinking too about the fact that, sometimes when I'm really pushing him to be angry at me and even if we're having a kind of fight where I'm wanting to hurt him physically, he's never—I've, I've sometimes sort of been afraid, well, he is stronger than me and he could hurt me. I've been sort of afraid of it. But I think I'm much more, I fee—, I feel some kind of a pleasure out of the fact that he is much stronger and I like something to happen so I'm made aware of it, very immediately aware of the fact that he's much stronger and, and even though I might be frustrated at this sometimes, if he can just hold me and I can't even move, there's, I think there's something I like very much about that.

This segment of patient speech was scored just below the patient's mean anxiety score for all random segments on Mahl's Speech Disturbance Ratio, and similarly on the Gottschalk–Gleser Anxiety Scale. The segment was rated slightly lower by the experienced clinical judges listening to audio tapes; specifically, about one standard deviation below the mean anxiety rating for all random segments.

We compared the anxiety level on each of these three measures when highly warded off contents emerged, with the anxiety level accompanying the appearance of randomly selected statements. The patient was significantly *less anxious* on the Mahl score when warded off contents emerged than when random statements emerged; the other two measures of anxiety showed no differences in anxiety level in the two circumstances.

Thus the patient became conscious of a number of clinically meaningful unconscious contents, without interpretation, and without evidence of intensified anxiety or conflict.

Finally, we used the Experiencing Scale to determine whether the patient permitted herself fully to experience the previously warded off contents which she was bringing forth. This scale measures the degree to which the patient is experiencing the mental contents which she is discussing. [We may illustrate the application of the Experiencing Scale to case material by noting how the brief segment of patient speech reported above was scored. The segment received a Mode Experiencing Score of 3.25 (mean for all random segments is 3.0, standard deviation .79), and a Peak Experiencing Score of 3.75 (mean for all random segments is 3.61, standard deviation is .75). The segment was thus scored just slightly above the mean for all random segments on the two Experiencing Scale measures.]

The patient's material (speech, associations), when previously warded-off contents emerged, was rated significantly higher on the Experiencing Scale than her material when randomly selected statements were made. This means that the patient was more involved with the feelings she was associating with the warded-off contents than she was at randomly selected times.

This combination of results is in agreement with predictions based on Theory B hypotheses. The patient, according to these hypotheses, maintained her defenses against certain mental contents until she unconsciously judged that she could safely experience these contents. She then made these contents conscious, and worked with the contents to increase her understanding and control over her mental life. These ideas readily account for our findings that the patient regularly became aware of previously warded off contents which had not been interpreted; that she was not anxious when she became aware of these contents; and that she experienced these contents vividly rather than attempting to isolate them or rerepress them.

In contrast, the combination of findings is not in agreement with predictions based on Theory A hypotheses. Indeed, Theory A hypotheses cannot readily account for these results. Theory A hypotheses could explain the patient's becoming aware of uninterpreted warded-off contents by the idea that these contents had become intensified and so thrust their way into awareness. However, if the contents became conscious, because of their thrust, the patient would either be anxious when these contents came into awareness, or, if the contents were sufficiently disguised or isolated, she would be calm, but she would not experience the contents vividly and would not work with them to further her self-understanding and self-control. In contrast to these expectations, Mrs. C. was not particularly anxious when previously warded-off contents came into awareness, she experienced these contents vividly, and she worked with these contents.

We conclude that Theory A hypotheses *cannot* provide a complete explanation for how unconscious mental life is regulated. Further research is needed to test whether Theory B hypotheses can provide a complete explanation, or whether a combined A plus B Theory, or yet some other theory, best accounts for the pertinent observations.

Concluding Remarks

We have described and illustrated a research approach based on a distinctive set of hypotheses about the behavior of the patient in psychotherapy, and how that behavior is affected by the therapist. We have tested certain of these hypotheses by reliable, rigorous, and case-specific methods. Because these hypotheses purport to offer a comprehensive account of psychotherapy, further research on their accuracy and power may cast considerable light on how therapy works, or fails to work.

Members of our research group are carrying out such studies at this time. They are studying both long-term therapies and brief therapies; therapies both with the young adult patient typically seen in community clinics or private practice, and with middle-aged and elderly patients; and therapies with patients varying in pathology from the well-functioning neurotic to the more seriously disturbed and even borderline or psychotic patient.

Our hypotheses and methods may be applied to the study of treatment carried out by therapists of any theoretical orientation,[5] and most of our own research is being car-

---

5. For example, we may study a patient's testing of the therapist, whether and to what extent the therapist's response passes the test, and how the patient responds to a passed or failed test, regardless of whether the therapist conceptualizes the patient's behavior or his own in these terms.

ried out on cases treated by therapists who are not members of our research group, and who are unfamiliar with its ideas.

Acknowledgment

This work was supported in part by the Research Support Program of the Mount Zion Hospital and Medical Center, San Francisco, California.

References

Cronbach, L. J., Gleser, G. C., Nand, A. H., & Rajaratnam, N. *The dependability of behavioral measures.* New York: Wiley, 1972.

Dahl, H. A new psychoanalytic model of motivation: Emotions as appetites and messages. *Psychoanalysis and Contemporary Thought,* 1978, *1*(3), 373–408.

Dahl, H. & Stengel, B. A classification of emotion words. *Psychoanalysis and Contemporary Thought,* 1978, *1*(3), 269–312.

Ebel, R. L. Estimation of the reliability of ratings. *Psychometrika,* 1951, *16,* 407–424.

Freud, S. The dynamics of transference, (1912). *Standard Edition,* 1958, *12,* 97–108.

Freud, S. Observations on transference-love, (1915). *Standard Edition,* 1958, *12,* 157–171.

Freud, S. Beyond the pleasure principle, (1920). *Standard Edition,* 1955, *18,* 3–64.

Freud, S. The ego and the id, (1923). *Standard Edition,* 1955, *19,* 3–66.

Freud, S. Inhibitions, symptoms, and anxiety, (1926). *Standard Edition,* 1959, *20,* 77–175.

Freud, S. Analysis terminable and interminable, (1937). *Standard Edition,* 1964, *23,* 209–253.

Freud, S. An outline of psychoanalysis, (1940). *Standard Edition,* 1964, *23,* 141–207.

Gassner, S., Sampson, H., Weiss, J., & Brumer, S. The emergence of warded-off contents. *Psychoanalysis and Contemporary Thought,* 1982, *5*(1), 55–75.

Gendlin, E. T. Experiencing: A variable in the process of psychotherapeutic change. *American Journal of Psychotherapy,* 1961, *15,* 233–245.

Gottschalk, L. A. The application of a method of content analysis to psychotherapy research. *American Journal of Psychotherapy,* 1974, *28*(4), 488–499. (a)

Gottschalk, L. A. Quantification and psychological indicators of emotions: The content analysis of speech and other objective measures of psychological states. *International Journal of Psychiatry in Medicine,* 1974, *5*(4), 587–610. (b)

Gottschalk, L. A., & Gleser, G. C. *The measurement of psychological states through the content analysis of verbal behavior.* Berkeley: University of California Press, 1969.

Guilford, J. P. *Psychometric Methods* (2nd ed.). New York: McGraw-Hill, 1954.

Horowitz, L. M., Sampson, H., Siegelman, E. Y., Wolfson, A., & Weiss, J. On the identification of warded-off mental contents: An empirical and methodological contribution. *Journal of Abnormal and Social Psychology,* 1975, *84,* 545–558.

Kasl, S., & Mahl, G. F. Disturbance and hesitations in speech. *Journal of Personality and Social Psychology,* 1965, *1,* 425–433.

Klein, M. H., Mathieu, P. L., Gendlin, E. T., & Kiesler, D. J. *The experiencing scale: A research and training manual,* (Vols. 1 and 2). Madison: Wisconsin Psychiatric Institute, Bureau of Audio Visual Instruction, 1970.

Kuhn, T. S. *The structure of scientific revolutions* (2nd ed., Enlarged). Chicago: University of Chicago Press, 1970.

Mahl, G. F. Disturbances and silences in the patient's speech in psychotherapy. *Journal of Abnormal and Social Psychology,* 1956, *53,* 1–15.

Mahl, G. F. Exploring emotional states by content analysis. In I. de S. Pool (Ed.), *Trends in content analysis.* Urbana: University of Illinois Press, 1959. (a)

Mahl, G. F. Measuring the patient's anxiety during interviews from ''expressive'' aspects of his speech. *Transaction of the New York Academy of Sciences*, 1959, 21(3), 249–257. (b)

Rosenberg, S., & Silberschatz, G. Role of the therapist in brief psychotherapy. National Institute of Mental Health Grant No. MH34052, 1982.

Sampson, H., & Wallerstein, R. S. New research directions: Comment from a psychoanalytic perspective. In H. H. Strupp & E. Bergin (Eds.), *Changing frontiers in the science of psychotherapy*. New York and Chicago: Aldine-Atherton, 1972.

Sargent, H. D., Horwitz, L., Wallerstein, R., & Appelbaum, A. Prediction in psychotherapy research: A method for the transformation of clinical judgments into testable hypotheses. *Psychological Issues*, 1968, 4(1), Monograph 21.

Silberschatz, G. Effects of the analyst's neutrality on patient's feelings and behavior in the psychoanalytic situation. Dissertation at New York University, 1978.

Silberschatz, G., & Curtis, J. Process and outcome of psychotherapy with older adults. National Institute of Mental Health Grant No. MH35230, 1982.

Tinsley, H. E., & Weiss, D. J. Interrater reliability and agreement of subjective judgments. *Journal of Counseling Psychology*, 1975, 22, 358–376.

Weiss, J. Crying at the happy ending. *Psychoanalytic Review*, 1952, 39(4), 338.

Weiss, J. The emergence of new themes: A contribution to the psychoanalytic theory of therapy. *International Journal of Psycho-Analysis* 1971, 52(4), 459–467.

Weiss, J., Sampson, H., Gassner, S., & Caston, J. Further research on the psychoanalytic process. Bulletin #4, June 1980. The Psychotherapy Research Group, Department of Psychiatry, Mount Zion Hospital and Medical Center. (Based on the presentations to the George S. Klein Research Forum, held in conjunction with the American Psychoanalytic Association Spring Meeting, St. Francis Hotel, San Francisco, May 1, 1980.)

Weiss, J., & Sampson, H. Psychotherapy research: Theory and findings. Bulletin #5, February 1982. The Psychotherapy Research Group, Department of Psychiatry, Mount Zion Hospital and Medical Center. (Based on presentations to the Mini-Series sponsored by the Post-Graduate Education Committee of the San Francisco Psychoanalytic Institute, January 19, 1982.)

Weiss, J., Sampson, H., & the Mount Zion Psychotherapy Research Group. *The psychoanalytic process: Theory, clinical observations, and empirical research*. In press, Guilford Press, 1986.

The Search for Phases in Group Development: Designing Process Analysis Measures of Group Interaction

Ariadne P. Beck
Private practice
Indian Head Park and Des Plaines, Illinois

James M. Dugo
Private practice
Forest Institute of Professional Psychology
Des Plaines, Illinois

Albert M. Eng
Palo Alto Veterans Administration
Palo Alto, California

Carol M. Lewis
Community Guidance Center
Mercy Hospital
Chicago, Illinois

Introduction

This chapter presents work on the creation of measures which can model a process that has been described by Beck's (1974, 1981a, 1981b) theory of group development. It does not take the work to the step of defining how these measures would be used in a hypothesis-testing empirical design: that work lies in the future. The chapter addresses the creation of measures for the study of small-group phase development. To place our work in proper perspective, a word might be said here about the stages of scientific organization of a particular field of study. Usually they begin with casual observation of interesting phenomena and progress: to more intensive observation; to the formulation of concepts, quasitheories, or descriptive theories; to systematic observation and recording; to the formulation of theory; to the clarification of parameters; to the selection or creation of appropriate measures; to the reformulation or refinement of theory; to hypothesis-testing empirical studies that find relationships between parameters and confirm or further modify theory; to the stimulation of related research and/or alternative theories and from there to a general clarification of the critical aspects of a particular area of knowledge. Although this is not a strict sequence it describes the typical process. Our work is at the stage of clarification of parameters, selection, or creation of measures and refinement of theory.

The Study of Group Development

The study of developmental phases in the life of a small group has been pursued for a period of 30 years. Although there is a considerable degree of agreement among observers (Hare, 1973; Lacoursiere, 1980; Tuckman, 1965; Tuckman & Jensen, 1977) that there are phases, and that they probably appear in a particular sequence, no one in that period of time had produced convincing evidence of the substantive content of phases, of phase boundaries or of characteristic phase-related patterns of interaction. The Chicago Group Psychotherapy Research Team[1] has taken up this problem, guided by Beck's theoretical description of phases in the structural development of therapy and encounter groups (Beck, 1974, 1981a, 1981b; Beck & Keil, 1967). This theory describes nine phases in group development and the emergence of four leaders during this process.

The structural development of a group is only one of a number of systematic sources of influence on group process (Beck, 1981b). All of these influences would have to be described and measures developed for them if we were to have a comprehensive predictive model of group interaction processes and their outcome for the individual, the group itself, and the context in which it meets. The present work is an attempt to model and eventually to measure the structural development of the small group itself. We have chosen this focus for our efforts because we believe that all the other influences in the group are organized by and integrated through the developmental phases in building a group's structure. It is the skeleton, so to speak, on which the other dimensions hang. Because of this organizing influence, we believe that the phases in group development relate in powerful ways to the outcome of the group experience for the individual member, both in terms of overall change and in terms of the kinds of issues the member can address. Further, an understanding of group development is directly relevant to an understanding of leadership and the impact of different leaders on groups and their members. The viewpoint with which we work postulates four leaders in each group.

The Design of a Methodology

This chapter presents the story of the design of a methodology for the process analysis of group psychotherapy for the purpose of identifying phase boundaries, describing characteristic phase-relevant processes in the group, and aspects of the four leaders' behaviors. The methodology has been guided at every step by the theory. The data analyses in turn have led to more refined understandings of group process and contributed to the theory building. This methodological work is still in progress. The major goal has been to find a set of variables which can describe the structural development of a therapy group during the second and third phases of development and which

---

1. The Chicago Group Psychotherapy Research Team has been working on various aspects of theory and methodological design problems related to phase development and emergent leadership in group psychotherapy. The team has been composed of five members: Ariadne Beck, James Dugo, Albert Eng, Carol Lewis, and Lana Peters.

can identify the phase boundary between those two phases in a similar way across different groups. Throughout the work, a clinical analysis of each group was used as the primary criterion against which empirical analyses were compared. At this time methods have been designed for modeling the second and third phases in group development. The variables involved may or may not be adequate to describe other phases in group life—this is a question that we will attempt to answer during the next step in our research program. However, the general format of our techniques is seen to be relevant throughout the group's life, while the particular variables to be used may change somewhat.

We will describe a pilot study in which measures were first applied to one time-limited therapy group (Group A) which had a remarkable history of traversing nine phases in 15 sessions. Many different variables were used in an exploratory way on this group until we found those which most accurately reflected the process of phase development for the second and third phases. These variables were then applied to two other groups (Groups S and N) to check their generalizability. Both the variables and their application to all three groups will be presented in this chapter. Since the methodological work has emerged directly from the theoretical work, it will be necessary to give the reader a thumbnail version of the theory and a description of the first three phases of group development.

Overview of Beck's Theory of Group Development

This theory of group development applies to groups with a stable membership of up to 10 people. When membership changes, it is very likely that a group will recycle, beginning again at the first phase. Also, the theory assumes a style of therapist leadership which encourages group-as-a-whole processes (whether or not this is explicitly expressed), as well as individual or dyadic processes, for therapeutic change. Unless the theoretical orientation of the therapist is one that deliberately constrains the group at a particular phase of development, it is not assumed to be relevant within the scope of this model. However, an interesting question for future work will be to look at the effect of such differences in leadership on group development.

In this theory there are nine phases in the development of group structure. Structure refers to the roles in the group, the norms for functioning in the group, the limits and criteria for membership, the group-level organizational issues, and the group-level identity.[2] The nine phases emerge in an unvarying sequence as long as the membership remains stable and the group is able to handle the group-level issues of each phase in turn. Since not all groups are able to do that, many groups do not progress through all, or even many, of the phases. Table 18-1 presents a list of the major themes of the nine phases. Progress through the phases requires that the members possess various levels of skill, in order to deal with the relevant group-level issues. Groups may remain at a particular phase doing productive work on the development of the appropriate skills. There are other times, however, when a group may get stuck in a particular phase because it is neither able to resolve the group-level issues of that phase nor to work on the relevant developmental issues of individuals.

The evolution of group structure progresses via a dialectical process in which group-level issues are posed early in each phase and responded to by the members from their

---

2. The term *group-level* refers to issues or problems of structural significance which are particularly relevant to the group as a whole at a particular time in its development.

Table 18-1   Major Themes in Group Development

1. Creating a contract to become a group.
2. Survival: personal influence and survival in group/the resolution of competitive needs while forging a group identity, group norms and selecting leaders.
3. Disclosure of individual identity/defining individual goals to be pursued in the group/establishing a work style.
4. Exploration of intimacy and closeness.
5. Establishment of mutuality and equality.
6. Autonomy of members from formal leader.
7. Self-confrontation in the context of interdependence.
8. Pursuit of independence.
9. Coping with separation and termination.

own particular vantage points. If it is to stay intact, the group must find solutions to each set of group-level problems, solutions which must encompass the members' range of viewpoints. The four leaders who emerge from the group play important roles in articulating appropriate solutions, by sharing leadership of the dialectical discussion (Beck, 1981a). These leaders are called the Task Leader, the Emotional Leader, the Scapegoat Leader, and the Defiant Leader.

Table 18-2 gives brief descriptions of the four leadership roles in terms of their ongoing maintenance functions throughout most of the group's life. In a mature group at Phase 7, the significance of these roles dissipates and the functions are shared more fluidly among all of the members.

Each of the four leaders acts as a model for the rest of the group in a conflict that each of the other members feels to some extent simply by being a member of a group. The Task Leader, for example, models the conflict between exercising control in the group—taking and using his* own power—and releasing control—giving to or sharing power with the other group members. The Emotional Leader models the conflict between affiliation with other members and rejection of other members—the question of whether to form deep bonds with others or to deny the need for deep bonds. The Scapegoat Leader models the conflict between assertion of the self and conformity to the group, struggling with impulses toward aggression and submission, an emotional problem raised by joining the group. The Defiant Leader usually openly expresses ambivalence about dependence and independence throughout the group's life, and models that struggle for the rest; he struggles to protect and maintain himself in relation to others. Group members who are developmentally focused on one or another of these emotional conflicts probably tend to become candidates for the relevant leadership roles. This is conjecture at this point, but will be one of the questions for research to clarify.

So that the reader can better understand both the design of our methods and the results of the pilot study, a description of the first three phases will be presented at this point. (A more detailed description appears in Beck, 1974.)

---

*Note: The pronoun *he* is used in a generic sense only; sexist language is not intended.—Editor.

Table 18-2   Ongoing Leadership Roles

---

1. *The Task Leader*, who is usually the therapist in a therapy group; this is often the person who convenes the group and usually the one who acts as the guide to the task of the group. In a therapy group, he is the expert on communication and self-exploration. This person influences norm development, goal clarification, style of communication, and many other dimensions of group life. This leader deals with the group's boundaries in its relationship to the surrounding organization and world.

2. *The Emotional Leader*, usually one of the members of the group who is most prepared and motivated to participate in the task of the group. Acts as the manager of the group's emotional processing; acts as a model of the change process in a therapy group; is generally the best-liked person in the group and is the most important support person to other members, throughout the group's life.

3. *The Scapegoat Leader*, usually a member of the group, but therapists have also been known to take this role. He is often the object of either open attack or nonverbal negative feelings from group members. He helps to crystallize group-level issues regarding norms, goals, and leadership selection. He has an ongoing role by being the vehicle for the group's clarifying many issues, and plays an important role in the initiation and termination of phases in the group's development.

4. *The Defiant Leader*, who is usually a member of the group who openly expresses an ambivalence about participating in the group and models the struggle between dependence and independence for the group as a whole. The ambivalence is also expressed in terms of the development of closeness in the group, and autonomy in relation to the therapist.

Phase 1

Phase 1 usually requires the settlement of membership composition because the members will not make a contract to become a group until they know who all the participants will be. An important aspect of Phase 1 is that members assess each other, each one estimating his own ability to cope with the others. Some will leave at this point if they feel too uncomfortable to be able to work with the others present, or if they cannot find another member with whom they can in some degree identify (Dugo & Beck, 1983b).

During Phase 1, the Task Leader, usually the therapist, plays a very important role in establishng the emotional tone, the pace, and the structure of the group. He demonstrates the way in which he will work therapeutically with individuals in the group. In his ongoing role, this leader functions as the expert on communication and self-exploration, and he influences goal clarification and leadership selection. The Emotional Leader, also an important person, is selected during Phase 1. Generally the best-liked member of the group, the Emotional Leader acts as a monitor of the group's emotional processing and is ultimately perceived by other members of the group as the most important support person.

Sometime during Phase 1 the members usually find some common experience, on the basis of which they begin to feel that they can work together. This shared experience allows the first level of cohesion to form in the group.

Phase 2

In Phase 2 the group moves on to a testing of the assessments made in Phase 1. This is a stressful time during which major group organizational issues are worked out, such as the completion of leadership selection, the establishment of important norms, the management of negative emotion, the resolution of competitive needs, and the definition of an initial group identity and group goals. These issues must be initiated at a level which engages the entire group, in such a way that they can proceed cooperatively beyond this phase.

Phase 2 is the most difficult phase in group process. It is usually characterized by a conflict with one person in particular, the Scapegoat Leader, who serves as a reference point against which the rest of the group defines itself and works out its organizational issues. The Emotional Leader, the Task Leader, and the Scapegoat Leader usually play critical roles in this phase.

Phase 3

Assuming that the conflict is resolved, then, Phase 3 is the beginning of a cooperative work process, during which the members become more personally disclosing. This period also introduces the therapeutic methods for dealing with personal change and growth in greater depth. Each member takes a turn to discuss the issues that brought him to the group and is seen more clearly for himself. By the end of the phase the members are really individuals once more, having established a kind of equality as clients by participating in this shared self-disclosure. During this phase, the Emotional Leader begins a significant growth spurt and becomes a model of the change process to the group. The Defiant Leader begins to assume a therapist-like stance in relation to others during Phase 3, while offering a minimal amount of self-disclosure. Phase 2 is essentially a competitive phase, and Phase 3 begins the cooperative group process. Therefore, the shift of a group from Phase 2 to Phase 3 represents a major change in group-level process.

An Overview of the Methodological Pilot Study

Selection of Measures

From the brief descriptions above of the first three phases it is probably clear that the shift from Phase 2 to Phase 3 is a major change in the group's life, style, and focus. It is, in fact, one of two such major changes or reorganizations of the group. The second one comes later in the shift from Phase 5 to Phase 6. Since many groups do not reach that point in development, the literature has fewer observations of Phases 5 and 6 than of Phases 2 and 3. For this reason and because of an interest in illuminating the process by which a group becomes a "working organization," the decision was made to focus on the second and third phases of development and the boundary between those two phases as the first step in designing methods of analysis of group development based on Beck's theory (1977).

In preparation for this work, an extensive review of the literature on group phases was conducted. Beck's phases were used as a basis for organizing all the rest of the literature. This organization of the material pointed to an amazing degree of agreement in the observations of the nine phases (Beck, in preparation-a). Lists were then made of the characteristics of Phases 2 and 3 which were generally agreed upon by all the observers reviewed. By comparing the lists for the two phases, it was possible to define the major changes that took place when the groups moved from one phase to the other. Table 18-3 lists the three critical dimensions of change that were identified by this analysis.

Table 18-3   Major Differences Between Phases 2 and 3

Phase 2		Phase 3
1. Movement from a period of high tension, anger, criticism, or discomfort	to	a period of relatively positive feeling and mutual support.
2. Movement from relatively defensive (stereotyping, manipulating, deflecting, behavior)	to	more open, mutually exploratory behavior.
3. Movement from concern, apprehension, and struggle related to organizational and norm development issues	to	a focus on individual members and their personal concerns.

The next step was to select or invent measures which would track the group's processes in terms of these dimensions of change. The problem here was to identify the appropriate level of process which could be expected to be similar across groups, regardless of the actual content of their discourse (Beck, 1977). A number of scales that exist in the literature, as well as a number which we invented, were tried and discarded. Finally, three scales have been evaluated as promising and been used in a pilot study of three time-limited groups. Two of these scales, the Hostility/Support Scale and the Normative-Organizational/Personal Exploration Scale, are our own inventions; the third, the Experiencing Scale, is taken from the field of research on individual psychotherapy. All three scales have been applied to all of the verbal interaction in transcripts of sessions of group psychotherapy. In the case of the Hostility/Support and the Experiencing Scales, variables are then extracted from this data base. Variables are based upon subsets of the data or different kinds of measures using the same data. These variables have been chosen because they are capable of identifying the exact point in time when a group shifts from Phase 2 to Phase 3.

Figure 18-1 shows graphs plotting the three variables which have been chosen to reflect the three major dimensions of change in Table 18-3. The scales were applied to transcripts of the second through fifth sessions of Group A. The solid vertical lines indicate session endings and beginnings and the vertical broken lines indicate the phase boundaries. On the basis of the pilot study, we propose to define a phase shift empirically as a pattern of this kind—that is, a set of variables in tandem which will show the timing of the phase shift in terms pertinent to the characteristics of the phases involved, as determined by the theory and the literature review. These process analysis measures, developed for use on psychotherapy groups by Beck, Dugo, and Lewis, will be described in detail in this chapter. We see the use of these three measures as only a first step in a long-range research program. And, that first step will only be completed when all nine phases and their boundaries have been modeled.

A second step in our overall program has been the design of a sociometric test which is filled out by all the members of a group and used to identify the four leaders. This work has been described elsewhere (Beck & Peters, 1981; Peters & Beck, 1982). Although the sociometric test can be used as a repeated measure, we have used it early in the group and at the end of a group primarily and do not at this time think of it as a process measure.

A third step in our overall program has been the design of very basic speech behavior measures by Eng and Beck, for use in looking at overall communication differences be-

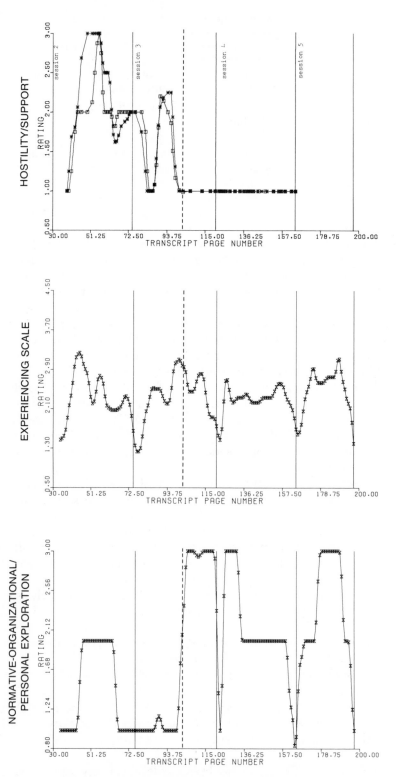

Figure 18-1   Three measures for analysis of group phase development. Group A, Sessions 2–5.

tween phases and more importantly for looking at, within—and between—phase behaviors of leaders and members. Several of the speech behavior measures will be presented in this chapter: (1) verbal participation (a measure of volume of verbal participation by person by phase); (2) speaker/spoken to (a measure of initiations by each person and of attention received by each person by phase); (3) we–group usage (a measure of the number of times group participants use the word "we" to refer to the group itself).

The Groups in the Pilot Study

The data base for the pilot study was generated by analyzing three time-limited psychotherapy groups, each of which met for a planned 15- or 20-session series. They were conducted at a university-based community clinic. The therapists, all working within the client-centered theoretical framework, were primarily focused on individual therapeutic change. None of them had a well-formulated focus on group-as-a-whole process. Groups A and S were composed of both male and female clients, all but two of whom were in or had been in individual therapy in the same clinic—the other two had been in therapy elsewhere. Group N was composed of five male graduate students who were in training as counselors and who had chosen the group format for their own therapy experience. They knew each other as classmates outside of the group. Each group was led by two therapists, one a beginner in training, the other a more experienced group leader from the staff of the clinic.

For presenting our measures in this handbook, a portion of the transcript of Group A has been selected and will be referred to whenever an example is needed of how the rating categories are used. The transcript appears as an appendix beginning on page 681.

The Group Development Process
Analysis Measures

The unique aspects of each of our measures as well as definitions of the categories will be presented in separate sections following this section. There are common aspects to all measures, however, and these will be presented first in this section.

Common Aspects of the Measures

Treatment Modalities and Therapy Orientations   The scales were all designed or modified for application to psychotherapy groups. However, they do not relate in any way to any particular modality or orientation of therapy. They would all be applicable to any form of group or family interaction. At this time, they have only been applied to the three client-centered, time-limited psychotherapy groups in our pilot study.

Access Strategy and Communication Channel   All the measures have been designed for use in rating the verbal statements in typed transcripts of audiotape recordings of group therapy sessions. Verbal and/or paralinguistic channels are used in making rating judgments. The measures could also be used directly with audio or videotape recordings as well, if methods were first devised for identifying statements and units of group interaction and if some other measure than the typed page were selected as the summarizing unit for data analysis of all of the graphed measures. There are problems, however, in using either audio or video recordings for rating since the number of speakers in a group creates a difficult task, especially when using audiotapes. It is, in fact, very hard to identify speakers accurately. This task was performed for us by the manuscript typist, who became quite familiar with each speaker's voice during the course of her work. The speed with which interaction occurs at times, and the interruptions or occasions when two members speak at once, also make the transcript essential. Presumably, videotapes would deal with some of these issues, but not all.

Data Format   All of the measures have been applied to typed transcripts of audiotape recordings of complete sessions of group psychotherapy. The typist identifies the speaker from voice, content, and context (see comments in paragraph above). Our transcripts were prepared by a BA-level psychology major who had an interest in counseling and communication and was an excellent listener.

The person spoken to has been determined by raters who read the transcripts (see section on speech behavior measures for details on rating "spoken to").

The transcripts list each burst of speech or expression as it occurs chronologically on the tape. Since people often interrupt each other, or sometimes speak simultaneously, these characteristics are also indicated, as are pauses, stutters, and laughter. Each speech on a page identified by a speaker is numbered, with numbers beginning at 1 on each new page of transcript. This numbering system makes it possible to identify each speech in the sequence in which it occurs by denoting page number and item number.

Finally, the transcript is read for the purpose of identifying statements. A statement may be the equivalent of a speech and it may not. Since people interrupt each other, overlap, or switch topics midstream, a judgment must be made about what constitutes a single statement. A statement may consist of an exclamation, a partial sentence, or many sentences. In the latter case, a statement is a period of speech in which complete thoughts, ideas, reactions, or themes are expressed by one individual. The statement is usually bounded by statements made by other group members, except in those instances where the person speaking is interrupted by someone else, but then continues with his own thought; or when two persons are speaking simultaneously through all or part of their speeches. In these cases, there may be several speeches on one or two pages that are considered part of the same statement. This judgment is made by raters who read and code the transcript. All statements in a transcript receive random code numbers as well as the number that indicates sequence on the page. Random code numbers are needed for the rating of the Hostility/Support Scale. This use of the random code will be explained in the section on that scale. When several speeches are considered part of one statement, they all receive the same random code number (e.g., items 7, 9, 10 in the excerpt from our working transcript, below). Reliability was established for each of the three groups between two raters who read the transcript in sequence and decided on assignment of random code numbers and therefore on statements. One entire session of each group was rated by two raters. The agreement was assessed by Pearson correlations (.91 for Group A; .93 for Group S, and .94 for Group N).

Following is a sample page of our working transcript (brackets indicate simultaneous speaking):

[802] 1. Diane: . . . operating with this . . . , yea . . .
[2432] 2. Helen: And that irritates you, it's like telling you there's something here but you can't get it. I'm not going to give it to you.
[1494] 3. Diane: Um. I-I-I was trying to think, trying to see if I really did feel ir-

ritation. This was what I was, when you said that irritates me . . .

^{8304} 4. Martha: That's not the feeling that I get from you . . .

^{1494} 5. Diane: Is irritati— . . .

^{8304} 6. Martha: No it's the thing I get from you that you feel is frus . . .

^{7371} 7. Diane: Frustra— . . .

^{8304} 8. Martha: . . . tration, I want in, or I wanna know you.

^{7371} 9. Diane: (unclear words here) Except I wanted to look at the irritation cuz sometimes I, I guess I want to really see if I . . .

^{7371} 10. Diane: But I think it is more frustration. It's more like, "Gee I'll spend 15 weeks with you and never really know you. I'll know all about what you think of racial prejudice and Marilyn Monroe and the, and the UN and that sort of thing but I'll never really know what is clickin' around inside you! (laugh)

^{5658} 11. ⌈ Joe: (unclear) I don't know myself. (laugh)

^{5994} 12. ⌊ Alice: And that, hurts some way that's . . .

^{4170} 13. Helen: There's something else now that I . . .

^{5994} 14. ⌈ Alice: It hurts in some way to . . .

^{7325} 15. ⌊ Diane: It doesn't hurt.

^{5994} 16. Alice: . . . think you won't know er . . .

^{971} 17. Diane: No it doesn't hurt, it's, I-I-I like your word frustration. (slight laugh)

^{5535} 18. Joe: Well like I say I mean it's . . .

^{5535} 19. ⌈ Joe: . . . a matter of personality.

^{3150} 20. ⌊ Diane: It seems wasteful! Almost.

^{5535} 21. Joe: It's a personal, a matter of personality. We're all different, develop different, we have different ideas, different thoughts, different inner thoughts.

As mentioned earlier, a portion of Group A's transcript appears as an appendix to this chapter. In comparison to our working transcript, the transcript in the appendix is a replica of our working transcript, but it has been simplified by giving all parts of a statement the same item number, and we have numbered statements continuously without respect to page numbers. Further, we have eliminated the random numbers. For comparison: the example above, page 96 of the working transcript, corresponds to statements 12 to 22 in the appendix transcript.

Selection of Events and Sampling   For the pilot study, entire sessions of group therapy were rated. In fact, we have used a number of succeeding sessions for each group that we have studied. Since we have chosen the study of phase developmental process and the phase shift between Phases 2 and 3, we have simply rated data from the early sessions of each group. But our location of this portion of group life was also based on an initial clinical analysis. This judgment was made by a member of the team who listened to the therapy tapes of each group, and was subsequently confirmed or modified by other team members as they worked with the transcripts.

None of the measures being presented here has been used in a context of taking samples from a group transcript. We do not feel that the phenomenon that we are trying to identify, namely phase processes or boundaries, can be meaningfully studied by sampling behavior in a group. Therefore, whole sessions are always rated.

Validity

Discriminant Validity   There are several issues to be discussed in this section. First is the question of discriminant validity as it relates to the measures' sensitivities to differences between Phase 2 and Phase 3 group processes; and their abilities to mark the phase boundary. To our knowledge no one has attempted to actually identify the specific boundary between two phases, although a number of studies have tried to differentiate different periods of time in a group in terms of a variety of dimensions, and by use of a variety of methods for aggregating data points. The entire purpose of the design of the process variables to be presented here has been precisely to track the processes of groups in Phases 2 and 3 and to accurately mark the boundary. In the course of our work, a number of measures were tried, which though they showed interesting aspects of the group process, were not able to track the group-as-a-whole behavior in terms that were relevant to the two phases or were not able to discriminate the phase boundary. These measures were all discarded. The three process variables we will present do seem to relate to and describe the differences between Phases 2 and 3 in expected ways and do identify the phase boundary between these two phases.

Second, these three variables, degree of hostility or support expressed to the Scapegoat Leader by other members; the level of experiencing of the group-as-a-whole; and the focus of the group-as-a-whole on either normative and organizational issues or on personal exploration issues, address quite different levels of the process. The Experiencing Scale is a measure applied to the individual's behavior and it addresses a dimension of an individual's intrapsychic life. The Hostility/Support Scale is based in the interpersonal sphere, assessing the attitude of one member toward another member. The Normative-Organizational/Personal Exploration Scale assesses the focus of the group-as-a-whole during any unit of group interaction.

Although based on a systems view of isomorphy, which expects these three realms to reflect each other to some degree, they are nevertheless three quite separate domains. Indeed, whole techniques of group therapy have been devised at one or another of these levels of group life. It is therefore some evidence of the discriminant validity of our method that all three measures behaved in expected ways and identified the phase boundary across groups.

To some extent this argument also applies to the speech behavior measures which tap the most basic level of verbal communication in the group, and which also differentiated between the phases and between leaders and nonleaders.

Construct Validity   An entirely different question is whether each of our scales measure what they purport to measure. With respect to the Hostility/Support Scale and the Normative-Organizational/Personal Exploration (NO/PE) Scale, both of which we invented, we have not as yet conducted a construct validity study. That step will be taken in the future. There are apparently several studies which have measured a dimension similar to the Hostility/Support Scale and a study correlating these scales would therefore be possible. At this time, we are not aware of any scale similar to the NO/PE scale but we will continue to search the literature for measures which address the same or similar constructs. Within our work on the speech behavior measures, however, the "we-group" measure to be described later in the chapter supports and corroborates the findings using the NO/PE scale.

Regarding the Experiencing Scale, the Klein, Mathieu-Coughlan, and Kiesler chapter in this book addresses the relationship of the EXP scale to a large number of other measures and concludes that it is related to measures of self-disclosure, problem expression, and internal focus and not related strongly to measures of patient concreteness, speech fluency, affective distress, or psychodynamically formulated judgment of productivity.

The Speech Behavior Coding System does not measure any constructs. The measures are behavioral and lexical counts.

Introduction to the Individual Scales   Now that the common aspects of the Group Development Process Analysis Measures have been presented, we will first present each of the scales relating to the Phase 2 to Phase 3 shift and the variables derived from them. Then we present the Speech Behavior Coding System, and, finally, the planned next steps in the completion of this methodology and the future plans for use of the measures in a larger-scale study.

The Hostility/Support Scale

The Scale   This nominal scale is a simple three-category measure that makes a gross assessment of a statement in terms of the basic supportiveness or negativity of the speaker in relation to the person being addressed (Beck, 1983). A brief form of the definitions of the three categories for rating the Hostility/Support Scale are presented below. A manual will present more detailed guidelines for rating (Beck, in preparation b).

Rating	Definition
1	Statement expresses acceptance, agreement, or neutrality toward the person addressed.
2	Statement expresses disagreement, mild or veiled negativity or criticism.
3	Statement expresses openly negative, angry, or aggressive feelings toward the person addressed.

Theoretical Base   This scale was designed to track the first major change listed in Table 18-3: the group shifts from a period of high tension, anger, criticism, or discomfort in Phase 2 to a period of relatively positive feeling and mutual support in Phase 3. In particular we have observed that the negative feelings in Phase 2 are directed most explicitly toward the Scapegoat Leader by the rest of the group members. If Phase 2 issues are resolved, one would therefore expect to see a change in the members' responses to this leader during Phase 3. One possible measure therefore of the shift from Phase 2 to Phase 3 would be the degree of support or negativity expressed by group members toward the Scapegoat Leader.

The Variable   Although the scale has been applied to the entire transcript of Group A, the variable which proved to be most relevant to the identification of the shift from Phase 2 to Phase 3 was based on the statements addressd to the Scapegoat Leader by group members (excluding therapists). This is the variable plotted in Figure 18-1. The Scapegoat Leader was identified by sociometric tests that all members filled out at the end of each group (Beck & Peters, 1981; Peters & Beck, 1982).

Units for Rating and for Data Analysis

Scoring Unit

The unit that was chosen for rating was one member's statement between two statements made by others, as the statement is defined by the preparation of our transcripts (see page 624). All statements addressed to the Scapegoat Leader by members (not therapists) were selected. Then, each statement from the typescript was retyped on 3×5 cards. Each card was identified by the random code number for the statement. No indication appears on the card of the speaker, the page number, or item number for that statement. The cards are organized numerically, which in effect randomizes them. Two raters rated each statement in terms of the three categories in the Hostility/Support Scale.

Contextual Unit

The rating of each statement is made totally out of context, based only on a careful reading of the statement itself. This is a severe test of the concept involved in this measure, since listening to the voice or rating in context would probably bring some seemingly innocuous verbal statements into the negative categories.

Summarizing Unit

After the raters rate each statement, they enter the code number and rating on a data sheet. The ratings are then transferred to another data sheet listing each item in the time order in which it appeared in the transcript, in terms of its page/item number and its code number. An average rating per page of transcript is then computed. This is the summarizing unit to which the statistical analysis is applied for the purpose of generating graphs such as Figure 18-1. The page of transcript was chosen as the time unit because pages of typescript tend to contain roughly equivalent amounts of communication.

Raters   The raters who have been selected for rating this variable were graduate students in training in counseling or psychotherapy. The only clinical orientation required was that the rater be someone attuned to emotional dimensions of communication, an individual who could easily identify emotional tone in written statement, particularly any subtle forms of negative response.

Reliability Data   Two methods of assessing the reliability of the two raters' ratings of the Hostility/Support Scale were used. First, a cross-tabulation assessed the percentage of complete agreement between the two raters. Second, a Pearson correlation was computed on the average rating per page of transcript, since these data enter the computer to be smoothed and to produce a graph. The results of both methods of assessment for the three groups in our study appear in Table 18-4.

In preparing raters, they are first trained to criterion, and then their ratings are compared by the two methods described above.

Data Analysis   With data such as these, it would be reasonable to expect a substantial degree of random fluctuation or noise. In order to reduce this noise and to extract any strong trends in the data, they have been smoothed by a nonlinear data smoother based on running medians (and referred to as hanning), which was developed by Tukey

Table 18-4   Reliability Data for Hostility/Support Scale

	Cross-tabulation % Complete Agreement (Item-by-Item)	Pearson Correlation (Average Rating/Page)	Level of Significance	N (Pages of Transcript)
Group A	74.32	.83	.000001	127
Group S	71.85	.66	.000001	200
Group N	75.78	.61	.000001	275

(Beaton & Tukey, 1974). The smoothed results are then plotted. In order to demonstrate the effect of the smoother on a set of data, several graphs are presented showing Group A (Beck, 1983).

Figure 18-2 shows a plot of the raw average rating per page of transcript. As you can see, the data are quite noisy. Figure 18-3 shows a simple moving average applied to the average rating per page. This reduces some of the noise.

Figure 18-4 shows Tukey's running median applied to the data. Virtually all the noise is removed and only major trends remain. This variable shows a clear shift in the group members' responses to the Scapegoat Leader from a fairly high degree of negativity in Phase 2 to acceptance in Phase 3. Figure 18-5 shows the two raters' smoothed ratings plotted on the same graph. On these computer-plotter-produced graphs, the solid vertical lines mark the end of one session and the beginning of the next. The vertical axis shows the smoothed average rating per page and the horizontal axis shows transcript page numbers (also smoothed). The plot is missing data points in Session 5 because the Scapegoat Leader was absent that day.

Since Tukey proposed the use of smoothers on exploratory data, a number of nonlinear data smoothers have been developed. A comparison of a number of these procedures indicated that the one we are using in this study, referred to as "53H, twice," was quite effective in "finding general smooth patterns for sequenced data confounded with long-tailed noise" (Velleman, 1980), without distorting the patterns in the data excessively.

Application of Scale to Transcript   The appendix presents two segments of group interaction from the transcript of Group A. The segments come from pages 95–102 and 187–188 in the original transcript. These page numbers will locate the material on the graph of Group A in Figures 18-1 through 18-5. Pages 95–102 include the phase shift from Phase 2 to Phase 3 in this group. Pages 187–188 take place within Phase 3. Each of our measures is being illustrated by application to this transcript.

The Hostility/Support Scale is used to rate all statements made by group members (not including therapists) to the Scapegoat Leader, who in Group A is Joe. As indicated above, the statements are rated out of context and in randomized order. We enter this transcript during the period when the group is in the final minutes of the second phase. There is still some anger and hostility being expressed toward Joe by Diane, who was one of two persons who attacked Joe for the style and content of his communication in the group. This is reflected in Diane's statements numbered 10 and 12 in the transcript, where she is criticizing Joe because he does not share his internal experience or feelings when he tells about incidents that concern him. This predominantly critical attitude of Diane's determined the rating of 2 for these statements. (See Table 18-5 for

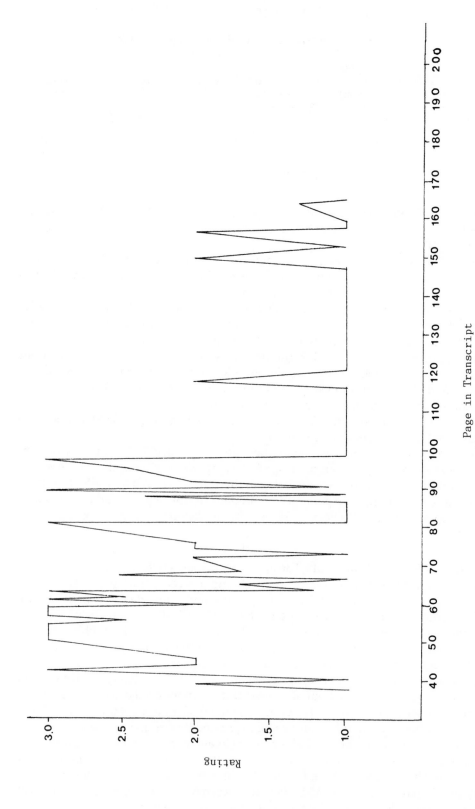

Figure 18-2 Average rating per page of transcript. Hostility/Support Scale, members' statements to SL. Group A, Sessions 2–5.

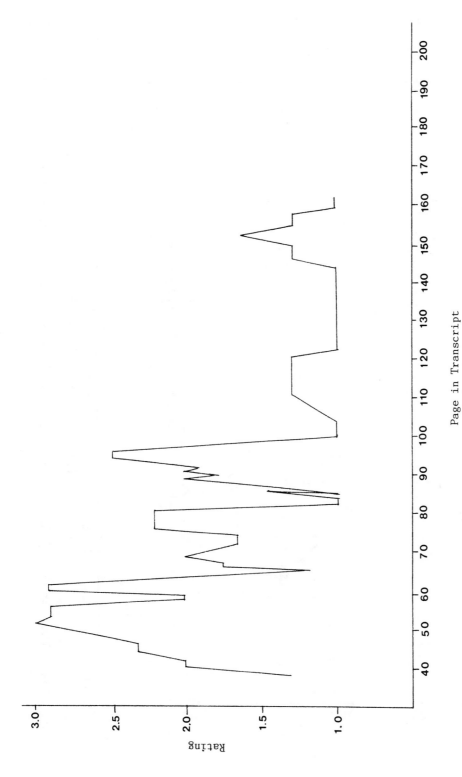

Figure 18-3 Moving average applied to average rating per page of transcript. Hostility/Support Scale, members' statements to SL. Group A, Sessions 2–5.

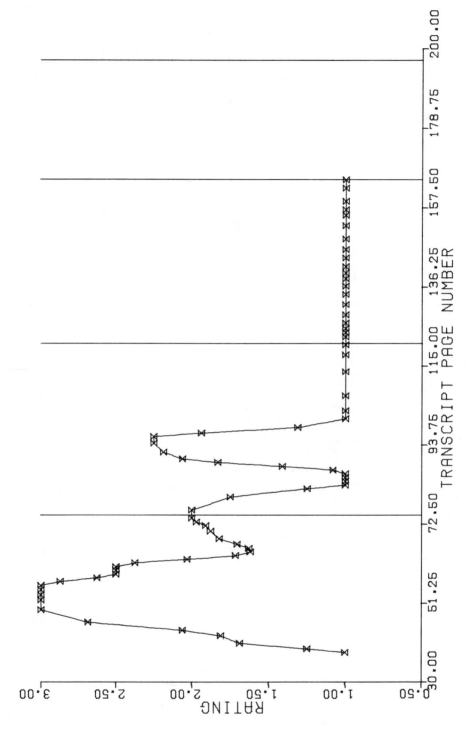

Figure 18-4 Tukey's smoother applied to average rating per page of transcript. Hostility/Support Scale, members' statements to SL. Group A, Sessions 2–5.

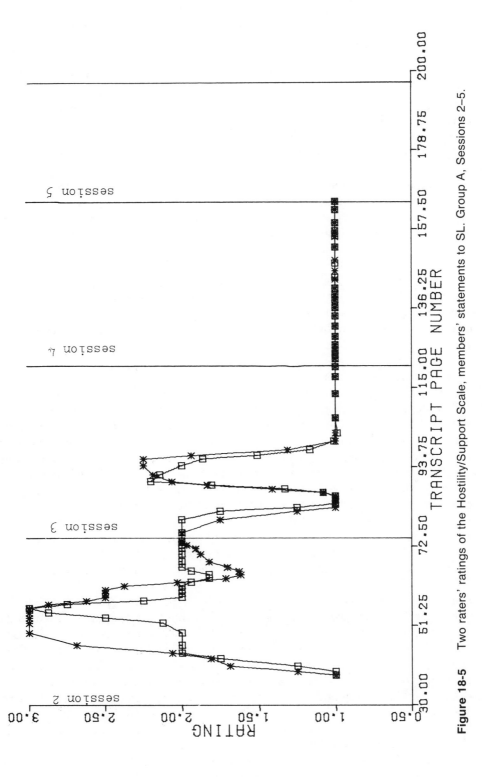

Figure 18-5 Two raters' ratings of the Hostility/Support Scale, members' statements to SL. Group A, Sessions 2–5.

rating definitions.) Then in statement 16, Diane for the first time acknowledges her irritation (born of frustration) with Joe. This open direct statement of her anger gets a rating of 3.

As the group approaches the resolution of their issues with Joe, and the end of Phase 2, Brad reflects on the fact that Joe has in fact revealed more about himself than has any other member of the group and wonders, "Why are we after him?" [statement 29]. This is the turning point in the group's viewing of Joe and the beginning of their group level awareness of themselves. This open, reflective, and accepting attitude toward Joe gets a rating of 1. After acknowledging their use of Joe in order to avoid self-disclosure, the group moves into Phase 3, where they are now free to begin their own self-explorations. Finally, at statement 70, Diane begins to relate to Joe from a more empathic position, drawing an analogy between her experience and his, and this statement is rated 1. These statements are reasonably clear examples of the three categories of the Hostility/Support Scale. The manual offers detailed definitions, clear examples, as well as examples that are more difficult to rate.

Research Results   The Hostility/Support Scale, used to rate statements that group members make to the Scapegoat Leader, was applied to three groups in our pilot study. Groups A and S successfully resolved their Phase 2 issues and moved into Phase 3. This is clearly reflected in the change from critical or hostile statements toward the respective Scapegoat Leaders to supportive statements in both of these groups. Figure 18-1 shows Group A and Figure 18-6 shows Group S.

Group N, on the other hand, was unable to make the shift from Phase 2 to Phase 3. This is reflected in the continuing, almost cyclical pattern of critical responses made to the Scapegoat Leader of this group. Figure 18-7 shows this phenomenon very nicely. Group N, as indicated earlier, was composed of male graduate students who had contact with each other outside the group, in courses on campus. They were all in training in a counseling practicum at the time. They had a competitive set of relationships in these other contexts and seemed to be unable to resolve competitive issues in order to move on to more self-disclosing group process. The level of trust in this group was inadequate, and the leaders were unable to facilitate a change.

These three groups show that the Hostility/Support variable is capable of reflecting a major change in group behavior, when the group moves from Phase 2 to Phase 3, and that it reflects this change in two different groups, A and S. Also, when a group is unable to resolve those differences, this variable nicely reflects that process as well, as in Group N.

The question arises as to how useful the Hostility/Support Scale will be to look at phases other than the second and third. We think that the same three measures that we are using for Phases 2 and 3 may be useful for identifying the phase boundaries between Phase 1 and Phase 2 as well. Since the relationship between the Scapegoat Leader and the rest of the group improves from Phase 3 on, it is unlikely that the Member to Scapegoat Leader variable will show any significant change. However, the scale may be useful in looking at the relationship between the Defiant Leader and the rest of the group in Phase 5, when that leader usually has a crisis. The scale is currently being applied to all statements in Group A for the entire life of that group, in order to check out its usefulness in later phases. The expectation, however, is that it will probably not be useful past Phase 3, and we will need a comparable variable that is unique to the processes of later phases. This general application will also allow us the opportunity to look at the responses of the group to other members during this period of time

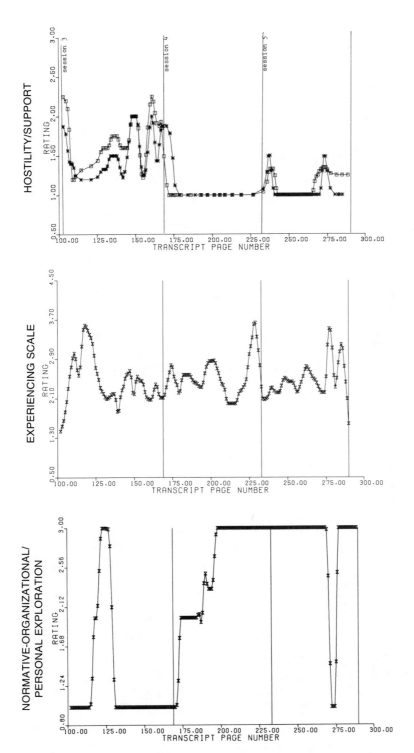

Figure 18-6   Three measures for analysis of group phase development. Group S, Sessions 3–5.

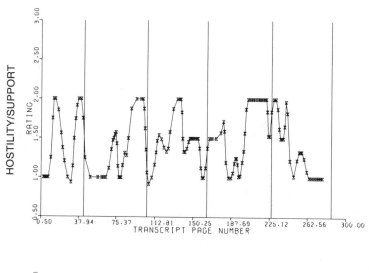

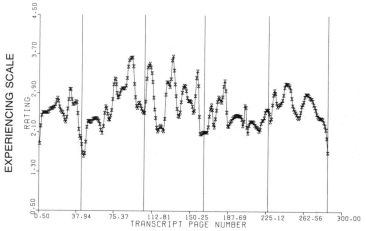

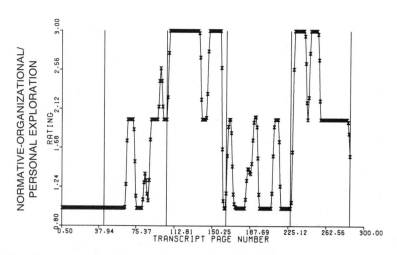

Figure 18-7   Three measures for analysis of group phase development. Group N, Sessions 3–7.

to assess whether the attitude being expressed toward the Scapegoat Leader is unique, or just part of a general atmosphere of negativity.

The Experiencing Scales

The Scales   There are separate scales for client and therapist statements. The Client Experiencing Scale is a research instrument designed to assess some aspects of a patient's degree of involvement in the process of self-exploration in psychotherapy through the use of tape recordings or transcripts of the therapy session. The Therapist Experiencing Scale assesses the therapist's statement in terms of the level of experiencing at which the client's exploration is represented, and the manner in which this is done.

Experiencing refers to an individual's ability to recognize and accept his feelings and their personal meanings. It also reflects the extent to which a person's awareness of his subjective experience is used as a referent for thought and action. The present Client Experiencing Scale, developed by Klein, Mathieu, Gendlin, and Kiesler in 1969, is a modified version of the scale originally developed by Gendlin and Tomlinson and published in 1967. The scale progresses from limited and externalized self-references toward inwardly elaborated descriptions of feelings. Recently, the Therapist Experiencing Scales have been developed as well (Mathieu-Coughlan & Klein, 1984), and this has made the application to group interaction feasible.

Brief descriptions of the scale points in the Client and Therapist Experiencing Scales will be presented below. These descriptions convey an initial idea of the range of exploratory behavior covered in the scales. For more detailed definitions, see Chapter 2 in this volume and the manuals on the Client Experiencing Scale (Klein, Mathieu, Gendlin, and Kiesler, 1969), and The Application of the Experiencing Scales to Group Interaction (Lewis & Beck, in preparation).

The Client Experiencing Scale

Stage 1: Experiences and events reported have an impersonal quality, and feelings are avoided. Often at this stage, the client is setting a clear limit on his willingness to be involved.

Stage 2: The individual's personal perspective emerges somewhat, manifested in his description of events around him, but even if the quality of his feeling response can be perceived by another through his manner, or through affect present during the description of events, the feelings are not referred to directly by the client.

Stage 3: Feelings become clearly defined in reference to particular situations or external events. The client notes what his internal reaction was, but anchors it within the context of the external events which stimulated his response.

Stage 4: The quality of the client's experiencing shifts from being anchored externally in some way to becoming predominantly concerned with a description of his inner feelings and reactions.

Stage 5: These inner referents are organized to pose a problem or question about the self, and are used by the client to explore an aspect of his experience.

Stage 6: Changing and emerging feelings are directly sensed. Self-exploration focuses on perception of emerging feelings and on integration of their meaning and impact.

Stage 7: Steady awareness of inner referents facilitates modifying concepts and perceptions of the self and feelings in light of immediately felt nuances.

For the client scale, both the content and the manner in which the speaker is using his feelings are taken into account in forming a judgment about level of experiencing, and assigning a rating to a sample segment.

For the Therapist Experiencing Scale, two ratings are made, treating content and manner separately. The Patient Content Referent is directly related to the Client Experiencing Scale, and rates the level of experiencing at which the content of the client's exploration is represented in the therapist's response. The Therapist Manner Scale rates the mode in which the therapist engages in the exploratory therapy process as this is reflected in his response to the client. The therapist manner ranges from an impersonal and detached stance, through various stages in which the therapist's feeling judgment and perceptual skills are focused and lent to the client's self-exploration. The stages represent different ways in which the client's process is shared by the client and therapist.

The Therapist Experiencing Scales

Stage 1: Referent: The therapist responds with ideas or events which are impersonal and which are external to the patient. *Manner:* The therapist is detached or withdrawn, and may show lack of involvement or attention.

Stage 2: Referent: The response refers to events in which the patient is directly involved, and the patient's behavior or thinking in relation to events, but does not verbally refer to or represent the patient's feelings. *Manner:* The therapist's interest and attention are made clear by his intellectual involvement, but any disclosure of the therapist's own response does not refer to his feelings or personal reactions.

Stage 3: Referent: The patient's feeling or inner awareness in reaction to an event are noted. *Manner:* The therapist's affect is a part of his response. He may express a feeling as an aspect of his response.

Stage 4: Referent: The therapist refers to the patient's feelings within the context of the patient's inner awareness and personal perspective. *Manner:* The therapist follows along the patient's frame of reference with his own feelings and reactions. He follows the patient's awareness with his feelings as well as with his intellect.

Stage 5: Referent: The response engages or assists the patient in identifying and representing a problem or proposition about himself from the viewpoint of his inner awareness. *Manner:* The therapist uses his own feelings in working on the problem or conflict at hand to facilitate the exploration and struggle which take place at this level with the feeling and attention turned inward.

Stage 6: Referent: The therapist refers to changing or emerging feelings and experience which occur as a result of the work at Stage 5. *Manner:* The therapist's affective responses and feelings are working as a kind of extension of the patient so that they confirm and extend the patient's awareness.

Stage 7: Referent: The response focuses on movement in the patient from one inner referent to another, with referents being used with facility as building blocks to further awareness. *Manner:* The therapist's responses continue to be integrated with those of the patient, so that feelings flow and build from one to the other.

At the time when we applied the scales to our material, the Therapist Manner Scale was still in the process of development. Therefore, only the data from the Patient Content Referent Scale of the therapist scales has been used in our data analysis at this time.

Since the Experiencing Scales are described in an earlier chapter, we will confine our presentation here to the adaptations and procedures necessitated by the application of the scales to group psychotherapy data. This application of the Experiencing Scales was made possible by the help of Klein and Mathieu-Coughlan, who taught us to use the Therapist Experiencing Scales while these scales were still being developed, and who consulted with us on the general application of the scales to group psychotherapy data, and collaborated on specific rating tasks.

Adapting the Experiencing Scales to Group Therapy Interaction

In order to apply the Experiencing Scales to group interaction, two other scales had to be developed: the Length of Statement Scale and the Client–Therapist Scale. Before each statement is rated on the Experiencing Scales, it is first coded for length. This scale was instituted in order to correct for what otherwise would have been a bias against long statements.

Length of Statement Scale

Code	Length
1	Statements of 1 to 5 lines in the transcript
2	Statements of 6 to 10 lines
3	Statements with 11 or more lines

Each statement is also classified as either a client or therapist type of statement, regardless of who is speaking. Based on this decision, the statement is then rated on the appropriate Experiencing Scale. For a statement to be rated on the therapist scale, it must be an effort on the part of the speaker to present his understanding or perception of another group member's experience or behavior, representing that person's feelings, thoughts, actions, or outlook. A statement which shows interest in finding out more about another person's experience, encourages another person to explore further, or asks a question about some aspect of another person's experience may also be rated on the therapist scale. After a statement has been classified as either a client or therapist type of statement, it is ready to be rated using the appropriate Experiencing Scale: the client or therapist scale.

Theoretical Base   Two constructs from the theory of group development with which we are working are pertinent.

Since the Experiencing Scale is designed to assess the process of self-exploration in psychotherapy, we chose it to study the second dimension of change (see Table 18-3) which occurs as the group develops from Phase 2 to Phase 3: the movement from relatively defensive behavior to more open self-exploration. Our initial idea was that the level of experiencing would rise in Phase 3. Our application to the first group, Group A, showed that experiencing peaked at the phase shifts. This finding, which we had not anticipated, seemed to us to have important implications for understanding phase processes, so we went ahead with the use of this set of scales (Lewis & Beck, 1983), applying them to the two other groups in the study.

The Experiencing Scale data also reflect an aspect of the developmental process which is common to all phases of group development. Beck (1981a, 1981b) notes that group structure evolves through a dialectical process of differentiation and integration during each phase. Each phase brings a set of group-level issues or problems to the group's attention. These group-level issues for each phase of development are probably similar across groups, but the way in which the issues are perceived and expressed is unique to each group, being affected by the personality characteristics, needs, and personal issues of each group member. To complete the developmental task for each phase of group development, the members must succeed in forming a shared and integrated perception and understanding of the issues that the phase has posed for them (Lewis, 1985). The Experiencing Scale data reflect this process of integration, as the group as a whole achieves resolution of a phase task.

The Variables The Experiencing Scales are part of our methodology for identifying phase boundaries or shifts. In addition, we are studying individual patterns of self-exploration within each phase of the group process. We are looking at how these patterns are affected by the developmental process of the group, and also at how the behavior of individuals contributes to the group-level process. In an exploratory way we are looking at what the Experiencing Scale data may tell us about leadership behavior and its growth during the life of a group. We are also identifying and rating therapeutic responses made by group members, and plan to study this aspect of the group therapy process.

We have in fact extracted a number of variables from the ratings of the three groups in our study, using the EXP scales. Following is a list of variables that we have actually explored by data analysis and computer-plotted graphs:

1. Group-as-a-whole level of experiencing: average rating per page of transcript, including clients and therapists, using both scales.
2. Clients' level of experiencing on the client scale: average rating per page, using client's statements on the client scale, including all clients.
3. Therapists' level of experiencing: average rating per page, using both scales, including both therapists.
4. Clients' level of experiencing on therapist scale: average rating per page, using clients' statements rated on Therapist Experiencing Scale (Patient Content Referent Scale), combining all clients.
5. Rate of therapist responses by clients: number of client statements rated on the Therapist Experiencing Scale per page.
6. Therapist level of experiencing: average rating per page, using both scales, individually graphed for each therapist.
7. Client level of experiencing on therapist scale: average rating per page, using client's statements rated on Therapist Experiencing Scale (Patient Content Referent Scale), individually graphed for each client.
8. Client level of experiencing: average rating per page, using both scales, graphed individually for each client.
9. Client level of experiencing on client scale: average rating per page, using client's statements rated on Client Experiencing Scale, individually graphed for each client.

For the analysis of phase development and the identification of the phase shift from Phase 2 to Phase 3 the variable which we have found most useful is the group-as-a-whole level of experiencing (number 1 above): see Figure 18-1.

What Is Rated, and Type of Scale Statements (see page 624) are rated in context by continuous reading of the transcripts of entire sessions of group therapy. Each statement is rated in three basic ways: the length of the statement (an ordinal scale); whether it is a client or a therapist statement (a nominal scale); and on the appropriate Experiencing Scale (an ordinal scale—see in Chapter 2). For the Experiencing Scales, every statement in the transcript is rated (except for statements that are too short or have been interrupted too prematurely to be rated with the Experiencing Scales). The behavior of every member of the group is rated, including both clients and therapists.

Units for Rating and Data Analysis

Scoring Unit

The scoring unit is the individual statement. The identification of a statement is described on page 628. For the Experiencing Scale application the statements are rated in context by two raters for length, for client/therapist type, and on one of the Experiencing Scales.

Contextual Unit

Each statement is rated in sequence in the context of the material which precedes it in that session of group therapy. This procedure is advised by Klein, Mathieu-Coughlan and Kiesler when rating whole sessions using the individual statement as a scoring unit (see Chapter 2).

Summarizing Unit

Our summarizing unit is the page of transcript. The data sheet lists each item in the order of its initial appearance in the transcript. The individual statements for each page are averaged, after being weighted for length. A number of variables have been created from the Experiencing Scale ratings, but each uses the page as the summarizing unit. For example, to obtain the level of experiencing for the group as a whole, an average is made of the ratings of all of the items on one page, regardless of who is speaking, or which scale—client or therapist—was used. The average rating per page is the summarizing unit used in the statistical smoothing process, which generates graphs such as Figure 18-1.

Other variables are prepared by selecting appropriate ratings. For instance, to look at an individual's ratings, an average is made from the ratings of each statement that that member made on each page. In this way, we can look at the individual level, group level, and subgroup level processes in the group. We can also separate the data according to which scale was used to rate each statement, client or therapist, and observe the members' performance in these two roles over time and in relation to other group-level variables.

Raters   Persons with graduate training in counseling or psychotherapy were selected as raters for the Experiencing Scales. We felt that this background was facilitative to their learning how to use the scales in the context of group interaction, though this is a different viewpoint than that expressed by Klein, Mathieu-Coughlan, and Kiesler in Chapter 2. We also needed to use raters with some training as psychotherapists in order to apply the Therapist Experiencing Scales, which are still being refined and developed.

Of primary importance for this modified application of the Experiencing Scales is thorough training and experience in the use of the scales, with the traditional materials and rating methods presented in the Experiencing Scales Research and Training Manual

(Klein *et al.*, 1969). In addition, practice is needed to apply the scale accurately with this somewhat more complex and difficult method.

Reliability   Inter-rater reliability has been assessed for both the selection of client or therapist scale for each statement, and for the rating on the selected Experiencing Scale. For the choice of client or therapist scale in the current study, the degree of agreement between raters regarding the selection has been addressed with a cross-tabulation. Results are shown in Table 18-5.

The degree of agreement between two independent ratings on the Experiencing Scales has been assessed with two methods. A cross-tabulation was used to compare the ratings of the two raters on an item-by-item basis for the segment of transcript which was rated by both. In addition, the Pearson correlation was computed comparing the raters on their average ratings per page, which is the data which enter the computer to be smoothed and plotted on our graphs. The results for both analyses are shown in Table 18-5.

Data Analysis   The summarizing unit is the page. Before preparing an average rating for each page, each rating is multiplied by its code for length. The average rating-per-page data are smoothed and graphed by the procedure described on page 628.

Application of the Scales to the Transcript   The appendix presents two segments of group interaction from the transcript of Group A. We enter the transcript in the final minutes of the second phase. The two segments come from pages 95 through 102 and 187–188 in the original transcript. These page numbers will locate the material on the Experiencing Scale graph in Figure 18-1. The application of the Experiencing Scales to group therapy data will be illustrated by reference to items in this transcript.

Full definitions of the client and therapist scales have been presented in Chapter 2 by Klein, Mathieu-Coughlan, and Kiesler and in the training manual for the client scale (Klein *et al.*, 1969).

Here, brief definitions of the most frequently occurring levels of the scales will be accompanied by examples from the transcript.

Table 18-5   Reliability Data for Experiencing Scale

	Cross-Tabulation: Selection of Client or Therapist Scale	Cross-Tabulation: % Complete Agreement (Item-by-Item EXP Rating)	Pearson Correlation (Average Rating/Page)	Level of Significance	N (Pages of Transcript)
Group A	.96	.67	.80	.000001	90
Group S	.99	.63	.74	.000001	121
Group N	.99	.66	.60	.000001	134

Client Experiencing Scale

1. At Stage 1, experiences and events reported have an impersonal quality, and feelings are avoided. Often at this stage the client is setting a clear limit on his willingness to be involved. Comments at the beginning and end of a therapy session which are oriented or informational somtimes occur in this category, as well as discussions which seem to take an intellectual bent for a time, lacking or temporarily losing a clear connection with personal experience. No ratings of Stage 1 appear in our sample of transcript. A brief example is included here from early in the second session of Group A:

Joe: . . . I suppose because it's connected with charity I think it's uh sort of a charitable organization it's more or less for families too, I think family groups or children that can't be controlled. I think they have a place over at 100th and Midge, I think, but they have branches all over. I think they have another one at 17th and Paint. I think it's partly run by the city. They're listed in the phone book.

Here Joe gives the group information about other sources of help with a different agency. He says nothing about his own experience with that agency or about his feelings or reactions to the group members he is addressing.

2. At Stage 2, the individual's personal perspective emerges in his description of events around him; but even if the quality of his feeling responses can be perceived by another person through his manner, or through affect present during the description of events, the feelings are not referred to directly by the client. This stage often lays the groundwork for further self-exploration, and is important in developing the context of feelings.

Items 10 and 12 in the appendix transcript are rated on the client scale at Level 2. Diane is attempting to express her own experience of and reaction to Joe, but she gets stuck instead on describing how Joe seems to her. She is unable in these two items to express her feelings listening to him.

3. At Stage 3, feelings become clearly defined in reference to particular situations or external events. The client notes what his internal reaction was, but anchors it within the context of the external events which stimulated his response. This could mean identifying feelings which are stimulated by interactions with others during the session, or his feelings specific to outside events and situations.

In item 37 of the appendix transcript Martha describes her feelings in reaction to a particular situation in the group. She expresses her feelings in reaction to the thought of coming to the group, and goes on to suggest that others in the group might be having feelings similar to hers.

4. At Stage 4, the quality of the client's experiencing shifts from being anchored externally in some way to becoming predominantly concerned with a description of his inner feelings and reactions.

In item 54, Martha describes an experience from her past which is pertinent to current issues in the group. She describes the external situation well enough to set the stage for others to understand, but her description of her feelings and of the response of others to her is unquestionably from an internal stance, as when she says ''the silence afterward was like a rebuke.''

Ratings of 1 to 4 are common in these early sessions of group interaction. As the group members begin to work in a more focused therapy process, ratings of 5 begin to come up.

5. At Stage 5, these inner perspectives and feelings are organized to pose a problem or question about the self, and used by the client to explore an aspect of his experience.

During Session 5 of Group A, Greg describes his thinking about going to Washington and questions what his feelings mean (item 18).

Greg: Yea, and I remember also saying that I was afraid going to Washington would be running away. I have sort of ambivalent feelings about it. Part of me feels it's running away and part of me feels that I sorta have to get out and fight something a little bit. At least this is a job. And, you know like I've been talking about this group as a poker game, I sort of, I sort of feel like I wanna spar a little bit with life for a while, and—and uh, feel me, I'm a master.

Stages 6 and 7 of the Experiencing Scales represent highly insightful and integrative phases of work, which have been less frequently found and identified in the course of work done with the scales. During these very early phases of group therapy, no examples of these two stages have occurred for the individual clients involved.

Therapist Experiencing Scale

For the current data analysis, only the Patient Content Referent Scale has been used. The definitions for levels of this scale closely follow those of the client scale, but refer to how the therapist represents the client's experience in his response. The scale has been applied to statements made by both therapists and clients to members of the group.

1. At Stage 1, the content of the therapist's response is composed of events which are impersonal, or which are external to the client, or where the client's involvement is minimal. These kinds of responses may occur at the beginning and end of a therapy session, as the attention of the participants shifts from an inner focus to external events and concerns.

At the beginning of Session 2, Alice gives these remarks in response to a question from a group member:

Alice: No I didn't. Um, I really didn't have time, frankly. So we'll just have to ask him when he gets here. Also, Helen and I were, gee I should have come about five minutes earlier.

2. At Stage 2, the content of the therapist's response refers to events in which the patient is personally involved, but remains with the description of events, a picture of what has happened. Or the remarks may be intellectual, where feelings are not articulated or identified. A therapist's comments at Stage 2 are often in keeping with the purpose of eliciting more of the background and factual or historical information which grounds and helps define personal experience.

In items 9 and 11, Alice's response to Diane is rated at Level 2. She does not make any reference to feeling in her response to Diane. Her response stays within Diane's frame of reference, which is at Level 2, and she tries to make sure that she understands Diane's frame of reference, as for example when she asks whether Diane is responding to something that Joe has said that day.

3. Therapist responses at Level 3 refer to the client's feelings or reactions to a specific situation or external event. The client's reaction may be described behaviorally, or with limited descriptive or identifying references to his feelings.

Items 13 and 15 follow the preceding example and highlight the difference between Stage 2 and Stage 3 of the scale. Helen and Martha each respond to Diane by identifying and naming the feeling that they think she is having. Diane considers both of these responses in the exploration that follows, and with the help of this input and the work of other group members, later succeeds in clearly and fully expressing her feelings from an internal standpoint (Level 4), in item 39.

4. At Stage 4, the therapist's response refers directly to the client's feelings and personal perceptions of himself. The events or situations used are a context to develop the focus of this inner description.

Items 85 and 88 are examples of this level of therapist response. Greg offers his understanding of that aspect of herself on which Diane is working. He focuses on an inner frame of reference, on what the sequence of feelings is like, rather than describing them in any situational context. Greg notes that he is using his own feelings in formulating his response, feelings associated with his mother as well as with Diane.

5. At Stage 5, the therapist's response is focused at a questioning or struggling aspect of the patient's self-exploration. The therapist helps to pose questions or clarify the relationship among aspects of the client's feelings and self-perceptions.

An example of therapist response at this stage occurs somewhat earlier in the transcript, as Alice helps an individual group member, and the whole group as well, focus on the difficult feelings accompanying self-disclosure. She suggests that feelings of fear of hurting others are closely connected to fear of being hurt as well.

Alice: Maybe I'm wrong. I mean I felt a little like you were saying, "Maybe when you're saying you're afraid to hurt someone or you're afraid to say something 'cause you think it might hurt them, what you're also saying is 'because if they get hurt they'll get mad and then they'll hurt you back' and you don't want to get hurt yourself."

As was noted with the examples for the client scale, no instances of Stage 6 therapist responses were found during the early stages of group treatment that we have studied.

Research Results   The Experiencing Scales which have been applied to the three groups in our pilot study have yielded a number of different views of the group's process.

Group as a Whole

First, the group-as-a-whole level of experiencing has been found to peak at phase shifts, and is one of the three variables for identifying the phase boundary between Phases 2 and 3. The group-as-a-whole graph is produced by averaging the ratings for each page of transcript. This includes both clients and therapists and both scales. Figure 18-1 shows the graph for Group A. Vertical lines indicate session beginnings and endings, and pages in the transcript are indicated along the horizontal axis. Rating on the Experiencing Scales is indicated on the vertical axis. The averages have been processed by Tukey's smoothing technique (see page 628). The Experiencing level is relatively low at the beginnings and endings of sessions when information is being exchanged or organizational issues are being discussed briefly. During the sessions the EXP level peaks and dips at various points. The Hostility/Support graph in Figure 18-1 shows a shift from Phase 2 to Phase 3 at around page 100. Here we see that the Experiencing level has a major peak at this same point in time. In fact, we think there are two other phase shifts shown in this graph as well: the peak early in Session 2 is the shift from Phase 1 to Phase 2; and the peak in the latter half of Session 5 is the shift from Phase 3 to Phase 4 (Lewis & Beck, 1983).

Moving on to Figure 18-6, which shows Group S, we see the Hostility/Support variable showing the phase shift at around p. 175. The Experiencing Scale also shows a peak above 2.5 (which we consider a cutoff point for significant peaks) and another, more substantial peak at around p. 200. Neither of these peaks is as high as peaks at other points in the process, but we believe that the phase shift did occur at p. 186. This and all other phase shifts have been corroborated by re-reading the transcripts and by discussion of the results from all three of the variables. The current understanding of the distance between the shift shown in the Hostility/Support variable and the peak in the center of Session 4 on the Experiencing Scale, is that this group had several other issues to resolve after they resolved the scapegoating process and before they were finished with Phase 2 group-level issues.

Group N, which is shown in Figure 18-7, never succeeded in resolving Phase 2 issues. The Experiencing Scale shows a high level of activity throughout their Phase 2 process. We have been interested in the way these ratings peak during a period of competitive process when critical or hostile feelings are being expressed in the three groups.

Client Level of Experiencing on Client Scale

In making the initial choice to use the Experiencing Scales as part of our methodology for identifying the shift from Phase 2 to Phase 3 in group development, we had in mind the second dimension of change which characterizes that shift (see Table 18-3): the movement from defensive behavior to more open and mutually exploratory behavior. We found that resolution of Phase 2 issues does allow for self-disclosing behavior and constructive periods of individual self-exploration. This can be observed in the data for Group A.

Figure 18-8 presents the Experiencing Scale ratings for all statements which were rated on the client scale in Group A, graphed for each client separately. The dotted line indicates the phase shift from Phase 2 to Phase 3 of group development for this group. These individual graphs illustrate a phenomenon characteristic of Phase 3, where each member in turn participates in a process of self-disclosure. Phase 3, in contrast to Phase 2, offers an atmosphere of supportiveness and attentiveness to each member's issues. In Figure 18-8 the peaks in the individual Experiencing Scale graphs, which represent this process of successive self-exploration, are numbered, and the graphs are arranged in order with the first member to work in this way during Phase 3 at the top, and the last at the bottom. The periods of self-exploration are fairly lengthy in this group, and occur over a period of about two and one-half sessions.

This succession of peaks differs from the pattern of the data in the sessions prior to the shift. In the earlier sessions of the group, peaks in the individual Experiencing Scale graphs occur at about the same time in the data. The two major points when peaks occur are early in Session 1 and early in Session 2.

This same pattern of turn-taking occurs in Phase 3 of Group S as well. Group N, on the other hand, does not evidence a comparable period of self-exploratory behavior, and this is consistent with its inability to resolve Phase 2 issues.

The group-as-a-whole Experiencing Scale graph peaks at phase shifts, while the individual Experiencing Scale graphs peak at times when individuals are engaged in productive self-exploratory work, or when they are expressing their feelings toward others, as they are working on group-level issues, as in Phase 2. In some ways, the data on the individual level are like the scores for individual instruments in a chamber music piece or a symphony, with significant differences between the contributions of each of the players.

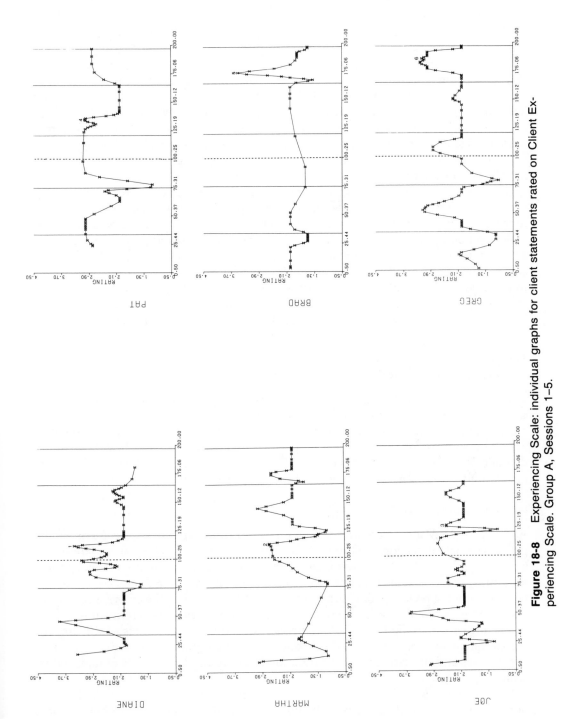

Figure 18-8 Experiencing Scale: individual graphs for client statements rated on Client Experiencing Scale. Group A, Sessions 1–5.

Therapists' Experiencing Levels

For our last example of Experiencing Scale data, we present the individual graphs of the two therapists in Group A, along with the graph of Experiencing data for the group as a whole, in Figure 18-9. The individual graphs can tell us something about the differences in the style of participation of each of these therapists. Alice, the senior therapist and primary leader, closely follows the pattern of Experiencing of the group as a whole. The levels of Experiencing in her graph are for the most part just below the levels of the group as a whole. We believe these data indicate that Alice took a supportive role in relation to the group's process and attended to it rather closely. The graph of Helen, a student coleader, peaks less frequently, but shows that Helen is active during peak periods of group work and sometimes highlights the process with responses at a high level of Experiencing.

The results presented here on the Experiencing Scales do not cover all the interesting variables which we have extracted but are a sample of what we discovered when we found a way to apply the scales to group psychotherapy data. We anticipate that these scales will be relevant to the study of the other seven phases in group development and plan to pursue that idea by analyzing all of Group A in the next stage of our research program. In addition to this exploration, we believe these scales lend themselves to the study of how individual self-exploration is affected by the group as a whole's developmental process, and also to the study of how facilitative or therapeutic behavior develops among group members over the course of the group's life.

The Normative-Organizational/
Personal Exploration Scale

The Scale   The Normative-Organizational/Personal Exploration Scale is a simple three-category nominal scale which allows us to observe the extent, sequence, and rhythm of the group's attention to group-level structural development, as compared to focusing on the exploration of the members' personal issues. Below is the brief form of the definitions of the three categories for rating with this scale. A manual will present more detailed guidelines for rating (Dugo & Beck, in preparation).

Definitions of Ratings

A rating of *1—Mainly Normative-Organizational Concerns*—refers to the focus of the group's verbal interactions on problems involving group organizational or planning issues; on guidelines for the operation of the group or the accomplishment of the group's task; on generating rules for appropriate behavior; on clarifying tolerances for differences or creating pressure for conformity to group norms. Also, the emergence of leaders in the group, and the interactions surrounding that process, are included here.

A rating of *2—Equally NO and PE concerns*—is used where the focus of the group's verbal statements appears to be equally addressing the exploration of individual's personal issues and the exploration or resolution of group-level normative organizational issues.

A rating of *3—Mainly Personal Exploration Issues*—refers, on the other hand, to the focus of the group's verbal statements on helping an individual explore his or her personal issues in order to attain more insight, further define the problem, bring about behavioral change, and/or understand the similarity between his or her experiences and that of other group members.

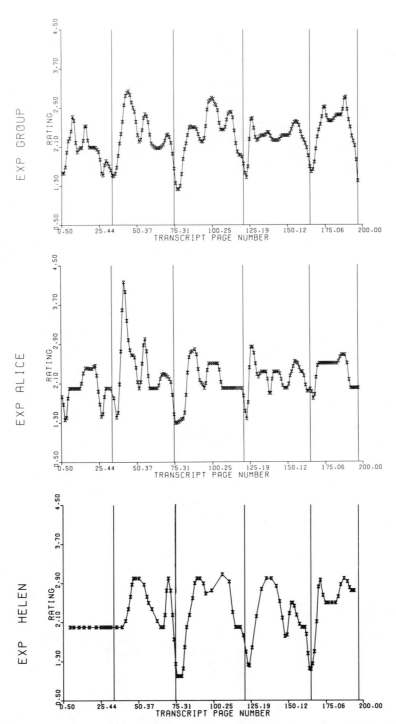

Figure 18-9   Experiencing Scale: graphs showing group as a whole and each therapist. Group A, Sessions 1–5.

Theoretical Base   The Normative-Organizational/Personal Exploration (NO/PE) variable was created in order to track the third major dimension of change in group life when the group moves from Phase 2 to Phase 3, as this is shown in Table 18-3: movement from concern, apprehension, and struggle related to organizational and norm development issues to a focus on individual members and their personal or interpersonal concerns. According to the theory (Beck, 1974, 1981a, 1981b), Phase 2 is a period when the primary effort of the group is on setting up its basic structure, in terms of leadership selection and confirmation, establishment of long-term goals, agreement on norms for behavior in the group, and the initial forging of an identity. As the group moves into Phase 3 there is a major shift in focus to the personal issues which brought members into the group. Often this work deals with historical issues with parents. For this reason, the NO/PE scale was designed to reflect that shift. The measure has been applied to the three groups in our pilot study (Dugo & Beck, 1983b).

A number of different systems of group psychotherapy seem to stress interactions by the leader at one end of the NO/PE continuum or the other. The NO/PE scale was designed on the assumption that groups in different phases or different points within a phase will naturally move from one level of focus to the other, unless they are constrained by the orientation of the Task Leader. For this reason we expect that this scale will be relevant to the study of the other phases of group development as well.

What Is Rated?   For phase analysis the entire session of a psychotherapy group is rated. Any segment of interaction that is long enough to be unitized can be rated with this scale. The behavior of all members is relevant.

Units for Rating and Data Analysis

Scoring Unit

An original procedure for unitizing group interaction has been designed for use with this scale. This became necessary when we discovered that an appropriate method could not be found in the literature. In order to use the NO/PE scale we needed units of group interaction which were process oriented; determined by the group's focus on a topic of discussion (preferably which had a beginning and an ending); and, which were based on the manifest content of the interaction, rather than inference about underlying meaning. The design of this procedure is a significant step in its own right and will be described in detail following the discussion on the NO/PE scale.

For the purposes of discussing the NO/PE scale, it is important to say that the unitizing is done prior to and separately from the rating on the scale. Units that emerge from this system are varied in length, being determined by the focus of the group's attention on a topic.

Contextual Unit

Units are rated in the context of the session in which they occur and in the sequence in which they occur. Therefore, all the preceding material in the session is part of the contextual unit.

Summarizing Unit

An average rating per page of transcript is the basic data used in the data analysis. Sometimes a page will be part of a longer unit and therefore receives the rating of that unit; sometimes several short units appear on one page and they are weighted by number of statements and averaged; sometimes the boundary between two units appears mid-page, in which case each part is weighted by the number of statements and then averaged.

Raters   Raters have to be experienced and sophisticated group therapists who are able to evaluate a unit of interaction and meaningfully apply the three-category system to it. The raters must have a knowledge of both group-as-a-whole levels and individual levels of process, and be capable of differentiating these.

Reliability   Reliability for the rating of the units using the variable was computed using the Pearson correlation. Table 18-6 shows the correlations and levels of significance for all three groups.

Data Analysis   The summarizing unit is the page. The average rating-per-page data are smoothed and graphed by the procedure described on page 628.

Application of Scale to Transcript   The appendix presents a transcript from Group A, plus the ratings for the NO/PE scale and the boundaries for the units. The rationale for the units will be presented in the next section of this chapter as part of the description of the unitizing procedure.

We enter the transcript midstream in a very long unit. In order to conserve space, we did not include the entire unit. The main focus of this unit is Diane's concern with Joe's style of communication in the group. She tries to exert pressure on Joe to conform to a style that she would find more comfortable. In items 10, 16, and 23, she tells Joe to be more internally and less externally focused in his discourse with the group. In item 24, Joe seems to understand that one can have difficulty tolerating someone else's style and shares his own stress when faced with long detailed jokes. He also tries to placate Diane by presenting his view that everyone is different, with different styles and personalities, and that he is not in fact trying to withhold himself with the way he talks. Finally, in item 28, Diane acknowledges her own intolerance in her unwillingness to accept Joe as he is, bringing this unit to a close. This unit was rated 1 (Normative-Organizational) because the group members are focused on normative issues regarding behavior in the group.

In the second unit (items 29 through 43), Brad and Greg (items 29, 32) expose the role that Joe has played for the group. The group has used Joe as a scapegoat and, in fact, in spite of Diane's complaints, Joe has revealed a great deal about himself while

Table 18-6   Reliability of Unitizing Transcript and Rating of the Normative-Organizational/ Personal Exploration Scale

| | Choice of Units | | Determination of Exact Boundaries | | Pearson Correlation of Ratings on NO/PE | Level of Significance | N (Pages of Transcript) |
	Rater 1	Rater 2	Rater 1	Rater 2			
Group A	89%	83%	98.2%	98.5%	.808	.000001	46
Group S	100%	90%	99.6%	99.9%	.846	.000001	68
Group N	97%	85%	99.9%	99.7%	.808	.000001	105

others have remained relatively hidden. Diane confirms the group's fears about self-disclosure in item 39 where she acknowledges that she too might do something that would not be acceptable to the group—that is, bore them. This unit was also rated 1, since it is dealing quite explicitly with normative concerns and with leadership and structural issues.

In the third unit (items 44 through 48), also rated 1, Diane tells of her fear of opening up in this group, further expanding on the theme that the group could not tolerate certain kinds of behavior.

In the fourth unit (items 49 through 58), Martha gives her version of being rejected by another group for inappropriate behavior. In units 3 and 4, even though Diane and Martha present personal information about themselves, the major focus of their presentation is in effect to reshape this group into an organism that will tolerate and accept their own idiosyncratic styles.

In unit 5 (items 59 through 68), Brad, Greg, and Martha indicate that the group acted as though it needed to have a fight with someone (i.e., Joe). Martha (item 68) concludes that "we don't have to fight and maybe we should encourage Diane to open up." This unit is rated 1 (NO).

In unit 6 (items 69 through 92), there is some attempt for the first time to help Diane explore her experience of having the "wrong values" in situations which have brought her conflict. In this unit, the members are still also trying to create space and understanding for individual differences. This unit is rated a 2 (both NO and PE), to reflect this dual concern.

With the shift of attention from unit 5 to unit 6, the group has also shifted from Phase 2 to Phase 3. In units 1–5, the group members put the final cap on the major group-level issues of Phase 2 and acknowledge their defensive behavior in constantly keeping after Joe. With unit 6, the group members begin a serious effort to address and work on the personal issues that brought them to the group.

Finally, a unit is presented from much further into Phase 3. In this last unit, Pat and Greg are able to explore some of their experiences with being alone in a new environment. The group in this unit is mainly dealing with personal exploration and the sharing of parallel issues with one another. This unit is rated 3.

Results   The Normative-Organizational/Personal Exploration Scale has been applied to the three groups in our pilot study: A, S, and N. Figure 18-1 shows Group A in the bottom graph; Figure 18-6 shows Group S and Figure 18-7, Group N. The graphs of Groups A and S show Phases 2 and 3; and, the graph of Group N shows Phase 2. The graphs of groups A and S showed a similar picture. Both groups moved from mainly Normative-Organizational concerns in Phase 2 to a focus on Personal Exploration in Phase 3 at the same point in time as the shifts are indicated on the Hostility/Support and the Experiencing Scales, and as indicated by a clinical analysis of the transcripts. Group N did not exhibit the same pattern and intensive analysis shows this group to remain stuck in Phase 2 behavior, unable to resolve their competitive relationships.

As a result of the analysis of these three groups, we have concluded that the Normative-Organization/Personal Exploration Scale is valuable for the study of phase shifts and further that it contributes a considerable amount of clarity to the study of group process by differentiating periods when the group is addressing group-as-a-whole structural issues from periods focused on personal exploration. This structural picture of the group tends to support the idea that groups develop in a systematic manner and that the group pays attention to different kinds of concerns in different phases at least for these two phases. The graphs of the three groups in our pilot study seem to indicate that groups sustain a particular focus either Normative-Organizational, Personal Exploration, or both over a considerable length of time during any particular session (Dugo & Beck, 1983b).

Currently we are analyzing Phase 1 and the shift to Phase 2 in all three groups and expect this scale to be helpful in that delineation as well. In fact, we are hopeful that this scale will be useful for the study of all nine phases of the group's life.

The Topic-Oriented Group Focus Unitizing Procedure

Rationale   Most unitizing systems used in studying group interaction have been either arbitrary in nature, such as a standard amount of time measured in either minutes or pages of transcript, or based on an individual's statement, which may comprise one or more sentences. We hunted in vain for an appropriate unit for rating with the Normative-Organizational/Personal Exploration Scale. In order to use this scale it became necessary to find a way to reflect the group-as-a-whole process in the unitizing procedure (Dugo & Beck, 1983b).

In trying to solve our problem, we believe that we have designed a unitizing procedure that will make it possible to study a wide range of questions in addition to those we are pursuing in our study. For example, no empirical study has ever been done which tells us what it is in fact that therapy groups work on. Our procedure will make it fairly simple to address that question.

Characteristics   For this scale our concern is with the focus of the group's verbal behavior. To achieve this, we felt that the unitizing procedure should have four major characteristics:

1. It should be process oriented—that is, determined by its context within the particular group.
2. It should be group centered—that is, determined by the *group*'s focus, not by the focus of any one member (the group at any particular time being defined as those who are participating verbally).
3. It should use *manifest* content—that is, be as free as possible from inference(s) regarding underlying motivation.
4. It should be a completed interaction, with a beginning and an ending—or be an interaction which is cut off before achieving an ending in order to start a new unit (Dugo & Beck, 1983b).

The procedure was developed for use with typed transcripts of group sessions, although it can be applied to video- or audiotape recordings directly as well. The topic-oriented, group-focused system was devised by Dugo with assistance from Mayer and Beck (Manual, in preparation). Following are brief definitions of critical terms and a description of the procedure for defining a unit.

Terms Used in Defining a Unit

Topic   The manifest content that group members are discussing and upon which they are focusing.

Focus   The sustained direction that the group members take in relation to a topic.

Sustained   When a group continues to stay with a particular topic by further defining, or refining it, by sharing views or experiences in relation to it, or by helping or letting the individual who raised it to discuss it further, until they reach closure.

Closure   When a topic ends, either because it is summed up with an integrative statement or a punch line, or because it is interrupted by the introduction of a new, sustained topic. The ending of a topic can mean an emotional release or simply a sense that the group can go no further with it.

Unit   The total number of statements that demonstrate a sustained focus in relation to a topic.

A Description of the Process of Defining a Unit   Using the terms just defined, a unit is identified in the following way:

1. A new topic, or a new idea building on the previous or even earlier topic, is raised.
2. The group focuses on some aspect of the new topic and shares in pursuing it. (*Group* means at least one other person.)
3. The topic is sustained through clarification, elaboration, and sharing of different versions, to some form of closure. In some units the progress of a topic is curtailed by an interruption and diversion of the group's attention, thus ending the unit at hand.
4. Finally a new topic is raised (or a new idea building on the previous one is raised), and the unit under study has ended.

The unitizer notes the boundaries of the unit, gives it a number, and attaches a brief statement which describes the manifest content. Boundaries of each unit are identified by page number and statement number. The unitizer then proceeds to identify the next unit. The unitizer takes into account the two previous units as well as the boundaries and topics for the preceding unit, and the unit that follows, and its boundaries in arriving at a final decision. Detailed instructions are available in the manual on the unitizing procedure (Dugo, Mayer, & Beck, in preparation).

Rater (Unitizer)   The unitizer needs to be someone who has a good command of the written language. He or she needs to be able to follow the essential components of a story (beginning, middle, and ending). The rater should at least have a college education. This person does not need to have inherent knowledge of psychotherapy groups. Although unitizing would appear to be a complex procedure, it was found that an intelligent nontherapist with high verbal skills could be trained in approximately 9 hours.

Reliability   In assessing reliability in unitizing, methods have been devised for evaluating two kinds of decisions which are made about each unit (Wiley, 1980). The first major decision has to do with the basic unit. Did the two raters see the same basic unit, or did one see two units where the other saw one? The decisions made by each rater were compared to the final units arrived at by the consensus of the two raters. Table 18-6 shows the rate of correct choice of units for each of two raters in the first column. The second major decision regards the determination of the exact boundaries of a unit. This is assessed for all agreed-upon units. The second column in Table 18-6 shows the rate of overlap between each rater and the final boundaries arrived at by consensus. One might conclude from the results that it is easier to determine the exact boundary of a unit than to agree on whether a segment constitutes one or two units. The exact procedures used to assess the percentages are described in detail in the manual on this procedure for unitizing (Dugo, Mayer, & Beck, in preparation).

Application of Unitizing Procedure to Transcript   As indicated earlier, we enter the transcript of Group A in the appendix midstream in a long unit which ends at item 28. A brief description for this unit is "Diane's difficulty with Joe." In item 29 a new topic is introduced by Brad and further defined and focused on by Greg in item 32: "Joe has revealed a lot and the group has used him." This topic is sustained by Martha, Greg, Diane, and Alice. This topic is concluded as Joe in item 43 tells Diane to use the group for herself: "Speak, get your money's worth."

Diane in item 44 introduces a new topic: "I am afraid I will bore the group." This topic is focused on and sustained by Alice. This topic is brought to a close in items 47 and 48 as Alice and Diane confirm that Diane really felt she was boring.

In item 49 Martha introduces a new topic which gets further clarified in item 54: "I have had bad experiences in groups also." This topic is sustained by Diane and Alice. Martha concludes the topic in item 58, stating that her experience was "really something." In item 59 Brad introduces a new topic: "Diane was really ready for a fight." In item 61 Greg focuses on the topic. Joe and Martha sustain the topic until item 68, where Martha brings the topic to a close by saying in effect, "We don't have to fight."

Joe introduces a new topic in item 69 which gets further defined by Diane in items 70 and 72: "Diane's having wrong values." This topic is sustained and finally brought to a close by Greg in item 92.

In item 93, which begins a segment further into the transcript, Alice introduces a topic: "Greg going away, being on his own." This topic is sustained by Greg, Alice, and Helen. In item 109 and 110 the topic is closed.

Results   The Topic-Oriented Group Focus Unitizing Procedure has been applied to the three groups in our study and the units thus created have been rated with the Normative-Organizational/Personal Exploration Scale. The results can be seen in Figures 18-1, 18-6, and 18-7. Now that these units exist, we will plan to explore their characteristics in a variety of other ways in the future.

The Use of the Measures in Relationship to Each Other

A Criterion for Phase Shift   Now that we have presented all three of the scales and the process variables developed from them, we would like to address the question of how to formulate a criterion for a phase shift—with the focus still being on the shift from Phase 2 to Phase 3. The analysis of the three groups in the pilot study has only just been completed—and we are in the process of the analysis of Phase 1 for each of the three groups. As a result, we have not yet fully defined the criterion for the phase shift. At this time, we are considering the use of the three variables, graphed in tandem, as such a criterion. That is, the phase boundary between Phases 2 and 3 would be identified as a place in the group where all three variables behaved in the expected manner. For example, if we look again at Figure 18-1, at the results for Group A, we see that page 100 is such a place. The Hostility/Support variable shifts from critical or hostile responses to supportive responses toward the Scapegoat Leader at this point. The Experiencing, Group-as-a-whole variable peaks at this point. And, the Normative-Organizational/Personal Exploration Scale shifts from Normative and Combination ratings to Personal Exploration ratings at this point. A similar pattern exists in the Group S graphs shown in Figure 18-6. And, in Group N, in Figure 18-7 we see a group that was unable to resolve the Phase 2 competitive issues, and we do not find a comparable pattern to the one we see in Groups A and S.

We will, of course, need to go beyond this visual, graphic form of the criterion to the use of statistical measures. This step will be pursued as soon as our analysis of Phase 1 is complete, since we are hopeful that these three measures will also identify the phase boundary between Phases 1 and 2 as well.

The analyses of these three groups in our pilot study have produced the first empirical evidence of phase boundaries in the literature. In the main, the characteristics of the process described by the graphs fits our expectations, based upon the theory—namely that the Scapegoat Leader is the object of hostile feelings during Phase 2, while the group is primarily working on normative and organizational issues—and that this hostility subsides when the group is able to resolve its Phase 2 group-level issues and move on to a cooperative period of self-exploration and self-disclosure. Also, we see from the Experiencing Scale, Group-as-a-whole that a high level of Experiencing characterizes phase shifts, indicating that these are times when a heightened self-awareness accompanies an integrative group-level process.

Identifying Critical Events   Two exploratory analyses have been conducted of the relationships between the Experiencing, Group-as-a-whole variable and the Normative-Organizational/Personal Exploration Scale which contribute to the intensive study of within-phase and across-phase processes.

1. The first analysis notes the frequency with which peaks in the Experiencing, Group-as-a-whole graph coincide with shifts in group focus on the NO/PE scale (Lewis, Dugo, & Beck, 1981). The data analysis was done with a Z test formula for large sample tests concerning proportions. The test compares the proportion of peaks and shifts which occur together to the proportion which may be expected to occur in the same amount of time if the shifts and peaks occurred independently and equally across time in the group. Five sessions in each of the three groups in the pilot study were analyzed. Fifty-four percent of all peaks observed occurred with shifts; 63% of all shifts observed occurred with peaks; and 58% of the total number of peaks and shifts in the data occurred together. The Z was significant at or above the .01 level for all of these proportions, when compared with the expected proportions.

We think that these two variables together identify special times in the group's process when structural issues are being addressed and when members are working on understanding the meaning of these issues in a very personal manner. The shift periods are times when the group's focus is a mixture of both Normative issues and Personal concerns. When accompanied by a peak in Experiencing, we think a shared understanding of an aspect of group process is being formed or worked on. These points in group process may identify integrative processes in the structural development of a group. We hope that with further study these variables will help us to understand more about the process of integration and differentiation in the group's development, and about the differences in this process as it occurs in successful groups as compared to groups which are unsuccessful in resolving group-level structural issues.

2. The second analysis shows some interesting evidence of the function of the four leaders during the change periods of the group-level processes (Beck, Dugo, Eng, Lewis, & Peters, 1983). It measures the proportion of these change periods in which leaders versus nonleaders participate with a significant contribution. *Leaders* here refers to the four leadership roles identified by the theory. Criteria have been defined for selecting the significant peaks in the Experiencing, Group-as-a-whole curve and for the significant shifts in the Normative-Organizational/Personal Exploration Scale. We are using these two criteria to identify important group-level change periods in terms of the pages of transcript which are involved in the peaks and shifts (Lewis, Dugo, & Beck, 1981). Since the level of experiencing measures the degree of attention to inner experience and the degree of quality of processing by the speaker, we think of it as a measure of the quality of participation of the individual member in the group therapy process. This measure looks at the Experiencing level for the individual members of the group in those pages in the transcript which were earlier identified as the significant peaks and shifts in Group-as-a-whole process. The Experiencing ratings which were above criterion during the significant change periods were recorded.

Table 18-7 shows the average proportion of leaders versus nonleaders whose individual peaks in experiencing coincide with significant group-level changes. The chart further breaks down group-level change times into those that occur during the group shift from one phase to another and those that occur at all other times during the group's process. The data have been summarized for two of the groups in our pilot study. The trend is clear that the four leaders have higher rates of participation at a significant level of experiencing during group-level change periods than nonleaders across both categories of change periods, in both groups.

As can be seen from these examples, there are ways in which the three process scales can be used in relationship to each other which produce important new insights into the group's process.

As we mentioned in the introduction, the process measures we have just described are only one part of a larger set of studies. Those measures were originally focused on the identification of phase boundaries and have subsequently been shown to be useful in describing within-phase processes as well. In the next section of this chapter we will present another set of measures which allow us to differentiate the behavior of the members and the leaders in these groups in terms of their speech behavior.

The Speech Behavior Coding System

The Scales The Speech Behavior Coding System is comprised of measures concerning relatively simple aspects of speech behavior among group members, including the length of statements; the identification of the speaker, the person(s) to whom a statement is addressed, and the person(s) spoken about; the use of selected pronouns, namely, "I," "we," and "you"; and disturbances in the flow of speech, such as stammers,

Table 18-7   Average Proportion of Leaders' and Nonleaders' Participation in EXP Peaks and NO/PE Shifts

	Peaks During Phase Changes	Peaks During Nonphase Changes	Overall Average	Shifts During Phase Changes	Shifts During Nonphase Changes	Overall Average
Group A						
Leaders	81.25	77.29	79.29	91.50	52.00	71.75
Nonleaders	68.75	53.57	61.16	75.00	50.00	62.50
Group S						
Leaders	81.25	71.15	76.20	75.00	55.36	65.18
Nonleaders	75.00	51.23	63.13	50.00	35.64	42.82

laughter, and interruptions. The specific measures which will be discussed in this section are (1) the length of statements; (2) the use of the pronoun "we" referring to the group or a subgroup within the group and hereafter referred to as "we–group"; (3) the speaker; and (4) the person(s) toward whom a statement is directed, hereafter referred to as "spoken-to." All four measures are used in our attempt to discern differences in speech behavior among members and differences across phases of group development (Eng & Beck, 1981, 1982).

Following are brief definitions of the four measures:

Speaker—The person identified in the transcript who makes each statement. This identification was made by the original transcriber who worked with the audiotape recordings to produce the typed transcripts.

Spoken-to—The person or persons to whom a particular statement is directed. A group member is designated as speaking to an individual group member, a specific subgroup, or the group as a whole.

Length of statement—A count of words, pauses, laughs, and other verbal utterances in each statement.

We–group—A count of the number of times the pronoun 'we' is used in a particular statement to refer to the group or a subgroup within the group.

Specific instructions for the application of these measures are provided in a manual (Eng & Beck, in preparation).

Theoretical Base The research questions which have guided the development of the measures of group process to be discussed in this section arose out of a curiosity about differences and changes in relatively simple aspects of speech behavior among group members. In 1979 a careful reading of Beck's (1974) theory of group development led us to generate an extensive list of exploratory questions which pertained to the speech behavior of individual members. In particular we were interested in the behavior of the emergent leaders, as compared to the rest of the group, and the behavior of the group-as-a-whole across phases. It was felt that all of these questions could be pursued by the application of relatively simple behavioral measures to transcripts of group sessions. From this group of measures it was hoped that a few simple behavioral measures would emerge as powerful, useful methods for tracing and analyzing group process.

Examples will be provided below of the kind of exploratory questions which have guided this methodological pilot study. In order to place those questions into a meaningful context, a further description of Phase 2 of Beck's theory of group development and emergent leadership will be helpful, in addition to what has already been stated about Phases 1, 2, and 3 in the introductory part of this chapter.

During Phase 2, various members of the group compete for leadership status, including the Scapegoat Leader. As noted earlier, this individual often feels under attack from other members. In response, he will tend to behave defensively. This leader often seems unable to tune in to the nonverbal aspects of the group's communication and often appears to be in disagreement with them regarding certain aspects of their verbal communication. He tends to be assertive and seems to flaunt his own style and his seeming lack of sensitivity. Under attack, he tends to become fairly verbal in an effort to defend himself and his viewpoint. At the same time, the Task Leader is likely to experience a strong desire to work hard at helping his factionalized group to resolve its differences. He may attempt to do this either by joining in the group's attack on the

Scapegoat Leader, or by taking sides with him; or he may attempt to act as mediator. The Emotional Leader often plays a critical role in this phase by representing the dominant view in the group in positive rather than angry terms. In any case, the group must resolve its conflict with the Scapegoat Leader and address the critical issues of this phase before it is able to move on to the next phase. Many groups, in fact, fail to accomplish this set of conditions and become stuck in Phase 2 (Beck, 1974).

From this brief description of Phase 2, as well as the descriptions in the introduction to this chapter, one can formulate a series of empirical questions regarding the rate of verbal participation of specific group members. For instance, we might expect that the Scapegoat Leader would tend to talk more than other members during Phase 2 because he feels that they have not heard or understood him. For this reason, and out of some wish to control the Scapegoat Leader in Phase 2 because of their annoyance with him, other members may address him more than they do one another. Since Phase 3 is typically an intensive work phase in which clients begin their cooperative process together, the Phase 2 negativity toward the Scapegoat Leader subsides in Phase 3. Also, since the theory posits a more significant structural role for the Scapegoat Leader in Phase 2 than in Phase 3, again we might expect that the Scapegoat Leader would tend to be more verbal in Phase 2 than in 3. Some of the empirical questions we could ask about the Scapegoat Leader then are as follows:

1. Does the Scapegoat leader tend to speak more than other group clients in Phase 2, in terms of the amount of time he speaks?
2. Are more remarks addressed to the Scapegoat Leader than to other group clients in Phase 2?
3. Is more attention given to the Scapegoat Leader in Phase 2 than in Phase 3?
4. Is the Scapegoat Leader's rate of participation higher in Phase 2 than in Phase 3?

Similar questions can be formulated about the other leadership roles. To the extent that the Task Leader plays a critical role in helping to shape the norms of the group in early group development, we might expect the Task Leader to make many comments about the group in Phases 2 and 3. With respect to the total amount of time that the Task Leader speaks, one might extrapolate from the theory that his participation is greatest in Phase 2, when he feels the strongest pressure to intervene in the group process. Presumably the Task Leader talks less during Phase 3 than in 2, once the group is able to begin a cooperative work process in which members present their individual issues and the Emotional Leader begins to assume some important modeling functions for all the other group clients. On the basis of this description of the Task Leader's behavior, the following empirical questions can be generated:

5. Does the Task Leader tend to be a highly verbal member in Phase 2, both in the amount of time he speaks and the number of times?
6. Does the Task Leader tend to speak more in Phase 2 than in 3?
7. Does the Task Leader make a large number of references to the group during Phases 2 and 3 in comparison to other group members?

According to the theory, the Emotional Leader is a well-liked member who assumes a major leadership role in Phase 3. We might expect this role to be reflected in relatively high verbal participation rates for the Emotional Leader in this phase. We might also expect this Leader, as one of the support persons in the group, to address a large number of remarks to others when they are working on their own issues as well. This description of the Emotional Leader's behavior yields the following empirical questions:

8. Is the Emotional Leader one of the most verbally active members during Phase 3 in terms of the amount of time he speaks?
9. Does the Emotional Leader tend to be verbally active in Phase 3 with respect to the number of times he speaks?
10. In Phase 3 does the Emotional Leader speak to other members more than they speak to one another?

On the basis of the theory, we might expect relatively low verbal participation rates for the Defiant Leader in Phases 1 and 2. Since the Defiant Leader presumably begins to assume some important functions in Phase 3, we might expect to find a moderate amount of verbal participation on the part of the Defiant Leader during this phase and certainly more than in Phase 2. However, in general, questions regarding the Defiant Leader's unique behavior are more meaningfully asked with respect to later phases of group development.

Questions 1–10 represent a sample of the questions that can be asked about the four group leadership roles. Also, questions regarding verbal participation can be asked about other aspects of member/member, member/leader, or leader/leader interactions.

In order to explore these questions by analysis of the three groups in our pilot study, we selected the following measures: the speaker; the person spoken to; the length of statement; and the number of statements (see brief definitions on page 658).

Besides looking at the speech behavior of individual members, one can use simple behavioral measures to track the speech behavior of the group as a whole. This would be especially interesting to observe in the contrast between Phase 2, which is so involved with normative and organizational business, and Phase 3, which involves exploring personal business. It would seem reasonable to suppose that during discussions of group-level issues group members would make a relatively large number of statements which refer to the group as a whole or various subgroupings within the group. One question that can be asked about collective speech behavior is:

11. Do group members collectively make more references to the group in Phase 2 than in Phase 3?

In order to address the question we chose to measure the use of the pronoun "we" in reference to the group itself (see brief definition on page 658).

Table 18-8 shows the variables which have been designed to address each of the 11 questions.

What is Rated?   At this time the Speech Behavior Coding System has been applied to all statements in all sessions which constitute the second and third phases of group development in Groups A and S. Due to our clinical interpretation of Group N as not having successfully traversed Phase 2, we have not yet completed the speech behavior data analysis of Group N. This will be reported at a later date.

Number and Type of Scales   Ratings of length of statement yield interval data in the form of frequency counts of all uttered words and pauses. Ratings of who speaks and to whom a statement is addressed yield nominal data: each separate speaker has been

Table 18-8 Measures Used to Answer the Exploratory Questions

Question	Speaker	Spoken-to	Length of Statement	Number of Statements	We-Group	Role Compared to Rest of Group	Within Phase 2 or 3	Comparison of Phases 2 and 3
1	X		X			X	X	
2		X	X			X	X	
3		X	X			X		X
4	X		X			X		X
5	X		X	X		X	X	
6	X		X			X		X
7	X				X	X		X
8	X		X			X	X	
9	X			X		X	X	
10	X	X		X		X	X	
11					X			X

identified, and all individuals to whom a statement is addressed are recorded, including the group-as-a-whole. The pronoun "we" is first rated on a nominal basis. Three separate usages of the pronoun "we" can be interpreted to be (1) the group itself (or a subgroup within the group); (2) persons or groups outside of the therapy group; or (3) an impersonal or "editorial" use of "we" when the speaker is actually expressing his or her own philosophy or viewpoint. Within each category of "we" usage, a frequency count is made, thus yielding interval data within each category per statement.

Units for Scoring and for Data Analysis

Scoring Units

The scoring unit for the length of statement measure is each individual word, pause, or laugh within a statement. Similarly, each utterance of the pronoun "we" with reference to the group is scored. With respect to the speaker and spoken-to measures, the scoring units are statements, as the statement is defined in the beginning of this chapter (see page 624).

Contextual Units

The contextual unit for the we–group measure is the statement. For the speaker and spoken-to measures, the contextual unit is every statement which precedes the statement being rated.

Summarizing Units

The summarizing unit for the length of statement measure is the total word count per group member per group phase. We–group usage is summarized both by the frequency per page of transcript and by member per group phase. The speaker and spoken-to data are summarized by each speaker and spoken-to pairing within a group phase.

Raters High school students were trained to count words, pauses, and other utterances on transcripts and, hence, make ratings on the lengths of statements. The background of the original transcriber who identified the speaker in each statement was described above in the introduction to the chapter. Both of the raters who applied the we-group and spoken-to measures were college graduates. One had a degree in psychology; the other in special education. Both were careful readers with an interest in English literature.

Reliability A Pearson product–moment correlation of 0.99 was obtained between two raters who used the length of statement measure on selected transcript material from each of the three therapy groups under study. Reliability was established by both raters rating sections from each of the groups in the pilot study: 10 pages from Group A; 15 pages from Group S.

   Two raters were trained to interpret the three referents of the pronoun "we." Their ratings were compared by a cross-tabulation, resulting in complete agreement on the referents of "we" in 95% of its occurrences in Group A; 90% of the time in Group S. Twenty pages of transcript in each group were used for the reliability measure.

   The inter-rater reliability for the application of the spoken-to measure was also assessed. Two raters were trained to identify the specific individuals to whom a statement was addressed, as well as the group-as-a-whole when it was addressed. The two sets of ratings, compared by a cross-tabulation, were in perfect agreement for 81% of the total number of ratings for sampled transcript material from group A; and 76% for Group S. Ten pages of transcript in Group A and 12 pages in Group S were used for the reliability measure. For all three measures, the coders were first trained to criterion on sampled material and then assessed on other sampled material for the determination of actual reliability.

Statistical Procedures Used to Correct for Absences of Members

Spoken-to Measure

Raw numbers of statements addressed to each member by other members were tabulated. The number of opportunities that a given member had of being addressed by another member during a group phase was taken to be the total number of statements made by the group membership during the specific sessions that a given combination of speaker and person spoken to were both present. Ratios were established for each combination of speaker and person addressed by dividing the raw number of statements addressed to a person by the number of opportunities for being addressed (Wiley, 1980).

Estimates of Speakers' Rates of Verbal Participation and We–Group Usage

Actual numbers of words spoken were calculated for each speaker for each session. Percentages of total words spoken were calculated for each speaker for those sessions when all members were present in a group phase. A second set of percentages of total words spoken by each member was calculated for all sessions comprising that group phase after first subtracting all the words spoken by a given member who was absent during part of that phase. These two sets of percentages were compared to determine if the absence of one member from a session had influenced the rates of participation of those who were present. If there appeared to be no such influence, then the overall rate of participation of the member absent during a given session was assumed to be that found when he or she was actually present. The rates of the other members were then adjusted. In particular, their estimated percentages of verbal participation were calculated, in turn, by multiplying their actual rates of participation by a constant derived from the absent member's estimated participation (Wiley, 1980).

The same procedure was employed to estimate we–group usage.

Application of the Speech Behavior Coding System to Transcript   The application of the length of statement, we–group, and spoken-to measures will be illustrated by working through two selected statements from the transcript material in the appendix, namely statements 29 and 82. First, each complete word in the statement is counted. In addition, the utterance of "um" counts as one word, as does each incomplete word which ends a phrase, namely "des," which follows "curious." Since statement 29 is an interrupted statement, the word counts from each part are added together for a total of 57 words. There are two occurrences of the pronoun "we" in statement 29. In both instances, the speaker, Brad, refers to the whole group. He first describes and then questions the group's behavior toward another member, Joe. Brad begins his statement by addressing Joe directly through use of the second person pronoun "you." The referent of "you" is made clear through the content of the first sentence. Brad is directly addressing someone who tells jokes in the group. In an earlier statement, #24, Joe talked about his propensity to tell jokes. Hence, the rater can infer that Brad begins statement 29 by addressing Joe directly. Then Brad shifts and refers to Joe in the third person. It is apparent that he is no longer addressing Joe but someone else. Now he is either addressing a particular person or a few persons other than Joe, or he is addressing the group as a whole. Several clues suggest that he appears to be speaking to the whole group in the latter part of statement 29. First, he is interrupted in statement 29 by two individuals, namely, Alice and Helen. Second, his comment is further amplified by a third individual, Greg, immediately after he has finally completed his statement. Hence, the rater records both "Joe" and "Group" in the spoken-to column of the data table for statement 29.

Statement 82 will serve as a second example of the application of the Speech Behavior measures. In comparison to the previous example, statement 82 is much easier to rate, since there are no interruptions. All words are counted separately. The contraction "I'm" is counted as one word. The length of this statement is 24 words. There is one occurrence of the pronoun "we." It is counted under the "we–group" heading, inasmuch as the speaker, Martha, is requesting another member, Diane, to reveal something which the whole group can then try to understand. The context of this statement makes it very clear that Martha is speaking to Diane. They have been having a dialogue for several statements prior to this point. Also, Martha's comment in #29 is a direct response to a question that Diane asks in #28.

The kinds of specific rules and contextual clues which have been mentioned in these two examples govern the application of the Speech Behavior measures to all of the other statements in the transcript. Length of statement and we–group can be rated with a high degree of reliability between two raters. Although application of the Spoken-to measure is quite problematic at times, we believe that it can be done with sufficient reliability to offer useful information.

Results   Some of our results obtained through application of the length of statement, speaker, spoken-to, and we–group measures will be reported.

Length of Statement

The length of statement measure was applied to every statement in Phases 2 and 3 of Groups A and S. Within the boundaries of previously identified group phases, a statistical procedure was used to correct for absences of various members in group sessions. Estimates were then formulated of the verbal participation of each speaker by group phase for each of the two groups (Wiley, 1980). Group members were then rank ordered according to their percentages of verbal participation. Phase boundaries had been identified by the use of a set of three process variables (Beck, 1983; Dugo & Beck, 1983b, Lewis & Beck, 1983). Also, the four leaders in each group had been identified by a sociometric questionnaire and confirmed through a clinical analysis of the group's transcripts (Beck & Peters, 1981; Peters & Beck, 1982). Data pertaining to all members' percentages of verbal participation in Phases 2 and 3 of Groups A and S appear in Tables 18-9 and 18-10.

The Scapegoat Leader is among the top three speakers in terms of length of statement in Phase 2 of both groups. In Group A, he is number 1; in Group S, she is number 3, with the Task Leader as number 2 and a nonleader member as number 1. Just how typical this pattern will be can only be known after many other groups are checked. In Phase 3, the Scapegoat Leader is number one in Group A, while in Group S she has slipped to fifth position. We see the Task Leader ranked two in Phase 2 of both

Table 18-9   Best Estimates of Percentages of Verbal Participation in Phases 2 and 3 of Group A, Based upon Length of Statement

		Phase 2		Phase 3	
Role	Member	Best Estimate of Percentage	Rank Order	Best Estimate of Percentage	Rank Order
TL	A	16.4	2	14.1	5
EL	G	11.8	4	15.0	2
SL	J	29.8	1	18.9	1
DL	M	11.1	5	14.8	3
	B	5.3	8	9.5	6
	D	12.0	3	14.2	4
	P	8.1	6	8.8	7
CoTh	H	5.5	7	4.6	8

TL=Task Leader; EL=Emotional Leader; SL=Scapegoat Leader; DL=Defiant Leader; CoTh=Cotherapist.

Table 18-10   Best Estimates of Percentages of Verbal Participation in Phases 2 and 3 of Group S, Based upon Length of Statement

		Phase 2		Phase 3	
Role	Member	Best Estimate of Percentage	Rank Order	Best Estimate of Percentage	Rank Order
TL	H	21.98	2	16.52	3
EL	Bb	14.30	4	26.44	1
SL	V	18.51	3	12.38	5
DL	T	8.69	5	17.81	2
	Bl	21.99	1	13.22	4
	R	3.31	8	3.23	7
	A	7.90	6	8.50	6
CoTh	M	3.34	7	1.90	8

TL=Task Leader; EL=Emotional Leader; SL=Scapegoat Leader; DL=Defiant Leader; CoTh=Cotherapist.

groups. The Emotional Leader, as expected, is highly ranked in both groups in Phase 3, *viz.*, numbers 2 and 1 in Groups A and S, respectively.

Another way of looking at the data on verbal participation rates is to plot the point of intersection of rate of participation in Phase 2 by rate of participation in Phase 3 for each member of the group.

Figures 18-10 and 18-11 present this information for Groups A and S. Points lying to the right of the equality line represent individuals who speak more in Phase 2 than in Phase 3. Points left of the line represent individuals who speak more in Phase 3 than

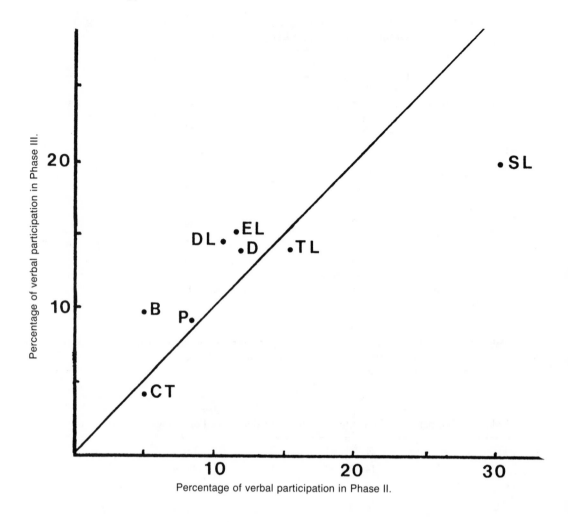

Figure 18-10   Comparison of percentages of verbal participation in Phases 2 and 3 for all members of Group A. CT = Cotherapist; TL = Task Leader; EL = Emotional Leader; SL = Scapegoat Leader; DL = Defiant Leader. Other initials stand for members' names.

in Phase 2. In the interest of seeking a method of data analysis which may be applied to many groups, we looked at these graphs with a concern for those characteristics which were similar in both groups. For the two groups in this pilot study, both the Task Leader (the therapist in each case) and the student cotherapist talk more in Phase 2 than in 3. The reverse is true for the Emotional Leaders who speak more in Phase 3 than 2 in both groups. In Groups A and S, the Scapegoat Leader talks more in Phase 2 than in Phase 3, and the Defiant Leader's rate is higher in 3 than 2, as we anticipated on the basis of Beck's theory.

Speaker/Spoken-to

The next measure to be discussed is the speaker by person-spoken-to measure. A group member is designated as speaking to an individual group member, a specific subgroup, or the group-as-a-whole. Every statement in what has been clinically identified as Phases

2 and 3 in both groups has been rated. Using these ratings, speaker by person-spoken-to matrices were constructed. These matrices are similar to the interaction matrices devised by Robert Bales (1970) to analyze who speaks to whom in a live group session. A statistical procedure has been used to correct for the absences of members in certain sessions (Wiley, 1980). From the speaker by person-spoken-to matrices, summary tables have been constructed.

Speaker

Tables 18-11 and 18-12 list the percentages of statements initiated by each member for Groups A and S.

The Task Leader initiated more statements than all other group members in both phases of the two groups. In Phase 2 of both groups, the Scapegoat Leaders initiated more statements than all other group members, except the Task Leaders. The Emotional Leader appears within the top three ranks in Phases 2 and 3.

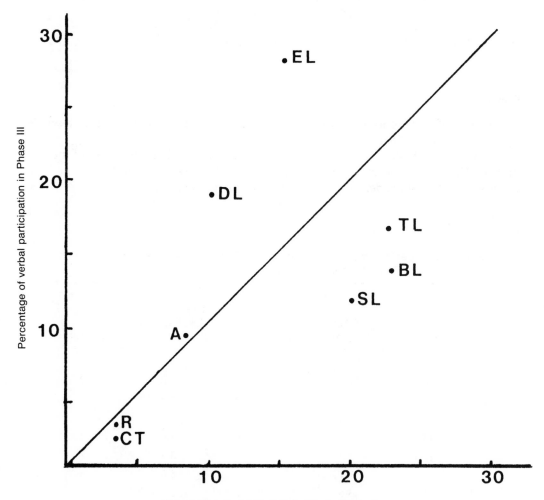

Percentage of verbal participation in Phase II.

Figure 18-11   Comparison of percentages of verbal participation in Phases 2 and 3 for all members of Group S. CT = Cotherapist; TL = Task Leader; EL = Emotional Leader; SL = Scapegoat Leader; DL = Defiant Leader. Other initials stand for members' names.

Table 18-11   Best Estimates of Percentages of Statements Initiated by Each Member in Phases 2 and 3 of Group A

| | | Phase 2 | | Phase 3 | |
Role	Member	Best Estimate of Percentage	Rank Order	Best Estimate of Percentage	Rank Order
TL	A	25.7	1	20.8	1
EL	G	13.8	3	12.8	3
SL	J	14.8	2	11.6	5
DL	M	14.7	4	18.2	2
	B	3.0	8	6.1	8
	D	11.4	5	12.4	4
	P	9.4	6	9.0	6
CoTh	H	7.2	7	8.9	7

TL=Task Leader; EL=Emotional Leader; SL=Scapegoat Leader; DL=Defiant Leader; CoTh=Cotherapist.

Spoken-to

Percentages of statements addressed to each group member and the Group-as-a-whole are found in Tables 18-13 and 18-14.

We see that the Task Leader appears in the top three ranks in both phases of the two groups. The Scapegoat Leader also appears in the top three ranks in Phase 2 of both groups. The Defiant Leaders appear in the top four ranks of Phase 3 in Groups A and S.

Table 18-12   Best Estimates of Percentages of Statements Initiated by Each Member in Phases 2 and 3 of Group S

| | | Phase 2 | | Phase 3 | |
Role	Member	Best Estimate of Percentage	Rank Order	Best Estimate of Percentage	Rank Order
TL	H	24.2	1	27.1	1
EL	Bb	14.6	4	26.0	2
SL	V	18.9	2	11.5	4
DL	T	8.0	6	8.4	5
	Bl	18.6	3	14.0	3
	R	3.9	7	3.4	7
	A	8.1	5	6.6	6
CoTh	M	3.6	8	2.9	8

TL=Task Leader; EL=Emotional Leader; SL=Scapegoat Leader; DL=Defiant Leader; CoTh=Cotherapist.

Table 18-13   Best Estimates of Percentages of Statements Received by Each Member and the Group in Phases 2 and 3 of Group A

		Phase 2		Phase 3	
Role	Member	Best Estimate of Percentage	Rank Order	Best Estimate of Percentage	Rank Order
TL	A	16.8	2	14.6	2
EL	G	10.2	6	11.0	6
SL	J	16.4	3	11.2	5
DL	M	11.0	4	11.7	4
	B	2.1	9	7.0	8
	D	10.3	5	14.5	3
	P	7.6	7	10.8	7
CoTh	H	5.6	8	3.9	9
	Group	19.9	1	15.5	1

TL = Task Leader; EL = Emotional Leader; SL = Scapegoat Leader; DL = Defiant Leader; CoTh = Cotherapist.

We–Group

The next section of this report deals with the use of we–group. The actual number of utterances of the pronoun "we" per page of transcript were plotted for Phases 2 and 3. All the utterances of "we" when used in reference to the group-as-a-whole or a sub-grouping within the group were counted for all participants in the group. Figures 18-12 and 18-13 present this data for Groups A and S, respectively.

Table 18-14   Best Estimates of Percentages of Statements Received by Each Member and the Group in Phases 2 and 3 of Group S

		Phase 2		Phase 3	
Role	Member	Best Estimate of Percentage	Rank Order	Best Estimate of Percentage	Rank Order
TL	H	18.2	2	16.4	3
EL	Bb	11.3	4	21.9	1
SL	V	25.1	1	14.7	4
DL	T	7.4	6	18.2	2
	Bl	15.3	3	11.3	5
	R	3.8	9	3.9	7
	A	10.6	5	9.1	6
CoTh	M	3.9	8	2.8	8
	Group	4.2	7	1.6	9

TL = Task Leader; EL = Emotional Leader; SL = Scapegoat Leader; DL = Defiant Leader; CoTh = Cotherapist.

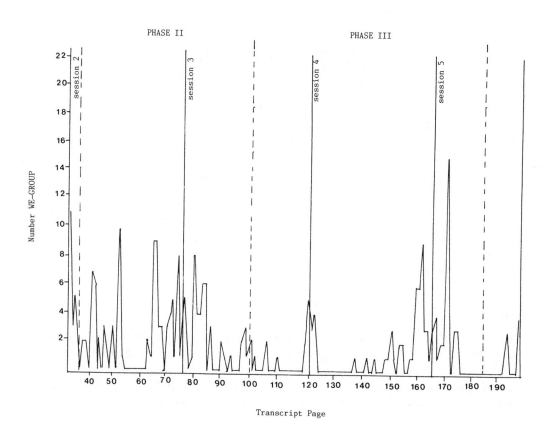

Figure 18-12   Use of the pronoun we–group. Group A, entire membership.

The horizontal axis on each graph shows transcript pages; the vertical axis shows the frequency of use of the pronoun we–group by all group members. Vertical solid lines represent session breaks, and dotted lines represent phase boundaries.

The graphs show rather dramatically that there is a greater use of the pronoun we–group in Phase 2 than there is in Phase 3, and that this pattern is the same in both groups.

Table 18-15 summarizes the same information numerically and shows that the average number of we–group used per page is consistently higher in Phase 2 than in Phase 3 in both groups. We might expect this kind of pattern, given the large number of group-level tasks that need to be discussed and resolved in Phase 2 in contrast to the third phase, which is primarily a period of exploration of personal issues and defining personal goals.

Another analysis of the we–group data was conducted in which we–group usage was calculated for each group member for each of the three group phases. First, a statistical procedure was used to correct for the absences of various members in group sessions (Wiley, 1980). Group members were then rank ordered according to their rates

Table 18-15   Average Number of We–Group per
Page per Phase

Group	Phase II	Phase III
A	2.16	1.14
S	1.69	0.39

of we-group usage. Data pertaining to all members' percentages of we-group usage
in Phases 2 and 3 of Groups A and S appear in Tables 18-16 and 18-17.

The Scapegoat Leader is in the top two ranks during Phase 2 in both groups in the
use of the pronoun we-group. Only the Task Leader (therapist) makes more use of
we-group during this phase. During Phase 3 the Scapegoat Leaders' ranks drop to 6
and 4 respectively for Groups A and S. The Task Leader shows high we-group usage

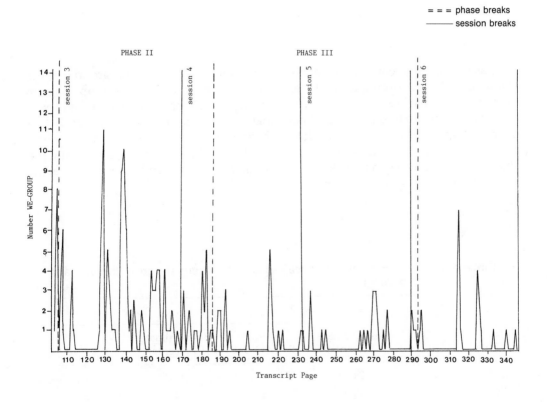

Figure 18-13   Use of the pronoun we–group. Group S, entire membership.

Table 18-16   Best Estimates of Percentages of We–Group Usage in Phases 2 and 3 of Group A

Role	Member	Phase 2 Best Estimate of Percentage	Phase 2 Rank Order	Phase 3 Best Estimate of Percentage	Phase 3 Rank Order
TL	A	18.2	1	23.1	1
EL	G	10.4	5	5.0	7
SL	J	17.6	2	9.5	6
DL	M	12.2	4	17.1	3
	B	9.8	6	18.1	2
	D	15.0	3	10.1	5
	P	7.8	7	1.0	8
CoTh	H	5.2	8	16.1	4

in Phases 2 and 3. According to the theory, we would expect high we–group usage in Phases 2 and 3. According to the theory, we would expect high we–group usage by both the Scapegoat Leader and the Task Leader in Phase 2 for the same types of reasons that we expected to find high verbal participation, and because during this period the primary responsibilities of these leaders *vis-à-vis* the group have to do with group-level issues. The Defiant Leader is ranked 3 in both groups during Phase 3, suggesting that this individual may begin to make his or her impact upon group-level structure at this point in the group's development.

Table 18-17   Best Estimates of Percentages of We–Group Usage in Phases 2 and 3 of Group S

Role	Member	Phase 2 Best Estimate of Percentage	Phase 2 Rank Order	Phase 3 Best Estimate of Percentage	Phase 3 Rank Order
TL	H	21.4	2	31.0	1
EL	Bb	9.3	5	24.4	2
SL	V	33.6	1	15.5	4
DL	T	13.6	3	15.8	3
	Bl	10.0	4	6.7	5
	R	2.9	8	0	8
	A	5.0	6	4.4	6
CoTh	M	4.3	7	2.2	7

Summary of Results

Four Speech Behavior measures, namely, speaker, spoken-to, length of statement, and we-group, were applied to transcripts of Phases 2 and 3 of Groups A and S. Their application yielded data relevant to questions 1–11, which were derived from Beck's theory and cited earlier in this chapter. Questions 1–4, which pertained to the Scapegoat Leader, were answered in the affirmative for both Groups A and S. The Scapegoat Leader tended to speak more than other group clients in Phase 2. More attention was given to the Scapegoat Leader in Phase 2 than 3, as measured by the number of statements addressed to him or her. In both groups, the Scapegoat Leader's rate of participation was higher in Phase 2 than in Phase 3. Questions 5–7, regarding the Task Leader, were also answered in the affirmative for the two groups. We note that the Task Leaders were highly verbal members in Phase 2. They spoke more in Phase 2 than in Phase 3 and made a large number of references to the group during both phases in comparison to other members. The Emotional Leader, the focus of questions 8–10, turned out to be one of the most verbally active members in Phase 3. In addition, the speaker by person-spoken-to matrices for Groups A and S revealed that the Emotional Leader tended to address more remarks to other members than other members did to each other in Phase 3. Lastly, the speech behavior data yielded an affirmative answer to question 11 for both groups. That is, in Groups A and S the members collectively made more references to the group in Phase 2 than in Phase 3, as measured by the average number of we-group references per transcript page per phase. These preliminary answers to questions 1–11 are encouraging, since they suggest that at least four measures of the Speech Behavior Coding System may be used in ways which meaningfully increase our knowledge of group psychotherapy process.

Clinical Applications   To the extent that the scapegoating phase is typically the most difficult phase of early group development for all members, including the therapist, it is important for the therapist to be able to identify the Scapegoat Leader and the group-level tensions that surround him or her. Data collected thus far on two groups using the length of statement measure suggest that the Scapegoat Leader tends to be one of the most talkative members during this phase. Hence, degree of talkativeness may be one of the indicators that the clinician can use in identifying this leader. Also, our data suggest that members who are less talkative during early phases may, nonetheless, become important leaders during later phases. It is possible that Defiant Leaders who are relatively quiet during early phases may become more talkative during the middle phases of a group.

By consciously using pronouns, such as we, our, and us, during early stages of group development, a group leader promotes awareness of group-level issues. It is likely that group members will imitate such behavior and, thus, promote the group's development.

Current Status of Development of the Measures

As the first phase in our design of a methodology for the process analysis of group development, we have focused on a particular and early step in the group's development—the shift from Phase 2 to Phase 3. This focus enabled us to begin the defining and operationalizing of the concepts which we thought would enable us then to model the group-level process. Even though our efforts were guided by theoretical issues pertinent to the Phase 2/Phase 3 process, our measures and methodology will probably be useful in the study of group development in later phases and with respect to questions other than phase analysis because we have chosen a method that allows us to study group process in a very detailed manner.

One strength of our methods of data analysis is their proven usefulness in refining the theory of group development and the group therapy process: both how groups grow and how individuals grow within groups. Also, our methods have now evolved to a point where we may either question or substantiate purely subjective or clinical judgments about the group development process.

From the application of the measures to the three groups in our pilot study, we have begun to refine our understanding of the phases, the phase shifts, and some of the aspects of structural development which are created during each of these processes. For instance, we have an increased appreciation of the role of each member during the resolution of developmentally relevant issues in a group. This is based upon the observation that during critical periods of the resolution of issues or the integration of perceptions in the group, there is input from all or almost all group members.

As we continue to develop our methodology, our next step will be to apply our current set of measures to the later phases of group process. Currently, we are completing work on Phase 1 for all three of the groups. This will be followed by analysis of all of Group A, since, in our clinical judgment, this group completed all nine phases of group development. We anticipate that the Experiencing Scale, the Normative-Organizational/Personal Exploration Scale, and the Speech Behavior Coding System will all be useful in the analysis of later phases and may become the backbone of the overall methodology. The Hostility/Support Scale will probably be useful in the analysis of Phases 4 and 5 specifically, where certain negative-feeling interactions are critically related to group developmental issues, but it will probably not be useful beyond that point. However, we think that we may also need to design or select other measures which address specific change dimensions that are uniquely characteristic of each later phase or pair of phases in the same way that the Hostility/Support Scale is pertinent to Phases 2 and 3, if we are to accurately define other phase boundaries and shifts.

Since we have clinically identified Group N in our data base as a group which did not succeed in resolving Phase 2 issues, we will be interested in completing the analysis on that group as well in order to further pursue questions about the significant differences between successful and unsuccessful group-level development.

Finally, the Speech Behavior Coding System is still incomplete in terms of the original plans for its development. We intend to pilot study the rest of the measures, namely, to look at the use of the pronouns I and you, and at the relationships of disturbances in the flow of speech, such as interruptions and stammers, to other aspects of the group and its process. We also intend to evolve a measure of what is spoken about, perhaps in collaboration with the project to identify topics of units in the Topic Oriented Group Focus Unitizing Procedure.

Other Uses of the Measures

There are a great many ways in which the data we have generated could be analyzed. Our focus in this initial round of work has been on a process analysis of group development which shows important differences between phases, and which describes the group-as-a-whole behavior during Phases 2 and 3. We would like to indicate in this section some of the other kinds of analyses that are possible.

First, the Topic Oriented Group Focus Unitizing Procedure has been shown to be a reliable method for creating units of interaction which reflect the attention of the group. This method breaks up the mass of data in a psychotherapy session into a natural series of segments of interaction, called units. Such units, which are relatively free of any theoretical assumptions, allow the researcher then to apply a variety of rating systems for the study of a wide range of issues in psychotherapy or any other small groups. For example, in the group psychotherapy area, no one has addressed the question of what it is that people actually discuss or work on in such settings. While the units were being identified by raters in our pilot study, they also wrote cryptic descriptions of the topic being addressed in each unit. We plan to define a set of theme or topic categories for analyzing the units in our groups. In addition we would like to look at the way themes are developed within units. For instance, there are units that have a beginning, a middle, and an ending as in a story, while in other units there is a quality of moving back and forth over a topic. Whether there is a relationship between such characteristics and phase of development or stage in the process of discussing a group-level issue is not clear at this time. Further, the communication patterns within units can be explored in a variety of ways. For example, we are interested in comparing the frequencies of ratings (on the measures we have already developed) across the kinds of units, over time, or across phases. The relationship of leaders to the proposing of topics and the development of topics can be explored.

The Normative-Organizational/Personal Exploration Scale makes no attempt to address the quality of the members' participation or the manner or style with which members focus on one area of concern or the other; or, the quality or comprehensiveness of resolutions to group-level concerns and to individuals' problems. All of these dimensions could be explored in relationship to the three kinds of units defined by the NO/PE scale.

We believe that both this variable and the unitizing technique have opened up important new areas for exploration of group process. Further, we believe that they will illuminate a number of issues, such as (1) outcome, (2) the implications for group structure of differences in leadership style or group composition, and (3) the comparative study of short-term and open-ended groups. The analysis of the substantive content of units will also allow us to see how norms and goals evolve in a group.

Second, from our experience so far in applying the Experiencing Scales to groups, a member may reflect upon the phenomena of group process, in addition to speaking about something specific to his own personal life. Specifically, we have noted that many statements are perceptions of the group itself and its process together, or are perceptions of an individual or subset of members regarding the way they are participating in the group at a particular time. These perceptions and comments have the same range of EXP stages as an individual's perception of himself or another member. Rating these statements separately from personal exploration may help us to identify and study more clearly the members' perceptions of the group's inner workings and development. In order to pursue this we hope to develop a "Group" Experiencing Scale in the near future.

The Experiencing Scales may be used in connection with our sociometric data to study roles in the group and the effect of leadership roles on individual self-exploration. Clinically, we would expect the group experience to be quite different for the Emotional Leader or for the Scapegoat Leader than for other members. We may look at a sample of each type of group leader and explore how the role affects their personal growth within the group process.

The analysis of client statements which were rated on the Therapist Experiencing Scale offers a rare opportunity to study how clients learn new interpersonal skills in the group, such as the ability to empathize with others—to respond in useful, facilitative ways to others' efforts to work in the group. Tracking this evolution of skills over time would be of interest.

As indicated in an earlier section, the Experiencing, Group-as-a-whole, and the Normative-Organizational/Personal Exploration graphs have been used in relation to each other to identify certain segments of group process where we think that structurally important group-level events are occurring. Methods of analysis that have been used in the study of critical incidents could be used to further study such events. Also, sequential analysis may lend itself to the intensive study of critical change periods in a group.

Third, the Hostility/Support Scale has been used in a circumscribed way for the phases on which we focused in our pilot study. The measure can also be applied to all the statements in the transcript, not just those addressed to the Scapegoat Leader. By using the Spoken-to measure in the Speech Behavior Coding System analyses to select all statements addressed to any particular member of the group, graphs could be produced for each member of the group. Further, tables can be prepared showing the proportions of critical or hostile comments addressed to each member of a group during any particular period in group process. We would anticipate that the patterns in such a table would differ between phases; and between groups which are progressing effectively and groups which are stuck in their developmental process.

Fourth, the measures in the Speech Behavior Coding System have as yet to be explored in their relationship to the other measures we have developed. For example, length of statement can be aggregated in relation to the units of the TOGF Unitizing Procedure and in relation to the NO/PE ratings of such units to tell us how much each member contributes to the Normative-Organizational or Personal Exploration aspects of the group's process. Length of statement can also be related to the ratings for each statement on the Experiencing Scales for a look at the relationship between the quantity and quality of input by each member; or by aggregates of members within certain time units that are of particular interest, such as TOGF units or critical incidents.

This list of possibilities is endless. In general, our problem will be to select the potentially most useful and/or most illuminating further analyses of our measures. This, of course, will be guided by our overall research plans and program, to be discussed below.

Future Plans for Our Research Program

In this section we would like to discuss our longer-term research program. We have several goals in this area: to deepen our clinical and theoretical understanding of group processes and further refine the specific theory of group development which has guided our research effort; to complete the methodology for all nine phases of group development; to apply our measures to a new set of groups in the context of a hypothesis testing study; and to broaden our horizons with some new research issues.

Clinical/Theoretical

Our work as clinicians and group leaders has always stimulated our intellectual curiosity about the dynamics in both individuals and groups. Now we are finding that the kind of research analyses we have produced also point out issues and dynamics that we had missed as clinicians. One example of this might be illustrative. In the Normative-Organizational/Personal Exploration graphs for Groups A and S (see Figures 18-1 and 18-6), we noticed a short period of time during Phase 3 when the ratings of the units moved away from Personal Exploration (3) to either Normative-Organizational (1) or Combination NO/PE (2). During this period of time there is also a peak on the Group-as-a-whole Experiencing Scale graph. Re-reading the transcripts at these pages revealed the fact that there was a period in each of these groups when the issues that were central to the earlier, Phase 2 conflict with the Scapegoat Leader are discussed again, except that during Phase 3 it was done in an exploratory way, with a good deal of self-reflectiveness and with each participant owning his part of the problem. It appears that the group revisits the problem in a more constructive way during Phase 3, resolves what was left unfinished in Phase 2, and then begins the process of reintegrating the Scapegoat Leader into the group as a positive person. This insight into the group's process has been very helpful in our current clinical work with groups, and has added further data to the process surrounding the Scapegoat Leader's role in the group.

As the work progresses, new clinical insights facilitate the research effort, and vice versa. Generally, our goals are to understand how group process facilitates or hinders individual growth or constructive change; but we also want to know how group interactions—whether they may have occurred in families, peer groups, or work contexts—create dysfunction in individuals who then become our clients. We see the effects of these past experiences in the issues that group members raise to work on in groups and, more powerfully, we see them in the dynamics of the relationships they create in the groups and which they must then work through (Dugo & Beck, 1984).

Further, we are interested in which group conditions do or do not facilitate work by individual members on their growth issues or by the group-as-a-whole on group-level issues. We are particularly interested in the specific kinds of changes that clients are able to make in groups. Finally, we want to know more about leaders' interventions and how they affect groups in either facilitative or disruptive ways. In particular, we think there are certain Task Leader behaviors that are more useful at one phase than another, and we wonder what happens when they are not provided or when the Task Leader is at odds with the group and/or the group-level needs at each phase.

As in the work we have reported in this chapter, we expect that the new clinical understandings and the continued empirical efforts will contribute to the evolution and refinement of our theory of group development. In the process we hope we are contributing also to a general theory of group interaction, since we consider our work on the structural development of a group to be a study of only one of many significant systematic sources of influence on group process (Beck, 1981b).

Currently, our main efforts in the theory-building area are being devoted to three topics. One, the theory is being rewritten for the small work group with interesting new insights emerging from this effort about both leaders and group-level processes (Beck, 1982). Second, we are interested in addressing the question of how the patterns we have observed in short-term groups apply to the long-term ongoing group which may have periodic changes in membership, but where certain members continue from one round of the group to the next. This pattern of group process is typical of the groups which are most commonly found in the field, especially in private practice and mental health center outpatient groups. Third, we are focusing attention on the cotherapy relationship with special interest in the changes in the leadership roles (Task Leader role, especially) when there are two therapists in a group. Also, we are writing a theory of the phases of development of a long-term cotherapy relationship and looking at the interaction of the phase of development of the cotherapists as a team with the phase of development of the group (Dugo & Beck, 1983a; in preparation, b).

Research Plans

As is clear from the interests we listed above, our clinical questions lead directly to research questions. We have more of these than we will be able to pursue in the immediate future. Our first goals in the further development of our research program are:

1. To develop and refine the measures further, including the use of other methods of statistical analysis. In particular, we must finalize our criterion for the phase boundary between Phases 2 and 3, and as we complete our data analysis on Phase 1 for our three groups to deal with the phase boundary between Phases 1 and 2 as well.

2. To extend our analysis to all nine phases of the group process. If necessary, this may mean designing some new variables for use with phases 4 through 9.

3. To pursue intensive analyses of critical events or change points in a group, picking up on the pilot studies in this area reported earlier in the chapter.

4. To make use of the units defined by the Topic Oriented Group Focus Unitizing Procedure to explore a variety of topics outlined earlier in the chapter, including the content of what is dealt with in groups.

5. To relate our view of group development and leadership emergence to outcome for the individual client in the group. Outcome issues that interest us include those cited in the literature on individual therapy but also include our idea that certain individual changes are facilitated more easily in groups and may even be unique to experiences in groups. We would like to see measures developed for these changes.

6. To design or adapt outcome measures for groups *qua* groups that relate to measures of the structural and qualitative aspects of group process. This would have implications for leadership evaluation as well as identifying the conditions to which the client was exposed.

7. To develop a method of evaluating the usefulness of particular leadership interventions from both the viewpoint of the therapeutic process for individuals and the group-level developmental process of groups-as-a-whole.

8. And, most important of all will be the opportunity to evaluate the usefulness of our methodology for identifying phases and their boundaries by applying it to a new set of groups in a larger-scale and hypothesis-testing study. This step, of course, depends on the completion of the methodology for all nine phases, and on completing at least some of the other steps outlined above.

References

Beaton, A. E., & Tukey, J. W. The fitting of power series, meaning polynomials, illustrated on band-spectroscopic data. *Technometrics*, 1974, *16*(2), 147–192.

Beck, A. P. Phases in the development of structure in therapy and encounter groups. In D. Wexler & L. N. Rice (Eds.), *Innovations in client-centered therapy*. New York: Wiley Interscience, 1974.

Beck, A. P. *On the development of a rating system for the identification of group phase boundaries.* Presented at the Society for Psychotherapy Research, Madison, Wisconsin, 1977.

Beck, A. P. Developmental characteristics of the system forming process. In J. Durkin (Ed.), *Living groups: group psychotherapy and general system theory*. New York: Brunner-Mazel, 1981. (a)

Beck, A. P. The study of group phase development and emergent leadership. *Group*, Winter 1981, 5(4), 48–54. (b)

Beck, A. P. *Phases in the development of work teams*. Presented at the 48th Plenary conference of the Diebold Research Group, Scottsdale, Arizona, 1982.

Beck, A. P. A process analysis of group development. *Group*, Spring 1983, 7(1), 19–26.

Beck, A. P. *A review of theories and research on group development*. In preparation. (a)

Beck, A. P. *A manual for rating group interaction with the Hostility/Support Scale*. In preparation. (b)

Beck, A. P., Dugo, J. M., Eng, A. M., Lewis, C. M., & Peters, L. M. The participation of leaders in the structural development of therapy groups. In R. R. Dies and K. R. MacKenzie (Eds.), *Advances in group psychotherapy: integrating research and practice*. New York: International Universities Press, 1983.

Beck, A. P., & Keil, A. V. Observations on the development of client centered, time-limited, therapy groups. *Counseling Center Discussion Papers, 13*(5). Chicago: University of Chicago Library, 1967.

Beck, A. P., & Peters, L. N. The research evidence for distributed leadership in therapy groups. *International Journal of Group Psychotherapy*, 1981, 31(1), 43–71.

Dugo, J. M., & Beck, A. P. *The art of co-therapy*. Presented at the Illinois Group Psychotherapy Society, Chicago, 1983. (a)

Dugo, J. M., & Beck, A. P. Tracking a group's focus on Normative/Organizational or Personal Exploration issues. *Group*, Winter 1983, 7(4), 17–26. (b)

Dugo, J. M., & Beck, A. P. Issues of intimacy and hostility viewed as group level phenomena. *International Journal of Group Psychotherapy*, January 1984, 34(1), 25–45.

Dugo, J. M., & Beck, A. P. *A manual for rating group process in terms of Normative/Organizational or Personal Exploration issues*. In preparation. (a)

Dugo, J. M., & Beck, A. P. The phases of development of the cotherapy relationship. In W. L. Roller & V. Nelson (Eds.), *The art of cotherapy: on the nature of coleadership*. In preparation. (b)

Dugo, J. M., Mayer, P., & Beck, A. P. *A manual for the topic-oriented group-focus procedure for unitizing group interaction*. In preparation.

Eng, A. M., & Beck, A. P. *Use of verbal participation measures and pronoun counts in the analysis of group development*. Presented at the Society for Psychotherapy Research Annual Conference, Aspen, Colorado, 1981.

Eng, A. M., & Beck, A. P. Speech behavior measures of group psychotherapy process. *Group*, Fall 1982, 6(3), 37–48.

Eng, A. M., & Beck, A. P. *The speech behavior coding system manual*. In preparation.

Gendlin, E. T., & Tomlinson, T. M. The process conception and its measurement. In C. R. Rogers, E. T. Gendlin, D. J. Kiesler, & C. B. Truax (Eds.), *The therapeutic relationship and its impact: A study of psychotherapy with schizophrenics*. Madison: University of Wisconsin Press, 1967.

Hare, A. P. Theories of group development and categories for interaction analysis. *Small Group Behavior*, 1973, 4(3), 259–304.

Klein, M. H., Mathieu, P. L., Gendlin, E. T., & Kiesler, D. J. *The Experiencing Scale: A research and training manual* (Vols. I & II). Madison: Wisconsin Psychiatric Institute, 1969.

Lacoursiere, R. B. *The life cycle of groups*. New York: Human Sciences Press, 1980.

Lewis, C. M. Symbolization of experience in the process of group development. *Group*, Summer, 1985 9(2), 29–34.

Lewis, C. M., & Beck, A. P. Experiencing level in the process of group development. *Group*, Spring 1983, 7(2), 18–26.

Lewis, C. M., & Beck, A. P. *The application of the experiencing scales to group interaction: A manual*. In preparation.

Lewis, C. M., Dugo, J. M., & Beck, A. P. *The application of two process variables to the analysis of structural development in small groups*. Presented at the Society for Psychotherapy Research Annual Conference, Aspen, Colorado, 1981.

Mathieu-Coughlan, P. L. & Klein, M. H. Experiential psychotherapy: key events in client-therapist interaction. In L. N. Rice & L. S. Greenberg (Eds.), *Patterns of change: intensive analysis of psychotherapy process*. New York: Guilford Press, 1984.

Peters, L. N., & Beck, A. P. Identifying emergent leaders in psychotherapy groups. *Group*, Spring 1982, *6*(1), 35–40.

Tuckman, B. W. Developmental sequence in small groups. *Psychological Bulletin*, 1965, *63*, 384–399.

Tuckman, B., & Jensen, M. Stages of small group development revisited. *Group and Organization Studies*, 1977, *2*, 419–427.

Velleman, P. F. Definition and comparison of robust nonlinear data smoothing algorithms. *Journal of the American Statistical Association*, September 1980, *75*(371), Theory and Methods Section, 609–615.

Wiley, D. Personal communication. Consultant regarding assessment, 1980.

Appendix: Transcript and Ratings: Group A

The reader enters the transcript in the middle of session 3. The following section corresponds to pages 95 through 102 in the original transcript. Also, we enter the transcript during a long unit in the Normative-Organizational/Personal Exploration analysis.

Guide to Notations in the Transcript

⌈ Helen ⌊ Diane	Bracketed statements indicate that they were spoken simultaneously.
. . .	Dots at the beginning or end of statement indicate interrupted statements, or a pause during a statement.
(laugh)	Indicates that the speaker laughed.
(unclear)	Indicates that the transcriber could tell the person was speaking but could not hear the words.

1.   Helen: You can only know the outside of him, and that's how *you* hear his . . .
1. ⌜ Helen: . . . saying, "You can know me, as I appear."

2. ⌊ Diane: This is how I hear it, yea . . .
2.   Diane: . . . this is how I hear it . . .
2. ⌜ Diane: . . . yea, now he may not be saying that.

3. ⌊ Helen: And he was saying, I thought . . .
3.   Helen: . . . exactly the opposite thing. I think he was saying, "I'm telling you some of the most important things about myself of the inner things about myself, that this is the way I, I can tell them to you. Now this is *my* way, and I think also he was saying, "I get disturbed about your way too, as you get disturbed by my way.

4.   Diane: Mm hm, mm hm. Yea, and I guess there is an element of judgment in here or evaluation on my part, in that what the things that Joe was telling last week for me were not, were not his internals they were his externals (*laugh*).

4. ⌜ Diane: This is a matter of judgment on my part.

5. ⌊ Alice: But what about the things he's said *today*.

6.   What about . . .?

7.   Diane: Hmm?

8. ⌜ Helen: What about today?

9. ⌊ Alice: What about the things . . .

9.   Alice: . . . that are being said today? That's what I keep wanting to ask you.

10.   Diane: Well all right. I'd be, now for instance when, when he talked, when, when you talked about the uh, the Negro, somehow for me you were staying again almost with the externals because, you fringed on your internals but you emphasized your externals . . .

11.   Alice: You mean you wondered how he really felt about the Negro himself.

12.   Diane: . . . because, yea because you drifted into racial prejudice. Uh, then when you talked about um, a-about this incident of, of the, the friend who played this rotten deal on you, um, you fringed on your internals but you really stayed with the externals. This is what I mean, by . . .

	Speech Behavior Measures				Hostility/ Support	Experiencing Scale			Normative/ Organizational Personal Exploration	
Item Number	Speaker	Spoken-to	# We–Group	Word Count	Rating	Item Length Rating	Scale Used	Rating	Unit Bound-aries	Rating
1	Helen	Diane	0	21		1	T	2	pre item 1	1
2	Diane	Helen	0	21		1	C	2	through item 28	
3	Helen	Diane	0	70		2	T	3		
4	Diane	Helen Group	0	54		1	C	2		
5	Alice	Diane	0	8		1	T	2		
6	Helen	Diane	0	2						
7	Diane	Helen	0	1						
8	Helen	Diane	0	3						
9	Alice	Diane	0	17		1	T	2		
10	Diane	Alice Joe	0	43	2	1	C	2		
11	Alice	Diane	0	12		1	T	2		
12	Diane	Joe	0	54	2	1	C or T	2		

12. Diane: . . . operating with this . . . yea . . .

13. Helen: And that irritates you, it's like telling you, "There's something here but you can't get it, I'm not going to give it to you."

14. Diane: Um, I-I-I was trying to think, trying to see if I really did feel irritation. This was what I was, when you said that irritates me . . .

15. Martha: That's not the feeling that I get from you . . .

14. Diane: Is irritati— . . .

15. Martha: No it's the thing I get from you that you feel is frus . . .

16. Diane: Frustra— . . .

15. Martha: . . . tration, I want in, or I wanna know you.

16. Diane: Yea that feels more like it.

15. Martha: uh huh

16. Diane: (*unclear words here*) . . . except I wanted to look at the irritation cuz sometimes I, I guess I want to really see if I . . . But I think it is more frustration. It's more like, "Gee I'll spend 15 weeks with you and never really know . . . you. I'll know all about what you think of racial prejudice and Marilyn Monroe and the, and the UN and that sort of thing but I'll never really know what is clickin' around inside you!" (*laugh*)

17. ⌈ Joe: (*unclear*) I don't know myself. (*laugh*)

18. ⌊ Alice: And that, hurts some way that's . . .

19. Helen: There's something else now that I . . .

18. ⌈ Alice: It hurts in some way to . . .

20. ⌊ Diane: It doesn't hurt.

19. Alice: . . . think you won't know er . . .

21. Diane: No it doesn't hurt, it's, I, I, I like your word frustration (*silent laugh*)

Item Number	Speech Behavior Measures				Hostility/ Support	Experiencing Scale			Normative/ Organizational Personal Exploration	
	Speaker	Spoken-to	# We-Group	Word Count	Rating	Item Length Rating	Scale Used	Rating	Unit Bound-aries	Rating
13	Helen	Diane	0	24		1	T	3		
14	Diane	Helen	0	30		1	C	2		
15	Martha	Diane	0	32		1	T	3		
14										
15										
16	Diane	Martha Joe	0	87	3	1	C or T	3		
15										
16										
15										
16										
17	Joe	Diane	0	6						
18	Alice	Diane	0	17		1	T	3		
19	Helen	Diane	0	6						
18										
20	Diane	Alice	0	3		1	C	2		
19										
21	Diane	Alice Martha	0	13		1	C	3		

22.	Joe:	Well like I say I mean it's . . .
22. ⌈	Joe:	. . . a matter of personality.
23. ⌊	Diane:	It seems wasteful! . . . Almost.

22.   Joe: It's a personal, a matter of personality. We're all different, develop different, we have different ideas, different thoughts, different inner thoughts.

23.   Diane: Again, you're, now you're giving me your, your, your *(laugh)* opinion of personality, you see and . . .

24.   Joe: Yea, well one thing uuuh, I'll say is well like if I'm at a party sometime and uh, you know everybody is drinkin' and tellin' jokes, well it'll go around and it's my tell, time to tell a joke, I'll tell, I don't have much patience on goin' into detail. I'll tell a real quick joke. I mean it's over you know, and everybody'll say, "Well you told a quickie again, and the, then the fella next to me, he'll go into some real long detailed joke and uh, I'll listen I mean I'm interested but I don't uh, have the patience for long details. I'm pro . . . I'm probably doin' the same thing. I don't know, I'm just uh, well I am the executive type er, I don't have the patience, I talk a few words and get it off my chest. I mean that's, I think that's the way I'm going here. And somebody else, they can tell it real long and detailed and I'm interested, I'll sit and listen, listen by the hour . . .

25.   Alice: Yea, it sounds like you're saying, "I'm not holding things back . . .

24.   Joe: No

25.   Alice: . . . and tryin' to keep you from knowing who . . .

24.   Joe: I mean that's just my na– . . .

25.   Alice: It's just my way of telling . . .

24.   Joe: It's just my nature uh . . .

26.   Diane: I think [Greg, then Brad start then stop] I think Helen really hit it right on the head when she said to me, I mean, that, it can, as you started to talk again, it hit me what you said *(laugh)*.

27.   Martha: Um, well, what?

Item Number	Speaker	Spoken-to	# We-Group	Word Count	Rating	Item Length Rating	Scale Used	Rating	Unit Bound-aries	Rating
		Speech Behavior Measures			Hostility/ Support	Experiencing Scale			Normative/ Organizational Personal Exploration	
22	Joe	Diane	2	32		1	C	2		
23	Diane	Joe	0	21	3	1	C	2		
22										
23						1	T	2		
24	Joe	Diane Alice Group	0	187		3	C	4		
25	Alice	Joe	0	25		1	T	4		
24										
25										
24										
25										
24										
26	Diane	Group, Martha	0	35		1	C	3		
27	Martha	Diane	0	3						

28.   Diane: You're absolutely right, I'm not willing to accept him on his terms cuz that's who he is.

27.   Martha: That's right.

29.   Brad: I'm just a little curious des-, um, despite what you do when you tell jokes I suppose that measured in minutes Joe has, mostly because we kept after him, has probably talked the most and said the most, uh revealed I think the most . . .

30.   Alice: And expressed . . .

31.   Helen: Yes.

29.   Brad: . . . in both sessions and, all three sessions now. Why are we after him?

32.   Greg: Every generation needs its scapegoat.

      Group: (*laughter*)

33.   Martha: Ah, you're crazy.

34.   Brad: Well I mean . . .
34.   Brad: . . . I suppose he's the only one in a way who has sort of begun to, you know, open up at all.

35.   Alice: Mm hm, in a way he's really put himself out and what we're doing is sitting around saying, "Well, put out more, Joe, put out more." (*laughs*)

36.   Greg: Well, the very fact that he's external makes it easier to jump on that than it is to jump on something that might hurt someone.

37.   Martha: Well, isn't?, didn't you expect?, I thought of this before I came, that there would be a certain amount of sparring to begin with. I mean on the way over I thought about things that I might bring up and I thought, "Well, I don't, that's kinda personal," you know? . . .

38.   Alice: Mm hm.

37. ⌈ Martha: . . . and it's usually . . .

38. ⌊ Alice: about yourself.

	Speech Behavior Measures				Hostility/ Support	Experiencing Scale			Normative/ Organizational Personal Exploration	
Item Number	Speaker	Spoken-to	# We–Group	Word Count	Rating	Item Length Rating	Scale Used	Rating	Unit Bound-aries	Rating
28	Diane	Group	0	17		1	C	3		
27										
29	Brad	Joe Group	2	57	1	1	T	3	item 29 through item 43	1
30	Alice	Brad	0	2						
31	Helen	Brad	0	1						
29										
32	Greg	Group	0	5		1	C	2		
33	Martha	Greg	0	3						
34	Brad	Group	0	24		1	T	3		
35	Alice	Brad Group	1	27		1	T	3		
36	Greg	Group	0	25		1	C	2		
37	Martha	Group Alice	2	85		1	C	3		
38	Alice	Martha	0	4		1	T	3		
37										
38										

37.   Martha: Yea. (*unclear words here*) . . . what I might have to offer. And it seems to me that we're not all quite sure just how, you know, we're gonna jump in and bare our secrets . . .

39.   Diane: You know one thing . . .

40.   Alice: Are you saying something like maybe it's almost easier to deal with whoever has put himself out than to put yourself out then?

41.   Martha: Yea. Uh huh.

39.   Diane: You know one thought occurs to me from your saying that. It . . . it just came to me and I'll bet there's more in this than I realize. I bet you in a way I'm envious, because it occurred to me it's occurred to me again. I seem to get a lot of thoughts when I'm writing up my journal (*laughs*), but it occurred to me when I was writing up my journal. And I thought, "You know there are a lot of things I'd like to tell about me in this group, and I'll betcha it's just because I don't have nerve enough to come right out and tell [*Diane, then Alice, laugh*], tell things. I mean I'm afraid for instance that it'll bore them, the group. You won't really wanta hear about it you know and, and maybe . . .

42.   Alice: Mm hm.

39. ⌈ Diane: I just wish I could . . . (*laughs*)

43. ⌊ Joe: Well, speak, get your . . .

43.   Joe: Speak, get your money's worth. (*laughter, especially Joe's*)

39.   Diane: (*unclear words*) . . . worth lookin' at. (*laughs*)

42.   Alice: (*unclear words*) . . . you could say about yourself *is* there.

44.   Diane: Yea. I know it's there when I'm away, you know, cuz I think "Oh gee, there's some things I really would like to look at in this group," and I always come . . . fast on this comes the thought, "Oh well, they don't want to hear about me, they'll be bored," you know.

45.   Alice: Yea, and yet here's somebody else who's putting himself . . .

46.   Diane: Joe is doing it, yea.

	Speech Behavior Measures				Hostility/ Support	Experiencing Scale			Normative/ Organizational Personal Exploration	
Item Number	Speaker	Spoken-to	# We-Group	Word Count	Rating	Item Length Rating	Scale Used	Rating	Unit Boundaries	Rating
37						1	T	3		
39	Diane	Martha Group	0	153		2	C	4		
40	Alice	Diane	0	23		1	T	3		
41	Martha	Alice	0	3						
39										
42	Alice	Diane	0	11						
39										
43	Joe	Diane	0	10		1	T	2		
43										
39										
42										
44	Diane	Alice Group	0	53		1	C	4	item 44 through item 48	1
45	Alice	Diane	0	29		1	T	3		
46	Diane	Alice	0	5						

45.   Alice: . . . now, and what you're in essence saying, "Yea, but I don't wanta hear about that part of you . . . "

47.   Diane: That's right.

45.   Alice: " . . . that's boring."

48.   Diane: That's right, yea.

49.   Martha: It's interesting because you're the one person in the group that I've thought most of since I've been away. The, the one thing that struck me that you said the first night we were here was that uh, reaction that you said you had gotten from groups, and the question I wanted to ask you was, whether you felt you had gotten that same reaction now being a part of this group, or not.

50.   Diane: Uh, I haven't yet, but this is primarily because I haven't really pushed forward on my own . . . (laughs)

51.   Alice: She hasn't put herself out yet, in the way that she's saying . . .

52.   Diane: Yea, well I . . . I . . .

51.   Alice: . . . that you haven't put yourself out.

52.   Diane: I haven't, I haven't taken a chance yet. (laughs)
[Unclear words from another member]

53.   Diane: I don't know.

54.   Martha: Something like that happened to me recently in the group that I go to and uh, something the speaker said I thought was perfectly adorable, just a delightful sense of humor, and I just burst out laughing, and I was the only one in the whole group that laughed, and the silence afterwards was like a rebuke . . .

55.   Alice: uh huh.

54.   Martha: and I thought of you because I think that's, at least as I got it from you, that was the reaction that you get from groups, cuz I was just thoroughly spontaneously, you know, delighted with what he said and the group was, is quite a cold self-conscious analyzing type of group, you know, very studious and all that academic . . .

	Speech Behavior Measures				Hostility/ Support	Experiencing Scale			Normative/ Organizational Personal Exploration	
Item Number	Speaker	Spoken-to	# We–Group	Word Count	Rating	Item Length Rating	Scale Used	Rating	Unit Bound-aries	Rating
45										
47	Diane	Alice	0	2						
45										
48	Diane	Alice	0	3						
49	Martha	Diane	1	74		2	T	3	item 49 through item 58	1
50	Diane	Martha	0	18		1	C	2		
51	Alice	Martha, Diane	0	18		1	T	3		
52	Diane	Alice	0	14		1	C	3		
51										
52										
53	Diane	Alice	0	3						
54	Martha	Alice, Diane, Group	0	177		3	C	4		
55	Alice	Martha	0	16		1	T	2		
54										

55.   Alice: jazz. (*laughs*)

54.   Martha: Yea, and uh, I just sort of cut across the feeling, you know, of the group and uh, the guilt that I felt and anxiety and all that sorta stuff afterwards I thought about, and I thought about you . . .

54. ⌈ Martha: It was tough, it was it was one of the . . .

55. ⌊ Alice: Seemed to you like this was exactly the sort of thing that . . .

54.   Martha: . . . one of the, almost like a crack across the face.

56.   Alice: Their silence.

57.   Martha: It was an active, it was as if that, you know . . .

57.   Martha: It was a rebuke, oh boy was it a rebuke.

58.   Martha: And they were, they were just as, and I was actually I was just as threatened by them as they had been threatened by me because, boy that was, that was really somethin'.

59.   Brad: Well, I uh, I was almost moved to say, uh, when you were first getting into it about Joe, how he wouldn't talk. And . . . and you, on the other hand, wanna pick a fight. And, uh, I don't think I really meant this. I was partly thinking of what, uh, well I mean who knows what, um, I was thinking partly of the fact that you yourself had said this the week before that this is partly what you are doing. But it seemed that one of the factors in why you were a little angry at Joe was that he was being so, uh, Byronic and er um, so uh peaceful, you know, and uh, and I guess that let's say I, I thought you wanted to keep the waters rough and rumpled up. [*Alice laughs*]

60.   Martha: Aha!

61.   Greg: She was ready for a fight.

62.   Joe: Yea, she wanted . . . [*general laughter*]

63.   Greg: I am, too, as a matter of fact. [*laughter and unclear voices throughout*]

64.   Martha: Do you have . . . are you feeling this way, too? [*Alice laughs throughout*]

Item Number	Speaker	Spoken-to	# We-Group	Word Count	Rating	Item Length Rating	Scale Used	Rating	Unit Bound-aries	Rating
		Speech Behavior Measures			Hostility/ Support	Experiencing Scale			Normative/ Organizational Personal Exploration	
55										
54										
54										
55										
54										
56	Alice	Martha	0	2						
57	Martha	Group	0	21		1	C	4		
57										
58	Martha	Group	0	33		1	C	3		
59	Brad	Diane	0	136		2	T	3	item 59 through item 68	1
60	Martha	Group	0	1						
61	Greg	Group	0	6		1	T	3		
62	Joe	Group	0	3						
63	Greg	Group	0	8		1	C	3		
64	Martha	Greg	0	10		1	T	2		

65. Greg: Oh, I'm, I've been ready for a fight all week, and that I'm, I sort of feel like I, a . . . clam [*laughter*] . . . in a shell, or maybe a hermit cra-crab. [*laughter*]

66. Martha: All right! Who's gonna start it!?

67. Greg: I just went back in. [*loud laughter*]

67. Greg: Why don't we pick somebody to attack—somebody else?

68. Martha: Do we have to attack? For heaven's sakes, why did you bring it up? Do you feel like it?

67. Greg: Why not?

68. Martha: This is like putting you on the spot. (*to Diane*) Do you feel like bringing up any of the things that you were thinking about?

69. Joe: (*unclear*) . . . group you said when you're (*unclear*) . . . you're dealing with groups there's irritation or you say there isn't harmony. I was wondering, uh, what is it that, you say were entertaining or you were with a group and there was friction or, uh, you didn't get along. I was wonderin' what, uh . . . what the details of that were.

70. Diane: Well, I'm, I'm not sure if it's possible to recreate it. It—it's almost like your experience, it has to be spontaneous because when it happens it, when it has happened it's so unexpected and yet, you know, so damaging—

71. Alice: The situation like with Joe, where you had a spontaneous [*Diane starts to interrupt*] feeling in the group . . .

72. Diane: Where I have offered myself spontaneously with a very deep-seated value at the bottom of it (*laughs*) always. It's something that is based on something that is *real* important to me, and um, uh, a-and then when I come out with whatever I'm offering that has, it—it is rooted in that value, a-and then when I'm faced with this active kind of re-buke (*laughs*) of course those aren't my terms but still, they—they feel familiar, um . . .

73. Greg: Well, this is, is this bothering you, something which might make you irritating to other people?

Item Number	Speaker	Spoken-to	# We-Group	Word Count	Rating	Item Length Rating	Scale Used	Rating	Unit Boundaries	Rating
		Speech Behavior Measures			Hostility/ Support	Experiencing Scale			Normative/ Organizational Personal Exploration	
65	Greg	Martha Group	0	31		1	C	4		
66	Martha	Group	0	6		1	C	2		
67	Greg	Group Martha	1	16		1	C	3		
67										
68	Martha	Greg Diane	1	42		1	T	3		
67										
68										
69	Joe	Diane	0	62		1	T	3	item 69 through item 92	2
70	Diane	Joe	0	40	1	1	C	3		
71	Alice	Diane	0	14		1	T	3		
72	Diane	Group	0	78		2	C	4		
73	Greg	Diane	0	16		1	T	4		

74. ⌈ Diane: Oh yes.

75. ⌊ Greg: I mean . . . yes, I mean like . . .

76.   Diane: (unclear, loud laugh throughout)

75.   Greg: . . . you rarely . . .

76.   Diane: (continues to laugh)

75.   Greg: You . . .

76.   Diane: (laughs)

77.   Alice: Do you mean you really feel they all are or because in this kind of ex-
                perience you've come to the conclusion they must all be?

78.   Martha: Well . . .

79.   Diane: I would say that, that all of my really major values are, uh, this kind,
                and I don't know how many they would be, I've never tried to list
                them, but I know the ones that are real important to me meet this kind
                of resistance.

80.   Martha: Can you think of just one instance? I mean that . . .

81.   Diane: One of my values? (laughs)

82.   Martha: No, I'm not saying just, naming a value, but you know, one time that
                something happened so that we could understand what it was.

83.   Diane: Well, I can almost go into any, any, um, any area—politics, uh, phi-
                losophy—

84. ⌈ Martha: You mean you're on the opposite side of the fence always?

85. ⌊ Greg: Is there . . . is there . . .

86.   Diane: Always.

85.   Greg: Is there any, is there any chance, now I'm just protecting from some-
                body else, my mother, as a matter of fact, but is there, is there any
                chance that it, that it's sort of, these are deepseated but most of the

Item Number	Speaker	Spoken-to	# We-Group	Word Count	Hostility/Support Rating	Experiencing Scale Item Length Rating	Scale Used	Rating	Normative/Organizational Personal Exploration Unit Boundaries	Rating
74	Diane	Greg	0	2						
75	Greg	Diane	0	10						
76	Diane	Group	0	10						
75										
76										
75										
76										
77	Alice	Diane	0	25		1	T	2		
78	Martha	Diane	0	1						
79	Diane	Alice	0	46		1	C	4		
80	Martha	Diane	0	10		1	T	2		
81	Diane	Martha	0	5		1	C	2		
82	Martha	Diane	1	24		1	T	2		
83	Diane	Martha	0	14		1	C	2		
84	Martha	Diane	0	11		1	T	2		
85	Greg	Diane	0	87		2	T	4		
86	Diane	Martha, Greg	0	27		1	C	4		
85										

time you don't, you don't, uh, it sort of stays veiled quite a bit, and then it sort of comes out, so that they feel all of a sudden as if it, it shot out, a-and it was threatening them.

86.	Diane:	Yes, I do, I have learned to veil them, because they have—see, my feeling is they have threatened people . . .
86.	Diane:	. . . at least I have been attacked.
87.	Alice:	. . . It's almost a shock . . .
88.	Greg:	I'm suggesting that it might . . .
88.	Greg:	Yea, it's sort of a shock a-a-and in some sense that you that you are that that you might without realizing be trying to flank them a little all of a sudden you know, tryin' . . .
89.	Diane:	It doesn't feel that way . . .
88.	Greg:	Um, I'm . . .
89.	Diane:	. . . I mean usually when I, when I do come out, I'm aware I'm coming out because it's . . .
89. ⌈	Diane:	. . . you know I'm not, uh, it's spontane- . . .
90. ⌊	Alice:	I think what you're trying to . . .
91. ⌈	Brad:	Well, what . . .
90. ⌊	Alice:	I'm sorry . . .
90.	Alice:	I think what you're trying to say is maybe you haven't indicated at all for a while . . .
90. ⌈	Alice:	. . . what
92. ⌊	Greg:	Maybe if it was less . . .
90.	Alice:	. . . and all of a sudden there it is.
92.	Greg:	Maybe if it was less veiled it, it, people would, it would, you know maybe it's, uh, it's the sudden change rather than actually the value

| Item Number | Speech Behavior Measures | | | | Hostility/ Support | Experiencing Scale | | | Normative/ Organizational Personal Exploration | |
	Speaker	Spoken-to	# We–Group	Word Count	Rating	Item Length Rating	Scale Used	Rating	Unit Bound-aries	Rating
86										
86										
87	Alice	Diane	0	4		1	T	3		
88	Greg	Alice, Diane	0	42		1	T	4		
88										
89	Diane	Greg	0	29		1	C	3		
88										
89										
89										
90	Alice	Diane, Brad	0	34		1	T	4		
91	Brad	Diane	0	2						
90										
90										
90										
92	Greg	Diane	0	31		1	T	2		
90										
92										

In this next segment the reader enters the transcript midstream in Session 4. The following section corresponds to pages 187 and part of page 188 in the original transcript.

93.   Alice: And I guess you've got, you've got an image of yourself being able to get to the point where you'll be free to let yourself take the chance because it's what you want. And your trip to California is, is not really, uh, an attempt to begin this process, but it'll be a kind of trying yourself in a new place.

94.   Pat: Uh huh.

95.   Greg: A little preview.

96.   Pat: Well, yea, like uh, I've never, I've never, um, well in the last five years I have never been able really to go anyplace much, except a year ago, uh, this last fall, I took a trip on a Greyhound Bus to Colorado. And I went by myself, and most of the way I went by myself and I, I really felt like, uh, I was testing myself i-in, in being able (*sighs*) to, uh, feel secure maybe, or to, uh, take care of myself, I guess.

97. ⌈ Alice: Mm hm. Alone.

98. ⌊ Helen: Be alone.

99.   Pat: Yea, yea, and, and to speak up when I needed something, and, and if I wasn't comfortable to do something about it—things like that. But I, I know I couldn't take it for an extended period, I mean a week is all right, at least that point I, I realized that, and I was very glad to get back here to familiar things and . . . or people that I . . .

100.   Alice: Kind of what's frightening for you is simply the physical, uh, alienness.

101.   Pat: Separateness, yes, the separation and, from familiar things and a real sense of insecurity, which, which is almost insurmountable, uh, in terms of getting my, my, my energy replenished with, with any kind of, um rest or security from others.

102.   Helen: Mm. I had a feeling that if you were doing that you wouldn't know when to stop to eat or if, if the schedule was not . . .

103.   Pat: Yea . . .

102.   Helen: . . . and you wouldn't know when, when to eat or when to go to sleep . . .

Item Number	Speaker	Spoken-to	# We-Group	Word Count	Hostility/Support Rating	Experiencing Scale Item Length Rating	Scale Used	Rating	Normative/Organizational Personal Exploration Unit Boundaries	Rating
93	Alice	Pat	0	61		1	T	4	item 93 through item 110	3
94	Pat	Alice	0	2						
95	Greg	Pat	0	3		1	C	4		
96	Pat	Alice, Group	0	88		2	C	2		
97	Alice	Pat	0	3						
98	Helen	Pat	0	2		1	T	2		
99	Pat	Group	0	70		1	C	3		
100	Alice	Pat	0	12		1	T	3		
101	Pat	Alice	0	40		1	C	4		
102	Helen	Pat	0	40		1	T	3		
103	Pat	Helen	0	32		1	C	4		
102										

103. Pat: Yea, because I just am a-all wound up inside with this feeling of, of, uh (*sighs*), well, I wanna say danger but I don't—that is, that's a little too strong.

104. Helen: Mm hm, but I am alone and I have to be on my guard.

105. Pat: Yea, that's right. That's the way I feel.

106. Greg: Sort of interesting, when I first came to school, I drove from Seattle and had most of my goods in my car. And uh, I came here and in my, my usual deliberate lack of foresight, I hadn't made any arrangements for a room at the University (*clears throat*), and uh, so for a few days, and for a week or two, for about a week, I went through a tremendous period of anxiety because I didn't know anybody and I was staying at a YMCA and carrying my hi-fi and stuff up and down to put it someplace. And then when I finally, and then I started looking for apartments, and I suddenly realized that, "God, if I feel like this, how am I gonna be able to stay all by myself in an apartment," and uh, finally I-I started looking through the . . . the, the places and found this, uh, room with this family, and I just sort of jumped at it, you know (*laughs*), and here was a, here was a new family tree to put myself under.

107. Alice: Mm hm, mm hm—a tremendous relief.

108. Greg: It took me six months . . . before I . . . got mad and wanted to move out. (*laughs*) But I've changed a lot since then—I don't think that my reactions would be that, that strong.

109. Alice: The sense of aloneness would still be there but not as frightening.

110. Greg: Right.

Item Number	Speech Behavior Measures				Hostility/ Support	Experiencing Scale			Normative/ Organizational Personal Exploration	
	Speaker	Spoken-to	# We-Group	Word Count	Rating	Item Length Rating	Scale Used	Rating	Unit Bound-aries	Rating
103										
104	Helen	Pat	0	14		1	T	4		
105	Pat	Helen	0	8						
106	Greg	Pat, Group	0	181		3	C	2 P3		
107	Alice	Greg	0	7		1	T	3		
108	Greg	Group	0	35		1	C	3		
109	Alice	Greg	0	12		1	T	4		
110	Greg	Alice	0	1						

Strategies and Methods

19

Research Strategies

Leslie S. Greenberg
Department of Psychology
York University
North York, Ontario

Intellectual Strategy

Strategic Choices

At certain points in the development of a science, questions of *intellectual strategy* arise which become a matter of judgment rather than a strictly logical dictate of ones scientific method (Kuhn, 1973; Toulmin, 1974). In routine cases, the scientists working in any particular discipline, to a large degree, share the same ideas and have a sufficiently agreed upon conception of what constitutes adequate description, explanation, and verification to allow knowledge to be accumulated. This agreed upon set of rules defines current standards and serves as the framework for deciding which of the variants and innovations circulating in the discipline at the time are scientifically acceptable.

Even during periods when the operating intellectual strategies in a field are not in question, the tactical choices of which direction to take are still hard to make because there are always multiple criteria by which to evaluate proposed innovation. However, when the intellectual strategy is temporarily in doubt, as must occur for any major scientific development to take place (Kuhn, 1973), the field is thrown into a state of reinspection and the conditions that normally apply, cease to hold good. There is no longer a collective agreement on conceptions of what constitutes adequate "explanation" in the science concerned and so the criteria for developing and judging new ideas are no longer unambiguous.

There is, at these times, a corresponding opportunity for greater individual difference in the practice of the science and for the exercising of individual judgment of a kind that does not exist in the routine exercise of the science. Toulmin (1976), in analyzing the history of change in scientific strategies, points out that the questions in the field at this stage shift toward asking what the general intellectual goals should be, what tasks should be undertaken, and how these tasks should be carried out. Questions such as these require us not so much to continue the game of science by the old familiar set of rules but to reappraise the whole theoretical context. It is at this point that strategic choices come to play a major role in the scientific discipline.

Psychotherapy Research

Psychotherapy and counseling research appear currently to be at the point where strategic choices as to the goals need to be made. Having, to date, emphasized methodological strategies based solely in the empiricist tradition (Feigl, 1973), psychotherapy

707

research methodology has neglected the possible contributions from rationalist and subjectivist positions which have gained in strength considerably in the last decade. The "theory laden" character of observation and empirical laws has been generally accepted as has the human element in the evolution of science (Brown, 1977; Feyerabend, 1975; Hanson, 1958, 1971; Harré, 1975; Kuhn, 1973; Lakatos, 1970; Manicas & Secord, 1983; McMullen, 1974 a & b; Polanyi, 1958).

The older belief that science must begin from irrefutable foundations, whether these be first principles or sense datum, has come under intense questioning. Operationism has been abandoned. Inductivism, whereby one progresses from observation to generalization, as the mode of inference proper to science, has failed to stand up to the scrutiny of time. It has been shown that *explanation* cannot easily be reduced to inductivist terms, thus rendering inductivism lame in aiding explanation of phenomena. Popper (1963) has stressed the *conjectural* aspects of laws and attacked the view that laws are arrived at by something called inductive inference. Feigl (1974), a defender of empiricism, admits that laws are frequently revised "from above," that is, from the level of theory and admits that observation statements depend in part upon the theories presupposed in their formulation. All this has put the accepted empiricist intellectual strategies into question. This questioning of empiricist strategies has been paralleled in psychotherapy and personality research (Bergin & Strupp, 1972; Gottman & Markman, 1978; Meehl, 1978; Rice & Greenberg, 1984; Rorer & Widiger, 1983; Singer, 1980). There has been a disaffection with verification and hypothesis testing as the only mode of investigation in psychotherapy and a call for greater emphasis on discovering mechanisms of change by studying experts and using theory to guide observation (Greenberg, 1975; Rice & Greenberg, 1984).

As Horowitz (1982), in his presidential address to the Society for Psychotherapy Research pointed out, investigators in psychotherapy research have been socialized into valuing a "contrast group" approach to therapy research over relational and descriptive paradigms. The contrast group approach involves a controlled experiment in which variables are systematically altered and subjects are randomly assigned to groups. By contrast, the relational paradigm involves the examination of associations or correlations among variables, often involving the examination of the relationships between input variables, process variables, and outcome variables. In the descriptive paradigm, one intensively observes phenomena in a particular domain of interest and develops classification or coding systems to describe the domain of interest. A reinspection of strategy in the field will at least need to address the ordering of these paradigms.

Differential treatment designs have not yielded as much as was expected (Frank, 1979) and this has led to a revival of interest in establishing general factors involved in therapeutic change and in discovering mechanisms of change by means of process research. Suggestions to be made in this chapter on research strategy will focus on the place of process research in a newly conceived approach to psychotherapy research aimed at identifying mechanisms of change. This newly emerging approach emphasizes *description* and *explanation* as important intellectual goals. It suggests that tasks which are designed to achieve these goals should often be carried out before contrast group designs. True prediction is seen as possible only with the aid of improved description and explanation. It is not that prediction is an unimportant goal but rather that we need rigorous description and explanation to illuminate prediction—to define what it is that leads to positive outcomes in psychotherapy.

Prediction, Explanation, and Description

The orthodox empiricist approach at the base of current research strategies rests on questionable assumptions such as the possibility of identifying basic "facts of observation" independent of theoretical considerations. Critical analysis of these assumptions has made it apparent that, although gathering evidence of an empirical nature is still crucial to science, the inductive logic approach is not the only legitimate approach to science. The positivists' earlier preoccupation with "prediction," which was regarded as the mark of scientific knowledge, has been supplemented by a concern with *explanation* as the core of scientific understanding (Kaplan, 1964; Toulmin, 1972). It is worthwhile here to pursue for a moment the nature of prediction and explanation for it will serve as a base for the suggestions on research strategy in the remainder of this chapter. If we look at the actual workings of science, we shall find, as Toulmin (1961) points out, that not all prediction (such as horseracing) is scientific and that not all science is predictive (such as evolutionary biology). New attention to the role of explanation in science has brought about important changes in the conception of science. In the empiricist tradition phenomena were explained by producing a universal proposition such as "All ravens are black" to explain a particular observation such as this raven is black. This model however, does not have any real relevance to the explanations of working science. To count as a scientific explanation, the account of a raven's blackness must shift to another conceptual level, involving theoretical reinterpretations which appeal, for example, to facts about pigments or evolutionary adaptiveness of color.

It is at this level, of providing explanations, that psychotherapy research strategy has been inadequate. Little, if anything, in the form of explanation has been able to emerge from current research strategy, because all efforts have been focused on predicting or more correctly forecasting (Toulmin, 1961). Forecasting is a craft or technology, an application of science rather than the kernel of science. If one is able to forecast successfully, this is a fact which needs explaining. Forecasting that sucking the bark of a tree will cure malaria is not a science but craft. Similarly, forecasting that snake phobias will be cured by desensitization or that self-esteem will be increased by a supportive relationship adds little to a scientific understanding of how this occurs. Only when outcome predictions of this type can be explained in terms of the active ingredients of treatment, how change takes place, and when and with whom specific treatments are effective, will psychotherapy research move from a prescientific to a scientific stage of development.

Once the important distinctions between explanation and prediction have been explicated, it is important to discuss the nature of description and its relation to explanation. It is the purpose of the empirical sciences "to describe, to explain and to predict the occurrences in the world we live in" (Hempel, 1966, p. 1). Describing is the first member of the triad which constitutes the fundamental tasks of scientific exploration. It seems to be generally agreed among philosophers now, that the ideal of a descriptive vocabulary applicable to observations, which is entirely free of theoretical influence, is unrealizable (Harré, 1975). Hanson (1969, 1971) has argued persuasively that scientific observation is a "theory-laden" activity. Knowledge is always presupposed in making sense of sense data. This does not mean that the incoming signals from the "subject matter" are unimportant but it must be recognized that even in the physical sciences the conceptual element and one's presuppositions determine where observations have to be "cleaned up" (Hanson, 1971), in order to fit into the intelligible structure. In addition, understanding of actual phenomena is often advanced by studies of nonexistent ideal cases such as frictionless planes, point particles perfectly rigid or elastic bodies, and so on. Understanding of ideal cases guides the investigator through the rough terrain of actual observation.

The epistemological position referred to by Bhaskar (1979) as transcendental realism best exemplifies the position suggested here as an alternative to either the standard empiricist view (Hempel, 1966) or a paradigmatic view (Kuhn, 1973). In this fallibilist realism one holds that knowledge is a social process but that there is a world that exists independently of cognizing experience. The task of science is to invent theories which aim to represent the world, and since theories are constitutive of the *known* world but not of the world as such, we may be wrong but not anything goes. Because there is a world out there, rational criteria do exist for evaluating our theories. This new philosophy of science has strong implications for psychology (Manicas & Secord, 1983) and for psychotherapy research in which the scientist must construct consensually reliable descriptions which attempt to approximate what is "out there." Even though observations are theory laden, science does not make facts out of thin air, although it may shape them or draw attention to some particular features they show. Significant observations within a science are ones which meet the criteria of relevance to current conceptions, but are also capable of providing evidence that can change theory.

Physical sciences, as Hanson (1969) points out, are not just methods of systematic exposure of the sense to the world, however, but also are a way of thinking about the world and what one sees. The scientist is the person who sees in familiar situations what no one else has seen before. As Toulmin (1961) suggests, scientists rely on ideals and paradigms to make nature intelligible. Science therefore progresses not by recognizing the truth of new observations but by *making sense* of these observations. To this task of interpretation are brought all one's working assumptions such as principles of regularity, conceptions of natural order, ideals, or intellectual patterns which define the range of things we can accept.

In general, the hypothetical entities which constitute the causal mechanism referred to in scientific explanation are not discovered initially by observation alone. They are first imagined and their attributes are derived by analogy with entities already known. A search for them is then undertaken. Observation, guided by these ideas, leads to the discovery of nonrandom patterns which then call for explanation. Their explanation is provided by the description of causal mechanisms, in general unobservable, whose functioning generates the observed pattern (Herbst, 1970; Polanyi, 1966). This process of *imagining, observing, and explaining* continues in the search for more fundamental relations. Psychotherapy research requires an emphasis on providing explanations by means of procedures which utilize both imagination and observation. Given that description and explanation, if they are not more basic to science (which they may be), are at least necessary and essential steps in a scientific investigation, it is crucial that more rigorous research to promote these goals be done and more sophisticated procedures be developed to promote this effort.

A Study of Phenomena

Discovery   The philosophy of science has taken as its central preoccupation how scientific theories are tested and verified, or how choices are made among competing theories. How theories are discovered in the first place has generally been neglected. Although in the past few years this position has been challenged (Hanson, 1971;

Kuhn, 1973; Lakatos, 1970), the "logic of a discovery" is still an underdeveloped domain.

The emphasis upon verification rather than discovery which is characteristic of contemporary psychotherapy research seems to be a distortion of the actual emphases in the practice of true science. Research in many of the physical sciences seems to devote much more time to seeking out possible regularities in phenomena than simply to proving that regularities they have noted are really there. Competition between theories, for example, the wave theory of light versus the particle theory, occurs only occasionally even in the physical sciences, yet our research strategies in psychotherapy are designed totally to deal with this contingency. Much more often, scientists are faced with a set of interesting phenomena and no theory that explains them in even a minimally acceptable way. In this more typical situation, the scientific task is not to verify or falsify theories, or to choose between alternative theories, but to discover candidate theories that might help explain the facts (Simon, 1973). Science is an endeavour of trying to figure out what phenomena are about.

All of this leads to the crucial question of what should be the focus of psychotherapy research. A predictive technology orients us toward counting frequencies of occurrences; but, if an important thrust of science is discovery and explanation, the subject matter of psychotherapy research must be *phenomena*. For scientists a phenomenon is a special event, possibly an unexpected or interesting event, whose cause is in question. What makes a phenomenon important for a scientist is that it is not yet *quite* intelligible but can possibly be mastered by taking a further intellectual step. Usually scientists have the beginnings of an idea about certain laws and mechanisms of nature and they are on the lookout for evidence that will show them how to further develop these ideas so they will more adequately fit the phenomena which which they are wrestling. The labeling of an event as a *phenomenon* is therefore an act of great significance and is the first step in a scientific enterprise. The description of phenomena in order to reveal underlying regularities then becomes a central task. Models of phenomena are then built and theory constructed to account for perceived regularities.

Phenomena therefore should be the primary data of psychotherapy research (Rice & Greenberg, 1984). Every step of scientific procedure from the initial identification of "phenomena" requiring explanation, to the decision that the explanation is satisfactory is, however, governed and directed by the fundamental concepts of the theory guiding the researcher. The problem is that scientists who accept different ideals and paradigms have no common theoretical terms in which to discuss their problems fruitfully. They will not even focus on the same phenomena since events which are phenomena from one point of view will be ignored from another viewpoint.

One of the realities in psychotherapy is that we are still in a preparadigmatic stage of development (Orlinsky & Howard, 1978) with no single governing paradigm, no common theory, and therefore no shared set of phenomena, no common descriptive language, and often rather different intellectual goals. If the investigators in the field began to work seriously at describing phenomena of interest and developing candidate theories to explain them we would begin to move closer to a goal of description and explanation and would be able to discuss these phenomena as a common set of reliable terms. The possibility of developing a valid descriptive methodology for psychotherapy research has not had sufficient attention. Fields such as astronomy, geology, botany, and even chemistry are based on a shared descriptive framework which took great time and effort to develop. This description eventually led to a theoretical framework that could be shared.

Descriptive Studies   Descriptive studies in psychotherapy have not been systematically and there has been a dearth of conceptually clarifying classification schemes. The construction of comprehensive classification schemes which describe and define different therapeutic phenomena would provide a basis for observationally based psychotherapy research. It is only through the study of *what is consensually agreed to actually occur* in therapy that we will advance our understanding of how change takes place.

In psychotherapy research the construction of a consensually reliable taxonomy of patient conditions or problem states and processes requiring change, plus an accompanying "dictionary" or "handbook" of therapeutic interventions applicable for each problem element, plus an interactional classification scheme, characterizing interpersonal qualities and interactional stances that two people can take *vis à vis* each other in therapy, would be invaluable in studying psychotherapeutic change. To these could be added the study of such person/situation individual difference variables that appeared important to different in-therapy performances from particular points of view. The individual difference variable could also be taken into account by taking measures of specific in-situation process measures for specific personality types, for example, measures of change in the specific resistances of obsessive clients or the specific behaviors by which an hysteric client leaks anxiety, rather than measures of change in resistance or anxiety in general.

This type of descriptive endeavour would result in a glossary of terms for classification of observed phenomena. Descriptive efforts of this nature would in and of itself be sufficient to elevate psychotherapy to a science with principles, theory, and predictions governing this descriptive domain. This type of descriptive enterprise would induce students and investigators to explore the actual phenomena and determine whether or not the phenomena operated as predicted by their theories. Effort at this level would yield much needed clarification of the phenomena of therapy. A distillation of those phenomena worthy of continued study would occur and continued investigation of these phenomena would produce empirically grounded candidate theories for inspection and testing.

Psychotherapy research can benefit greatly by paying much more attention to phenomena. Although social science methodology should not necessarily be based on the methodology of the physical sciences and should develop its own methodology, the study of psychotherapy is similar to the study of the natural events (especially in modern physics) in a number of ways. The phenomena of therapy are like those in physics, in that they are extremely complex and interactive, with layer upon layer of structure. Like the phenomena of physics they are best described multidimensionally by a large number of variables. As in physics, advances will be made only by an intensive analysis of the complex *phenomena* themselves. It is only once these phenomena have been reliably described and measured that the emphasis can shift from description to explanation of phenomena, model building, and finally prediction.

Mechanisms of Change   Exploration of mechanisms of change is of the greatest importance in psychotherapy process research, although exploration of mechanisms of symptom formation, pathology, and so on, are also important. It is the client who changes and the goal of psychotherapy research should be explaining how this change comes about. The phenomena of interest therefore, will be predominantly client change performances, although certain therapist phenomena will also be of interest. In observing client performances in therapy it becomes possible to identify specific types of in-therapy processes that lead to change. Processes that lead to change can be observed as they are taking place. This observation of in-therapy change is the closest one can get to observing therapeutic change. From close observation of phenomena the investigator can then infer what internal mechanisms appear to be operating. The advent of the "cognitive" revolution in psychology has made it possible for investigators from a variety of different theoretical orientations to discuss these observationally based changes in terms of the internal mental operation taking place and to do this in a common information processing language. A descriptively rigorous study of psychotherapy process will therefore enhance the search for mechanisms of change and the possibility of developing a universal language for describing previously disparate approaches to therapy.

In the study of therapeutic phenomena aimed at isolating mechanisms of change one does not have to be a master clinician to be able to see change or recognize relevant phenomena in psychotherapy. The attitudes that only the great clinicians "know" what is really going on in therapy only adds to the mystification of psychotherapy and its research. Phenomena important to change are easily observable by students of psychotherapy when they directly observe the process of psychotherapy. Concrete phenomena such as avoiding talking about something, anxious or hostile reactions to particular situations, increased self-disclosure, deeper experiencing, and even more abstract phenomena such as transference or insight can all be observed and studied. Some phenomena require special training to improve the reliability of their detection but others do not. None seem to demand extra special unique sensitivities or abilities.

A process research which focuses on therapeutic phenomena and concentrates its efforts on the description and explanation of what actually occurs in therapy offers a promise of returning pscyhotherapy research to its scientific roots. A new type of process research which actively focuses on providing an understanding of some of the specific mechanisms of change in different psychotherapeutic episodes could begin to help in the search for explanations of the active ingredients in therapeutic change.

Description in Psychotherapy Research

In studying psychotherapy, detailed description of a phenomenon and its context are essential in order to ensure that researchers can reliably identify the phenomenon across situations. The development of coding systems of varying complexity to describe and categorize different phenomena that therapists pay attention to in therapy (and in case conferences) represents an important step in transforming psychotherapy into a descriptive science.

Presumably, it has been the perceived difficulty of the task of describing in-situation performances that has deterred many researchers from attempting this undertaking. We would however be much further ahead in the 1980s, if this attempt had been made and either proved to be unworkable at this stage or provided us with a systematic framework. The advent of accessible videorecordings of therapy now makes this descriptive endeavour inevitable, its omission much more blatant, and its achievement more possible. Pioneers in the field are now able to provide us not only with their theories but with visual records of their practice. This gives us first-hand examples of what these therapists and their clients are actually doing in therapy. We are able to observe the actual practice and subject the process to detailed analysis. Therapist classification schemes (Hill, this volume; Pinsof, this volume; Stiles, this volume) have already been used to rate therapist behaviors and enable a differential description of different therapeutic styles. This is just a beginning. Only verbal content has so far been rated and only that of the therapist. Nonverbal coding schemes are being introduced (Gottman, Markman, & Notarius, 1977; Hill, Siegelman, Gronsky, Sturniolo, & Fretz, 1981) though they need to be further developed and new interactional and client coding systems need to be developed.

Multidimensional Coding

A number of recent process studies have shown the value of multiple measures of process in revealing patterns (Gottman *et al.*, 1977; Greenberg, 1980, 1983). What is needed now is a more complex multidimensional and context sensitive approach to process research in which a profile of measures is used to describe behaviors across time. The fallacy in studies which rate process on single variables in isolation from their context is that all client or therapist behaviors receiving the same rating on a single dimension (such as level of empathy, or self-disclosure) are assumed to have the same therapeutic significance and the same effect on outcome. An empathic reflection focused on a client's feeling of confusion, delivered in a "warm" voice by a therapist leaning toward the client, following a confrontation of a discrepancy in what the client is saying and doing, delivered in a supportive manner, by a therapist shifting position is a far more accurate description of a therapist intervention than a single dimensional description such as empathic reflection.

All performance, to be coded accurately, must be treated as multifaceted and must be described multidimensionally. As Pinsof (this volume) has pointed out, reconstructivity, the ability to reconstruct what has occurred is an important principle of coding. The greatest reconstructivity will be achieved by combining a number of different ratings of a performance. For example, even on existing systems in this book a therapist statement could be rated as a reflection (Hill, this volume; Stiles, this volume) and as being delivered in a warm voice (Rice & Kerr, this volume), focusing on the client's inner experience (Klein, Mathieu-Coughlin, & Kiesler, this volume). This degree of descriptive specificity greatly enhances our ability to depict what is actually occurring. Similarly a client statement could be rated as a reevaluation (Toukmanian, this volume), as a Level 5 on the Experiencing Scale (Klein, Mathieu, Kiesler, & Gendlin, 1969), and as being spoken in a focused voice (Rice & Kerr, this volume). Once some further nonverbal indices are able to be rated a type of description which matches the degree of complexity and differentiation of the human observer will have been obtained. At this point our coding systems should be able to pick up the subtle therapeutic cues that therapists respond to.

The first goal then of research should be the development of further systems to enable a more comprehensive description of therapeutic process. The more systems that exist, the more researchers will be able to provide profile scores describing in-therapy performance. And it is these comprehensive multidimensional descriptions of process that will enable reliable description of phenomena at a level of clinical relevance.

Level of Description

An issue which has troubled and perplexed process researchers has been the problem of level of description. This issue of level covers both the size of rating unit and possibly more important, the nature of the unit. In addressing the problem of choice of unit Kiesler (1973) concludes that "in process research there are as many different units as there are distinct constructs requiring separate measurement." In this view the unit chosen, be it word, phrase, utterance, problem area, initial period of therapy, and so on, will depend on the constructs of interest and on the questions being asked by a particular study.

An overall conceptualization of levels of units of study would help to coordinate all these different process measurements and would greatly enhance process research. Pearce and Cronen (1980) have recently proposed a hierarchical model of meaning which suggests that a complex network of relations exists among various hierarchical levels of meaning and that several levels of this hierarchy need to be described in order to understand the meaning of a communicative act. Drawing on their studies of the levels of this hierarchy, it appears that psychotherapy process research would benefit by using at least three or possibly four hierarchically arranged levels to describe process. The levels which appear to be most relevant are the levels of Content, Speech Act, Episode, and Relationship, arranged in the order given as shown in Figure 19-1. *Content* is possibly the most dispensable of the levels. It refers to the *actual content being talked about* without reference to the kind of message being used.

The level of *Speech Acts* represents *what one person is doing to another by saying or doing something*. This level refers to the pragmatics of discourse (Austin, 1962; Searles, 1969). Pragmatics here refers to the function or effect of messages in human affairs. Speech Acts according to these linguists involve such things as inform, advise, promise, threaten, insult, direct, and so on. A number of coding systems of this level are reported in the literature and in this book but more systems focusing on this level of client process are needed.

Episodes are "communicative routines which (the participants) view as distinct wholes, separate from other types of discourse, characterized by special rules of speed and nonverbal behavior and often distinguished by clearly recognizable opening or closing sequences" (Gumperz, 1972, p. 17). As Pearce and Cronen (1980) point out, recognition of Episodes has come independently from several lines of inquiry. Tedeschi, Heister, and Gahagan (1969) have shown that meaning of behaviors arise from patterns of sequential behavior rather than single acts. The Episode unit has been used in descriptive studies in anthropology, sociology, and social psychology. An example of this comes from the componential analysis of ethnoscience in which investigators attempt to locate and describe the Episodes by which a culture defines itself. In conversational analysis the concept of Episode has been used to describe how conversants fill in missing meanings by drawing on their knowledge of the structure of Episodes (Schank & Abelson, 1977). In this area an Episode is defined as a meaningful sequence of interaction that forms a unit.

The *Relationship level* describes the particular *qualities that people attribute to the ongoing relationship* which go beyond any particular content, act, or episode. These are un-

Figure 19-1   Hierarchical levels of process ratings.

Relationship
↑
Episode
↑
Speech Act
↑
Content

derstandings, usually implicit, that make up a collective sense of the attributes of the Relationship, the sense of "we." Relationship has been discussed in detail in the therapeutic literature and various measures of the relationship have been devised (Lambert, 1983). A construct currently generating a lot of interest at this level is that of the Working Alliance (Bordin, 1979) of which a number of new measures appear in this book.

This hierarchical model is suggested as a heuristic device for identifying levels of meaning for understanding communication in psychotherapy. Pearce and Cronen (1980) suggest that the different levels provide a context for each other and this helps define the meaning of any communication. The same act in a different context will have a different meaning. For example, the statement "you are beautiful" counts as a speech act of "compliment" in the episodic context of "dating" or in the relationship context of "being friends." However the episodic context "argument" or the relationship context "enemies" may lead to identifying the statement as "sarcastic insult." Similarly in psychotherapy a statement, "I feel like a small child" counts as "self-exploration" or Level 4 "experiencing" in the episodic context of working on resolving a specific problem or in the relationship context of a good Working Alliance. However in the Episode context of "discussing the relationship" or a Relationship context of "poor alliance" (in which goals and tasks were not agreed upon and there was no sense of working together) this statement counts as an "accusation" or "complaint."

Social meanings therefore are context dependent. With the perspective that systems of meaning are organized hierarchically, researchers will have to contend with the complexities of doing research on phenomena that are viewed as hierarchical systems. The following notation system devised by Pearce and Cronen (1980) helps depict this method of analysis.

Using the symbol ———➤ to mean "implies," and the symbol ——————| to mean "in the context of" one can represent hierarchically structured communicative acts as follows:

Relationship	Trusting
Episode	Play
Speech Act	Insult ———➤ Good humor

This means that the Speech Act of insult in the context of a play Episode in a safe Relationship implies good humor.

It appears from much psychotherapy and communication research that the Relationship level is very important in understanding messages between people. Psychotherapy process research must therefore pay attention to this level of process as a primary context for other levels. A suggested approach to the problem of choice of unit is to treat psychotherapeutic process as a three or four level phenomena (depending on the relevance of Context) in which Content and/or Speech Acts are given meaning by their Episode and Relationship contexts.

Rather than implyng that Content or Speech Acts are the fundamental data of process research to the exclusion of other variables such as stylistic, kinesic, or paralinguistic variables, the intent here is to suggest that context is of great importance in psychotherapy process research and should be incorporated in our research strategy. This framework of rating process, in the context of episodes, in the context of relationship defines a type of process research in which one uses a battery of process instruments of different types in order to ensure that one captures the three levels discussed above. This type of research would enable one to describe both client and therapist process in such a way as to allow the meaning of the act to be more clearly described.

What emerges from this discussion of description then is a type of multidimensional approach to process as shown in Figure 19-2, in which one uses a battery of instruments to describe both different levels in the hierarchy and a profile of different variables at the same level in order to capture different facets of the performance. How many profile variables are needed at each level would be determined in general by the research question being asked.

Explanation in Psychotherapy Research

Events

A major strategy shift is required in psychotherapy research in order to increase knowledge of what occurs in situations that produce therapeutic change. We need to explain the mechanisms of change. Theories of practice which are tied to the actual performance of therapist and client in therapy need to be spelled out and tested, in order to help explain how change actually occurs in specific therapeutic situations. With this goal in mind an events-based investigation of psychotherapy has been suggested (Rice & Greenberg, 1974, 1984). An event consists of a client in-therapy state or condition called a marker, the therapist response or intervention at this point, called the therapist operation, and the subsequent client response referred to as the client performance. These events can vary in size from a three statement client–therapist–client interchange, to an event occupying a complete session or possibly a few sessions. Events are best selected for study because they are regarded as potent change episodes or because they have relevance to understanding what occurs in therapy. Using this events framework, the investigator attempts to answer the following questions about potent events in therapy.

1. What client in-therapy performances suggest themselves as problem states requiring and ready for intervention?
2. What therapist operations are appropriate at these markers? What therapist performances will best facilitate a process of change?
3. What client performances following the markers lead to change? What are the aspects of the client performance that seem to carry the change process and what does the final in-therapy performance, that is, problem resolution, look like?

This set of questions brings the investigator much closer to studying what people actually do in therapy. Increased understanding of therapy will emerge by discovering

Figure 19-2   A scheme for comprehensive process analysis.

Coding Level	Dimensions
Relationship	Variable A, B, C
Episode	Variable X, Y, Z
Speech Act	Variable I, II, III

what interventions make what type of impact at what particular client "moments" in therapy. Research on this question in the descriptive framework of multilevel, multidimensional descriptions would allow a description of specific therapist activities (such as reflection or interpretation) in strategic Episode contexts (such as challenging irrational beliefs or reliving a critical incident from the past) in specific Relationship contexts (a good Working Alliance or therapist perceived as empathic). Similarly, client process could be coded in the context of higher-level descriptions. Attempts at this type of explanation-oriented events research leads to a number of different types of studies of psychotherapy.

First, differential intervention studies in which the focus is on in-therapy outcomes for particular problem states can provide evidence on what interventions are most effective at particular points in therapy. Second, studies which identify what problems clients actually discuss in therapy which suggest a readiness for intervention, will begin the delineation of different types of client problem states. This will lead, as was suggested earlier, to the construction of a typology of problem states or conditions that would help to organize the domain of client process. Third, studies of client resolution performance will lead to understanding how clients actually change in therapy. Single-change events can be studied to see what client statements relate to what preceding client and/or therapist statements. Similar events from different clients can be inspected for regularities in client performance across clients. Questions of what influence the client has on the therapist, and vice versa, can be answered. In these studies of resolution performances, both investigative single-case studies and group verification studies can be performed. This will lead to improved understanding and explanation of change both by intensive discovery-oriented investigation and by testing of hypotheses. Information concerning the effects on client process of specific therapist actions at particular moments will greatly improve our theory of practice and our ability to explain how change actually occurs.

In addition to the above three questions related to the process in specific change events, questions regarding individual differences and outcome are placed in a different perspective by the study of potent change events. Two further highly researchable questions present themselves:

1. What are the specific outcome effects of in-therapy resolutions? This leads to studies of specific session outcomes and their relationship to encurring change.
2. What client individual difference variables are related to the production of different types of in-therapy "markers" and to the different types of in-therapy performances and problem resolutions?

These questions would lead to a clearer understanding of what kind of in-therapy performances/outcomes lead to what type of extra-therapy changes, and would sharpen outcome research by providing a basis for the study of extra-therapy change. Rather than outcome being seen as a single unitary event, the process of daily and weekly impact of therapy would come into focus and studies of outcome as a process would result. In addition, a study of more person/situation intervention variables of significance to therapeutic change would emerge.

An events-based research would therefore pose a set of questions much closer to the practice of psychotherapy and would lead to research which could more directly affect practice. Once we knew what interventions were most appropriate for which client states and what resulting client performances led to problem resolution, we would be much closer to describing how change actually takes place in therapy. We would then be able to identify the active ingredients of change and explain the mechanisms that lead to this change.

Patterns

Initial attempts at explanation in psychotherapy process research generally sought associations between single variables in isolation from their contexts, such as the relationship between therapist activity and client productivity (Pope, 1977). This approach relies on a view of explanation in which, rather than interpretation of pattern, notions of prediction and entailment predominate, that is, if *x* then *y*. This framework for explanation emphasizes the sense of the term explanation in which something explains why some event is true or highly confirmed, *rather than explaining the nature or properties of the phenomena*. Explanation and prediction in this framework are therefore identical and differ only in the time at which the arguments are formulated—before or after the observation. These explanations are, therefore, casual explanations which settle, with evidence, the question of which of two prefigured explanations is a correct one, rather than providing something which was previously unknown.

It is rather the notion of explanation which involves revealing something previously unknown, namely, *the nature and structure of phenomena and their operation* in specific situations in which they manifest their properties, which is of interest to us. It is important to note that in this type of discovery-oriented explanation it is always possible and permissible to attempt a "higher-order" explanation (Hanson, 1971) which explains why the phenomenon has a particular nature or structure. It is not a requirement for an explanation that it be a "complete" one. Completeness is never possible (Kaplan, 1964).

A promising strategy which will aid improved explanation is the identification and discovery of *patterns* of in-session client and therapist behaviors (Gottman & Markman, 1978; Rice & Greenberg, 1984). Data require interpretation in order for them to have meaning and explanatory significance. Identification of pattern in the data is a step on the path toward attributing, to the data, meanings which have a bearing on reality (Polanyi, 1958). Appearance of a pattern in the data does not yet provide an explanation, but the rigorous identification of the occurrence of the pattern is an aid to comprehension and explanation by providing observable properties which require explanations. *Interpretation* is inherent in explanation. Different investigators may perceive the same pattern without finding the same meaning in the pattern. This is well illustrated in interpretation of X-rays or microbiology slides. First one needs skills to even see the patterns. Second, the pattern has particular meanings to the trained observer. Explanation of a pattern is therefore arrived at by a human act of interpretation in which the observed pattern and the constructed meaning are used to help in the discovery of new features of reality.

Clearly process varies over time and different processes have different meanings in different in-session contexts. Aggregating processes, as though all processes during sessions or across therapy are the same, perpetuates a uniformity myth from which psychotherapy research must escape. Particular processes occur at different times in therapy and different meanings in different contexts. It is more the occurrence of a particular *pattern* of variables than their simple presence or frequency of occurrence that indicates the therapeutic significance of what is occurring in therapy. Typically, however, frequency data have been used as the basis of process research. Percentage of occurrence of the number of statements in a particular category in relation to total number of statements has been the summary figure (e.g., percentage of interpretations, head nods, etc.). The assumption is that all behaviors are equivalent regardless of context, timing, appropriateness, and quality. Clearly the timing, context, and pattern of interpretations or confrontations is of much greater significance than their frequency.

In studying patterns of client behavior, the major strategy is one of looking for covarying relationships over time between variables of the same level of description. In addition, this pattern may need to be viewed as being of particular significance in a particular higher-level context. For example, a series of covarying indices at the level of Speech Acts and observable stylistic indicators such as *client statement of problem and a request for help*, followed by a differentiation of *meaning with newly expressed feeling*, and all this in the context of an Episode of "seeking insight" (Elliott, 1984) would begin to describe some steps in the process. It is the ability to detect these patterns which distinguishes the sensitive clinician. Knowledge of the patterns provide clinicians with ideas of what they are aiming to facilitate.

An example of covariations over time, at the episode level, has been described by Horowitz (1979). His group tracks, over time, the relationship between states of mind such as "hurt," "superficial," "angry and withdrawn," and "hurt but working" states, and so on. The sequencing of these states during early or late sessions can be used to show change and can be investigated in order to understand how this change took place. Here we have sequences, at the episodic level, which then need to be understood in the context of higher-order relationship variables.

What is being suggested then is that it is the pattern of occurrence and nonoccurrence of particular performance which reveals what is transpiring in the process of change. One instance of "hurt but working" or "differentiation with a pondering quality" at a crucial point in an exploratory sequence may far outweigh the significance of its rate of occurrence. In addition, the tracking of observable variables over time reveals patterns which are there in the data, which clinicians respond to in doing therapy, and which most importantly serve to explicate what is occurring in the process of change. Once one knows the pattern that occurs it is possible to more easily facilitate it as well as study how to enhance the facilitation process.

Three Research Approaches

Performance Analysis   Rice and Greenberg (1984) have suggested that certain core assumptions seem to underlie approaches which use an intensive analysis of process to find patterns and explain mechanisms of change in therapy. Two of the major assumptions are (1) the targeting of recurrent phenomena, and (2) the use of implicit theory to guide observation. The goal of pattern identification and the consequent rejection of aggregate external variable designs, which do not attend to the internal pattern of variables, need not leave researchers in the position of dealing with an infinite series of idiosyncratic interchanges. Clearly there are episodes or events in therapy that are similar to each other and have some clearly identifiable structural similarities. They recur sufficiently often within and across clients to merit intensive investigation.

The first strategy decision in an explanation-oriented investigation of this type is to select particular episodes for study rather than sampling randomly. There are many different ways in which such recurring events could be selected. Some of the most promising phenomena to select for study are points in the process at which some particular kind of client change is taking place. These are the points about which thoughtful therapists ponder and develop hypothesess; the points at which theoretical issues often come into focus.

Using a task analytic approach (Greenberg, 1984b) the investigator selects a particular kind of recurring event for intensive analysis in which the client is working on solving an affective task such as conflict. These recurring tasks are selected on the basis of both theory and observation. An important aspect of this approach is that a general theory of therapy and personality change often informs one's thinking about the phenomena and guides one's selection of phenomena. The rationalist recognition of the theory-laden nature of observation is built in. Rather than attempts being made to expunge the theory bias of the observer, the investigator attempts to explicate the cognitive map of the observer, that is, the expert clinician, in order to make theoretical assumptions available, to guide the investigation. In this approach, the cognitive map of the observer serves as part of the data of science.

In a task analysis of therapeutic events, a hypothetical *idealized* client performance, which represents the clinician's best understanding of how resolution takes place, is compared with descriptions of *actual* client resolution performances from a series of intensive single-case analyses. This is done in an iterative manner, moving back and forth between idealized and actual performances until a refined proposed model of a resolution performance is built. This postdictive, discovery-oriented, aspect of the approach involves a process of moving from the clinical/theoretical expectations to observation and back again until the investigator is satisfied that the phenomena at hand have been described. The model constructed by this method is then subjected to appropriate verification procedures, such as relating these performances to outcome. This iterative procedure of comparing actual and possible performances represents a rigorous form of inductive clinical theorizing which results in the construction of a model in terms which can be tested by process measurement.

New information is generated at a number of levels in this approach. First, the comparison of actual performances illuminates where one's ideas were incorrect and provides information on new phenomena and patterns. This is where observation of actual performance helps to confront theoretical preconceptions. Secondly, the approach is truly constructive in the domain of measurement (Coombs, Dawes, & Tversky, 1970) for one is continually required to develop or refine one's measurement system based on what one finds. Measurement has to be developed to initially capture what one thinks might be there (i.e., required by one's rational model) but then needs to be refined to capture what one actually finds (i.e., required by one's empirical model) until one is able to depict what is really there. The observation of actual performance highlights what our measurement systems are missing. This approach is highly similar to a conjoint measurement approach suggested by Krantz & Tversky (1971), and reflects some of the actual processes of measurement construction in psychotherapy research (Greenberg, 1975).

Using this task analytic approach to the study of therapeutic events, a model of the steps of intrapsychic conflict resolution have been constructed (Greenberg, 1984a) as well as a model of the resolution of problematic reactions (Rice, 1984). In a task analysis of a number of conflict resolution events using two-chair dialogue, Greenberg (1975, 1980, 1983, 1984a) found, for each side of the conflict, a characteristic pattern of voice quality, depth of experiencing, and dominance and affiliation behaviors were associated with resolution. It appeared that an essential aspect of resolution was the change in a previously externally focused, harsh critic, to a more internally focused affiliative stance.

Horowitz and coworkers (Horowitz, 1979; Horowitz, Marmar, & Wilner, 1979), using a method called configurational analysis, have been studying in-therapy performance by observing patient states and state transitions. In this method the problem states of a person are carefully described in terms of behavior and reported subjective experiences and are then distinguished from other states both before, during, and after therapy. In addition to identification of states, this configurational analysis involves the description from two additional points of view labeled "Relationship" and "Information Processing." "Relationship" refers to an analysis of the key images of self and other which underlie and relate to states. Here the self and object role attributes and role relationships that characterize each state are listed. "Information Processing" refers to how data on self, other, and environment are processed by the person and involves describing defenses and style of processing. States and state transitions can then be related to in-therapy events. For example, Horowitz (1979) showed that marked change in the pattern of states, relationship, and information processing occurred over time in a brief therapy of a single client and related the change to developments in the Therapeutic Alliance.

In another rational–empiricist analysis of performance patterns in therapy, the first 100 hours of a psychoanalytic treatment of a woman whose presenting complaint was sexual frigidity were studied (Horowitz, Sampson, Siegelman, Weiss, & Goodfriend, 1978). The sequence of change in two classes of behavior, cohesive (closeness) and dispersal (fighting) behaviors, were tracked. It was shown that both these classes of behavior decreased over the therapy but that progress in dispersal-type behaviors preceded progress in cohesive-type behaviors. It was also shown that complaints of the form of "I can't do something" or "I have to do something" declined in frequency during treatment.

These intensive studies of process indicate how, *as one gets closer to the data and identifies patterns, one gets closer to possible explanation of mechanism of change.* Once one has a refined model of change, the possibility exists of testing components of the model in a manner which will truly enhance our understanding of how change takes place in psychotherapy. These approaches are all based on some form of discovery of patterns of process variables and their rigorous identification. In addition, these performance analysis methods all emphasize empirically based theory construction and explanation of mechanisms of change.

Empirical Pattern Identification　A more purely empirical approach to pattern identification utilizes pattern analysis or sequential analysis methods such as Markov chain analysis, lag sequential analysis, and uncertainty analysis (Sackett, 1978; Garner, 1962; Attneave, 1959). In this approach statistical methods are used to find sequences, usually probabilistic sequences, collapsing the occurrence of sequences over time to provide an overall picture of what occurs in a session. Although this approach, because of its aggregation of data, does not provide an opportunity for isolating the unique phenomena that represent change, that is, occurrence of a unique pattern, it is a useful one for moving beyond frequency counts of variables in isolation, toward identification of sequential dependencies among a number of variables.

Sequential analysis utilizes conditional probabilities (the probability of x occurring given y has occurred) to describe the effects of antecedents on consequents. In psychotherapy research, however, analysis of two responses in a sequence rarely represents a meaningful interaction sequence. Two-step contingencies, say a client statement followed by a therapist statement or vice versa, may not be an ideal unit for investigation of all therapeutic change. Longer sequences need to be considered. The difficulty in analyzing longer sequences by simple conditional probabilities is the increasing paucity of data points that occurs by combining events together. Increasing the chain to include three events (the probability of z following x, given y has occurred) leads to a sizable increase in sampling error, since the N at each data point decreases with the addition of each new step in the sequence.

One proposed solution to this problem is the use of lagged sequential analysis, where responses are considered in relation to antecedents more than one step back in time, *irrespective of what happens in between*. As Revenstorf, Hahlweg, Schindler, and Vogel (1984) have pointed out, the problem with this approach is that it does not really consider chains of behavior but events which are simply more distant from the initial antecedents. Some authors infer characteristics of behavior sequences from these lagged probabilities (Gottman & Bakeman, 1979; Patterson & Moore, 1979). This seems to neglect what is occurring in the time between the antecedent and the lagged response.

Pattern analysis of this type is not as fully a discovery oriented approach, as is the "rational–empiricist" approach. One can discover dependencies only in the behaviors captured by the coding systems one starts with. There is no possibility of refining or modifying one's category systems as one goes along. Investigators can, however, discover patterns among selected variables and once these patterns have been identified, further variables for coding might be suggested by the understanding provided by the revealed patterns.

In an empirical pattern analysis of actual performances, Gottman and colleagues (Gottman, 1979; Gottman, Markman, & Notarius, 1977) showed that nonclinic couples differed from clinic couples in the pattern of their communication on problem-solving tasks. Analyses of the sequential interaction patterns using Markov chain analysis, revealed that clinic couples entered into a "cross-complaining" loop at the beginning of a discussion and were subsequently likely to enter into a negative exchange. A negative exchange involved "mindreading," with negative affect, by one partner which was taken as a blaming criticism by the other partner, which was then refuted with negative affect. On the other hand nonclinic couples were likely to begin the discussion with a validation sequence characterized by agreement with neutral affect. They also avoided negative exchanges and ended the discussion with a contract sequence, characterized by agreement interspersed with problem-solving proposals. Gottman *et al.* (1977) stress that the two groups differ in pattern, "they do not simply differ in response frequencies but they traverse essentially different terrains in their interaction."

Theory Testing   A third type of approach to explanation is one in which one intensively analyzes process patterns at specific points in therapy in order to explicitly test theoretically generated hypotheses. This is a theory testing approach, as opposed to the two preceding approaches, which were theory construction approaches. This approach is, however, an approach to testing hypotheses in which highly specified properties that closely describe *observable phenomena* are being explored in order to enhance *explanation* of underlying mechanisms. This approach involves those more rare and elegant studies in the true spirit of the hypothetico-deductive model of science in which competing theories are contrasted by subjecting theoretically derived hypothesis to a critical test. What is important here is that the hypotheses are as closely and carefully linked to theory as possible and the measurements of the dependent and independent variables are clear, precise, and possess face validity in terms of the theoretical propositions being tested. The best example of an intensive approach to theory testing comes from the work of the Mount Zion group reported in this book (Sampson & Weiss, this volume). They propose alternative hypotheses about the specific effects of specific interventions at particular client moments are tested as a means of evaluating theoretical propositions. They show, for example, that contrary to expectation of classical psychoanalytic theory, frustration of a transference demand does not lead to increased anxiety and regression but rather to greater boldness in exploration and progress. This is more consistent with their theory of the passing of an unconscious test than the attempt to seek gratification of fixated impulses. This type of intensive analysis of process in highly specified contexts illuminates the path for improving the understanding and explanation of therapeutic phenomena by theory testing.

Luborsky (1967) developed the symptom context method in which the in-session context of recurring behaviors or symptoms is examined to test theoretical propositions. Critical segments in which a recurrent symptom appears such as momentary forgetting, a headache, or stomach pain (Luborsky & Auerbach, 1969) are matched with segments of therapy from the same patient in which the critical event did not occur. The two sets of events are then rated to see on which variables the context of the symptoms differ. In work on momentary forgetting 37 pairs of critical and control segments were rated on 12 categories. Luborsky (1978) found that some categories that discriminated critical from control segments were: new attitude or behavior, guilt, and feeling of lack of control. Another comparison was tried on a symptom that did not require a self-report as did those above. Petit-mal epileptic attacks signaled by an EEG wave were studied as the symptom of interest. For a single patient in psychotherapy significant differences were found for critical and control segments especially on helplessness and related variables. Five intensive single-case analyses of different symptoms have shown that patient helplessness, considered central by Freud in his theory of symptom formation, was discriminating (Luborsky, 1978). A factor of crucial importance in this work is the selection of categories for rating contexts, for it is these categories that will ultimately determine the findings. This method, which has been used primarily for understanding conditions leading to symptom formation, can be applied to any recurrent behavior of therapists or clients in therapy to understand the condition leading to this behavior. This method has the capacity for both theory construction, identifying what patterns actually occur, and theory testing, confirming whether particular theoretically expected patterns distinguish critical and control segments.

Finally, a further avenue for theory testing is opened by the discovery and identification of significant patterns of process variables. Once certain patterned behaviors, related to a particular phenomena, have been identified, these configurations can be used as dependent variables to more accurately track what is occurring in the therapeutic process. They can be used to test the effects of interventions or to test hypothesized sequences of client process related to change or dysfunction. Both Horowitz and coworkers and Luborsky and coworkers have used their identification of patterns of client process to begin testing certain analytic propositions relating to the effect of transference interpretations and the process related to onset of symptoms.

Relevance of These Approaches

All of these studies of intrapsychic processes have relied on precise descriptions of verbal and nonverbal behaviors and analyzed them with regard to the context in which they occurred, not by aggregate analyses but by a rigorous intensive structural analysis (Greenberg, 1982) in which elements were identified and the rules governing the relationship of these elements were statistically demonstrated. Process research of this type which identifies the patterned characteristics of successful in-therapy performances holds promise for increasing our understanding of mechanisms of client change in psychotherapy. More studies of the type described above, which compare the performance of people engaged in therapeutic change episodes to the performance of others who are less successful in the episode under study, will greatly enhance the explanatory power of research findings. This type of study of the characteristics of in-session performances that lead to change, will, by providing descriptions of how "things are" in successful performances, also provide clinicians with evidence of how things "ought to be" with their clients. This provision of normative standards based on the empirical description of patterns of effective functioning can provide a factual base to guide the action of practitioners.

Validity of Models

In order to increase understanding of what is occurring in psychotherapy, we have argued that it is essential to investigate phenomena in their contexts and to identify the occurrences of patterns of variables that describe the phenomena. The next step essential to research programs oriented toward explanation is demonstration of the validity of the models developed by these methods. If the patterns of variables which describe the in-therapy change phenomena are found to correlate with therapeutic outcome, both short-term specific outcomes and long-term global outcomes, the validity of the models will be enhanced. In order to validate explanatory models of change it is therefore necessary to *relate in-session process to extra-therapy outcome*.

This brings into focus the nature of the relationship between process and outcome researchers which has often been conflictual rather than supportive. As Kiesler (1971) has noted, "Process research begins with the in-the-interview behavior of the patient; outcome investigation begins with his outside the interview improvement. The crucial point is that for either to be maximally useful, the other focus or perspective must be considered" (p. 46). It is necessary for investigators to combine these perspectives and to relate in-therapy variables to extra-therapy variables. This synthesis of the descriptive and explanatory, and the predictive aspects of psychotherapy research, in studies which relate process to outcome, represents an important direction for process research.

Relating Process to Outcome

In the development of psychotherapy research, investigators, concerned with demonstrating the efficacy of psychotherapy, placed an emphasis on evaluation or prediction; and, this influenced the field so significantly that the necessary systematic description and subsequent explanation of the many phenomena observed by therapists to be important to change did not take place. In the desire to demonstrate efficacy, outcome research prevailed and process research of phenomena of interest fell into the background. It is becoming increasingly apparent that a new style of research which integrates both process and outcome must be developed. Outcome research, without a rigorous study of the process associated with outcomes, is inadequate. Outcome research alone misses fundamental scientific issues such as providing for explanation of phenomena. In addition existing outcome research unaided by process description has neglected certain control issues and has therefore been unable to specify what procedures and processes are causally connected to outcome.

Outcome studies over the last decade have tended to ask whether a particular treatment is effective for a specified population. In these studies however the various components and the essential ingredients of the treatment were not clearly specified and have remained unclear. Even if an effect were found in these studies there is no scientific implication, no clear guide for explanation, for it is inherently unclear what in the complex treatment produced the effect. Something was effective; but without a clear theoretical underpinning of how the treatment worked, without a testing of specified variables and known processes, and without the establishment of a clear relationship between the active ingredients of the treatment and specific effects, we do not have any scientific knowledge about psychotherapy.

Process and outcome can be related in both naturalistic, correlational designs, and in experimental designs in which the presence of the process under study is related to outcome. Studies that relate process to outcome enhance our ability to both explain and predict treatment effects. A study of the relationship between the three variables therapist intervention (T), client process (C), and outcome (O), however, poses a difficult "three-variable" problem for traditional experimental designs. Although it is possible to study the relationship between any two in both correlational and experimental designs, the task of relating all three at the same time is difficult. As was attempted in the studies of Rogerian variables, relationships were sought between therapist level of empathy (T) and outcome(O) both correlationally and then in experimental designs attempting to show causal relationships. Similarly, attempts were made to relate empathy to depth of experiencing and exploration (C), and finally the most difficult task of relating these client process variables to outcome was also attempted.

When links between T, C, and O can be shown, between two variables at a time, this procedure still leaves certain questions unanswered, the major question being that unless T is shown to cause C and cause O at the same time, the nature of the *direction* of the causal relationship between T and C always remains in doubt and one never knows whether it is T or C which leads to O. The strongest causal design therefore would experimentally compare two therapist interventions T_1 and T_2 and attempt to show they produced differential processes C_1 and C_2 and differential outcomes O_1 and O_2. The possibility of this type of differential process/outcome design at the level of complex treatment approaches appears beyond the capabilities of current research procedures mainly because of our lack of adequately specific instruments with which to measure the *interventions and processes*. The lack of clear explanations of mechanisms of change in different therapies leaves us with fuzzy notions of what we should be attempting to measure. This problem would be solved by the type of task analysis and structural modeling suggested earlier. A more circumscribed type of study relating T, C, and O in which more specific interventions at specific times in therapy and their effect on specific processes and outcomes are compared, seems to be promising (Greenberg & Rice, 1981; Greenberg & Dompierre, 1981), but still leaves unanswered the question of how to compare broader and more complex treatments over the course of a complete therapy.

Therapist Manuals

Recently the notion of providing training and treatment *manuals* to describe the treatment more clearly has evoked a lot of interest. It is clear that manual-described treatments *combined with checks that the treatments were implemented* will provide greater control over the nature of the treatment actually delivered and will allow specification of what the independent variable is, in experimental studies of treatment effect.

Although attempts to describe therapies by manuals (Luborsky, Woody, McLellan, O'Brian, & Rosenzweig, 1982; DeRubeis, Hollon, Evans, & Bernis, 1982) show some possibility of being able to discriminate among different approach, the real task, of describing what is actually occurring in a particular therapy, remains unaddressed by manual-guided research. Manuals do not provide sufficient control of the variables affecting treatment delivery nor do they allow any statement as to the nature of the active ingredients of the treatment. Although the manuals specify the components, they do not sequence or prioritize these components. Nor do they provide adequate descriptions of the complex, multidimensional variables involved in the therapist behaviors which are needed to describe not only the type but also the manner and the quality of the behaviors. Even designs involving ideal manuals with detailed intervention rules do not provide sufficient control unless there is a detailed check that the components were administered as specified in the manual.

Recently, Schaffer (1982) emphasized the importance of separating therapist variables into at least three separate dimensions. These dimensions include therapist tactic, skill, and manner. He suggests that a productive strategy for future research would involve clearly specifying and measuring each of these dimensions. First, the tactic or type of intervention would be identified. Next, the researcher would estimate both the level of competence illustrated in carrying out this tactic and the manner in which the therapist related to the patient during this interchange. Manuals, in order to control some of the variability in treatment delivery, would at least need to specify manner and skill in addition to tactic.

The current recognition of the greater need for descriptive specificity in the form of therapist manuals still does not address the need for the description and explanation of phenomena and processes of change. The manuals are being used in the spirit of the experimental designs and evaluations of which they are part. These manuals are being used as "implementation checks" rather than as systematic descriptions of the occurrence of change phenomena. They will improve group contrast designs by defining more clearly the treatments being contrasted and by describing and specifying some of the variables under study. The use of these manuals, although they may improve experimental control by checking that something is being done, add little to the aim of relating process to outcome, or to the explanation of mechanisms of change. A valid cause–effect relationship will be demonstrated only with a process analysis which adequately describes what actually occurred in the therapy and relates this therapeutic treatment to outcome. Even if therapies based on manuals are shown to be effective, we still will not know which therapist interventions led to change.

Outcome

Research relating process to outcome, in addition to specifying process in greater detail will need to answer a number of questions concerning the specificity, time of application, and sequencing of outcome measures. Ideally, a study relating process to outcome would specify the treatment intervention and the client process related to outcome and would link in-therapy change to specific extra-therapy change at a session-by-session level. These sessional outcomes in turn would be linked to overall treatment outcome. It is important, in order to truly understand both the process and outcome of psychotherapy, to focus not only on the complex whole treatment but also on the smaller units which go up to make the whole treatment. In the desire to evaluate the efficacy of psychotherapy we often overlook the fact that we possess little knowledge of the effects on each other of the smaller component parts that constitute the total complex treatment. Three smaller units that suggest themselves as natural units of study are the "change event" (Rice & Greenberg, 1984), the "session" (Orlinsky & Howard, this volume; Stiles, this volume) and the "phase" of treatment (McCullough, 1979). By focusing on these smaller units a number of interesting research questions arise concerning issues such as:

1. The nature of the relationship between "general factors" such as empathy, warmth, bond, rapport, and so on, and more "specific" technical aspects of the treatment in these smaller units, that is, differences between an interpretation in the context of different relationships or delivered in a different manner.
2. The relationship of immediate session outcome to duration over the week and to reports before the next session—using daily ratings, weekly goals, and so on.
3. The relationship of intermediate outcomes to final treatment outcomes plus questions concerning the process of outcome.

These more specific questions relating process to outcome will provide a detailed understanding of how change takes place. Studies relating general process variables to overall outcomes in large group designs will, in contrast to the detailed studies suggested above, provide a perspective on some important pantheoretical processes which are related to outcome, for example, client involvement, hope and degree of collaboration or bond between client and therapist, and so on. It is also important to search for relationships between specific processes and specific outcomes. This is where the "general" versus "specific" factors issue affects process research. Research which relates process to outcome across clients and therapies will probably eventually result in the specification of general process variables which cut across modalities and relate to aspects of the enduring effectiveness of therapy. These would be the processes underlying the general principles of therapy. In addition to these general factors, there exists a potential for describing specific processes involved in different change events and relating these to specific outcomes. Investigation of both general and specific processes will provide the fullest picture of all the processes in therapy that relate to outcome.

Intensive Analysis

The intensive analysis of a few single cases of successful whole therapies, potent change episodes, and moments of change is probably the method of choice for those who want to tackle questions about specific mechanisms of change. It is through the intensive analysis of process that one comes face to face with what is occurring in psychotherapy and with the process of change (Greenberg, 1980; Hill, Carter, & O'Farrel, 1983; Strupp, 1980a, b, & c). It has long been one of the anomalies of psychotherapy research that change in process has not been recognized or utilized as a viable measure of change. It is probably true that it will only be when we can relate change in in-session process to immediate postsession outcome and this in turn to longer-term outcome that we will be in a position to truly explain the process of change.

In intensive analysis one is able to observe changes and differences in verbal and nonverbal processes which the client uses to express thoughts, feelings, and actions.

These observable client processes are the primary targets of therapy, and change in these should be guides to therapeutic behavior. With a developed set of descriptive process systems, psychological processes can be measured in a systematic fashion and this will allow for investigatory research which will provide explanations of how change occurs.

Intensive analysis can be used to investigate mechanisms of change in a number of different ways. One manner which has already been suggested is to study the effect of specific interventions at specific points in client performance, by comparing instances at which one implements the intervention with times when one does not. The means by which client process is modified by the interventions is studied intensively in order to reveal what is occurring in this change process.

Another method is to compare instances in which change took place with those in which it did not, either over the total therapy (Strupp, 1980a, 1980b, 1980c), or over particular sessions or episodes and to identify distinguishing characteristics of successful and unsuccessful performances. This is a type of task analysis. The important issue here is that intensive analysis leads to the possibility of discerning patterns in their own context. It allows more adequate description of what occurs between client and therapist in therapy and improved understanding of what processes are related to positive and negative outcomes in this client.

The researcher, by intensively analyzing recurring instances in addition to closely observing the phenomenon, can adopt a truly investigative approach which is a process in itself (Rice & Greenberg, 1984). One starts with an initial tentative hypothesis and looks closely at the data in the first case. This results in a revision, reformulation, or refining of the hypothesis which is then tested against new cases which represent both positive and negative instances of the phenomena. The investigation is therefore an iterative process of formulation and testing of hypothesis on a series of new cases until the investigator arrives at an understanding of the phenomena. This is somewhat similar to the formative evaluations being suggested in evaluation research. Rather than jumping into a large-scale study at the start of a research program, from which one gleans only information about group averages and about overall effects, the investigator can, by intensive analysis, discern from the beginning if something worth studying is occurring and what this "something" is. This requires not only being close to the phenomena and identifying potent variables by intensive observation of the actual situation but generating and testing hypotheses on each new case. Once this has been done and one has improved one's understanding of the situation so as to be able to enhance the possibility, demonstrating what is occurring, only then does one move to verifying that these potent factors generalize across situations.

Once one has built a model of what is occurring in these situations, one determines to what extent the findings on the original cases are confirmed in similar instances or in similar individuals. Thus replication becomes an essential requirement of intensive analysis. The issue is not so much whether one uses replicated single-case studies or group studies to verify findings, but rather that intensive analysis allows for the identification of much more complex relationships and patterns of variables related to change. This occurs both because one is closer to the data and because one is looking at a large number of variables in one or a few cases rather than a few variables in a large number of individuals. If one discovers a possibly significant pattern then it is checked out further by whatever means are appropriate. It is the opportunity of identifying patterns afforded by intensive analysis which is its strength and makes it a valuable approach in an explanation-oriented science.

Once one enters the domain of intensive analysis all sorts of benefits arise from the specificity of description. Those of most immediate benefit are the use of individualized repeated outcome measures and the much more detailed description of conditions under which particular treatments work. A promising new approach to obtaining individualized outcome measures involves individualized diagnostic assessment, prior to treatment, of clients core conflicts or dynamic issues which require change, and specification of predicted indices of improvement based on these diagnostic assessments (Malan, 1976). Using this approach changes in individualized, complex dynamics which would be expected to occur in a particular therapy can be evoked. This is a vast improvement over the measurement of change on general standardized instrument which may miss the issues on which clients work and change in their therapy.

In addition to encouraging the tracking of individual outcomes, intensive analysis can be used to deal with the problem of individual differences in response to treatment by different clients. In single-case studies, the population to which the study refers is so well specified (initially the single case) that tests of hypotheses concerning treatment effects in relation to individual difference variables can be made directly. The variation among individuals in responses to treatment is an essential reason for studying processes on a single-case basis. Until one can show with some degree of certainty that the differences in responses among people to treatment are due to experimental error (whatever that might be) one should not combine the data from a number of individuals. Each case should be studied individually until descriptions and explanations of behavior of a sufficiently high degree of fidelity are obtained to allow a combination of data which will not obscure essential phenomena or patterns in the data.

Although single-case studies are important in intensive analysis, group studies can play a role in the intensive analysis endeavour by providing clues for what to study more intensively. Group studies, which relate process to outcome, can be seen as a means of discovering phenomena worthy of more intensive study. Group comparison studies, rather than focusing solely on the differential efficacy question of ''what treatment for whom by whom and to what end,'' can attempt to identify processes which on the average seem to correlate with change. The approach here is one of first establishing that some treatment is differentially effective and then looking for the processes induced by this treatment which seem related to some type of change. This would mean that large-scale group studies relating process to outcome could be a source of phenomena in need of explanation. In this approach, change phenomena are identified empirically by using measures of outcome as independent variables in a design in which good and poor outcome cases are studied by the methods of intensive pattern analysis discussed above. This type of study could be done by first administering a large number of existing coding schemes and identifying general processes which correlate with change by checking hunches about particular processes. Specific instances in which active change processes occurred would be isolated and investigated more intensively, in order to discover in greater detail the mechanisms involved in these processes. Once the change processes have been identified the investigator can then proceed to study what therapist interventions brought about these processes. This would eventually provide sufficient information for controlled experimental studies of the effects of therapist interventions (T) on client process (C) and outcome (O).

Conclusion

Process research therefore, is best concerned with describing, explaining, and predicting therapeutic change. Although certain internal aspects of the ongoing process of therapy may be worthy of study for particular purposes, it is the investigation of the *process of change* which, at this time, will provide the greatest yield in psychotherapy research. With this view on the importance of studying the process of therapuetic change, the dichotomy between outcome research and process research breaks down; both process measures and measures of change are necessary in any study and can only be defined as either process or outcome, relative to each other. Some in-session "process" measures may be viewed as interim measures of outcome, whereas some postsession "outcome" measures may be viewed as process measures in studies of the process of change over time. In measuring extra-therapy change, we should ensure that sessional and weekly changes, the "small" outcomes of therapy, are collected as well as the final outcomes at termination and follow-up.

With the process of change as the phenomenon under study, recurring significant change events in the session become an important focus. Taxonomies of change events need to be developed and minitheories explaining the specific change processes in these events constructed. To do this, in-session processes should be studied in context, in a multidimensional, multilevel fashion. In addition to understanding specific change processes, further work on general processes of the change are needed to help us understand processes that are helpful across all therapies. When the general and specific process of in-session change can be reliably described in a detailed fashion, we will be in a good position to demonstrate relationships between in-session processes and extra-therapy outcomes.

In terms of overall approach, it appears that both quantitative verification-oriented study and more open, qualitative, discovery-oriented study is required to promote knowledge. Recognition by an observer, in a relatively open inquiry, of patterns, consistencies, and covariations without previously rigorously specifying what the elements or variables will be, allows for discovery of important phenomena. This is followed by hypothesizing relationships among variables and seeking to support or reject anticipated patterns, contingencies, or covariations. To conduct this type of combined study, the open discovery-oriented aspect which requires observation and interpretation requires astute observers of human performance who can differentiate relevant patterns. The latter, more closed, verification-oriented studies require more sophisticated logical thinking concerning design and analyses and rigorous data analysts. If either of these approaches or skills is given predominance, as the only right way, it will be the advancement of the scientific knowledge of psychotherapy which will suffer.

References

Attneave, F. *Applications of information theory to psychology.* New York: Holt, Rinehart & Winston, 1959.
Austin, J. L. *How to do things in words.* New York: Oxford, 1962.
Bhaskar, R. *The possibility of naturalism.* Atlantic Highlands, N.J.: Hamanities Press, 1979.
Bergin, A., & Strupp, H. *Changing frontiers in the science of psychotherapy.* Hawthorne, NY: Aldine, 1972.
Bordin, E. S. The generalizability of the psychoanalytic concept of the working alliance. *Psychotherapy: Theory, Research & Practice,* 1979, 16, 252–259.
Brown, H. *Perception theory & committment.* Chicago: Chicago University Press, 1977.
Coombs, C., Dawes, R., & Tversky, A. *Mathematical psychology.* Englewood Cliffs, N.J.: Prentice-Hall, 1970.
DeRubeis, R., Hollon, S., Evans, M., & Bemis, K. Can psychotherapies for depression be discriminated? A systematic investigation of cognitive therapy & interpersonal therapy. *Journal of Consulting & Clinical Psychology,* 1982, 50, 744–756.
Elliott, R. A discovery-oriented approach to significant events in psychotherapy: Interpersonal

Process Recall and Comprehensive Process Analysis. In L. Rice & L. Greenberg (Eds.), *Patterns of Change. Intensive analysis of psychotherapy process.* New York: Guilford Press, 1984.

Feigl, H. Empiricism at bay?: Revisions and a new defense. In R. S. Cohen & M. W. Wartofsky (Eds.), *Methodological & historical essays in the natural and social sciences.* Boston: D. Reidel Publishing Co., 1973.

Feyerabend, P. K. *Against Method.* London: NLB, 1975.

Frank, J. The present status of outcome studies. *Journal of Consulting and Clinical Psychology,* 1979, 47, 310–317.

Garner, W. *Uncertainty & structure as psychological concepts.* New York: Wiley, 1962.

Gottman, J. M. *Marital interaction.* New York: Academic Press, 1979.

Gottman, J., & Bakeman, R. The sequential analysis of observational data. In M. Lamb, S. Suomi, & G. Stephenson (Eds.), *Social interaction methodology.* Madison: University of Wisconsin Press, 1979.

Gottman, J. M., & Markman, H. J. Experimental designs in psychotherapy research. In S. L. Garfield & A. E. Bergin (Eds.), *Handbook of psychotherapy and behaviour change.* New York: Wiley, 1978.

Gottman, J., Markman, H., & Notarius, C. The topography of marital conflict: A sequential analysis of verbal and non-verbal behaviour. *Journal of Marriage and the Family,* 1977, August, 461–477.

Greenberg, L. *Task analysis of psychotherapeutic events.* Unpublished Doctoral Dissertation, York University, 1975.

Greenberg, L. The intensive analysis of recurring events from the practice of Gestalt therapy. *Psychotherapy Theory Research & Practice,* 1980, 17, 143–152.

Greenberg, L. Psychotherapy process research. In E. Walker (Ed.), *Handbook of Clinical Psychology.* Homewood, Ill.: Dorsey Press, 1982.

Greenberg, L. Toward a task analysis of conflict resolution in Gestalt therapy. *Psychotherapy Theory Research & Practice,* 1983, 2, 190–201.

Greenberg, L. A task analysis of interpersonal conflict resolution. In L. Rice & L. Greenberg (Eds.), *Patterns of change: An intensive analyses of the psychotherapy process.* New York: Guilford Press, 1984. (a)

Greenberg, L. Task analysis: the general approach. *Patterns of change: An intensive analysis of psychotherapy process.* New York: Guilford Press, 1984. (b)

Greenberg, L. S., & Dompierre, L. The specific effects of Gestalt two-chair dialogue on intrapsychic conflict in counselling. *Journal of Counseling Psychology,* 1981, 27, 221–225.

Greenberg, L. S., & Rice, L. The specific effects of a Gestalt intervention. *Psychotherapy Theory Research & Practice,* 1981, 18, 210–216.

Gumperz, J. J. "Intro." *Directions in sociolinguistics.* In J. J. Gumperz & D. Hymes (Eds.), New York: Holt, Rhinehardt & Winston, 1972.

Gurman, A. S. Instability of therapeutic conditions of psychotherapy. *Journal of Counseling Psychology,* 1973, 20, 16–24.

Hanson, N. R. *Patterns of discovery.* Cambridge: Cambridge University Press, 1958.

Hanson, N. R. *Perception & discovery. An introduction to scientific inquiry.* San Francisco: Freeman, 1969.

Hanson, N. R. *Observation and explanation: A guide to philosophy of science.* New York: Harper & Row, 1971.

Harré, R. (Ed.) *Problems of scientific revolution. Progress and obstacles to progress in the sciences.* Clarenden Press, Oxford, 1975.

Hempel, C. G. *Philosophy of natural science.* Englewood Cliffs, N.J.: Prentice-Hall, 1966.

Herbst, P. *Behavioral worlds. The study of single cases.* London: Tavistock Publications, 1970.

Hill, C., Carter, J., & O'Farrel, M. A case study of the process and outcome of time limited counseling. *Journal of Counseling Psychology,* 1983, 30, 26–30.

Hill, C., Siegelman, L., Gronsky, B., Sturniolo, F., & Fretz, G. Nonverbal communication & counseling outcome: *Journal of Counseling Psychology,* 1981, 28, 203–212.

Horowitz, M. J. *States of mind.* New York: Plenum Press, 1979.

Horowitz, M. Strategic dilemmas and the socialization of psychotherapy researchers. *British Journal of Clinical Psychology*, 1982, *21*, 119–127.

Horowitz, M. J., Marmar, C., & Wilner, N. Analysis of patient states and state transitions. *Journal of Nervous and Mental Disease*, 1979, *167*, 91–99.

Horowitz, L. M., Sampson, H., Siegelman, E. Y., Weiss, J., & Goodfriend, S. Cohesive and dispersal behaviours: Two classes of concomitant change in psychotherapy. *Journal of Consulting and Clinical Psychology*, 1978, *46*, 336–564.

Kaplan, A. *The conduct of inquiry*. San Francisco: Chandler, 1964.

Kiesler, D. J. Experimental designs in psychotherapy research. In A. E. Bergin & S. L. Garfield (Eds.), *Handbook of psychotherapy and behaviour change*. New York: Wiley, 1971.

Kiesler, D. *The process of psychotherapy: Empirical foundations and systems of analysis*. Hawthorne, N.Y.: Aldine, 1973.

Klein, M., Mathieu, P., Keisler, O., & Gendlin, E. *The experiencing scale*. Madison, Wis.: Wisconsin Psychiatric Inst., 1969.

Krantz, D., & Tversky, A. Conjoint measurement analysis of composition rules in psychology. *Psychological Review*, 1971, *78*, 151–169.

Kuhn, T. S. *The structure of scientific revolution*. Chicago: University of Chicago Press, 1973.

Lakatos, I. Falsification and the methodology of scientific research programmes. In I. Lakatos & A. Musgrove (Eds.), *Criticism and the Growth of Knowledge*. Cambridge: Cambridge University Press, 1970.

Lambert, M. *Psychotherapy and patient relationships*. Homewood, Ill.: Dow Jones Irwin, 1983.

Luborsky, L. Momentary forgetting during psychotherapy and psychoanalysis: A theory and research method. In R. Holt (Ed.), Motives and thought: Psychoanalytic essays in honor of David Rappaport. *Psychological Issues*, 1967, *5*, 177–217.

Luborsky, L. Research cannot yet influence clinical practice. In A. Bergin & H. Strupp (Eds.), *Changing frontiers in the science of psychotherapy*. Hawthorne, N.Y.: Aldine, 1972.

Luborsky, L. Quantitative research on psychoanalytic therapy. In S. L. Garfield & A. E. Bergin (Eds.), *Handbook of psychotherapy and behaviour change*. New York: Wiley, 1978.

Luborsky, L., & Auerbach, A. The symptom-context method: Quantitative studies of symptom formation in psychotherapy. *Journal of American Psychoanalytic Association*, 1969, *17*, 68–99.

Luborsky, L., Woody, G., McLellan, A., O'Brian, C., & Rosenzweig, J. Can independent judges recognize different psychotherapies? An experience with manual guided therapies. *Journal of Consulting & Clinical Psychology*, 1982, *50*, 49–62.

Malan, D. *Toward the validation of dynamic psychotherapy*. New York: Plenum Press, 1976.

Manicas, P., & Secord, P. Implications for psychology of the new philosophy of science. *American Psychologist*, 1983, *38*, 399–413.

McCullough, J. *Cognitive-behavioral analysis system of psychotherapy*. Unpublished paper, Virginia Commonwealth, University Richmond, Virginia, 1979.

McMullin, E. Empiricism at sea. In R. S. Cohen & M. W. Wartofsky (Eds.), *Methodological & historical essays in the natural and social sciences*. Boston: D. Reidel Publishing Co., 1974. (a)

McMullin, E. Logicality and rationality: A comment on Toulmin's theory of science. In R. Seeger & R. Cohen (Eds.), *Philosophical foundations of science*. Boston Studies in the Philosophy of Science. Vol. XI, Derdrecht Holland: D. Reidel Publishing Co., 1974. (b)

Meehl, P. Theoretical risks & tabular asterisks: Sir Karl, Sir Ronald and the slow progress of soft psychology. *Journal of Consulting & Clinical Psychology*, 1978, *46*, 806–834.

Orlinsky, D. E., & Howard, K. I. The relation of process to outcome in psychotherapy. In S. L. Garfield & A. E. Bergin (Eds.), *Handbook of psychotherapy and behaviour change*. New York: Wiley, 1978.

Patterson, G., & Moore, D. Interactive patterns as units of behavior. In M. E. Lamb (Ed.), *Social interaction analysis*. Madison, Wis.: University of Wisconsin Press, 1979.

Pearce, W., & Cronen, V. *Communication action and meaning*. New York: Praeger, 1980.

Polanyi, M. *Personal knowledge: Towards a post-critical philosophy*. Chicago: University of Chicago Press, 1958.

Polanyi, M. The tacit dimension. Garden City: Doubleday, 1966.

Pope, B. Research on therapeutic style. In A. S. Gurman & A. M. Razin (Eds.), *Effective psychotherapy*. Elmsford, N.Y.: Pergamon Press, 1977.

Popper, K. *Conjectures & refutations*. London: Routledge & Kegan Paul, 1963.

Revenstorf, D., Hahlweg, K., Schindler, L., & Vogel, B. Interaction Analysis of marital conflict. In K. Hahlweg & N. Jacobson (Eds.), *Marital interaction: Analysis & modification*. New York: Guilford Press, 1984.

Rice, L. A task analysis of the resolution of problematic reactions. In L. Rice & L. Greenberg (Eds.), *Patterns of change: Intensive analysis of psycholotherapeutic process*. New York: Guilford Press, 1984.

Rice, L. N., & Greenberg, L. S. *A method for studying the active ingredients in psychotherapy: Application to client-centred and Gestalt therapy*. Paper presented to the Society for Psychotherapy Research, Denver, 1974.

Rice, L., & Greenberg, L. (Eds.). *Patterns of change: Intensive analysis of psychotherapy process*. New York: Guilford Press, 1984.

Rorer, L., & Widiger, T. Personality structure and assessment. In M. Rosenzweig & L. Porter (Eds.), *Annual Review of Psychology*, 1983, *34*, 431–464.

Sackett, G. (Ed.) *Observing behavior. Vol. II. Data collection and analysis methods*. Baltimore: University Park Press, 1978.

Schaffer, N. Multidimensional measures of therapist behavior as predictors of outcome. *Psychological Bulletin*, 1982, *92*, 670–681.

Schank, R., & Abelson, R. *Scripts, plans, goals, & understanding*. Hillsdale, N.J.: Erlbaum, 1977.

Searles, J. *Speech acts; An essay on the philosophy of language*. New York: Oxford, 1969.

Simon, H. Does scientific discovery have a logic? *Philosophy of Science*, 1973, *49*, 471–480. In *Models of discovery. Boston studies in the philosophy of science, Vol. 54*. Dordrecht, Holland: D. Reidl Publishing Co., 1977.

Singer, J. The scientific basis of psychotherapeutic practice: A question of values and ethics. *Psychotherapy Theory Research and Practice*, 1980, *17*, 369–375.

Strupp, H. Success and failure in time-limited psychotherapy. *Archives of General Psychiatry*, 1980, *37*, 545–603. (a)

Strupp, H. Success & failure in time limited psychotherapy: A systematic comparison of two cases: Comparison 2. *Archives of General Psychiatry*, 1980, *37*, 708–716. (b)

Strupp, H. Success & failure in time limited psychotherapy. Further evidence: Comparison 4. *Archives of General Psychiatry*, 1980, *37*, 947–954. (c)

Tedteschi, J., Heister, D., & Gahagan, J. Trust and the prisoner's dilemma game. *Journal of Personality and Social Psychology*, 1969, *79*, 43–50.

Toulmin, S. *Philosophy of science*. London: Hutchinson's University Library, 1953.

Toulmin, S. *Foresight & understanding*. Watford, Ind.: Indiana University Press, 1961.

Toulmin, S. *Human understanding* (Vol. 1). Oxford: Clarendon Press, 1972.

Toulmin, S. Scientific strategies and historical change. In R. J. Seeger & R. S. Cohen (Eds.), *Philosophical foundations of science: Boston studies in the philosophy of science*. Boston: D. Reidel Publishing Co., 1974.

Toulmin, S. From form to function. *Encounter*, 1976, *21*, 150–164.

Index